The Oxford Business Spanish Dictionary
El Diccionario de Negocios Oxford

El Diccionario de Negocios Oxford

Español ⟶ Inglés
Inglés ⟶ Español

Dirección editorial
Sinda López
Donald Watt

OXFORD
UNIVERSITY PRESS

The Oxford Business Spanish Dictionary

Spanish ⟶ English
English ⟶ Spanish

Chief editors
Sinda López
Donald Watt

OXFORD
UNIVERSITY PRESS

OXFORD
UNIVERSITY PRESS

Great Clarendon Street, Oxford OX2 6DP

Oxford University Press is a department of the University of Oxford.
It furthers the University's objective of excellence in research, scholarship,
and education by publishing worldwide in

Oxford New York

Auckland Bangkok Buenos Aires Cape Town Chennai
Dar es Salaam Delhi Hong Kong Istanbul Karachi Kolkata
Kuala Lumpur Madrid Melbourne Mexico City Mumbai Nairobi
São Paulo Singapore Taipei Tokyo Toronto

with an associated company in Berlin

Oxford is a registered trade mark of Oxford University Press
in the UK and in certain other countries

Published in the United States
by Oxford University Press Inc., New York

British Library Cataloguing in Publication Data
Data available

Library of Congress Cataloging in Publication Data
Data available

ISBN 0-19-860481-5

10 9 8 7 6 5 4 3 2 1

Typeset in Nimrod, Arial and Meta
by Morton Word Processing Ltd
Printed in Great Britain by Clays Ltd, Bungay, Suffolk

Preface

The *Oxford Business Spanish Dictionary* has been written to meet the challenges of the new economy and to embrace the changes taking place in business practices with the rise of new information and communications technologies. Designed to meet the needs of the business studies student, the business professional, and all who need to understand the language of business, it combines an extensive word list with clearly presented examples of business language in use.

The dictionary offers the user comprehensive coverage of core business vocabulary from a wide range of fields, including accountancy, banking, economics, human resource management, law, sales and marketing, the stock market, management, taxation, insurance, and information technology. The word list is further enhanced by the addition of vocabulary generated by the Internet revolution and the growth of the digital economy. Where appropriate, American variations in spelling and usage are highlighted.

Presentation of the entries is streamlined to provide ease of reference. Essential information is provided in brackets to guide the user to the most appropriate translation. Field labels, e.g. **Fin, Ins, Comp**, help the user navigate through the entry to the relevant category of information. Examples of typical structures and phrases in which a word is frequently found allow the user to deploy the term accurately and effectively in a sentence. Compounds are grouped alphabetically in a block for ease of consultation. Where a compound contains a preposition, the preposition is ignored for the purposes of alphabetical ordering.

English compounds and adjective-noun combinations are listed under their first elements.

In recognition of the greater degree of mobility within the labour market, a section of the dictionary is devoted to the presentation of curricula vitae with covering letters in English and Spanish. This section equips the user with a wide variety of expressions and vocabulary for describing their career path, achievements, and skills which can be tailored to suit individual requirements.

An additional feature of the dictionary is the sample business correspondence. The letters are presented in pairs on similar themes for ease of comparison and exemplify the different conventions prevalent in each language. The material covers standard business correspondence as well as e-mail, memoranda, faxes, invoices, and statements of account.

'Using the telephone' provides a wealth of information on the vocabulary of telecommunications, including mobile communications. A list of the world's major countries, nationalities, languages, and currencies is also supplied in the central section of the dictionary, as is an overview of the euro and details on conversion.

The dictionary is designed to be a practical, effective, and user-friendly tool both for study purposes and for tackling business assignments.

Prólogo

Esta primera edición del *Diccionario de Negocios Oxford* ha sido creada para enfrentar los retos de la nueva economía y para adoptar los cambios que han surgido en el mundo de los negocios con las nuevas tecnologías informáticas y de comunicaciones. Ha sido concebida tanto para los estudiantes de ciencias empresariales como para los empresarios y todo aquel que necesite entender el lenguaje del comercio. Además de una amplia lista de entradas, incluye también ejemplos del uso del lenguaje de negocios.

El diccionario ofrece al usuario una cobertura completa del vocabulario esencial de negocios, abarcando los campos de contabilidad, banca, economía, gestión de recursos humanos, derecho, ventas y marketing, la bolsa, gestiones, impuestos, seguros e informática. La lista de entradas se ve enriquecida por el vocabulario que se ha generado por la revolución de Internet y el crecimiento de la economía digital. Se cubre tanto el español europeo como el latinoamericano y, donde corresponda, se destacan las variantes de ortografía y de uso del inglés norteamericano.

Las entradas se presentan de una manera que hace fácil su consulta. A fin de guiar el usuario para seleccionar la mejor traducción, la información esencial aparece entre paréntesis. Los indicadores de campo semántico, p. ej. Fin, Ins, Comp, sirven para encontrar la categoría relevante de la traducción que se busca. Los ejemplos de frases y estructuras típicas permiten al usuario utilizar el término en forma precisa y eficaz.

Las palabras compuestas y las combinaciones de adjetivo-sustantivo inglesas están ordenadas alfabéticamente, de acuerdo a su primer elemento. Si un compuesto contiene una preposición, ésta se ignora en el orden alfabético.

En vista de la mayor movilidad que existe dentro del mercado laboral, se ha dedicado una sección del diccionario a la presentación de los curriculums vitae con cartas de presentación en español y en inglés. Esta sección proporciona al usuario una gran variedad de expresiones y vocabulario para describir una carrera, logros y aptitudes, lo cual se puede adaptar a las necesidades de cada persona.

Una característica adicional del diccionario es la sección de ejemplos de correspondencia de negocios. Las cartas están agrupadas en pares, de acuerdo a su tema, para facilitar la comparación y para destacar las diferentes convenciones de cada lenguaje. Este material cubre la correspondencia típica de negocios y también el correo electrónico, memorándums, faxes, facturas e informes.

'El teléfono' contiene abundante información sobre el lenguaje de las telecomunicaciones, incluyendo la telefonía móvil. En la sección central del diccionario se encontrará una lista de los países, nacionalidades, lenguas y monedas principales del mundo y también una introducción al euro y detalles sobre conversión.

Este diccionario ha sido concebido para ser una herramienta práctica, eficaz y fácil de usar, tanto para el estudio como para enfrentar todo lo relacionado con los negocios.

Contributors/Colaboradores

Chief Editors/Dirección editorial
Sinda López
Donald Watt

Business correspondence, curriculum vitae, using the telephone/
correspondencia comercial, currículum vitae, el teléfono
Antonio Fortin

Proprietary names/Marcas registradas

This dictionary includes some words which have, or are asserted to have, proprietary status as trademarks or otherwise. Their inclusion does not imply that they have acquired for legal purposes a non-proprietary or general significance, nor any other judgement concerning their legal status. In cases where the editorial staff have some evidence that a word has proprietary status, this is indicated in the entry for that word by the symbol ®, but no judgement concerning the legal status of such words is made or implied thereby.

Este diccionario incluye palabras que constituyen, o se afirma que constituyen, marcas registradas o nombres comerciales. Su inclusión no significa que a efectos legales hayan dejado de tener ese carácter, ni supone un pronunciamiento respecto de su situación legal. Cuando al editor le consta que una palabra es una marca registrada o un nombre comercial, esto se indica por medio del símbolo ®, lo que tampoco supone un pronunciamiento acerca de la situación legal de esa palabra.

Contents/Índice

Abbreviations/Abreviaturas

English/Inglés	Abbreviation/Abreviatura	Spanish/Español
abbreviation	abbr, abr	abreviatura
Accountancy	Acc	Contabilidad
adjective	adj	adjetivo
Business Administration	Admin	Administración de Empresas
adverb	adv	adverbio
American English	AmE	Inglés americano
Latin America	AmL	América Latina
Banking	Banca, Bank	Banca
Stock Market	Bolsa	Bolsa
British English	BrE	Inglés británico
Communications	Comms	Comunicaciones
Computing	Comp	Informática
Communications	Coms	Comunicaciones
conjunction	conj	conjunción
Accountancy	Cont	Contabilidad
Law	Der	Derecho
Economics	Econ	Economía
Environment	Envir	Medio Ambiente
Spain	Esp	España
feminine	f	femenino
feminine plural	f pl	femenino plural
Finance	Fin	Finanzas
Taxation	Fisc	Fiscalidad
phrase	fra	frase
formal	frml	formal
Management	Ges	Gestión
Human Resource Management	HRM	Gestión de Recursos Humanos
Import & Export	Imp/Exp	Importación y Exportación
Industry	Ind	Industria
Computing	Info	Informática
informal	infrml	informal
Property	Inmob	Inmobiliarios
Insurance	Ins	Seguros
jargon	jarg	jerga
Law	Law	Derecho
Leisure & Tourism	Leis	Ocio y Turismo
masculine	m	masculino
masculine or feminine	mf	masculino o femenino

Abbreviations/Abreviaturas

English/Inglés	Abbreviation/Abreviatura	Spanish/Español
masculine, feminine	m,f	masculino, femenino
masculine plural	m pl	masculino plural
Environment	Med Amb	Medio Ambiente
Mass Media	Media, Medios	Medios de Comunicación
Management	Mgmnt	Gestión
noun	n	sustantivo
noun plural	n pl	sustantivo plural
obsolete	obs	obsoleto
Leisure & Tourism	Ocio	Ocio y Turismo
Patents	Patent	Patentes
phrase	phr	frase
Politics	Pol	Política
prefix	pref	prefijo
preposition	prep	preposición
Property	Prop	Inmobiliarios
Welfare & Safety	Prot Soc	Protección Social
Human Resource Management	RRHH	Gestión de Recursos Humanos
Sales & Marketing	S&M	Ventas y Marketing
somebody	sb	alguien
Insurance	Seg	Seguros
something	sth	algo
Stock Market	Stock	Bolsa
Taxation	Tax	Fiscalidad
also	tb	también
Transport	Transp	Transporte
Sales & Marketing	V&M	Ventas y Marketing
intransitive verb	vi	verbo intransitivo
pronominal verb	v pron	verbo pronominal
transitive verb	vt	verbo transitivo
transitive and intransitive verb	vti	verbo transitivo e intransitivo

Aa

abajo *adv* below; **hacia** ∼ *adv* downwards BrE, downward AmE; ∼ **mencionado** undermentioned

abajofirmante *m,f*: **el/la** ∼ the undersigned

abandonado *adj* (plan, opción) abandoned; (negocio, posibilidad) neglected

abandonar *vt* (plan, opción) abandon; (Info) quit; (programa) abort; ∼ **el buque** abandon ship

abandono *m* (de plan, opción) abandonment; ∼ **del servicio** dereliction of duty

abanico *m* (gama) range; (surtido) product line; ∼ **salarial** *or* **de salarios** wage scale

abaratamiento *m* drop *o* fall in price; (Fin) undertrading

abaratar *vt* (coste, precio) lower, bring down; (Fin) undertrade; **esta subvención abarata el coste de producción** this subsidy brings down production costs

abaratarse *v pron* (artículo) become cheaper; (coste, precio) come down

abarcar *vt* cover, comprise; (tarea) undertake, take on

abastecedor, a *m,f* supplier

abastecer *vt* supply; ∼ **el mercado** supply the market; ∼ **a alguien de algo** supply sb with sth

abastecimiento *m* (acto) supplying; (servicio) supply; **suficiente** ∼ **de algo** plentiful supply of sth; ∼ **electrónico** power supply; ∼ **fijo** fixed supply

abierto *adj* (comercio, carácter) open; (enfoque) outward-looking; ∼ **al público de 10 a 2** open to the public from 10 to 2; ∼ **las 24 horas** open 24 hours

abogacía *f* legal profession; (oficio) law; **ejercer** *or* **practicar la** ∼ practise BrE *o* practice AmE law

abogado, -a *m,f* lawyer, solicitor BrE, attorney-at-law AmE, attorney AmE; (en una corte) barrister BrE, court lawyer AmE; **ejercer de** ∼ practise BrE *o* practice AmE law; ∼ **administrativista** public administration lawyer; ∼ **civilista** civil lawyer; ∼ **de empresa** in-house lawyer, company lawyer; ∼ **del Estado** public prosecutor, Government lawyer; ∼

jurídico militar military lawyer; ∼ **laborista** labour BrE *o* labor AmE law lawyer; ∼ **matrimonialista** divorce lawyer; ∼ **mercantilista** commercial lawyer; ∼ **de oficio** duty solicitor BrE, court-appointed attorney AmE; ∼ **penalista** criminal lawyer; ∼ **tributarista** tax lawyer

abogar *vi* plead; ∼ **por** *or* **en favor de** defend, plead for; (ser partidario de) advocate

abolición *f* abolition

abolir *vt* abolish; (mandamiento judicial) quash

abonable *adj* payable; ∼ **en cuotas trimestrales** payable in three-monthly instalments BrE *o* installments AmE; ∼ **a fin de mes** payable at the end of the month *or* at month end

abonado, -a *m,f* customer; (al teléfono) subscriber; (Transp) season-ticket holder; **no** ∼**s** *m pl* general public; (a un servicio) non-subscribers; ∼ **a prueba** trial subscriber

abonar *vt* (deuda, factura) pay; (préstamo) credit; (cheque) cash; ∼ **un cheque en cuenta** pay in a cheque BrE *o* check AmE, credit a cheque BrE *o* check AmE to an account

abono *m* (pago) payment; (crédito) credit; (plazo) instalment BrE, installment AmE; (Cont) credit entry; (boleto) season ticket BrE, commutation ticket AmE; ∼ **trimestral** quarterly instalment BrE, quarterly installment AmE

abordar *vt* (problema) tackle, deal with; ∼ **a alguien sobre algo** approach sb about sth

abreviar *vt* abbreviate

abreviatura *f* abbreviation

abrir *vt* (negociaciones, cuenta) open; (negocio) set up, start; (mercado, posibilidades) open up; ∼ **brecha** break new ground; ∼ **brecha en un mercado** break into a market; ∼ **un expediente a alguien** start proceedings against sb; ∼ **el mercado a la competencia** open up the market to competition

abrogación *f* (Fin) defeasance; (Der) abrogation, repeal

abrogar *vt* abrogate, repeal

absentismo *m* absenteeism

absentista *m* absentee

absolución *f* (Der) acquittal

absolver *vt* acquit, clear; **el juez absolvió al acusado** the defendant was acquitted by the judge

absorber *vt* (costes, beneficios) absorb; (compañía) take over; ~ **gastos generales** absorb overheads

absorbido *adj* (costes) absorbed; (compañía) taken over

absorción *f* (de costes) absorption; (de compañía) takeover; ~ **supranacional** offshore takeover

abstención *f* abstention

abstenerse *v pron* (en elección) abstain; ~ **intermediarios** (en anuncios) no dealers, no agencies

abundancia *f* (de recursos) abundance, wealth; (prosperidad) affluence; ~ **de oportunidades** wealth of opportunities

abundante *adj* abundant

abusar *vi* take advantage; ~ **de algo/ alguien** take advantage of sth/sb

abuso *m* abuse; ~ **de autoridad** abuse of authority; ~ **de confianza** breach of trust; ~ **de poder** abuse of power

acabado *m* finish

academia *f* academy; (de enseñanza) (private) school *o* college; ~ **comercial** *or* **de negocios** business school *o* college

académico *adj* academic

acaparado *adj* (mercado) monopolized, cornered

acaparador, a *m,f* (de negocio, mercado) cornerer, monopolizer; (de beneficios) profiteer; (de capital) monopolizer

acaparamiento *m* (de negocio, mercado) cornering, monopolization; (de capital) monopolization; (de bienes) hoarding, stockpiling

acaparar *vt* (mercado) corner, monopolize; (bienes) hoard, stockpile

acatar *vt* observe

acceder *vi*: ~ **a algo** (ceder) agree *o* consent to sth; (a mercado) gain *o* have access to sth; (información, base de datos) access; ~ **a hacer algo** agree *o* consent to do sth

accesibilidad *f* accessibility; ~ **a algo** accessibility to sth

accesible *adj* (información, lenguaje) accessible; (persona) approachable; (precio) affordable; ~ **a todos los bolsillos** within everyone's price range

acceso *m* access; (acierto) hit; **tener** ~ **a algo** have access to sth; **sin** ~ **al mar** landlocked; ~ **aleatorio** random access; ~ **conmutado** dial-up access *o* connection; ~ **directo** direct access; ~ **a distancia** remote access; ~ **a Internet** Internet access; ~ **en línea** online access; ~ **a los mercados** market access; ~ **no restringido** unrestricted access; ~ **en paralelo** parallel access; ~ **público** public access; ~ **remoto** remote access; ~ **secuencial** sequential access; ~ **en serie** serial access

accesorio *adj* accessory; (gastos) incidental

accesorios *m pl* equipment; ~ **de escritorio** office equipment ~ **e instalaciones** fixtures and fittings

accidente *m* accident; **tener** *or* **sufrir un** ~ have an accident; ~ **industrial** industrial accident

acción *f* action; (Bolsa) stock; (titularidad pública) share, equity; **acciones** stocks, shares; **emitir acciones** issue shares *or* stock; **los precios de las acciones alcanzaron un máximo histórico** share prices reached an all time high; **por** ~ per share; ~ **admitida** approved share BrE, approved stock AmE; ~ **adquirida** acquired share BrE, acquired stock AmE; ~ **alfa** alpha share; **acciones de alto rendimiento** high-yielding *o* performance stock; **acciones amortizables** redeemable shares; **acciones apalancadas** leveraged stock; **acciones de base** base stock; ~ **beta** beta share; **acciones en circulación** issued shares, issued stock; ~ **de clase A** class A share; **acciones clasificadas** classified stock; ~ **coercitiva** enforcement action; **acciones de compensación** compensation stocks; **A**~ **Comunitaria** (UE) Community Action; ~ **congelada** stopped stock; ~ **conjunta** joint action; **acciones cotizables** listed shares; **acciones con cotización oficial** listed *o* quoted shares, listed *o* quoted stock; **acciones sin cotización oficial** unlisted *o* unquoted shares, unlisted *o* unquoted stock; ~ **con/sin derecho de voto** voting/nonvoting share; **acciones emitidas** issued stock; **acciones no emitidas** unissued stock; ~ **ficticia** phantom share; **acciones flotantes** floating stock; ~ **ilegal** unlawful act; **acciones indexadas** index-linked stock; ~ **industrial** industrial action; ~

judicial legal action, law suit; ~ **legal** legal action; **acciones liberadas** bonus shares, bonus stock; **acciones nominales, acciones nominativas** registered shares, registered stock; ~ **ordinaria** ordinary share BrE, common stock AmE; **acciones a la par** par stock; ~ **al portador** bearer stock; **acciones preferentes** preference shares, preference stock; **acciones de primer orden** blue-chip stock; ~ **judicial** legal action, law suit; **acciones selectas** blue chips; ~ **sin valor nominal** no-par-value share BrE, no-par stock AmE

accionariado *m* shareholding BrE, stockholding AmE; (personas) shareholders BrE, stockholders AmE; ~ **mayoritario/minoritario** majority/minority shareholding BrE *o* stockholding AmE

accionista *mf* shareholder BrE, stockholder AmE; ~ **mayoritario(-a)** *m,f* majority shareholder BrE, majority stockholder AmE; ~ **minoritario(-a)** *m,f* minority shareholder BrE, minority stockholder AmE; ~ **nominativo(-a)** *m,f* registered shareholder BrE, registered stockholder AmE; ~ **ordinario(-a)** *m,f* common *o* ordinary shareholder BrE, common *o* ordinary stockholder AmE; ~ **principal** principal shareholder BrE, principal stockholder AmE

aceleración *f* acceleration

acelerado *adj* (paso) accelerated, fast; (cursos de formación) intensive, crash (jarg)

acelerador *m* (Econ) accelerator

acelerar 1 *vt* speed up
2 *vi* accelerate, put on a spurt (infrml)

acento *m* emphasis; **poner el ~ en algo** emphasize *o* stress sth

aceptabilidad *f* acceptability

aceptable *adj* acceptable

aceptación *f* acceptance; (éxito) success; **tener gran ~ entre los jóvenes** be very successful with young people; ~ **condicionada** qualified acceptance; ~ **condicional** conditional acceptance; ~ **del consumidor** consumer acceptance; ~ **de marca** brand acceptance; ~ **del mercado** market acceptance; ~ **del producto** product acceptance

aceptado *adj* accepted

aceptante *m,f* (de letra) acceptor

aceptar *vt* (oferta, pago) accept; (cuentas, libros) agree; (trabajo, tarjeta) take; **aceptamos tarjetas de crédito** we take credit cards; **no aceptamos devoluciones** no refunds; ~

asesoramiento jurídico take legal advice; ~ **la obligación** accept liability

acerca de *prep* about, regarding

acertado *adj* (respuesta) right, correct; (idea) clever; (comentario) appropriate, relevant

acertar *vi* be right; ~ **a hacer algo** manage to do sth

acíclico *adj* noncyclical

acierto *m* good decision, right choice; (en el Internet) hit; **con ~** skilfully BrE, skillfully AmE

aclaración *f* clarification, explanation; **hacer una ~** clarify sth

aclarar *vt* clarify, explain

acometer *vt* (problemas) tackle; (trabajos) undertake

acomodadizo *adj* adaptable, accommodating

acomodar *vt* accommodate; ~ **algo a algo** adapt sth to sth, bring sth in line with sth

acompañado *adj* (persona) accompanied; ~ **de algo/alguien** accompanied by sth/sb; **venir ~ de algo** (producto) come with sth

acompañante *mf* escort

acompañar *vt* accompany, go with; (adjuntar) attach, enclose

aconsejable *adj* advisable; **poco ~** inadvisable

aconsejado *adj*: **estar bien/mal ~** be well/ill advised

aconsejar *vt* advise; ~ **a alguien (no) hacer algo** advise sb (not) to do sth; ~ **a alguien que (no) haga algo** advise sb (not) to do sth

acontecer *vi* happen

acontecimiento *m* event; ~ **mediático** media event; ~ **patrocinado** sponsored event

acopiado *adj* accumulated, gathered together

acopiar *vt* accumulate, gather together

acopio *m* accumulation, collection; ~ **de efectivo** cash collection

acordado *adj* agreed; **según lo ~** as agreed

acordar *vt* (términos, precio) agree; (transacciones) settle; (diferencias) resolve; ~ **hacer algo** agree to do sth

acorde *adj* agreed; **estar ~s** be agreed *o* in agreement; ~ **con algo** in line with sth

acortar *vt* (texto, artículo) shorten; (vacaciones, reunión) cut short

a

acoso *m* harassment; ~ **sexual** sexual harassment

acrecentamiento *m* increase, growth; ~ **del crédito** credit enhancement

acrecentar *vt* increase

acrecentarse *v pron* increase, grow

acrecimiento *m* increase, growth

acreditación *f* accreditation; ~ **de prensa** press pass

acreditado *adj* (periodista) accredited; (casa) reputable; (distribuidor) approved

acreditar *vt* (garantizar) accredit; (autorizar) authorize; **este documento le acredita como propietario** this document confirms him as the owner

acreedor, a *m,f* creditor; ~ **asegurado(-a)** *m,f* secured creditor; ~ **hipotecario(-a)** *m,f* mortgagee; ~ **no asegurado(-a)** *m,f* unsecured creditor; ~ **ordinario(-a)** *m,f* general creditor; ~ **privilegiado(-a)** *m,f* preferred creditor

acta *f* (de congreso) proceedings *pl*; (de reunión) minutes *pl*; **levantar** ~ take the minutes; **constar en** ~ be in the minutes, be minuted; ~ **de acusación** bill of indictment; ~ **notarial** affidavit; ~ **oficial** official document *o* record; **A~ Única Europea** Single European Act

actitud *f* attitude; ~ **del usuario** user attitude

activado *adj* activated; ~ **por el tacto** touch-activated; ~ **por la voz** voice-activated, voice-actuated

activador *m* activator; ~ **de ajuste** *m* adjustment trigger

activar *vt* (dispositivo, alarma) activate; (programas) enable; (mercado) stimulate

actividad *f* activity; ~**es de apoyo** support activities; ~ **bancaria** banking business; ~ **comercial** commercial activity; ~ **económica** economic activity; ~ **inversionista** investment activity; ~ **profesional** work; ~ **secundaria** subactivity, secondary activity

activista *mf* activist

activo¹ *adj* active

activo² *m* assets; ~ **acumulado** accrued assets; ~ **amortizable** depreciable assets; ~**s bloqueados** frozen assets; ~**s de capital** (inversiones) capital assets; ~ **circulante** current assets; ~**s congelados** frozen assets; ~ **consumible** wasting assets; ~ **corriente** current assets; ~ **devengado** accrued assets; ~ **diferido** deferred assets; ~ **disponible** (en valores) available assets; (en efectivo) cash available; ~ **de explotación** operating assets; ~ **fijo** (tierras, propiedades, edificios) fixed assets; ~ **fungible** fungible assets; ~**s imponibles** chargeable assets; ~ **inmovilizado** fixed assets; ~ **intangible** intangible assets; ~ **invisible** invisible assets; ~**s líquidos** cash assets, liquid assets; ~ **neto** net assets; ~**s no fungibles** nonfungible assets; ~ **oculto** concealed assets, hidden assets; ~ **y pasivo** assets and liabilities; ~ **social** corporate assets; ~ **tangible** tangible assets

acto *m* act; ~ **de cesión** act of cession; ~ **ilícito civil** tort; ~ **de quiebra** act of bankruptcy; ~ **de reconocimiento** act of acknowledgement

actuación *f* performance; (acción) action; ~ **judicial** legal action

actual *adj* current, present; (técnica) up-to-date, up-to-the-minute

actualidad *f*: **de** ~ evergreen; **en la** ~ at the present time, currently; ~**es** *or* **la** ~ current affairs

actualizable *adj* updatable

actualización *f* update; (acto) updating

actualizado *adj* up-to-date

actualizar *vt* update

actuar *vi* act; ~ **de buena fe** act in good faith; ~ **en calidad de** act in the capacity of; ~ **en nombre de** act on behalf of; ~ **sobre algo** act upon sth

actuarial *adj* actuarial

actuario, -a *m,f* actuary

acudir *vi* (venir) come; (ir) go; ~ **a las urnas** go to the polls; ~ **a votar** turn out to vote; ~ **a la ley** resort to the law; ~ **a los tribunales** go to court; **acudo a ustedes para informarles que...** I am writing to you to inform you that...

acuerdo *m* agreement; (comercial) deal; (en el trato) arrangement; (del programa) resolution; (tratado) alliance; **cerrar un** ~ close *o* conclude a deal; **de** ~ **con** according to, in accordance with; **de** ~ **con el programa** according to schedule; **de** ~ **con sus instrucciones** in accordance with your instructions; **de común** ~ by common consent, by mutual agreement; **estar de** ~ **con algo** agree with sth; **estar de** ~ **en algo** agree on sth; **llegar a un** ~ reach *o* come to an agreement; **no llegar a un**

~ fail to reach an agreement; **ponerse de ~ para hacer algo** agree to do sth; **por ~** by arrangement; **por ~ mutuo** by mutual consent; **por ~ tácito** by tacit agreement; **~ de arrendamiento** lease agreement; **~ de asistencia técnica** know-how agreement; **~ de coalición** coalition alliance; **~ de cobro** collection agreement; **~ comercial** trade agreement; (V&M) marketing agreement; **~ comercial bilateral** bilateral trade agreement; **~ complementario** supplementary agreement; **~ de compraventa** buy-and-sell agreement; **~ sin condiciones** unconditional agreement; **~ de confidencialidad** confidentiality agreement; **~ de contrato** contract agreement; **~ de cooperación** cooperation agreement; **~ por escrito** written agreement; **~ estándar** standard agreement; **~ exclusivo** exclusive agreement; **~ de fábrica** Esp (*cf* ▸**contrato de fábrica** AmL) shop-floor agreement; **~ de fideicomiso** trust agreement; **~ formal** formal agreement; **~ de franquicia** franchise agreement; **A~ GATT** (▸**Acuerdo General sobre Aranceles y Comercio**) GATT (General Agreement on Tariffs and Trade); **~ general** blanket agreement; **~ de gestión** management agreement; **~ de indemnización** compensation settlement; **~ de Libre Comercio** (entre países europeos) Free Trade Agreement; **~ de licencia** licensing agreement; **~ marco** outline agreement, framework agreement; **~ modelo** pattern agreement; **~ monetario** monetary agreement; **~ de ocupación limitada** limited occupancy agreement; **~ de paz** peace agreement; **~ en plica** escrow agreement; **~ prematrimonial** prenuptial agreement; **~ privado** private arrangement; **~ de productividad** productivity agreement; **~ provisional** interim agreement; **~ de recompra** (comercio internacional) buy-back agreement; **~ sindical** union agreement; **~ unánime** unanimous agreement; **~ unilateral** unilateral agreement; **~ verbal** verbal agreement; **~ vinculante** binding agreement

acumulación *f* accumulation; (Cont) accrual; (de trabajo) backlog; **~ de existencias** stockpiling; **~ de intereses** accrual of interest

acumulado *adj* (interés) accrued

acumular *vt* (capital) accumulate; (interés) accrue; (datos) gather, amass; **~ deudas** run up debts

acumularse *v pron* accumulate; (trabajo) pile up

acumulativo *adj* cumulative; **no ~** noncumulative

acuñación *f* (de moneda) minting; (de frase) coining

acuñar *vt* mint; (frase) coin

acusación *f* accusation; (Der) charge; (fiscal) prosecution; **formular una ~ contra alguien** bring charges against sb; **la ~ no se mantuvo en el tribunal** the charge did not stand up in court; **negar la ~** deny the charge; **~ particular** private prosecution

acusador, a *m,f* accuser; **~ público(-a)** *m,f* public prosecutor BrE, district attorney AmE

acusar *vt* accuse; **~ a alguien de algo** accuse sb of sth; (Der) charge sb with sth; **~ recibo de algo** acknowledge receipt of sth; **~ recibo por carta** acknowledge receipt in writing

acuse de recibo *m* acknowledgement of receipt; **enviar un paquete con ~** send a parcel by recorded delivery

AD *abr* (▸**automatización del dibujo**) DA (design *o* drawing automation)

ADA *abr* (▸**Ayuda del Automovilista**) *Spanish motorists' organisation* ≈ AA BrE, ≈ RAC BrE, ≈ AAA AmE

adaptabilidad *f* adaptability

adaptable *adj* adaptable

adaptación *f* (proceso) adaptation; (arreglo) tuning, adjustment; **~ especial** tailoring; **~ del producto** product adaptation

adaptado *adj* adapted; (al cliente, mercado) tailored

adaptador *m* adaptor; **~ color/gráficos** colour/graphics adaptor BrE, color/graphics adaptor AmE; **~ de corriente** mains adaptor BrE, current adaptor AmE; **~ de gráficos de vídeo** Esp *or* **video** AmL video graphics adaptor; **~ en serie** serial adaptor; **~ videográfico** video graphics adaptor

adaptar *vt* adapt; (al cliente, mercado) tailor

adaptarse *v pron* adapt; **~ a algo** adapt to sth; **hay que saber ~** you have to be able to adapt

adecuación *f* adaptation; (a una situación) adjustment

a

adecuado *adj* appropriate, suitable;
(fondos, provisiones) adequate; ∼ **para algo**
suitable *o* appropriate for sth

adelantado *adj* advanced; **ir** ∼ be
ahead of schedule, be well advanced; **por**
∼ in advance, up front; **pagar algo por**
∼ pay for sth up front *o* in advance

adelantamiento *m* advancement

adelantar ▢1 *vt* (fecha, reunión) bring
forward; (dinero, sueldo) advance;
(información) reveal
▢2 *vi* make progress; **parece que no**
adelantamos nada we don't seem to be
making any progress

adelanto *m* (progreso, anticipo) advance;
con un ∼ **de 10 minutos** 10 minutes
early; **pedir un** ∼ ask for an advance; ∼
a cuenta down payment

además *adv* also, moreover; ∼ **de** in
addition to, as well as

adeudar *vt* owe; (cuenta) debit

adherir *vt* (etiqueta) affix; (Der) comply;
∼ **a** *vt* (contrato) adhere to, comply with

adhesión *f* adhesion; (apoyo) support; (a
la UE) accession; ∼ **a alguien** support for
sb; **desde su** ∼ **a la UE** since joining the
EU

adición *f* addition; (Medios) addendum;
sin ∼, **sin corrección** no addition, no
correction

adicto¹ *adj* addicted; ∼ **a algo** addicted
to sth; **ser** ∼ **a las compras** be a
shopaholic; **ser** ∼ **al trabajo** be a
workaholic

adicto², **-a** *m,f* addict

ad interim *adj* (juicio) ad interim

aditivo *m* additive; **sin** ∼ free of all
additives, additive-free

adj. *abr* (▸**adjunto**) encl. (enclosed)

adjudicación *f* awarding; (Bolsa)
allocation; (de fondos) appropriation; (Der)
adjudication; ∼ **por licitación**
allocation by tender; ∼ **prioritaria**
priority allocation; ∼ **de recursos**
resource allocation

adjudicador, a *m,f* adjudicator

adjudicar *vt* award; (dinero, obligaciones)
allocate; (Der) adjudicate; (contratos)
award; (fondos) appropriate, allocate

adjuntar *vt* attach

adjunto¹ *adj* attached; (ayudante)
assistant; **adjunta copia de la carta** copy
of letter enclosed; **director** ∼ assistant
director

adjunto² *adv* enclosed; **les envío** ∼
una copia de la factura please find
enclosed a copy of the invoice

adjunto³: ∼, **-a al director** *m,f*
assistant *o* deputy director

administración *f* administration;
(gestión) management; **bajo nueva** ∼
under new management; ∼ **de activos**
asset management; ∼ **de la calidad** AmL
(*cf* ▸**gestión de la calidad** Esp) quality
control; ∼ **de carteras** portfolio
management; **A**∼ **central** central
government; ∼ **por crisis** crisis
management; ∼ **de una cuenta** account
management; ∼ **de la deuda pública**
national debt management BrE, public
debt management AmE; ∼ **de empresas**
business administration, business
management; (curso) Business
Administration; ∼ **financiera** financial
administration, financial management;
∼ **de fondos** fund management; ∼
general general management; ∼ **de**
información information management;
∼ **de inversiones** investment
management; ∼ **local** local government;
mala ∼ mismanagement; ∼ **de**
menudeo AmL (*cf* ▸**gestión al por**
menor Esp, *cf* ▸**gestión minorista** Esp)
retail management; ∼ **por objetivos**
management by objectives; ∼ **del**
personal personnel management, staff
management; ∼ **de la producción**
production management; ∼ **de**
proyectos project management; ∼
pública civil service BrE, public
administration AmE; ∼ **del riesgo** risk
management; ∼ **de los recursos**
informáticos facilities management

administrador¹, **a** *m,f* administrator;
(de empresa) manager; (de quiebra) official
receiver; (de propiedades) bailiff; ∼ **de**
activos asset manager; ∼ **de aduanas**
customs officer; ∼ **de bienes** estate
manager; ∼ **de la cobertura** hedge
manager; ∼ **de la deuda** debt manager;
∼ **de fincas** land agent BrE, realtor
AmE; ∼ **de herencia** appointed
executor, estate manager; ∼ **de**
marketing Esp *or* **mercadotecnia** AmL
m,f marketing officer; ∼ **de pasivos**
liability manager; ∼ **de propiedades**
estate manager; ∼ **de red** network
manager; ∼ **del sistema** systems
administrator

administrador²: ∼ **del correo**
electrónico *m* postmaster; **A**∼ **de**
Programas *m* Program Manager

administrar *vt* (personal) manage;
(negocio) run; (capital) administer; ∼ **mal**
mismanage; ∼ **los negocios de alguien**
manage sb's affairs

administrativo¹ *adj* administrative; **gastos ~s** administrative expenses

administrativo², **-a** *m,f* administrator

admisibilidad *f* admissibility

admisible *adj* admissible, allowable

admisión *f* admission; (entrada) intake; **por su propia ~** by his own admission; **plazo de ~ de solicitudes** application period; **~ a la cotización** admission to quotation; **~ gratuita** free admission *o* entrance

admitir *vt* admit, acknowledge; (tarjetas, socios) accept, take; **no lo han admitido en la empresa** he was turned down by the company; **no se admiten tarjetas de crédito** no credit cards; **no admite duda** it leaves no room for doubt

admón. *abr* (▶**administración**) admin. (administration)

admonición *f* warning; **~ por mora** formal notice

adopción *f* (de moneda única) adoption

adoptar *vt* adopt; (decisión, postura) take; **~ una postura diferente** take a different view

adquirido *adj* acquired; (beneficiario) vested

adquirir *vt* (acciones) acquire; (comprar) purchase; (compañía) take over; **~ una participación** acquire an interest

adquisición *f* (compra) purchase, acquisition; **~ apalancada** leveraged buyout; **~ de hipoteca** mortgage assumption

adscribir *vt* assign to; **~ a alguien a algo** assign sb to sth

adscripción *f* enrolment BrE, enrollment AmE; (a un trabajo) assignment

aduana *f* customs; **libre de ~** duty-free; **pasar la ~** go through customs

aduanero, **-a** *m,f* customs officer

aducir *vt* adduce, cite

ad valórem *adj* ad valorem

adversario, **-a** *m,f* adversary

adverso *adj* adverse

advertencia *f* warning, word of advice; **sin ~ previa** without previous warning; **~ escrita** written warning; **~ pública** public warning; **~s repetidas** repeated warnings; **~ verbal** verbal warning

advertir *vt* warn, advise; **~ a alguien de algo** warn sb about sth

AELC *abr* (▶**Asociación Europea de Libre Comercio**) EFTA (European Free Trade Association)

AENOR *abr* (▶**Asociación Española de Normalización y Certificación**) ≈ BSI (British Standards Institution), ≈ ASA (American Standards Association)

aéreo *adj* air; **correo ~** airmail; **tráfico ~** air traffic

aerofotogrametría, aerofotometría *f* aerial survey

aerograma *m* aerogram, airmail letter

aeroplano *m* aircraft, aeroplane BrE, airplane AmE

aeropuerto *m* airport

afectación *f* (de fondos) appropriation; (de dinero, cargas) allocation

afectado *adj* affected; **~ adversamente** adversely affected

afectar *vt* affect; (fondos) appropriate; (contrato) allocate; **en lo que afecta a** in reference to

afianzar *vt* guarantee; (ser fiador) stand surety for

afiliación *f* affiliation; **~ sindical** trade BrE *o* labor AmE union membership

afiliado¹ *adj* affiliated; **no ~** unaffiliated

afiliado², **-a** *m,f* affiliate, member

afiliar *vt* affiliate, join; **~ a alguien a algo** make sb a member of sth

afiliarse *v pron*: **~ a** become affiliated to; **~ a un sindicato** join a union

afirmación *f* statement, assertion; (respuesta afirmativa) affirmation; **hacer una ~** make a statement; **~ del mensaje publicitario** copy claim

afirmar *vt* state, assert

afirmarse *v pron* (moneda) firm up; (crecimiento económico) be consolidated

aflojar *vi* (negocio, economía) slow down; (ventas) tail off

afluencia *f* influx; **~ de capital** capital influx

afrontar *vt* (problemas) face, tackle; **~ los hechos** face the facts

agarrotarse *v pron* Esp (Seg) bind

agencia *f* agency; **~ de aduanas** customs agency; **~ de alojamiento** accommodation agency; **~ de cobro de deudas** debt collection agency; **~ de colocaciones** employment agency, recruitment agency; **~ de crédito** credit agency; **A~ de Desarrollo Internacional** International Development Agency; **~ donante** donor agency; **~ de empleo** employment agency, employment bureau; **~ de información** news agency; **~ inmobiliaria** estate agent's BrE, estate ⋯▷

agency BrE, real estate agency AmE; **A~ Internacional de la Energía** International Energy Agency; **A~ de las Naciones Unidas para la Ayuda a la Infancia** United Nations Children's Fund, UNICEF; **~ de noticias** news agency BrE, wire service AmE; **~ de prensa** press agency; **~ de protección de datos** data protection agency; **A~ de Protección del Medio Ambiente** Environmental Protection Agency AmE; **~ de publicidad** advertising agency; **~ publicitaria** advertising agency; **~ de referencias de crédito** credit reference agency; **~ de relaciones públicas** public relations agency; **~ de trabajo** employment agency, recruitment agency; **~ única** sole agency; **~ de venta de billetes** ticket agency; **~ de viajes** travel agency, travel agent's; **~ de voluntariado** voluntary agency

agenda *f* (programa) agenda; (libreta) diary; (para direcciones) address book; **estar en la ~** be on the agenda; **~ electrónica** personal organizer; **~ oculta** hidden agenda; **~ telefónica** telephone book

agentaria *f Spanish national savings trust,* ≈ National Savings Bank

agente *mf* agent; (de pólizas) broker; **~ administrador(-a)** *m,f* managing agent; **~ autorizado(-a)** *m,f* authorized dealer; **~ comercial** sales representative, sales rep ((infrml)); **~ de bolsa, ~ de cambio** stockbroker; **~ de comercio electrónico** e-broker; **~ de compensación** clearing agent; **~ de direcciones** list broker; **~ de exportación** export agent; **~ exterior** overseas agent; **~ financiero(-a)** *m,f* financial agent; **~ inmobiliario(-a)** *m,f* estate agent BrE, realtor AmE; **~ judicial** bailiff; **~ oficial** authorized agent; **~ de patentes** patent agent; **~ de prensa** press agent; **~ de publicidad** media broker, publicity agent; **~ de seguros** insurance broker; **~ de seguros en línea** e-broker; **~ único** sole agent; **~ de ventas** sales agent; **~ de viajes** travel agent

agio *m* agio, speculation

agiotaje *m* agiotage, speculation

agitación *f* unrest

agitar *vt* stir up, disturb; (Banca) churn

aglomeración *f* (mercado) congestion; (Econ) agglomeration; **~ urbana** built-up area

agobiar *vt* (oprimir) stress; (molestar) harass; **estar agobiado** be stressed; **tanto trabajo me agobia** I'm really stressed (out) by all this work

agobio *m* stress

agotado *adj* sold out; (Cont) overspent; (sin existencias) out of stock

agotamiento *m* exhaustion; **~ del ozono** ozone depletion

agotar *vt* (recursos) exhaust; (existencias) sell out

agotarse *v pron* (recursos) run out; (existencias) sell out, run out

agradecer *vt* thank; **quisiera agradecer la ayuda de todos los participantes** I would like to thank all those involved for their help; **agradecemos su carta de ayer** thank you for your letter of yesterday

agradecido *adj* grateful; **estar ~ por algo** be grateful for sth

agrario *adj* agricultural; **productos ~s** agricultural produce

agravar *vt* aggravate, compound

agravio *m* (Der) grievance

agregado[1] *adj* aggregate

agregado[2]**, -a** *m,f* attaché; **~, -a cultural** cultural attaché; **~, -a de defensa** defence attaché BrE, defense attaché AmE; **~, -a militar** military attaché; **~, -a de prensa** press officer

agregar *vt* add; **~ a alguien a algo** attach *o* appoint sb to sth

agresión *f* aggression; (ataque) assault; **una ~** *or* **un acto de ~** an act of aggression; **una ~ a la libertad** an affront to freedom; **~ sexual** sexual assault

agresivo *adj* aggressive; **venta agresiva** hard sell

agrícola *adj* agricultural

agricultor, a *m,f* farmer, agriculturalist; **pequeño ~** smallholder

agricultura *f* agriculture, farming; **~ orgánica** organic farming

agrimensor, a *m,f* surveyor

agroindustria *f* agribusiness, agroindustry

agronomía *f* agriculture, agronomy

agrónomo, -a *m,f* agriculturalist, agronomist

agrosilvicultura *f* agroforestry

agroturismo *m* rural tourism

agrupación *f* (acción) grouping; (grupo) group; (V&M) clustering; **~ por aptitud** ability grouping; **~ en bloque** blocking;

agrupaciones económicas mundiales world economic groupings

agrupamiento *m* grouping; (de productos) bundling

agua *f* water; **hacer** ~ founder; **estar** *or* **nadar entre dos** ~**s** sit on the fence; ~**s jurisdiccionales** territorial waters; ~**s residuales** waste water, sewage

aguacero *m* spate

agudizar *vt* (crisis, problema) aggravate

agudizarse *v pron* (problema) get worse; (competencia) intensify

ahorrar *vt* save; **no** ~ **esfuerzo** spare no effort; **que ahorra tiempo** time-saving

ahorro *m* saving; ~**s** savings; ~ **de patrimonio** life savings

AIE *abr* (▸**Agencia Internacional de la Energía**) IEA (International Energy Agency)

AIF *abr* (▸**Asociación Internacional de Fomento**) IDA (International Development Association)

aire *m* air; **en el** ~ on the air

airear *vt* (opinión, observación) air

aislacionista *adj* isolationist

aislado *adj* insulated; (separado) isolated

aislamiento *m* insulation; (separación) insulation; ~ **acústico** soundproofing; ~ **del ruido** noise insulation; ~ **sonoro** sound insulation

aislar *vt* insulate; (separar) isolate

ajeno[1] *adj*: ~ **a** alien to; ~ **a mi voluntad** beyond my control; **personas ajenas a la empresa** unauthorized personnel

ajeno[2], **-a** *m,f* outsider

ajetreo *m* hustle and bustle

ajustable *adj* adjustable; (horas) flexible; (pensión) index-linked

ajustado *adj* adjusted; (descripción) accurate; (presupuesto) tight

ajustador, a *m,f* adjuster; ~ **independiente** independent adjuster; ~ **de reclamaciones** claims adjuster

ajustar *vt* adjust; ~ **algo a algo** adjust sth to sth; ~ **algo al alza/a la baja** adjust sth upwards/downwards; ~ **algo al valor del mercado** price sth to the market; ~ **cuentas pendientes** settle accounts

ajustarse *v pron*: ~ **a** (normas) conform to, comply with

ajuste *m* adjustment; (de organizaciones) fit; ~ **de amortización** depreciation adjustment; ~ **de apalancamiento** leverage adjustment, gearing adjustment BrE; ~ **de cierre de ejercicio** year-end

adjustment; ~ **del coste** Esp *or* **costo** AmL **de vida** cost-of-living adjustment; ~ **estacional** seasonal adjustment; ~ **estratégico** strategic fit; ~ **del mercado** market adjustment; ~ **de pantalla** screen shot; ~ **salarial** wage adjustment; ~ **de la tasa de interés** interest rate adjustment; ~ **del tipo de interés** interest rate adjustment

alargado *adj* extended, lengthened

alargar *vt* extend, lengthen; ~ **el plazo de presentación de solicitudes** extend the closing date for applications

albacea *mf* (m) executor; (f) executrix

albarán *m* packing slip

albergar *vt* (sitios web) host

albergue *m* (de sitios web) web hosting

alboroto *m* disturbance; ~**s populares** civil riots

alcance *m* scope; (V&M) reach; (importancia) extent, significance; **estar al** ~ **de alguien** be within sb's reach; **estar fuera de** ~ be out of range; **de gran** ~ far-reaching; **de largo** ~ (planificación) long-term; ~ **del acuerdo** scope of agreement; ~ **de mercado** market reach; ~ **de la negociación** bargaining scope

alcanzar *vt* reach; (objetivo) achieve; ~ **un acuerdo** come to *o* reach an agreement; ~ **un máximo de** reach a high of; **no** ~ (expectativas, metas) fall short of; **no** ~ **un objetivo** undershoot a target; ~ **el punto más bajo** hit rock bottom; ~ **el punto de saturación** reach saturation point

alcismo *m* bullishness

alcista[1] *adj* bullish; **una tendencia** ~ an upward trend; **mercado** ~ bull market

alcista[2] *mf* bull

aleatoriamente *adv* at random, randomly

aleatorio *adj* random; **elegidos de forma aleatoria** chosen at random

aleatorización *f* randomization

alegación *f* allegation; (argumentación) pleading; ~ **por deuda** libelling BrE, libeling AmE

alegar *vt* claim; (Der) allege; (razones, motivos) cite; ~ **exención fiscal** claim tax immunity; ~ **ignorancia** plead ignorance

alegato *m* declaration; (de testigo) statement; (oral) allegation; (en favor del acusado) plea

alentador *adj* encouraging

alentar *vt* encourage; ∼ **a alguien a hacer algo** encourage sb to do sth

alerta[1] *adj* alert; **estar** ∼ be on the alert

alerta[2] *f* alert; **en estado de** ∼ on the alert; **poner en** ∼ **a alguien** alert sb; ∼ **roja** red alert; ∼ **sanitaria** health warning

alertar *vt* alert; ∼ **a alguien de algo** alert sb to sth

alevosía *f* premeditation; **con** ∼ maliciously, with malicious intent

alfa *adj* alpha

alfanumérico *adj* alphanumeric

alfombrilla *f* (de ratón) mouse mat

álgebra *f* algebra; ∼ **de Boole** Boolean algebra

algoritmo *m* algorithm; ∼ **de conversión** conversion algorithm

alianza *f* alliance; ∼ **estratégica** strategic alliance; (de empresas) joint venture

alias[1] *adv* alias, also known as

alias[2] *m* alias

aliciente *m* incentive; **ofrecer un** ∼ **para hacer algo** offer an incentive to do sth

alienación *f* alienation

alienar *vt* alienate

alimentación *f* feed; ∼ **por fricción** friction feed; ∼ **del papel** paper feed

alimentador *m* feeder; ∼ **automático** automatic feeder, autofeeder; ∼ **de hojas** sheet feeder; ∼ **de papel** paper feeder

alimentar *vt* feed; (inflación) fuel

alimento *m* food; ∼s **básicos** basic foodstuffs; ∼s **en conserva** tinned BrE *o* canned AmE food; ∼s **frescos** fresh food; ∼s **naturales** health foods

alineación *f* alignment

alinear *vt* align

alinearse *v pron*: ∼ **con algo/alguien** align yourself with sth/sb, side with sth/sb

alistarse *v pron* (matricularse) enrol BrE, enroll AmE, sign up

alivio *m* relief; ∼ **de la deuda** debt relief

allanamiento *m* unlawful entry; ∼ **de morada** breaking and entering

allanar *vt* (problemas) resolve, overcome; ∼ **el camino para algo** smooth the way for sth

almacén *m* (existencias) storehouse, warehouse; **tener algo en** ∼ have sth in stock; **grandes almacenes** department store; ∼ **de datos** data warehouse

almacenaje *m* storage; ∼ **comercial** commercial storage; ∼ **frigorífico** cold storage

almacenamiento *m* warehousing; (Info) storage; ∼ **al aire libre** open storage; ∼ **de archivos** archive storage; ∼ **de datos** data storage; ∼ **intermedio** buffer storage; ∼ **masivo** mass storage; ∼ **refrigerado** cold storage

almacenar *vt* warehouse, stockpile; (datos, mercancías) store

almacenista *mf* trader; (de almacén) warehouseman

almohadilla *f* (de ratón) mat; ∼ **de toque** touch pad

almuerzo de negocios *m* business lunch

alojamiento *m* accommodation; (de sitios web) web hosting; **buscar** ∼ look for accommodation; ∼ **y comida** board and lodging; ∼ **compartido** shared accommodation; ∼ **exento** free lodging; ∼ **hotelero** hotel accommodation; ∼ **web** website hosting

alojar *vt* accommodate; (página web) host

alojarse *v pron* lodge; (Info) log; ∼ **en** stay at

alquilar *vt* (vivienda) hire, let, rent; **se alquila** to let BrE, for rent AmE

alquiler *m* hire, rental; (de propiedad) leasing; (coste de vivienda) rent; **coche de** ∼ hire car BrE, rental car AmE; **pagar el** ∼ pay the rent; ∼ **atrasado** back rent; ∼ **de coches** car hire BrE, auto rental AmE; ∼ **comercial** commercial letting; ∼ **de explotación** operating lease; ∼ **mensual/semanal** monthly/weekly rent; ∼ **de la tierra** ground rent, land rent

alrededor de *prep* around, in the region of

alta *f* membership; **dar de** ∼ **a alguien** discharge sb; **dar(se) de** ∼ join, register; **darse de** ∼ **en en consulado** register with the consulate

altamente *adv* highly; ∼ **competitivo** highly competitive; ∼ **cualificado** highly-qualified, highly-skilled

alteración *f* alteration

alterar *vt* alter

alternar *vt* alternate

alternativa *f* alternative, option; **la mejor** ∼ the best option; **no hay** ∼ there is no alternative

alternativo, -a *m,f* (suplente) substitute
BrE, alternate AmE

alterno *adj* alternate

alto *adj* high; **de alta calidad** high-
quality, up-market; **de ~ nivel** top-level;
de ~ potencial high-calibre BrE, high-
caliber AmE; **de ~ rendimiento** high-
return, high-yielding; **de ~ riesgo** high-
risk; **de ~ secreto** top-secret; **~ cargo**
high office; **~ coste** Esp *or* **costo** AmL
de la vida high cost of living; **alta
definición** high resolution; **alta
densidad** high density; **~ funcionario**
top-ranking official; **~s niveles** high
standards; **~ nivel de vida** high
standard of living; **~s niveles de
contaminación** high levels of pollution;
alta tecnología high technology

altruismo *m* altruism

aluminio *m* aluminium BrE, aluminum
AmE

alza *f* rise; (de economía) upturn,
upswing; **al** *or* **en ~** rising; **el precio de
las acciones sigue en ~** the share price
continues to rise; **~s y bajas** bull and
bear; **jugar al ~** speculate on a bull
market; **~ de capital** capital
appreciation

alzada *f* appeal

a.m. *abr* (▸**ante merídiem**) a.m.

amalgamación *f* amalgamation

amalgamar *vt* amalgamate

amañar *vt* (resultado) fix, rig; (documento)
falsify, tamper with; (cuentas) fiddle

amasar *vt* (fortuna) amass

ambición *f* ambition

ambicioso *adj* ambitious

ambiental *adj* environmental;
contaminación ~ enviromental
pollution; **música ~** mood music

ambientalismo *m* environmentalism

ambientalmente *adv*
environmentally; **~ protegido**
environmentally protected

ambiente *m* atmosphere; (entorno)
environment; **el medio ~** the
environment; **~ laboral** working
environment

ámbito *m* domain; (de demandas) scope;
de ~ nacional/europeo nationwide/
Europe-wide; **~ de cobertura** scope of
coverage

ambos *adj* both; **ambas fechas
inclusive** both dates inclusive

ambulatorio *m* health centre BrE,
health center AmE

amenaza *f* threat; **bajo ~** under
threat; **~ de bomba** bomb scare; **~ de
huelga** strike threat; **~ de muerte**
death threat

amenazar **1** *vt* threaten; **nos ~on
con acudir a los tribunales** they
threatened to take us to court
2 *vi*: **~ con hacer algo** threaten to do
sth; **amenazó con dimitir** he threatened
to resign

amigable *adj* amicable

amnistía fiscal *f* tax break

amortiguar *vt* (crecimiento) dampen

amortizable *adj* amortizable; (bono)
redeemable

amortización *f* depreciation,
amortization, write-off; (de un préstamo)
repayment; (de bono) redemption; **~
acelerada** accelerated amortization *o*
depreciation; **~ de un activo** asset
write-down; **~ acumulada** accumulated
depletion; **~ antes del vencimiento**
redemption before due date; **~
anticipada** (de deuda) anticipated
repayment, early redemption; **~ de
cuota fija** straight-line depreciation; **~
fiscal** tax write-off

amortizar *vt* amortize; (préstamo, deuda,
hipoteca) pay off, repay; (inversión)
depreciate, write down; (bono) redeem

amparar *vt* protect

amparo *m* aid, protection; **~ fiscal** tax
shield

ampliable *adj* open-ended; (equipo)
upgradeable; (programas) expandable

ampliación *f* expansion; (Info)
extension; **~ de la memoria** memory
extension

ampliamente *adv* largely; **~
reconocido** *adv* widely recognized

ampliar *vt* (actividades, empresa) expand;
(investigación, plazo) extend; (personal)
increase; (con incremento de personal)
upsize; **~ la base del impuesto** broaden
the tax base; **~ el límite de tiempo**
extend the time limit

amplio *adj* (margen) wide; (surtido)
extensive; **de amplia base** broad-based

amplitud *f* extent, size; **de gran ~** far-
reaching; **~ de banda** bandwidth; **~ de
cobertura** extent of cover; **~ del
mercado** market size

A/N *abr* (▸**alfanumérico**) A/N
(alphanumeric)

análisis *m* analysis; **hacer un ~ de
algo** carry out an analysis of sth; **~ de
ciclo de vida** life-cycle analysis; **~** ····⋗

comercial commercial analysis; ~ **de competidores** competitor analysis; ~ **de coste-beneficio** Esp *or* **costo-beneficio** AmL cost-benefit analysis; ~ **coste-efectividad** Esp *or* **costo-efectividad** AmL cost-effectiveness analysis; ~ **de los costes** Esp *or* **costos** AmL cost analysis; ~ **de cuentas** account analysis; ~ **financiero** financial analysis, financial review; ~ **a fondo** in-depth analysis; ~ **de mercado** market analysis; ~ **del producto** product analysis; ~ **de proyectos** project analysis; ~ **de riesgos** risk analysis; ~ **de sistemas** systems analysis; ~ **de tendencias** trend analysis; ~ **del valor** value engineering, value analysis; ~ **de ventas** sales analysis

analista *mf* analyst; ~ **de bolsa** chartist; ~ **de mercados** market analyst; ~ **de programas** program analyst; ~ **de sistemas** systems analyst

analítico *adj* analytical, analytic

analizador *m* (Info) analyser BrE, analyzer AmE

analizar *vt* analyse BrE, analyze AmE

analogía *f* analogy; **por** ~ by analogy

analógico *adj* analogical; ~ **a digital** *adj* analogue-to-digital BrE, analog-to-digital AmE

análogo *adj* analogue BrE, analog AmE

anarquía *f* anarchy

anchura *f* (de pensamiento) latitude; ~ **de banda** bandwidth

anexionar *vt* annex

anexo *m* enclosure, attached document; (edificio) annexe BrE, annex AmE; (Der) addendum; ~ **a los estados financieros** notes to the financial statements

angel caído *m* (Bolsa) fallen angel

anidado *adj* (Info) nested

anidamiento *m* (Info) nesting

anidar *vt* (Info) nest

anillo *m* (Info) (en Internet) circle; ~ **web** web ring

animación *f* animation

animar *vt* encourage; (reunión) liven up; (mercado) stimulate

ánimo *m* encouragement; (intención) intention; **con** ~ **de lucro** profit-making, profitable; **sin** ~ **de lucro** nonprofitable, nonprofit-making BrE, nonprofit AmE

aniversario *m* anniversary

anomalía *f* anomaly

anonimato *m* anonymity

anónimo *adj* anonymous; **sociedad anónima** limited company

anotación *f* note; (en texto) annotation; ~ **en cuenta** account entry; ~ **al margen** note in the margin, marginal note

anotar *vt* make a note of, jot down; (texto) annotate; ~ **una entrada** post an entry

ante *prep* before; (posibilidad, dificultad) faced with

antecedentes *m pl* record, background; **poner a alguien en** ~ put sb in the picture; **tener buenos** ~ have a good track record; ~ **crediticios** credit record; ~ **educativos** educational background; ~ **laborales** job history; ~ **penales** police *o* criminal record; **no tener** ~ **penales** have no criminal record, have no previous convictions

antecesor, a *m,f* predecessor; ~ **legal** legal predecessor

antedatar *vt* (cheque, contrato) backdate; (situación) predate

antemano: **de** ~ *adv* in advance, up front; **agradeciendo de** ~ **su respuesta** thanking you in advance for your reply

antememoria *f* cache buffer

ante meridiem *adv* ante meridiem, a.m.

anteproyecto *m* draft, blueprint; ~ **de ley** bill

anterior *adj* previous, preceding; ~ **a algo** prior to sth

anti-ajeno *m* antialiasing

anticíclico *adj* anticyclical

anticipación *f* anticipation; **con (una semana/un mes)** ~ (a week/month) in advance; **¿con cuánta** ~ **hay que pedirlo?** how far in advance does it have to be ordered?; **llegar con** ~ arrive early; **reservar con** ~ book in advance; ~ **del vencimiento** acceleration of maturity

anticipado *adj* (pago) early; (cliente) prospective; **por** ~ beforehand, in advance; **pagar por** ~ pay in advance

anticipar *vt* expect, anticipate; (dinero) advance; ~ **un pago** make an advance payment; ~ **un préstamo** advance a loan

anticiparse *v pron* happen before expected; ~ **a hacer algo** do sth ahead of time

anticipo *m* advance, sum advanced; (de compra) initial outlay; (V&M) retainer; **hacerle un** ~ **a alguien** give sb an

anticorrosivo *adj* corrosion-resistant

anticuado *adj* old-fashioned; (tecnología) outdated, antiquated

anticuarse *v pron* become obsolete

antideslumbrante *adj* (pantalla) antiglare

antidumping *adj* antidumping

antieconómico *adj* uneconomic

antiestatutario *adj* ultravires

antigüedad *f* (en el empleo) seniority

antiguo *adj* former, old; **mi antigua jefa** my former boss *o* ex-boss; **uno de nuestros más ∼s clientes** one of our oldest customers; **∼ cónyuge** former spouse

antiinflacionista *adj* anti-inflationary

antimercadista *adj* antimarket

antimonopolio, antimonopolista *adj* antitrust

antirecesión *adj* antirecession

ANU *abr* (▸**Asociación de las Naciones Unidas**) UNA (United Nations Association)

anual *adj* annual, yearly; **nos cuesta 200.000 euros anuales** it costs us 200,000 euros a year

anualidad *f* annuity; **(Fisc)** yearly allowance

anualizado *adj* annualized

anualizar *vt* annualize

anualmente *adv* annually, yearly

anuario *m* yearbook, annual

anulable *adj* voidable

anulación *f* (de decisión) annulment; (de contrato, prima) cancellation

anulado *adj* annulling

anular *vt* (decisión) annul; (contrato, prima) cancel; (factor) cancel out; (partida contable) write off; (sentencia) quash; **∼ una anotación** reverse an entry

anunciado *adj* advertised; **no ∼** unadvertised; **según ∼ en televisión** as advertised on TV

anunciante *mf* advertiser

anunciar *vt* advertise; (detalles, noticia) announce; **∼ un empleo** advertise a job; **∼ de nuevo** readvertise; **según se anuncia** as reported

anuncio *m* (publicidad) advertisement, commercial; (noticia) announcement; **los pequeños ∼s** the small ads; **poner un ∼ en el periódico** put an advert in the paper; **prohibido fijar ∼s** bill posters will be prosecuted; **∼s breves** *or* **clasificados** classified ads, small ads; **∼ comercial televisivo** television commercial; **∼ destacado** display advertisement; **∼ de dividendo** dividend announcement; **∼ a doble página** double-page advertisement; **∼ de empleo** job advertisement; **∼ de página entera** full-page advertisement; **∼ por palabras** classified ad, classified advertisement; **∼ en prensa** press advertisement

anverso *m* recto

añadido *m* add-on

añadir *vt* add; (detalles, figuras) add in; (números, resultados) add up; (documento) append

año *m* year; **al** *or* **por ∼** per annum, p.a., per year; **∼ hasta la fecha** year to date; **el ∼ a examen** the year under review; **en el ∼ de** in the year of; **a lo largo del ∼** during the course of the year; **segunda parte del ∼** second half of the year; **∼ de adquisición** year of acquisition; **∼ anterior** previous year; **∼ base** base year; **∼ bisiesto** leap year; **∼ de carestía** lean year; **∼ comercial** trading year; **∼ contable** accounting year; **∼ en curso** current year; **∼ de emisión** year of issue; **∼ financiero** financial year; **∼ fiscal** financial year, fiscal year, tax year; **∼ fiscal en curso** current tax year; **∼ fiscal finalizado** tax year ended; **∼ natural** calendar year; **∼ no impositivo** nontaxable year; **∼ nuevo** new year; **∼ pasado** past year; **el ∼ pasado** last year; **∼ pobre** lean year

año-hombre *m* man-year

apaciguar *vt* pacify

apalancamiento *m* leverage, gearing BrE; **∼ de capital** capital leverage, capital gearing BrE; **∼ inverso** reverse leverage, reverse gearing BrE

apalancar *vt* leverage up

aparato *m* device; (político, publicitario) machine; **el ∼ del partido** the party machine

aparejado *adj* (Der) appurtenant; **traer** *or* **llevar ∼** come with; **el puesto trae ∼ un buen salario** the job comes with a good salary

aparejador, a *m,f* quantity surveyor

apartado *m* paragraph; (Fin) subchapter; **∼ de correos** Esp (*cf* ▸**casilla postal** AmL) Post Office Box, P.O. Box; **∼ de defensa** defence ⋯⊳

advance; pedir un ∼ ask for an advance; **sin ∼** no deposit required; **∼ salarial** advance on salary

envelope BrE, defense envelope AmE; ∼ **postal** Esp (*cf* ▶**casilla postal** AmL) Post Office Box, P.O. Box

apartamento *m* AmL (*cf* ▶**piso** Esp) flat BrE, apartment AmE

Apdo. *abr* Esp (▶**apartado de correos**) P.O. Box

apelación *f* appeal; **presentar una** ∼ appeal, lodge an appeal; **ganar/perder en** ∼ win/lose on appeal

apelar *vi* appeal; ∼ **de** *or* **contra una decisión** appeal against a decision; ∼ **ante el tribunal** appeal to the court

apéndice *m* appendix; (**Der**) addendum

apercibimiento *n* notice; (advertencia) warning; **el restaurante fue multado con** ∼ **de cierre** the restaurant was fined and threatened with closure; ∼ **de mejoras** improvement notice; ∼ **de prohibición** prohibition notice

apertura *f* (de reunión) opening; (de plazo, curso) start, starting date; **ceremonia de** ∼ opening ceremony; ∼ **de plicas** bid opening

apilamiento *m* stacking, stockpiling

apilar *vt* stack, stockpile

aplazado *adj* (reunión) postponed; (pago, decisión) deferred

aplazamiento *m* (de reunión) postponement; (de pago, decisión) deferment

aplazar *vt* (reunión) postpone; (pago, decisión) defer; ∼ **la discusión de una enmienda** postpone discussion of an amendment BrE, table an amendment AmE; ∼ **el pago de impuestos** defer tax payment; ∼ **un proyecto** shelve a project

aplicable *adj* applicable; ∼ **a** applicable to; **no** ∼ not applicable

aplicación *f* application; (de medidas) implementation; (de fondos) allocation; **de** ∼ **general** general-purpose; ∼ **de autoservicio** self-service application; ∼ **informática** application; ∼ **de la ley** law enforcement; ∼ **web** web application, web-based application, web-enabled application

aplicado *adj* (ciencias, tecnología) applied; (persona) hard-working; **no** ∼ unappropriated

aplicar *vt* (principio, ley) apply; (costes, fondos) allocate, assign; (medidas) implement; (sanción) impose; (descuento) give; ∼ **la ley contra alguien** bring the law to bear against sb; ∼ **ingresos a un periodo** apply revenues to a period

aplicarse *v pron* come into force; (norma) apply

apoderado, -a *m,f* agent, manager; (en ley civil) proxy; ∼ **en bancarrota** assignee in bankruptcy

apoderar *vt* authorize; (**Der**) grant power of attorney to

apoderarse *v pron*: ∼ **de algo** appropriate sth, take control of sth

apología *f* defence BrE, defense AmE, justification; **hacer una** ∼ **del terrorismo** make a statement defending *o* justifying terrorism

aportación *f* contribution; **aportaciones de los empleados** employee contributions

aportar *vt* contribute; (aval) pledge; (ingresos) bring in; ∼ **algo a algo** contribute sth to sth; ∼ **capital** *or* **fondos** provide capital; ∼ **una contribución** make a contribution; ∼ **una garantía** supply collateral

apostar *vt* bet; ∼ **algo a algo/alguien** bet sth on sth/sb

apoyar *vt* (moneda) support; (moción) second, back; (idea) buy into

apoyo *m* support; **apoyo a algo** support for sth; **el** ∼ **popular** popular support, the support of the people; **retirar el** ∼ **a algo** withdraw support for sth; ∼ **financiero** backing, financial support; ∼ **gerencial** management support; ∼ **del gobierno** government support; ∼ **del mercado** market support; ∼ **de reserva** backup support; ∼ **técnico** technical support; **sin** ∼ **técnico** unsupported; ∼ **por teléfono** telephone support

applet *m* (Info) applet

apreciable *adj* appreciable, substantial

apreciación *f* (de acciones, propiedades) appreciation; ∼ **de méritos** merit rating

apreciar *vt* appreciate; (valorar) value; **apreciamos su ayuda en el asunto** we appreciate your help in the matter; **apreciaron mucho las ideas que aportó a la compañía** they valued highly the ideas he contributed to the company

apremio *m* pressure; (**Der**) court order; ∼ **de tiempo** time pressure

aprendiz, a *m,f* apprentice, trainee BrE, intern AmE; **estar de** ∼ **con alguien** be apprenticed to sb

aprendizaje *m* apprenticeship; (en compañía) training period BrE, internship AmE; ∼ **asistido por computadora** AmL *or* **ordenador** Esp *m* computer-aided learning; ∼ **programado** programmed learning

apresurar *vt* hurry

apretado *adj* (plan de trabajo) tight; (época) difficult, hard; **andamos apretados de dinero** money's a bit short *o* tight

aprobación *f* (de cuentas, préstamo, decisión) approval; (Der) enactment; (producto) endorsement; ∼ **del proyecto** project approval

aprobado *adj* (cuentas, decisión, préstamo) approved

aprobar *vt* (ley) pass; (cuentas, préstamo, decisión) approve; (producto, plan) endorse; **sin** ∼ (opciones) nonapproved; ∼ **una emisión** subscribe to an issue

apropiación *f* appropriation; ∼ **indebida** illegal seizure, misappropriation; **apropiaciones legales** statutory appropriations

apropiar *vt* adapt

apropiarse *v pron*: ∼ **de algo** appropriate sth

aprovechar *vt* take advantage of, make the most of; ∼ **una oportunidad** take advantage of an opportunity; ∼ **el tiempo bien** make the best use of one's time

aprovisionamiento *m* supply; ∼ **del Estado** (UE) public procurement

aprovisionar *vt* supply

aproximación *f* approximation; ∼ **a algo** (acercamiento) approach to sth; ∼ **de coste** Esp *or* **de costo** AmL *f* cost approach

aproximadamente *adv* approximately

Apt. *abr* AmL (▶**apartamento**) flat BrE, apartment AmE

aptitud *f* ability, aptitude; (Cont) qualification; **tener** ∼ **para los negocios** have a flair for business; ∼**es** abilities; ∼ **administrativa** management competence; ∼ **legal** legal competence

apto *adj* (Der) fit and proper; ∼ **para el trabajo** able to work; **ser** ∼ **para hacer algo** be qualified to do sth

Apto. *abr* AmL (▶**apartamento**) flat BrE, apartment AmE

apuesta *f* bet; **hacerle una apuesta a alguien** bet sb sth

apuntalar *vt* (divisa) underpin, prop up

apuntar *vt* note down, make a note of

apuntarse *v pron* put one's name down; ∼ **a un curso** enrol BrE *o* enroll AmE on a course

apunte *m* note; (Cont) entry; ∼ **compuesto** compound entry; ∼ **contable** book entry; ∼ **en el libro diario** journal entry

aquiescencia *f* (del parlamento) assent

arancel *m* tariff; ∼ **aduanero** customs tariff

arancelario *adj* protected by tariffs

arbitraje *m* arbitration; (Bolsa) arbitrage; ∼ **de acciones** stock arbitrage; ∼ **de agravios** grievance arbitration; ∼ **fiscal** tax straddle; ∼ **industrial** industrial arbitration; ∼ **salarial** wage arbitration

arbitrajista *mf* arbitrage dealer, arbitrageur

arbitral *adj* arbitral

arbitrar ⬜1 *vt* (disputa) arbitrate in ⬜2 *vi* arbitrate, act as arbitrator

arbitrario *adj* arbitrary

árbitro, -a *m,f* arbitrator; (Bolsa) arbitrageur; ∼ **judicial** judicial arbitrator

árbol *m* tree; ∼ **de correspondencia** pertinence tree; ∼ **de decisión** decision tree; ∼ **genealógico** family tree

archivado *adj* filed; (Info) archived

archivador[1] *m* filing cabinet

archivador[2]**, a** *m,f* filing clerk BrE, file clerk AmE, archivist

archivar *vt* file; (documentos históricos, ficheros) archive; ∼ **una declaración** (Fisc) file a return

archivero, -a *m,f* filing clerk BrE, file clerk AmE, archivist

archivista *mf* filing clerk BrE, file clerk AmE, archivist

archivo *m* file; (de documentos, ficheros) archive; (ocupación) filing, archiving; ∼ **en anaqueles** open-shelf filing; ∼ **ASCII** ASCII file; ∼ **de auditoría** audit file; ∼ **de caracteres** character file; ∼ **de comandos** command file; ∼ **de firma** signature file; ∼ **fuente** source file; ∼ **gráfico** graphics file; ∼ **índice** index file; ∼ **por materias** subject filing; **A**∼ **Nacional** ≈ Public Record Office BrE; ∼**s policíacos** police files *o* records; ∼ **positivo** positive file; ∼ **de programa** program file; ∼ **de protección** backup file; ∼ **de registro** log file; ∼ **de salida** output file

ardid *m* scheme, stratagem

área *f* area; ~ **de almacenamiento** storage area; ~ **comercial** market place; ~ **de comercio** trading area; ~ **de desarrollo** development area; ~ **edificada** built-up area; ~ **de influencia del dólar** dollar area; ~ **de libre comercio** free-trade area; ~ **de recepción** reception area; ~ **de responsabilidad** area of responsibility; ~ **restringida** restricted area; ~ **rural** rural area; ~ **de trabajo** workspace; ~ **urbana** urban area

arenga *f* harangue

argot *m* slang; ~ **burocrático** officialese

argumento *m* argument; ~ **de supuesto óptimo/pésimo** best-case/worst-case scenario

arma *f* weapon; ~ **de doble filo** double-edged sword BrE, whipsaw AmE; ~ **publicitaria** advertising weapon

armonización *f* harmonization; (de diferencias) reconciliation; ~ **legal** (EU) legal harmonization; ~ **mundial** global harmonization

armonizar *vt* harmonize; (diferencias) reconcile; ~ **algo con algo** bring sth into line with sth

arquitecto, -a *m,f* architect; ~ **de red** network architect

arraigado *adj* long-established, deep-rooted

arrancar *vt* (compañía) start, start up; (ordenador) boot up; (programa) set up

arranque *m* start, start-up; ~ **en caliente** restart, reboot; ~ **en frío** cold start; (Info) cold boot

arrastrar *vt* (atraer) attract; ~ **hacia abajo** (precio) drive down; ~ **una pérdida** carry a loss; ~ **y soltar** drag and drop

arrebatar *vt* snatch; (cautivar) captivate, capture

arreglar *vt* fix; (disputa) settle; ~ **las cosas** sort things out; ~ **cuentas** settle the bill

arreglo *m* agreement, arrangement; (de disputa) settlement; (con un acreedor) composition; **con ~ a** in accordance with; **llegar a un ~ con alguien** come to an agreement *o* arrangement with sb; **que no tiene ~** beyond repair; **tener fácil ~** be easy (enough) to sort out; ~ **extrajudicial** out-of-court settlement; ~ **financiero** financial settlement

arrendado *adj* leased; **no ~** untenanted

arrendador, a *m,f* landlord, lessor

arrendamiento *m* (precio, acuerdo) lease; (de apartamento) leasing, tenancy; ~ **al mes** month-to-month tenancy; ~ **de capital** capital lease agreement; ~ **comercial** business lease, commercial lease; ~ **conjunto** co-tenancy; ~ **de equipo** equipment leasing; ~ **fijo** fixed rent; ~ **perpetuo** perpetual lease; ~ **sin plazo fijo** tenancy at will; ~ **de tierras** land lease

arrendar *vt* let, lease

arrendatario, -a *m,f* leaseholder, lessee, tenant

arriba-abajo *adj* top-down

arriba mencionado *adj* above-mentioned

arribar *vi* arrive; ~ **a** reach, arrive at; ~ **a una conclusión** reach a conclusion

arriendo *m* tenancy, lease, leasehold; ~ **de mercado** market rent

arriesgado *adj* risky

arriesgar *vt* risk; (situación) jeopardize

arroba *f* (en direcciones de e-mail) at (sign)

arruinado *adj* (en quiebra) bankrupt

arruinar *vt* spoil, wreck

arruinarse *v pron* go bankrupt, go broke (infrml); (negocio) go under, go to the wall (infrml)

arte *m* art; (habilidad) skill; **el ~ de lo posible** the art of the possible; ~ **de vender** salesmanship

artículo *m* article; (Fin) item; (de acta) Article; ~**s** goods; ~**s de calidad** quality goods; ~**s de consumo** consumer goods; ~**s de consumo corriente** convenience goods; ~**s cualificados** qualifying items; ~**s defectuosos** faulty goods; ~**s devueltos** returned goods; ~**s de escritorio** stationery; ~**s especializados** speciality goods BrE, specialty goods AmE; ~**s de fin de serie** end-of-line goods; ~ **de fondo** editorial; ~ **gravable** taxable item; ~**s de lujo** luxury goods; ~**s de marca** branded goods; ~**s no desgravables** disallowable items; ~ **de primera necesidad** essential item; ~ **de reclamo** loss leader; ~**s de relleno** (imprenta) fillers; ~**s de valor** valuables; ~**s varios** sundry articles; ~**s de venta difícil** slow-moving goods; ~**s de venta fácil** fast-moving goods

artificial *adj* artificial, man-made

artilugio *m* gadget

asalariado, -a *m,f* salaried person, salary *o* wage earner

asamblea f (reunión) meeting; (cuerpo) assembly; ~ **de accionistas** shareholders' meeting; ~ **de acreedores** creditors' meeting; ~ **anual** annual meeting; ~ **general** general assembly; ~ **general anual** annual general meeting

ascendente adj ascending; (Info) upward

ascender [1] vt advance; (a un empleado) promote; ~ **un puesto** upgrade a post [2] vi (precios) rise; ~ **a** amount to, come to; (empleado) be promoted to

ascensión f promotion; ~ **rápida** fast tracking

ascenso m promotion

asediar vt (mercado) blitz

asegurabilidad f insurability; ~ **garantizada** guaranteed insurability

aseguración f securitization

asegurado adj insured; (garantizado) assured; **no** ~ uninsured; **estar** ~ be insured

asegurador, a m,f insurer, underwriter; ~ **de bienes** property insurer; ~ **de vida** life insurer

asegurar vt (vida, bienes) insure; (precio) secure; (garantizar) guarantee, assure; ~ **algo contra incendios** insure sth against fire; **asegurar algo a** or **contra todo riesgo** take out a fully-comprehensive insurance policy on sth

asentir vi agree; ~ **a algo** agree to sth

asesinato m murder; ~ **en primer grado** murder in the first degree BrE, first-degree murder AmE

asesor, a m,f advisor, consultant; ~ **administrativo(-a)** m,f management consultant; ~ **de crédito** credit adviser; ~ **financiero(-a)** m,f financial adviser; ~ **fiscal** tax adviser; ~ **de imagen** image consultant; ~ **de informática** computer consultant; ~ **jurídico(-a)** m,f (en empresa) in-house lawyer; ~ **legal** counsel, legal adviser; ~ **de marketing** marketing consultant; ~ **político(-a)** m,f spin doctor; ~ **privado(-a)** m,f aide; ~ **de relaciones públicas** public relations consultant; ~ **de selección** recruitment consultant; ~ **técnico(-a)** m,f technical consultant

asesoramiento m advice; (Der) counsel; ~ **bancario** bank advice; ~ **a los empleados** employee counseling AmE, employee counselling BrE; ~ **financiero** financial advice; ~ **jurídico** legal advice

asesorar vt advise, give advice to; ~ **a alguien** (Der) counsel sb

asesoría f consultancy; ~ **de empresas** f management consultancy; ~ **jurídica** legal consultancy; ~ **de relaciones públicas** public relations consultancy

asiento m (para sentarse) seat; (Cont) entry; ~ **de abono** credit entry; ~ **de ajuste** adjusting entry; ~ **de apertura** book of first entry, opening entry; ~ **de cargo** debit entry; ~ **de cierre** closing entry; ~ **de cierre de ejercicio** year-end closing entry; ~ **contable** book entry, accounting entry; ~ **contable suplementario** supplementary entry; ~ **en el libro diario** journal entry; ~ **del mayor** ledger entry; ~ **posterior** post-entry

asignación f allocation, assignment; (Fin) allowance; **sin** ~ ex allotment; ~ **de activos** asset allocation; ~ **de costes** Esp or **costos** AmL f cost allocation; ~ **de empleo** job assignment; ~ **familiar** child benefit BrE, child allowance AmE; ~ **de recursos** resource allocation; ~ **de responsabilidades** allocation of responsibilities; ~ **para vivienda** housing allowance, accommodation allowance

asignado adj allocated; **no** ~ unallocated

asignar vt (tareas, recursos) allocate, allot; (Cont) break down; ~ **fondos** earmark funds

así llamado adj so-called

asilo m asylum; ~ **político** political asylum

asimilación f assimilation

asincrónico adj asynchronous

asistencia f (ayuda) aid, assistance; (a empleo, espectáculo) attendance; ~ **financiera** financial assistance; ~ **de jornada completa** full-time attendance; ~ **jurídica** legal services; ~ **pública** public welfare; ~ **sanitaria** medical care; ~ **social** social security benefit BrE, welfare payment AmE; ~ **técnica** technical assistance, technical support, product support; ~ **a los usuarios** user support

asistente, -a m,f assistant; **los** ~**s** those present; ~ **personal** personal assistant; ~ **técnico(-a)** m,f technical assistant

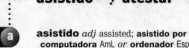

asistido *adj* assisted; **asistido por computadora** AmL *or* **ordenador** Esp *adj* computer-aided, computer-assisted

asistir ① *vt* (personas) assist, aid ② *vi* (a una reunión, junta) attend; **¿cuántos miembros asistieron?** how many members were there *o* attended?; **¿vas a ~ a la reunión?** are you going to the meeting?, will you be attending the meeting?; **~ a una cita** keep an appointment

asociación *f* association; **en ~ con alguien** in association with sb; **A~ de Agentes y Corredores de Futuros** Association of Futures Brokers and Dealers; **~ agrícola** farmers' association; **~ caritiva** charity; **A~ Española de Normalización y Certificación** ≈ British Standards Institution, ≈ American Standards Association; **~ Europea de Libre Comercio** European Free Trade Association; **~ sin fines lucrativos** nonprofit-making association BrE, nonprofit association AmE; **A~ para la Formación y Desarrollo Empresarial** Esp *training and business development association*; **A~ Internacional de Fomento** International Development Association; **~ de marca** brand association; **A~ de Mercados de Negociación** Secondary Market Association; **A~ de las Naciones Unidas** United Nations Association; **~ mutua** mutual association; **~ no lucrativa** nonprofit-making association BrE, nonprofit association AmE; **~ de propietarios** homeowners' association; **~ sindical** trade union (BrE), labor union (AmE); **~ de vecinos** community association

asociado¹ *adj* associated; **~ a** affiliated to; **~ con** in association with; **no ~** unaffiliated

asociado², **-a** *m,f* associate; **~ extranjero(-a)** *m,f* foreign affiliate

asociarse *v pron* collaborate; **~ con alguien** go into partnership with sb; **~ a algo** become a member of sth, affiliate to sth

aspecto *m* aspect; **en ciertos ~s** in certain respects

aspirante *m* candidate, applicant; **~s al puesto** candidates for the post; **~s al poder** those who aspire to power

aspirar *vi*: **~ a algo** aspire to sth; **~ a ser director** he aspires *o* hopes to become director

astilla *f* (infrml) sweetener (infrml), backhander (infrml)

astucia *f* shrewdness, astuteness

asumir *vt* (riesgo) take; (responsabilidad) assume, take on; (poder) assume; (cargo) take up; **~ el control** take over; **~ los costes** Esp *or* **costos** AmL bear the costs; **~ una pérdida** take a loss; **~ el poder** come to power

asunto *m* issue, matter; (incidente, acontecimiento) affair; (Der) case; **el ~ de que se trata** the matter in hand; **el ~ está concluido** the matter is closed; **un ~ en marcha** an ongoing concern; **~s de la agenda** items on the agenda; **~s de la compañía** company affairs *o* matters; **~s corporativos** corporate affairs; **~s económicos** economic affairs; **~ estratégico** strategic issue; **~s europeos** European affairs; **~s exteriores** foreign affairs; **~s internos** domestic affairs, home affairs; **~s pendientes** outstanding matters; **~s políticos** political affairs

atacar *vt* (problema) tackle; **~ a una compañía** raid a company

ataque *m* attack; **ataque a** *or* **contra algo/alguien** attack on sth/sb

atareado *adj* (persona) busy

atasco *m* (de impresora) jam

atención *f* attention; **a la ~ del Sr García** Attention: Mr García; **hora de ~ al público** (de oficina) hours of business; (de tienda) opening times; **para ~ inmediata** for immediate attention; **~ al cliente** customer services; **~ a los pasajeros** passenger care; **~ de la salud** health care

atender *vt* (asunto) deal with; (deuda) honour BrE, honor AmE; (necesidades, gastos) meet; (norma) abide by, comply with; **~ a un cliente** attend to *o* serve a customer; **¿le atienden, Señora?** are you being served, Madam?; **~ una reclamación** meet a claim; **~ a sus obligaciones** meet one's obligations

atenerse *v pron*: **~ a** adhere to; **~ a las reglas** abide by the rules

atentamente *adv* carefully; (en correspondencia) sincerely; **le saluda ~** yours sincerely BrE, sincerely yours AmE

atenuación *f* mitigation

atenuar *vt* weaken; (fluctuaciones) smooth

aterrizaje *m* landing; **~ forzoso** forced *o* emergency landing

atesorar *vt* amass, hoard

atestar *vt* vouch for; (Der) attest

atestiguar *vt* witness; ~ **la firma de alguien** witness sb's signature

atmósfera *f* atmosphere; ~ **controlada** controlled atmosphere

atolladero *m* stumbling block; **salir del** ~ get out of a sticky situation

atracción *f* attraction, appeal; ~ **masiva** mass appeal; ~ **turística** tourist attraction

atractivo¹ *adj* (oferta) attractive

atractivo² *m* appeal; ~ **emocional** emotional appeal; ~ **de las ventas** sales appeal; ~ **visual** visual appeal

atraer *vt* attract; ~ **la atención de alguien** attract *o* grab sb's attention; ~ **nuevos negocios** attract new business

atrapar *vt* (internautas) attract

atrasar *vt* (salida) delay; (reunión) postpone

atrasarse *v pron* fall behind; ~ **en los pagos** fall behind *o* into arrears with payments

atraso *m* delay; ~**s** *m pl* arrears; (de sueldo) back payment; **tener** ~**s** be in arrears

atribución *f* attribution; ~ **de poder** empowerment; **atribuciones** powers; **atribuciones de emergencia** emergency powers

atribuible *adj*: ~ **a algo** attributable to sth; **no** ~ nonattributable

atribuido *adj*: ~ **a algo** attributed to sth

atribuir *vt*: ~ **algo a algo** attribute sth to sth; ~ **algo a alguien** ascribe *o* attribute sth to sb

atributo *m* attribute

audiencia *f* audience; (Der) hearing; **la** ~ **está abierta** the court is now in session; **índice de** ~ ratings; ~ **cautiva** captive audience; **A**~ **Nacional** Esp ≈ High Court BrE; ≈ Supreme Court AmE; ~ **pública** public hearing; ~ **a puerta cerrada** private hearing

audioconferencia *f* audio conference; (acción) audio conferencing

audiomecanografía *f* audiotyping

audiomensajería *f* voice mail

audiovisual *adj* audiovisual

auditabilidad *f* auditability

auditable *adj* auditable

auditado *adj* audited; **no** ~ unaudited

auditar *vt* audit

auditor, a *m,f* auditor; ~**es independientes** independent auditors

auditoría *f* audit; (acción) auditing; ~ **administrativa** administrative audit, management audit; ~ **de cierre de ejercicio** year-end audit; ~ **de cumplimiento** compliance audit; ~ **externa** external audit; ~ **de gestión** management audit; ~ **interina** interim audit; ~ **interna** internal audit; ~ **legal** statutory audit; ~ **medioambiental** environmental audit

AUE *abr* (►**Acta Unica Europea**) SEA (Single European Act)

auge *m* boom; ~ **económico** economic boom; ~ **de posguerra** post-war boom

aumentar **1** *vt* (valor) gain; (salarios, producción) increase; (poder adquisitivo) enhance; (memoria) upgrade; (precios) put up; (ventas) boost; ~ **un déficit** run up a deficit; ~ **la plantilla** *or* **el personal** staff up

2 *vi* increase; ~ **diez veces** increase tenfold; ~ **el doble** double; ~ **lentamente** (precios) edge up; ~ **de valor** gain value

aumento *m* increase, rise; (Bolsa) accretion; ~ **del crédito** credit increase; ~ **del precio** price increase; ~ **salarial** wage *o* salary increase; ~ **salarial retroactivo** backdated pay increase

aunar *vt* (recursos, capacidades) pool

ausencia *f* absence; (falta) lack; **ante la** ~ **de** (información) in the absence of; **en** ~ **de alguien** in sb's absence; ~ **por enfermedad** sick leave; ~ **con permiso** leave of absence; ~ **sin permiso** absence without leave

ausentado, -a *m,f* absentee

ausente *adj* absent; ~ **por enfermedad** absent, off sick (infrml)

austeridad *f* austerity; ~ **económica** economic austerity

autarquía *f* autarchy

autentificación *f* authentification

autentificado *adj* authenticated; **no** ~ unauthenticated; ~ **como copia fiel** certified as a true copy

autentificar *vt* authenticate

auto *m* edict; (Der) court order, decree; ~**s** *m pl* proceedings; ~**s de apelación** appeal proceedings; ~ **de embargo** writ of sequestration; ~ **interlocutorio** interlocutory decree; ~ **de procesamiento** indictment; ~ **de requerimiento** writ of subpoena

autoabastecimiento *m* self-sufficiency

autoactualización *f* self-actualization

autoalmacenamiento *m* (Info) autosave

autoarranque *m* autoboot, autostart

autoayuda *f* self-help

autocargador *m* autoloader

autocartera *f shares in a company held by the company itself*

autoconsumo *m* home consumption

autocontrato *m* self-dealing

autocorrelación *f* autocorrelation

autodirección *f* self-management

autodominio *m* self-control, self-restraint

autoedición *f* desktop publishing, DTP

autoempleo *m* self-employment

autoestable *adj* self-supporting

autoevaluación *f* self-appraisal

autofinanciación *f* self-financing; ~ **de enriquecimiento** retained earnings

autofinanciamiento *m* self-financing

autofinanciarse *v pron* self-finance, finance oneself

autogenerado *adj* self-generated

autogestión *f* self-management

autogobierno *m* self-government

autoimagen *f* self-image

autoliquidación *f* self-liquidation; (tributaria) self-assessment

automáticamente *adv* automatically

automático *adj* automatic

automatización *f* automation; ~ **del dibujo** design automation, drawing automation; ~ **de oficinas** office automation

automatizado *adj* automated; (Info) computerized

automatizar *vt* automate; (Info) computerize

automotivación *f* self-motivation

automóvil *m* car; ~ **de alquiler** hire car BrE, rental car AmE; ~ **de la empresa** company car

autonomía *f* autonomy

autónomo *adj* (departamento, entidad) autonomous; (ordenador) stand-alone, offline; **trabajador** ~ freelance, freelancer

autopista *f* motorway BrE, freeway AmE; ~ **de la información** information highway

autorregulado *adj* self-governing

autoridad *f* authority; ~**es** *f pl* authorities; **tener** ~ **para hacer algo** have the authority *o* power to do sth; **tener** ~ **para firmar** have signing authority; ~ **competente** statutory authority; ~ **para comprar** authority to buy; ~ **expedidora** issuing authority; ~**es fiscales** tax *o* fiscal authorities; ~**es monetarias** monetary authorities; ~**es reguladoras** regulatory authorities

autoritativo *adj* authoritative

autorización *f* authorization, approval; ~ **de pago** payment authorization

autorizado *adj* authorsized; (Patent) licensed

autorizar *vt* authorize; (persona, acción) allow; (editar) release; ~ **a alguien a** *or* **para hacer algo** authorize sb to do sth

autorregulación *f* self-regulation

autoseguro *m* self-insurance

autoselección *f* self-selection

autoservicio *m* self-service

autosostenido *adj* (crecimiento) self-sustained

autosuficiencia *f* self-sufficiency

autosuficiente *adj* self-sufficient

auxiliar[1] *adj* auxiliary; (costes) ancillary

auxiliar[2] *mf* (empleado) junior; ~ **administrativo(-a)** *m,f* administrative assistant

auxiliar[3] *m* assistant; ~ **personal digital** personal digital assistant, PDA

aval *m* guarantee; (Econ) collateral; ~ **bancario** bank guarantee, bank reference; ~ **de la firma** guarantee of signature

avalar *vt* (documento) guarantee; ~ **a alguien** act as guarantor for sb; ~ **un préstamo** secure a loan

avalista *mf* guarantor

avalúo *m* AmL (*cf* ▸**tasación** Esp) appraisal; ~ **de gastos de capital** AmL (*cf* ▸**valuación de gastos de capital** Esp) capital expenditure appraisal; ~ **del proyecto** AmL (*cf* ▸**valoración de proyecto** Esp) project assessment

avance *m* advance; **no hubo** ~**s en las negociaciones** no progress was made in the negotiations; ~ **económico** economic advance; ~ **extraordinario** breakthrough; ~ **de formato** form feed; ~ **de línea** line feed; ~ **de noticias** news flash; ~ **tecnológico** technological progress

avanzado *adj* (aplicaciones, sistemas) advanced

avanzar *vti* advance; ~ **hacia algo** move towards sth

avatar *m* (étapa) phase; (Info) avatar

aventajar *vt* (sobrepasar) surpass

aventurar *vt* (opinión) venture; (dinero) risk, stake; ~ **la causa de algo** speculate on the cause of sth

aventurarse *v pron* dare; ~ **a hacer algo** venture to do sth

avería *f* breakdown, fault; (Cont) average; ~ **común** general average

averiado *adj* not working, out of order

averiarse *v pron* break down, fail

averiguación *f* inquiry; **hacer averiguaciones** make inquiries

averiguar *vt* find out; (hecho) ascertain, establish

aversión *f* aversion; ~ **al riesgo** risk aversion

aviación civil *f* civil aviation

avión *m* aeroplane BrE, airplane AmE, aircraft; **por** ~ by air; ~ **chárter** charter plane; ~ **de línea** airliner; ~ **de pasajeros** airliner, passenger aircraft

avisar *vt* inform, tell; (advertir) warn

aviso *m* (notificación) notice; (advertencia) warning; **dar** ~ **a alguien (de algo)** notify sb (about sth); **estar sobre** ~ be on the alert; **hasta nuevo** ~ until further notice; **según** ~ as per advice; **sin (previo)** ~ without warning *o* notice; ~ **de bomba** bomb alert; ~ **de cancelación** cancellation notice; ~ **de cobertura** cover note; ~ **escrito** written notice; ~ **de mora** notice of arrears; ~ **de objeción** notice of objection; ~ **público** (causa civil) posting; ~ **de quiebra** bankruptcy notice; ~ **de recibo de mercancías** goods received note; ~ **de remesa** remittance slip; ~ **de retirada de fondos** withdrawal notice

ayuda *f* assistance, help; ~**s** *f pl* aids; ~ **alimentaria** *or* **alimenticia** food aid; ~**s audiovisuales** audiovisual aids; **A~ del Automovilista** *Spanish motorists' Organization,* ≈ Automobile Association BrE, ≈ Royal Automobile Club BrE, ≈ American Automobile Association; ~ **compensatoria** ≈ income support BrE, ≈ welfare AmE; **A~ Comunitaria** (UE) Community Aid; ~ **al desarrollo** development aid; ~ **a distancia** remote support; ~ **económica** economic aid; ~ **de emergencia** emergency aid; ~ **del Estado** government assistance; ~ **exterior** foreign aid, overseas aid; ~ **federal** federal aid; ~ **financiera** financial aid; ~ **fiscal** tax assistance; ~ **técnica** technical assistance; ~ **a usuario** help, helpdesk; ~ **vinculada** tied aid

ayudante, -a *m,f* assistant; ~ **general** handyman; ~ **personal** personal assistant; ~ **postal** postal assistant

ayudar *vt* help; (financieramente) aid; ~ **a alguien a hacer algo** help sb do sth; ~ **a alguien con algo** help sb with sth

Ayuntamiento *m* city council, ≈ District Council BrE; (sede de la alcaldía) town hall BrE, city hall AmE

azar *m* chance; **al** ~ at random, randomly; **por** ~ by chance

b

Bb

bache *m* gap; (mal momento) bad patch; ∼ **económico** economic slump; ∼ **inflacionista** inflationary gap

baja *f* fall, drop; (en el mercado) downswing, downturn; (Cont) writing-off; (de plan de pensiones) deregistration; (permiso) leave; (certificado) doctor's *o* medical certificate; **abrir/cerrar a la** ∼ (Bolsa) open/close down; **dar de** ∼ (a empleado) dismiss; (teléfono) have disconnected *o* cut off; **darse de** ∼ (de club, consulado) leave; (de servicio, subscripción) cancel; **estar a la** ∼ (Bolsa) be bearish; **estar de** ∼ be on sick leave; **presentar la** ∼ produce a medical certificate; **seguir a la** ∼ continue to fall; ∼ **densidad por una cara** single-sided single density; ∼ **por enfermedad** sick leave; ∼ **incentivada** voluntary redundancy (*with redundancy pay*) BrE; ∼ **por maternidad** maternity leave; ∼ **médica** sick leave; ∼ **por paternidad** paternity leave; ∼ **presión** low pressure; ∼ **repentina** slump; ∼ **voluntaria** voluntary redundancy BrE

bajada *f* (de precio) fall; ∼ **de las ventas** sales slump

bajar [1] *vi* (valor, acciones, ventas) drop, fall; ∼ **un 10%** fall by 10%, be down 10%; ∼ **de precio** come down in price; **el euro bajó frente al dólar** the euro fell against the dollar
[2] *vt* (precios) lower, reduce, bring down; ∼ **el promedio** average down; ∼ **el tipo de interés** lower interest rates; ∼ **a alguien de categoría** demote sb

bajista¹ *adj* bearish

bajista² *mf* bear

bajo *adj* (interés) low; (comercio) light; **de baja calidad** low-quality, low-grade; **de baja categoría** low-quality; **de baja gama** (producto) down-market; **mantener los precios** ∼**s** keep prices low

bajón *m* (de precios) sharp fall *o* drop; (en el mercado) slump

balance *m* balance; (estado de cuentas) balance sheet, financial statement; **cuadrar un** ∼ balance the accounts; ∼ **de activo y pasivo** assets and liabilities statement; ∼ **de apertura** opening balance; ∼ **de la cartera** portfolio balance; ∼ **de cierre** closing balance; ∼ **de comprobación** trial balance; ∼ **de comprobación ajustado/vencido** adjusted/aged trial balance; ∼ **consolidado** consolidated balance sheet; ∼ **de una cuenta corriente** balance on current account; ∼ **a cuenta nueva** balance brought down; ∼ **descubierto** overdraft; ∼ **de ejercicio** balance sheet; ∼ **final** ending balance; (Cont) bottom line; ∼ **general** balance sheet; ∼ **hipotecario** mortgage statement; ∼ **del mayor** ledger balance; ∼ **de pagos** balance of payments; ∼ **provisional** interim balance; ∼ **de resultados** income statement, earnings report; ∼ **de situación** balance sheet; ∼ **de situación consolidado** consolidated balance sheet

balanza *f* balance; **inclinar la** ∼ tilt the balance, tip the scales; ∼ **comercial** balance of trade; ∼ **por cuenta corriente** current account balance; ∼ **de pagos** balance of payments

banca *f* banking; ∼ **automática** computerized banking; ∼ **automatizada** self-service banking; ∼ **comercial** commercial banking; ∼ **computerizada** computerized banking; ∼ **corporativa** corporate banking; ∼ **directa** direct banking; ∼ **domiciliaria electrónica** electronic home banking; ∼ **electrónica** electronic banking, e-banking, online banking; ∼ **externa** offshore banking; ∼ **financiera** investment banking, merchant banking BrE; ∼ **internacional** international banking; ∼ **libre** free banking; ∼ **mercantil** investment banking, merchant banking BrE; ∼ **telefónica** telebanking, telephone banking, home banking

bancario *adj* bank, banking; **cuenta bancaria** bank account

bancarrota *f* bankruptcy; **al borde de la** ∼ on the verge of bankrupcy; **declararse en** ∼ declare oneself bankrupt; **ir a la** ∼ go bankrupt; ∼ **voluntaria** voluntary bankruptcy

banco *m* bank; ∼ **de ahorros** savings bank; ∼ **central** central bank; **B**∼

Central Europeo (UE) European Central Bank; ~ **comercial** business *o* commercial bank; ~ **de comercio** merchant bank BrE, investment bank AmE; ~ **de consorcio** consortium bank; ~ **de crédito** credit bank; ~ **de datos** database, data bank; ~ **electrónico** e-bank, electronic bank, online bank, Internet bank; ~ **de emisión** issuing bank; ~ **emisor** issuing bank; ~ **de ensayos** test bench; **B**~ **de España** Esp *national bank of Spain,* ≈ Bank of England; **B**~ **Europeo de Inversiones** (mercantil) European Investment Bank; **B**~ **Europeo para la Reconstrucción y el Desarrollo** European Bank for Reconstruction and Development; **B**~ **Exterior de España** *Spanish bank for international trade;* ~ **fiduciario** trust bank; ~ **fusionado** amalgamated bank; ~ **hipotecario** ≈ building society BrE, savings and loan association AmE; **B**~ **Hipotecario de España** *Spanish mortgage bank;* **B**~ **Internacional de Pagos** Bank for International Settlements; ~ **de inversiones** investment bank; ~ **de memoria** memory bank; ~ **mercantil** merchant bank; ~ **multinacional** multinational bank; **B**~ **Mundial** World Bank; ~ **mutualista de ahorros** mutual savings bank; ~ **nacional** national bank; ~ **pagador** paying bank; ~ **de pruebas** test bed; ~ **receptor** receiving bank, recipient bank; ~ **registrado** chartered bank; ~ **de la Reserva Federal** Federal Reserve Bank AmE; ~ **de trabajo** job bank

banda *f* band; ~ **ancha** broadband; ~ **de base** baseband; ~ **fiscal** tax band; ~ **de ingresos** income band; ~ **de sonido** sound track; ~ **sonora magnética** magnetic soundtrack

bandeja *f* tray; ~ **de entrada** in-tray; ~ **de pendientes** pending tray; ~ **de salida** out-tray

bandera *f* flag; ~ **de conveniencia** flag of convenience

banner *m* banner; ~ **publicitario** banner advertisement

banquero, -a *m,f* banker; ~ **comercial** investment banker AmE, merchant banker BrE

barata *f* AmL (*cf* ▸**rebaja** Esp) sale

barato[1] *adj* cheap, low-cost

barato[2] *adv* cheaply; **comprar/vender algo** ~ buy/sell sth cheap

barco *m* boat; (grande) ship; ~ **de cabotaje** coaster; ~ **de carga** cargo boat; ~ **mercante** trading vessel; ~ **de pasajeros** passenger liner

baremo *m* scale

barómetro *m* barometer; ~ **económico** business barometer

barra *f* (en tipografía) slash; ~ **de desplazamiento** scroll bar; ~ **de dirección** address bar; ~ **espaciadora** space bar; ~ **de estado** status bar; ~ **inversa** backslash; ~ **de menús** menu bar; ~ **de navegación** navigation bar; ~ **oblicua** forward slash; ~ **de trabajo** tool bar

barraca *f* stall, booth

barrera *f* barrier; ~ **aduanera** customs barrier; ~ **al comercio** barrier to trade; ~ **arancelaria** tariff barrier; ~ **comercial** trade barrier; **imponer/levantar una** ~ **comercial** impose/lift a trade barrier; ~ **de comunicación** communication barrier; ~ **de entrada** entry barrier; ~ **fiscal** tax barrier; ~ **no arancelaria** nontariff barrier; ~ **protectora** *or* **de seguridad** safety barrier; ~ **de salida** exit barrier

barrio *m* area; (fuera del centro) suburb; (en Londres) borough; **los** ~ **exteriores** the suburbs

basado *adj*: ~ **en** based on, on the basis of; ~ **en nuestras previsiones de ventas** based on our sales forecasts; ~ **en computadora** AmL *or* **ordenador** Esp computer-based; ~ **en PC** (programas, equipamiento, servicio) PC-based

basar *vt*: ~ **algo en algo** base sth on sth

bascular *vi* (Info) toggle

base *f* basis; (sede, fundamento) base; **las** ~**s** *f pl* the rank and file; **con** ~ **en Londres** London-based; **en** ~ **a algo** on the basis of sth; **sobre la** ~ **de que...** on the premise that...; **sobre una** ~ **sólida** on a sound footing, on solid ground; **sobre** ~ **consolidadas** on a consolidated basis; ~ **A** (Cont) A-base; ~ **de un acuerdo** basis of an agreement; ~ **de acumulación** accrual basis; ~ **de capital** capital base; ~ **cero** ground zero; ~ **de clientes** client base, customer base; ~ **del coste** Esp *or* **costo** AmL cost base; ~ **de datos** database; ~ **de datos compartida** shared database; ~ **de datos distribuida** distributed database; ~ **de datos en línea** online database; ~ **de datos relacional** relational database; ~ ⋯›

para la discusión basis for discussion; ～ **económica** economic base; ～ **de efectivo** cash basis; ～ **imponible** tax base, taxable income; ～ **del mercado** market base; ～ **monetaria** monetary base, deposit base; ～ **salarial** salary base; ～ **de valoración** valuation basis

BASIC *abr* (*código de instrucciones simbólicas de carácter general para principiantes*) BASIC (Beginner's All-Purpose Symbolic Instruction Code)

básico *adj* basic; (equipo) base

bastardilla *f* italics; **en** ～ in italics

basura *f* rubbish BrE, garbage AmE, waste; (Info) trash

batería *f* battery; ～ **de seguridad** backup battery

baudio *m* (Info) baud

BCE *abr* (▸**Banco Central Europeo**) ECB (European Central Bank)

BDI *abr* (**beneficio del ejercicio después de impuestos**) profit for the year after tax

BDR *abr* (▸**base de datos relacional**) RDB (relational database)

beca *f* grant, scholarship; ～ **de investigación** research grant

becario, -a *m,f* grant holder; ～ **de investigación** research student

BEE *abr* (▸**Banco Exterior de España**) *Spanish bank for international trade*

BEI *abr* (▸**Banco Europeo de Inversiones**) EIB (European Investment Bank)

beneficiar *vt* benefit; **salir beneficiado de algo** be better off with sth, benefit from sth

beneficiario, -a *m,f* beneficiary; (de cheque) payee; (de subsidio) recipient; (con poder notarial) grantee; (Bolsa) allottee; ～ **designado(-a)** designated beneficiary; ～ **de una renta** annuitant; ～ **de un testamento** beneficiary of a will

beneficiarse *v pron* benefit; ～ **de algo** benefit from sth

beneficiencia *f* charity; **asociación de** ～ charitable organization; ～ **pública** public welfare

beneficio *m* benefit; (ganancia) profit; (de inversiones) return, yield; (de despedida) payoff; **con** ～ **de** at a profit of; **obtener** ～ make a profit; **sin** ～ nonprofit-making BrE, nonprofit AmE, nonprofitable; **sin** ～ **ni pérdida** at-the-money; **sacarle** ～ **a algo** benefit from sth; **vender algo con** ～ sell sth at a profit; ～ **por acción**

earning per share; ～ **acumulado** accumulated profit, earned surplus; ～ **al vencimiento** maturity yield; ～ **antes de impuestos** pre-tax profit; ～ **bruto** gross profit, gross earnings; ～ **bruto de explotación** gross operating income; ～ **a corto plazo** short-term gain; ～ **después de impuestos** after-tax profit; ～s **diferidos** deferred revenue; ～ **del ejercicio** accounting profit; ～ **de explotación** operating profit; ～ **fiscal** tax benefit; ～ **gravable** taxable profit; ～ **imponible** taxable benefit; ～ **de justicia gratuita** entitlement to legal aid; ～ **libre de impuestos** tax-free benefit; ～ **según libros** book profit; ～ **mutuo** mutual benefit; ～ **neto** net profit, net earnings; ～s **retenidos** retained earnings, retained profits

benevolente *adj* benevolent

benévolo *adj* benevolent

best seller *m* bestseller

BHE *abr* (▸**Banco Hipotecario de España**) *Spanish mortgage bank*

bianual *adj* biannual

biblioteca *f* library; ～ **empresarial** business library; ～ **de programas** program library

bidireccional *adj* bidirectional; (impresión) duplex

bien[1] *adv* well; ～ **colocado** well-positioned; ～ **informado** well-informed; ～ **pagado** well-paid; ～ **preparado** well-educated; ～ **situado** well-placed; ～ **surtido** well-stocked

bien[2] *m* asset, commodity; ～es *m pl* goods; (Cont) assets; ～es **de baja calidad** low-quality goods; ～es **de capital** capital goods, capital assets; ～es **en consignación** goods on consignment; ～es **consumibles** expendable goods, wasting assets; ～es **de consumo** consumer goods; ～es **de consumo duraderos** consumer durables, hard goods; ～es **de consumo perecederos** soft goods; ～es **domésticos** household commodities; ～es **duraderos** consumer durables; ～es **de equipo** capital goods, capital assets; ～es **fungibles** fungibles, replaceable goods; ～es **inmuebles** property, real estate AmE; ～es **intangibles** intangible assets; ～es **libres de impuestos** duty-free goods; ～es **de lujo** luxury goods; ～es **manufacturados** manufactured goods; ～es **muebles** moveables; (Der) chattels; ～es **no duraderos** consumer nondurables, nondurable goods; ~**es no fungibles** nonfungible goods; ~**es perecederos** perishable goods; ~**es personales** personal estate; ~**es primarios** primary commodities; ~**es raíces** property, real estate AmE; ~**es semiperecederos** semidurable goods; ~ **sociales** corporate assets; ~**es tangibles** tangible goods

bienal *adj* biennial

bienalmente *adv* biennially, every two years

bienestar *m* welfare; ~ **económico** economic well-being, economic welfare; ~ **social** social welfare

bienintencionado *adj* well-meaning

bifurcación *f* (Info) branch; ~ **condicional** conditional branch

bilateral *adj* bilateral

bilaterales *m pl* (Econ) bilaterals

bilateralismo *m* bilateralism

billete *m* (Banca) bill AmE, note BrE; (Transp) ticket; ~ **abierto** open ticket; ~ **de banco** (bank) bill AmE, banknote BrE, note BrE; ~ **completo** full fare; ~ **económico** economy ticket; ~ **de entrada** entrance ticket; ~ **falso** counterfeit *o* forged bill AmE, forged note BrE; ~ **grande** large denomination bill AmE *o* note BrE; ~ **de grupo** party ticket; ~ **de ida** single ticket; ~ **de ida y vuelta** return ticket BrE, round-trip ticket AmE; ~ **en lista de espera** standby ticket; ~ **pequeño** small denomination bill AmE *o* note BrE; ~ **sencillo** single ticket; ~ **de temporada baja** off-peak ticket

billetero *m* wallet; ~ **electrónico** e-wallet

billón *m* (en GB) billion; (en EEUU) trillion

bimensual *adj* bimonthly, twice a month, fortnightly

bimensualmente *adv* fortnightly

binario *adj* binary

bioagricultura *f* organic farming

biobasura *f* organic waste

biocarburante *m* organic fuel

biodegradabilidad *f* biodegradability

bioeconomía *f* bioeconomics

biogás *m* biogas

biometría *f* biometrics

biotecnología *f* biotechnology

bipolar *adj* bipolar

bisemanal *adj* biweekly, twice a week

bisemanalmente *adv* twice a week, twice-weekly

bit *m* (Info) bit

bitio *m* (Info) bit; ~ **de control** check bit; ~ **de datos** data bit; ~ **de detención** stop bit; ~ **de información** information bit; ~ **de inicio** start bit; ~ **de paridad** parity bit; ~**s por pulgada** bits per inch; ~**s por segundo** bits per second

blanco *m* target; **dar en el** ~ hit the target, be spot on; **en** ~ blank; **dejar algo en** ~ leave sth blank

blanqueo *m* laundering; ~ **de dinero** money laundering

bloque *m* block; ~ **del Este** Eastern Bloc; ~ **comercial** trading block; ~ **de edificios** tower block; ~ **monetario** monetary bloc

bloqueado *adj* blocked

bloquear *vt* block, inhibit

bloqueo *m* blockade; (en negociaciones) deadlock; ~ **de los precios** price freeze

Bluetooth® *m* Bluetooth®

bobina *f* spool; ~ **receptora** takeup reel

bobinar *vt* spool

BOE *abr* (▶**Boletín Oficial del Estado**) *Spanish official gazette*

boicot *m* boycott; **hacer el** ~ **a algo** boycott sth

boicotear *vt* boycott

boicoteo *m* boycott

bola *f* ball; ~ **rodante** (dispositivo señalador) control ball, trackball

boleta *f* AmL (*cf* ▶**vale canjeable** Esp) dealing slip, voucher; (*cf* ▶**papeleta de votación** Esp) (elección sindical) ballot paper, voting paper; (recibo) receipt; ~ **del banco** AmL (*cf* ▶**recibo bancario** Esp) banker's ticket; ~ **de despido** AmL (*cf* ▶**carta de despido** Esp) redundancy letter BrE, pink slip AmL

boletín *m* newsletter, report, bulletin; ~ **comercial** trade report; ~ **de cotizaciones en bolsa** stock list; ~ **de empresa** house journal; **B**~ **Oficial del Estado** *Spanish official gazette*; ~ **de prensa** press release; ~ **de suscripción** registration form

boleto *m* coupon; AmL ticket; ~ **de lotería** *m* lottery ticket

bolsa *f* exchange; **la B**~ the Stock Exchange; ~ **de comercio** commodity exchange, securities exchange; ~ **de contratación** commodity market, commodity exchange; ~ **de divisas** ⋯⟩

b

foreign currency market; **B∼ Internacional** International Stock Exchange; **∼ de Nueva York** New York Stock Exchange; **∼ de pobreza** poverty pocket; **∼ de trabajo** labour pool BrE, labor pool AmE; **∼ de valores** Stock Exchange, Stock Market, securities exchange

bomba *f* bomb; **∼ electrónica** *or* **e-mail** e-mail bomb

bonificable *adj* rebatable

bonificación *f* bonus; (descuento) discount; (Cont) allowance; (devolución) rebate; **∼ fiscal** tax credit; **∼ de interés** interest rebate; **∼ libre de impuestos** tax-free allowance; **∼ por maternidad** maternity allowance; **∼ por traslado** relocation allowance

bonificar *vt* discount

bono *m* voucher; (Fin) bond; **∼ en acciones** share bond; **∼ alcista y bajista** bull-and-bear bond; **∼ de amortización** redemption bond; **∼ de arbitraje** arbitrage bond; **∼ autorizado** authorized bond; **∼ en bancarrota** default bond; **∼ basura** junk bond; **∼ bloqueado** stopped bond; **∼ de capitalización** capitalization bond; **∼ clase AAA** AAA bond, triple A bond; **∼ consolidado** consolidated bond; **∼ convertible** convertible bond; **∼ cupón cero** zero coupon bond; **∼ depositario** bail bond; **∼ descontado** discount bond; **∼ del Estado** government bond AmE; **∼ en mora** defaulted bond; **∼ de paridad** parity bond; **∼ al portador** bearer bond; **∼ del Tesoro** Treasury bond

booleano *adj* Boolean

boom *m* boom; **∼ económico** economic boom

borderó *m* slip; **∼ de aceptación** acceptance slip

borrador *m* draft, working copy; (publicidad) rough; **en ∼** in draft form; **∼ de artículo** *or* **cláusula** draft clause; **∼ de un contrato** draft contract; **∼ de decreto** draft order; **∼ de directiva** (UE) draft directive; **∼ de impresión** print preview; **∼ de presupuesto** draft budget; **∼ de prospecto** draft prospectus; **∼ de riesgo** exposure draft

borrar *vt* delete, erase; **∼ algo de una cinta** wipe sth from a tape; **∼ a alguien de la lista** take *o* strike sb off the list

bosquejo *m* outline, sketch

botiquín *m* first-aid kit; **∼ de emergencia** *or* **primeros auxilios** first-aid kit

botón *m* button; **darle al ∼** press the button; **∼ de privacidad** secrecy button; **∼ del ratón** mouse button; **∼ de rellamada** redial button; **∼ del volumen** volume control

botones *m* office boy

boutique *f* boutique

bóveda *f* vault; **∼ de seguridad** AmL safe-deposit vault, strong room

boyante *adj* (mercado) buoyant; **el negocio está ∼** business is doing really well

BPA *abr* (▸**beneficio por acción**) EPS (earning per share)

BPI *abr* (▸**Banco de Pagos Internacionales**) BIS (Bank for International Settlements)

bpp *abr* (**bitios por pulgada**) bpi (bits per inch)

bps *abr* (**bitios por segundo**) bps (bits per second)

brainstorming *m*: **tener una sesión de ∼** have a brainstorming session

brazo *m* arm

brecha *f* gap; **∼ deflacionaria** deflationary gap; **∼ inflacionaria** inflationary gap; **∼ en el mercado** gap in the market; **∼ tecnológica** technological gap

breve *adj* short; **en ∼** shortly; **en ∼s palabras** in short, briefly; **un ∼ resumen** a brief summary

brevedad *f* brevity; **con la mayor ∼ posible** as soon as possible, a.s.a.p.

broker *mf* AmL broker, stockbroker

browse: **hacer un ∼** *fra* (Internet) browse

brusco *adj* (descenso) sudden, sharp

bruto *adj* gross; **beneficio ∼** gross profit

bucle *m* loop; **∼ local** local loop

bueno *adj* good; **en buen estado** in good repair; **∼s antecedentes mercantiles** *m pl* good business background; **buen negocio** good business; **en buena posición** in a good position; (economicamente) well off; **buenas noticias** good news

bufete *m* law firm

buhonero *m* huckster (infrml)

buque *m* vessel, ship; **∼ de carga** Esp (*cf* ▸**fletero** AmL) cargo ship BrE, freighter AmE; **∼ cisterna** tanker; **∼ costero** coaster; **∼ mercante** merchant

ship, merchant vessel; ~ **nodriza**
mother ship; ~ **de pasajeros** passenger
liner

burocracia *f* bureaucracy; (papeleo) red
tape

burócrata *mf* bureaucrat

burocrático *adj* bureaucratic

burocratización *m* bureaucratization

burocratizar *vt* bureaucratize

buromática *f* office automation

burótica *f* office automation

bursátil *adj* stock-exchange, stock-
market; **mercado** ~ stock market

bus *m* (equipo) bus; ~ **común de
dirección** address bus; ~ **de datos**
data bus

buscador *m* browser; ~ **fuera de
línea** offline browser

buscar *vt* search, look for; (ayuda) seek;
(ejecutivo) headhunt; ~ **averías**
troubleshoot; ~ **clientes** seek clients,
tout for custom; ~ **a alguien por medios
publicitarios** advertise for sb; ~ **un
mercado** seek a market; ~ **trabajo** look
for a job, job-hunt; **se busca** wanted

busca y cambia *fra* (Info) search and
replace

búsqueda *f* search; **hacer una** ~ do a
search; **en** ~ **de algo** in search of sth; ~
automática global search; ~ **avanzada**
advanced search; ~ **de Boole** Boolean
search; ~ **ejecutiva** executive search;
~ **de empleo** job hunting; ~ **genérica**
generic search; ~ **en el Internet**
Internet search; ~ **de palabra clave**
keyword search; ~ **de puesto de
trabajo** job search; ~ **y sustitución**
search and replace

bustos parlantes *m pl* (en televisión)
talking heads

butaca *f pl* (en teatro) seat; ~ **de
patio** seat in the stalls BrE *o* orchestra
AmE

buzón *m* letter box BrE, postbox BrE,
mailbox AmE; (de e-mail) inbox, mailbox;
~ **de e-mail** *or* **correo electrónico**
inbox, mailbox; ~ **de envío** outbox;
~ **de sugerencias** suggestion box;
~ **telefónico** *or* **de voz** voice
mailbox

buzoneo *m* AmL (*cf* ▶**lista de
direcciones** Esp) mailing list; ~ **de
propaganda** AmL (*cf* ▶**envío
publicitario, propaganda por correo**
Esp) mailing

Cc

CA *abr* Esp (▸**Comunidad Autónoma**) *territory governed as a unit with a certain degree of autonomy,* ≈ county BrE

caballaje *m* AmL, **caballo de vapor** *m* Esp horsepower

cabalmente *adv* accurately, exactly

cabecera *f* header; (de periódico) headline; (página) head

cabeza *f* head; **estar a la ∼ de la lista** be top of the list; **ir en ∼** be in the lead; **por ∼** per capita, per head; **∼ de borrado** erase head; **∼ de familia** head of household; **∼ lectora-grabadora** read-write head; **∼ de lectura** read head; **∼ de la liga** top of the league; **∼ de lista** front-runner; **∼ magnética** magnetic head; **∼ de turco** (infrml) scapegoat, fall guy (infrml) AmE

cabina *f* booth; **∼ electoral** polling booth, voting booth; **∼ de portazgo** tollbooth; **∼ de teléfono** Esp (*cf* ▸**locutorio** AmL) telephone box BrE, call box AmE

cable *m* cable; **televisión por ∼** cable tv; **∼ coaxial** Esp *or* **coaxil** AmL pipeline; (Info) coaxial cable **∼ de conexión a tierra** grounding cord; **∼ de fibra óptica** fibre-optic cable BrE, fiber-optic cable AmE; **∼ de suspensión** carrying cable, running cable; **∼ de sustentación** light cable

CAC *abr* (▸**compromiso de aseguramiento continuado**) RUF (revolving underwriting facility)

CAD *abr* (*diseño asistido por computadora* AmL *or* *ordenador* Esp) CAD (computer-aided design)

CADD *abr* (*diseño y dibujo asistido por computadora* AmL *or* *ordenador* Esp) CADD (computer-aided design and drafting)

cadena *f* (de almacenes, restaurantes) chain; (Info) string; (de radiodifusión) network; **∼ afiliada** affiliated chain; **∼ alimenticia** food chain; **∼ de bancos** banking group BrE, bank group AmE; **∼ de bitios** bit string; **∼ de caracteres** character string; **∼ continua de montaje** line production; **∼ de distribución** chain of distribution, distribution chain; **∼ de ensamblaje**
assembly line; **∼ de fabricación** production line; **∼ de grandes almacenes** department store chain; **∼ de marketing** marketing chain; **∼ de montaje** assembly line; **∼ de órdenes** chain of command; **∼ perpetua** life sentence, life imprisonment; **∼ de producción** flow line, production line; **∼ de suministro** supply chain; **∼ de televisión** television network; **∼ de tiendas** retail chain

caducado *adj* expired, lapsed

caducar *vi* expire, lapse

caducidad *f* expiry BrE, expiration AmE; **fecha de ∼** expiry date BrE, expiration date AmE; (de alimento) sell-by date; **∼ artificial** artificial obsolescence; **∼ programada** built-in obsolescence

caer *vi* (precios, gobierno) fall; **∼ en desuso** fall into abeyance; **∼ en picado** plummet, fall sharply

CAI *abr* (*instrucción asistida por computadora* AmL *or* *ordenador* Esp) CAI (computer-aided instruction)

caída *f* collapse, fall; (de tensión eléctrica) brownout; **∼ en desuso** obsolescence; **∼ en desuso artificial** artificial obsolescence; **∼ en desuso dinámica** dynamic obsolescence; **∼ en desuso funcional** functional obsolescence; **∼ de la demanda** fall in demand; **∼ de la divisa** currency fall; **∼ del dolar** fall (in the value) of the dolar; **∼ en las inversiones** drop in investments; **∼ en picado** collapse, sharp fall; **∼ en picado del mercado** market dive; **∼ de la producción** fall in production; **∼ de tensión** power failure; **∼ de ventas** slump in sales

caja *f* box; (en tienda) cash desk, till; (en banco) window; (en supermercado) checkout; **abonar/pagar un cheque en ∼** cash/pay in a cheque BrE *o* check AmE at the desk; **hacer la ∼** cash up; **∼ de ahorros** savings and loan association AmE, building society BrE; **∼ de alquiler** safe-deposit box, safety-deposit box; **∼ de caudales** safe, strongbox; **∼ chica** petty cash; **∼ para depósitos de seguridad** safety-deposit box; **∼ de diálogo** dialogue box BrE, dialog box

AmE; ~ **de fichas** card catalogue BrE, card catalog AmE; ~ **fuerte** safe, strongbox; ~ **negra** black box; ~ **de pensiones** (state) pension fund; ~ **registradora** cash register; ~ **de seguridad** safe-deposit box, safety-deposit box

cajero¹, -a *m,f* cashier, checkout assistant BrE, checkout clerk AmE; ~ **adjunto(-a)** *m,f* assistant cashier BrE, assistant teller AmE; ~ **bancario(-a)** *m,f* bank teller

cajero²: ~ **automático** *or* **bancario** *m* cashpoint BrE, (automated) cash dispenser BrE, automated teller machine AmE

calculadora *f* calculator; ~ **de bolsillo** pocket calculator; ~ **electrónica** electronic calculator

calcular *vt* calculate; (anticipar) estimate, forecast; ~ **que...** estimate that...; ~ **el espacio tipográfico** cast off; ~ **mal** miscalculate

cálculo *m* calculation; (Cont) reckoning; **hacer un** ~ **(aproximado)** calculate (roughly), make a (rough) estimate; **hoja de** ~ spreadsheet; **según mis** ~**s** according to my calculations; ~ **de costes** Esp *or* **costos** AmL costing; ~ **de costes** Esp *or* **costos** AmL **diferenciales** marginal costing; ~ **de costes** Esp *or* **costos** AmL **funcionales** functional costing; ~ **de costes** Esp *or* **costos** AmL **marginales** marginal costing; ~ **del impuesto sobre la renta** income tax assessment; ~ **de precios** pricing; ~ **de ventas** sales estimate

calderilla *f* small change

calendario *m* calendar; (de un proyecto) schedule; ~ **de pagos** schedule of repayments; ~ **de taco** tear-off calendar

calibración *f* calibration; **calibraciones personales** *f pl* (Info) preference settings

calibre *m* (del personal) calibre BrE, caliber AmE

calidad *f* quality; (función) capacity; **de** ~ **aceptable** of acceptable quality; **control de** ~ quality control; **en** ~ **de asesor** in an advisory capacity; **en su** ~ **de director** in his capacity as director; **de poca** ~ poor-quality, third-rate; **de primera** ~ high-quality, top-quality; **productos de** ~ quality goods; ~ **de letra** letter quality; ~ **de la mano de obra** quality of the labour BrE *or* labor AmE force; ~ **normal** basic grade; ~ **de**

vida quality of life; ~ **de vida en el trabajo** quality of working life

calificación *f* qualification; (RRHH) banding; ~ **de méritos** merit rating; ~ **mínima** (requerida en un examen) minimum mark BrE *o* grade AmE; ~ **del personal** personnel rating; ~ **de solvencia** credit score; ~ **triple A** triple-A rating

calificar *vt* describe, rate; ~ **algo/a alguien de algo** describe sth/sb as sth; **la califican de buena jefa** they rate her as a boss

calificatorio *adj* qualifying

calle *f* street; ~ **comercial** shopping street; ~ **mayor** *or* **principal** high street BrE, main street AmE

callejón *m* alley; ~ **sin salida** impasse, dead end; (en una calle) cul-de-sac

calma *f* lull, calm; (en negocio) quiet patch

columnia *f* defamation, calumny (frml); (oral) slander; (escrita) libel

calumniar *vi* (oralmente) slander; (por escrito) libel

calumnioso *adj* slanderous; (artículo) libellous BrE, libelous AmE

calzada *f* carriageway

CAM *abr* (*fabricación asistida por computadora* AmL *or* *ordenador* Esp) CAM (computer-aided manufacturing)

cámara *f* (de reuniones, juicios) chamber; ~ **de abogados** (barristers') chambers BrE; ~ **acorazada** (bank) vault, strong room; **C~ Alta** Esp ≈ House of Lords BrE, ≈ Senate AmE; **C~ Baja** Esp ≈ House of Commons BrE, ≈ House of Representatives AmE; ~ **del circuito cerrado de televisión** CCTV camera, closed-circuit TV camera; ~ **de comercio** trading room; **C~ de Comercio** Chamber of Commerce; **C~ de Comercio Americana** American Board of Trade, American Chamber of Commerce; **C~ de Comercio Española** Spanish Chamber of Commerce; **C~ de Comercio e Industria** Chamber of Commerce and Industry; **C~ de Comercio Internacional** International Chamber of Commerce; ~ **de compensación** clearing house; ~ **de compensación internacional** international clearing house; ~ **lenta** slow-motion safe; ~ **de movimiento ocular** eye-movement camera; ~ **de observación ocular** eye-observation camera

cambiar **1** *vt* change, exchange; (viejo modelo por el nuevo) trade in; (sustituir) ⋯✦

replace; ~ **algo por algo** change *o* exchange sth for sth; ~ **euros a dólares** change euros into dollars; ~ **materias primas por bienes manufacturados** trade raw materials for manufactured goods

2 *vi* change; ~ **de dueño** change hands; ~ **de idea** change one's mind; ~ **de imagen** re-image; ~ **de tema** change the subject; ~ **de trabajo** change jobs

cambio *m* change; (Bolsa) swop, amendment; (monedas) small change; (de moneda extranjera) bureau de change, change; (de precio) change; (Pol) (a izquierda o derecha) swing; **a ~** in exchange; **a ~ de algo** in return for sth; **sobre el ~** (acciones) at a premium; ~ **al contado** spot price; ~ **completo** turnaround, U-turn; ~ **de control** change in power; ~ **de dirección** change of address; (en negocio) change of management; ~ **de empleo** change of job; ~ **estacional** seasonal swing; ~ **estructural** structural change; ~ **fijo** fixed *o* pegged exchange rate; ~ **flotante** floating exchange; ~ **de marca** (por consumidores) brand switching; (por empresa) rebranding; ~ **oficial** official rate; ~ **organizacional** organizational change; ~ **de página** page break; ~ **a la par** par trading; ~ **a plazo** forward price, forward rate; ~ **político** political change; ~ **porcentual** percentage change; ~ **de profesión** career change; ~ **de propietario** under new ownership; ~ **de rescate** (UE) buying-in price; ~ **del tipo de interés** interest rate movement; ~ **de turno** change of shift; ~ **de venta** selling rate

cambista *mf* arbitrageur, foreign exchange dealer

camino *m* path; ~ **crítico** critical path

camión *m* lorry BrE, truck AmE; ~ **cisterna** tanker (lorry) BrE, tank truck AmE; ~ **de mudanza** removal van; ~ **de reparto** delivery truck, delivery lorry BrE

camionero, -a *m,f* lorry driver BrE, teamster AmE

campaña *f* campaign; ~ **alcista** bull campaign; ~ **bajista** bear campaign; ~ **electoral** election campaign; ~ **de limpieza** cleanup campaign; ~ **de marketing** marketing campaign; ~ **nacional** national campaign; ~ **de pancartas publicitarias** poster campaign; ~ **de prensa** press campaign; ~ **de productividad** productivity drive; ~ **promocional**

promotional campaign; ~ **publicitaria** advertising campaign; ~ **publicitaria mediante banners** (en el Internet) banner campaign; ~ **de ventas** sales drive

campo *m* area, field; **en un ~ limitado** in a limited sphere; ~ **de actividad** sphere of activity; ~ **de almacenamiento** storage field; ~ **de datos** data field; ~ **de dirección** address field; ~ **de identificación** tag; ~ **petrolífero** oil field; ~ **de referencia** target field; ~ **técnico** technical field

canal *m* channel; (marítimo) canal; **cambiar de** ~ change channels; ~ **analógico** analogue BrE *o* analog AmE channel; ~ **comercial** trade channel; ~ **de comercialización** distribution channel, marketing channel; ~ **de comunicación** channel of communication; ~ **de distribución** distribution channel; ~ **de información** information channel; ~ **de pago** subscription channel; ~ **de pedidos** channel for orders; ~ **publicitario** advertising channel; ~ **selector** selector channel; ~ **de televisión** television channel; ~ **de ventas** sales channel

canalizar *vt* channel; ~ **algo a través de algo** channel sth through sth; ~ **algo debidamente** put sth through the proper channels; ~ **fondos hacia un proyecto** channel funds into a project

canasta *f* basket; ~ **de dinero** basket of rates; ~ **familiar** AmL (▶**cesta de la compra** Esp) shopping basket; ~ **de monedas** AmL (▶**cesta de monedas** Esp) basket of currencies

cancelación *f* (de pedido) cancellation; (de contrato) annulment; (Cont) write-off; ~ **de la deuda** debt cancellation; ~ **de una hipoteca** discharge of mortgage; ~ **de un pagaré** redemption of a promissory note; ~ **parcial** part-cancellation; ~ **de préstamo** loan write-off; ~ **total** write-off

cancelar *vt* cancel; (contrato) annul; (deuda) settle, pay off; (Cont) charge off; (partida contable) write off; (hipoteca) pay off

cancillería *f* chancery

candidato, -a *m,f* candidate; ~ **propuesto(-a)** *m,f* nominee

candidatura *f* candidature, candidacy

canje *m* exchange, swop; ~ **de activos** asset swop; ~ **de bonos** bond switch

canjeabilidad *f* convertibility

canjeable *adj* exchangeable, redeemable

canjear *vt* exchange, redeem; ~ **algo por algo** exchange sth for sth

canon *m* royalty, royalties

cantidad *f* quantity; (Cont) volume; (de bienes) amount; ~ **a abonar** amount due; **esta ~ no figura en las cuentas** this sum does not appear in the accounts; ~ **adeudada** amount due; ~ **amortizable** depreciable amount; ~ **aplazada** deferred amount; ~ **base** base amount; ~ **básica** basic amount; ~ **cargada** amount charged; ~ **en descubierto** overdrawn amount; ~ **desembolsada** amount paid out; ~ **específica** specific amount; ~ **en exceso** excess amount; ~ **exenta** exempted amount; ~ **ingresada en una cuenta** amount credited to an account; ~ **inicial** initial quantity; ~ **por invertir** amount to be invested; ~ **llevada a cuenta nueva** amount carried forward; ~ **media** average amount; ~ **mínima** minimum amount; ~ **pagada** amount paid; ~ **pagada a plazos** amount paid by instalments BrE *o* installments AmE; ~ **pagadera** amount payable; ~ **a pagar** amount due; ~ **de pedido** order quantity; ~ **pendiente** amount outstanding; ~ **de punto muerto** break-even quantity; ~ **reembolsable** amount repayable

cantón *m* canton

capa *f* (Info) layer; ~ **de conexiones seguras** secure sockets layer; ~ **de ozono** ozone layer

capacidad *f* ability, capability, aptitude; (profesional) capacity; **a plena ~** at full capacity; ~ **de hacer algo** ability to do sth; ~ **de ganar dinero** earning capacity; **tener gran ~ para algo** have an aptitude for sth; ~ **adquisitiva** purchasing power; ~ **de almacenamiento** storage capacity; ~ **de ampliación** extensibility; ~ **asesora** advisory capacity; ~ **de beneficio** earning power; ~ **de cálculo** computing power; ~ **competitiva** competitiveness; ~ **contributiva** taxpaying ability; ~ **crediticia** creditworthiness; ~ **económica** economic capacity; ~ **empresarial** entrepreneurship; ~ **de endeudamiento** borrowing capacity; ~ **excedente** spare capacity, surplus capacity; ~ **máxima** maximum capacity; ~ **de memoria** storage capacity, memory capacity; ~ **normal**

normal capacity; ~ **de pago** ability to pay; ~ **de producción** production capacity; ~ **profesional** job skills; ~ **para el puesto** competence for the job; ~ **sobrante** spare capacity

capacitación *f* training; ~ **asertiva** assertiveness training; ~ **complementaria** booster training; ~ **por computadora** AmL *or* **ordenador** Esp computer-based training; ~ **dentro de la empresa** in-house training, training within industry; ~ **gerencial** management training; ~ **grupal** group training; ~ **interna** in-company training, in-house training; ~ **en multimedia** multimedia training; ~ **ocupacional** employment training; ~ **por ordenador** Esp *or* **computadora** AmL computer-based training; ~ **de personal** staff training; ~ **profesional** vocational training; ~ **en el trabajo** in-service training, on-the-job training

capacitado *adj* qualified; ~ **para algo/hacer algo** qualified for sth/to do sth; ~ **para el trabajo** qualified for the job

capacitar *vt* train, qualify; ~ **a algn para algo** qualify sb for sth

capataz, a *m,f* overseer, foreman; ~ **a pie de obra** site foreman

CAPE *abr* (▶**compra apalancada por ejecutivos**) LMBO (leveraged management buyout)

capear *vt* weather; ~ **la recesión** weather the recession

capillas *f pl* proofs

capitación *f* capitation

capital *m* capital; ~ **accionario** share capital; ~ **en acciones diferidas** deferred stock; ~ **de los accionistas** shareholders' equity; ~ **amortizado** amortized capital, sunk capital; ~ **aportado** contributed capital; ~ **de arranque** start-up capital; ~ **de base consolidado** consolidated base capital; ~ **bloqueado** frozen capital; ~ **circulante** circulating capital, working capital; ~ **contable** shareholders' equity; ~ **declarado** stated capital; ~ **desembolsado** paid-out capital, paid-up capital; ~ **emitido** issued capital; ~ **de empréstito** loan capital; ~ **fijo** fixed assets, fixed capital; ~ **flotante** floating capital; ~ **de inversión** investment capital; ~ **invertido** invested capital; ~ **de negocio** business assets; ~ **pagado** paid-in capital, paid-up capital; ~ **retraído** locked-in capital; ~ **(de)** ···⟶

riesgo risk capital, venture capital; ∼ **(de) riesgo de una corporación** corporate venture capital, CVC; ∼ **social** (Bolsa) share capital, stockholders' equity; (Econ) social capital; ∼ **social en acciones** equity capital BrE, capital stock AmE; ∼ **social emitido** issued share capital; ∼ **social fijo** overhead capital; ∼ **variable** variable capital; ∼ **vencido** matured capital; ∼ **a la vista** callable capital

capitalismo m capitalism; ∼ **benevolente** benevolent capitalism; ∼ **de Estado** state capitalism; ∼ **salvaje** or **tardío** black capitalism

capitalista¹ adj capitalist

capitalista² mf capitalist; ∼ **de riesgo** venture capitalist

capitalización f capitalization; ∼ **del impuesto** tax capitalization; ∼ **del interés** capitalization of interest; ∼ **de mercado** market capitalization

capitalizado adj capitalized

capitalizar vt capitalize; (interest) compound

capitán m captain; ∼ **de empresa** captain of industry

capítulo m chapter, budget item

captación f (Medios) pick-up; ∼ **de datos** data acquisition

captura f capture; ∼ **de datos** data capture; ∼ **total permitida** (Med amb) total allowable catches

cara f (de hoja) side; **de una** ∼ single-sided; **de** ∼ **a** vis-à-vis

carácter m character; **con** ∼ **oficioso** on-the-record; **sin** ∼ **oficial** off-the-record; ∼ **alfanumérico** alphanumeric character; ∼ **en blanco** blank character; ∼ **de borrado** delete character; ∼ **de cambio de código** escape character; ∼ **comodín** wildcard character; ∼ **de control** check character; ∼ **de encuadramiento** justification character, layout character; ∼ **gráfico** graphic character; ∼ **ilegal** illegal character; ∼ **en negrita** bold character; ∼ **numérico** numeric character; ∼ **de retroceso** backspace character; ∼ **de tabulación** tabulation character; ∼ **de verificación** control character

característica f feature, characteristic; ∼ **adicional** additional feature; ∼ **especial** special feature; ∼ **principal** main feature; ∼**s del puesto** job features

carate m AmL (cf ▸**quilate** Esp) carat

carátula f (de vídeo) case; (de libro) title page; AmL covering letter

carburante m fuel; ∼ **sin plomo** lead-free fuel

carecer vi: ∼ **de** lack

carencia f lack, shortage; ∼ **de personal** manpower shortage

careo m (en un tribunal) confrontation

carestía f high cost; ∼ **de liquidez** liquidity famine; ∼ **de la vida** high cost of living

carga f load; (Fin) charge; (Fisc) burden; (Transp) cargo, freight; **libre de** ∼ unencumbered; ∼**s** charges; ∼ **adicional** additional charge; ∼ **automática** (Info) autologin; ∼**s comerciales** business charges; ∼ **de la deuda** debt burden; ∼**s extraordinarias** extraordinary charges; ∼ **familiar** dependant; ∼ **fijas** fixed charges; ∼ **fiscal** tax burden; ∼ **de polución** pollution charge; ∼ **de la prueba** burden of proof; **la** ∼ **de la prueba recae en la acusación** the burden of proof lies with the prosecution; ∼ **real** encumbrance; ∼ **de trabajo** workload

cargable adj loadable; ∼ **por teleproceso** adj downloadable

cargar **1** vt (cuenta) debit; (cobrar) charge; (Info) (datos) upload; (programa) load; ∼ **algo a algo** charge sth to sth; ∼ **un gasto a una cuenta** charge an expense to an account; ∼ **instrucciones** bootstrap; ∼ **interés** charge interest **2** vi load; ∼ **con la responsabilidad** shoulder the responsibility

cargo m charge; (puesto) post, position; **hacerse** ∼ **de algo** take charge of sth; **hacerse** ∼ **de la cuenta** take care of the bill BrE o check AmE; **correr a** ∼ **de algn** be sb's responsibility; **los gastos corren a** ∼ **de la empresa** expenses will be paid by the company; **sin** ∼ **adicional** without additional charge; **negar todos los** ∼**s** deny all charges; ∼ **auxiliar** junior position; ∼**s bancarios** bank charges; ∼**s de la deuda** debt charges; ∼ **devengado** accrued charge; ∼ **diferido** deferred charge; ∼ **directivo** or **de director** managerial position; ∼ **directo** direct debit; ∼ **ejecutivo** managerial position; ∼ **elegido** elected office; ∼ **por el empréstito** borrowing fee; ∼**s estimados** estimated charges; ∼ **por exceso de equipaje** excess baggage charge; ∼ **fijo** fixed charge; ∼ **importante** important office; ∼ **de**

llamadas call charge; ~ **de mantenimiento** maintenance fee; ~ **por operaciones** operating charge; ~ **público** (UE) public office; ~ **por servicios** service charge; ~ **al superávit** surplus charge; ~**s por tramitación** handling charges; ~ **al usuario** charge-back

carnet, **carné** *m* membership card; (de identidad) identity card; ~ **de conducir** Esp (*cf* ▸**licencia de conducir** AmL) driving licence BrE, driver's license AmE; ~ **de identidad** identity card

caro *adj* expensive; **vender/comprar algo muy** ~ charge/pay a lot for sth

carpeta *f* folder; **cerrar la** ~ close the file; ~ **de antecedentes** case history

carpetazo *m*: **dar** ~ **a algo** shelve sth, close sth; **dar** ~ **a un proyecto** shelve a project

carrete *m* reel; (de película) film, roll of film; ~ **G** G-spool

carretera *f* road; ~ **de circunvalación** ring road BrE, beltway AmE; ~ **general** main road; ~ **nacional** *or* **principal** A-road BrE, highway AmE

carril *m* lane; ~ **de tránsito** traffic lane

carrito *m* trolley; ~ **electrónico** electronic shopping trolley *o* cart

carro *m* trolley; ~ **para equipaje** baggage trolley BrE, baggage cart AmE

carta *f* letter; ~ **al director** (prensa) letters to the editor; **escribir una** ~ write a letter; **echar una** ~ **(al correo)** post BrE *o* mail AmE a letter; ~ **abierta** open letter; ~ **de aceptación** letter of agreement; **C**~ **de Acuerdo del Cliente** Client Agreement Letter; ~ **adjunta** covering letter; ~ **de agradecimiento** thank-you letter; ~ **de asignación** letter of assignment; (Fin) allotment letter; ~ **de autorización** letter of authority; ~ **de aviso** advice note; ~ **blanca** carte-blanche; **darle** ~ **blanca a alguien (para hacer algo)** give sb carte-blanche (to do sth); ~ **bomba** letter bomb; ~ **certificada** registered letter; ~ **de cesión** (de negocio) letter of assignment; ~ **circular** circular; ~ **de cobranza** dunning letter; ~ **de cobro** collection letter; ~ **comercial** business letter; ~ **de compañía** accompanying letter; ~ **de compromiso** letter of undertaking; ~ **de confirmación** confirmation letter; ~ **de cooperación** letter of cooperation; ~ **por correo aéreo** airmail letter; ~ **de crédito** letter of credit; ~ **de declaración**

representation letter; **C**~ **de Derechos del Ciudadano** Citizen's Charter; ~ **de despido** Esp (*cf* ▸**boleta de despido** AmL) redundancy letter BrE, pink slip AmE; ~ **de dimisión** letter of resignation; ~ **de disculpas** letter of apology; ~ **estándar** standard letter; ~ **fiduciaria** trust letter; ~ **franqueada** franked letter; ~ **de garantía** letter of commitment; ~ **de gracia** letter of respite; ~ **de indemnización** letter of indemnity; ~ **de insistencia** follow-up letter; ~ **de intención** letter of intent; ~ **de introducción** letter of introduction; ~ **de moratoria** letter of respite; ~ **de pago** receipt (*confirming payment in full*); ~ **personalizada** personalized letter; ~ **poder** letter of attorney, proxy; ~ **de presentación** letter of introduction; ~ **de rechazo** rejection letter; ~ **de reclamación** letter of complaint; ~ **de recomendación** reference, letter of recommendation; ~ **recordatoria** follow-up letter; ~ **rehusada** dead letter; ~ **de renuncia** resignation letter; ~ **de seguimiento** follow-up letter; **C**~ **Social** (UE) Social Charter; **C**~ **Social Europea** European Social Charter; ~ **de solicitud** letter of application; ~ **verde** green card; ~ **por vía aérea** airmail letter; ~ **de vinos** (restaurantes) wine list

cartel *m* poster; (consorcio) cartel; **prohibido fijar** ~**es** bill posters will be prosecuted; **lleva seis semanas en** ~ it has been on for six weeks; ~ **internacional** international cartel; ~ **luminoso** neon sign

cartelera *f* AmL bulletin board AmE, noticeboard BrE

cartelización *f* cartelization

cartelón *m* (hombre-anuncio) sandwich board

carteo *m* correspondence; ~ **masivo** mass mailing

cartera *f* (de actividad del gobierno) portfolio; (para documentos) briefcase; **ministro sin** ~ minister without portfolio; **tener algo en** ~ have sth in the pipeline; ~ **de acciones** stock *o* share portfolio; ~ **de activos** asset portfolio; ~ **de bonos** holding of bonds; ~ **de clientes** client portfolio, portfolio of clients; ~ **comercial** trading portfolio; ~ **empresarial** business portfolio; ~ **de existencias** stock portfolio; ~ **de inversiones** investment portfolio; ~ **de pedidos** order book; **la** ⋯⋮

cartero ···❖ causahabiente

C~ **de Salud** the Department of Health, the Health portfolio; ~ **de valores** equity holdings, stock portfolio

cartero *m* postman BrE, mailman AmE

cartilla de ahorros *f* savings book

cartón *m* cardboard; (de embalaje) strawboard; ~ **duro** fibreboard BrE, fiberboard AmE; ~ **ondulado** corrugated board; ~ **ordinario** chipboard

cartoné: **en** ~ *adj* hardback, casebound

cartucho *m* cartridge; ~ **de cinta** ribbon cartridge; ~ **de monedas** coin wrapper

casa *f* house; (empresa) company, firm; **buscar** ~ look for somewhere to live; **cambiarse** *or* **mudarse de** ~ move (house); ~ **de** care of, c/o; **invita la** ~ it's on the house; **vino de la** ~ house wine; ~ **de aceptaciones** accepting house; ~ **adosada** semidetached house BrE, duplex AmE; ~ **de arbitraje** arbitrage house; **la C**~ **Blanca** the White House; ~ **de cambio** exchange office; ~ **compradora** buying house; ~ **discográfica** record company; ~ **editorial** publishing house; ~ **emisora** issuing house; ~ **de empeño** pawnshop; ~ **familiar** family house; ~ **filial** affiliated firm; ~ **franca** free house; ~ **de liquidación** clearing house; ~ **matriz** head office; ~ **matriz financiera** financial holding company; ~ **minorista** retail house; ~ **modelo** show house; **C**~ **de la Moneda** Mint; ~ **móvil** mobile home; ~ **prefabricada** manufactured home, prefabricated house; ~ **principal** head office; ~ **de valores** securities house

casado *adj* married; ~ **legalmente** legally married; **estar** ~ **con alguien** be married to sb

casar *vt* marry

casarse *v pron* get married; ~ **con alguien** marry sb, get married to sb

cascada: **en** ~ *adj* cascading, in cascade; **ventanas en** ~ cascading windows

casco *m* (de obrero) safety helmet, hard hat; (de ciclista) crash helmet; (zona) area; ~ **protector** hard hat; ~ **urbano** built-up area; ~ **viejo** old quarter

casete *f* cassette; (grabador) cassette recorder

cash-flow *m* cash flow; ~ **negativo/positivo** negative/positive cash flow

casilla *f* (de formulario) box BrE, check box AmE; ~ **de correos** *or* **postal** AmL (*cf*

▸**apartado de correos** Esp) Post Office Box, P.O. Box; ~ **electrónica** e-mail address

casillero *m* (compartimento) pigeonhole; ~ **para fichas** card bin; (mueble) set of pigeonholes

caso *m* case; **en el** ~ **de** with reference to; **en** ~**s como ese** in situations like that; **en ningún** ~ on no account; **en último** ~ as a last resort; **hacer** ~ **de algo** take notice of sth; **hacer** ~ **omiso de algo** ignore sth, take no notice of sth; **hacerle** ~ **a alguien** take notice of sb, pay attention to sb; **pongamos por** ~ **que...** let's suppose *o* assume that...; **se ha dado el** ~ **de** there have been cases of; ~ **cuestionable** *or* **límite** borderline case; ~ **fortuito** act of God; ~ **modelo** textbook case

castigar *vt* punish; (penar) penalize

catalizador *m* catalyst; **servir de** ~ act as a catalyst

catalogar *vt* catalog AmE, catalogue BrE; (clasificar) classify; (en una lista) record

catálogo *m* catalogue BrE, catalog AmE; **compra por** ~ mail order shopping; ~ **en línea** e-catalogue BrE, e-catalog AmE; ~**s en línea** brochureware; ~ **de venta por correo** mail order catalog AmE *o* catalogue BrE

catastral *adj* cadastral

catastro *m* land register *o* registry, cadastre

catedrático-a *m,f* professor

categoría *f* category; **de** ~ quality; **de primera** ~ first-class, top-quality; **de** ~ **superior** (posición) senior; ~ **fiscal** *or* **impositiva** tax bracket; ~ **de la inversión** investment grade; ~ **profesional** professional status; ~ **salarial** wage bracket; ~ **social** social category; ~ **única** single status

categórico *adj* categorical

categorización *f* categorization

caución *f* security, guarantee

caudal *m* volume, flow; ~ **de transferencia de datos** data transfer rate

causa *f* cause, reason; (Der) lawsuit, trial; **por** ~ **de** because of, on account of; **ver una** ~ **a puerta cerrada** hear a case in camera; ~ **de acción** cause of action; ~ **civil** lawsuit; ~ **criminal** criminal case

causahabiente *m* successor

causar *vt* (problema, inquietud) cause; **me causó muy buena impresión** I was very impressed with her

cautelar *adj* cautionary

cauteloso *adj* cautious

cazade talentos *f* headhunting

cazador, a: ~ **de gangas** *m,f* bargain hunter

cazatalentos *mf* (de ejecutivos) headhunter; (de modelos, artistas) talent scout

cc *abr* (▸**copia carbón**) cc (carbon copy)

c/c *abr* (▸**cuenta corriente**) c/a (current account) BrE, checking account AmE

CCI *abr* (▸**Cámara de Comercio e Industria**) CCI (Chamber of Commerce and Industry)

c.d. *abr* (▸**certificado de depósito**) c.d. (certificate of deposit)

c/d *abr* (▸**casa de**) c/o (care of)

CD-I *abr* (▸**disco compacto interactivo**) CD-I (compact disc BrE *o* disk AmE interactive)

CD-ROM *abr* (▸**disco compacto con memoria sólo de lectura**) CD-ROM (compact disc BrE *o* disk AmE read-only memory)

CDTI *abr* (▸**Centro para el Desarrollo Tecnológico Industrial**) *Spanish centre for industrial and technological research*

CE *abr* (▸**Comunidad Europea**) (obs) EC (European Community); (▸**Consejo de Europa**) CE (Council of Europe)

CECA *abr* (▸**Confederación Española de Cajas de Ahorro**) *Spanish savings banks' association*

cedente *mf* assignor

ceder ⓵ *vt* give up; (Der) transfer, cede, assign; ~ **tierras al Estado** transfer *o* cede land to the State
⓶ *vi* (en negociaciones) give in, give way; (Pol) stand down

cédula *f* licence BrE, license AmE; ~ **de caducidad** (Cont) lapsing schedule

CEE *abr* (obs) (▸**Comunidad Económica Europea**) (obs) EEC (European Economic Community)

celda *f* cell; ~ **binaria** bit location

celebrar *vt* celebrate; (reunión, cumbre) hold; ~ **una conferencia** hold a conference; ~ **un convenio** enter into an agreement; ~ **juicio** sit in judgment

celebrarse *v pron* take place; **el congreso se celebrará en Barcelona**

the conference will take place *o* be held in Barcelona

célula *f* cell

CEN *abr* (▸**Comité Europeo para la Normalización**) CEN (European Committee for Standardization)

censo *m* census; **hacer un** ~ conduct a census; ~ **demográfico** population census; ~ **electoral** electoral register, electoral roll; ~ **de población** (estadística) population census

censor *m* censor, watchdog; ~ **jurado de cuentas** chartered accountant BrE, certified accountant BrE, certified public accountant AmE

censura *f* censorship; **censura de cuentas** audit, auditing

censurar *vt* censor; (criticar) strongly criticize; (Cont) audit

centavo *m* cent; **estar sin un** ~ be broke (infrml)

centímetro *m* centimetre BrE, centimeter AmE; ~**s de columna** (Medios) column inches BrE, column centimeters AmE; ~**-columna** single column centimetre BrE, single column centimeter AmE

central¹ *adj* central; (Info) front-end

central² *f* (oficina principal) head office; (de energía) station; ~ **eléctrica** power station; ~ **de energía nuclear** nuclear power station; ~ **hidroeléctrica** hydroelectric power station; ~ **telefónica** telephone exchange

centralita *f* switchboard

centralización *f* centralization

centralizado *adj* centralized; (Internet) host-driven

centralizar *vt* centralize

centrar *vt* centre BrE, center AmE; (investigación) focus; ~ **algo en algo** focus sth on sth

céntrico *adj* central

centro *m* centre BrE, center AmE; ~ **de actividad** hub of activity; ~ **administrativo** administrative centre BrE, administrative center AmE; ~ **de beneficios** profit centre BrE, profit center AmE; ~ **de cálculo** computer centre BrE, computer center AmE; ~ **de capacitación** training centre BrE, training center AmE; ~ **ciudad** town centre BrE, city centre BrE, downtown AmE; ~ **comercial** shopping centre BrE, shopping precinct BrE, shopping mall AmE; ~ **comercial electrónico** *or* **virtual** cybermall, e-mall; **C**~ **del** ⋯>

Comercio Mundial World Trade Center; ~ **de compensación** clearing centre BrE, clearing center BrE; ~ **de costes** Esp or **costos** AmL m cost centre BrE, cost center AmE; ~ **cultural** cultural centre BrE, cultural center AmE; ~ **de datos corporativos** corporate data centre BrE, corporate data center AmE; **C**~ **para el Desarrollo Tecnológico Industrial** Spanish centre for industrial and technological research; ~ **de descuento** discount centre BrE, discount center AmE; ~ **de distribución** distribution centre BrE, distribution center AmE; ~ **de educación a distancia** correspondence school, distance learning centre BrE, distance learning center AmE; ~ **de educación técnica** technical college; ~ **de exposición** exhibition centre BrE, exhibition center AmE; ~ **financiero** financial centre BrE, financial center AmE; ~ **de formación (profesional)** training centre BrE, training center AmE; ~ **de gastos** cost centre BrE, cost center AmE; ~ **de ingresos** revenue centre BrE, revenue center AmE; **C**~ **de Investigaciones Sociológicas** Spanish social studies institute; ~ **de llamadas** call centre BrE, call center AmE; ~ **de negocios** business centre BrE, business center AmE; ~ **neurálgico** nerve centre BrE, nerve center AmE; ~ **de ocio** leisure centre BrE, leisure center AmE; ~ **de procesamiento de datos** computer centre BrE, computer center AmE; ~ **de procesamiento de texto** word-processing centre BrE, word-processing center AmE; ~ **de responsabilidad** responsibility centre BrE, responsibility center AmE; ~ **de salud** health centre BrE, health center AmE; ~ **de ultramar** offshore centre BrE, offshore center AmE; ~ **urbano** urban centre BrE, urban center AmE

CEOE abr (▸**Confederación Española de Organizaciones Empresariales**) Spanish association of business organizations, ≈ CBI (Confederation of British Industry)

CEPAL abr (▸**Comisión Económica para América Latina**) UN-ECLA (United Nations Economic Commission for Latin America)

CEPE abr (▸**Comisión Económica para Europa**) ECE (Economic Commission for Europe)

CEPYME abr Esp (▸**Confederación Española de la Pequeña y Mediana Empresa**) Spanish confederation of small and medium sized companies

cerca f (Bolsa) hedge

cercanías f pl commuter belt

cerrado adj (Com gen) closed; ~ **por reformas** closed for refurbishment; ~ **al público** closed to the public

cerradura f lock; (Info) keylock; ~ **de seguridad** safety lock; (Info) keylock

cerrar 1 vt (tienda, negocio) close; (definitivamente) close down; (salida) seal off; ~ **un acuerdo** close a deal; ~ **una posición** close a position; ~ **un trato** make a deal; ~ **una venta** complete o close a sale
2 vi close down

certidumbre f certainty

certificación f certification; ~ **de cuentas** accounts certification

certificado¹ adj (carta, paquete) registered; (fotocopia) certified

certificado² m certificate; ~ **de acciones** share certificate BrE, stock certificate AmE; ~ **de adeudo** debt certificate; ~ **de aeronavegabilidad** airworthiness certification; ~ **de ahorro** savings certificate; ~ **de bono** bond certificate; ~ **de caja** cash certificate; ~ **de cobertura** covering warrant; ~ **de competencia** certificate of competency; ~ **de defunción** death certificate; ~ **de depósito** certificate of deposit; ~ **de despacho** clearance papers; ~ **digital** digital certificate; ~ **de dividendo diferido** scrip dividend; ~ **de estudios** school-leaving certificate; ~ **de exención** exemption certificate; ~ **de fideicomiso de tierras** m land trust certificate; ~ **de franqueo** certificate of posting, postage certificate; ~ **de impedimento legal** estoppel certificate; ~ **impositivo** tax certificate; ~ **de inversión** investment certificate; ~ **médico** medical certificate; ~ **de nacimiento** birth certificate; ~ **de origen** certificate of origin; ~ **al portador** bearer certificate; ~ **de registro** (de propiedad intelectual) certificate of registration; ~ **de salud** certificate of health; ~ **de título** certificate of title; ~ **tributario** tax certificate

cesación f (de interés, pago) suspension, cessation

cesar 1 vt (personal) dismiss, make redundant BrE, sack; (pagos) suspend, stop; ~ **a alguien (en** or **de su puesto)** dismiss sb (from his/her job), sack sb (from his/her job); ⁓ **el trabajo** leave work

2 *vi* stop, cease; (empleado) resign, leave one's job; ⁓ **de hacer algo** stop doing sth; **sin** ⁓ without stopping, nonstop; **trabajar sin** ⁓ work nonstop

cese *m* (despido) dismissal, termination; (dimisión) resignation; (interrupción) stoppage, cessation; **darle el** ⁓ **a alguien** dismiss *o* sack sb; ⁓ **con preaviso** termination with notice; ⁓ **de pagos** suspension of payments

cesión *f* (de bienes, derechos) transfer, assignment, cession (frml); (**Fisc**) disposal, release; ⁓ **de arriendo** assignment of lease; ⁓ **de cartera** cession of portfolio; ⁓ **de derechos** assignment of rights; ⁓ **del excedente** surplus stripping; ⁓ **de una patente** surrender of a patent

cesionario, -a *m,f* assignee; (poder notarial) grantee

cesión-arrendamiento *f* leaseback

cesionista *m,f* grantor; (derechos de sucesión) transferor

cesta *f* basket; ⁓ **de la compra** Esp (▸**canasta familiar** AmL) shopping basket; ⁓ **electrónica** electronic shopping basket; ⁓ **de monedas** Esp (▸**canasta de monedas** AmL) basket of currencies; ⁓ **de productos** basket of goods; ⁓ **de tipos** basket of rates; ⁓ **virtual** electronic shopping basket, virtual shopping basket

cestillade archivo *f* filing basket

CFC *abr* (▸**clorofluorocarbono**) CFC (chlorofluorocarbon)

CFI *abr* (▸**Corporación de Finanzas Internacionales**) IFC (International Finance Corporation)

CGA *abr* (▸**adaptador color/gráficos**) CGA (colour/graphics adaptor BrE, color/graphics adaptor AmE)

chanchullo *m* price rigging, racket (infrml)

chantaje *m* blackmail; **hacerle** ⁓ **a alguien** blackmail sb

chantajear *vt* blackmail

chantajista *mf* blackmailer

chapa *f* (de un profesional) nameplate, plaque; ⁓ **de matrícula** numberplate BrE, license plate AmE

chapucero, -a *m,f* (infrml) cowboy (infrml)

chaquetero *adj* (infrml) turncoat (infrml)

charla *f* (en Internet) chat; **C**⁓ **Interactiva Internet** Internet Relay Chat; ⁓ **en línea** online chat, Web chat; ⁓ **en tiempo real** real-time chat

charlar *vi* (en Internet) chat

charola *f* AmL tray; ⁓ **de pendientes** pending tray; ⁓ **de salida** out-tray

chárter *m* charter (flight)

chartismo *m* chartism

chat *m* (en Internet) chat room

chatarra *f* spoilage; (**Med amb**) scrap metal

chatarrero, -a *m,f* scrap dealer

chatear *vi* (en el Internet) chat

checar *vt* AmL (*cf* ▸**fichar** Esp) check in; ⁓ **la tarjeta** AmL (*cf* ▸**fichar la entrada** Esp) clock in, clock on BrE, punch in AmE; (*cf* ▸**fichar la salida** Esp) clock out, clock off BrE, punch out AmE

cheque *m* cheque BrE, check AmE; **cobrar un** ⁓ cash a cheque BrE *o* check AmE; **pagar con** ⁓ pay by cheque BrE *o* check AmE; **un** ⁓ **a nombre de alguien** a cheque BrE *o* check AmE made out to sb; ⁓ **abierto** open cheque BrE, open check AmE; ⁓ **anulado** cancelled cheque BrE, canceled check AmE; ⁓ **bancario** (*cf* ▸**cheque de gerencia** AmL) bank *or* banker's cheque BrE, bank *o* banker's check AmE; ⁓ **barrado** crossed cheque BrE, crossed check AmE; ⁓ **en blanco** blank cheque BrE, blank check AmE; ⁓ **bloqueado** stopped cheque BrE, stopped check AmE; ⁓ **de caja** cashier's cheque BrE, officer's cheque BrE, officer's check AmE; ⁓ **cancelado** cancelled cheque BrE, canceled check AmE; ⁓ **por la cantidad de** cheque BrE *o* check AmE to the amount of; ⁓ **certificado** certified cheque BrE, certified check AmE; ⁓ **no cobrado** uncashed cheque BrE, uncashed check AmE; ⁓ **sin cobrar** unpresented cheque BrE, unpresented check AmE; ⁓ **para cobrar en efectivo** cheque BrE *o* check AmE made to cash; ⁓ **compensado** cleared cheque BrE, cleared check AmE; ⁓ **confirmado** marked cheque BrE, marked check AmE; ⁓ **conformado** certified cheque BrE, certified check AmE; ⁓ **cruzado** crossed cheque BrE, crossed check AmE; ⁓ **no cruzado** uncrossed cheque BrE, uncrossed check AmE, open cheque BrE, open check AmE; ⁓ **sin cruzar** uncrossed cheque BrE, uncrossed check AmE; ⁓ **devuelto** returned cheque BrE, returned check AmE, bounced cheque BrE (infrml), bounced check AmE (infrml); ⁓ **de dividendos** dividends cheque BrE, dividends check AmE; ⁓ **endosado** ⋯⋗

third-party cheque BrE, third-party check AmE; ~ **falsificado** or **falso** forged cheque BrE, forged check AmE; ~ **a favor de** cheque in favour of BrE, check in favor of AmE; ~ **de fecha atrasada** stale-dated cheque BrE, stale-dated check AmE; ~ **sin fondos** bad cheque BrE, bad check AmE, uncovered cheque BrE, uncovered check AmE; ~ **en garantía** memorandum cheque BrE, memorandum check AmE; ~ **de gerencia** AmL (cf ►**cheque bancario**) bank or banker's cheque BrE, bank o banker's check AmE; ~ **impagado** dishonoured cheque BrE, dishonored check AmE, unpaid cheque BrE, unpaid check AmE; ~ **incobrable** bad cheque BrE, bad check AmE; ~ **no librable** undeliverable cheque BrE, undeliverable check AmE; ~ **libre** open cheque BrE, open check AmE; ~ **limitado** limited cheque BrE, limited check AmE; ~ **de mostrador** counter cheque BrE, counter check AmE; ~ **nominativo** pay-self cheque BrE, pay-self check AmE; ~ **a la orden** negotiable cheque BrE, negotiable check AmE; ~ **de la paga** pay cheque BrE, pay check AmE; ~ **no pagado** dishonoured cheque BrE, dishonored check AmE, unpaid cheque BrE, unpaid check AmE; ~ **en pago de dividendos** dividend warrant; ~ **al portador** bearer cheque BrE, bearer check AmE; ~ **posdatado** or **posfechado** postdated cheque BrE, postdated check AmE; ~ **postal** postal cheque BrE, postal check AmE; ~ **no presentado** unpresented cheque BrE, unpresented check AmE; ~ **regalo** gift certificate; ~ **registrado** registered cheque BrE, registered check AmE; ~ **rehusado** dishonoured cheque BrE, dishonored check AmE; ~ **por valor de** cheque to the amount of BrE, check to the amount of AmE; ~ **sin valor** worthless cheque BrE, worthless check AmE; ~ **vencido** overdue cheque BrE, overdue check AmE; ~ **de ventanilla** counter cheque BrE, counter check AmE; ~ **de viajero** traveller's cheque BrE, traveler's check AmE

chequera f chequebook BrE, checkbook AmE

chip m chip; ~ **biológico** biochip; ~ **de memoria** memory chip; ~ **de silicio** silicon chip

chocar 1 vi (coches) crash; ~ **con algo** collide with sth; (enfrentarse) come up against sth; ~ **con alguien** clash with sb; ~ **con los derechos de alguien** impinge on sb's rights; ~ **con la ley** fall foul of the law; ~ **con un obstáculo** come up against an obstacle, hit a problem
2 vt (asombrar) shock

choque m shock; (conflicto) clash; ~ **cultural** culture shock; ~ **de oferta** supply shock; ~ **de personalidades** personality clash; ~ **de productividad** productivity shock

CI abr (►**circuito integrado**) IC (integrated circuit)

Cía. abr (►**compañía**) Co. (Company)

ciberadicto mf cyberholic

cibercafé m cybercafe

ciberciudadano, -a m,f cybercitizen

cibercomercio m Web commerce

cibercomprador, -a m,f Internet shopper, cybershopper

ciberconsumidor, a m,f cyberconsumer, Internet shopper, online shopper

cibercrimen m cybercrime

cibercriminal mf cybercriminal

cibercultura f cyberculture

ciberespacio m cyberspace

ciberguerra m information war o warfare

ciberintermediario, -a m,f cyberintermediary

ciberlibrería f online bookshop o bookstore

cibermercado m e-marketplace, Internet o online marketplace

cibermercadotecnia f cybermarketing

cibernauta mf cybernaut, surfer

cibernética f cybernetics

ciberocupa mf cybersquatter

ciberpirata m,f hacker

ciberpiratería f cyberpiracy

ciberrevista f cybermagazine, webzine

cibersubasta f cyberauction

cibertecario, -a m,f cybrarian

cíclico adj cyclical

ciclo m cycle; ~ **de acceso** access cycle; ~ **del activo circulante** current asset cycle; ~ **administrativo** management cycle; ~ **de búsqueda** search cycle; ~ **comercial** trade cycle; ~ **contable** accounting cycle; ~ **de control** control cycle; ~ **económico** business cycle, economic cycle; ~ **de existencias** stock cycle; ~ **de negocios** business cycle; ~ **de operación** operating cycle; ~ **del**

producto product cycle; ~ **de trabajo** work cycle; ~ **de vida** (de producto) life cycle; ~ **de visitas** calling cycle

ciencia *f* science; ~ **administrativa** management science; ~ **del comportamiento** behavioral science AmE, behavioural science BrE; ~**s empresariales** Business Studies

científico, -a *m,f* scientist

ciento *m* hundred; **por** ~ per cent

cierre *m* closure, close; (de acuerdo) conclusion; **al** ~ at closing; **hora de** ~ closing time; ~ **anual** annual closing; ~ **del año fiscal** end of the tax year; ~ **a la baja** bear closing; ~ **bancario** bank holiday BrE, legal holiday AmE; ~ **de la bolsa** closing of the stock exchange; ~ **centralizado** central locking; ~ **de edición** copy deadline; ~ **de ejercicio** year-end closing; ~ **de la emisión** closedown; ~ **empresarial** lockout; ~ **de libros** cut-off; ~ **de licitación** bid closing; ~ **del mercado** market close, market sealing; ~ **del negocio** close of business; ~ **de operaciones** close of business

ciervo *m* (Bolsa) stag

cifra *f* figure; (mensaje codificado) cipher; ~**s** figures; **en** ~**s desajustadas** in unadjusted figures; **en** ~**s reales** in real terms; **en** ~**s redondas** in round figures; **sus** ~**s concuerdan con las nuestras** your figures are in agreement with ours; ~**s ajustadas estacionalmente** seasonally-adjusted figures; ~**s comerciales** trade figures; ~**s consolidadas** consolidated figures; ~**s de crecimiento** growth figures; ~**s de desempleo** unemployment figures; ~**s de empleo** employment figures; ~**s de exportación** export figures; ~ **de negocios** *or* **ventas anual** annual turnover; ~**s oficiales** official figures; ~**s reales** actual figures; ~**s revisadas** revised figures; ~**s de ventas** sales figures, sales turnover

cifrado *m* encryption, encoding

cifrar *vt* encrypt, encode

cilindro *m* cylinder

cine *m* cinema; **hacer** ~ make films BrE *o* movies AmE

cineasta *mf* filmmaker BrE, moviemaker AmE

cinta *f* ribbon, tape; ~ **de audio digital** digital audiotape; ~ **magnética** magnetic tape; ~ **para medir** measuring tape; ~ **de serpentina** streamer; ~ **de teletipo** tickertape; ~

transbordadora travelator AmE; ~

transportadora conveyor belt; ~ **de vídeo** Esp *or* **video** AmL videocassette, videotape

cinturón *m* belt; **apretarse el** ~ tighten one's belt; ~ **ecológico** green belt; ~ **de ronda** ring road BrE, beltway AmE; ~ **de seguridad** safety belt, seat belt; ~ **verde** green belt

circuito *m* circuit; **causar corto** ~ **en algo** short-circuit sth; ~ **adicionador** adding circuit; ~ **de alimentación** feed circuit; ~ **de arranque** driver; ~ **biestable** flip-flop, ~ **cerrado** closed circuit; **televisión de** ~ **cerrado** closed-circuit television; ~ **integrado** integrated circuit; ~ **lógico** logic circuit

circulación *f* circulation; ~ **por carretera** road traffic; ~ **fiduciaria** fiduciary money, fiat money AmE, token money BrE; ~ **de la información** information flow

circular[1] *f* circular (letter), round robin

circular[2] [1] *vi* (dinero, billete) be in circulation; (noticia, rumor) circulate, go around
[2] *vt* circulate

círculo *m* circle; ~**s bancarios** banking circles; ~**s económicos** business circles; ~**s financieros** financial circles; ~**s informáticos** computer circles; ~ **vicioso** vicious circle

circunflejo *m* circumflex

circunstancia *f* circumstance; **en estas** ~**s** under the circumstances; **en** *or* **bajo ninguna** ~ under no circumstances; ~**s atenuantes** extenuating circumstances, mitigating circumstances; ~**s especiales** special circumstances; ~**s familiares** family circumstances; ~**s hipotéticas** hypothetical circumstances; ~ **material** (Seg) material circumstance

CIS *abr* (▸**Centro de Investigaciones Sociológicas**) *Spanish social studies institute*

cita *f* appointment; (reunión) meeting; **pedir** ~ make an appointment; **sólo con** ~ **previa** by appointment only

citación *f* citation, subpoena; ~ **judicial** citation, judicial notice

citado: **antes** ~ *adj* above-mentioned, previously-mentioned

citar *vt* quote; (Der) cite; ~ **a alguien** take out a summons against sb; ~ **a alguien como testigo** call sb as a witness

City: la ~ (de Londres) the City

ciudad f city; ~ **anfitriona** host city; ~ **dormitorio** dormitory town BrE, bedroom community AmE, commuter suburb; ~ **generatriz** generative city; ~ **metropolitana** metropolitan town; ~ **óptima** optimum city; ~ **parasitaria** parasitic city; ~ **satélite** satellite town; ~ **universitaria** university campus

ciudadanía f citizenship

ciudadano, -a m,f citizen; **el ~ medio** or **de a pie** the man in the street; ~ **de segunda clase** second-class citizen

civil adj civil; **casarse por lo ~** get married in a register o registry office BrE, be married in a civil ceremony AmE

clamor m clamour BrE, clamor AmE; ~ **público** public outcry

claridad f clarity; **con ~** clearly

clase f class; (RRHH) grade; **dar ~s** teach; **de primera ~** first-class; ~ **alta** upper class; ~ **baja** lower class; ~ **capitalista** capitalist class; ~ **club** club class; ~ **dominante** ruling class; ~ **económica** economy class; ~ **ejecutiva** business class; ~ **de empleo** class of employment; ~ **media** middle class; ~ **de negocio** class of business; ~ **nocturna** evening class; ~ **obrera** working class; ~**s particulares** private lessons; ~ **preferente** business class; ~ **social** social class; ~ **trabajadora** working class; ~ **turista** tourist class

clasificación f classification, rating; (Info) arrangement, sorting; (RRHH) ranking; ~ **AAA** AAA rating; ~ **de acciones** share classification, share rating; ~ **por cribadura** (ramación) bubble sort, sifting sort; ~ **de cuentas** classification of accounts; ~ **industrial común** standard industrial classification; ~ **laboral** work classification; ~ **numérica** digital sort; ~ **de productos** product classification; ~ **del puesto de trabajo** job classification; ~ **retroactiva** retroactive classification; ~ **de títulos** bond rating

clasificado adj classified; **no ~** adj unclassified

clasificador, a m,f sorter

clasificadora f sorter; ~ **de tarjetas** card sorter

clasificados m pl small ads, classifieds

clasificar vt classify, categorize; ~ **por fecha** (cuentas) age; ~ **incorrectamente** misfile; **sin ~** unsorted

clasificarse vi rank

claudicar vi give up; ~ **de algo** renounce sth

claustro m staff meeting

cláusula f clause; ~ **abrogatoria** (en un contrato) cancelling clause BrE, canceling clause AmE; ~ **de aceleración** acceleration clause; ~ **adicional** additional clause; ~ **al portador** bearer clause; ~ **de arbitraje** arbitration clause; ~ **de autorización** enabling clause; ~ **de buena fe** bona fide clause; ~ **de caducidad** lapse clause, obsolescence clause; ~ **condicional** contingency clause; ~ **derogatoria** overriding clause; ~ **de disponibilidad** availability clause; ~ **disputable** contestable clause; ~ **de elusión** escape clause; ~ **de errores y omisiones** errors and omissions clause; ~ **de evasión** escape clause; ~ **de excepción** exceptions clause; ~ **de exclusiones generales** general exclusions clause; ~ **de exención** exemption clause; ~ **de huelga** strike clause; ~ **de insolvencia** insolvency clause; ~ **laboral** labour clause BrE, labor clause AmE; ~ **de negligencia** negligence clause; ~ **de pagos simultáneos** simultaneous payments clause; ~ **de penalización** penalty clause; ~ **punitiva** penalty clause; ~ **de renuncia** waiver clause; ~ **de rescisión** termination clause; ~ **de retrocompra** buy-back clause; ~ **de revisión** trigger clause; ~ **de salvaguardia** disaster clause, escape clause; ~ **sobre paridad** parity clause

clausura f (de edificio) closure; (de reunión) adjournment; **discurso de ~** closing speech

clausurar vt (edificio) close (down); (reunión) adjourn; (debate, sesión) close, bring to a close

clave f (código) key, code element; **en ~** in code; ~ **de acceso** password; ~ **de búsqueda** search key, keyword; ~ **de clasificación** sort key; ~ **directa** hot key; ~ **de registro** record key

clic m (del ratón) click; **hacer ~** (en algo) click (on sth); **hacer ~ con el botón derecho** right-click; **hacer doble ~** double-click; **proporción de ~s** click-through rate; **secuencia de ~s** click stream

cliché m (en tipografía) plate, boilerplate

cliente m,f client, customer; **atención al ~** customer services; **atender a un ~**

serve a customer; ∼ **de auditoría** audit client; ∼ **corporativo(-a)** *m,f* corporate client, corporate customer; ∼ **de cuenta corriente** current account customer BrE, checking account customer AmE; ∼ **extranjero(-a)** *m,f* overseas customer; ∼ **fijo(-a)** *m,f* permanent customer; ∼ **futuro(-a)** *m,f* prospective customer; ∼ **habitual** regular customer; ∼ **importante** big customer; ∼ **nominativo(-a)** *m,f* named client; ∼ **potencial** prospective client; ∼ **de primer orden** blue-chip customer; ∼ **principal** main client; ∼ **privado(-a)** *m,f* private client; ∼ **web** Web client

clientela *f* custom, clientele

cliente/servidor *m* client/server

clima *m* climate; ∼ **económico** economic climate; ∼ **económico favorable** favourable BrE *o* favorable AmE economic climate; ∼ **financiero** financial climate; ∼ **inversor** investment climate; ∼ **laboral sano** positive labour BrE *o* labor AmE relations; ∼ **político** political climate; ∼ **socioeconómico** socioeconomic climate

climatización *f* air conditioning

climatizado *adj* air-conditioned

cliquear *vi* (con el ratón) click; ∼ **con el botón derecho del ratón en algo** right-click (on) sth

clon *m* clone

clonar *vt* clone

clorofluorocarbono *m pl* chlorofluorocarbon

club *m* club; ∼ **de beneficios mutuos** benefit club; ∼ **de salud** health club

CNMV *abr* (▸**Comisión Nacional del Mercado de Valores**) ≈ SEC (Securities and Exchange Commission) AmE, ≈ SIB (Securities and Investments Board) BrE

coacción *f* coercion, duress; **bajo** ∼ under duress

coactivo *adj* coercive; **por medios** ∼**s** by coercion

coadyuvar *vt* aid and abet

coalición *f* coalition

coarriendo *m* joint tenancy

coasegurado *adj* coinsured

coasegurador, a *m,f* coinsurer

coaseguro *m* coinsurance

coasociación *f* joint partnership

coauditor, a *m,f* joint auditor

cobertura *f* (Seg) cover BrE, coverage AmE; (en prensa, televisión) coverage; (Bolsa, Info) margin; **de amplia** ∼ wide-ranging; **una** ∼ **frente a la inflación** a hedge against inflation; ∼ **ampliada** extended cover BrE *o* coverage AmE; ∼ **contra todo riesgo** all-risks cover; ∼ **de dependientes** dependent cover BrE *o* coverage AmE; ∼ **fiscal** tax umbrella; ∼ **informativa** news coverage; ∼ **en los medios de comunicación** media coverage; ∼ **periodística** press coverage; ∼ **del seguro** insurance cover BrE *o* coverage AmE; ∼ **televisiva** television coverage; ∼ **total** fully comprehensive cover BrE *o* coverage AmE; ∼ **de ventas** sales coverage

COBOL *abr* (*lenguaje común orientado a la gestión y los negocios*) COBOL (Common Business Oriented Language)

cobrable *adj* (cheque) cashable; (fondos) recoverable

cobrado *adj* (cheque) cashed; ∼ **y entregado** collected and delivered; **no** ∼ uncashed

cobrador, a *m,f* collector; ∼ **de alquileres** rent collector; ∼ **de deudas** debt collector

cobranza *f* collection; ∼ **de primas** collection of premiums

cobrar ⓵ *vt* charge; (cheque) cash; (sueldo) earn; ∼ **comisión** collect commission; ∼ **una deuda** collect a debt; ∼ **impulso** gain momentum; ∼ **la jornada y media** be on time and a half; ∼ **un precio excesivo** overcharge ⓶ *vi* cash up; ∼ **al contado** accept cash payments only; ∼ **a destajo** be paid by the hour; ∼ **de más** overcharge; **¿me cobra, por favor?** can I have the bill BrE *o* check AmE, please?; **no he cobrado todavía** I haven't been paid yet

cobro *m* (de salario, pensión, deuda) collection; (de cheque) cashing, encashment; ∼**s** cash receipts, monies paid in; **llamar a** ∼ **revertido** reverse the charges BrE, call collect AmE; ∼ **por adelantado** advanced charge; ∼ **antes de la entrega** cash before delivery; ∼ **anticipado** advanced collection; ∼ **automático de tarifas** automatic fare collection; ∼ **coercitivo** enforced collection; ∼ **de cuentas** collection of accounts; ∼ **excesivo** overcharge; ∼ **a la par** par collection; ∼ **de primas** collection of premiums

coche *m* car; ∼ **cama** sleeper, sleeping car; ∼ **de alquiler** hire car BrE, rental car AmE; ∼ **de la empresa** company car

cociente *m* quotient, ratio; ~ **intelectual** *or* **de inteligencia** IQ, intelligence quotient

coconsulta *f* joint consultation

codeterminación *f* codetermination

codicilo *m* codicil

codicioso *adj* (compañía) acquisitive

codificación *f* coding, encryption; ~ **binaria** binary coding; ~ **de cuentas** coding of accounts

codificado *m* encoding

codificador-descodificador *m* codec

código *m* code; ~ **de acceso** access code; ~ **de autorización** authorization code; ~ **bancario** bank code; ~ **de barras** bar code; ~ **binario** binary code; ~ **de bloques** block code; ~ **bursátil** stock symbol; ~ **de calculadora** computer code; ~ **cifrado** cipher code; ~ **civil** civil code, civil law; ~ **de comercio** code of commerce, commercial code, commercial law; ~ **de conducta** code of practice; ~ **del documento** document code; C~ **de Empresa** Companies Code; ~ **de ética** code of ethics, code of practice; ~ **fiscal** tax code; ~ **fuente** source code; ~ **impositivo** tax code; ~ **inventarial** schedule code; ~**s legales** statute book; ~ **legible por máquina** machine-readable code; ~ **de orden** operation code; ~ **de país** country code; ~ **postal** postcode BrE, postal code BrE, zip code AmE; ~ **de práctica** code of practice; ~ **de procedimiento** code of procedure; ~ **de respuesta** reply code, answerback code

codirección *f* joint management

codirector, a *m,f* co-director, co-manager, joint director

codueño, -a *m,f* co-owner, joint owner

coeficiente *m* ratio, factor, coefficient; ~ **de amortización** depreciation rate; ~ **de caja** cash ration, liquidity ratio; ~ **de desembolso de dividendos** dividend payout ratio; ~ **de endeudamiento** capital-debt ratio; ~ **de incremento** coefficient of increase; ~ **intelectual** *or* **de inteligencia** intelligence quotient, IQ; ~ **del pasivo** liability ratio; ~ **tributario** tax ratio; ~ **de utilidad bruta** gross profit ratio; ~ **de volumen de beneficios** profit-volume ratio

coercitivo *adj* enforced, coercive; (poder) compulsory

cofinanciación *f* joint financing, co-financing

cofinanciar *vt* co-finance

cogerente *mf* joint manager

cogestión *f* joint management

cognición *f* cognition

cohacedor, a *m,f* briber

cohacer *vt* bribe

cohecho *m* (*cf* ►**coima** AmL) bribe

coherencia *f* consistency

coherente *adj* consistent

cohesión *f* cohesion

coima *f* AmL bribe

coincidir *vi* coincide

coinversión *f* joint venture

cola *f* queue; (de una lista) bottom; **hacer** ~ queue (up) BrE, wait in line AmE; ~ **de espera de trabajos** job queue

colaboración *f* collaboration

colaborador[1] *adj* collaborative

colaborador[2], **-a** *m,f* collaborator, co-worker; (en una revista) contributor

colaborar *vi* collaborate, work together; ~ **en algo** help with sth; ~ **en una revista** contribute to *o* write for a magazine

colapso *m* (de mercado, empresa) collapse; (de operaciones) breakdown

colateral[1] *adj* collateral

colateral[2] *m* collateral, security

colectivamente *adv* collectively

colectivización *f* collectivization

colectivo[1] *adj* collective

colectivo[2] *m* group; ~ **de trabajadores** workers' collective

colector, a *m,f* collector

colegio *m* college; C~ **de Abogados** ≈ Law Society BrE, ≈ Bar Association AmE; ~ **electoral** polling station; (electores) electoral college

colgar *vi* hang up; **no cuelgue, por favor** please hold (the line)

colocación *f* (de acciones) placement; (empleo) job; ~ **en espera de llamadas** call queuing; ~ **segura** safe investment

co-localizar *vt* co-locate

colocar *vt* place; ~ **a alguien** get sb a job; ~ **progresivamente** (Info) phase in; ~ **un producto en el mercado** launch a product onto the market

colocarse *v pron* get a job; **se colocó como redactor** he got a job as an editor

colonización *f* settlement

coloquio *m* symposium, colloquium

color *m* colour BrE, color AmE; **a dos ~es** two-colour BrE, two-color AmE; **~ de fondo** background colour BrE, background color AmE

columna *f* column; **a dos ~s** two-column; **la ~ vertebral de la economía** the backbone of the economy; **~ del debe** debit column; **~ derecha** right column, right-hand column; **~ editorial** editorial column; **~ del haber** credit column; **~ izquierda** left column, left-hand column; **~ publicitaria** advertising tower

colusión *f* collusion; **actuar en ~** be in collusion

coma *f* comma; **dos ~ cinco** two point five; **~ decimal** decimal point

comandita *f* limited company

comanditario[1] *adj* (sociedad) limited; (socio) sleeping BrE, silent AmE

comanditario[2], **-a** *m,f* sleeping BrE *o* silent AmE partner

comando *m* (Info) command; **~ de control** control command; **~ integrado** built-in command

combatir *vt* (inflación) fight, combat; (proyecto, propuesta) fight

combinación *f* combination; **~ de activos** asset mix; **~ de divisas** currency mix; **~ de estrategias de comunicación** communication mix; **~ de estrategias de precios** pricing mix; **~ de estrategias de productos** product mix; **~ de estrategias promocionales** promotional mix; **~ mercantil** business combination; **~ de políticas** policy mix

combinar *vt* combine; (recursos) pool; **~ algo con algo** combine sth with sth

combustible *m* fuel; **~ pesado** heavy fuel

comentar *vt* (decir) mention, comment on; (discutir) discuss; **~le algo a alguien** mention sth to sb; **~ que...** mention that..., comment that...

comentario *m* comment, remark; (en radio, televisión) commentary; **hacer ~s sobre algo** comment on sth; **no hay** *or* **sin ~s** no comment; **~ de textos** critical commentary

comentarista *mf* announcer, commentator; **~ de radio** radio announcer; **~ de televisión** television announcer

comenzar *vti* begin, start; **~ a hacer algo** start doing sth; **~ por algo** begin with sth; **~ por hacer algo** begin by doing sth; **comenzó por saludar a todos**

los presentes he began by greeting all those present

comerciabilidad *f* marketability, saleability BrE, salability AmE

comerciable *adj* marketable, saleable BrE, salable AmE

comercial[1] *adj* commercial, business; **carta ~** business letter; **departamento ~** sales department; **zona ~** shopping area

comercial[2] *m* AmL commercial, advertisement

comercialidad *f* commercialism

comercializable *adj* marketable, saleable BrE, salable AmE

comercialización *f* commercialization; (de productos) marketing; (de subproductos) merchandising; **costes** Esp *or* **costos** AmL **de ~** marketing costs; **~ directa** direct marketing

comercializar *vt* commercialize; (producto) market

comercialmente *adv* commercially; **~ viable** *adv* commercially viable

comerciante *mf* trader, businessman, businesswoman; (Bolsa) dealer; **~ activo(-a)** *m,f* active trader; **~ callejero(-a)** *m,f* street trader BrE, street vendor AmE; **~ individual** sole trader; **~ mayorista** wholesale trader; **~ minorista** retail trader; **~ al por mayor** wholesale merchant *o* trader; **~ al por menor** retail merchant *o* trader

comerciar *vi* trade; **~ en algo** trade *o* deal in sth; **~ con alguien** trade *o* do business with sb; **~ bajo nombre de** trade under the name of; **~ por cuenta propia** trade on one's account

comercio *m* commerce, business, trade; (acción) trading; (tienda) shop BrE, store AmE; (Bolsa) dealing, trading; **el mundo del comercio** the business world; **~ activo** active business; **~ clandestino** illegal trading; **~ colaborativo** c-commerce, collaborative commerce; **~ competitivo** competitive trading; **~ electrónico** e-commerce, e-business, electronic commerce, Internet commerce; **~ electrónico por móvil** m-commerce, m-business; **~ electrónico sin cables** wireless e-commerce; **~ equitativo** fair trade; **~ especializado** speciality trade BrE, specialty trade AmE; **~ especulativo** speculative trading; **~ de exportación** export trade; **~ exterior** foreign trade; **~ de importación** import trade; **~** ⋯⟩

informático computer trading; ∼
intercomunitario (UE) intercommunity
trade; ∼ **interindustrial** interindustry
trade; ∼ **interior** domestic trade; ∼
interior de la UE intra-EU trade; ∼
internacional international trade; ∼
interno domestic trade; ∼
intracomunitario intra-Community
trade; ∼ **invisible** invisible trade; ∼
legal fair trading; ∼ **en línea** Web
commerce, on-line business; ∼
mayorista wholesale trade; ∼ **al
menudeo** retail trade; ∼ **en mercado
libre** open market trading; ∼ **minorista**
retail trade; ∼ **mundial** world trade; ∼
al por mayor wholesale trade,
wholesale business; ∼ **al por menor**
retail trade, retail business; ∼ **de
productos** commodity trading; ∼
recíproco reciprocal trading; ∼
transfronterizo cross-border trading; ∼
de trueque bartering

cometer *vt* (crimen, delito) commit; (error,
falta) make

comida *f* food; ∼ **de negocios**
business lunch; ∼ **preparada** ready-
made meal; ∼ **rápida** fast food

comienzo *m* beginning, start; **al** ∼ at
first, at the outset; **cuyo** ∼ **está previsto
para** scheduled to begin in; **dar** ∼ **a algo**
begin sth; ∼ **del año** beginning of the
year; ∼ **de una tarea** (Info) task
initiation

comillas *f pl* quotation marks, inverted
commas BrE; **poner algo entre** ∼ put sth
in quotation marks *o* inverted commas
BrE

comisario *m* commissary; (Bolsa)
shareholder's auditor

comisión *f* (pago) commission, fee;
(junta) committee; **cobrar un 15% de** ∼
charge 15% commission; **en** ∼ on
consignment; **trabajar a** ∼ work on a
commission basis, be on commision; ∼
comisiones (sobre operaciones bancarias)
charges; ∼ **de aceptación** acceptance
fee; ∼ **de administración** management
fee; ∼ **de adquisición** acquisition fee;
∼ **del agente** agent's commission; ∼
de arbitraje board of arbitration; ∼
asesora advisory committee BrE,
prudential committee AmE; ∼ **bancaria**
banking commission; ∼ **de
compromiso** commitment fee; **C**∼ **de
las Comunidades Europeas**
Commission of the European
Communities; ∼ **de corretaje**
brokerage fee; ∼ **dividida** split
commission; **C**∼ **Económica para**

América Latina Economic Commission
for Latin America; **C**∼ **Económica
para Europa** Economic Commission for
Europe; ∼ **ejecutiva** executive
committee; **C**∼ **de la Energía y el
Medio Ambiente** Commission on
Energy and the Environment; **C**∼ **de
Estudios del Mercado Monetario**
*Spanish commission of main institutions
that regulate the monetary market*; **C**∼
Europea European Commission; ∼ **fija**
flat fee; **C**∼ **Forestal** Forestry
Commission BrE, Forestry Service AmE;
∼ **de gestión** (pago) agency fee; (comité)
management committee; ∼ **gestora**
management committee; ∼ **de
incentivo** incentive commission; ∼ **de
mantenimiento de cuenta** account
maintenance fee; ∼ **mixta** joint
committee; **C**∼ **Nacional del Mercado
de Valores** ≈ Securities and
Investments Board BrE, ≈ Securities and
Exchange Commission AmE; ∼ **de
operarios** (UE) Works Council; ∼
permanente (en Parlamento Europeo)
standing committee; ∼ **de
planificación** planning commission; ∼
reguladora (UE) regulatory committee;
∼ **por servicio bancario** bank service
charge; ∼ **de ventas** sales commission

comisionar *vt* (requerir, apoderar)
commission

comisionario, -a *m,f* commissionaire

comisionista *mf* commission agent;
(Bolsa) broker; ∼ **en colocaciones**
investment dealer; ∼ **de exportación**
export agent

comité *m* committee, board; ∼
administrativo management committee;
∼ **de arbitraje** arbitration committee;
∼ **asesor** advisory committee BrE,
prudential committee AmE; ∼ **de
dirección** steering committee; ∼
ejecutivo executive committee; **C**∼
Europeo para la Normalización
European Committee for
Standardization; ∼ **de gerencia**
management committee; ∼ **de
inspección** committee of inspection; ∼
paritario joint committee; ∼ **de
planificación** planning committee; ∼
de vigilancia supervisory board

comodidades *f pl* amenities

comodín *m* (Info) wild card

compaginadorade documentos *f*
collator

compaginar *vt* combine; (documentos)
collate

compañero, -a m,f companion; ~ **de equipo** fellow team member; ~ **de trabajo** colleague, workmate, coworker

compañía f company; **fundar una** ~ set up a company; **y** ~ and Co.; ~ **de acciones de primera clase** blue-chip company; ~ **adquirente** purchasing company; (toma de control) acquiring company; ~ **adquirida** purchased company; ~ **apalancada** leveraged company; ~ **aseguradora** insurance company; ~ **asociada** affiliated company; ~ **de capital de riesgo** venture capital corporation; ~ **cedente** ceding company; ~ **central** parent company; ~ **cerrada** closed corporation AmE; ~ **de coinversión** joint-venture company; ~ **cotizable** listed company; ~ **de cotización oficial pública** publicly listed company; ~ **desaparecida** defunct company; ~ **disuelta** defunct company; ~ **emisora** issuing company; ~ **excluida** excluded corporation; ~ **exenta** exempt corporation; ~ **fiduciaria** trust company; ~ **filial** affiliated company, subsidiary company BrE, subsidiary corporation AmE; ~ **financiera** financial company; ~ **sin fines de lucro** nonprofit-making company BrE, nonprofit corporation AmE; ~ **fundadora** founding company; ~ **de fusión** merger company; ~ **fusionada** amalgamated corporation, merged company; ~ **de gestión de activos** asset management company; ~ **integrada** integrated company; ~ **de Internet** Internet company; ~ **de inversión conjunta** joint-venture company; ~ **inversionista** investment company; ~ **matriz** parent company; ~ **mutua** mutual company, mutual corporation; ~ **mutua de seguros** mutual insurance company; ~ **no cotizable** unlisted company; ~ **prestamista** loan company; ~ **privada** private company; ~ **privatizada** privatized company; ~ **pública** insurance company; ~ **de seguros** insurance company; ~ **de seguros mutuos** mutual insurance company; ~ **de seguros de vida** life insurance company; ~ **subsidiaria** subsidiary; ~ **de telecomunicaciones** telecommunications company; **C~ Telefónica Nacional de España** *Spanish national telecommunications network,* ≈ British Telecom; ~ **tenedora** holding company

comparabilidad f comparability; ~ **de pagos** pay comparability

comparable adj comparable; ~ **a** or **con algo** comparable to o with sth

comparables m pl (Inmob) comparables

comparación f comparison; **hacer** or **establecer una** ~ **entre algo y algo** make o draw a comparison between sth and sth; **no tiene ni punto de** ~ there's no comparison

comparar vt compare; ~ **precios/ cifras** compare prices/figures; ~ **algo/a alguien a algo** compare sth/sb with sth; **comparado con ayer** compared with yesterday

comparativamente adv comparatively

comparativo adj comparative

comparecer vi appear; ~ **ante un tribunal** come before a court

compartimentación f compartmentalization

compartimentalizar vt compartmentalize

compartimiento m sharing; ~ **de conocimientos** knowledge sharing; ~ **de recursos** resource sharing

compartir vt share; ~ **algo con alguien** share sth with sb; ~ **un piso** share a flat; ~ **el trabajo** job-share

compatibilidad f compatibility; ~ **ascendente** upward compatibility; ~ **descendente** downward compatibility; ~ **de equipos** hardware compatibility; ~ **del PC** PC-compatibility; ~ **de productos** product compatibility

compatible adj compatible; **ser** ~ **con algo** be compatible with sth; (encajar) fit in well with sth; ~ **con PC** PC-compatible

compendio m abstract, compendium

compensación f compensation; (de cheques) clearing; (Cont) offset; (de pérdidas) making-up; (Econ) trade-off, equalization; (Imp/Exp) countervailing; ~ **por daños y perjuicios** compensation for damages; ~ **por defunción** death benefit; ~ **por despido** severance pay, redundancy pay BrE; ~ **de deudas** settlement per contra; ~ **de ingresos y gastos** equalization of revenue and expenditure; ~ **en lugar de preaviso** pay in lieu of notice; ~ **media** average compensation; ~ **del riesgo** risk-reward

compensado adj (cheque) cleared; (Cont) balanced; **no** ~ uncleared

compensar *vt* compensate, make up for; (indemnizar) pay compensation to; (cheque) clear; (precio de valores) average up; (dividendos) equalize; (pérdidas y ganancias) offset, balance out; ~ **a alguien por algo** compensate sb for sth; **le** ~**on con 25.000 euros por el accidente** they gave *o* paid him 25,000 euros compensation for the accident; ~ **algo contra algo** offset sth against sth; ~ **un débito a cuenta de un crédito** set off a debit against a credit; ~ **la diferencia** make up the difference; ~ **una pérdida** offset a loss

compensatorio *adj* compensating, compensatory

competencia *f* competition; (nacional) authority; (Pol) jurisdiction; (habilidad) competence; ~**s** powers; **la** ~ the competition; **hacerle la** ~ **a alguien** compete with sb, be in competition with sb; **trabajar para la** ~ work for the competition; ~ **abierta** open competition; ~ **desleal** unfair competition; ~ **dura** stiff competition; ~ **ejecutiva** executive competence; ~ **entre industrias** interindustry competition; ~ **equitativa** fair competition; ~ **leal** fair competition; ~ **legislativa** law-making power

competente *adj* competent; ~ **en la informática** computer-literate

competido *adj* (mercado) contested

competidor, a *m,f* competitor

competir *vi* compete; ~ **con alguien (por algo)** compete with sb (for sth); ~ **contra alguien** compete against sb; ~ **ventajosamente con alguien** have a competitive advantage over sb; **los dos productos compiten en calidad y precio** both products rival each other in quality and price

competitividad *f* competitiveness; ~ **de los precios** price competitiveness

competitivo *adj* (precio) competitive; **no** ~ non-competitive; **sumamente** ~ highly competitive

compilación *f* (de datos) compilation

compilador, a *m,f* compiler

compilar *vt* compile

complejidad *f* complexity, sophistication

complejo¹ *adj* (sistema, problema) complex

complejo² *m* complex; ~ **deportivo** sports complex; ~ **para espectáculos** entertainment complex; ~ **industrial** industrial complex; ~ **residencial** housing complex

complementado *adj* supplemented

complementar *vt* supplement

complementario *adj* complementary; (adicional) supplementary, additional

complemento *m* complement; ~ **salarial** perquisite, perk (infrml)

completar *vt* complete; AmL (formulario) fill in

completo *adj* (plan, informe) comprehensive; (pedido) complete; (lleno) full; **completo** no vacancies; **por** ~ completely; **a tiempo** ~ full-time

complicación *f* complication; **sin** ~ straightforward

complicado *adj* complicated, complex

complicar *vt* (situación, asunto) complicate

componente¹ *adj* component

componente² *m* component; ~ **de capital** capital component; ~ **electrónico** electronic component; ~ **de un equipo** team member; ~ **del precio de coste** Esp *or* **costo** AmL *m* cost factor; ~ **tiempo** time component; ~ **tributario** tax component

componer *vt* make up; ~ **una deuda** compound a debt

comportamiento *m* behaviour BrE, behavior AmE; (de empresa, valores) performance; ~ **de los beneficios** earnings performance; ~ **cognitivo** cognitive behaviour BrE, cognitive behavior AmE; ~ **de compra** buying behaviour BrE, buying behavior AmE; ~ **del consumidor** consumer behaviour BrE, consumer behavior AmE; ~ **del mercado** market behaviour BrE, market behavior AmE; ~ **no profesional** unprofessional behaviour BrE, unprofessional behavior AmE

composición *f* composition; (en imprenta) typesetting; ~ **amigable** amicable settlement; ~ **fotográfica** filmsetting; ~ **de página** page setting; ~ **tipográfica** typesetting

compra *f* purchase, purchasing, buying; (para la casa) shopping; (de una compañía) acquisition; **hacer una** ~ make a purchase; **una buena/mala** ~ a good/bad buy; ~ **de acciones** share buying; ~ **de acciones propias** share buyback; ~ **de acciones con sus dividendos** pyramiding; ~ **acelerada** accelerated purchase; ~ **de activos** purchase of assets; ~ **agresiva a la baja** bear raid; ~ **al cierre** closing purchase; ~ **al**

contado cash purchase; ~ **anticipada** forward buying; ~ **apalancada** leveraged buyout; ~ **apalancada por ejecutivos** leveraged management buyout; ~ **por catálogo** catalog buying AmE, catalogue buying BrE; ~ **compulsiva** compulsive buying; ~ **de conjunto** basket purchase; ~ **de contrapartida** counter purchase; ~ **de control** buyout; ~ **a corto** short call; ~ **con derecho a devolución** sale or return; ~ **por ejecutivos** management buyout; ~ **electrónica** online shopping, cybershopping, electronic shopping; ~ **escalonada de acciones** (con ganancias) pyramiding; ~ **de espacios publicitarios** buying of advertising space; ~ **especulativa** speculative buying; ~ **sin garantía** naked call; ~**s a granel** bulk buying; ~ **impulsiva** impulse buy; ~ **obligatoria** compulsory purchase; ~ **on-line** online shopping, home shopping; ~ **por placer** pleasure shopping; ~ **a plazos** hire purchase BrE, installment plan AmE; ~ **a precio corriente** at-the-money call; ~ **a precios escalonados** scale buying; ~ **de prueba** trial purchase; ~ **repetida** repeat buying; ~ **telefónica** teleshopping

comprador, a *m,f* buyer, purchaser; (en tienda) shopper; **buscar un** ~ look for a buyer; ~ **al contado** cash buyer; ~ **a crédito** credit buyer; ~ **de espacio publicitario** advertising space buyer; ~ **en firme** firm buyer; ~ **de graneles** bulk buyer; ~ **por impulso** impulse buyer

comprar [1] *vt* buy, purchase; ~**le algo a alguien** (a quien lo vende) buy sth from sb; (para dárselo a alguien) buy sth for sb; ~ **acciones** buy shares; ~ **acciones de una compañía** buy into a company, buy a company's shares; ~ **algo barato** buy *o* get sth cheap; ~ **algo caro** pay a lot for sth; ~ **algo a condición** buy sth on approval; ~ **algo al contado** buy sth for cash, pay cash for sth; ~ **algo al crédito** buy sth on credit; ~ **algo en el mercado negro** buy sth on the black market; ~ **algo a plazos** buy sth on hire purchase BrE, pay for sth in instalments BrE, buy sth in installments AmE; ~ **algo a precio alto** buy sth at the top of the market; ~ **algo a precio de mercado** buy sth at market price; ~ **a precio reducido** buy sth at a reduced price; ~ **algo a prueba** buy sth on approval

[2] *vi* buy, shop; ~ **al alza** buy on a rise; ~ **a la baja** buy on a fall; ~ **a la baja y vender al alza** buy low and sell high; ~ **al cierre** buy on close

compraventa *f* buying and selling; ~ **de billetes bancarios** banknote BrE *o* bank bill AmE trading; ~ **de futuros** futures trading

comprendido *adj* inclusive, included; **todo** ~ all-in

compresión *f* compression; ~ **de datos** data compression; ~ **de fichero** file compression

comprimir *vt* (fichero) compress, zip

comprobación *f* check; ~ **al azar** spot check; ~ **asistida por computadora** AmL *or* **ordenador** Esp computer-assisted testing; ~ **automática** (Econ) automatic check-off; (Info) automatic check, built-in check; ~ **de beneficios** (Cont) profit test; (Fisc) earnings test; ~ **en bucle** message feedback; ~ **de los ingresos** income test; ~ **de paridad** parity check; ~ **de validez** validity check

comprobador *m* tester; ~ **de código** code checker

comprobante *m* proof; (de pago) receipt; (de crédito, dividendo) voucher; (Banca) slip; ~ **de caja** cash voucher; ~ **de caja chica** petty cash voucher; ~ **de compra** proof of purchase; ~ **de envío** proof of postage; ~ **de pago** proof of payment, receipt; ~ **de retiro** withdrawal slip

comprobar *vt* check; (confirmar) prove; (verificar) verify; **necesitamos algún documento que compruebe su identidad** we need some proof of identity

comprometer *vt* compromise; (situación) jeopardize; (capital) invest, tie up; ~ **a alguien a algo** commit sb to sth; ~ **a alguien en algo** implicate sb in sth; **los doucumentos le comprometían** the documents compromised him

comprometerse *v pron* commit oneself; ~ **a hacer algo** commit oneself to doing sth, undertake to do sth

comprometido *adj* committed; **estar** ~ **en algo** be implicated in sth; **ya estoy** ~ **para un trabajo este mes** I've already got a job on this month

compromisario, -a *m,f* delegate

compromiso *m* (promesa) commitment, undertaking; (obligación) obligation; (cita) engagement; (acuerdo) agreement; **hacer algo por** ~ be obliged to do sth, do sth out of duty; **llegar a un** ~ reach an ⸽⸽⸽⸽

agreement; **poner a alguien en un** ∼ put sb in an embarrassing *o* awkward position; **sin** ∼ without *o* no obligation; **una solución de** ∼ a compromise solution; **tener otro** ∼ have a prior engagement; ∼ **de aseguramiento continuado** revolving underwriting facility; ∼ **de fianza** bail bond; ∼ **no librado** *or* **pagado** undischarged commitment; ∼**s de pago** payment commitments; ∼ **pendiente** outstanding commitment

compuesto *adj* composite; (interés) compound; ∼ **de algo** *adj* composed of sth

computación *f* (*cf* ▸**informática** Esp) computing

computadora *f* AmL, **computador** *m* AmL (*cf* ▸**ordenador** Esp) computer; ∼ **activa** AmL active computer; ∼ **analógica** AmL analogue BrE *o* analog AmE computer; ∼ **de bolsillo** AmL pocket computer; ∼ **central** AmL central computer; ∼ **comercial** AmL business computer, commercial computer; ∼ **de cuarta generación** AmL fourth-generation computer; ∼ **destinataria** AmL target computer; ∼ **doméstica** AmL home computer; ∼ **frontal** AmL front-end computer; ∼ **fuente** AmL source computer; ∼ **híbrida** AmL hybrid computer; ∼ **por lotes** AmL batch computer; ∼ **de mano** AmL hand-held computer; ∼ **de mesa** desktop computer; ∼ **de nivel superior** AmL high-end computer; ∼ **periférica** AmL peripheral computer; ∼ **personal** AmL personal computer; ∼ **portátil** AmL laptop, portable computer, notebook; ∼ **de primera generación** AmL first-generation computer; ∼ **de quinta generación** AmL fifth-generation computer; ∼ **de red** AmL netsurfer; ∼ **satélite** AmL satellite computer; ∼ **de segunda generación** AmL second-generation computer; ∼ **en serie** AmL serial computer; ∼ **en tándem** AmL duplex computer; ∼ **de tercera generación** AmL third-generation computer; ∼ **terminal** AmL terminal computer; ∼ **vectorial** AmL array processor

computadorizado *adj* AmL (*cf* ▸**informatizado** Esp) computerized, computer-based

computadorizar *vt* AmL (*cf* ▸**informatizar** Esp) computerize

computar *vt* (cálculos) calculate, compute

computerizado *adj* computerized

computerizar *vt* computerize

cómputo *m* computation, reckoning; ∼ **de inventario** inventory computation

común *adj* common; ∼ **a todos** shared by all; **en** ∼ in common; **cuenta en** ∼ joint bank account; **gastos comunes** joint expenses; **por lo** ∼ as a rule

comuna *f* commune

comunal *adj* communal

comunicación *f* communication; (contacto) contact; (por teléfono) call; **comunicaciones** communications; **establecer** ∼ **con alguien** establish contact with sb; **cortarse la** ∼ (telefónica) get cut off; **estar en** ∼ **con alguien** be in contact *o* touch with sb; **ponerse en** ∼ **con alguien** get in contact *o* touch with sb; ∼ **de cobro revertido** (por teléfono) reverse-charge call BrE, collect call AmE; **comunicaciones digitales inalámbricas** cordless digital telecommunications; ∼ **formal** formal communication; **comunicaciones globales** global communications; **comunicaciones internas** internal communications; ∼ **interurbana** trunk call BrE, toll call AmE; ∼ **de masas** mass communication; **comunicaciones móviles** mobile communications; ∼ **no verbal** non-verbal communication; ∼ **oficial** official statement; ∼ **verbal** verbal communication; ∼ **por vía satélite** satellite communication

comunicado *m* communiqué; ∼ **de prensa** press release; ∼ **radiofónico** radio announcement

comunicante *m* speaker; (por teléfono) caller; (informador) source; **un** ∼ **anónimo** an anonymous source

comunicar **1** *vt* communicate; (informar) inform; **se comunica que...** please note that...; **sentimos tener que** ∼**les que...** we regret to have to inform you that...; ∼**le algo a alguien por teléfono** inform sb of sth by phone **2** *vi*: **estar comunicando** Esp (teléfono) be engaged

comunidad *f* community; **C**∼ **Autónoma** Esp *autonomous region*, ≈ county BrE; ∼ **bancaria** banking community; ∼ **dormitorio** dormitory town BrE, bedroom community AmE; **C**∼ **Económica Europea** (obs) European Economic Community (obs); ∼ **electrónica** e-community, electronic community; **C**∼ **Europea** (obs) European Community (obs); ∼ **rural**

rural community; ~ **virtual**
e-community, online community

comunismo *m* communism

comunización *f* (de tierras)
communization

comunizar *vt* (tierras) communize

con *prep* with; (Bolsa) cum; ~
dividendo cum dividend; ~ **cupón** cum
coupon

concatenación *f* concatenation

concebir *vt* (plan, proyecto) conceive,
devise; **concebido en función del niño**
child-centred BrE, child-centered AmE;
concebido para el usuario user-oriented

concedente *mf* licensor

conceder *vt* (contrato) award; (permiso,
prórroga) grant; (reconocer) concede, admit;
~ **un aumento salarial** award a salary
increase; ~ **un crédito** extend a loan; ~
una entrevista agree to an interview *o*
to being interviewed; ~ **demasiada
importancia a** give *o* attach too much
importance to

concejal *mf* town councillor BrE, town
councilor AmE

concentración *f* concentration; ~
absoluta absolute concentration; ~
agregada aggregate concentration; ~
de compradores buyer concentration;
~ **industrial** concentration of industry;
~ **de temporada** seasonal
concentration

concentrar *vt* (esfuerzos) concentrate;
(atención) focus

concepción *f* conception,
understanding; **una clara** ~ **de los
hechos** a clear understanding of the
facts; ~ **del producto** product
conception

concepto *m* concept; **bajo ningún** ~
under no circumstances, not on any
terms; ~ **de acumulación** accrual
concept; ~ **básico** basic concept; ~ **de
empresa establecida** *or* **en
funcionamiento** going-concern concept;
~ **de estilo de vida** lifestyle concept;
~ **de marketing** marketing concept; ~
publicitario advertising concept

concertar *vt* arrange; (precio) agree; ~
una cita make an appointment; ~ **una
deuda** compound a debt; ~ **una
entrevista** arrange *o* set up an
interview; ~ **hacer algo** agree to do sth

concesión *f* concession; (de patente,
crédito) granting; **hacer concesiones**
make concessions; ~ **de distribución**
distribution allowance; **concesiones
económicas** economic grants; ~ **de**

explotación operating grant; ~ **fiscal**
tax concession

concesionario¹ *adj* concessionary;
no ~ nonconcessional

concesionario², -a *m,f* licence BrE *o*
license AmE holder, licensee; (V&M)
authorized dealer

concesionario³ *m* franchise

conciencia *f* awareness,
consciousness; (moral) conscience; **a** ~
conscientiously; **con** ~ **ecológica**
(consumidores) green-conscious; **a plena** ~
de que... fully aware that...; **tomar** ~ **de
algo** become aware of sth; ~ **del cliente**
customer awareness; ~ **fiscal** *or*
tributaria tax awareness; ~ **social**
social conscience

concierto *m* accord; **de** ~ **con** in
agreement with; ~ **de voluntades**
meeting of minds

conciliable *adj* reconcilable

conciliación *f* conciliation,
reconciliation; ~ **de cuentas** account
reconciliation

conciliador, a *m,f* (de disputas laborales)
conciliator; (de problemas) troubleshooter

conciliar *vt* conciliate; (diferencias)
reconcile

concluir **1** *vt* conclude; (reunión) wind
up, round off; (proyecto) complete; ~
que... conclude that...; ~ **la emisión**
sign off
2 *vi* end, finish

conclusión *f* completion; (de contrato)
conclusion; (de reunión) winding-up;
conclusiones *f pl* findings; **llegar a la** ~
de que... reach the conclusion that...

conclusivo *adj* conclusive

concretar *vt* (fecha, precio) fix, set;
(términos, detalles) agree; (precisar) specify;
~ **los términos de un contrato** agree
the terms of a contract

concurrencia *f* (asistencia) attendance;
(en una elección) turnout

concurrente *m* participant; **los** ~**s**
those present

concurrir *vi*: ~ **a algo** attend sth;
(tomar parte) take part in sth; ~ **a las
urnas** turn out to vote; ~ **en algo**
(confluir) contribute to sth

concurso *m* contest, competition;
(licitación) tender; **presentarse a un** ~
take part in a competition; **presentar** *or*
sacar algo a ~ put sth out to tender; ~
eliminatorio knockout competition; ~
de ventas sales contest

condena *f* sentence; **cumplir una ∼** serve a sentence; **∼ condicional** suspended sentence

condenar *vt* (desaprobar) condemn; (Der) sentence, convict; **∼ una acción terrorista** condemn an act of terrorism; **∼ a alguien a cinco años de cárcel** sentence sb to five years in prison; **la ∼on en costas** she was ordered to pay costs, costs were awarded against her

condensado *adj* condensed

condescender *vi* agree, acquiesce; **∼ a algo** agree *o* consent to sth

condición *f* condition; **a ∼ de que...** on condition that..., provided that...; **con una ∼** on one condition; **condiciones** *f pl* conditions, terms; **sin condiciones** unconditionally; **en condiciones de hacer algo** in a position to do sth; **en condiciones normales** under normal circumstances; **en condiciones de vuelo** airworthy; **condiciones de aceptación** terms of acceptance; **condiciones adversas** adverse weather conditions; **condiciones ambientales** environmental conditions; **condiciones atractivas** attractive terms; **condiciones del contrato** terms of the contract; **condiciones crediticias** *or* **de crédito** credit terms; **condiciones económicas** economic conditions; (de acuerdo) financial terms; **condiciones de empleo** conditions of employment, terms of employment; **condiciones de entrega** terms of delivery; **∼ expresa** express condition, express term; **∼ implícita** implied condition; **∼ indispensable** essential condition; **condiciones del intercambio** terms of trade; **condiciones limitadas** limited terms; **condiciones del mercado** market conditions; **condiciones favorables** *or* **de favor** concessionary terms; **condiciones de pago** payment terms; **condiciones de pago aplazado** credit facilities; **∼ previa** precondition; **condiciones de trabajo** working conditions; **condiciones de uso** conditions of use; **condiciones de venta** conditions of sale, terms of sale; **condiciones de vida** living conditions

condicional *adj* conditional; **una oferta ∼** a conditional offer

condominio *m* (de una propiedad) joint ownership; (edificio) condominium, block of flats BrE

condómino, -a *m,f* co-owner, joint owner

condonar *vt* (deuda) cancel, write off; **∼ una pena** lift a sentence

conducente: **∼ a** *adj* conducive to

conducir *vt* drive; (dirigir) conduct; (equipo, empresa) run; **∼ a algo** lead to sth

conducta *f* conduct, behaviour BrE, behavior AmE; **∼ intachable** unimpeachable conduct

conducto *m* (medio) channel; **por ∼ oficial** through the official channels

conectado *adj* (switched) on; (al Internet) connected

conectar *vti* connect; **∼ al Internet** connect to the Internet, log onto the Internet

conexión *f* connection; (de televisión, teléfono) link; **en ∼** online; **∼ al Internet** Internet connection; **perder la ∼ al Internet** lose one's Internet connection; **∼ comercial** business connection; **∼ en directo** live link-up; **∼ ferroviaria** rail link; **∼ por línea conmutada** dial-up connection; **∼ en el mercado** market connection; **∼ de módem** modem link; **∼ permanente** (al Internet) always-on connection; **∼ a la red** Web link; **∼ de redes** (Info) networking

confección *f* (de ropa) dressmaking; (industria) clothing industry; **de ∼** ready-to-wear, off-the-peg; **∼ del presupuesto** budgeting

confeccionar *vt* make; (lista) draw up; (factura) make out

confederación *f* confederation; **C∼ Española de Cajas de Ahorro** *Spanish savings banks' association*; **C∼ Española de Organizaciones Empresariales** *Spanish association of business organizations*; ≈ Confederation of British Industry; **C∼ Española de la Pequeña y Mediana Empresa** Esp *Spanish confederation of small and medium sized companies*; **C∼ de Sindicatos Europeos** European Trade Union Confederation

conferencia *f* conference; (discurso) lecture; (telefónica) (telephone) call; **celebrar una ∼** hold a conference; **∼ a cobro revertido** reverse-charge call BrE, collect call AmE; **∼ por Internet** Internet conference *o* conferencing; **∼ interurbana** trunk call BrE, toll call AmE; **∼ de larga distancia** long-distance telephone call; **∼ de marketing** marketing conference; **∼ de prensa** press conference; **∼ de ventas** sales conference

conferenciante, conferencista
AmL *mf* speaker

conferir *vt* (derechos) confer

confesión *f* (de delito) admission, confession

confiable *adj* reliable

confianza *f* confidence; (fe) trust; ~ **en algo/alguien** confidence in sth/sb; **de ~** trustworthy, reliable; **tener plena ~ que...** have every confidence that...; **en ~** in confidence; ~ **del cliente** customer confidence; ~ **del mercado** market confidence

confiar ⟨1⟩ *vi*: ~ **en** trust, rely on; ~ **en algo/alguien** trust sth/sb; ~ **en que...** be confident that... ⟨2⟩ *vt* entrust; (secreto) confide; ~**le algo a alguien** entrust sth to sb, trust sb with sth

confidencial *adj* confidential

confidencialidad *f* confidentiality; **la ~ de algo** the confidential nature of sth

configuración *f* shape; (Info) configuration; **la ~ de la economía mundial** shape of the world economy; **la ~ del futuro** the shape of the future; **la ~ del terreno** the lie of the land; ~ **básica** base configuration; ~ **binaria** bit configuration; ~ **del equipo** hardware configuration

configurado *adj* shaped, tailored; (Info) configured

configurar *vt* shape, tailor; (Info) configure

confirmación *f* confirmation; ~ **de lectura** read notification; ~ **de pedido** acknowledgement *o* confirmation of order; ~ **de renovación** confirmation of renewal

confirmar *vt* confirm; (llegada) acknowledge; ~ **una reserva/un vuelo** confirm a booking/flight; **por ~** to be confirmed, TBC; **sin ~** (noticia) unconfirmed; (rumor) unsubstantiated

confiscación *f* confiscation; (Der) forfeiture

confiscador, a *m,f* sequestrator

confiscar *vt* confiscate; (contrabando/armas) seize; (propiedad) repossess, sequestrate

conflictivo *adj* (relaciones industriales) difficult

conflicto *m* conflict; (laboral) dispute; ~ **contable** account conflict; ~ **industrial** industrial conflict; ~ **de intereses** conflict of interests; ~ **laboral** industrial dispute, labour dispute BrE,

labor dispute AmE; ~ **de papeles** conflict of roles

confluencia *f* (de intereses) convergence, confluence

conforme *adj* in agreement; ~ **a** according to; (requerimientos) in compliance with; ~ **al auto de procesamiento** by indictment; ~ **al plan** according to plan; ~ **al programa** on schedule; ~ **exige la ley** as required by law; ~ **a la muestra** true to sample; ~ **a la norma** according to the norm; ~ **a su petición** as requested; **un sueldo ~ a sus responsabilidades** a salary in keeping with your responsibilities

conformemente *adv* consistently

conformidad *f* conformity; (aceptación) approval; (Der) compliance; **de ~** accordingly; **de ~ con** in accordance with, in conformity with; (Der) pursuant to

confrontación *f* confrontation

confundir *vt* confuse; (mezclar) mix up; ~ **algo/a alguien con algo/alguien** confuse sth/sb with sth/sb, mistake sth/sb for sth/sb

confusión *f* confusion; (equivocación) mistake; **crear ~** cause confusion; **para evitar confusiones** to avoid confusion

congelación *f* (de salarios, precios, crédito) freeze; ~ **de alquileres** rent freeze; ~ **de créditos/depósitos** credit/deposit freeze; ~ **de empleo** job freeze; ~ **de precios** price freeze

congelado *adj* (activos, créditos) frozen

congelar *vt* (salarios, precios, crédito) freeze; ~ **una cuenta** freeze an account

congestión *f* (del mercado) congestion; ~ **del tráfico** traffic congestion

conglomeración *f* conglomerate; ~ **financiera** financial conglomerate

conglomerado *m* conglomerate; ~ **de empresas** conglomerate

congreso *m* congress; (conferencia) conference; **actas de ~** conference proceedings; **asistir a un ~** attend a conference; **C~ de los Diputados** Esp *lower house of the Spanish parliament,* ≈ House of Commons BrE, ≈ House of Representatives AmE

congruencia *f* congruence; ~ **de objetivos** goal congruence

conjetura *f* conjecture; **hacer ~s** speculate

conjugar *vt* combine

conjunción *f* combination; **en ~ con algo** in conjunction with sth

conjunto¹ *adj* joint

conjunto² *m* set, group; **en ~** on the whole; **~ de caracteres** character array, character set; **~ de código** code set; **~ de datos** data set; **~ finito** finite set; **~ de gráficos de supervídeo** Esp *or* **supervideo** AmL *m* super video graphics array; **~ de medidas** set of measures; **~ de opciones** set of options; **~ de programas** software package, program suite; **~ de reglas** set of rules

conmutabilidad *f* commutability

conmutable *adj* commutable

conmutación *f* commutation, switching; **~ de bancos** bank switching; **~ de bonos** bond switching; **~ de mensajes** message switching

conmutado *adj* dial-up; **acceso ~** dial-up access

conmutador *m* (Info) commuter

conmutar *vt* (pena) commute; **~ algo a algo** convert sth to sth; **~ algo por algo** exchange sth for sth; Esp (convalidar) recognize sth as equivalent to sth

conocer *vt* know; (alguien por primera vez) meet; **~ el mercado** know the market; **dar a ~ algo** make sth known

conocido¹ *adj* known; (famoso) well-known; **también ~ como** alias, also known as, a.k.a.; **~ por su nombre** known by name

conocido², -**a** *m,f* acquaintance

conocimiento *m* knowledge; **con ~ de causa** in full knowledge of the facts; **dar ~ de algo a alguien** inform sb of sth; **pongo en su ~ que...** I am writing to inform you that...; **tener ~ de algo** be aware of sth; **tener un ~ práctico de algo** have a working knowledge of sth; **~ de embarque** bill of lading; **~ especializado** specialist knowledge; **~ experto** expertise; **~ de marca** brand awareness; **~ del mercado** market awareness; **~ del producto** product awareness, product knowledge; **~ tácito** tacit knowledge

consciencia *f* ▸**conciencia**

consciente *adj* aware; **ser** *or* **estar consciente de algo** be aware of sth

consecución *f* (de objetivos) achievement; **~ de un contrato** securing of a contract

consecuencia *f* consequence; **~s** *f pl* implications, repercussions; **a** *or* **como ~** as a result; **por ~** therefore; **pagar** *or* **sufrir las ~s** suffer the consequences; **tener** *or* **traer ~s graves** have serious

consequences *o* repercussions; **traer algo como ~** result in sth; **la decisión trajo como ~ su renuncia** the decision resulted in her resignation *o* brought about her resignation

consecuente *adj* consistent; **~ con** consistent with

consecutivo *adj* consecutive, successive

conseguir *vt* get; (reputación) build up; (meta, objetivo) achieve, realize; (contrato) win; **~ un aumento de sueldo** get a pay rise; **~ hacer algo** manage to do sth; **~ acceso a** gain entry to; **~ un buen valor por el dinero** get good value for money; **~ comunicarse con alguien** get through to sb; **~ un equilibrio** find a balance; **~ nuevos pedidos** secure new orders; **~ una primicia informativa** get a scoop; **~ resultados** get results; **~ un trato** secure a deal

consejería *f* Esp ministry (in some autonomous governments); **C~ de Juventud y Deportes** Esp *autonomous body in charge of promoting sports and youth programmes,* ≈ Sports Council BrE

consejero, -**a** *m,f* (asesor) adviser, consultant; (de compañía) director; **~ de administración** director; **~ de crédito** credit adviser; **~ delegado(-a)** *m,f* managing director; **~ fiscal** tax adviser; **~ de inversiones** investment adviser; **~ técnico(-a)** *m,f* technical adviser

consejo *m* board; (organismo) council; (información) piece of advice; **darle un ~ a alguien** give sb some advice; **pedirle un ~ a alguien** ask sb for advice; **~ de administración** board (of directors); **~ asesor** advisory board; **~ directivo** (*cf* ▸**mesa directiva** AmL) board of directors, management board; **C~ Económico y Social** Economic and Social Council; **~ ejecutivo** executive board; **C~ de Europa** Council of Europe; **~ de fideicomisarios** board of trustees; **~ de ministros** cabinet; **~ de Ministros** (UE) Council of Ministers; **C~ Oficial de Normas Contables** ≈ Governmental Accounting Standards Board; **~ de redacción** editorial board; **~ de selección** screening board, selection board; **C~ Superior de Investigaciones Científicas** *Spanish institute for scientific research;* **~ de supervisión** supervisory board

consenso *m* consensus; **llegar a un ~** reach a consensus

consensuar *vt* agree by consensus, reach a consensus on

consentimiento *m* consent; **por ∼ mutuo** by mutual consent

consentir 1 *vt* allow
2 *vi*: **∼ en algo/hacer algo** agree to sth/do sth

conservación *f* conservation; (de hábitats) preservation; **∼ económica** economic conservation; **∼ de la energía** energy conservation; **∼ del margen** (Bolsa) margin maintenance; **∼ de la naturaleza** nature conservation; **∼ ordinaria** routine maintenance

conservacionista *mf* conservationist

conservador *adj* (gasto, estimación) conservative

conservadurismo *m* conservatism

conservantes *m pl* preservatives; **sin ∼** no preservatives; **sin ∼ ni aditivos** no preservatives or additives

conservar *vt* conserve, preserve

consideración *f* consideration; **tomar algo en ∼** take sth into consideration; **∼ condicional** contingent consideration; **∼ parcial** partial consideration

considerando *m* legal reason; **los ∼s** the whereas clauses

considerar *vt* consider; (ver, juzgar) regard; **∼ los pros y los contras** weigh up the pros and cons; **∼ a alguien culpable de algo** consider sb to be guilty of sth; **bien considerado** all things considered; **considerándolo más detenidamente** upon further consideration

consigna *f* left-luggage office BrE, checkroom AmE; **∼s partidarias** party line

consignación *f* (de mercancías) consignment; (asignación) allotment, apportionment; (de fondos) appropriation; **en ∼** on consignment; **∼ neta** net remittance

consignador, a *m,f* consigner

consignar *vt* (mercancías) consign; (asignar) allocate, allot; **∼ la autoridad que hace el gasto** set forth the spending authority; **∼ fondos presupuestarios** apportion budget funds

consignatario, -a *m,f* consignee; (de paquete) recipient

consistencia *f* consistency

consistente *adj* (argumentación) sound; (conducta, persona) consistent; **∼ en algo** consisting of sth

consistir *vi*: **∼ en algo** consist of sth; **∼ en hacer algo** involve *o* entail doing sth; **el trabajo consiste en atender al público** the job entails dealing with the public

consolidación *f* consolidation; **∼ de acciones** consolidation of shares; **∼ de balances** consolidation of balances; **∼ del capital** capital consolidation; **∼ de la deuda** debt consolidation; **∼ de empresas** merger; **∼ de fondos** consolidation of funds

consolidado *adj* consolidated, well-established; **no ∼** nonconsolidated; **poco ∼** underfunded

consolidar *vt* (posición, acuerdo) consolidate; (deuda) fund

consorcio *m* consortium, syndicate; (deuda) fund; (Fisc) pool; **∼ de aseguradores** underwriting syndicate; **∼ de bancos** consortium of banks

consorte *mf* spouse

constante¹ *adj* constant; (aumento) steady

constante² *f* constant; **∼ de comparación** criterion; **∼ hipotecaria** mortgage constant

constantemente *adv* constantly; (aumentar) steadily

constar *vi*: **∼ de** comprise, consist of; **como** *or* **según consta en** as can be seen from; **∼ en acta** be noted, be placed on record; **hacer ∼ algo** place sth on record; **que conste que…** note that…, let it be known that…

constitución *f* constitution; (establecimiento) setting up; **∼ de una compañía** formation *o* setting up of a company

constituido *adj* (sociedad) incorporated; (fideicomiso) constituted

constituir *vt* (componer, formar) form, make up; (representar) constitute; **∼ una comisión** set up a commission; **∼ una custodia en una cuenta** place a hold on an account; **∼ quorum** form a quorum; **∼ una sociedad** form a partnership; **esa acción no constituye delito** that action does not constitute a crime

construcción *f* construction; **en ∼** under construction; **∼ y uso** construction and use; **∼ de red** network building

constructor, a *m,f* builder, building contractor; **∼ por encargo** custom builder

construir *vt* build, construct; **construido de encargo** purpose-built

cónsul *mf* consul; ∼ **general** consul general

consulado *m* consulate

consulta *f* consultation; (pregunta) enquiry, query; **en ∼ con** in consultation with; ∼ **colectiva** *or* **en común** joint consultation; ∼ **unilateral** unilateral reference

consultar *vt* consult

consulting *m* consulting firm

consultivo *adj* consultative; (papel) advisory

consultor, a *m,f* consultant; ∼ **en administración de empresas** management consultant; ∼ **administrativo(-a)** *m,f* management consultant; ∼ **financiero (-a)** *m,f* financial adviser; ∼ **de publicidad (-a)** *m,f* advertising consultant

consultoría *f* consultancy, consulting firm; ∼ **de gestión** management consultancy

consumado *adj* consummate, accomplished

consumar *vt* consummate; (delito) carry out

consumible *adj* consumable, expendable; **bienes ∼s** consumer goods

consumibles *m pl* consumables, expendables

consumidor, a *m,f* consumer; **entre ∼es** consumer to consumer, C2C; ∼ **electrónico** e-consumer; ∼ **final** end user

consumir *vt* consume; ∼ **preferentemente antes de** (alimentos) best before

consumismo *m* consumerism

consumista[1] *adj* consumer, consumerist; **sociedad ∼** consumer society

consumista[2] *mf* consumer

consumo *m* consumption; **de ∼** consumer; **artículos de ∼** consumer goods; **de bajo ∼** low-energy; **gran ∼** mass consumption; **sociedad ∼** consumer society; **no apto para el ∼** unfit for consumption; ∼ **de capital** capital spending; ∼ **domestico** domestic consumption; ∼ **de electricidad** electricity consumption; ∼ **humano** human consumption; ∼ **interior** domestic consumption; ∼ **intermedio** intermediate consumption; ∼ **mundial** world consumption; ∼ **por persona** consumption per capita; ∼

privado consumer spending; ∼ **público** public spending

contabilidad *f* (práctica) accounting, bookkeeping; (profesión) accountancy; ∼ **acumulativa** accrual accounting; ∼ **administrativa** managerial accounting; ∼ **de un centro de beneficio** profit centre BrE *o* center AmE accounting; ∼ **de compras** acquisition accounting; ∼ **por computadora** AmL (*cf* ▸**contabilidad por ordenador** Esp) computer accounting, electronic accounting; ∼ **computadorizada** AmL (*cf* ▸**contabilidad informatizada** Esp) computer accounting, electronic accounting; ∼ **de costes** Esp *or* **costos** AmL *f* cost accounting; ∼ **de costes** Esp *or* **costos** AmL **normalizados** standard cost accounting; ∼ **creativa** creative accounting; ∼ **directiva** (práctica) management accounting; (profesión) management accountancy; ∼ **financiera** financial accounting; ∼ **fiscal** tax accounting; ∼ **del flujo de efectivo** cash flow accounting; ∼ **de gestión** (práctica) management accounting; (profesión) management accountancy; ∼ **informatizada** Esp (*cf* ▸**contabilidad computadorizada** AmL) computer accounting, electronic accounting; ∼ **medioambiental** environmental accounting, green accounting; ∼ **por ordenador** Esp (*cf* ▸**contabilidad por computadora** AmL) computer accounting, electronic accounting; ∼ **por partida doble** double-entry bookkeeping; ∼ **por partida simple** single-entry bookkeeping; ∼ **de responsabilidad** responsibility accounting; ∼ **social** social accounting; ∼ **verde** environmental accounting, green accounting

contabilización *f* accounting

contabilizar *vt* (en el libro diario) enter in the accounts; ∼ **el margen** post margin

contable *mf* Esp (*cf* ▸**contador** AmL) accountant; ∼ **autorizado(-a)** *m,f* Esp qualified accountant; ∼ **cualificado(-a)** *m,f* Esp qualified accountant; ∼ **diplomado(-a)** *m,f* Esp qualified accountant; ∼ **financiero(-a)** *m,f* Esp financial accountant; ∼ **de gestión** Esp management accountant; ∼ **habilitado(-a)** *m,f* qualified accountant; ∼ **jefe(-a)** *m,f* Esp chief accountant; ∼ **principal** Esp chief clerk, senior clerk; ∼ **público(-a)** *m,f* Esp chartered accountant BrE, certified public accountant AmE

contacto *m* contact; **estar en** ∼ be in contact *o* touch; **mantener el** ∼ **con alguien** keep in touch with sb; **ponerse en** ∼ **con alguien** get in touch with sb; **póngase en** ∼ **con el consulado** get in contact *o* touch with the consulate

contado *m* cash; **al** ∼ for cash

contador, a *m,f* AmL (*cf* ▸**contable** Esp) accountant; ∼ **autorizado(-a)** *m,f* AmL qualified accountant; ∼ **autorizado(-a) colegiado(-a)** *m,f* Accredited Chartered Accountant; ∼ **cualificado(-a)** *m,f* AmL qualified accountant; ∼ **diplomado(-a)** *m,f* AmL qualified accountant; ∼ **financiero(-a)** *m,f* AmL financial accountant; ∼ **de gestión** AmL management accountant; ∼ **habilitado(-a)** *m,f* qualified accountant; ∼ **jefe(-a)** *m,f* AmL chief accountant; ∼ **principal** AmL chief clerk, senior clerk; ∼ **público(-a)** *m,f* AmL chartered accountant BrE, certified public accountant AmE

contaduría *f* (profesión) AmL accountancy; (departamento) accounts department; (oficina de contabilidad) accounting office

contaminación *f* (de producto) contamination; (del medio ambiente) pollution; ∼ **del agua** water pollution; ∼ **del aire** air pollution; ∼ **ambiental** environmental pollution; ∼ **atmosférica** air pollution; ∼ **de las costas** coastal pollution; ∼ **por crudos** oil pollution; ∼ **por lluvia ácida** acid rain pollution; ∼ **por petróleo** oil pollution; ∼ **por radiación** radiation pollution; ∼ **de los ríos** river pollution

contaminado *adj* contaminated, polluted

contaminador, -a *m,f* polluter

contaminante *f* pollutant

contaminar *vt* (aire, atmósfera, agua) pollute; (alimentos) contaminate

contar *vti* count; ∼ **con algo** count on sth; ∼ **con alguien para algo** rely *o* count on sb for sth; ∼ **con el apoyo de alguien** count on sb's support; ∼ **con la aprobación de alguien** have the approval of sb; ∼ **con los medios para hacer algo** have the means to do sth

contención *f* (de demanda) containment; (de gastos) restriction; (de política monetaria) constraint; ∼ **de los costes** Esp *or* **costos** AmL *f* cost containment

contener *vt* contain; (demanda, inflación) control, contain; ∼ **un informe** carry a report; **contiene carta de aviso** advice enclosed

contenido *m* content, subject matter; ∼ **del puesto** job content; ∼ **de la red** Web content

contestación *f* answer, response; **en** ∼ **a su carta** in reply to your letter; ∼ **a la demanda** defence BrE *o* defense AmE plea

contestador *m* answerphone, answering machine; ∼ **automático** answerphone, answering machine

contestar ⓵ *vt* answer, reply to; ∼ **el teléfono** answer the telephone ⓶ *vi* answer, reply; ∼ **por carta** write back; ∼ **a vuelta de correo** reply by return of post BrE *o* by return mail AmE; **no contestan** there's no reply

contexto *m* context; **fuera de** ∼ out of context; **poner algo en** ∼ put sth in context

contiguo *adj* adjoining; (Info) contiguous

continental *adj* continental

continente: **el** ∼ (Europa continental) the Continent

contingencia *f* contingency; **prever cualquier** ∼ make contingency plans; ∼ **de beneficio** *or* **ganancia** gain contingency; ∼ **de pérdidas** loss contingency

contingente¹ *adj* incidental; (responsabilidad) contingent

contingente² *m* quota; ∼ **arancelario** import quota, tariff quota; ∼ **arancelario comunitario** community tariff quota

continuación *f* continuation; **a** ∼ next; (en carta) below; **a** ∼ **de** after, following

continuamente *adv* around-the-clock, round-the-clock BrE

continuar *vi* continue; **continúa** (documentos escritos) continued, cont.; ∼ **con algo** continue with sth

continuidad *f* continuity; ∼ **en el empleo** continuity of employment

continuo *adj* continuous, constant; (interés, apoyo) continuing

contraargumento *m* counter-argument

contraasiento *m* contra entry, reversing entry, correcting entry

contraatacar *vi* counter-attack, fight back

contraataque *m* counter-attack, fightback

contrabandear *vt* smuggle

contrabandista *mf* smuggler

contrabando *m* (mercancías) contraband; (actividad) smuggling

contracción *f* contraction; ∼ **de la demanda** contraction of demand, shrinkage; ∼ **de la economía** economic slowdown

contracomercio *m* counter trade

contracorriente *f* cross-current; **ir a** ∼ swim against the tide

contracubierta *f* (de un libro) back cover

contradecir *vt* contradict; (Der) traverse

contrademanda *f* counterclaim; (Fisc) cross demand

contradicción *f* contradiction; (Der) traverse

contradictorio *adj* contradictory; (Der) traversable

contraer *vt* contract; (deudas) incur

contraerse *v pron* (crecimiento) contract

contralor, a *m,f* AmL (*cf* ▸**interventor** Esp) controller, financial accountant

contramedida *f* countermeasure

contraoferta *f* counteroffer, contra-deal

contrapaquete *m* counterpack

contrapartida *f* adjusting entry; (Econ) balancing item; ∼ **de un contrato** consideration

contraportada *f* (de libro) back cover; (de revista) back page

contraprestación *f* consideration, compensation

contrario *adj* contrary, opposite; **al** ∼ on the contrary; **de lo** ∼ otherwise; **llevar la contraria** disagree; **si no se especifica lo** ∼ unless otherwise specified

contrarrestar *vt* counteract; (Econ) counterbalance

contraseña *f* password

contraste *m* contrast; **en** ∼ **con** in contrast to

contratación *f* contract hire, engagement; ∼ **automática por computadora** AmL *or* **ordenador** Esp *f* program trading; ∼ **pública** public engagement; ∼ **y selección** recruitment and selection; ∼ **de servicios externos** outsourcing

contratante, a *m,f* contractor; ∼ **comprador (a)** *m,f* bargaining party

contratar *vt* contract; (personal) engage, hire, take on; ∼ **a alguien para hacer algo** contract sb to do sth; ∼ **y despedir personal** hire and fire staff; ∼ **los servicios de alguien** hire sb's services

contratista *mf* contractor; ∼ **independiente** independent contractor

contrato *m* contract, agreement; **condiciones del** ∼ terms of the contract; **firmar un** ∼ sign a contract; **incumplimiento de** ∼ breach of contract; **rescindir un** ∼ cancel a contract; ∼ **abierto** open contract; ∼ **de alquiler** rental agreement; ∼ **anual por horas** annual hours contract; ∼ **de anualidad** annuity contract; ∼ **basura** *employment contract for poorly paid temporary work*; ∼ **bilateral** bilateral agreement; ∼ **blindado** golden parachute; ∼ **colectivo** collective bargaining agreement; ∼ **comercial** commercial contract; ∼ **de compra a plazos** hire purchase agreement BrE, installment plan AmE; ∼ **de compraventa** contract of sale and purchase; ∼ **condicional** conditional contract; ∼ **de corretaje** broker's note; ∼ **a corto plazo** short-term contract; ∼ **de divisas a plazo** forward exchange contract; ∼ **de emisión de bonos** bond indenture; ∼ **de empresa** company agreement; ∼ **de exclusividad** exclusive contract; ∼ **de fábrica** AmL (*cf* ▸**acuerdo de fábrica** Esp) shop-floor agreement; ∼ **de fideicomiso** trust deal; ∼ **de futuros** futures contract; ∼ **de futuros financieros** financial futures contract; ∼ **de gestión** management contract; ∼ **de mantenimiento** service agreement, maintenance contract; ∼ **marco** *or* **modelo** standard contract, skeleton contract; ∼ **nulo** void contract; ∼ **a plazo** forward contract; ∼ **de plazo fijo** fixed-term contract; ∼ **a precio fijado** fixed-price contract; ∼ **a precio global** lump-sum contract; ∼ **prematrimonial** prenuptial agreement; ∼ **de representación** agency agreement; ∼ **de servicios** service contract; ∼ **social** social contract; ∼ **de sociedad** partnership agreement; ∼ **de trabajo** contract of employment; ∼ **de trabajo a destajo** piecework contract; ∼ **de venta** sales agreement, sales contract; ∼ **verbal** verbal agreement, oral contract; ∼ **vinculante** binding contract

contravalor *m* exchange value

contribución *f* contribution; (Fisc) tax; (Imp/Exp) levy; **pagar las contribuciones** pay one's taxes; **exento de contribuciones** tax-free; ~ **a la avería gruesa** general average contribution; ~ **urbana** local property tax, ≈ council tax BrE

contribuir *vi* contribute; ~ **a algo** contribute to sth

contribuyente[1] *adj* contributory

contribuyente[2] *mf* taxpayer; ~ **de bajos ingresos** low-income taxpayer; ~ **de ingresos elevados** high-income taxpayer; ~ **de ingresos medios** middle-income taxpayer; ~ **moroso(-a)** *m,f* delinquent taxpayer

control *m* control; (inspección) check; **estar bajo** ~ be under control; **llevar el** ~ **de algo** run *o* manage sth; **perder el** ~ lose control; ~ **de acceso** (Info) access control; ~ **de actuación** performance monitoring; ~ **administrativo** managerial control; ~ **aleatorio** random check; ~ **ambiental** environmental control; ~ **de caja** cash control; ~ **de calidad** quality control; ~ **de la contaminación** pollution control; ~ **de costes** Esp *or* **costos** AmL *m* cost control; ~ **de crédito** credit control; ~**es cualitativos** qualitative controls; ~**es cuantitativos** quantitative controls; ~ **de errores** error control; ~**es estrictos** tight controls; ~ **de existencias** inventory control, stock control; ~ **financiero** financial control; ~ **de funcionamiento** performance monitoring; ~ **del gasto público** public expenditure control; ~ **de inmigración** immigration control; ~ **interno** internal control; ~ **de paridad** parity check; ~ **de pasaportes** passport control; ~ **de precios** price control, price regulation; ~ **del riesgo** risk monitoring; ~ **de rutina** routine check; ~ **de salarios** wage control; ~ **de tiempo** time-keeping; ~ **de tráfico aéreo** air-traffic control; ~ **de ventas** sales control

controlado *adj* controlled; ~ **por computadora** AmL *or* **ordenador** Esp computer-controlled; ~ **a distancia** remote-controlled

controlador, a *m,f* controller; ~ **de almacén** *or* **existencias** stock controller; ~ **de grupo** (Info) cluster controller; ~ **de tráfico aéreo** air-traffic controller

Control-Alternar-Suprimir *m* Control-Alt-Delete

controlar *vt* control; ~ **los gastos** control spending; ~ **un mercado** control a market; (V&M) monitor a market

controversia *f* controversy, issue

controvertido *adj* controversial

contumacia *f* (Der) nonappearance, contempt of court

convalidación *f* (Der) validation; **obtener la** ~ **de títulos** get one's qualifications recognized *o* validated

convencer *vt* convince; (persuadir) persuade; ~ **a alguien de algo** convince sb of sth; ~ **a alguien para hacer algo** persuade sb to do sth; **no me convence** I'm not convinced

convención *f* convention; ~ **de negocios** business convention, business conference

convenido *adj* agreed; **según lo** ~ as agreed

conveniente *adj* advisable; (cómodo) convenient

convenio *m* agreement; **de** ~ **mutuo** by mutual agreement; ~ **antidumping** antidumping agreement; ~ **bilateral** bilateral agreement; ~ **colectivo** collective agreement; ~ **comercial** trade agreement; ~ **de compensación** clearing agreement; ~ **de crédito** credit agreement; ~ **financiero** financial settlement; ~ **fiscal** tax agreement; ~ **laboral** collective agreement on wages and working conditions; ~ **de restricción del comercio** restrictive covenant; ~ **salarial** wage agreement

convenir [1] *vt* (precio, fecha) agree (upon); **a la hora convenida** at the appointed time; ~ **hacer algo** agree to do sth; **sueldo a** ~ salary negotiable [2] *vi* suit, be convenient; **el martes no me conviene** Tuesday doesn't suit me, Tuesday isn't convenient (for me); ~ **que: no conviene que esté presente** I shouldn't be there; **no conviene venderlo a ese precio** it's not worth selling at that price; ~ **en algo** agree on sth

convergencia *f* convergence; ~ **digital** digital convergence

converger *vi* converge; ~ **en algo** concur on sth

conversación *f* conversation; **conversaciones** *f pl* talks; **conversaciones de alto nivel** top level talks

conversión f conversion; **tasa de ~**
conversion rate; **~ acelerada**
accelerated conversion; **~ de datos**
data conversion; **~ de la deuda** debt
conversion; **~ de fichero** file
conversion; **~ de un préstamo**
refunding of a loan

conversor m converter; **~ de**
analógico a digital analogue-to-digital
converter BrE, analog-to-digital converter
AmE; **~ catalítico** catalytic converter

convertible adj (bonos, divisa, moneda)
convertible; **no ~** (bono) nonconvertible;
~ en efectivo encashable

convertido adj converted; **no ~**
unconverted

convertidor m converter; **~**
catalítico catalytic converter; **~ de**
analógico a digital analogue-to-digital
converter BrE, analog-to-digital converter
AmE

convertir vt convert; **~ algo en algo**
convert sth into sth; **~ algo en dinero**
convert sth into cash

convocar vt (elecciones, huelga) call for;
(reunión, asamblea) convene

convocatoria f call; (aviso)
notification; **una ~ a elecciones** a call
for elections

cónyuge mf spouse; **~ divorciado(-a)**
m,f divorced spouse; **~ de hecho**
common-law spouse; **~ separado(-a)**
m,f estranged spouse; **~ superviviente**
surviving spouse

cookie m (en Internet) cookie

cooperación f cooperation; **C~**
Europea en Ciencia y Tecnología
European Cooperation in Science and
Technology; **~ monetaria europea**
European monetary cooperation; **~**
política (UE) political cooperation; **~**
técnica technical cooperation; **~**
tecnológica technological cooperation

cooperador, a m,f joint operator

cooperar vi cooperate; **~ con alguien**
en algo cooperate with sb in sth; **~ en**
la lucha contra el terrorismo cooperate
in the fight against terrorism

cooperativa f cooperative, co-op
(infrml); (vivienda) housing association; **~**
agrícola agricultural cooperative; **~ de**
crédito credit union; **~ de inversiones**
investment trust; **~ de trabajadores**
workers' cooperative

coordenadas f pl (en curriculum vitae)
particulars

coordinación f coordination

coordinado adj coordinated

coordinador, a m,f coordinator,
organizer

coordinar vt coordinate

copia f copy; **~ de la carta adjunta**
copy of letter attached; **enviarle una ~ a**
alguien copy sb in; **hacer una ~ de algo**
make a copy of sth; **~ para archivo** file
copy; **~ autentificada** legally validated
copy; **~ carbón** carbon copy, cc; **~**
certificada certified true copy; **~ ciega**
(en e-mail) blind copy, bcc; **~ directa en**
papel hard copy; **~ fiel** true copy; **~**
fiel y auténtica certified true copy; **~**
heliográfica blueprint; **~ impresa**
printed copy, hard copy; **~ invisible**
blind carbon copy, bcc; **~ legalizada**
legally validated copy; **~ maestra**
master copy; **~ original** original copy,
top copy; **~ de la pantalla** screen copy;
~ pirata pirate copy; **~ de reserva** or
respaldo or **seguridad** backup copy; **~**
de seguridad temporizada timed
backup

copiadora f copier, photocopier

copiar vti copy; **~ del original** copy
from the original; **~ y pegar** copy and
paste

coprocesador m coprocessor

coproducto m coproduct

copropiedad f joint ownership, co-
ownership

copropietario, -a m,f joint owner, co-
owner

copyright m copyright

corchetes m pl square brackets

corp. abr (▶**corporación**) corp.
(corporation)

corporación f corporation; **~ afiliada**
affiliated company; **~ de capital de**
riesgo venture capital corporation; **C~**
de Finanzas Internacionales
International Finance Corporation; **~**
fusionada amalgamated corporation; **~**
transnacional transnational
corporation

corporativismo m corporatism

corporativo adj corporate

corpóreo m corporeal

correa f belt; **~ transportadora**
conveyor belt

corrección f correction; (de tasación)
adjustment; **~ del mercado** market
correction; **~ monetaria** indexation; **~**
de pruebas proofreading

correcto adj correct, exact

corrector¹, a *m,f* copy editor; ∼ **de estilo** copy editor; ∼ **de pruebas** proofreader

corrector² *m* correcting fluid; ∼ **ortográfico** spellchecker

corredor, a *m,f* broker, trader; ∼ **de apuestas** bookmaker; ∼ **de bolsa** broker, trader; ∼ **de comercio** sales representative, sales rep; (Bolsa) bond broker; ∼ **de divisas** foreign exchange trader; ∼ **de propiedades** estate agent BrE, realtor AmE; ∼ **de espacio publicitario** advertising space seller; ∼ **de fincas** estate agent BrE, realtor AmE; ∼ **de hipotecas** mortgage broker; ∼ **de mercancías** commodity broker; ∼ **de productos** commodity broker; ∼ **de seguros** insurance broker; ∼ **titulado(-a)** *m,f* registered broker; ∼ **de valores** security dealer

correduría *f* brokerage, broking; ∼ **de bolsa** stockbroking; ∼ **de seguros** insurance broking

corregido *adj* corrected, amended

corregir *vt* (errores) correct, amend; (cifras) adjust; **sin** ∼ uncorrected; ∼ **algo a la baja** revise sth downwards BrE *o* downward AmE; ∼ **pruebas** proofread

correlación *f* correlation

correlacionar *vt* correlate

correo *m* post BrE, mail AmE; **Correos** Esp ≈ Post Office BrE, Postal Service AmE; **echar algo al** ∼ post BrE *o* mail AmE sth; **por** ∼ by post BrE, by mail AmE; **por** ∼ **aéreo** by airmail; **por** ∼ **marítimo o terrestre** by surface mail; ∼ **aéreo** airmail; ∼ **asegurado** insured post BrE, insured mail AmE; ∼ **basura** junk mail; (Info) junk e-mail; ∼ **por caracol** snail mail; ∼ **certificado** registered post BrE, certified mail AmE; ∼ **directo** direct mail; ∼ **electrónico** e-mail, electronic mail; **mandarle algo a alguien por** ∼ **electrónico** e-mail sb sth, send sb sth by e-mail; ∼ **entrante** incoming post BrE, incoming mail AmE; ∼ **normal** snail mail; ∼ **ordinario** second-class post BrE, second-class mail AmE; ∼ **preferencial** first-class post BrE, first-class mail AmE; ∼ **de respuesta comercial** business reply mail; ∼ **saliente** outgoing post BrE, outgoing mail AmE

correr ① *vt* (riesgo) run

② *vi* (sueldo, intereses) be payable; ∼ **con** bear, meet; ∼ **con el coste** Esp *or* **costo** AmL **de** bear *o* meet the cost of; ∼ **por cuenta de la empresa** be at the company's expense; **los gastos corren por cuenta de la empresa** the company is paying

correspondencia *f* correspondence; **tener** ∼ **con alguien** correspond with sb; ∼ **comercial** business correspondence

corresponder *vi* correspond; ∼ **a algo** pertain *o* correspond to sth; ∼ **con alguien** correspond with sb; **la decisión le corresponde al director** the decision rests with the director

correspondiente *adj* corresponding; ∼ **a algo** pertaining to sth

corresponsal *mf* correspondent; ∼ **en el extranjero** foreign correspondent

corretaje *m* brokerage, broking; ∼ **de bolsa** stockbroking; ∼ **de información** information brokering

corrida *f* run; ∼ **de producción** AmL production run; ∼ **sobre un banco** bank run

corriente¹ *adj* current; **del** ∼ of the current month; (en correspondencia) instant, inst.; **su carta del 15 del** ∼ your letter of the 15th instant *o* inst.; ∼ **y moliente** (infrml) run-of-the-mill; **precio** ∼ going price *o* rate

corriente² *f* trend; ∼ **de capital** capital flow; ∼ **empresarial** business stream; ∼ **financiera** financial flow; ∼ **de fondos** cash flow

corro *m* (Bolsa) ring, pit; ∼ **de contratación** trading desk

corrosión *f* corrosion

corrupción *f* corruption

cortapisa *f* restriction, condition; **sin** ∼**s** no strings attached

cortar ① *vt* cut; (teléfono, agua, luz) cut off; ∼ **la comunicación** hang up ② *vi* AmL hang up; ∼ **y pegar** cut and paste; ∼ **por lo sano** cut one's losses

corte¹ *m* cut; ∼ **de corriente** power cut *o* failure

corte² *f* court; **Las C**∼**s** Esp *legislative assembly*, ≈ Parliament BrE, ≈ Congress AmE; **C**∼ **Europea** European Court; **C**∼**s Generales** *Spanish Parliament*; **C**∼ **Suprema** Supreme Court AmE

corto *adj* short; **de** ∼ **alcance** short-range; **a** ∼ **plazo** short-term

cosa *f* thing; ∼ **juzgada** res judicata; ∼ **de nadie** res nullius; ∼ **nullius** estate in abeyance; ∼ **pública** res publica

cosecha *f* crop; **nueva** ∼ new crop; ∼ **vieja** old crop; ∼ **de vino** vintage

coseguro *m* coinsurance

COST *abr* (▶**Cooperación Europea en Ciencia y Tecnología**) COST (European Cooperation in Science and Technology)

costa *f*: ~s costs; **a** ~ **de** at the expense of; **a toda** ~ at all costs; **condenar a alguien en** ~s order sb to pay costs; ~s **judiciales** legal expenses; (concedidas por el tribunal) legal costs

costar *vt* cost; (tiempo) take; ~ **caro/ barato** be expensive/cheap; **cueste lo que cueste** at all costs

coste *m* Esp, **costo** AmL cost; **al** ~ at cost; ~ **absorbido** absorbed cost; ~ **de acatamiento** cost of compliance; ~ **adicional** additional charge; ~s **administrados** managed costs; ~ **administrativo** administrative cost; ~ **de adquisición** acquisition cost; ~s **agregados** add-on costs; ~ **amortizable** depreciable cost; ~ **amortizado** amortized cost, depreciated cost; ~ **aplicado** applied cost; ~ **autónomo** stand-alone cost BrE; ~ **de capital** cost of capital; ~ **por clic** (en Internet) cost per click, CPC; ~ **creciente** rising cost; ~ **de cumplimiento** compliance cost; ~ **de depreciación** depreciable cost; ~ **depreciado** amortized cost, depreciated cost; ~ **directo** direct cost; ~ **directo de las ventas** direct cost of sales; ~s **de distribución** distribution costs; ~s **elevados** high costs; ~ **estimado** estimated cost; ~s **evitables** avoidable costs; ~ **explícito** explicit cost; ~s **de explotación** operating costs; ~ **de fabricación** manufacturing cost; ~ **fijo** fixed cost; ~s **financieros** financial costs; ~ **de flotación** flotation cost; ~s **de funcionamiento** operating costs; ~ **hundido** sunk cost; ~ **implícito** implicit cost; ~s **incurridos** incurred costs; ~s **indirectos** indirect costs, overheads; ~s **inevitables** unavoidable costs; ~ **laboral** labour cost BrE, labor cost AmE; ~ **de manipulación** handling charge; ~ **de la mano de obra** cost of labour BrE, cost of labor AmE, manpower cost; ~ **de marketing** marketing cost; ~ **medio** average cost, mean cost; ~ **por mil páginas vistas** (en Internet) cost per mille, CPM; ~ **no depreciado** undepreciated cost; ~s **de nómina** payroll costs; ~s **obligados** committed costs; ~s **ocultos** hidden costs; ~s **de operación** running costs; ~ **previsto** anticipated cost; ~ **de producción** production cost; ~ **promedio** average

cost; ~ **real** actual cost, real cost; ~ **recuperable** recoverable cost; ~ **de reemplazo** replacement cost; ~ **salarial** wage cost; ~s **semivariables** semivariable costs; ~s **sumergidos** sunk costs; ~ **suplementario** supplementary cost; ~ **unitario** unit cost; ~ **de ventas** cost of sales; ~s **variables** variable costs; ~ **de la vida** cost of living

coste-eficiente Esp, **costo-eficiente** AmL *adj* cost-efficient

costoso *adj* costly

costumbre *f* custom; (Fin) usance; **de** ~ usual; **en contra de** ~ against policy

cotejar *vt* check, collate; ~ **algo con algo** check sth against sth

cotizable *adj* quotable

cotización *f* quotation, price; **sin** ~ unlisted, unquoted; ~ **de acciones** stock quotation; ~ **al contado** spot price; ~ **de apertura** opening price; ~ **de cierre** closing price; ~ **del dólar** dollar price; ~ **mecanizada** automated quotation; ~ **de valores** securities listing

cotizado *adj* quoted, listed; ~ **en la bolsa** listed on the stock exchange

cotizar ⓵ *vt* (acciones) quote; (cuota) pay; **las acciones se cotizan a 50 euros** the shares are quoted at *o* are worth 50 euros, the share price is 50 euros
⓶ *vi* (contribuir) pay contributions; ~ **al máximo** (tipo, precio, coste) top out; ~ **en bolsa** be listed *o* quoted on the stock exchange, go public; **al cierre cotizaba a 20,57 euros** it closed at 20.57 euros; ~ **a una pensión** pay pension contributions, pay into a pension

C.O.U. *abr* (**Curso de Orientación Universitaria**) *Spanish university entrance examination,* ≈ A level

covarianza *f* covariance

coyuntura *f* situation; ~ **económica** economic situation, economic climate

CPE *abr* (▶**compra por ejecutivos**) MBO (management buyout)

crac *m* (Bolsa) crash

cracker *m* (Info) cracker

creación *f* creation; ~ **comercial** business creation, trade creation; ~ **de empleos** job creation; ~ **de mercado** market creation; ~ **de páginas web** Web authoring; ~ **de producto** product creation; ~ **de prototipos** prototyping

crear *vt* (oportunidades, demanda) create; (problemas) cause; (sistema) set up; (subsidiaria) form, launch; (prototipo, modelo nuevo) develop

creatividad *f* creativity

creativo[1] *adj* creative

creativo[2], **-a** *m,f* copywriter

crecer *vi* grow, increase; (inflación, gastos) rise; **el número de desempleados** *or* **parados** Esp **sigue creciendo** the number of unemployed continues to rise

crecimiento *m* growth, increase; **de** ~ **rápido** fast-growing; **de** ~ **bajo** low-growth; **economías con** ~**s negativos** negative-growth economies; **una industria en** ~ a growth industry; **sin** ~ no-growth; ~ **anual compuesto** compound annual growth; ~ **del capital** capital growth; ~ **cero** zero growth; ~ **constante** steady growth; ~ **corporativo** corporate growth; ~ **del desempleo** rise in unemployment; ~ **económico** economic growth; ~ **nulo** zero growth; ~ **orgánico** organic growth; ~ **rápido** rapid growth; ~ **sostenible** sustainable growth; ~ **sostenido** steady growth

credibilidad *f* credibility; ~ **de la fuente** source credibility

crédito *m* credit; (reputación) standing; ~**s** *m pl* credits; **comprar algo a** ~ buy sth on credit; **concederle a alguien un** ~ grant sb a loan; ~ **abierto** open credit; ~ **al consumo** consumer credit; ~ **ampliado** extended credit; ~ **autorizado** authorized credit; ~ **comercial** goodwill; ~ **corporativo** corporate credit; ~ **a corto plazo** short-term credit; ~ **cubierto/descubierto** secured/unsecured credit; ~ **en cuenta corriente** overdraft facility; ~ **diferido** deferred credit; ~ **hipotecario** mortgage loan; ~ **inmediato** instant credit; ~ **a largo plazo** long-term credit; ~ **puente** bridging loan BrE, bridge loan AmE; ~ **no utilizado** unused credit; ~ **de vivienda** mortgage

creer *vt* believe, think; ~ **que...** think that...

crimen *m* crime; ~ **organizado** organized crime

criminal *adj* criminal

crisis *f* crisis; **la economía está en** ~ the economy is in crisis; ~ **económica** economic slump; ~ **financiera** financial crisis; ~ **nerviosa** nervous breakdown; ~ **del petróleo** oil crisis

criterio *m* criterion; (opinión) opinion, view; ~**s** criteria; ~**s económicos** economic criteria; ~ **de referencia** benchmark; ~**s de selección** selection criteria

crítica *f* criticism; (Medios) review, critique; **duras** ~**s** harsh criticism; **lanzar** *or* **dirigir duras** ~**s contra alguien** launch a fierce attack on sb

criticar *vt* criticize; (libro, película) review

crítico[1] *adj* critical

crítico[2] *m* critic; ~ **de cine** film critic; ~ **de salón** armchair critic

crónica *f* (en periódico) article, feature, report; ~ **financiera** financial news

cronometrador, a *m,f* timekeeper

cronometraje *m* timekeeping

cronómetro *m* chronometer

crudo *m* crude oil

cruzar *vt* cross; ~ **una fila de manifestantes** cross a picket line

CSIC *abr* (▶**Consejo Superior de Investigaciones Científicas**) *Spanish institute for scientific research*

cta. *abr* (▶**cuenta**) a/c (account)

ctdad *abr* (▶**cantidad**) qnty, qty, (quantity)

cte. *abr* (▶**corriente**) inst. (instant)

CTNE *abr* (▶**Compañía Telefónica Nacional de España**) *Spanish national telecommunications network,* ≈ BT (British Telecom)

cuadrado *adj* square

cuadrar *vi* (cuentas, libros) tally; ~ **con algo** tally with sth

cuadratín *m* em dash

cuadrícula *f* grid; ~ **administrativa** managerial grid

cuadro *m* (en un documento) table, chart; (lista) schedule; ~**s** *m pl* (en organización) management; ~ **de amortización** amortization schedule, depreciation schedule; ~ **de diálogo** dialogue box BrE, dialog box AmE, message window; ~ **de depreciación** depreciation schedule; ~ **directivo** board of directors; ~**s dirigentes** senior management; ~ **de mandos** control panel; (en coche) dashboard; ~**s de mando** management; ~**s medios** middle management; ~ **de periodificación** lapsing schedule; ~ **repartidor** switchboard, tagboard AmE

cuadruplicado: **en** ~ *adj* in quadruplicate

cualificación *f* qualification; ~ **doble** dual skilling; ~ **múltiple** multiskilling; ⋯⟶

cualificaciones profesionales professional qualifications

cualificado *adj* qualified, skilled; **no ~** unskilled, unqualified; **estar debidamente ~ para el puesto** have the right qualifications for the job; **estar ~ para hacer algo** be qualified to do sth

cualitativamente *adv* qualitatively

cualitativo *adj* qualitative

cuantía *f* amount; (de pérdidas) extent; **~ no pagada al vencimiento** amount overdue

cuantificación *f* quantification; **~ de la indemnización** measure of indemnity

cuantificar *vt* quantify

cuantitativo *adj* quantitative

cuanto: **en ~ a** *prep* as regards, with reference to

cuarentena *f* (número) about forty; (aislamiento) quarantine

cuartil *m* quartile

cuarto¹ *adj* fourth; **~ mercado** fourth market; **~ mundo** Fourth World; **~ trimestre** fourth quarter

cuarto² *m* (habitación) room; (cuarta parte) quarter

cuasi *pref* quasi; **~ contrato** nearly contract, quasi-contract; **~ dinero** near money

cuatro *m* four; **~ libertades** *f pl* (Econ) four freedoms

cúbico *adj* cubic

cubierta *f* cover; (de libro) jacket; (Info) hood

cubierto *adj* covered; **~ en exceso** oversubscribed

cubrir *vt* (costes, pérdidas) cover; (demanda) meet; (vacante) fill; **~ un puesto** fill a position; **~ el riesgo** hedge the risk

cuenca *f* basin; **~ del Mediterráneo** Mediterranean basin

cuenta *f* account; (cargos) bill BrE, check AmE; (cálculo) calculation; **~s** *f pl* accounts; **a ~** on account; **a ~ de** on account of; **darse ~ de algo** realize sth; **en resumidas ~s** in short; **hacer** *or* **echar ~s** do some sums *o* calculations; **depositar** *or* **ingresar** Esp **dinero en una ~** pay money into an account; **llevar la ~ de algo** keep account of sth; **llevar las ~s** do the accounts; **por ~ propia** at one's own risk; **sacar dinero de una ~** withdraw money from an account; **tener** *or* **tomar algo en ~** take sth into account; **trabajar por ~ propia** work freelance; **~ administrada** managed account; **~ de ahorros** savings account, deposit account; **~ de ajuste** adjustment account; **~s anuales** annual accounts; **~ bancaria** bank account; **~ bancaria conjunta** joint bank account; **~ bloqueada** frozen account, blocked account; **~ cancelada** closed account; **~ de cargo** charge account; **~ cerrada** closed account; **~ de cheques** current account BrE, checking account AmE; **~ de cliente** client account, customer account; **~s de clientes por cobrar/pagar** trade accounts receivable/payable; **~ comercial** business account; **~ de compensación** clearing account; **~ conjunta** joint account; **~ corriente** current account BrE, checking account AmE; **~ de débito directo** cash account; **~ de depósito** deposit account; **~ en descubierto** overdrawn account; **~ deudora** debit account; **~s diversas** sundry accounts; **~s de la empresa** company accounts; **~s estatutarias** statutory accounts; **~ de explotación** operating account; **~ de fideicomiso** trust account; **~s finales** final accounts; **~s fiscalizadas** certified accounts; **~ de gastos** expense account; **~s de gestión** management accounts; **~ de gestión de activos** asset management account; **~ hipotecaria** mortgage account; **~ de ingresos y gastos** income and expenditure account; **~s interinas** *or* **intermedias** interim accounts; **~ de Internet** Internet account; **~s intervenidas** certified accounts; **~ de inversiones** investment account; **~ de negocios** business account; **~s a pagar** accounts payable; **~ de pagos** disbursing account; **~ de pérdidas y ganancias** profit and loss account BrE *o* statement AmE; **~ a plazo fijo** fixed-term deposit BrE, time deposit AmE; **~ presupuestaria** budget account; **~s publicadas** published accounts; **~ saldada** closed account; **~ de valores** securities account; **~s de varios** sundry accounts; **~ vencida** aged account; **~ de ventas** sales account; **~ a la vista** call account, demand account

cuerpo *m* body; (Der) corpus; (de letra impresa) point size; **~ del delito** (piece of) evidence; **~ de la demanda** statement of claim; **~ electoral** electorate; **~ de inspectores** inspectorate; **~ legislativo** legislative body; **~ del mensaje** e-mail text; **~ político** body politik; **~ profesional**

reconocido recognized professional body; **~ del texto** body of the text; **~ de voluntarios** voluntary body

cuestión *f* issue, matter; **poner algo en ~** call sth into question; **~ clave** key issue; **~ de derecho** point of law; **~ estratégica** strategic issue; **~ política** political issue; **~ técnica** technical point

cuestionario *m* questionnaire; **rellenar un ~** fill in a questionnaire; **~ de evaluación** evaluation questionnaire

cuidado *m* care

culminar *vi*: **~ en** culminate in

culpa *f* fault; (Der) guilt; **echarle la ~ a alguien de algo** blame sb for sth; **sin ~ de** no fault of; **~ grave** gross negligence

culpabilidad *f* guilt, culpability (frml)

culpable¹ *adj* guilty, culpable (frml); **declarar ~ a alguien** find sb guilty

culpable² *mf* guilty party

culpar *vt* blame; **~ a alguien de algo/ de hacer algo** blame sb for sth/for doing sth

culposo *adj* guilty, culpable

cultivo *m* (de tierra) farming, cultivation; **~ comercial** cash crop; (de plantas) growing, cultivation; (cosecha) crop; **~ extensivo** extensive farming; **~ industrializado** factory farming; **~ intensivo** intensive farming; **~s marinos** seafarming; **~ no intensivo** deintensified farming; **~ orgánico** organic farming; **~ de subsistencia** subsistence farming

culto *adj* educated; (literatura, música) highbrow

cultura *f* culture; **~ corporativa** corporate culture; **~ de la dependencia** dependency culture; **~ de organización** organization culture; **~ popular** popular culture

cultural *adj* cultural; **identidad ~** cultural identity

cumbre *f* summit; **el momento ~** the high point, the peak; **~ económica** economic summit

cumplido¹ *adj* complete, full

cumplido² *m* compliment; **visita de ~** courtesy call

cumplimentación *f* (de suscripciones) fulfilment BrE, fulfillment AmE

cumplimentar *vt* (formulario) fill in

cumplimiento *m* (de normas, leyes) observance, compliance; (de empresa) performance; (de suscripciones, obligaciones) fulfilment BrE, fulfillment AmE; **en ~ de algo** in compliance with sth; **~ de contrato** contract compliance; **~ de la ley** law enforcement; **~ tributario** tax compliance

cumplir ① *vt* (orden) carry out; (compromiso, requisito) fulfil BrE, fulfill AmE; (norma, condiciones) comply with; (objetivo) achieve, meet; (condena) serve; **~ todos los requisitos para el puesto** have the right qualifications for the job; **hacer ~ un contrato** enforce a contract ② *vi* (plazo) expire; **~ con** (compromiso) honour BrE, honor AmE, fulfil BrE, fulfill AmE; (condición) comply with; **~ con una cláusula** comply with a clause; **~ con sus obligaciones** fulfil BrE o fulfill AmE one's obligations; **~ con su deber** do one's duty

cuña *f* quoin; **~ publicitaria** advertisement; (emisión) commercial break

cuota *f* quota; (parte) share; **~s** dues, fees; **en ~s mensuales** in monthly instalments BrE o installments AmE; **~ administrativa** management fee; **~ anual** annual fee, annual instalment BrE, annual installment AmE; **~s de asistencia** attendance fees; **~ de conexión** (al Internet) connection charge; **~ inicial** AmL deposit, down payment; **~ de mantenimiento de cuenta** account maintenance fee; **~ de marca** brand share; **~ mensual** monthly instalment BrE, monthly installment AmE; **~ de mercado** market share, share of market, slice of the market; **~ de pantalla** audience share; **~ no reembolsable** nonrefundable fee; **~ patronal** employer's contribution; **~ de la seguridad social** social security contribution, ≈ National Insurance contribution BrE; **~s sindicales** union dues; **~ de socio** membership fee; **~ del usuario** user fee

cupo *m* quota; **~ de ventas** sales quota

cupón *m* coupon; **~ al portador** bearer coupon; **~ para arrancar** tear-off coupon; **~ de dividendo** dividend coupon; **~ de intereses** interest coupon; **~ de regalo** gift token o voucher BrE, gift certificate AmE; **~ de respuesta pagada** reply-paid card; **~ vencido** matured coupon; **~ de vuelo** flight coupon

cúpula *f* (de organización) top

curriculum *m* curriculum; ∼ **vitae** curriculum vitae BrE, CV BrE, résumé AmE

cursar 1 *vt* (tramitar) deal with; (Patent) file

2 *vi*: **el mes que cursa** the current month

cursiva *f* italics; **en** ∼ in italics

curso *m* course; **en** ∼ underway, current; **en el** ∼ **de** in the course of; **hacer un** ∼ do a course; **ser de** ∼ **legal** be legal tender; ∼ **de acción** course of action; ∼ **acelerado** (de formación) accelerated training course; ∼ **de capacitación** *or* **formación** training course; ∼ **de introducción** induction course; ∼ **introductorio** introductory course; ∼ **legal** legal tender; ∼

monetario monetary course; ∼ **preliminar** introductory course; ∼ **de reactualización profesional** retraining course; ∼ **de reciclaje** retraining course; ∼ **a tiempo completo** full-time course

cursor *m* cursor

curva *f* curve; ∼ **de aprendizaje** learning curve; ∼ **campaniforme** bell curve; ∼ **de costes** Esp *or* **costos** AmL cost curve; ∼ **de crecimiento** growth curve; ∼ **de demanda** demand curve; ∼ **de experiencia** experience curve

custodia *f* (de niño) custody; ∼ **de acciones** custody of shares; ∼ **conjunta** joint custody; ∼ **de haberes** safekeeping of assets

Dd

d

D/A *abr* (▸**digital/analógico**) D/A (digital/analogue BrE, digital/analog AmE)

dador, a *m,f* (Fin) drawer

dañar *vt* (imagen, reputación) damage, harm; **dañado en tránsito** damaged in transit

daño *m* (a empresa, reputación) damage; **causar** *or* **hacer** ∼ cause *o* do damage; **calcular los** ∼s assess the damage; ∼ **por agua** water damage; ∼ **ambiental** environmental damage; ∼ **corporal** bodily injury; ∼ **irreparable** irreparable damage, irreparable harm; ∼ **material** damage to property; ∼**s y perjuicios** damages; **pagar/reclamar** ∼**s y perjuicios** pay/claim damages; ∼**s y perjuicios incidentales** incidental damages; ∼**s punitivos** punitive damages

dar ① *vt* give, grant; (precio) quote; ∼**le a alguien hasta el final del mes** give sb until the end of the month; ∼**le la bienvenida a alguien** welcome sb; **dar algo por:** ∼ **un trabajo por terminado** consider a job finished; **dieron el dinero por perdido** they wrote the money off, they considered the money lost ② *vi*: **darle a algo** press sth, hit sth; ∼ **con algo** find sth, hit on sth; **dieron con una buena solución** they hit on a good solution

datación *f* dating

datáfono *m* dataphone

datos *m pl* data; **disponer de todos los** ∼ have all the necessary information; **por falta de** ∼ because of a lack of information; **un dato importante** an important piece of information; **procesamiento de** ∼ data processing; **recuperación de** ∼ data retrieval; ∼ **de aceptación de entrada** entry acceptance data; ∼ **agregados** aggregate data; ∼ **básicos** key data; ∼ **biográficos** biographical data, curriculum vitae BrE, CV BrE, résumé AmE; ∼ **brutos** raw data; ∼ **de control** control data; ∼ **digitales** digital data; ∼ **económicos** economic data; ∼ **de entrada** input data; ∼ **estadísticos** statistical returns; ∼ **de fuente** source data; ∼ **justificativos** supporting data;

∼ **mecánicos** mechanical data; ∼ **de muestra** sample data; ∼ **no procesados** raw data; ∼ **primarios** primary data; ∼ **personales** personal details, particulars; ∼ **de salida** output data; ∼ **secundarios** secondary data; ∼ **técnicos** technical data

DCB *abr* Esp (▸**Diseño Curricular Base**) ≈ NC (≈ National Curriculum) BrE

DDB *abr* (▸**base de datos distribuida**) DDB (distributed database)

debajo *adv* underneath; ∼ **de** under, below; **por** ∼ **del cambio** at a discount; **por** ∼ **de la media** below average; **por** ∼ **del 20%** under 20%

debate *m* debate; (menos formal) discussion; **tener un** ∼ have a discussion

debatir *vt* debate; (problema, asunto) discuss

debe *m* debit; ∼ **y haber** debit and credit

deber ① *vt* owe; ∼ **algo a alguien** owe sb sth ② *vi* should, ought to; **deberías ir a la reunión** you should go to the meeting

debido *adj* due; ∼ **a** due to, on account of; ∼ **a que...** due to the fact that...; **a su** ∼ **tiempo** in due course; **con el** ∼ **respeto** with all due respect; **debida diligencia** due diligence

débil *adj* weak; (mercado, demanda) sluggish; (moneda) soft

debilidad *f* weakness; (de demanda) sluggishness

debilitar *vt* weaken

débito *m* debit, debit entry; ∼ **bancario** direct debit; **pagar por** ∼ **bancario** pay by direct debit; ∼ **neto** net debit

década *f* decade

decaer *vi* (demanda) decline, wane; (comercio) fall away; **el prestigio de la compañía ha decaído mucho** the company's prestige has declined considerably

decaimiento *m* (de interés) fall, decline; ∼ **de la memoria** memory decay

decepcionante *adj* disappointing

decibelio *m* decibel

decidir *vti* decide; **~ entre dos cosas** decide between two things; **~ hacer algo** decide to do sth; **~ que no** decide against sth; **~ sobre algo** decide on sth, take a decision on sth

decir *vt* say; **~le algo a alguien** tell sb sth; **decir que sí/no** say yes/no; **diga** *or* **dígame** (hablando por teléfono) hello; **es ~** in other words; **~ unas palabras en favor de alguien** put in a word for sb; **~ unas palabras de bienvenida** say a few words of welcome

decisión *f* decision; **tomar una ~** make *o* take a decision; **llegar a una ~** reach a decision; **~ de alto nivel** high-level decision; **~ comercial** business decision; **~ de compra** purchase decision; **~ de compromiso** compromise decision; **~ de fabricar o comprar** make-or-buy decision; **~ judicial** judgment; **~ mayoritaria** majority decision; **~ presupuestaria** budget resolution; **~ salarial nacional** national wage award; **~ de última hora** last-minute decision

decisivo *adj* decisive; (resultado) conclusive

declaración *f* announcement; (Der) declaration, statement; **hacer una ~** make a statement; **hacer una ~ jurada** swear an affidavit; **presentar la ~** file one's tax return; **no haber presentado la ~** be in default in filing one's tax return; **sin ~ de valor** no value declared; **~ de abandono** notice of abandonment; **~ de la acusación** prosecution statement; **~ de aduana** bill of entry, customs declaration; **~ arancelaria** customs declaration; **~ de bancarrota** declaration of bankruptcy; **~ por computadora** AmL (*cf* ▸**declaración por ordenador** Esp) computer return, online return; **~ de condiciones** statement of terms and conditions; **~ conjunta** joint statement; **~ conjunta de interés** joint declaration of interest; **~ de derechos** bill of rights; **~ de dividendo** dividend declaration; **~ del editor** publisher's statement; **~ por escrito** written statement; **~ falsa** false statement; (Fisc) false declaration, false return; **~ fraudulenta** fraudulent misrepresentation; **~ a hacienda** tax return; **~ del impuesto sobre la renta** tax return; **~ incompleta** (Fisc) underdeclaration; **~ incorrecta** (Fisc) misdeclaration; **~ de los ingresos** reporting of income; **~ del IVA** VAT return; **~ jurada por escrito** affidavit, sworn statement; **~ morosa** delinquent return; **~ negativa** debit return; **~ por ordenador** Esp (*cf* ▸**declaración por computadora** AmL) computer return, online return; **~ de origen** declaration of origin; **~ de política** policy statement; **~ presupuestaria** budgetary statement; **~ previa** preliminary entry; **~ de quiebra** declaration of bankruptcy; **~ de la renta** tax return; **~ de un testigo** witness statement

declarante *mf* deponent; (Fisc) filer; **~ fuera de plazo** late filer

declarar **1** *vt* (apoyo, oposición) declare, state; (noticia, decisión) announce, state; (bienes, ingresos) declare; (huelga) call; **~ a alguien en bancarrota** *or* **quiebra** declare sb bankrupt; **¿algo que declarar?** anything to declare?; **~ a alguien culpable/inocente** find sb guilty/not guilty
2 *vi* give evidence, testify; **~ bajo juramento** give evidence on oath, swear on affidavit

declinación *f* decline; **~ de responsabilidad** disclaimer

declinar *vt* decline; **~ una oferta/invitación** decline an offer/invitation; **~ responsabilidad** not accept reponsibility *o* liability

decodificación *f* decoding

decodificador *m* decoder

decodificar *vt* decode

decomisación *f* decommissioning

decomisar *vt* decommission

decretar *vt* decree

decreto *m* decree; **D~ de Presupuestos** Appropriation Act BrE, Appropriation Bill AmE; **D~ de Sociedades Mercantiles** Companies Act BrE, Companies Bill AmE

dedicación *f* dedication; **~ a algo** dedication to sth; **~ parcial/plena** part-time/full-time

dedicado *adj* dedicated

dedicar *vt* dedicate, devote; **~ algo a algo** dedicate *o* devote sth to sth; **dedicó su vida a la empresa** he devoted his life to the company

dedicarse *v pron*: **~ a** devote oneself to; **¿a qué se dedica Usted?** what do you do?

deducción *f* allowance; (Fisc) deduction, relief; **hacer una ~** make a deduction; **~ admisible** allowable deduction; **~ por amortización**

allowance for depreciation; ∼ **autorizada** allowable deduction; ∼ **de capital** capital deduction; ∼ **por carga familiar** dependant tax credit; ∼ **por cargas familiares** childcare expense deduction; ∼ **de crédito básica** basic credit allowance; ∼ **de la cuota permitida** allowable tax credit; ∼ **por doble imposición** double taxation relief; ∼ **por la esposa** spouse's allowance; ∼ **de gastos** expense allowance; ∼ **por gastos corrientes** allowance for living expenses; ∼ **por gastos de viaje** allowance for traveling AmE o travelling BrE expenses; ∼ **impositiva** tax deduction; ∼ **por incapacidad** disability tax credit; ∼ **por invalidez** disability allowance; ∼ **por matrimonio** married person's allowance; ∼ **no utilizada** unused relief; ∼ **en nómina** payroll deduction; ∼ **en origen** deduction at source; ∼ **personal** personal allowance BrE, personal exemption AmE

deducibilidad f deductibility

deducible adj deducible; (Fisc) deductible; ∼ **a efectos impositivos** tax-deductible; **gastos** ∼**s** allowable expenses

deducir vt (razonar) deduce; (descontar) deduct; ∼ **de** net against; **antes/después de** ∼ **los impuestos** before/after tax

deduplicado adj de-duped

defecto m flaw; **por** ∼ by default; **sin** ∼ flawless; **el plan tiene muchos** ∼**s** it's a flawed plan, there are a lot of things wrong with the plan; ∼ **de fábrica** manufacturing fault; **tener un** ∼ **de fábrica** be faulty; ∼ **inherente** inherent defect

defectuoso adj faulty, flawed, defective

defender vt stand up for; ∼ **el propio caso** argue one's own case, defend oneself

defensa f defence BrE, defense AmE; **acudir** or **salir en defensa de algo/ alguien** come out in sth's/sb's defence BrE o defense AmE, stand up for sth/sb

defensor, a m,f defender, champion; ∼ **del estado del bienestar** welfarist

deficiencia f deficiency, shortfall; ∼ **de experiencia** experience deficiency

deficiente adj deficient, poor

déficit m deficit, shortfall; ∼ **de la balanza comercial** trade gap; ∼ **de la balanza de pagos** balance of payments deficit; ∼ **de caja** cash deficit; ∼

comercial trade deficit; ∼ **deflacionario** deflationary gap; ∼ **inflacionario** inflationary gap; ∼ **presupuestario** budget deficit; ∼ **de recursos** resources gap

deficitario adj deficit; **balance** ∼ negative balance

definición f definition; ∼ **de artículos** definition of items; ∼ **básica** basic definition

definitivo adj definite, final; (mandamiento judicial, decreto) absolute; **en definitiva** finally, in short

deflación f deflation

deflacionar vt deflate

deflacionario adj deflationary; **medidas deflacionarias** deflationary measures

deformación f deformation, distortion

deformante adj distorting

deformar vt distort

defraudación f fraud; ∼ **fiscal** tax fraud

defraudador, a: ∼ **de impuestos** m,f tax evader, tax dodger (infrml)

defraudar vt (fisco) defraud; (impuestos) evade, dodge (infrml)

DEG abr (▸**derechos especiales de giro**) (special drawing rights)

degradación f (de ciudades) degradation; ∼ **del suelo** soil degradation

degradar vt degrade; (RRHH) demote

dejación f surrender

dejar **1** vt leave; ∼ **abierto** (tema) leave open; ∼ **acumular** (deuda) run up; ∼ **algo de lado** pass sth over; ∼ **algo atrás** leave sth behind; ∼ **algo claro** make sth clear; ∼ **constancia de algo** (gastos, déficit) provide a record of sth; ∼ **una cuenta en descubierto** overdraw an account; ∼ **el trabajo** leave one's job **2** vi cease, stop; ∼ **de hacer algo** stop doing sth; ∼ **de tener efecto** (contrato) cease to have effect; ∼ **de trabajar** stop o give up work

delegación f delegation; ∼ **comercial** trade delegation; ∼ **del gobierno** *office of the government representative responsible for liaising with an autonomous region*; ∼ **de Hacienda** tax office; ∼ **de poderes** (del gobierno) devolution; (de votos) proxy

delegado, -a m,f delegate, representative; ∼ **a una conferencia** conference delegate; ∼ **del gobierno** government representative; ∼ **gremial** ····⟩

shop steward; ~ **sindical** union
representative

delegar *vt* delegate; ~ **algo en alguien**
delegate sth to sb; ~ **la autoridad en**
alguien delegate authority to sb

delimitación *f* demarcation; (RRHH)
(de responsabilidades) definition

delimitar *vt* delimit, demarcate; (RRHH)
(responsabilidades) define

delito *m* crime, criminal offence BrE,
criminal offense AmE; **cometer un** ~
commit a crime; **cuerpo del** ~ corpus
delicti, (piece of) evidence; ~
económico economic crime; ~ **de**
guante blanco white-collar crime; ~
menor misdemeanour BrE, misdemeanor
AmE

delta *m* delta; **delta-neutral** delta-
neutral; ~ **de una opción de**
compra/venta delta call/put

demanda *f* demand; (derecho penal)
complaint; (judicial) lawsuit, (legal) action;
(de capital) call; (Seg) claim; **en** ~ (trabajos)
in demand; **ley de la oferta y** ~ law of
supply and demand; **por** ~ **popular** by
popular demand; **presentar una** ~
contra alguien sue sb, bring a lawsuit
against sb; **el producto no tiene** ~ the
product does not sell well; **según** ~ Esp
(*cf* ▸**justo a tiempo** AmL) just-in-time;
según la ~ at the market call; **sobre** ~
at call; ~ **actual** current demand; ~
animada brisk demand; ~ **aplazada**
deferred demand; ~ **civil** civil action; ~
de los consumidores consumer
demand; ~ **creciente** growing demand;
~ **por daños** claim for damages; ~ **por**
difamación libel action; ~ **estacional**
seasonal demand; ~ **legal** civil action;
~ **de mercado** market demand; ~**s y**
obligaciones claims and liabilities; ~
persistente repeat demand; ~ **prevista**
anticipated demand; ~ **salarial** wage
demand

demandado, -a *m,f* defendant

demandante *mf* plaintiff, claimant

demandar *vt* claim; (Der) sue; **precio**
demandado y ofertado asked and bid
price; ~ **a alguien por difamación** sue
sb for libel; ~ **a alguien por daños y**
perjuicios sue sb for damages; ~ **a**
alguien por violar una patente sue sb
for infringement of patent

demo *m* demo

democracia *f* democracy; ~ **popular**
people's democracy; ~ **social** social
democracy

democráticamente *adv*
democratically

democrático *adj* democratic

demografía *f* demography

demográfico *adj* demographic

demolición *m* demolition; (de un
sistema) destruction

demora *f* delay; (Econ) lag; **sin** ~
without delay; **una** ~ **de dos horas** a
two-hour delay; ~ **en el pago**
arrearage; ~**s de trámite** procedural
delays

Demoscopia *m Spanish market
research institute,* ≈MORI (Market and
Opinion Research International)

demostración *f* demonstration; (de
productos) show; ~ **en tienda** in-store
demonstration

demostrar *vt* show, demonstrate

denegación *f* denial, refusal

denegar *vt* refuse; ~ **una fianza** refuse
bail; ~ **información** withhold
information

denominación *f* (de artículos) title; ~
de una cuenta account title; ~ **legal**
(administrativa) legal name; **D**~ **de Origen**
(Protegida) (Protected) Designation of
Origin, *official guarantee of origin and
quality of a product;* ~ **del puesto** job
title

denominador *m* denominator; ~
común common denominator

densidad *f* density; ~ **de**
almacenamiento (de datos) packing
density; ~ **en dígitos binarios** bit
density; ~ **de población** population
density; ~ **simple** single density

densímetro *m* hydrometer

dentro *adv* inside; **aquí** ~ herein; ~ **de**
within; **estar** ~ **del alcance de** fall
within the scope of; ~ **de los límites**
prescritos within the prescribed limits;
~ **del plazo especificado** *or* **fijado**
within the specified time; ~ **del precio**
in-the-money; ~ **de una semana** this
time next week, within a week; ~ **del**
tiempo permitido within the allotted
time frame, within the time allowed

denuncia *f* (acción civil) complaint;
presentar *or* **hacer una** ~ **contra**
alguien report sb, make a formal
complaint against sb

departamento *m* (de una impresa,
institución) department; (AmL, *cf* ▸**piso** Esp)
flat BrE, apartment AmE; ~ **acreedor**
creditor department; **D**~ **de Aduanas y**
Tributos ≈ Customs & Excise

Department BrE; ~ **de atención al cliente** customer services department; ~ **de bienestar social** welfare department; ~ **de caja** cash office; ~ **de cambios** exchange department; ~ **de circulación** (Medios) circulation department; ~ **de compras** purchasing department; ~ **de contabilidad** accounts department; **D**~ **de Control de Prácticas Comerciales** ≈ Office of Fair Trading; ~ **creativo** creative department; ~ **de crédito** credit department; ~ **de facturación** invoicing department BrE, billing department AmE; ~ **financiero** finance department; ~ **fiscal** revenue department; ~ **gráfico** art department; ~ **de hipotecas** mortgage department; ~ **de impuestos** tax department; ~ **jurídico** legal department; ~ **de marketing** marketing department; ~ **de nóminas** payroll department; ~ **de personal** personnel department; ~ **de planificación** planning department; ~ **de producción** manufacturing department, production department; ~ **de publicidad** advertising department, publicity department; ~ **de reclamaciones** claims department; ~ **de servicio al cliente** customer services (department); ~ **de ventas** sales department

dependencia f dependence; ~ **del gobierno** government agency

depender: ~ **de** vt depend on; ~ **de alguien** (en jerarquía) report to sb

dependiente[1] adj dependent; ~ **de algo/alguien** dependent on sth/sb

dependiente[2], **-a** m,f assistant; ~ **de tienda** shop assistant BrE, sales clerk AmE

deposición f deposition

depositante mf bailer, depositor

depositar vt deposit, pay in; ~ **dinero en una cuenta** pay money into an account

depositario, -a m,f depository; (Der) escrow; ~ **de una apuesta** stakeholder; ~ **de bienes embargados** garnishee; ~ **judicial** receiver; ~ **legal de documentos** escrow agent

depósito m deposit; (edificio) depot, storeroom; (Der) bailment; **en** ~ in bond; (cantidad) as a deposit; ~ **aduanero** or **afianzado** bonded warehouse; ~ **al por menor** retail deposit; ~ **de averías** average deposit; ~ **bancario** bank deposit; ~ **en caja de seguridad** safe

deposit; ~ **de claves** key escrow; ~**s en divisas** currency deposits; ~ **de mercancías** goods depot; ~ **de muebles** furniture depot; ~ **a plazo fijo** fixed-term deposit BrE, time deposit AmE; ~ **sujeto a preaviso** notice deposit; ~ **a la vista** sight deposit

depreciación f depreciation; (Cont) amortizement, write-off; **tasa de** ~ depreciation rate; ~ **acelerada** accelerated depreciation; ~ **de un activo** write-down; ~ **de activos fijos** depreciation of fixed assets; ~ **acumulada** accumulated depletion, accumulated depreciation; ~ **anual** annual depreciation; ~ **de balance decreciente** declining balance depreciation; ~ **física** (cuentas anuales) physical depreciation; ~ **monetaria** currency depreciation; ~ **planeada** planned obsolescence

depreciado adj depreciated; **no** ~ undepreciated

depreciar vt depreciate, write off; (trabajo) downgrade

depreciarse v pron depreciate

depredador, a m,f predator

depresión f depression; (de curva, gráfico) trough; ~ **económica** economic slump

deprimido adj (mercado, región) depressed

depuración f (Info) debugging; (Med amb) purification; ~ **del agua** water purification; ~ **de aguas residuales** sewage treatment, waste-water treatment

depurador m (Info) debugger

depurar vt (Info) debug; (Med amb) depurate, purify; ~ **las aguas residuales** treat sewage, treat waste-water

derechas: **de** ~ adj right-wing

derechismo m rightism, right-wing tendencies

derecho m (permiso) right, entitlement; (carrera) law; ~**s** rights; (honorarios) royalties; **con** ~ **a adjudicar** eligible to adjudicate; **de** ~ de jure; **por** ~ ex claim; **por** ~ **propio** in its own right; **reservados todos los** ~**s** all rights reserved, copyright; **reservado el** ~ **de admisión** the management reserves the right to refuse admission; **sin** ~ **a apelar** with no right of appeal; **sin** ~ **a dividendo** ex dividend; **tener** ~ **a** be eligible for, be entitled to; ~ **absoluto** (pertenencia) absolute title; ~ **de acceso** access right; ~ **administrativo** administrative law; ~**s de admisión** ⋯⟩

admission fee; ~ **adquirido** vested interest; ~s **de aduana** or **arancelarios** customs duty, excise duty; ~ **aeronáutico** aviation law; ~ **angloamericano** common law; ~s **de antena** broadcasting rights; ~ **antiguo** old law; ~ **de apelación** right of appeal; ~ **de arrendamiento** rental right; ~ **de arrendamiento vitalicio** life tenancy; ~ **del arrendatario** tenant's rights; ~s **de autor** copyright; (honorarios) royalties; ~s **de certificación** registration fee; ~s **cinematográficos** film BrE o movie AmE rights; ~ **civil** civil law; ~s **civiles** civil rights; ~ **de compensación** right of redress; ~s **compensatorios** (Imp/Exp) countervailing duties; ~s **conferidos** rights afforded; ~ **constitucional** constitutional law; ~ **consuetudinario** common law; ~s **de conversión** conversion rights; ~ **de devolución** right of return; ~s **editoriales** or **de edición** publishing rights; ~s **de ejecución** performing rights; ~s **elevados** heavy duties; ~s **de emisión** broadcasting rights; ~ **empresarial** business law; ~ **de entrada** right of entry; ~s **de entrada** entrance fee; ~ **escrito** statute law; ~s **especiales de giro** special drawing rights; ~ **exclusivo** exclusive right; ~s **exclusivos de negociación** sole bargaining rights; ~s **de exportación** export duty; ~ **fiscal** fiscal law, tax law; ~ **general de retención** general lien; ~s **humanos** or **del hombre** human rights; ~ **a la huelga** right to strike; ~s **de importación** import duties; ~s **inalienables** vested rights; ~s **individuales** rights of the individual; ~ **internacional** international law; ~s **de interpretación** performing rights; ~ **jurisprudencial** case law; ~ **laboral** labour law BrE, labor law AmE; ~ **legal** legal right, statutory right; ~s **de llave** (de una propiedad) premium; (de un negocio) goodwill; ~ **marítimo** maritime law; ~ **mercantil** business law, commercial law, mercantile law; ~ **parlamentario** statute law; ~ **penal** criminal law; ~ **positivo** statute law; ~ **prendario** lien; ~ **de prioridad** pre-emption right, priority right; ~ **privado** private law; ~ **procesal** procedural law; ~ **público** public law; ~ **de réplica** right of reply; ~ **de reproducción** copyright; ~ **de retracto** right of repurchase; ~ **de reventa** right of resale; ~ **de sociedades** company law, corporation

law; ~ **de sucesión** succession law; ~ **de sucesión** inheritance tax; ~ **de tanteo** or **del tanto** (comercial) pre-emptive right; ~ **a trabajar** right to work; ~ **del trabajo** labour law BrE, labor law AmE; ~s **de traspaso** transfer fees; ~ **a vacaciones** holiday entitlement BrE, vacation entitlement AmE; ~ **de voto** voting right, right to vote

deriva f drift; **a la** ~ adrift; **la empresa va a la** ~ the company has lost its direction o way; ~ **salarial** (jarg) wage drift (jarg)

derivada f derivative

derivador m (Bolsa) shunter

derivar vt (conversación, llamada) divert; (Econ) spin off

derogación f abolition; (Der) repeal

derogar vt abolish; (Der) repeal

derrama f apportionment

derrumbarse v pron (edificios) fall down; (planes, sistema) collapse

desacato m contempt; ~ **a las normas** failure to comply with the regulations; ~ **al tribunal** contempt of court

desaceleración f deceleration

desacelerar vi decelerate; (proceso) slow down

desactivado adj disabled

desactivar vt (Info) disable, lock; (caja) uncheck AmE, untick BrE

desacuerdo m disagreement; **estar en** ~ be in disagreement; ~ **sobre algo** disagreement over sth

desafiar vt challenge; (autoridad) defy

desagregar vt (costes) break down

desaguar vt run off

desagüe m run-off; (Med amb) effluence; (para residuos peligrosos) outlet; ~ **industrial** industrial discharge

desahogo m (Info) flame

desahorro m dissaving

desahuciar vt evict, dispossess

desahucio m eviction

desajustado adj (números, estadísticas) unadjusted

desajuste m imbalance; ~ **de precios** price gap

desalentar vt discourage

desaliento m discouragement; ~ **mercantil** slackening

desalineación f misalignment; (Cont) mismatch

desalojar *vt* (inquilino) evict; (edificio) vacate; (por peligro) evacuate

desalojo *m* (de inquilino) eviction; (evacuación) evacuation

desanimar *vt* demotivate

desánimo *m* demotivation; ~ **comercial** slackening

desarmonizar *vt* (Fin) degear

desarrollado *adj* (mercado, país, región) developed; **poco** ~ underdeveloped

desarrollador, a *m,f* developer; ~ **de programas** software *o* program developer; ~ **web** Web developer

desarrollar *vt* (mercado, país, región) develop

desarrollarse *v pron* (economía, mercado, país) develop, grow

desarrollo *m* (de operaciones) development; **en (vía de)** ~ developing; **países en vía de** ~ developing countries; **zona de** ~ development area; ~ **administrativo** management development; ~ **comercial** commercial development; ~ **económico** economic development; ~ **educativo** educational development; ~ **empresarial** business development; ~ **insostenible** unsustainable development; ~ **de marca** brand development; ~ **de mercado** market development; ~ **de nuevo producto** new-product development; ~ **del personal** staff development; ~ **personal** personal growth; ~ **de producto** product development; ~ **profesional** career development; ~ **de recursos humanos** Human Resource Development; ~ **regional** regional development; ~ **del sistema** system development; ~ **sostenible** sustainable development

desastre *m* disaster; ~ **económico** economic disaster

desatendido *adj* unattended

desbaratar *vt* (planes) ruin; (sistema) disrupt

desbloquear *vt* (fondos) release, unfreeze; (negociaciones) break the deadlock *o* stalemate in; (teclado) unlock

desbloqueo *m* (de cuenta) unblocking, unfreezing; ~ **de los sueldos** release of pay cheques BrE *o* checks AmE

desbordamiento *m* spillover; (Info) overflow

desbordarse *v pron* spill over

descalificación *f* disqualification; (RRHH) deskilling

descapitalización *f* undercapitalization

descapitalizado *adj* undercapitalized

descargar *vt* (carga) unload; (responsabilidad, trabajo) offload; (Der) acquit; ~ **a alguien de una responsabilidad** relieve sb of a responsibility

descargo *m* offloading; (de deuda) acquittance; (del acusado) acquittal

descartar *vt* (idea, proyecto) rule out

descendente *adj* (tendencia) downward

descender *vi* (acciones, ventas) fall; (en jerarquía) be demoted

descendiente *mf* descendant; **morir sin** ~**s** die without issue

descenso *m* downswing, downturn, fall; ~ **en picado** sharp dive; ~ **de la población** fall in population; ~ **de suministros** fall in supplies

descentralización *f* decentralization

descentralizar *vt* decentralize

descifrado *m* (de programa) decryption

descifrar *vt* (programa) decrypt, unscramble

descolgar *vt* (teléfono) answer, pick up; **dejar el teléfono descolgado** leave the phone off the hook

descompartimentalización *f* decompartmentalization

descomponer *vt* break down

descomposición *f* breakdown; ~ **del trabajo en fases** breakdown of tasks

descompresión *f* (de datos, archivos) decompression

descomprimir *vt* (datos, archivos) decompress, unzip

desconectado *adj* (del Internet) disconnected, offline

desconectar *vti* (del Internet) disconnect

descongelar *vt* unfreeze

desconocido *adj* unknown; ~ **en esta dirección** unknown at this address

descontable *adj* discountable; **no** ~ indiscountable

descontado *adj* (precio) discounted

descontar *vt* (letra, pagaré) discount; (deducir) deduct; **me descontó el 15%** he gave me a discount of 15% *o* a 15% discount; **me descuentan un 25% del sueldo** they deduct 25% of my salary

descontento *m* discontent; ~ **del personal** labour unrest BrE, labor unrest AmE

descontratación *f* decruitment

d

describir *vt* describe

descripción *f* description; **hacer una ∼** give a description; **∼ comercial** trade description; **∼ de la patente** patent specification; **∼ de puesto** job description

descriptivo *adj* descriptive

descuadre *m* mismatch

descubierto *m* overdraft; **estar en ∼** be overdrawn; **∼ no garantizado** unsecured overdraft

descubrir *vt* discover, find out; (planes, intenciones) reveal

descuento *m* discount; **con ∼** at a discount, on special offer; **hacer un ∼** give a discount; **sin ∼** no discount; **un ∼ del 10%** a 10% discount; **∼ comercial** trade discount; **∼ por compra a granel** bulk discount; **∼ corporativo** corporate discount; **∼ de deudas** debt factoring; **∼ por pago al contado** cash discount; **∼ de temporada** seasonal discount; **∼ por volumen** volume discount

descuidado *adj* in a state of neglect

descuido *m* mistake; (falta de cuidado) negligence

desdomiciliación *f* dedomiciling

desechos *m pl* waste; **∼ industriales** industrial waste

deseconomía *f* diseconomy; **∼ de aglomeración** agglomeration diseconomy; **∼ de escala** diseconomy of scale

desembolsable *adj* disbursable

desembolsar *vt* disburse, pay out

desembolso *m* disbursement, outlay; **∼s de caja** cash disbursement; **∼ de capital** capital outlay; **∼ inicial** initial outlay

desempaquetado *adj* unpacked

desempaquetar *vt* unpack

desempeñar *vt* (cargo) hold; **∼ un cometido** carry out a duty; **∼ un papel en** play a part in; **desempeñó un papel muy importante en las negociaciones** she played a very important role in the negotiations

desempeño *m* (de una función) execution; **∼ económico** economic performance; **∼ del puesto** job performance; **durante el ∼ de su cargo como director** during his time as director

desempleado *adj* unemployed, out of work; **los ∼** the unemployed; **los ∼ crónicos** the long-term unemployed

desempleo *m* unemployment; **∼ creciente** rising unemployment; **∼ crónico** long-term unemployment; **∼ encubierto** concealed unemployment, hidden unemployment; **∼ estacional** seasonal unemployment; **∼ de larga duración** long-term unemployment; **∼ masivo** mass unemployment

desequilibrado *adj* unbalanced

desequilibrar *vt* upset the balance of

desequilibrio *m* disequilibrium, imbalance; **∼ comercial** trade imbalance; **∼ económico** economic disequilibrium; **∼ de intercambios** imbalance of trade; **∼ monetario** financial disequilibrium

desertización *f* desertification

desestabilizar *vt* destabilize

desestacionalizado *adj* seasonally-adjusted

desestructurado *adj* unstructured

desfalcador, a *m,f* embezzler

desfalcar *vt* embezzle

desfalco *m* embezzlement

desfasado *adj* jet-lagged

desfase *m* lag; **∼ cronológico** time lag; **∼ entre generaciones** generation gap; **∼ horario** jet lag; **∼ salarial** Esp (*cf* ▸**rezago salarial** AmL) wage lag

desfavorable *adj* unfavourable BrE, unfavorable AmE

desfavorecido *adj* underprivileged

desfiguración *f* misrepresentation; **∼ voluntaria de los hechos** wilful misrepresentation of facts

desforestación *f* deforestation

desgaste *m* wear and tear; (del poder) loss, decline; **∼ del mercado** market attrition; **∼ natural** natural wear and tear

desglosar *vt* (costes) break down

desglose *m* (de cifras, costes) breakdown; **∼ de activos** asset stripping; **∼ de gastos** cost trimming; **∼ de operaciones** operations breakdown; **∼ del trabajo** job breakdown

desgravable *adj* tax-deductible

desgravación *f* allowance, tax relief; **∼ básica** basic relief; **∼ de los costes** Esp *or* **costos** AmL **de inversión** capital cost allowance; **∼ de dividendo** dividend tax credit; **∼ empresarial** corporate tax credit; **∼ fiscal** tax allowance; **∼ fiscal del empleo** employment tax credit; **∼ fiscal en origen** tax relief at source; **∼ fiscal de**

la propiedad property tax allowance; ∼ **fiscal reembolsable** refundable tax credit; ∼ **de gastos personales** allowance for personal expenses; ∼ **hipotecaria** mortgage relief; ∼ **de los ingresos personales** personal income tax allowance; ∼ **de los intereses** interest relief; ∼ **de pensión** pension tax credit

desgravar **1** *vt* claim tax relief on; (producto, importación) eliminate the tax *o* duty on; ∼ **hasta 20.000 euros** claim tax relief on up to 20,000 euros **2** *vi* (bonos) be tax-deductible, qualify for tax relief

deshacerse: ∼ **de** *v pron* divest oneself of; ∼ **de las existencias** dispose of stock

designación *f* appointment, designation; ∼ **conjunta** joint designation

designado, -a *m,f* appointee

designar *vt* (empleado) appoint, designate (frml); **ha sido designado presidente** he has been appointed chairman

desigualdad *f* (Cont) mismatch; (Pol) inequality; ∼**es sociales** social inequality; **en** ∼ **de condiciones** non-arm's-length

desincentivo *m* disincentive

desindicalización *f* de-unionization

desindustrialización *f* deindustrialization

desinflación *f* deflation

desinformación *f* disinformation

desinstalación *f* uninstallation, deinstallation

desinstalar *vt* uninstall, deinstall

desintegración *f* disintegration

desintermediación *f* nonintervention

desinversión *f* disinvestment

desinversor, a *m,f* disinvestor

desinvertir *vt* disinvest

desistimiento *m* waiver; ∼ **de contrato** anticipatory breach

desistir *vi* desist; ∼ **de una apelación** abandon *o* drop an appeal

desmarketing *m* demarketing

desmaterialización *f* dematerialization

desmaterializado *adj* (certificados de depósito) dematerialized

desmonetización *f* demonetization; ∼ **del oro** gold demonetization

desmoralizar *vt* demoralize, demotivate

desmotivación *f* demotivation

desmotivar *vt* demotivate

desmutualización *f* demutualization

desmutualizar *vt* demutualize

desnacionalización *f* denationalization

desnacionalizar *vt* denationalize

desnudo *adj* bare

desobediencia *f* disobedience; (en tribunal) contempt of court; ∼ **civil** civil disobedience

desocupación *f* dismissal, dehiring AmE

desordenado *adj* disorganized; **estar** ∼ be in a mess

despachador, a *m,f* clearer

despachar *vt* (asunto) deal with; (en tienda) serve; (carta) send, dispatch; ∼ **un pedido** deal with an order; ∼ **por favor** please forward

despacho *m* office; (envío) dispatch; ∼ **de aduanas** customs clearance; ∼ **de billetes** (Ocio) box office; (Transp) ticket office; ∼ **de consultoría** consulting office; ∼ **de pedidos** fulfilment BrE *o* fulfillment AmE of orders

despedida *f* (al final de carta) ending; (fiesta) leaving party, leaving do BrE (infrml); **una cena de** ∼ a farewell dinner; ∼ **y cierre** (de empresa, fábrica) closedown

despedido *adj* fired, sacked (infrml); **ser** ∼ be fired, be dismissed

despedir *vt* (personal) fire, dismiss; (por no ser necesario) lay off, make redundant BrE, dehire AmE

despedirse *v pron* say goodbye, take one's leave (frml)

despegar **1** *vt* (quitar) remove, peel off **2** *vi* (avión) take off

despegue *m* takeoff; ∼ **y aterrizaje corto** short takeoff and landing

desperdicio *m* waste product; ∼**s domésticos** domestic waste

despido *m* dismissal, firing (infrml); (por no ser necesario) laying off; ∼ **por causa justa** just cause dismissal; ∼ **colectivo** collective dismissal, mass dismissal; ∼ **constructivo** constructive dismissal; ∼ **disciplinario** disciplinary dismissal; ∼ **implícito** constructive dismissal; ∼ **improcedente** wrongful dismissal; ∼ **injustificado** unfair dismissal; ∼ **justificado** fair dismissal; ∼ **masivo** mass dismissal, mass redundancy BrE; ⋯⟩

∼ **con notificación** termination with notice; ∼ **obligatorio** compulsory redundancy BrE; ∼ **sumario** summary dismissal; ∼ **voluntario** voluntary redundancy BrE

despilfarro *m* waste

desplazamiento *m* move, shift; **gastos de** ∼ travel expenses; ∼ **de bloque** (procesamiento de datos, textos) block move; ∼ **de la demanda** shift in demand; ∼ **a la derecha/izquierda** right/left shift; ∼ **hacia abajo/arriba** scrolling down/up; ∼ **en pantalla** scrolling

desplazar ⌐1⌐ *vt* replace; (información, datos) scroll up/down; (trasladar) relocate; ∼ **a alguien de su cargo** remove sb from his/her post, replace sb; **el e-mail ha desplazado varias otras formas de comunicación** e-mail has replaced various other methods of communication ⌐2⌐ *vi* scroll

desplazarse *v pron* scroll; ∼ **hacia arriba/abajo** scroll up/down

desplegable *m* (en libro, revista) gatefold; **menú** ∼ drop-down menu

desplegar *vt* (hoja) unfold, open out; (equipo) deploy

despliegue *m* deployment

desplome *m* (Bolsa) crash; (de divisa) collapse; (del comercio mundial) slump

despoblación *f* depopulation; ∼ **forestal** Esp deforestation

despojar *vt* evict; ∼ **a alguien de algo** strip sb of sth

desposeimiento *m* divestiture

despreciar *vt* (oferta, ayuda) reject

desprenderse: ∼ **de** *v pron* (trabajadores, existencias) shed, get rid of

desprovisto *adj*: ∼ **de algo** devoid of sth, lacking in sth

desreconocimiento *m* derecognition

desregulación *f* deregulation; ∼ **global** global deregulation; ∼ **de precios** price deregulation

desregular *vt* deregulate

destacado *adj* outstanding

destacar *vt* (diferencias) highlight, underline; (Info) highlight

destajo *m* piecework; **trabajar a** ∼ do piecework; **cobrar a** ∼ be paid a rate for the job

destilación *f* distilling

destinar *vt* (fondos) allocate, earmark; (persona) post; **lo han destinado a Londres** he's been posted to London

destinatario, -a *m,f* recipient, receiver, addressee; **si no se entrega al** ∼, **por favor devuélvase al remitente** if undelivered, please return to sender

destino *m* destination; (puesto) posting; **con** ∼ **a** bound for; ∼ **de los impuestos** revenue allocation

destituir *vt* dismiss; ∼ **al consejo** unseat the board

destreza *f* skill; **con** ∼ skilfully BrE, skillfully AmE

destrucción *f* destruction; **la** ∼ **de las selvas pluviales** the destruction of the rain forests

destructorade documentos *f* shredder

destruir *vt* destroy; (reputación, plan) ruin; ∼ **el medio ambiente** damage the environment

desuso *m* disuse; **en** ∼ in abeyance; **caer en** ∼ fall into disuse *o* abeyance

desutilidad *f* disutility

desvalorización *f* devaluation; ∼ **del capital propio** dilution of equity

desvalorizar *vt* devalue

desventaja *f* disadvantage; ∼ **competitiva** competitive disadvantage

desventajado *adj* disadvantaged

desventajoso *adj* disadvantageous

desviación *f* discrepancy; (Cont) variance; (en la ley) deviation; (Econ) shift; ∼ **salarial** wage drift

desviar *vt* (vuelo, fondos) divert; (pregunta) deflect

desvío *m* detour; (Info) switch; (de tráfico) diversion; ∼ **de llamada** (telefonía) call diversion

detalle *m* detail; (de factura) item; **sin entrar en** ∼**s** without going into detail; **al** ∼ retail; **venta al** ∼ retail sale; ∼ **del balance** balance item; ∼ **de los empleados** personnel specification

detallista *mf* retailer

detección *f* detection; ∼ **de averías** diagnostic

detención *f* detention

detener *vt* stop; (competición) block; (arrestar) detain

detenido *adj* under arrest

detentado: **no** ∼ *adj* (Bolsa) not held

deteriorar *vt* damage; (moneda) impair; **deteriorado en tránsito** damaged in transit

deteriorarse *v pron* deteriorate

deteriorización *f* deterioration; ∼ **de precios** price deterioration

deterioro *m* deterioration; (Fisc) impairment; ~ **físico** (en cuentas anuales) physical deterioration

determinación *f* determination; (evaluación) assessment; ~ **del activo fijo** fixed asset assessment; ~ **del activo neto** net worth assessment; ~ **de beneficios** profit splitting; ~ **de los costes** Esp *or* **costos** AmL fixing of costs; ~ **de costes** Esp *or* **costos** AmL **estándar** standard costing; ~ **de los hechos** fact-finding; ~ **del impuesto** tax assessment; ~ **de objetivos** target setting, objective setting; ~ **de precios** price determination; ~ **de precios del mercado** market pricing; ~ **de tareas** task setting; ~ **del valor neto** net worth assessment

determinante *m* determinant; ~ **de precio** price determinant

determinar *vt* (precio) ascertain, determine; (valor) set; ~ **judicialmente** (demanda) adjudicate

detonador *m* detonator

detrimento *m* detriment; **en ~ de** to the detriment of

deuda *f* debt, liability; **cobrar una ~** collect a debt; **pagar una ~** pay off *o* clear a debt; ~ **activa** uncancelled debt BrE, uncanceled debt AmE; ~ **amortizable** amortizable debt; ~ **anulada** cancelled debt BrE, canceled debt AmE; ~ **atrasada** arrears; ~ **bruta** gross debt; ~ **comercial** trading debt; ~ **consolidada** consolidated debt; ~ **del estado** (títulos emitidos) government stock; (suma adeudada) public sector borrowing; ~ **externa** foreign debt; ~ **fallida** bad debt; ~ **fiscal** tax liability; ~ **flotante** floating debt; ~ **garantizada** secured debt; ~ **incobrable** bad debt; ~ **interna** internal debt; ~ **morosa** doubtful debt; ~ **nacional** national debt BrE, public debt AmE; ~ **per capita** per-capita debt; ~ **precedente** underlying debt; ~ **privada** private debt; ~ **pública** national debt BrE, public debt AmE; ~ **pública bruta** gross national debt; ~ **de recurso limitado** limited-recourse debt; ~ **vencida** liquid debt, matured debt

deudor, a *m,f* debtor; ~ **comercial** trade debtor; ~ **dudoso(-a)** *m,f* doubtful debtor; ~ **fiscal** tax debtor; ~ **hipotecario** mortgager; ~ **moroso(-a)** *m,f* bad debtor

devaluación *f* devaluation; ~ **monetaria** currency devaluation

devaluar *vt* devalue; ~ **una moneda** devalue a currency

devaluarse *v pron* (moneda) devalue

devengado *adj* (intereses) accrued, accruing

devengar *vt* accrue, bear; ~ **intereses** earn interest

devengo *m* accrual; ~ **modificado** modified accrual

devolución *f* refund; (de impuestos, alquiler) rebate; (de sueldo) back payment; ~ **anual** annual repayment; ~ **de compras** purchase returns; ~ **económica** economic devolution; ~ **de préstamo** loan repayment; ~ **en un solo pago** balloon repayment; ~ **de ventas** sales returns

devolver *vt* return; (dinero) repay, pay back; ~ **al remitente** return to sender; ~ **una llamada telefónica** return a phone call

DG *abr* (▸**director general**) CEO (chief executive officer)

DHTML *abr* (*lenguaje de referencia de hipertexto dinámico*) DHTML (Dynamic Hypertext Mark-up Language)

día *m* day; **efectivo desde el ~** with effect from; **en el ~** same-day; **en ~s alternos** on alternate days; **en ~s laborables** on weekdays; **estar al ~ en el pago de la hipoteca** be up to date with one's mortgage repayments; **estar en el orden del ~** be on the agenda; **por ~** per day, daily; ~ **a día** day by day; ~ **de asueto** (frml) public holiday, bank holiday BrE, legal holiday AmE; ~ **de aviso** reporting day; ~ **de bancos** banking day; ~ **de calendario** calendar day; ~ **de cesión** (de opciones) assignment day; ~ **de compensación** clearing day; ~**s completos** clear days; ~**s consecutivos** consecutive days, successive days; ~ **de cuenta** account day; ~ **designado** appointed day; ~ **de elecciones** polling day; ~ **de entrega** delivery day; ~ **de estudio** study day; ~ **de facturación** billing day; ~ **festivo** *or* **feriado** public holiday; ~**s de gracia** grace days; ~ **hábil** working day; ~**s hasta el vencimiento** days to maturity; ~ **inhábil** non-working day, bank holiday BrE, legal holiday AmE; ~ **laborable** workday, working day BrE; ~ **libre** day off; ~ **del mercado** market day; ~ **natural** (en contrato) calendar day; ~ **de pago** payment date; (de jornales) payday; ~ **de temporada alta** peak day; ~ **de temporada baja** ⋯⃗

off-peak day; ∼ **de trabajo** working day
BrE, workday AmE

diagnosis *f* diagnosis

diagnóstico *m* diagnostic; ∼
ambiental environmental assessment

diagrama *m* diagram, chart; **hacer un**
∼ **de algo** draw a diagram of sth; ∼ **de**
actividad activity chart; ∼ **de barras**
bar chart; ∼ **circular** pie chart; ∼ **de**
dispersión scatter diagram,
scattergram; ∼ **de flujo** flowchart; ∼ **de**
flujo de datos data flow chart; ∼ **de**
frecuencia histogram; ∼ **de Gantt**
Gantt chart; ∼ **de gestión** management
chart; ∼ **de procedimientos** process
chart; ∼ **sectorial** pie chart

diálogo *m* dialogue BrE, dialog AmE

diamantista, -a *m,f* diamond
merchant; (tallador) diamond cutter

diariamente *adv* daily

diario¹ *adj* (de todos los días) daily; (al día)
a day; **tres horas diarias** three hours a
day

diario² *m* (periódico) newspaper; (agenda)
journal, diary; (en oficina) daybook; **a** ∼
every day; ∼ **de caja** cash journal, cash
book; ∼ **de caja chica** petty cash book;
∼ **de cobros al contado** cash receipts
journal; ∼ **comercial** trade journal; ∼
de compras purchases journal; ∼
electrónico e-journal; ∼ **de entradas**
en caja cash receipts journal; ∼ **de**
máquina computer log; ∼ **de**
navegación ship's log; ∼ **de**
operaciones log; ∼ **de pagos al**
contado cash payments journal; ∼ **de**
ventas sales journal, sold daybook

dibujante *mf* designer; ∼
publicitario(-a) *m,f* commercial artist

dibujar *vt* draw

dibujo *m* drawing; ∼ **lineal** line
drawing

dictamen *m* opinion; (informe) report; ∼
de auditoría auditor's certificate; ∼
jurídico legal opinion; ∼ **de propiedad**
opinion of title; ∼ **con salvedades**
qualified opinion

dictar *vt* (carta, texto) dictate; (leyes,
medidas) announce; (sentencia) pronounce,
pass; ∼ **un auto** pronounce an order; ∼
un auto contra alguien issue a writ
against sb; ∼ **un auto de prisión**
preventiva remand in custody

diente *m* (alimentador de papel) pin

diesel-eléctrico *adj* diesel-electric

dieselización *f* dieselization

dieta *f* per diem allowance, subsistence
allowance; ∼**s de viaje** (*cf* ▶**viáticos**
AmL) travelling expenses BrE, traveling
expenses AmE

difamación *f* defamation

difamatorio *adj* libellous BrE, libelous
AmE

diferencia *f* difference, gap; **a** ∼ **de**
unlike; **la** ∼ **entre las dos compañías**
the difference between the two
companies; ∼ **a la baja** bear spread; ∼
de cambio exchange difference; ∼
debida al género gender gap; ∼
deflacionaria deflationary gap; ∼ **de**
precio difference in price; ∼ **de**
rendimiento yield gap; ∼ **salarial** wage
differential, wage gap

diferenciación *f* (mercadotecnia)
differentiation; ∼ **de marca** brand
differentiation

diferencial *m* gap; (beneficio)
differential; ∼ **al alza/a la baja**
bullish/bearish spread; ∼ **fiscal** tax gap;
∼ **de habilidad** skill differential; ∼ **de**
opciones option spread; ∼ **de pago**
pay differential; ∼ **de precios** price
differential; ∼ **de rendimiento** yield
gap; ∼ **de salarios** wage differential,
wage gap; ∼ **de sueldo** earnings
differential; ∼ **de tipos de interés**
interest rate differential

diferenciar *vt* differentiate

diferido *adj* deferred; **en** ∼ prerecorded; **una transmisión en** ∼ a prerecorded broadcast

diferir ⓵ *vt* defer; ∼ **una deuda** defer a
debt; ∼ **el pago** defer payment; ∼
sentencia adjourn sentence
⓶ *vi* differ; ∼ **de algo** differ from sth

difícil *adj* difficult, hard; **le resultó** ∼
adaptarse a la nueva compañía he
found it hard to settle in the new
company; **ser** ∼ **de utilizar** not be user-
friendly

dificultad *f* difficulty, problem; **superar**
or **vencer** ∼**es** overcome problems; ∼
imprevista unforeseen problem, snag
(infrml); ∼ **técnica** technical hitch

difundido: **muy** ∼ *adj* widespread

difunto *adj* deceased

difusión *f* (de ideas, información)
spreading, dissemination (frml); (de prensa)
circulation; **los medios de** ∼ the media;
∼ **auditada** audited circulation; ∼ **en**
red webcasting, netcasting; ∼ **salarial**
wage diffusion

digeratos *m pl* (Info) digerati

digital *adj* digital; **brecha ~** technology gap; **mercado ~** digital marketplace

digital/analógico *adj* digital/analogue BrE, digital/analog AmE

digitalización *f* digitalization

digitalizar *vt* digitize

dígito *m* digit; **~ binario** binary digit; **~ de comprobación** check digit; **~ decimal** decimal digit

digno *adj* honourable BrE, honorable AmE; **~ de confianza** trustworthy; **ser ~ de mención/verse** be worth mentioning/seeing

dilapidación *f* dilapidation

dilema *m* dilemma

diligencia *f* (Der) procedure; **hacer las ~s necesarias para algo** take the necessary steps to do sth; **instruir ~s** institute proceedings; **~s judiciales** legal proceedings; **~s de lanzamiento** eviction proceedings

dilución *f* dilution; **~ del capital** equity dilution

dimensión *f* size, dimension; **~ nominal** basic size

dimensionar *vt* (pantalla) size

dimisión *f* resignation; **presentar la ~** hand in *o* tender one's resignation; **~ sumaria** summary dismissal

dinámica *f* dynamics; **~ de grupo** group dynamics; **~ de producto** product dynamics

dinámico *adj* dynamic; **HTML ~** dynamic HTML

dinamismo *m* dynamism; (Bolsa) buoyancy

dinero *m* money, cash; **gastar ~** spend money; **hacer ~** make money; **el restaurante les da mucho ~** the restaurant is a nice little earner; **tener ~ en mano** have cash in hand; **~ abundante** easy money; **~ de ayuda** aid money; **~ bancario** bank money; **~ barato** cheap money; **~ en caja** float, till money; **~ caliente** hot money; **~ en circulación**, **~ circulante** money in circulation; **~ de compensación** compensation money; **~ contante** specie; **~ en depósito** deposit money; **~ en efectivo** cash; **~ electrónico** e-money, digital cash; **~ generador** seed money; **~ inactivo** idle cash, idle money; **~ inicial** front-end money; **~ de mercancía** commodity currency; **~ en metálico** cash, ready money; **~ negro** undeclared money; **~ no convertible** inconvertible money; **~**

personal personal money; **~ prestado** borrowed money; **~ productivo** active money; **~ rápido** smart money; **~ recibido** monies received; **~ para sobornos** slush fund; **~ sucio** dirty money; **~ suelto** change; **~ a la vista** day-to-day money; (Econ) money at call

diodo *m* diode; **~ electroluminiscente** light-emitting diode

diploma *m* diploma; **D~ en Comercio** ≈ Diploma of Commerce

diplomacia *f* diplomacy

diplomático[1] *adj* diplomatic; **inmunidad diplomática** diplomatic immunity

diplomático[2], **-a** *m,f* diplomat

diputación *f* delegation, deputation; **~ permanente** standing committee; **~ provincial** ≈ county council

diputado, -a *m,f* (delegado) delegate; (del gobierno) ≈ Member of Parliament BrE, ≈ MP BrE, ≈ Congressman AmE, ≈ Congresswoman AmE, ≈ Member of Congress AmE

dirección *f* (señas) address; (de compañía) management; (sentido) direction; **bajo nueva ~** under new management; **de una ~** one-way; **de ~ sur** southbound; **la ~ se disculpa por las molestias causadas** the management regrets any inconvenience caused; **la ~ indicada arriba** the above address; **~ absoluta** absolute address; **~ ascendente** bottom-up management; **~ para avisos** notify address; **~ de carteras** portfolio management; **~ central** (de empresa) headquarters; **~ codificada** code address; **~ comercial** business address; **~ corporativa** corporate management; **~ de correo electrónico** e-mail address; **~ por crisis** crisis management; **~ deficiente** mismanagement; **~ por departamentos** departmental management; **~ de devolución** return address; **~ electrónica** e-mail address; **~ de empresas** business administration, business management; **~ de energía** energy management; **~ por excepción** management by exception; **~ de fábrica** plant management; **~ financiera** financial management; **~ general** general management; **D~ General de Correos y Telégrafos** ≈ Post Office BrE, ≈ Postal Service AmE; **D~ General de Tributos** Esp ≈ Inland Revenue BrE, ≈ Internal Revenue Service AmE; **~ intermedia** ⋯▶

middle management; ~ **Internet** Internet address; ~ **de inversiones** investment management; ~ **IP** IP address; ~ **del mercado** market management; ~ **por objetivos** management by objectives; ~ **de oficina** office management; ~ **de operaciones** operations management; ~ **de origen** source address; ~ **de particular** home address; ~ **de personal** personnel management, staff management; ~ **postal** postal address; ~ **de primera línea** first-line management; ~ **del producto** product management; ~ **profesional** business address; ~ **de proyectos** project management; ~ **de recursos** resource management; ~ **de recursos humanos** human resource management; ~ **de reenvío** forwarding address; ~ **de riesgos** risk management; ~ **de sistemas** systems management; ~ **de tarea** task management; ~ **de la tesorería** cash management; ~ **de ventas** sales management

direccionable *adj* addressable

direccionamiento *m* addressing; ~ **absoluto** absolute addressing

directamente *adv* directly; ~ **relacionado con** directly related to; ~ **responsable de** directly responsible for

directiva *f* (directriz) directive; (comité) management committee; ~ **común** common directive; ~ **de la UE** EU directive

directivo¹ *adj* managing

directivo², -a *m,f* (gerente) manager; (ejecutivo) executive, director

directo *adj* direct; (tren) through; **en ~** live; **banca/comercialización directa** direct banking/marketing

director, a *m,f* manager; (de la junta directiva) director; ~ **adjunto(-a)** *m,f* assistant manager; (de la junta directiva) deputy director; ~ **artístico(-a)** *m,f* artistic director; ~ **de atención al cliente** customer relations manager; ~ **de banco** bank manager; ~ **comercial** business manager; ~ **comercial y de desarrollo** business development manager; ~ **de compras** purchasing manager, head buyer; ~ **de comunicaciones de marketing** marketing communications manager; ~ **de cuentas** account manager; ~ **de departamento** head of department; ~ **de desarrollo (comercial)** (business) development manager; ~ **de distribución** distribution manager; ~

de división division head, division manager; ~ **editorial** publishing director; ~ **ejecutivo(-a)** *m,f* chief executive; ~ **de empresa** company director; ~ **de exportación** export manager; ~ **financiero(-a)** *m,f* financial director, financial controller; ~ **de formación** training manager; ~ **sin funciones ejecutivas** nonexecutive director; ~ **general** chief executive officer; ~ **general de información** chief information officer; ~ **gerente** managing director; ~ **de importación** import manager; ~ **interino(-a)** *m,f* acting manager; ~ **jurídico(-a)** *m,f* head of legal department BrE, general counsel AmE; ~ **de marketing** marketing manager; (jefe de división) marketing director; ~ **de modas** fashion editor; ~ **de oficina** office manager; ~ **de operaciones** operations manager; ~ **de personal** head of personnel, personnel manager; ~ **de la planta** works manager; ~ **de postventa** after-sales manager; ~ **principal** senior manager; ~ **provincial** regional manager; ~ **de proyecto** project manager; ~ **de publicidad** publicity manager; ~ **de recursos humanos** human resources director; ~ **regional** regional manager; ~ **de relaciones públicas** public relations manager; ~ **residente** resident manager; ~ **sectorial** division manager; ~ **de sucursal** branch manager; ~ **técnico(-a)** *m,f* technical manager; ~ **de ventas** sales manager; (jefe de división) sales director

directora *f* manager(ess)

directorio *m* directory; ~ **comercial** trade directory; ~ **electrónico** electronic directory; ~ **de ficheros** file directory; ~ **raíz** root directory

directriz *f* directive; **directrices** guidelines; ~ **común** common directive; **directrices fiscales** tax guidelines; ~ **de paga igual** equal pay directive

dirigente *mf* leader; ~ **sindical** union officer

dirigido *adj* targeted; **no ~** untargeted; ~ **por computadora** AmL *or* **ordenador** Esp computer-driven

dirigir *vt* (empresa) manage, run; (crítica, producto) direct, target, aim; (discurso, palabras) address; ~ **algo a alguien** address sth to sb; ~ **la atención hacia** turn one's attention to; ~ **sus reclamaciones a** address complaints to; **un producto dirigido al mercado**

comercial a product aimed o targeted at the business market

dirigirse: ~ **a** v pron (referirse a alguien) address; ~ **al librador** refer to drawer

discado m AmL dialling BrE, dialing AmE; ~ **directo** or **automático** AmL direct dialling BrE, direct dialing AmE; ~ **internacional directo** AmL international direct dialling BrE o dialing AmE

disciplina f discipline; ~**s análogas** cognate disciplines

disciplinar vt discipline

disco m disk; ~ **de alta densidad** high-density disk; ~ **de arranque** boot disk; ~ **de una cara** single-sided disk; ~ **compacto** compact disc BrE, compact disk AmE; ~ **compacto interactivo** compact disc interactive BrE, compact disk interactive AmE; ~ **compacto con memoria sólo de lectura** compact disc read-only memory BrE, compact disk read-only memory AmE; ~ **compacto reescribible** compact disc rewritable BrE, compact disk rewritable AmE; ~ **compacto registrable** compact disc recordable BrE, compact disk recordable AmE; ~ **de dos caras** double-sided disk; ~ **duro** hard disk; ~ **fijo** hard disk; ~ **flexible** floppy (disk); ~ **magnético** magnetic disk; ~ **de origen** source disk; ~ **protegido contra copias** copy-protected disk; ~ **de RAM** RAM disk; ~ **de sistema** system disk; ~ **de trabajo** scratch disk; ~ **versátil digital** digital versatile disc BrE, digital versatile disk AmE, DVD; ~ **vídeo** Esp or **video** AmL **digital** digital videodisc BrE, digital videodisk AmE, DVD

disconformidad f nonconformity

discrecional adj discretionary

discrepancia f discrepancy; ~ **entre dos cosas** discrepancy between two things

discreto adj discreet, low-profile

discriminación f discrimination; ~ **antes de la entrada** pre-entry discrimination; ~ **directa** direct discrimination; ~ **por edad** age discrimination; ~ **por motivo de edad** ageism; ~ **positiva** positive discrimination; ~ **racial** race discrimination, racial discrimination; ~ **por religión** religious discrimination; ~ **sexual** sex discrimination, gender discrimination

discriminar 1 ~ **a** vt discriminate against

2 vi discriminate

disculpa f apology; **pedirle** ~**s a alguien por algo** apologize to sb for sth; **no admite** ~ there's no excuse, it's inexcusable

disculparse v pron apologize; ~ **(ante alguien) por algo** apologize (to sb) for sth

discurso m speech; ~ **de bienvenida** welcome speech

discusión f discussion; **en** ~ under discussion; **discusiones francas** frank discussions; ~ **de grupo** group discussion; ~ **en profundidad** in-depth discussion

discutir vt discuss; ~ **algo a fondo** discuss sth in depth

diseminar vt disseminate

disentir vi disagree; ~ **en algo** disagree about sth

diseñador, a m,f designer; ~ **comercial** commercial designer; ~ **gráfico(-a)** m,f graphic designer; ~ **de modas** fashion designer; ~ **de sitios web** Web designer

diseño m design; **de** ~ **ergonómico** (estación de trabajo) ergonomically designed; ~ **asistido por computadora** AmL or **ordenador** Esp m computer-aided design; **D**~ **Curricular Base** Esp ≈ National Curriculum BrE; ~ **y dibujo asistido por computadora** AmL or **ordenador** Esp m computer-assisted design and drafting; ~ **y composición** design and layout; ~ **del envase** package design; ~ **gráfico** graphic design; ~ **industrial** industrial design; ~ **de producto** product design; ~ **de sistemas** systems design; ~ **de sitios web** Web design

disminución f decrease, decline; (en tipos de interés) fall; (del mercado) shrinkage; ~ **de un cargo** charge-off; ~ **de las inversiones** decline in investments; ~ **de la prima** rate cutting; ~ **del valor** decrease in value

disminuir 1 vt decrease, lower; (negocio, demanda) diminish, lessen; (activos líquidos) run down; ~ **la producción proporcionalmente** scale down production

2 vi diminish; ~ **gradualmente** taper off

disolución f breakup; (del parlamento) dissolution

disolver vt (sociedad, parlamento) dissolve; (junta) break up

disolverse *v pron* (fiesta, reunión) break up

disparidad *f* disparity

disparo *m* shot; **~ a ciegas** shot in the dark

dispensa *f* dispensation

dispensador *m* dispenser; **~ de cambio** change dispenser; **~ de dinero en efectivo** cashpoint BrE, (automatic) cash dispenser BrE, automated teller machine AmE

dispensar *vt* exempt; **~ a alguien de algo** exempt sb from sth

disponer 1 *vt* arrange; **~ un préstamo** arrange a loan
2 *vi*: **~ de** dispose of, use; **~ de las existencias** dispose of stock

disponibilidad *f* availability; **~es** liquid assets; **~ en efectivo** cash holdings, cash in hand; **~ de recursos** resource availability

disponible *adj* available; **no ~** not available, unavailable; **~ a corto plazo** available at short notice; **~ en el mejor tiempo** best time available

disposición *f* regulation; (Cont) layout; (Der) provision; (Fisc) disposal, disposition; **con ~ al riesgo** risk-oriented; **disposiciones aduaneras** customs regulations; **~ legal** legal enactment; **~ de la liquidez** cash drawdown

dispositivo *m* appliance, device; **~ de alerta** warning device; **~ de alimentación de documentos** document feeder; **~ de almacenamiento** storage device; **~ antirrobo** antitheft device; **~ de entrada** input device; **~ externo** external device; **~ de fijación de precios** pegging device; **~ lógico** logic device; **~ para teléfonos de manos libres** hands-free headset; **~ periférico** peripheral device; **~ de salida** output device

disputa *f* dispute; **~ jurisdiccional** jurisdiction dispute

disputar *vt* dispute; **~ un testamento** dispute a will; **~le algo a alguien** dispute sb's right to sth, fight sb for sth

disquete *m* diskette; **~ flexible** floppy (disk); **~ de instalación** installation diskette

disquetera *f* disk drive

distancia *f* distance; **a ~** remote; **enseñanza a ~** distance learning; **a larga ~** long-distance

distanciamiento *m* distancing

distinción *f* distinction; **hacer una ~ entre** make a distinction between

distinguir 1 *vt* distinguish
2 *vi* tell the difference; **~ entre** distinguish between, tell the difference between

distintivo *adj* (rasgo, característica) distinctive; (factor) distinguishing

distorsión *f* distortion; **~ comercial** trade distortion; **~ del mercado** market distortion

distorsionar *vt* (cifras) distort

distribución *f* (de mercancías) distribution; (de fondos, recursos) allocation; **~ de costes** Esp *or* **costos** AmL *f* cost distribution; **~ de dividendos** distribution of dividends; **~ de las ganancias** allocation of earnings; **~ de ingresos** income distribution; **~ masiva** mass distribution; **~ de la nómina** payroll distribution; **~ de plusvalías** capital gains distribution; **~ de los recursos** resource allocation; **~ de responsabilidades** allocation of responsibilities; **~ de riesgos** distribution of risks; **~ de la riqueza** wealth distribution; **~ de trabajo** allocation of work

distribuido *adj* distributed; **no ~** (acciones) unallotted; **~ íntegramente** fully distributed

distribuidor, a *m,f* distributor; **~ designado(-a)** *m,f* appointed distributor

distribuir *vt* distribute; (fondos, recursos) allocate; **~ en ejercicios posteriores** carry forward

distrito *m* district; **~ financiero** financial district; **~ fiscal** tax district; **~ municipal** municipal borough; **~ postal** postal zone

disuadir *vt* deter, dissuade; **~ a alguien de hacer algo** deter *o* dissuade sb from doing sth

divergencia *f* divergence

divergir *vi* (tipo de cambio) diverge

diversidad *f* diversity; **~ de activos** asset mix

diversificación *f* diversification; **~ de activos** asset mix; **~ excesiva** overdiversification; **~ mixta** (del riesgo) composite spread; **~ de los negocios** business diversification; **~ de productos** product diversification

diversificar *vt* diversify; ~ **riesgos** diversify risks

diverso *adj* (variado) diverse; (Cont) miscellaneous; **en diversas ocasiones** on several occasions

dividendo *m* dividend; **con** ~ (todavía sin pagar) cum dividend; **sin** ~ ex dividend; ~ **de una acción** share dividend; ~ **por acción** dividend per share; ~ **de acción ordinaria** common share BrE *o* stock AmE dividend; ~ **acumulado** accrued dividend; ~ **acumulativo** cumulative dividend; ~ **anticipado** interim dividend; ~ **anual** annual dividend; ~ **bruto** gross dividend; ~ **complementario de fin de año** year-end dividend; ~ **a cuenta** interim dividend; ~ **declarado** declared dividend; ~ **devengado** accrued dividend; ~ **diferido** deferred dividend; ~ **en efectivo** cash dividend; ~ **en especie** dividend in kind; ~ **exento** exempt dividend; ~ **final** final dividend; ~ **imponible** taxable dividend; ~ **no repartido** passed dividend

dividir *vt* divide; ~ **algo en compartimentos** compartmentalize sth; ~ **algo en dos partes** halve sth; ~ **un proyecto** carve up a project

divisa *f* currency; **mercados de** ~s foreign exchange markets; **pagar en** ~s pay in foreign currency; ~s **comerciales** trading currencies; ~ **controlada** managed currency; ~ **débil** soft currency; ~ **por encima de la par** currency at a premium; ~ **extranjera** foreign currency, foreign exchange; ~ **fluctuante** fluctuating currency; ~ **de pago** payment device; ~ **principal** major currency; ~ **de referencia** reference currency; (internacional) key currency; ~ **única** single currency

divisibilidad *f* divisibility

divisible *adj* divisible

división *f* division; ~ **de cartera de valores** portfolio split; ~ **de consultoría** consulting division; ~ **departamental** departmentalization; ~ **inversa** reverse split; ~ **en tercios** three-way split; ~ **del trabajo** division of labour BrE *o* labor AmE

divulgación *f* filtering down; ~ **completa** full disclosure; ~ **de información financiera** financial disclosure

divulgar *vt* (opinión, observación) air; (información, noticias) circulate; ~ **la noticia** break the news; ~ **las propias opiniones** air one's opinions; ~ **los propios puntos de vista** air one's views

DNI *abr* (▸**documento nacional de identidad**) ID card

D.O. *abr* (▸**Denominación de Origen**) *official guarantee of origin and quality of a product*

doblaje *m* dubbing

doble¹ *adj* double; **de** ~ **acción** (maquinaria) double-action, double-acting; **de** ~ **cara** double-sided; **de** ~ **ingreso** (familia, matrimonio) double-income; **de** ~ **precisión** double-precision; ~ **arbitraje** double switching; ~ **bonificación** reallowance; ~ **clic** double click; **hacer** ~ **clic en** *or* **sobre algo** double-click on sth; ~ **columna** double column; ~ **densidad** double density; ~ **densidad por una cara** single-sided double density; ~ **distribución** double distribution; ~ **entrada** double entry; ~ **espacio** double space; ~ **imposición** double taxation; ~ **opción** double option; ~ **residencia** dual residency; ~ **responsabilidad** (UE) dual responsibility; ~ **tecleo** (Info) double strike

doble²: **el** ~ (doble cantidad) twice as much as; (doble tiempo) twice as long as; **costar el** ~ be *o* cost twice as much; **tardar el** ~ be *o* take twice as long

doctor, a *m,f* doctor; (título) Doctor; **D**~ **en Comercio** Doctor of Commerce

doctrina *f* doctrine; ~s **contables** accounting doctrines

documentación *f* documentation; ~ **de viaje** travel documents

documental *m* documentary

documento *m* document; (Der) instrument; (prueba en un juicio) exhibit; ~ **de aceptación** acknowledgement; ~ **adjunto** enclosed document; ~ **al portador** bearer form; ~ **de antecedentes** background paper; ~s **del caso** case papers; ~ **fuente** source document; ~ **de garantía** accommodation paper; ~s **justificantes** supporting documents; ~ **legal** legal document; ~ **maestro** master document; ~ **marco de la política** policy framework paper; ~ **nacional de identidad** identity card; ~ **oficial** official document; ~ **de origen** original document; ~ **original** source document; ~ **de título** muniment; ~ **de trabajo** working paper

dólar *m* dollar

dolarización *f* dollarization

dolo *m* fraud

domiciliación *f* automatic payment;
~ **(bancaria) de pagos** direct debit,
banker's order; ~ **de la nómina**
*payment of salary direct into bank
account*

domicilio *m* address, domicile (frml);
cambio de ~ change of address;
servicio a ~ home delivery service; **sin**
~ **fijo** of no fixed abode; **trabajador a** ~
homeworker; ~ **bancario** bank address;
~ **familiar** family home; ~ **fiscal** tax
domicile; ~ **legal** legal residence; ~
particular private address; ~ **postal**
mailing address; ~ **social** registered
address, registered office; ~ **social fijo**
fixed place of business

dominación *f* domination

dominante *adj* dominant

dominar *vt* (mercado) dominate; ~ **la
situación** be in control of a situation

dominio *m* domain; **nombre de** ~ (en
Internet) domain name; ~ **del consumo**
consumer sovereignty; ~ **del mercado**
market holding; ~ **vitalicio** life estate

don *m* gift, skill; ~ **de gentes** social
skills

donación *f* donation, gift; (del estado)
grant; **hacer** ~ **de algo** donate sth; ~ **a
un centro benéfico** charitable gift *o*
donation; ~ **gubernamental**
government grant

donado *adj* donated

donante *mf* donor; ~ **de ayuda** aid
donor

donar *vt* donate

donatario, -a *m,f* donee

donativo *m* donation; ~ **benéfico**
charitable donation

dongle *m* (Info) dongle

dorso *m* back; **véase al** ~ see overleaf,
P.T.O. please turn over

dos *adj* two; **de** ~ **caras** two-sided; **de**
~ **direcciones** (Info) two-way

DOS *abr* (▸**sistema operativo de
discos**) DOS

dotación *f* appropriation, endowment;
~ **de ayuda** aid package; ~ **de capital**
capital endorsement; ~ **de factores**
factor endowment; ~ **de personal**
staffing

dotado *adj* gifted; ~ **de personal**
staffed; (servicio) manned

dote *f* dowry

download: **hacer un** ~ **de** *vt*
download

dpto. *abr* (▸**departamento**) dept.;
(Inmob) (AmL) flat BrE, apartment AmE

Dr *abr* (▸**deudor**) Dr, debtor; (▸**Doctor**)
Dr

drawback *m* drawback

drenaje *m* (de recursos) drain

DRH *abr* (▸**desarrollo de recursos
humanos**) HRD (Human Resource
Development)

droga *f* drug

DTML *abr* (▸**lenguaje de referencia
dinámico**) DHTML (Dynamic Hypertext
Mark-up Language)

dto. *abr* (▸**descuento**) disc. (discount)

dueño, -a *m,f* owner; ~ **de
restaurante** restaurateur, restaurant
proprietor; ~ **único(-a)** *m,f* sole owner

duopolio *m* duopoly; ~ **espacial**
spatial duopoly

dupdo. *abr* (▸**duplicado**) copy; (Info)
duplicate

dúplex *m* penthouse

duplicación *f* duplication; ~ **de
prestaciones** duplication of benefits

duplicado¹ *adj* duplicate; **por** ~ in
duplicate

duplicado² *m* (▸**dupdo.**) copy; (Info)
duplicate

duplicar *vt* duplicate; (copiar) copy

duración *f* duration; (de cargo, del
gobierno) term; **de corta/larga** ~ short/
long; ~ **de la garantía** duration of
guarantee; ~ **media de vida** average
life expectancy; ~ **de la patente** term
of patent; ~ **del servicio** length of
service; ~ **de vida** (de producto) shelf life

durar *vi* last; **¿cuánto durará la
reunión?** how long will the meeting
take?

duro *adj* (condiciones) tough

DVD *m* (▸**disco vídeo digital** Esp *or*
digital AmL) DVD; ~**-audio** DVD-audio;
~**-ROM** DVD-ROM

Ee

Easdaq *m* (*sistema automático de cotización de la Asociación Europea de Operadores de Bolsa*) Easdaq (European Association of Securities Dealers Automated Quotation)

e-broker *m* e-broker, electronic broker

echar *vt* (persona) fire, sack; (enviar) post BrE, mail AmE; ∼ **una carta al correo** post BrE *o* mail AmE a letter

echarse *v pron*: ∼ **atrás** backtrack, go back on one's word

ecoauditoría *f* environmental audit, eco-audit

ecoetiquetado *m* ecolabelling BrE, ecolabeling AmE

ECOFIN *abr* (▸**Consejo Europeo de los Ministros de Finanzas**) ECOFIN (European Community Finance Ministers)

ecoindustria *f* green industry

ecología *f* ecology

ecológico *adj* ecological, environmentally friendly

ecologista *mf* ecologist, environmentalist

ecomárketing *m* green marketing, eco-marketing

econometría *f* econometrics

econométrico *adj* econometric

econometrista *mf* econometrician

economía *f* (de un país) economy; (ciencia) economics; ∼**s** savings; **hacer** ∼**s** economize; ∼ **abierta** open economy; ∼ **aplicada** applied economics; ∼ **de asedio** siege economy; ∼ **de autoservicio** self-service economy; ∼ **avanzada** advanced economy; ∼ **del bienestar** welfare economics; ∼ **cerrada** closed economy; ∼ **clandestina** black economy, underground economy; ∼ **competitiva** free enterprise economy; ∼ **del conocimiento** knowledge economy; ∼ **dependiente** branch economy, dependent economy; ∼ **del desarrollo** development economics; ∼ **digital** digital economy; ∼ **dirigida** managed economy; ∼ **dual** dual economy; ∼ **emergente** tiger economy; ∼ **de empresa** business economics; ∼ **de**

escala economy of scale; ∼**s de escala** economies of scale; ∼ **falsa** false economy; ∼ **financiera** financial economy; ∼ **formal** formal economy; ∼ **sin fricción** frictionless economy; ∼ **de información** information economy; ∼ **informal** black economy; ∼ **interna** internal economy; ∼ **intervenida** managed economy; ∼ **de libre mercado** free-market economy; ∼ **madura** mature economy; ∼ **de mercado** market economy, free enterprise economy; ∼ **mixta** mixed economy; ∼ **monetaria** cash economy; (ciencia) monetary economics; ∼ **mundial** world economy, global economy; ∼ **nueva** new economy; ∼ **de oferta** supply side economics; ∼ **paralela** black economy, parallel economy; ∼ **participada** share economy; ∼ **participativa** stakeholder economy; ∼ **planificada** planned economy; ∼ **del pluriempleo** moonlight economy; ∼ **recalentada** overheated economy; ∼ **de servicios** service economy; ∼ **sumergida** black economy, underground economy; ∼ **urbana** urban economics

económicamente *adv* economically; ∼ **sólido** financially sound; **depender** ∼ **de alguien** be financially dependent on sb

económico *adj* economic; (barato) cheap, economical; **tener problemas** ∼**s** have financial problems; **política económica** economic policy; **viajar en clase económica** travel economy class

economista *mf* economist; ∼ **jefe(-a)** *m,f* chief economist; ∼ **mercantil** business economist

economizar *vti* economize; (tiempo) save

ecosistema *m* ecosystem

ECOSOC *abr* (▸**Consejo Económico y Social**) ECOSOC (Economic and Social Council)

ecotasa *f* green tax, ecotax, environmental tax

ecotoxicológico *adj* ecotoxicological

ECU *abr* (▸**Unidad Monetaria
Europea**) (obs) ECU (European Currency
Unit) (obs)

ecuación *f* equation; ∼ **del balance**
balance sheet equation

ED *abr* (▸**eurodólar**) ED (Eurodollar)

edad *f* age; **la tercera** ∼ (personas)
senior citizens, the elderly; (fase de vida)
old age; ∼ **al vencimiento** age at
expiry; ∼ **de jubilación** retirement age;
∼ **límite** age limit, maximum age; ∼
penal age of criminal responsibility

edición *f* edition; (número) issue;
(industria) publishing; (corrección) editing;
∼ **ampliada** enlarged edition; ∼
atrasada (de diario o revista) back issue,
back number; ∼ **electrónica** electronic
edition *o* version; (proceso, industria)
electronic publishing; ∼ **de prensa**
press edition; ∼ **limitada** limited
edition; ∼ **en pantalla** onscreen editing;
∼ **revisada** revised edition; ∼ **de texto**
text editing

edificar *vt* build

edificio *m* building; ∼ **de
apartamentos** apartment building,
block of flats BrE; ∼ **en copropiedad**
condominium, cooperative; ∼ **de
oficinas** office building, office block BrE

editado *adj* published; (corregido) edited

editar *vt* (revista, periódico) publish;
(corregir) edit

editor, a *m,f* (de textos, programas) editor;
(empresario) publisher; ∼ **de diseño**
design editor; ∼ **de pantalla** onscreen
editor; ∼ **de textos** text editor

editorial[1] *adj* publishing; (política,
reunión) editorial; **casa** ∼ publishing
house

editorial[2] *m* editorial, leading article

editorial[3] *f* publisher, publishing house

editorialista *mf* leader writer

educación *f* education; ∼
administrativa management education;
∼ **a distancia** distance learning; ∼ **a
distancia por Internet** e-learning,
online learning, virtual learning; ∼ **en
línea** e-learning, online learning, virtual
learning; ∼ **secundaria** secondary
education; ∼ **superior** higher education;
∼ **terciaria** tertiary education

efectivamente *adv* (verdaderamente)
really; (con efectividad) effectively

efectividad *f* effectiveness

efectivo[1] *adj* effective; **hacer** ∼
(cheque) cash; (pago) make; **hacerse** ∼
take effect, come into effect; **las reglas**
se harán efectivas desde junio the rules
will come into effect from June; **el
abono se hará** ∼ **por mensualidades**
the payment will be made in monthly
instalments BrE *o* installments AmE

efectivo[2] *m* (fondos) cash, hard cash,
ready cash; ∼**s** *m pl* actuals; **pago en** ∼
cash payment; **con** ∼ **abundante** cash
rich; **con** ∼ **insuficiente** cash poor;
pagar en ∼ pay cash; **venta en** ∼ cash
sale; ∼ **de caja** cash in hand; ∼
disponible *or* **en caja** (en banco) till
money; (fondo) float; (Cont) available cash

efecto *m* effect, impact; (pagadero,
cobrable) bill; ∼**s** *m pl* personal
belongings *o* effects; **a** ∼**s contables/
fiscales** for accounting/tax purposes;
con ∼ **retroactivo** backdated; **por** ∼ **de
algo** as a result of sth; **tener** ∼ take
effect; **tener** ∼ **legal** have statutory
effect; **la nueva legislación no tuvo el** ∼
deseado the new legislation did not
have the desired effect; ∼ **de alcance**
catch-up effect; ∼ **anticipado** advance
bill; ∼ **de aplazamiento** holdover
effect; ∼ **de aprendizaje** learning
effect; ∼**s bancarios** bank bills; ∼
cambiario bill of exchange; ∼**s a
cobrar** bills receivable; **otros** ∼**s por
cobrar** other receivables; ∼**s por
cobrar congelados** frozen receivables;
∼ **colateral** side effect; ∼ **como aval**
billback; ∼ **contable** accounting effect;
∼ **desincentivador** disincentive effect;
∼ **dominó** domino effect; (Bolsa)
butterfly effect; ∼ **incentivador**
incentive effect; ∼ **indirecto** spill-over
effect; ∼ **de ingreso** income effect;
∼**invernadero**, ∼ **de invernadero**
(Med amb) greenhouse effect; ∼ **legal**
legal effect; ∼ **negociable** trading
security; ∼ **a pagar** bill payable,
amount payable; ∼**s personales**
personal effects; ∼ **palanca** ratchet
effect; ∼ **al portador** bearer bill; ∼
residual ripple effect; ∼ **secundario**
side effect, knock-on effect; ∼
subsidiario spillover effect; ∼ **tardío**
after-effect

efectuar *vt* accomplish, carry out;
(pago) effect, make; (anotación, asiento,
registro) pass; **los dividendos serán
efectuados a fin de año** dividends will
be paid (out) at the year end

eficacia *f* efficiency; (de política, solución)
effectiveness; ∼ **administrativa**
managerial effectiveness; ∼
organizacional organizational

effectiveness; ~ **publicitaria** advertising effectiveness

eficaz *adj* effective; ~ **en relación con el coste** Esp *or* **costo** AmL cost-effective

eficiencia *f* efficiency; ~ **bancaria** bank efficiency; ~ **de la energía** energy efficiency; ~ **laboral** labour efficiency BrE, labor efficiency AmE

eficiente *adj* efficient

efímero *adj* shortlived

egreso *m* expenditure, outgoings

ej. *abr* (▸**ejemplo**) ex.; **p.ej.** e.g.

ejecución *f* execution, carrying out; (de la empresa) performance; **poner algo en ~** carry out sth; ~ **de la cadena de suministros** supply chain execution; ~ **de prueba** (de sistema, máquina) test run; ~ **rápida** summary application; ~ **del trabajo** job performance

ejecutable *adj* exercisable, practicable; (Der) enforceable; **no ~** irredeemable

ejecutado *adj* executed, completed; **no ~** unexecuted

ejecutante *mf* (Econ) performer

ejecutar *vt* execute, perform, carry out; (Info) run; ~ **una opción** declare an option; ~ **órdenes** carry out orders; ~ **el procedimiento de entrada** log in

ejecutivo¹ *adj* executive; **no ~** nonexecutive

ejecutivo² *m* executive; **el E~** *m* the Executive

ejecutivo³, -a *m,f* executive; ~ **de la compañía** company executive; ~ **de cuentas** account executive; (en publicidad) account manager; ~ **de empresa** corporate executive; ~ **de marketing** *m,f* marketing executive; ~ **de reclutamiento** recruitment officer; ~ **de ventas** sales executive

ejecutor, a *m,f* (m) executor; (f) executrix; **los ~es testamentarios** the executors of a will

ejecutorio *adj* enforceable, executory

ejemplar *m* example; (de libro) copy; (de revista) issue; ~ **gratuito** free copy (para prensa) presentation copy, press copy; ~ **obsequio** *or* **de regalo** complimentary copy

ejemplo *m* example; **por ~** for example; **poner** *or* **dar un ~** give an example; **servir de ~** serve as an example

ejercer *vt* (profesión) practise BrE, practice AmE; (opción, poder, derecho) exercise; (efecto, influencia) exert; ~ **la**

abogacía practise BrE *o* practice AmE law; ~ **influencia sobre alguien** exert influence on sb, have influence over sb; ~ **presión sobre alguien** exert *o* put pressure on sb

ejercicio *m* exercise; (Fin) financial year; (de profesión) practice; (de cargo) tenure, holding; **abogado en ~** practising BrE *or* practicing AmE lawyer; **cierre del ~** year end; **durante el ~ actual** during the current financial year; ~ **de adquisición** year of acquisition; ~ **anterior** prior period; ~ **anual** business year; ~ **contable** accounting period, financial period; ~ **contable terminado** accounting year then ended; ~ **económico** financial period, financial year, fiscal year; ~ **económico actual** *or* **vigente** *or* **en curso** current business *o* financial year; ~ **fiscal** financial year, fiscal year, tax year; ~ **hasta la fecha** year to date; ~ **de la opción** option exercise; ~ **de una opción de compra/venta** call's/put's strike; ~ **presupuestario** budget year

elaboración *f* processing; (de informe) preparation, drawing up; ~ **del presupuesto** budget preparation, budgeting

elaborar *vt* produce; (plan, informe) prepare, draw up

elasticidad *f* elasticity, resilience; ~ **de la demanda y del suministro** elasticity of demand and supply; ~ **precio-demanda** price-demand elasticity

elección *f* choice; (Pol) election; **convocar elecciones** call an election; ~ **del consumidor** consumer choice; ~ **federal** federal election; ~ **local** local election; ~ **parcial** by-election

electivo *adj* elective

electorado *m* electorate

electricidad *f* electricity

eléctrico *adj* (máquina, luz) electric; (aparato) electrical; **suministro ~** electricity supply

electrificación *f* (de ferrocarriles) electrification

electrodomésticos *m pl* domestic appliances, electrical appliances; (televisión, etc) brown goods; (lavadora, etc) white goods

electrónica *f* electronics

electrónico *adj* electronic; **agenda electrónica** personal organizer; **banco ~** e-bank; **comercio ~** e-commerce, e-business; **dinero ~** e-money

electrostático *adj* electrostatic

electrotipo *m* electrotype

elegibilidad *f* eligibility

elegible *adj* eligible

elegido *adj* elected; **~ recientemente** newly elected

elegir *vt* choose, select; (votar) elect; **~ a alguien para la junta** elect sb to the board; **le eligieron presidente** he was elected president

elemento *m* element; **~ del activo** asset; **~s comunes** (de condominio) common elements; **~ del coste** Esp *or* **costo** AmL *m* cost factor; **~ excepcional** exceptional item; **~ de información** piece of information; **~s no fungibles** nonfungible goods; **~ optativo** optional item; **~ de riesgo** element of risk

elevación *f* (acción) raising; (aumento) rise, increase

elevar *vt* raise; (incremento) step up; (sanciones) lift; (reclamación) file, submit; **precios muy elevados** very high prices

elevarse *v pron* (beneficios, precios) rise; (mucho) soar

eliminación *f* elimination, removal; (de errores) deletion, editing-out; (Cont) writing-off; **~ de desperdicios** waste disposal; **~ de una deuda** deletion of a debt

eliminar *vt* eliminate; (redactar) delete, edit out; (restricciones) remove; (partida contable) write off; (inflación) stamp out; **~ progresivamente** (tecnología, servicio, sistema) phase out

eliminatorio *adj* (examen, fase) qualifying

ELIO *abr* (▸**estimador lineal insesgado óptimo**) BLUE (best linear unbiased estimator)

eludir *vt* avoid; **eludió las preguntas de los periodistas** she avoided the reporters' questions

elusión *f* avoidance; **~ legal de impuestos** tax avoidance

e-mail *m* e-mail; **tener ~** (sistema) have e-mail, be on e-mail; (recibir correo) have e-mail *o* e-mails; **enviarle un ~ a alguien** send sb an e-mail; **mandarle** *or* **enviarle algo a alguien por ~** e-mail sth to sb, send sb sth by e-mail; **~ marketing** e-mail marketing

emancipación *f* emancipation

embajada *f* embassy

embajador, a *m,f* ambassador

embalador, a *m,f* packer

embalaje *m* (acción) packing; (envoltura) packaging; **~ por contracción** shrink wrapping; **~ defectuoso** defective packaging; **~ impermeable** waterproof packing; **~ con papel de burbujas** blister packaging

embalar *vt* pack, package; **embalado al vacío** vacuum-packed

embarcar *vt* (personas) embark; (fletes, carga) ship

embarcarse *v pron* embark, board; **~ en** (curso de acción) embark on

embargado *adj* restrained

embargador, a *m,f* sequestrator

embargar *vt* (Der) garnish; (Inmob) distrain

embargo *m* (Der) garnishment; (Inmob) distraint; (Imp/Exp) embargo; **sin ~** however, nonetheless; **~ comercial** trade embargo; **~ preventivo** lien; **~ de propiedad** distraint of property

embarque *m* (de mercancías) shipment; (de pasajeros) boarding, embarkation; **tarjeta de ~** boarding card

embaucador, a *m,f* confidence trickster

embaucar *vt* deceive, trick

embotellamiento *m* bottleneck; (de tráfico) traffic jam

emergencia *f* emergency; **medidas de ~** emergency measures; **salida de ~** emergency exit

emergente *adj* (mercado) emerging; **menú ~** pop-up menu

emigración *f* (de personas) emigration; (de datos) migration

emigrante *mf* emigrant; **~ económico** economic migrant

emilio *m* (infrml) (mensaje) e-mail; **mandarle un ~ a alguien** e-mail sb, send sb an e-mail; **tienes un ~** you've got an e-mail

eminente *adj* (carrera) distinguished

emisario *m* effluent

emisión *f* (Bolsa) (share) issue; (de gases) emission; (Info) output; (Medios) broadcast; **la ~ no fue suscrita en su totalidad** the issue was undersubscribed; **~ de acciones** share issue, flotation; **~ de bonos** bond issue, flotation; **~ de carbono** carbon emission; **~ de cheques** cheque issue BrE, check issue AmE; **~ de cheques de sueldos** release of pay cheques BrE *or* checks AmE; **~ convertible** conversion issue; **~ de derechos** rights issue; **~ de dióxido de carbono** carbon dioxide emission; ~ **garantizada** warrant issue; ~ **de gases** (de vehículos automotores) exhaust emission; ~ **de radio** radio broadcast; ~ **por la red** (video) webcast; ~ **de títulos** equity issue; ~ **de valores** share issue, flotation

emisor, a *m,f* issuer, writer; (Coms) transmitter; ~ **de una opción** option writer; ~ **de opciones de compra** call option writer; ~ **de pasivos** liability issuer; ~ **de tarjetas de crédito** credit card issuer

emisora *f* radio station; ~ **de radio** radio station

emitido *adj* issued; ~ **y en circulación** issued and in circulation

emitir *vt* (acciones) issue; (opción) write; (veredicto) deliver; (prensa, radio) broadcast; ~ **acciones a la par** issue shares at par; ~ **billetes** issue banknotes BrE *o* bank bills AmE; ~ **un cheque a favor de alguien** make out a cheque BrE *or* check AmE to sb; ~ **un empréstito** issue a loan; ~ **de nuevo** reissue

emolumento *m* perk (infrml), perquisite

emoticón *m* emoticon

empantanar *vt* swamp, bog down (infrml)

empantanarse *v pron* get bogged down (infrml)

empaquetado¹ *adj* (mercancías) packaged

empaquetado² *m* packing, packaging

empaquetar *vt* package

emparejado *adj*: ~ **con** coupled with

empeñar *vt* pawn

empeñarse *v pron* get into debt; (insistir) insist; ~ **en algo/hacer algo** insist on sth/on doing sth

empeño *m* (recomendación, objeto) pledge, undertaking; **poner ~ en algo/hacer algo** put a lot of effort into sth/doing sth; **tener ~ en algo** be insistent on sth; **tener ~ en hacer algo** be insistent on doing sth

empeorar ⒈ *vi* worsen ⒉ *vt* make worse

empezar ⒈ *vi* begin, start; ~ **a avanzar** (economía) gain momentum; ~ **desde cero** start from scratch; ~ **a destacar** come to the fore; ~ **a hacer algo** set about doing sth; ~ **haciendo algo** start by doing sth; **para ~** to start *o* begin with; ~ **por algo/alguien** start with sth/sb ⒉ *vt* (trabajo, reunión) start; ~ **algo mal** get sth off to a bad start

empírico¹ *adj* empirical

empírico², -a *m,f* empiricist

emplazamiento *m* site; (de fábrica) location; (acción) siting, positioning; ~ **de huelga** strike call; ~ **judicial** summons; ~ **de primer orden** prime site

emplazar *vt* summons; (edificio) site; ~ **a alguien a hacer algo** call upon sb to do sth

empleado¹ *adj* employed

empleado², -a *m,f* employee; **~s** employees, personnel, staff; ~ **administrativo(-a)** *m,f* clerical worker, desk clerk; ~ **de banco** bank employee; ~ **de contabilidad** accounting clerk; ~ **de correos** postal worker; ~ **de cuentas a pagar** accounts payable clerk; ~ **diplomado(-a)** *m,f* certifying officer; ~ **eventual** temporary worker, temp (infrml); ~ **fijo** permanent member of staff; ~ **de oficina** office worker, white-collar worker; ~ **del parquet** (Bolsa) floor official; ~ **postal** postal clerk BrE, mail clerk AmE; ~ **de primera línea** front-line employee; ~ **a prueba** probationary employee; ~ **de seguridad** safety officer; **~s sin cargo** rank-and-file; ~ **sindical** union official; ~ **a sueldo** salaried employee; ~ **a tiempo completo** full-time employee, full-timer (infrml); ~ **a tiempo parcial** part-time employee, part-timer (infrml)

emplear *vt* (método) use; (trabajador) employ; (tiempo) spend; ~ **a alguien de nuevo** rehire sb; **emplearon tres años en el proyecto** the project took them three years, they spent three years on the project

empleo *m* employment; (puesto) job; (uso) use; (de recursos naturales) utilization; **buscar ~** look for a job; **conseguir ~** get *o* find a job; **estar sin ~** be out of work, be unemployed; **en ~ activo** in active employment; **en el ámbito del ~** on the employment front; **pleno ~** full employment; **modo de ~** instructions for use; **tener ~** have a job; ~ **comunitario** community work; ~ **encubierto** concealed employment; ~ **eventual** temporary employment; ~ **fijo** permanent employment; ~ **involuntario** involuntary employment; ~ **de media jornada** *or* **medio tiempo** part-time employment; (puesto) part-time job; ~ **permanente** permanent employment; ~ **protegido** sheltered employment; ~ **en el sector público** public sector employment; ~ **secundario** secondary ⋯⟶

employment; ∼ **sumergido** underground employment; ∼ **temporal** temporary employment; ∼ **a tiempo parcial** part-time employment; ∼**s vacantes** appointments, situations vacant; ∼ **vitalicio** lifetime employment, job for life

empobrecido *adj* impoverished

emprendedor *adj* enterprising

emprender *vt* (tarea) undertake; ∼ **acción legal** take legal action; ∼ **acciones laborales** take industrial action; ∼ **una campaña** conduct a campaign, embark on a campaign

empresa *f* (compañía) company, business; (organización empresarial) concern; (proyecto) enterprise; (tarea, labor) undertaking; ∼ **al consumidor** business-to-consumer, B2C; ∼ **a** ∼ business-to-business, B2B; ∼ **a** ∼ **a consumidor** business-to-business-to-consumer, B2B2C; ∼ **al gobierno** business-to-government, B2G; ∼ **absorbente** (en fusión) absorbing company; ∼ **accionista** corporate shareholder BrE o stockholder AmE; ∼ **adquirida** acquired company; ∼ **afiliada** affiliated company; ∼ **de alquiler de computadoras** AmL *or* **ordenadores** Esp computer leasing business; ∼ **de alto riesgo** high-risk venture; ∼ **aseguradora** insurance carrier, underwriter; ∼ **asociada** associate company; ∼ **cedente** transferor company; ∼ **comercial** business enterprise; ∼ **comercial sin cotización oficial** unquoted trading company; ∼ **conjunta** joint venture company; ∼ **constructora** construction company; ∼ **controlada por el gobierno** government-controlled corporation; ∼ **de conveniencia** off-the-shelf company; ∼ **con cotización pública** publicly listed company; ∼ **cotizada en bolsa** quoted company; ∼ **diversificada** diversified company; ∼ **dominante** dominant firm; ∼ **estatal** government enterprise, state-owned enterprise; ∼ **filial** associate company; ∼ **financiera** finance house, financial enterprise; ∼ **en funcionamiento** going concern; ∼ **de gestión pública** publicly traded company; ∼ **de hecho** de facto corporation; ∼ **inmobiliaria** real estate company AmE; ∼ **de intermediación** brokerage firm; ∼ **de inversión regulada** regulated investment company; ∼ **en marcha** going concern; ∼ **matriz** parent

company; ∼ **de mensajería** courier firm; ∼ **mercantil** business corporation; ∼ **multinacional** multinational corporation; ∼ **no lucrativa** non-profit-making enterprise BrE, nonprofit enterprise AmE; ∼ **objetivo** target company; ∼ **paraestatal** government-controlled corporation; ∼ **pequeña** small firm; ∼ **privada** private sector company; ∼ **de programación** software company; ∼ **pública** public sector company; ∼ **regulada** regulated firm; ∼ **rentable** profit-making enterprise; (compañía) profitable firm; ∼ **de segunda fila** second-tier company; ∼ **de servicios** service enterprise; ∼ **de servicios públicos** public utility company; ∼ **situada en zona verde** greenfield site company; ∼ **subsidiaria** subsidiary company BrE, subsidiary corporation AmE; ∼ **de titularidad privada** private holding corporation; ∼ **transnacional** transnational corporation; ∼ **de transporte aéreo/ interior/marítimo** air/inland/sea carrier; ∼ **vendedora** vendor company

empresariado *m* management, managers

empresarial *adj* business-oriented, entrepreneurial

empresario, -a *m,f* entrepreneur; (m) businessman; (f) businesswoman; (de espectáculos) promoter; ∼ **de Internet** entrepreneur

empresólogo(-a) *m,f* business consultant

empréstito *m* loan; (acción) borrowing; ∼ **calificado** qualified borrowing; ∼ **consolidado** consolidated loan; ∼ **de contrapartida** back-to-back loan; ∼ **convertible** convertible loan; ∼ **corporativo** corporate lending; ∼ **extranjero** foreign borrowing; ∼ **con garantía** secured loan; ∼ **sin garantía** unsecured loan; ∼ **público** public borrowing

empuje *m* (entusiasmo) drive; ∼ **de ventas** sales push

emulación *f* emulation

emulador *m* emulator; ∼ **de terminal** terminal emulator

emular *vt* (programa) emulate

enajenable *adj* alienable

enajenación *f* alienation

enajenar *vt* alienate

encabezamiento *m* (de carta) heading; (de periódico) headline; (Info) header; ∼ **de columnas** column

heading; ∼ **de mensaje** (en e-mail)
message header

encabezar *vt* (carta, artículo) head; (lista)
be at the top of

encajar *vi* fit, tally; ∼ **con algo** tally
with sth; ∼ **con alguien** fit in with sb; ∼
en el trabajo fit in at work

encaje *m* reserve; ∼ **excedente** cash
reserve; ∼ **legal** legal reserve; ∼ **de
primas** premium income

encaminar *vt* (esfuerzos) direct,
channel; (Info) route, dispatch; ∼**on sus
esfuerzos a la conclusión del proyecto**
they chanelled all their efforts into
completing the project

encarar *vt* face up to, confront

encarcelamiento *m* imprisonment

encarcelar *vt* imprison, put away

encargado¹ *adj* (persona) responsible;
(trabajo) commissioned; ∼ **de algo** in
charge of sth

encargado², -a *m,f* person in charge,
manager; **quiero hablar con el** ∼ I'd like
to speak to the person in charge; ∼ **de
facturación** invoice clerk; ∼ **de la
planta** plant operator; ∼ **de prensa**
press officer

encargar *vt* (pedir) order; (encomendar)
entrust; ∼**le algo a alguien** entrust sb
with sth, ask sb to do sth; ∼ **a alguien
de algo** give sb responsibility for sth

encargo *m* (pedido) order; (recado)
errand; (comisión) commission; **hacer un**
∼ (pedido) place an order; (recado) run an
errand; **por** ∼ to order; **hecho de** ∼
made to order

encarte *m* (periódicos, revistas) tip-in,
loose insert

encender *vt* turn on, switch on; (Info)
enable

enchufado *adj* well-connected; **estar**
∼ have useful contacts, be well
connected

enchufar *vt* plug in; (recomendar) pull
some strings for; ∼ **y usar** plug and
play; **equipo de** ∼ **y usar** plug and play;
su padre lo enchufó en la empresa his
father pulled some strings to get him a
job in the company

enchufe *f* plug; (influencia): **tener** ∼ have
useful contacts, have friends in the right
places; **entró en la empresa por** ∼
someone pulled some strings to get him
a job in the company

enchufismo *m* (infrml) string-pulling
(infrml)

enclave *m* enclave; ∼ **industrial**
industrial site

encontrar *vt* find; (problema, dificultad)
encounter, come up against; ∼ **algo
deficiente** find sth wanting; ∼ **defectos
en algo** find fault with sth

encriptación *f* encryption; ∼ **de
clave pública/privada** public-key/
private-key encryption

encriptar *vt* encrypt

encuadernación *f* binding

encuadre *m* (Info) frame

encubrimiento *m* cover-up; (acción)
covering up; (Der) nondisclosure

encuentro *m* meeting; ∼ **de
negocios** business meeting

encuesta *f* inquiry; (en investigación de
mercado) survey, poll; **efectuar** *or*
realizar una ∼ carry out a survey; ∼ **de
campo** field survey; ∼ **de
consumidores** consumer survey; ∼ **de
opinión** opinion poll

endémico *adj* endemic

endeudado *adj* indebted; ∼ **con**
indebted to

endeudamiento *m* indebtedness; ∼
externo borrowing abroad

endeudarse *v pron* get into debt
(infrml)

endosador, a *m,f* endorser

endosante *mf* endorser; ∼ **por aval**
accommodation endorser

endosar *vt* (cheque, certificado) endorse,
guarantee

endosatario, -a *m,f* endorsee

endoso *m* endorsement; **sin** ∼
unendorsed; ∼ **absoluto** absolute
endorsement; ∼ **por aval**
accommodation endorsement; ∼
bancario bank endorsement; ∼
especial special endorsement; ∼ **de un
tercero** third-party endorsement

endurecer *vt* (normas) tighten up

endurecimiento *m* (de normas)
tightening-up

energía *f* energy; (corriente) power; **con**
∼ energetically, vigorously; **consumo
de** ∼ energy consumption; ∼
alternativa alternative energy; ∼
atómica atomic energy, nuclear power;
∼ **ecológica** green energy; ∼ **eléctrica**
electric power; ∼ **eólica** wind power; ∼
hidráulica hydraulic power, water
power; ∼ **hidroeléctrica** hydroelectric
power; ∼ **maremotriz** tidal power; ∼
nuclear nuclear energy; ∼ **solar** solar
energy; ∼ **térmica** thermal energy

enfatizar *vt* emphasize

enfermedad *f* disease, illness; **estar ausente por** ∼ be off sick; ∼ **ficticia** malingering; ∼ **laboral** industrial disease; ∼ **profesional** occupational illness

enfiteusis *f* long lease

enfoque *m* approach; **depende del** ∼ **que se le de** it depends on the way you look at it; ∼ **cualitativo** qualitative approach; ∼ **de productos** commodity approach; ∼ **de sistemas** systems approach

enfrentar *vt* (situación, problema) face up to, confront

enfriar *vt* (relaciones) cool down

enganchar *vt* hook up; ∼ **al Internet** log onto the Net

enganche *m* (Info) hook-up, connection

engañar *vt* mislead, deceive; **no dejarse** ∼ not be taken in

engaño *m* deception

engañoso *adj* misleading, deceptive

engranaje *m* gears; (sistema) mechanism, machinery

enlace¹ *m* link, liaison; ∼ **con el cliente** customer liaison; ∼ **común de datos** data bus; ∼ **de comunicación** communication link; ∼ **de datos** data link; ∼ **de hipertexto** hypertext link, hotlink; ∼ **de hipertexto local** local link; ∼ **rail-avión** rail-air link; ∼ **de transporte** transport link

enlace²: ∼ **sindical** *mf* shop steward

enlazar *vt* (periféricos, conexiones) link

enmendado *adj* amended; **voto** ∼ spoiled ballot paper

enmendar *vt* amend; (corregir) correct

enmienda *f* amendment; (corrección) correction; ∼s **al borrador** draft amendments

enmiendado *adj* amended

enriquecimiento *m* (de trabajo, empleo) enrichment

enrollar *vt* scroll up

ensamblador *m* (Info) assembler; ∼ **cruzado** *or* **de referencias cruzadas** cross-reference assembler

ensamblaje *m* (acción) assembling; (lenguaje) assembly language

ensanchamiento, **ensanche** *m* widening, expansion

ensayar *vt* try, test out

ensayo *m* test; ∼ **en banco de pruebas** benchmark test; ∼ **clínico**

clinical trial; ∼ **piloto** pilot run, pilot test

enseñanza *f* teaching; (aprendizaje) learning; ∼ **en línea** online learning, open learning

enseres *m pl* equipment, furniture and fittings; ∼ **domésticos** household effects

entablar *vt* (discusión) start; (negociaciones) enter into; ∼ **demanda contra alguien** take out a summons against sb; ∼ **una demanda por daños y perjuicios** file a claim for damages; ∼ **un pleito contra alguien** bring a lawsuit against sb

ente *m* body, organization; ∼ **público** public body

entender *vt* understand; **dar algo a** ∼ imply *o* suggest sth; **me dió a** ∼ **que no estaba feliz en su puesto** she led me to believe that she wasn't happy in her job; ∼ **mal** misunderstand

entendido: **en el** ∼ **de que...** on the understanding that..., provided that...

entendimiento *m* understanding; **llegar a un** ∼ reach an understanding

enterado *adj* well-informed; **estar** ∼ **de algo** be well-informed about sth

enterarse *v pron* find out; ∼ **de algo** find out *o* hear about sth; **tenemos que enterarnos de lo que piensan pagar** we have to find out what they're prepared to pay

entero *m* (Bolsa) point; **las acciones perdieron tres** ∼s the shares went down *o* have lost three points; ∼ **natural** natural number

entibar *vt* (economía) prop up, shore up

entidad *f* entity; (organización) body, organization; (compañía) company; ∼ **de ahorro y préstamo** savings institution BrE, thrift institution AmE; ∼ **comercial** business concern; ∼ **de crédito** credit association; ∼ **exenta** exempt organization; ∼ **financiera** financial institution; ∼ **sin fines de lucro** nonprofit-making association BrE, nonprofit association AmE; ∼ **jurídica** legal entity; ∼ **pública** public body

entorno *m* environment; ∼ **económico** economic framework; ∼ **del mercado** market environment; ∼ **de red** network environment; ∼ **de trabajo** working environment; ∼ **virtual** virtual environment

entrada *f* entrance; (de datos) entry, input; (de nuevos pedidos) intake; (de fondos) inflow; (pago inicial) down payment;

(recaudación) admission, gate; (billete) ticket; ~s f pl tickets; **sacar** ~s buy tickets; **prohibida la** ~ no entry; **tuvimos que dar 10.000 euros de** ~ we had to put down 10,000 euros; ~ **automática al sistema** autologon; ~ **bruta** gross revenue; ~s **de caja** cash receipts; ~ **de capital** capital inflow; ~ **comercial** trade entrance BrE, service entrance AmE; ~ **en compensación** clearing entry; ~ **de datos** data entry; ~ **descontrolada/salida descontrolada** (Info) garbage-in/garbage-out; ~ **de divisas** inflow of currency; ~ **en efectivo** cash inflow; ~ **falsa** false entry; ~ **fraudulenta** deceptive entry; ~ **inmediata** immediate possession; ~ **libre** (espectáculos) free admission; ~ **en el mercado** market entry; ~s **netas** net receipts; ~ **de pedido** order entry; ~ **pendiente** outstanding entry; ~ **de proveedores** tradesman's entrance; ~s **y salidas** income and expenditure; ~ **de trabajo** job entry; ~ **en vigor** coming into force

entrada/salida f input/output; ~ **masivas** bulk input/output

entradilla f (en prensa) lead

entrar vi enter; ~ **en** enter into, be part of; **eso no entra en el precio** that's not included in the price; ~ **en bolsa** go public; ~ **con buen pie** (negocios, proyecto) get off to a flying start; ~ **en funcionamiento** come into operation; ~ **en juego** (factores) come into play; ~ **en máquina** (prensa, publicación) go to press; ~ **en el mercado** come onto the market; ~ **en el mercado de trabajo** enter the job BrE o labor AmE market; ~ **en negocios** go into business; ~ **en pérdidas** run into debt; ~ **en política** go into o enter politics; ~ **en un programa** access a program; ~ **en recesión** go into recession; ~ **en el sistema** access the system; ~ **a trabajar** start work; ~ **en vigencia** or **vigor** come into effect, come into force; ~ **en vigor desde** take effect from

entrega f (de mercancías, acciones) delivery; **para** ~ **inmediata** for immediate delivery; ~ **aplazada** delayed delivery; ~ **bruta** gross taking; ~ **contra reembolso** cash on delivery ; ~ **en el día** same-day delivery; ~ **a domicilio** home delivery (service); ~ **exenta** free delivery; ~ **gratuita** free delivery; ~ **inicial** (de compra) initial outlay; (pago) down payment; ~

inmediata immediate occupancy; ~ **a la par** par delivery

entregado adj delivered

entregar vt (mercancías, carta, paquete) deliver; (solicitud, impreso) submit; (llaves, dinero) give, hand over; (notificación) serve

entretanto adv in the interim

entretenimiento m entertainment; ~ **didáctico** edutainment; ~s **públicos** public amenities

entrevista f interview; **dar una** ~ (a la prensa) give an interview; ~ **dirigida** directed interview; ~ **estructurada** structured interview; ~ **de evaluación del desempeño** performance appraisal interview; ~ **informal** informal interview; ~ **personal** personal interview; ~ **en profundidad** in-depth interview; ~ **de salida** exit interview; ~ **telefónica** telephone interview; ~ **de ventas** sales interview

entrevistado, -a m,f interviewee; (en encuesta) respondent

entrevistador, a m,f interviewer

enumeración f enumeration

enumerar vt enumerate, list

envase m packaging; ~ **burbuja** bubble wrap, blister pack; ~ **conjunto** (para el mismo producto) banded pack, bundled pack; ~ **con incentivo** incentive pack; ~ **engañoso** deceptive packaging; ~ **primario** primary package; ~ **reutilizable** reusable pack; ~ **de tamaño familiar** family-size package; ~ **unitario** unit pack; ~ **vacío** vacuum packaging

enverdecimiento m (de la opinión pública) greening

envergadura f (del problema) scale, importance; **de cierta** ~ considerable, substantial

enviar vt send; ~ **por correo** post BrE, send by post BrE, mail AmE; ~ **por correo aéreo** send by airmail; ~ **por fax** fax, send by fax; ~ **una petición por escrito** send a written request

envío m (de correo) delivery; ~ **en bus** bus mailing; ~ **por correo** mailing; ~ **múltiple** crossposting; ~ **postal** postal remittance; ~ **publicitario** mailing; ~ **urgente** express delivery

envoltorio m package

envolver vt wrap (up); (involucrar) involve; **está envuelto en el asunto** he's involved in the matter

epígrafe m Esp (hoja de balance) heading

época f period; **hacer ~** be a landmark; **un proceso que hizo ~** a landmark trial

equidad f (legalidad) equity; **~ entre los contribuyentes** taxpayers' equity

equilibrado adj balanced, well-balanced

equilibrar ① vt balance; **~ el balance** redress the balance; **~ la balanza comercial** restore the balance of trade; **~ gastos e ingresos** balance income and expenditure; **~ el presupuesto** balance the budget ② vi break even

equilibrio m balance, equilibrium; **estar en ~** be balanced; **~ estable** stable equilibrium; **~ inestable** unstable equilibrium; **~ interno** internal balance; **~ del mercado** market equilibrium; **~ presupuestario** budget equilibrium; **~ sostenido** steady-state equilibrium; **~ temporal** temporary equilibrium

equipaje m baggage, luggage; **facturar el ~** check in one's luggage; **~ acompañado** accompanied baggage; **~ facturado** checked-in luggage; **~ de mano** hand luggage; **~ no acompañado** unaccompanied baggage; **~ permitido** baggage allowance

equipamiento m equipment

equipar vt equip, fit out; **la compañía está bien equipada para este volumen de pedidos** the company is well-equipped to deal with this amount of orders; **~ a alguien con** or **de algo** equip sb with sth

equiparación f comparison; **~ fiscal** tax equalization

equipo m (de trabajadores) team; (máquinas, materiales) equipment; **trabajar en ~** work as (part of) a team; **~ administrativo** management team; **~ agrícola** farm equipment; **~ de apoyo financiero** financial support staff; **~ audiovisual** audiovisual equipment; **~ de auditores** audit team; **~ auxiliar** auxiliary equipment; **~ de ayuda** helpware; **~ complementario** add-on equipment; **~ físico** hardware; **~ flexible** flexible plant; **~ de gestión** management team; **~ humano** human resources team; **~ de investigación** research team; **~ lógico** software; **~ de mantenimiento** (maquinaria) maintenance equipment; (personal) maintenance staff; **~ de oficina** office equipment; **~ periférico** peripheral equipment; **~ de prueba** test equipment; **~ de**

reparación repair kit; **~ terminal de datos** data terminal equipment; **~ de trabajo** team; **~ de venta** sales force

equitativo adj equitable

equivalencia f equivalence; **~ de las cargas fiscales** commensurate taxation; **~ en efectivo** cash equivalence; **~ de rendimiento** yield equivalence

equivalente m equivalent; **~ de acciones ordinarias** common shares BrE o stock AmE equivalent; **~s de caja** cash equivalents

equivaler vi: **~ a** be equivalent to

equivocación f mistake; (descuido) oversight; **por ~** by mistake

equivocar vt mix up, get mixed up; **~ a alguien** make sb go wrong, make sb make a mistake

equivocarse v pron be mistaken o wrong; **~ de algo** get sth wrong; **se ha equivocado de número** (de teléfono) you've got the wrong number

era f age, era; **~ de las computadoras** AmL or **de los ordenadores** Esp f computer age

erario m Treasury; **~ público** public monies, public treasury

ergofobia f ergophobia

ergonometría f ergonometrics

ergonométrico adj ergonometric

ergonomía f ergonomics; **~ cognitiva** cognitive ergonomics

ergonómicamente adv ergonomically

ergonómico adj ergonomic

ergonomista mf ergonomist

erosión f (del suelo) erosion; **~ fiscal** tax erosion

erosionar vt (poder) erode

erradicar vt eradicate

errar vt (en una decisión) be mistaken, err

errata f misprint, typo (infrml), literal (jarg), erratum (frml); **fe de ~s** errata

erróneo adj erroneous, mistaken

error m error, mistake; (ramación) bug; **cometer un ~** make a mistake; **~es y omisiones** errors and admissions; **salvo ~ u omisión** errors and omissions excepted; **por ~** by mistake; **sin ~es** error-free; **~ aleatorio** (estadística) random error; **~ de cálculo** miscalculation; (Info) computational error; **~ de codificación** coding error; **~ de compensación** compensating error; **~ contable** accounting error; **~ de derecho** error of law, legal error; **~**

grave fatal error; **~ de hecho** factual error; **~ de imprenta** misprint; **~ inherente** inherent error; **~ judicial de envergadura** gross miscarriage of justice; **~ mecanográfico** typing error; **~ de memoria** memory lapse; **~ de muestreo** sampling error; **~ de oficina** clerical error; **~ de pase** posting error; **~ permitido** permissible error; **~ de programa** software *o* programming error; **~ del programa** program bug; **~ de programación** miscoding, programming error; **~ de pulsación** keying error; **~ recuperable** recoverable error; **~ de registro** posting error; **~ de sintaxis** syntax error; **~ de sistema** system error; **~ tipográfico** typographic error, typo (infrml)

E/S *abr* (▸**entrada/salida**) I/O (input/output)

esbozar *vt* outline

esbozo *m* sketch; **~ de anuncio** animatic

escala *f* scale; **a ~ internacional** on an international scale; **a ~ mundial** on a worldwide scale; **a gran ~** on a large scale; **un proyecto a gran ~** a large-scale project; **a pequeña ~** on a small scale; **hacer ~** (vuelo) stop over; **~ de actitudes** (en investigación de mercado) attitude scale; **~ de amortización de activos** asset depreciation range; **~ de cargos** scale of charges; **~ de la comisión** scale of commission; **~ del impuesto sobre la renta** income tax scale; **~ intermedia** (de vuelo) stopover; **~ móvil** sliding scale; **~ móvil de salarios** sliding wage scale; **~ nominal** nominal scale; **~ de precios** price range; **~ progresiva** (Fisc) progressive scale; (RRHH) incremental scale; **~ de promoción** promotion ladder; **~ salarial** salary scale; **~ de salarios** *or* **sueldos** salary scale; **~ de valoración** rating scale

escalar *vt* climb, scale up; **~ posiciones** scale *o* move up the career ladder

escalón *m* echelon

escalonado *adj* stepped

escalonamiento *m* staggering; **~ de las vacaciones** staggering of holidays BrE *o* vacations AmE

escalonar *vt* (costes, pagos) stagger

escándalo *m* scandal

escáner *m* (aparato) scanner; (imagen) scan

escaño *m* (en el Parlamento) seat

escaparate *m* shop window, window display; **mirar los ~s** window-shop; **~ electrónico** electronic storefront; **~ virtual** virtual storefront

escape *m* (Info) escape key

escasear *vi* run low, be in short supply

escasez *f* (de existencias, fondos) shortage; (de demanda) lack; **~ de capital** capital shortage; **~ de mano de obra** shortage of manpower; **~ de personal** understaffing; **~ de petróleo** oil shortage; **~ de viviendas** housing shortage

escaso *adj* in short supply; (recursos) scarce; **~ de** short of; **~ de personal** *or* **plantilla** Esp *adj* understaffed

escatimar *vt* skimp on

escenario *m* scene; (de negociaciones) stage

escepticismo *m* scepticism BrE, skepticism AmE

esclarecer *vt* throw light on

escogido *adj* chosen, selected; (Bolsa) top-rated

escope *m* scoop

escribir *vti* write; **~ pidiendo algo** send away for sth; **~ a máquina** type; **una carta escrita a máquina** a typed letter; **por escrito** in writing

escrito *m* document; **~ de súplica** petition

escritor, a *m,f* writer; **~ freelance** *or* **independiente** freelance writer

escritorio *m* desk; (en pantalla) desktop; **de ~** desktop

escritura *f* deed; **~ de autorización** (comercial) licence bond BrE, license bond AmE; **~ de la casa** title deeds; **~ de caución** bail bond; **~ de cesión** deed of assignation; **~ de cesión de un derecho** quitclaim deed; **~ de compraventa** bought contract; **~ de donación** gift deed; **~ de fianza** bail bond; **~ de fideicomiso** deed of trust; **~ de garantía** guarantee deed, deed of covenant BrE; **~ de hipoteca** mortgage deed; **~ en negrilla** bold printing; **~ de propiedad** title deed; **~ pública** public instrument, deed; **~ de transmisión** transfer deed; **~ de traslación de dominio** deed of conveyance; **~ única lectura múltiple**, write once read many, WORM

escriturado *adj* under article

escriturar *vt* bind

escrutinio *m* (de cuentas) scrutiny; ∼ **en profundidad** depth polling

escucha *f* monitoring; ∼ **telefónica** *f* wiretapping

escuela *f* school; ∼ **del estado** state school BrE, public school AmE; ∼ **de formación profesional** vocational school; ∼ **de negocios** business school; ∼ **preescolar** nursery school BrE, preschool BrE, preschool center AmE; ∼ **privada** private school, public school BrE; ∼ **pública** state school BrE, public school AmE

esfera *f* sphere; **altas** ∼**s** upper echelons; ∼ **de actividad** sphere of activity

esfuerzo *m* effort; **hacer un** ∼ make an effort; ∼ **concertado** concerted effort; ∼ **fiscal** tax effort; ∼ **a toda potencia** all-out effort; ∼ **de venta** sales effort

eslabonar *m* link, connect

eslogan *m* (anuncios) slogan, tagline; ∼ **publicitario** advertising slogan

esp. *abr* (▸**especialmente**) esp. (especially)

espaciado *m* pitch; ∼ **doble** dual pitch; ∼ **de letras** letter spacing

espaciar *vt* (devoluciones, riesgos) spread

espacio *m* space; (Medios) slot (jarg); (publicitario) spot (jarg); **a un** ∼ single-spaced; **a doble** ∼ double-spaced; ∼ **abierto** open space; ∼ **adjudicado** appointed space; ∼ **designado** (en publicidad) appointed space; ∼ **del disco** disk space; ∼ **disponible** spare capacity; **E**∼ **Económico Europeo** European Economic Space; ∼ **de la eme** (en tipografía) em space; ∼ **entre líneas** line spacing; ∼ **en estante** shelf space; ∼ **favorable** window of opportunity; ∼ **fijo** (TV, radio) fixed spot; ∼ **informativo** news bulletin; ∼ **para oficina** office space; ∼ **publicitario** (radiodifusión) advertising spot; ∼ **de ventas** selling space; ∼ **vital** living space; ∼ **web** Internet presence, Internet site, Web space

especialidad *f* speciality BrE, specialty AmE; (de estudio) specialization

especialista *mf* specialist; ∼ **en bonos** bond specialist; ∼ **en equipo físico** hardware specialist; ∼ **en informática** computer scientist

especialización *f* specialization; ∼ **laboral** job specialization

especializado *adj* specialized; (revista) specialist; ∼ **en** specializing in; **usuarios no** ∼**s** general users

especializarse *v pron*: ∼ **en** specialize in; **se especializó en Dirección Empresarial** he specialized in Business Management

especialmente *adv* especially

especie: **en** ∼ *adj* (pago, ganancias) in kind, in specie

especificación *f* specification; **especificaciones contractuales** contract specifications

especificar *vt* specify; **no especificado en otro punto** not elsewhere specified

específico *adj* specific; ∼ **del país** country-specific; ∼ **de un dispositivo** device-specific

especifidad *f* specificity; ∼ **de activos** *f* asset specificity

espécimen *m* specimen copy

espectáculo *m* show; ∼**s** *m pl* entertainment; (en periódicos) listings, entertainment guide; ∼**s durante el vuelo** in-flight entertainment

espectador, a *m,f* spectator; (de televisión, Internet) viewer

especulación *f* speculation; **por** ∼ on speculation, on spec (infrml); ∼ **alcista** bull speculation; ∼ **a la baja** bear speculation; ∼ **bursátil** speculation on the Stock Exchange; ∼ **eventual** venture; ∼ **fuerte** plunge; ∼ **inmobiliaria** property speculation

especulador, a *m,f* speculator; (Bolsa) stag; ∼ **alcista** bull speculator; ∼ **en bolsa** dabbler; ∼ **corporativo(-a)** *m,f* corporate raider; ∼ **fuerte** plunger; ∼ **inmobiliario(-a)** *m,f* property speculator; ∼ **insolvente** lame duck

especular *vi* speculate; ∼ **en la bolsa** speculate on the Stock Exchange

especulativo *adj* speculative

espera *f* wait; **una** ∼ **de tres horas** a three-hour wait; **llamada en** ∼ call waiting; **en** ∼ **de algo** pending sth; **en** ∼ **de la decisión del comité** pending the committee's decision; **en** ∼ **de su respuesta** I look forward to hearing from you

esperado *adj* (resultado, final) expected

esperanza *f* hope, expectation; ∼ **de vida** life expectancy; ∼ **de vida del producto** product life expectancy

esperar **1** *vt* (persona, órden) wait for; (contar con) expect; (expresando deseo) hope;

estoy esperando una llamada I'm expecting a call; ～ **algo de algo/alguien** expect sth of sth/sb; **era de** ～ it was to be expected; **no hay que** ～ **mucho de las conversaciones** we shouldn't expect too much from the talks
[2] *vi* (aguardar) wait; **hacer** ～ **a alguien** keep sb waiting

espigar *vi* shoot up

espionaje *m* espionage; ～ **comercial** *or* **industrial** industrial espionage

espiral *f* (de precios) spiral; ～ **ascendente/descendente** (en sueldos, precios) upward/downward spiral; ～ **inflacionista** inflationary spiral; ～ **inflacionista de salarios y precios** wage-price inflation spiral; ～ **precios-salarios** wage-price spiral

espíritu *m* spirit; ～ **comunitario** community spirit; ～ **empresarial** entrepreneurial spirit; ～ **de equipo** team spirit

esponsorización *f* sponsorship

esponsorizar *f* sponsor

esporádico *adj* sporadic

esposa *f* wife; ～ **de hecho** common-law wife

esquema *m* outline; ～ **de la computadora** AmL *m* (cf ▸**esquema del ordenador** Esp) computer map; ～ **de disposición** organization chart, organigram; ～ **económico** economic pattern; ～ **funcional** block diagram; ～ **del ordenador** Esp (cf ▸**esquema de la computadora** AmL) computer map; ～ **de pensión contributoria** contributory pension scheme; ～ **de sugerencias** suggestion scheme

esquemático *adj* schematic

esquilmar *vt* (riquezas, recursos) exhaust; (mercado) skim

esquirol *mf* (infrml) scab (infrml), blackleg (infrml) BrE

esquirolismo *m* (infrml) strikebreaking

esquivar *vt* (evitar) avoid; (evadir) sidestep, dodge

estabilidad *f* stability; **tener** ～ **en el cargo** have security of tenure; ～ **económica** economic stability; ～ **financiera** financial stability; ～ **política** political stability; ～ **de precios** price stability

estabilización *f* stabilization; ～ **económica** economic stabilization; ～ **artificial de precios** pegging system; ～ **de precios** price stabilization; (V&M)

price fixing; ～ **salarial** wage stabilization

estabilizador *m* stabilizer; ～**es incorporados** (Econ) built-in stabilizers; ～ **automático** (Econ) automatic stabilizer

estabilizar *vt* stabilize, peg

estabilizarse *v pron* stabilize, become stable

estable *adj* stable, steady

establecer *vt* (hecho) establish, ascertain; (negocio) set up; (reglas) lay down; (registro, criterio) set; ～ **comunicación directa con** establish a direct link with; ～ **un contrato con** enter into a contract with; ～ **una diferencia entre** draw a distinction between; ～ **los estándares** set the standards; ～ **la lista final** shortlist; ～ **las normas** set the rules; ～ **un nuevo máximo** set a new high; ～ **un orden** establish an order; ～ **un orden del día** draw up an agenda; ～ **la sede** set up headquarters; ～ **vínculos con** build links with

establecerse *v pron* (en trabajo, residencia, país) settle; ～ **por cuenta propia** set up on one's own account

establecido *adj* established

establecimiento *m* establishment; ～ **bancario** banking establishment; ～ **comercial** business establishment; ～ **docente** educational establishment; ～ **de metas** goal setting; ～ **de normas de contabilidad** accounting standard setting; ～ **de objetivos** target setting; ～ **de la política** policymaking

estación *f* station; ～ **emisora** transmitting station; ～ **de ferrocarril** railway station BrE, train station BrE, railroad station AmE; ～ **generadora** generating station; ～ **de máxima actividad** peak season; ～ **de servicio** service station, petrol station BrE, gas station AmE; ～ **de sondeos** drilling installation; ～ **de trabajo** (espacio físico) workstation; ～ **turística** tourist resort

estacional *adj* seasonal

estacionalidad *f*: ～ **de la demanda** seasonal nature of demand

estacionamiento *m* car park BrE, parking lot AmE; ～ **automático** (disco duro) autopark

estadística *f* (ciencia) statistics; (figura) statistic; **las últimas** ～**s muestran que ...** the latest statistics show that ...; ～ **demográfica** (estadística) population ⋯⋮

statistics; ~ **de desempleo** unemployment statistics; ~**s de publicidad** advertising statistics; ~**s de referencia** benchmark statistics

estadístico[1] *adj* statistical

estadístico[2], **-a** *m,f* statistician

estado *m* state, condition; (informe) statement; (Info) status; (nación) state; **el E~** the State; **asuntos de** ~ affairs of state; **estar en buen** ~ be in good condition; (máquina) be in good working order; **estar en mal** ~ be in poor condition; **la seguridad del E~** state security; ~ **de activos y pasivos** statement of assets and liabilities; ~ **de ánimo** frame of mind; ~ **anual** annual statement; ~ **auditado** audited statement; ~ **autoritario** authoritarian state; ~ **benefactor** welfare state; ~ **del bienestar** welfare state; ~ **de cash-flow** cash flow statement; ~ **civil** marital status; ~ **de conciliación** reconciliation statement; ~ **condensado** condensed statement; ~ **consolidado** consolidated statement; ~ **de contabilidad consolidado** consolidated statement of condition; ~ **contable** financial statement, accounting report; ~ **corporativo** corporate state; ~ **de cosas** state of affairs; ~ **de cuenta** account *o* bank statement, balance of account; ~ **de cuenta pormenorizado** itemized statement; ~ **de cuentas a cobrar** accounts receivable statement; ~ **de cuentas de compensación** clearing balance statement; (Cont) aggregate statement; ~ **de la economía** state of the economy; ~ **del efectivo (de caja)** cash statement; ~ **de excepción** state of emergency; ~ **de existencias** inventory sheet; ~ **financiero** financial statement; ~ **financiero consolidado** consolidated financial statement; ~ **de flujos de caja** cash flow statement; ~ **de ganancias** statement of earnings; ~ **de ingresos y gastos** statement of income and expenses; ~ **legal** legal status; ~ **mensual** monthly statement; ~ **miembro** (UE) member state; ~ **de pérdidas y ganancias** profit and loss statement; ~ **presupuestario** (gubernamental) budgetary statement; ~ **protector** buffer state; ~ **de reconciliación** reconciliation statement; ~ **de resultados de operación** operating statement; ~ **resumido** summary statement; ~ **revisado** audited statement; ~

temporal temporary status; ~ **verificado** audited statement

estafa *f* swindle

estafador, a *m,f* swindler, con artist (infml)

estafar *vt* swindle, defraud; ~ **algo a alguien** swindle sb out of sth, defraud sb of sth

estafeta[1] *mf* courier

estafeta[2] *f*: ~ **de correos** sub-post office

estagnación *f* stagnation

estallar *vi* (bomba) explode, go off; (máquina) blow up

estampación *f* embossing; ~ **sobre metal** foil stamping

estampar *vt* stamp; (sello) affix; ~ **la fecha** (en impreso) stamp the date

estampilla *f* AmL postage stamp; (sello de goma) rubber stamp

estancado *adj* (conversaciones) deadlocked; (economía) stagnant

estancamiento *f* stagnation; ~ **económico** economic slowdown

estancar *vt* deadlock, bring to a standstill

estancarse *v pron* (economía) stagnate; (negociaciones) come to a standstill

estándar[1] *adj* standard

estándar[2] *m* standard; ~ **de emisión** emission standard; ~ **de igualdad** equality standard; ~ **nacional de ruido** national noise standard; ~ **presupuestario** budget standard

estandarización *f* standardization

estandarizante *adj* standardizing

estandarizar *vt* standardize

estandarte *m* standard, banner; ~ **aéreo** aeroplane banner BrE, airplane banner AmE

estanflación *f* stagflation

estar *vi* be; (estar listo) be ready; **¿está José?** is José there *o* in?; **el director no está** the manager's not here; **el director está fuera** the manager is out; (de viaje) the manager is away; **las fotos estarán para mañana** the photos will be ready tomorrow; **¡ya está!** that's it!, it's done; **¿a cuántos estamos hoy?** what's the date today?; **estamos a 12 de mayo** it's the 12th of May; ~ **en ello** be working on it, be on the case; ~ **con alguien** (apoyar) support sb; **para eso estamos** (en respuesta a gracias) that's what we're here for, you're welcome

estatal *adj* (empresa) government-owned, state-owned; **apoyo ~** government backing

estatalización *f* Esp nationalization

estatalizar *vt* Esp nationalize

estático *adj* (producción, precios) static

estatización *f* AmL nationalization

estatizar *vt* AmL nationalize

estatus *m* status; **~ social** social status

estatutario *adj* statutory

estatuto *m* statute; (Der) enactment; **~s** articles of association; **~s sociales** by-laws

estenografía *f* stenography

estenógrafo, -a *m,f* stenographer

estenotipista *mf* shorthand typist

estereotipación, estereotipia *f* stereotyping; **~ de los sexos** sexual stereotyping

estereotipo *m* stereotype

esterilización *f* sterilization

esterilizar *vt* sterilize

estilete *m* stylus

estilista *mf* stylist; (Medios) designer

estilizar *vt* stylize; (Medios) design

estilo *m* style; **de ~ occidental** western-style; **por el ~** along similar lines; **compañías por el ~** companies of that type; **~ de la casa** (imprenta) house style; **~ de gerencia** management style; **~ de vida** lifestyle, way of life; **~ de vida familiar** family lifestyle

estima *f* esteem, respect; **tener a alguien en gran ~** have a high regard for sb

estimación *f* estimate, assessment; (evaluación) appraisal; (previsión) forecast; (respeto) respect; **última ~** latest estimate; **ganar la ~ de alguien** earn sb's respect; **~ aproximativa** rough estimate; **~ de la base imponible** *or* **impositiva** tax assessment; **~ de caja** cash forecast; **~ contable** accounts appraisal; **~ de costes** Esp *or* **costos** AmL cost estimate; **~ de empleo** job appraisal; **~ financiera** financial forecast; **~ de ganancias** earnings forecast; **~ de gastos** estimate of expenditure; **~ de gastos de capital** capital expenditure appraisal; **~ del mercado** market appraisal; **~ objetiva** objective evaluation; **~ óptima** best estimate; **~ presupuestaria** budget estimate; **~ propia** self-esteem; **~ de riesgos** risk assessment; **~ de ventas** sales estimate

estimado *adj* (en correspondencia) dear; **Estimada Señora García** Dear Mrs García

estimador *m* estimator; **~ lineal insesgado óptimo** best linear unbiased estimator

estimar *vt* (calcular) estimate, gauge BrE; gage AmE; (respetar) hold in esteem; (considerar) deem, consider; **~ por aproximación** guesstimate (infrml); **~ necesario** deem necessary; **el banco sufrió pérdidas estimadas en varios millones** the bank's losses were estimated at several million

estimulante *adj* stimulating

estimular *vt* stimulate, boost; **~ un avance** fuel an advance; **~ la inflación** fuel inflation

estímulo *m* stimulus; (incentivo) incentive; **~ competitivo** competitive stimulus; **servir de ~ a la inversión** serve *o* act as an incentive for investment

estipular *vt* stipulate; **~ las bases para** provide the base for

estorbo *m* hindrance, obstacle

estrangulamiento *m* bottleneck

estraperlo *m* black market; **comprar algo de ~** buy sth on the black market

estrategia *f* strategy; **~ de beneficios** profit strategy; **~ comercial** business strategy; **~ competitiva** competitive strategy; **~ de comunicación** communication strategy; **~ corporativa** corporate strategy; **~ de crecimiento** growth strategy; **~ de desarrollo** development strategy; **~ de diversificación** diversification strategy; **~ económica** economic strategy; **~ de la empresa** company strategy; **~ de expansión** expansion strategy; **~ financiera** financial strategy; **~ fiscal** tax strategy; **~ global** global strategy; **~ informática** computer strategy; **~ de inversión** investment strategy; **~ de marketing** marketing strategy; **~ de los medios de comunicación** media strategy; **~ de negocios** business strategy; **~ de precios** pricing strategy; **~ publicitaria** advertising strategy; **~ de supervivencia** survival strategy; **~ de tira y afloja** push/pull strategy; **~ de ventas** sales strategy

estratégico *adj* strategic

estratificación *f* stratification; **~ social** social stratification

estrato *m* stratum; **~ de petróleo** oil deposit

estrechamiento *m* (de relaciones) strengthening; (de margen) narrowing, reduction; ∼ **del crédito** credit squeeze; ∼ **del margen de beneficios** reduction of the profit margin

estrechar *vt* (relaciones) strengthen; (brecha, margen) narrow, reduce; ∼**le la mano a alguien** shake sb's hand

estrecho *adj* (cooperación, relación) close; **en** ∼ **contacto** in close contact; **mantener estrechas relaciones con algo/alguien** maintain close ties with sth/sb

estrenar *vt* launch; (película) premiere; **oficinas a** ∼ (en anuncio) brand new offices

estreno *m* (de producto) launch; (de película) premiere

estrés *m* stress; **tener** ∼ be stressed, be suffering from stress; ∼ **del ejecutivo** executive stress; ∼ **laboral** work-related stress

estresar *vt* stress (out); **estar muy estresado** be under a lot of stress

estrictamente *adv* strictly, stringently

estricto *adj* (medidas, programa) strict, stringent; (normas) hard and fast; **estricta adhesión al contrato** strict adherence to the contract

estructura *f* structure; ∼ **administrativa** management structure; ∼ **en árbol** tree structure; ∼ **de capital** capital structure; ∼ **del consumo** consumption pattern; ∼ **corporativa** corporate structure; ∼ **del coste** Esp *or* **costo** AmL *f* cost structure; ∼ **de datos** data structure; ∼ **directiva** management structure; ∼ **económica** economic structure; ∼ **de la empresa** company structure; ∼ **financiera** financial structure; ∼ **fiscal** tax structure; ∼ **de la gestión** management structure; ∼ **de grupo** group structure; ∼ **impositiva** tax structure; ∼ **de la inversión** pattern of investment; ∼ **de matriz** grid structure; ∼ **del mercado** market structure; ∼ **de la organización** organization structure; ∼ **de precios** price structure; ∼ **del programa** programme structure BrE, program structure AmE; ∼ **en rejilla** grid structure; ∼ **salarial** salary structure; ∼ **sindical** union structure; ∼ **de votos** vote structure

estructuración *f* structuring; ∼ **del trabajo** work structuring

estructurado *adj* structured

estructurar *vt* structure

estruendo *m* outcry; (alboroto) uproar

estudiante *mf* student; ∼ **extranjero(-a)** *m,f* foreign student; ∼ **universitario(-a)** *m,f* undergraduate, university student

estudiar *vt* study; (en la universidad) read; (examinar) consider, examine; **el informe estudia las causas de la recesión** the report examines *o* looks into the causes of the recession

estudio *m* (actividad) study; (lugar) studio; (investigación de mercado) survey; ∼ **de actitudes** attitude survey; ∼ **de casos** case study; ∼ **del déficit** gap study; ∼ **de desplazamientos y tiempos** time and motion study; ∼ **de diseño** design engineering; ∼**s económicos** *or* **empresariales** business studies; ∼ **empírico** empirical study; ∼ **de factibilidad** feasibility study; ∼ **del gasto del consumidor** consumer expenditure survey; ∼ **de gerencia** management survey; ∼ **de impacto** impact study; ∼ **laboral** job study; ∼ **de medios de comunicación** media research; ∼ **de mercado** (actividad) market research; (sondeo) market survey; ∼ **de movimientos** motion study; ∼ **de muestra** sample study; ∼ **piloto** pilot study; ∼ **pormenorizado** in-depth study; ∼ **preliminar** reconnaissance survey; ∼ **de un proyecto** project study; ∼ **de rentabilidad** profitability study; ∼**s sociales** social studies; ∼ **de sueldos y salarios** wage and salary survey; ∼ **de viabilidad** feasibility study

etapa *f* stage; **en determinada** ∼ at some stage; **hacer algo por** ∼**s** do sth in stages; ∼ **alfa** alpha stage; ∼ **del proceso** process stage; ∼ **de prueba** test stage; ∼ **de transición** (de mercado) transition stage

Ethernet® *m* (red) Ethernet®

ética *f* ethics; (Der) moral law; ∼ **comercial** business ethics; ∼ **profesional** professional ethics; ∼ **del trabajo** work ethic

ético *adj* ethical

etiqueta *f* (identificación de carga) label, tag; (formalidad) etiquette; **de** ∼ formal; **traje de** ∼ formal dress; ∼ **adhesiva** stick-on label; ∼ **de calidad** quality label; ∼ **comercial** business etiquette; ∼ **de equipaje** luggage label, baggage tag; ∼ **equivalente** alias; ∼ **postal** address label; ∼ **de precio** price tag; ∼

propia own label; ~ **de quita y pon** Post-it®, sticky label

etiquetado *m* labelling BrE, labeling AmE; ~ **ecológico** ecolabelling BrE, ecolabeling AmE; ~ **ecologista** ecolabelling BrE, ecolabeling AmE

etiquetar *vt* label

euro *m* (moneda) euro; **zona** ~ euro zone

eurobono *m* Eurobond

eurocartera *f* Europortfolio

eurocéntrico *adj* Eurocentric

eurocheque *m* Eurocheque

eurócrata *mf* Eurocrat

eurodiputado, -a *m,f* Euro MP

eurodivisa *f* Eurocurrency

eurodólar *m* Eurodollar

euroemisión *f* Eurocurrency issue

euroequidad *f* Euroequity

euroescéptico[1] *adj* Eurosceptic

euroescéptico[2], **-a** *m,f* Eurosceptic

eurófilo, -a *adj, m,f* Europhile

eurófobo *adj* Europhobic

euromercado *m* Euromarket

euromoneda *f* Euromoney

Euronet *f* Euronet

europeo, -a *adj, m,f* European

eurorrebelde *mf* Eurorebel

eurotasas *f pl* Eurorates

eurotúnel *m* Eurotunnel

euroventana *f* Eurowindow

Eurovisión *f* Eurovision

evacuación *f* evacuation; ~ **de residuos** refuse disposal

evadir *vt* (impuestos, problema) evade

evaluación *f* assessment, evaluation; (de experto) appraisal; (Inmob) survey, valuation; ~ **del activo fijo** fixed asset assessment; ~ **de la actuación** performance appraisal; ~ **del ciclo vital** Life Cycle Assessment; ~ **continua** continuous assessment; ~ **al coste** Esp *or* **costo** AmL **estándar** valuation at standard cost; ~ **del daño** appraisal of damage; ~ **de la demanda** demand assessment; ~ **del desempeño** performance evaluation; ~ **económica** economic appraisal; ~ **de existencias** valuation of stocks; ~ **financiera** financial appraisal; ~ **fiscal** tax assessment; ~ **de impacto medioambiental** environmental impact assessment; ~ **interna** in-house valuation; ~ **de inversiones** investment appraisal; ~ **del mercado** market evaluation; ~ **del personal** staff appraisal; ~ **del problema** problem

assessment; ~ **del producto** product evaluation; ~ **del proyecto** project assessment; ~ **prudente** conservative estimate; ~ **del puesto** job appraisal; ~ **de riesgos** risk assessment; ~ **de tareas** task analysis; ~ **del valor neto** net worth assessment; ~ **de valores** security rating

evaluador, a *m,f* assessor

evaluar *vt* (daños, situación, pérdidas) assess; (datos) evaluate; **no** ~ unassessed

evasión *f* evasion; ~ **fiscal** *or* **de impuestos** tax evasion

evasivo *adj* (respuesta, acción) evasive

evasor, a: ~ **de impuestos** *m,f* tax evader

evento *m* event

eventual *adj* (trabajo) temporary; (posible) possible; **cliente** ~ potential client

eventualidad *f* eventuality

eventualmente *adv* possibly

evidencia *f* evidence; **negar la** ~ deny the facts; **rendirse ante la** ~ face the facts; ~ **de auditoría** audit evidence

evidenciar *vt* show, prove

evidente *adj* evident, obvious

evitar *vt* avoid; (impedir) prevent; ~ **riesgos** not take any risks, play safe

evolución *f* (de precios) evolution, movement; (Info) upgrading; ~ **adversa de los precios** adverse price movement

evolutivo *adj* developmental

exacerbar *vt* compound, exacerbate

exactitud *f* accuracy; **con** ~ accurately

exacto *adj* correct, exact

exagerar *vt* exaggerate

examen *m* examination, exam; (de sistema) overhaul; **hacer un** ~ do *o* take *o* sit BrE an exam; ~ **de aptitud** aptitude test; ~ **atento** close examination; ~ **de auditoría** audit examination; ~ **de ingreso** entrance examination; ~ **de ingresos** revenue test; ~ **para licencia** licensing examination; ~ **médico** medical examination; ~ **público** public examination

examinador, a *m,f* examiner

examinar *vt* examine, look at; ~ **algo en profundidad** study sth in depth

excedente *m* surplus; ~ **de acciones** excess shares; ~ **del activo sobre el pasivo** surplus of assets over liabilities; ~ **acumulado** accumulated surplus; ~**s alimentarios** food surplus; ⸱⸱⸱⟩

∼ **de capacidad** excess capacity; ∼ **de capital** capital surplus; ∼ **de capital disponible** capital surplus on hand; ∼ **de efectivo** cash surplus; ∼ **de explotación** earned surplus; ∼ **de exportación** export surplus; ∼ **de importación** import surplus; ∼ **de inversiones** investment surplus; ∼ **neto diario** net daily surplus; ∼ **presupuestario** budgetary surplus; ∼ **de producción** production surplus

exceder *vt* exceed; (sobrepasar) surpass; **sin que exceda** not exceeding; **las ganancias excedieron cinco millones de euros** profits were in excess of *o* exceeded five million euros

excelente *adj* excellent, first-rate

excepción *f* exception; **con la ∼ de** with the exception of; **de ∼** extraordinary, exceptional; **hacer una ∼** make an exception; **sin ∼** without exception

excepcional *adj* (caso, circunstancias) exceptional

excepto *prep* except, excluding

excesivamente *adv* excessively; (gravado) heavily

excesivo *adj* excessive

exceso *m* excess; (Fin) surplus; **con ∼ de personal** overstaffed; ∼ **de capacidad** excess capacity; ∼ **de comercialización** overtrading; ∼ **de compromisos** overcommitment; **tener un ∼ de compromisos** be overcommitted; ∼ **de demanda** excess demand; ∼ **de depósito** excess bank reserves; ∼ **de desembolso** disbursement excess; ∼ **de emisión** overissue; ∼ **de empleo** overemployment; ∼ **de equipaje** baggage excess; ∼ **de información** information overload, infoglut; ∼ **de inversión** overtrading; ∼ **de liquidez** excess cash; ∼ **de pedidos** backlog of orders; ∼ **de personal** overstaffing; ∼ **de rendimiento sobre la deuda** reverse yield gap; ∼ **de suministro** excess supply

excluir *vt* exclude; (descartar) rule out; (prestamistas, inversores), crowd out; ∼ **a alguien de algo** exclude sb from sth

exclusión *f* exclusion; (Fin) crowding out; **con la ∼ de** excluding, to the exclusion of; ∼ **del dividendo** dividend exclusion; ∼ **estatutaria** statutory exclusion; ∼ **general** blanket ban; ∼ **legal** statutory exclusion; ∼ **de riesgos**

comerciales business risk exclusion; ∼ **social** social exclusion

exclusiva *f* exclusive rights, sole rights; **tener la ∼ de algo** have the exclusive rights to sth, be the sole agent for sth

exclusividad *f* exclusivity; (V&M) exclusive rights, sole rights

exclusivismo *m* exclusivism

exclusivo *adj* exclusive, sole; **distribuidor ∼** sole distributor

excursión *f* trip; **ir de ∼** go on a trip

excusa *f* excuse; **buscar una ∼** look for an excuse; **poner una ∼** make an excuse; **presentar** *or* **ofrecer sus ∼s** make one's apologies

excusar *vt* excuse; ∼ **a alguien de algo/hacer algo** excuse sb from sth/ doing sth

excusarse *v pron* apologize, excuse oneself; ∼ **por no hacer algo** apologize for not doing sth

ex-empleado, -a *m,f* ex-employee

exención *f* exemption; (renuncia) waiver; ∼ **admisible** allowable exemption; ∼ **anual** annual exemption; ∼ **básica** basic exemption; ∼ **por edad** age exemption; ∼ **fiscal** *or* **de impuestos** tax exemption; ∼ **personal** personal allowance BrE, personal exemption AmE

exento *adj* exempt; **no ∼** nonexempt; ∼ **de derechos** duty-free; ∼ **de impuestos** tax-free; ∼ **de todo impuesto** completely tax-free

exhaustivo *adj* exhaustive, comprehensive

exhibición *f* exhibition; ∼ **audiovisual** audiovisual display

exhortar *vt* exhort, urge; ∼ **a alguien a hacer algo** urge sb to do sth

exigencia *f* requirement; ∼ **de capital** capital requirement; ∼ **de dividendos** dividend requirement; ∼ **de impuestos** levying of taxes; ∼ **de rentabilidad** profitability requirement

exigible *adj*: ∼ **sin previo aviso** repayable on demand

exigir *vt* demand, require; ∼ **algo de alguien** require sth of sb; ∼ **una cantidad** claim an amount; ∼ **compensación** claim compensation, seek redress; ∼ **un impuesto** levy a tax; ∼ **indemnización por daños** claim damages

exilio *m* exile; ∼ **fiscal** tax exile

eximente *adj* exculpatory

eximir *vt* exempt; (Der) discharge; (Fisc) waive

existencias *f pl* stock, goods; **liquidación de** ∼ stock clearance; **mientras duren las** ∼ while stocks last; **renovar** ∼ restock; **sin** ∼ out of stock; **tener algo en** ∼ have sth in stock; ∼ **en almacén** stock in; ∼ **en caja** cash in hand; ∼ **de capital** equity capital BrE, capital stock AmE; ∼ **disponibles** stock in hand; ∼ **en efectivo** cash reserve; ∼ **inmovilizadas** dead stock; ∼ **en inventario** inventory count; ∼ **de productos básicos** staple stock; ∼ **reales** actual stock

éxito *m* success; (en búsqueda de Internet) match; **de** ∼ successful; **ser un gran** ∼ be a big success; **tener** ∼ be successful; **no tener** ∼ be unsuccessful; **una decisión/situación que será el** ∼ **o la ruina** a make-or-break decision/situation; ∼ **crítico** critical success; ∼ **inesperado** (V&M) sleeper; ∼ **permanente** continued success

exitoso *adj* successful

exoneración *f* (del impuesto) remission; ∼ **de gastos** remission of charges; ∼ **de impuestos** tax remission

exorbitante *adj* exorbitant, steep

exóticas *f pl* (Bolsa) exotics

expandir *vt* (mercado) expand, enlarge

expansión *f* expansion; (de la UE) enlargement; ∼ **del crédito** credit expansion; ∼ **del crédito interior** domestic credit expansion; ∼ **de la demanda** expansion of demand; ∼ **económica** economic expansion *o* growth; ∼ **industrial** industrial expansion; ∼ **de las inversiones** investment expansion; ∼ **del mercado** market expansion; ∼ **del negocio** business expansion

expansionario *adj* expanding

expansionista *adj* (política fiscal) expansionist, expansionary

expansivo *adj* expanding, expansive

expatriado, -a *m,f* expatriate

expectativa *f* expectation, prospect; **estar a la** ∼ **de algo/hacer algo** be waiting for sth/to do sth; ∼ **de beneficio** profit outlook; ∼**s del consumidor** consumer expectations; ∼**s económicas** economic prospects; ∼**s de empleo** job prospects; ∼**s profesionales** career expectations

expedidor, a *m,f* forwarder

expediente *m* file, case notes; (historial) record; ∼ **académico** career record; ∼

administrativo administrative file; ∼ **de antecedentes** case history; ∼ **personal** personal file

expendedor automático *m* vending machine; (para billetes) ticket machine

experiencia *f* experience; **aprender por** ∼ learn by experience; ∼ **comercial** business experience; ∼ **comprobada** proven experience, track record; ∼ **en la dirección** management experience; ∼ **laboral** work experience; ∼ **práctica** hands-on experience

experimentado *adj* experienced

experimentar *vt* (probar) experiment with, try out; (crecimiento) experience; (baja) record; (pérdida) suffer; **la inflación ha experimentado un alza de tres puntos** inflation has risen three points

experimento *m* experiment; **como** ∼ as a experiment; **hacer** *or* **realizar un** ∼ do *o* carry out an experiment

experto[1] *adj* expert; **ser** ∼ **en algo/hacer algo** be an expert at sth/doing sth

experto[2]**, -a** *m,f* expert; **ser un** ∼ **en algo** be an expert in *o* on sth; ∼ **en comercio** trade expert; ∼ **contable** chartered accountant BrE, certified public accountant AmE; ∼ **fiscal** tax expert; ∼ **en informática** computer expert; ∼ **en inversiones** investment expert; ∼ **en marketing** *or* **mercadotecnia** *m,f* marketing expert, marketeer

expiración *f* expiry BrE, expiration AmE; ∼ **de una patente** expiry BrE *o* expiration AmE of a policy

expirar *vi* (plazo) expire, run out

explicación *f* explanation; **dar explicaciones de algo** give an explanation *o* reason for sth

explicar *vt* explain

explícito *adj* explicit

exploración *f* exploration; (por la red) surfing, netsurfing; (electrónica) scanning; ∼ **medioambiental** environmental scanning; ∼ **del mercado** market exploration

explorador[1] *m* scanner; ∼ **medioambiental** environmental scanner; ∼ **óptico** optical scanner

explorador[2]**, a** *m,f* explorer

explorar *vt* explore; (electronicamente) scan

explosión *f* explosion; ∼ **demográfica** population explosion; ∼ **salarial** wage explosion

explotación *f* exploitation; **gastos de** ~ running *o* operating costs; **margen de** ~ operating margin; ~ **de datos** data mining; ~ **de recursos petrolíferos** tapping of oil resources; ~ **de la tierra** land development

explotador *m* owner-operator

explotar *vt* exploit; **sin** ~ (recursos, mercados) untapped

exponente *m* exponent; (buen ejemplo) prime example

exponer *vt* (condiciones, razones, problemas) set out, state; (productos) show, exhibit; (en tienda, vitrina) display; (plan, vida) risk, put at risk; ~ **algo/a alguien a algo** expose sth/sb to sth; ~ **lo obvio** state the obvious; ~ **un proyecto** put a project at risk; ~ **una sugerencia ante un comité** put a suggestion before a committee

exportación *f* (acción) exportation; (mercancía) export; **exportaciones** exports; ~ **invisible** invisible export; ~ **de materias primas** staple export; **exportaciones subvencionadas** subsidized exports; ~ **visible** visible export

exportado *adj* exported

exportador[1] *adj* exporting; **mercado** ~ export market; **países** ~**es de petróleo** oil-exporting countries

exportador[2]**, a** *m,f* exporter; ~ **a gran escala** large-scale exporter

exposición *f* exhibition, display; (Bolsa) exposition; (Der) representation; (publicidad) exposure; ~ **ambulante** travelling exhibition BrE, traveling exhibit AmE; ~ **comercial** trade exhibition BrE, trade exhibit AmE, trade show; ~ **en estantes** shelf display; ~ **industrial** trade fair; ~ **en nota al pie** footnote disclosure; ~ **de pre-campaña** pre-campaign exposure; ~ **al riesgo** risk exposure; ~ **universal** world fair

expositor *m* (persona) exhibitor; (mueble) stand

expreícono *m* emoticon

expresar *vt* express, show; (Econ) denominate; ~ **algo en dólares** make sth out in dollars

expresión *f tb* (Info) expression; **como** ~ **de nuestro agradecimiento** as a token of our gratitude

expreso *adj* (intención) express, specific

expropriar *vt* expropriate

expulsar *vt* evict; (tarjeta, disco) eject

expulsión *f* eviction; (Info) ejection; ~ **constructiva** constructive eviction; ~

efectiva actual eviction; ~ **parcial** partial eviction

extemporáneo *adj* untimely

extender *vt* (poder, derecho, plazo) extend; (cheque) make out; ~ **cheques sin fondos** issue bad cheques BrE *o* checks AmE; ~ **una factura** raise an invoice; ~ **un pagaré** make out a promissory note; ~ **una póliza** issue a policy; **quieren** ~ **los derechos a todos sus empleados** they want to extend the rights to all their employees

extensión *f* extension; (de tiendas) spread; **por** ~ by extension; **¿puede ponerme con la** ~ **201?** could you put me through to extension 201, please?; **pidieron una** ~ **del plazo** they asked for an extension *o* for the deadline to be extended; ~ **del daño** extent of damage; ~ **del empleo** scope of employment; ~ **de la línea de productos** line-stretching; ~ **de la marca** brand extension; ~ **del riesgo** exposure; ~ **telefónica** telephone extension

exterior[1] *adj* foreign; **asuntos** ~**es** foreign affairs; **comercio** ~ foreign trade

exterior[2] *m* outside, exterior; **el** ~ foreign countries; **relaciones con el** ~ relations with countries abroad; **E**~**es** the Foreign Office BrE, the State Department AmE

externalidad *f* externality

externalización *f* externalization; (of services) outsourcing

externalizar *vt* externalize; (servicios) outsource

extinción *f* abatement, discharge; (Fisc) burnout; ~ **de una obligación** *or* **deuda** forfeiture of a debt

extinguir *vt* abate, discharge

extorno *m* rebate; ~ **del activo** charge-off

extorsión *vt* extorsion; **hacerle** ~ **a alguien** extort money from sb

extorsionar *vt* extort; ~ **a alguien** extort money from sb

extra[1] *adj* extra; **horas** ~ overtime; **paga** ~ double pay

extra[2] *m* additional expense; (pago) bonus

extracción *f* extraction

extracto *m* (sumario) abstract, summary; (de documento) extract; ~ **de cuentas** statement of accounts

extraer *vt* extract; (datos, texto) output

extrajudicial *adj* extrajudicial

extrajudicialmente *adv* extrajudicially

extramarginal *adj* extramarginal

extranet *m* extranet

extranjero[1] *adj* foreign, offshore; **mercados ∼s** overseas markets

extranjero[2], **-a** *m,f* foreigner; (Der) alien; **∼ ilegal** illegal alien; **∼ residente** resident alien

extranjero[3] *m*: **en el ∼** abroad; **trabajó dos años en el ∼** he worked abroad for six years

extraoficial *adj* extraofficial, unofficial; **con carácter ∼** in an unofficial capacity

extraoficialmente *adv* extraofficially

extraordinaria *f* double pay received by employees in the summer and at Christmas

extraordinario *adj* extraordinary; **en circunstancias extraordinarias** in extraordinary circumstances; **horas extraordinarias** overtime

extrapolación *f* extrapolation

extrapolar *vt* extrapolate

extrared *f* extranet

extrarradio *m* outskirts; **del ∼** out-of-town

extraterritorial *adj* extraterritorial

extratipo *m* tip

extremado *adj* exaggerated

extremo *m* extreme; **∼ alto/bajo de la banda** top/bottom end of the range

e

Ff

fábrica *f* factory; precio de ~ factory price, wholesale price, price ex-works; **tienda de ~** factory outlet; **~ de gas** gas works; **~ de la moneda** mint; **~ multisindical** multiunion plant; **~ de productos químicos** chemical works

fabricación *f* manufacture; **coches de ~ española** Spanish-built cars, cars built in Spain; **en ~** in production; **~ asistida por computadora** AmL *or* **ordenador** Esp *f* computer-aided manufacturing; **~ en cadena** flow production; **~ integrada por computadora** AmL *or* **ordenador** Esp *f* computer-integrated manufacture; **~ con licencia** manufacturing under licence BrE *o* license AmE; **~ en serie** mass production

fabricado *adj* manufactured; **~ en el Reino Unido** made in the UK

fabricante *mf* manufacturer; **~ de coches** car manufacturer; **~ de electrodomésticos** makers of domestic appliances; **~ de herramientas** toolmaker

fabricar *vt* manufacture, produce; **~ en serie** mass-produce; **~ bajo licencia** manufacture under licence BrE *o* license AmE

fabril *adj* manufacturing

facción *f* faction

face-time *m* (Info) face-time

fachada *f* (de edificio) facade, frontage

fácil *adj* easy; **~ de utilizar** *or* **de ~ manejo** user-friendly

facilidad *f* facility; **~ bancaria internacional** international banking facility; **~es de crédito** credit facilities; **~ de crédito autorrenovable** revolving underwriting facility; **~ de manejo** ease of handling; (Info) user-friendliness; **~ monetaria** monetary ease; **~es de pago** easy payment terms, credit terms; **~ de sobregiro** overdraft facility; **~ de uso** ease of handling; (Info) user-friendliness; **~ de venta** saleability BrE, salability AmE

facilitación *f* facilitation; **~ comercial** trade facilitation

facilitador, a *m,f* facilitator, arranger; **~ del comercio electrónico** electronic business facilitator

facilitar *vt* facilitate; (controles de crédito) ease; **~ algo a alguien** provide sb with sth; **e-mail ha facilitado mucho la comunicación** e-mail has made communicating a lot easier

facsímil *m* facsimile

factible *adj* feasible, achievable

fáctico *adj* factual, real

factor *m* factor; **ser un ~ de** be a factor in; **~ de actividad** activity factor; **~ de acumulación** accumulation factor; **~ aleatorio** random factor; **~ de atención** attention factor; **~ de capacidad** capacity factor; **~ común de distinción** common distinguishing factor; **~ constrictor** constraining factor; **~ de conversión** conversion factor; **~ del coste** Esp *or* **costo** AmL *m* cost factor; **~ estacional** seasonal factor; **~ fijo** fixed factor; **~ impositivo** tax factor; **~ de lealtad** loyalty factor; **~ precio** price factor; **~ de riesgo** risk factor

factoraje *m* factoring

factoría *f* factory

factorial *m* factorial

factorización *f* factoring

factótum *m* factotum, odd-job man

factura *f* invoice; (de teléfono, electricidad) bill; **según ~** as per invoice; **pasarle ~ a alguien** invoice sb, send sb an invoice; **~ de aduanas** customs invoice; **~ certificada** certified invoice; **~ a cobrar** invoice receivable; **~ de compra** purchase invoice; **~ de conciliación** reconciliation bill; **~ detallada** itemized invoice; **~ electrónica** e-bill, electronic bill; **~ de embarque** shipping bill; **~ impagada** unpaid bill; **~ en línea** online bill; **~ de muestra** specimen invoice; **~ original** original bill; **~ a pagar** invoice payable; **~ pendiente** outstanding bill; **~ proforma** pro forma invoice; **~ provisional** provisional invoice; **~ de prueba** convenience bill; **~ rectificada** corrected invoice; **~ telefónica** telephone bill

facturación *f* (acción) billing, invoicing; (volumen) turnover; (en aeropuerto) check-in (desk); ∼ **al cliente** customer billing; ∼ **anticipada** advance billing; ∼ **anual** annual turnover; ∼ **bruta** gross billing; ∼ **diferida** deferred billing; ∼ **electrónica** e-billing, electronic billing; ∼ **de exportación** export turnover; ∼ **extra** extra billing; ∼ **en línea** e-billing, online billing; ∼ **de publicidad** advertising turnover; ∼ **de ventas** sales revenue, sales turnover

facturador *m* (máquina) biller

facturar *vti* (cliente) invoice; (equipaje) check in; **volver a** ∼ reinvoice; **la empresa factura más de $500 millones al año** the company has a turnover of more than $500 million a year

facultad *f* faculty; (autoridad) authority; **tener** ∼ **para hacer algo** be authorized to do sth, have the power *o* authority to do sth; **F**∼ **de Derecho** Faculty of Law; ∼ **de vender** power of sale

facultativo *adj* optional

faena *f* task; **la dura** ∼ **diaria** the daily grind

fajo *m* (de billetes) wad (infrml)

falacia *f* fallacy

falibilidad *f* fallibility

falible *adj* fallible

falla *f* flaw; ∼ **de seguridad** security breach

fallar *vi* fail; (Der) pass judgment; ∼ **en favor de alguien** give a ruling in favour BrE *o* favor AmE of sb

fallecimiento *m* death, demise

fallo *m* failure, fault; (Der) ruling, sentence; (RRHH) award; ∼ **de deficiencia** (Der) deficiency judgment; ∼ **de divorcio condicional** decree nisi; ∼ **del equipo** hardware failure; ∼ **de funcionamiento** malfunction; ∼ **humano** human error; ∼ **del mercado** market failure; ∼ **del sistema** (Info) system failure

falseamiento *m* (de datos) falsification; (de cuentas) window-dressing; ∼ **de la competencia** misrepresentation of competition

falsear *vt* (cuentas, datos) falsify; (competencia) misrepresent

falsificación *f* falsification; (de billetes, firma) forgery; ∼ **de actas** adulteration of proceedings; ∼ **de elecciones** gerrymandering

falsificar *vt* (cuentas) falsify; (competencia) misrepresent; (firma, billete) forge

falso *adj* false; (billete, documento) forged; (dinero) counterfeit; (respuesta) wrong; ∼ **alarma** false alarm; ∼ **enfermo** malingerer; ∼ **llamada** (de teléfono) wrong number; ∼ **testimonio** false testimony, perjury; **dar** ∼ **testimonio** commit perjury

falta *f* (en sistema) fault; (carencia) lack, shortage; **a** ∼ **de** (noticias) in the absence of; **a** ∼ **de pruebas en contra** in the absence of evidence to the contrary; **por** ∼ **de** owing to a lack of; **con** ∼ **de liquidez** cash strapped; **hacer** ∼ need; ∼ **de aceptación** failure to accept; ∼ **de competencia** lack of competence; ∼ **de consideración** lack of consideration; ∼ **de cumplimiento** failure to comply; ∼ **de entrega** failure to deliver; ∼ **de existencias** lack of inventory; ∼ **de fondos** insufficient funds; ∼ **grave** gross misconduct; ∼ **de materia prima** lack of raw material; ∼ **de pago** default of payment; ∼ **con permiso** leave of absence; ∼ **de presentación** (de declaración, formulario) nonfiling

faltar *vi* (fondos) be lacking; (no estar) be missing; **¿falta alguien?** is anyone missing?; **¿falta algo?** anything else?; **faltan tres recibos** there are three receipts missing; ∼ **a algo** not attend sth; ∼ **a una cita/reunión** miss an appointment/meeting; **nos faltan los fondos necesarios** we lack the necessary funds; ∼ **a la obligación** fail in one's duty

falto *adj*: ∼ **de algo** lacking in sth; ∼ **de personal** short-staffed, undermanned

familia *f* family; ∼ **monoparental** single-parent family; ∼ **numerosa** large family (*entitled to special benefits*); ∼ **de productos** product family; ∼ **residual** residual family; ∼ **de tipos** (en tipografía) font family

familiaridad *f* familiarity

familiarización *f* familiarization; ∼ **con la informática** computer literacy

farmacéutico *adj* pharmaceutical

fase *f* phase, stage; **en** ∼ **de pruebas** at proof stage; ∼ **de acabado** stage of completion; ∼ **ascendente** upswing, upturn; ∼ **de borrador** draft stage; ∼ **clave** key stage; ∼ **de crecimiento económico** stage of economic growth; ∼ **de depresión del mercado** market downturn; ∼ **descendente** downswing, ····⟩

downturn; ~ **de ejecución** production stage; ~ **de expansión** upswing, upturn; (en actividad) upsurge; ~ **intermedia** intermediate stage; ~ **de lanzamiento** launch phase; ~ **de promoción** promotional phase; ~ **de recesión** recessionary phase; ~ **de redacción** draft stage; ~ **de verificación** verification phase

fatalidad f fate; (desgracia) misfortune

fatiga f fatigue; ~ **industrial** industrial fatigue

favor m favour BrE, favor AmE; **a ~** in favour BrE o favor AmE; **15 votos a ~, 3 en contra**; 15 votes for, 3 against; **a ~ de** in favour BrE o favor AmE of; **a ~ de los cambios** in favour BrE o favor AmE of the changes; **en ~ de** in favour BrE o favor AmE of; **actuó en ~ de la empresa** she acted in the interests of the company; **hacerle un ~ a alguien** do sb a favour BrE o favor AmE; **¿me puedes hacer un ~?** could you do me a favour BrE o favor AmE?; **haga el ~ de llamar más tarde** would you mind calling back later?; **pedirle un ~ a alguien** ask sb (for) a favour BrE o favor AmE; **por ~** please; **por ~, envíe su confirmación por fax** please fax your confirmation; **por ~, expongan sus presupuestos** please submit your quotations

favorabilidad f favourability BrE, favorability AmE

favorable adj (precio, condiciones) favourable BrE, favorable AmE

favorecer vt favour BrE, favor AmE; (desarrollo, comprensión) help, aid

favorito m (marcador) favourite BrE, favorite AmE; **lista de ~s** hotlist

fax m fax; **mandar un ~** send a fax; **mandarle algo a alguien por ~** fax sb sth

FDA abr (▸**fin de archivo**) EOF (end of file)

FDM abr (▸**fin de mensaje**) EOM (end of message)

fe f belief, faith; **de buena ~** bona fide, in good faith; **de mala ~** mala fide, in bad faith; **en ~ de lo cual** in witness whereof; **tener ~ en algo/alguien** have faith in sth/sb; ~ **ciega** blind faith; ~ **de erratas** errata

febril adj (actividad) feverish; (debate) heated; ~ **competitividad** rat race (infrml)

fecha f date; **a ~** as at; **con ~ adelantada** postdated; **después de ~** after date; **en una ~ por determinar** at some future date; **en ~ posterior** at a

later date, at a subsequent date; **hasta la ~** to date; **poner la ~ en una carta/un cheque** date a letter/cheque BrE o check AmE; **sin ~** undated; **la carta tiene ~ del 20 de junio** the letter is dated 20th June; ~ **abierta** open dating; ~ **de acumulación** accrual date; ~ **de adquisición** date of acquisition; ~ **de amortización** redemption date; ~ **de ampliación** roll-over date; ~ **de apertura** opening date; ~ **base** base date; ~ **de caducidad** expiry date BrE, expiration date AmE; (en productos) use-by date; (de caducidad de venta) sell-by date; ~ **de cambio de interés** interest rollover date; ~ **de cierre** closing date; ~ **de cierre de licitación** bid-closing date; ~ **de conservación** retention date; ~ **de consumo preferente** best-before date; ~ **de conversión** conversion date; ~ **de desembolso** pay-out date; ~ **de devengo** accrual date; ~ **sin dividendos** ex-dividend date; ~ **de emisión** date of issue; ~ **de entrada en vigor** effective date; ~ **de entrega** delivery date; ~ **esperada** expected date; ~ **exigible** recoverable date; ~ **de la factura** date of invoice; ~ **de facturación** invoice date BrE, billing date AmE; ~ **de liberación** (Bolsa) release date; ~ **límite** cutoff date, deadline; ~ **límite de presentación** (de declaración) due date of filing; ~ **de liquidación** settlement date; ~ **de oferta** (de nueva emisión) offering date; ~ **de operación** transaction date, trade date; ~ **de pago** payment date; ~ **de presentación** (Fisc) date of filing; ~ **prevista** expected date; ~ **de prioridad** priority date; ~ **propuesta** target date; ~ **de publicación** press date, publication date; ~ **de puesta a la venta** (Medios) on-sale date; ~ **de redacción** copy date; ~ **de registro** date of registration; ~ **de rescate** redemption date; ~ **de retirada de la venta** off-sale date; ~ **de terminación** completion date; ~ **tope** closing date, cut-off date, deadline; ~ **de valor** value date; ~ **de vencimiento** date of maturity; (Banca) call date; ~ **de vencimiento de la prima** due date of premium

fechado m dating, date-marking

fechador m date stamp

fechar vt date; (mercaderías) age

FECOM abr (▸**Fondo Europeo para la Cooperación Monetaria**) EMCF (European Monetary Cooperation Fund)

FEDER *abr* (▸**Fondo Europeo para el Desarrollo Regional**) ERDF (European Regional Development Fund)

federación *f* federation; ∼ **de mutualidades** federation of mutual societies; ∼ **de sindicatos** federation of trade unions

federal *adj* federal

federalismo *m* federalism; ∼ **económico** economic federalism

feedback *m* (Info) feedback

feria *f* show, fair; ∼ **agrícola** agricultural show; ∼ **de artesanía** crafts fair; ∼ **comercial** trade fair; ∼ **especializada** specialized fair; ∼ **de la exportación** export goods fair; ∼ **itinerante** travelling fair BrE, traveling fair AmE; ∼ **mundial** world fair

ferrocarril *m* railway BrE, railroad AmE; ∼ **subterráneo** tube BrE, underground BrE, subway AmE

ferrocarrilero *m* railwayman BrE, railman AmE

ferroso *adj* ferrous

ferroviario *m* railwayman BrE, railman AmE

fertilizante *m* fertilizer

fertilizar *vt* fertilize

festival *m* festival; ∼ **de cine** film festival

festivo *adj* festive; **día** ∼ public holiday

feudalismo *m* feudalism

fiabilidad *f* reliability; ∼ **del producto** product reliability

fiable *adj* reliable

fiador, a *m,f* guarantor; (Fin) sponsor; **salir** ∼ **por alguien** act as a guarantor for sb

FIAMM *abr* (▸**fondo de inversión en activos del mercado monetario**) MMF (money market fund), MMMF (money market mutual fund)

fianza *f* bail; (Seg) fidelity bond; **pagar la** ∼ **de alguien** stand bail for sb; **salir bajo** ∼ be released on bail; ∼ **de apelación** appeal bond; ∼ **de avería** average bond; ∼ **de bonos** bond guarantee; ∼ **comercial** guarantee bond; ∼ **de conservación** maintenance bond; ∼ **de contratista** contract bond; ∼ **de cumplimiento** maintenance bond; ∼ **en efectivo** surety in cash; ∼ **de entredicho** injunction bond; ∼ **de garantía** guarantee bond; ∼ **de incumplimiento** performance bond; ∼ **de indemnización** indemnity bond; ∼

judicial judicial bond; ∼ **de licitación** bid bond

fiar *vi* give credit; **no se fía** no credit; **(no) ser de** ∼ be (un)reliable

fiarse *v pron*: ∼ **de algo/alguien** trust sth/sb; ∼ **de que...** believe that...

fibra *f* fibre BrE, fiber AmE; ∼ **sintética** man-made fibre BrE *o* fiber AmE, synthetic fibre BrE *o* fiber AmE; ∼ **de vidrio** fibreglass BrE, fiberglass AmE

fibroóptica *f* fibre optics BrE, fiber optics AmE

ficha *m* (tarjeta) card; (de archivo) index card; (en préstamos comerciales) point; ∼ **de almacén** stock control card; ∼ **contable** ledger card; ∼ **de control** time card; ∼ **de cuenta** account card; ∼ **de datos** data card; ∼ **de existencias** stock card; ∼ **de firmas** signing slip; ∼ **magnética** magnetic card; ∼ **de pago** credit slip

fichar *vt* (*cf* ▸**checar** AmL) check in; ∼ **la entrada** Esp (*cf* ▸**checar la tarjeta** AmL) clock in BrE, clock on BrE, punch in AmE; ∼ **la salida** Esp (*cf* ▸**checar la tarjeta** AmL) clock off BrE, clock out BrE, punch out AmE

fichero *m* file; (caja) card index; ∼ **no encontrado** file not found; ∼ **activo** active file; ∼ **archivado** archive file; ∼ **de clasificación** sort file; ∼ **de computadora** AmL (*cf* ▸**fichero de ordenador** Esp) computer file; ∼ **contable** accounting file; ∼ **de datos** data file; ∼ **de direcciones** address file; ∼ **de edición** report file; ∼ **de espera** spool file; ∼ **con etiqueta** labelled file BrE, labeled file AmE; ∼ **de existencias** inventory file; ∼ **de imagen** image file; ∼ **de impresión** output file; ∼ **indexado** indexed file; ∼ **informatizado** computerized file; ∼ **de lectura** ReadMe file; ∼ **maestro** master file; ∼ **de movimientos** transaction file; ∼ **oculto** hidden file; ∼ **de ordenador** Esp (*cf* ▸**fichero de computadora** AmL) computer file; ∼ **padre** father file; ∼ **principal** main file; ∼ **de programa** program file; ∼ **de referencias** reference file; ∼ **de reserva** backup file; ∼ **secuencial** batch file; ∼ **de tarjetas** card file; ∼ **transitorio** scratch file; ∼ **zip** zip file

ficticio *adj* ficticious

fidedigno *adj* reliable

fideicomisario *m,f* trustee

fideicomiso *m* trust, trusteeship; ∼ **activo** living trust; ∼ **benéfico** charitable trust; ∼ **de bienes** land trust

fidelidad *f* fidelity; (de cliente, empleado) loyalty; ∼ **a una marca** brand loyalty

fidelización *f* creation of customer loyalty; **programa de** ∼ loyalty programme BrE, loyalty program AmE

fidelizar (clientela, usuario) cultivate the loyalty of

fiduciaria *f* trusteeship, fiduciary

fiduciariamente *adv* fiduciarily

fiduciario¹ *adj* fiduciary

fiduciario², **-a** *m,f* trustee

fiel *adj* faithful; (copia) exact

fiero *adj* (competencia) fierce

fiesta *f* (día festivo) holiday; ∼ **de lanzamiento** (de libro) launch party; ∼ **nacional** *or* **oficial** public holiday, bank holiday BrE, legal holiday AmE

figurar *vti* (en documento) be, appear; ∼ **por debajo/encima de** rank below/above

fijación *f* fixing; ∼ **del coste** Esp *or* **costo** AmL *f* cost pricing; ∼ **de cuotas** quota fixing; ∼ **diferencial de precios** differential pricing; ∼ **estratégica de precios** strategic pricing; ∼ **de objetivos** goal setting, objective-setting; (V&M) target setting; ∼ **de precios** price fixing; ∼ **de precios agresiva** aggressive pricing; ∼ **de precios para cubrir los gastos** break-even pricing; ∼ **de precios indicativos** target pricing; ∼ **de precios de paridad** parity pricing; ∼ **de precios por unidad** unit pricing; ∼ **de tarifas** rate fixing

fijador de precios *m* price leader

fijar *vt* (precio, fecha) fix, set; (carteles) put up; ∼ **el cambio** peg the exchange; ∼ **contingentes** fix quotas; ∼ **una fecha** set a date; ∼ **la indemnización** settle the claim; ∼ **los parámetros** set the parameters; ∼ **un precio** set *o* fix a price; ∼ **el presupuesto** set the budget; **prohibido** ∼ **carteles** bill stickers will be prosecuted

fijo¹ *adj* (precio, cantidad) fixed, set; (trabajo, empleado) permanent; **activo** ∼ fixed assets; **bienes** ∼**s** tangible assets; **¿estás fijo en la empresa?** are you permanent at the company?, have you got a permanent job with the company?

fijo² *m* fix; ∼ **disponible** quick fix

fila *f* (de números) row; **de primera/segunda fila** first-rate/second-rate; ∼ **de caja** checkout lane

filial¹ *adj* subsidiary

filial² *f* subsidiary, affiliated company, branch office; ∼ **bancaria** banking subsidiary; ∼ **consolidada** consolidated branch

filigrana *f* watermark

filigranado *adj* watermarked

filme *m* film; ∼ **magnético** magnetic film

filón *m* (Med amb) seam; (negocio) (infrml) gold mine (infrml)

filosofía *f* philosophy; ∼ **del derecho** jurisprudence; ∼ **de la empresa** company philosophy

filtración *f* filtering

filtrar *vt* (llamadas) screen; (información) leak (infrml)

filtro *m* filter; ∼ **de llamadas** call-screening

fin *m* (final) end; (objetivo) goal; ∼**es** *m pl* purposes; **a** ∼ **de** in order to; **a** ∼**es de mayo** at the end of May; **a tal** ∼ to this end; **con el** ∼ **de hacer algo** in order to do sth; **dar** ∼ **a algo** bring sth to a close; **en** ∼ in short, anyway; **llevar algo a buen** ∼ bring sth to a successful conclusion; **poner** ∼ **a algo** put an end to sth; ∼ **de año** year end; ∼ **de archivo** end of file; ∼**es benéficos** charitable purposes; ∼ **de ejercicio** year end; ∼**es fiscales** tax purposes; ∼ **de mensaje** end of message; ∼ **de mes** month end; ∼ **de trimestre** quarter-end

final *adj* final; **dar los toques** ∼**es a algo** put the finishing touches to sth

finalidad *f* purpose, goal; **¿con qué** ∼ **montaron el nuevo equipo?** what is the purpose of the new team?; ∼ **especulativa** speculation motive

finalización *f* completion; (de reunión) winding-up

finalizar **1** *vt* (reunión) finish, end; ∼ **la comunicación** *or* **sesión** (Info) log off, log out
2 *vi* (reunión, contrato) end, come to an end

finalmente *adv* finally

financiable *adj* bankable

financiación *f* financing, funding; (facilidades) credit facilities; **financiaciones** *f pl* capital; ∼ **activa** active financing; ∼ **de la administración local** local government financing; ∼ **de alto rendimiento** high-yield financing; ∼ **bancaria** bank financing; ∼ **basada en activos** asset-based financing; ∼ **básica** core funding;

~ **del capital** capital financing; ~ **comercial** business financing; ~ **conjunta** joint financing; ~ **corporativa** corporate financing; ~ **a corto plazo** short-term financing; ~ **de la deuda** debt financing; ~ **a largo plazo** long-term financing; ~ **de un proyecto** project financing, project funding

financiado *adj* financed, funded; ~ **con dineros públicos** publicly funded; ~ **por un banco** bank-financed; ~ **por el Estado** government-financed, state-funded

financiamiento *m* financing, funding *ver tb* ▸**financiación**

financiar *vt* finance, fund; ~ **la diferencia** finance the difference; ~ **directamente** finance directly

financiera *f* finance company

financiero *adj* financial; **apoyo** ~ financial backing; **ayuda financiera** financial assistance

financista *mf* financier

finanzas *f pl* finance; **el mundo de las** ~ the world of finance; ~ **corporativas** corporate finance; ~ **públicas** public finance

finca *f* farm; (terreno) plot (of land); (propiedad) property

finiquitar *vt* settle, pay off

finiquito *m* settlement; (Der) quitclaim; (de jubilación) termination payment

finito *adj* finite

firma *f* (empresa) business, firm; (identificación) signature; **tener** ~ **autorizada** be authorized to sign; ~ **de alquiler de computadoras** AmL *or* **ordenadores** Esp *f* computer leasing firm; ~ **autenticada** authenticated signature; ~ **autorizada** authorized signature; ~ **en bancarrota** bankrupt firm; ~ **en blanco** blank signature; ~ **certificada** authenticated signature; ~ **cliente** client firm; ~ **conjunta** joint signature; ~ **consultora** consulting firm; ~ **contable** accounting firm; ~ **de corretaje en bolsa** brokerage house; ~ **digital** digital signature; ~ **electrónica** electronic signature; ~ **financiera** financial firm; ~ **de inversión** brokerage house; ~ **no autorizada** unauthorized signature; ~ **social** firm signature

firmado *adj* signed

firmante *mf* signatory; **devuélvase al** ~ refer to drawer; **el abajo** ~**, declara que...** I, the undersigned, declare that...;

~ **del cheque** cheque signatory BrE, check signatory AmE

firmar *vti* sign; ~ **conjuntamente** cosign; ~ **a la entrada** book in; ~ **al entrar a la empresa** sign in; ~ **un contrato** sign a contract; ~ **el registro** book in; (en un hotel) check in; ~ **a la salida** book out; (en un hotel) check out; **sin** ~ unsigned

firme *adj* firm; (rígido) hard; (contrato) absolute; **pedido en** ~ firm order

fiscal[1] *adj* fiscal, tax; **fraude** ~ tax fraud; **año** ~ tax year, financial year

fiscal[2] *mf* public prosecutor, District Attorney AmE, DA AmE

fiscalidad *f* taxation; (sistema) tax system; (normas) tax regulations

fiscalista *mf* fiscalist, tax specialist

fiscalización *f* (inspección fiscal) audit; (impuestos) taxation; ~ **continua** continuous audit; ~ **directa e indirecta** direct and indirect taxation

fisco *m* ≈ Exchequer BrE, Treasury AmE; (declaración de la renta) Inland Revenue BrE, Internal Revenue Service AmE

fisgoneo *m* (en Internet) lurking; **estar de** ~ lurk

físicamente *adv* physically

físico *adj* physical

flamante *adj* brand-new

flamewars *m pl* (Info) flamewars

flecha *f* arrow; ~ **hacia abajo/arriba** (en teclado) down/up arrow; ~ **de desplazamiento** scroll arrow; ~ **de retroceso/avance** back/forward arrow

fletador, a *m,f* charterer

fletamento *m*, **fletamiento** *m* chartering

fletante *mf* charterer

fletar *vt* (vehículos) charter

flete *m* freight; ~ **aéreo** air cargo, air freight; ~ **ferroviario** rail freight; ~ **marítimo** ocean freight; ~ **pagado** advance freight; ~ **por cobrar** freight forward

fletero *m* cargo ship BrE, freighter AmE

flexibilidad *f* flexibility; ~ **de horario** flexitime

flexible *adj* flexible; **horario** ~ flexible working hours, flexitime

flexografía *f* flexography

flojo[1] *adj* (mercado) slack; (precio) weak

flojo[2]**, -a** *m,f* (infrml) shirker (infrml)

florecer *vi* flourish, thrive; **el negocio está floreciendo** business is thriving

flota *f* fleet

flotación *f* (de moneda) flotation, floating

flotante *adj* floating

flotar *vt* float

fluctuación *f* (de precios, tipos de interés) fluctuation; ~ **de clientela** customer flow; ~ **de costes** Esp *or* **costos** AmL *f* cost flow; ~ **económica** economic fluctuation; ~ **estacional** seasonal fluctuation; ~ **financiera** financial flow; ~ **de inversiones** flow of investments; ~ **máxima del precio** maximum price fluctuation; ~ **de mercado** market fluctuation; ~ **del tipo de cambio** exchange rate fluctuation

fluctuar *vi* (precio de acciones, tipo de cambio) fluctuate

flujo *m* (de fondos, datos) flow; ~ **anual de tesorería** annual cash flow; ~ **de bienes** commodity flow; ~ **de caja** cash flow; ~ **de caja positivo/ negativo** positive/negative cash flow; ~ **comercial** trade flow; ~ **de datos** data flow, data stream; ~ **de efectivo en aumento** incremental cash flow; ~ **de efectivo descontado** discounted cash flow; ~ **de ingresos** income stream; ~ **monetario** flow of money; ~ **neto de caja** net cash flow; ~ **de operaciones** (Info) work flow; ~ **de trabajo** work flow

flujograma *m* flowchart

FMI *abr* (▸**Fondo Monetario Internacional**) IMF (International Monetary Fund)

fobia *f* phobia; ~ **informática** computer phobia, technophobia

foco *m* focus, source; ~ **industrial** (de polución) industrial source; ~ **de perturbaciones** trouble spot

folio *m* folio; (tamaño) ~ A4 size; (tamaño) **doble** ~ A3 size; **un** ~ a sheet of A4; ~ **único de referencia** unique reference number

folleto *m* leaflet; (promocional) handout, flier; (Ocio) brochure; ~ **electrónico** e-zine; ~ **de instrucciones** instruction leaflet; ~ **publicitario** sales brochure

fomentar *vt* promote, encourage; (aumentar) boost

fomento *m* encouragement; ~ **del comercio** (publicidad) trade promotion; ~ **del medio ambiente** environmental development; ~ **del tiempo libre** leisure development

fondo *m* (parte más baja) bottom; (dinero) fund; **investigación a** ~ in-depth *o* thorough investigation; ~**s** *m pl* funds;

apartar ~**s** set aside funds; **con** ~**s adecuados** adequately funded; **recaudar** ~**s** raise money; **cheque sin** ~**s** rubber cheque BrE *o* check AmE (infrml); **tocar** ~ bottom out; ~ **de acciones ordinarias** common shares BrE *o* stock AmE fund; ~ **acumulativo** accumulating fund; ~ **de agencia** agency fund; ~ **de alto rendimiento** high-performance fund; ~ **de amortización** amortization fund, sinking fund; ~ **de anualidad** annuity fund; ~ **de bienestar** welfare fund; ~ **de caja chica** petty cash fund; ~ **de cambio** exchange fund; ~ **de comercio** goodwill; ~ **de comercio de la consolidación** goodwill on consolidation; ~ **de comercio negativo** bad will; ~ **de comercio positivo** goodwill; ~ **de compensación** compensation fund; ~ **de compras** purchase fund; ~ **consolidado** consolidated fund; ~ **de contingencia** umbrella fund; **F**~ **para la Cooperación Económica Exterior** Overseas Economic Cooperation Fund; ~ **de crecimiento** growth fund; ~ **en custodia** trust fund; **F**~ **de Desarrollo para Mercados Emergentes** Emerging Markets Growth Fund; ~**s disponibles** available funds; ~ **de dividendo** dividend fund; ~**s en efectivo** liquid funds; ~ **especulativo** speculative fund; **F**~ **Europeo para la Cooperación Monetaria** European Monetary Cooperation Fund; **F**~ **Europeo de Desarrollo** European Development Fund, EDF; **F**~ **Europeo para el Desarrollo Regional** European Regional Development Fund; ~ **fiduciario** *or* **de fideicomiso** trust fund; ~ **de garantía de depósitos** deposit guarantee fund; ~ **de huelga** strike fund; ~ **de imprevistos** contingency fund; ~ **indexado** indexed fund; ~**s insuficientes** insufficient funds; ~ **de inversión** investment fund; ~ **de inversión en activos del mercado monetario** money market fund, money market mutual fund; ~ **de inversión indexado** *or* **en índices** tracker fund; ~ **de inversión de renta variable** variable yield fund; **F**~ **Monetario Europeo** European Monetary Fund; **F**~ **Monetario Internacional** International Monetary Fund; ~ **mutuo** mutual fund; ~ **de pensión contributivo** contributory pension fund; ~ **de pensión no contributivo** noncontributory pension fund; ~ **de pensiones** pension fund;

~s públicos public funds; **~ de reptiles** slush fund; **~ de retiros** retirement fund; **F~ Social Europeo** European Social Fund; **~ de solidaridad** fighting fund; **~s en títulos** equity funds

fonocaptor *m* sound pick-up

fontesoro *m* treasury bond

forfeiting *m* forfeiting

forma *f* form; (modo) way; **de ~ inmediata** immediately; **de ~ que** so as, in such a way as; **de todas ~s** anyway, in any case; **en ~ de** in the form of; **su ~ de trabajar** his way of working, his approach to work; **la ~ de las cosas por venir** the shape of things to come; **en ~ de tabla** in a table, in tabulated form; **tomar ~** take shape; **el proyecto empieza a tomar ~** the project is beginning to take shape

formación *f* formation; (profesional) training; **con una ~ adecuada** well-educated; **~ asertiva** assertiveness training; **~ dentro de la empresa** in-house training, training within industry; **~ de una empresa** company formation; **~ en la empresa** on-the-job training; **~ de equipo** team building; **~ específica** specific training; **~ gerencial** management training; **~ grupal** group training; **~ de imágenes** (Info) imaging; **~ interna** in-company training, in-house training; **~ en línea** online training, online learning, teletraining; **~ ocupacional** employment training; **~ por computadora** AmL *or* **por ordenador** Esp computer-based training; **~ de personal** staff training; **~ profesional** vocational training; **~ profesional en la empresa** on-the-job training; **~ en el puesto de trabajo** job training, in-service training; **~ de sensibilidad** sensitivity training

formal *adj* (responsable) responsible, reliable; (lenguaje, situación) formal

formalidad *f* formality; (fiabilidad) reliability; **~ aduanera** customs formality; **~ legal** legal formality

formalización *f* formalization

formalizar *vt* formalize

formar *vt* (sociedad, alianza) form; (plan) lay; (RRHH) train; (constituir) make up; **~ parte de algo** form part of sth; **el jurado está formado por nueve personas** the jury is made up of nine people

formarse *v pron* (RRHH) train; (idea, opinión) form

formateado *m* formatting

formatear *vt* (disco) format; **sin ~** unformatted

formato *m* (de documento, fichero) format; **de ~ libre** free format; **~ apaisado** landscape; **~ de cuenta** account format; **~ de documento transferible** portable document format; **~ de fichero** file format; **~ gráfico** graphics format; **~ horizontal** landscape; **~ de interfaz de gráficos** Graphics Interchange Format, GIF; **~ MPEG** *or* **MPG** MPG, MPEG; **~ PDF** PDF; **~ de registro** record format; **~ vertical** portrait

fórmula *f* formula; **~ de cortesía** polite expression; (en correspondencia) complimentary close; **~ de interés** interest formula; **~ del promedio** *or* **término medio** averaging formula

formulación *f* formulation; **~ de una política** policy formulation

formular *vt* draw up; (política) formulate

fornido *adj* robust

foro *m* forum; **~ de interés** (en Internet) newsgroup

forzar *vt* force; **~ a alguien a hacer algo** force sb to do sth; **~ el descenso de** (tipos de interés) force down; **~ una salida** force an issue

foto *f* photo, picture; **hacer** *or* **sacar una ~** take a photo

fotocomposición *f* typesetting; (imprenta) filmsetting

fotocopia *f* photocopy; **hacer** *or* **sacar una ~ de algo** photocopy sth, make a photocopy of sth

fotocopiado *f* photocopying

fotocopiar *vt* photocopy

fotocopista *mf* photocopier operator, photocopying assistant

fotograbado *m* photogravure

fotografía *f* photograph, picture; **hacer** *or* **sacar una ~** take a photograph; **~s de prensa** news pictures

fotógrafo, -a *m,f* photographer; **~ de prensa** press photographer

fotollamada *f* photo call

fracasar *vi* fail; (negociaciones) break down

fracaso *m* failure; **el ~ de las negociaciones** the breakdown of the negotiations; **su última película fue un ~** his last film flopped *o* was a flop

fraccionamiento *m* splitting up; **~ de los honorarios** fee split

fraccionar *vt* (cantidad) split up; ∼ **los pagos** pay by instalments BrE *o* installments AmE

frágil *adj* fragile

fragmentación *f* (de mercado, disco) fragmentation, splitting

fraguar *vt* (falsedad) make; ∼ **un complot** hatch a plot

franco *adj* free

franja *f* fringe; (geográfica) strip; ∼ **competitiva** competitive fringe; ∼ **de edad** age-group; ∼ **horaria** (en publicidad) time segment

franqueadora *f* franking machine BrE, postage meter AmE

franquear *vt* frank

franqueo *m* postage; ∼ **en destino** postage-due stamp; ∼ **pagado** postage paid

franquicia *f* exemption; (Seg) excess; (negocio) franchise; ∼ **de equipaje** free baggage allowance; ∼ **fiscal** tax holiday

franquiciado, -a *m,f* franchisee, franchise holder

franquiciador, a *m,f* franchisor

fraude *m* fraud; ∼ **fiscal** tax fraud; ∼ **informático** computer fraud

fraudulencia *f* fraudulence

fraudulentamente *adv* fraudulently

fraudulente *adj* fraudulent; **por medios** ∼**s** by fraudulent means

frecuencia *f* frequency; **con** ∼ frequently; ∼ **alta** high frequency; ∼ **absoluta** absolute frequency; ∼ **de fallos** failure rate

freelance *mf* freelance

frenar *vt* (inflación) curb

frenazo *m* (de subvenciones) sharp reduction; ∼ **y expansión** (Econ) stop-go

frontera *f* frontier; ∼ **común** common border; ∼ **exterior** external border; ∼ **interna** internal frontier; ∼**s nacionales** national borders, national boundaries

frustración *f* frustration; ∼ **de contrato** frustration of contract

FSE *abr* (▸**Fondo Social Europeo**) ESF (European Social Fund)

fuente *f* (de fondos, información) source; **según** ∼**s cercanas al gobierno** according to sources close to the government; ∼ **de alimentación** (Info) power supply; ∼ **autorizada** reliable source; ∼ **de capital** source of capital; ∼ **de dinero** moneymaker, money-spinner (infrml); ∼ **energética** energy

source; ∼**s externas** outsources; **recurrir a** ∼**s externas** outsource (work); ∼ **de fondos** source of funds; ∼ **de ingresos** source of income; ∼ **de mensajes** message source; ∼ **de recursos** source of funds; ∼ **de tipos** type font; ∼ **única** single sourcing

fuera *adv* out; **estar** ∼ (de viaje de negocios) be away; **el director está** ∼ the manager is away (on business); **llevamos a los clientes a comer** ∼ we took the clients out for a meal *o* out for lunch/dinner; ∼ **de acta** off-the-record; ∼ **del balance general** off the balance sheet; ∼ **del centro de la ciudad** out of town; ∼ **de cotización** off-the-board; ∼ **de funcionamiento** (sistema) down; ∼ **de la ley** outside the law, illegal

fuerte *adj* strong; (precio, deuda) hefty (infrml); ∼ **caída** sharp drop; ∼ **demanda** heavy demand

fuertemente *adv* (aumentar, bajar) sharply

fuerza *f* (de moneda) strength; (potencia) force; **con** ∼ **legal** legally binding; **con toda la** ∼ **de la ley** with the full force of the law; **cobrar** ∼ gather *o* gain strength; **por** ∼ inevitably; ∼ **financiera** financial muscle; ∼ **legal de un acuerdo** legal enforceability of an agreement; ∼ **mayor** force majeure; ∼ **del mercado** strength of the market; ∼**s del mercado** market forces; ∼ **motriz** driving force; ∼ **pública** police force; ∼ **de trabajo** work force, human resources; ∼ **de trabajo cualificada** skilled labour BrE *o* labor AmE force

fuga *f* escape; ∼ **de capital** *or* **divisas** flight of capital; ∼ **de cerebros** brain drain

fugarse *v pron* flee, escape; **se ha fugado del país** he's fled the country; **se fugó con el dinero de los inversores** she ran off with the investors' money

fulcro *m* fulcrum

fumar *vti* smoke; **prohibido** ∼ no smoking

función *f* function; (papel) role; (espectáculo) performance; **funciones** *f pl* duties; **desempeñar la** ∼ **de director** hold the position *o* post of director; **en** ∼ **de** according to, on the basis of; **el precio se determina en** ∼ **de la oferta y la demanda** the price is fixed according to supply and demand; **salario en** ∼ **de la experiencia** salary according to experience; **en el ejercicio de sus funciones** while carrying out her duties;

la **función del comité** the role of the committee; **gerente en funciones** acting manager; **un gobierno en funciones** an interim government; ∼ **asesora** advisory function; ∼ **benéfica** charity performance; ∼ **directiva** managerial function; ∼ **exponencial** (Info) exponential function; ∼ **fiscalizadora** audit function; ∼ **de gastos** expenditure function; ∼ **de inversión** investment function; ∼ **de oferta** supply function; ∼ **programable** programmable function; ∼ **de respuesta** response function

funcional *adj* functional

funcionalidad *f* functionality; (para el usuario) usability

funcionamiento *m* (del mercado) functioning, performance; **en** ∼ in use *o* operation, up and running (infrml); ∼ **de una sucursal** branch operation

funcionar *vt* operate, work; **¿cómo funciona esto?** how does this work?; **el sistema no puede** ∼ **con tan poco personal** the system cannot operate with such a small staff; **no funciona** out of order

funcionariado *m* government employees, civil service BrE

funcionario, -a *m,f* government employee, civil servant BrE; ∼ **de capacitación** *or* **formación** training officer; ∼ **de inmigración** immigration officer; ∼ **judicial** legal officer; ∼ **público(-a)** *m,f* government employee, civil servant BrE; ∼ **de relaciones públicas** public relations officer

fundación *f* foundation; ∼ **benéfica** charitable foundation; ∼ **privada** private foundation; ∼ **pública** public foundation

fundador, a *m,f* founder; (empresario) promoter

fundamental *adj* fundamental

fundamentalmente *adv* (afectar, interesar) principally; (alterar) fundamentally

fundamento *m* foundation, basis, grounds; ∼**s** basics, fundamentals; ∼ **constitucional** constitutional foundation

fundar *vt* (compañía) set up, found

fungibilidad *f* fungibility

fungible *adj* fungible; **bienes** ∼**s** fungibles

fusión *f* fusion; (de compañías) merger, amalgamation; (Info) merge; **fusiones y adquisiciones** mergers and acquisitions; ∼ **de conglomerados** conglomerate merger; ∼ **de correo** mailmerge; ∼ **extranjera** foreign merger; ∼ **horizontal** horizontal merger; ∼ **horizontal/vertical** horizontal-vertical merger; ∼ **de intereses** (Cont) merger accounting BrE, pooling of interests AmE; ∼ **inversa** reverse takeover; ∼ **transfronteriza** cross-border merger; ∼ **vertical** vertical merger

fusionar *vt* (compañías) merge, amalgamate

fusionarse *v pron* (compañías) merge, amalgamate; (archivos) merge; ∼ **a** merge into; ∼ **con** merge with

futuro¹ *adj* future

futuro² *m* future; ∼**s** futures; **en el** ∼ in the future; **en un** ∼ **próximo** in the near future; **poner la mira en el** ∼ look to the future; ∼ **financiero** financial future; ∼ **inmediato** near future; ∼**s sobre divisa** currency futures; ∼**s sobre índices** index futures; ∼**s sobre productos básicos** commodities futures

Gg

G-7 *abr* (▸**Grupo de los Siete**) G-7 (Group of Seven)

G-8 *abr* (▸**Grupo de los Ocho**) G-8 (Group of Eight)

gabinete *m* cabinet; (conjunto de profesionales) department, office; ∼ **de estrategia** think-tank; ∼ **de prensa** press office

gacetilla *f* press release; (en periódico) News in Brief

gafete *m*: ∼ **de identificación** name badge

gajes *m pl* (beneficios) perquisites; ∼ **y emolumentos** perquisites; ∼ **del oficio** (infrml) *m pl* occupational hazards; **son los** ∼ **del oficio** it's part and parcel of the job

galera *f* (de prensa) galley

galería *f* (de compras) mall, arcade BrE; ∼ **comercial** shopping mall; ∼ **de la muerte** death row

gallinero: **el** ∼ (Ocio) the gods

gama *f* range, line; **de** ∼ **alta** top-of-the-range, upmarket; **de** ∼ **baja** bottom-of-the-range, downmarket; ∼ **alta/baja del mercado** top/bottom end of the market; ∼ **media del mercado** middle range of the market; ∼ **de opciones** range of options; ∼ **de productos** product range

gamma *f* gamma

ganadería *f* stockbreeding; ∼ **intensiva** intensive livestock farming

ganadero, -a *m,f* stockbreeder, rancher AmE

ganador, a *m,f* winner; (Fin) earner; **todo para el** ∼ winner takes all

ganancia *f* profit, return; **sacarle** ∼ **a algo** make a profit from sth; ∼**s** earnings; ∼ **por acción** earning per share; ∼ **antes de impuestos** pretax earnings; ∼**s anuales** annual earnings; ∼ **bruta** gross profit, trading income; ∼**s de capital** capital gains; ∼**s exentas** exempt earnings; ∼ **imponible** taxable gain; ∼ **inesperada** *or* **imprevista** windfall profit; ∼**s invisibles** invisible earnings; ∼ **líquida** *or* **neta** net profit, net gain; ∼ **neta imponible** taxable net gain; ∼

ordinaria ordinary gain; ∼ **total** gross profits; ∼**s y pérdidas** profit and loss

ganar ⨋**1** *vt* (sueldo) earn; (clientes) win; (mercado) capture; ∼ **dinero con algo** earn money on sth; ∼ **importancia/popularidad** gain in importance/popularity; ∼ **terreno** gain ground; ∼ **valor** increase in value

⨋**2** *vi* benefit; **salir ganando** do well; **los empleados han salido ganando tras la fusión** the staff have done well out of the merger

ganarse *v pron* earn; ∼ **el favor de alguien** win sb's favour BrE *o* favor AmE; ∼ **la vida** earn a living

ganga *f* bargain; **precios de** ∼ bargain prices

gap *m* (Econ) gap

GAP *abr* (▸**gestión de activos y pasivos**) ALM (asset-liability management)

garante *mf* guarantor; (Der) warranter; ∼ **de un crédito** credit guarantor

garantía *f* guarantee, warranty; (fianza) surety; **con** ∼ cum warrant; **bajo** *or* **en** ∼ under guarantee; **sin** ∼ unsecured; **sin** ∼ **de compra** ex-warrant; ∼ **de actuación** performance guarantee; ∼ **adicional** collateral security; ∼ **de una aprobación** seal of approval; ∼ **bancaria** bank guarantee, bank security; ∼ **de calidad** quality assurance; ∼ **de crédito** credit guarantee; ∼ **de depósitos** deposit insurance; ∼ **de deuda** debt security; ∼ **fiscal** revenue guarantee; ∼ **implícita** implied warranty; ∼**s materiales** physical collateral; ∼ **de pago** payment guarantee; ∼ **prolongada** extended guarantee, extended warranty; ∼ **tácita** implied warranty

garantizado *adj* guaranteed, warranted; **no** ∼ (Banca) unendorsed

garantizar *vt* (préstamo) guarantee, warrant; ∼ **la ampliación de un crédito** grant extended credit; ∼ **una deuda con una hipoteca** secure a debt by mortgage

gas *m* gas; ∼ **de escape** (de vehículos) exhaust gas; ∼ **licuado de petróleo**

liquid petroleum gas; ~ **natural** natural gas; ~ **nocivo** noxious gas

gasoil *m* diesel oil

gasóleo *m* diesel oil

gasolina *f* petrol BrE, gasoline AmE; ~ **para aviación** aviation fuel; ~ **para motores** motor spirit; ~ **sin plomo** unleaded *o* lead-free petrol BrE, unleaded *o* lead-free gasoline AmE

gasolinera *f* petrol station BrE, gas station AmE

gastar *vti* spend; (consumir) use; **no gastado** unexpended, unspent; ~ **de menos** *or* **por debajo del presupuesto** underspend

gasto *m* expenditure; (Cont) charge; ~**s** expenses, costs; **cubrir los** ~**s** cover costs; **reducir los** ~**s** reduce costs *o* spending; **el cambio de sistema nos supondría un** ~ **de un millón de euros** changing systems would cost us a million euros; **tener muchos** ~**s** have a lot of expenses *o* outgoings; **todos los** ~**s pagados** all expenses paid; ~ **acumulado** accrued expense; ~ **adicional** additional charge; ~**s administrativos** *or* **de administración** administrative costs; ~**s de adquisición** acquisition costs; ~ **de agencia** agency fee; ~**s anticipados** prepaid expenses; ~**s autorizables** allowable expenses; ~**s bancarios** bank charges; ~**s de calle mayor** high-street spending BrE, main-street spending AmE; ~**s de cancelación** cancellation fee; ~ **de capital** capital expenditure, capital spending; ~**s de comunidad** service charges; ~ **computable** eligible expense; ~**s de conservación** maintenance charges; ~ **de consumo** consumer spending; ~**s contingentes** contingent expenses; ~**s de correo** postage; ~**s deducibles** allowable expenses; ~**s deficitarios** deficit spending; ~**s de depreciación** depreciation expenses; ~**s de desarrollo** development expenditure; ~**s de desplazamiento** (por viaje) travelling BrE *o* traveling AmE expenses; (por mudanza) relocation allowance; ~**s de la deuda** debt charges; ~**s devengados** accrued expenses; ~**s diferidos** deferred charges; ~**s diversos** miscellaneous expenses; ~**s en efectivo** out-of-pocket expenses, petty expenses; ~**s de embalaje** packing costs; ~**s de emisión** flotation costs; ~**s de empleo** employment expenses; ~**s de envío** postage and

packing BrE, postage and handling AmE; ~**s estimados** estimated charges; ~**s estructuales** fixed costs, fixed expenses; ~**s de explotación** operating costs; ~**s extraordinarios** extraordinary expenses; ~**s de fabricación** manufacturing expenses, manufacturing overheads; ~**s fijos** fixed expenses; ~**s de financiación** financing costs; ~**s de franqueo y empaquetado** postage and packing; ~**s de funcionamiento** operating costs; ~**s de fusión** merger expenses; ~ **general del Estado** general government expenditure; ~**s generales** general expenses, overheads; ~**s generales fijos** fixed overheads; ~**s incurridos** incurred expenses; ~**s indirectos** indirect expenses; ~**s de instalación** initial expenditure; ~**s de inversión** investment expenditure; ~**s judiciales** legal costs; ~**s de mantenimiento** maintenancecosts, running costs; (de vida) living expenses; ~**s médicos** medical expenses; ~**s menores** out-of-pocket expenses, petty expenses; ~**s mensuales** monthly expenses; ~ **nacional bruto** Gross National Expenditure; ~**s del negocio** business expenses; ~**s de oficina** office expenses; ~**s personales** personal expenses; ~ **público** public spending; ~**s realizados** incurred expenses; ~**s de representación** entertainment expenses; ~ **de sociedad** corporate spending; ~**s de tramitación** negotiation fee; ~**s de transacción** transaction fee; ~**s de transferencia** handling charges; ~**s de traslado** relocation expenses; ~**s variables** variable expenses; ~**s varios** sundry expenses, miscellaneous expenses, sundries; ~**s de viaje** travel expenses

GATT *abr* (*Acuerdo General sobre Aranceles Aduaneros y Comercio*) GATT (General Agreement on Tariffs and Trade)

generación *f* generation; **tercera/ cuarta** ~ *f* (Info) third/fourth generation; ~ **de energía** power generation; ~ **de estados** report generation; ~ **Internet** Internet generation; ~ **de producto** product generation

generador *m* generator

general *adj* general; **en** ~ *or* **por lo** ~ in general, on the whole; **temas de interés** ~ subjects of general interest; ⋯⋗

nos dieron una visión ∼ **de la situación** they gave us a general overview of the situation

generalista *mf* generalist

generalmente *adv* generally

generar *vt* (energía, beneficios, ideas) generate; (empleo) create; ∼ **ingresos** generate income; **un proyecto destinado a** ∼ **puestos de trabajo** a project intended to create *o* generate jobs

genérico *adj* generic

género *m* kind, type; ∼**s** goods, stock; (mercancías) commodities; **trabajos de ese** ∼ jobs of that type, that type of job; ∼**s a condición** goods on approval; ∼ **trasladado** forward stock

generoso *adj* generous

geodemografía *f* geodemography

geografía *f* geography; ∼ **económica** economic geography; ∼ **política** political geography

geográfico *adj* geographic, geographical

geopolítico *adj* geopolitical

gerencia *f* management; ∼ **de calidad** quality management; ∼ **de carteras** portfolio management; ∼ **de las comunicaciones** communication management; ∼ **corporativa** corporate management; ∼ **departamental** departmental management; ∼ **de energía** energy management; ∼ **de fábrica** plant management; ∼ **financiera** financial management; ∼ **general** general management; ∼ **intermedia** middle management; ∼ **de inversiones** investment management; ∼ **de línea** line management; ∼ **del medio ambiente** environmental management; ∼ **del mercado** market management; ∼ **de oficina** office management; ∼ **de operaciones** operations management; ∼ **del personal** personnel management, staff management; ∼ **de primera línea** first-line management; ∼ **del producto** product management; ∼ **de recursos** resource management; ∼ **de riesgos** risk management; ∼ **de sistemas** systems management; ∼ **de tarea** task management; ∼ **de la tesorería** cash management; ∼ **de ventas** sales management

gerencial *adj* managerial

gerente *mf* manager; (f) manageress; (director) director; ∼ **adjunto(-a)** *m,f* deputy manager, junior manager; ∼ **de área** section manager, area manager; ∼

de banco bank manager; ∼ **de capacitación** training manager; ∼ **comercial** business manager; ∼ **de contratación** recruitment manager; ∼ **de cuentas** (Medios) account manager; ∼ **departamental** departmental manager; ∼ **de distrito** area manager; ∼ **de división** division head, division manager; ∼ **de fábrica** plant manager; ∼ **de fabricación** production manager; ∼ **financiero(-a)** *m,f* financial manager; ∼ **de formación** training manager; ∼ **en funciones** acting manager; ∼ **general** general manager; ∼ **intermedio(-a)** *m,f* middle manager; ∼ **de línea** line manager; ∼ **de marcas** brand manager; ∼ **medio(-a)** *m,f* middle manager; ∼ **de operaciones** operations manager; ∼ **de personal** personnel manager; ∼ **de producción** production manager; ∼**-propietario(-a)** *m* owner-manager; ∼ **de publicidad** advertising manager; ∼ **técnico(-a)** *m,f* technical manager; ∼ **de ventas** sales manager

gestión *f* management, administration; **gestiones** *f pl* negotiations; ∼ **de activos** asset management; ∼ **de activos y pasivos** asset-liability management; ∼ **de la cadena de suministros** supply chain management; ∼ **de caja** cash management; ∼ **de la calidad** quality control; ∼ **de la calidad total** total quality management, TQM; ∼ **de carteras** portfolio management; ∼ **de la configuración** configuration management; ∼ **del conocimiento** knowledge management; ∼ **del contenido de la web** Web content management; ∼ **del correo electrónico** mail management; ∼ **de crédito** credit management; ∼ **de crisis** crisis management; ∼ **de una cuenta** account management; ∼ **de datos** data management; ∼ **deficiente** mismanagement; ∼ **de desempeño** performance management; ∼ **de la deuda** debt management; ∼ **de la deuda pública** national debt management BrE, public debt management AmE; ∼ **del dinero** money management; ∼ **directa** first-line management; ∼ **efectiva** effective management; ∼ **de empresas** business administration, business management; ∼ **de ficheros** file management; ∼ **fiduciaria** trusteeship; ∼ **financiera** financial management; ∼ **fiscal** fiscal planning; ∼ **de los flujos de trabajo**

workflow planning; ∼ **de fondos** fund management; ∼ **inmobiliaria** property management; ∼ **de inversiones** investment management; ∼ **de liquidez** cash management; ∼ **de la marca** brand management; ∼ **del mercado** market management; ∼ **minorista** retail management; ∼ **al por menor** retail management; ∼ **por objetivos** management by objectives; ∼ **del pasivo** liability management; ∼ **del personal** personnel management; ∼ **presupuestaria** budget management; ∼ **de la producción** production management; ∼ **de proyectos** project management; ∼ **de recursos** resource management; ∼ **de recursos humanos** human resource management; ∼ **de los recursos naturales** natural resources management; ∼ **de recursos y políticas** policy and resource management; ∼ **de la red** *or* **de redes** (Info) networking; ∼ **de las relaciones con los clientes** customer relationship management, CRM; ∼ **de los residuos** waste management; ∼ **de riesgos** risk management; ∼ **de sistemas** systems management; ∼ **de tareas** task management; ∼ **de tesorería** cash management; ∼ **de versiones** version control; ∼ **vertical** top-down management

gestionado *adj* managed; ∼ **por programa** software-driven

gestor, a *m,f* manager; (f) manageress; (negociador) agent; (de programas) administrator; ∼ **administrativo(-a)** *m,f* administrative agent; ∼ **de la cartera de valores** portfolio manager; ∼ **de centro de responsabilidad** responsibility centre BrE *o* center AmE manager; ∼ **de cuentas** account manager; ∼ **de fondos** fund manager; ∼ **de riesgos** risk manager

gestoría *f* agency dealing with official legal documents

GGE *abr* Esp (▸**gasto general del Estado**) GGE (general government expenditure)

gigaocteto *m* gigabyte

GIGO *abr* (▸**entrada descontrolada/salida descontrolada**) GIGO (garbage-in/garbage-out)

gira *f* tour; **de** ∼ on tour; ∼ **publicitaria** advertising tour

girado, -a *m,f* drawee

girador, a *m,f* drawer, cheque signer BrE, check signer AmE

girar ⓵ *vt* (cheque, letra de cambio) draw; (dinero) send; (a través de un banco) transfer. ⓶ *vi* draw; ∼ **contra los ahorros** draw on savings; ∼ **en descubierto** draw money from an overdrawn account

giro *m* draft, money order; ∼ **bancario** banker's draft, bank giro BrE; ∼ **cablegráfico** cable transfer; ∼ **en divisas** currency draft; ∼ **monetario internacional** international money draft; ∼ **postal** giro, postal order BrE, postal money order AmE; ∼ **postal internacional** international money order; ∼ **telegráfico** telegraphic money order, wire transfer; ∼ **a la vista** demand draft, sight draft

global *adj* global; (respuesta) comprehensive, blanket; (cantidad) total; **cantidad** ∼ **a abonar** total amount due

globalización *f* globalization

globalizar *vt* globalize

glorieta *f* roundabout BrE, traffic circle AmE

glosario *m* glossary

Gobernador, a *m,f* (de banco) Governor

gobierno *m* government; (dirección) management; **el G**∼ the Government; **el buen/mal** ∼ **de algo** the good/bad management of sth; ∼ **a consumidor** government to consumer, G2C; ∼ **a empresa** government to business, G2B; ∼ **a** ∼ government to government, G2G; ∼ **central** central government; ∼ **de coalición** coalition government; ∼ **descentralizado** decentralized government; ∼ **electrónico** e-government, electronic government, online government; ∼ **federal** federal government; ∼ **en funciones** caretaker *o* interim government; ∼ **inestable** unstable government; ∼ **municipal** local government, municipal government; ∼ **de transición** general manager

golpe *m* knock; ∼ **de estado** coup d'état; ∼ **de inspiración** flash of inspiration; ∼ **rápido** (Fisc) quick flip; ∼ **de suerte** (infrml) (lucky) break (infrml)

gotear *vt* (información) leak (infrml)

goteo *m* drip; **un** ∼ **constante de algo** a steady flow of sth

grabación *f* recording; ∼ **en cinta** tape recording; ∼ **digital** digital recording; ∼ **en directo** live recording; ∼ **en vídeo** Esp *or* **video** AmL videotape recording

grabado *m* illustration; **con ∼s** illustrated

grabador, a *m,f*: **∼ de datos** data entry operator

grabadora *f* recorder; **∼ de casetes** *or* **cintas** tape recorder

grabar *vt* tape, record; **∼ en vídeo** Esp *or* **video** AmL **una entrevista** record *o* tape an interview

gracias *f pl* thanks; **darle las ∼ a alguien (por algo)** thank sb (for sth); **¡∼!** thank you!, thanks! **muchas ∼** thank you very much, many thanks; **∼ a algo/ alguien** thanks to sth/sb; **∼ anticipadas** *or* **por anticipado** thanking you in advance *o* anticipation

grado *m* (medida) degree; (de protección) extent; (etapa) stage; **en mayor o menor ∼** to a greater or lesser extent; **en sumo ∼** in the extreme; **∼ de consumo** level of consumption; **∼ del daño** degree of damage; **∼ de exactitud** degree of accuracy; **∼ óptimo** optimal rate; **∼ de rendimiento** earning capacity; **∼ de riesgo** degree of risk; **∼ de solvencia estimado** credit rating

graduado, -a *m,f* graduate

gradual *adj* gradual

gradualismo *m* gradualism

gradualmente *adv* gradually

gráfica *f* (diagrama, gráfico) chart, graph; **∼s** graphics; **∼ de utilidad** profit graph

graficar *vt* chart, plot

gráfico *m* graphic; (diagrama) chart; **∼ de actividades múltiples** multiple-activity chart; **∼ de barras** bar chart; **∼ de circulación** flowchart; **∼ circular** pie chart; **∼s comerciales** *or* **de gestión** business graphics; **∼ de correspondencia** pertinence chart; **∼ de puntos** dot chart; **∼ de ratios** ratio chart; **∼ de sectores** pie chart

grafista *mf* graphic artist *o* designer; **∼ de bolsa** chartist

gran *adj* ▸**grande**

grande *adj* big; **a ∼s rasgos** in broad terms; **de gran volumen** high-volume; **en gran parte** to a large extent; **∼s almacenes** department store; **Gran Bretaña** Great Britain; **la Gran Depresión** the Great Depression; **la gran explosión** the Big Bang

granel *m* bulk; **a ∼ in** bulk

grapa *f* staple

grapadora *f* stapler

grapar *vt* staple

GRASEFI *abr* (▸**Gravamen sobre los Servicios Financieros**) *financial services tax*

gratificación *f* perquisite, perk (infrml); **∼ de capital** capital bonus; **∼ intangible** intangible reward

gratificante *adj* rewarding

gratis *adv* free, gratis, without charge

gratuito *adj* free

gravable *adj* taxable; (valor) rateable

gravado *adj* taxable; (sujeto a gravamen) taxed; **no ∼** tax-free; (Inmob) free and clear AmE; **∼ en origen** taxed at source

gravamen *m* tax; (sobre propiedad) encumbrance; (sobre exportaciones) levy; (carga) burden; (derecho de retención) lien; **∼ estatutario** statutory lien; **∼ financiero** financial encumbrance; **G∼ sobre los Servicios Financieros** *financial services tax*; **∼ superpuesto** superimposed tax

gravar *vt* tax; (con carga) burden, encumber; **∼ algo con un impuesto** levy a tax on sth; **∼ los ingresos de las personas** tax people's incomes

grotesca *f* (tipografía) sans serif

grúa *f* crane; (para retirar coches) tow truck AmE, breakdown van BrE; **vehículos abandonados serán retirados por la ∼** abandoned vehicles will be towed away

grueso *m* (de la cartera de valores) bulk; **el ∼ de** most of, the bulk of

grupo *m* group; **∼ analizado** focus group; **∼ asesor** advisory group; **∼ asociado** affiliated group; **∼ bancario** banking group BrE, bank group AmE; **∼ de compañías** group of companies; **∼ consultivo** consultative group; **∼ de control** control group; **∼ creativo** creative group; **∼ de cuentas** set of accounts; **∼ de dirección** management group; **∼ de discusión** discussion group; **∼ disidente** splinter group; **∼ estratégico** target group; **∼ de estudios** study group; **∼ etario** age group, age bracket; **∼ de expertos** panel of experts, think-tank; **∼ de expertos fotográficos** Joint Photographic Experts Group, JPEG; **∼ de ingresos** income bracket; **∼ de interés** interest group; **G∼ de los Ocho** Group of Eight; **∼ paritario** peer group; **∼ de presión** pressure group, lobby; **∼ de presión ecologista** environmental lobby; **∼ de productos** product group; **G∼ de los Siete** Group of Seven; **∼ socioeconómico** socioeconomic group; **∼ de tiendas**

store group; ~ **de trabajo** working party, working group; ~ **de usuarios** user group

gte. *abr* (▶**gerente**) dir. (director)

guardamuebles *m* furniture warehouse; **llevar algo a un** ~ put sth in storage

guardapolvo *m* dust cover

guardar *vt* (meter) put; (conservar) keep; (dinero, archivo) save; ~**le el puesto a alguien** keep sb's job open for them; ~ **el anónimato** remain anonymous; ~ **algo en depósito** warehouse sth; ~ **algo en reserva** keep sth in reserve

guardarropa *m* cloakroom

gubernamental *adj* governmental

gubernamentalización *f* extension of government control

guerra *f* war; ~ **comercial** trade war; ~ **de patentes** patent war; ~ **de precios** price war; ~ **de territorios** turf war

GUI *abr* (**interfaz de usuario gráfica**) GUI (Graphical User Interface)

guía[1] *f* (libro, telefónica) telephone directory, phone book; ~ **administrativa** management guide; ~ **aproximada** rough guide; ~ **de**

carrera career guidance; ~ **clasificada** classified directory; ~ **de coste** Esp *or* **costo** AmL *f* cost leader; ~ **del DOS** DOS prompt; ~ **de servicios** service handbook; ~ **de sites** *or* **sitios web** site directory; ~ **telefónica** telephone directory, phone book; ~ **de usuario** user guide

guía[2] *mf* leader

guión *m* script; (en tipografía) dash; ~ **cinematográfico** film script; ~ **gráfico** (para publicidad) storyboard; ~ **de rodaje** shooting script

guionado *m* hyphenation

guionista *mf* scriptwriter

gusano *m* (Info) worm

gustar *vi*: **no me gusta** I don't like it; **como guste** as you wish; **pásese por nuestras oficinas cuando usted guste** please call in at our offices whenever convenient *o* at your convenience

gusto *m* taste; **a** ~ **del consumidor** to suit the consumer; **mucho** *or* **tanto** ~ pleased to meet you; **tengo el** ~ **de presentarles el equipo ganador** I have pleasure in introducing the winning team, I am pleased to introduce the winning team

Hh

habeas corpus *m* habeas corpus

haber *m* credit side; ~es (bienes) assets; (ingresos) income, earnings

habilidad *f* skill; **con** ~ skilfully BrE, skillfully AmE; **tener mucha** ~ **para algo** be very good at sth; **tiene mucha** ~ **para los negocios** she has a very good business sense, she is a very good businesswoman; ~ **administrativa** management skill; ~ **manual** manual skill; ~**es sociales** social skills

habilitación *f* eligibility

habitante *mf* inhabitant

hábitat *m* (de vida salvaje) habitat

hábito *m* habit; ~**s del consumidor** consumer habits

habituar *vt*: ~ **a alguien a algo/hacer algo** get sb used to sth/doing sth

hablar ⓵ *vi* talk; ~ **de algo/alguien** talk about sth/sb, discuss sth/sb; ~ **de negocios** talk business; ~ **del trabajo** talk about work, talk shop (infrml); **se habla de que...** it is rumored that..., people are saying that...; ~ **por teléfono** speak on the phone; **¿quién habla?** (al teléfono) who's calling?
⓶ *vt* (tratar) discuss, talk about; (idioma) speak; **habla muy bien el inglés** he speaks very good English; **se habla inglés** English spoken; **no hay (nada) más que** ~ there's nothing more to be said; **ya lo hablaremos cuando tengamos más tiempo** we'll talk about it when we have more time

hacedor, a *m,f* maker; ~ **de política** policy maker

hacendado-a *m,f* landowner

hacer ⓵ *vt* (efectuar) do; (crear) make; (pregunta) ask; (objeción) raise; **¿qué hace tu marido?** what does your husband do?; ~ **un curso** do a course; ~ **(la carrera de) Derecho** do a Law degree, do Law; ~ **dinero** make money; ~ **negocios** do business; ~ **un trato** do a deal; ~ **bajar los precios/la tasa de inflación** bring prices/the rate of inflation down; ~ **efectivo** (cheque) cash; (bonos) cash in; (contrato) implement; ~**le un favor a alguien** do sb a favour BrE *o* favor AmE; ~ **frente a** (problemas) confront;

(responsabilidades) face up to; (críticas, futuro) face
⓶ *vi*: ~ **constar algo** put sth on record; **por lo que hace a** *or* **en cuanto hace a su solicitud** as far as your application is concerned, as regards your application

hacerse *v pron*: ~ **a algo** get used to sth; ~ **con lo mejor** (dinero, demanda) cream off the best (infrml); ~ **con una fortuna** amass a fortune; ~ **rico** get rich

hacienda *f* (finca) estate; (dedicada a la ganadería) ranch; ~ **pública** government funds; **la H**~ ≈ Inland Revenue BrE, ≈ Internal Revenue Service AmE; **H**~ **Pública** ≈ Treasury BrE, ≈ Treasury Department AmE

halagüeño *adj* (perspectivas) rosy

hardware *m* hardware

hecho[1] *adj* made; ~ **para durar** made to last; ~ **de encargo** custom-made; ~ **a mano** handmade; ~ **a máquina** machine-made; ~ **a medida** customized, tailor-made, made to measure

hecho[2] *m* (suceso) event; (realidad) fact; **de** ~ in fact; (Der) de facto; ~ **consumado** fait accompli; ~ **fortuito** fortuitous event; ~ **imponible** taxable event; ~ **material** material fact; ~**s y números** facts and figures; ~ **posterior** subsequent event; ~ **sin precedentes** unprecedented event; ~ **verificado** ascertained fact

hedging *m* hedging

hegemonía *f* hegemony

heliestación *f* helistop

heliográfica *f* blueprint

helipuerto *m* heliport

heredar *vt* inherit; ~ **algo de alguien** inherit sth from sb

heredero, -a *m,f* heir; ~ **legítimo(-a)** *m,f* rightful heir; ~**s y sucesores** heirs and assigns

herencia *f* inheritance; **dejarle algo a alguien en** ~ leave sb sth

hermético *adj* (envase, precinto) airtight

herramienta *f* tool; ~ **de marketing** marketing tool; ~ **de producción** production implement; ~ **de trabajo** tool of the trade; ~ **de ventas** sales tool

heterogéneo *adj* heterogeneous

heurística *f* heuristics
heurístico *adj* heuristic
híbrido *adj* hybrid
hidrocarburo *m* hydrocarbon
hidroeléctrico *adj* (energía) hydroelectric
hidrogenerado *adj* (electricidad) water-generated
higiene *f* hygiene; **∼ industrial** industrial hygiene; **∼ medioambiental** environmental hygiene
hijo *m* child; **Lucas e H∼s** Lucas & Sons; **∼ dependiente** dependent child
hiperdocumento *m* hyperdocument
hiperenlace *m* hyperlink; **∼ empotrado** embedded hyperlink
hiperenlazar *vt* hyperlink
hiperinflación *f* hyperinflation
hiperinflacionista *adj* hyperinflationist
hipermedia *f* hypermedia
hipermercado *m* hypermarket, superstore
hipertexto *m* hypertext; **enlace de ∼** hypertext link
hipoteca *f* mortgage; **redimir una ∼** pay off a mortgage; **∼ abierta** open mortgage; **∼ dotal** endowment mortgage; **∼ fiduciaria** trust mortgage; **∼ en segundo grado** second mortgage BrE, junior mortgage AmE; **∼ de tasa variable** variable-rate mortgage
hipotecar *vt* mortgage; **(Der)** hypothecate
hipótesis *f* hypothesis
hipotético *adj* hypothetical
histéresis *f* hysteresis
histograma *m* histogram
historia *f* story; (historial) history; **∼ documental** (imprenta, periódico) background story; **∼ de éxito** success story; **∼ financiera** financial history
historial *m* track record; (en el Internet) history; (de carrera) curriculum vitae BrE, CV BrE, résumé AmE; **tener un ∼ de algo** have a history of sth; **∼ del crédito** credit history; **∼ de inversión** investment history; **∼ laboral** work history, career history; **∼ médico** health record, medical history; **∼ previo** previous history; **∼ probado** proven track record
históricamente *adv* historically
histórico *adj* (fecha, suceso) historic; (hecho) historical

hito *m* signpost; (acontecimiento) milestone, landmark; **∼s financieros** financial highlights
hoja *f* sheet; **de ∼ suelta** loose-leaf; **∼ de almacén** stock sheet; **∼ de asistencia** time sheet; **∼ de balance** balance sheet; **∼ de cálculo** spreadsheet; **∼ de costes** Esp *or* **costos** AmL **por órdenes de trabajo** job cost sheet; **∼ de cumplido** compliments slip; **∼ de datos** data sheet; **∼ electrónica** spreadsheet; **∼ de embarque** consignment note; **∼ de estilo** style sheet; **∼ de montaje** base sheet; **∼ de pedido** order form; **∼ de pedido electrónica** electronic order form; **∼ de programación** work sheet; **∼s de prueba** proofs; **∼ de reclamación** relcamation form; **∼ de registro** tally sheet; **∼ de ruta** waybill; **∼ de servicios** service record; **∼ de trabajo** worksheet
hojear *vt* (documentos) browse; (leer rápido) glance through
holding *m* holding company, holding corporation
hombre *m* man; **∼ anuncio** advertising man; **∼ de la calle** the man in the street; **∼ casado** married man; **∼ de negocios** businessman
homogéneo *adj* homogeneous
homologación *f* certification mark, official recognition; **la ∼ de los títulos sudamericanos con los españoles** recognition of South American qualifications which are equivalent to Spanish ones
homólogo, -a *m,f* (en otra organización) counterpart, opposite number
honor *m* honour BrE, honor AmE; **en ∼ a la verdad** to be perfectly honest; **hacer ∼ a algo** honour BrE *o* honor AmE sth; **hacer ∼ a un compromiso** honour BrE *o* honor AmE a commitment; **tener el ∼ de hacer algo** to have the honour BrE *o* honor AmE of doing sth; **tengo el honor de presentarles al nuevo director** it gives me great pleasure to introduce the new director
honorarios *m pl* fee, honorarium (frml); **∼ de administración** management fee; **∼ fijos** fixed fee; **∼ de incentivo** incentive fee; **∼ del letrado** legal fees
honradez *f* trustworthiness
honrar *vt* honour BrE, honor AmE
hora *f* hour; (horario) time; (cita) appointment; **a la ∼ fijada** at the appointed time; **a la ∼ prevista** on ⸱⸱⸱⟩

h

schedule; **antes/después de** ~**s de oficina** before/after (office) hours; **cobrar/trabajar por** ~**s** get paid/work by the hour; **pedir** ~ **para algo** get an appointment for sth; **poner muchas** ~**s en algo** put a lot of hours *o* time into sth; **de última** ~ last-minute; ~ **de apertura** opening time; ~**s centrales** core hours; ~ **central establecida** Central Standard Time; ~ **centroeuropea** Central European Time; ~ **de cierre** closing time; ~ **de comer** lunch-hour; ~**s de comercio** business hours; ~ **contada doble** double time; ~ **estándar del este** Eastern Standard Time; ~**s extra** *or* **extraordinarias** overtime; ~**-hombre** man-hour; ~**s laborables** office hours; ~ **legal** standard time; ~ **límite** deadline; ~ **límite de redacción** copy deadline; ~ **local** local time; ~ **de máxima audiencia** prime time; ~ **media de Greenwich** Greenwich Mean Time; ~**s de oficina** office hours, hours of business; ~ **pico** AmL (*cf* ▸**hora punta** Esp) peak time; (Transp) rush hour; ~ **prevista de llegada** estimated time of arrival; ~ **prevista de salida** estimated time of departure; ~ **punta** Esp (*cf* ▸**hora pico** AmL) peak time; (Transp) rush hour; ~ **de salida** departure time; ~**s de trabajo** working hours; ~ **universal coordinada** coordinated universal time

horario *m* schedule, timetable; **según el** ~ according to the schedule; ~ **de apertura** opening hours; ~ **bancario** banking hours; ~ **de la bolsa** stock exchange hours; ~ **de contratación** trading hours; ~ **flexible** flexitime, flexible working hours; ~ **intensivo** *working day with an early start and no breaks in order to finish early, especially in the summer*; ~ **del mercado** market hours; ~ **móvil** flexible working hours, flexitime; ~ **de oficina** office hours; ~ **partido** split shift (*working day with a long break for lunch*); ~ **al público** opening hours; ~**s regulares** regular hours; ~ **selecto** prime time; ~ **de trabajo** (programa) schedule; (horas) working time; ~ **de trenes** train timetable; ~ **de verano** daylight saving time

horizontal *adj* horizontal; (formato) landscape

horizonte *m* horizon; ~ **de inversión** investment horizon; ~ **de planificación** planning horizon

hortelano, -a *m,f* market gardener BrE, truck farmer AmE

horticultura *f* horticulture, gardening; ~ **comercial** market gardening BrE, truck farming AmE

hospedaje *m* accommodation BrE, accommodations AmE; **dar** ~ **a alguien** provide accommodation BrE *o* accommodations AmE for sb

hospedar *vt* provide accommodation BrE *o* accommodations AmE for; (en el Internet) host

hospedarse *v pron* stay at

hostelería *f* hotel and catering business

hotelero(a) *m,f* hotelier

HTML *abr* (*lenguaje de referencia de hipertexto*) HTML (Hypertext Mark-up Language); ~ **dinámico** DHTML (Dynamic Hypertext Mark-up Language)

hub *m* hub; ~ **del comercio electrónico** e-commerce hub

HUC *abr* (▸**hora universal coordinada**) UTC (coordinated universal time)

hueco *m* (en inventario) pitfall; ~ **en el mercado** gap in the market; ~ **de oportunidad** window of opportunity

huecograbado *m* rotogravure

huelga *f* industrial action, strike; **estar en** ~ be on strike; **ir a la** ~ go on strike, go out on strike BrE; **hacer** ~ strike; **hacer** ~ **por solidaridad** strike in sympathy; **se canceló la** ~ the strike was called off; ~ **de brazos caídos** sit-down strike; ~ **de celo** work-to-rule; ~ **ferroviaria** rail strike; ~ **general** general strike; ~ **ilegal** illegal strike; ~ **legal** legal strike, official strike; ~ **de ocupación** sit-in; ~ **oficial** official strike; ~ **política** political strike; ~ **de protesta** protest strike; ~ **rápida** snap strike; ~ **relámpago** lightning strike; ~ **salvaje** wildcat strike; ~ **de solidaridad** sympathy strike

huelguista *mf* striker

huésped *mf* paying guest

huida *f* flight; ~ **de capitales** flight of capital

hulla *f* coal; ~ **blanca** white coal

humo *m* fumes

hundido *adj* (mercado, empresa) collapsed

hundimiento *m* collapse; ~ **del mercado** market collapse

hundirse *v pron* (mercado) collapse; (precios) crash

hurto *m* theft; ~ **mayor** serious crime

BrE, grand larceny AmE; ~ **en tiendas** shoplifting

husmeador *m* (programa) sniffer

Ii

IA *abr* (▸**inteligencia artificial**) AI (artificial intelligence)

I&D *abr* (▸**investigación y desarrollo**) R&D (research and development)

IATA *abr* (**Asociación Internacional de Transporte Aéreo**) IATA (International Air Transport Association)

ibíd *abbr* (**ibídem**) ibid. (ibidem)

ICB *abr* (▸**índice de capitalización bursátil**) market capitalization index

ICO *abr* (▸**Instituto de Crédito Oficial**) *Spanish official credit institute*

icono *m* icon

íd. *abr* (▸**ídem**) do. (ditto)

idea *f* idea; **formarse una ∼ de algo/ alguien** form an opinion about sth/sb; **hacerse una ∼ de algo** get an idea of sth; **tener una ∼** have an idea; **∼ genial** brilliant idea, brainwave

idear *vt* devise, think up; (invento) design

ídem *adj* ditto

identidad *f* identity; **carné de ∼** identity card; **∼ contable** accounting identity; **∼ corporativa** corporate identity

identificación *f* (de declaraciones) identification; **∼ desde tierra** ground control; **∼ de marca** brand identification

identificador *m* identifier

identificar *vt* (sospechoso, víctima, problema) identify; **∼ a alguien con algo** identify *o* associate sb with sth; **sin ∼** unidentified

idoneidad *f* eligibility, suitability

idóneo *adj* eligible, suitable

IEF *abr* (▸**Instituto de Estudios Financieros**) *Spanish financial research institute*

ignífugo *adj* fire-resistant

igual[1] *adj* equal; **igual a** *o* **que** the same as; **en ∼es condiciones** on an equal footing; **∼ y opuesto** equal and opposite; **∼ para todas las categorías** across-the-board; **por ∼** equally

igual[2] *m* equal; (signo) equals sign; **sin ∼** unrivalled BrE, unrivaled AmE

iguala *f* agreed fee; (para asegurar los servicios de alguien) retainer

igualación *f* equalization; **∼ de diferencias salariales** equalization of wage differentials

igualar *vt* (precios) even out; (oferta, resultados) match, equal

igualdad *f* equality; **en ∼ de condiciones** on equal terms; **∼ de derechos de voto** equal voting rights; **∼ de oportunidad de empleo** equal employment opportunities; **∼ de oportunidades** equal opportunities BrE *or* opportunity AmE

igualitarismo *m* egalitarianism

igualmente *adv* equally

ilegal *adj* illegal, unlawful

ilegalmente *adv* illegally, unlawfully

ilícito *adj* illicit

ilimitado *adj* unlimited

iliquidez *f* liquidity squeeze

ilíquido *adj* illiquid

ILT *abr* (▸**incapacidad laboral transitoria**) temporary disability benefit

ilusión *f* illusion; **con ∼** hopefully; **poner su ∼ en algo** pin one's hopes on sth; **∼ fiscal** fiscal illusion

ilustración *f* (ejemplo, imagen) illustration; **ilustraciones** (imprenta) artwork

ilustrar *vt* illustrate; (tema) explain

IMAC *abr* (▸**Instituto de Mediación, Arbitraje y Conciliación**) Esp *independent conciliation service, involved in disputes between trade unions and management,* ≈ ACAS BrE

imagen *f* image; **∼ consolidada** established image; **∼ corporativa** corporate image; **∼ fiel** true and fair view BrE, fair representation AmE; **∼ fija** still; **∼ global** global image; **∼ de marca** brand image; **∼ de pantalla** soft copy; **∼ del producto** product image; **∼ secundaria** (publicidad) afterimage; **∼ sobresaliente** high image; **∼ virtual** virtual image

IME *abr* (▸**Instituto Monetario Europeo**) EMI (European Monetary Institute)

imitación *f* imitation; (brillante) fake; **de ~ fake; una cartera ~ cuero** an imitation leather wallet; **imitaciones ilegales** counterfeit goods

impacto *m* impact; **~ ambiental** environmental impact; **~ del beneficio** profit impact; **~ de una pérdida** impact of a loss; **~ visual** visual impact

impagado *adj* unpaid, outstanding

impago *m* nonpayment

impar[1] *adj* odd

impar[2] *m* odd number

imparcial *adj* impartial

impedimento *m* obstacle, impediment; **~ legal** estoppel

impedir *vt* prevent, stop; **~ el paso** block the way; **~le a alguien hacer algo** prevent sb from doing sth

imperialismo *m* imperialism; **~ capitalista** capitalist imperialism

implantación *f* (de métodos, reformas) introduction, establishment

implantar *vt* (métodos, reformas, normas) introduce, institute; (sistema, red) install

implementación *f* implementation; **~ de un artículo** (Fin) implementation of an article; **~ desfasada** implementation lag; **~ estratégica** strategy implementation

implementar *vt* (medidas, plan) implement

implicación *f* involvement; (consecuencia) implication; **~ del beneficio** profit implication; **~ de los empleados** employee involvement; **~ financiera** financial involvement; **~ del lector** reader involvement; **implicaciones plenas** full implications

implicar *vt* involve; (bajo sospecha) implicate; (significar) imply; **estar implicado en algo** be involved in sth

implícito *adj* (condiciones) implicit

imponer *vt* (pena, sanciones, impuesto) impose; (embargo) put, place, lay; (moda) set; (depositar) deposit; **~ la moda** set the trend

imponerse *v pron* be necessary; (hacerse respetar) assert oneself *o* one's authority; (prevalecer) prevail; **se impone tomar una decisión inmediata** it it essential *o* imperative that a decision is taken today; **se impuso la justicia** justice prevailed

imponible *adj* taxable; **no ~** nontaxable

importación *f* (artículo) import; (acción) importation; **de ~** imported; **~ de**

capital capital import; **importaciones de la Comunidad** Community imports; **~-exportación** import-export; **~ invisible/visible** invisible/visible import

importado *adj* imported

importador, a *m,f* importer

importancia *f* importance; **de gran ~** very important, of great importance; **darle mucha ~ a algo** attach a lot of importance to sth, make much of sth; **no tiene ~** it's not important; **quitar ~ a algo** play down the importance of sth; **detalles sin ~** minor details

importante *adj* important; (cantidad) significant, considerable; **lo más ~** the most important thing

importar [1] *vt* (productos, datos) import; (gastos, beneficios) amount to [2] *vi* (ser importante) matter, be important; **no importa** never mind, it doesn't matter; **¿le importaría esperar?** would you mind waiting?

importe *m* (de factura) amount; (precio) cost; **el ~ de la deuda asciende a 20.000 euros** the debt amounts to 20,000 euros; **rogamos abonen de inmediato el ~ total de la factura adjunta** we request immediate payment in full of the enclosed invoice; **por un ~ de** to the value of; **~ atrasado** arrears; **~ bruto** gross amount; **~ deducible** deduction; **~ efectivo** actual amount; **~ específico** specific amount; **~ de la factura** invoice amount; **~ pagado** amount paid; **~ total** full amount; **~ de las ventas** sales value, value of sales

imposible *adj* impossible; **es ~ terminarlo en ese tiempo** it is impossible to finish it in that time; **hicieron lo ~ para tratar de salvar la compañía** they did everything they could to try and save the company

imposición *f* taxation; (carga, requisito) imposition; (depósito) deposit; **~ directa** direct taxation; **~ excesiva** overtaxation; **~ indirecta** indirect taxation; **~ múltiple** multiple taxation; **~ a plazo** fixed-term deposit BrE, time deposit AmE; **~ regresiva** regressive taxation

impositivo *adj* tax; **sistema ~** tax system

impresión *f* (opinión) impression; (acción) printing; (resultado) printout; (tirada) print run; **hacer** *or* **causar una buena/mala ~** make a good/bad impression; **dar la ~ de que** look as if; **~ por** ⋯⋗

computadora AmL (*cf* ▸**impresión por ordenador** Esp) computer printout; ~ **de control** machine proof; ~ **digital** fingerprint; ~ **inversa** reverse printing; ~ **de la memoria** memory printout; ~ **por ordenador** Esp (*cf* ▸**impresión por computadora** AmL) computer printout; ~ **de pantalla** print screen; ~ **sin prioridad** background printing

impresionante *adj* (aumento) impressive

impreso¹ *adj* printed; ~ **en negrita** printed in bold

impreso² *m* printed form; ~**s** *m pl* (prensa) printed matter; **rellenar un** ~ fill in a form; ~ **al portador** bearer form; ~ **de ingreso** Esp paying-in slip BrE, pay-in slip AmE

impresor, a *m,f* (persona) printer

impresora *f* printer; (de tarjeta de crédito) imprinter; ~ **de alta calidad** letter-quality printer; ~ **de alta velocidad** high-speed printer; ~ **bidireccional** bidirectional printer; ~ **a chorro de tinta** ink-jet printer; ~ **de gráficos** graphics printer; ~ **de inyección de burbujas** bubble-jet printer; ~ **láser** laser printer; ~ **de líneas** line printer; ~ **de margarita** daisywheel printer; ~ **matriz** dot-matrix printer; ~ **de percusión** impact printer; ~ **de rayo láser** laser printer; ~ **en serie** serial printer; ~ **de tambor** drum printer

imprevisible *adj* unpredictable, unforeseeable

imprevisto *adj* unforeseen, unanticipated

imprevistos *m pl* incidental *o* unforeseen expenses

imprimir *vt* print, print out, output

ímprobo *adj* (esfuerzo) enormous, huge; (deshonesto) dishonest

improcedente *adj* (conducta) inappropriate; (Der) inadmissible; **despido** ~ unfair dismissal

improcesable *adj* unworkable

improductivo *adj* unproductive

imprudencia *f* negligence; ~ **temeraria** criminal negligence

impuesto *m* tax; ~**s** *m pl* taxes, taxation; **antes/después de deducidos los** ~**s** before/after tax; **beneficios antes de** ~**s** pretax profits; **beneficios después de** ~**s** profits after tax; **libre de** ~**s** tax-free; ~ **acumulado** accrued tax; ~ **acumulativo** cumulative tax; ~ **ad valórem** ad valorem tax; ~ **adicional** surtax; ~**s aduaneros** customs duties;

~ **afectado** earmarked tax; ~ **agrario** agricultural levy; ~ **ambiental** environmental tax; ~ **aplazado** deferred tax; ~ **atrasado** back tax; ~ **básico** basic tax; ~ **sobre beneficios** profits tax; ~ **de circulación** road tax; ~ **sobre compras** purchase tax; ~ **comercial** business tax; ~ **sobre el consumo** consumption tax; ~ **por contaminación** pollution tax; ~**s debidos** taxes due; ~ **después de beneficios** after-profits tax; ~ **diferido** deferred tax; ~ **directo** direct tax; ~ **sobre dividendos** dividend tax; ~ **sobre donaciones** gift tax; ~ **sobre el empleo** employment tax; ~ **encubierto** hidden tax; ~ **escalonado** graduated tax; ~ **sobre la exportación** export tax; ~ **extraordinario** windfall tax; ~ **ficticio** phantom tax; ~ **fijo** fixed duty; ~ **a la fuente** source tax; ~ **general sobre la renta** general income tax; ~ **general sobre las ventas** general sales tax; ~ **global** lump-sum tax; ~ **sobre herencias** estate duty, inheritance tax; ~ **impagado** unpaid tax; ~ **indirecto** indirect tax; ~ **sobre las inversiones** investment income tax; ~ **de lujo** luxury tax; ~ **sobre mercancías** commodity tax; ~ **municipal** local tax, ≈ council tax BrE; ~ **sobre la nómina** payroll tax; ~ **sobre el patrimonio** wealth tax, general property tax; ~ **por persona** capitation tax; ~ **sobre la plusvalía** capital gains tax; ~ **sobre la renta** ≈ Income Tax; ~ **sobre la renta de sociedades** corporate tax; ~ **retenido en origen** tax deducted at source; ~ **de rodaje** road tax; ~ **sobre sucesiones** death tax, estate duty, inheritance tax; ~ **de tipo básico** basic-rate tax; ~ **de tipo estándar** standard-rate tax; ~ **de tipo fijo** flat-rate tax; ~ **sobre el tráfico de empresas** turnover tax; ~ **sobre el transporte aéreo** air transportation tax; ~ **sobre el valor añadido** Esp *or* **agregado** AmL ≈ Value Added Tax BrE; ~ **sobre las ventas** sales tax

impugnar *vt* (decisión) challenge; (testamento) contest; (reclamación) dispute

impulsado *adj* driven; ~ **por** driven by; ~ **por el mercado** market-driven

impulsar *vt* (mercado) drive; ~ **una subida** fuel an advance

impulso *m* impetus, momentum; (esfuerzo concertado) drive; **un fuerte** ~ **para el comercio** a major boost for trade; ∼ **competitivo** competitive thrust; ∼ **económico** economic thrust

impulsor, a *m,f* (persona) driving force; ∼ **de algo** driving force behind sth; **fue la ∼a de las reformas** she was the driving force behind the reforms

imputable *adj* chargeable; ∼ **a impuestos** chargeable to tax

imputación *f* (de dinero, cargas) allocation, apportionment; ∼ **de costes** Esp *or* **costos** AmL cost allocation; ∼ **de fondos** (de organismo, proyecto gubernamental) apportionment of funds

imputar *vt* (costes) assign, allocate; ∼**le algo a alguien** attribute sth to sb

inaccesibilidad *f* unavailability

inaceptación *f* nonacceptance

inaceptado *adj* (factura) unaccepted

inactivo *adj* inactive, idle

inadecuado *adj* (recursos, fondos) inadequate

inadvertidamente *adv* inadvertently

inadvertido *adj* unnoticed; **el error pasó ∼** the mistake went unnoticed

inalámbrico[1] *adj* cordless, wireless

inalámbrico[2] *m* cordless telephone

inalcanzable *adj* (objetivo) unachievable, unattainable

inalienable *adj* unalienable

inalterado *adj* unaltered

inanimado *adj* (mercado) lifeless

inapreciable *adj* invaluable

inarchivado *adj* unrecorded

inasegurable *adj* uninsurable

inatacable *adj* unassailable

inauguración *f* opening, inauguration; **ceremonia de ∼** opening ceremony

INB *abr* (▸**ingreso nacional bruto**) GNI (gross national income)

incambiable *adj* unexchangeable

incapacidad *f* (para actividad) inability; (para trabajar) incapacity; (física) disability; ∼ **laboral transitoria** temporary disability benefit; ∼ **para trabajar** incapacity to work

incapacitado *adj* unfit; ∼ **para trabajar** unfit for work

incapaz *adj* (inepto) incompetent; (Der) unfit

incautación *f* confiscation, seizure, impounding

incautar *vt* confiscate, seize, impound

incautarse: ∼ **de** *v pron* (fondos) appropriate

incendio *m* fire; **peligro de ∼** fire hazard; ∼ **forestal** forest fire; ∼ **provocado** arson

incentivación *f* incentive scheme

incentivar *vt* encourage, provide an incentive for; **baja incentivada** voluntary redundancy BrE

incentivo *m* incentive; **baja por ∼** voluntary redundancy BrE; **ofrecer algo como ∼** offer sth as an incentive; ∼ **económico** economic incentive; ∼ **financiero** financial incentive; ∼ **fiscal** tax incentive; ∼ **fiscal sobre opciones** incentive shares option BrE, incentive stock option AmE; ∼ **por productividad** output bonus; ∼ **de ventas** sales incentive

incidencia *f* incidence; ∼ **económica** economic incidence; ∼ **fiscal** tax incidence

incidente *m* incident

incineración *f* (de residuos) incineration

incitación *f* prompt; ∼ **a algo** incitement to sth

incitar *vt* (dar lugar a) incite; ∼ **a alguien a algo** incite sb to sth

incluido *adj* included, including; (en correspondencia) enclosed; ∼ **en la lista negra** blacklisted; **todo ∼** all-in, inclusive; **servicio no ∼** service not included; **con el IVA ∼** including VAT, inclusive of VAT

incluir *vt* include; **sin ∼ algo** exclusive of sth; ∼ **un asunto en el orden del día** place an item on the agenda; ∼ **algo en el presupuesto** budget for sth

inclusión *f* inclusion

inclusive *adj* inclusive; **del 7 al 10, ambos ∼** from the 7th to the 10th inclusive; **domingos ∼** including Sundays

incobrable *adj* uncollectable

incobrables *m pl* bad debts

incombustible *adj* fireproof

incomparecencia *f* nonappearance, failure to appear

incompatible *adj* incompatible

incompetencia *f* incompetence

incompetente *adj* incompetent, unqualified

incompleto *adj* incomplete

incondicional *adj* unconditional

incongruencia *f* inconsistency

inconsumible *adj* unfit for consumption

inconveniente *m* problem, drawback; (desventaja) disadvantage; **si no surge ningún** ∼ if no problems arise; **tener ventajas e** ∼**s** have advantages and disadvantages; **poner** ∼**s** raise objections; **si hay algún** ∼ if there is any problem

incorporable *adj* (Info) add-on

incorporación *f* incorporation; **dos meses después de su** ∼ **a la compañía** two months after she joined the company; ∼ **inmediata** (en anuncio de trabajo) start immediately; ∼ **de reservas** capitalization of reserves

incorporado *adj* incorporated; (Info) built-in; ∼ **al R.U.** UK-incorporated

incorporar *vt* incorporate; ∼ **algo en un contrato** build sth into a contract

incorporarse *v pron*: ∼ **a algo** join sth; ∼ **a un puesto** start a job

incorpóreo *adj* incorporeal

incorrecto *adj* wrong; (irregular) improper

INCOTERM *abr* (*cláusula comercial internacional*) INCOTERM (International Commercial Term)

incremental *adj* incremental

incrementar *vt* increase; ∼ **la producción** increase production

incrementarse *v pron* increase

incremento *m* increase; ∼ **de pedidos** increase in orders; ∼ **en los precios** price increase; ∼ **salarial** salary increase, pay rise BrE, raise AmE

incumbencia *f* term of office; (obligación) duty

incumplimiento *m* nonfulfilment BrE, nonfulfillment AmE; (de la ley) noncompliance; (infracción) breach; ∼ **de contrato** breach of contract; ∼ **del deber** breach of duty; ∼ **de garantía** breach of warranty; ∼ **voluntario** wilful default BrE, willful default AmE

incumplir *vt* breach; (pagos) default on; ∼ **la ley** fail to observe the law

incuria *f* negligence

incurrir *vi*: **incurrir en** (gastos) incur; (error) make; ∼ **en gastos excesivos** incur heavy costs; ∼ **en pérdidas de millones de euros** suffer losses of millions of euros

incursión *f* raid; ∼ **al amanecer** (Bolsa) dawn raid

indebidamente *adv* unduly

indeciso¹ *adj* (ser) indecisive; (estar) undecided

indeciso², **-a** *m,f* (en encuesta) don't know; (en votación) undecided voter

indefinido *adj* indefinite

indemne *adj* undamaged

indemnidad *f* indemnity

indemnizable *adj* indemnifiable

indemnización *f* compensation, indemnity; (por despido) redundancy pay BrE, severance pay; (por mercancías dañadas o perdidas) allowance; **cobrar una** ∼ receive compensation; ∼ **compensatoria** compensatory damages, financial compensation; ∼ **por daños y perjuicios** damages; ∼ **por desempleo** unemployment benefit BrE, unemployment compensation AmE; ∼ **por despido** redundancy pay BrE; ∼ **diaria** daily allowance, daily compensation; ∼ **en especie** allowance in kind; ∼ **por fallecimiento** death benefit; ∼ **de invalidez** disability benefit; ∼ **por pérdida de ingresos** compensation for loss of earnings; ∼ **por traslado** relocation package

indemnizar *vt* compensate, indemnify; ∼ **por daños y perjuicios** compensate for damages

independencia *f* independence; ∼ **en auditoría** audit independence; **con** ∼ **de** independent of, irrespective of

independiente¹ *adj* independent; (asesor) outside; ∼ **de** independent of; **trabajador** ∼ freelance

independiente² *mf* freelance

indexación *f* index-linking, indexation; ∼ **formal** formal indexation

indexado *adj* indexed, index-linked; ∼ **de la moneda** currency-linked

indicación *f* (guía) prompt; **indicaciones** *f pl* directions, instructions; **por** ∼ **de alguien** at the suggestion of sb; ∼ **geográfica protegida** (UE) protected geographic indication, PGI; ∼ **del grupo objetivo** target group index; ∼ **de interés** indication of interest; ∼ **de precio** price cue

indicado *adj* suitable, appropriate; **la persona indicada para el puesto** the best *o* right person for the job

indicador *m* (tendencias) gauge BrE, gage AmE; (econometría) indicator; (Info) flag; ∼ **anticipado** leading indicator; ∼ **de aviso** warning indicator; ∼ **básico** leading indicator; ∼ **de la bolsa** stock index and average; ∼ **comercial** business indicator; ∼ **de desempeño** performance indicator; ∼ **económico**

economic indicator; ∼ **de empleo** employment figure; ∼ **del mercado** market indicator; ∼ **de prosperidad** prosperity o wealth indicator

indicar vt indicate, show; (Info) flag; **como indican los resultados** as the results show

indicativo¹ adj: **ser** ∼ **de** be indicative of

indicativo² m (en radiodifusión) signature tune

índice m index; (tasa, coeficiente) rate; (de audiencia) rating; ∼ **de absorción** absorption rate; ∼ **de audiencia televisiva** audience ratings; ∼ **bursátil** stock market index; ∼ **bursátil del Financial Times** Financial Times Stock-Exchange Index; ∼ **de capitalización bursátil** market capitalization index; ∼ **compuesto** composite index; ∼ **de conversión publicitaria** advertising conversion rate; ∼ **del coste** Esp or **costo** AmL **de la vida** cost-of-living index; ∼ **de cotización de acciones** share index; ∼ **de cotización de valores** stock price index; ∼ **de crecimiento** growth index, growth rate; ∼ **de decadencia** rate of decay; ∼ **de desempleo** unemployment rate; ∼ **Dow Jones** Dow Jones index; ∼ **del Financial Times** Financial Times Index, FT Index; ∼ **Footsie** Footsie, FTSE 100; ∼ **Hang Seng** Hang Seng Index; ∼ **de indicadores anticipados** index of leading indicators; ∼ **de indicadores coincidentes** index of coincident indicators; ∼ **de indicadores retardados** index of lagging indicators; ∼ **de materias** subject index; (en libro) table of contents; ∼ **del mercado monetario** money market rate; ∼ **del mercado de valores** stock market index; ∼ **Nikkei** Nikkei Index; ∼ **de penetración** penetration rate; ∼ **de popularidad** popularity rating; ∼ **de precios** price index; ∼ **de precios al detalle** or **al por menor** retail price index BrE, consumer price index AmE; ∼ **de rendimiento** rate of return; ∼ **de repetición** repeat rate; ∼ **de rotación de existencias** stock turnover rate; ∼ **salarial** salary rate; ∼ **superior** (tipografía) superscript; ∼ **de utilidad bruta** gross profit ratio

indicios m pl evidence; ∼ **concretos** concrete evidence; ∼ **indudables** conclusive evidence

indiferente adj (mercado, comercio) listless

indirectamente adv indirectly

indirecto adj (impuesto) indirect

indiscutible adj unquestionable

indisponerse v pron: ∼ **con algo** fall foul of sth; ∼ **con alguien** fall out with sb

indisponible adj unavailable

individual adj individual; (habitación) single

individualismo m individualism

individualización f individualization

individualmente adv individually

individuo¹ adj individual

individuo² m individual; ∼ **computable** (Fisc) eligible individual

indivisibilidad f indivisibility

indización f index-linking; (Info) indexing; ∼ **salarial** wage indexation

indizar vt index-link; (Info) index

industria f industry; (V&M) trade; **entre** ∼**s** industry to industry; ∼ **abastecedora** upstream industry; ∼ **del acero** steel industry; ∼ **agrícola-alimentaria** agrifood industry; ∼ **agropecuaria** agribusiness; ∼ **alimenticia** food-processing industry; ∼ **artesanal** cottage industry; ∼ **automotriz** or **de la automoción**, ∼ **automovilística** car industry BrE, automotive industry AmE; ∼**s avanzadas** leading industries; ∼ **bancaria** banking industry; ∼**s básicas** staple industries; ∼ **caída en desgracia** out-of-favour industry BrE, out-of-favor industry AmE; ∼ **del carbón** coal industry; ∼ **casera** cottage industry; ∼ **cíclica** cyclical industry; ∼ **cinematográfica** film industry BrE, motion-picture industry AmE; ∼ **clave** key industry; ∼ **consolidada** sunset industry; ∼ **en crecimiento** growth industry; ∼ **decadente** ailing industry; ∼ **en desaparición** declining industry; ∼ **en desarrollo** growth industry; ∼ **farmacéutica** pharmaceutical industry; ∼ **financiera** financial industry; ∼ **incipiente** infant industry, sunrise industry; ∼ **ligera** light industry; ∼ **manufacturera** manufacturing industry; ∼ **militar** arms industry, defence industry BrE, defense industry AmE; ∼ **nacional** domestic industry; ∼ **nacionalizada** nationalized industry; ∼ **del ocio** leisure industry; ∼ **pesada** heavy industry; ∼ **pesquera** fishing industry; ∼ **petrolera** oil industry; ∼**s** ⋯⋗

protegidas sheltered industries; ∼ **de la publicidad** advertising industry; ∼ **de recreación** leisure industry; ∼ **regulada** regulated industry; ∼ **de servicios** service industry; ∼ **de servicios financieros** financial services industry; ∼ **siderúrgica** iron and steel industry; ∼ **de las telecomunicaciones** telecommunications industry; ∼ **turística** tourist trade

industrial *adj* industrial

industrialismo *m* industrialism

industrialista *mf* industrialist

industrialización *f* industrialization

industrializado *adj* industrialized

industrializar *vt* industrialize

INE *abr* (▸**Instituto Nacional de Estadística**) ≈ CSO (≈ Central Statistical Office) BrE

ineficacia *f* (de persona, máquina, organización) inefficiency

ineficiencia *f* inefficiency

ineficiente *adj* inefficient

inelasticidad *f* inelasticity; ∼ **de la oferta/demanda** inelasticity of supply/demand

INEM *abr* (▸**Instituto Nacional de Empleo**) ≈ Employment Service BrE

inercia *f* inertia; ∼ **industrial** industrial inertia

inestable *adj* (mercado bursátil) volatile, jumpy

inevitable *adj* unavoidable

inevitablemente *adv* inevitably

inexactitud *f* inaccuracy

inexigible *adj* unenforceable

inexplicado *adj* unaccounted for

infalible *adj* unfailing

infectado *adj* (Info) infected; **no** ∼ uninfected

inferior *adj* (producto) inferior, down-market; ∼ **al nivel medio** substandard; ∼ **al precio de mercado** below-market price

infidelidad *f* (Der) misfeasance; ∼ **reincidente** double-dipping

infidencia *f* (acto) misfeasance, breach of trust

infiltración *f* infiltration, seepage

infiltrarse *v pron* infiltrate; (en sistema informático) hack into

infinito *adj* infinite; **hasta lo** ∼ ad infinitum

inflación *f* inflation; ∼ **básica** core inflation; ∼ **contenida** suppressed

inflation; ∼ **controlada** administered inflation; ∼ **de costes** Esp *or* **costos** AmL cost-push inflation; ∼ **creciente** rising inflation; ∼ **de demanda** demand-pull inflation; ∼ **desenfrenada** runaway inflation; ∼ **fiscal** taxflation; ∼ **galopante** galloping inflation; ∼ **inerte** inertial inflation; ∼ **larvada** hidden inflation; ∼ **mundial** world inflation; ∼ **reptante** creeping inflation; ∼ **de salarios** wage inflation; ∼ **subyacente** underlying inflation

inflacionario *adj* inflationary

inflacionista *adj* inflationist

inflar *vt* (economía) inflate; (cuentas, fondos) swell; ∼ **la bolsa** *or* **el mercado** churn the market

inflexible *adj* inflexible

influencia *f* influence, leverage; ∼ **fiscal** tax influence; ∼ **personal** personal influence

influenciar *vt* influence

influir ☐ *vt* (decisión) influence ☐ *vi*: ∼ **en** (resultado) influence, sway

influyente *adj* influential

infografía *f* computer graphics

infopista *f* information highway

información *f* information; (noticias) news; **obtener** ∼ get information; **para más** ∼ for further details, for further information; **para su** ∼ for your information, FYI; ∼ **actualizada** up-to-date information; ∼ **básica** background information; ∼ **sobre competidores** competitor intelligence; ∼ **confidencial** confidential information; ∼ **de control** control information; ∼ **sobre créditos** credit information; ∼ **durante el vuelo** in-flight information; ∼ **equívoca** misleading information; ∼ **falsa** false information; ∼ **financiera** financial information, white information; ∼ **general** personal particulars; ∼ **de la gestión** management information; ∼ **de marketing** marketing intelligence; ∼ **personal** particulars; ∼ **privilegiada** inside information, privileged information; ∼ **publicada** published information; ∼ **de vuelo** flight information

informado *adj* (decisión, argumento) informed; **estar** ∼ **de algo** be informed about sth; **mantener a alguien** ∼ keep sb informed; **estar mal** ∼ be misinformed

informal *adj* informal

informalidad *f* informality

informante *mf* (de prensa) source; (de policía) informer

informar ① *vt* inform, brief; ~ **a alguien de algo** inform sb of sth, tell sb about sth

② *vi* report; **según** ~**on en la prensa** according to newspaper reports; ~ **sobre algo** report on sth

informática *f* computing, information technology, IT; ~ **gráfica** computer graphics

informático¹ *adj* computer; **sistema** ~ computer system; **servicios** ~**s** computer services

informático², **-a** *m,f* computer expert

informatización *f* computing

informatizado *adj* computer-based, computerized

informatizar *vt* computerize

informe *m* report; (Cont) statement, reporting; ~ **de la actividad diaria** daily activity report; ~ **anual** annual report; ~ **de auditoría** audit report; ~ **de averías** survey report; ~ **de la conferencia** conference report; ~ **confidencial** insider report; ~ **crediticio** credit report; ~ **del ejercicio** debriefing; ~ **de evaluación** appraisal report; ~ **externo** external report; ~ **del gobierno** government report; ~ **intermedio** interim report; ~ **legal** statutory report; ~ **de la posición neta** net position report; ~ **provisional** interim statement, interim report; ~ **provisional de riesgo** exposure draft; ~ **resumido** summary report, condensed report; ~ **con salvedades** qualified report; ~ **de la situación** situation report, status report; ~ **sobre el mercado** market report; ~ **de viabilidad** feasibility report; ~ **de visita** call report, contact report

infovía *f* information highway

infra- *pref* infra-

infracapitalizado *adj* undercapitalized

infracción *f* infringement, unlawful trespass; ~ **fiscal** tax offence BrE, tax offense AmE

infractor, a *m,f* infringer, offender; ~**es de la ley tributaria** tax offenders

infraestructura *f* infrastructure; ~ **de clave pública** public key infrastructure, PKI

infraocupado *adj* underemployed

infrautilizar *vt* underuse; (recursos) underutilize

infravaloración *f* underestimation, undervaluation

infravalorado *adj* undervalued

infravalorar *vt* undervalue

infringir *vt* break, violate, infringe

infructuoso *adj* fruitless, unprofitable

infundado *adj* groundless

ingeniería *f* engineering; ~ **asistida por computadora** AmL *or* **ordenador** Esp computer-assisted engineering; ~ **aeronáutica** aeronautical engineering; ~ **civil** civil engineering; ~ **del conocimiento** knowledge engineering; ~ **eléctrica** electrical engineering; ~ **estructural** structural engineering; ~ **financiera** financial engineering; ~ **genética** genetic engineering; ~ **industrial** industrial engineering; ~ **informática** computer technology; ~ **invertida** reverse engineering; ~ **mecánica** mechanical engineering; ~ **de precisión** precision engineering; ~ **química** chemical engineering; ~ **de producción** production engineering; ~ **de programas** software engineering; ~ **de sistemas** systems engineering

ingeniero, -a *m,f* engineer; ~ **aeronáutico(a)** aeronautical engineer; ~ **de calidad** quality engineer; ~ **civil** civil engineer; ~ **del conocimiento** knowledge engineer; ~ **consultor(a)** *m,f* consultant engineer; ~ **de diseño** design engineer; ~ **industrial** civil engineer, industrial engineer; ~ **informático(-a)** *m,f* computer engineer; ~ **de mantenimiento** maintenance engineer; ~ **de obra** site engineer; ~ **de producto** product engineer; ~ **de programación** software engineer; ~ **de red** network engineer; ~ **de reparaciones** service engineer; ~ **de servicio** service engineer; ~**, -a de sistemas** systems engineer

ingeniosidad *f* ingenuity

ingresar ① *vt* (Esp dinero) pay in, bank, deposit; (al hospital) admit

② *vi* (en la Universidad) start; ~ **al mercado del trabajo** enter the labour BrE *o* labor AmE market

ingreso *m* (Esp depósito) deposit; (ganancia) income; (en una organización) entry; (en hospital) admission; ~**s** income, revenue; (futuros) receipts; **de bajo** ~ low-paid; **fecha de** ~ **en la empresa** date of joining the company; **otros** ~**s** *mpl* other income; **tras su** ~ **en el hospital** after he was admitted to hospital, following his admission to ⋯⋗

hospital; ~**s accesorios** additional income; ~ **activo** active income; ~**s acumulados** accrued income; ~ **ajustado** adjusted income; ~ **ajustado a la inflación** inflation-adjusted income; ~ **bajo** low pay; ~ **básico** basic income; ~ **bruto** gross revenue, gross income; ~ **compuesto** compound yield; ~**s corrientes** actual earnings; ~**s después de impuestos** income after tax; ~**s diferidos** deferred income; ~ **disponible** disposable income; ~ **por dividendos** dividend income; ~**s en efectivo** cash earnings; ~**s y egresos** income and expenditure, ingress and egress; ~**s estimados** estimated revenue; ~**s fiscales** tax receipts; ~**s y gastos** income and outgoings, income and expenditure; ~**s libres de impuestos** tax-exempt income; ~**s netos** net receipts; ~**s de operación** operating costs; ~ **percibido** earned income; ~ **principal** prime entry; ~ **promedio** average revenue; ~**s publicitarios** advertising revenue; ~**s reales** actual earnings; ~**s sujetos a imposición** income subject to tax; ~ **total** total revenue; ~**s por ventas** sales revenue

inhibidor m inhibitor

inhóspito adj inhospitable

iniciación f beginning; (introducción) introduction; ~ **del producto** product initiation

iniciador, a m,f initiator; ~ **de una moda** trendsetter

inicial adj initial; (salario, capital) starting

inicializar vt (sistemas operativos) initialize, boot up

iniciar vt (programas) start, initiate; (V&M) launch; ~ **a alguien en algo** initiate sb into sth; (empleo) start sb off as sth; **que inicia una moda** trendsetting; ~ **la conexión** log on; (al Internet) connect; ~ **el despegue de algo** (de negocios, proyecto) set sth up, get sth off the ground; ~ **un juicio** bring an action; ~ **la sesión** log in o on

iniciativa f initiative; **actuar por** ~ **propia** act on one's own initiative; **tomar la** ~ take the initiative; **tener** ~ show initiative; **una nueva** ~ a new initiative; ~ **privada** private enterprise

inicio m start, commencement (frml); ~ **de la cobertura** commencement of cover BrE o coverage AmE; ~ **de texto** start of text

injuriador, a m,f tortfeasor

injusticia f injustice; (Der) miscarriage of justice

injusto adj unjust, unfair

inmanejable adj unmanageable

inmigración f (internacional) immigration; ~ **ilegal** illegal immigration

inmigrante mf immigrant; ~ **ilegal** illegal immigrant

inmobiliaria f estate agent's BrE, real-estate agency AmE; (Banca) credit bank, Spanish mortgage bank

inmodificado adj unchanged

inmovilizado m capital assets; ~ **inmaterial** intangible assets; ~ **material** tangible fixed assets

inmueble m building, property; ~ **inmueble comercial** trading estate; ~**s personales** personal property

inmunidad f immunity; ~ **diplomática** diplomatic immunity; ~ **fiscal** tax exemption; ~ **legal** legal immunity; (de sindicatos) statutory immunity

inmunización f immunization

inmunizar vt immunize

innecesario adj unnecessary

innegociable adj unnegotiable

innominado adj (Info) (disco, archivo) unnamed

innovación f innovation; ~ **estratégica** strategic innovation; ~ **tecnológica** technological innovation

innovador[1] adj innovative

innovador[2]**, a** m,f innovator

innovar vi innovate

inobservancia f (de condiciones) nonobservance; (de ley) violation

inocente adj innocent; **lo declararon** ~ he was found not guilty

input m (Info) input; ~**-output** input-output

inquietud f unrest; ~ **laboral** labour unrest BrE, labor unrest AmE

inquilinato m tenancy; (contrato) tenancy agreement

inquilino, -a m,f tenant; ~ **inamovible** anchor tenant; ~ **en posesión** sitting tenant BrE, holdover tenant AmE; ~ **vitalicio(-a)** m,f life tenant

inscribir vt register; (en curso) enrol BrE, enroll AmE

inscribirse v pron register, put one's name down; (en curso) enrol BrE, enroll AmE; (en concurso) enter; ~ **en el censo**

electoral put one's name down on the
electoral register, register to vote

inscripción *f* enrolment BrE,
enrollment AmE, registration; (en concurso)
entry

inscrito, -a *m,f* registrant; **no ∼** *m,f*
nonregistrant; **sólo los ∼s en el censo
electoral tendrán el derecho a votar**
only people on the electoral register will
have the right to vote

insensible *adj* (mercado) unresponsive;
∼ a los fallos fault-tolerant

insertar *vt* insert; (Info) paste; **∼ un
anuncio en algo** place an ad in sth

insignificante *adj* insignificant

insistir *vi* insist; **es inútil insistir** there
is no point insisting *o* going on about it;
insiste, al final alguien te contestará
keep trying, someone will have to
answer in the end; **∼ en que ...** insist
that ...; **∼ en un precio más alto** hold
out for a higher price

insoluble *adj* insoluble

insoluto *adj* (deuda) outstanding

insolvencia *f* insolvency, bankruptcy

insolvente *adj* bankrupt, insolvent

inspección *f* inspection, examination;
∼ aduanera customs inspection; **∼
catastral** cadastral survey; **∼ de
expedientes** inspection of files; **∼ de
Hacienda** tax inspection; **∼ de
personal** staff inspection; **∼ de
seguridad** safety check; **I∼ Técnica de
Vehículos** ≈ MOT BrE, ≈ Ministry of
Transport Test BrE

inspeccionar *vt* inspect; (personal)
supervise; **∼ la situación** survey the
situation

inspector, a *m,f* inspector, controller;
(supervisor) supervisor; (Inmob) surveyor;
∼ de aduanas customs officer; **∼ de
calidad** quality controller; **∼ de
cantidades** quantity surveyor; **∼ de
Hacienda** tax inspector; **∼
recaudador(a)** *m,f* collection agent,
encashing agent; **∼ de sanidad** health
officer; **∼ de trabajo** labour inspector
BrE, labor inspector AmE

instalación *f* (activo fijo) plant; (Info)
facility; (Inmob) fixture; **instalaciones**
fpl facilities; **∼ de almacenamiento**
storage facility; **∼ de apoyo** backup
facility; **instalaciones de atención
infantil** childcare facilities; **∼
comercial** trade fixture; **∼ de crédito**
credit *o* borrowing facility; **∼
defectuosa** faulty installation;
instalaciones para el ocio leisure

facilities; **∼ recreativa** recreational
facility

instalado *adj* installed BrE, instaled
AmE

instalador, -a *m,f* installer, fitter

instalar *vt* (programa, periféricos) install
BrE, instal AmE; (ordenador, vídeo, oficina) set
up

instancia *f* official request; (Der)
petition; (autoridad) authority; **a ∼ de** at
the request of; **en esta ∼** in this
instance; **en última ∼** as a last resort;
las más altas ∼s the highest authorities

instantánea *f* (publicidad, sesión
fotográfica) shoot

instante *m* moment; **al ∼** right away;
información al ∼ up-to-the-minute
information

instar *vt* urge; **∼ a alguien a hacer
algo** urge sb to do sth; **lo ∼on a asistir**
they urged him to attend

instigar *vt* incite; **∼ a alguien a algo/
hacer algo** incite sb to sth/do sth

instinto *m* instinct; **por ∼**
instinctively; **tener ∼ para los negocios**
have a good business instinct *o* sense; **∼
adquisitivo** acquisitive instinct

institución *f* institution; **∼ de ahorro
y préstamo** savings institution BrE,
thrift institution AmE; **∼ bancaria**
banking institution; **∼ benéfica**
charity; **∼ de crédito** lending
institution; **∼ financiera** financial
institution; **∼ política** political
institution; **∼ privada** private
institution

instituto *m* institute; **I∼ de Crédito
Oficial** *Spanish official credit institute*;
I∼ de Estudios Financieros *Spanish
financial research institute*; **I∼ Europeo
de Normas de Telecomunicaciones**
European Telecommunications
Standards Institute; **I∼ de Mediación,
Arbitraje y Conciliación** Esp
*independent conciliation service, involved
in disputes between trade unions and
management*; **I∼ Monetario Europeo**
European Monetary Institute; **I∼
Nacional de Empleo** *government office
for employment*, ≈ Employment Service
BrE; **∼ Nacional de Estadística** ≈
Central Statistical Office BrE

instrucción *f* instruction; (formación)
training; (Info) command; **instrucciones**
f pl instructions; **∼ asistida por
computadora** AmL *or* **ordenador** Esp
computer-aided instruction; **∼ de
embalaje** packing instruction; **∼ de** ⋯⋗

envío forwarding instruction; ~ **de máquina** computer instruction; **instrucciones de uso** directions for use

instructor, a *m,f* instructor; (para capacitación) trainer

instruir *vt* (capacitar) train; (informar) brief; (Der) try, hear; ~ **a alguien sobre algo** brief sb on sth; ~ **una causa** try *o* hear a case

instrumental *adj* instrumental; (Der) documentary; **prueba** ~ documentary evidence

instrumentalidad *f* instrumentality

instrumentar *vt* (sistema, plan) implement

instrumento *m* instrument; ~ **de descuento** discount instrument; ~ **financiero** financial instrument; ~ **legal** statutory instrument; ~ **liberado** paid instrument; ~ **del mercado monetario** money market instrument; ~ **al portador** bearer instrument

insuficiencia *f* shortfall; (de personal) shortage; ~ **de medios** lack of resources; ~**s del sistema** inadequacies of the system

insumos *m pl* consumables, inputs

insurrecto, -a *m,f* insurgent

intangible *adj* intangible; **activos** ~**s** intangible assets

integración *f* integration; ~ **de algo/ alguien en algo** integration of sth/sb into sth; **la** ~ **de grupos minoritarios en la sociedad** the integration of minority groups into society; ~ **económica** economic integration; ~ **de E/S** spooling; ~ **informática-telefonía** computer-telephony integration; ~ **progresiva/regresiva** forward/ backward integration

integrado *adj* integrated; (Info) built-in

integral *adj* integral; (total) comprehensive; (incorporado) built-in; **una reforma** ~ a comprehensive reform

integrar *vt* (formar) make up; (incorporar) incorporate; (en un grupo) integrate; **los países que integran la UE** the countries which make up the EU; ~ **algo/ alguien en algo** integrate sth/sb into sth; **dos empresas más integradas al grupo** two more companies incorporated into the group; ~ **los nuevos socios en el grupo** integrate the new members into the group

integrarse *v pron* integrate; (unirse) join; ~ **en algo** integrate into sth, fit into sth; **se integró muy rápido en el**

equipo he fitted into the team very quickly; **países deseando** ~ **a la UE** countries wishing to join the EU

integridad *f* integrity; (Cont) completeness; **en su** ~ completely; ~ **de los datos** data integrity; ~ **fiscal** fiscal rectitude; ~ **física** personal safety; **han garantizado la** ~ **física de los detenidos** the prisoners' safety has been guaranteed

íntegro *adj* complete, whole; (edición) unabridged; (película) uncut; **comprar algo a precio** ~ pay full price for sth; **versión íntegra** full-length version

intelectual[1] *adj* intellectual

intelectual[2] *mf* intellectual

inteligencia *f* intelligence; ~ **artificial** artificial intelligence; ~ **económica** economic intelligence; ~ **electrónica** electronic intelligence

inteligente *adj* intelligent, clever; **tarjeta** ~ smart card

intempestivo *adj* (visita) untimely, inopportune; (fuera de estación) unseasonal

intención *f* intention; **con** ~ deliberately; **con mala** ~ maliciously; **con la** ~ **de hacer algo** with the intention of doing sth; **tener (la)** ~ **de hacer algo** intend to do sth; **lo hizo con buena** ~ she meant well

intensificación *f* intensification; ~ **del capital** capital deepening

intensificar *vt* (esfuerzo) intensify; (Econ) tighten; (huelga) step up; ~ **las restricciones monetarias** tighten the monetary reins

intensificarse *v pron* intensify

intensivo *adj* intensive; **cursos** ~**s** crash courses; ~ **en capital** capital-intensive; ~ **en conocimientos** knowledge-intensive; ~ **en trabajo** labour-intensive BrE, labor-intensive AmE *ver tb* ▸**jornada**

intentar *vt* attempt, try; ~ **hacer algo** try to do sth

intento *m* (tentativa) attempt; **al segundo** ~ at the second attempt, second time around; ~ **de asesinato** attempted murder; ~ **fracasado** failed attempt

interactividad *f* interactivity

interactivo *adj* interactive; **televisión/computación interactiva** interactive television/computing

intercalación *f* (con clasificación) collation

intercalado *adj* (en texto) inserted; (páginas) collated; (Info) embedded

intercalar *vt* insert; (Info) embed; ~ **ilustraciones en el texto** insert illustrations in *o* into the text

intercambiar *vt* (información, puntos de vista) exchange

intercambio *m* exchange; ~ **de cartas** exchange of letters; ~ **de cartera** portfolio switching; ~ **comercial** trade; ~ **de contratos** exchange of contracts; ~ **electrónico de datos** electronic data interchange; ~ **de la deuda** debt swap; ~ **electrónico de documentos** electronic document interchange; ~ **de ideas** exchange of ideas; ~ **de información** exchange of information; ~ **de monedas** currency swap; ~ **de opciones** options exchange

interceptar *vt* (carta) intercept; (teléfono) tap; (carretera) block off

interclasificadora *f* collator

interconectar *vt* interconnect; (Info) network

interconectarse *v pron* (Info) attach

interconexión *f* interconnection; (Info) attachment; ~ **de sistemas abiertos** open systems interconnection

intercontinental *adj* intercontinental

interdepartamental *adj* interdepartmental

interdependencia *f* interdependence; ~ **estratégica** strategic interdependence

interdependiente *adj* interdependent

interdicto *m* interdiction, prohibition, ban; ~ **mandatario** mandatory injunction

interempresa *adj* business-to-business, B2B

interés *m* interest; **cobrar intereses** charge interest; **con** ~ interest-bearing; **devengar** *or* **ganar** ~ earn interest; **pagan un 10% de** ~ they pay 10% interest; **poner** ~ **en algo** take an interest in sth; **que no devenga** ~ noninterest-bearing; **sin** ~ noninterest-bearing; (préstamo) interest-free; **tasa** *or* **tipo de** ~ interest rate; **tener** ~ **en algo** be interested in sth; **un conflicto de intereses** a conflict of interests; ~ **acumulado** accrued interest, accumulated interest; ~ **aditivo** add-on interest; ~ **anual** annual interest; ~ **bancario** bank interest; ~ **base** base rate interest; ~ **comercial** commercial interest, business interest; ~ **compuesto** compound interest; ~ **compuesto acumulado** accrued

compound interest; **intereses creados** vested interests; ~ **devengado** earned interest, accrued interest; ~ **fijo** fixed interest; ~ **material** (en empresa) material interest; ~ **mayoritario/minoritario** majority/minority interest

interesado, -a *m,f* interested party; **los** ~**s deben rellenar un formulario** anyone interested should fill in a form

interesar ⓵ *vi* be of interest; **este anuncio podría** ~**te** this advert could be of interest to you, you might be interested in this advert; ~**ía comprobar los datos** it would be interesting *o* useful to check the data ⓶ *vt*: ~ **a alguien en algo** interest sb in sth, get sb interested in sth; **logramos** ~**los en la idea** we managed to get them interested in the idea

interestatal *adj* (en los EEUU) interstate; **comercio** ~ interstate trade

interfaz *m* interface; ~ **de buscador** browser interface; ~ **común de pasarela** Common Gateway Interface, CGI; ~ **paralelo** parallel interface; ~ **para programas de aplicación** application program interface, API; ~ **de usuario** user interface; ~ **usuario gráfico** Graphical User Interface, GUI; ~ **usuario web** Web front end

interferencia *f* interference; (Info) glitch

interferir *vi* interfere; ~ **en algo** interfere in sth

interfondo *m* (internacional) interfund

intergrupal *adj* intergroup

intergubernamental *adj* intergovernmental

interín *m* interim; **en el** ~ in the interim

interino *adj* (trabajador, cargo) temporary; (medida) interim; **gobierno** ~ interim government; **director** ~ acting manager; **profesor** ~ supply teacher

interior *m* interior, inside; **en el** ~ **del partido** within the party; ~ **de la contraportada** inside back cover; ~ **de la portada** inside front cover

interlínea *f* (imprenta) line space

interlocutorio *adj* interlocutory

intermediación *f* mediation; (Fin) brokerage; ~ **electrónica** e-brokering, electronic brokering; ~ **financiera** financial intermediation

intermediario¹ *adj* intermediary

intermediario², -a *m,f* intermediary, middleman; (mediador) mediator; (Bolsa) ⋯⋗

broker, dealer, trader; ~ **autorizado(-a)** *m,f* authorized dealer; ~ **electrónico(-a)** *m,f* e-broker, electronic broker; ~ **financiero(-a)** *m,f* financial mediator; (Bolsa) broker; ~ **fiscal** fiscal agent; ~ **del mercado monetario** money market trader; ~ **de la publicidad en línea** Web (ad) broker; ~ **de renta fija** bond trader

intermedio *adj* intermediate; **de precio** ~ medium-priced

intermitente *adj* intermittent

intermodal *adj* intermodal

internacional *adj* international; noticias ~es foreign news

internacionalización *f* internationalization

internacionalizar *vt* internationalize

internalización *f* internalization

internalizar *vt* internalize

internauta *mf* Internet user, surfer; **de** ~ **a** ~ by word of mouse; ~ **mayor** silver surfer

Internet *m* Internet, Net; **de** ~ Internet; **compañía de** ~ Internet company; **en el** ~ on the Internet; **estar conectado al** ~ be connected to the Internet; **encontrar algo en el** ~ find sth on the Internet; ~ **de alta velocidad** high-speed Internet; ~ **de banda ancha** broadband Internet; ~ **móvil** mobile Internet; ~ **sin cables** wireless Internet *o* Web

interno¹ *adj* (llamada, departamento) internal; (comercio) domestic; (traductor, servicio) in-house

interno² *m* AmL telephone extension

interoperabilidad *f* interoperability

interponer *vt* (demanda, denuncia) lodge; ~ **una acción** bring an action

interpretación *f* interpretation; (profesión) interpreting; ~ **simultánea** simultaneous interpreting

interpretador *m* (Info) interpreter

interpretar *vti* interpret; ~ **mal** misinterpret, misunderstand

intérprete *mf* (de lenguas) interpreter; **servir de** ~ act as interpreter

interrogación *f* interrogation; (Info) query; **signo de** ~ question mark

interrogar *vt* (testigo) question; (por policía) interrogate; (Info) query

interrogatorio *m* interrogation, questioning

interrumpir *vt* (persona, reunión, emisión) interrupt; (negociaciones) break off; (suministro) cut off; (misión, despegue,

operación) abort; (acortar) cut short; ~ **el subsidio de alguien** stop sb's allowance

interrupción *f* interruption; (de negociaciones) breakdown; ~ **de actividades** interruption of business; ~ **de la carrera profesional** career interruption; ~ **natural** natural break; ~ **de las operaciones** operations breakdown; ~ **del pago** payment holiday, pay pause; ~ **del trabajo** work stoppage

interruptor *m* (dispositivo) switch; (Info) toggle; ~ **basculante** *or* **de palanca** toggle switch

interurbano *adj* inter-city; **llamada interurbana** long-distance call

intervalo *m* interval; **a** ~**s de cuatro horas** at four-hour intervals

intervención *f* intervention; (Cont) audit; (de teléfono) tapping; **de no** ~ nonintervention; **política de no** ~ policy of nonintervention; ~ **continua** continuous audit; ~ **estatal** state intervention, government intervention; ~ **fiscal** tax audit; ~ **interior de cuentas** internal audit; ~ **a posteriori** post-audit; ~ **a priori** pre-audit

intervencionista *adj* interventionist

intervenir ⓵ *vt* (cuentas) audit; (llamada telefónica) tap into; (armas, droga) seize ⓶ *vi* intervene; ~ **en algo** (mediar) intervene in sth; (influir) play a part in sth; **diversos factores intervinieron en la decisión** various factors played a part in the decision

interventor, a *m,f* inspector; ~ **de cuentas** auditor

intestado *adj* intestate; **morir** ~ die intestate

intimidación *f* intimidation; **ser objecto de** ~ be subjected to intimidation

intracomunitario *adj* (UE) intra-Community, within the EU

intradepartamental *adj* intradepartmental

intraestatal *adj* (en los EEUU) intrastate

intranet *m* intranet

intransferible *adj* untransferable, not transferable; (Der) unassignable

introducción *f* (de libro, conferencia) introduction; ~ **a algo** introduction to sth; **la** ~ **del euro** the introduction of the euro; **la** ~ **del producto en el mercado** the launch of the product on the market; ~ **de datos** data input

introducir *vt* introduce; (Info) imput; ~ **progresivamente** (tecnología, servicios, sistema) phase in; ~ **un nuevo producto en el mercado** bring a new product out onto the market; ~ **por teclado** key in, input

introducirse: ~ **en** *v pron* enter; ~ **en el mercado** get into *o* enter the market

intrusión *f* intrusion; (Der) encroachment

intruso[1] *adj* intrusive

intruso[2]**, -a** *m,f* intruder; (en organización) outsider

inutilizable *adj* unusable, unfit for use

inutilizado *adj* (línea de crédito) non-utilized

invalidación *f* invalidation

invalidar *vt* invalidate; (contrato) void

invariable *adj* (precio) constant, stable; (mercado) flat, steady

invasión *f* invasion; (Der) encroachment; (de propiedad) trespassing

invención *f* invention

invendible *adj* unmarketable, unsaleable

invendido *adj* unsold

inventar *vt* invent

inventario *m* (lista) inventory; (actividad) stocktaking; **cerrado por** ~ closed for stocktaking; **hacer un** ~ to do a stocktake; ~ **de apertura/cierre** beginning/closing inventory; ~ **contable** detailed account; ~ **de existencias** stock inventory

inventor, a *m,f* inventor; ~ **único(-a)** *m,f* sole inventor

inversamente *adv* inversely

inversión *f* investment; **inversiones** *f pl* investments; ~ **en acciones ordinarias** common share investment BrE, common stock investment AmE; ~ **activa** active investment; ~ **de capital** capital investment; ~ **ética** ethical investment; ~ **extranjera** foreign investment, offshore investment; ~ **financiera** financial investment; ~ **del sector privado** private-sector investment; ~ **segura** secure investment

inversionista *mf* investor

inverso *adj* reverse; **a la inversa** conversely; **en orden** ~ in reverse order

inversor, a *m,f* investor; ~ **en acciones** equity investor; ~ **corporativo(-a)** *m,f* corporate investor; ~ **extranjero(-a)** *m,f* foreign investor,

overseas investor; ~ **hostil** greenmailer; ~ **individual** individual investor; ~ **inmobiliario(-a)** *m,f* property investor; ~ **potencial** potential investor; ~ **privado(-a)** *m,f* private investor; ~ **público(-a)** *m,f* public investor

invertido *adj* (dinero) invested; (imagen) inverted; **orden** ~ reverse order

invertir *vti* invest; (tendencia) reverse; (imagen) invert; ~ **en acciones** invest in shares; ~ **con cobertura** hedge one's bets; ~ **dinero en algo** invest money in sth; ~ **en obligaciones** invest in bonds; ~ **en propiedades** invest in property

invertirse *v pron* (tendencia) reverse

investigación *f* investigation; (académica, científica) research; **llevar a cabo** *or* **realizar una** ~ **sobre algo** (caso, delito) conduct an investigation into sth; (académica, científica) research into sth; ~ **académica** academic research; ~ **de antecedentes** (del solicitante) background check; ~ **aplicada** applied research; ~ **básica** basic research; ~ **de campo** field research; ~ **científica** scientific research; ~ **de clientes** customer research; ~ **conductista** behavioural research BrE, behavioral research AmE; ~ **del consumidor** consumer research; ~ **cualitativa** qualitative research; ~ **cuantitativa** quantitative research; ~ **de datos ya existentes** desk research; ~ **y desarrollo** research and development; ~ **económica** economic research; ~ **por encuestas** survey research; ~ **independiente** independent inquiry; ~ **de mercado** market research; ~ **permanente** ongoing research; ~ **del producto** product research; ~ **pura** blue-sky research

investigador, a *m,f* investigator; (académico) researcher; ~ **de campo** field researcher

investigar *vt* (delito) investigate; (V&M) research; (posibilidad) explore, look into

investir *vt* inaugurate; ~ **a alguien de algo** invest sb with sth

invitación *f* invitation

invocar *vt* (ley, penalización) invoke

inyección *f* (de dinero) injection; ~ **de capital** capital injection

inyectar *vt* (fondos) inject

IPD *abr* (▸**índice de precios al detalle**) RPI (Retail Price Index) BrE, CPI (Consumer Price Index) AmE

ir *vi* go; ~ **por buen/mal camino** be on the right/wrong track; ~ **en contra de** ⋯▸

algo go against sth; ∼ **a contracorriente** go against the tide; ∼ **con la corriente** go with the flow; ∼ **cuesta abajo** (negocios) go downhill; ∼ **directo a** go straight to; ∼ **al grano** get straight to the point; ∼**se a pique** (infrml) (negocio) go to the wall (infrml); ∼ **a la quiebra** go out of business, go bankrupt

IRPF *abr* (►**impuesto sobre la renta**) ≈ IT (Income Tax)

irrealizable *adj* unfeasible

irrebatible *adj* irrefutable

irrecuperable *adj* (datos) unrecoverable, irretrievable

irredimible *adj* irredeemable

irreductible *adj* (actitud) unyielding

irreemplazable *adj* irreplaceable

irrefutable *adj* (indicio) irrefutable

irregular *adj* (procedimiento, acción) irregular; (tendencia) abnormal

irregularidad *f* irregularity; ∼**es en el proceso electoral** irregularities in the electoral process

irrelevante *adj* irrelevant

irreparable *adj* (pérdida, daño) irreparable

irreprochable *adj* (contrato, evidencia) unimpeachable

irrescatable *adj* irredeemable

irreversible *adj* (estrategia) irreversible

irrevocable *adj* (decisión) irrevocable

irrumpir *vi*: ∼ **en algo** (mercado) break into sth

ISBN *abr* (►**Numeración Internacional Normalizada de Libros**) ISBN (International Standard Book Number)

isocosto *m* isocost

isocuanta *f* isoquant

ISRS *abr* (►**impuesto sobre la renta de sociedades**) corporate tax

ITE *abr* (►**impuesto sobre el tráfico de empresas**) turnover tax

ítem *m* item

itemizar *vt* itemize

iteración *f* iteration

itinerario *m* itinerary

ITV *abr* (►**Inspección Técnica de Vehículos**) ≈ MOT (Ministry of Transport test) BrE

IVA *abr* (►**impuesto sobre el valor añadido** Esp *or* **agregado** AmL) VAT (Value Added Tax) BrE

izquierda *f* left; **de** ∼ left-wing

izquierdismo *m* leftism

izquierdista *mf* left-winger

Jj

japonización *f* japanization

jefe, -a *m,f* (encargado) boss; (de negocio) manager; (de sección) head; (de equipo) leader; ~ **administrativo(-a)** *m,f* administration officer; (Der) senior clerk; ~ **de almacén** stock controller; ~ **de auditoría** audit head; ~ **de caja** cash manager; ~ **de capacitación** training officer; ~ **de cobros** (Banca) drawing officer; ~ **comercial** commercial director, commercial manager; ~ **de compras** chief buyer; ~ **de contabilidad** chief accountant; ~ **contable** Esp, ~ **contador(-a)** *m,f* AmL head accountant; ~ **de contratación** recruitment officer; ~ **de control de tráfico** chief traffic controller; ~ **de créditos** credit officer; ~ **de departamento** head of department; (de grandes almacenes) department manager; ~ **de distribución** distribution manager; ~ **de distrito** district manager; ~ **de división** division head; ~ **ejecutivo(-a)** *m,f* chief executive officer; ~ **de equipo** team leader; ~ **de estación** stationmaster; ~ **de estado** head of state; ~ **de estudios** Director of Studies; ~ **de exportación** export manager; ~ **de flota** fleet manager; ~ **de flotilla** fleet manager; ~ **de formación** training officer; ~ **de grupo** group leader; ~ **de información** chief information officer; ~ **de inmigración** chief immigration officer; ~ **de lista** list manager; ~ **de movimiento** traffic manager; ~ **de negociado** head of department; ~ **de obra** site manager; ~ **de oficina** office manager; (Der) head clerk; ~ **de oficina de ventas** sales office manager; ~ **de personal** personnel manager; ~ **del producto** product manager; ~ **de proyecto** project leader, project manager; ~ **de publicidad** advertising manager; ~ **de reclamaciones** claims manager; ~ **de reclutamiento** recruitment officer; ~ **de redacción** editor-in-chief; ~ **de redacción adjunto(-a)** *m,f* associate editor, deputy editor; ~ **de sección** head of department; (de grandes almacenes) floor manager BrE, floorwalker AmE; ~

de servicio departmental manager; ~ **del servicio al cliente** customer services manager; ~ **de taller** head foreman; ~ **de unidad** head of unit; ~ **de ventas** sales manager; ~ **de ventas de exportación** export sales manager

jerarquía *f* hierarchy; ~ **piramidal** pyramid hierarchy; ~ **profesional** career ladder

jerárquico *adj* hierarchical

jerga *f* jargon; ~ **de vendedor** sales jargon (infrml); ~ **de publicidad** advertising jargon

jingle *m* jingle; ~ **publicitario** advertising jingle

JIT *abr* AmL (▸**justo a tiempo**) JIT (just-in-time)

jornada *f* day; (laboral) working day BrE, workday AmE; **media** ~ half day; **una** ~ **de siete horas** a seven-hour day; **a** ~ **completa** full-time; **trabajar a** ~ **completa** work full-time; **tener** ~ **reducida** be on short time; ~ **intensiva** *working day with an early start and no breaks to allow an early finish*; ~ **de huelga** day of industrial action; ~ **informativa** open day BrE, open house AmE; ~ **laboral** working day BrE, workday AmE; ~ **partida** split shift (*working day with long break for lunch*))

jornal *m* (pago) day's wages; (trabajo) day's work; **trabajar a** ~ be paid by the day

jornalero, -a *m,f* casual worker (*paid by the day*)

JPEG *abr* (*grupo de expertos fotográficos*) JPEG (Joint Photographic Experts Group)

jubilación *f* (pensión) (retirement) pension; (retiro) retirement; ~ **anticipada** early retirement; ~ **diferida** deferred retirement; ~ **forzosa** *or* **obligatoria** compulsory retirement BrE, mandatory retirement AmE; ~ **profesional** occupational pension; ~ **temprana** early retirement; ~ **voluntaria** voluntary retirement

jubilado[1] *adj* retired

jubilado[2]**, -a** *m,f* pensioner, retired person

jubilarse *v pron* retire; ~ **anticipadamente** take early retirement; ~ **con pensión** retire on a pension

judicatura *f* judiciary

judicial *adj* judicial; **por lo** ~ through the courts; **proceso** ~ legal process

judicialización *f* juridification

juego *m* game; **el** ~ gambling; **estar en** ~ be at stake; **su credibilidad estaba en** ~ his credibility was at stake; ~ **terminado** game over; **poner algo en** ~ put sth at stake; ~ **de la administración** management game; ~ **de caracteres** character set; **(tipografía)** font; ~ **de computadora** AmL (*cf* ►**juego de ordenador** Esp) *m* computer game; ~**s de guerra** war games; ~ **limpio** fair play; ~ **de ordenador** Esp (*cf* ►**juego de computadora** AmL) *m* computer game; ~**s de rol** (de empresa) role-playing

jueves *m* Thursday; ~ **negro** Black Thursday

juez, a *m,f* judge; ~ **árbitro(-a)** *m,f* arbitrator; ~ **de paz** Justice of the Peace; ~ **de instrucción** examining magistrate; ~ **de turno** presiding judge

jugada *f* move; **hacer una** ~ make a move

jugador, a *m,f* gambler

jugar *vi* play; ~ **en bolsa** bet *o* speculate on the stock market; ~ **al alza/a la baja** bet on a bull/bear market; ~ **algo a algo** bet sth on sth; ~ **a favor de alguien** work in sb's favour BrE *o* favor AmE; ~ **en contra de alguien** work against sb; **el no hablar inglés juega en contra suya** the fact that she doesn't speak English works against her *o* doesn't help her

jugarse *v pron* bet, risk, stake; ~ **todo** risk *o* stake everything; ~ **la reputación** stake one's reputation, put one's reputation on the line

juicio *m* judgment; **(Der)** trial; **a mi** ~ in my opinion; **llevar a alguien a** ~ take sb to court; ~ **civil** civil action; ~ **criminal** criminal proceedings; ~ **por difamación** libel proceedings; ~ **incidental** special case; ~ **con jurado** jury trial; ~ **oral** trial (*where witnesses testify in person*); ~ **a priori** a priori statement; ~ **de valor** value judgment

junta *f* (reunión) meeting; (comité) committee; **celebrar una** ~ hold a meeting; ~ **de accionistas** shareholders' meeting; **convocar una** ~ **de accionistas** call a shareholders'

meeting; ~ **anual** annual meeting; ~ **anual de accionistas** annual shareholders' meeting; ~ **arbitral** arbitration board; **J**~ **de Comercio** Board of Trade BrE; ~ **de conciliación** board of conciliation; ~ **de conferencias** conference board; ~ **del consejo de administración** board meeting; ~ **consultiva** advisory board; ~ **directiva** *or* **de directores** board of directors; ~ **general anual** annual general meeting; ~ **general extraordinaria** extraordinary general meeting; ~ **general ordinaria** (de accionistas) ordinary general meeting; ~ **ordinaria** regular meeting; ~ **de revisión** review board

jurado¹ *adj* (traductor) sworn; **una declaración jurada** a sworn statement, an affidavit

jurado² *m* jury; (en concurso) panel; ~ **de acusación** grand jury AmE; ~ **ordinario** trial jury

juramento *m* oath; **bajo** ~ under oath

jurar *vt* swear; ~ **el cargo** be sworn in

jurídico *adj* legal; **el sistema** ~ the legal system

jurisdicción *f* (geográfica, política) jurisdiction; **caer dentro/fuera de la** ~ **de alguien** fall within/beyond sb's jurisdiction; ~ **aduanera** customs jurisdiction; ~ **fiscal** tax jurisdiction

jurisprudencia *f* (legislación) jurisprudence; (criterio) case law; ~ **antigua** old law; ~ **reciente** new law

jurista *mf* jurist

justicia *f* justice; **pedir** ~ ask for justice; **recurrir a la** ~ have recourse to the law; ~ **social** social justice

justiciable *adj* (reclamación) actionable

justificable *adj* justifiable

justificación *f* (razón) justification; ~ **de título** proof of title

justificado *adj* justified; ~ **a la derecha** right-justified, flush right; ~ **a la izquierda** left-justified, flush left; **no** ~ unjustified

justificante *m* receipt; ~ **de depósito** trust receipt; ~ **fiscal** tax voucher

justificar *vt* (acción) justify, explain, account for; (excusar) excuse; ~ **a la derecha/izquierda** right-/left-justify

justiprecio *m* (valoración) valuation; (del personal) appraisal

justo *adj* fair, accurate; (exacto) exact; **andamos ~s de dinero** money is a bit tight; **andamos ~s de tiempo** we're a bit pushed for time; **~ a tiempo** AmL (*cf* ▸**según demanda** Esp) just-in-time

juzgado *m* court; **~ para la bancarrota** bankruptcy court; **~ de distrito** district court AmE; **~ de instrucción** *or* **de**

primera instancia court of first instance; **J~ de Menores** juvenile court; **~ de paz** magistrates' court; **~ de lo penal** criminal court; **~ de segunda instancia** court of appeal; **J~ de lo Social** Esp industrial tribunal BrE

juzgar *vt* judge; (acusado, caso) try; **a ~ por** judging by

keynesianismo *m* Keynesianism

kilometraje *m* distance in kilometres BrE *o* kilometers AmE, ≈ mileage BrE

kilómetro *m* kilometre BrE, kilometer AmE

kiloocteto *m* kilobyte, KB

kiosco *m* kiosk; (de periódicos) newspaper kiosk

km *abr* (▸**kilómetro**) km (kilometre BrE, kilometer AmE)

Ll

labor *f* work; **profesión: sus ~es** occupation: housewife; **~ de equipo** teamwork; **~es de tabaco** tobacco products

laborable *adj* work, working; **días ~s** work days, weekdays; **días no ~s** non-working days

laboral *adj* (condiciones) working; (disputos) labour BrE, labor AmE; **accidente ~** industrial accident

laborar *vi* work; (intrigar) scheme, plot; **~ por algo** strive to achieve sth

laboratorio *m* laboratory; **~ de investigación** research laboratory

laborismo *m* labour movement BrE, labor movement AmE

labrador, a *m,f* farmhand

labranza *f* farming

labrar *vt* (metales) work; (tierra) work, farm

lacre *m* sealing wax

lado *m* side; **al ~ de** alongside; **por un ~ ..., por otro ~ ...** on one hand ..., on the other hand ...; **dejar algo/a alguien de ~** (cosa, diferencias) put sth aside; (persona) leave sb out; **del ~ comprador** (Info) buy-side; **del ~ vendedor** (Info) sell-side

laissez faire *m* laissez-faire

LAN *abr* (▶**lenguaje de alto nivel**) HLL (high-level language)

lanzamiento *m* (de programa, producto) launch, release; (Bolsa) flotation; **oferta de ~** promotional offer; **~ al mercado** release to market, RTM; **~ piloto** pilot launch; **~ del producto** product launch

lanzar *vt* (producto, campaña) launch, bring out; (Bolsa) float; (mensaje) issue, deliver; **~ un producto al mercado** launch a new product onto the market; **~ una emisión de bonos** launch a bond issue

lanzarse *v pron* start; (decidirse) take the plunge; **~se a algo** rush to do sth; (dedicarse a) embark upon sth; **se lanzaron a una campaña larga de publicidad** they embarked on a long advertising campaign; **se lanzó al mundo de las finanzas** she got into the world of finance

lápiz *m* pencil; **~ óptico** optical pen, light pen; **~ trazador** plotting pen

lapso *m* lapse; **en el ~ de una semana** in the space of a week; **~ ojo-mano** hand-eye span; **~ ojo-voz** voice-eye span; **~ de tiempo** space of time

laptop *m* laptop, portable computer

larga *f*: **a la ~** in the long term

largo *adj* long; **a lo ~ de** throughout; **a lo ~ de los años** over the years; **a ~ plazo** in the long term; **va** *or* **tenemos para ~** it's going to be a while; **venir de ~** go back a long way; **el problema viene de ~** the problem goes back a long way

largometraje *m* feature film

latigazo *m* (Bolsa) whiplash

latitud *f* latitude; **~es** parts; **en estas ~es** in these parts

laudo *m* decision, findings; **~ arbitral** judgment; **dictar ~** announce a judgment; **~ de obligado cumplimiento** binding decision

lavado *m* (Fin) laundering; **~ de bonos** bond washing; **~ de dinero** money laundering

lavar *vt* (dinero) launder

lealtad *f* loyalty; **~ del cliente** customer loyalty; **~ a una marca** brand loyalty

leasing *m* (contrato) lease; (sistema) leasing; **~ de material** equipment leasing

lector[1]**,** *a m,f* reader; **~es múltiples** *m pl* multiple readership

lector[2] *m* (dispositivo) scanner, reader; **~ de código de barras** bar code scanner; **~ digital** digital scanner; **~ de discos compactos** CD player; **~ de documentos** document reader; **~ DVD** DVD player; **~ de etiquetas** tag reader; **~ de microfichas** microfiche reader; **~ óptico** laser scanner; **~ óptico de caracteres** optical character reader; **~ óptico de precios** price scanner; **~ en serie** serial reader; **~ de tarjetas** card swipe

lector/escritor *m* read/write

lectura *f* reading; **dar** ∼ **a un documento** read out a document; **segunda** ∼ (de decreto, directiva) second reading

leer *vti* read; (pruebas) read, edit; **no leído** (e-mail) unread

legado *m* legacy, bequest

legajo *m* dossier, file

legal *adj* (trámite, documento) legal; (permitido) lawful; (persona) with no previous convictions; **por la vía** ∼ through legal channels

legalidad *f* legality; (legislación) legislation, law; **estar dentro de la** ∼ **vigente** comply with current legislation, be within the existing law

legalista *adj* legalistic

legalización *f* legalization; (documento) validation

legalizar *vt* legalize; (documento) validate

legalmente *adv* legally; ∼ **obligado** legally bound; ∼ **vinculante** legally binding

legar *vt* bequeath, leave; **los problemas que nos ha legado el gobierno anterior** the problems we've inherited from the previous government

legatario, -a *m,f* devisee, legatee; ∼ **residual** residuary legatee; ∼ **único(-a)** *m,f* sole legatee

legible *adj* legible; ∼ **mecánicamente** *or* **por máquina** machine-readable

legislación *f* legislation, laws; **según la** ∼ **vigente** as the law stands at present; ∼ **antimonopolio** antitrust laws; ∼ **concatenada** piggyback legislation; ∼ **económica** economic law; ∼ **sobre insolvencia** insolvency legislation; ∼ **laboral** employment law; ∼ **de protección al consumidor** consumer-protection legislation; ∼ **sobre construcciones** building regulations; ∼ **sobre insolvencia** insolvency legislation; ∼ **social** social welfare legislation; ∼ **de tarifas** tariff legislation; ∼ **tributaria** tax laws

legislar *vt* legislate

legislativo *adj* legislative

legislatura *f* legislature

legitimar *vt* legitimize; (documento) authenticate; (situación, divorcio) legalize

legítimo *adj* (heredero) legitimate, rightful; (acción) lawful, above-board; (cuero) real, genuine

lengua *f* language; ∼ **de destino** target language; ∼ **franca** lingua franca; ∼

madre *or* **materna** mother tongue; ∼ **minoritaria** minority language; ∼ **oficial** official language; ∼ **de origen** source language

lenguaje *m* language; **en** ∼ **claro** in plain language; ∼ **de alto nivel** high-level language; ∼ **autor** *or* **de componer** authoring language; ∼ **avanzado** advanced language; ∼ **común orientado a la gestión y los negocios** Common Business Oriented Language, COBOL; ∼ **de consulta** query language; ∼ **corporal** body language; ∼ **de ensamblador** assembly language; ∼ **estandarizado y generalizado de marcado** Standard Generalized Mark-up Language; ∼ **fuente** source language; ∼ **HTML** Hypertext Mark-up Language, HTML; ∼ **de interrogación** query language; ∼ **de máquina** computer language, machine language; ∼ **de marcado** mark-up anguage; ∼ **de marcado ampliable** *or* **extensible** XML, eXtensible Mark-Up Language; ∼ **de marcado sin cables** Wireless Mark-up Language; ∼ **de modelación de realidad virtual** virtual reality modelling BrE *o* modeling AmE language, VRML; ∼ **no verbal** body language; ∼ **objeto** target language; ∼ **de orden superior** high-order language; ∼ **de programación** program *o* programming language, software language; ∼ **de referencia** mark-up language; ∼ **de referencia dinámico** Dynamic Text Mark-up Language, DTML; ∼ **de referencia de hipertexto dinámico** Dynamic Hypertext Mark-up Language, DHTML; ∼ **de referencia para computadoras** AmL *or* **ordenadores** Esp **de mano** Handheld Device Mark-up Language, HDML; ∼ **SGML** SGML, Standard Generalized Mark-up Language

lento *adj* (recuperación económica) slow; (mercado) sluggish

lesión *m* injury; ∼**es graves** serious injuries; ∼ **laboral** industrial injury; ∼ **personal** personal injury

letra *f* letter; (de imprenta) print, script; (Fin) bill; **la** ∼ **de la ley** the letter of the law; ∼ **aceptada** acceptance bill; ∼ **bastardilla** italics, italic script; ∼ **avalada** guaranteed bill; ∼ **bancaria** banker's bill; ∼ **de cambio** bill of exchange; ∼ **de cambio al uso** usance bill; ∼ **de cambio al vencimiento** term draft; ∼**s a cobrar** bills receivable; ∼ **comercial** trade bill; ∼ **cursiva** ····❖

italics, italic script; ~ **descontable** bankable bill; ~ **de descuento** discount bill; ~ **documentaria** documentary draft; ~ **extranjera** foreign bill; ~ **impagada** dishonoured bill BrE, dishonored bill AmE; ~ **de imprenta** print; **escribir en ~ de imprenta** please print in block capitals *o* letters; ~ **limpia** clean bill; ~ **de liquidación** settlement draft; ~ **mayúscula** capital letter, upper-case letter; ~ **minúscula** small letter, lower-case letter; ~ **de molde** print, block letters; **escriba el nombre en ~ de molde** print your name; ~ **negrita** *or* **negrilla** bold (type); ~ **pagadera a la vista** bill payable at sight; ~ **pequeña** *or* **menuda** *or* **chica** AmL small print, fine print; ~ **a plazo** time bill, usance bill; ~ **redonda** roman (type); ~ **de tesorería** Treasury bond, Treasury bill; ~ **a la vista** sight bill

letrado, -a *m,f* lawyer

levantamiento *m* (de objecto) raising; (de restricciones, sanciones) lifting; ~ **de embargo** discharge of lien

levantar *vt* (alarma, finanzas) raise; (restricción, sanción) lift; (acta, informe) prepare; (industria, economía) boost, build up; (polémica) cause; (sospecha) arouse; (muro, edificio) erect; ~ **acta** take minutes; ~ **ánimos** raise spirits; ~ **el embargo sobre la importación/exportación de algo** lift the embargo on importing/exporting sth; ~ **la moral** boost morale; ~ **la sesión** (cerrar) close the proceedings; (posponer) adjourn; **se levanta la sesión** the court is adjourned

leve *adj* (sospecha, duda) slight; (infracción, herida) minor

ley *f* (sistema, legislación) law; **aprobar una ~** pass a law; **atenerse a la ~** abide by the law; **conforme a la ~** in accordance with the law; **dictar una ~** issue a law; **dentro/fuera de la ~** within/outside the law; **violar la ~** break the law; **~es antilibelo** libel laws; **~es antimonopolio** antimonopoly laws; **L~ Arancelaria** Import Duty Act; ~ **bancaria** banking law; ~ **bancaria internacional** International Banking Act; **L~ de Comercio Internacional** (UE) International Trade Law; ~ **de competencia** competition act; ~ **de contabilidad** accounting law; ~ **de la demanda recíproca** law of reciprocal demand; **L~ de Derechos de Autor** Copyright Act; **L~ de los Derechos Civiles** Civil Rights Act; ~ **de empleo** employment law; ~ **fiscal** tax law; ~ **de inmigración** immigration law; ~ **internacional** international law; ~ **laboral** labour law BrE, labor law AmE; ~ **moral** moral law; **L~ de Murphy** Murphy's Law; ~ **de la oferta y demanda** law of supply and demand; ~ **parlamentaria** act, statute; **L~ de Protección Ambiental** Environmental Protection Act; **L~ de Protección de Datos** Data Protection Act BrE; ~ **de protección de la intimidad** privacy law; **L~ de Quiebras** Bankruptcy Act; ~ **reformada** amended act; ~ **de reglamentación bursátil** blue-sky law; ~ **de rendimientos decrecientes** law of diminishing returns; ~ **de representación** agency law; **L~ de Sociedades Mercantiles** Company Law, Companies Act BrE, Companies Bill AmE; ~ **del trabajo** employment law; ~ **de ventaja comparativa** (en comercio internacional) law of comparative advantage

libelo *m* (demanda) lawsuit; (escrito difamatorio) libellous BrE *o* libelous AmE article

liberal *adj* liberal

liberalismo *m* liberalism; ~ **social** social liberalism

liberalización *f* liberalization; (del mercado) deregulation; **la ~ del comercio exterior** the relaxing of restrictions on foreign trade; ~ **comercial** trade liberalization; ~ **de precios** abolition of price controls

liberalizador *adj* liberalizing

liberalizar *vt* (comercio, importaciones) liberalize; (compañías, servicios) deregulate

liberar *vt* (preso, rehén) free; (país) liberate; (dividendos, recursos) release; (precios) deregulate; ~ **a alguien de algo** free *o* release sb from sth; ~ **a alguien bajo fianza** release sb on bail; ~ **fondos** unlock funds

libertad *f* freedom; **~es** *f pl* rights; **estar en ~** be free; **quedar en ~** be free to go; **poner a alguien en ~** release sb; ~ **de acción** freedom of action; ~ **de asociación** freedom of association; ~ **bajo fianza** release on bail; ~ **bajo palabra** parole; **~es civiles** *f pl* civil liberties; ~ **de comercio** free trade; ~ **de competencia** freedom of competition; ~ **condicional** probation; ~ **económica** economic freedom; ~ **de elección** freedom of choice; ~ **de establecimiento** (UE) freedom of establishment; ∼ **de expresión** freedom of speech; ∼ **de prensa** freedom of the press

libra *f* pound; **un billete de veinte** ∼**s** a twenty-pound note; ∼ **esterlina** pound sterling

librado, -a *m,f* drawee

librador, a *m,f* drawer

libramiento *m* (Fin) order of payment; ∼ **de cheques** issue of cheques BrE *o* checks AmE

libranza *f* (de cheque, giro) order of payment, draft

librar ① *vt* (liberar) free; (cheque) draw; ∼ **a alguien de algo** free sb from *o* of sth; **no librado** undischarged; **un cheque librado contra un banco irlandés** a cheque drawn on an Irish bank; ∼ **una batalla perdida contra algo/alguien** fight a losing battle against sth/sb ② *vi* be off; **libro los martes** I'm off on Tuesdays, I have Tuesdays off; **libro a las cinco** I get off at five, I finish work at five

librarse *v pron*: ∼ **de algo** get out of sth; ∼ **de algo/alguien** (deshacerse de) get rid of sth/sb

libre *adj* free; **día** ∼ day off; **trabajar por** ∼ (work) freelance, work on a freelance basis; ∼ **de contribución** tax-exempt; ∼ **de deudas** clear of debts; ∼ **de gastos** free of charge; ∼ **de gravamen** unencumbered; ∼ **de hipotecas** mortgage-free, unmortgaged; ∼ **de impuestos** tax-free, duty-free; ∼ **de peaje** toll-free; ∼ **de riesgo** risk-free; ∼ **cambio** free trade; ∼ **circulación de capitales** (UE) free movement of capital; ∼ **circulación de mano de obra** (UE) free movement of labour BrE *o* labor AmE; ∼ **circulación de mercancías** (UE) free movement of goods; ∼ **comercio** free trade; ∼ **competencia** free competition; ∼ **economía** free economy; ∼ **empresa** free enterprise

librecambismo *m* free trade

librecambista *mf* free trader

libreta *f* notebook; (de cuenta) account book, passbook; ∼ **de ahorro** savings passbook; ∼ **de calificaciones** report card; ∼ **de depósitos** deposit passbook

libro *m* book; **comprobar los** ∼**s** check the books; **lleva los** ∼**s de la empresa** he does *o* keeps the company's books; ∼ **de actas** minute book; ∼ **de almacén** inventory book; ∼ **de balances** balance book; **L**∼ **Blanco** consultation

document, White Paper BrE; ∼ **de caja** cash book; ∼ **comercial** trade book; ∼ **de compras** (Cont) bought book; (V&M) purchase book; ∼ **de cuentas** account book; ∼ **devuelto** returned book; ∼ **diario** daybook; ∼ **diario de compras** bought journal; ∼ **de direcciones** address book; ∼ **electrónico** e-book; ∼ **de entradas y salidas** daybook; ∼ **de facturas** invoice book, bill book; ∼ **de familia** *family record of marriage, birth of children, deaths, etc*; ∼ **de inventario** inventory book; ∼ **de letras** bill book; ∼ **de letras aceptadas** acceptance ledger; ∼ **mayor** ledger; ∼ **mayor de clientes** accounts receivable ledger; ∼ **mayor de compras** accounts payable ledger, bought ledger; ∼ **mayor de cuentas a cobrar** accounts receivable ledger; ∼ **mayor de cuentas a pagar** accounts payable ledger; ∼ **mayor del pasivo** liability ledger; ∼ **mayor de ventas** sales ledger; ∼ **de normas** rule book; ∼ **de pedidos** order book; ∼ **de reclamaciones** complaints book; ∼ **registro** register; ∼ **de rendimiento** yield book; ∼ **en rústica** paperback; ∼ **de ventas** sales book; ∼ **de vuelos** (de avión) logbook

licencia *f* licence BrE, license AmE; (AmL de trabajo) leave; **con** ∼ under licence BrE, under license AmE; **estar de** ∼ be on leave; ∼ **de apertura** opening licence BrE, opening license AmE, licence to open BrE, license to open AmE; ∼ **de conducir** driver's licence BrE, driver's license AmE; ∼ **de conducir internacional** international driver's licence BrE, international driver's license AmE; ∼ **exclusiva** exclusive licence BrE, exclusive license AmE; ∼ **de exportación/importación** export/import licence BrE, export/import license AmE; ∼ **fiscal** business licence BrE, business license AmE (*authorizing the holder to engage in a specific trade or occupation*); ∼ **de instalación** (Info) site licence BrE, site license AmE; ∼ **de maternidad** AmL (*cf* ▸**baja por maternidad** Esp) maternity leave; ∼ **de multiusuarios** multi-user licence BrE, multi-user license AmE; ∼ **de obras** planning permission BrE, planning approval AmE; ∼ **de paternidad** AmL (*cf* ▸**baja por paternidad** Esp) paternity leave; ∼ **de programas de computadora** AmL *or* **ordenador** Esp computer software licence BrE *o* license ⋯⋗

AmE; ~ **de urbanización** planning permission BrE, planning approval AmE

licenciado[1] *adj* licensed

licenciado, -a[2] *m,f* graduate; ~ **en Ciencias** ≈ Bachelor of Science, BSc; ~ **en Humanidades** ≈ Bachelor of Arts, BA

licenciarse *v pron* (de la Universidad) graduate; ~ **en Ciencias Empresariales** graduate in Business Studies, get a degree in Business Studies

licenciatario, -a *m,f* licensee

licitación *f* tender; (presentación de ofertas) tendering; (en subasta) bidding; **llamar a ~ para algo** put sth out to tender; **presentarse a una ~** submit a tender; **ganar una ~** win a contract; ~ **abierta** open tendering; ~ **competitiva** competitive tendering

licitar *vt* (llamar a concurso) tender, invite tenders for; (presentar una propuesta) submit a tender for; (en subasta) bid for

lícito *adj* lawful, legal; **medios ~s** legal means

líder[1] *adj* (marca, empresa) leading

líder[2] *mf* leader; ~ **del equipo** team leader; ~ **del grupo** group leader; ~ **del mercado** market leader; ~ **mundial** world leader; ~ **nato(-a)** *m,f* born leader; ~ **de opinión** opinion leader

liderazgo *m* leadership; ~ **del mercado** market leadership

liga *f* league

ligero *adj* (paquete) light; (aumento) slight; (inconveniente) minor

light *adj* light

limitación *f* limitation, restriction; ~ **al libre comercio** restraint of trade; ~ **de los daños** damage limitation; ~ **de una escritura** deed restriction; ~ **de la pérdida** loss limitation; ~ **a la urbanización** planning restriction

limitar *vt* (riesgo) limit; (funciones, crédito) restrict

límite *m* limit; (de propiedad) boundary; **fecha ~** deadline; (para solicitudes) closing date; **poner un ~ a algo** put a limit on sth, limit sth; **sin ~** unlimited; **tiempo ~** time limit; ~ **de carga** maximum load; ~ **de construcción** building line; ~ **del crédito** credit limit; ~ **diario** daily limit; ~ **discrecional** discretionary limit; ~ **de edad** age limit; ~ **de efectivo** cash limit; ~ **de emisión** emission limit; ~ **de endeudamiento** borrowing limit; ~ **del gasto** expenditure limit, spending

limit; ~ **de liquidez** cash limit; ~ **máximo** maximum limit, ceiling; ~ **máximo de hipoteca** mortgage ceiling; ~ **de negocio diario** daily trading limit; ~ **de precio** price limit; ~ **de propiedad** boundary, property line; ~**s de seguridad** safety limits; ~ **superior** (en valor de acciones) upper limit; (de salario) wage ceiling; ~ **de tiempo** time limit

limpiar *vt* (Med amb) clean up

limpio *adj* clean; (ganancia) clear; **pasar algo a ~** make a fair copy of sth; **saca unos mil euros ~s al mes** she clears a thousand euros a month

linaje *m* lineage

linde *f* boundary, property line

línea *f* line; **se cortó la ~** (de teléfono) we were cut off; **en ~** online; **estar en ~** be online; **ayuda en ~** online help; **buscar/comprar en ~** search/shop online; **fuera de ~** offline; **funcionamiento/almacenamiento fuera de ~** offline working/storage; **de primera ~** first-rate, high-profile; ~ **aérea** airline; ~ **aérea de cabotaje** commuter airline; ~ **aérea interna** domestic airline; ~ **aérea internacional** international airline; ~ **de apoyo** (Fin) backup line; ~ **de ataque** line of attack; ~ **de ayuda** helpline; ~ **blanca** white goods; ~ **central** mainstream; ~ **de código** code line; ~ **de comandos** command line; ~ **compartida** party line; ~ **de compraventa de divisas** swop line; ~ **de comunicación directa** hotline; ~ **de condición** status line; ~ **de conducta** (en microeconomía) behaviour line BrE, behavior line AmE; ~ **de crédito** credit line, line of credit; ~ **directa** direct line; ~ **directa de consulta** support hotline; ~ **externa** outside line; ~ **jerárquica** line of command; ~ **marrón** brown goods; ~ **de montaje** assembly line; ~ **de parcelación** lot line; ~ **principal** mains BrE, supply network AmE; ~ **de prioridad** (de teléfono) hotline; ~ **del producto** product line; ~ **punteada** dotted line; ~ **de referencia** baseline; ~ **telefónica común** party line

lingote *m* ingot

liquidación *f* (de negocio) liquidation, winding-up; (de cuenta) settlement; (cuenta final) final account; (V&M) clearance (sale); (por despido) redundancy pay BrE; **entrar en ~** go into liquidation; ~ **de activos** asset stripping; ~ **de balances** clearing; ~ **por cierre** closing down BrE *o* up AmE sale; ~ **de daños** claim settlement; ~ **de deudas** settlement of debts; ~ **diaria** daily settlement; ~ **de existencias** clearance sale; ~ **de fin de año** yearly settlement; ~ **forzosa** compulsory liquidation; ~ **de una hipoteca** final mortgage payment; ~ **involuntaria** involuntary liquidation; ~ **obligatoria** compulsory liquidation; ~ **salarial** wage settlement; ~ **del seguro** insurance settlement; ~ **de siniestro** claim settlement; ~ **total** clearance sale; ~ **voluntaria** voluntary liquidation

liquidado *adj* (opciones) liquidated; (deuda, cuenta) settled

liquidador, a *m,f* liquidator

liquidar *vt* (cuenta) clear, settle, liquidate (frml); (negocio) wind up; (deuda) pay off; (mercancías) sell off; (posición, activo) liquidate; (títulos) clear; ~ **en metálico** settle in cash

liquidez *f* liquidity; (cantidad disponible) cash; ~ **de un banco** bank liquidity; ~ **de la empresa** company liquidity; ~ **negativa** negative cash flow; ~ **del sector privado** private sector liquidity

líquido[1] *adj* (fondos) liquid; (sueldo, renta) net

líquido[2] *m* (capital disponible) cash; ~ **disponible** disposable income; ~ **imponible** taxable income

lista *f* list; **hacer una** ~ make a list; ~ **aprobada** (de inversiones) approved list; ~ **de control** checklist; ~ **de deseos** wish list; ~ **de direcciones** mailing list; ~ **de distribución** distribution list; ~ **de errores** catalogue BrE *o* catalog AmE of errors; (Info) error report; ~ **de espera** waiting list; ~ **de existencias** stocklist; ~ **de éxitos** hit list; (de libros) bestseller list; ~ **de favoritos** (Info) favourites BrE, favorites AmE, hot list; ~ **negra** blacklist; **poner a alguien en la** ~ **negra** blacklist sb; ~ **de pasajeros** passenger list; ~ **de precios** price list; ~ **de remisiones** cross-reference list; ~ **de seleccionados** shortlist; ~ **de turnos** roster

listado[1] *adj* listed

listado[2] *m* listing; (Info) report

listar *vt* list; (Info) report

listo *adj* ready, prepared; ~ **para fotografiar** camera-ready; **el trabajo debe estar** ~ **para el viernes** the job needs to be finished by Friday

litigación *f* litigation

litigante *mf* litigant

litigio *m* litigation; (pleito) lawsuit; **en** ~ at issue, in dispute; **someter un** ~ **a arbitraje** take a dispute to arbitration

litigioso *adj* litigious, contentious

llamada *f* call; **devolver una** ~ phone sb back; **gracias por la** ~ thank you for calling; **hacer una** ~ make a (phone) call; **hacer una** ~ **a algo** call for sth; **hacer una** ~ **a la huelga** call for strike action; **pasar una** ~ (de teléfono) put a call through; **si hay una** ~ **de Nueva York, pásamela en seguida** if there's a call from New York, put it through straight away; ~ **de alarma** alarm call; ~ **a cobro revertido** reverse-charge call BrE, collect call AmE; ~ **en conferencia** conference call, teleconference; ~ **directa** direct call; ~ **de entrada** incoming call; ~ **en espera** call waiting; ~ **internacional** international call; ~ **interurbana** trunk call BrE (obs), toll call AmE; ~ **interurbana de abonado** subscriber trunk dialling BrE; ~ **de larga distancia** long-distance call; ~ **a licitación** call for tenders; ~ **de negocios** business call; ~ **al orden** call to order; ~ **de persona a persona** person-to-person call; ~ **selectiva digital** digital selective calling; ~ **telefónica** phone call; ~ **tridireccional** three-way call, conference call; ~ **urbana** local call

llamar [1] *vt* call; **¿quién llama, por favor?** who's calling, please?; ~ **a alguien** call sb; ~ **a alguien a algo/a hacer algo** call sb to sth/do sth; **nos** ~**on a declarar** we were called to give evidence; ~ **a alguien como testigo** call sb as a witness; ~ **algo al orden** call sth to order; ~ **a alguien por el intercomunicador** call sb over the intercom; ~ **la atención de alguien** attract sb's attention; ~ **sin pagar tasas** call on a Freefone® number BrE, call toll-free AmE
[2] *vi* call; ~ **a cobro revertido** reverse the charges BrE, call collect AmE; ~ **a la huelga** call for strike action

llamarada *f* (en Internet) flamewar

llamativo *adj* (comercialización) eye-catching, attractive

llave *f* key; ~ **en mano** vacant possession

llegada *f* arrival; ~**s** (en el aeropuerto) arrivals; **tiene prevista la** ~ **para las ocho** the estimated time of arrival is eight o'clock

llegar *vi* arrive; (bastar) be enough; **un millón de euros no llega para cubrir los gastos** a million euros is not enough to cover costs; **~ a** (alcanzar) reach; (sumar) come to; **~ a un acuerdo** reach an agreement, strike a deal; **~ a un compromiso** reach a compromise; **~ a una conclusión/decisión** reach a conclusion/decision; **~ a un entendimiento** come to an understanding; **~ al vencimiento** come to maturity; **~ a concretarse** come to fruition; **los gastos ~on a 10.000 euros** the costs came to 10,000 euros; **hacer ~ el sueldo a fin de mes** make one's salary last until the end of the month

llenar *vt* (vacante) fill; (brecha) bridge; (cumplimentar) fill in, fill out; **~ los requisitos** fulfil BrE *o* fulfill AmE the requirements; **~ un vacío** *o* **hueco en el mercado** fill a gap in the market

lleno *adj* full; **~ de** full of; **de ~** fully; **se dedicó de ~ a su carrera** she threw herself into her career, she dedicated herself entirely to her career

llevar *vt* take; (dirigir) run, be in charge of; (cobrar) charge; (fecha, nombre) bear; **¿cuánto te llevaron por arreglarlo?** how much did they charge you to fix it?; **no es para ~** not to be removed; **~ a cabo** carry out; **~ a cabo una conferencia** hold a conference; **~ a cabo una negociación** pull off a deal; **~ un caso** handle a case; **~on los clientes a cenar/a un restaurante** they took the clients to dinner/to a restaurant; **~ un control de** keep track of; **~ la cuenta de** keep a tally of; **~ a cuenta nueva** bring forward, bring down; **~ las cuentas de la empresa** do the company's accounts *o* books; **~ la defensa** lead for the defence BrE *o* defense AmE; **¿llevas dinero?** do you have any money on you?; **~ información sobre algo** carry information on sth; **~ a alguien hasta el límite** push sb to the limit; **~ las negociaciones** conduct the negotiations; **~ nota** keep a note; **~ tiempo** take time; **el proyecto llevó cinco años** the project took five years; **lleva diez años en la empresa** she's been with the company (for) five years; **~ a alguien a los tribunales** take sb to court; **~le la ventaja a alguien** have the edge over sb; **~ la voz cantante** run the show

lluvia *f* rain; **~ ácida** acid rain

local¹ *adj* local

local² *m* premises; **~ alquilado** hired premises; **~ autorizado** approved premises; **~ comercial** business premises; **~ para oficina** office premises; **~ sin trastienda** lock-up premises BrE

localización *f* location, siting; (Info) localization; **~ de averías** troubleshooting; **~ dinámica** dynamic positioning

localizador¹, a *m,f* localizer; **~ de averías** troubleshooter

localizador² *m* pager, beeper; **~ uniforme de recursos** Uniform Resource Locator, URL

localizar *vt* locate; (pago) trace, track down; (Info) localize

locutor, a *m,f* announcer; **~ de radio/televisión** radio/television announcer

locutorio *m* AmL (cf ►**cabina de teléfono** Esp) call box AmE, telephone box BrE; **~ radiofónico** media studio

lógica *f* logic; **~ difusa** fuzzy logic

logical *m* software; **~ de sistemas** systems software

lógico *adj* logical; **componentes ~s** software

logística *f* logistics

logísticamente *adv* logistically

logístico *adj* logistical

logo, logotipo *m* logo, logotype; **~ de la empresa** company logo

lograr *vt* (aumento, nivel, objetivo) achieve; (acuerdo) reach, work out; **~ hacer algo** manage to do sth, succeed in doing sth

logro *m* achievement, accomplishment; **~ profesional** professional achievement

longitud *f* length; **~ de página** page length; **~ de palabra** word length

longitudinal *adj* longitudinal

lonja *f* (comercio) exchange; **~ de transacciones** (Bolsa) pit

lote *m* batch; (en subasta) lot; **procesamiento por ~s** batch processing

lotería *f* lottery; **L~ Nacional** National Lottery

LSI *abr* (*gran escala de integración*) LSI (large-scale integration)

lucha *f* fight, conflict, struggle; **abandonar la ~** give up the fight; **~ antiinflacionista** fight against inflation; **~ de clases** class war; **~ contra algo** fight against sth; **~ por el poder** power struggle

luchar *vi* fight; **~ contra algo** fight (against) sth; **~ contra el terrorismo** fight terrorism

lucrativo *adj* lucrative, profitable; **no
~** unprofitable; **sin fines ~s** non-profit-
making BrE, nonprofit AmE

lucro *m* profit; **afán** *or* **ánimo de ~**
profit motive; **~ cesante** shortfall in
earnings

lugar *m* place; (puesto) position; **dar ~ a
algo** cause sth, give rise to sth; **en ~ de
algo/alguien** instead of sth/sb; **en ~ de
paga** in lieu of pay; **ponerse en el ~ de
alguien** put oneself in sb's position;
primer/segundo ~ first/second place;
tener ~ take place; **~ de la
conferencia** conference venue; **~**
contaminado contaminated site; **~ del
crimen** scene of the crime; **~ de
destino** destination; **~ de empleo**
place of employment; **~ de origen** place
of origin; **~ de residencia** place of
abode; **~ de trabajo** workplace

lujo *m* luxury; **de ~** luxury; **artículos
de ~** luxury goods

lunes *m* Monday; **~ negro** (Bolsa)
Black Monday

luz *f* light; **~ verde** (autorización) green
light

Mm

MAC *abr* (▸**mecanismo de ajuste de cambios**) ERM (Exchange Rate Mechanism)

macro *m* macro

macroambiente *m* macroenvironment

macrodistribución *f* macrodistribution

macroeconomía *f* macroeconomics

macroeconómico *adj* macroeconomic

macroempresa *f* macrocompany

macroinformática *f* macrocomputing

macroinstrucción *f* macroinstruction, macro

macromarketing *m* macromarketing

macroproyecto *m* macroproject

macrosegmentación *f* macrosegmentation

macrosegmento *m* macrosegment

madre *f* mother; ∼ **soltera** single mother, single parent

madrina *f* (de fundación, función) patron

magistrado, -a *m,f* magistrate

magistratura *f* (cargo) judgeship; (jueces) judges; **M∼ de Trabajo** Esp industrial tribunal BrE

magnate *mf* magnate, tycoon; ∼ **financiero(-a)** *m,f* financial magnate

magnetofón *m* tape recorder; ∼ **de bolsillo** personal stereo

magnitud *f* magnitude; **de gran ∼** major; **una crisis de primera ∼** a full-scale crisis

mailing *m* mailing; (de publicidad) mailshot; **hacer un ∼** do a mailshot

mal[1] *adj* bad (cf ▸**malo**)

mal[2] *adv* badly; **estar ∼** be wrong; **la fecha está ∼** the date is wrong; **el negocio les va muy ∼** their business isn't doing very well; ∼ **pagado** low-paid

maledicencia *f* backbiting, gossip

malentendido *m* misunderstanding; **ha habido un ∼** there's been a misunderstanding

maleta *f* suitcase; ∼ **de muestra** sample case

malfuncionar *vi* break down

malgastar *vt* (dinero, tiempo) waste, squander

malo *adj* bad, poor; **mala administración** bad management, mismanagement; **mala compra** bad buy; **mala cosecha** crop failure; **mal negocio** bad business; **malas noticias** bad news

maltusianismo *m* Malthusianism

malvender *vt* sell at a loss, sell off cheaply

malvenderse *v pron* undersell oneself, sell oneself short

malversación *f* misappropriation; ∼ **de dinero/fondos** misappropriation of money/funds

malversar *vt* misappropriate

mánager *mf* manager

mancha *f* mark, stain; ∼ **oleosa** oil slick

mancheta *f* (de periódico) masthead; (de libro) blurb

mancomunadamente *adv* jointly

mancomunado *adj* (propiedad, bienes) joint; (deudores) jointly responsible

mancomunidad *adj* community; (Der) joint responsibility

mandamiento *m* (de los tribunales) court order; ∼ **de embargo** writ of attachment, sequestration order; ∼ **judicial** court order

mandar [1] *vt* (dar órdenes) tell, order; (enviar) send; ∼**le hacer algo a alguien** tell *o* order sb to do sth; ∼ **una carta** post BrE *o* mail AmE a letter; ∼ **un e-mail** send an e-mail; ∼ **a alguien por algo** send sb for sth; ∼ **algo por correo** post BrE *o* mail AmE sth; ∼ **algo mediante un representante** send sth via an agent [2] *vi* be in charge; **¿quién manda aquí?** who is in charge here?

mandarín *m* (en gobierno) mandarin, government official

mandatario, -a *m,f* leader; (representante) agent; (con poder de voto) proxyholder

mandato *m* mandate; **expedir un ∼** issue a writ; **notificarle un ∼ a alguien** serve a writ on sb; ∼ **judicial** writ; ∼ **de pago** warrant for payment

mando *m* leadership; **con la Señora Lago al** ~ with Mrs Lago in charge *o* as leader; **poner a alguien al** ~ **de algo** put sb in charge of sth; ~ **a distancia** remote control; ~**s intermedios** middle management

manejable *adj* manageable; (de uso fácil) easy to use

manejado *adj* operated; ~ **por computadora** AmL *or* **ordenador** Esp computer-operated; ~ **mediante teclado** keyboard-operated

manejar *vt* (máquina) use, operate; (negocio) manage; (asuntos, dinero, personal) handle; ~ **con cuidado** (inscripción en paquetes frágiles) handle with care; ~ **un déficit** run a deficit; ~ **grandes sumas de dinero** handle large sums of money; ~ **un superávit** run a surplus

manejo *m* handling; **mal** ~ mishandling; **de fácil** ~ easy to use, user-friendly; **facilitar el** ~ **de algo** make sth easier to use *o* more user-friendly; ~ **de la computadora** AmL (*cf* ▸**manejo del ordenador** Esp) computer operation; ~ **de una cuenta** account operation; ~ **de la información** information handling; ~ **de mensajes** message handling; ~ **del ordenador** Esp (*cf* ▸**manejo de la computadora** AmL) computer operation

manera *f* way; **de esa** ~ that way; **a** ~ **de ejemplo** by way of example; **de** ~ **que** so that; **de una** ~ **u otra** one way or another; **de todas** ~**s, lo haré** I'll do it anyway *o* in any case

manifestación *f* demonstration; **asistir a una** ~ take part in *o* go on a demonstration; **dispersar una** ~ break up a demonstration

manifestar *vt* state, express; **manifestó su condena del atentado** he expressed his condemnation of the attack

manifiesto *m* manifesto

manipulación *f* (de información, cifras) manipulation; (de votos) rigging; (de mercancías) handling; ~ **a la baja** bear raiding; ~ **de la cobertura** hedge management; ~ **de la contabilidad** window-dressing; ~ **de precios** price fixing

manipulador, -a *m,f* manipulator

manipular *vt* (información, cifras) manipulate; (precios) fix; (votos) rig; ~ **una contabilidad** manipulate *o* fix the accounts

mano *f* hand; **a** ~ by hand; **darse** *o* **estrecharse la** ~ shake hands; **lo dejo**

en tus ~**s** I'll leave it with you *o* in your hands; **estar en buenas** ~**s** be in good hands; **estar en (las)** ~**s de alguien** be in the hands of sb; **estar en** ~ **de un liquidador** be in the hands of a receiver; **poner algo en las** ~**s de alguien** put sth in sb's hands; **poner un asunto en las** ~**s de un abogado** put a matter in the hands of a lawyer; ~ **invisible** (Econ) invisible hand; ~**s limpias** (en conducta profesional) clean hands; ~ **de obra** work force; ~ **de obra contratada** contract labour BrE, contract labor AmE; ~ **de obra cualificada** skilled labour BrE, skilled labor AmE; ~ **de obra directa** direct labour BrE, direct labor AmE; ~ **de obra especializada** skilled labour BrE, skilled labor AmE; ~ **de obra explotada** sweated labour BrE, sweated labor AmE; ~ **de obra migratoria** migrant labour BrE, migrant labor AmE; ~ **de obra no cualificada** unskilled labour BrE, unskilled labor AmE

mantenedor, a *m,f* (m) chairman; (f) chairwoman; ~ **de la familia** breadwinner

mantener *vt* keep, maintain; (familiar dependiente) support; (fondos, posición) hold; (medio ambiente, parentesco) foster; ~ **el archivo al día** keep the filing up to date; ~ **baja la inflación** keep inflation down; ~ **algo en secreto** keep sth secret, keep sth under wraps (infml); ~ **algo como garantía** hold sth as a security; ~ **informado a alguien** keep sb informed; ~ **los márgenes** hold margins; ~ **el orden** keep *o* maintain order; ~ **los precios a raya** hold prices in check

mantenerse *v pron* (económicamente) support oneself; (permanecer) keep, stay; ~ **al corriente de algo** keep abreast of sth; ~ **en contacto con alguien** keep in touch with sb; ~ **dentro de la ley** keep within the law; ~ **firme** stand firm, hold one's ground; ~ **a flote** (negocio) keep afloat; ~ **en sus trece** stand one's ground; ~ **en vigor** remain in effect

mantenimiento *m* maintenance; **gastos de** ~ maintenance costs; ~ **del contrato** contract maintenance; ~ **a distancia** remote maintenance; ~ **de los precios** price maintenance

manual[1] *adj* manual

manual[2] *m* manual; ~ **de auditoría** auditing manual; ~ **de instrucciones** instruction manual; ~ **de mantenimiento** service manual; ~ **de** ⋯⟫

procedimiento rule book; ~ **de ventas** sales manual

manualmente *adv* manually

manufactura *f* manufacture

manufacturado *adj* manufactured; **artículos** ~**s** manufactured goods

manufacturar *vt* manufacture, make

manuscrito[1] *adj* handwritten

manuscrito[2] *m* manuscript

manutención *f* maintenance; **gastos de** ~ maintenance costs

manzana *f* (de edificios) block; ~ **de la discordia** bone of contention

mapa *m* (Info) map; **el** ~ **político** the political scene *o* climate; ~ **de un sitio web** website plan

maqueta *f* scale model

maquetación *f* layout, page makeup

maquiladora *f* AmL assembly plant

maquillar *vt* (cifras) massage

máquina *f* machine; **escribir** *or* **pasar algo a** ~ type sth (up); ~ **calculadora** calculating machine; ~ **dispensadora de dinero** cashpoint BrE, automated teller machine AmE, cash dispenser, cash-dispensing machine; ~ **de escribir** typewriter; ~ **expendedora** vending machine; ~ **expendedora de sellos** stamp vending machine; ~ **franqueadora** franking machine BrE, postage meter AmE; ~ **de sumar** adding machine; ~ **tragamonedas** *or* **tragaperras** slot machine

maquinaria *f* machinery; ~ **administrativa** wheels of government

maquinista *mf* machine operator

mar *m* sea; **por** ~ by sea

marca *f* (de producto, servicio) brand; (de vehículo) make; (señal) mark; **artículos de** ~ brand products; **ropa de** ~ designer clothes; ~ **de agua** watermark; ~ **de aleación** (en oro y plata) hallmark BrE, assay mark AmE; ~ **de aprobación** (vehículos) approval mark; ~ **blanda** own brand; ~ **de calidad** quality brand; ~ **de certificación** certification mark; ~ **comercial** trademark; (Patent) certification mark; (V&M) store brand; ~ **comercializable** marketable brand; ~ **conocida** well-known brand *o* label; ~ **establecida** established brand; ~ **exclusiva** proprietary brand; ~ **familiar** family brand; ~ **de fin de archivo** end-of-file mark; ~ **genérica** generic brand; ~ **de identificación** certification mark; ~ **industrial registrada** registered trademark; ~ **de**

ley hallmark BrE, assay mark AmE; ~ **líder** brand leader; ~ **no registrada** unregistered trademark; ~ **propia** own brand; ~ **registrada** registered trademark; ~ **rival** rival brand; ~ **de la UE** (para juguetes) EU-mark

marcación *f* marking

marcado *adj* (descenso, diferencia) marked

marcador *m* (en Internet) bookmark

marcaje marking; ~ **con código de barras** bar code marking

marcar **1** *vt* mark; (en una lista) tick off BrE, check off AmE; (número de teléfono) dial (up); (sitio web) bookmark; ~ **un hito** score a hit; ~ **la tónica** set a trend; **un descuento del 10% sobre el precio marcado** 10% off the marked price. **2** *vi* dial; ~ **mal** dial the wrong number, dial incorrectly

marcha *f* operation, running; (desarrollo) course; **en** ~ (proceso, máquina) in operation; (negocios) up and running; **poner algo en** ~ set sth in motion; **las negociaciones se han puesto en** ~ the negotiations have been set in motion; **la** ~ **de los acontecimientos** the course of events; ~ **atrás** reverse (gear); **dar** ~ **atrás a algo** pull *o* back out of sth

marchamo *m* label, tag; ~ **de calidad** label of quality

marco *m* framework; **en un** ~ **ideal/acogedor** in an ideal/friendly setting; ~ **conceptual** (de valores) conceptual framework; ~ **jurídico** legal framework; ~ **temporal** time frame

margen *m* margin; **márgenes** *m pl* fringes; **al** ~ marginally; **darle un** ~ **razonable de tiempo a alguien (para hacer algo)** allow sb a reasonable amount of time to do sth; ~ **adicional** additional margin; (de precio) additional mark-up; ~ **alcista** bull spread; ~ **de beneficio** profit margin; ~ **de beneficio bruto/neto** gross/net profit margin; ~ **bruto** gross margin; ~ **comercial** profit margin; ~ **de compra a la alza/baja** bull/bear call spread; ~ **diferencial** differential margin; ~ **entre los precios** price differential; ~ **de error** margin of error; ~ **escaso** narrow margin; ~ **estrecho** narrow margin; ~ **de explotación** operating profit; ~ **favorable competitivo** competitive edge; ~ **de fluctuación** rate of variation; ~ **futuro** forward margin; ~ **de ganancia** profit margin; ~ **de mantenimiento** maintenance

margin; ∼ **mínimo** minimum margin;
∼ **del minorista** retail margin; ∼ **neto**
net margin; ∼ **obligatorio** compulsory
margin; ∼ **operacional** operational
margin; ∼ **de resultado de ejercicio**
bottom-line profit margin; ∼ **de**
seguridad safety margin; ∼ **de**
solvencia solvency margin; ∼ **de**
tiempo time spread; (para mercancías) lead
time; ∼ **de tolerancia** tolerance; ∼ **de**
variación rate of variation; ∼ **de venta**
al alza/a la baja bull/bear put spread

marginal *adj* marginal

marginalismo *m* marginalism

marginalizar *vt* marginalize

mariposa *f* (Bolsa) butterfly; ∼
comprada/vendida long/short butterfly

marketing, **márketing** *m*
marketing; ∼ **agresivo** aggressive
marketing; ∼ **blando** soft marketing; ∼
boca a boca word-of-mouth marketing;
∼ **de consumo** consumer marketing; ∼
cooperativo cooperative marketing; ∼
creativo creative marketing; ∼
diferenciado differentiated marketing;
∼ **directo** direct marketing; ∼ **directo**
a contracorriente upstream direct
marketing; ∼ **divergente** divergent
marketing; ∼ **ecológico** ecomarketing;
∼ **electrónico** electronic marketing, e-
mail marketing; ∼ **especializado** niche
marketing; ∼ **de exportación** export
marketing; ∼ **global** global marketing;
∼ **industrial** industrial marketing; ∼
interactivo interactive marketing; ∼
internacional international marketing;
∼ **por Internet** Internet marketing; ∼
de marca brand marketing; ∼ **de**
masa mass marketing; ∼ **negocio a**
negocio business-to-business marketing,
b2b marketing; ∼ **de objetivos** target
marketing; ∼ **con permiso previo**
permission marketing, opt-in marketing;
∼ **personalizado** one-to-one marketing;
∼ **del producto** product marketing; ∼
de red network marketing; ∼ **de**
relaciones relationship marketing; ∼
de rendimiento performance
marketing; ∼ **de respuesta directa**
direct response marketing; ∼
simbiótico symbiotic marketing; ∼ **de**
situación situational marketing; ∼
telefónico telemarketing; ∼ **viral** viral
marketing

marquesina *f* awning

márquetin *m* marketing

martillo *m* (de subastador) hammer, gavel

marxismo *m* Marxism

más[1] *adj/adv* (uso comparativo) more
(than); (uso superlativo) most; **ganar** ∼
(dinero) earn more (money); ∼ **abajo**
hereunder; **el** ∼ **caro** the most
expensive; **la marca** ∼ **vendida** the top-
selling brand; **tres días** ∼ three more
days

más[2] *prep* plus

masa *f* mass; **comprar en** ∼ buy in
bulk; **producción en** ∼ mass production;
∼ **de acreedores** body of creditors; ∼
bruta gross mass; ∼ **crítica** critical
mass

masivo *adj* massive; **protesta masiva**
mass protest

master *m* master's degree; **M**∼ **de**
Ciencias Master of Science, MSc; **M**∼
en Administración de Empresas
Master of Business Administration,
MBA

materia *f* matter; (material) material; **ser**
un experto en la ∼ be an expert on the
subject; ∼ **orgánica** organic matter; ∼**s**
primas raw materials; ∼**s primas**
agrícolas agrifoodstuffs

material[1] *adj* substantial, material;
bienes ∼**es** material possessions; **daños**
∼**es** damage to property

material[2] *m* material; **reunir** ∼**es para**
un artículo collect *o* gather material for
an article; ∼ **de apoyo** backup
material; ∼ **editorial** editorial matter;
∼ **a granel** bulk material; ∼ **impreso**
printed matter; ∼**es de oficina** office
supplies; ∼ **de presentación**
presentation pack; ∼ **de promoción**
promotional material *o* literature; ∼
publicitario publicity material; ∼ **de**
punto de venta point-of-sale material;
∼ **recuperable** (Med amb) recoverable
material; ∼ **de referencia** reference
material

materialidad *f* (informes contables)
materiality

materialismo *m* materialism

materializarse *v pron* materialize;
(proyecto) come to fruition

maternidad *f* maternity; **estar de baja**
por ∼ be on maternity leave; **subsidio**
de ∼ maternity benefit

matrícula *f* registration; (tasa)
registration fee; (de coche) numberplate
BrE, license plate AmE; **hacer la** ∼
register; ∼ **reducida** concessional fee

matriculación *f* registration

matriz *f* grid, matrix; (Info) array; (de
talonario) stub, counterfoil; ∼ **de cheque**
cheque counterfoil BrE, check counterfoil ⋯▸

AmE; ~ **de gráficos realzada** enhanced graphics array; ~ **interactiva** interaction matrix; ~ **de medida variable** variable-size font; ~ **de registro** record locking; ~ **de vídeo** Esp *or* **video** AmL **gráfico** video graphics array

maximización *f* maximization; ~ **del beneficio** revenue maximization; ~ **de beneficios** *or* **ganancias** profit maximization; ~ **de las ventas** sales maximization

maximizar *vt* maximize

máximo¹ *adj* maximum; **máxima eficiencia** maximum efficiency

máximo² *m* maximum; **hasta un ~ de** up to a maximum of; **al ~** to the limit; **aprovechar los recursos/las oportunidades al ~** make the most of one's resources/opportunities; ~ **histórico** all-time high

mayor¹ *adj* (usos comparativos) bigger; (en importancia) greater; (en edad) older; (usos superlativos) biggest; (en importancia) greatest; (en edad) oldest; **al por ~** wholesale; **ser ~ de edad** be an adult, be a grown-up, be over 18

mayor² *m* (libro) ledger; (persona) adult, grown-up; **los ~es** *m pl* adults, grown-ups; ~ **de acreedores** creditors' ledger; ~ **de clientes** client ledger; ~ **de compras** bought ledger; ~ **de edad** adult, grown-up; ~ **privado** private ledger

mayoría *f* majority; **la ~ de los negocios** most businesses; **estar en ~** be in the majority; ~ **absoluta** absolute majority; ~ **calificada** qualified majority; ~ **precoz** (de consumidores) early majority; ~ **silenciosa** silent majority; ~ **tardía** late majority

mayorista *mf* wholesaler; ~ **de venta al contado** cash and carry wholesaler

mayúscula *f* capital letter, upper-case letter; **en ~s** in capitals

Mb *abr* (►**megabyte**) Mb (megabyte)

MBA *abr* (►**Master en Administración de Empresas**) MBA (Master of Business Administration)

mecanismo *m* mechanism; ~ **de ajuste de cambios** Exchange Rate Mechanism, ERM; ~ **de cambios** Exchange Rate Mechanism; ~ **de descuento** discount mechanism; ~ **del disparador** trigger mechanism; ~ **de emisión** issuance facility; ~ **impulsor de disco** disk drive; ~ **del mercado** market mechanism; ~ **de precios** price

mechanism; ~**s de votación** voting procedures

mecanización *f* mechanization

mecanizado *adj* mechanized, machine-based

mecanizar *vt* mechanize

mecanografía *f* typing

mecanografiado *adj* typed, typewritten

mecanografiar *vt* type, typewrite; ~ **al tacto** touch-type

mecanógrafo, -a *m,f* typist

media *f* average, mean; **una ~ diaria de** a daily average of; ~ **móvil** moving average; ~ **nacional** national average; ~ **de vida** lifetime averaging

mediación *f* mediation; **por ~ de alguien** through sb; **consiguió el puesto por ~ de su padre** she got the job through her father; ~ **por necesidad** (Der) agency by necessity

mediador, a *m,f* mediator

mediana *f* median

medianil *m* gutter

mediar *vi* mediate; ~ **en algo** mediate in sth, act as a mediator in sth; ~ **por alguien** intervene on sb's behalf

medicamento *m* drug; ~ **de marca registrada** proprietary drug; ~ **sin receta** over-the-counter medicine

medición *f* measurement; ~ **de ejecución** performance measurement; ~ **de líquidos** liquid measure; ~ **monetaria** money measurement; ~ **de la productividad** productivity measurement; ~ **del rendimiento** performance measurement; ~ **del trabajo** work measurement

médico¹ *adj* medical; **un reconocimiento ~** a medical (examination)

médico², -a *m,f* doctor; ~ **de cabecera** family doctor, GP, general practitioner

medida *f* measure, measurement; **a la ~ de sus aptitudes** to suit his abilities, commensurate with his abilities (frml); **en cierta ~** to an extent; **a la ~ del cliente** customized, tailored to the customer; **como ~ precautoria** as a precautionary measure; **en mayor ~** to a greater extent; **en menor ~** to a lesser extent; **hacer algo a ~** make sth to order; **tomar la ~ de algo** measure sth; **tomar ~s** take steps *o* measures; ~ **para áridos** dry measure; ~ **de control** (de precios) measure of control; ~

disciplinaria disciplinary measure; ∼
drástica drastic measure; ∼
estimulante stimulative measure; ∼
fiscal tax measure; ∼ **de huelga** strike
action; ∼ **de presión** form of pressure;
la huelga y otras ∼**s de presión** strikes
and other forms of pressure; ∼
preventiva preventive measure; ∼
reguladora regulatory measure; ∼ **de**
represalia retaliatory measure; ∼ **de**
seguridad security measure, safety
measure, safety precaution; ∼
unilateral unilateral measure

medidor *m* gauge BrE, gage AmE; ∼ **de**
neumático tyre gauge BrE, tire gage AmE

medio[1] *adj* (la mitad de) half; (promedio)
average; **a media jornada** on half-time;
media pensión half board; **media**
tarifa half fare

medio[2] *m* (de comunicación) medium;
(centro) middle; ∼**s** *m pl* means; **como** ∼
de as a means of; **contar con los** ∼**s**
necesarios para hacer algo have the
necessary means to do sth; **por** ∼ **de** via,
through; **el** ∼ **ambiente** the
environment; ∼ **básico** basic medium;
∼ **de cambio** medium of exchange; ∼**s**
por caudales push media, streaming
media; ∼ **comercial** business
environment; ∼**s de comunicación**
media; ∼**s de comunicación al**
público mass media; ∼ **de eliminación**
(de desperdicios) disposal facility; ∼**s**
financieros financial means; ∼
interactivo lean-forward medium; ∼**s**
mezclados mixed media; ∼**s de pago**
means of payment; ∼ **pasivo** lean-back
medium; ∼**s políticos** political circles;
∼ **publicitario** advertising medium; ∼
de respuesta reply vehicle; ∼ **de**
transporte means of transport

mediodía *m* midday, noon; **a** ∼ at
midday *o* noon

medir *vt* measure; (consecuencias, ventajas)
consider, weigh up; (Inmob) survey; ∼ **el**
desempeño de alguien measure sb's
performance; ∼ **las palabras** choose
one's words carefully; ∼ **las ventajas y**
los inconvenientes de algo weigh up
the pros and cons of sth

MEFF *abr* (▸**Mercado Español de**
Futuros Financieros) *Spanish financial*
futures market

megabyte *m* megabyte

megaempresa *f* mega-corporation

mejor *adj* (uso comparativo) better; (uso
superlativo) best; **cuanto antes** ∼ the
sooner the better; ∼ **alternativa** best

alternative; ∼ **oferta** best bid; ∼ **precio**
best price

mejora *f* improvement; (aumento de valor)
betterment; ∼ **de beneficios** profit
improvement; ∼ **de la casa** home
improvement; ∼ **del producto** product
improvement

mejorado *adj* (calidad) improved

mejoramiento *m* (de sistema)
improvement; ∼ **de la tierra** land
improvement

mejorar *vt* (calidad) improve; ∼ **las**
condiciones de trabajo improve
working conditions; ∼ **la oferta** make a
better offer

melodía *f* melody, tune; ∼ **publicitaria**
advertising jingle

membresía *f* AmL membership; ∼
honoraria AmL honorary membership

membrete *m* letterhead; **papel con** ∼
headed paper; ∼ **oficial** official
letterhead

memorándum *m* memo,
memorandum (frml); ∼ **de crédito** credit
memorandum; ∼ **de débito** debit
memorandum; ∼ **de intención**
memorandum of intent

memoria *f* memory; (informe) report;
(Cont) financial statement; ∼ **de acceso**
aleatorio RAM (random access
memory); ∼ **adicional** add-on memory;
∼ **de alta velocidad** high-speed
memory; ∼ **anual** annual report; ∼ **de**
apoyo backup memory; ∼ **auxiliar**
auxiliary memory; (equipo) auxiliary
storage; ∼ **baja** low memory; ∼ **de**
burbujas bubble memory; ∼ **de la**
computadora AmL (*cf* ▸**memoria del**
ordenador Esp) computer memory; ∼
externa add-on memory; ∼ **global**
global memory; ∼ **interfaz** buffer store;
∼ **interna** internal storage; ∼
magnética magnetic storage; ∼ **de**
masa mass memory; ∼ **de núcleos**
core storage, core memory; ∼ **del**
ordenador Esp (*cf* ▸**memoria de la**
computadora AmL) computer memory;
∼ **presupuestaria** budgetary statement;
∼ **real** real storage; ∼ **de sólo lectura**
ROM (read only memory); ∼ **tampón**
buffer; ∼ **temporal** cache memory; ∼
de tránsito buffer store; ∼ **virtual**
virtual memory

mención *f* mention; ∼ **editorial**
editorial mention, acknowledgement

mencionar *vt* mention; **antes**
mencionado aforementioned; **sin** ∼ not
to mention

m

menor[1] *adj* (uso comparativo) less, smaller; (gastos) minor; (precios) lower; (uso superlativo) least; (en tamaño) smallest; ∼ **que algo** smaller *o* lower than sth; **en** ∼ **grado** to a lesser extent; **en mayor** *o* ∼ **grado** to a greater or lesser extent; **al por** ∼ retail; **venta al por** ∼ retail sales; **suceder con** ∼ **frecuencia que** happen less often *o* frequently than

menor[2] *mf* (persona) minor; **no se admiten** ∼**es** over 18s only; ∼ **de edad** minor

menos[1] *adj/adv* (uso comparativo) less; (uso superlativo) least; ∼ **caro** less expensive; **al** ∼ at least; ∼ **que** less than; **a** ∼ **que** unless; ∼ **de** less than, under; **cada vez** ∼ less and less; **poco** ∼ **que perfecto** less-than-perfect; **por lo** ∼ at least; **a** ∼ **que se disponga lo contrario** unless otherwise provided

menos[2] *prep* (excepto) except, apart from; (en restas) minus; ∼ **un descuento del 10%** minus *o* less a 10% discount

menos[3] *m* (símbolo) minus (sign)

menoscabo *m* impairment, damage; **en** ∼ **de algo** to the detriment of sth

menospreciar *vt* (valor) underestimate; (persona) underrate

mensaje *m* message; ∼ **de bienvenida** welcome message; ∼ **cifrado** (por satélite) scrambled message; ∼ **de correo electrónico** e-mail message; ∼ **de diagnóstico** diagnostic message; ∼ **de entrada** input message; ∼ **de error** error message; ∼ **de intervención** action message; ∼ **publicitario** advertising message; ∼ **sms** text message, sms message; ∼ **telefónico** telephone message; ∼ **texto** text message; ∼ **vocal** *or* **por voz** voice message

mensajería *f* messaging; ∼ **electrónica** electronic messaging; ∼ **instantánea** instant messaging; ∼ **vocal** *or* **por voz** voice messaging

mensajero, -a *m,f* messenger, courier BrE; **servicio de** ∼**s** messenger service, courier service BrE

mensual *adj* monthly; **gana 2.000 euros** ∼**es** he earns 2,000 euros a month

mensualidad *f* monthly instalment BrE, monthly installment AmE

mensualmente *adv* monthly, every month

menú *m* menu; ∼ **de archivos** file menu; ∼ **desplegable** drop-down menu; ∼ **emergente** pop-up menu; ∼ **de**

ficheros file menu; ∼ **de funciones** pop-up menu; ∼ **principal** main menu

mercadería *f* merchandise; ∼**s** goods; ∼**s futuras** future goods

mercado *m* market; **en el** ∼ on the market; **se ha derrumbado** *or* **hundido el** ∼ the bottom has fallen out of the market; **inundar el** ∼ flood the market; **salir al** ∼ come onto the market

(**mercado a...**) ∼ **abierto** open market; ∼ **activo** active market; ∼ **de los adolescentes** teenage market; ∼ **alcista** *or* **al alza** bull market, buoyant market; ∼ **amplio** broad market, large market; ∼ **átono** flat market

(**b...**) ∼ **bajista** bear market, declining market; ∼ **de bienes raíces** property market, real-estate market AmE; ∼ **de bonos** bond market

(**c...**) ∼ **de calidad** quality market; ∼ **cambiario** foreign exchange market; ∼ **de capitales** capital market; ∼ **cautivo** captive market; ∼ **comercial** commercial market; ∼ **de compradores** buyers' market; ∼ **común** (obs) Common Market (obs); ∼ **consolidado** established market; ∼ **de consumo** consumer market; ∼ **al contado** cash market, spot market; ∼ **contingente** contingent market; ∼ **continuo** all-day trading; ∼ **a corto plazo** short-term market; ∼ **sin cotización oficial** unlisted market; ∼ **crediticio** credit market; ∼ **de crédito al consumo** consumer credit market; ∼ **de créditos recíprocos** swap market

(**d...**) ∼ **débil** weak market; ∼ **de derivados** derivatives market; ∼ **desanimado** stale market; ∼ **desarrollado** developed market; ∼ **de descuento** discount market; ∼ **digital** digital marketplace; ∼ **dinerario** money market; ∼ **de dinero** money market; ∼ **de dinero doméstico** *or* **interno** domestic money market; ∼ **de divisas** foreign exchange market, currency market; ∼ **de divisas al contado** spot currency market; ∼ **doméstico** domestic market

(**e...**) ∼ **electrónico** e-marketplace, electronic marketplace; ∼ **electrónico colaborador** collaborative e-marketplace; ∼ **emergente** emerging market; ∼ **de emisiones** issue market; ∼ **equitativo** fair trading; ∼ **escaso** tight market; **M**∼ **Español de Futuros Financieros** *Spanish financial futures market*; **M**∼ **Español de Opciones y Futuros** *Spanish options and futures*

stock market; ~ **estable** stable market; ~ **exclusivo** exclusive market, market of one; ~ **de exportación** export market; ~ **exterior** overseas market

f... ~ **financiero** financial market; ~ **flojo** dull market, narrow market; ~ **fragmentado** fragmented market; ~ **de futuros** futures market; ~ **de futuros en divisas** currency futures market

g... ~ **genérico** generic market; ~ **gris** grey market BrE, gray market AmE

h... ~ **hipotecario** mortgage market

i... ~ **inactivo** quiet market; ~ **inestable** disorderly market; ~ **inmobiliario** property market, real-estate market AmE; ~ **inmovilizado** locked market; ~ **de intercambio** replacement market; ~ **interempresarial** intercompany market; M~ **Internacional de Opciones** International Options Market; ~ **interno** internal market, domestic market; ~ **sin intervención** free market; ~ **intervenido** controlled market; ~ **irregular** irregular market

j... ~ **de jóvenes** youth market

l... ~ **laboral** job market, labour market BrE, labor market AmE; ~ **legalizado** white market; ~ **de letras** bill market; ~ **libre** free market; ~ **de libre empresa** free enterprise market; ~ **de liquidación** clearing market

m... ~ **maduro** mature market; ~ **manipulado** rigged market; ~ **marginal** fringe market; ~ **de masas** mass market; ~ **de materias primas** commodities market; ~ **al por mayor** wholesale market; ~ **al por menor** retail market; ~ **monetario** money market; M~ **Monetario Internacional** International Monetary Market; ~ **muerto** graveyard market; ~ **mundial** world market

n... ~ **nacional** domestic market; ~ **negro** black market; ~ **no existente** missing market; ~ **no intervenido** free enterprise market

o... ~ **objetivo** target market; ~ **oficial** official market; ~ **de opciones** options market

p... ~ **paralelo** parallel market; ~ **periférico** fringe market; ~ **a plazo** future trading market; ~ **de préstamos** loan market; ~ **de préstamos corporativos** corporate lending market; ~ **de propiedades** property market, real-estate market AmE

r... ~ **rápido** fast market; ~ **regional** regional market; ~ **regulado** regulated market; ~ **restringido** restricted market; ~ **retraído** shrinking market; ~ **de reventa** reseller market

s... ~ **saturado** flooded market, saturated market; ~ **secundario** secondary market, aftermarket; ~ **de segunda mano** second-hand market; ~ **de seguros** insurance market; ~ **seminegro** semiblack market; ~ **sensible** sensitive market; ~ **socialista** socialist market; ~ **sostenido** bull market, buoyant market; ~ **superficial** shallow market; ~ **de swaps** swap market

t... ~ **técnico** technical market; ~ **de trabajo** job market, labour BrE *o* labor AmE market; ~ **de tránsito** transit market

u... ~ **único** (de UE) Single Market; ~ **único laboral** single labour BrE *o* labor AmE market

v... ~ **de valores** equity market; ~ **de valores de primera** (títulos del Estado) gilt-edged market; ~ **de vendedores** sellers' market; ~ **virtual** virtual marketplace; ~ **de la vivienda** housing market

mercadotecnia *f* marketing

mercancía *f* commodity; ~**s** goods, merchandise; ~**s de auxilio** relief goods; ~ **al contado** cash commodity; ~ **básica** primary commodity; ~ **blanda** soft commodity; ~**s en bruto** crude goods; ~ **estándar** standard commodity; ~ **física** physical commodity; ~**s a granel** bulk goods; ~**s imponibles** dutiable goods; ~**s importadas** imported goods; ~**s al por mayor** wholesale goods; ~**s al por menor** retail goods; ~**s no vendidas** unsold goods; ~**s peligrosas** dangerous goods; ~**s perecederas** perishable goods, perishables; ~**s prohibidas** prohibited goods; ~**s restituibles** returnable goods; ~**s de venta fácil** fast-moving consumer goods

mercante *adj* merchant

mercantil *adj* mercantile

mercantilismo *m* mercantilism

mercantilización *f* commercialization, commercial exploitation

mercantilizar *vt* commercialize, exploit commercially

meridiano *m* meridian

mérito *m* merit, worth; **quitar** *or* **restar ∼s a alguien** take the credit away from sb

meritocracia *f* meritocracy

merma *f* leakage; **∼s de las existencias** stock shortage; **∼ natural** natural wastage

mermar [1] *vt* (capital) reduce; (suministro, provisión) reduce, cut down on [2] *vi* (nivel, arcas) diminish

mes *m* month; **al ∼** a *o* per month, p.c.m., per calendar month; **el ∼ pasado/que viene** last/next month; **del ∼ corriente** of the current month; **dentro de un ∼** in a month *o* in a month's time; **a primeros/últimos de ∼** at the beginning/end of the month; **una vez al ∼** once a month; **∼ calendario** calendar month; **∼ de entrega** delivery month; **∼es vencidos** months after sight; **∼ de vencimiento** expiry month BrE, expiration month AmE

mesa *f* table; (de trabajo) desk; **de ∼** (agenda) desk; (Info) desktop; **sobre la ∼** (propuesta) on the table; **∼ de cambios** foreign exchange desk; **∼ de conferencias** conference table; **∼ directiva** board of directors, management board; **∼ de negociaciones** negotiating table; **∼ redonda** round table

mesoeconomía *f* mesoeconomy

meta *f* goal, target; **alcanzar una ∼** achieve a goal, meet a target; **∼ de beneficios** profit goal; **∼ comercial** business goal; **∼ corporativa** corporate goal; **∼ de desempeño** performance target; **∼ de la empresa** company goal; **∼ de ingreso** income target; **∼ profesional** career goal; **∼ de rendimiento** performance target; **∼ de ventas** sales target

metabúsqueda *f* metasearch

metadatos *m pl* metadata

metadispositivo de búsqueda *m* metasearch engine

metálico *m* cash; **pagar en ∼** pay (in) cash

metalista *mf* (escuelas monetarias) metallist

metamarketing *m* metamarketing

meter *vt* put; **∼ en máquina** pass for press; **∼ una solicitud** AmL put in an application

método *m* method; **∼ de acumulación** accrual method; **∼ administrativo** management method; **∼ de amortización** amortization method;

∼ de amortización lineal straight-line method of depreciation; **∼ de caja** cash basis; **∼ del cambio de cierre** (traducción a divisas) closing rate method BrE, current rate method AmE; **∼ del camino crítico** critical path method; **∼ del cinco por ciento** five-percent rule; **∼ de clasificación por puntos** points-rating method; **∼ de comparación** benchmark method; **∼ de comparación de mercados** market comparison approach; **∼ de compra** purchase method; **∼ de comprobación** benchmark method; **∼ de consolidación** consolidation method; **∼ contable** accounting method; **∼ de coste** Esp *or* **costo** AmL cost method, cost approach; **∼ de crecimiento sostenido** steady-growth method; **∼ de cultivo** farming method; **∼ de la cuota** (de impuestos diferidos) liability method; **∼ de descuento directo** direct charge-off method; **∼ de la deuda** liability method; **∼ económico** economic method; **∼ de efectivo** cash basis; **∼ lineal** *or* **de la línea recta** (en amortización) straight-line method; **∼ de pago** method of payment; **∼ de partida doble** double-entry method; **∼ de porcentaje de ventas** percentage-of-sales method; **∼ de precio de compra** purchase price method; **∼ de rendimiento** income approach; **∼ de restituir** pay-back method; **∼ del salario real** closing rate method BrE, current rate method AmE; **∼ de saldo decreciente** diminishing-balance method; **∼ de tanteo** trial-and-error method; **∼ de tributación** method of taxation

metodología *f* methodology; **∼ cualitativa** qualitative methodology; **∼ cuantitativa** quantitative methodology

metraje *m* yardage; (de película) footage; **película de corto ∼** short, short film BrE *o* movie AmE; **película de largo ∼** feature, feature-length film BrE *o* movie AmE

metro *m* underground BrE, tube BrE (infrml), subway AmE

metropolitano *adj* metropolitan

mezcla *f* mix; (de valores) commingling; **∼ de estrategias marketing** marketing mix; **∼ de estrategias de productos** product mix; **∼ de estrategias de ventas** sales mix

micro *m* micro

microbuscador *m* microbrowser

microchip *m* microchip

microcomputadora f AmL (cf
▸**microordenador** Esp) microcomputer
microcrédito m microcredit
microdecisión f microdecision
microdisco m microdisk
microeconomía f microeconomics
microeconómico adj microeconomic
microelectrónica f microelectronics
microelectrónico adj
microelectronic
microficha f microfiche
microfilm m microfilm
microinformática f microcomputing
micromárketing m micromarketing
micromercado m micromarketplace
microordenador m Esp (cf
▸**microcomputadora** AmL)
microcomputer
micropago m micropayment
microplaqueta f chip; ~ **de silicio**
silicon chip
microprocesador m microprocessor
microprograma m microprogram
microprogramación f firmware
microsegmentación f
microsegmentation
microtransacción f
microtransaction
miembro mf (de empresa, sindicato)
member; **hacerse** ~ **de algo** become a
member of sth; **los países** ~s member
countries; ~ **afiliado(-a)** m,f affiliate
member; ~ **aliado(-a)** m,f allied
member; ~ **del comité** committee
member; ~ **de conferencia** conference
member; **M**~ **del Congreso** ≈ MP BrE,
≈ Member of Parliament BrE, Member of
Congress AmE, (m) ≈ Congressman AmE;
(f) ≈ Congresswoman AmE; ~
corporativo(-a) m,f corporate member;
~ **especificado(-a)** m,f specified
member; ~ **fundador(a)** m,f founder
member; ~ **de un grupo de trabajo**
team member; ~ **de la junta directiva**
member of the board; **M**~ **del
Parlamento Europeo** Member of the
European Parliament, MEP; ~ **en
plantilla** Esp staff member; ~ **de pleno
derecho** full member
miércoles m Wednesday; ~ **negro**
Black Wednesday
migración f migration; ~ **circular**
circular migration
mil m thousand
milésima f thousandth; (tipos fiscales)
mill

militante¹ adj militant
militante² mf activist
millón m million
millonario, -a m,f millionaire; (tb f)
millionairess; ~ **en el papel** paper
millionaire
mina f mine; **ser una** ~ **de información**
be a mine of information; **ser una** ~ **(de
oro)** be a goldmine
mineral m mineral; (de un metal) ore
minería f mining; ~ **del carbón** coal
mining
minicomputadora f AmL (cf
▸**miniordenador** Esp) minicomputer
minifundista mf small farmer
minifurgoneta f minivan
minimización f minimization; ~ **de
costes** cost minimization
minimizar vt (riesgos, ventana) minimize;
(gravedad, problema) play down
mínimo¹ adj minimum; **tarifa mínima**
minimum charge
mínimo² m minimum; ~ **de coste** Esp
or **costo** AmL (balance general) minimum
cost; ~ **histórico** (Bolsa) all-time low
miniordenador m Esp (cf
▸**minicomputadora** AmL) minicomputer
minipágina f (en publicidad) mini-page
miniserie f mini-series
Ministerio m Ministry, Department; ~
de Economía y Hacienda ≈ The
Treasury BrE, ≈ Treasury Department
AmE; ~ **de Relaciones Exteriores** ≈
Foreign Office BrE, ≈ State Department
AmE; ~ **de la Seguridad Social** ≈
Department of Social Security BrE,
Welfare Department AmE
ministro, -a m,f minister; (en GB)
Secretary; **M**~ **de Asuntos Exteriores**
≈ Foreign Secretary BrE, ≈ Secretary of
State AmE; **M**~ **de Economía y
Hacienda** Esp ≈ Chancellor of the
Exchequer BrE, ≈ Secretary of the
Treasury AmE; **M**~ **sin cartera** Minister
without portfolio
minoría f minority; **estar en** ~ be in
the minority
minorista m,f retailer; ~ **afiliado(-a)**
m,f affiliated retailer; ~
especializado(-a) m,f speciality
retailer BrE, specialty retailer AmE; ~
independiente independent retailer
minucias f pl minutiae
minuciosamente adv painstakingly
minucioso adj meticulous, thorough

m

minusvalía *f* disability; (Fin) depreciation, fall; ~ **física/mental** physical/mental disability

minusvaloración *f* undervaluation

minuta *f* (de abogado) bill; (borrador) draft copy

minuto *m* minute

miope *adj* (decisión) short-sighted

mira *f* aim, intention; **con** ~ **a** with a view to; **con** ~ **a reducir los gastos** with a view to reducing costs

mirón, -ona *m,f* (Info) (en salas de charla) lurker

mironeo *m* (Info) (en salas de charla) lurking; **estar de** ~ lurk

misceláneo *adj* miscellaneous, misc.

miseria *f* poverty; ~ **absoluta** absolute poverty

misión *f* mission; **cumplir una** ~ accomplish a mission; ~ **corporativa** corporate mission; ~ **diplomática** diplomatic mission; ~ **económica** economic mission; ~ **de investigación** fact-finding mission

mismo *adj* same; **del** ~ **género** of the same kind

mitigación *f* mitigation

mitigar *vt* (problemas) mitigate; **para** ~ **los efectos de la crisis económica** to mitigate the effects of the economic crisis

mixto *adj* (comisión, comité) joint; (economía, capitales) mixed; (educación) mixed, coeducational

MMTC *abr* (▸**modelo multilateral de tipos de cambio**) MERM (Multilateral Exchange Rate Model)

mobiliario *m* furniture; ~ **y efectos domésticos** household goods; ~ **e instalación** furniture and fittings

moción *f* motion; **aceptar/rechazar una** ~ pass/reject a motion; **apoyar una** ~ support a motion; **presentar una** ~ propose *o* table BrE a motion; ~ **de censura** motion of censure

mod. *abr* (▸**modificado**) alt. (altered)

moda *f* mode; (V&M) fashion; **estar de** ~ be in fashion; **última** ~ latest fashion

modalidad *f* (tipo) kind; (Info) mode; (Econ) terms; ~ **americana** American terms; ~ **aplazada** instalment base BrE, installment base AmE; ~ **byte a byte** byte mode; ~ **dialogada** conversational mode; ~ **de edición** edit mode; ~**es de una emisión** terms and conditions of an issue; ~ **europea** European terms; ~ **interactiva** interactive mode; ~

normal de inversión normal investment practice; ~ **en ráfagas** burst mode; ~ **de respuesta** answer mode; ~ **textual** text mode

modelado *m* paste-up

modelo *m* model; **tomar algo como** ~ take sth as a model; ~ **bimetálico** bimetallic standard; ~ **clásico** classical model; ~ **de compra** purchasing pattern; ~ **de consumo** consumer pattern; ~ **contable** accounting model; ~ **corporativo** corporate model; ~ **de costes** Esp *or* **costos** AmL cost standard; ~ **de decisión** decision model; ~ **económico** economic model; ~ **de empresa** company model; ~ **de estado financiero** financial reporting standard; ~ **estático** static model; ~ **estructural** structural model; ~ **de fijación de precios de los activos de capital** capital asset pricing model; ~ **flexible** soft modelling BrE, soft modeling AmE; ~ **de gran escala** large-scale model; ~ **de gravedad** gravity model; ~ **de indicación de salida** point-output model; ~ **de justo a tiempo** AmL just-in-time model; ~ **de marketing** marketing model; ~ **matemático** mathematical model; ~ **multilateral de tipos de cambio** Multilateral Exchange Rate Model, MERM; ~ **de multiplicador-acelerador** multiplier-accelerator model; ~ **de negociación** trading pattern; ~ **de peaje** toll model; ~ **de simulación** simulation model; ~ **de valoración** pricing model

módem *m* modem

moderación *f* moderation; ~ **del ritmo** slowdown; ~ **salarial** wage restraint

moderado *adj* moderate; (precios) reasonable; (buzoneo) moderated

moderador, a *m,f* moderator

moderar *vt* moderate; (palabras) tone down; (entusiasmo) dampen; (reducir) cut, reduce; (inflación) curb

modernización *f* modernization, updating; (Info) upgrading

modernizado *adj* modernized, updated; (Info) upgraded

modernizar *vt* modernize, update; (Info) upgrade; (imagen del producto) revamp

moderno *adj* (equipos) modern, up-to-date

modestamente *adv* modestly

modesto *adj* modest

modificación f (de datos) modification; (en un plan) amendment, change; ~ **de la conducta** behaviour modification BrE, behavior modification AmE; ~ **contable** accounting change; **modificaciones y mejoras** (Cont) alterations and improvements

modificado adj modified; ~ **genéticamente** genetically modified

modificar vt modify; (términos) vary, amend; **sin** ~ unchanged

modo m way; (Info) mode; **a mi** ~ **de ver** in my opinion; **de cualquier** ~ anyway, in any case; **de ningún** ~ under no circumstances, in no way; ~ **de ayuda** help mode; ~ **borrador** draft mode; ~ **de consulta** query mode; ~ **conversación** conversational mode; ~ **edición** edit mode; ~ **de empleo** directions for use; ~ **gráfico** graphics mode; ~ **interactivo** interactive mode; ~ **de interrogación** query mode; ~ **manual** (de cálculo) manual mode; ~ **de pago** method of payment; ~ **en ráfagas** burst mode; ~ **respuesta** answer mode; ~ **texto** text mode; ~ **de transporte** mode of transport BrE, mode of transportation AmE

modulación f modulation; ~ **de frecuencias** frequency modulation

modulador-desmodulador m modulator/demodulator, modem

modularidad f modularity

módulo m (Info) module; ~ **de gestión** (Info) driver

MOFIPAC abr (▸**modelo de fijación de precios de los activos de capital**) CAPM (capital asset pricing model)

moldear vt (opinión pública) mould BrE, mold AmE

momento m moment; (periodo, ocasión) time; **en algún** ~ **futuro** at some point in the future; **por el** ~ for the time being; ~ **concertado** appointed time

moneda f (pieza) coin; (de un país) currency; ~ **agropecuaria** green currency; ~ **artificial** artificial currency; ~ **blanda** soft currency; ~ **circulante** currency; ~**s combinadas** or **compuestas** composite currency; ~ **común** common currency; ~ **convertible** convertible currency; ~ **de curso legal** legal tender; ~ **débil** soft currency; ~ **despreciada** token money BrE, fiat money AmE; ~ **falsa** counterfeit; ~ **fiduciaria** fiduciary currency; ~ **flotante** floating currency; ~ **forzada** forced currency; ~ **fuerte** hard

currency; ~ **funcional** functional currency; ~ **de intervención** intervention currency; ~ **de inversión** investment currency; ~ **nacional** national currency, local currency; ~ **nominal** token money BrE, fiat money AmE; ~ **de reserva** reserve currency; ~ **sin respaldo estatal** stateless currency; ~ **sobrevalorada** overvalued currency; ~ **solvente** sound currency; ~ **subvalorada** undervalued currency; ~ **única** single currency; ~ **única europea** single European currency

monetario adj monetary

monetarismo m monetarism; ~ **global** global monetarism

monetarista¹ adj monetarist

monetarista² mf monetarist

monetización f monetization

monitor m (Info) monitor; ~ **analógico** analogue BrE o analog AmE monitor; ~ **visualizador** display monitor

monocromo adj (pantalla) monochrome

monoeconomía f monoeconomics

monograma m monogram

monopolio m monopoly; ~ **absoluto** absolute monopoly; ~ **bilateral** bilateral monopoly; ~ **compartido** shared monopoly; ~ **discriminante** discriminating monopoly; ~ **espacial** spatial monopoly; ~ **exclusivo** exclusive monopoly; ~ **legal** legal monopoly; ~ **puro** pure monopoly; ~ **sindical** closed shop; ~ **total** absolute monopoly

monopolista mf monopolist

monopolístico adj monopolistic

monopolización f monopolization

monopolizar vt (negocio, sector) monopolize

monopsónico adj monopsonic

monopsonio m monopsony

monorrail m monorail

monóxido m monoxide; ~ **de carbono** carbon monoxide

montaje m assembly; (de película) editing; (publicidad) montage, paste-up; **cadena de** ~ assembly line; ~ **final** final assembly

montante m total, total amount; ~ **neto del activo** net asset amount

montar 1 vt (establecer, instalar) set up 2 vi: ~ **a** (sumar) amount o come to

monto m total, total amount; ~ **global** aggregate; ~ **insoluto** amount outstanding; ~ **neto de los activos** net ⋯⟶

asset amount; ∼ **de la pérdida** amount
of loss

mora f default; **en** ∼ in arrears

moral f (del personal) morale; **subir** or
levantar la ∼ boost morale

moralidad f morality; ∼ **corporativa**
corporate morality

moratoria f moratorium

morir vi die; ∼ **intestado** die intestate

morosidad f (Der) delinquency; (Fin)
arrears

moroso, -a m,f slow payer

mortalidad f mortality; ∼ **infantil**
infant mortality; ∼ **prevista** expected
mortality

mostrador m (en tienda) counter; (de
facturación) check-in (desk); ∼ **de
recepción** front desk; ∼ **de reservas**
reservation desk

mostrar vt (pérdida, remanente) show;
(artículos) exhibit; ∼ **claramente** (auditoría)
present fairly

motivación f motivation; ∼ **del
activo** asset motive; ∼ **extrínseca**
extrinsic motivation; ∼ **intrínseca**
intrinsic motivation

motivacional adj motivational

motivador¹, a m,f motivator

motivador² m: ∼ **de compras**
purchasing motivator

motivar vt (estimular) motivate; (causar)
cause; **motivado por** caused by

motivo m motive; (causa) reason; **por
∼s de mala salud** on grounds of ill
health; **ser** ∼ **de interés** excite interest;
∼ **de compra** buying motive; ∼ **de
despido** grounds for dismissal; ∼ **de
salvaguarda** precautionary motive

motor m engine; ∼ **de búsqueda**
search engine; ∼ **del crecimiento**
engine of growth; ∼ **diesel-eléctrico**
diesel-electric engine

mover vt move; **la Bolsa movió unos
100 millones de euros** 100 million euros
were moved o handled on the Stock
Market

moverse v pron move; ∼ **en serie**
move in tandem

móvil¹ adj (teléfono, comunicaciones)
mobile; **teléfono** ∼ mobile phone BrE,
cellphone AmE; **escala** ∼ sliding scale

móvil² m mobile (phone) BrE, cellphone
AmE

movilidad f mobility; ∼ **fiscal** fiscal
mobility; ∼ **laboral** job mobility

movimiento m movement; **sin** ∼
(mercado) flat; ∼ **de activos** asset

turnover; ∼ **adverso** adverse
movement; ∼ **alcista** bullish movement;
∼ **a la baja** bearish movement; ∼ **de
base popular** grass-roots movement; ∼
crediticio credit swing; ∼ **de la
cuenta** account activity; ∼
descendente downward movement; ∼
de impuesto único single tax
movement; ∼ **de la mano de obra**
movement of labour BrE o labor AmE; ∼
de precios price move; ∼ **sindical**
union movement

MP3 abr (*Imagen en Movimiento nivel 3*)
MP3 (Moving Pictures Audio Layer 3);
archivo ∼ MP3 file

MPEG abr (*Grupo de expertos de Imagen
en Movimiento*) MPEG (Moving Pictures
Expert Group); **formato** ∼ MPEG format

mudarse v pron move; ∼ **de casa**
move house; ∼ **a un local más grande**
move to larger premises

muelle m (puerto) quay; ∼ **franco** or
libre free dock

muerto adj (mercado) dead; (maquinaria)
idle

muestra f sample; ∼ **aleatoria**
random sample; ∼ **comercial**
commercial sample; ∼ **de firma**
specimen signature; ∼ **gratuita** free
sample; ∼ **de probabilidad** probability
sample; ∼ **de promocional**
promotional sample; ∼ **regular** fair
sample; ∼ **representativa**
representative sample

muestrario m swatch

muestreo m sampling; ∼ **para
aceptación** (en control de calidad)
acceptance sampling; ∼ **de una
actividad** activity sampling; ∼ **al azar**
or **aleatorio** random sampling; ∼ **en
bloque** block sampling; ∼
característico attribute sampling; ∼
por cuotas quota sampling; ∼
domiciliario house-to-house sampling;
∼ **estadístico** statistical sampling; ∼
sistemático systematic sampling; ∼
del trabajo work sampling; ∼ **por
universos** cluster sampling

mujer f woman; ∼ **de negocios**
businesswoman

multa f penalty, fine; **ponerle una** ∼ **a
alguien por algo/hacer algo** fine sb for
sth/doing sth; ∼ **ilimitada** unlimited
fine

multar vt fine; ∼ **a alguien (con algo)
por algo/hacer algo** fine sb (sth) for
sth/doing sth; **le** ∼**on con 500.000**

euros por fraude fiscal he was fined 500,000 euros for tax evasion

multiacceso *m* multiaccess

multianual *adj* multiannual, multiyear

multicanal *adj* (distribución, estrategia) multichannel

multicentro *m* shopping complex, shopping mall

multidivisa *adj* multicurrency

multifuncional *adj* multifunctional

multihabilidades *f pl* dual skilling

multijurisdiccional *adj* multijurisdictional

multilateral *adj* multilateral

multilateralismo *m* multilateralism

multilingüe *adj* multilingual

multimedia *adj* multimedia

multimillonario, -a *m,f* multimillionaire

multimodal *adj* multimodal

multinacional[1] *adj* multinational

multinacional[2] *f* multinational (corporation)

multinacionalmente *adv* multinationally

multiplataforma *adj* multiplatform

multiplicador *m* multiplier; ∼ **del arrendamiento bruto** gross rent multiplier; ∼ **del comercio exterior** foreign trade multiplier; ∼ **del crédito** credit multiplier; ∼ **de depósitos** deposit multiplier; ∼ **de empleo** employment multiplier; ∼ **fiscal** fiscal multiplier; ∼ **de inversión** investment multiplier; ∼ **monetario** money multiplier

multiplicar *vt* multiply

multiplicarse *v pron* (beneficios, costes) multiply, increase significantly

multiprocesador *m* multiprocessor

multiproceso *m* multiprocessing

multiprogramación *f* multiprogramming

multipropiedad *f* timeshare (property)

multiregional *adj* multiregional

multiruta *adj* multiroute

multisectorial *adj* multisector

multisindicalismo *m* multiunionism

multitarea *f* multitasking

multiuso *adj* multipurpose

multivía *adj* (distribución, estrategia) multichannel

mundial *adj* worldwide, global; **a escala** ∼ globally; **mercado** ∼ world market; **ventas** ∼**es** worldwide sales

mundialización *f* globalization

mundo *m* world; ∼ **comercial** business world; ∼ **del espectáculo** show business; ∼ **de las finanzas** world of finance; ∼ **de habla inglesa** English-speaking world; ∼ **hispanohablante** Spanish-speaking world; ∼ **de los negocios** business world

municipal *adj* municipal

municipio *m* (municipal) borough

mutualidad *f* friendly society BrE, benefit society AmE

mutuamente *adv* mutually; ∼ **excluyente** mutually exclusive

mutuo *adj* mutual; **de** ∼ **acuerdo** by mutual agreement

Nn

N *abr* (▸**carretera nacional**) A-road BrE, Interstate (highway) AmE

N.A. *abr* (▸**nota del autor**) author's note

nación *f* nation; ~ **industrializada** industrial nation

nacional *adj* national, domestic; **una campaña a nivel** ~ a nationwide campaign; **de origen** ~ home-grown

nacionalidad *f* nationality

nacionalismo *m* nationalism

nacionalización *f* (de una industria) nationalization

nacionalizar *vt* nationalize

nafta *f* AmL petrol BrE, gasoline AmE; ~ **ecológica** *or* **sin plomo** AmL lead-free petrol BrE o gasoline AmE

narcodólares *m pl* (infrml) drug money

narcotráfico *m* drug trafficking

naturaleza *f* nature

naufragar *vi* (compañía) go under; (plan) fall through

navegación *f* navigation; ~ **por la red** netsurfing, Internet surfing

navegador *m* (Web) browser; ~ **gráfico** graphics-based browser

navegante *m* surfer, Internet user

navegar *vi* (por Internet) surf (the Net)

necesidad *f* need; ~**es** requirements, needs; **de primera** ~ essential; ~ **básica** basic need; ~**es de caja** *or* **efectivo** cash needs; ~ **de capacitación** *or* **formación** training needs; ~**es financieras** financial requirements

negación *f* denial

negar *vt* (rumor, alegación, hecho) deny; (no conceder) refuse; ~**le la entrada a alguien** refuse sb entry; **el banco le negó el préstamo** the bank refused him the loan

negativa *f* refusal; (ante una acusación) denial; ~ **rotunda** flat refusal

negativo *adj* negative

negligencia *f* negligence; ~ **concurrente** contributory negligence; ~ **criminal** criminal negligence; ~ **grave** gross negligence; ~ **profesional** malpractice; ~ **temeraria** gross negligence

negligente *adj* negligent

negociabilidad *f* negotiability

negociable *adj* negotiable; **no** ~ non-negotiable; **valores** ~**s** negotiable securities

negociación *f* negotiation; (transacción) deal; **entablar negociaciones** enter into negotiations; **la ruptura de las negociaciones** the breakdown of negotiations; ~ **activa** active dealing, active trading; ~ **colectiva** collective bargaining; ~ **conjunta** joint negotiation; ~ **de contrato** contract bargaining; ~ **del día** day trading; ~ **dura** hard bargaining; ~ **de empresa** company bargaining; ~ **interrumpida** suspended trading; ~ **multisindical** multiunion bargaining; ~ **del pago** settlement bargaining; ~ **paralela** side-by-side trading; ~ **de planta** plant bargaining; ~ **de posiciones** position trading; ~ **regional de salarios** regional wage bargaining; ~ **rotativa** switch trading; **negociaciones salariales** pay talks; ~ **sobre la productividad** productivity bargaining; ~ **tras el cierre** after-hours trading

negociador, a *m,f* negotiator

negociante *mf* (m) businessman; (f) businesswoman; (comerciante) trader; ~ **al por mayor** wholesaler; ~ **al por menor** retailer

negociar ① *vt* (acuerdo, valores) negotiate
② *vi* negotiate; (Bolsa) trade; ~ **con alguien** negotiate with sb; ~ **en bolsa** trade on the Stock Exchange; ~ **con valores y bonos** trade in stocks and bonds

negocio *m* business, trade; **estar de** ~**s** be on business; **hacer** ~ make a profit; **hacer** ~**s** do business; **hacer** ~**s por teléfono** do business over the phone; **hicieron un buen/mal** ~ it was a good/bad deal for them; ~ **por tramitar** business to be transacted; ~ **básico** core business; ~ **comercial** commercial concern; ~ **competitivo** competitive business; ~ **por correspondencia** mail order business; ~ **electrónico** e-business, electronic business; ~ **familiar** family business; ~ **granel** bulk business; ~ **habitual** (Fisc) ordinary business; ~ **Internet** Internet business; ~ **principal** main o principal business; ~ **recíproco** reciprocal trading; ~ **sucio** unfair trade

negrita f bold (type), boldface; **en ~** in bold

negro[1] adj (mercado, economía) black

negro[2], **-a** m,f ghostwriter

neocorporativismo m neocorporatism

nepotismo m nepotism

netiqueta m (de Internet) netiquette

neto adj (sueldo, beneficio) net

neurolingüístico adj neurolinguistic

neutral adj neutral

neutralidad f neutrality; ~ **del dinero** neutrality of money; ~ **fiscal** fiscal neutrality; ~ **positiva** positive neutrality

neutralismo m neutralism

neutralizar vt neutralize; (Cont) balance out

nicho m niche; ~ **de mercado** market niche

NIF abr (▸**número de identificación fiscal**) taxpayer number

nivel m level; (calidad) standard; (Fisc) threshold; **de alto ~** high-level; **de bajo ~** low-level; **de ~ inicial** entry-level; **a ~ internacional** at (an) international level; **ser del ~ requerido** be up to standard, be up to scratch (infrml); ~ **de absentismo** absentee rate; ~ **de actividad** activity rate; ~ **de apoyo** support level; ~ **arancelario** tariff level; ~ **de beneficios** level of return; ~ **de capacidad** ability level; ~ **de confianza** confidence level; ~ **crítico** critical level; ~ **de desempleo** level of unemployment; ~ **de gasto** level of expenditure; ~ **general de precios** general price level; ~ **del índice de precios** price index level; ~ **de ingresos** income threshold; ~ **de ingresos básicos** basic income level; ~ **de los ingresos familiares** family income threshold; ~ **de inscripción** (del IVA) registration threshold; ~ **de inversiones** level of investment; ~ **de materialidad** materiality level; ~ **máximo** peak level; ~ **de negociación** bargaining level; ~ **de ocupación** occupancy level; ~ **de participación** participation rate; ~ **de pedidos** level

of orders; ~ **de personal** staffing level; ~ **de precios** price level; ~ **presupuestario** budget level; ~ **de renta** income range; ~ **de resistencia** resistance level; ~ **del ruido** noise level; ~ **sostenible** sustainable level; ~ **de subsistencia** subsistence level, breadline (infrml); ~ **de sueldo** salary level; ~ **de tolerancia** tolerance level; ~ **de tributación** tax threshold; ~ **de vida** standard of living

nivelación f levelling-out BrE, leveling-out AmE; ~ **exponencial** exponential smoothing

nivelado m levelling BrE, leveling AmE; ~ **de precio** pricing plateau

nivelar vt (fase de ejecución) level out; (presupuesto) balance

noción f notion; **tener nociones de algo** have a basic grasp of sth

nodo m node

nombrado adj appointed

nombramiento m (de persona) appointment; ~ **permanente** permanent appointment

nombrar vt (para un cargo) appoint

nombre m name; **a ~ de** (carta) addressed to; (cheque) made out o payable to; **en ~ de** on behalf of; (delante de una firma) pp, per pro; **en mi ~ y representación** in my name and on my behalf; ~ **y apellidos** full name; ~ **codificado** code name; ~ **comercial** trading name; ~ **de cuenta** account name; ~ **del documento** document name; ~ **del dominio** domain name; ~ **familiar** family name; ~ **habitual** usual first name; ~ **legal** legal name; ~ **de marca** brand name; ~ **del nominatario** or **titular** nominee name; ~ **registrado** proprietary name

nómina f (lista de empleados asalariados) payroll; (recibo de pago) pay slip; **estar en ~** be on the payroll

nominación f nomination

nominal adj nominal

nominatario, -a m,f nominee

nominativo adj nominal; (acciones) registered; **un cheque ~ a alguien** a cheque BrE o check AmE payable o made out to sb

norma f rule, regulation; (estándar) standard; **bajo la ~** below the norm; **por encima de la ~** above the norm; **observar las ~s de seguridad** observe the safety regulations; **según las ~s** by the book; **ser la ~** be the norm, be standard practice; ~ **aceptada** ⋯▸

n

convention; ∼ **aplicable** (Fisc) deemed disposition; ∼ **de atribución** attribution rule; ∼ **de auditoría** audit standard; ∼ **básica** ground rule; ∼ **de calidad** quality standard; ∼ **de calidad ambiental** environmental quality standard; ∼ **comercial** trading standard; ∼ **de contabilidad** accounting standard; ∼ **de costes** Esp *or* **costos** AmL cost standard; ∼ **de cumplimiento** performance standard; ∼ **del derechohabiente** successor rule; ∼ **disciplinaria** disciplinary rule; ∼ **de la elegibilidad** eligibility rule; ∼ **establecida** (Fisc) carve-out rule; ∼ **de fabricación** product standard; ∼ **financiera** financial standard; ∼ **fiscal** tax rule; ∼ **de higiene** hygiene standard; ∼ **industrial** industry standard; ∼ **de informes financieros** financial reporting standard; ∼ **internacional** international standard; ∼ **del medio año** half-year rule; ∼ **medioambiental** environmental standard; ∼ **mínima de calidad** minimum quality standard; ∼ **presupuestaria** budget standard; ∼ **primaria** primary standard; ∼ **procesal** court procedure; ∼ **de producción** production standard; ∼ **de producto** product standard; ∼**s y reglamentos** *f pl* rules and regulations; ∼ **de rendimiento** performance standard; ∼ **de riesgo** at-risk rule; ∼ **sanitaria** health regulation; ∼ **de seguridad** safety regulation; (estándar) safety standard; ∼ **sindical** union rule; ∼ **técnica** technical standard; ∼**s de urbanismo** planning regulations; ∼**s vigentes** current regulations

normalización *f* (de servicio, relaciones) normalization; (de productos) standardization

normalizado *adj* (productos) standardized

normalizar *vt* (servicio, relaciones) normalize, return to normal; (productos) standardize

normativa *f* regulations; (Der) legislation; ∼ **comercial** business regulations; ∼ **vigente** current regulations

nota *f* note; ∼ **bene** nota bene, NB; **tomar** ∼ **de algo** note sth, take *o* note sth down; **hemos tomado** ∼ **de su queja** we have noted your complaint; ∼ **de abono** credit note; ∼ **del autor** author's note; ∼ **de aviso** advised bill; ∼ **de cargo** debit note; ∼ **de contrato**

contract note; ∼ **de crédito** credit slip, credit note; ∼**s a las cuentas** notes to the accounts; ∼ **de entrega** delivery note; ∼ **de envío** dispatch note; ∼ **de inspección** jerque note; ∼ **marginal** margin note; ∼ **no emisible** unissuable note; ∼ **a pie de página** footnote; ∼ **de prensa** press release; ∼ **de quita y pon** Post-it®; ∼ **de la redacción** editor's note; ∼ **del traductor** translator's note

notar *vt* notice; **dejarse** ∼ be noticeable; **hacer** ∼ **algo** point sth out

notario, -a *m,f* notary, solicitor BrE; ∼ **público(-a)** *m,f* notary public, solicitor BrE

noticia *f* piece of news; ∼**s** news; **las** ∼ (en periódico, TV) the news; **tener** ∼**s de algo/alguien** have (some) news about sth/sb; **tener buenas/malas** ∼**s** have good/bad news; **¿quién les va a dar la** ∼**?** who is going to tell them (the news)?; **¿hay alguna** ∼**?** is there any news?; ∼**s de actualidad** current affairs; ∼ **bomba** bombshell; ∼**s de portada** *or* **primera plana** front-page news

notificación *f* notice, notification; ∼ **de apelación** notice of appeal; ∼ **de cancelación** notice of cancellation; ∼ **de despido** notice, pink slip AmE; ∼ **de envío** remittance advice; ∼ **de expiración** (de póliza) expiry notice BrE, expiration notice AmE; ∼ **de inversión** investment advice; ∼ **legal** legal notice, statutory notice; ∼ **de quiebra** bankruptcy notice

notificar *vt* inform, notify; ∼ **algo a alguien** notify sb of sth; ∼ **un giro** advise a draft; ∼ **a alguien una orden de detención** *or* **de registro** serve sb with a warrant

novato, -a *m,f* beginner; (de Internet) newbie (infrml)

novedad *f* (cualidad) novelty; (cosa nueva) innovation; (elemento nuevo) new feature; ∼**es** news; **sin** ∼ (llegar) safely; (terminar, transcurrir) without incident

NPI *abr* (▸**número personal de identificación**) PIN, PIN number

N.R. *abr* (▸**nota de la redacción**) editor's note

N.T. *abr* (▸**nota del traductor**) translator's note

núcleo *m* core; ∼ **duro** (de accionistas) hard core; ∼ **de la economía** core economy; ∼ **familiar** family unit; ∼ **magnético** magnetic core; ∼ **de población** population centre BrE, population center AmE

nuevo *adj* new; **de** ~ again; **nueva edición** new edition; ~ **enfoque** refocussing BrE, refocusing AmE; ~ **federalismo** new federalism; **nueva generación** next generation; ~ **giro** new business; ~ **mecanismo económico** new economic mechanism; ~ **orden mundial** new world order; ~ **pedido** incoming order; ~ **realismo** new realism; **nuevas tecnologías** new technology; ~ **trato** new deal; **nueva versión** new version; (de película) remake

nulo *adj* null and void

numeración *f* numbering; (números) numerals; **de** ~ **par** even-numbered; ~ **arábiga/romana** Arabic/Roman numerals; **N~ Internacional Normalizada de Libros** International Standard Book Number, ISBN

numerar *vt* number; ~ **consecutivamente** number consecutively; **sin** ~ unnumbered

numerario *adj* (empleado) permanent; (miembro) full

numérico *adj* numeric, numerical

número *m* number; (de fascículo) issue; **en** ~**s redondos** in round numbers; **estar en** ~**s rojos** (infrml) be in the red (infrml); ~ **aleatorio** random number; ~ **atrasado** (de diario, revista) back issue, back number; ~ **de autorización** authorization number; ~ **de base total** total base number; ~ **binario** binary

number; ~ **de bono** bond number; ~ **consecutivo** running number; ~ **de cotejo** collator number; ~ **de cuenta** account number; ~ **decimal** decimal number; ~ **de empleados** number of employees; ~ **especial** *or* **extraordinario** special issue; ~ **de identificación fiscal** taxpayer number; ~ **de identificación personal** personal identification number, PIN (number); ~ **índice** index number; ~ **de inscripción del IVA** VAT registration number BrE; ~ **Internet** Internet number; ~ **interno** intra number; ~ **de lectores** (de periódicos, libros) readership; ~ **de matrícula** registration number BrE, license number AmE; ~ **oficial** official number; ~ **de orden** serial number; ~ **de página** page number; ~ **paralelo de lectores** parallel readership; ~ **de pedido** order number; ~ **primario de lectores** primary readership; ~ **de puerta** (de embarque) gate number; ~ **real** real number; ~ **de referencia** reference number; ~ **de registro** registration number; ~ **de secuencia** sequence number; ~ **de serie** serial number; ~ **de serie de la Norma Internacional** International Standard Serial Number, ISSN; ~ **de sucursal** branch number; ~ **de teléfono** telephone number; ~ **de votantes** voter turnout

n

Oo

obedecer [1] *vt* (persona, ley) obey.
[2] *vi* (persona) obey; (mecanismo) respond;
~ **a algo** arise from sth, be due to sth; **el
retraso del proyecto obedece a un
cambio de sistema** the delay in the
project is due to the system being
changed, the reason for the delay is that
the system was changed

objeción *f* objection; **hacer** *or* **poner
una** ~ raise an objection, object; **no
poner ninguna** ~ raise no objections;
sin ~ no objections; ~ **denegada**
objection overruled; ~ **justificada**
objection sustained; ~ **de conciencia**
conscientious objection

objetar [1] *vi* object, raise objections
[2] *vt* (plan) object to

objetivo[1] *adj* objective

objetivo[2] *m* objective, target; **la
empresa** ~ the target company; **fijar** ~s
set objectives *o* targets; ~ **de
beneficios** profit target; ~ **de
cobertura** hedging goal; ~ **de
comunicación** communication
objective; ~ **corporativo** corporate
objective; ~ **a corto plazo** short-term
objective; ~ **de costes** Esp *or* **costos**
AmL cost objective; ~ **departamental**
depart mental objective; ~ **de la
empresa** company objective; ~ **de
inversiones** investment objective; ~ **de
investigación** research objective; ~ **a
largo plazo** long-term objective; ~ **de
marketing** marketing objective; ~ **de
mercado** market objective; ~ **de
negocios** business objective; ~ **de
ventas** sales target

objeto *m* (cosa) object; (meta) aim,
purpose; (tema) theme; (Der) exhibit; **con
el único** ~ **de** with the sole aim *o*
purpose of, in order to; **con el** ~ **de
coordinar los esfuerzos** with a view to
coordinating efforts; **esta reunión tiene
por** ~ **fijar el presupuesto** the purpose
of this meeting is to set the budget; ~
fuente source object; ~ **del informe**
reporting object; ~ **de la línea** line
object

obligación *f* obligation; (Banca)
debenture, debt; (Bolsa) bond; (Fin)
obligation, liability; **cumplir con sus**
obligaciones fulfil BrE *o* fulfill AmE one's
obligations; **es su** ~ **hacerlo** it is his
duty to do it; **sin** ~ without obligation;
sin ~ **de compra** no obligation to buy;
(en promoción de ventas) no purchase
necessary; ~ **amortizable** redeemable
bond; ~ **bancaria** bank debenture; ~
contingente contingent obligation; ~
contractual contractual obligation; ~
convertible convertible bond; ~ **de la
deuda** debt obligation; ~ **de empresa**
corporate debenture; ~ **del Estado**
government obligation; ~ **excluida**
excluded obligation; ~ **fuera del
balance general** off-balance sheet
commitment; ~ **sin garantía** unsecured
bond; ~ **con garantía hipotecaria**
general mortgage bond; ~ **garantizada**
secured debenture; ~ **hipotecaria**
mortgage commitment; ~ **imperfecta**
imperfect obligation; ~ **implícita**
implied obligation; ~ **imponible** taxable
obligation; **obligaciones de impuestos
diferidos** deferred tax liabilities; ~ **de
interés compuesto** compound interest
bond; ~ **de interés variable** floating-
rate note; ~ **internacional**
international bond; ~ **a largo plazo**
long-term security; ~ **legal** legal
obligation; ~ **municipal** municipal
bond; ~ **no imponible** nontaxable
obligation; ~ **ordinaria** marketable
bond; ~ **pagadera** amount payable; ~
de pago (de préstamo) payment
commitment; (Fisc) burden of payment;
~ **pendiente** outstanding commitment;
~ **perfecta** perfect obligation; ~
preferente participating bond; ~ **con
prima** premium bond; ~ **de renta fija**
fixed-interest bond; ~ **rescatada**
redeemed debenture; ~ **sin sellar**
unstamped debenture; ~ **solidaria** joint
obligation; ~ **subordinada**
subordinated debenture; ~ **de tipo
flotante** floating-rate debenture; ~
vencida matured bond

obligacionista *mf* bondholder,
debenture holder

obligado[1] *adj* obliged; **de** ~
cumplimiento legally-binding; **estar** ~ **a
hacer algo** be obliged to do sth; **estar** ~
legalmente a hacer algo be under a

legal obligation to do sth; **no estar ~ a hacer algo** be under no obligation to do sth; **quedar** *or* **estar ~ a alguien** be obliged to sb, remain *o* be in sb's debt

obligado², -a *m,f* obligor

obligar *vt* force, oblige; **~ a alguien a hacer algo** force sb to do sth; **el contrato nos obliga a pagar** the contract requires us to pay; **~ a alguien a una jubilación anticipada** force sb to take early retirement; **esta ley obliga a todos los negocios** the law applies to all businesses, all businesses are legally bound by this law

obligatorio *adj* compulsory, obligatory; (acuerdo) binding; (Der) statutory; **no ~** noncompulsory, nonobligatory; (Der) nonstatutory; **la asistencia es obligatoria** attendance is compulsory

obra *f* work; (de construcción) building site; **~ benéfica** charity, charitable organization; **~ en carretera** roadworks; **~ maestra** (de una colección) showpiece; **~ pública** public work

obrero¹ *adj* (familia) working-class; **la clase obrera** the working class; **el movimiento ~** the labour BrE *o* labor AmE movement

obrero², -a *m,f* worker; **~ de la construcción** construction worker; **~ cualificado(-a)** *m,f* skilled worker; **~ de línea** assembly-line worker; **~ manual** manual worker

observación *f* observation; (Fisc) monitoring; **observaciones** remarks; **hacer una ~** comment; **~ telefónica** telephone tappping

observador, a *m,f* observer; **~ del mercado** market watcher

obsolescencia *f* obsolescence; **~ económica** economic obsolescence; **~ incorporada** built-in obsolescence; **~ planificada** planned obsolescence; **~ progresiva** progress obsolescence; **~ tecnológica** technological obsolescence

obsoleto *adj* obsolete

obstaculizar *vt* hinder, hamper

obstáculo *m* obstacle, hurdle; **salvar ~s** overcome obstacles

obstante: **no ~** *adv* nevertheless, however

obstruir *vt* obstruct; (proceso, plan) hamper

obtención *f* procurement; **facilitar la ~ de algo** make it easier to obtain sth; **~ de fondos** raising of funds

obtener *vt* (resultado, cualificación) obtain, get; (meta) achieve; (Patent) take out; **~ la aprobación formal de** gain formal approval from; **~ beneficio** make a profit; **~ el favor de alguien** win sb's favour BrE *o* favor AmE; **~ algo fraudulentamente** obtain sth by fraud; **~ justicia** get justice; **~ permiso por escrito** obtain permission in writing; **~ una respuesta** receive a reply

O/C *abr* (▸**orden de compra**) P.O. (purchase order)

ocasión *f* (circunstancia) occasion; (oportunidad) opportunity, chance; (motivo) cause; **aprovechar una ~ para hacer algo** take advantage of an opportunity to do sth; **de ~** bargain; **precios de ~** bargain prices

ocasionar *vt* cause; (gastos) incur

occidentalizado *adj* westernized

occidentalizarse *v pron* become westernized

ocio *m* leisure

octavilla *f* pamphlet, leaflet; (publicidad) flyer

octeto *m* byte

OCU *abr* (▸**Organización de Consumidores y Usuarios**) *consumer protection advisory bureau*, ≈ CA (Consumers' Association) BrE, ≈ CAC (Consumers' Advisory Council) AmE

ocultación *f* (de información) concealment; (Info) blanking; **~ de pérdidas** concealment of losses

ocultar *vt* (información) conceal, hide; (Info) blank; (Pol) cover up; (publicidad) mask

ocupación *f* (trabajo) occupation; (actividad) activity; (de propiedad) occupancy; **~ comercial** commercial occupancy; **~ conjunta** joint occupancy; **~ residencial** residential occupancy; **~ vitalicia** life tenancy

ocupado *adj* (persona) busy; (señal) engaged BrE, busy AmE; (sitio) taken (aparato, lugar) in use; **estar ~ con algo/ haciendo algo** be busy with sth/doing sth

ocupante *mf* occupant

ocupar *vt* (tiempo, espacio) take up; (cargo, puesto) hold; (vacante) fill; (trabajadores) provide employment for; (edificio, oficina) occupy; **la empresa ocupa el primer puesto en el mundo financiero** the company is the leader *o* ranks top in the world of finance; **la nueva fábrica ~á a unos 1.000 trabajadores** the new factory will provide employment for about 1,000 ···⟩

workers; **el proyecto le ocupa demasiado tiempo** the project takes up too much of his time; **la redacción de la carta me ocupó toda la tarde** it took me all afternoon to write the letter; **ocupó la presidencia del club durante varios años** she was president of the club for several years

ocuparse: ∼ **de** *v pron* take care of; (asunto, problema, crisis) deal with; ∼ **de las cosas diarias** take care of day-to-day business; **nuestro departamento se ocupa de la facturación** our department deals with invoicing; **no nos ocupamos de préstamos personales** we don't deal with personal loans

ocurrir *vi* happen, occur; **ocurre que ...** it so happens that ...; **¿ha ocurrido algo?** is something wrong?, has something happened?; **lo peor que puede ∼ es que ...** the worst that can happen is that ...; **ocurra lo que ocurra** come what may, whatever happens; **¿qué ocurre?** what's up?, what's going on?; **volver a ∼** happen again

ofensiva *f* offensive; **tomar la ∼** go on the offensive; ∼ **comercial** sales offensive

oferta *f* offer; (en licitación) tender, bid; (V&M) special offer; **en ∼** (casa) under offer; (V&M) on offer; **estar de ∼** be on special offer; **hacer/rechazar una ∼** make/reject an offer; **u ∼ próxima** or near offer, o.n.o.; ∼ **y aceptación** offer and acceptance; ∼ **afianzada** hedged tender; ∼ **agregada** aggregate supply; ∼ **apalancada** leveraged bid; ∼ **de apertura** opening bid; ∼ **asociada** banded offer; ∼ **atractiva** attractive offer; ∼ **de buena fe** bona fide offer; ∼ **sin competencia** noncompetitive bid; ∼ **competitiva** competitive tendering; ∼ **de compra de dólares** dollar bid; ∼ **de compras** buyout; ∼ **condicional** conditional offer; ∼ **definitiva** closing bid; ∼ **y demanda** supply and demand; ∼ **de dinero** money supply; ∼ **de divisas** exchange offer; ∼ **elástica** elastic supply; ∼**s de empleo** job vacancies; ∼ **por escrito** written offer; ∼ **especial** special offer; ∼ **excesiva** oversupply; ∼ **en firme** firm offer; ∼ **garantizada** hedged tender; ∼ **invisible** invisible supply; ∼ **de lanzamiento** introductory offer, launch offer; ∼ **más alta** highest tender; ∼ **más baja** lowest tender; ∼ **más próxima** nearest offer; ∼ **minorista** retail offer; ∼ **de muestras** sampling offer; ∼ **original**

original bid; ∼ **de pago al contado** cash tender offer; ∼ **en pliego cerrado** sealed tender; ∼ **preferente** pre-emptive bid; ∼ **sin presión** soft offer; ∼ **de prueba** trial offer; ∼ **pública de adquisición** takeover bid; ∼ **pública de adquisición hostil** hostile takeover bid; ∼ **pública de compra** takeover bid; ∼ **pública inicial** initial public offering; ∼ **pública de venta** public offering; ∼ **de reembolso total** full refund offer; ∼ **regresiva** regressive supply; ∼ **de trabajo** job offer; ∼**s de trabajo** (en periódico) job vacancies, situations vacant BrE; ∼ **verbal** verbal offer; ∼ **vinculante** binding offer; ∼ **viscosa** viscous supply

ofertado *adj* (Fin) bid, tendered; **productos ∼s** products on offer

ofertar *vt* (en licitación) bid, tender; (V&M) sell on special offer

oficial¹ *adj* official; **fuentes ∼es** official sources; **no ∼** unofficial

oficial², **a** *m,f* officer, official; ∼ **de aduanas** customs officer; ∼ **administrativo** administrative officer; ∼ **de almacén** warehouse officer; ∼ **de formación** *or* **capacitación** training officer; ∼ **de guardia** duty officer; ∼ **de prensa** press officer

oficialmente *adv* officially

oficina *f* office; **horas de ∼** office hours; ∼ **de alojamiento** accommodation bureau; ∼ **de apoyo** back office; ∼ **bancaria extraterritorial** (para inversiones) offshore banking unit; ∼ **de bienestar social** welfare agency; ∼ **de cambio** foreign exchange office; ∼ **del catastro** land office; ∼ **central** head office; ∼ **central de reservas** central reservation office; ∼ **de colocaciones** employment agency; ∼ **comercial** business office; **O∼ de Comercio Internacional** Office of International Trade; ∼ **de contabilidad** accounting office; ∼ **corporativa** head office; ∼ **de correos** post office; ∼ **de crédito** credit bureau; ∼ **designada** designated office; ∼ **de distribución** distribution office; ∼ **electrónica** electronic office; ∼ **de empleo** employment agency, recruitment agency; **O∼ Europea para el Medio Ambiente** European Environment Bureau; ∼ **de exportación** export office; ∼ **del gerente** manager's office; ∼ **de información** information office, information desk; ∼ **de información**

turística tourist information office; ~ **de investigaciones** enquiry desk; ~ **matriz** head office; ~ **del paro** Esp (infrml) ≈ Social Security Office BrE, ≈ Welfare Office AmE; ~ **de planificación abierta** open-plan office; ~ **de prensa** press office; ~ **principal** head office; ~ **privada** private office; **O~ de Protección al Consumidor** ≈ Office of Fair Trading; ~ **de proyectos** design office; ~ **pública** government office; ~ **de recaudación de impuestos** revenue office; ~ **de recepción** receiving office; ~ **de reclutamiento** recruiting office; ~ **regional** regional office; ~ **de registro** registration office; ~ **del Registro Civil** register office BrE, registry office BrE; ~ **de trabajo** recruitment agency; **O~ de Turismo** *Spanish national tourism office,* ≈ English Tourist Board; ~ **de ventas** sales office; ~ **virtual** virtual office; ~ **de zona** area office

oficinista *mf* clerk, office worker

oficio *m* profession, occupation; **aprender un** ~ learn a trade; **es ingeniero de** ~ he is an engineer by trade; **saber su** ~ know one's job

ofimática *f* office automation *o* computerization

ofrecer *vt* (ayuda, empleo, préstamo) offer; (información) volunteer; (en TV) show; (fiesta, comida) hold, give; (imagen) present; (pujar) bid; ~ **hacer algo** offer to do sth; **el plan ofrece varias posibilidades** the plan offers various possibilities; **ofrecieron una fiesta de despedida en su honor** they gave him a leaving party; ~ **acciones al público** go public

OIC *abr* (▸**Organización Internacional de Comercio**) ITO (International Trade Organization)

OIN *abr* (▸**Organización Internacional de Normalización**) ISO (International Standards Organization)

OIT *abr* (▸**Organización Internacional de Trabajo**) ILO (International Labour Organization BrE, International Labor Organization AmE)

OL *abr* (▸**onda larga**) LW (long wave)

oleada *f* wave, surge; ~ **de gastos** spending surge; ~ **de huelgas** wave *o* spate of strikes

oleoducto *m* oil pipeline

oligopolio *m* oligopoly; ~ **colusorio** collusive oligopoly; ~ **espacial** spatial oligopoly; ~ **homogéneo** homogeneous oligopoly

oligopolístico *adj* oligopolistic

oligopsonio *m* oligopsony

OMC *abr* (▸**Organización Mundial del Comercio**) WTO (World Trade Organization)

omisión *f* omission; (comercial) nonfeasance; ~ **de hacer algo** failure to do sth

omitir *vt* omit, leave out; ~ **un dividendo** pass a dividend (jarg); ~ **hacer algo** omit *o* fail to do sth; ~ **un pago** miss a payment

OMS *abr* (▸**Organización Mundial de la Salud**) WHO (World Health Organization)

onda *f* wave; ~ **corta/larga** short/long wave

ONG *abr* (▸**organización no gubernamental**) NGO (nongovernmental organization)

ONU *abr* (▸**Organización de las Naciones Unidas**) UNO (United Nations Organization)

OPA *abr* (▸**oferta pública de adquisición**) TOB (takeover bid)

OPAH *abr* (▸**oferta pública de adquisición hostil**) hostile takeover bid

OPC *abr* (▸**oferta pública de compra**) TOB (takeover bid)

opción *f* option; **la** ~ **fácil** the easy option; **no les queda más** ~ **que vender el negocio** they have no option but to sell the business; **¿no hay otra** ~? is there no other option?; **de** ~ **múltiple** (pregunta, examen) multiple-choice; ~ **sobre acciones** share option; ~ **admitida a cotización** listed option; ~ **al contado** cash-delivery option; ~ **de arrendamiento** lease option; ~ **de base** fallback option; ~ **con beneficio potencial** in-the-money option; ~ **de bonos** bond option; ~ **de bonos a largo plazo** long-term bond option; ~ **caducada** lapsed option; ~ **de cambio negociada** traded exchange option; ~ **de cierre** (en absorción de sociedad) lock-up option; ~ **de compra** option to buy; (Bolsa) call option; ~ **de compra de acciones** share option, stock option; ~ **de compra al portador** bearer warrant; ~ **de compra de bonos** bond call option; ~ **de compra sin cobertura** uncovered call option; ~ **de compra cubierta** covered call option; ~ **de compra de divisas** currency call option; ~ **de compra emitida** written call; ~ **de compra a largo plazo** long call; ~ **de compra a precio corriente** ⋯⟩

at-the-money call option; ∼ **de compra** call option; ∼ **de compra y venta** call and put option; ∼ **del consumidor** consumer choice; ∼ **cotizada** listed option; ∼ **sin cubrir** uncovered option; ∼ **por defecto** default option; ∼ **sobre divisas** currency option; ∼ **doble a corto** short straddle; ∼ **doble sin garantía** naked put; ∼ **emitida** written option; ∼ **de entrada en el mercado** market entry option; ∼ **ficticia sobre acciones** phantom share option; ∼ **de futuro** futures option; ∼ **sobre futuros de divisas** option on currency futures; ∼ **con garantía** covered option; ∼ **sin garantía** naked option; ∼ **índice** index option; ∼ **sobre el índice bursátil** stock index option; ∼ **indiferente** at-the-money option; ∼ **inmovilizada** (en absorción de empresa) lock-up option; ∼ **intercalada** embedded option; ∼ **librada al contado** cash-delivery option; ∼ **negativa** negative option; ∼ **negociada** traded option; ∼ **sobre el neto** equity option; ∼ **objeto de comercio** traded option; ∼ **pagada al contado** cash-settled option; ∼ **sobre permuta financiera** swap option; ∼ **de recompra** buy-back option; ∼ **de renovación** (de contrato de arrendamiento) renewal option; ∼ **de reserva** fallback option; ∼ **de tipo de interés** interest-rate option; ∼ **de venta** put option; ∼ **de venta de bonos** bond put option; ∼ **de venta sin cobertura** uncovered put; ∼ **de venta cubierta** covered put; ∼ **de venta en descubierto** short put; ∼ **de venta de divisas** currency put option; ∼ **de venta emitida** written put; ∼ **de venta indiferente** in-the-money put

opcional *adj* optional

opcional/obligatorio *adj* optional/ mandatory

operación *f* operation; (Fin) transaction; ∼ **administrativa** management operation; ∼ **al alza** bull operation *o* transaction; ∼ **al cierre** closing trade; ∼ **al contado** cash operation; ∼ **de arbitraje** arbitrage dealing; ∼ **auxiliar** ancillary operation; ∼ **a la baja** bear operation *o* transaction; ∼ **bancaria** banking operation; ∼ **con bonos** bond trading; ∼ **bursátil** stock exchange transaction; ∼ **de cobertura** hedge trading, hedging operation; ∼ **comercial** trading operation, commercial trade; ∼ **de compensación** clearing process; ∼ **de**

compra-venta extranjera forex trading; ∼ **de contado** spot trading; ∼ **de corrección** corrective action; ∼ **discontinua** discontinued operation; ∼ **de dobles** swap; ∼ **con dobles primas** put and call; ∼ **de emisión de bonos** bond issue operation; ∼ **de emplazamiento** site operation; ∼ **fiduciaria** fiduciary operation; ∼ **a futuros** forward dealing; ∼ **con intereses** interest operation; ∼ **interna** in-house operation; ∼ **de limpieza** cleaning-up operation; ∼ **con margen** spread trading; ∼ **de la memoria** memory operation; ∼ **de mercado** market dealing; ∼ **modelo** textbook operation; ∼ **no continuada** discontinued operation; ∼ **no válida** illegal operation; ∼ **a plazo** forward operation; ∼ **a precio puesto** blackboard trading; ∼ **de préstamo** lending business; ∼ **de protección cambiaria** hedging operation; ∼ **de rescate** bailout; ∼ **retorno** *the journey home after a public holiday*; ∼ **en serie** serial operation; ∼ **subsidiaria** ancillary operation; ∼ **a término** forward dealing

operacional *adj* operational

operador¹ *m* operator; ∼ **binario** binary operator; ∼ **de satélite** satellite operator

operador², **a** *m,f* operator; ∼ **alcista** bull operator; ∼ **de arbitraje** arbitrage dealer; ∼ **de bolsa** dealer; ∼ **cambiario(-a)** *m,f* forward exchange dealer; ∼ **de consola** keyboarder; ∼ **de descuento** value broker; ∼ **informático(-a)** *m,f* computer operator; ∼ **del mercado** marketer; ∼ **de opciones autorizado(-a)** *m,f* registered options trader; ∼ **de posición** position trader; ∼ **de posiciones diarias** day trader; ∼ **de teclado** keyboard operator; ∼ **de teléfonos** switchboard operator; ∼ **de terminal** terminal operator

operar *vi* (funcionar) operate; (empresa) do business, deal; ∼ **en la bolsa** deal on the Stock Exchange; **el vuelo** ∼**á de lunes a viernes** the flight will operate Mondays to Fridays

operario, -a *m,f* worker, labourer BrE, laborer AmE; ∼ **de fábrica** factory worker

operativo, -a *m,f* operative

OPI *abr* (▸**oferta pública inicial**) IPO (initial public offering)

opinar *vt* think; ~ **que ...** think that ...; **¿qué opinas de la situación?** what do you think about the situation?, what are your views on the situation?

opinión *f* opinion; **cambiar de** ~ change one's mind *o* point of view; **en mi** ~ in my opinion; **formar una** ~ form an opinion; **ser de la** ~ **que ...** be of the opinion that ...; **sondeo de** ~ opinion poll; ~ **del auditor** auditor's opinion; ~ **legal** legal opinion; ~ **pública** public opinion; ~ **de título** (Inmob) opinion of title

oponerse *v pron* be opposed, object; ~ **a algo** oppose sth, object to sth; **nadie se opuso al plan** nobody objected to *o* opposed the plan

oportunidad *f* opportunity; **aprovechar una** ~ make the most of an opportunity; **dar a alguien la oportunidad de hacer algo** give sb the opportunity to do sth; **tener la** ~ **de hacer algo** have a chance *o* an opportunity to do sth; ~ **comercial** business opportunity; ~ **de empleo** job opportunity; ~ **de inversión** investment opportunity; ~ **de mercado** market opportunity; ~ **de negocios** business opportunity; ~ **de ventas** sales opportunity

oportunismo *m* opportunism

oportunista *mf* opportunist

oportuno *adj* (momento) opportune; (indicado) appropriate; **llegó en el momento** ~ she arrived just at the right moment; **se tomarán las medidas que se estimen oportunas** appropriate measures will be taken; **sería** ~ **avisarles de antemano** it would be wise to let them know beforehand

oposición *f* opposition; (*tb* **oposiciones** Esp) (examen) *competitive examination for a public-sector job*; ~ **a algo** opposition to sth; **hacer oposiciones** a sit *o* take an exam for

optar *vi*: ~ **por algo/por hacer algo** opt for sth/to do sth; ~ **a algo** apply for sth; **sólo los licenciados en Ciencias Empresariales pueden** ~ **a esta plaza** only graduates in Business Studies are eligible for this post

optimismo *m* optimism; ~ **cauto** cautious optimism

optimización *f* optimization; ~ **de beneficios** profit optimization

optimizar *vt* optimize; ~ **la función objetiva** optimize the objective function

óptimo *adj* optimum; **de óptima calidad** top-quality; **condiciones óptimas** ideal conditions; ~**s resultados** top *o* best results

opulencia *f* affluence, wealth

OPV *abr* (▸**oferta pública de venta**) public offering

oráculo *m* oracle

orador, a *m,f* speaker

orden[1] *f* order; **hasta nueva** ~ until further notice; **mi** ~ my order; ~ **de** order of; **cheques a la** ~ **de** cheques BrE *o* checks AmE made out *o* payable to; ~ **abierta** open order; ~ **bancaria** banker's order; ~ **administrativa** administration order; ~ **al mercado** market order; ~ **de bloqueo** stop order; ~ **de cancelación** cancel order; **órdenes casadas** matched orders; ~ **de cobro de deudas** debt collection order; ~ **de compra** purchase order; ~ **de compra abierta** blanket order; ~ **de compraventa a crédito** spread order; ~ **de desahucio** eviction order; ~ **del día** agenda; ~ **de disolución** winding-up order; ~ **ejecutoria** enforcement order; **órdenes emparejadas** matched orders; ~ **de entrega** delivery order; ~ **de exención** order of discharge; ~ **judicial** court order; ~ **de moneda extranjera** foreign money order; ~ **de pago** payment order, order to pay; ~ **de pago internacional** international payment order; ~ **de popularidad** popularity rating; ~ **de registro** search warrant; ~ **de reserva** booking order; ~ **de trabajo** job order; ~ **de transferencia de dinero** money transfer order; ~ **del tribunal** court order; ~ **de venta anticipada** presale order

orden[2] *m* order; **del** ~ **de** in the order *o* region of; **de primer** ~ (empresa) leading, major; **estar en** ~ be in order; **todo está en** ~ everything is in order; **en** *or* **por** ~ **alfabético** in alphabetical order; **en** *or* **por** ~ **ascendente/decreciente** in ascending/descending order; **en** *or* **por** ~ **de importancia/prioridad** in order of importance/priority; **en el** ~ **señalado** in the order shown; **mantener el** ~ keep order; **poner algo en** ~ sort sth out; **restablecer el** ~ restore order; ~ **público** public order

ordenador *m* Esp (*cf* ▸**computadora** AmL) computer; ~ **activo** Esp active computer; ~ **agenda** Esp palmtop; ~ **analógico** Esp analogue BrE *o* analog ⋯⋯▸

AmE computer; ~ **auxiliar** Esp satellite
computer; ~ **de bolsillo** Esp pocket
computer; ~ **central** central computer;
~ **comercial** Esp business computer,
commercial computer; ~ **de cuarta
generación** Esp fourth-generation
computer; ~ **destinatario** Esp target
computer; ~ **doméstico** Esp home
computer; ~ **frontal** Esp front-end
computer; ~ **fuente** Esp source
computer; ~ **híbrido** Esp hybrid
computer; ~ **por lotes** Esp batch
computer; ~ **de mano** Esp hand-held
computer; ~ **de mesa** Esp desktop
computer; ~ **de nivel superior** Esp
high-end computer, high-spec computer;
~ **periférico** Esp peripheral computer;
~ **personal** Esp personal computer; ~
portátil Esp laptop, notebook, notepad;
~ **de primera generación** Esp first-
generation computer; ~ **de quinta
generación** Esp fifth-generation
computer; ~ **de red** Esp Internet surfer;
~ **de segunda generación** Esp
second-generation computer; ~ **en serie**
Esp serial computer; ~ **en tándem** Esp
duplex computer; ~ **de tercera
generación** Esp third-generation
computer; ~ **terminal** Esp terminal
computer; ~ **vectorial** Esp array
processor

ordenamiento *m* legislation; ~
jurídico legal system

ordenanza¹ *f* ordinance; ~ **comercial**
trade regulation; ~s **municipales** by-
laws

ordenanza² *m* office boy

ordenar *vt* (arreglar, colocar bien) arrange,
sort out; (clasificar) put in order; (dar una
orden) order; (Info) sort; ~ **las fichas** put
the cards in order; ~ **algo por
antigüedad** *or* **fecha** put sth in date
order; **la policía ordenó el cierre del
local** the police ordered the closure of
the establishment

organigrama *m* (de empresa)
organigram, organization chart; (gráfico)
flowchart; ~ **de correspondencia**
pertinence chart; ~ **funcional** flowchart

organismo *m* body, authority; ~
consultivo consultative body; ~ **de
financiación** funding agency; ~
gubernamental public authority; ~
internacional international agency; ~
legal statutory body; ~ **de
planificación** planning authority; ~
profesional professional body; ~
público public body; ~ **regulador**
regulatory body; ~ **de revisión** review

body; ~ **del sector público** public
sector body; ~ **de servicio público**
public service body

organización *f* (acción, compañía)
organization; ~ **sin ánimo de lucro**
non-profit-making organization BrE,
nonprofit organization AmE; ~
autorreguladora self-regulatory
organization; ~ **benéfica** charitable
organization; ~ **comercial** trade
organization; ~ **del consumidor**
consumer organization; O~ **de
Consumidores y Usuarios** *consumer
protection advisory bureau,* ≈
Consumers' Association BrE, ≈
Consumers' Advisory Council AmE; ~
educativa educational organization; ~
de la empresa business organization;
~ **funcional** functional organization; ~
de la gestión management
organization; ~ **horizontal** flat
organization; ~ **industrial** industrial
organization; O~ **Internacional de
Comercio** International Trade
Organization; O~ **Internacional de
Normalización** International Standards
Organization; O~ **Internacional
Reguladora de Valores** International
Securities Regulatory Organization; ~
Internacional de Trabajo International
Labour BrE *o* Labor AmE Organization; ~
lineal line organization; O~ **Marítima
Internacional** International Maritime
Organization; ~ **matriz** matrix
organization; O~ **Mundial de la Salud**
World Health Organization; O~
Mundial del Comercio World Trade
Organization; O~ **de las Naciones
Unidas** United Nations Organization; ~
de negocios business organization; ~
no gubernamental nongovernmental
organization; ~ **del personal** staff
organization; ~ **de un proyecto** project
planning; ~ **regional** regional
organization; ~ **religiosa** religious
organization; ~ **sindical** trade union
BrE, labor union AmE; ~ **social** social
organization; ~ **del Tratado del
Atlántico Norte** North Atlantic Treaty
Organization; ~ **de ventas** sales
organization; ~ **vertical** vertical
organization

organizador¹ *m,f* organizer

organizador² *m* organizer; ~
electrónico electronic organizer; ~
personal personal organizer; ~ **de
escritorio** desk planner; ~ **del tráfico**
(de sitio web) traffic manager

organizar *vt* organize; ~ **una huelga** stage a strike

órgano *m* body; ~ **consultivo** advisory body

orientación *f* orientation; (posición) position; (consejo) guidance; **de ~ comercial** business-oriented; **de ~ profesional** career-oriented; ~ **del cliente** customer orientation; ~ **del consumo** consumer orientation; ~ **de marketing** marketing orientation; ~ **profesional** professional *o* vocational guidance; ~ **de ventas** sales orientation

orientado *adj* oriented; ~ **al cliente** customer-oriented; ~ **al consumidor** consumer-oriented; ~ **al mercado** market-oriented; ~ **al usuario** user-oriented; ~ **hacia los negocios** business-oriented; ~ **a la investigación** research-oriented

orientador, a *m,f* careers adviser *o* officer; ~ **vocacional** careers adviser *o* officer

orientar *vt* (enfocar) direct; (guiar) advise; ~ **algo hacia algo** gear sth towards BrE *o* toward AmE sth; **orientemos nuestros esfuerzos hacia ese objetivo** let's direct our efforts towards BrE *o* toward AmE that objective; **una política orientada a combatir la inflación** a policy designed to combat inflation

original[1] *adj* (copia) original; (coste) historical; **en su forma ~** in the original

original[2] *m* original; (radiodifusión) master

oriundo *adj* native; ~ **de** native to

oro *m* gold; ~ **en custodia** earmarked gold; ~ **negro** (petróleo) black gold; ~ **puro** solid gold

oscilación *f* (de precios) fluctuation; **oscilaciones estacionales** seasonal fluctuations; **oscilaciones de los tipos de cambio** exchange rate movements

oscilar *vt* (precios) fluctuate; **la cotización osciló entre $50 y $65** the share price fluctuated between $50 and $65

OSI *abr* (▸**interconexión de sistemas abiertos**) OSI (open systems interconnection)

ostentar *vt* (cargo, posición) hold; (exhibir) flaunt; **la empresa ostenta el liderazgo en su especialidad** the company is the market leader in its field

OTAN *abr* (▸**Organización del Tratado del Atlántico Norte**) NATO (North Atlantic Treaty Organization)

otorgante *mf* grantor

otorgar *vt* (permiso, préstamo) grant; (derecho, poderes) bestow, confer; (contrato, plan) draw up; ~ **a alguien el derecho a** give sb the right to; ~ **ante notario** notarize; ~ **importancia a** (argumento, suposición) lend weight to

o

Pp

p *abr* (▸**página**) p. *o* pg. (page)

PAC *abr* (▸**Política Agrícola Común**) CAP (Common Agricultural Policy)

paciente, -a *mf* patient; ~ **privado** private patient

pactar 1 *vt* (acuerdo, tregua) negotiate; (plazo) agree on
2 *vi* come to an agreement

pacto *m* agreement, pact; **cumplir un** ~ abide by the terms of an agreement; **hacer un** ~ make a deal; **romper un** ~ break a deal *o* an agreement; **P~ Andino** Andean Pact (*agreement on economic cooperation between Andean countries*); ~ **de ayuda mutua** mutual aid pact; ~ **de caballeros** gentleman's agreement; ~ **de no competencia** no-competition agreement; ~ **de protección** protective covenant; ~ **de recompra** repurchase agreement; ~ **de retrocompra** buy-back agreement; ~ **social** social contract

PAD *abr* (▸**proceso automático de datos**) ADP (automatic data processing)

padre *m* (pariente) father; (título) senior; (Info) parent; ~ **soltero** single father, single parent

PAF *abr* (▸**porcentaje anual fijo**) FAP (fixed annual percentage)

pág *abr* (▸**página**) p. *o* pg. (page)

paga *f* pay; (sueldo) salary; (semanal) wages; **recibir la** ~ receive one's salary, get paid; ~ **adicional** extra pay; ~ **de antigüedad** long-service pay; ~ **según desempeño** performance-related pay; ~ **extra** *or* **extraordinaria** *double pay received twice a year, in the summer and at Christmas*; ~ **extraordinaria de Navidad** *double pay given at Christmas*, ≈ Christmas bonus; ~ **por horas extra** *or* **extraordinarias** overtime pay; ~ **de huelga** strike pay; ~ **por incentivos** incentive pay scheme; ~ **por maternidad** maternity benefit; ~ **por mérito** merit pay; ~ **retrospectiva** back pay; ~ **de vacaciones** holiday pay BrE, vacation pay AmE

pagadero *adj* payable; **hacer** ~ **a** make payable to; ~ **anticipadamente** payable in advance; ~ **en cuotas mensuales** payable in monthly

instalments BrE *o* installments AmE; ~ **después del aviso** payable after notice; ~ **el día 25 de cada mes** payable *o* due on the 25th of every month; ~ **en tres años** payable over three years; ~ **mensualmente a plazo vencido** payable monthly in arrears; ~ **al vencimiento** payable at maturity

pagado *adj* (dividendos, vacaciones, factura) paid; **no** ~ unpaid; ~ **por adelantado** paid in advance, prepaid; ~ **al contado** paid in cash; ~ **por hora** paid by the hour; ~ **por pieza** on piece rates; **totalmente** ~ fully paid; ~ **por unidad** paid by the piece

pagador, a *m,f* payer; (Fin) disburser; (RRHH) paymaster; ~ **moroso(-a)** *m,f* slow payer

pagar 1 *vt* pay; (deuda) pay back; (préstamo) repay, pay off; (en una cuenta) pay in; **no** ~ **un cheque** dishonour a cheque BrE, dishonor a check AmE; ~ **la cuenta** pay the bill BrE *o* check AmE; ~ **una cuota** pay an instalment BrE *o* installment AmE; ~ **una fianza a alguien** bail sb out; ~ **los gastos** pay expenses; ~ **una letra** take up a bill; ~ **a la orden de** pay to the order of; ~ **un plazo** pay an instalment BrE *o* installment AmE
2 *vi* pay; **a** *or* **por** ~ due, payable; **pagan bien** they pay well; **el negocio no paga** the business doesn't pay; ~ **anualmente** pay yearly; ~ **por completo** pay in full; ~ **al contado** Esp *or* **de contado** AmL pay (in) cash; ~ **en efectivo** pay in cash; ~ **en especie** pay in kind; ~ **por giro** pay by giro; ~ **por hora** pay by the hour; ~ **en metálico** pay cash; ~ **a plazos** pay in instalments BrE *o* installments AmE; ~ **semanalmente** pay weekly; ~ **con tarjeta** pay by (credit/debit) card; ~ **trimestralmente** pay quarterly

pagaré *m* promissory note, I owe you, IOU (infrml); ~ **avalado** accommodation note; ~ **bancario** bank bill; ~ **de empresa** corporate bond; ~ **especial** balloon note; ~ **de favor** accommodation bill; ~ **negociable** tradeable promissory note; ~ **solidario** joint promissory note; ~ **del tesoro**

Treasury bill; ~ **a la vista** demand note

página *f* page; **a toda** ~ full-page; **P~s Amarillas**® Yellow Pages®; ~ **asabanada** (imprenta) broadsheet; ~ **de bienvenida** (en Internet) welcome page; ~ **frontal** *or* **inicial** (en Internet) home page; ~**s de negocios** (de los periódicos) business pages; ~ **de portada** title page; ~ **principal** (en Internet) home page; ~ **visitada** *or* **vista** viewed page; ~ **web** Web page; ~ **web interactiva** interactive Web page; ~ **web personal** personal Web page

paginación *f* pagination

paginar *vt* paginate; **sin** ~ unnumbered

pago *m* payment; **atrasarse en los** ~**s** get *o* fall behind with payments, be in arrears; **contra** ~ against payment; **efectuar** *or* **hacer un pago** make a payment; **en** ~ **de** (deuda) in settlement of; **forma de** ~ method of payment; **suspender** ~**s** stop payments; ~ **a favor de** payment made to; ~ **adelantado** advance payment, cash in advance, money up front; ~ **de amortización** amortization payment; ~ **antes de la entrega** cash before delivery; ~ **antes del vencimiento** prepayment; ~ **anticipado** advance payment; ~ **anticipado de derechos** advance royalty payment; ~ **anual** annual *o* yearly payment; ~ **de anualidad** annuity payment; ~ **aplazado** instalment BrE *o* installment AmE payment; ~ **atrasado** outstanding payment, payment in arrears; ~ **de atrasos** back pay; ~ **por aval** accommodation payment; ~ **bajo protesta** payment under protest; ~ **por clic** click payment, pay-per-clic; ~ **del cliente** user fee; ~ **compensatorio** compensation payment; ~ **al contado** cash payment; ~ **contingente** contingency payment; ~ **contra documentación** cash against documents; ~ **contractual** contract payment; ~ **contra entrega** cash on delivery; ~ **a cuenta** payment on account; ~ **y declaración** (Fisc) pay and file; ~ **de una deuda** satisfaction of a debt; ~ **diferido** deferred payment; ~ **directo** direct payment; ~ **electrónico** electronic payment; ~ **escalonado** staggered payment; ~ **especial** balloon payment; ~ **en especie** payment in kind; ~ **específico** specific payment; ~ **eventual** contingency payment; ~ **ex**

gratia ex gratia payment; ~ **en exceso** overpayment; ~ **por exceso de equipaje** excess baggage charge; ~ **externo** outward payment; ~ **extraordinario** balloon payment; ~ **de facturas** settlement of account; ~ **fraccionario del impuesto** tax instalment BrE, tax installment AmE; ~ **de garantía** guarantee payment; ~ **global** single payment; ~ **de hipoteca** mortgage payment; ~ **por horas** hourly rate; ~ **igual** equal pay; ~ **de incentivo** inducement payment; ~ **inicial** down payment; ~ **íntegro** settlement in full; ~ **de intereses** interest payment; ~ **interno** inward payment; ~ **del IVA** VAT payment BrE; ~ **en línea** online payment; ~ **móvil** mobile payment; ~ **no efectivo** noncash payment; ~ **nominal** nominal payment; ~ **parcial** part payment; ~ **pendiente** amount outstanding; ~ **de la pensión** pension payment; ~ **a plazos** instalment payment BrE, installment payment AmE; ~ **preautorizado** pre-authorized payment; ~ **presupuestario** budget payment; ~ **de prima** premium payment; ~ **progresivo** incremental payment; ~ **puntual** prompt payment; ~ **de la reclamación** claim payment; ~ **regular** regular payment; ~ **retenido** (de cheques, letras) stopped payment; ~ **seguro** secure payment; ~ **simple** clean payment; ~ **por subsidio familiar** family allowance payment; ~ **tardío** late payment; ~ **con tarjeta de crédito** credit card payment; ~ **de transferencia** transfer payment; ~ **de transfronterizo** cross-border payment; ~ **trimestral** quarterly instalment BrE, quarterly installment AmE; ~ **del usuario** user charge; ~ **por vista** (en el Internet) pay-per-view; ~ **por visión** (por programas de televisión) *m* pay-per-view

págs. *abr* (▸**páginas**) pp. (pages)

país *m* country; ~ **acreedor** creditor country; ~ **anfitrión** host country; ~ **autónomo** self-governing nation; ~ **desarrollado** developed country, First World country; ~ **en desarrollo** developing country; ~ **de destino** country of destination; ~ **donante** (de ayuda internacional) donor country; ~ **dotado de autogobierno** self-governing nation; ~ **de economía planificada** Second World country; ~ **exportador de petróleo** oil-exporting country; ~ **industrializado** ┄┄┊›

p

industrialized country; ∼ **sin litoral**
landlocked country; ∼**es miembros**
member countries; ∼ **de origen** country
of origin; ∼ **prestatario** borrower
country; ∼ **productor de petróleo** oil-
producing country; ∼ **recientemente**
industrializado newly industrialized
country; ∼ **de residencia** country of
residence; ∼ **sede** home country; ∼
subdesarrollado underdeveloped
country; ∼ **del tercer mundo** Third
World country; ∼ **vecino** neighbouring
country BrE, neighboring country AmE; ∼
en vías de desarrollo developing
country

palabra f word; **dar su** ∼ give one's
word; **faltar a su** ∼ go back on one's
word, break one's promise; **darle** or
cederle la ∼ **a alguien** hand over to sb;
pedir la ∼ request permission to speak;
tener la ∼ (en reunión, ceremonia) have the
floor; ∼ **clave** keyword; ∼**s por**
minuto words per minute, wpm; ∼ **de**
moda buzzword (infrml)

palanca f lever; (influencia) influence;
tener ∼ know people in the right places;
∼ **basculante** toggle; ∼ **financiera**
leverage; ∼ **de mando** joystick

pancarta f (publicitaria) banner

panel m panel; ∼ **de consumidores**
consumer panel; ∼ **de ofertas** tender
panel

paneuropeo adj pan-European

panfleto m pamphlet

pánico m panic; ∼ **financiero**
financial panic

panorama m view; (expectativas,
perspectivas) outlook; ∼ **del mercado**
market view

pantalla f screen; (de ordenador) screen,
display; **a toda** ∼ full screen; ∼ **a color**
colour display BrE, color display AmE; ∼
de computadora AmL (cf ▸**pantalla de**
ordenador Esp) computer screen; ∼
cortafuegos firewall; ∼ **dividida** split
screen; ∼ **de ordenador** Esp (cf
▸**pantalla de computadora** AmL)
computer screen; ∼ **plana** flat screen; ∼
de precios electrónica electronic
posting board; ∼ **protectora de**
seguridad protective safety screen; ∼
táctil touch screen; ∼ **de televisión**
television screen; ∼ **terminal** terminal
screen; ∼ **de vídeo** Esp or **video** AmL
video display

papá-estado m nanny state

papel m paper; (Fin) bond; ∼**es**
documents, papers; **hoja de** ∼ sheet of

paper; ∼ **avalado** accommodation
paper; ∼ **avitelado** wove paper; ∼ **de**
borrador scrap paper; ∼ **carbón**
carbon paper; ∼ **comercial** commercial
paper; ∼**es contables** accounting
papers; ∼ **continuo** continuous feed
paper; ∼ **para correo aéreo** airmail
paper; ∼ **mojado** worthless piece of
paper; **el contrato es** ∼ **mojado** the
contract isn't worth the paper it's
written on; ∼ **moneda** paper money; ∼
de pago money order; ∼ **de regalo**
wrapping paper; ∼ **reciclado** recycled
paper; ∼ **satinado** glossy paper; ∼**es**
de trabajo working papers

papeleo m paperwork; (burocrático) red
tape

papelera f waste paper basket BrE,
waste basket AmE

papelería m pl stationery; **artículos de**
∼ stationery

papelero, -a m,f (vendedor) stationer;
(fabricante) paper manufacturer

papeleta f slip of paper; (en elección
sindical) ballot paper, voting paper; ∼
anulada spoilt ballot paper; ∼ **de**
saludos compliments slip; ∼ **de**
votación or **voto** (en elección sindical)
ballot paper, voting paper; (Bolsa)
dealing slip

papelote m waste paper

paquete m parcel, package; (de reformas,
incentivos) package; (de viajes) package
deal; ∼ **de acciones** block of shares; ∼
de aplicaciones applications package;
∼ **bomba** parcel bomb; ∼ **comercial**
business package; ∼ **de contabilidad**
accounting package; ∼ **de exposición**
display pack; ∼ **familiar** family-size
pack; ∼ **financiero** finance package; ∼
informativo press pack; ∼ **de medidas**
package of measures; ∼ **de medidas**
urgentes or **de medidas de**
salvamento rescue package; ∼ **postal**
parcel (sent by mail); ∼ **de programas**
software package; ∼ **de programas de**
presentación presentation package; ∼
de prueba (Info) testdeck; ∼ **de**
reformas package of reforms; ∼ **de**
reivindicaciones (RRHH) package deal;
∼ **de remuneración** remuneration
package

par¹ adj even

par² f (Fin) par; **a la** ∼ at par; **bajo/**
sobre la ∼ below/above par

par³ m (igual) peer; (pareja) pair; **de** ∼ **a**
∼ peer-to-peer, P2P

parada f (de fábrica, ordenador) shutdown

paradigma *m* paradigm; ~ **económico** economic paradigm

parado[1] *adj* Esp out of work, unemployed; **estar** ~ Esp (persona) be unemployed, be out of work; (producción, fábrica) be at a standstill

parado[2], **-a** *m,f* Esp unemployed person; **los** ~**s** the unemployed

paraestatal *adj* (organismo) public

paraíso *m* haven; **el** ~ (en teatro) the gods; ~ **fiscal** tax haven

paralegal *adj* paralegal

paralización *f* standstill; **provocar la** ~ **de algo** bring sth to a standstill, paralyze sth

paralizar *vt* (obras, producción) bring to a standstill, paralyze

parámetro *m* parameter

parar *vt* stop; **sin** ~ non-stop

parcela *f* plot; ~ **y bloque** plot and block

parcelar *vt* parcel out

parcial *adj* partial; (partidista) biased; **a tiempo** ~ part-time; **pago** ~ part payment

parcialidad *f* bias, partiality; ~ **del entrevistador** interviewer bias

parcialmente *adj* partially; (pagado) partly

parecer[1] *vi* seem, appear; **al** ~ apparently; ~ **que ...** look as though ...; **parece ser que ...** it would seem that ...; **según parece** apparently

parecer[2] *m* opinion, view; **a mi** ~ in my opinion; **ser del mismo** ~ be of the same opinion, share the same view; **ser del** ~ **de que la ley debería cambiarse** be of the opinion that the law should be changed

pared *f* wall; ~ **china** Chinese wall; ~ **medianera** party wall

parentesco *m* relationship

paréntesis *m pl* brackets, parenthesis; **entre** ~ in brackets

paridad *f* parity; ~ **adquisitiva** purchasing parity; ~ **competitiva** competitive parity; ~ **de conversión** conversion parity; ~ **móvil** sliding parity; ~ **par** even parity; ~ **de poder adquisitivo** purchasing power parity; ~ **de tipo de cambio** parity of exchange

parlamentario, -a *m,f* Member of Parliament; ~ **europeo(-a)** *m,f* European Member of Parliament, Euro MP

parlamento *m* parliament

paro *m* Esp unemployment; (subsidio) unemployment benefit BrE, unemployment compensation AmE; (huelga) strike; (de máquina, producción) stoppage; **cobrar el** ~ get unemployment benefit BrE, receive unemployment compensation AmE; **estar en el** ~ be unemployed, be on the dole (infrml) BrE; ~ **encubierto** Esp concealed unemployment; ~ **general** general strike; ~ **de larga duración** Esp long-term unemployment; ~ **parcial** Esp partial unemployment; ~ **registrado** Esp registered unemployment; ~ **voluntario** Esp voluntary unemployment

parpadear *vi* (pantalla) flicker

parpadeo *m* (de pantalla) flickering

parque *m* park; (de coches de empresa) fleet; ~ **de atracciones** theme park; ~ **científico** science park; ~ **comercial** retail park; ~ **de desguace** scrap yard; ~ **empresarial** business park; ~ **industrial** industrial estate BrE, industrial park AmE; ~ **móvil** car *o* motor fleet; ~ **tecnológico** technological park; ~ **de vivienda móvil** trailer park AmE

parqué *m* (Bolsa) trading floor

párrafo *m* paragraph; ~ **inicial** leader, lead article

parrilla *f* grid; ~ **de gestión** managerial grid

parte[1] *f* part; (en contrato) party; (dividendo, cantidad) portion; **de** ~ **de alguien** on behalf of sb; **¿de** ~ **de quién?** who's calling, please?; **en** ~ partly; **en gran** ~ to a large extent; **formar** ~ **de algo** be part of sth; **ponerse de** ~ **de alguien** take sb's side, side with sb; **por mi** ~ as far as I am concerned; **por una** ~ **..., por otra** ~ **...** on one hand ..., on the other (hand) ...; **tomar** ~ **en algo** take part in sth, play a part in sth; ~ **de un acuerdo** party to an agreement; ~ **agraviada** injured party; ~ **alta de la gama** top end of the range; ~ **del crédito** credit tranche; ~ **cualificada** (en contrato) competent party; ~ **de horas trabajadas** time sheet; ~ **imponible** taxable quota; ~ **integrante** integral part; ~ **interesada** interested party; ~ **de la jurisprudencia** piece of legislation; ~ **de la negociación** trading party; ~ **no utilizada** unused part; ~ **ofendida** *or* **perjudicada** injured party; ~ **predominante** prevailing party; ~ **recortable** tear-off slip; (de chequera) stub

parte² *m* report; **dar ∼ de algo** report sth; **llamar para dar ∼ de enfermo** call in sick

partición *f* (reparto) division, sharing out; (Info, Inmob) partition; **∼ de acciones** share split

participación *f* participation; (parte) share, holding; **∼ en algo** (colaboración) participation in sth; (parte) interest *o* share in sth; **tuvo una destacada ∼ en las negociaciones** she played an important role in the negotiations; **exigen ∼ en los beneficios** they are demanding a share in the profits; **∼ accionaria** shareholding; **∼ en los beneficios** profit sharing; **∼ en el capital social** equity ownership; **∼ en una compañía** interest in a company; **∼ controladora** controlling interest; **∼ discrecional** discretionary share; **∼ en una empresa** stake in a business; **∼ horizontal** horizontal equity; **∼ inmobiliaria** stake in property BrE, stake in real estate AmE; **∼ mayoritaria** majority holding; **∼ en el mercado** market share; **∼ recíproca** (entre empresas) cross-holding; **∼ de la renta** income splitting

participado *m* (Fin) investee

participante *mf* participant; (en negociaciones) player

participar *vt* participate; **∼ en algo** (tomar parte) participate in sth; (en ganancias, empresa) have a share *o* interest in sth

participativo *adj* participating, participative

particular¹ *adj* (aspecto) particular, special; (privado) private; (estilo) individual, personal; (teléfono) home; **en ∼** in particular, particularly; **no tiene nada de ∼** there's nothing special about it

particular² *m* matter; **sin otro ∼, le saluda atentamente** ≈ yours faithfully

particularidad *f* peculiarity; (rasgo distintivo) special feature

partida *f* (en registro) entry; (documento) certificate; (de presupuesto) item; **∼ de activo** asset item; **∼ del balance** balance sheet item; **∼ compensatoria** offsetting entry; **∼ doble** double entry; **∼ de defunción** death certificate; **∼ extraordinaria** extraordinary item, below-the-line item; **∼ de gastos** item of expenditure; **∼s invisibles** invisibles; **∼ monetaria** monetary item; **∼ de nacimiento** birth certificate; **∼ del**

pasivo liability item; **∼ pendiente** outstanding item; **∼ presupuestaria** budget item; **∼ de reserva** reserve entry; **∼ simple** single entry

partidario¹ *adj*: **ser ∼ de algo** be in favour BrE or favor AmE of sth; **no soy ∼ de los cambios propuestos** I'm not in favour BrE o favor AmE of the proposed changes

partidario², **-a** *m,f* supporter, follower

partido *m* party; (comarca) administrative area; **sacar ∼ de una situación** take advantage of a situation; **tener mucho ∼** enjoy wide support; **tomar ∼** take sides; **∼ de la oposición** opposition party; **∼ político** political party

partir *vi* set off, depart; **∼ de algo** start from sth; **∼ de la base de que ...** start from the premise that ...; **a ∼ de** from; **a ∼ de mayo/del mes que viene** from May/next month; **a ∼ de la implementación de esas medidas** since those measures were implemented

pasada *f* run; **∼ de comprobación** trial run; **∼ en computadora** AmL or **ordenador** Esp computer run; **∼ de máquina** machine run

pasajero, **-a** *m,f* passenger; **∼ en tránsito** transit passenger; **∼ de vía aérea** air traveller BrE, air traveler AmE

pasante *mf* trainee; (Der) pupil, articled clerk

pasantería *f* traineeship; (Der) pupillage

pasapáginas *m* page-turner

pasaporte *m* passport; **darle el ∼ a alguien** (infrml) give sb his/her cards (infrml) BrE, give sb a pink slip (infrml) AmE; **sacar el ∼** get a passport

pasar **1** *vi* (ocurrir) happen; (entrar) go in; (transcurrir) pass, go by; **el tiempo pasa** time is ticking away; **ya ha pasado lo peor de la recesión** the worst of the recession is over; **pase lo que pase** come what may, whatever happens; **¿qué pasa?** what's up?, what's going on?; **le paso con el director** I'll put you through to the manager; **∼ por** (oficina) drop by, stop off at; (ciudad, dificultades) go through; (lector de tarjetas) swipe; **la empresa está pasando por una racha difícil** the company is going through a bad patch; **∼ por caja** pay at the desk; **∼ por los canales debidos** go through the proper channels; **no está perfecto, pero puede ∼** it's not perfect, but it'll do; ~ **a ser** become; ~ **sin algo** manage without something

[2] *vt* (dar, aprobar) pass; (tiempo) spend; (página) turn; ~ **las pruebas** pass the proofs; **pasé el fin de semana trabajando** I worked all weekend, I spent the weekend working; ~ **a cuenta nueva** carry forward; ~ **factura a alguien** invoice sb; ~ **algo a limpio** make a clean copy of sth, write sth out again; ~ **algo a máquina** type sth up; ~ **algo por alto** overlook sth

pase *m* pass; ~ **de asientos** posting; ~ **de asientos al libro mayor** ledger posting

pasivo[1] *adj* (publicidad) passive

pasivo[2] *m* liability; ~ **aceptado** accepted liability; ~ **acumulado** accrued liability; ~ **asegurado** insured liability; ~ **consolidado** funded debt; ~ **contingente** contingent liability; ~ **corriente** current liability; ~ **a corto plazo** short-term liability; ~ **devengado** accrued liability; ~ **eventual** contingent liability; ~ **fijo consolidado** fixed liability; ~ **flotante** floating debt; ~ **de garantía** guaranteed liability; ~ **interno** domestic liability; ~ **a largo plazo** long-term liability; ~ **de obligaciones** bond liability; ~ **protegido** hedged liability; ~ **subordinado** subordinated liability; ~ **total** total liability

paso *m* step; **a este** ~ at this rate; **dar los** ~**s necesarios** take the necessary steps; **dar los primeros** ~**s** take the first steps; **dejar** ~ **a alguien** make way for sb; **mencionar algo de** ~ mention sth in passing; **archiva estas fichas y de** ~ **comprueba todas las direcciones** file these cards and while you're at it check all the addresses; ~ **a** step by step; **prohibido el** ~ no entry

pasta *f* (infrml) (dinero) dough (infrml); ~ **gansa** (infrml) megabucks (infrml)

patentabilidad *f* patentability

patentable *adj* (propiedad intelectual) patentable

patentado *adj* patented; **no** ~ unpatented

patentar *vt* patent

patente *f* patent; **sacar la** ~ take out a patent; ~ **dependiente** dependent patent; ~ **nacional** national patent; ~ **regional** regional patent; ~ **en tramitación** patent pending

patrimonial *adj* patrimonial, hereditary

patrimonio *m* wealth; (herencia) inheritance; (del causante) estate; ~ **bruto** gross estate; ~ **nacional** national heritage; ~ **neto** net worth; ~ **personal** personal wealth *o* assets; ~ **social** corporate assets; ~ **sucesorio** decedent's estate, estate of the deceased

patrocinador, a *m,f* sponsor; ~ **de arte** arts sponsor; ~ **de un proyecto** project sponsor

patrocinar *vt* sponsor; **patrocinado por el Estado** government-sponsored

patrocinio *m* sponsorship; (de beneficencia) patronage; **bajo el** ~ **de** sponsored by; ~ **de arte** arts sponsorship; ~ **corporativo** corporate sponsorship

patrón[1] *m* (de medida) standard; (Info) pattern; ~ **de cambio del oro** gold exchange standard; ~ **dólar** dollar standard; ~ **lingote oro** gold bullion standard; ~ **monetario** monetary standard; ~ **oro** gold standard; ~ **plata** silver standard

patrón[2], **-ona** *m,f* employer

pausa *f* break; **tras una breve** ~ after a short break; ~ **publicitaria** commercial break

pauta *f* pattern; **dar la** ~ set the pace; **establecer las** ~**s** establish pattern; ~ **de la demanda** demand pattern; ~ **de gastos** spending pattern; ~ **de trabajo** work pattern

p.c. *abr* (▸**por ciento**) p.c. (per cent)

PC *abr* (▸**ordenador personal** Esp, ▸**computadora personal** AmL) PC (personal computer)

PCGA *abr* (▸**Principios de Contabilidad Generalmente Aceptados**) GAAP (Generally Accepted Accounting Principles)

P.D. *abr* (▸**posdata**) P.S. (postscript)

pdo. *abr* (**pasado**) ult. (ultimo)

peaje *m* toll

peatón *m* pedestrian

peculiar *adj* (característico) particular; (raro) peculiar

pecuniario *adj* pecuniary

PED *abr* (▸**procesamiento electrónico de datos**) EDP (electronic data processing)

pedido *m* order; **entregar** *o* **servir un** ~ supply an order; **hacer un** ~ place an order; **mi** ~ my order; ~ **acumulado** backlogged order; ~ **al contado** cash order; ~ **anual** annual order; ~ **en blanco** blank order; ~ **del corredor de** ···⟫

comercio broker's order; ∼ **por correo** or **correspondencia** mail order; ∼ **a crédito** credit order; ∼ **sin entregar** outstanding order; ∼ **en espera** back order; ∼ **de fabricación** manufacturing order; ∼ **en firme** firm order; ∼ **futuro** future order; ∼ **a granel** bulk order; ∼ **importante** large order; ∼ **imprevisto** contingent order; ∼ **no despachado** unfulfilled order; ∼ **original** original order; ∼s **pendientes** outstanding orders; ∼ **de prueba** trial order; ∼ **retrasado** back order; ∼ **urgente** rush order

pedir [1] *vt* (solicitar) ask for, request; (encargar) order; (consejo) seek; ∼le **a alguien que haga algo** ask sb to do sth; ∼le **disculpas** *or* **perdón a alguien por algo/hacer algo** apologize to sb for sth/ doing sth; ∼ **hora** make an appointment; ∼ **la palabra** ask to speak; ∼ **permiso** ask for permission; ∼ **algo prestado** borrow sth
[2] *vi* (mendigar) beg; (para una causa) collect money

pegar *vt* (etiqueta) stick; (sello) affix

p.ej. *abr* (▸**por ejemplo**) e.g. (for example)

pelea *f* (lucha) fight; (discusión) row

película *f* film BrE, movie AmE; ∼ **durante el vuelo** in-flight film BrE, in-flight movie AmE; ∼ **de la serie B** B-movie; ∼ **taquillera** (jarg) box-office hit

peligro *m* danger; **correr** ∼ be in danger; **en** ∼ **de** in danger of; **poner algo en** ∼ endanger sth; (plan) jeopardize; ∼ **de incendio** fire hazard

pelota *f*: **pasar la** ∼ **(a alguien)** pass the buck (to sb)

pelotazo *m* (Fin) scoop

penalización *f* penalty; ∼ **por incumplimiento de contrato** penalty for breach of contract; ∼ **por pago anticipado** early repayment penalty; ∼ **por primera incidencia** first occurrence penalty; ∼ **por reembolso anticipado** early redemption penalty; ∼ **por retirada anticipada** early withdrawal penalty

pendiente *adj* (asunto, caso) pending; (cuenta, reclamación) outstanding; **dejar algo** ∼ leave sth for later *o* another time; **quedó** ∼ **hasta la próxima reunión** it was left for the next meeting; **aún tenemos algunos asuntos** ∼s we still have some unfinished business; ∼ **de amortizar** unamortized; ∼ **de aprobación** subject to approval; ∼ **de**

pago outstanding; ∼ **de resolución judicial** sub judice; ∼ **de respuesta** pending a reply

penetración *f* penetration; ∼ **en el mercado** market penetration; ∼ **de ventas** sales penetration

penetrar *vt* (mercado) penetrate

pensado *adj* (plan, decisión) thought-out; **fue muy bien** ∼ it was very well thought-out *o* thought through; **poco** ∼ badly thought-out

pensamiento *m* (razonamiento) thinking; (facultad, cosa pensada) thought; ∼ **creativo** creative thinking; ∼ **lateral** lateral thinking

pensar [1] *vt* (opinar) think; (considerar) think about; **piénsalo bien** think about it carefully, think it through properly; **déjame** ∼**lo** let me (have a) think about it; **pensándolo bien** on second thoughts BrE *o* thought AmE; ∼ **hacer algo** think of doing sth; **¿piensas ir al congreso?** are you thinking of going to the conference?; **tengo pensado hacerlo mañana** I'm thinking of doing it tomorrow
[2] *vi* (razonar) think; **después de mucho** ∼, **decidió no aceptar el puesto** after a lot of thought, she decided not to take the job; **actuar sin** ∼ do things *o* act without thinking; ∼ **en algo/hacer algo** think about sth/doing sth

pensión *f* pension; (alojamiento) accomodation BrE, accomodations AmE; (para huéspedes) guesthouse; **cobrar la** ∼ draw one's pension; **media** ∼ half board; ∼ **alimenticia** alimony, maintenance allowance; ∼ **completa** full board; ∼ **del Estado** state pension BrE; ∼ **interina** interim pension; ∼ **de invalidez** disability pension; ∼ **de jubilación** retirement pension; ∼ **de vejez** old age pension; ∼ **vitalicia** annuity; ∼ **de viudedad** *or* **viudez** widow's pension

pensionista *m,f* pensioner; (por jubilación) old age pensioner BrE

PEPS *abr* (▸**primero en entrar, primero en salir**) FIFO (first in, first out)

pequeño *adj* small; **pequeña empresa** *f* small business; ∼ **inversor, a** *m,f* small investor; **pequeña y mediana empresa** *f* small and medium-size enterprise

per cápita *adj* per capita; **gastos** ∼ per capita spending

percentil *m* percentile

percepción *f* perception; ~ **selectiva** selective perception; ~ **subjetiva** subjective perception

perder *vt* (clientes, control, dinero) lose; (oportunidad) miss; (tiempo) waste; ~ **el empleo** lose one's job; ~ **terreno** (en la competencia) lose ground; ~ **valor** lose value, depreciate

pérdida *f* loss; (Der) damage; ~**s** losses; ~ **actuarial** actuarial loss; ~ **de beneficios** revenue loss; ~ **de capital** capital loss; ~ **de capital reembolsable** allowable capital loss; ~ **de la clientela** loss of custom; ~ **compensatoria** compensating loss; ~ **a corto plazo** short-term loss; ~ **de credibilidad** credibility gap; ~ **de crédito** credit loss; ~**s de cuentas incobrables** bad-debt losses; ~**s del ejercicio** trading losses; ~ **elemental** elementary loss; ~ **del excedente** deadweight loss; ~ **de la explotación** operating loss; ~ **extraordinaria** extraordinary loss; ~**s financieras** financial losses; ~**s y ganancias** profit and loss; ~ **inesperada** windfall loss; ~ **de información** (Info) drop-out; ~ **líquida** clear loss; ~**s llevadas a cuenta nueva** losses carried forward; ~**s materiales** damage; ~ **por mortalidad** mortality loss; ~ **neta** net loss; ~**s no realizadas** unrealized losses; ~ **ordinaria** ordinary loss; ~ **parcial** partial loss; ~ **potencial** paper loss; ~ **real** actual loss; ~ **de remuneración** loss of pay; ~ **de salvamento** salvage loss; ~ **de sueldo** loss of earnings; ~**s sufridas** losses suffered; ~ **de tiempo** waste of time; ~ **total** total loss; ~ **de traducción** (comercio internacional) translation loss; ~ **en la transacción** transaction loss; ~ **en tránsito** loss in transit

perdonar *vt* forgive; ~ **una deuda** forgo collection of a debt

perecedero *adj* (producto) perishable; **no** ~ non-perishable

perecederos *m pl* perishables

perfil *m* profile; **de** ~ **discreto** low-profile; ~ **de adquisición** acquisition profile; ~ **del cliente** customer profile; ~ **del consumidor** consumer profile; ~ **discreto** low profile; ~ **del empleado** employee profile; ~ **de la empresa** company profile; ~ **de los lectores** readership profile; ~ **de marketing** marketing profile; ~ **del modelo** model profile; ~ **del producto** product profile; ~ **del puesto** job profile, job

specification, job spec (infrml); ~ **de recursos** resource profile; ~ **de riesgo** risk profile; ~ **técnico** technical profile; ~ **del usuario** user profile

perforación *f* (acción) drilling; (en papel) perforation; (con perforadora) punch-hole; ~ **costera** offshore drilling; ~ **exploratoria** wildcat drilling

perforadora *f* hole punch; ~ **de cinta** tape punch; ~ **de tarjetas** card punch; ~ **de teclado** key punch

perforista *mf* keypuncher

pericia *f* (experiencia) expertise; (habilidad) skill

periférico[1] *adj* peripheral; **los barrios** ~**s** the suburbs

periférico[2] *m* peripheral

periódico[1] *adj* periodic

periódico[2] *m* newspaper; ~ **de calidad** (imprenta) quality newspaper, broadsheet BrE; ~ **económico** economic journal; ~ **local** local newspaper; ~ **nacional** national newspaper

periodismo *m* journalism; ~ **electrónico** electronic news gathering; ~ **financiero** financial journalism; ~ **gráfico** photojournalism; ~ **financiero** financial journalism; ~ **sensacionalista** chequebook BrE *o* checkbook AmE journalism (infrml)

periodista *mf* journalist

periodo, período *m* period; **durante el** ~ **de** over the period of; **durante un** ~ **de tiempo** over a period of time; **en el** ~ **subsiguiente de** in the aftermath of; **en un** ~ **de** within a period of; **para el** ~ **de** for the period of; ~ **del alquiler** rental term; ~ **anterior** prior period; ~ **aplicable** relevant period; ~ **de aviso** notice period; ~ **base** base period; ~ **de beneficios** earnings period; ~ **de carencia** qualifying period; ~ **de conservación** (para acciones adjudicadas a empleados) retention period; ~ **contable** accounting period; ~ **de declaración** (Fisc) reporting period; ~ **con derechos** cum-rights period; ~ **sin derechos** ex-rights period; ~ **de discreción** discretionary period; ~ **de emisión** float time; ~ **de espera** waiting period; ~ **estimado** estimated lapse; ~ **excluido** excluded period; ~ **exento** exempt period; ~ **financiero** financial period, fiscal period; ~ **flojo** (en ventas) slack period; ~ **de formación** (Prot Soc) qualification period; ~ **de gestación** gestation period; ~ **de gracia** period of ⋯⋗

grace, grace period; ~ **intermedio** intermediate term; ~ **largo** long period; ~ **de notificación** notice period; ~ **de ocupación gratuita** rent-free period; ~ **de opción** option period; ~ **de pago** repayment term; ~ **de la póliza** policy term; ~ **de posguerra** postwar period; ~ **presupuestario** budgetary period; ~ **de producción** production time; ~ **de prueba** trial period; (en un empleo) probationary period; ~ **de recesión** recession; ~ **de recuperación** payback period; ~ **de recuperación de la deuda** debt recovery period; ~ **de reembolso** repayment term; ~ **de reflexión** cooling-off period; ~ **de respaldo financiero** bailout period; ~ **de rodaje** running-in period; ~**s semestrales** six-monthly periods; ~ **de tenencia** holding period; ~ **de tiempo** time frame; ~ **de transición** transition period; ~ **de vacaciones** holiday period BrE, vacation period AmE

peritaje *m* expert's report; (Inmob) survey; (Seg) loss adjuster's report

perito, -a *m,f* expert; ~ **mercantil** chartered accountant BrE, Certified Public Accountant AmE

perjudicar *vt* harm, be detrimental to; (intereses, derechos) prejudice

perjudicial *adj* prejudicial

perjuicio *m* (daño) damage; (Fin) loss; **en** ~ **de algo** to the detriment of sth; **redundar en** ~ **de algo** be detrimental to sth, have an adverse effect on sth; **sin** ~ **de** without prejudice *o* detriment to sth

perjurar *vi* perjure oneself, commit perjury

perjurio *m* perjury

permanecer *vi* remain; ~ **en un valor** (Bolsa) stay in the money; **permaneciendo invariable todo lo demás** all things being equal

permanente *adj* permanent

permisible *adj* permissible; (gastos) allowable; (exportación) licensable

permiso *m* permission, authorization; (documento) permit; (de conducir) licence BrE, license AmE; (tiempo libre) leave; **con su** ~ if you'll excuse me; **darle** ~ **a alguien para hacer algo** give *o* grant sb permission to do sth; **de** ~ (civil) on leave; ~ **de conducir** driving licence BrE, driver's license AmE; ~ **de construcción** planning permission BrE, planning approval AmE; ~ **de entrada** entry permit; ~ **de exportación** export

licence BrE, export license AmE; ~ **de importación** import licence BrE, import license AmE; ~ **pagado** paid leave; ~ **privilegiado** privilege leave; ~ **de residencia** residence permit; ~ **residencia temporal** temporary residence permit; ~ **de trabajo** work permit, green card AmE; ~ **de vacaciones** holiday leave BrE, vacation leave AmE

permitir *vt* allow, permit; ~**le a alguien hacer algo** allow *o* permit sb to do sth; ~ **a alguien el acceso a algo** give sb access to sth; ~ **un margen de error** allow for a margin of error; **no se permite la entrada a menores** no under 18s

permitirse *v pron* allow oneself; (gastos) afford; **se permiten el lujo de viajar en primera** they can afford to travel first class; **no pueden permitirse más empleados** they can't afford to take on more staff

permuta *f* exchange; ~ **financiera** swap

permutación *f* permutation

permutar *vt* exchange, swap; **vendo o permuto** for sale or exchange

perpetuidad *f* perpetuity; **a** ~ in perpetuity

perpetuo *adj* perpetual

persecución *f* persecution; (RRHH) victimization

persistente *adj* persistent

persona *f* person; **de** ~ **a** ~ person-to-person; **en** ~ in person; **miles de** ~**s** thousands of people; **por** ~ per person, per head; ~ **afiliada** affiliated person; ~ **asociada** associated person; ~ **autorizada** authorized person; ~ **de bajo rendimiento** low achiever, low-flier; ~ **a cargo** dependant; ~ **designada** appointee, named person; ~ **dinámica** self-starter; ~ **emprendedora** self-starter; ~ **especificada** specified person; ~ **fallecida** deceased person; ~ **física** individual; ~ **jubilada** retired person; ~ **jurídica** legal entity; ~ **mundana** socialite; ~ **de nacionalidad extranjera** foreign national; ~ **en prácticas** trainee; ~ **privada** private individual; ~ **relacionada** related person

personaje *mf* important figure, big name (infrml); ~ **taquillero** (jarg) box-office draw (jarg)

personal¹ *adj* personal; **llamada/ asunto ~** personal call/matter

personal² *m* personnel, staff; **con exceso de ~** overstaffed; **con poco ~** short-staffed; **reducir ~** reduce the number of staff; **~ administrativo** administrative staff; **~ de alta dirección** top management personnel; **~ asalariado** salaried staff; **~ de auditoría** audit staff; **~ de cabina** cabin crew; **~ de campo** field staff; **~ directivo** management staff; **~ de fábrica** manufacturing workforce; **~ obrero** workforce; **~ de oficina** office staff, clerical staff; **~ permanente** permanent staff; **~ profesional** professional staff; **~ reducido** skeleton staff; **con ~ reducido** lean; **~ de secretaría** secretarial staff; **~ de supervisión** supervisory personnel; **~ de tierra** ground crew *o* staff; **~ de ventas** sales force

personalidad *f* personality; **~ jurídica** legal entity

personalizado *adj* (servicio) personalized; (a medida del usuario) customized; **plan ~ de ahorro** personal savings plan

personalizar *vi* (servicio) personalize; (sistema, producto) customize

personalmente *adv* personally; **personalmente responsable** personally responsible; **(Der)** personally liable

perspectiva *f* (punto de vista) perspective; (posibilidad) prospect; (económica) outlook; **~s** *f pl* prospects; **desde una ~ comercial** from a commercial perspective *o* viewpoint; **en ~** on the horizon; **hay ~s de mejoría** things look like they will improve, there's hope for improvement; **tener buenas ~s** look promising, have good prospects; **~s de beneficio** profit outlook; **~s de empleo** job prospects; **~ empresarial** business outlook; **~s de mercado** market forecast, market prospects; **~s de ventas** sales prospects

perspicacia *f* acumen; **~ comercial** *or* **empresarial** commercial *o* business acumen

perspicaz *adj* far-sighted

persuadir *vt* persuade; **~ a alguien de algo/para que haga algo** persuade sb of sth/to do sth; **fueron incapaces de ~le** they were unable to persuade him; **le persuadieron para que no dimitiese** they persuaded him not to resign

persuasión *f* persuasion; **~ moral** moral persuasion

persuasivo *adj* persuasive

pertenecer *vi*: **~ a algo/alguien** belong to sth/sb

pertenencia *f* (posesión) ownership; (a una organización) membership; **~s** belongings, possessions; (de una finca) appurtenances (frml)

pertinente *adj* (relevante) relevant; (adecuado) appropriate; **en lo ~ a** as regards; **no ~** not relevant, irrelevant; (en formulario) not applicable, N/A; **tomar las medidas ~s** take the appropriate measures

perturbar *vt* (trastornar) disturb; (interrumpir) disrupt; **~ el orden público** disturb the peace; **~ la marcha de las negociaciones** disrupt the progress of the negotiations; **~ las actividades comerciales** disrupt business

pesar *vi* (objeto) weigh; **le pesa mucha responsabilidad** she has a lot of responsibility on her shoulders; **su opinión sigue pesando en la compañía** his opinion still counts in the company; **los argumentos que pesaron en la decisión** the arguments which played an important part in the decision; **pese a** despite, in spite of; **firmó el contrato pese a no estar seguro** he signed the contract even though he wasn't sure about it; **pese a que** even though

peseta *f* peseta, *Spanish unit of currency replaced by the euro in 2002*

pesimismo *m* pessimism; (en mercado) gloom

pesimista¹ *adj* pessimistic

pesimista² *mf* pessimist

peso *m* weight; **(Fin)** burden; **tener ~** carry weight; **tener poco ~** not be very important; **todo el ~ de la ley** the full weight of the law; **quitarle un ~ de encima a alguien** take a load off sb's mind; **~ bruto** gross weight; **~ de la deuda** debt burden; **~ muerto** deadweight; **~ neto** net weight; **~ de la prueba** burden of proof; **el ~ de la prueba recae en la acusación** the burden of proof lies with the prosecution

petición *f* (solicitud) request; (instancia) petition; (de desgravación fiscal) claim; **a ~** on request; **a ~ del público** by popular demand; **respondiendo a su ~** in response to your request; **~ de crédito** credit demand; **~ de divorcio** petition for divorce; **~ de extradición** application for extradition; **~** ⸺⸽

financiera financial claim; ~ **de indulto** plea for exemption; ~ **de patente** patent application

petrobono m petrobond

petrodivisa f petrocurrency

petrodólar m petrodollar

petróleo m oil, petroleum; ~ **crudo** crude oil

petrolero m oil tanker

petrolífero adj (país) oil-producing; **compañía petrolífera** oil company

PEUS abr (▸**primero en entrar, último en salir**) FILO (first in, last out)

pez gordo mf (infrml) fat cat (infrml)

PIB abr (▸**producto interior bruto**) GDP (gross domestic product); ~ **per capita** GDP per capita

picapleitos mf litigious person

pie m foot; **a** ~ **de página** at the foot of the page; **al** ~ **de la letra** (cumplir) to the letter; (repetir) word for word, verbatim; **en** ~ **de igualdad** on an equal footing; ~ **de autor** by-line; ~ **de foto** caption; ~ **de imprenta** imprint

piedra f stone; ~ **de escándalo** source of scandal; ~ **de toque** touchstone

pieza f part, component; **la** ~ **clave de algo** the key element of sth; ~ **legislativa** piece of legislation; ~ **de recambio** or **repuesto** spare part

pignoración f pledge

pila f (de papeles) pile, stack; (Info) stack; (para radio, aparato) battery; **tengo una** ~ **de trabajo** I have stacks o loads of work (to do)

piloto[1] adj (programa, producto) pilot

piloto[2] mf pilot

piloto[3] m pilot; (luz) pilot light; ~ **automático** autopilot

PIN abr (▸**producto interior neto**) NDP (net domestic product)

pionero, -a m,f pioneer

piquete m (en huelga) picket; ~ **móvil** flying picket

piramidación f pyramiding; ~ **fiscal** tax pyramiding

piramidal adj pyramidal

pirámide f pyramid; ~ **financiera** financial pyramid; ~ **de población** age pyramid

pirata[1] adj pirate; **edición/copia** ~ pirate edition/copy

pirata[2] mf pirate; ~ **aéreo(-a)** m,f hijacker; ~ **informático(-a)** m,f hacker

pirateado adj (edición) pirated; (sistema) hacked into

piratear vt (edición) pirate; (sistema) hack into

pirateo informático m hacking

piratería f piracy; (Info) hacking; ~ **informática** hacking; ~ **de líneas telefónicas** phreakage; ~ **de vídeos** Esp or **videos** AmL video piracy

pirómetro m pyrometer

piscicultura f fish farming

piscifactoría f fish farm

piso m Esp (cf ▸**apartamento** cf ▸**departamento** AmL) flat BrE, apartment AmE; (planta) floor, storey BrE, story AmE; **de varios** ~**s** (aparcamiento) multistorey BrE, multistory AmE; **en el primer** ~ on the first BrE o second AmE floor; **se alquila** ~ flat to let BrE, apartment for rent AmE; **un edificio de 12** ~**s** a 12-storey BrE o 12-story AmE building; ~ **franco** safe house; ~ **modelo** show flat BrE, show apartment AmE; ~ **piloto** Esp show flat BrE, show apartment AmE; ~ **de producción** shop floor; ~ **de remates** (Bolsa) front office

pista f (dato) clue, hint; (huella) trail, track; **darle una** ~ **a alguien** give sb a clue o hint; **estar sobre la** ~ be on the right track; ~ **de aterrizaje** runway; ~ **de rodaje** taxiway

pixel m pixel

pizarra f blackboard; ~ **blanca** whiteboard

placa f plate; (Info) board; ~ **base** (Info) motherboard; ~ **de matrícula** numberplate BrE, license plate AmE; ~ **sensible al tacto** (Info) touchpad

plagiar vt plagiarize

plagio m plagiarism

plan m plan; **hacer** ~**es** make plans; **cambiar de** ~**es** change plans; ~ **de acción** plan of action, action plan; ~ **de ahorro** savings plan; ~ **de ahorros en nómina** payroll savings plan; ~ **de amortización** (de préstamo) repayment schedule; (Cont) amortization schedule; ~ **anual de auditoría** annual audit plan; ~ **de anualidades** annuity plan; ~ **de auditoría** audit plan; ~ **de bonificaciones** bonus scheme; ~ **de campaña** campaign plan, plan of campaign; ~ **de capacitación** training scheme; ~ **a cinco años** five-year plan; ~ **comercial** business plan; ~ **de contabilidad** accounting plan; ~ **de contingencia** contingency plan; ~ **de continuidad de negocio** business continuity plan; ~ **de contribución diferida** deferred contribution plan; ~

departamental departmental plan; ∼ **de desarrollo** development plan; ∼ **de emergencia** contingency plan; ∼ **estratégico** strategic plan; ∼ **de estudios** curriculum; ∼ **de etiquetado ecológico** green labelling BrE o labeling AmE scheme; ∼ **de evaluación del programa** programme BrE o program AmE evaluation plan; ∼ **de financiación** financing plan; ∼ **de formación** training scheme; ∼ **genérico de negocios** generic business plan; ∼ **de hospitalización** hospitalization plan; ∼ **de incentivo** incentive plan; ∼ **de jubilación** pension fund, retirement plan o scheme; ∼ **de jubilación profesional** occupational pension scheme BrE; ∼ **de liquidación fiscal** tax equalization scheme; ∼ **maestro** master plan; ∼ **de marketing** marketing plan; ∼ **de marketing y ventas** sales and marketing plan; ∼ **de medios de comunicación** media plan; ∼ **mensual de inversión** monthly investment plan; ∼ **de mercado** market plan; ∼ **de negocios** business plan; ∼ **de opción de acciones** share option scheme; ∼ **de pago a plazos** instalment BrE o installment AmE repayment schedule; ∼ **de participación en beneficios** profit-sharing scheme; ∼ **de pensión contributiva** contributory pension scheme; ∼ **de pensión para los empleados** employee pension plan; ∼ **de pensión laboral del empresario** employer's occupational pension scheme; ∼ **de pensión no contributivo** noncontributory pension scheme; ∼ **de pensiones** pension plan, pension scheme; ∼ **personal de jubilación** personal pension plan; ∼ **piloto** pilot scheme; ∼ **provisional** tentative plan; ∼ **quinquenal** five-year plan; ∼ **de recompra de acciones** share repurchase plan; ∼ **de recuperación de catástrofes** disaster recovery plan, DRP; ∼ **de rehabilitación** recovery plan; ∼ **de revisión anual** annual audit plan; ∼ **salarial** salary scheme; ∼ **de saneamiento** (de compañía) reorganization plan; ∼ **de seguros de enfermedad** health insurance scheme; ∼ **táctico** tactical plan; ∼ **de trabajo** work plan; ∼ **de vivienda** housing scheme

plana f (de periódico) page; **aparecer en primera** ∼ be on o make the front page; **noticias de primera** ∼ front-page news;

∼ **doble** centre spread BrE, center spread AmE

planear vt plan; **tener planeado hacer algo** plan to do sth

planificación f planning; ∼ **anticipada** forward planning; ∼ **de beneficios** profit planning; ∼ **de capacidad** capacity planning; ∼ **central** central planning; ∼ **de contingencia** contingency planning; ∼ **y control** planning and control; ∼ **corporativa** corporate planning; ∼ **a corto plazo** short-term planning; ∼ **del desarrollo** development planning; ∼ **económica** economic planning; ∼ **de emergencia** contingency planning; ∼ **empresarial** corporate planning; ∼ **estratégica** strategic planning; ∼ **estratégica corporativa** corporate strategic planning; ∼ **financiera** financial planning; ∼ **fiscal estratégica** strategic tax planning; ∼ **de las instalaciones** site planning; ∼ **del inventario** inventory planning; ∼ **a largo plazo** long-term planning; ∼ **de la mano de obra** manpower planning; ∼ **de medios** media planning; ∼ **de mercado** market planning; ∼ **de negocios** business planning; ∼ **de la oficina** office planning; ∼ **operacional** operational planning; ∼ **de la organización** organization planning; ∼ **del personal** staff planning; ∼ **presupuestaria** budgetary planning; ∼ **previa** preplanning; ∼ **de la producción** production planning; ∼ **de los productos** product planning; ∼ **de un proyecto** project planning; ∼ **de los recursos humanos** human resource planning; ∼ **de recursos de fabricación** manufacturing resource planning, MRP; ∼ **de sistemas** systems planning; ∼ **táctica** tactical planning; ∼ **de tierras** land-use planning; ∼ **urbana** town planning; ∼ **de utilidad** profit planning; ∼ **de las ventas** sales planning

planificador, a m,f planner; ∼ **financiero(-a)** m,f financial planner; ∼ **de medios de comunicación** media planner

planificar vt plan

planilla f AmL (lista) payroll; (recibo de pago) pay slip; **estar en** ∼ be on the payroll

plano¹ adj flat

plano² m (de edificio) plan; (de ciudad) map; (en cine, foto) shot; (nivel) level; **en el** ∼ **laboral** as far as employment is ···⟶

concerned; **estar en otro** ~ be in a different class; **negar algo de** ~ flatly deny sth; **rechazar algo de** ~ reject sth outright; **equivocarse de** ~ be totally wrong *o* mistaken; ~ **corto** close-up; ~ **largo** long shot; ~ **maestro** master plan; ~ **de terreno** plot *o* site plan

planta *f* (instalación) plant; (de edificio) floor, storey BrE, story AmE; (de empleados) staff, personnel; **a** ~ **baja** on ground level BrE, at first-floor level AmE; **un edificio de tres** ~**s** a three-storey building BrE, a three-story building AmE; ~ **depuradora** purification plant; ~ **de electricidad** power station; ~ **de ensamblado** assembly plant; ~ **fija** fixed plant; ~ **de incineración** incineration plant; ~ **industrial** industrial plant; ~ **y maquinaria** plant and machinery; ~ **de montaje** assembly plant; ~ **nuclear** nuclear plant; ~ **de procesado** processing plant; ~ **de producto fijo** fixed plant; ~ **de producto flexible** flexible plant; ~ **de pruebas** testing plant

plantación *f* plantation

planteamiento *m* (enfoque) approach; (análisis) analysis; **hacer un** ~ **de algo** give an analysis of sth

plantear *vt* (cuestión, objeción) raise, bring up; (problema, dificultad) cause; ~**le algo a alguien** suggest *o* put sth to sb; **su dimisión les** ~**ía graves problemas** her resignation would cause them serious problems

plantilla *f* Esp personnel, staff; (lista de empleados asalariados) payroll; (patrón) template; **estar en** ~ be on the payroll, be a member of staff; **de** ~ **escasa** short-staffed

plástico *m* plastic

plataforma *f* platform; ~ **electoral** electoral platform; ~ **de lanzamiento** launch pad; ~ **de perforación** drilling platform; ~ **petrolífera** oil platform, oil rig; ~ **de ventas** sales platform

plato *m* (utensilio) plate; (receta) dish; ~**s precocinados** ready-made meals, convenience food

plaza *f* (puesto) post; (asiento) seat; ~ **comercial** marketplace; ~ **vacante** vacancy

plazo *m* (de tiempo) period; (cuota) instalment BrE, installment AmE; **a corto/largo/medio** ~ in the short/long/medium term; **antes del** ~ **previsto** ahead of schedule; **a** ~ **fijo** fixed-term; **a** ~**s (mensuales)** in (monthly)

instalments BrE *o* installments AmE; **comprar algo a** ~**s** pay for sth in instalments BrE *o* installments AmE, buy sth on credit terms; **el** ~ **de admisión finaliza el día 25** the closing date *o* deadline for entries is the 25th; **en un** ~ **de treinta días** at thirty days' usance; **tener un** ~ **de un mes para pagar** have a month (in which) to pay; ~ **alargado** extended term; ~ **de amortización** payback period; ~ **anual** annual instalment BrE, annual installment AmE; ~ **de comercialización** time to market; ~ **de entrega** delivery time; (V&M) lead time; ~ **final** final instalment BrE, final installment AmE; ~ **de gracia** period of grace; ~ **mensual** monthly instalment BrE, monthly installment AmE; ~ **de pago de una letra** usance; ~ **de recuperación** payback period; ~ **de validez** validity period; ~ **para el vencimiento** term to maturity

pleito *m* lawsuit; **entablar un** ~ **contra alguien** bring a lawsuit against sb, take legal action against sb; **ganar/perder un** ~ win/lose a case *o* lawsuit; **ponerle un** ~ **a alguien** take sb to court; **tener un** ~ **con alguien** be involved in a legal dispute with sb

plenario *adj* (sesión parlamentaria) plenary

pluralismo *m* pluralism

pluriempleado, -a *m,f* person with more than one job; (en secreto) moonlighter (infrml); **una cultura de** ~ a culture where having more than one job is the norm

pluriempleo *m* holding of more than one job; (en secreto) moonlighting (infrml)

plusmarquista *mf* record holder

plusvalía *f* added value; (de capital) capital gain(s); **impuesto sobre la** ~ capital gain(s) tax; ~ **acumulada** accumulated surplus; ~**s netas** net capital gain; ~ **restringida** undistributable reserve BrE, restricted surplus AmE

pmo. *abr* (▸**próximo**) prox. proximo

PNB *abr* (▸**producto nacional bruto**) GNP (gross national product)

población *f* population; ~ **activa** working population; ~ **adulta** adult population; ~ **flotante** floating population; ~ **ocupada** working population; ~ **pasiva** non-working population; ~ **residente** resident population

poblado *adj* populated; **densamente ~** densely-populated; **poco ~** sparsely populated

pobre¹ *adj* poor

pobre² *mf* poor person; **los ~s** the poor, poor people

pobreza *f* poverty; **~ absoluta** absolute *o* abject poverty

poder *m* (control) power; (autoridad) authority; (Der) power of attorney; (posesión) possession; **estar en el ~** be in power; **estar en ~ de las autoridades** be in the hands of the authorities; **por ~** (Der) by proxy; **tomar el ~** seize power; **~ adquisitivo** purchasing power; **~ al portador** bearer proxy; **~ compensador** countervailing power; **~ ejecutivo** executive power; **~ general** power of attorney; **~ judicial** judiciary; **~ legal** statutory power; (de procuración) power of attorney; **~ legislativo** legislative power; **~ de mercado** market power; **~ monopolístico** monopoly power; **~ de negociación** bargaining power; **~es notariales** power of attorney; **~ obrero** labour power BrE, labor power AmE; **~ para pleitos** power of recourse; **~ policial** police power; **los ~es públicos** the authorities; **~ regulador** regulatory authority

poderoso *adj* powerful

polarización *f* polarization

policentrismo *m* polycentrism

policultivo *m* mixed farming

polígono *m* Esp (zona) area, zone; (urbanización) development; **~ industrial** industrial zone

política *f* politics; (postura) policy; **~ de adquisición** acquisition policy; **~ agraria** agricultural policy; **~ agrícola** farming policy; **P~ Agrícola Común** (UE) Common Agricultural Policy; **~ ambiental** environmental policy; **~ comercial** trade policy; **~ crediticia** credit policy; **~ de desarrollo** development policy; **~ discrecional** discretionary policy; **~ de distribución** distribution policy; **~ de dividendos** dividend policy; **~ de la empresa** company policy; **~ exterior** foreign policy; **~ financiera** financial policy; **~ fiscal** fiscal policy; **~ de igualdad de oportunidades** equal opportunities policy; **~ de inmigración** immigration policy; **~ interior** domestic policy; **~ de inversión** investment policy; **~ legal** statutory policy; **~ macroeconómica** macroeconomic policy; **~ medioambiental** environmental policy; **~ monetaria** monetary policy; **~ de no intervención** (Pol) policy of nonintervention; (RRHH) hands-off policy; **~ de personal** personnel policy; **~ de precios** pricing policy; **~ presupuestaria** budgetary policy; **~ de promoción** promotional policy; **~ publicitaria** advertising policy; **~ regional** regional policy; **~ de rentas** incomes policy; **~ salarial** wage policy; **~ social** social policy; **~ superficial** (V&M) skimming policy; **~ de uso aceptable** acceptable-use policy; **~ de ventas** sales policy

políticamente *adv* politically; **~ correcto** politically correct

político¹ *adj* political

político², a *m,f* politician

politizar *vt* politicize

polivalencia *f* versatility; (RRHH) multiskilling

polivalente *adj* multipurpose

póliza *f* policy; **~ abierta** blanket policy; **~ de anualidades** annuity policy; **~ en blanco** sample policy; **~ combinada** comprehensive policy; **~ de compra** share certificate BrE, stock certificate AmE; **~ conjunta** block policy; **~ cubierta** (de vida) fully-paid policy; **~ nula** void policy; **~ de seguro** insurance policy; **~ de seguro a todo riesgo** comprehensive insurance policy; **~ de seguro de vida** life insurance *o* BrE assurance policy

polución *f* pollution; **~ ambiental** environmental pollution; **~ base** background pollution; **~ marítima** marine pollution

ponderado *adj* (acciones) considered; (índice, promedio) weighted; (votación) proportional

ponderar *vt* (considerar) weigh up; (Econ) weight

ponente *mf* speaker

pool *m* (de empleados) pool; (Fin) consortium

populista¹ *adj* populist

populista² *mf* populist

porcentaje *m* percentage; **~ de accesos** (Info) hit rate; **~ anual fijo** fixed annual percentage; **~ de devolución** rate of return; **~ de dividendo** pay-out; **~ exento** exempt percentage; **~ de la muestra** sample rate; **~ de respuesta** response rate

porcentual *adj* percentage; **un aumento** ∼ a percentage rise

porqué *m* reason; **el** ∼ **de la huelga** the reason for the strike; **los** ∼**s** the whys and wherefores

portada *f* (cubierta) cover; (de periódico) front page; (página de libro) title page

portador, a *m,f* bearer; **páguese al** ∼ pay the bearer

portal *m* (Info) portal; ∼ **gobierno a cliente** government to client portal, G2C portal; ∼ **gobierno a empresa** government to business portal, G2B portal; ∼ **sin cables** wireless portal; ∼ **vertical** vertical portal; ∼ **WAP** WAP portal

portátil[1] *adj* (equipo, programas) portable

portátil[2] *m* portable computer

portavoz *mf* spokesperson; (m) spokesman; (f) spokeswoman

porte *m* carriage; ∼ **debido** carriage forward; ∼ **pagado** postage *o* carriage paid

portilla *f* gateway

poscompra *adj* post-purchase

poscomunista *adj* post-Communist

posdata *f* postscript

poseer *vt* own; (acciones, bonos) hold

posesión *f* possession; **estar en** ∼ **de algo** (carta, pago) be in receipt of sth; **tomar** ∼ **de algo** take possession of sth; (puesto) take over sth; ∼ **segura** safe asset; ∼ **sumaria** summary possession

posfechado *adj* postdated

posfechar *vt* postdate

posgraduado, -a *m,f* postgraduate

posguerra *f* postwar period; **de** ∼ postwar

posibilidad *f* possibility; (oportunidad) chance; **prever todas las** ∼**es** anticipate every eventuality; **tener muchas** ∼**es de algo** stand a good chance of sth; **tener varias** ∼**es** have several options; **vivir dentro/por encima de sus** ∼**es** live within/beyond one's means; ∼**es económicas** means; ∼**es de pago** payment options; (de deuda) repayment options; ∼ **remota** remote possibility

posibilismo *m* possibilism

posible *adj* possible, potential; **hacer algo** ∼ make sth possible; **hacer todo lo** ∼ do everything one can, do one's best; **lo más pronto** ∼ as soon as possible; **si es** ∼ if possible; ∼ **cliente** potential customer

posición *f* position; **adoptó una** ∼ **crítica frente a la propuesta** she adopted a critical stance on the proposal **dejar clara su** ∼ make one's position clear; **en una** ∼ **peligrosa** in an dangerous position; **en última** ∼ in last position; **tomar** ∼ take a position; ∼ **abierta** open position; ∼ **acreedora** creditor position; ∼ **alcista** bull position; ∼ **alfa** alpha position; ∼ **de apertura** opening position; ∼ **de autoridad** position of authority; ∼ **bajista** bear position; ∼ **cerrada** closed position; ∼ **de compensación** clearing position; ∼ **competitiva** competitive position; ∼ **al contado** spot position; ∼ **corta** short position; ∼ **cubierta** covered position; ∼ **en descubierto** naked position; ∼ **dominante** dominant position; ∼ **dura** tough stance; ∼ **económica** economic position; ∼ **financiera** financial position; ∼ **fiscal** fiscal *o* tax position; ∼ **futura neta** net forward position; ∼ **de futuros** futures position; ∼ **de inversión neta** net investment position; ∼ **jurídica** legal position; ∼ **larga** long position; ∼ **en el mercado** market position; ∼ **mixta** straddle position; ∼ **negociadora** negotiating position, bargaining position; ∼ **neta** net position; ∼ **a plazo** forward position; ∼ **de riesgo** risk position; ∼ **social** social standing

posicionamiento *m* (acción) positioning; (posición) position; (postura) stance; ∼**s** (Info) settings; ∼ **de marca** brand positioning; ∼ **en el mercado** market positioning; ∼ **del producto** product placement

posponer *vt* postpone

posterior *adj* later, subsequent; ∼ **a la elección** post-election, following the election

postor *m* bidder; **vender algo al mejor** ∼ sell sth to the highest bidder

postura *f* (actitud) position, stance; **dejar clara su** ∼ make one's position clear; **reconsiderar su** ∼ reconsider one's position; **tener** ∼**s encontradas** *or* **enfrentadas** hold opposing views; **tomar** ∼ take a stand; ∼ **alcista** bullish stance; ∼ **antiinflacionaria** anti-inflationary stance; ∼ **fiscal** fiscal stance

posventa *adj* after-sales; **servicio** ∼ after-sales service

potencia *f* power; **en** ∼ potential; **ser un director en** ∼ be a potential manager, have the makings of a manager

potencial[1] *adj* potential

potencial² *m* potential; ~ **de beneficio** profit potential; ~ **de crecimiento** growth potential; ~ **del mercado** market potential; ~ **de ventas** sales potential

potencialmente *adv* potentially

potentado, -a *m,f* tycoon, big shot (infrml); ~ **comercial** business magnate *o* tycoon

potestad *f* authority, power; ~ **administrativa** administrative authority

ppm *abr* (▸**palabras por minuto**) wpm (words per minute)

ppp *abr* (▸**puntos por pie**) dpi (dots per inch)

práctica *f* practice; **en la** ~ in practice; **es la** ~ **habitual** it is standard *o* common practice; **poner algo en** ~ put sth into practice, implement sth; ~ **comercial restrictiva** restrictive business practice; ~ **ilegal** illegal practice; ~ **restrictiva** restrictive practice

practicable *adj* practicable, workable

practicar *vt* practise BrE, practice AmE

práctico *adj* practical

pragmáticamente *adv* pragmatically

pragmático¹ *adj* pragmatic

pragmático², -a *m,f* pragmatist

pragmatismo *m* pragmatism

preacuerdo *m* draft agreement

preámbulo *m* preamble

prearrendar *vt* prelease

preaviso *m* notice; **con un** ~ **de 2 días** at 2 days' notice; **dar un mes de** ~ give a month's notice

prebenda *f* (privilegio) privilege; (gaje) perk (infrml); (RRHH) sinecure

precario *adj* (situación) precarious

precaución *f* precaution; **por** ~ as a precaution; **tomar medidas de** ~ take precautionary measures

precedente¹ *adj* preceding, previous

precedente² *m* precedent; **establecer** *or* **sentar** *or* **marcar un** ~ set a precedent; **sin** ~**s** unprecedented

preceder *vt* precede; ~ **en prioridad a algo** take priority over sth

preceptivo *adj* mandatory; **no** ~ (directrices) nonmandatory

precepto *m* rule

precio *m* price; **a** ~ **de fábrica** at cost price; **a** ~ **de mercado** at the market price; **al** ~ **(de contado)** at-the-money; **a**

un ~ **de** at a price of; **a un** ~ **muy bajo** at a very low price; **bajar/subir los** ~**s** cut/raise prices; **los** ~**s han sido ajustados a la baja** prices have been marked down; ~ **en aplicación** price on application

(**precio a...**) ~ **de abastecimiento** supply price; ~ **abierto** open price; ~ **aceptable** acceptable price; ~ **de adquisición** acquisition price; ~ **al mercado** at-market price; ~ **de apertura** opening price; ~ **de apoyo** support price; ~ **aprobado** approved price; ~ **asequible** affordable price

(**b...**) ~ **bajo** low price

(**c...**) ~ **de la calle** street price; ~ **de catálogo** catalogue price BrE, catalog price AmE; (minorista) list price; ~ **cerrado** fixed price; ~ **de cesión** transfer price; ~ **de cierre** closing price; ~ **competitivo** competitive price; ~ **de compra** purchase price; ~ **comprador** bid price; ~ **de compraventa** bid-and-offered price; ~ **compuesto** composite price; ~ **al contado** cash price; ~ **convenido** agreed price; ~ **de conversión** conversion price; ~ **de coste** Esp *or* **costo** AmL cost price; ~ **de cotización** quoted price

(**d...**) ~ **descendente** falling price; ~ **con descuento** discount price; ~ **sin descuento** full rate

(**e...**) ~ **económico** cheap price; ~ **elevado** high price; ~ **de emisión** (Bolsa) issue price; (Med amb) emission charge; ~ **de entrada** entry price; ~ **de equilibrio** break-even price; ~ **estable** pegged price; ~ **estándar** standard price; ~ **de exportación** export price

(**f...**) ~ **del fabricante** manufacturer's price; ~ **de factura** invoice price; ~ **fijo** fixed price; (Econ) pegged price; ~ **franco (de) fábrica** factory-gate price

(**g...**) ~ **garantizado** guaranteed price; ~ **global** all-inclusive price; ~ **guía** guide price

(**i...**) ~ **de importación** import price; ~ **de incentivo** premium price; ~ **indicativo** target price; ~ **índice** index price; ~ **inicial** starting price; ~ **de intervención** trigger price; ~ **de introducción** introductory price

(**j...**) ~ **justo** fair price

(**l...**) ~ **de lanzamiento** launch price; ~ **de liquidación** settlement price

p

m... ~ **máximo** maximum price, ceiling price; ~ **medio** average price; ~ **de mercado** market price; ~ **mínimo** minimum price

n... ~ **negociado** negotiated price; ~ **neto** net price; ~ **nominal** nominal price; ~ **normal** normal price

o... ~ **de oferta** sale price; ~ **de oportunidad** bargain price

p... ~ **de paridad** parity price; ~ **al por mayor** wholesale price; ~ **al por menor** retail price; ~ **por pieza** unit price; (pago) piece rate; ~ **prescrito** prescribed price; ~ **publicado** published price; ~ **de punto muerto** break-even price

r... ~ **razonable** reasonable price; ~ **rebajado** reduced price; ~ **reducido** (Ocio) concessionary rate; ~ **regulado** (Ocio) controlled price; ~ **de reventa** resale price

s... ~ **de saldo** sale price; ~ **de subasta** auction price, hammer price (jarg); ~ **de suscripción** subscription price

t... ~ **a tipo fijo** flat-rate price; ~ **todo incluido** all-inclusive price

u... ~ **umbral** threshold price; ~ **unitario** unit price

v... ~ **de valoración** valuation price; ~ **del vendedor** asking price; ~ **de venta** selling price; ~ **de venta al público** retail price; ~ **de venta recomendado** recommended retail price

precisión f (exactitud) precision, accuracy

preciso adj (exacto, detallado) precise

precodificado adj precoded

precursor, a m,f precursor, forerunner

predador, a m,f predator

predecesor, a m,f predecessor

predecir vt predict, forecast

predefinido adj (Info) preset

predeterminado adj predetermined

predeterminar vt predetermine

predicción f forecast

predominante adj (dominante, extendido) predominant; (opinión, pauta) prevailing; (Fin) (interés) controlling

predominar vi (dominar) predominate, dominate; (opinión, pauta) prevail

preeminente adj pre-eminent

preestablecido adj pre-established

preestreno m preview

prefabricado adj prefabricated

prefacio m preface

preferencia f (predilección) preference; (prioridad) precedence, priority; ~**s** (Info) preferences; **dar** ~ **a algo/alguien** give priority to sth/sb; **de** ~ preferably; **tener una** ~ **por algo/alguien** have a preference for o prefer sth/sb; ~ **del consumidor** consumer preference; ~ **de marca** brand preference

preferencial adj preferential; (Info) foreground

preferir vt prefer; ~ **algo a algo** prefer sth to sth; ~ **hacer algo** prefer doing o to do sth, rather do sth; **prefiero trabajar sola** I prefer working on my own

pregunta f question; **contestar a una** ~ answer a question; **hacer una** ~ ask a question; ~ **abierta** open-ended question; ~ **cerrada** closed question; ~ **de control** control question; ~ **hipotética** hypothetical question; ~**s más frequentes** frequently asked questions, FAQs; ~ **de opción múltiple** multiple-choice question

preguntar vt ask; ~**le algo a alguien** ask sb sth; ~ **por algo/alguien** (buscando algo/a alguien) ask for sth/sb; (interesándose por algo/alguien) ask about sth/ask after sb

prejuicio m (preferencia) prejudice; (idea preconcebida) preconception; **sin** ~ without prejudice; **tener** ~**s hacia** or **contra alguien** be prejudiced against sb; ~**s sexistas** gender bias

prejuzgar vt prejudge

prematuro adj premature

premio m prize; **de** or **como** ~ as a prize; **ganar un** ~ win a prize; **el** ~ **al mejor libro** the prize for best book; **ese boleto lleva** ~ that's a prizewinning ticket; ~ **de consolación** consolation prize; ~ **gordo** jackpot; ~ **de promoción** free gift

premisa f premise

prenda f pledge, security; **dejar algo en** ~ give sth as security o surety

prensa f press; (periódicos) papers; **comprar/leer la** ~ buy/read the newspapers; **conferencia** or **rueda de** ~ press conference; **en** ~ at the printer's; **tener buena/mala** ~ get a good/bad press; ~ **amarilla** gutter press, tabloid press; ~ **especializada** trade press; ~ **de imprimir** printing press; ~ **local** local press; ~ **nacional** national press; ~ **regional** regional press; ~ **sensacionalista** gutter press, tabloid press

prepago m prepayment

preparación f preparation; (para un trabajo) qualifications; (Info) setup; **con mucha** ~ highly trained; **sin** ~ untrained; ~ **de datos** data preparation; ~ **del presupuesto** budget preparation; ~ **del terreno** (vaciamiento) site development

preparar vt prepare; ~ **una declaración** (Fisc) prepare a return; ~ **el terreno para algo** pave the way for sth; **preparado para el Internet** Net-enabled, Internet-enabled

prerrogativa f prerogative

prescribir vt prescribe

prescripción f prescription

prescrito adj prescribed

preselección f initial selection; (de candidatos) shortlist; **hacer una** ~ draw up a shortlist

preseleccionar vt make an initial selection of; (candidatos) shortlist

presencia f presence; ~ **en Internet** Internet presence; ~ **en el mercado** market presence

presentación f (acción, demostración) presentation; (de documento procesado) layout; (Fisc) filing; **presentaciones** introductions; **hacer las presentaciones** do the introductions, introduce everybody; ~ **comercial** sales presentation; ~ **leal** (Cont) fair presentation AmE; ~ **de ofertas** submission of bids; ~ **visual del número llamado** caller display

presentador, a m,f presenter; ~ **de noticias** newscaster; (m) anchorman; (f) anchorwoman; ~ **de televisión** television presenter

presentar vt present; (mostrar) show; (entregar) submit, hand in; (queja) lodge; (moción) propose, table BrE; (producto) launch; (apelación) enter; (declaración de renta) file; (solicitud) put in; (a una persona) introduce; **al** ~ **algo** on presentation of sth; **bien presentado** well presented; ~ **la dimisión** hand in one's resignation; **permítame** ~**le al director del proyecto** allow me to introduce the project manager (to you); ~ **una propuesta de nuevo** resubmit a proposal

presentarse v pron (aparecer) appear; (a un concurso) enter; (a un examen) sit BrE, take; (a un trabajo) apply for; (a elecciones) stand in; (oportunidad) arise; (problema) come up; (darse a conocer) introduce oneself; **cuando se presente la oportunidad** when the opportunity

arises; **permítame que me presente** allow me to introduce myself

presente adj present; **el día 20 del** ~ **mes** the 20th of this month, the 20th inst.; **estar** ~ **en algo** be present at sth; **hacerle** ~ **a alguien que ...** notify sb that ...; **por la** ~ **testifico que ...** I hereby testify that ...; **tener** ~ bear in mind

presidente, -a m,f chair; (m) chairman; (f) chairwoman; (de comisión) president; ~ **del consejo** chairman of the board; ~ **del consejo de administración** chairman of the board of directors; ~ **honorario** honorary president; ~ **de la junta directiva** chairman of the executive board

presidir vt (reunión, comité) chair; (jurado) preside over

presión f pressure; (Pol) lobbying; **trabajar bajo** ~ work under pressure; **confesar/firmar bajo** ~ confess/sign under duress; ~ **del consumidor** consumer pressure; ~ **fiscal** tax burden; ~ **inflacionista** inflationary pressure

presionar vt put pressure on, pressure, pressurize BrE; ~ **a alguien para que haga algo** put pressure on sb to do sth

prestación f (ayuda económica) benefit; (de servicios) provision; **agradecemos la** ~ **de ayuda** we are grateful for all the help we have received; ~ **en especie** (del empleo) benefit in kind; ~ **ex gratia** ex gratia payment; ~ **de juramento** (de presidente) swearing in; **prestaciones de la seguridad social** social security benefits BrE, welfare payments AmE; **prestaciones sanitarias** health services

prestamista mf lender; ~ **hipotecario(-a)** m,f mortgage lender; ~ **del sector privado** private sector lender

préstamo m (dinero prestado) loan; (acción) lending; **conceder un** ~ grant a loan; **pedir un** ~ ask for a loan; **tener algo en** ~ have sth on loan; ~ **acreditado** seasoned loan; ~ **amortizable** redeemable loan; ~ **atado** tied loan; ~ **bancario** bank loan; ~ **barato** low-cost loan; ~ **con caución** secured loan; ~ **de estudiante** student loan; ~ **fiduciario** uncovered loan; ~ **con/sin garantía** secured/unsecured loan; ~ **hipotecario** mortgage loan; ~ **incobrable** bad loan; ~ **indexado** indexed loan; ~ **interbancario** bank-to-bank lending; ~ **a interés fijo** fixed-interest loan; ~ **sin intereses** interest- ⋯⟩

free loan; ~ **a largo plazo** long-term loan; ~ **mancomunado** joint loan; ~ **pendiente** outstanding loan; ~ **a plazo fijo** fixed-term loan; ~ **puente** bridging loan BrE, bridge loan AmE; ~ **reestructurado** restructured loan; ~ **reincidente** repeater loan; ~ **sobregirado** overdraft loan

prestar *vt* lend; (servicio, ayuda) provide; ~ **declaración** (Der) give evidence; ~ **una fianza a alguien** stand surety for sb; ~ **juramento** (Der) swear an oath; ~ **testimonio en nombre de** give witness on behalf of

prestatario, -a *m,f* borrower

prestigio *m* prestige; **de ~** prestigious

prestigioso *adj* prestigious

presunción *f* presumption

presunto *adj* alleged; ~ **terrorista** alleged terrorist

presupuestar *vt* budget

presupuestario[1] *adj* (reforma, política) budgetary; (déficit) budget; **no ~** nonbudgetary

presupuestario[2] *m* budget item

presupuesto *m* budget; (cálculo aproximado) estimate; (cálculo exacto) quotation, quote; **pedir un ~** ask for an estimate, get a quote; ~ **ajustado** tight budget; ~ **anual** annual budget; ~ **base cero** zero-base budget; ~ **comunitario** (UE) Community budget; ~ **contingente** contingent budget; ~ **equilibrado** balanced budget; ~ **eventual** contingent budget; ~ **de explotación** operating budget; ~ **familiar** family budget; ~ **de gastos** expense budget; ~ **de gastos de capital** capital expenditure budget; ~ **de ingresos** revenue budget; ~ **de inversiones** investment budget; ~ **para la investigación** research budget; ~ **de marketing** marketing budget; ~ **promocional** promotional budget; ~ **publicitario** advertising budget

pretensión *f* (reclamación) claim; ~ **competitiva** competitive claim

prevención *f* prevention; **en ~ de algo** in order to prevent sth; ~ **de accidentes** accident prevention; ~ **de incendios** fire prevention; ~ **de reclamaciones** claims prevention

prevenir *vt* prevent; (advertir) warn; ~ **a alguien de algo** warn sb about sth

preventa *f* presale

prever *vt* (predecir) forecast, predict; (proyectar) plan; (problema, retraso) anticipate, foresee; (ventas) project; **como se preveía** as predicted *o* expected; **el** proyecto costó más de lo que se había previsto the project cost more than expected *o* planned; **estar previsto para** be planned *o* scheduled for; **el proyecto está previsto para el año que viene** the project is due *o* scheduled to start next year; **se prevé un aumento de precio** a price increase is predicted; **según lo previsto** according to plan; **tal como previsto** as planned; **tener previsto** plan; **tengo previsto viajar a los Estados Unidos el mes que viene** I am planning to go to the States next month; **terminaron antes de lo previsto** they finished ahead of schedule; **ventas previstas** projected sales

previo *adj* previous; **no se necesita experiencia previa** no previous experience required; ~ **a** prior to; **un compromiso ~** a previous engagement; **sin ~ aviso** without prior warning

previsión *f* (pronóstico) forecast; (precaución) precaution; (anticipación) foresight; **con ~ de futuro** forward-thinking; **en ~ de** as a precaution against; **por falta de ~** owing to a lack of foresight; ~ **de beneficios** profit forecast; ~ **a corto plazo** short-range forecast; ~ **de la demanda** demand forecast; ~ **económica** economic forecast; ~ **de fondos** cash flow forecast; ~ **a largo plazo** long-range forecast; ~ **social** social security BrE, welfare AmE; ~ **de ventas** sales forecast

previsor *adj* farsighted

previsualizar *vt* (documento) preview

PRH *abr* (▸**planificación de los recursos humanos**) HRP (human resource planning)

prima *f* (de un seguro) premium; (paga extra) bonus; **estar a ~** be at a premium; ~ **anual** annual premium; ~ **base** basic premium; ~ **de cancelación** redemption premium; ~ **complementaria** additional premium; ~ **devengada** earned premium; ~ **de ejecución** performance bonus; ~ **de emisión** share premium BrE; ~ **fija** fixed premium; ~ **de incentivo** incentive bonus; ~ **por lealtad** loyalty bonus; ~ **del riesgo** risk premium; ~ **de seguros** insurance premium; ~ **de traslado** relocation allowance; ~ **única** single premium

primario *adj* primary

primer *adj* first *cf* ▸**primero**

primeramente *adv* primarily

primero *adj* first; **el ~** the first; **de primera calidad** high-quality; **de primera generación** first-generation; **en primera instancia** in the first instance; **en primer lugar** first of all; **~ en entrar, ~ en salir** first in, first out; **~ en entrar, último en salir** first in, last out; **primer año** initial year; **primer borrador** first draft; **primera clase** first class; **el primer mundo** the First World; **primera opción** right of first refusal; **primera plana** (de periódico) front page; **primer plano** close-up; **primer trimestre** first quarter

primicia *f* exclusive, big story; **~ informativa** scoop

principal¹ *adj* main

principal² *m* (Fin) principal, capital

principio *m* principle; (comienzo) beginning; **de ~** on principle; **~ del acelerador** accelerator principle; **~ de antigüedad** seniority principle; **~ de auditoría** auditing principle; **~ de contabilidad** accounting principle; **P~s de Contabilidad Generalmente Aceptados** Generally Accepted Accounting Principles; **~ del devengo** accrual principle; **~ de equilibrio** matching principle; **~ de exclusión** exclusion principle

priori: a ~ *fra* a priori

prioridad *f* priority; **dar ~ a algo** prioritize sth, give priority to sth; **tener ~** have *o* take priority

prioritario *adj* priority, prime; (Info) foreground

priorizar *vt* prioritize, give priority to

privado *adj* private; **en ~** in private, privately

privar *vt*: **~ a alguien de algo** deprive sb of sth; (de licencia, permiso) take sth away from sb; **le ~on del permiso de trabajo** they took away his work permit

privatización *f* privatization

privatizar *vt* privatize

privilegiado *adj* privileged

privilegio *m* privilege; **disfrutar de un ~** enjoy a privilege; **~ fiscal** tax privilege; **~ general** general lien; **~ del puesto** perk (infrml) of the job; **~ de reinversión** reinvestment privilege; **~ de suscripción** subscription privilege

pro *m* plus, advantage; **el ~ y el contra** the pros and cons; **sopesar el ~ y el contra** weigh up the pros and cons; **en ~ de** in favour BrE *o* favor AmE of

pro- *pref* pro-; **~-europeo** pro-European; **~-gobierno** pro-government

proactivo *adj* proactive

probabilidad *f* probability; (oportunidad) chance; **existe poca ~ de que sea reelegido** there is little prospect *o* chance of his being reelected

probable *adj* probable; (cliente) prospective; **es ~ que le renueven el contrato** they are likely to renew her contract

probar *vt* (teoría, inocencia) prove; (poner a prueba) test, try out; **~ a alguien** give sb a trial; **~ una reclamación** substantiate a claim

probatorio *adj* evidenciary

problema *m* problem; **crear ~s** cause problems; **resolver un ~** solve a problem; **sin ~** problem-free; **~s económicos** financial difficulties *o* problems; **~ de liquidez** cash flow problem; **~ medioambiental** environmental problem; **~ técnico** technical problem

procedimiento *m* (método) procedure; (proceso) process, method; (Der) proceedings; **el ~ a seguir en tales casos** the procedure to be followed in such cases; **los resultados obtenidos mediante este ~** the results obtained using this process; **~ de agravio** grievance procedure; **~ de apelación** appeals procedure; **~ de auditoría** auditing procedure; **~s de la conferencia** conference proceedings; **~ de control** control procedure; **~ de despido** dismissal procedure; **~ disciplinario** disciplinary procedure; **~ judicial** legal proceedings; **~ parlamentario** parliamentary procedure; **~ de reclamación** complaints procedure; (Seg) claims procedure

procesable *adj* actionable

procesador *m* processor; **~ de datos** data processor; **~ frontal** front-end computer; **~ de textos** word processor; **~ vectorial** array processor

procesal *adj* procedural; **derecho ~** procedural law

procesamiento *f* processing; (Der) prosecution; (juicio) trial; **~ de alimentos** food processing; **~ de datos** data processing; **~ electrónico de datos** electronic data processing; **~ por lotes** batch processing; **~ de pagos** payment processing; **~ remoto** remote processing; **~ de textos** word processing

procesar *vt* (datos, cheques) process; (Der) prosecute; (juicio) try; ~ **a alguien por algo/hacer algo** prosecute sb for sth/doing sth; **fue procesado por fraude fiscal** he was prosecuted for tax fraud; **sin** ~ unprocessed

proceso *m* (serie de acciones) process; (Der) action, proceedings; (juicio) trial; (Info) processing; (transcurso) course; **entablar** ~ **a alguien** bring a lawsuit against sb; **estar en** ~ be in process; ~ **contra alguien** action against sb; ~ **analítico** analytical process; ~ **de armonización** harmonization process; ~ **automático de datos** automatic data processing; ~ **civil** civil action; ~ **de compra** buying process; ~ **de computadora** AmL (*cf* ▸**proceso de ordenador** Esp) computer processing; ~ **criminal** criminal proceedings; ~ **de datos** data processing; ~ **de decisión** decision-making process; ~ **de fabricación** manufacturing process; ~ **legal** legal suit; ~ **por lotes** batch processing; ~ **por lotes a distancia** remote batch processing; ~ **no prioritario** background processing; ~ **de ordenador** Esp (*cf* ▸**proceso de computadora** AmL) computer processing; ~ **de paz** peace process; ~ **prioritario** foreground processing; ~ **de producción** production process; ~ **de selección** selection process; ~ **de textos** text processing, word processing; ~ **verbal** written report

procomunista *adj* pro-communist

procuración *f* procurement; (Der) power of attorney, proxy

procurador, a *m,f* (de trámites burocráticos) solicitor BrE, attorney AmE

producción *f* production; (rendimiento) output; (Info) throughput; ~ **ajustada** lean production; ~ **en cadena** mass production, assembly-line production; ~ **conjunta** joint production; ~ **deficitaria** underproduction, production shortfall; ~ **integrada por computadora** AmL *or* **ordenador** Esp computer-integrated manufacturing; ~ **intensiva** intensive production; ~ **interior** domestic output; ~ **justo a tiempo** AmL (*cf* ▸**producción según demanda** Esp) just-in-time production; ~ **en lotes** batch production; ~ **máxima** maximum output; ~ **nacional** home production; ~ **neta** net output; ~ **según demanda** Esp (*cf* ▸**producción justo a tiempo** AmL) just-in-time production; ~ **en serie** mass production

producir *vt* (petróleo, artículos, coches) produce; (causar) cause; (beneficios, interés) yield; ~ **algo en serie** mass-produce sth; ~ **un beneficio/una pérdida** yield a profit/loss; **la nueva ley produjo reacciones violentas** the new law provoked a violent reaction; **esta cuenta produce un 7% de interés** this account yields 7% interest

productividad *f* productivity; **aumentar la** ~ increase productivity

productivo *adj* productive; (Fin) profitable, lucrative; **no** ~ unproductive; (Fin) unprofitable

producto *m* (artículo) product; (resultado) result; (Bolsa) commodity; (Fin) yield, profit; **ser el** ~ **de algo** be the result *o* product of sth; **el acuerdo es el** ~ **de meses de negociaciones** the agreement is the result *o* product of months of negotiations; ~ **acabado** finished product; ~ **agrícola** agricultural produce; ~**s comunitarios** Community goods; ~ **al contado** spot commodity; ~ **alimenticio** foodstuff; ~ **auténtico** genuine article; ~ **básico** commodity; (V&M) core product; ~ **de belleza** beauty product; ~ **de calidad** quality product; ~**s de consumo** consumer goods; ~**s de conveniencia** convenience goods; ~ **derivado** derivative product, by-product; ~ **duradero** hard commodity; ~ **ecológico** environmentally-friendly product; ~**s elaborados** manufactured goods; ~ **de gancho** appeal product; ~ **interior bruto** gross domestic product, GDP; ~ **interior neto** net domestic product, NDP; ~**s lácteos** dairy products, dairy produce; ~ **manufacturado** manufactured product; ~ **de marca** brand-name product; ~ **nacional bruto** gross national product, GNP; ~**s perecederos** perishable goods, nondurables; ~ **primario** primary *o* basic commodity; ~ **secundario** by-product, spin-off product; ~ **de segunda generación** second-generation product; ~ **de las ventas** proceeds of sales

productor, a *m,f* producer; ~ **cinematográfico(-a)** *m,f* film BrE *o* movie AmE producer

profesión *f* profession; (en formularios) occupation; **un ingeniero de** ~ an engineer by profession; ~ **contable** accountancy profession

profesional[1] *adj* professional; **poco** ~ unprofessional

profesional² *mf* professional
profesionalismo *m* professionalism
profesionalización *f*
professionalization
profesor, a *m,f* (de universidad) lecturer;
(de escuela) teacher
pro forma *adj* pro forma
programa *m* programme BrE, program
AmE; (Info) program; (horario) schedule;
~**s** (Info) software; ~ **de actuación**
development programme BrE,
development program AmE; ~ **del**
afiliado affiliate program; ~ **antivirus**
antivirus software, virus checker; ~**s**
de base systems software; ~ **de**
capacitación training programme BrE,
training program AmE; ~ **comunitario**
(UE) Community Programme BrE,
Community Program AmE; ~ **de**
consulta inquiry program; ~ **de**
control control program; ~ **de**
creación de páginas web Web-
authoring program; ~ **en directo** live
programme BrE, live program AmE; ~**s**
de estantería shelfware; ~ **de**
fiscalización audit programme BrE,
audit program AmE; ~ **de formación**
training programme BrE, training
program AmE; ~ **fuente** source program;
~ **de gestión de redes** networking
software; ~ **informático** computer
program; ~ **de instalación** set-up
program; ~ **de inversión** investment
programme BrE, investment program
AmE; ~ **de investigación** research
programme BrE, research program AmE;
~ **de perforaciones** drilling
programme BrE, drilling program AmE; ~
de privatización privatization
programme BrE, privatization program
AmE; ~ **de procesamiento de textos**
word-processing software; ~ **de**
proceso de mensajes message
processing program; ~ **de producción**
production schedule; ~ **de rearranque**
restart program; ~ **de reconocimiento**
de la voz speech *o* voice recognition
software; ~ **de trabajo** work schedule;
~ **de traducción** translation software;
~ **de utilidades** utility program; ~
vapor vapourware BrE, vaporware AmE;
~ **de vencimiento** lapsing schedule; ~
en vivo live programme BrE, live
program AmE
programación *f* (Info) programming;
(conjunto de programas) programs;
(planeamiento) scheduling, programme BrE
o program AmE planning; (guía de
programas) listings; ~ **de computadoras**

AmL (*cf* ▸**programación de**
ordenadores Esp) computer
programming; ~ **informática** computer
programming; ~ **neurolingüística**
neurolinguistic programming, NLP; ~
de objetivos goal programming *o*
setting; ~ **de ordenadores** Esp (*cf*
▸**programación de computadoras**
AmL) computer programming; ~ **de la**
producción production scheduling; ~
de sistemas systems programming; ~
de tareas task scheduling
programado *adj* scheduled; (Info)
programmed; **no** ~ unscheduled
programador, a *m,f* programmer; ~
de aplicaciones applications
programmer; ~ **de computadoras** AmL
or **ordenadores** Esp computer
programmer; ~ **de contenido de la**
web Web content developer; ~ **de**
sistemas systems programmer; ~ **de**
vuelos flight scheduler
programar *vt* (actividades, eventos) plan;
(trabajo, programas) schedule; (Info)
program
progresismo ideológico *m*
political correctness
progresivamente *adv* progressively
progresivo *adj* progressive
progreso *m* progress; **hacer** ~**s** make
progress; ~ **técnico** technical progress;
~ **tecnológico rápido** rapid
technological progress
prohibición *f* ban; (de exportaciones)
embargo; **levantar la** ~ **de algo** lift the
ban on sth
prohibir *vt* ban, forbid, prohibit; **una**
ley que prohíbe la huelga en los
servicios públicos a law which
prohibits *o* bans strikes in the public
services; ~**le algo/hacer algo a alguien**
ban sb from sth/doing sth; **queda**
terminantemente prohibido it is strictly
forbidden *o* prohibited; **prohibido fumar**
or **se prohíbe fumar** no smoking;
prohibido el paso no entry; **prohibida la**
entrada no admittance; **prohibido fijar**
carteles no bill stickers, bill stickers
will be prosecuted
proletariado *m* proletariat
prolongación *f* extension
prolongar *vt* (contrato) extend; (visita)
prolong
promediador, a *m,f* averager
promediar *vt* (coste, beneficio) average
out; ~ **al alza/a la baja** average up/
down

P

promedio *m* average; **como ~** on average; **las ventas alcanzaron un ~ de 150.000 en tres años** sales averaged 150,000 over three years; **gana un ~ de 1.000 euros a la semana** she earns on average *o* averages 1,000 euros a week; **~ Nikkei** Nikkei Average

promesa *f* promise; **cumplir/romper una ~** keep/break a promise; **faltó a su ~** he went back on his word; **fue fiel a su ~** he kept his word, he was as good as his word; **~ de pago** promise to pay; **~ de vender** promise to sell; **~ vinculante** binding promise

prometer **1** *vt* promise; **promete ser un gran éxito** it promises to be a huge success.
2 *vi* show promise, be promising; **el nuevo empleado promete** the new recruit shows promise

prominente *adj* (importante) prominent; (actividad, visita) high-profile

promoción *f* (ascenso) promotion; (V&M) special offer, promotion; **hacer la ~ de un nuevo producto** promote a new product; **esta semana tenemos una ~** we have a special offer this week; **~ combinada** tie-in promotion; **~ de marca** brand promotion; **~ de un producto** product promotion; **~ en el punto de venta** point-of-sale promotion; **~ rápida** (RRHH) fast tracking; **~ en tienda** in-store promotion; **~ de ventas** sales promotion

promocional *adj* promotional

promocionar *vt* promote

promotor, a *m,f* promoter; (Inmob) developer; **~ comercial** commercial developer; **~ financiero(-a)** *m,f* financial backer; **~ inmobiliario(-a)** property developer

promover *vt* (instigar) promote; (causar) provoke; **~ un acuerdo** promote an agreement; **el comunicado promovió una ola de protestas** the announcement caused *o* provoked a wave of protest

promulgación *f* (de ley) enactment

promulgar *vt* enact; **promulgado por** enacted by

pronóstico *m* forecast, prediction; **~ ambiental** environmental forecast; **~ empresarial** business forecast; **~ del mercado** market forecast

pronto[1] *adj* prompt; **esperamos una pronta respuesta** we look forward to your prompt *o* early reply; **~ pago de las facturas** prompt payment of invoices

pronto[2] *adv* soon; **lo más ~ posible** as soon as possible, a.s.a.p.; **tan ~ como** as soon as; **por lo ~** for the time being

pronunciar *vt* (decir) say; (discurso) make, deliver; (Der) pronounce; **~ un discurso** make a speech; **~ un fallo favorable a alguien** give a ruling in favour BrE *o* favor AmE of sb; **~ una sentencia** pass judgment; **~ unas palabras de bienvenida** say a few words of welcome; **~ una sentencia condenatoria** pass sentence; **~ un veredicto** return a verdict

propaganda *f* advertising; (material publicitario) advertising leaflets; (Pol) propaganda; **~ de buzón** junk mail; (por correo electrónico) junk e-mail; **~ por correo** Esp (*cf* ▸**buzoneo** AmL) mailing

propensión *f* tendency, inclination, propensity (frml); **~ a ahorrar/invertir** propensity to save/invest

propenso *adj*: **ser ~ a** be prone to

propiedad *f* property; (pertenencia) ownership; (Fisc) estate; **ser ~ de alguien** belong to sb; **no es de mi ~** it isn't mine, it doesn't belong to me; **tener en ~** own; **~ absoluta** freehold property; **~ alquilada** let property, rented property; **~ amortizable** depreciable property; **~ arrendada** leasehold property; **~ del capital** capital property; **~ comercial** commercial property; **~ compartida** joint ownership; **~ horizontal** (sistema) joint freehold BrE, condominium AmE; (edificio) *building owned under joint freehold, condominium* AmE; **~ inmobiliaria** property, real estate AmE; **~ industrial** patent rights; **~ intelectual** intellectual property; **~ mancomunada** joint property, property held in joint names; **~ privada** private property; **~ pública** public property

propietario, -a *m,f* (de comercio, negocio) proprietor, owner; (de vivienda) homeowner, property owner; **ser ~ de un negocio** have one's own business, own a business; **~ absentista** Esp *or* **ausentista** absentee landlord; **~ absoluto(-a)** *m,f* freehold owner, freeholder; **~ nominal** (de bono) registered owner; **~-ocupante** owner-occupier; **~ de una patente** patent proprietor; **~ registrado(-a)** *m,f* registered proprietor; **~ único(-a)** *m,f* sole proprietor

propina *f* tip; **darle una ~ a alguien** give sb a tip; **dar algo de ~** leave sth as a tip; **dar** *or* **dejar una** ∼ **de diez euros** leave a ten euro tip

proponente *mf* proposer

proponer *vt* (sugerir) propose, suggest; (recomendar a alguien) propose, nominate; ∼ **una moción** propose a motion; ∼ **un trato** propose a deal; **propuse a Juan como candidato** I proposed Juan as a candidate; ∼ **que ...** propose that ...; **propuso que aceptaramos la oferta** he proposed that we should accept the offer

proporción *f* proportion; (de población) size; **de grandes proporciones** huge; **en** ∼ **a** in proportion to, commensurate with; **como** ∼ **de** as a proportion of; **en diferentes proporciones** in varying degrees; **en iguales proporciones** in equal proportions; **no guardar** ∼ **con algo** be out of proportion to sth; **los sueldos no han subido en** ∼ **a la inflación** salaries have not risen in line *o* kept pace with inflation; ∼ **beneficio- volumen** profit-volume ratio; ∼ **de clics** click-through rate, CTR; ∼ **de conversión** conversion ratio; ∼ **de coste** Esp *or* **costo** AmL cost ratio; ∼ **de crecimiento económico sostenible** sustainable economic growth rate; ∼ **de desembolso de dividendos** dividend payout ratio; ∼ **directiva** management ratio; ∼ **de eficiencia** efficiency ratio; ∼ **de existencias** stock ratio; ∼ **de inflación básica** core inflation rate; ∼ **de inflación subyacente** underlying inflation rate; ∼ **principal** (de inflación) headline rate; ∼ **de pérdida de clientes/abonados** customer/ subscriber churn rate; ∼ **de rentabilidad** profitability ratio; ∼ **de ventas** sales ratio

proporcionado *adj* proportionate, commensurate

proporcional *adj* proportional, proportionate; ∼ **a los ingresos** commensurate with earnings

proporcionalmente *adv* proportionately

proporcionar *vt* provide, supply; ∼ **algo a alguien** provide sb with sth; **me** ∼**on toda la información necesaria** they provided me with all the necessary information; ∼ **un mercado para** provide a market for

proposición *f* (sugerencia) proposal; (oferta) proposition; **mi** ∼ **es que levantemos la sesión** I propose that we adjourn; **nuestra** ∼ **sigue en pie** our proposal still stands; ∼ **alternativa**

alternative proposal; ∼ **única de venta** unique selling proposition *o* point, USP

propósito *m* purpose, aim, goal; (intención) intention; **a** ∼ on purpose; **a** ∼ **de** with regard to; **con el** ∼ **de** with the intention of, in order to; **el** ∼ **de la reunión era de buscar maneras de mejorar las ventas** the purpose of the meeting was to find ways of improving sales; ∼ **especificado** specified purpose

propuesta *f* proposal; **aprobar una** ∼ approve a proposal; **desestimar** *or* **rechazar una** ∼ reject *o* turn down a proposal; **presentar una** ∼ put forward a proposal; ∼**s fiscales** tax proposals; ∼ **de ley** bill; ∼ **de negocio** business proposition

prorrata *f* pro rata share, proration; **a** ∼ pro rata, on a pro rata basis; **lo calcularon a** ∼ they calculated it pro rata *o* on a pro rata basis

prorratear *vt* (costes, propiedades) apportion, share on a pro rata basis

prorrateo *m* averaging; (de propiedades, bienes) apportionment; ∼ **del coste** Esp *or* **costo** AmL cost apportionment

prórroga *f* (extensión) extension; (aplazamiento) deferment

prorrogar *vt* (alargar) extend; (aplazar) defer

proscribir *vt* ban, prohibit

proseguir ⟨1⟩ *vi* continue, proceed; **prosiga, por favor** please proceed; ∼ **con algo** proceed *o* continue with sth. ⟨2⟩ *vt* continue; ∼ **la discusión** continue the discussion

prospección *f* (de petróleo) prospecting; (V&M) research; ∼ **de mercado** market research

prospecto *m* prospectus; (de propaganda) leaflet, pamphlet; ∼ **definitivo** (Bolsa) final prospectus

prosperar *vi* (negocio) prosper, thrive; (tener éxito) be successful; (persona) do well

prosperidad *f* prosperity

próspero *adj* prosperous, thriving

protección *f* protection; (Fin) hedge; **bajo** ∼ **policial** under police protection; ∼ **del consumidor** consumer protection; ∼ **de datos** data protection; ∼ **de ficheros** file protection; ∼ **del medio ambiente** environmental protection; ∼ **de patentes** patent protection

proteccionismo *m* protectionism

proteccionista¹ *adj* protectionist

proteccionista² *mf* protectionist

P

proteger *vt* protect; (Bolsa) hedge; (intereses) safeguard; (derechos) defend; (moneda) shadow; ∼ **algo/a alguien de** *or* **contra algo/alguien** protect sth/sb from *o* against sth/sb; ∼ **de escritura** write-protect; ∼ **lós intereses del país** protect *o* safeguard the country's interests

protegido *adj* protected; (económicamente) secure; (disquete) write-protected; ∼ **copia** copy-protected; ∼ **por contraseña** password protected

protesta *f* protest; **bajo** ∼ under protest; **hacer una** ∼ **(contra algo)** protest (against sth); **una campaña de** ∼ a protest campaign; **en señal de** ∼ in protest

protestar *vi* protest; (quejarse) complain; ∼ **contra** *or* **por algo** protest against *o* about sth; ∼**on por el trato recibido** they complained about the way they had been treated; **¡protesto, Señoría!** (en tribunal) objection, Your Honour BrE *o* Honor! AmE

protocolo *m* protocol; ∼ **de aplicación inalámbrica** *or* **sin cables** wireless application protocol, WAP; ∼ **de Internet** Internet protocol; ∼ **de transferencia de archivos** file transfer protocol, FTP

prototipo *m* prototype

provecho *m* benefit; **sacarle mucho** ∼ **a algo** benefit from sth, profit by sth

provechoso *adj* profitable, lucrative; **un contrato muy** ∼ a very lucrative contract

proveedor[1]**, a** *m,f* supplier, dealer; (Econ) provider; ∼ **de fondos** financial backer; ∼ **de servicios mercantiles** merchant services provider

proveedor[2] *m* (de Internet) provider; ∼ **de acceso de Internet** Internet Access provider, IAP; ∼ **de contenido** content provider; ∼ **de espacio web** Internet presence provider, Web space provider; ∼ **de servicio de aplicaciones** application service provider, ASP; ∼ **de servicios de almacenamiento** storage services provider, SSP; ∼ **de servicios Internet** Internet service provider, ISP, online service provider, OSP; ∼ **de servicios Internet gratis** subscription-free ISP; ∼ **de servicios WAP** wireless application service provider, WASP

proveer *vt* (fondos) provide; (suministrar) supply; (Der) decree; ∼ **a alguien de algo** provide sb with sth; ∼ **los recursos necesarios para un proyecto** adequately

resource a project, provide the necessary funds for a project

provenir *vi*: ∼ **de** come from; (tener origen en) stem from; **el vuelo proveniente de Madrid** the flight from Madrid

providencia *f* (Der) ruling; ∼**s** measures, steps; **tomar** ∼**s para hacer algo** take steps to do sth

provincia *f* province, region, county

provincial *adj* provincial, county

provisión *f* provision; ∼ **fiscal** tax provision; ∼ **para pérdidas** loss provision

provisional *adj* provisional, interim

provisionalmente *adv* provisionally; (Der) ad interim

provocar *vt* cause, start; (coste) trigger

próximo *adj* next; (en correspondencia) proximo; **de la próxima generación** (ordenadores, software) next-generation; **el** ∼ **lunes** next Monday; **la próxima reunión** the next meeting; **el 20** ∼ on 20th proximo

proyección *f* projection; ∼ **de beneficios** profit projection; ∼ **fiscal** fiscal projection; ∼ **de imagen** image projection; ∼ **de ventas** sales projection

proyectar *vt* plan; ∼ **hacer algo** plan to do sth; **tienen proyectado ampliar el negocio** they have plans *o* are planning to expand the business

proyecto *m* project, plan; **tener** ∼**s para algo** have plans for sth; **tener algo en** ∼ be planning sth; **tenemos varios productos en** ∼ we have several products in the pipeline; ∼ **aprobado** approved project; ∼ **de ley** bill; ∼ **piloto** pilot project; ∼ **de resolución** draft resolution; ∼ **de riesgo** exposure draft; ∼ **de sugerencias** suggestion scheme

proyector *m* projector; ∼ **de acetatos** overhead projector; ∼ **de diapositivas** slide projector; ∼ **de luz concentrada** spotlight; ∼ **de video** Esp *or* **video** AmL **portátil** portable video projector, PVP

prudente *adj* prudent, sensible; (proyección) cautious

prudentemente *adv* prudently, sensibly

prueba *f* proof; (Der) evidence; (examen) test; (de imprenta) page proof; ∼**s** evidence; **a** ∼ on a trial basis, on approval; (empleado) on probation; **a** ∼ **de balas** bulletproof; **un argumento a** ∼ **de balas** a cast iron argument; **a** ∼ **de**

destrozos tamper-proof; **a ~ de humedad** damp-proof; **a ~ de incendios** fire-resistant; **a ~ de piratas** hacker-proof; **a ~ de robo** theft-proof; **corregir ~s** proofread; **falta de ~s** lack of evidence; **poner algo a ~** put sth to the test; **presentar ~s** present evidence; **ser ~ de algo** prove sth; **~ alfa** alpha-test; **~ de aptitud** aptitude test; **~ beta** beta-test; **~ de capacidad** eligibility test; **~ de carretera** test drive; **~ a ciegas** blind test; **~ cinematográfica** screen test; **~ circunstancial** circumstancial evidence; **~ de comparación** comparison test; **~ del consumidor** consumer test; **~ documental** documentary evidence; **~ de entrega** proof of delivery; **~ escrita** written evidence; **~ de fiabilidad** reliability test; **~ de fuego** acid test; **~ de memorización asistida** aided recall test; **~ de mercado** market test; **~ de panel** panel testing; **~ preliminar** pre-testing; **~ presunta** prima facie evidence; **~ del producto** product testing; **~ del programa** program testing; **~ de propiedad** proof of title; **~ psicológica** psychological test; **~ psicométrica** psychometric test; **~ de reconocimiento** recognition test; **~ de referencia** benchmark test; **~ de rendimiento** performance testing; **~ de sonido** sound check

psicográficos *m pl* psychographics

psicología *f* psychology; **~ industrial** industrial psychology; (RRHH) personnel *o* occupational psychology; **~ de mercado** market psychology

psicometría *f* psychometrics

PTU *abr* (**participación de las trabajadores en las utilidades**) profit sharing

publicación *f* publication; **una revista de ~ mensual/semanal** a monthly/weekly magazine; **fecha de ~** publication date; **~ anticipada** early publication; **~ comercial** trade publication; **~ de dividendo** declaration of dividend; **~ electrónica** electronic publishing, Internet publishing; **~ periódica** periodical

publicar *vt* publish; (software, productos) release

publicidad *f* (propaganda) advertising; (material) advertising material; (anuncio) advertisement; (divulgación) publicity; **dar ~ a algo** publicize sth; **hacer ~ de algo** advertise sth; **agencia/campaña de ~** advertising agency/campaign; **~**

agresiva hard sell; **~ de ambiente** mood advertising; **~ anticipada** advance publicity; **~ comercial** trade advertising; **~ corporativa** corporate advertising; **~ directa** direct advertising; **~ directa por correo** direct-mail advertising; **~ de una empresa a otra** business-to-business advertising; **~ especializada** speciality advertising BrE, specialty advertising AmE; **~ estática** billboard advertising; **~ ética** ethical advertising; **~ en Internet** Internet advertising; **~ en línea** online advertising; (anuncio) online advertisement; **~ poscompra** post-purchase advertising; **~ en la prensa** press advertising; **~ del producto** product advertising; **~ en el punto de venta** point-of-sale advertising; **~ en la radio** radio advertising; **~ de reclutamiento** recruitment advertising; **~ de respuesta directa** direct-response advertising; **~ subliminal** subliminal advertising; **~ televisiva** television advertising

publicista *mf* publicist

publicitario[1] *adj* advertising; **anuncio ~** advertisement, commercial; **campaña publicitaria** advertising campaign

publicitario[2], **-a** *m,f* advertising executive

público[1] *adj* public; **hacer algo ~** announce sth, make sth public; **ser de dominio ~** be in the public domain, be public knowledge

público[2] *m* public; (espectadores) crowd, people; (en teatro) audience; **abierto al ~** open to the public; **el gran ~** the general public; **~ objetivo** target audience; (V&M) target market

publireportaje *m* advertorial

puente *m* bridge; (vacaciones) *short break provided by an extra day's leave in between a public holiday and the weekend*, ≈ long weekend; **hacer ~** have a long weekend; **~ aéreo** (vuelo) shuttle; **~ de peaje** tollbridge

puericultura *f* childcare

puerta *f* door, entrance; (Info) port; (de embarque) gate; **abrir/cerrar la ~ a algo** open/close the door to sth; **a ~ cerrada** behind closed doors; (Der) in camera; **de ~s adentro** behind closed doors; **de ~s afuera** in public; **de ~ a ~** door-to-door; **~ de embarque** boarding gate; **~ de impresora** printer port; **~ a puerta** cold canvass; **~ en serie** serial port; **~** ⋯⟩

P

de servicio tradesman's entrance BrE, service entrance AmE

puerto *m* port, harbour BrE, harbor AmE

puesta *f*: ~ **a cero** reset; ~ **en común** round table discussion; (para ideas nuevas) brainstorm; ~ **al día** updating; ~ **en escena** production, staging; ~ **en marcha** start-up; ~ **en práctica** implementation; **la ~ en práctica del plan** putting the plan into action; ~ **a punto** fine tuning; ~ **en vigor** coming into force; **la ~ en vigor de la nueva ley se prevé para enero** the new law is expected to come into force in January

puesto *m* position, post, job; (de mercado) stall; **solicitar un ~** apply for a job; ~ **directivo** management post; ~ **fijo** permanent job; ~ **menor** junior position; ~ **de oficinista** office job; ~ **de periódicos** newspaper stand; ~ **vacante** vacancy

puja *f* (en subasta) bidding; (cantidad) bid; (lucha) struggle, fight; **la ~ por mejorar las condiciones de trabajo** the fight to improve working conditions; ~ **de salida** opening bid

pujar *vi* bid; (luchar) struggle, fight; ~ **por hacer algo** struggle to do sth

pulgada *f* inch; ~ **de columna** column inch

pulsación *f* keystroke

pulsar *vt* (mercado) tap; (tecla, botón) press

punta¹ *adj* leading-edge, state-of-the-art; (máximo) peak; **tecnología ~** state-of-the-art technology; **hora ~** Esp (*cf* ▸**hora pico** AmL) rush hour; **horas ~** Esp (*cf* ▸**horas pico** AmL) peak times

punta² *f* end, tip; ~ **nocturna** evening peak

puntero¹ *adj* (empresa) leading; (tecnología) state-of-the-art

puntero² *m* pointer

punto *m* point; (señal) dot; (signo de puntuación) full stop BrE, period AmE;

(Cont) item; (Info) dot; **poner a ~** (programa) fine-tune; **poner ~ final a algo** put an end to sth; ~ **central** focus; ~ **clave** key point; ~ **de control** check point; ~ **crítico** critical point; ~ **débil** weak point; ~ **de entrada** (en país) point of entry; ~ **de equilibrio** breakeven point; ~ **de flexión** turning point; ~ **grueso** bullet point; ~ **de índice** index point; ~ **límite** cutoff point; ~ **máximo** peak; ~ **muerto** deadlock, stalemate; **las negociaciones han llegado a un ~ muerto** the negotiations have reached deadlock; ~ **neurálgico** nerve centre BrE, nerve center AmE; ~ **de origen** point of origin; ~ **de partida** starting point; (de viaje) point of departure; ~ **peligroso** danger point; ~**s por pie** dots per inch; ~ **porcentual** percentage point; ~ **de presencia** point of presence, POP; ~ **prominente** landmark; ~ **de provocación** trigger point; ~ **de referencia** benchmark; ~ **de rentabilidad** breakeven point; ~ **de retención** sticking point; ~ **de saturación** saturation point; ~ **de umbral** threshold point; ~ **de venta** point of sale; ~ **de venta electrónico** electronic point of sale, e-point of sale; ~ **de vista** point of view; **desde un ~ de vista técnico** from a technical point of view

puntocom *f* dot-com

puntual *adj* punctual, on time; (detallado); (exacto) specific; **llegar/empezar ~** arrive/start on time *o* punctually; **ser ~** be punctual; **un informe ~** a detailed report

puntualidad *f* punctuality

P.V.P. *abr* (▸**precio de venta al público**) R.R.P (recommended retail price)

PYME *abr* (▸**pequeña y mediana empresa**) S.M.E. (small and medium-size enterprise)

Qq

quebrado *adj* (Fin) bankrupt

quebrar *vi* (Fin) go bankrupt, go out of business

quebrarse *v pron* (Info) crash (jarg)

quedar *vi* be, remain; (faltar) be left; (acordar) agree; (citarse) arrange to meet; **quedan cinco minutos** there are five minutes left *o* to go; **quedan tres días para las vacaciones** there are three days left till the holidays; **quedamos para el lunes** we arranged to meet next Monday; **¿a qué hora quedamos?** when *o* what time shall we meet?; ~ **en algo/hacer algo** agree sth/to do sth, arrange to do sth; **quedó en venir mañana** she said she would come tomorrow; **quedamos a la espera de su respuesta** (en correspondencia) we look forward to hearing from you

quedarse *v pron*: ~ **sin** run out of; ~ **atrás** lag behind, be left behind; **la empresa se está quedando atrás** the company is getting left behind

queja *f* complaint; (RRHH) grievance; **dar** ~ **de algo/alguien** complain about sth/sb; **no tener** ~ **de algo/alguien** have no complaints about sth/sb; **presentar una** ~ make *o* lodge a complaint

quejarse *v pron* complain; ~ **de algo/alguien** complain about sth/sb; ~ **de que ...** complain that ...

querella *f* lawsuit; **poner** *or* **presentar una** ~ **contra algo/alguien** sue sth/sb, take legal action against sth/sb; ~ **por difamación** libel suit *o* action

quid *m* crux; **el** ~ **de la cuestión** the crux of the matter

quiebra *f* bankruptcy; (Bolsa, Info) crash; **en** ~ bankrupt; **declararse en** ~ go into liquidation, file for bankruptcy; **ir a la** ~ go bankrupt, go bust (infrml); ~ **comercial** business failure; ~ **involuntaria** involuntary bankruptcy; ~ **voluntaria** voluntary bankruptcy

quilate *m* Esp carat

quincena *f* two weeks, fortnight BrE

quincenal *adj* fortnightly BrE, bimonthly AmE

quincenalmente *adv* fortnightly BrE, bimonthly AmE

quinielas *f pl* Esp ≈ (football) pools BrE, ≈ sports lottery AmE

quinquenio *m* five-year period

quiosco *m* kiosk

quita *f* deduction; **de** ~ **y pon** detachable; **etiqueta de** ~ **y pon** Post-it®

quórum *m* quorum; **no se pudo votar en la reunión por falta de** ~ we could not vote at the meeting because we did not have a quorum *o* because the meeting was inquorate BrE

Rr

RACE *abr* (▸**Real Automóvil Club de España**) *Spanish motorists' organization*, ≈ AA BrE, ≈ RAC BrE, ≈ AAA AmE

racha *f* run, patch; **buena/mala ∼** good/bad patch; **∼ de suerte** run of good luck; **∼ de triunfos** winning streak

ración *f* share

racional *adj* rational

racionalización *f* rationalization, streamlining; **∼ de la marca** brand rationalization

racionalizar *vt* rationalize, streamline

racionamiento *m* rationing; **∼ del capital** capital rationing; **∼ del crédito** credit rationing

radiación *f* (nuclear) fallout, radiation

radicación *f* location

radicado *adj*: **∼ en** based in; **∼ en Madrid** based in Madrid

radical *adj* radical; (cambio) sweeping

radicar *vi*: **∼ en** (estar localizado en) be in; (venir de) lie in, stem from; **el éxito de la compañía radica en su originalidad** the company's success lies in its originality

radio¹ *f* radio; **∼ comercial** commercial radio; **∼ pirata** pirate radio; **R∼ Televisión Española** *Spanish national broadcasting company*

radio² *m* (área) sphere; **∼ de acción** sphere of action

radiodifusión *f* broadcasting

radiotelefonía *f* radiotelephony

radioteléfono *m* radiotelephone; **∼ portátil** walkie-talkie

radiotelegrafía *f* radiotelegraphy

radioyente *mf* listener

raíz *f* root; **a ∼ de algo** as a result of sth; **echar raíces** take root, catch on; **ir a la ∼ de algo** get to the bottom of sth; **la ∼ del problema**

RAL *abr* (▸**red de área local**) LAN (local area network)

ralentizar *vt* slow down

ralentizarse *v pron* decelerate, slow down

RAM *abr* (*memoria de acceso aleatorio*) RAM (random access memory); **∼ dinámica** DRAM (dynamic random access memory)

rama *f* branch; **irse por las ∼s** go off at a tangent; **∼ principal** main branch

ramo *m* sector; **el ∼ de las finanzas** the finance sector

rampa *f* ramp; **∼ de acceso** access ramp; **∼ de lanzamiento** launch pad

rango *m* rank; (nivel) level; **de alto ∼** of high standing; **∼ percentil** percentile ranking

ranura *f* slot; **∼ de expansión** expansion slot

rápido¹ *adj* fast; **∼ aumento** (Bolsa) sharp rise

rápido² *adv* quickly; **tan ∼ como pueda** as fast as you can

rasgo *m* feature, characteristic; **a grandes ∼s** broadly speaking; **∼ clave** key feature; **∼ saliente** highlight

rastreador *m* (Info) crawler

rastrear *vt* trawl, search

rastreo *m* (de la Red) trawl, search; (de satélite) tracking; **∼ de auditoría** audit trail

ratificación *f* ratification

ratificar *vt* (tratado) ratify; (puesto, noticia) confirm

ratio *m* ratio; **∼ de cobertura** coverage ratio; **∼ de cuentas a cobrar** collection ratio; **∼ precio-beneficio** price-earnings ratio; **∼ de ventas a crédito** accounts receivable turnover

ratón *m* (Info) mouse

rayo *m* ray; **∼ láser** laser beam

razón *f* reason; **a ∼ de** at a rate of; **con ∼** with good reason; **dar la ∼ a alguien** agree that sb is right; **dar ∼ de algo/alguien** give information about sth/sb; **en ∼ de la conveniencia** on grounds of expediency; **la ∼ por la que** the reason why; **la ∼ de su dimisión** the reason for her resignation; **por ninguna ∼** for no reason; **quitar la ∼ a alguien** say that sb is wrong; **∼: recepción** inquire at reception; **∼ de más para hacer algo** all the more reason to do sth; **sin ∼** wrongly; **tener ∼** be right, be in the right; **tener toda la** ∼ **del mundo** be absolutely right; ∼ **de estado** national interest; **razones médicas** medical grounds; ∼ **social** business name, registered name

razonable *adj* reasonable

razonablemente *adv* reasonably

razonamiento *m* reasoning, thinking; ∼ **deductivo** deductive reasoning; ∼ **horizontal** lateral thinking; ∼ **lúcido** clear thinking

RD *abr* (*dirigirse al librador*) RD (refer to drawer)

reabrir *vt* reopen; (Cont) bring down

reacción *f* reaction; (respuesta) response; ∼ **en cadena** chain reaction; ∼ **del consumidor** consumer reaction; ∼ **negativa/positiva** negative/positive feedback

reaccionar *vi* (ante noticia, situación) react; (responder) respond; ∼ **bien/mal frente a algo** react well/badly to sth

reaccionario[1] *adj* reactionary

reaccionario[2], **-a** *m,f* reactionary

reacio *adj* reluctant; **ser** *or* **mostrarse** ∼ **a hacer algo** be reluctant to do sth

reacondicionado *adj* (renovado) reconditioned, refurbished; (adaptado) adpated, converted

reacondicionar *vt* (renovar) recondition, refurbish; (adaptar) adapt, convert

reactivación *f* (recuperación) recovery; (de economía, mercado) growth, revival; (de programas) reactivation

reactivar *vt* (economía) revive, reflate; (programas) reactivate

reactivarse *v pron* (Bolsa) rally

reactor *m* reactor; ∼ **nuclear** nuclear reactor

readmitir *vt* (empleado) reinstate; (en club, grupo) readmit

reafirmar *vt* reaffirm, reassert; **esto reafirma su autoridad** this reasserts his authority

reagrupar *vt* regroup

reagruparse *v pron* regroup

reajustar *vt* (precios) adjust; (cambiar de nuevo) readjust

reajuste *m* adjustment; (cambio nuevo) readjustment; (de organización, personal) reorganization; ∼ **de financiación** financing adjustment; ∼ **impositivo** tax adjustment; ∼ **ministerial** cabinet reshuffle; ∼ **salarial** wage settlement

real *adj* (coste) actual; (salario) real; (de la realeza) royal; **R**∼ **Automóvil Club de**

España *Spanish motorists' organization*, ≈ Automobile Association BrE, ≈ Royal Automobile Club BrE, ≈ American Automobile Association AmE

realista[1] *adj* realistic

realista[2] *mf* realist

realizable *adj* feasible, practicable; (Fin) realizable; (activo) liquid; **activo no** ∼ illiquid assets

realización *f* (de propósito, bienes) realization; (de objetivos) achievement; (de empresa) performance; (de película) production; (liquidación) sale, clearance; ∼ **de activos** realization of assets; ∼ **de beneficios** profit-taking; ∼ **personal** fulfilment BrE *o* fulfillment AmE of professional ambitions

realizar *vt* (bienes) realize; (beneficios) take; (compromiso, obligación) fulfil BrE, fulfill AmE; (objetivo) achieve; (plan, encuesta) carry out; (película) produce; (deuda) clear, pay; (pago) make; ∼ **una conferencia** hold a conference; ∼ **indagaciones** make enquiries; ∼ **órdenes** execute orders; ∼ **pruebas en el mercado** market-test, test-market; ∼ **una transacción** make a transaction

realzar *vt* (hacer notar) emphasize, enhance, make stand out; (Info) highlight

reanudación *f* (de conversaciones, negociaciones) resumption

reanudar *vt* (conversaciones, negociaciones) resume; (Info) restart

reapertura *f* reopening

reaprovisionar *vt* (tienda) restock

rearrancar *vt* restart

rearranque *m* restart

rearriendo *m* (al vendedor) leaseback

reasegurar *vt* reinsure; (póliza) underwrite

reaseguro *m* reinsurance; (de póliza) underwriting

reasentamiento *m* resettlement

reasignación *f* reallocation; (Info) reassignment

reasignar *vt* reallocate; (Info) reassign

rebaja *f* reduction; (descuento) discount; ∼**s** sale, sales; **estar de** ∼ be reduced; **estar de** ∼**s** have a sale on; **hacer una** ∼ **(del 10%)** give a (10%) discount; **una** ∼ **de los tipos de interés** a reduction in interest rates; ∼ **de precios** price cut

rebajar *vt* (impuestos, precios) reduce, cut; (límite) lower; **me rebajó 100 euros** he took off 100 euros, he reduced the price by 100 euros; ∼ **un cargo** charge off; ∼ ⋯⇝

de categoría relegate to a lower category, downgrade

rebasamiento *m* (de presupuesto) overspend

rebasar *vt* (sobrepasar) exceed; (presupuesto) overspend; (plazo) overrun; (tomar la delantera) overtake; **los resultados ∼on todas las expectativas** the results exceeded all expectations

rebeldía *f* defiance; (Der) default; **estar en ∼** be in default; **fue juzgado en ∼** he was tried in his absence

rebobinar *vt* (cinta) rewind

recadero, -a *m,f* messenger; (en oficina (m) office boy; (f) office girl

recado *m* message; (encargo) errand; **coger** *or* **tomar un ∼** take a message; **dejar un ∼ (a alguien)** leave a message for sb; **¿quiere dejarle algún ∼?** would you like to leave a message for her?; **hacer un ∼** run an errand

recaer *vi* (situación, delincuente) relapse; **∼ en** *or* **sobre alguien** fall on sb; **toda la responsabilidad del negocio recae en él** he shoulders all the responsibility for the business

recalcular *vt* recalculate

recapitalización *f* recapitalization

recapitalizar *vt* recapitalize

recargar *vt* (programa) reload; (precio) mark up; (aparato) recharge; **le ∼on un 10%** they charged him an extra 10% *o* a 10% surcharge; **∼ a alguien de algo** overload sb with sth

recargo *m* extra charge, surcharge; (por mora) penalty; **sin ∼** at no extra cost *o* charge

recaudación *f* collection; **∼ de fondos** fundraising; **∼ tributaria** *or* **de impuestos** tax collection

recaudador, a *m,f* receiver; (Fisc) tax collector

recaudar *vt* (fondos, dinero) raise; (deuda) collect, recover; **∼ un impuesto** levy a tax; **∼ pagos** collect payments

recepción *f* (de pedido) receipt; (de empresa, hotel) reception (desk); **a la ∼ de** on receipt of

recepcionista *mf* receptionist

receptividad *f* receptiveness; **∼ del mercado** market receptiveness

receptivo *adj* receptive

receptor¹, -a *m,f* (persona) recipient

receptor² *m* (aparato) receiver

recesión *f* recession; **estar/entrar en ∼** be in/go into a recession; **∼ económica** economic recession

recesionario *adj* recessionary

receso *m* recess; **∼ estival** (del Parlamento) summer recess

rechazado *adj* (idea, propuesta) rejected; (cheque) dishonoured BrE, dishonored AmE

rechazar *vt* (idea, propuesta) reject; (cheque) dishonour BrE, dishonor AmE, bounce (infrml); (pasajero) refuse

rechazo *m* rejection; (de letra o pagaré) nonacceptance

recibí *m* receipt

recibido *adj* received

recibimiento *m* reception; **un caluroso ∼** a warm reception *o* welcome

recibir *vt* receive, get; (visita) see; (acoger) welcome; (dar hospitalidad) entertain; **¿recibiste el recado?** did you get the message; **salió a ∼ a los clientes** she came out to greet *o* welcome the clients; **recibieron los clientes en la sala de juntas** the clients were entertained in the conference room; **el director la ∼á enseguida** the manager will be with you right away; **reciba un atento saludo de** yours sincerely BrE, sincerely yours AmE

recibo *m* receipt; (de teléfono) bill; **acusar ∼ de algo** acknowledge receipt of sth; **al ∼ de esta carta** on receipt of this letter; **∼ bancario** banker's ticket; **∼ en blanco** blank receipt; **∼ de caja** (till) receipt; **∼ de cajero automático** automated teller machine statement AmE, cashpoint receipt *o* slip BrE; **∼ de reintegro** refund slip; **∼ de ventas** sales receipt

reciclable *adj* recyclable; **no ∼** nonrecyclable

reciclado¹ *adj* recycled

reciclado² *m* recycling; **∼ de residuos** waste recycling

reciclaje *m* recycling; **∼ profesional** retraining, reskilling

reciclar *vt* recycle; (RRHH) retrain, reskill

recién llegado, -a *m,f* newcomer

reciprocidad *f* reciprocity; **∼ del contrato** mutuality of contract

recíproco *adj* (acuerdo, ventajas) reciprocal, mutual

reclamación *f* (petición, demanda) claim; (queja) complaint; **desistir de una ∼** abandon a claim; **formular** *or* **presentar una ∼** make *o* lodge a complaint; **liquidar una ∼** settle a claim; **∼ de compensación** compensation claim; **∼ contingente** contingent claim; **∼ de devolución** repayment claim; **∼**

financiera financial claim; ~ **fiscal** tax claim; ~ **legal** legal claim; ~ **máxima** maximum claim; ~ **retrospectiva** retrospective claim; ~ **salarial** wage claim; ~ **solventada** adjusted claim; ~ **a terceros** third-party claim

reclamante *mf* claimant

reclamar [1] *vt* (derecho, indemnización) claim; (tierras) reclaim; (requerir) require; (exigir) demand; ~ **a alguien como carga familiar** claim sb as a dependant; ~ **daños y perjuicios** claim damages; ~ **una exención personal** claim personal exemption; **la situación reclama una solución inmediata** the situation requires *o* demands an immediate solution; ~ **justicia** demand justice [2] *vi* complain; **tiene derecho a** ~ **si no está satisfecho** you have the right to make a complaint if you are not satisfied; ~ **ante los tribunales** take a matter to court; ~ **contra algo** complain about sth; (Der) appeal against sth

reclame *m* AmL (publicidad) advertisement, advert, commercial; (aviso) announcement

reclamo *m* (Der) claim; (atractivo) lure; **artículo de** ~ loss-leader; (publicidad) advertisement, advert; ~ **publicitario** advertising appeal

reclasificación *f* reclassification

reclasificar *vt* reclassify

reclutamiento *m* (de personal) recruitment; ~ **en línea** online recruitment, e-cruitment

reclutar *vt* (personal) recruit; (obreros) contract, take on; ~ **en línea** recruit online

recobrar *vt* (dinero, posición) recover; (control, confianza) regain; ~ **la normalidad** return to normal

recobro *m* (de deuda) recovery; (de propiedad) repossession

recoger *vt* (recolectar) collect; (datos) gather; (incluir) include; (retirar) withdraw; (periódico) seize; (moneda vieja) call in; **el informe recoge las últimas estadísticas** the report includes the latest statistics

recogida *f* collection; ~ **de basuras** refuse collection; ~ **de datos** data collection, data gathering

recolección *f* (de dinero, datos) collection

recolocación *f* relocation

recolocar *vt* relocate

recomendación *f* recommendation; (para empleo) reference; **carta de** ~ letter

of introduction *o* recommendation; **por la** ~ **de alguien** on sb's recommendation; **consiguió el puesto por** ~ **de su antiguo jefe** she was recommended for the job by her former boss; **tener excelentes recomendaciones** have excellent references

recomendar *vt* recommend; ~ **a alguien para un puesto** recommend sb for a job; ~**le a alguien que haga algo** recommend that sb should do sth; **no te lo** ~**ía** I wouldn't recommend it

recomercializar *vt* remarket

recompensa *f* reward; **dar algo como** *or* **de** *or* **en** ~ **por algo** give sth as a reward for sth; **ofrecer una** ~ offer a reward

recompra *f* (de opción) recall; ~ **inversa** reverse repurchase

recomprar *vt* buy back; (opción) recall

reconciliación *f* reconciliation; ~ **de cuentas** reconciliation of accounts

reconciliar *vt* reconcile

reconfiguración *f* reconfiguration

reconfigurar *vt* (sistema) reconfigure; (estructura empresarial) re-engineer

reconocer *vt* (conocer) recognize; (error, culpa) admit, acknowledge; **hay que** ~ **que está bien redactado** you can't deny that it is well written; **reconozco que va a ser difícil** I admit that it won't be easy

reconocido *adj* recognized, acknowledged; **no** ~ unrecognized, unacknowledged; **estar** *or* **quedar muy** ~ be very much obliged

reconocimiento *m* recognition, acknowledgement; (inspección) examination; ~ **de deuda** acknowledgement of debt; ~ **legal** legal recognition; ~ **de marca** brand recognition; ~ **de mercado** market recognition; ~ **mutuo** (de leyes nacionales dentro de la UE) mutual recognition; ~ **óptico de caracteres** optical character recognition, OCR; ~ **de pérdidas** recognition of loss; ~ **de la voz** voice recognition, speech recognition

reconsiderar *vt* reconsider

reconstrucción *f* reconstruction

reconstruido *adj* rebuilt

reconstruir *vt* rebuild; (suceso, hechos) reconstruct

reconversión *f* (reestructuración) restructuring; (de divisas) retranslation; (Info) reconversion; ~ **profesional** retraining; ~ **urbana** urban renewal

r

reconvertir *vt* restructure; (Info) reconvert; (personal) retrain

recopilación *f* compilation, collection; ∼ **de datos** data collection *o* gathering

recopilar *vt* (datos) compile, collect

récord[1] *adj* record, record-breaking; **se completó el proyecto en un tiempo** ∼ the project was completed in record time

récord[2] *m* record; **batir un** ∼ beat a record

recordatorio *m* reminder, aide-mémoire

récordman *m* record holder

recorrido *m* (viaje) journey; (distancia) distance; **de corto** ∼ short-haul; **de largo** ∼ long-haul; **hacer un** ∼ **por Europa** travel around Europe; ∼ **electoral** campaign trail

recortar *vt* (presupuesto, gastos) cut; (personal) reduce; ∼ **el programa de inversión** trim the investment programme BrE *o* program AmE

recorte *m* cut; (Bolsa) killing (infrml); (de periódico) cutting BrE, clipping AmE; ∼ **de gastos** cut in spending; ∼ **de precios** price cut; ∼ **de prensa** press cutting BrE, press clipping AmE; ∼ **presupuestario** budget cut; ∼ **en tipos de interés** reduction in interest rates

rectificación *f* (de información, error) correction, rectification

rectificar *vt* (información, error) correct, rectify; ∼ **un asiento** rectify an entry

recto *m* recto

rector, a *m,f* vice-chancellor BrE, rector AmE

recuadro *m* box BrE, check box AmE

recuento *m* count; ∼ **de existencias** stocktaking; ∼ **de palabras** word count

recuerdo asistido *m* (V&M) aided recall

recuperable *adj* (pérdidas) recoverable; (datos, fichero) retrievable; **no** ∼ non-recoverable

recuperación *f* (de economía) recovery; (de fichero) retrieval; ∼ **de la base** base recovery; ∼ **de datos** data retrieval; ∼ **de desastre** disaster recovery; ∼ **de deudas incobrables** bad-debt recovery; ∼ **de energía** energy recovery; ∼ **de errores** error recovery; ∼ **de gastos** recovery of expenses; ∼ **de la información** information retrieval; ∼ **de mensajes** message retrieval; ∼ **del mercado** rally, market recovery

recuperar *vt* (dinero, inversión) recover, recoup; (datos, archivos) retrieve; (cuota de mercado) regain; ∼ **el tiempo perdido** make up for lost time

recuperarse *v pron* (de una enfermedad) recover; (mercado) rally, pick up

recurrir [1] *vi*: ∼ **a** resort to, fall back on; ∼ **a fuentes internas/externas** insource/outsource

[2] *vt* appeal against; ∼ **una sentencia** appeal against a judgment

recurso *m* (medio) resort; (Der) appeal; **agotar todos los** ∼**s** exhaust all the options; **como último** ∼ as a last resort; ∼**s** resources; (Fin) capital, means; ∼**s agotables** depletable resources; ∼**s disponibles** available funds; ∼**s económicos** economic resources, financial resources; ∼ **explotado** exploited resource; ∼ **fiscal** tax appeal; ∼ **a fuentes externas** outsourcing; ∼**s humanos** human resources; ∼ **a fuentes internas** insourcing; ∼**s naturales** natural resources; ∼ **primario** primary resource; ∼ **renovable** renewable resource; ∼ **no renovable** nonrenewable resource

recusación *f* challenge

recusar *vt* (juez, juzgado) challenge; (rechazar) reject

red *f* network; **la R**∼ *f* the Net, the Internet, the Web; **navegar por la R**∼ surf the net; ∼ **de alimentación** mains BrE, supply network AmE; ∼ **de área extendida** wide area network, WAN; ∼ **de área local** local area network, LAN; ∼ **bancaria** banking network; ∼ **de carreteras** road network; ∼ **de computadoras** AmL (*cf* ▸**red de ordenadores** Esp) computer network; ∼ **de comunicaciones** communications network; ∼ **comunitaria** community network; ∼ **corporativa** corporate network; ∼ **de corredores de bolsa** dealer network; ∼ **de créditos recíprocos** swap network; ∼ **de datos** data network; ∼ **digital de servicios integrados** integrated services digital network, ISDN; ∼ **de distribución** distribution network; ∼ **en estrella** star network; ∼ **de expertos** expert network; ∼ **de ferrocarriles** railway network BrE, railroad network AmE; ∼ **de gran amplitud** wide area network, WAN; ∼ **de información** information network; ∼ **informática** computer network; ∼ **de minoristas** retail network; **R**∼ **Nacional de Ferrocarriles Españoles** *Spanish national rail network*; ∼ **neural** *or* **neurológica** neural network; ∼ **de**

ordenadores Esp (*cf* ▸**red de computadoras** AmL) computer network; ~ **privada virtual** virtual private network, VPN; ~ **de sucursales** branch network; ~ **de swops** swap network; ~ **de telecomunicaciones** telecommunications network; ~ **de ventas** sales network

redacción *f* editorial staff; (de un contrato) wording; (Medios) newsroom

redactado *adj* drafted; (corregido) edited

redactar *vt* (escribir) write, draft; (periódico) edit; (contrato, testamento) draw up

redactor, a *m,f* (escritor) writer; (de textos, periódico) editor; ~ **jefe(-a)** *m,f* (en imprenta) editor-in-chief; ~ **de textos publicitarios** copywriter

redención *f* redemption; (de deuda, hipoteca) repayment

redepositar *vt* redeposit

redescontable *adj* rediscountable

redescontador *m* rediscounter

redescuento *m* discount rate BrE, discount window AmE, rediscounting

redimensionamiento *m* resizing

redimensionar *vt* resize

redimible *adj* redeemable; (bono) amortizable; **no** ~ non amortizable

rediseñar *vt* redesign

redistribución *f* redistribution; (de personal) redeployment

redistribuir *vt* redistribute; (personal) redeploy; (fondos) reallocate

rédito *m* interest, return; ~ **anual** (de acciones) annual return; ~ **corriente** current yield

redondear *vt* (números) round off; (por lo alto) round up; (por lo bajo) round down; ~ **por exceso/defecto** round up/down

reducción *f* (de precios, cantidad) reduction; (de pago al contado) rebate; (Fisc) abatement; (RRHH) downsizing; ~ **de capital** reduction of capital; ~ **de categoría laboral** downgrading; ~ **de costes** Esp *or* **costos** AmL cost reduction, reduction in costs; ~ **impositiva** tax reduction; ~ **de impuestos** tax cut; ~ **de ingresos** revenue dilution; ~ **de intereses** interest cut; ~ **del margen** margin shrinkage; ~ **de personal** downsizing, staff cutback; ~ **de precios** price cut; ~ **presupuestaria** budget cut; ~ **del riesgo** decrease of risk; ~ **de los tipos de interés** reduction in interest rates

reducido *adj* (precio, cantidad) reduced; (grupo, número) small; **a precios** ~**s** at reduced prices; **un grupo** ~ **de personas** a small group of people

reducir *vt* (gastos, personal) reduce, cut; (Bolsa) scale down; (pena) commute, shorten; ~ **ligeramente** (tasa, precio) shade; ~ **el valor contable de** write down; ~ **algo a algo** reduce sth to sth; **todas sus ideas quedaron reducidas a nada** nothing came of any of his ideas; ~ **algo en algo** reduce sth by sth; **pretenden** ~ **el gasto en cinco millones** they are aiming to reduce costs by five million

reducirse *v pron* (inflación) fall; ~ **a algo** amount to sth; **todo se reduce a saber interpretar las cifras** it all comes down to knowing how to interpret the figures

redundancia *f* (superfluidad) redundancy

redundante *adj* (superfluo) redundant, superfluous

reeditar *vt* republish; (reimprimir) reprint

reeducar *vt* re-educate, retrain

reejecución *f* rerun

reejecutar *vt* rerun

reelección *f* re-election

reembarcarse *v pron* re-embark

reembolsable *adj* redeemable, refundable, repayable; **no** ~ nonrefundable

reembolsar *vt* (gastos) reimburse; (depósito) refund, return; (préstamo) repay

reembolso *m* (de gastos) reimbursement; (de depósito) refund, return; (de préstamo) repayment

reempaquetar *vt* repack

reemplazar *vt* replace; (durante un periodo limitado) stand in for; **el e-mail está reemplazando otros medios de comunicación** e-mail is taking over other methods of communication; ~ **algo/a alguien** replace sb/sth; **nadie lo podrá reemplazar** nobody will be able to replace him *o* take his place; **¿quién te reemplazará en la reunión?** who will be standing in for you at the meeting?; ~ **algo con** *or* **por algo** replace sth with sth; ~ **a alguien con** *or* **por alguien** replace sb by sb

reemplazo *m* replacement; **mandar a alguien en su** ~ send someone in one's place

reempleo *m* re-employment

reenvío *m* cross-reference; ~ **automático** automatic call forwarding

reescribir *vt* rewrite

reestructuración *f* (de empresa, deuda) restructuring; (de préstamo) rescheduling

reestructurado *adj* (empresa, deuda) restructured; (préstamo) rescheduled

reestructurar *vt* (empresa, deuda) restructure; (préstamo) reschedule

reevaluación *m* revaluation, reassessment; ~ **de impuestos** reassessment of tax

reevaluar *vt* reassess

reexamen *m* re-examination; (de directrices) revision

reexaminar *vt* re-examine; (directrices) revise

referencia *f* reference; **con** ~ **a** with reference to, regarding; **de** ~ baseline; **publicidad de** ~ baseline advertising; **su** ~ your reference; ~ **del banco** banker's reference

referéndum *m* referendum

referir *vt* relate; ~ **a alguien a algo** refer sb to sth; **referido a** referring to; ~ **al aceptante** refer to acceptor

referirse: ~ **a** *v pron* refer to; **en** *or* **por lo que se refiere a su pregunta** with regard to your question, as far as your question is concerned

refinación *f* refining

refinado *adj* refined

refinanciación *f* refinancing

refinanciar *vt* refinance

refinar *vt* (búsqueda en la Red) refine

reflejar *vt* reflect

reflejarse: ~ **en** *v pron* be reflected in

reflexión *f* reflection; **periodo de** ~ cooling-off period; **sin** ~ without thinking

reflexionar *vi* reflect; ~ **sobre algo** reflect on sth, think about sth, give some thought to sth; **sin** ~ without thinking

reflotamiento *m* refloating

reforestación *f* reforestation, reafforestation BrE

reforma *f* reform; **cerrado por** ~**s** closed for refurbishment; ~ **agraria** land reform; ~ **económica** economic reform; ~ **fiscal** tax reform; ~ **monetaria** currency reform

reformado *adj* reformed; (Der) amended

reformar *vt* reform; (Der) amend

reformatear *vt* reformat

reformismo *m* reformism

reforzado *adj* reinforced, strengthened

reforzamiento *m* reinforcement; (de moneda) strengthening; ~ **de marca** brand reinforcement

reforzar *vt* (relaciones) boost, strengthen; (efecto, impacto) reinforce; (control, medidas de seguridad) tighten; ~ **la confianza de alguien** boost *o* bolster sb's confidence

refrescar *vt* (conocimientos) brush up on; (memoria) refresh

refrigeración *f* (de alimentos) refrigeration

refrigerar *vt* (alimentos) refrigerate

refuerzo *m* reinforcement; ~ **continuo** continuous reinforcement

refugiado, -a *m,f* refugee

refugio *m* shelter; ~ **fiscal** tax shelter

regalar *vt* give away; (vender barato) sell very cheaply; **regalamos un perfume con cada compra** we're giving away a bottle of perfume with every purchase, a free bottle of perfume with every purchase; **compre dos y le regalamos otra** buy two and get one free

regalías *f pl* royalties

regalo *m* free gift, giveaway; **compre dos y llévese otro de** ~ buy two and get one free

regatear ① *vi* haggle; ~ **sobre algo** haggle over sth
② *vt* (precio) haggle over; **no** ~**on esfuerzos** no effort was spared; **no se puede** ~ **horas en este tipo de trabajo** you can't rush this type of work

regenerar *vi* (Info) refresh

régimen *m* regime; (sistema) system; **en** ~ **de descuento** on a discount basis; ~ **comercial** trade regime; ~ **político** political system; ~ **temporal** temporary status; ~ **de vida** lifestyle

región *f* (área) region, area; (Pol) county; ~ **deprimida** depressed region; ~ **desarrollada** developed region; ~ **designada** designated region

regional *adj* regional

regir ① *vt* govern, rule; (negocio) manage, run
② *vi* (ley) be in force, be valid; **ese horario ya no rige** that timetable is no longer valid *o* no longer applies; **el mes/año que rige** the current month/year

registrado *adj* registered; **no** ~ unregistered

registrador[1] *m* (aparato) recording instrument; ~ **ambiental** environment scan; ~ **de video** AmL *or* **vídeo** Esp videotape recorder

registrador[2]**, a** *m,f* registrant

registrar *vt* register, record; (equipaje, persona) search; **el mercado apenas ha registrado variación** there has been hardly any change in the market; ~ **un alza** register a rise; ~ **una escritura** start an entry

registrarse *v pron* (apuntarse) register; (en asistencia social) sign on BrE; (en un hotel) check in; (incidente) be recorded; **no se registraron víctimas mortales** there were no fatalities

registro *m* (libro) register; (acción) registration; (lista) record; (Inmob) valuation; (examinación) search; **~s** records; **firmar el** ~ sign the register; ~ **de acciones** share register, stock register; ~ **de automóviles** car registration; ~ **catastral** land registry; ~ **de cheques** cheque register BrE, check register AmE; ~ **civil** (libro) register of births, marriages and deaths; (oficina) registry *or* register office BrE; ~ **de clientes** customer records; ~ **de comercio** trade register; ~ **de contabilidad** accounting records; ~ **contable** book entry; ~ **domiciliario** house search; ~ **duplicado** duplicated record; ~ **electoral** electoral register *o* roll; ~ **de empleo** employment record; ~ **de escrituras** registry of deeds; **R~ Europeo de Comercio** European Registry of Commerce; ~ **fiscal** tax record; ~ **de Información Fiscal** Tax Information Registry; ~ **internacional** international registration; ~ **de letras** bill diary; ~ **mercantil** register of companies; ~ **de la propiedad** land registry BrE, land office AmE; ~ **de la propiedad industrial** patent office; ~ **de socios** register of members; ~ **telefónico** phone-in poll; ~ **de ventas** sales record

regla *f* rule; **en** ~ in order; **por** ~ **general** as a general rule; ~ **del cinco por ciento** five percent rule; ~ **cuantitativa** quantitative rule; ~ **de la mayoría** majority rule; ~ **de oro** golden rule

reglamentación *f* regulation; (conjunto de reglas) regulations; ~ **de exportación** export regulations; ~ **de precios** price fixing

reglamentar *vt* regulate

reglamentario *adj* (que reglamenta) regulatory; (vacaciones, periodo) statutory; (preceptivo) regulation; **uniforme** ~ regulation uniform; **trabajar más de las horas reglamentarias** work more than the set *o* stipulated number of hours

reglamento *m* regulations, rules; (municipal) by-law; **R~ del Impuesto sobre la Renta** Income Tax regulations

regulable *adj* adjustable

regulación *f* regulation; (control) control; (ajuste) adjustment; ~ **bancaria** banking regulation; ~ **de plantilla** Esp downsizing; ~ **de precios** price regulation; ~ **salarial** wage control

regulador *m* regulator; (de aparato, volumen) control

regular¹ *adj* (uniforme) regular; (mediano) medium, average; **el rendimiento de la compañía ha sido** ~ the company's performance has been average; **a intervalos** ~**es** at regular intervals; **por lo** ~ as a general rule

regular² *vt* adjust, regulate; **las leyes que regulan la industria** the laws governing the industry; **regulado por el Estado** government-regulated

regularización *f* year-end adjustment

rehabilitación *f* (de empresa, reputación, delincuente) rehabilitation; (en un cargo) reinstatement; (de local) renovation; ~ **del quebrado** discharge of bankruptcy

rehabilitar *vt* (reputación, empresa, delincuente) rehabilitate; (en un cargo) reinstate; (local) renovate; ~ **a alguien en un cargo** reinstate sb in a post

rehusar *vt* refuse; ~ **hacer algo** refuse to do sth; ~ **la aceptación de una letra** refuse acceptance of a draft

reimportación *f* reimportation

reimportar *vt* reimport

reinado *m* reign

reincidencia *f* recidivism; **hay un alto nivel de** ~ **entre estos delincuentes** a high rate of these criminals reoffend *o* are reoffenders

reincorporación *f* (depués de ausencia) return; (a un cargo) reinstatement

reincorporar *vt* (a un cargo) reinstate

reincorporarse *v pron* return; ~ **al trabajo** return to work

reingeniería *f* (de sistema) reconfiguration; (de estructura empresarial) re-engineering

reingresar *vi*: ~ **en** rejoin, return to; **reingresó en el departamento** she returned to *o* rejoined the department

reiniciación *f* reinitiation; (Info) rebooting

reinicialización *f* rebooting

reinicializar *vt* reboot

reiniciar *vt* reinitiate; (Info) reboot

r

reintegrable *adj* (bono) refundable; **no** ~ nonrefundable

reintegrar *vt* (deuda, préstamo) pay back, repay; (depósito) refund; (gastos) reimburse; (persona a un cargo) reinstate; ~ **a alguien en un puesto** reinstate sb in a post

reintegrarse *v pron* return; ~ **a algo** return to sth; ~ **al trabajo** return to work

reintegro *m* refund; (de préstamo) repayment; (de lotería) return of stake; ~ **de bonos** bond refunding

reintroducción *f* reintroduction

reinversión *f* reinvestment; ~ **automática** automatic reinvestment; ~ **de dividendos** dividend reinvestment

reinvertir *vt* reinvest

reiterar *vt* reiterate, repeat

reivindicación *f* claim, demand; (Der) replevin; ~ **independiente** independent claim

relación *f* (trato) relationship; (conexión) connection, relation; (proporción) ratio; **relaciones** relations; **en ~ con** in relation to, with regard to; **romper las relaciones con alguien** break off relations with sb; **tener una buena ~ con alguien** have a good relationship with sb; ~ **de apalancamiento** gearing ratio BrE, leverage ratio; ~ **calidad-precio** value for money; **tener buena ~ calidad-precio** be good value for money; ~ **capital-producto** capital-output ratio; **relaciones con los clientes** customer relations; **relaciones comerciales** trade relations; ~ **coste-eficacia** Esp, **relación costo-eficacia** AmL cost effectiveness; ~ **de débito** debit ratio; **relaciones diplomáticas** diplomatic relations; ~ **dividendo-precio** dividend-price ratio; **relaciones humanas** human relations; **relaciones laborales** labour relations BrE, labor relations AmE; ~ **de paridad** parity ratio; ~ **precio-beneficio** price-earnings ratio; **relaciones públicas** public relations; ~ **de rentabilidad** profitability ratio

relacionado *adj* related; ~ **con** related to, connected with; ~ **con el comercio** trade-related

relacionar *vt* (asociar) connect; (tipos de cambio) link

relajación *f* relaxation; **una ~ de la tensión entre los dos países** an easing of tension between the two countries

relajar *vt* relax; (tensión) relieve, ease

relanzamiento *m* relaunch

relanzar *vt* relaunch

relativamente *adv* relatively

relativo *adj* relative; ~ **a** relating to; **en lo ~ a** with regard to

rellenar *vt* (formulario) fill in *o* out; ~ **un cheque** make out a cheque BrE *o* check AmE

relleno *m* padding; (prensa) filler; ~ **de formularios** form-filling

relocalizable *adj* (área de memoria) relocatable

relocalización *f* relocation

remanente *m* surplus; (Fisc) carry-over; ~**s** remnants; ~ **de impuestos mínimo** minimum tax carry-over

remapeo *m* remapping

rematar *vt* round off; (negocio) conclude; (en subasta) AmL auction

remesa *f* (de dinero) remittance; (de facturas) batch; ~ **bancaria** bank remittance

remisión *f* remission; (referencia) cross-reference; ~ **de un impuesto** remission of tax

remite *m* return *o* sender's address

remitente *mf* (en correspondencia) sender; **devuélvase al ~** return to sender

remitir *vt* (enviar) send; (paquete, sobre) address; (condena) remit; (referir) refer; ~ **a alguien a algo** refer sb to sth; ~ **al aceptante** refer to acceptor

remoción *f* removal; ~ **de escombro** debris removal

remodelación *f* (de organización) reorganization, restructuring; ~ **urbana** urban renewal

remodelar *vt* (organización) reorganize, restructure

rémora hindrance *f*; ~ **fiscal** taxflation

remoto *adj* remote

remuneración *f* remuneration; (Bolsa) consideration; ~ **a convenir** salary to be agreed; ~ **por acción** return on equity; ~ **bruta** gross pay; ~ **por despido** severance pay, redundancy pay BrE; ~ **igual** equal pay; ~ **media** average pay; ~ **mensual** monthly salary; ~ **según rendimiento** performance-related pay; ~ **igual** equal pay

remunerado *adj* paid; **bien ~** well-paid; **mal ~** badly-paid

remunerador *adj* remunerative; **poco ~** unremunerative

rendimiento *m* (de persona, empresa) performance; (producción) output; (Fin) yield, return; **con ∼ de intereses** interest-bearing; **sin ∼ de intereses** noninterest-bearing; **tener bajo ∼** underperform; **∼ de los activos** return on assets; **∼ actual** current yield; **∼ alto/bajo** high/low return; **∼ anual** annual return; **∼ del bono** bond yield; **∼ del capital** return on capital; **∼ decreciente** diminishing returns; **∼ en dividendos** dividend yield; **∼ de explotación** operating income; **∼ fiscal** tax yield; **∼ de la inversión** return on investment, ROI; **∼ mixto** composite yield; **∼ neto del capital** net capital gain; **∼ del precio de una acción** share price performance; **∼ del producto** product performance; **∼ sobre acción** return on equity; **∼ sobre el capital** return on capital; **∼ de ventas** return on sales

rendir ☐1 *vt* (producir) produce; (beneficios) yield; **∼ cuentas de** account for ☐2 *vi* perform well; **la empresa no rinde** the company isn't performing well; **me rindió mucho la mañana** I had a very productive morning; **trabaja mucho pero no le rinde** she works very hard but doesn't have much to show for it

rendirse *v pron* give up

renegociación *f* renegotiation

renegociar *vt* renegotiate

RENFE *abr* (▸**Red Nacional de Ferrocarriles Españoles**) *Spanish national rail network*

renombrado *adj* renowned, well-known

renombrar *vt* rename

renombre *m* renown; **de ∼** renowned, well-known

renovación *f* (de pasaporte, contrato) renewal; (Fisc) rollover; (Info) (de sistema informático) upgrading; (de memoria) wraparound; (Inmob) renovation; (de interiores) refurbishment; **∼ de hipoteca** renewal of mortgage

renovado *adj* renewed; **con ∼ interés** with renewed interest

renovar *vt* (contrato, suscripción, poliza) renew; (Inmob) renovate; (interiores) refurbish; (sistema) update, bring up to date; (sistema informático) upgrade; (imagen del producto) revamp, repackage; **∼ existencias** restock

renta *f* (ingresos) income; (alquiler) rent; **pagar la ∼** pay the rent; **∼s** private income *o* means; **vivir de las ∼s** live on a private income; **∼ de aduanas** customs duties; **∼ antigua** fixed rent; **∼**

anual annuity income; **∼ baja** low rent; **∼ bruta** gross earnings, gross income; **∼ directa** direct yield; **∼ empresarial** business income; **∼ del Estado** government annuity; **∼ de explotación** operating income; **∼ fija** fixed income; **∼ gravable** *or* **imponible** taxable income; **∼ nacional bruta** gross national income; **∼ pasiva** passive income; **∼ per cápita** per capita income; **∼ personal** personal income; **∼ de la propiedad** income from property; **∼ de publicidad** advertising revenue; **∼ de terreno** land rent; **∼ vitalicia** life annuity

rentabilidad *f* cost-effectiveness; (ganancia) profitability; **de baja ∼** low-yielding; **∼ de los activos** return on assets; **∼ del capital** return on equity; **∼ económica** earning power; **∼ del producto** product profitability

rentable *adj* cost-effective; (lucrativo) profitable; **no** *or* **poco ∼** unprofitable

rentista *mf* annuitant

renuncia *f* (a derecho) renunciation; (limitación de responsabilidad) disclaimer; (dimisión) resignation; (de sentencia, deuda) remittal; (Patent) waiver; **presentar su ∼** tender one's resignation

renunciar *vt* (derecho) renounce; (dimitir) resign; (poder, libertad) relinquish; (proyecto, demanda) abandon; (pago) waive; **∼ (a) una herencia** forgo an inheritance

reoferta *f* retendering

reordenación *f* (monetaria) realignment

reorganización *f* reorganization; (Inmob) redevelopment; **∼ de la dirección** management reshuffle; **∼ gubernamental** cabinet reshuffle

reorganizar *vt* reorganize; (dirección, gabinete) reshuffle; (Inmob) redevelop

reorientación *f* (de política, enfoque) reorientation; (de recursos) redeployment; **∼ profesional** retraining

reparación *f* repair; (de daño) redress; **∼ de edificios** building repairs; **∼ legal** legal redress

reparar *vt* repair; (ofensa, agravio) make amends for; (perjuicios) compensate, give compensation for

repartición *f* (distribución) distribution; (división) sharing out; (Seg) adjustment, apportionment; **∼ inmobiliaria** estate distribution

repartir *vt* (distribuir) distribute; (dividir) share out; (tareas, recursos) allocate, allot; (dividendos) pay out; **∼ acciones** allot ····⟶

shares; ~ **el coste** Esp or **costo** AmL
spread the cost; ~ **el riesgo** spread the
risk

repartirse v pron (comisión, ganancias)
share out

reparto m (distribución) distribution;
(división) sharing out; (de dividendos,
obligaciones) allocation, allotment; (de
mercancías, correo) delivery; ~ **a**
domicilio home delivery service; ~ **de**
beneficios profit sharing; ~ **de**
trabajo allocation of work

repasar vt review, look over; (comprobar)
check ~ **un trabajo** check a piece of
work

repaso m (revisión) review; (comprobar)
check; **darle un ~ a algo** give sth a
quick chéck, look over sth; **un ~ de los**
puntos principales a run-through o
review of the main points

repatriación f repatriation; ~ **de**
fondos repatriation of funds

repatriar vt repatriate

repercusión f repercussion; **tener**
amplias repercusiones have widespread
repercussions

repercutir vi: ~ **en algo** have
repercussions on sth, have an effect on
sth

repertorio m (de instrucciones)
repertoire; (guía) directory

repetición f repetition; (en TV)
playback; ~ **automática del último**
número last number redial

repetir vt repeat

réplica f (respuesta) reply; (copia) replica

repo m repo, repurchase agreement

repoblación f repopulation; ~
forestal reforestation, reafforestation
BrE

reponer vt (existencias) replace,
replenish; ~ **los ahorros** replenish one's
savings

reportaje m (en TV) report, news item;
(en prensa) article

reportar 1 vt (beneficios, pérdidas)
produce, yield; (dar cuenta de) report; **el**
negocio le reportó grandes ganancias
the business made him large profits
2 vi: ~ **a alguien** report to sb

reporte m AmL report; (Cont) statement;
~ **de los auditores** AmL auditor's
report; ~ **confidencial** AmL (Bolsa)
insider report; ~ **crediticio** AmL credit
report; ~ **del estado** AmL status report;
~ **del gobierno** AmL government report;
~ **legal** AmL statutory report; ~ **sobre**

el mercado AmL market report; ~ **de**
viabilidad AmL feasibility study

reposición f (reemplazo) replacement;
(de asientos) reversal; (de obra de teatro)
revival; (de empleado) reinstatement

reposicionamiento m repositioning

reposicionar vt reposition

reposo m rest; **en** ~ (Info) on standby

represalia m reprisal; ~**s** (RRHH)
victimization; **como ~ por algo** in
retaliation for sth; **tomar ~s contra**
alguien retaliate against sb

representación f representation; **en**
~ **de algo/alguien** on sth's/sb's behalf,
on behalf of sth/sb; ~ **comercial**
commercial representation; ~ **conjunta**
joint representation; ~ **exclusiva** sole
agency; ~ **proporcional** proportional
representation; ~ **de los trabajadores**
worker representation; ~ **visual** visual
display

representante mf representative,
agent; ~ **autorizado(-a)** m,f authorized
representative; ~ **de centro de**
llamadas call centre BrE o center AmE
agent; ~ **de comercio** commercial
agent, trade representative; ~
exclusivo(-a) m,f sole o exclusive
agent; ~ **legal** legal representative; ~
del personal staff representative; ~
sindical union representative; ~
único(-a) m,f sole agent; ~ **de ventas**
sales representative, sales rep

representar vt (cliente, organización)
represent; (significar) mean; (amenaza) pose;
representa un incremento del 7% it
represents a 7% increase; **introducir las**
modificaciones ~ía tres días de
trabajo making the changes would mean
three days' work

representativo adj (sistema, cifras)
representative

represivo adj (política) repressive

reprivatización f reprivatization

reprivatizar vt reprivatize

reprocesar vt rerun

reproducción f reproduction

reprografía f reprography

reprogramación f (Info)
programming, rescheduling; ~ **de la**
deuda debt rescheduling o restructuring

reprogramar vt (Info) reprogram;
(deuda, pagos) reschedule

reproyección f (Info) remapping

repudiar vt (violencia) repudiate,
condemn

reputación f reputation

requerimiento *m* (petición) request; (Der) subpoena; (requisito) requirement; **a ～ on demand; a ～ de alguien** at sb's request, at the request of sb; **～ de caja** cash requirement; **～ de cheque** cheque requisition BrE, check requisition AmE; **～ de equipo** hardware requirement; **～ de sistema** system requirement

requerir *vt* require, demand; (Der) summon; **～ el pago** demand payment; **este tema requiere atención** this matter requires attention

requisa *f* (de bienes) seizure; (inspección) inspection

requisito *m* requirement; **satisfacer** *or* **reunir los ～s** satisfy *o* meet the requirements; (para un puesto) have the necessary qualifications; **～ financiero** financial requirement; **～ legal** legal requirement, statutory requirement; **～ previo** prerequisite; **～ del puesto** job requirement; **～ de revelación** disclosure requirement; **～ de seguridad** safety requirement

resaltar *vt* (calidad, rasgos) bring out, stress; (Info) highlight

resarcir *vt* (indemnizar) compensate; (reembolsar) reimburse; **fue resarcido por los daños sufridos** he received compensation for the damage caused; **～ a alguien de algo** reimburse sb for sth

resarcirse: ～ de *v pron* (compensar) compensate for

rescatar *vt* (acción) redeem; (dinero) recover

rescate *m* rescue; (de bienes) recovery; (de póliza) redemption; **equipo/operación de ～** rescue team/operation; **valor de ～** surrender value; **～ anticipado** early redemption

rescindible *adj* rescindible; **el contrato es ～** the contract may be terminated

rescindir *vt* (contrato) rescind, cancel, terminate; (oferta) withdraw; **～ el contrato a alguien** terminate sb's employment

rescisión *f* (de contrato) cancellation, termination; (de oferta) withdrawal; (Der) rescission

reseña *f* (de libro) review; (impresa en funda) back-cover copy, blurb (infrml)

reserva *f* (de divisas) reserve; (de habitación, hotel) reservation; (de entradas) booking; (discreción) confidence; **～s** reservations; **a ～ de** except for; **de ～** in reserve, stand-by; **la más absoluta ～** the strictest confidence; **hablar sin ～s**

speak freely; **～ anticipada** advance reservation AmE, advance booking BrE; **～ en bloque** block booking; **～ de capital** (sin distribuir) capital reserve; **～ de divisas** foreign exchange reserve; **～ de efectivo** cash reserve; **～ energética** energy reserve; **R～ Federal** Federal Reserve AmE; **～ de fondos** earmarking of funds; **～ para impuestos** tax provision; **～ monetaria** monetary reserve; **～ con tarjeta de crédito** credit-card reservation AmE, credit-card booking BrE; **～ por teléfono** telephone reservation AmE, telephone booking BrE

reservable *adj* reservable

reservado *adj* reserved; (entradas) booked; (tema) confidential

reservar *vt* reserve; (entradas) book; (fondos) set aside, earmark; **～ con antelación** book in advance; **～ contra un riesgo** provide against a risk

reservarse *v pron* reserve; **～ el derecho de** reserve the right to; **～ el fallo** *or* **la opinión** reserve judgment

resguardo *m* receipt; **～ de ingreso** Esp paying-in stub; **～ de ventas** sales receipt

residencia *f* residency; (vivienda) residence; **～ de ancianos** old people's home, nursing home *(for the elderly)*; **～ permanente** (permiso) permanent residency; (vivienda) permanent residence; **～ principal** main residence; **～ temporal** (permiso) temporary residency; (vivienda) temporary residence

residencial *adj* residential

residente¹ *adj* resident; **no ～** nonresident; **～ en memoria** (Info) memory-resident

residente² *mf* resident; **no ～** nonresident; **～ ordinario(-a)** *m,f* ordinary resident; **～ permanente** permanent resident; **～ temporal** temporary resident

residir *vi*: **～ en** (vivir en) live in; (radicar en) lie in; **el problema reside en la falta de organización** the problem lies in poor organization

residualización *f* residualization

residuos *m pl* (de producción industrial) waste; **～ industriales** industrial waste; **～ peligrosos** dangerous waste; **～ tóxicos** toxic waste

resistencia *f* resistance; **de gran ～** high-strength; **～ a algo** resistance to sth; **～ del mercado** market resistance

resistente *adj* resistant; (fuerte) strong; **～ al fuego** *adj* fire-resistant

resolución *f* (de situación, problema) resolution; (decisión) decision; (Der) ruling; ∼ **judicial** legal ruling

resolver *vt* (problema) solve; (conflicto, disputa) resolve, settle; **por** ∼ outstanding, pending; ∼ **hacer algo** resolve to do sth; ∼ **a favor de algo/alguien** rule in favour BrE *o* favor AmE of sth/sb; ∼ **una disputa mediante arbitraje** settle a dispute by arbitration

respaldar *vt* support, back; **la moneda está respaldada por las reservas del banco central** the currency is supported by the reserves of the central bank; **respaldado por el Gobierno** government-backed

respaldo *m* support, backing; ∼ **financiero** financial backing

respectivamente *adv* respectively

respectivo *adj* respective; **en lo** ∼ **a** as regards, with regard to

respecto *m*: **al** ∼ on the matter *o* subject; **a este** ∼ in this respect; **con** ∼ **a** *or* **a** ∼ **de** with regard to, in connection with; **supone el 25%** ∼ **a la inversión total** it represents 25% of the total investment

respetar *vt* respect; (ley, norma) observe; ∼ **los márgenes** hold margins

respeto *m* respect; **con el debido** ∼ with all due respect

respiro *m* (descanso) break; (alivio) respite; **trabajar sin** ∼ work nonstop *o* without respite

responder [1] *vi* reply, respond; (a pregunta) answer; ∼ **a algo** (contestar) reply to sth; (a petición) respond to sth; (a necesidades, exigencias) meet; (corresponder) correspond to sth; **responde a las exigencias del usuario** it meets users' demands; ∼ **de algo** answer for sth, be held responsible for sth.
[2] *vt* (pregunta) answer, reply; ∼ **que sí/no** say yes/no

responsabilidad *f* responsibility; (Der) liability; **un puesto de mucha** ∼ a job with a lot of responsibility; ∼ **civil** civil liability; ∼ **civil de terceros** third-party liability; ∼ **conjunta** joint liability; ∼ **fiscal** tax liability; ∼ **jurídica** legal liability; ∼ **penal** criminal liability; ∼ **personal** personal liability; ∼ **profesional** professional liability

responsable[1] *adj* responsible; (Der) liable; ∼ **de algo** responsible for sth; (encargado) in charge of sth; **hacerse** ∼ **de algo** take responsibility for sth; ∼

por daños liable for damages; ∼ **ante la ley** responsible in law; ∼ **mancomunadamente** jointly responsible; ∼ **solidariamente** (Der) severally liable

responsable[2] *mf* person in charge; ∼ **de compras** head buyer; ∼ **de información** information officer

respuesta *f* answer, response; **en** ∼ **a su carta/llamada telefónica** further to your letter/telephone call; ∼ **del consumidor** consumer response; ∼ **desfasada** lag response; ∼ **directa** direct response; ∼ **eficiente al consumidor** efficient consumer response; ∼ **positiva** positive response; ∼ **publicitaria** advertising response

resquicio *m* opportunity, opening; ∼ **de oportunidad** window of opportunity

restablecer *vt* re-establish, restore; ∼ **el equilibrio** redress the balance; ∼ **el orden público** restore law and order

restablecimiento *m* re-establishment, restoration; ∼ **automático** (Info) automatic reset

restar *vt* (gastos) deduct, take away; ∼ **importancia a** detract from

restauración *f* restoration; (Info) reset

restaurar *vt* (fichero, directorio) restore

restitución *f* (restablecimiento) restoration; (Der) restitution

restituir *vt* restore, return; (en un cargo) reinstate; (Info) undo

resto *m* remainder; **el** ∼ the rest, the remainder; ∼**s de edición** remaindered books; ∼**s de temporada** end-of-season goods

restricción *f* restriction; ∼ **comercial** trade restriction; ∼ **del crédito** credit squeeze; ∼ **de planificación** planning restriction; ∼ **presupuestaria** budgetary constraint; ∼ **de tiempo** time constraint; ∼ **de venta** sales restriction

restringido *adj* restricted

restringir *vt* restrict; (márgen, crédito) squeeze

resuelto *adj* resolved; ∼ **a hacer algo** determined to do sth

resultado *m* result; (Info) hit, match; **como** ∼ as a result; **con el** ∼ **de que ...** with the result that ...; **dar/no dar** ∼ be successful/unsuccessful; **el plan dió** ∼ the plan worked; ∼ **de beneficios** profit performance; ∼ **bruto** gross earnings; ∼**s de la compañía** company results, company performance; ∼ **electoral** election result; ∼ **de los exámenes** exam result; ∼ **de**

explotación operating income; ~ **final** end result

resultar *vi* be, turn out; (dar resultado) work; ~ **bien/mal** turn out well/badly; ~ **fácil/difícil** be easy/difficult; **me resultó muy difícil darles la noticia** I found it very difficult to tell them the news; ~ **acertado/equivocado** prove right/wrong; **comprándolo al por mayor resulta más barato** it works out cheaper if you buy it wholesale; **el proyecto resultó más caro de lo que pensaban** the project worked out more expensive than they had thought; ~ **ser** turn out to be; **resulta que …** it turns out that …

resumen *m* summary, abstract; **en** ~ in short; **hacer un** ~ **de algo** summarize sth; ~ **financiero** financial summary; ~ **informativo** news round-up

resumido *adj* summarized; **en resumidas cuentas** in short

resumir *vt* summarize; (recapitular) sum up

resurgimiento *m* resurgence; (de la economía) revival

retardar *vt* (recuperación) delay, slow down

retardo *m* delay, lag

retención *f* retention; (de información) withholding; (del salario) deduction; ~ **de garantía** retention money

retener *vt* (acciones, tarjeta) retain; (información) withhold; (impuestos) deduct

retirada *f* withdrawal; ~ **de dividendos** profit taking; ~ **de una objeción** withdrawal of an objection

retirado *adj* retired

retirar *vt* withdraw; ~ **el apoyo** withdraw support; ~ **un cheque** draw a cheque BrE *o* check AmE; ~ **un producto del mercado** take a product off the market

retirarse *v pron* withdraw; (jubilarse) retire; (Pol) stand down; ~ **de algo** (de acuerdo) pull out of sth

retiro *m* withdrawal; (jubilación) retirement; **cobrar el** ~ draw a pension; ~ **de fondos** cash withdrawal; ~ **prematuro** early retirement

reto *m* challenge; ~ **del trabajo** job challenge

retocar *vt* tweak

retórica *f* rhetoric

retornable *adj* (botellas) returnable; **no** ~ non-returnable

retorno *m* return; ~ **de cursor** wraparound; ~ **manual** hard return

retractable *adj* retractable

retractación *f* retraction

retractar *vt* (acusación, propuesta) withdraw

retraerse *v pron* withdraw

retransmisión *f* transmission; ~ **en diferido** prerecorded broadcast

retrasado *adj* delayed; **ir** ~ **con el trabajo** be behind with one's work; **tener trabajo** ~ have a backlog of work

retrasar *vt* (retardar) delay; (aplazar) postpone

retrasarse *v pron* be late; ~ **en algo** fall behind with sth

retraso *m* (demora) delay; (aplazamiento) postponement; (tardanza) lateness; **con** ~ late; **empezar/llegar con diez minutos de** ~ start/arrive ten minutes late; **pagar con un mes de** ~ pay one month in arrears; **llevar** *or* **tener un mes de retraso sobre el programa previsto** be a month behind schedule; ~ **en el plazo de entrega** lead-time delay

retribución *f* fee, payment; (sueldo) salary; ~ **a convenir** salary negotiable; **retribuciones y beneficios gravables** taxable allowances and benefits; ~ **por hora** hourly fee

retroactividad *f* (de ley) retroactively; (Fisc) reachback; **un aumento con** ~ **desde enero** an increase backdated to January

retroactivo *adj* retroactive; **un aumento con efecto** ~ **desde enero** an increase backdated to January

retroalimentación *f* (Info) feedback

retroceder *vi* (en la competencia) lose ground; (retirarse) step back; (abandonar, renunciar) give up; (Info) backspace; **no** ~ stand firm

retrocesión *f* (de asientos) reversal

retroceso *m* setback; (económico) recession; (Info) backspace

retrogresión *f* retrogression

retrospectiva *f* retrospective; **en** ~ in *o* with hindsight

retroventa *f* resale

reubicación *f* (Info) reallocation; AmL (de trabajadores) redeployment; (de empresas) relocation

reunión *f* meeting; (de datos, información) gathering; **celebrar una** ~ hold a meeting; **la** ~ **se disolvió** the meeting broke up; ~ **del comité** committee meeting; ~ **cumbre** summit meeting; ~ **del directorio** board meeting; ~ **del G-7** G-7 meeting; ~ **informativa** ⋯⟩

briefing; ~ **de trabajo colectiva** joint working party

reunir *vt* (información, datos) gather; (dinero) collect, raise; (condiciones, requisitos) satisfy; ~ **esfuerzos** join forces; ~ **pruebas contra alguien** gather evidence against sb; ~ **todos los requisitos** fulfil BrE *o* fulfill AmE *o* satisfy all the requirements

reunirse *v pron* meet, have a meeting; ~ **con alguien** meet (with) sb; ~ **en sesión parlamentaria** sit

reutilizable *adj* reusable; **no** ~ nonreusable

reutilizar *vt* reuse

revaloración, **revalorización** *f* (de divisa) revaluation; (de activo) appreciation; (de propiedad) increase in value

revalorar, **revalorizar** *vt* revalue

revaluación *f* (de divisa) revaluation; (de activo) appreciation; (de propiedad) increase in value; ~ **del capital** capital appreciation

revaluar *vt* (bienes, divisa) revalue; (Cont) write up; (situación) reassess, reevaluate

revelación *f* revelation, disclosure; ~ **de información** disclosure of information

revelar *vt* reveal, disclose; (fotografía) develop

revendedor, a *m,f* retailer; (de billetes) ticket tout BrE, scalper AmE; ~ **de valor agregado** *or* **añadido** Esp value-added reseller

revender *vt* resell; (acciones) sell back

reventa *f* resale

reversible *adj* reversible

reversión *f* reversion; ~ **de tendencia** trend reversal

revientasistemas *m* cracker

revisable *adj* (auditoría) auditable

revisado *adj* examined, checked

revisar *vt* (examinar, comprobar) examine, check; (cuentas) inspect; (Cont) audit; (repasar) look through; (edición) revise; (sueldos, descuentos) review

revisión *f* (inspección) examination, checking; (Cont) audit; (de sueldos, descuentos) review; **bajo** ~ under review; **etapa de** ~ checking phase; ~ **de cuentas** accounts audit; ~ **de cumplimiento** performance review; ~ **del mercado** market review; ~ **de precios** pricing review; ~ **presupuestaria** budget review; ~ **de rendimientos** performance review; ~

del salario pay review, salary review; ~ **de ventas** sales review

revisionismo *m* revisionism

revista *f* magazine; (de una profesión) journal; ~ **de abordo** in-flight magazine; ~ **de admiradores** fanzine; ~ **comercial** trade magazine; ~ **del consumidor** consumer magazine; ~ **de distribución gratuita** free circulation magazine; ~ **económica** economic journal; ~ **electrónica** e-zine, cybermagazine; ~ **de empresa** house magazine; ~ **de lujo** glossy magazine; ~ **de modas** fashion magazine

revitalización *f* revitalization

revocable *adj* revocable

revocación *f* revocation

revocar *vt* (testamento, fallo) revoke

revolución *f* revolution; ~ **cultural** cultural revolution; ~ **ecológica** green revolution; ~ **electrónica** electronic revolution; ~ **gerencial** managerial revolution; ~ **industrial** industrial revolution; ~ **de la información** information revolution; ~ **Internet** Internet revolution; ~ **verde** green revolution

revuelta *f* uprising, riot; ~ **popular** civil riot

rezagado *m* (Bolsa) laggard (jarg)

rezagarse *v pron* fall behind; **nos hemos rezagado en el trabajo** we have fallen behind schedule with the work

rezago *m* unused *or* surplus material; ~ **salarial** AmL wage lag

rico[1] *adj* rich; **países** ~**s en petróleo** oil-rich countries

rico[2], **-a** *m,f* rich person; **los** ~**s** rich people

rienda *f* rein; **dar** ~ **suelta a alguien** give free rein to sb, give sb a free hand; **llevar las** ~**s de algo** be in charge of sth; **tomar las** ~**s de un negocio** take over (the running of) a business

riesgo *m* risk; **a** ~ **de hacer algo** at the risk of doing sth; **a** *or* **contra todo** ~ all-risks; **a** ~ **del comprador** at buyer's risk; **correr el** ~ **de hacer algo** run the risk of doing sth; **correr** ~**s** take risks; **los** ~**s son altos** the stakes are high; **poner algo/a alguien en** ~ put sth/sb at risk; ~ **de activos** asset exposure; ~ **asegurable** insurable risk; ~ **de cambio** exchange risk; ~ **calculado** calculated risk; ~ **comercial** business risk, commercial risk; ~ **compartido** joint venture; ~ **cubierto** covered peril;

~ **empresarial** business venture; ~ **excluido** (en póliza) exclusion clause; ~ **financiero** financial risk; ~ **laboral** occupational hazard; ~ **limitado** limited risk; ~ **de mercado** market risk; ~ **de no pago** risk of nonrepayment; ~ **para la salud** health risk, health hazard; ~ **de seguridad** security risk; ~ **de la tasa de interés** interest rate risk

RIF *abr* (▸**Registro de Información Fiscal**) Tax Information Registry

rigidez *f* rigidity; (de ley, norma) inflexibility; ~ **de precios** price rigidity

riqueza *f* wealth; ~ **intangible** intangible wealth; ~ **nacional** national wealth; ~ **tangible** tangible wealth

ritmo *m* pace, rate; **a este** ~ at this rate; ~ **de crecimiento** growth rate; ~ **de trabajo** work rate; ~ **de vida** lifestyle; **llevan un** ~ **de vida muy ajetreado** they have a very hectic lifestyle

robar *vt* (dinero, propiedad) steal; (clientes, empleados) poach; (tiempo) take up; **no quiero** ~**le más tiempo** I don't want to take up any more of your time

robo *m* (de dinero, propiedad) theft; (de personal) poaching; ~ **con escalo** burglary

robot *m* robot; ~ **de conocimiento** knowbot

robótica *f* robotics

robotizar *vt* (producción, fábrica) automate, robotize

rodaje *m* (de publicidad, películas) shooting

rodar *vt* (películas, publicidad) shoot

rodillo *m* power politics, machtpolitik

rogar *vt* appeal to, plead with; **se ruega no fumar** no smoking; **rogamos respondan a la brevedad** please reply at your earliest convenience

rol *m* role

rollo *m* (infrml) spiel; ~ **publicitario** sales pitch

rompehuelgas *mf* strikebreaker, blackleg BrE (infrml)

romper *vt* (contrato) break; (negociaciones) break off; ~ **el estancamiento** break the stalemate; ~ **filas** break ranks; ~ **una**

huelga break a strike; ~ **relaciones con** sever links with

romperse *v pron* (negociaciones, relaciones) break down

ronda *f* round; **una nueva** ~ **de negociaciones** a new round of negotiations

rotación *f* rotation; ~ **de activos** asset turnover; ~ **de existencias** stock turnover; ~ **de trabajos** job rotation

rotafolios *m* flip chart

rotulación *f* (letra) lettering

rótulo *m* show card; (letra) lettering; (letrero) sign; ~ **comercial** trade sign; ~ **de neón** neon sign

rotura *f* break; ~ **de cabeza** (jarg) (Info) head crash (jarg)

rozamiento *m* friction

RRHH *abr* (▸**recursos humanos**) HR (human resources); (dirección) HRM (human resource management)

rte. *abr* (▸**remitente**) (en sobre) sender

RTVE *abr* (▸**Radio Televisión Española**) *Spanish national broadcasting company,* ≈ BBC BrE

rueda *f* wheel; ~ **de prensa** press conference

ruego *m* request; **atendiendo a los** ~**s de numerosas personas** in response to popular demand; ~**s y preguntas** (al final de una reunión) any other business, A.O.B.

ruido *m* noise; **hacer** ~ make a noise; **la impresora hace demasiado** ~ the printer is very noisy; ~ **blanco** white noise; ~ **de fondo** background noise

rumor *m* rumour BrE, rumor AmE

ruptura *f* (de relaciones) breaking-off; (de contrato) breaking; (negociaciones) breakdown; **la** ~ **del contrato traería consecuencias muy graves** breaking the contract would have serious consequences

ruta *f* route; ~ **comercial** trade route

rutina *f* routine; **por** ~ as a routine; ~ **de diagnóstico** diagnostic routine; ~ **de oficina** office routine

rutinario *adj* routine; **inspección rutinaria** routine inspection

r

Ss

S.A. *abr* (▶**sociedad anónima**) ≈ Ltd BrE, ≈ plc BrE, ≈ Corp. AmE, ≈ Inc. AmE

S.A.A. *abr* (▶**sociedad anónima por acciones**) ≈ plc BrE, ≈ Inc. AmE

sacar *vt* take out; (al mercado) bring out; (conclusión) draw; (idea, información) get; (ganancia, dinero) make; ~ **algo de algo** get sth out of sth; **saqué los datos del informe oficial** I got the information from the official report; ~ **a alguien de algo** get sb out of sth; **el préstamo nos sacó de una situación muy difícil** the loan got us out of a very difficult situation *o* a tight spot; ~ **algo adelante** get sth off the ground; ~ **beneficio** *or* **provecho de algo** capitalize on sth; ~ **dinero del banco** get *o* take *o* draw money out of the bank; ~ **en la tele** show on TV; ~**on el reportaje en primera plana** they published the report on the front page

sacrificar *vt* (carrera, vida) sacrifice

sagaz *adj* shrewd

sala *f* room; (Der) chamber; ~ **de computadoras** AmL (*cf* ▶**sala de ordenadores** Esp) computer room; ~ **de conferencias** conference hall; ~ **del consejo** boardroom; ~ **de embarque** departure lounge; ~ **de espera** waiting room; ~ **de exposiciones** exhibition hall; ~ **de juntas** boardroom; ~ **de muestras** showroom; ~ **de ordenadores** Esp (*cf* ▶**sala de computadoras** AmL) computer room; ~ **de pasajeros** passenger lounge; ~ **de preembarque** departure lounge; ~ **de subastas** auction room; ~ **de visionado** viewing room

salario *m* salary, wage; ~ **anual** annual salary; ~ **bajo** low pay; ~ **base** basic salary; ~ **bruto** gross salary; ~ **a destajo** piece wage; ~ **fijo** fixed salary; ~ **por horas** hourly rate; ~ **inicial** starting salary; ~ **medio** average wage; ~ **mensual** monthly salary; ~ **mínimo** minimum wage; ~ **mínimo interprofesional** statutory minimum wage; ~ **neto** net pay; ~ **semanal** weekly wage; ~ **social** *social*

improvements in lieu of larger wage increases; ~ **tope** earnings ceiling

saldar *vt* (cuenta) settle; (factura) pay; (empleado) pay off; (existencias) sell off; ~ **costes** Esp *or* **costos** AmL meet costs

saldo *m* (de cuenta) balance; (liquidación) clearance sale; **precios de** ~ sale prices; ~ **acreedor** credit balance; ~ **anterior** carry-over balance; ~ **de apertura** opening balance; ~ **de caja** cash balance; ~ **de cierre** closing balance; ~ **de cuenta** balance of account, account statement; ~ **a cuenta nueva** balance carried forward; ~ **deudor** debit balance; ~ **disponible** available balance; ~ **insuficiente** insufficient funds; ~ **del mayor** ledger balance; ~ **medio diario** average daily balance; ~ **negativo** debit balance; ~ **pendiente** outstanding balance; ~ **positivo** credit balance

salida *f* (de edificio) exit, way out; (de fondos) outflow; (Info) output; (de producto) outlet; (de avión, tren) departure; (solución) way out, solution; ~**s** outgoings, expenditure; (en trabajo) openings, job opportunities; **no le veo ninguna** ~ **a esta situación** I can't see a way out of this situation; **tener mucha** ~ sell very well, be very popular; **no tener mucha** ~ not sell very well, not be very popular; **tener muchas** ~**s** offer a lot of opportunities, have a lot of openings; **la informática tiene muchas** ~**s** there are a lot of job opportunities in computing; ~ **de datos** data output; ~ **en efectivo** cash outflow; ~ **de emergencia** emergency exit; ~ **impresa** printout; ~ **de incendios** fire exit

salir *vi* leave, depart; (programa) exit, quit; (emitirse) be broadcast; (producto, revista) come out, appear; (puesto, plaza) come up; **no salgo de trabajar hasta las siete** I don't leave work until seven; ~ **a** work out at; ~ **para** leave for; **han salido varias plazas** several vacancies have come up; **los libros salen a cinco euros por unidad** the books work out at five euros each; ~ **de apuros** get out of trouble; ~ **en el periódico** be in the papers; ~ **por la tele** be on TV; ~ **en titulares** hit the headlines

S

salón *m* room; ~ **de fumar** smoking room

salpicadura *f* (en prensa) splash

saltar ⟦1⟧ *vt* (pregunta, página) skip, miss out; ~ **las normas** flout the rules. ⟦2⟧ *vi* jump; **su nombre me saltó a la vista** his name jumped out at me

salto *m* jump; **dar un ~ adelante/atrás** take a leap forward AmE *o* forwards BrE/ step backward AmE *o* backwards BrE; **los precios han dado un ~** prices have shot up; ~ **de línea** line break; ~ **de página forzado** hard page break

salud *f* health; **tener ~** be healthy, enjoy good health; ~ **ocupacional** occupational health; ~ **pública** public health

saludar *vt* greet, say hello to; **le saluda atentamente** Yours sincerely BrE, Sincerely yours AmE

saludo *m* greeting; ~**s** *m pl* (en correspondencia) best wishes; **reciba un cordial ~** with best wishes

salvaguardar *vt* (activos) safeguard; ~ **contra la inflación** safeguard against inflation

salvamento *m* rescue, salvage; **equipo/operación de ~** rescue team/ operation

salvar *vt* (situación) rescue, salvage; (Info) save; (dificultad, obstáculo) overcome; ~ **a alguien de algo** save sb from sth; **salvando unos cuantos** apart from a few, with a few exceptions

salvedad *f* (condición) proviso, condition; (excepción) exception; **con la ~ de que ...** with the proviso that ...; **con una ~** on one condition; **no podemos hacer ~es** we cannot make any exceptions; **sin ~** without reservation

salvo¹ *adj* safe

salvo² *prep* except (for); ~ **domingos y días festivos** Sundays and holidays excepted; ~ **error u omisión** errors and omissions excepted; ~ **que se acuerde lo contrario** unless otherwise agreed

salvo³: **a ~** *adv* safe; **estar a ~** be out of danger, be out of the woods; **poner algo a ~** put sth in a safe place; **consiguió poner los documentos a ~** she managed to put the documents in a safe place

sanción *f* sanction; **imponer/levantar sanciones** impose/lift sanctions; ~ **comercial** trade sanction; ~ **económica** economic sanction

sancionar *vt* (acuerdo) sanction, approve; (penalizar) penalize

saneamiento *m* (de zona, río) cleaning up; (de organización, economía) restructuring

sanear *vt* (zona, río) clean up; (organización, economía) restructure; **el gobierno presentó sus planes para ~ la economía** the government set out its plans for getting the economy back on track

sangrar ⟦1⟧ *vt* (párrafo) indent; (ilustración) bleed ⟦2⟧ *vi* (ilustración) bleed

sangría *f* (de párrafo) indentation; (de ilustración) bleed

sano *adj* healthy; (idea) sound, sensible; **cortar por lo ~** take drastic action; ~ **y salvo** safe and sound

satélite *m* satellite; **por** *or* **vía ~** by satellite; **una conexión vía ~** a satellite link; ~ **de comunicaciones** communications satellite

satisfacción *f* satisfaction; ~ **del consumidor** consumer satisfaction; ~ **profesional** job satisfaction

satisfacer *vt* (persona) satisfy; (deuda) settle, pay off; (condiciones, requisitos) fulfil BrE *o* fulfill AmE; (gastos) meet

satisfactorio *adj* satisfactory

satisfecho *adj* (complacido, contento) satisfied, pleased

saturación *f* (del mercado) saturation; (de producto) glut

saturado *adj* (economía, mercado) saturated; (producto, acciones) oversold; (líneas telefónicas) busy AmE, engaged BrE; ~ **de trabajo** snowed under *o* overloaded with work

saturar *vt* (economía, mercado) saturate, flood

sección *f* section; (de una empresa) department; ~ **de cartera** portfolio section; ~ **extranjera** foreign section; ~ **transversal** cross section

secretaría *f* (cargo) post of secretary; (oficina) secretary's office; (departamento administrativo) secretariat

secretariado *m* (departamento administrativo) secretariat

secretario, -a *m,f* secretary; ~ **de asuntos sociales** social secretary; ~ **ejecutivo(-a)** *m,f* executive secretary; ~ **de la empresa** company secretary; **S~ de Estado** Secretary of State; ~ **general** general secretary; ~ **particular** private secretary; ~ **personal** personal secretary, personal assistant, PA; ~ **de prensa** press secretary; ~ **de redacción** deputy editor

S

secreto¹ *adj* secret

secreto² *m* secret; (Pol) cover-up; **en ~** secretly, in secret; **~ de fabricación** trade secret; **~ sumario** *confidentiality surrounding legal proceedings*; **no podemos dar más detalles debido al ~ sumario** we are unable to disclose any further details because the matter is sub judice

sector *m* sector; **~ bancario** banking sector; **~ empresarial** business sector; **~ de exportación** export sector; **~ financiero** financial sector; **~ manufacturero** manufacturing sector; **~ de mercado** market sector; **~ al por menor** retail sector; **~ primario** primary sector; **~ privado** private sector; **~ público** public sector; **~ rural** rural sector; **~ sanitario** health sector; **~ secundario** secondary sector; **~ de servicios** service sector; **~ de servicios públicos** utilities sector; **~ terciario** tertiary sector

sectorial *adj* sectorial

sectorización *f* sectoring; **~ lógica** (Info) soft sectoring

sectorizar *vt* (disco) sector

secuencia *f* sequence; **~ de abandono** escape sequence; **~ de arranque** start-up sequence *o* routine; **~ de clics** click stream; **~ de entrada** job stream; **~ de intercalación** collating sequence

secuencial *adj* sequential

secuestrar *vt* (bienes) seize, sequestrate; (avión) hijack; (persona) kidnap

secuestro *m* (de bienes) sequestration; (de avión) hijacking; (de persona) kidnapping; **~ de páginas** page-jacking

secundar *vt* (moción) second; (huelga, proyecto) support

sede *f* head office, headquarters; **~ social** head office, registered office

segmentación *f* segmentation; (Info) partition; **~ de mercado** market segmentation

segmentar *vt* segment; (desgravación fiscal) taper; (Info) partition

segmento *m* segment; **~ de base** (Info) root segment; **~ de edad** age group; **~ objetivo** (V&M) target segment

segregación *f* segregation; **~ laboral** occupational segregation; **~ racial** racial segregation

segregado *adj* segregated

seguido *adj* continuous; (consecutivo) in a row, one after the other; **tres días ~s** three days in a row

seguidor, a *m,f* follower

seguimiento *m* (de proceso) tracking, monitoring; **de ~ rápido** fast-tracked

seguir **1** *vt* (persona, instrucciones, camino) follow; (gasto, proceso) track, monitor; (curso) do; (política) pursue; **está siguiendo un curso de contabilidad** she's doing a course in accountancy; **~ su curso** carry on *o* continue as expected; **~ el ejemplo** follow suit; **~ haciendo algo** carry on *o* continue doing sth; **~ un modelo similar** follow a similar pattern; **~ el ritmo de** keep up with **2** *vi* (continuar) go on, carry on; **sigue** continued, cont.; **sigue al dorso** continued overleaf, P.T.O.; **siguen sin tomar una decisión** they still haven't come to a decision; **~ adelante** carry on, go ahead; **la oferta sigue en pie** the offer still stands

segundo *adj* second; **de ~ grado** second-grade; **en ~ lugar** secondly; **el ~** the latter; **de segunda mano** second-hand; **segunda generación** second generation; **segunda hipoteca** second mortgage BrE, junior mortgage AmE

seguridad *f* (contra peligro) safety; (contra riesgo) security; (confianza) confidence, self-confidence; (garantía) assurance; (certeza) certainty; **con ~** for certain; **controles de ~** security checks; **darle ~es a alguien de que ...** assure sb that ...; **medidas de ~** (contra peligro) safety measures; (contra riesgo) security measures; **tenga la ~ de que ...** rest assured that ...; **~ de los datos** data security; **~ del estado** state security; **~ e higiene** health and safety; **~ industrial** industrial safety; **~ de Internet** Internet security; **~ de posesión** security of tenure; **~ del producto** product safety; **S~ Social** (sistema de bienestar) Social Security BrE, Welfare AmE; (sistema de salud) ≈ National Health Service BrE, ≈ Medicaid AmE; (cotizaciones) ≈ National Insurance BrE

seguro¹ *adj* (convencido) sure; (sin riesgo) safe; (estable) secure; (fiable) reliable; (fecha) definite; **estar ~ de que ...** be sure that ...; **es un método bastante ~** it is a reasonably reliable method; **tener un trabajo ~** have a secure job; **lo más ~ es que cierre la empresa** the company will probably shut down

seguro² *m* insurance; **el S~** ≈ the NHS BrE, ≈ Medicaid AmE; **cubierto por**

~ covered by insurance; **hacerse** *or* **sacar un** ~ take out insurance *o* an insurance policy; ~ **abierto** blanket insurance; ~ **de abonado** subscriber's insurance policy; ~ **de accidentes** accident insurance; ~ **de automóviles** car insurance BrE, automobile insurance AmE; ~ **de cartera** portfolio insurance; ~ **colectivo** collective insurance; ~ **de decesos** AmL life insurance, life assurance BrE; ~ **de desempleo** unemployment insurance; ~ **de enfermedad** health insurance; ~ **de gastos jurídicos** legal expense insurance; ~ **de hipotecas** mortgage insurance; ~ **de incendios** fire insurance; ~ **inmobiliario** property insurance, building insurance; ~ **médico** medical insurance; ~ **de paro** Esp unemployment insurance; ~ **de pérdidas de ingresos** loss of income insurance; ~ **de préstamo** loan insurance; ~ **de responsabilidad** liability insurance; ~ **contra** *or* **a todo riesgo** all-risks insurance, comprehensive insurance; ~ **social** Social Security benefit BrE, Welfare AmE; ~ **contra terceros** third-party insurance; ~ **de viaje** travel insurance; ~ **de vida** life insurance, life assurance BrE

seguro³ *adv* for certain; ~ **que venden la compañía** they will almost certainly sell the company

selección *f* selection; **hacer una** ~ **de candidatos** draw up a shortlist of candidates; ~ **al azar** random selection; ~ **automática internacional** international direct dialling BrE *o* dialing AmE; ~ **múltiple** multiple choice

seleccionado *adj* selected

seleccionar *vt* select; (valor predefinido) set

Selectividad *f Spanish university entrance examination*

sellar *vt* (sobre, pasaporte) stamp; (acuerdo, pacto) seal

sello *m* (postage) stamp; (marca) seal; (de compañía discográfica) (record) label; ~ **de calidad** seal of quality; ~ **de correos** Esp postage stamp; ~ **de la empresa** company seal; ~ **de endoso** endorsement stamp; ~ **de entrada** (en pasaporte) entry stamp; ~ **fiscal** fiscal stamp, revenue stamp; ~ **de goma** rubber stamp; ~ **de recibo** receipt stamp

selva *f* forest; ~ **tropical** rainforest

semana *f* week; **a la** ~ *a o* per week; **de aquí a una** ~ a week from now; **entre** ~ during the week; **la** ~ **pasada** last week; **la** ~ **próxima** *or* **que viene** next week; **una** ~ **por adelantado** a week in advance; ~ **laborable (media)** (average) working week BrE, (average) workweek AmE

semestral *adj* half-yearly, six-monthly, biannual

semestralmente *adv* half-yearly, every six months, biannually

semestre *m* (period of six months); **el balance del segundo** ~ the balance for the second half of the year

semianual *adj* semiannual

semicualificado *adj* semiskilled

semidúplex *adj* half-duplex

semifabricante *m* quasi-manufacturer

semiindustrializado *adj* semi-industrialized

seminario *m* seminar

seminuevo *adj* nearly-new; (automóvil) second-hand, pre-owned AmE

Senado *m upper house of the Spanish parliament*, ≈ Senate AmE

senador, -a *m,f* senator

sencillo *adj* straightforward; (billete) single, one-way

sensación *f* (percepción) feeling; (conmoción) sensation; **causar una** ~ cause a sensation; ~ **de bienestar** feelgood factor

sensibilidad *f* sensitivity; ~ **al precio** price sensitivity; ~ **del mercado** market sensitivity

sensibilizar *vt* raise awareness of; **una campaña para** ~ **a los ciudadanos** a campaign to raise public awareness

sensible *adj* (mercado) sensitive; (grande) noticeable, significant; ~ **al coste** Esp *or* **costo** AmL cost-sensitive; ~ **al mercado** market-sensitive; ~ **al precio** price-sensitive

sentada *f* (acción laboral) sit-in, sit-down protest

sentencia *f tb* (Der) sentence; **dictar** *or* **pronunciar** ~ pass *o* pronounce sentence; ~ **de bancarrota** decree of bankruptcy; ~ **de embargo** garnishment; ~ **de muerte** death sentence

sentido *m* sense; **en cierto** ~, **tienen razón** in a way *o* sense, they're right; **tener** ~ make sense; **la decisión no tiene** ~ the decision doesn't make any ···⟩

S

sense; ~ **comercial** business sense; ~ **común** common sense; ~ **de deber** sense of duty; ~ **de justicia** sense of justice; ~ **del mercado** feel of the market; ~ **de responsabilidad** sense of responsibility

sentir *vt* (emoción) feel; (lamentar) regret, be sorry for; **dejarse** *or* **hacerse** ~ be felt; **los efectos de la recesión se dejaron** ~ **durante varios años** the effects of the recession were felt for several years; **nuestro departamento no ha sentido el cambio de dirección** our department hasn't been affected by the change in management; **sentimos no poder ayudarles** we regret we cannot be of any help

señal *f* (indicación) signal; (marca) mark; (en teléfono) tone; (depósito) deposit; **dejar algo como** ~ leave sth as a deposit; **en** ~ **de algo** as a sign of sth; **ser buena/ mala** ~ be a good/bad sign; **ser** ~ **de que ...** be a sign that ...; **es** ~ **de que la compañía va mal** it's a sign that the company isn't doing very well; ~ **de alerta** alarm signal; ~ **de compra** buying signal; ~ **de llamada** ringing tone; ~ **de ocupado** engaged tone BrE, busy signal AmE; ~ **de peligro** warning sign; ~ **sonora** (de aviso) beep; ~ **de tráfico** traffic sign

señalar *vt* (fecha, lugar) set, fix; (indicar) show, point out; (marcar) mark; **a la hora señalada** at the appointed time; **el informe señala la necesidad de cambiar de sistema** the report points out the need to change systems; ~ **algo con una cruz** mark sth with a cross, put a cross by sth; ~**on el día 20 para la reunión** they set the meeting for the 20th; ~ **algo con el puntero y hacer clic** point and click on sth; ~ **que ...** point out that ...

señalización *f* (acto) signalling BrE, signaling AmE; (conjunto de señales) signs

señor, a *m,f* (m) man; (f) lady; **S**~ Sir; (delante de apellido) Mr; **S**~**a** Madam; (delante de apellido) Mrs; **S**~ **don** (título de encabezamiento de carta) Esquire; **S**~**as y S**~**es** ladies and gentlemen; **ahora mismo le atiendo, S**~/**S**~**a** I'll be with you in just a moment, Sir/Madam; **Buenos días, S**~ **López** Good morning, Mr López; **Estimado S**~ *or* **Muy S**~ **mío** Dear Sir; **Muy S**~**a mía** Dear Madam; **Estimado S**~ **Martínez** Dear Mr Martínez; **Estimados S**~**es** *or* **Muy S**~**es nuestros** Dear Sirs

separación *f* separation; (de empresas) demerger; (de tierras) severance; ~ **de bienes** division of property; ~ **de colores** colour separation BrE, color separation AmE; ~ **de deberes** segregation of duties; ~ **legal** legal separation

separadamente *adv* separately

separador *m* (Info) separator; (de carpeta) divider

separar *vt* (Com gen) separate; ~ **algo de algo** separate sth from sth

sequía *f* drought

ser *vi* be; **a no** ~ **que** unless; **de** ~ **así** if that's the case; **de no** ~ **así** otherwise; **o sea** that's to say; **sea como sea** whatever happens, come what may

SER *abr* (▸**Sociedad Española de Radiodifusión**) *Spanish broadcasting association*

serial-paralelo *adj* serial-parallel

serie *f* series; **en** ~ (fabricado) mass-produced; (Info) serial; ~ **cronológica** time series; ~ **de opciones** series of options

serio *adj* serious; (sensato) responsible, reliable; **en** ~ seriously; **tomar algo en** ~ take sth seriously; **ponerse** ~ get *o* become serious; **la situación se está poniendo seria** the situation is becoming serious

serpiente *f* (Econ) snake

servicio *m* service; **estar de** ~ be on duty; **fuera de** ~ (máquina) out of service; **por** ~**s prestados** for services rendered; ~ **no incluido** service not included; ~ **de apoyo** support service; ~ **de atención al cliente** customer services; ~ **de banca electrónica** electronic banking service; ~ **bancario** banking service; ~ **bancario personal** personal banking service; ~ **de bienestar social** welfare service; ~ **de consulta** advisory service; ~ **de consultoría** consulting service; ~ **contable** accountancy service; ~ **de correos** postal service; ~ **de datos directo** online data service; ~ **deficiente** poor service; **S**~ **Diplomático** ≈ Diplomatic Service BrE; ~ **de distribución** distribution service; ~ **de documentación** cuttings service BrE, clippings service AmE; ~ **a domicilio** home-delivery service; ~ **durante el vuelo** in-flight facilities; ~ **electrónico de noticias** online news service, newsfeed; ~ **de emergencia** emergency service; ~ **de envío urgente** express delivery service; ~ **financiero** financial service; ~ **de giro** drawing facility; ~ **gobierno a cliente** government-to-client service, G2C service; ~ **gobierno a empresa** government-to-business service, G2B service; ~ **a habitaciones** room service; ~ **de informática** IT services o department; ~**s informativos** news services; **S~s Integrados para el Empleo** ≈ Jobcentre BrE; ~ **interno** memorandum; ~ **de mantenimiento** maintenance service; **con/sin ~ de mantenimiento** supported/unsupported; ~ **de marketing** marketing services; ~ **de mensajería** courier service; ~ **mínimo** skeleton service; ~ **permanente** permanent service, 24-hour service; ~ **personalizado** customized service; ~ **de posventa** after-sales service; ~ **de preventa** presales service; ~ **programado** scheduled service; ~ **público** public utility, public service; ~ **regular** regular service, scheduled service; ~ **de reparto** delivery service; ~ **de respuesta comercial** business reply service; ~ **de respuesta telefónica** telephone answering service; ~ **de seguridad** security service; ~ **de seguros en línea** e-brokering; ~**s sociales** social services; ~ **técnico** technical assistance; ~ **telefónico de atención al cliente** customer careline; ~ **urgente de correos** express mail service; ~ **de valor agregado** or **añadido** Esp added-value service; ~ **de 24 horas** 24-hour service, round-the-clock service BrE, around-the-clock service; ~ **de ventas** sales service; ~ **de viajeros** passenger service

servidor m (Info) server, mainframe, host computer; ~ **de alojamiento** Web hosting server; ~ **del anuncio** ad server; ~ **de aplicaciones** application server; ~ **de correo** or **e-mail** mail server, e-mail server; ~ **de ficheros** file server; ~ **de Internet** Internet server; ~ **en segundo plano** backend server; ~ **WAP** WAP server; ~ **web** Web server

servidumbre f easement; ~ **de paso** right-of-way; ~ **tácita** implied easement

servir [1] vt (cliente) serve; (pedido) fill, process
[2] vi (ser útil) be useful; **sin firma no sirve** it's no use o good without a signature; **¿esto sirve para algo?** is this any use?; ~ **de** or **como** serve o act as; ~ **para el caso** serve the purpose; ~

como garante de alguien stand as guarantor for sb

sesgo m bias; **dar un ~ positivo a algo** put a positive spin on sth

sesión f session; **abrir/levantar la ~** open/close the session; ~ **de cierre** closing session; ~ **de contratación** trading session; ~ **informativa** briefing session; ~ **de Internet** Internet o Web session; ~ **de noche** evening performance, late show; ~ **plenaria** plenary session; ~ **práctica** hands-on session; ~ **de trabajo** working session; **última ~ bursátil** last trading day

sesionar vi be in session

seudónimo m pseudonym; (Info) alias

s.e.u.o. abr (►**salvo error u omisión**) e.&o.e. (errors and omissions excepted)

SGBD abr (►**sistema de gestión de base de datos**) DBMS (database management system)

SGML abr (lenguaje estandarizado y generalizado de marcado) SGML (Standard Generalized Mark-up Language)

SICAV abr (►**sociedad de inversión de capital variable**) unit trust

siempre adv always; ~ **y cuando ...** provided that ...

SIG abr (►**sistema de información para la gestión**) MIS (management information system)

sigla f (acrónimo) acronym; (abreviatura) abbreviation

signatario, -a m,f signatory

significación f significance; ~ **marginal** marginal significance

significado m (sentido) meaning; (importancia) significance; ~ **secundario** secondary meaning

significante adj significant

significar vt mean

significativo adj significant

signo m sign; ~ **de inserción** caret

silvicultura f forestry

símbolo m symbol; ~ **corporativo** corporate symbol; ~ **monetario** currency symbol; ~ **de prestigio** status symbol

simpatizante mf sympathiser, supporter

simplificar vt simplify

simposio m symposium

simulación f simulation; ~ **por computadora** AmL or **ordenador** Esp computer simulation

simular *vt* simulate

simultáneo *adj* simultaneous

sinceridad *f* sincerity; **con toda ~** in all sincerity

sincero *adj* sincere; **ser ~ con alguien** be honest with sb

sincronización *f* synchronization; **~ del mercado** market timing

sincronizado *adj* synchronized; **no ~** out of sync

sincronizar *vt* synchronize; (Bolsa) lock in

síncrono *adj* synchronous

sindicación *f* syndication

sindicado *adj* unionized; **no ~** non-union

sindicalismo *m* unionism, trade unionism BrE

sindicalista *mf* union member

sindicalización *f* unionization

sindicato *m* union, trade union BrE, labor union AmE; (consorcio) syndicate; **~ de accionistas** shareholders' *o* stockholders' syndicate; **~ afiliado** affiliated trade BrE *o* labor AmE union; **~ bancario** banking syndicate; **~ de compra** buying syndicate; **~ esquirol** (infrml) scab union (infrml); **~ no afiliado** unaffiliated union; **~ de periódicos** newspaper syndicate; **~ reconocido** recognized trade BrE *o* labor AmE union

síndico, -a *m,f* trustee; (de quiebras) official receiver

síndrome *m* syndrome

sinecura *f* sinecure

sinergia *f* synergy

sinergismo *m* synergism

siniestro *m* disaster; **~ al contado** cash loss; **~ pagado** claim paid; **~ total** write-off

sinopsis *f* synopsis

sintaxis *f* syntax

síntesis *f* (de ideas, políticas) synthesis; (resumen) summary; **en ~** in short

sintético *adj* synthetic, man-made

sintonización *f* tuning; **~ fina automática** automatic fine tuning; **~ precisa** fine tuning

SIPE *abr* (▸**Servicios Integrados para el Empleo**) ≈ Jobcentre BrE

sistema *m* system; **con ~** systematically; **~ de apoyo** support system; **~ de archivo** filing system; **~ de autoliquidación** (Fisc) self-assessment system; **~ autónomo** stand-alone system; **~ autor** authoring

system; **~ bancario** banking system; **~ de bienestar social** welfare system; **~ central de reservas** central reservation system; **~ de codificación** coding system; **~ de compensación** clearing system; **~ común** (UE) common system; **~ de contabilidad automatizado** computerized accounting system; **~ contable** accounting system; **~ de control de tráfico aéreo** air-traffic control system; **~ de distribución** distribution system; **~ de dos niveles** two-tier system; **~ electrónico de transferencia de fondos** electronic funds transfer system; **~ experto** expert system, knowledge-based system; **~ de gestión ambiental** environmental management system; **~ de gestión de base de datos** database management system; **~ de gestión financiera** financial management system; **~ global de comunicaciones móviles** global system for mobile, GSM; **~ impositivo** tax system, taxation system; **~ de información** information system; **~ de información administrativo**, **~ de información para la gestión** management information system; **~ informático** computer system; **~ interactivo** interactive system; **~ legado** legacy system; **~ legal** legal system; **~ de libre empresa** free-enterprise system; **~ de libre mercado** free-market system; **~ de límite de crédito** credit-rating system; **~ en línea** online system; **~ manual** manual system; **~ mayoritario** majority rule; **S~ Monetario Europeo** European Monetary System, EMS; **~ monetario mundial** world monetary system; **~ de nombres de dominio** domain-name system; **~ operativo** operating system; **~ operativo de administración** management operating system; **~ operativo de discos** disk operating system, DOS; **~ de pagos** payment system; **~ de planificación avanzado** advanced planning system, APS; **~s y procedimientos** systems and procedures; **~ de procesamiento de datos** data processing system; **~ de procesamiento de texto** word-processing system; **~ propietario** *or* **propio** proprietary system, in-house system; **~ de recuperación acelerada de costes** Esp *or* **costos** AmL *m* accelerated cost recovery system; **~ de recuperación de documentos** document retrieval system; **~ de**

recuperación de información information retrieval system; ~

regulador regulatory system; ~ **de remitente** (en correo electrónico) remailer; ~ **de reserva** reservation system, booking system; ~**s en segundo plano** backend systems; ~ **de sugerencias** suggestion scheme; ~ **de tablón de anuncios** bulletin board system; ~ **de transporte** transport system; ~ **tributario** tax system; ~ **universal de telecomunicaciones móviles** Universal Mobile Telecommunication System, UMTS; ~ **de usuarios múltiples** multiuser system

sistemático *adj* systematic

sistematización *f* systematization; ~ **de datos** information processing

sistematizar *vt* systematize

site *m* site, website; (*ver tb* ▸**sitio**)

SITF *abr* (▸**Sociedad Internacional de Telecomunicaciones Financieras**) SWIFT (Society for Worldwide Interbank Financial Telecommunications)

sitio *m* site; ~ **comercial** merchant site; ~ **especular** mirror site; ~ **fantasma** ghost site; ~ **web** website; ~ **web interactivo** interactive website; ~ **web promocional** promotional site

situación *f* situation; (económica, legal) position; (de local) position, location; **en la ~ actual** in the current situation; **tener la ~ bajo control** have the situation under control; ~ **económica** financial position; ~ **de efectivo** cash position; ~ **jurídica** legal status; ~ **laboral** employment situation; ~ **de liquidez y deudas** cash and debt position

S.L. *abr* (▸**sociedad limitada**) ≈ Ltd. (limited company BrE), ≈ Inc. (incorporated business company AmE)

slogan *m* advertising slogan, slogan

SME *abr* (▸**Sistema Monetario Europeo**) EMS (European Monetary System)

SMMD *abr* (▸**sociedad mediadora en el mercado de dinero**) discount house BrE

SMS *abr* (▸**subred de gestión de jerarquía digital síncrona**) SMS (Synchronous Digital Hierarchy Management Subnetwork)

s/n *abr* (**sin número**) no number

SO *abr* (▸**sistema operativo**) OS (operating system)

sobornar *vt* bribe, buy (infrml)

soborno *m* Esp bribe; **aceptar ~s** take bribes

sobrante *m* excess, surplus; **con ~ de liquidez** cash-rich

sobre *m* envelope; **en ~ cerrado** in a sealed envelope; **en ~s separados** under separate cover; ~ **acolchado** Jiffy bag®; ~ **de bolsillo** pocket envelope; ~ **con ventanilla** window envelope

sobreacumulación *f* overaccumulation

sobreasegurado *adj* overinsured

sobrecapitalización *f* overcapitalization

sobrecapitalizado *adj* overcapitalized

sobrecarga *f* (de sistema, circuito) overload; (recargo) surcharge; (congestión) congestion

sobrecomprado *adj* overbought

sobrecontratado *adj* (vuelo) overbooked

sobrecoste *m* Esp, **sobrecosto** AmL cost overrun

sobrecubierta *f* jacket

sobredependencia *f* overdependence

sobreestimar *vt* overestimate

sobreexplotación *f* overexploitation

sobreextendido *adj* overextended

sobregirado *adj* overdrawn

sobregirar *vt* overdraw

sobregiro *m* overdraft; ~ **no garantizado** unsecured overdraft

sobreimpresión *f* overprint

sobreinversión *f* overtrading

sobrepasar *vt* exceed; ~ **el límite máximo** break the ceiling

sobrepastoreo *m* overgrazing

sobreproducir *vt* overproduce

sobrepujar *vt* outbid

sobrerrepresentación *f* (en el mercado) overrepresentation

sobrerrepresentar *vt* overrepresent

sobresuscrito *adj* oversubscribed

sobretasa *f* surcharge; (Fisc) surtax; ~ **por congestión** congestion surcharge; ~ **de gasóleo** fuel surcharge; ~ **postal** additional postage

sobreurbanización *f* overurbanization

sobrevaloración *f* overvaluation

sobrevalorado *adj* overvalued

sobrevaluar *vt* overvalue

sobreventa *f* overbooking

s

sobrevivir *vi* survive

socavar *vt* (a un competidor) undercut

social *adj* social; (corporativo) company;
sede ~ company headquarters

socialdemocracia *f* social
democracy

socialismo *m* socialism

socialista¹ *adj* socialist

socialista² *mf* socialist

sociedad *f* society; (compañía) company;
(de socios) partnership; **formar una** ~ set
up *o* form a company; **la** ~ **del
despilfarro** the waste society; ~
anónima ≈ limited company BrE, ≈
incorporated business company AmE; ~
anónima por acciones ≈ public
limited company BrE, ≈ public
corporation AmE; ~ **de arrendamiento**
leasing company; ~ **de cartera
financiera** financial holding company;
~ **comanditaria** limited partnership; ~
comercial trading company; ~ **de
consumo** consumer society; ~
cooperativa cooperative society; ~
disuelta defunct company; **S~
Española de Radiodifusión** *Spanish
broadcasting association*; ~ **estatal** state
corporation; ~ **fantasma** bogus
company; ~ **financiera** finance
company, finance house; ~ **inmobiliaria**
property company, real estate company
(AmE); **S~ Internacional de
Telecomunicaciones Financieras**
Society for Worldwide Interbank
Financial Telecommunications; ~ **de
inversión de capital variable** unit
trust; ~ **limitada** ≈ limited company
BrE, ≈ incorporated business company
AmE; ~ **mediadora en el mercado de
dinero** discount house BrE; ~ **mercantil**
trading company; ~ **mixta** joint
venture; ~ **personal** partnership; ~
pública public corporation; ~
puntocom dot-com, pure player; ~ **de
responsabilidad limitada** ≈ limited
company BrE, ≈ incorporated business
company AmE; ~ **de servicios
públicos** public utility company; ~ **de
socorros mutuos** friendly society BrE,
mutual society AmE

socio, -a *m,f* (RRHH) partner; (de un club)
member; **ser/hacerse** ~ **de algo** be/
become a member of sth; ~
accionista(-a) *m,f* shareholder; ~
activo(-a) *m,f* active partner; (de bolsa)
trading member; ~ **capitalista(-a)** *m,f*
silent partner; ~ **comanditario(-a)** *m,f*
limited liability partner; ~ **comercial**
trading partner; ~ **inactivo(-a)** *m,f*

sleeping partner BrE, silent partner AmE;
~ **limitado(-a)** *m,f* limited partner; ~
mayoritorio(-a) majority shareholder;
~ **menor** junior partner

sociocultural *adj* sociocultural

socioeconómico *adj* socioeconomic

sociometría *f* sociometry

sociométrico *adj* sociometric

sofisticación *f* sophistication

sofisticado *adj* (sistema, tecnología)
sophisticated

software *m* software; ~ **antivirus**
virus checker, anti-virus software; ~ **de
aplicación** application software; ~ **de
auditoría** audit software; ~ **de
bloqueo** blocking software; ~ **de
censura** censorware; ~ **de la
computadora** AmL (*cf* ▸**software del
ordenador** Esp) computer software; ~
del conocimiento knowledgeware; ~
de contabilidad accounting software;
~ **del contenido** contentware; ~
didáctico educational software,
courseware; ~ **de dominio público**
freeware; ~ **de estadística** statistical
software; ~ **de filtración** filtering
software, nanny software; ~ **de gestión
de redes** networking software; ~ **de
grupo** groupware; ~ **legado** legacy
software; ~ **libre** freeware; ~ **del
ordenador** Esp (*cf* ▸**software de la
computadora** AmL) computer software;
~ **de presentación** presentation
software; ~ **de procesamiento de
textos** word-processing software; ~ **de
productividad** productivity software; ~
de reconocimiento de la voz speech *o*
voice recognition software

solapamiento *f* aliasing

solar *m* site, plot BrE, lot AmE

solicitación *f* solicitation

solicitado *adj* sought-after; **no** ~
unsolicited

solicitante *mf* applicant

solicitar *vt* (información, permiso) request,
ask for; (puesto, préstamo, acciones) apply
for; ~ **ofertas** invite tenders

solicitud *f* (petición) application; (formulario)
application form; **presentar una** ~
submit an application; **rechazar una** ~
reject an application; **rellenar una** ~ fill
in an application form; ~ **admisible**
admissible claim; ~ **de cheque** cheque
requisition BrE, check requisition AmE; ~
de cotización (Bolsa) application for
listing; ~ **de empleo** job application; ~
de exención bill of sufferance; ~ **de**

fondos application for funds; ~ **de préstamo** loan application

solidariamente *adv* jointly, mutually

solidaridad *f* solidarity; (**Der**) joint and several liability; **en** ~ **con** in support of, in solidarity with

solidario *adj* (obligación) mutually binding; (participante) jointly and severally liable

solidez *f* (de mercado, acciones) firmness; (financiera) soundness

sólido *adj* (argumento) solid, sound

solución *f* solution; **buscar/encontrar una** ~ look for/find a solution; **la** ~ **a todos sus problemas** the solution *o* answer to all their problems; ~ **alternativa** alternative solution; ~ **de compromiso** compromise solution; ~ **de e-commerce** e-commerce solution; ~ **improvisada** makeshift solution; ~ **llaves en mano** turnkey solution

solucionar *vt* (problema) solve; (conflicto, asunto) resolve, settle, sort out

solvencia *f* solvency; ~ **crediticia** credit scoring

solventar *vt* (gastos) pay; (cuenta, deuda) settle; (reclamación) adjust

solvente *adj* solvent

sombreado *m* (en ilustración) shading

someter *vt* submit; ~ **algo a algo** (exponer) subject sth to sth; (buscar aprobación) submit sth to sth; ~ **algo a votación** put sth to the vote; ~ **un producto a pruebas de calidad** put a product through quality control tests

sondear *vt* sound out; (**Pol**) canvass; (mercado) test

sondeo *m* survey, poll; ~ **de opinión** opinion poll

sonido *m* sound

sonoemisión *f* noise emission

sopesar *vt* weigh up; ~ **los pros y los contras** weigh up the pros and cons

soportar *vt* (carga, responsabilidad) bear; (pérdida, daño) sustain

soporte *m* (**Info**) medium; ~ **de comunicación** communications medium; ~ **de datos** data carrier; ~ **físico** hardware; ~ **lógico** software; ~ **de navegación** (**Info**) navigation aid; ~ **de producto** product support; ~ **publicitario** advertising medium

sostén *m* (de dependiente) support

sostener *vt* (sustentar) support; (mercado) hold; (gastos, objetivos) meet; (pérdidas) sustain; (opinar) maintain; **siempre ha**

sostenido que... he has always maintained that...

spam *m* (en correo electrónico) spam, bulk e-mail

spammer *mf* (en correo electrónico) spammer

spot *m* ad, advert

S.R.L. *abr* (▸**sociedad de responsabilidad limitada**) ≈ Ltd (limited company) BrE, ≈ Inc. (incorporated business company) AmE

stagflación *f* stagflation

stand *m* (en exposición) stand

stock *m* (**Bolsa**) stock

strip *m* (**Bolsa**) strip bond

suavizar *vt* (situación) ease, smooth over; (ley, régimen) relax; (tono) tone down

subactividad *f* subactivity

subagente *mf* subagent

subalterno *adj* subordinate

subarchivo *m* subfile

subarrendar *vt* sublet

subarrendatario, -a *m,f* subtenant

subarriendo *m* (acción) subletting; (acuerdo) sublease, sublet

subasta *f* auction; **sacar algo a** ~ put sth up for auction

subastar *vt* auction off; (contrato) put out to tender

subcapacidad *f* undercapacity

subcapitalizado *adj* undercapitalized

subcapítulo *m* subchapter

subclase *f* underclass

subcomité *m* subcommittee

subconcesión *f* sublicence BrE, sublicense AmE

subconjunto *m* subset

subcontratación *f* subcontracting, contracting out

subcontratar *vt* subcontract, contract out, farm out (infrml)

subcontratista *mf* subcontractor

subcontrato *m* subcontract

subcuenta *f* subsidiary account

subdirección *f* junior management

subdirector, a *m,f* assistant manager, deputy manager

subdirectorio *m* subdirectory

subdividido *adj* subdivided

subdivisión *f* subdivision

subempleado *adj* (persona) underemployed; (recursos) underused

subempleo *m* underemployment

subentrada *f* sub-entry

subestimación *f* (de acciones) undervaluation; ~ **de la renta** understatement of income

subestimar *vt* (acciones, bienes, propiedad) undervalue; (cantidad, capacidad) underestimate

subgerente *mf* assistant manager

subgrupo *m* subgroup

subida *f* (de precios) rise, increase

subinciso *m* subparagraph

subíndice *m* subscript

subinversión *f* underinvestment

subir ⟦1⟧ *vt* (precios) increase, raise, put up; (oferta) up (infrml); ~ **los tipos de interés** increase interest rates; **nos han subido muy poco este año** our salaries have gone up by very little this year ⟦2⟧ *vi* (aumentar) rise, go up; **ha subido el dólar con respecto al euro** the dollar has risen against the euro; ~ **a** come to

sublicencia *f* sublicence BrE, sublicense AmE

suboficina *f* suboffice

suboptimización *f* suboptimization

subordinado[1] *adj* subordinate

subordinado[2], **-a** *m,f* subordinate

subordinar *vt* subordinate; ~ **algo a algo** subordinate sth to sth

subproducción *f* underproduction

subproducto *m* byproduct, spinoff

subprograma *m* subprogram

subrayar *vt* (texto) underline; (recalcar) emphasize

subred *f* subnetwork; ~ **de gestión de jerarquía digital síncrona** Synchronous Digital Hierarchy Management Subnetwork, SMS

subrutina *f* subroutine; (Info) subprogram

subsecretario, -a *mf* undersecretary

subsector *m* subsector

subsidiado *adj* subsidized

subsidiar *vt* subsidize

subsidiaria *f* subsidiary; ~ **bancaria** bank subsidiary

subsidiario *adj* (compañía) subsidiary; (Bolsa) underlying; (Der) accessory

subsidio *m* subsidy, grant; (de seguridad social) benefit, allowance; ~ **de alojamiento** accommodation allowance, ≈ housing benefit BrE; ~ **de bienestar social** social security benefit BrE, welfare benefit AmE; ~ **de desempleo** unemployment benefit BrE, unemployment compensation AmE; ~ **de enfermedad** sickness benefit; ~

estatal state subsidy; ~ **a la exportación** export subsidy; ~ **familiar** family allowance; ~ **de huelga** strike pay; ~ **imponible** taxable alowance; ~ **por maternidad** maternity benefit; ~ **de la seguridad social** social security benefit BrE, welfare benefit AmE; ~ **transitorio** transitional relief

subsistencia *f* subsistence

subtítulo *m* sub-head

subtotal *m* subtotal

subvaloración *f* undervaluation

subvalorar *vt* undervalue

subvención *f* subsidy, grant; ~ **del gobierno** government grant

subvencionado *adj* subsidized; **no** ~ unsubsidized

subvencionar *vt* subsidize

subyacente *adj* underlying

sucedáneo *m* substitute

suceder ⟦1⟧ *vi* (ocurrir) happen; **lo peor que puede** ~ **es que...** the worst that can happen is that...; **suceda lo que suceda** come what may, whatever happens ⟦2⟧ *vt* (persona) succeed; **¿quién le** ~**á cuando se vaya?** who will succeed her when she goes?

sucesión *f* (serie) succession; (herencia) inheritance; **morir sin** ~ die without issue; ~ **vacante** estate in abeyance

sucesivo *adj* successive; **en lo** ~ in future; **gobiernos** ~**s** successive governments

suceso *m* event; (resultado) outcome; **de** ~ **arriesgado** touch and go

sucesor, a *m,f* successor

sucursal *f* branch; ~ **en el extranjero** overseas branch; ~ **principal** main branch

sueldo *m* salary, wage; **cobrar un buen** ~ earn a good salary; ~ **negociable** salary negotiable; ~ **base** basic pay BrE, base pay AmE; ~ **base más comisión** on-target earnings, OTE; ~ **y condiciones** pay and conditions; ~ **inicial** starting salary; ~ **neto** net salary *o* pay, take-home pay

suelo *m* floor; ~ **industrial** factory floor; ~ **de operaciones** dealing floor

suficiencia *f* aptitude; **prueba de** ~ aptutude test

sufragar ⟦1⟧ *vt* (costes) meet, defray ⟦2⟧ *vi* AmL vote

sufrir *vt* (consecuencias, daños) suffer; (cambio) undergo; ~ **una pérdida/un revés** suffer a loss/setback

sugerencia *f* suggestion; **hacer una ~** make a suggestion; **a ~ de alguien** at sb's suggestion

sugerir *vt* suggest; **~ hacer algo** suggest doing sth; **sugiero dejarlo para mañana** I suggest we leave it *o* I suggest leaving it until tomorrow; **~ que...** suggest that...; **me sugirió que lo consultara con un especialista** he suggested that I should consult a specialist about it

sujeción *f* (Inmob) binder AmE; **con ~ a las normas** subject to the regulations

sujeto *adj*: **~ a** subject to, liable to; **~ a aprobación** subject to approval; **~ al cambio** subject to change; **~ a gravamen** encumbered; **~ a hipoteca** subject to mortgage; **~ a impuesto** liable for tax

suma *f* addition; **en ~** in short; **~ y sigue** brought forward, carried down, carried forward; **~ de aportación** amount contributed; **~ asegurada** sum assured; **~ convenida** agreed sum; **~ invertida** amount invested; **~ de verificación** (Info) checksum

sumadora *f* adding machine

sumamente *adv* (gravado) heavily

sumar *vt* (cantidades) add up; (totalizar) add up to, come to

sumario *m* summary; **~ del proceso** summary of the proceedings

suministrar *vt* (información) supply; **~ bienes a crédito** supply goods on credit

suministro *m* supply; **~ de agua** water supply; **~ elástico** elastic supply; **~ de energía** energy supply; **~ de servicios** supply of services

superabundancia *f* superabundance

superadaptador videográfico *m* super video graphics adaptor, SVGA

superar *vt* (obstáculo) overcome; (demanda, expectativas) exceed; **las ventas ~on todas las expectativas** sales exceeded all expectations; **~ a los competidores** beat *o* outperform the competition

superávit *m* surplus; **~ acumulado** accumulated surplus; **~ de la balanza comercial** trade surplus; **~ de capital** capital surplus; **~ presupuestario** budget surplus

supercapacidad *f* overcapacity

supercomputadora *f* AmL (*cf* ▶**superordenador** Esp) supercomputer

superestructura *f* superstructure

superficie *f* surface; **~ habitable** floor space

superior¹ *adj* (producto) upmarket, superior

superior² *mf* superior

supermercado *m* supermarket; **~ financiero** financial supermarket

superneutralidad *f* superneutrality

supernumerario, -a *m,f* supernumerary

superordenador *m* Esp (*cf* ▶**supercomputadora** AmL) supercomputer

superposición *f* overlap

superpotencia *f* superpower

superproducción *f* overproduction

superutilización *f* overuse

supervisar *vt* supervise, oversee

supervisión *f* supervision; **de ~** supervisory; **~ del desempeño** performance monitoring; **~ del riesgo** risk monitoring

supervisor, a *m,f* supervisor, line manager

supervivencia *f* survivorship

suplantar *vt* supersede

suplementario *adj* supplementary, extra

suplemento *m* supplement; (Der) addendum; (tarifa) excess fare; **~ por habitación individual** single-room supplement

suplente *mf* (RRHH) stand-in, replacement; **~ interno(-a)** *mf* inplacement

súplica *f* (ruego) plea; (Der) petition

suplicar 1 *vt* (Der) petition, appeal to 2 *vi* plead

suplir *vt* (compensar) make up for

SUPR *abr* (▶**carácter de borrado**) DEL (delete character)

supra *adv* supra

supranacional *adj* supranational

supraorganización *f* supraorganization

supremacía *f* supremacy

supresión *f* (de controles, impuestos) abolition; (de noticias) suppression; (de párrafo) deletion; (de barreras, sanciones) lifting

suprimir *vt* (controles, impuestos) abolish; (noticias) suppress; (párrafo) delete, edit out; (barreras, sanciones) lift

surfear *vt* (Internet) surf

surtido *m* assortment, range; **~ de mercancías** range of goods

susceptible *adj* susceptible; ∼ **de diversas interpretaciones** open to several interpretations

suscitar *vt* (asunto) bring up; (dudas) raise; (sospechas, interés) arouse; (polémica, debate) provoke, cause

suscribir 1 *vt* (tratado, convenio) sign; (opinión) agree with, subscribe to; (préstamo) take out; ∼ **acciones** subscribe for shares; ∼ **una póliza de seguros** take out an insurance policy
2 *vi*: ∼ **a algo** subscribe to sth, take out a subscription to sth

suscribirse *v pron*: **suscribirse a algo** subscribe to sth, take out a subscription to sth

suscripción *f* subscription; (de tratado) signing; (de seguro) underwriting; ∼ **de acciones** subscription for shares; ∼ **anual** annual subscription

suscriptor, a *m,f* subscriber; (de seguros) underwriter

suscrito *adj* underwritten

susodicho *adj* above-mentioned

suspender *vt* suspend; (caso, reunión) adjourn; ∼ **el pago de un cheque** stop payment of a cheque BrE *o* check AmE

suspensión *f* suspension; (de caso, reunión) adjournment; ∼ **de la apelación** stay of appeal; ∼ **de arancel** duty suspension; ∼ **de cotización** delisting; ∼ **del negocio** stoppage of trade; ∼ **de operaciones** suspension of trading; ∼ **de pagos** bankruptcy protection; **solicitar la** ∼ **de pagos** file for bankruptcy protection

sustancia *f* substance; ∼ **contaminante** pollutant; ∼ **peligrosa** dangerous substance

sustitución *f* replacement, substitution; (de asientos) reversal

sustituir *vt* stand in for; (permanentemente) replace

sustituto, -a *m,f* (RRHH) stand-in; (permanente) replacement

SVGA *abr* (▸*conjunto de gráficos de supervídeo* Esp *or* supervídeo AmL) SVGA (super video graphics array)

swap *m* swap; ∼ **futuro** forward swap

Tt

T. *abr* (▶**tara**) t. (tare)

tabla *f* table; **acabar** *or* **quedar en** ∼**s** end in stalemate; ∼ **de consulta** (Info) lookup table

tablero *m* (Info) board; ∼ **de avisos** bulletin board AmE, noticeboard BrE; ∼ **de control** control panel; ∼ **de cotización** quotation board; ∼ **de dibujo** drawing board; (Info) plotting board; ∼ **de diseño** (publicidad) art board; ∼ **de distribución** switchboard

tablón *m* bulletin board AmE, noticeboard BrE; ∼ **de anuncios** Esp (*cf* ▶**cartelera** AmL) bulletin board, noticeboard BrE

tabulación *f* tabulation

tabulador *m* (Info) tab

tabular¹ *adj* tabular; **en forma** ∼ in tabular *o* table form

tabular² *vt* (Info) tab

TAC *abr* (▶**tasa anual compuesta**) CAR (compound annual rate)

tachar *vt* (escrito) cross out; (criticar) fault

táctica *f* tactic; **cambiar de** ∼ change tactics; ∼ **competitiva** competitive tactic; ∼ **dilatoria** delaying tactic; ∼ **publicitaria** advertising tactic

táctil *adj* (pantalla) touch-sensitive

TAE *abr* (▶**tasa anual equivalente**) effective annual rate of interest

talento *m* talent; **con** *or* **de** ∼ talented; **tener** ∼ **para algo** have a talent for sth, be good at sth; **no tiene** ∼ **para ese tipo de trabajo** he's not right for that sort of work; **no tiene** ∼ **para presentaciones** he doesn't have good presentation skills

talla *f* size; **de** ∼ **estándar** standard-size

taller *m* workshop

talón *m* (de cheque) stub; (cheque) cheque BrE, check AmE; (vale) chit; **depositar** *or* **ingresar un** ∼ Esp pay in a cheque BrE *o* check AmE

talonario *m* (de cheques) chequebook BrE, checkbook AmE; (de billetes) book; ∼ **de recibos** receipt book

tamaño *m* size; **de** ∼ **medio** medium-sized; **(de)** ∼ **carné** passport-size; ∼ **aleatorio** random size; ∼ **base** basic size; ∼ **económico** economy size

tambaleante *adj* (recuperación) shaky

tambor *m* barrel; (Info) drum

tampón *m* (para sellos) ink *o* stamp pad

tangible *adj* tangible; **bienes** ∼**s** tangible assets

tanteo *m* rough estimate, guesstimate (infrml)

tanto *m* certain amount, so much; **estar al** ∼ **de algo** be abreast of sth, know about sth; **poner a alguien al** ∼ **de algo** fill sb in on sth; **un** ∼ **porciento** a certain percentage

tapa *f* cover; **con** *or* **de** ∼ **dura** (libro) hardback

tapar *vt* (encubrir) cover up

taquigrafía *f* shorthand, stenography

taquigrafiar *vt* take down in shorthand

taquígrafo, -a *m,f* stenographer

taquilla *f* ticket office; (para espectáculos) box office; (recaudación) takings; **ser un éxito/fracaso de** ∼ be a box-office hit/flop; ∼ **de venta anticipada** advance booking office

taquimecanógrafo, -a *m,f* shorthand typist

tara *f* (peso) tare; (defecto) fault

tarea *f* task, undertaking; (Info) task; (por lote) job; ∼ **secundaria** (Info) background task

tarifa *f* (baremo, escala) rate; (de transporte) fare; (lista de precios) price list, tariff BrE; **pagar una** ∼ **reducida** pay a reduced fare; ∼**s** fees, honorarium (frml); (precios) prices; ∼ **de adulto** adult fare; ∼ **alta** peak rate; ∼ **económica** economy rate; (de vuelo) economy *o* cheap fare; ∼ **fija** flat-rate fee; ∼ **mínima** minimum charge; ∼ **de precios** price list, tariff BrE; ∼ **reducida** reduced fare; ∼ **de temporada** seasonal rate

tarjeta *f* card; **pagar con** ∼ pay by card; ∼ **bancaria** bank card; ∼ **de cajero bancario** *or* **automático** cashpoint card BrE, ATM card AmE, automated teller card AmE; ∼ **de caracteres** (Info) character card; ∼ **de cargo** charge card; ∼ **de cheque** check card AmE, cheque card BrE; ∼ **con chip** chip card; ∼ **comercial** business card; ∼ **de cobro automático** debit card; ∼ ⋯⋗

de crédito credit card; ~ **de crédito corporativa** corporate *o* company credit card; ~ **de débito** debit card; ~ **de desembarque** landing card; ~ **electrónica** e-card, electronic card; ~ **de embarque** boarding card; ~ **de emulación** emulation card; ~ **de expansión** expansion card; ~ **de expansión de memoria** memory expansion card; ~ **externa** add-on card; ~ **de fichar** time card; ~ **de gráficos** graphics card; ~ **de identificación** identity card; ~ **inteligente** smart card; ~ **de lealtad** loyalty card; (de supermercado) reward card; ~ **maestra** master card; ~ **magnética** magnetic card; ~ **magnética de acceso** swipe card; ~ **de memoria** memory card; ~ **multifilar** (Info) cage card; ~ **oro** gold card; ~ **de pedido** order card; ~ **perforada** punch card, punched card; ~ **prepagada** prepaid card; (para teléfono) phonecard; ~ **de presentación** business card; ~ **de respuesta comercial** business reply card; ~ **de servicio** (Info) service card; ~ **de sonido** sound card; ~ **telefónica** phonecard; ~ **VGA** VGA card; ~ **de vídeo** Esp *or* **video** AmL *f* video card; ~ **de visita** (business) card, visiting card BrE, calling card AmE

tasa *f* (índice) rate; (impuesto) tax, duty; ~ **a acordar** rate to be agreed; ~ **de adopción** adoption rate; ~ **anual** annual rate; ~ **bancaria** bank rate; ~ **base** base rate; ~ **de cambio al contado** spot rate; ~ **combinada** (de interés) blended rate; ~ **de comisión** commission rate; ~ **de compra** buyer's rate; ~ **compuesta** compound rate; ~ **de conversión** conversion rate; ~ **corriente** going rate; ~ **de crecimiento** growth rate; ~ **de crecimiento compuesto** compound growth rate; ~ **de crecimiento prevista** anticipated growth rate; ~ **de depreciación** rate of depreciation; ~ **de descuento** discount rate BrE, discount window AmE; ~ **de desempleo** unemployment rate; ~ **de desgaste** attrition rate; ~ **de devolución** rate of return; ~ **de empresa preferencial** prime business rate; ~ **de error** error rate; ~ **de financiación** financing rate; ~ **flotante** floating rate; ~ **hipotecaria** mortgage rate; ~ **de incremento** rate of increase; ~ **de inflación** rate of inflation, inflation rate; ~ **de interés** rate of interest, interest rate; ~ **de**

interés acumulado accumulated rate of interest, accrued interest rate; ~ **de interés flotante** floating interest rate; ~ **de interés preferencial** preferential interest rate, prime rate; ~ **de interés variable** variable interest rate; ~ **interna de descuento** internal rate of discount; ~ **de letras de cambio** bill rate; ~ **máxima** maximum rate; (Fin) ceiling rate; ~ **media** average rate; **media ponderada** average weighted rate; ~ **mínima** minimum rate; (de futuros) floor rate; ~ **de mortalidad** mortality rate; ~ **de natalidad** birth rate; ~ **nominal de interés** nominal interest rate; ~ **de porcentaje anual** annualized percentage rate; ~ **preferencial** preferential rate; ~ **de préstamo variable** variable lending rate; ~ **de préstamos** borrowing rate; ~ **de prima** premium rate; ~ **prorrateada** proration rate; ~ **de recompra** repurchase rate; ~ **de rendimiento** *or* **rentabilidad** rate of return; ~ **de rotación de personal** turnover rate; ~ **variable** variable rate

tasación *f* (de acciones) valuation; (de propiedades) appreciation; ~ **excesiva** overvaluation

tasador, a *m,f* appraiser; (Seg) adjuster; ~ **de Hacienda** tax assessor; ~ **de pérdidas** (seguros) loss adjuster

tasar *vt* (bienes) value; (fijar el precio de) fix the price of

TAV *abr* (▶**Tren de Alta Velocidad**) ≈ HST (high-speed train)

techo *m* ceiling; (de tipo de interés) cap; ~ **de crédito** credit ceiling

tecla *f* key; ~ **activación** hot key; ~ **alt** Alt key; ~ **de ayuda** help key; ~ **de barra inversa** backslash key; ~ **de comando** command key; ~ **de contacto** touch key; ~ **CTRL** control key; ~ **de función** function key; ~ **maestra** master key; ~ **de mando** control key; ~ **de mayúsculas** shift key

teclado *m* keyboard; ~ **de entrada** input keyboard; ~ **en función programable** soft keyboard; ~ **numérico** numeric keypad; ~ **personalizado** customized keyboard; ~ **QWERTY** QWERTY keyboard; ~ **táctil** tactile keyboard

teclear *vt* key in; (tecla) press; (botón del ratón) click

técnica *f* technique; (tecnología) technology; (habilidad) skill; ~ **de**

búsqueda push technology; ∼ **de comunicación** communication skill; ∼ **de extracción** pull technology; ∼ **de fabricación** process engineering; ∼ **interpersonal** interpersonal skill; ∼ **de producción** production technique; ∼ **de las relaciones humanas** human engineering; ∼ **de secretariado** secretarial skill; ∼ **de subasta** bidding technique; ∼ **de ventas** sales technique

tecnicidad *f* technicality

técnico[1] *adj* technical; **poco** ∼ low-tech

técnico[2], **-a** *m,f* engineer; (experto) expert, specialist; ∼ **asesor(a)** *m,f* consulting engineer; ∼ **electrónico(-a)** *m,f* electronics *o* electronic engineer; ∼ **informático(-a)** *m,f* computer specialist

tecnocracia *f* technocracy

tecnócrata *mf* technocrat

tecnocrático *adj* technocratic

tecnoestructura *f* technostructure

tecnófobo, -a *m,f* technophobe

tecnología *f* technology; ∼ **de alimentos** food technology; ∼ **alternativa** alternative technology; ∼ **avanzada** advanced technology; ∼ **de la comunicación** communications *o* communication technology; ∼ **flexible** soft technology; ∼ **informática** computer *o* information technology; ∼ **limpia** clean technology; ∼ **nueva** new technology; ∼ **de oficina** office technology; ∼ **PAL/SECAM** PAL/SECAM technology; ∼ **punta** state-of-the-art technology; ∼ **transferible** transferable technology; ∼ **WAP** WAP technology

tecnológicamente technologically; ∼ **avanzado** technologically advanced

Telaraña *f* Web, Net; ∼ **mundial** World Wide Web, WWW

telebanca *f* telebanking

telecom *m* telecoms

telecompra *f* teleshopping

telecomunicaciones *f pl* telecommunications; ∼ **por satélite** satellite communications

teleconferencia *f* (proceso) teleconferencing; (conferencia) teleconference; ∼ **por computadora** AmL *or* **ordenador** Esp *f* computer conferencing

telecopiadora *f* telewriter

teléf. *abr* (▶**teléfono**) tel. (telephone)

telefonía *f* telephony; ∼ **por Internet** Internet telephony; ∼ **móvil** mobile telephony

telefónico *adj* telephone; **llamada telefónica** telephone call

telefonista *mf* telephone operator, switchboard operator

teléfono *m* telephone; (número) telephone number; **colgar el** ∼ hang up; **constestar al** ∼ *or* **coger el** ∼ answer the phone; **darle el** ∼ **a alguien** give sb one's phone number; **estar al** ∼ **con alguien** be on the phone to sb; **hablar por** ∼ **con alguien** speak to sb on the phone; **llamar por** ∼ phone, call; **por** ∼ by phone; **tener** ∼ have a phone, be on the phone BrE; ∼ **de botones** push-button telephone; ∼ **celular** mobile phone BrE, cellphone AmE; ∼ **Internet** Internet phone, Web phone; ∼ **móvil** mobile phone BrE, cellphone AmE; ∼ **de pago** pay phone BrE, pay station AmE; ∼ **portátil** portable phone; ∼ **público** public telephone; ∼ **con** *or* **de teclado** touch-tone phone; ∼ **WAP** WAP phone

telegrafiar *vt* telegraph

telegrama *m* telegram

teleimpresión *f* remote printing

teleimpresora *f* teleprinter

teleinformática *f* computer communication

telemando *m* remote control

telemarketing, telemárketing *m* telemarketing

telemática *f* telematics

telemercado *m* telemarketing

telepago *m* remote payment, telepayment, electronic payment

telepedido *m* (pedido) teleorder; (acción) teleordering

teleproceso *m* teleprocessing

telepromoción *m* infomercial

teleregistro *m* telerecording

telesondeo *m* telecanvassing

telespectadores *m pl* television audience, viewers

teletexto *m* teletext

teletrabajador, a *m,f* teleworker

teletrabajo *m* telework, teleworking

teletranscripción *f* telewriting

teletranscriptor *m* telex machine

televentas *f pl* telesales

televisión *f* television; **por** ∼ on television; **salir en** *or* **por la** ∼ be on television; **ver la** ∼ watch television; ∼ **por abonadas** subscription television; ⸱⸱⸱⟩

∼ **de alta definición** high-definition television; ∼ **por cable** cable television; ∼ **a la carta** pay-per-view TV, PPV; ∼ **en circuito cerrado** closed-circuit television; ∼ **comercial** commercial television; ∼ **patrocinada** sponsored television; ∼ **por satélite** satellite television; ∼ **privada de pago** pay-per-view TV

telón *m* curtain; ∼ **de bambú** bamboo curtain; ∼ **de fondo** (de una situación) background

tema *m* (asunto) subject, matter; (motivo) theme; **discutir un** ∼ discuss a matter; **sacar un** ∼ bring a subject up; **salirse del** ∼ digress, get sidetracked; ∼**s medioambientales** environmental issues; ∼ **musical** theme tune; ∼ **publicitario** advertising theme

temperatura *f* temperature; ∼ **ambiente** room temperature

temporada *f* season; **fuera de** ∼ off season, out of season; **de** ∼ **baja** off-peak; ∼ **alta** high season, peak season; ∼ **baja** low season, off season

temporero[1] *adj* temporary

temporero[2], **-a** *m,f* casual worker; (en oficina) temp., temporary worker

tendencia *f* tendency; (moda) trend; ∼ **a algo** trend towards BrE *o* toward AmE sth; **tener** ∼ **a hacer algo** have a tendency to do sth; ∼ **al alza** bullish tendency, upward trend; ∼ **a la baja** bearish tendency, downward trend; ∼ **comercial** business trend; ∼ **de las compras** purchasing pattern; ∼ **de consumo** consumer trend; ∼ **declinante** downtrend; ∼ **del mercado** market trend; ∼**s políticas** political tendencies *o* leanings; ∼ **subyacente** underlying trend

tender *vi*: ∼ **a** tend towards BrE *o* toward AmE; ∼ **a hacer algo** tend to do sth; **la economía tiende a recuperarse** the economy is showing signs of recovery, the economy is on an upward trend

tendero, -a *m,f* shopkeeper BrE, storekeeper AmE

tenedor, a *m,f* (Banca) bearer; (Bolsa) holder; ∼ **de libros** bookkeeper; ∼ **de una opción** option holder; ∼ **de seguro** policyholder; ∼ **de títulos** security holder

teneduría de libros *f* bookkeeping

tenencia *f* holding; ∼ **de bonos** bond holding; ∼ **por el propietario** owner

occupation; ∼ **de valores** security holding

tensión *f* (de una situación) tension; (estrés) stress

tenso *adj* (situación) tense; (relaciones) strained

teorema *m* theorem

teoría *f* theory; **en** ∼ in theory; ∼ **del camino crítico** critical path theory; ∼ **del caos** chaos theory; ∼ **de la probabilidad** probability theory

teórico *adj* theoretical

tercero[1] *adj* third; **tercera edad** the third age; (personas) senior citizens; **Tercer Mundo** Third World

tercero[2], **-a** *m,f* third party; ∼ **de confianza** trusted third party

terminación *f* completion

terminado *adj* finished

terminal[1] *m* (Info) (de aviones) terminal; ∼ **de aplicaciones** applications terminal; ∼ **básico** dumb terminal; ∼ **de computadora** AmL (*cf* ▸**terminal de ordenador** Esp) computer terminal; ∼ **de información** report terminal; ∼ **inteligente** intelligent terminal, smart terminal; ∼ **mudo** *or* **no inteligente** dumb terminal; ∼ **de ordenador** Esp (*cf* ▸**terminal de computadora** AmL) computer terminal; ∼ **de pago electrónico** electronic payment terminal; ∼ **con pantalla de visualización** visual display terminal AmE, visual display unit BrE; ∼ **en punto de venta** point-of-sale terminal; ∼ **de representación gráfica** graphic display terminal; ∼ **de vídeo** Esp *or* **video** AmL video terminal

terminal[2] *f* (de aviones) terminal; (de autobuses) terminus; ∼ **de carga** freight terminal; ∼ **de pasajeros** passenger terminal

terminar [1] *vt* finish; ∼ **la comunicación** (Info) log out; ∼ **su alegato** rest one's case [2] *vi* end

término *m* (palabra) term; (final) end; (posición) place, position; ∼**s** (condiciones) terms; **en los mismos** ∼**s** in the same terms, on equal terms; **en primer/ segundo** ∼ firstly/secondly; **en** ∼**s absolutos** in absolute terms; **en** ∼**s generales** generally speaking; **en** ∼**s relativos** in relative terms; **llevar algo a buen** ∼ bring sth to a successful conclusion; **poner** ∼ **a algo** put an end to sth; **por** ∼ **medio** at an average; **según los** ∼**s del contrato** under the

terms of the contract; ~ **explícito** or
expreso (de contrato) express term; ~
implícito (de contrato) implied term; ~**s**
del intercambio terms of trade; ~
medio happy medium

terminología f terminology

terrateniente mf landowner

terreno m land; (lote) plot BrE, lot AmE;
~ **de abono** dumping ground; ~
agrícola agricultural land; ~**s,**
viviendas y herencias land, tenements
and hereditaments

terrestre adj (transportes, comunicaciones)
land, terrestrial; (transmisión) terrestrial

territorio m territory; ~ **de ventas**
sales territory

terrorismo m terrorism

tesis f (opinión) view, theory; (trabajo)
thesis

tesorería f (activo disponible) liquid assets

tesorero, -a m,f treasurer

Tesoro m Treasury, Exchequer BrE

test m test; ~ **de respuesta** recall test

testaferro m dummy

testamento m will, last will and
testament

testificación f attestation

testificar vi testify, give evidence

testigo m witness; ~ **de cargo**
witness for the prosecution; ~ **de**
descargo or **de la defensa** witness for
the defence BrE o defense AmE; ~ **ocular**
eye witness; ~ **pericial** expert witness

testimonio m testimony; **dar** ~
testify; **en** ~ **de algo** as proof of sth; **en**
~ **de lo cual** (Der) in witness whereof;
~ **contradictorio** conflicting evidence;
~ **falso** false testimony; ~ **irrefutable**
irrefutable evidence

tetrapak® m Tetra Pak®

texto m text; (mensaje por móvil) text
message, text; **enviarle un** ~ **a alguien**
text sb; ~ **completo** text in full; ~
publicitario advertising copy; ~ **sms**
text message

tiburón m raider; ~ **corporativo**
corporate raider

tiempo m time; **a** ~ on time; **a** ~
completo/parcial full-time/part-time;
con ~ in good time; **con** ~ **de sobra**
with time to spare; **el** ~ **apremia** time is
pressing; **el** ~ **es oro** time is money; **en**
un ~ **determinado** at a given time; **en**
un ~ **futuro** some time in the future;
llevar mucho ~ take a long time; **tener/**
no tener ~ have/not have time; ~ **de**
acceso access time; ~ **de acceso**

múltiple multiple access time; ~ **de**
antena airtime; ~ **de audiencia**
primaria prime listening time; ~
compartido time-sharing; ~ **de**
conexión connection time; ~ **de**
contacto personal face time; ~
disponible available time; ~ **de**
ejecución operation time; (Info)
execution time; ~ **de emisión** airtime;
~ **de espera** waiting time; ~ **inactivo**
(Info) downtime, idle time; ~ **libre** free
time, time off; ~ **de operación** uptime;
~ **previsto de llegada** estimated time
of arrival, ETA; ~ **de proceso** run
time; ~ **productivo** uptime; ~ **real** real
time; **en** ~ **real** in real time; ~ **de**
recuperación retrieval time; ~
transcurrido elapsed time

tienda f shop BrE, store AmE; ~ **de**
autoservicio self-service shop BrE, self-
service store AmE; ~ **de barrio** local
shop BrE, corner shop BrE, neighborhood
store AmE; ~ **de una cadena**
chainstore; ~ **de descuento** discount
house AmE, discount store; ~
franquiciada franchise; ~ **insignia**
flagship store; ~ **libre de impuestos**
duty-free shop; ~ **en línea** or **on-line**
online shop BrE o store AmE, Web shop
BrE o store AmE; ~ **de venta al público**
retail outlet; ~ **virtual** virtual store

tierra f land; ~ **baldía** waste land; ~**s**
sin titular land in abeyance

timador, a m,f confidence trickster,
con artist (infrml)

timbre m (para llamar) bell; (sello fiscal)
fiscal stamp; ~ **postal** postmark

timo m confidence trick BrE, confidence
game AmE

típicamente adv typically

típico adj typical

tipificación f (de productos)
standardization

tipificar vt (clasificar) classify, categorize;
(producto) standardize; (ser representativo de)
typify

tipo m type, sort, kind; (de cambio) rate;
(en imprenta) typeface; **a un** ~ **actual** at a
current rate; **a un** ~ **anual** at an annual
rate; **ser** ~ **cero para el IVA** be zero-
rated for VAT; ~ **de cambio** exchange
rate, rate of exchange; ~ **combinado**
composite rate; ~ **competitivo**
competitive rate; ~ **concedido**
concessionary rate; ~ **de depreciación**
rate of depreciation; ~ **fijo** flat rate; ~
fijo de cambio pegged exchange rate; ~
flotante (de cambio) floating rate; ~ ⋯▸

impositivo tax rate; ~ **del impuesto sobre la renta** income tax rate; ~ **de interés** interest rate; ~ **máximo** ceiling rate; ~ **mínimo** floor rate; ~ **negrita** bold type; ~ **preferencial** preferential rate; ~ **preferencial para préstamos** prime lending rate

tipografía *f* typography

tipología *f* typology

tira *f* strip; ~ **de película** film strip; ~ **posterior** backstrip; ~ **de rasgado** tear strip

tirada *f* print run; **de una** ~ in one go; **tener una gran** ~ have a large circulation; ~ **controlada** controlled circulation; ~ **total** gross circulation

tirón *m* pull; ~ **de los precios** pull of prices

titulación *f* qualifications; **se exige** ~ **universitaria** must be a graduate, graduate required

titular[1] *mf* (de pasaporte, de puesto de trabajo) holder; (de patente) owner; ~ **del cargo** incumbent; ~ **de una cuenta** account holder; ~ **de derechos** rights holder; ~ **de una licencia** licence holder BrE, license holder AmE; ~ **de tarjeta** cardholder

titular[2] *m* (de periódico) headline; ~ **en bandera** streamer; ~ **sensacionalista** screamline

titularidad *f* ownership; ~ **de acciones** share ownership, stock ownership

titulizar *vt* securitize

título *m* (de libro) title; (encabezamiento) heading; (Fin) security; (Bolsa) bond; (académico) degree, qualification; **a** ~ **de advertencia** by way of warning; **a** ~ **de ensayo** on approval; **a** ~ **honorífico** in an honorary capacity; **a** ~ **informativo** for your information; **a** ~ **personal** in a private capacity; ~**s acreditativos** (Inmob) muniments of title; ~ **cotizado** listed security, quoted security; ~ **al portador** bearer security; ~ **de propiedad** (Inmob) title deed; ~**s valores** securities, shares

TLC *abr* (▸**Tratado de Libre Comercio**) NAFTA (North American Free Trade Agreement)

TM *abr* (▸**tiempo medio**) MT (mean time)

TNC *abr* (▸**corporación transnacional**) TNC (transnational corporation)

todólogo, -a *m,f* business generalist

tolerancia *f* tolerance

tolerante *adj* tolerant; ~ **a fallos** fault-tolerant

toma *f* (de datos) capture; (de película) shot; (secuencia) take; ~ **de datos** data capture; ~ **de decisiones** decision-making; ~ **de postura** stance

tomador, a *m,f* payee; ~ **de seguro** policyholder

tomar *vt* take; ~ **algo mal** take sth badly; ~ **algo en cuenta** take sth into consideration; ~ **una decisión** make *o* take a decision; ~ **forma** take shape; ~ **medidas** take measures; ~ **nota de algo** take account of sth; ~ **parte en algo** play a part in sth, take part in sth; ~ **partido por alguien** take sides with sb; ~ **posición** take a position; ~ **tiempo** take time; **me tomó todo el día** it took me all day

tonalidad *f* tone; ~ **de llamada** ringtone

tonalizador *m* (para fax, fotocopiadora) toner

tono *m* tone; **cambiar el** ~ **de algo** change the tone of sth; ~ **alcista** bullish tone; ~ **bajista** bearish tone; ~ **de llamada** ringtone; ~ **de marcar** dialling tone BrE, dial tone AmE; ~ **de ocupado** engaged tone BrE, busy signal AmE

tope *m* limit; (Fin) ceiling; **fecha** ~ deadline; **trabajar a** ~ work flat out

topógrafo, -a *m,f* surveyor

total[1] *adj* total

total[2] *m* total, total number; ~ **general** grand total; ~ **hasta la fecha** total to date

totalidad *f* totality; (de datos) completeness; **en su** ~ in its entirety

totalizador *m* totalizator BrE, pari-mutuel AmE

totalizar *vt* add up, total

totalmente *adv* totally, completely

toxicidad *f* toxicity

tóxico[1] *adj* toxic

tóxico[2] *m* toxin, poison

trabajador, a *m,f* worker; ~ **autónomo(-a)** *m,f* self-employed person, freelance worker; (utilizando medios electrónicos) e-lancer; ~ **clandestino(-a)** *m,f* moonlighter (infrml); ~ **del conocimiento** knowledge worker; ~ **por cuenta ajena** employee; ~ **por cuenta propia** self-employed person, freelance worker; ~ **a distancia** teleworker, telecommuter; ~ **diurno(-a)** *m,f* dayworker; ~ **domiciliario(-a)** *m,f*

t

homeworker; (para una compañía) outworker; ~ **fronterizo(-a)** *m,f* border worker; ~ **eventual** casual labourer BrE, casual laborer AmE; ~ **por horas** pieceworker; ~ **incapacitado(-a)** *m,f* disabled worker; ~ **independiente** self-employed person; ~ **inmigrante** immigrant worker; ~ **manual** manual worker; ~ **migratorio(-a)** *m,f* migrant worker; ~ **no declarado(-a)** *m,f* moonlighter (infrml); ~ **de oficina** office worker; ~ **semiespecializado(-a)** *m,f* semiskilled worker; ~ **social** social worker; ~ **de temporada** seasonal worker; ~ **a tiempo completo** full-time worker, full-timer; ~ **a tiempo parcial** part-time worker, part-timer; ~ **por turnos** shift worker

trabajar 1 *vi* work; ~ **en algo** work in sth; **trabaja en publicidad** she's in *o* she works in advertising; **¿en qué trabajas?** what do you do?; ~ **de algo** work as sth; ~ **como parte de un equipo** work as part of a team; ~ **por cuenta propia** be self-employed, work freelance; ~ **a destajo** (por pieza) do piecework; (mucho) work flat out; ~ **en estrecha colaboración con alguien** work closely with sb; ~ **horas extras** work overtime; ~ **para una compañía** work for a company; ~ **a pérdida** operate *o* run at a loss; ~ **en sociedad con alguien** work in partnership with sb; ~ **a tiempo completo/parcial** work full-time/part-time; ~ **por turnos** work shifts
2 *vt* (género, marca) handle; (máquina) operate; (tierra, cuero) work; **no trabajamos esa marca** we don't handle that brand

trabajo *m* work; (empleo) job; (tarea) task; (esfuerzo) effort; **buscar** ~ look for work *o* a job; **dar mucho** ~ be a lot of work *o* effort; **conseguir un** ~ get a job; **estar sin** ~ be out of work; **quedarse sin** ~ lose one's job; **me costó mucho** ~ it was a huge effort; **tener** ~ have a job; **tener mucho** ~ have a lot of work (on); ~ **agrícola** agricultural work; ~ **de asesor** consultancy work; ~ **atrasado** backlog of work; ~ **de baja categoría** menial work; ~ **bajo contrato** contract work; ~ **clandestino** moonlighting (infrml); ~ **compartido** job share; ~ **cualificado** skilled labour BrE, skilled labor AmE; ~ **por cuenta propia** self-employment; ~ **en curso** work-in-progress BrE, work-in-process AmE; ~ **a destajo** piecework; ~ **a distancia** (mediante teléfono, red) teleworking,

telecommuting; ~ **diurno** daywork; ~ **a domicilio** homeworking; (por red informática) telecommuting; ~ **en equipo** teamwork; ~ **eventual** casual labour BrE, casual labor AmE; ~ **fijo** steady *o* permanent job; ~ **manual** manual labour BrE, manual labor AmE; ~ **de medio tiempo** part-time work; ~ **nocturno** night work; ~ **ocasional** casual labour BrE, casual labor AmE, temporary work; ~ **de oficina** clerical work, office work; ~ **por pieza** Esp piecework; ~ **en proceso** work-in-progress BrE, work-in-process AmE; ~ **seguro** secure job; ~ **social** community job; ~ **temporal** temporary work; ~ **a tiempo completo/parcial** full-time/part-time job; ~ **por turnos** shift work; ~ **voluntario** voluntary work

trabajoadicto, -a *f* workaholic

tradición *f* tradition

tradicional *adj* traditional

traducción *f* translation; ~ **asistida por computadora** AmL *or* **ordenador** Esp computer-aided translation, computer-assisted translation; ~ **automática** machine-assisted translation; ~ **directa/inversa** *translation into/from one's native language*; ~ **simultánea** simultaneous translation

traducir *vt* translate

traductor, a *m,f* translator; ~ **jurado(-a)** *m,f* official *o* sworn translator

traficante *mf* trafficker

traficar *vi* trade; ~ **en** traffic in

tráfico *m* (en la Red) traffic; ~ **aéreo** air traffic; ~ **de drogas** drug trafficking, drug trade

trama *f* raster; ~ **gruesa** coarse screen

tramitación *f* processing; **los documentos necesarios para la** ~ **del visado** the necessary documents for processing the visa application

trámite *m* (de aplicación) processing; **en** ~ in the pipeline; ~ **de autorización** approval process; ~s **burocráticos** red tape; ~s **de cierre de ejercicio** year-end procedures

tramo *m* (de margen) leg; (impositivo, de precios) bracket; ~ **de crédito** credit tranche; ~ **de renta** income bracket

trampa *f* trap; ~ **del bienestar** welfare trap; ~ **de la pobreza** poverty trap

tranquilo *adj* (mercado, negocios) quiet

transacción f transaction; ~ **bancaria** bank transaction; ~ **comercial** business transaction; ~ **a cuenta** account transaction; ~ **electrónica segura** secure electronic transaction, SET; ~ **por Internet** Internet transaction; ~ **sin papel** paperless trading; ~ **con tarjeta de crédito** credit card transaction

transaccional adj transactional

transcodificador m transcoder

transcodificar vt transcode

transcribir vt transcribe

transcripción f transcription

transcurrir vi pass, elapse

transductor m transducer

transeúnte mf passer-by

transeuropeo adj transeuropean

transferencia f transfer; (Info) porting; ~ **automática** automatic transfer; ~ **bancaria** bank transfer; ~ **por cable** cable transfer; ~ **de compromiso** transfer of undertaking; ~ **de crédito** credit transfer; ~ **de fondos** funds transfer, transfer of funds; ~ **de fondos automática** automatic funds transfer; ~ **de fondos electrónica** electronic funds transfer; ~ **de informaciones** information transfer; ~ **de participación** share transfer; ~ **de tecnología** technology transfer

transferible adj (opciones) transferable; (programas) portable

transferidor, -a m,f transferor

transferir vt (fondos, dinero) transfer; (Info) port; ~ **por cable** transfer by cable

transformación f transformation, conversion

transformar vt transform, convert; ~ **algo en algo** transform o convert sth into sth

transfronterizo adj cross-border

transgénico adj genetically modified

transición f transition; **periodo de ~** transitional period

tránsito m transit; **en ~** in transit

transitorio adj (medida) provisional, temporary; (periodo) transitional

transmisibilidad f (de acciones nominales) transferability

transmisión f transmission; (Medios) broadcast; (Patent) assignment; ~ **en circuito** hookup; ~ **de datos** data transmission; ~ **electrónica de datos** electronic data transmission, EDT; ~ **en diferido** prerecorded broadcast; ~ **en directo** live broadcast; ~ **de dominio** transfer of ownership; ~ **multimedia continua** media streaming transmission; ~ **simultánea** (por radio y TV) simultaneous broadcast, simulcast; ~ **en tiempo real** real-time transmission; ~ **por vía satélite** satellite broadcasting

transmisor adj transmitting

transmitir vt transmit; (Inmob) assign; ~ **por la Red** webcast; ~ **por telecomunicaciones** telecommunicate

transnacional¹ adj transnational

transnacional² f transnational, multinational

transparencia f (de material) transparency; (claridad) openness; (de proyector) acetate, (overhead) transparency; **la ~ del gobierno** the government's policy of openness

transparente adj (dispositivo, red) transparent

transportabilidad f portability

transportable adj transportable

transportar vt transport

transporte m transport BrE, transportation AmE; ~ **público** public transport BrE, transportation AmE

transversal adj transverse

trasladar vt (cambiar de sitio) move; (empleado, oficina) relocate; (información) transfer; **trasladado a cuenta nueva** (balance de cuentas) carried forward

traslado m (de residencia) move; (de oficina, empleado) relocation; (de información) transfer; **gastos de ~** relocation expenses; ~ **de bloque** cut-and-paste operation

traspasar vt (negocio, poderes) transfer; (propiedad) assign; (local) sell; (arrendar) let, lease; ~ **al periodo anterior/futuro** carry back/forward

traspaso m transfer; (de acciones) delivery; (de propiedad, deudas) assignment; (de local) sale; (arrendamiento) letting, leasing; ~ **de propiedad** change of ownership

trasposición f (Der) transposal

trastienda f room at the back of a shop; (establecimientos) back office

trastornar vt shake up

tratado m (política) treaty, agreement; **firmar un ~** sign a treaty; ~ **comercial**, ~ **de comercio** trade agreement; **T~ de Libre Comercio** North American Free Trade Agreement; **T~ Monetario Europeo** European Monetary Agreement; **T~ de Roma** Treaty of

Rome; **T~ de la Unión Europea** European Union Treaty; **~ de paz** peace treaty

tratamiento *m* treatment; (Info) processing; **~ del agua** water treatment; **~ de datos** data processing; **~ de la imagen** image processing; **~ por lotes** batch processing; **~ de los residuos** waste treatment; **~ de textos** word processing

tratar ⓵ *vt* (tema) deal with, discuss; (Info) process; **~ a alguien** have dealings with sb; **no lo he tratado mucho todavía** I haven't had much to do with him yet; **~ a alguien de usted/tú** address sb formally/informally
⓶ *vi* try; **~ de hacer algo** try to do sth; **~ de** *o* **sobre algo** be about sth; **~ con alguien** deal with sb; **~ directamente con alguien** deal directly with sb; **~ en algo** deal in sth

trato *m* (acuerdo) deal; (relación) relations; (manera de ser) manner; (tratamiento) treatment; **hacer un ~** do a deal; **¡~ hecho!** (it's a) deal!; **cerrar un ~** close *o* clinch a deal; **~s** negotiations, dealings; **estar en ~s con alguien** be talking to sb, be in negotiations with sb; **ser de ~ agradable/desagradable** have a pleasant/an unpleasant manner; **tener poco ~ con alguien** not have much to do with sb; **~ comercial** business deal; **~ en firme** firm deal; **~ preferencial** preferential treatment; **darle un ~ preferencial a alguien** give sb preferential treatment

través: **a ~ de** *prep* through; **a ~ del sistema** across-the-network

travesía *f* (viaje) crossing; **~ por Internet** (Internet) surfing

trayecto *m* journey; **~ de ida/vuelta** outward/return journey

trayectoria *f* trajectory, path; **~ profesional** career

trazador *m* tracer; (Info) plotter; **~ de gráficos** graph plotter; **~ de tambor** drum plotter

trazar *vt* (gráfico) plot; (plan, proyecto) devise, draw up

tren *m* train; **T~ de Alta Velocidad** high-speed train; **~ de carga** goods train BrE, freight train AmE; **~ de cercanías** commuter train; **~ directo** through train; **~ de pasajeros** passenger train

trepar *vt* climb; **~ puestos** climb the ladder

TRI *abr* (▸**tasa de rendimiento interna**) IRR (internal rate of return)

triangular *adj* triangular

tribunal *m* court; **llevar algo/a alguien a los ~es** take sth/sb to court; **recurrir a los ~es** go to court; **el T~** the Bench; **~ de apelación** court of appeal; **~ de arbitraje** court of arbitration; **T~ Constitucional** Esp ≈ Employment Appeal Tribunal BrE; **~ de lo contencioso administrativo** court of claims *with jurisdiction in cases brought against the government*; **T~ Europeo** European Court; **T~ Europeo de Justicia** European Court of Justice; **~ federal** federal tribunal; **T~ de la Haya** Hague Tribunal; **T~ Internacional de Justicia** International Court of Justice; **~ judicial ordinario** court of law; **T~ de Justicia** Court of Justice; **~ de menores** juvenile court; **~ de primera instancia** court of first instance; **~ de quiebras** bankruptcy court; **~ de sucesiones** probate court; **T~ Supremo** High Court BrE, Supreme Court AmE

tributación *f* taxation; **~ directa/indirecta** direct/indirect taxation

tributo *m* (homenaje) tribute; (impuesto) tax; **rendir ~ a alguien** pay tribute to sb; **~ municipal** local tax

trimestral[1] *adj* quarterly

trimestral[2] *m* (prensa) quarterly

trimestralmente *adv* quarterly, every three months

trimestre *m* quarter; **pagar por ~s** pay quarterly; **~ fiscal** fiscal quarter; **segundo ~** second quarter

tripartismo *m* tripartism

triplicado *adj* triplicate; **por ~** in triplicate

triplicar *vt* triple; (precios, ventas) treble

tripulación *f* crew

triunfador, a *m,f* winner

triunfar *vi* succeed; (en la vida, profesión) be successful

triunfo *m* success

trocar *vt* barter

troica *f* (Pol) troika

tropiezo *m* (error) blunder; (contratiempo) setback, hitch; **sin ningún ~** without a hitch

truco *m* gimmick; **~ publicitario** publicity stunt, advertising gimmick

trueque *m* exchange; **a ~ de** in exchange for

truncamiento *m* truncation, shortening

truncar *vt* (acortar) truncate; (texto) cut, shorten; (planes) thwart

trust *m* trust

tumulto *m* turmoil; **∼s y agitaciones sociales** riots and civil commotions

túnel *m* tunnel; **T∼ del Canal de la Mancha** Channel Tunnel

turboeléctrico *adj* turbo-electric

turbulencias *f pl* (del mercado) ups and downs

Turespaña *f* Esp *Spanish tourist board*, ≈ English Tourist Board

turismo *m* tourism; **hacer ∼** travel, go on a sightseeing holiday; **∼ extranjero** overseas tourism; **∼ rural** rural tourism

turista *mf* tourist; **∼ extranjero(-a)** *m,f* overseas tourist

turno *m* (de trabajo) shift; (orden) turn; **estar de ∼** be on duty; **trabajar por ∼s** work shifts; **∼s alternos** alternating shifts; **∼ de día** day shift; **∼ de noche** night shift; **∼ de preguntas** question time; **∼ de relevo** relief shift; **∼ rotativo** rotating shift; **∼ vespertino** twilight shift

tutelar *vt* (intereses nacionales) protect

tutor, a *m,f* guardian

tutorial *m* tutorial; **∼ on-line** online training, online tutorial

TV *abr* (▸**televisión**) TV; **∼ digital interactiva** iDTV (interactive digital TV); **∼ privada de pago** pay-per-view TV

Uu

ubicación *f* location

UCP *abr* (▸**Unidad Central de Procesamiento**) CPU (Central Processing Unit)

UE *abr* (▸**Unión Europea**) EU (European Union)

UEPS *abr* (▸**último en entrar, primero en salir**) LIFO (last in, first out)

UIT *abr* (▸**Unión Internacional de Telecomunicaciones**) ITU (International Telecommunications Union)

último *adj* last; (más reciente) latest; ∼ **en entrar, primero en salir** last in, first out; **a última hora** at the last minute; **a ∼s de mes** at the end of the month; **de última hora** last-minute; **una reserva de última hora** a last-minute reservation; **en ∼ caso** as a last resort; **el ∼ modelo** the latest model; **por ∼** lastly; **última advertencia** final warning; **∼ día de operaciones** last day of trading; **última reclamación** final demand

ultramar *m*: **de ∼** overseas; (Banca) offshore

ultra-portátil *adj* ultraportable

umbral *m* threshold; **estar en los ∼es de algo** be on the verge of sth; **∼ impositivo** tax threshold; **∼ de pobreza** poverty line; **∼ de rentabilidad** break-even point

UME *abr* (▸**Unión Monetaria Europea**) EMU (European Monetary Union)

UMTS *abr* (▸**sistema universal de telecomunicaciones móviles**) UMTS (Universal Mobile Telecommunication System)

unánime *adj* (decisión) unanimous

unanimidad *f* unanimity; **por ∼** unanimously

UNED *abr* Esp (▸**Universidad Nacional de Educación a Distancia**) ≈ OU (Open University) BrE

UNICEF *abr* (▸**Agencia de las Naciones Unidas para la Ayuda a la Infancia**) UNICEF (United Nations Children's Fund)

único¹ *adj* only; (sin igual) unique

único², **-a** *m,f* only one; **es el ∼ que queda** it is the only one left

unidad *f* unit; **∼ central** mainframe computer; **∼ central de procesamiento** *or* **proceso** central processing unit; **∼ de discos** disk drive; **∼ de disco duro** hard disk drive; **∼ de disco flexible** floppy disk drive; **∼ de DVD** (en ordenador) DVD player, DVD drive; **∼ enchufable** plug-in; **∼ de escritorio** desktop unit; **∼ estratégica de negocio** strategic business unit; **∼ familiar** family unit; **∼ fiduciaria** trust unit; **∼ de impresión** print driver; **∼ monetaria** monetary unit; **∼ monetaria combinada** composite currency unit; **U∼ Monetaria Europea** (obs) European Currency Unit (obs); **∼ de negociación** bargaining unit; **∼ de negocios** business unit; **∼ de pantalla** screen driver; **∼es periféricas** peripherals; **∼ de ratón** mouse driver; **∼ de representación visual** visual display unit; **∼ salarial** wage unit; **∼ de tratamiento de entradas** entry processing unit; **∼ de venta** shop unit; **∼ de visualización** visual display unit BrE *o* terminal AmE; **∼ de visualización de vídeo** Esp *or* **video** AmL *f* visual display unit BrE, visual display terminal AmE

unidimensional *adj* unidimensional

unidireccional *adj* (transmisión) simplex

unificación *f* unification

unificar *vt* unify, unite

uniformar *vt* standardize

uniforme *adj* (criterios, precios, tarifas) uniform, standard; (Bolsa) flat

uniformidad *f* uniformity

unilateral *adj* unilateral

unilateralmente *adv* unilaterally

unión *f* union; (de empresas) merger; **con la ∼ de nuestros esfuerzos** by joining forces, by combining our efforts; **en ∼ con** in association with; **∼ aduanera** customs union; **∼ económica** economic union; **U∼ Económica y Monetaria** Economic and Monetary Union; **U∼ Europea** European Union; **U∼** ····⟩

Internacional de
Telecomunicaciones International
Telecommunications Union; **U~
Monetaria Europea** European
Monetary Union; **~ política** political
union; **~ de trabajadores** trade union
BrE, labor union AmE

unipersonal *adj* individual

unir *vt* unite; (atar) bind; (asociar)
combine; **~ fuerzas** join forces

universal *adj* universal; (mundial)
worldwide, world; **de fama ~** world
famous

universalismo *m* universalism

universalmente *adv* universally; **~
aceptado** universally accepted

universidad *f* university; **U~
Nacional de Educación a Distancia**
Esp ≈ Open University BrE

universo *m* universe

uñero *m* thumb index

urbanismo *m* town planning, urban
planning

urbanista *mf* town planner, urban
planner

urbanización *f* (proceso) urbanization;
(barrio) housing development

urbanizar *vt* urbanize, develop

urbano *adj* urban, town, city

urgencia *f* urgency; (caso urgente)
emergency; **con ~** urgently; **de ~**
urgent; **en caso de ~** in case of
emergency

urgente *adj* urgent; (servicio) express

URL *abr* (*localizador uniforme de
recursos*) URL (Uniform Resource
Locator)

urna *f* ballot box; **acudir a las ~s** go to
the polls; **~ electoral** ballot box

usar *vt* use; **fácil de ~** easy to use; **de
~ y tirar** disposable; **~ algo/a alguien
de** *or* **como algo** use sth/sb as sth;

quieren **~me de testigo** they want to
use me as a witness

USB *abr* (*bus serial universal*) USB
(Universal Serial Bus)

uso *m* use; (costumbre) custom; **estar en
~** be in use; **de ~ común** in common
use *o* usage; **de ~ fácil** user-friendly,
easy to use; **hacer ~ pleno de** make full
use of; **fuera de ~** not in use; (averiado)
out of order; **hacer ~ de algo** make use
of sth; **hacer ~ de un derecho** exercise
a right; **sólo para ~ interno** for office
use only; **~ y desgaste** wear and tear;
~ alternativo alternative use; **~
anterior** prior use; **~ compartido de
datos** data sharing; **~s de compra**
buying habits; **~s y costumbres**
custom and practice; **~ del Internet**
Internet use; **~ público** public use

usuario, -a *m,f* user; **~ continuo(-a)**
m,f heavy user; **~ final** end user; **~ de
Internet** Internet user; **~ potencial**
potential user; **~ registrado(-a)** *m,f*
registered user; **~ de terminal** terminal
user; **~ WAP** WAP user

usufructo *m* usufruct; **con derecho a
~** beneficially interested; **~ vitalicio de
algo** life interest in sth

usufructuador, a *m,f* usufructuary

usufructuario, -a *m,f* usufructuary

usura *f* usury

usurario *adj* usurious

usurero, -a *m,f* usurer

usurpar *vt* (poder) usurp; (fondos)
misappropriate; (tierras) seize

utilidad *f* usefulness; **~es** profit; **de
gran ~** very useful

utilitarismo *m* utilitarianism

utilización *f* use, utilization (frml); **~
en común de ficheros** file sharing

utilizar *vt* use, utilize (frml)

utillaje *m* tools, equipment

vacación *f*, **vacaciones** *f pl* holiday BrE, vacation AmE; **estar de vacaciones** be on holiday BrE *o* vacation AmE; **cogerse vacaciones** take time off; **ir de vacaciones** go on holiday BrE *o* vacation AmE; **vacaciones anuales** annual leave; **vacaciones pagadas** *or* **retribuidas** paid holiday BrE, paid vacation AmE

vacante¹ *adj* vacant; (puesto) unfilled

vacante² *f* vacancy, job opening; ~ **no cubierta** unfilled vacancy

vaciado *m* (Info) dump; ~ **de memoria** memory dump; ~ **de pantalla** screen dump

vaciar *vt* empty; (Info) dump

vacilación *f* hesitation; (transacción bursátil) halt

vacilar *vi* hesitate, falter; **sin** ~ without hesitating *o* hesitation; ~ **en hacer algo** hesitate to do sth; **vacilaba entre aceptar o no** she couldn't decide whether to accept or not

vacío¹ *adj* empty; (local) vacant

vacío² *m* vacuum; (espacio) gap; **envasado al** ~ vacuum-packed; ~ **de comunicación** communication gap; ~ **legal** loophole; ~ **tecnológico** technological gap

vacunación *f* vaccination

vagón *m* carriage BrE, car AmE, coach

vaivén *m* (de gente) toing and froing; **vaivenes** *m pl* ups and downs; (del mercado) swings

vale *m* (cupón) voucher; (recibo) receipt; (Fin) promissory note; ~ **canjeable** dealing slip, voucher; ~ **de comida** luncheon voucher BrE, LV BrE, meal ticket AmE; ~ **de descuento** discount voucher; (para una compra) money-off coupon; ~ **electrónico** virtual coupon; ~ **de regalo** gift voucher *o* token *o* certificate AmE

valer 1 *vt* (costar) cost; (tener valor) be worth; **¿cuánto** *or* **qué vale?** how much is it?; **vale 20.000 euros** it costs 20,000 euros; ~ **la pena** be worthwhile; ~ **un potosí** be worth a mint
2 *vi* (costar) cost; (pasaporte, documento) be valid; (moneda) be legal tender; **hacer** ~ **un argumento** get a point across; **hizo** ~

sus derechos she asserted her rights; **más vale terminarlo hoy** it would be better to finish it today; **más vale que no se enteren** they'd better not find out; **no** ~ **para nada** be useless; **ese documento no vale para nada** that document is useless *o* isn't worth anything; ~ **mucho** be very expensive, cost a lot; (tener valía) be excellent; ~ **poco** be cheap, not cost very much; (no tener valía) not be very good

valía *f* worth; **de gran** ~ (personal) high-calibre BrE, high-caliber AmE

validación *f* validation

validar *vt* validate

validez *f* validity; **dar** ~ **a algo** validate sth; ~ **legal** legal force

válido *adj* (argumento) valid; ~ **hasta** valid until

valija *f* (correspondencia) mail AmE, post BrE; ~ **diplomática** diplomatic bag BrE, diplomatic pouch AmE

valla publicitaria *f* billboard AmE, hoarding BrE

valor *m* value; (validez) validity; ~**es** securities, stocks; **con** ~ **agregado** *or* **añadido** Esp added-value; **no tener** ~ not be valid; **por encima del** ~ **nominal** (Bolsa) above par; **por** ~ **de** to the value of; **sin** ~ worthless; **sin** ~ **comercial** no commercial value; **sin** ~ **nominal** *or* **a la par** no-par value; **sin** ~ **en aduana** no customs value; ~ **de activo** asset value; ~ **actual** current value; ~ **de adquisición** acquisition value; ~ **agregado** added value; ~ **al vencimiento** maturity value; ~ **amortizado** amortized value, written-down value; ~ **añadido** added value; ~ **en bolsa** stock market value; ~ **de cambio** exchange value; ~ **capital** capital value; ~**es en cartera** holdings; ~ **por cobrar** receivable; ~ **comerciable** marketable value; ~ **comercial** commercial value; ~ **comercial actual** current market value; ~**es cotizados** listed *o* quoted securities; ~ **disponible** cash assets; ~ **en efectivo** cash value; ~ **estrella** leading share, blue-chip share; ~ **facial** face value; ~ **de factura** invoice value; ⋯⟩

~ imponible (de propiedad) rateable value BrE (obs), taxable value BrE, assessed valuation AmE; **~ en libros** book value; **~ de mercado** market value; **~ monetario** monetary value; **~ del negocio establecido** or **en funcionamiento** going-concern value; **~ neto** net value; **~es no cotizados** unlisted o unquoted securities; **~ nominal** par value, nominal value; **~ nominal común** common par value; **~ a la par** par value; **~ de rescate** redemption value; (de póliza) surrender value; **~ de rescate al contado** cash surrender value; **~ residual** salvage value; **~ de reventa** resale value; **~ de venta** sale value

valoración f valuation; (de personal) appraisal; (de situación) assessment; **en la más alta/baja ~** at the highest/lowest estimate; **~ de la actuación** (Fin) performance rating; **~ de la calidad** quality assessment; **~ excesiva** overvaluation; **~ de existencias** stock valuation; **~ de mercado** market valuation; **~ de proyecto** project assessment; **~ tributaria** income tax assessment

valorador, a m,f appraiser

valorar vt (tasar) value; (daños, pérdidas) assess; **estar valorado en** be valued at

valorización f (tasación) valuation, valorization; (de situación) assessment

valuación f (de gastos) appraisal; (de situación, proyecto) assessment; **~ de gastos de capital** capital expenditure appraisal

valuador, a m,f AmL appraiser; (Seg) adjuster

VAN abr (▶**valor de activo neto**) NAV (net asset value); (▶**valor actual neto**) NPV (net present value)

vanguardia f vanguard, leading edge; **estar** or **ir a la ~** be in the vanguard o at the cutting edge; **de ~** state-of-the-art, leading-edge

vanguardista adj state-of-the-art, leading-edge

variable¹ adj variable; **no ~** nonvariable

variable² f variable; **~ aleatoria** random variable; **~ booleana** Boolean variable

variación f (de renta, gasto) variation; (discrepancia) variance; **~ aleatoria** random variation; **~ del coste** Esp or **costo** AmL cost variance; **~ estacional** seasonal variation; **~ del precio** price

variance; **~ presupuestaria** budget variance

variante f variant

varianza f variance; **~ de tipo** rate variance

variar vi vary; **~ según** vary according to; **el precio varía según la temporada** the price varies according to the season; **~ de precio** vary in price

vario adj (variado, diverso) varied; **~s** several, various

varios m pl sundries; (en hoja de balance) miscellaneous

vecindario m neighbourhood BrE, neighborhood AmE

vector m vector

vehículo m vehicle; **~ publicitario** advertising o media vehicle

velocidad f speed, velocity; (paso) rate, pace; **~ de arrastre** feed rate; **~ de cálculo** computing speed; **~ de impresión** printing speed; **~ mecanográfica** typing speed; **~ de regeneración** refresh rate; **~ de reloj** clock rate; **~ de transferencia** transfer rate; **~ de transferencia de bitios** bit rate

vencer vi (plazo, documento) expire; (pago) be due; (inversión) mature; (ganar) win; **el plazo para entregar el trabajo vence el 25** the deadline for returning the work is the 25th; **el viernes vence el plazo para la entrega de las solicitudes** Friday is the closing date for (submitting) applications; **¿cuándo vence la garantía?** when does the guarantee run out o expire?; **el pago del préstamo vence a final de mes** repayment of the loan is due at the end of the month

vencido adj (plazo, documento) expired; (pago, interés) due, payable; (inversión) matured; (persona) beaten; **tenía la visa vencida** her visa had run out o expired; **~ e impagado** due and unpaid; **darse por ~** give in o up; **pagar/cobrar a mes vencido** pay/get paid a month in arrears

vencimiento m (caducidad) expiry BrE, expiration AmE; (de préstamo) term; (de pago) due date; (de inversión) maturity; **al ~** at due date; **antes del ~** before maturity; **~ a fecha fija** fixed maturity

vendedor, a m,f salesperson; (m) salesman; (f) saleswoman; **~ al descubierto** short seller; **~ ambulante** pedlar BrE, huckster AmE; **~ callejero(-a)** m,f street vendor AmE, street trader BrE; **~ a comisión** commission salesman; **~ a domicilio** door-to-door salesman; ∼ **robotizado(-a)** *m,f* robot salesperson; ∼ **de televentas** telesales person

vender ⟦1⟧ *vt* sell; ∼ **algo a algo** sell sth at sth; **esa tienda lo vende a 50 euros** they sell it at 50 euros in that shop; ∼ **algo en** *or* **por algo** sell sth for sth; **lo he vendido en 2.500 euros** I've sold it for 2,500 euros; ∼ **al cierre** (futuros) sell on close; ∼ **al contado** sell for cash; (Bolsa) sell spot; ∼ **a comisión** sell on commission; ∼ **a crédito** sell on credit; ∼ **al descubierto** sell short; ∼ **directamente al público** sell directly to the public; ∼ **falsamente** miss-sell; ∼ **a futuro** sell forward; ∼ **a granel** sell in bulk; ∼ **en línea** *or* **on-line** sell online, e-tail; ∼ **con pérdida** sell at a loss; ∼ **al por mayor** sell wholesale; ∼ **al por menor** sell retail; ∼ **a precio de mercado** sell at market price; **se vende** for sale
⟦2⟧ *vi* (producto, línea) sell); **esa línea siempre ha vendido muy bien** that line has always sold well

vendible *adj* saleable BrE, marketable, salable AmE

venidero *adj* coming, future

venir *vi* come; (estar) be; **la semana/el lunes que viene** next week/Monday; **venía en el periódico de ayer** it was in yesterday's paper; **viene en el contrato** it's in the contract; ∼ **a parar en** result in

venta *f* sale; (acción) selling; ∼**s** sales; **en** ∼ on sale; **estar a la** ∼ be on sale; **poner algo a la** ∼ put sth up for sale; ∼ **acoplada** tie-in sale; ∼ **de activos** asset sale; ∼ **agresiva** hard sell; ∼ **al alza** long put; ∼ **asistida por la Red** Web-assisted selling; ∼ **anticipada** (de valores) advance selling; (para teatro, restaurante) advance booking BrE, advance reservation AmE; ∼ **bajo mano** under-the-counter sale; ∼ **bajo presión** pressure selling; ∼ **de billetes electrónica** e-ticketing, virtual ticketing; ∼**s brutas** gross sales; ∼ **por catálogo** mail-order selling; ∼ **condicional** conditional sale; ∼ **por consignación** consignment selling; ∼ **por contacto directo** face-to-face selling; ∼ **al contado** cash sale; ∼ **por correo** *or* **correspondencia** mail-order selling; ∼ **a crédito** credit sale; ∼ **al descubierto** short sale; ∼ **directa** direct selling; ∼ **domiciliaria** door-to-door selling; ∼**s de exportación** export sales; ∼ **fácil** quick sale; ∼ **falsa** mis-

selling; ∼ **en línea** (acción) online selling, e-tailing; (resultado) online sale; ∼ **de liquidación** winding-up sale; ∼ **mayorista** wholesaling; ∼ **mediante licitación pública** sale by tender; ∼ **mensual** monthly sale; ∼ **minorista** retailing; ∼**s netas** net sales; ∼ **on-line** online selling, e-tailing; ∼ **al por mayor** wholesaling; ∼ **al por menor** retailing; ∼ **por persuasión** soft sell; ∼ **piramidal** pyramid selling; ∼ **a plazos** hire purchase BrE, installment plan AmE; ∼ **precipitada** sell-off; ∼ **a prueba** sale on approval; ∼ **de rendimiento nulo** breakpoint sale; ∼**s repetidas** repeat sales; ∼ **secreta** backdoor selling; ∼ **telefónica** telephone selling, telesales

ventaja *f* advantage; (pro) plus, upside; **llevarle (la)** ∼ **a alguien/algo** have an advantage over sb/sth; **tener (la)** ∼ have an advantage; (avance) have a head start; ∼ **comercial** commercial advantage; ∼ **competitiva** competitive advantage; (V&M) competitive edge; ∼ **para el consumidor** consumer benefit; ∼ **para los empleados** employee benefit, fringe benefit; ∼ **fiscal** tax advantage

ventajista *mf* opportunist

ventajoso *adj* advantageous

ventana *f* window; **tirar algo por la** ∼ throw sth out of the window, squander sth; ∼**s en cascada** cascading windows; ∼ **de consulta** *or* **interrogación** query window; ∼ **de intervención** audit window

ventanilla *f* counter; (de sobre) window; ∼ **única** one-stop shop

ver *vti* see; **se ve que ...** (parece) it seems that ...; (está claro) it is clear that ...; **véase a la vuelta** see overleaf, please turn over, P.T.O.; **véase página 12** see page 12

veracidad *f* truthfulness

veraneante *mf* holidaymaker BrE, (summer) vacationer AmE

verbigracia *adv* for example, e.g.

verdadero *adj* real; (historia) true; ∼ **y equitativo** true and fair

verde *adj* green; **zona** ∼ green space

veredicto *m* verdict; **emitir** ∼ issue a verdict; ∼ **de culpabilidad/ inculpabilidad** guilty/not guilty verdict; ∼ **mayoritario** majority verdict

verificable *adj* verifiable; (Cont) auditable

verificación *f* verification; (Cont) audit; ∼ **de aduana** customs check; ∼ **retrospectiva** (Info) audit trail

verificado *adj* verified; **no ~** unverified

verificador¹, a *m,f* checker

verificador² *m*: **~ ortográfico** spellchecker

verificar *vt* verify; (Cont) audit; **~ la identidad de alguien** certify sb's identity

versal *f* capital letter

versatilidad *f* versatility

versión *f* version; **en ~ original/ española** in the original/in Spanish; **~ avanzada** advanced version; **~ beta** beta version; **~ electrónica** electronic version; **~ en línea** *or* **on-line** online version; **~ revisada** revised version

versus *prep* versus

vertedero *m* landfill site

verter *vt* (residuos) dump

vertical *adj* vertical

vertido *m* (de petróleo) spillage; (de residuos) (waste) dumping

vertiente *f* side, aspect; **tanto en su ~ nacional como en su ~ europea** both from a domestic and a European point of view; **~ tecnológica** technological edge

vertiginosamente *adv* steeply; **los precios subieron ~** prices rose sharply *o* spiralled upwards BrE *o* upwards AmE

vertiginoso *adj* (argumento, caída, cambio) rapid

vetar *vt* veto, put a veto on

veterano¹ *adj* veteran; **un abogado ~ en estas lides** a lawyer with a lot of experience in these matters

veterano², -a *m,f* veteran, old hand (infrml)

veto *m* veto; **poner el ~ a algo** veto sth; **tener el derecho de ~** have the right of veto

vez *f* time; **a la ~** at the same time; **a veces** sometimes; **cada ~ más/menos** more and more/less and less; **de ~ en cuando** from time to time; **en ~ de** instead of; **pocas veces** rarely; **tres veces al año** three times a year

VGA *abr* (▸**adaptador de gráficos de vídeo** Esp *or* **video** AmL) VGA (video graphics adaptor)

v.gr. *abr* (▸**verbigracia**) e.g. (for example)

VHF *abr* (*frecuencia muy alta*) VHF (very high frequency)

vía *f* road, way; **por la ~ amistosa** amicably; **por la ~ legal** by legal means; **por la ~ oficial** officially, through official channels

viabilidad *f* viability; **~ económica** economic viability

viable *adj* viable

viajante *mf* (m) travelling BrE *o* traveling AmE salesman; (f) travelling BrE *o* traveling AmE saleswoman

viajar *vi* travel; **~ en coche/avión** travel *o* go by car/plane

viaje *m* trip, journey; **¡buen ~!** have a good trip!; **estar de ~** be away; **~ de estudios** field trip; **~ en grupo** group travel; **~ de ida** outward journey; **~ de ida y vuelta** return trip BrE, round trip AmE; **~ de negocios** business trip; **~ relámpago** flying visit; **~ de vuelta** return journey

viajero, -a *m,f* traveller BrE, traveler AmE; **~ abonado(-a)** *m,f* commuter

viáticos *m pl* AmL travelling expenses BrE, traveling expenses AmE

vicepresidente, -a *m,f* (Pol) vice president; (de empresa, comité) (m) vice chairman BrE, (f) vice chairwoman BrE, vice president AmE

vicesecretario, -a *m,f* vice secretary

viceversa *adv* vice versa

vicio *m* (corrupción) vice; (defecto) defect, fault; (Der) error, flaw; **~ oculto** latent defect

víctima *f* victim; **~s de accidente** casualties; (mortales) fatalities

victoria *f* victory; **~ fácil** walkover (infrml)

vida *f* life; **de por ~** for life; **ganarse la ~** earn a living; **~ amortizable** depreciable life; **~ media** average life; **~ de un producto** product life

vídeo Esp, **video** AmL *m* video; (aparato) video recorder; **~ a la carta** *or* **a petición** video-on-demand, VOD; **~ promocional** promotional video; **~ RAM** video-RAM

videocámara *f* video camera

videoconferencia *f* (conferencia) videoconference; (proceso) videoconferencing; **~ por IP** videoconference over IP

videocorreo *m* video mail, v-mail

videodisco *m* video disk; **~ digital** DVD, digital video disk

videograbadora *f* video recorder

videojuego *m* video game

videopantalla *f* view screen

videopiratería *f* video piracy

videotelefonía *f* videotelephony

videoteléfono *m* videophone

videotex *Esp*, **videotexto** *Esp*, **videtex** *AmL m* videotex®

viejo *adj* old; **vieja economía** old economy

viernes *m* Friday; **~ y vacaciones incluidos** Fridays and holidays included; **~ negro** Black Friday

vigencia *f* (validez) validity; (de opción) life; **estar en ~** be valid; **entrar en ~** come into effect *o* force; **la nueva ley aún no ha entrado en ~** the new law has not yet come into effect *o* force; **perder ~** no longer be valid, be out of date

vigente *adj* valid, current, in force; **de acuerdo con la legislación ~** in accordance with current legislation; **el acuerdo continúa ~** the agreement is still valid; **precios ~s hasta fin de mes** prices valid until the end of the month

vigilancia *f* (atención) vigilance; (por guardias, cámaras) surveillance; (servicio) security; (observación) monitoring; **han extremado la ~** security has been tightened; **el edificio está bajo ~** (por guardias) guards patrol the building; (por cámaras) the building is under surveillance; **~ de la contaminación** pollution monitoring; **~ tecnológica** technology watch; **~ por vídeo** *Esp or* **video** *AmL* videosurveillance

vigilante *mf* guard; (en tienda) security guard; (de incógnito) store detective

vigilar *vt* (atender) watch; (custodiar) guard; **~ a alguien atentamente** keep a close watch on sb

vigor *m* vigour *BrE*, vigor *AmE*; **en ~** in force; **entrar en ~** come into force; **poner en ~** put into effect *o* operation

vinatero, -a *m,f* wine merchant, vintner

vinculado *adj* linked; **estar ~ a** be tied to

vinculante *adj* (decisión) binding

vincular *vt* link; (moneda, precios) peg; **~ a un índice** index-link

vínculo *m* link; **~ móvil** (Econ) crawling peg

viñeta *f* (publicidad) vignette

violación *f* (de derecho) violation; (de contrato) breach; (de ley, patente) infringement; **en ~ de** in violation of; **~ de la seguridad** breach of security

violar *vt* (ley, acuerdo) break, infringe; (derecho) violate

violencia *f* violence; **no ~** non-violence; **~ familiar** domestic violence

virtual *adj* virtual; **realidad ~** virtual reality

virtud *f* virtue; **en ~ de** by virtue of

virus *m* virus; **sin ~** virus-free

visado *m* visa; **~ de entrada** entry visa; **~ de entradas múltiples** multiple-entry visa; **~ de residencia** residence visa *BrE*, green card *AmE*; **~ de residencia temporal** temporary residence visa; **~ de salida** exit visa; **~ turístico** tourist visa

visar *vt* (pasaporte) visa, stamp with a visa; (documento) endorse, approve

viscosidad *f* viscosity

viscoso *adj* viscous

visible *adj* visible

visibles *m pl* visibles

visión *f* vision; **con ~ de futuro** (persona, proyecto) forward-looking

visionar *vt* view; (por adelantado) preview

visita *f* visit; **hacer una ~** a visit, pay a visit to; **horario de ~** visiting hours; **~ de cumplido** courtesy call; **~ de negocios** business call; **~ relámpago** flying visit; **~ de venta** sales call

visitante¹ *adj* visiting

visitante² *mf* visitor; **~ extranjero(-a)** *m,f* overseas visitor

visitar *vt* visit

vista *f* sight; (Der) hearing; **cuenta a la ~** instant access account, sight account; **pagar a la ~** pay at sight; **a la ~ de algo** in the light of sth; **a primera ~** at first sight; **con ~s a hacer algo** with a view to doing sth; **en ~ de que ...** in view of the fact that ...; **la ~ del juicio se celebrará el día 30** the hearing will take place on the 30th; **~ de conjunto** conspectus; **~ privada** private hearing

visual *adj* visual

visualización *f* visualization; (Info) display; **~ en color** color display *AmE*, colour display *BrE*

visualizador *m* visual display unit *BrE*, visual display terminal *AmE*

visualizar *vt* visualize; (Info) display

vitrina *f* (exposición) showcase

viudedad *f* (pensión) widow's pension

viudo, -a *m,f* (m) widower; (f) widow

vivienda *f* housing; **~ de protección oficial** government-subsidized housing, ≈ council house *BrE*; **~ unipersonal** single-person household

vivir *vi* live; **~ bien** have *o* enjoy a good standard of living; **~ al día** live from day to day; **~ de las rentas** have a ⋯⟩

private income; ~ **de subsidios sociales** be on benefits BrE o welfare AmE

vocación f vocation; **tener ~ por algo** have a vocation for sth

volante m (nota) note; (de publicidad) leaflet

volátil adj volatile

volatilidad f volatility

volcado m (Info) dump; (acción) dumping; ~ **de memoria** storage dump; ~ **de modificaciones** change dump

voltio m volt

volumen m volume; ~ **comercial** trade volume; ~ **de ingresos** income amount; ~ **de negocios** turnover; ~ **de pedidos** volume of orders; ~ **de producción** output volume; ~ **de siniestros** burden of losses; ~ **de ventas** sales volume

voluminoso adj bulky

voluntario¹ adj voluntary, noncompulsory

voluntario², -a m,f volunteer

volver vi return; ~ **a hacer algo** do sth again; ~ **a empezar** start again; ~ **dentro de una hora** be back within an hour; ~ **a llamar** call back

volverse v pron (darse la vuelta) turn, turn round; (regresar) turn back; (hacerse) become; ~ **atrás** back-pedal, go back on one's word; (en discusión) back down; (en negociaciones) pull out; **el Internet se ha vuelto muy popular** the Internet has become very popular

votación f (acto) voting; (voto) vote; (en sindicatos) ballot; **someter algo a ~** put sth to the vote, take a vote on sth; ~ **en bloque** block voting; ~ **de huelga** strike ballot; ~ **por poder** voting by proxy; ~ **secreta** secret ballot; ~ **táctica** tactical voting; ~ **de tanteo** straw poll; ~ **unánime** unanimous vote

votante mf voter; ~ **indeciso(-a)** m,f floating voter BrE, swing voter (jarg)

votar ① vt (candidato) vote for; (moción) approve, pass

② vi vote; ~ **a mano alzada** vote by a show of hands

voto m vote; **dar** or **emitir su ~** cast one's vote; **derecho al ~** right to vote;

ganaron por tres ~s they won by three votes; ~ **afirmativo** vote in favour BrE o favor AmE; ~ **en blanco** blank vote; ~ **en bloque** or **colectivo** block vote; ~ **de castigo** protest vote; ~ **de censura** vote of no confidence; ~ **de confianza** confidence vote; ~ **en contra** vote against; ~ **por correo** postal vote; ~ **decisivo** casting vote; ~ **de desconfianza** vote of no confidence; ~ **a favor** vote in favour BrE o favor AmE; ~ **mayoritario** majority vote; ~ **negativo** vote against; ~ **por poderes** proxy vote; ~ **de protesta** protest vote; ~ **secreto** secret ballot

voz f voice; **tener ~ y voto** have a say; (en votación) have a vote; **llevar la ~ cantante** call the tune o shots (infrml); ~ **en off** voice-over; ~ **pública** public opinion; **salir a la ~ pública** be made public

VP abr (▸**vicepresidente**) VP (vice president)

VPO abr (▸**vivienda de protección oficial**) ≈ council house BrE

VRAM abr (▸**vídeo RAM** Esp or **video RAM** AmL) VRAM (video-RAM)

VTR abr (▸**grabación en vídeo** Esp or **video** AmL) VTR (videotape recording)

vuelco m turnround BrE, turnaround; **dar un ~** change dramatically

vuelo m flight; ~ **chárter** charter flight; ~ **de conexión** connecting flight; ~ **económico** economy o cheap flight; ~ **internacional** international flight; ~ **sin escalas** direct o nonstop flight; ~ **inaugural** inaugural flight; ~ **nacional** internal o domestic flight; ~ **programado** scheduled flight; ~ **regular** scheduled flight

vuelta f (regreso) return; (de viaje) return journey; (cambio) change; **a ~ de correo** by return of post BrE, by return of mail AmE; **a la ~ de dos meses** after two months, two months later; ~ **rápida a la baja** bear squeeze; ~ **rápida a corto** short squeeze

vulnerable adj vulnerable

vulnerar vt (ley) infringe; (reputación) damage

Ww

WAP *abr* (*protocolo de aplicación sin cables*) WAP (wireless application protocol)

web *f* website; **la W~** the Net, the Web; **preparado para la W~** Web-enabled, Web-ready

webcam *m* webcam
webmaster *m* webmaster
website *f* website, site
WP *abr* (▸**procesador de textos**) WP (word processor)

Xx

xerocopia *f* photocopy, Xerox®
xerocopiar *vt* photocopy, Xerox®

xerografiar *vt* Xerox®
xerográfico *adj* xerographic

Yy

yacimiento *m* bed, deposit; **~ petrolífero** oilfield
yanquis *m pl* (bonos) yankees (jarg)

yarda *f* yard
yen *m* yen
yermo *m* waste land

Zz

zapear *vi* channel-hop
zapeo *m* channel-hopping
zapping *m* channel-hopping; **hacer ~** channel-hop
zócalo *m* plinth
zona *f* (región) area; **de ~ verde** greenfield; **~ azul** Esp *f restricted parking zone*; **~ de captación** catchment area; **~ catastrófica** disaster area; **~ del centro** city centre BrE, downtown AmE; **~ comercial** commercial district, business district; **~ comercial peatonal** shopping precinct BrE, shopping mall AmE; **~ densamente poblada** densely-populated area; **~ de desarrollo industrial** enterprise zone; **~ euro** euro zone; **~ forestal** woodland; **~ franca** free-trade zone; **~ industrial** industrial estate BrE, industrial park AmE; **~ intermedia** buffer area; **~ interactiva** (Info) hotspot; **~ de la libra esterlina** Sterling Area; **~ de libre comercio** free-trade zone; **~ de libre mercado** free-market zone; **~ monetaria** currency zone; **~ de pruebas** testbed; (en mercadotecnia) test area; **~ publicitaria** advertising zone; **~ residencial** residential area; **~ restringida** restricted area; **~ salarial** wage zone; **~ sensible** (Info) hotspot; (Med amb) sensitive zone; **~ turística** tourist area; **~ urbanizada** built-up area; **~ urbana** urban area; **~ verde** green area *o* space

z

● ●

El diseño de una carta de negocios

■ *membrete / dirección del remitente*   ■ *razón social*

Watchdog Technologies
Unit 7 Harwell Trading Park
London SE1 2JF
Tel: + 44 (0) 20 7132 4186   **Fax:** + 44 (0) 20 0745 8765
e-mail: pbrandon@watchdogtechs.co.uk

EH/PB/33 ·········· ■ *referencia*

19 January 2002 ·········· ■ *fecha*

Gabriel Kent
Head of Purchasing
Forest Security
15 The Avenue
Canterbury
CT3 9DN
·········· ■ *destinatario*

Dear Mr Kent ·········· ■ *fórmula de encabezamiento*

Catalogue request ·········· ■ *asunto*

Thank you for your interest in our new range of security products. I have pleasure in enclosing our current catalogue as well as a price list and order form.

If you would like a demonstration of the new models in the Z500 alarm series, I would be happy to arrange for our representative to call on you at your convenience. Full technical specifications for all our products can be found on our website at **www.watchdogtech.co.uk**

I would like to take this opportunity to draw your attention to the range of discounts currently on offer on orders placed before 1 March 2002. Please do not hesitate to contact me for any further information.

Yours sincerely ·········· ■ *fórmula de despedida*

J. Murphy ·········· ■ *firma*

John Murphy ·········· ■ *remitente*

Sales Manager ·········· ■ *posición*

enc. ·········· ■ *anexo(s)*

Head office: Watchdog Technologies
Unit 7 Harwell Trading Park London SE1 2JF
Registered in England: 750 63941
Vat no: 635 0895 41

■ *contenido de la carta*   *Número de registro de la compañía* ■

How to lay out a business letter

company registration number ■   date ■

company name ■

Servicios Infocomp S.A

letterhead/ ■
sender's address

Calle San Rafael 133
Madrid 14
Número de registro 32B 77
Teléfono: (91) 757 44 38   Fax: (91) 757 44 39

addressee ■

Sr. Manuel Moreno
Gerente General
Productos Omega
Avenida de las Americas 57
Madrid 20

Madrid, 17 marzo de 2002

reference ■   Referencia: 44-23MM

subject ■   Asunto: su pedido del 12 de enero

salutation ■   Estimado señor Moreno

body of ■
the letter

En respuesta a su carta del 12 de enero pasado, me place
informarle que, además de los repuestos que ha pedido,
también le podemos proporcionar un servicio completo de
apoyo técnico para la red interna de su empresa. Puede ver
que nuestros precios, que le envío como anexo, son muy
competitivos e incluyen el IVA.

Si decide seguir adelante con el servicio completo,
le haremos llegar los repuestos lo antes posible y nos
encargaremos de organizar una visita a sus oficinas para
que nuestros técnicos puedan asegurarse de que su red
esté funcionando óptimamente antes de comenzar el
servicio de apoyo.

complimentary ■
close

Quedando a su entera disposición para proseguir con la
pronta entrega de su pedido, le saluda atentamente,

signature ■

sender's name ■   Eduardo González Ortiz

organizational ■
role

Gerente Comercial

enclosures ■   Anexo: Tarifas de repuestos, enero 2002

El diseño de una carta de negocios en inglés

La práctica más común para las cartas de negocios es alinear el texto con el margen izquierdo y dejar un espacio doble entre cada párrafo. Para las fechas, las direcciones y las fórmulas de saludo y despedida, es cada vez más común omitir la puntuación.

El Membrete/remitente

La mayoría de las empresas usan papel con membrete, el cual indica el nombre, el logotipo y las señas de la compañía, en el centro o a la derecha de la página. Si el papel no tiene membrete, la dirección entera deberá ir arriba, al lado derecho de la hoja. En Gran Bretaña se escribe el código postal en una línea separada, después del nombre de la ciudad. En los Estados Unidos se escribe el 'ZIP code' inmediatamente después del nombre del estado: *Cleveland, OH 40101.*

La referencia

El número de referencia puede ser un código que clasifica la carta pero también puede dar información sobre cualquier correspondencia anterior y el número del cliente o del pedido. La referencia se debe poner a la izquierda de la hoja, antes de las señas del destinatario o a la derecha, antes de la fecha. Es común que la referencia esté indicada por la abreviación *Your ref:/Our ref:*

La fecha

En Gran Bretaña se escribe la fecha en el orden día/mes/año, sin coma después del día: *22 February 2002.* Los estadounidenses prefieren el orden mes/día/año, generalmente con una coma después del día: *February 22, 2002.* Se puede poner la fecha en el lado derecho de la hoja.

La dirección del destinatario

Las señas del destinatario deberán incluirse completamente y deberán indicar el cargo o la función de la persona en cuestión.

La fórmula de saludo

La fórmula de saludo que se usa para una carta de negocios es Dear.
- *Dear Sir* or *Madam* (si se sabe el título o el cargo de la persona pero no se sabe si se trata de un hombre o de una mujer)
- *Dear Sirs* (si se dirije a la empresa)
- *Dear Mr Dixon/Mrs Dixon* (si se sabe el nombre de la persona)
- *Dear Ms Dixon* (Ms se usa para dirigirse a las mujeres, estén casadas o solteras. Es mejor usar esta fórmula si no se sabe el estado civil de la persona. Siempre va seguida del apellido)
- *Dear Paul/Dear Martha* (para los amigos y los colegas)

El asunto

El asunto de la carta se indica brevemente antes de la fórmula de saludo y antes del cuerpo mismo de la carta. Se debe escribir en negrita, en mayúsculas o subrayado.

La fórmula de despido

Si se ha usado el nombre del destinatario en el saludo:
- *Yours sincerely*

Si no se sabe el nombre del destinatario:
- *Yours faithfully*

A un colega o a un conocido:
- *Best wishes/Yours/Regards*

La costumbre en EEUU es de usar *Sincerely yours* o simplemente *Sincerely*. La fórmula *Yours faithfully* casi no se usa.

The layout of a Spanish business letter

Letterhead/sender's address
Most companies have headed stationery with their full company name, logo, and contact details which are displayed at the top of the page or at the top left-hand side of the page. When not using pre-printed stationery it is customary for the sender to type their details at the top left-hand side of the page. In Spanish addresses, the name of the town is written in capitals preceded by the post code on the same line eg:
28080 MADRID

Reference
The reference line is usually placed on the left-hand side of the page, opposite or below the addressee's details. It may take the form:
Referencia:

Date
The date in Spanish is usually placed on the right-hand side of the page, above or below the addressee's address. It is always given in the following form, although brackets indicate that the town element is optional: (town,) day/month/year:
Lima, 28 de mayo de 2002; 5 de noviembre 2002.

Addressee
The addressee's full address is given on the right-hand side of the page beneath the letterhead.
The addressee's full title or organizational role is included in the address.

Salutation
The standard formulas for formal correspondence are:
- *Estimado/a señor/a*
- *Estimados señores/Señores/Muy señores míos*

Subject
The subject of the letter is given succinctly before the opening salutation e.g.:
Asunto: su pedido 456-8900

Complimentary closing
The standard complimentary close in Spanish is simply *Atentamente*. However, other, lengthier forms are also common, for example:
- *Los saluda atentamente,*
- *Reciba mi más atento saludo*
- *Sin más, quedo a la espera de su respuesta*
- *A la espera de sus prontas noticias los saludo cordialmente*

To a colleague or close personal contact:
- *Cordialmente/Afectuosamente/ Saludos*

Expresiones útiles

As requested I am forwarding you a [price list, catalogue]

As stated in your letter of [date] concerning...

Thank you for your letter of [date] concerning/requesting...

Thank you for sending me a [catalogue, price list, brochure]

Thank you for your enquiry of [date] concerning...

Further to our telephone conversation of [date]...

I am sorry to inform you that...

I am writing to confirm our telephone conversation of [date]

I am writing to enquire whether...

I am writing to express my dissatisfaction with...

I am writing to inform you that...

I am pleased to inform you that...

In reply to your letter/enquiry of [date]...

I refer to your letter of [date] concerning...

I wish to draw your attention to...

I wish to inform you that...

I would be grateful if you could forward me a [price list/catalogue]

Please find enclosed...

With reference to your letter/order of [date]

Fórmulas de despido

I look forward to hearing from you

I look forward to your response

I would be most grateful if you would look into this matter as soon as possible

I trust that you will give this matter your urgent attention

Please do not hesitate to contact me should you require any further information

Please let me know as soon as possible what action you propose to take

Abreviaciones y convenciones

ASAP (as soon as possible)—lo antes posible

bcc (blind carbon copy)—copia invisible

by return of post—a vuelta de correo

c (circa)—alrededor de

cc (carbon copy)—copia carbón

certified true copy—copia certificada

c/o (care of)—para entregar a

confidential—confidencial

cont'd overleaf—sigue al dorso

draft—borrador

enc(s)., encl(s)., (enclosure(s))—anexos, adjuntos

FAO (for the attention of)—a la atención de

FYI (for your information)—a título de información, para su información

incl. (including)—incluido

N/A (not applicable)—no corresponde

please forward—sírvase remitir

pp. (per procurationem)—p.p. (por poder)

printed matter—impresos

private—privado

ps (post-scriptum)—pd (post data)

PTO (please turn over)—sigue al dorso

registered—certificado

SAE (stamped addressed envelope)—sobre franqueado (a nuestro/su/mi nombre)

TBC (to be confirmed)—por confirmar

under separate cover—por separado

without prejudice—sin perjuicio de los derechos de los firmantes

Correspondence/La correspondencia

Useful phrases

Acusamos recibo de su [catálogo, respuesta]

Recibí, con fecha de [fecha], su carta con respecto a...

Le agradezco su carta y sus sugerencias acerca de...

En relación con la conversación telefónica de [fecha]...

Conforme a su carta/fax de [fecha]...

De acuerdo a lo convenido en nuestra conversación telefónica de hoy, le mando...

Me dirijo a ustedes a fin de solicitarles...

Le agradecería mucho si me pudiera mandar...

Rogamos que sirvan remitirnos su catálogo de...

Por la presente le informo de intención de...

Me permito informarle acerca de...

Le ruego tome nota de...

Adjunto les envío...

Closures

Confiando en que mi solicitud recibirá la debida atención y en que se dará rápida solución al problema...

Quedo a la espera de sus noticias, con la seguridad de que tomará el máximo interés en este asunto.

Rogamos que se sirvan acusar recibo.

Por favor no dude en ponerse en contacto conmigo si requiere más información.

Written conventions and abbreviations

por confirmar—TBC (to be confirmed)

a la atención de—FAO (for the attention of)

acusar recibo—to acknowledge receipt

a título de información—FYI (for your information)

para entregar a—c/o (care of)

borrador – draft

cc (copia carbon)—cc (carbon copy)

copia certificada—certified true copy

confidencial—confidential

copia invisible—bcc (blind carbon copy)

lo antes posible—ASAP (as soon as possible)

sobre franqueado (a nuestro/su/mi nombre)—SAE (stamped addressed envelope)

alrededor de—c (circa)

impresos—printed matter

incl. (incluidos)—including

a vuelta de correo—by return of post

anexo(s)—enc(s)., encl(s). (enclosure(s))

sírvase remitir—please forward

privado—private

pd (post data)—ps (post-scriptum)

p.p. (por poder—pp. (per procurationem)

certificado—registered

no corresponde—N/A (not applicable)

por separado—under separate cover

sin perjuicio a los derechos de los firmantes—without prejudice

sigue al dorso—cont'd overleaf, PTO (please turn over)

Petición de información

Herriot Consulting

18 Robert Adam Place
Edinburgh EH15 6YF

Tel: +44 (0) 131 339 8896
Fax: +44 (0) 131 339 8810

The Conference Manager
The Craiglochart Hotel
George Grove
GLASGOW G3 6DD

12th August 2002

Dear Sir or Madam

I am currently organizing a two-day residential staff-training event for 40 staff from our Scottish offices. In addition to accommodation and meals, our requirements would include a fully equipped conference room, and four syndicate rooms suitable for workshop sessions.

I would be very grateful if you would forward me information on your conference facilities and details of availability for early November.

I look forward to hearing from you.

E. Ashford-Leigh

Edward Ashford-Leigh

Professional Development Manager

Petición de muestras

THE FRANK COMPANY

22 BLOOMING PLACE
LONDON SW12

TEL: 020-8669 7868
FAX: 020-8669 7866

The Sales Director
June Office Supplies
55 Dewey Road
Wolverhampton WV12 HRR

5 June 2002

Dear Sir/Madam,

Thank you for sending us your brochures. We are particularly interested in the Dollis range, which would complement our existing stock.

We would be grateful if you could send us samples of the whole range promptly, as we are hoping to place an order soon for the autumn.

Thanking you in advance,

Yours faithfully,

Mr T Jones
Manager

Requesting information

Julie Collins
Sandford Publishing Co.
Dalton Street
Wantage OX12 6DP
Gran Bretaña
Teléfono: (++0044 1865) 57 32 45
Fax: (++0044 1865) 57 32 46

Servicio de Archivos de Cine
Centro Nacional de la Cinematografía

17 marzo de 2002

Señores

En este momento, Sandford Publishing Co. se prepara para publicar
una obra sobre el urbanismo en el cine europeo. Los autores quisieran
incluir algunas placas que pertenecen a sus archivos y por eso le
agradecería si me pudieran proporcionar documentación que indique
las condiciones y los costos de reproducción.

Los saludo atentamente y quedo a la espera de su respuesta

Julie Collins

Asking for samples

18 de abril 2002

Estudios Vázquez
Casa Matriz
Apdo. de correos 3588
04988 Valladolid
Registro de compañías: 87 E 22
Teléfono/Fax: 983 76 09 23
email: vazquez@estudios.com

Textiles Profom
Camino de los Alpes
027738 Granada

Señores

Acuso recibo de su catálogo y le agradezco su pronta atención. Antes de hacer
un pedido, le ruego que sirva remitirnos un lote de muestras de los géneros
presentados de las páginas 254 a 256, ref. TAF.10/54/5/6.

Lo saludo cordialmente y quedo a la espera de su respuesta

Juan Vázquez
Proprietario

Carta promocional

Fashion Statements

Wallace Road, Ellon, Aberdeenshire AB32 5BY

Tel: 01224 497214 Fax: 01224 497234

February 2002

Dear Mrs Evans

As one of our most valued customers, I wanted to make sure that you would have the opportunity to select your orders from the advance copy of our new Spring-Summer catalogue which I enclose.

More Choice

As you will see from our catalogue, we have more women's styles in more sizes than ever before, with a greater range of fittings to suit all our customers.

Top quality

We pride ourselves on the quality of our goods and will ensure that your order reaches you within 28 days in perfect condition. Our customer care team is on hand to deal with queries on our customer hotline and if you are not completely satisfied with your order they will arrange for an immediate refund.

Post your completed order form today, or call our team on **01224 445382** to enjoy next season's fashions today.

Faith Pickett

Faith Pickett
Customer Care Manager

Pedido

BUTLERS OF BATH LTD

Garrard Street Mall, Bath BA7 2JD
Tel: 01225 678 9865 Fax: 01225 678 9800

Joseph Hayes
Sales Manager, New Textiles Express
Bexford Way
Thatcham
RG18 2WS

21 March 2002

Dear Sir

Following our discussion last week I am pleased to confirm my order for an initial batch of 20 Harlequin bed linen sets at a unit price of £13.99.

A purchase order form is enclosed which takes into account a 10% trade discount. I would be grateful if you could send me confirmation of receipt of the order and dispatch details.

I look forward to hearing from you.

Yours faithfully

Amy Peterson

Amy Peterson
Manager

Sales promotion

Ventas Iberia
Camino de los Leones
93100 Málaga

Señor Costa
Calle Miguel de Cervantes 34
31300 Cáceres
20 de febrero 2002

Estimado Señor Costa

Ya está por llegar el buen tiempo y es hora de empezar a pensar en ropa para las vacaciones. Por esa razón le presentamos nuestro nuevo catálogo de primavera-verano. Este año y como siempre, tenemos el placer de ofrecerle un amplio surtido y un servicio de la más alta calidad, como lo demuestran nuestras novedades.

Mayor surtido y calidad:
Nueva colección infantil: ahora tenemos algo para toda la familia, gracias a nuestra línea de ropa para bebés, fácil de lavar y que, sobre todo, ¡le gusta a nuestros pequeños!
Amplia gama de artículos de sport para todas sus actividades deportivas. Vea nuestra nueva sección dedicada a nuestras bicicletas, cada una con dos años de garantía.

Mejor servicio:
- Nuevos recuadros con más información sobre nuestros electrodomésticos. Sabiendo más, comprará mejor.
- Pedido por Internet: la informática a su servicio. Podrá efectuar su pedido más fácil y rápidamente.
- Entrega más rápida: garantizamos recepción de su pedido en 48h.

Además de esto, le ofrecemos a usted, nuestro estimado cliente, cualquier artículo de nuestra colección de invierno que todavía esté disponible, con una rebaja del 20% (oferta válida hasta el 15 de abril 2002).

Gracias por su compra, le agradecemos su preferencia y su confianza en nuestros productos.

Cordialmente,

Ventas Iberia

Placing an order

Moncloa y Cía.
Avenida Gambetta
03000 Murcia
Tel: 968 21 19 03   Fax: 968 21 25 69

Señor Javier Quesada
Director Comercial
Muebles Modernos
Rosales 62
Madrid 4

4 de julio 2002

Asunto: pedido

Señor

Conforme a nuestra conversación telefónica, le confirmo el siguiente pedido:

Artículo	Referencia	Cantidad	Precio/unidad
silla 'dáctilo ergonómica'	Ref:SDE/423	2	126,00€
terminal de trabajo 130x90 cm	Ref:TDT/452	3	224,56€
escritorio base metal 120cm	Ref:EBM/567	1	198,50€

Como quedamos de acuerdo, el pago será efectuado al contado en cuanto recibamos la factura. Le agradeceríamos si pudiera concertar la entrega de los muebles para el fin del mes.

Rogando que se sirvan acusar recibo, les saludamos atentamente,

Daniel Schwinger

Daniel Schwinger
Director de compras

Factura

Art Decoratif

224 Haversham Road, Reading, Berkshire, RG32 5SE

VAT No 280 268690

Item	Quantity	Unit Price	£
gilt mirror (Regency)	10	£27.90	270.90
lampshade code 02345	7	£10	70.00
rug 120x75 code 0346	5	£62.45	312.25
		Carriage	18.75
		Total excluding VAT	671.90
		VAT @ 17.5 %	117.58
		Total including VAT	789.48

Charges are payable when this invoice is issued. The account is therefore due for settlement

---

The Round Place

2 Nighend High, Bristol, BS9 0UI
Tel: 0117 66900   Fax: 0117 55450

Famous Gourmet   4 June 2002
399 Old Green Road
Bristol
BS12 8TY

Dear Sirs,

Invoice no. B54/56/HP

We would be glad if you would amend your recent invoice (copy
enclosed).

The quantities of the last three items are incorrect, since they
refer to "24 dozen" instead of the correct quantity of "14 dozen"
in each case. In addition to this, our agreed discount of 4% has
not been allowed.

Please check your records and issue a revised invoice, which we
will then be happy to pay within the agreed time.

Yours faithfully,

M. R Edwardson

M. R Edwardson
Chief Supplies Officer

Encl.

• •

Invoice

Ediciones Verbatim

Calle Islas Baleares 523, 5ºA
FUENCARRAL
28083 MADRID
tel/fax: (+34) 91 243 55 64/5

Descripción	Cantidad	Precio/unidad	€ (euro)
manuales "Trato hecho"	10	5,75	57,50
caja de colección audio	1	48,50	48,50
CD-ROM	1	26,00	26,00
casete VHS "Viaje de negocios"	1	18,50	18,50

total sin el IVA:	150,50
Subtotal	150,50
IVA 18,2%	27,39
Total	177,89

"La Casa de la Ropa Interior"

Avenida Ramón y Cajal 120
06540 Barcelona
Tel: 93 66 22 00

12 de septiembre 2002
Industrias Vallatextil
Confección - Ventas de mayoreo
Camino de los Leones
4703 Valladolid

Referencia de pedido: 00/08/30-VAL

Señores

Acuso recibo de la partida, pero me veo obligado a devolvérsela, ya que las tallas no corresponden a las indicadas en el formulario de pedido.

Les agradecería mucho si pudieran corregir este error y hacerme llegar los artículos conforme a mi encargo, lo antes posible.

Aguardando sus prontas noticias, les saludamos atentamente,

A. Covarrubias
Gerente

Estado de cuenta

RBS Stationery Supplies

Unit 2, Maltby Way
Swindon
SN4 7JT
Tel: 0870 674 532
Fax: 0870 674 453

Customer No. BH/345/29

Date	INVOICE AND STATEMENT OF ACCOUNT	Amount
	Balance brought forward as at 06 Jul 01	132.95
20 Jul 01	Payment – thank you	132.95CR
25 Jul 01	25 x boxes A4 laser printer paper @4.99	124.75
25 Jul 01	2 x RBS toner @11.99	23.98
25 Jul 01	Carriage	7.00
Payments and transactions received after 06 Aug 01 are not shown		
	PAYMENT IS DUE WITHIN 10 DAYS OF RECEIPT *For details of how to pay, please see over*	£155.73

Head Office: 45 Glebe Rd, Swindon SN4 5 KT
Registered in England: 679 4289
Vat no: 562 9832 43

Recibo

Date 4 February   20 02   No. 5450
Customer's Name Mr Charles
Address 97 Lyon Terrace, Chichester

Stock No.	Description of Article Sold		Amount	
B78-54	Leather briefcase	£	95—	00
	10% discount	£	(9—	50)
		£	85—	50
	Paid in full – cheque			

Thank you for your custom
McCarthy's Limited — 50 Kingsgate, Chichester Tel: 643876

Statement of Account

Música de Allá

Calle Victor Jara 10
28056 Madrid
tel/fax 92 558 87 42/3

Medioteca Municipal
Peña Santa 10
28063 Madrid

N° de abonado YL 33209

Fecha	Descripción	Precio €	Fecha de pago
7/02/02	Estuche 3 CD Latinoamérica	30.00 €	30/01/02
7/03/02	Estuche 3 CD Medio Oriente	30.00 €	27/02/02
8/04/02	Estuche 3 CD Europa Oriental	30.00 €	
	Suma debida	30.00 €	

Si paga su factura por domiciliación de pagos, su cuenta será debitada el día 30 del
mes. Para todo pago por tarjeta de crédito, cheque bancario o cuenta de Caja Postal,
véase al dorso.

Receipt

Andrés Blanco y Cía

"Ultramarinos al por mayor"
Avenida Ramón y Cajal 42
47010 Valladolid
www.andresblanco.com

Daniel Clark
Westfare Stores Ltd
48 Eastbury Road
Kingston KT2 5BX

Fecha: 09/04/2002

RECIBO

Cantidad	Concepto	Referencia	Precio por Kg.	Importe
50 Kg.	Aceitunas rellenas de anchoa	6/334	15	750
20 Kg.	Mejillones en salsa picante	6/526	21	420
10 Kg.	Turrón de chocolate	3/52N	30	300
			Subtotal	€1470
			Gastos de envío	160
			IVA	297
			Total	€1927

Pago recibido, 08 de abril 2002

Fax

Cantata Publishing

55 Mill St
Liverpool L12 GH
Tel: +44 (0)151 234 8970
Fax: +44 (0)151 235 8744

FACSIMILE NUMBER:+ 44 (0)151 4497 8744

<u>Message for:</u> Peter Evans
<u>Address:</u> Boom Books, The Market Place
    Marville
    M33 7GH
<u>Fax number:</u> 0377 624 994
<u>From:</u> Mary Dunn
<u>Date:</u> 14 June 2002

Number of pages including this one: 2

Thank you for confirming that you will be able to exhibit at the New Age Book Fair on 12 July 2002. I have reserved a room on a bed-and-breakfast basis at the Consort Hotel, which is close to our venue (see attached plan), from 11 July–14 July inclusive.

We will need to receive all your promotional material, samples, books and posters by the 2 July at the very latest so that stands can be prepared on 11 July.

Can you confirm that the arrangements above are acceptable? If you require any further details, don't hesitate to get in touch.

Looking forward to meeting you again on 11 July.

Mary Dunn

Promotions Coordinator

Memorándum

Memorandum

```
To:        All staff
From:      F. Farnes, Expenses administrator
CC:        Head of Finance
Date:      3/3/2002
Subject:   Expense claims
```

Staff are reminded that all expense claims must be submitted by 14 March 2002 in time to be processed before the end of this financial year. Reimbursement of late claims will be delayed.

Fax

• •

INFORMÁTICA L.C.
CALLE SAN BERNARDO
86000 MEXICO DF
N° de teléfono: (210) 775-2688
N° de fax: (210) 775-2689

FAX

Fecha: 12 de agosto 2002

Por favor entregar este documento a: Juan Briones

Número de fax: (210) 866-5528

De parte de: Sara Ballinas

Número de páginas (incluyendo esta): 1

Mensaje: Por favor hágame llegar con urgencia, por Chronopost si es posible, los originales de sus boletos de avión y tren, para que pueda proceder con su reembolso.

También necesitaré sus recibos de hotel y de restaurante, pero no con tanta urgencia. Gracias.

Saludos cordiales,

Sara Ballinas

Sara Ballinas

Memorandum

MEMORÁNDUM

05/06/2002

Por razones de seguridad, se recuerda al personal que el acceso a los locales está estrictamente prohibido entre viernes a las 22h00 y lunes a las 6h00, excepto con la autorización especial otorgada por el Sr. Jiménez.

La dirección

Correspondence/La correspondencia

El correo electrónico

la barra de herramientas ■
destinatario ■
copia a ■
asunto ■
adjuntos ■

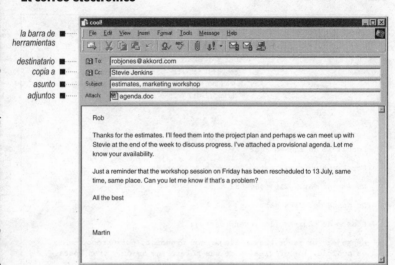

```
cool!                                                    _ □ ×
File  Edit  View  Insert  Format  Tools  Message  Help
To:      robjones@akkord.com
Cc:      Stevie Jenkins
Subject: estimates, marketing workshop
Attach:  agenda.doc

   Rob

   Thanks for the estimates. I'll feed them into the project plan and perhaps we can meet up with
   Stevie at the end of the week to discuss progress. I've attached a provisional agenda. Let me
   know your availability.

   Just a reminder that the workshop session on Friday has been rescheduled to 13 July, same
   time, same place. Can you let me know if that's a problem?

   All the best


   Martin
```

to be on e-mail	tener e-mail	to receive an attachment	recibir datos adjuntos *or* un anexo
an e-mail	un mensaje electrónico, un e-mail, un emilio (infrml)	to open an attachment	abrir los datos adjuntos *or* un anexo
an e-mail address	una dirección electrónica	to save a message to the desktop/hard disk	guardar un mensaje en el escritorio/disco duro
at at sign	una arroba	to delete a message	borrar un mensaje
an address book	una libreta de direcciones	an inbox	un bandeja de entrada
a mailing list	una lista de distribución	an outbox	una bandeja de salida
to send an e-mail	enviar un e-mail	freemail	un servicio de correo electrónico gratuito
to receive an e-mail	recibir un e-mail	snail mail	el correo postal
to forward an e-mail	hacer seguir un mensaje	to send/get spam	enviar/recibir spam *or* mensajes no solicitados
to copy somebody in, to cc somebody	enviar un mensaje a alguien como copia	spamming	envío masivo, la propaganda por e-mail
c.c. (carbon copy)	copia		
b.c.c. (blind carbon copy)	copia invisible	a mail bomb	una bomba (electrónica)
a file	un archivo	a modem	un módem
a signature file	un archivo firma		
an emoticon, a smiley	un emoticono, una carita sonriente, un smiley		
to attach a file	enviar datos adjuntos *or* un anexo		

Using e-mail

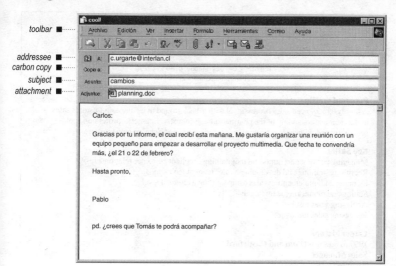

toolbar ■
addressee ■
carbon copy ■
subject ■
attachment ■

Archivo Edición Ver Insertar Formato Herramientas Correo Ayuda

A: c.urgarte@interlan.cl
Copia a:
Asunto: cambios
Adjuntos: planning.doc

Carlos:

Gracias por tu informe, el cual recibí esta mañana. Me gustaría organizar una reunión con un equipo pequeño para empezar a desarrollar el proyecto multimedia. Que fecha te convendría más, ¿el 21 o 22 de febrero?

Hasta pronto,

Pablo

pd. ¿crees que Tomás te podrá acompañar?

tener e-mail	to be on e-mail	recibir datos adjuntos *or* un anexo	to receive an attachment
un mensaje electrónico, un e-mail, un emilio (infrml)	an e-mail	abrir los datos adjuntos *or* un anexo	to open an attachment
una dirección electrónica	an e-mail address	guardar un mensaje en el escritorio/disco duro	to save a message to the desktop/hard disk
una arroba	an at sign	borrar un mensaje	to delete a message
una libreta de direcciones	an address book	una bandeja de entrada	an inbox
una lista de distribución	a mailing list	una bandeja de salida	an outbox
enviar un e-mail	to send an e-mail	un servicio de correo electrónico gratuito	freemail
recibir un e-mail	to receive an e-mail	el correo postal	snail mail
hacer seguir un mensaje	to forward an e-mail	enviar/recibir spam *or* mensajes no solicitados	to send/get spam
enviar un mensaje a alguien como copia	to copy somebody in, to cc somebody	envío masivo, la propaganda por e-mail	spamming
copia	c.c. (carbon copy)	una bomba (electrónica)	a mail bomb
copia invisible	b.c.c. (blind carbon copy)	un módem	a modem
un archivo	a file		
un archivo firma	a signature file		
un emoticono, una carita sonriente, un smiley	an emoticon, a smiley		
enviar datos adjuntos *or* un anexo	to attach a file		

Currículum vitae: ejecutivo británico

Madeleine Thompson

132 Albert Road, Brighton, BN1 7RF

Tel: 01273 455 942 Mobile: 0780 273 7414
E-mail: mthompson@fasternet.co.uk

Personal profile

A highly experienced sales professional with a background in business-to-business sales and a clear understanding of the pharmaceuticals industry. Energetic, professional and self-motivated with a proven ability to exceed targets and develop new business.

Key Skills

Managing customer accounts and maintaining excellent customer relationships
Recruiting, training and developing a sales team of ten members
Planning and implementing sales campaigns on a regional level
Setting and monitoring team targets
Analysing sales results
Increasing sales turnover

Career history

1997 to present   **Dunn and Castleford**
Sales Manager
Analysed target markets
Formulated long-term sales strategy
Negotiated major sales contracts worth in excess of £2 million over five years with national companies including The Drugstore chain, Chemco, and the High Street chemist Scotts
Managed major client accounts
Built up a sales team of ten and created an in-house training programme

1994-1997 **Trent Pharmaceuticals**
Sales Associate
Travelled throughout the South West revitalizing sales networks and establishing new contacts
Won Salesperson of the Year Award 1996
Produced quarterly sales analysis for head office

1992-1994 **Pharmwares**
Telesales Administrator
Responsible for running a telesales unit of five staff
Presented company products and services to prospective clients
Handled complaints and enquiries
Updated customer databases

Education and Training

1993-1994 London Business Institute - Postgraduate Diploma in Retail Marketing
1990-1993 Brighton College - Diploma in Sales and Marketing
Currently working towards a certificate in e-customer relationship management by open learning

Personal Details

Date of birth: 22 March 1972
Driving Licence: Full UK licence
Interests: horse-riding, travel, chess
References: Available on request

Curriculum vitae: Spanish executive

Armando Alonso Gutiérrez

ABOGADO

Manila 38
75013 Valencia

Formación académica

1988 Diploma de la Cámara de Comercio de Bruselas
1987 Curso de inglés de negocios, Cámara de Comercio de Londres
1986 Maestría en Derecho por la Universidad Autónoma de Barcelona
1985 Licenciado en Derecho por la Universidad Autónoma de Barcelona.
Premio Extraordinario de Licenciatura en la rama de Derecho Comercial.

Experiencia profesional

1994 al presente: Jefe del servicio jurídico de PRM Auditores, Madrid.

Responsabilidades:
- asegurar la preparación de dossiers jurídicos para la fusión de empresas y la creación de filiales
- asegurar el enlace entre los abogados empresariales y el Fiscal de Hacienda

Logros destacados:
- reorganización y uniformización de la gestión jurídica de las diferentes filiales del grupo
- desarrollo de un proyecto para la cuarta filial en París

1989-1994 Asistencia Jurídica para STTM, Barcelona
(Seguros de transporte terrestre y marítimo)

Responsabilidades:
- negociación de contratos de transporte y fletamento
- seguimiento de los avisos de siniestro
- elaboración de un programa interno de formación de personal

1987-1988 Experiencia profesional, tres meses con la Comisión Europea

Responsabilidades:
- preparación de dossiers con respecto a la uniformización de los sistemas de seguros para las empresas de los países miembros

Información personal

37 años, casado, un hijo
Trilingüe español, inglés, francés
Cineasta amateur
Aficionado del hockey sobre hielo
Referencias disponibles a petición

Currículum vitae: joven con título universitario

Alexander Joseph

23 Nevis Close
Carlisle
CL13 7HK
Tel: 01228 677 453

Personal profile

A hard-working, self-motivated and enthusiastic Information Technology graduate with a keen interest in the Internet and the digital economy. A good problem-solver with an ability to work well as part of a team.

Career objectives

I am looking for a position where I could further develop my strong IT skills in a business environment.

Education and training

1998-2002 **University of Aberdeen**
BSc Honours Computing Science (2:1)
1991-1998 **Carlisle Community College**
Obtained three 'A' levels (maths, physics, information technology) at grade A and seven 'O' levels including English
Programming languages: HTML,C, C++, Java,VRML, Oracle Forms 4
Environments: Microsoft Windows 98 & NT, Sun Solaris

Work experience

2001-2002 Weekend work as cashier and customer advisor - Buildit Discount Store, Carlisle
2001 Summer employment as junior programmer in a local software house writing browser-enabled customer billing and stock control software.

Achievements

Represented my university in the triathlon at the National Student Games 2000
Chair of the University Debating Society 2001
Editorial assistant on the student newspaper

Personal details

Date of birth: 14 December 1979
Full UK driving licence
Interests: athletics, music, travel
References: available on request

Curriculum vitae: Spanish graduate

Datos personales

NOMBRE Y APELLIDOS: María Luisa Márquez Blanco
FECHA DE NACIMIENTO: 26/2/77
LUGAR: Pina de Ebro (Zaragoza)
ESTADO CIVIL: Soltera
DOMICILIO ACTUAL: c/Islas Bermudas 18, 2º-B
                                    FUENCARRAL
                                    28080 MADRID
TELÉFONO: 2435394

Datos Académicos

1995-2000: Licenciatura en Ciencias de la Información,
                  Periodismo, por la Universidad Complutense de Madrid.

1991-1995: BUP/COU en el Colegio San Pablo, Fuencarral, Madrid.

Otros títulos

2002: Curso de OFIMÁTICA: MS-DOS, WP 5.1, DBASE III y LOTUS 1-2-3.

2000 y 2001: Seminario de Periodismo Deportivo en el Colegio Universitario
                     San Juan de Madrid.

Experiencia Profesional

2002: Adjunta del Jefe de Prensa en los Juegos Olímpicos de Barcelona.

2000-2002: Corresponsal deportiva en Madrid del periódico 'Correo de Aragón' de
                  Zaragoza.

1998, 1999, 2000: Adjunta del Jefe de Prensa en los Campeonatos del Circuito Europeo
                  de Tenis Profesional celebrados en España. Este trabajo consistía en
                  preparar toda la información para los periodistas, entrevistar a los
                  jugadores, traducciones, etc.

1998 y 1999: Responsable de la Sala de Prensa y de la organización de azafatas del Rally
                   de Valencia.

1997: Jefe de Prensa del Circuito de Profesionales de Tenis PRT.

1995, 1996 y 1997: Azafata en la Institución Ferial de Madrid, IFEMA.

Publicaciones y Colaboraciones

1998, 1999 y 2000: Colaboraciones en la revista MUNDO DEPORTIVO.

1997: Publicaciones en le periódico de la CÁMARA DE COMERCIO E
          INDUSTRIA DE ZARAGOZA.

Idiomas

INGLÉS: Dominio total, hablado y escrito.

FRANCÉS: Hablado y escrito.

Aficiones

Leer, viajar, esquí, tenis, baloncesto.

El diseño de un currículum vitae en inglés

En general, un currículum vitae no deberá exceder las dos páginas. Al mismo tiempo, deberá ser conciso y estar bien presentado. Es preferible no utilizar la primera persona singular al describir su carrera y habilidades. Cierta información personal, como por ejemplo, nombre de soltera o nacionalidad, no es necesaria, salvo cuando esta información tenga una relevancia directa al trabajo.

El formato más común para un CV es incluir los datos en orden cronológico, empezando por la experiencia profesional más reciente.

Cualidades personales/personal profile

Esta sección permite destacar sus cualidades personales e incluir cualquier punto de interés que no quepa en otra sección. Puede mencionar sus aspiraciones con una frase del tipo:
*I am looking for a position as a.../
I am looking for a role where...*
Ciertas frases y expresiones llaman más la atención que otras:
an established track record in [sales, retail]
proven administrative/staff management skills
articulate
able to work to deadlines
creative
dynamic
efficient
energetic
enthusiastic
experienced
flexible
highly motivated

innovative
organized
people-oriented
reliable
self-motivated
team-player
versatile

Aptitudes esenciales/key skills

Esta sección del CV permite al candidato proporcionar los detalles de las habilidades que ha adquirido a través de su formación y de su carrera. Las expresiones que siguen le podrán ser útiles:
a detailed knowledge of [financial planning, project management]
good analytical and problem-solving skills
good communication skills
team leadership skills
strategic thinking
commercial awareness
administrative experience
bookkeeping skills
good telephone manner
staff management experience
keyboard skills (60wpm)
shorthand
conversational/reading knowledge of German
fluent Italian
good written/spoken French
proficient in using spreadsheets/Excel/PowerPoint

Carrera profesional/career history

En la descripción de sus logros se recomienda usar el participio pasado, omitiendo el sujeto 'I'. Verbos útiles:

> analysed
> coordinated
> created
> delivered
> designed
> directed
> evaluated
> facilitated
> headed
> identified
> implemented
> launched
> liaised
> maintained
> managed
> monitored
> organized
> planned
> prepared
> produced
> provided
> researched
> reorganized
> resolved

Puede destacar la importancia de su propia contribución a los puestos que ha ocupado, usando ciertas expresiones positivas, como por ejemplo:

achieved [increase/improvement]
completed [the project on time and within budget]
drove forward [the implementation of]
exceeded [targets/objectives]
increased [profits/turnover/sales]
improved [efficiency/information flow]
maximized [impact/productivity]
negotiated [contract/deal]
pioneered [technique/system]
reduced [wastage/costs]
resolved [conflict/difficulty]
secured [contracts/customers]
upgraded [system/procedure]
streamlined [process/procedure]
successfully [delivered/implemented, completed/negotiated]
won [contract/tender]

The presentation of a Spanish curriculum vitae

A curriculum vitae should not generally exceed two pages in length and should be clearly laid out and succinctly worded. It is standard practice to avoid the use of the first person when describing one's career outline and skills. Personal details such as marital status, maiden name and nationality are now often omitted in a British curriculum vitae except where they have a direct bearing on the job for which one is applying. However, in Spain they are still often given. It is common for a Spanish job advertisement to request a handwritten letter (*carta a mano*) and a photograph. Advertisements for professional positions rarely give any indication of salary and a candidate is asked to state their current salary or their desired salary.

There are two common styles of presentation: the chronological CV with experience listed either in chronological order, starting with one's education, or in reverse chronological order, starting with the most recent or current position, and the functional CV, with experience grouped according to field and relevance to the job for which one is applying.

Personal profile/cualidades personales

The candidate has the opportunity in an opening statement to 'sell' the personal qualities and aptitudes which might not be evident elsewhere in the CV. It may be appropriate to state your career aspirations here with a phrase such as: *Busco un puesto en el cual…/*

Busco un puesto donde mi papel será de… Useful phrases might include:

    experiencia comprobada en gestión de personal
    administrador experimentado
    conocimiento a fondo de
    excelente comunicador
    creativo
    dinámico
    eficiente
    lleno de energía
    con entusiasmo
    flexible
    muy motivado
    espíritu de innovación
    sentido de la organización
    de fácil relación
    responsable
    espíritu de equipo

Key skills/aptitudes esenciales

The applicant will wish to provide details of general competencies acquired over the course of their education, training or career. Useful phrases could include:

    espíritu analítico y aptitud para resolver los problemas
    comunicador
    aptitud para dirigir un equipo
    aptitud para elaborar una estrategia
    espíritu comercial
    experiencia administrativa
    pericia en contabilidad
    experiencia en gestión de personal
    rapidez dactilográfica (60 ppm)
    conocimiento de estenografía
    alemán hablado/leído
    italiano cotidiano
    buen dominio del francés escrito/oral

Career history/carrera profesional

When listing one's achievements it is usual to employ action verbs in the past tense. Useful verbs might include:

diseñé
produje
concebí
dirigí
evalué
facilité
llevé a cabo
identifiqué
implementé
lancé
trabajé con
garanticé el mantenimiento
controlé
organicé
planifiqué
preparé
investigué
reorganicé
resolví

You can stress the benefits you have brought to the companies you have worked for with positive phrases such as:

aumenté
mejoré
llevé a cabo (el proyecto dentro de los límites del presupuesto)
aceleré (la implementación de)
superé (los objetivos)
aumenté (los beneficios/ventas)
aumenté (la eficiencia/la circulación de la información)
maximicé (el impacto/la productividad)
negocié (un contrato/un trato)
desarrollé (una técnica/un sistema)

reduje (pérdidas/costos)
resolví (un conflicto/una dificultad)
perfeccioné (el sistema/proceso)
simplifiqué (la técnica/proceso)
logré (implementar/producir)
garanticé (el contrato/la oferta)

Currículum Vitae

Carta de presentación

17 Roslyn Terrace,
London
NW2 3SQ

15th October 2002

Ms R. Klein,
Travis Consulting Group
44 Commercial Way
LONDON
E14 5BH

Dear Ms Klein,

Principal Consultant, E-business Strategy

I should like to apply for the above post, advertised in today's Sunday Times and have pleasure in enclosing my curriculum vitae for your attention.

MBA-qualified, I am a highly experienced information systems strategy consultant and have worked with a range of blue-chip clients, primarily in the financial services and retail sectors. In my most recent role, with Herriot Consulting, I have successfully led the development of a new e-business practice.

I am now seeking an opportunity to fulfil my career aspirations with a major management consultancy such as TCG, which has recognised the enormous potential of the e-business revolution. I believe I can offer TCG a combination of technical understanding, business insight and entrepreneurial flair.

I would be delighted to discuss this opportunity further with you at a future interview and look forward to hearing from you.

Yours sincerely,

Jane Penner

Jane Penner

enc

Expresiones útiles

I am writing in response to your advertisement in [publication] of [date]

I wish to enquire about the vacancy for a [job title]

I should like to apply for the post of [job title] advertised in [publication] of [date]

As you will see from the enclosed CV...

Please find enclosed a copy of my curriculum vitae/résumé (AmE)

Fórmulas de despedida

Thank you for considering this application

I should be pleased to attend an interview

Please do not hesitate to contact me on the above number if you should require any further information

I look forward to hearing from you

I look forward to discussing this position further with you at a future interview

· ·

Covering letter for a job application

Urbanización El Molino
Chalet 88
VILLANUEVA DE LA CAÑADA
(Madrid)
Tel. (91) 815 24 97

17 de abril de 2002

Director de Recursos Humanos
Textiles Echevarría
Torre Picasso 10–9
28080 MADRID

Estimado señor

En respuesta al anuncio publicado en el periódico "El País" de fecha 16 de abril en el que solicitan secretaria trilingüe, quisiera ser considerada al realizarse la selección de candidatos.

Como se desprende del currículum vitae que adjunto, estoy casada con un ciudadano británico y acabo de regresar a España después de haber vivido durante seis años en el Reino Unido, donde trabajé como secretaria de dirección en una empresa multinacional. Tengo perfecto dominio del idioma inglés, sólidos conocimientos de francés y amplia experiencia en procesamiento de textos.

Agradezco a Ud. la atención que me pueda dispensar y quedo a su entera disposición para cualquier aclaración y/o ampliación de antecedentes.

Sin otro particular, le saluda atentamente.

María José García

María José García
Anexo: Currículum vitae

Useful phrases

Con referencia al puesto de [puesto] anunciado recientemente en [publicación] del [fecha]...

Me dirijo a usted con el fin de expresarle mi interés en ser considerado para la posición de [posición]...

Mis credenciales están resumidas en mi currículum vitae, el cual estoy adjuntando para su mejor referencia.

Además de detallar mis datos personales y profesionales en el currículo vitae adjunto, me permito subrayar mi experiencia en el campo de...

Closing formulas

Quedo a su disposición para ampliar datos y ofrecer referencias

Sin otro particular, quedo a la espera de su respuesta...

A la espera de sus noticias, se despide con un cordial saludo...

Estoy a su disposición para realizar la entrevista en el momento que me digan...

Me sentiré muy honrado de poder concretar la fecha y hora de nuestra entrevista

Vocabulario útil

El teléfono y las llamadas telefónicas

the handset, the receiver	el auricular
the base	la base
the (numeric) keypad	el teclado (numérico)
the telephone cord	el cordón, el cable
to pick up the phone	descolgar
to hang up	colgar
a telephone call	una llamada telefónica
to make a phone call	hacer una llamada telefónica
a telephone number	un número de teléfono
an extension (phone)	un teléfono secundario
an extension (number)	una extensión
the dialling tone	la señal (de marcar)
the tone (in a recorded message)	la señal
to dial the number	marcar el número
to dial 999/911	marcar el 999/911
the area/country code	el código territorial
the operator	el operador/la operadora
the switchboard operator	el/la telefonista
a telephone company	una compañía de teléfonos
a digital phone	un teléfono digital
a tone-dialling phone	un teléfono de marcado multifrecuencia
a cordless phone	un teléfono sin cable
a digital cordless phone	un teléfono digital sin cable
an answering machine	un contestador (automático)
a fax machine	un fax
voice mail	el correo de voz
a phone book	una guía telefónica/de teléfonos
the Yellow Pages®	las Páginas Amarillas®

a business/residential number	un número profesional/personal
a Freefone number (GB)	una llamada gratuita
a toll-free number (US)	una llamada gratuita
the emergency services number (999 in the UK and 911 in the US for fire, police or ambulance services)	el número de emergencia
to hear the phone ring	oir sonar el teléfono
to let the phone ring 3/5…times	dejar sonar 3/5… veces
it's engaged/the line is engaged	esta ocupado/suena ocupado
there's no answer	no contestan
to leave a message on the answerphone	dejar un mensaje en el contestador

Expresiones útiles para el teléfono

Hello!	Dígame, ¿Aló? (AmL)
It's Rebecca Major	Habla Rebecca Major
May I speak to…?	¿Podría hablar con…?
Who's calling, please?	¿De parte de quien?
Speaking!	¡Con él/ella!
It's a business/personal call	Es una llamada profesional/personal
One moment please	Un momento por favor
Hold the line please	No cuelgue
I'll put you through (ie to their extension)	Le comunico con…
I'll put him/her on	Se lo/la paso
I'll put you on hold	No cuelgue
Mr Fowler cannot come to the phone at the moment	El Sr. Fowler está ocupado en este momento
May I take/leave a message?	¿Puedo tomar/dejar un mensaje?
I'll call back later	Llamaré más tarde
Please leave your message after the tone (on an answering machine)	Por favor deje un mensaje después de la señal

Useful vocabulary

The phone and calling procedures

el auricular	the handset, the receiver
la base	the base
el teclado (numérico)	the (numeric) keypad
el cordón, el cable	the telephone cord
descolgar	to pick up the phone
colgar	to hang up
una llamada telefónica	a telephone call
hacer una llamada telefónica	to make a phone call
un número de teléfono	a telephone number
un teléfono secundario	an extension (phone)
una extensión	an extension (number)
la señal (de marcar)	the dialling tone
la señal	the tone (in a recorded message)
marcar el número	to dial the number
marcar el 999/911	to dial 999/911
el código territorial	the area/country code
el operador/la operadora	the operator
el/la telefonista	the switchboard operator
una compañía de teléfonos	a telephone company
un teléfono digital	a digital phone
un teléfono de marcado multifrecuencia	a tone-dialling phone
un teléfono sin cable	a cordless phone
un teléfono digital sin cable	a digital cordless phone
un contestador (automático)	an answering machine
un fax	a fax machine
el correo de voz	voice mail
una guía telefónica/de teléfonos	a phone book
las Páginas Amarillas®	the Yellow Pages®
un número profesional/personal	a business/residential number
una llamada gratuita	a Freefone number (GB), a toll-free number (US)
el número de emergencia	the emergency services number (999 in the UK and 911 in the US for fire, police or ambulance services)
oír sonar el teléfono	to hear the phone ring
dejar sonar 3/5… veces	to let the phone ring 3/5…times
esta ocupado/suena ocupado	it's engaged/the line is engaged
no contestan	there's no answer
dejar un mensaje en el contestador	to leave a message on the answerphone

Common phrases used on the phone

Dígame, ¿Aló? (AmL)	Hello!
Habla Raquel García	It's Raquel García
¿Podría hablar con…?	May I speak to…?
¿De parte de quien?	Who's calling, please?
¡Con él/ella!	Speaking!
Es una llamada profesional/personal	It's a business/personal call
Un momento por favor	One moment please
No cuelgue	Hold the line please
Le comunico con…	I'll put you through (ie to their extension)
Se lo/la paso	I'll put him/her on
No cuelgue	I'll put you on hold
El Sr. Solana está ocupado en este momento	Mr Solana cannot come to the phone at the moment
¿Puedo tomar/dejar un mensaje?	May I take/leave a message?
Llamaré más tarde	I'll call back later
Por favor deje un mensaje después de la señal	Please leave your message after the tone (on an answering machine)

Funciones y servicios especiales

fault reporting	aviso de averías
directory enquiries (GB), directory assistance (US)	información
to be ex-directory	no figurar en la guía telefónica
to make a reverse charge call (GB), to call somebody collect (US)	llamar a cobro revertido
a three-way call	una llamada de tres en conferencia
an itemized bill	una factura detallada
call waiting	llamadas en espera, call waiting
call diversion	desvío de llamadas
caller display	identificación del llamador
last number redial	la remarca del último número
secrecy button	el botón de privacidad

Cuando no está en su casa

a phone booth (US), a phone box (GB)	una cabina (telefónica)
a payphone	un teléfono público
a coin-operated phone	un teléfono a monedas
a cardphone (GB)	un teléfono de tarjeta
a phonecard	una tarjeta telefónica (para llamar de un teléfono público)
a car phone	un teléfono de coche
a pager	un bíper

La telefonía móvil

a mobile (GB), a mobile phone (GB), a cellphone (US)	un teléfono móvil
mobile telephony	la telefonía móvil
an Internet phone	un teléfono Internet
a WAP phone	un teléfono WAP
call alert	un aviso de llamada
caller identification	la identificación del llamador
call credit	crédito prepagado
call charges	el costo de la llamada
a hands-free headset	un aparato manos libres
a hands-free kit	un kit manos libres
a phone charger	un cargador
a handset cover, a fascia	una carcasa
keypad locking	el bloqueo del teclado
a text alert	una alerta de texto
the ringtone	el tono, el ringtone
vibrate setting	el modo vibración
an SMS message	un mensaje SMS
a text message	un mensaje de texto
text sb	mandar un mensaje de texto a algn
a network	una red
dual-band	multi-red, dual-band
tri-band	multi-red, tri-band
a prepaid mobile phone voucher (GB)	una tarjeta telefónica prepagada (para teléfono móvil)

Some special functions and services

aviso de averías	fault reporting
información	directory enquiries (GB), directory assistance (US)
no figurar en la guía telefónica	to be ex-directory
llamar a cobro revertido	to make a reverse charge call (GB), to call somebody collect (US)
una llamada de tres en conferencia	a three-way call
una factura detallada	an itemized bill
llamadas en espera, call waiting	call waiting
desvío de llamadas	call diversion
identificación del llamador	caller display
la remarca del último número	last number redial
el botón de privacidad	secrecy button
crédito prepagado	call credit
el costo de la llamada	call charges
un aparato manos libres	a hands-free headset
un kit manos libres	a hands-free kit
un cargador	a phone charger
una carcasa	a handset cover, a fascia
el bloqueo del teclado	keypad locking
una alerta de texto	a text alert
el tono, el ringtone	the ringtone
el modo vibración	vibrate setting
un mensaje SMS	an SMS message
un mensaje de texto	a text message
mandar un mensaje de texto a algn	text sb
una red	a network
multi-red, dual-band	dual-band
multi-red, tri-band	tri-band
una tarjeta telefónica prepagada (para teléfono móvil)	a prepaid mobile phone voucher (GB)

When you are not at home

una cabina (telefónica)	a phone booth (US), a phone box (GB)
un teléfono público	a payphone
un teléfono a monedas	a coin-operated phone
un teléfono de tarjeta	a cardphone (GB)
una tarjeta telefónica (para llamar de un teléfono público)	a phonecard
un teléfono de coche	a car phone
un bíper	a pager

Mobile telephony

un teléfono móvil	a mobile (GB), a mobile phone (GB), a cellphone (US)
la telefonía móvil	mobile telephony
un teléfono Internet	an Internet phone
un teléfono WAP	a WAP phone
un aviso de llamada	call alert
la identificación del llamador	caller identification

Countries/Los países

Country/ País	Inhabitant/ Habitante	Official language(s)/ Lengua(s) oficial(es)	Currency/ Moneda
Afghanistan *Afganistán m*	Afghan *afgano(-a) m,f*	Pashto/Pushtu/Dari *pashtu/dari*	afghani *afganí m*
Albania *Albania m*	Albanian *albano(-a) m,f/ albanés(-esa) m,f*	Albanian *albanés*	lek *lek m*
Algeria *Argelia f*	Algerian *argelino(-a) m,f*	Arabic *árabe*	dinar *dinar argelino m*
Andorra *Andorra f*	Andorran *andorrano(-a) m,f*	Catalan/French/Spanish *catalán/francés/español*	euro *euro m*
Angola *Angola f*	Angolan *angoleño(-a) m,f*	Portuguese *portugués*	kwanza *kwanza f*
Antigua and Barbuda *Antigua y Barbuda f*	Antiguan/Barbudan *de Antigua y Barbuda*	English *inglés*	East Caribbean dollar *dólar del Caribe Oriental m*
Argentina *Argentina f*	Argentinian/Argentine *argentino(-a) m,f*	Spanish *español*	peso *peso m*
Armenia *Armenia f*	Armenian *armenio(-a) m,f*	Armenian *armenio*	dram *dram m*
Australia *Australia f*	Australian *australiano(-a) m,f*	English *inglés*	Australian dollar *dólar australiano m*
Austria *Austria f*	Austrian *austriaco(-a) m,f*	German *alemán*	euro *euro m*
Azerbaijan *Azerbaiyán m*	Azeri/Azerbaijani *azerbaiyano(-a) m,f*	Azeri/Russian *azerí/ruso*	manat *manat m*
Bahamas *Bahamas fpl*	Bahamian *bahamense mf/ bahamés(-esa) m,f/ bahameño(-a) m,f*	English *inglés*	Bahamian dollar *dólar de Bahamas m*
Bahrain/Bahrein *Bahrein m*	Bahraini *bahreiní mf*	Arabic *árabe*	Bahrain dinar *dinar de Bahrein m*
Bangladesh *Bangladesh m*	Bangladeshi *bangladesí mf*	Bengali/English *bengalí/inglés*	taka *taka m*
Barbados *Barbados m*	Barbadian *barbadense mf*	English *inglés*	Barbados dollar *dólar de Barbados m*
Belarus *Bielorrusia f*	Belarussian *bielorruso(-a) m,f*	Belarussian *bielorruso*	Belarussian rouble *rublo bielorruso m*
Belgium *Bélgica f*	Belgian *belga mf*	French/Flemish/German *francés/flamenco/alemán*	euro *euro m*
Belize *Belice m*	Belizean *beliceño(-a) m,f*	English/Spanish/Creole *inglés/español/criollo*	Belize dollar *dólar de Belice m*
Benin *Benín m*	Beninese *beninés(-esa) m,f/ aboense mf*	French *francés*	CFA franc *franco CFA m*
Burmuda *Bermudas f pl*	Burmudan/Burmudian *de Bermudas*	English *inglés*	Bermudian dollar *dólar de Bermudas m*
Bhutan *Bután m*	Bhutanese *butanés(-esa) m,f*	Dzongka *dzong-kha*	ngultrum, Indian rupee *ngultrum m, rupia india f*

Countries

Country/ País	Inhabitant/ Habitante	Official language(s)/ Lengua(s) oficial(es)	Currency/ Moneda
Bolivia *Bolivia f*	Bolivian *boliviano(-a) m,f*	Spanish/Quechua/Aymara *español/quechua/aimará*	boliviano *boliviano m*
Bosnia-Herzegovina *Bosnia-Herzegovina f*	Bosnian *bosnio(-a) m,f*	Serbian/Croatian/Bosnian *serbio/croata/bosnio*	convertible marka *marka convertible*
Botswana *Botswana f*	Botswanan *botsuano(-a) m,f/ botsuanés(-esa) m,f*	English/Setswana *inglés/setswana*	pula *pula m*
Brazil *Brasil m*	Brazilian *brasileño(-a) m,f*	Portuguese *portugués*	cruzeiro *cruzeiro m*
Brunei *Brunei m*	Bruneian *de Brunei*	Malay/English *malayo/inglés*	Brunei dollar *dólar de Brunei m*
Bulgaria *Bulgaria f*	Bulgarian *búlgaro(-a) m,f*	Bulgarian *búlgaro*	lev *lev m*
Burkina Faso *Burkina Faso f*	Burkinabe *voltense mf*	French/Mossi *francés/mossi*	CFA franc *franco CFA m*
Burma *Birmania f*	Burmese *birmano(-a) m,f*	Burmese *birmano*	kyat *kyat m*
Burundi *Burundi m*	Burundian *burundés(-esa) m,f*	Kirundi/French *kirundi/francés*	Burundi franc *franco burundés m*
Cambodia *Camboya f*	Cambodian *camboyano(-a) m,f*	Khmer *khmer*	riel *riel m*
Cameroon *Camerún*	Cameroonian *camerunés(-esa) m,f*	French/English *francés/inglés*	CFA franc *franco CFA m*
Canada *Canadá*	Canadian *canadiense mf*	English/French *inglés/francés*	Canadian dollar *dólar canadiense m*
Central African Republic *República Centroafricana*	person from the Central African Republic *centroafricano(-a) m,f/ habitante de la República Centroafricana mf*	French/Sangho *francés/sango*	CFA franc *franco CFA m*
Chad *Chad m*	Chadian *chadí mf/chadiano(-a) m,f*	Arabic/French *árabe/francés*	CFA franc *franco CFA m*
Chile *Chile m*	Chilean *chileno(-a) m,f*	Spanish *español*	Chilean peso *peso chileno m*
China *China f*	Chinese *chino(-a) m,f*	Chinese/Mandarin *chino/mandarín*	yuan *yuan m*
Colombia *Colombia f*	Colombian *colombiano(-a) m,f*	Spanish Colombian *español*	peso *peso colombiano m*
Comoros *Comoras fpl*	Comorian *comorano(-a) m,f*	French/Arabic *francés/árabe*	CFA franc *franco CFA m*
(Republic of the) Congo *(República del) Congo m*	Congolese *congoleño(-a) m,f/ congolés(-esa) m,f*	French *francés*	CFA franc *franco CFA m*
Costa Rica *Costa Rica f*	Costa Rican *costarricense mf*	Spanish *español*	colón *colón m*
Croatia *Croacia f*	Croat/Croatian *croata mf*	Croatian *croata*	kuna *kuna f*
Cuba *Cuba f*	Cuban *cubano(-a) m,f*	Spanish Cuban *español*	peso *peso cubano m*
Cyprus *Chipre m*	Cypriot *chipriota mf*	Greek/Turkish *griego/turco*	Cyprus pound *libra chipriota f*

Country/ País	Inhabitant/ Habitante	Official language(s)/ Lengua(s) oficial(es)	Currency/ Moneda
Czech Republic *República Checa f*	Czech *checo(-a) m,f*	Czech *checo*	czech koruna *corona checa f*
Denmark *Dinamarca f*	Dane *danés(-esa) m,f*	Danish *danés*	Danish krone *corona danesa f*
Djibouti *Yibuti m*	Djibuti/Djibutian *habitante de Yibut mf*	Arabic/French *árabe/francés*	Djibouti franc *franco de Yibuti m*
Dominica *Dominica f*	Dominican *dominicano(-a) m,f*	English *inglés*	East Caribbean dollar *dólar del Caribe Oriental m*
Dominican Republic *República Dominicana f*	Dominican *dominicano(-a) m,f*	Spanish *español*	Dominican peso *peso dominicano m*
Ecuador *Ecuador m*	Ecuadorian/Ecuadoran *ecuatoriano(-a) m,f*	Spanish *español*	sucre *sucre m*
Egypt *Egipto m*	Egyptian *egipcio(-a) m,f*	Arabic *árabe*	Egyptian pound *libra egipcia f*
El Salvador *El Salvador m*	Salvadoran *salvadoreño(-a) m,f*	Spanish *español*	colón *colón m*
England *Inglaterra f*	Englishman, Englishwoman *inglés(-esa) m,f*	English *inglés*	Sterling pound *libra esterlina f*
Equatorial Guinea *Guinea Ecuatorial f*	Equatorial Guinean *ecuatoguineano(-a) m,f*	Spanish *español*	CFA franc *franco CFA m*
Estonia *Estonia f*	Estonian *estoniano(-a) m,f*	Estonian *estonio*	kroon *corona f*
Ethiopia *Etiopía f*	Ethiopian *etíope mf/etiope mf/ abisinio(-a) m,f*	Amharic *amárico/amhárico*	birr *birr m*
Fiji *Fiji m*	Fijian *fijiano(-a) m,f*	English *inglés*	Fijian dollar *dólar de Fiji m*
Finland *Finlandia f*	Finn *finlandés(-esa) m,f/ finés(-esa) m,f*	Finnish/Swedish *finlandés/sueco*	euro *euro m*
France *Francia f*	Frenchman, Frenchwoman *francés(-esa) m,f*	French *francés*	euro *euro m*
Gabon *Gabón m*	Gabonese *gabonés(-esa) m,f*	French *francés*	CFA franc *franco CFA m*
Gambia *Gambia f*	Gambian *gambiano(-a) m,f*	English *inglés*	dalasi *dalasi m*
Georgia *Georgia f*	Georgian *georgiano(-a) m,f*	Georgian *georgiano*	lari *lari m*
Germany *Alemania f*	German *alemán(-ana) m,f*	German *alemán*	euro *euro m*
Ghana *Ghana f*	Ghanaian *ghanés(-esa) m,f*	English *inglés*	cedi *cedi m*
Greece *Grecia f*	Greek *griego(-a) m,f/heleno(-a) m,f*	Greek *griego*	euro *euro m*
Grenada *Granada f*	grenadian *granadino(-a) m,f*	English *inglés*	East Caribbean dollar *dólar del Caribe Oriental m*

Country/ País	Inhabitant/ Habitante	Official language(s)/ Lengua(s) oficial(es)	Currency/ Moneda
Guatemala *Guatemala f*	Guatemalan *guatemalteco(-a) m,f*	Spanish *español*	quetzal *quetzal m*
Guinea *Guinea f*	Guinean *guineo(-a) m,f/ guineano(-a) m,f*	French *francés*	Guinean franc *franco guineano m*
Guinea-Bissau *Guinea-Bissau f*	person from Guinea-Bissau *habitante de Guinea-Bissau mf*	Portuguese *portugués*	CFA franc *franco CFA m*
Guyana *Guyana f*	Guyanese *guyanés(-esa) m,f*	English *inglés*	Guyana dollar *dólar guyanés m*
Haiti *Haití m*	Haitian *haitiano(-a) m,f*	French *francés*	gourde *gourde m*
Honduras *Honduras fpl*	Honduran *hondureño(-a) m,f*	Spanish *español*	lempira *lempira f*
Hong Kong *Hong Kong m*	person from Hong Kong *hongkonés(-esa) m,f*	English/Chinese *inglés/chino*	Hong Kong dollar *dólar de Hong Kong m*
Hungary *Hungría f*	Hungarian *húngaro(-a) m,f*	Magyar/Hungarian *magyar/húngaro*	forint *florín m*
Iceland *Islandia f*	Icelander *islandés(-esa) m,f*	Icelandic *islandés*	Icelandic krona *corona f*
Ireland, Republic of *Irlanda, República de*	Irishman, Irishwoman *irlandés(-esa) m,f*	Irish Gaelic/English *gaélico irlandés/inglés*	euro *euro*
India *India f*	Indian *indio(-a) m,f*	Hindi/English *hindi/inglés*	Indian rupee *rupia india f*
Indonesia *Indonesia f*	Indonesian *indonesio(-a) m,f*	Bahasa Indonesian *bahasa indonesio*	Indonesian rupiah *rupia indonesia f*
Iran *Irán m*	Iranian *iraní mf*	Farsi *farsi*	Iranian rial *rial iraní m*
Iraq (also Irak) *Iraq m*	Iraqi/Iraki *iraquí mf*	Arabic *árabe*	Iraqi dinar/Iraki dinar *dinar iraquí m*
Israel *Israel m*	Israeli/Israelite *israelí mf/israelita mf*	Hebrew/Arabic *hebreo/árabe*	New Israeli shekel *nuevo shekel israelí m/ siclo m*
Italy *Italia f*	Italian *italiano(-a) m,f*	Italian *italiano*	euro *euro m*
Ivory Coast *Costa de Marfil f*	Ivoirian *marfileño(-a) m,f*	French *francés*	CFA franc *franco CFA m*
Jamaica *Jamaica f*	Jamaican *jamaicano(-a) m,f/ jamaiquino(-a) m,f*	English *inglés*	Jamaican dollar *dólar jamaicano m*
Japan *Japón m*	Japanese *japonés(-esa) m,f*	Japanese *japonés*	yen *yen m*
Jordan *Jordania f*	Jordanian *jordano(-a) m,f*	Arabic *árabe*	Jordanian dinar *dinar jordano m*
Kazakhstan *Kazajstán m*	Kazakh/Kazak *kazajo(-a) m,f*	Kazakh/Russian *kazajo/ruso*	Kazakhstani tenge *tenge kazajo m*
Kenya *Kenia/Kenya*	Kenyan *keniata mf/ kenyano(-a) m,f*	Swahili/English *suahili/inglés*	Kenyan shilling *chelín de Kenya m*

Country/País	Inhabitant/Habitante	Official language(s)/Lengua(s) oficial(es)	Currency/Moneda
Kuwait	Kuwaiti	Arabic	Kuwaiti dinar
Kuwait/Koweit m	*kuwaití mf*	*árabe*	*dinar kuwaití m*
Kyrgyzstan	Kyrgyzstani	Kyrgyz	som
Kirguizistán m	*kirguiz mf*	*kirguiz*	*som m*
Laos	Laotian	Lao	kip
Laos m	*lao(-a) m,f/laosiano(-a) m,f*	*laosiano*	*kip m*
Latvia	Latvian	Latvian/Lettish	lat
Letonia f	*letón(-ona) m,f*	*letón*	*lat m*
Lebanon	Lebanese	Arabic	Lebanese pound
Líbano m	*libanés(-esa) m,f*	*árabe*	*libra libanesa f*
Lesotho	Basotho	Sesotho/English	loti
Lesoto f	*basoto(-a) m,f*	*sesotho/inglés*	*loti m*
Liberia	Liberian	English	Liberian dollar
Liberia f	*liberiano(-a) m,f*	*inglés*	*dólar liberiano m*
Libya	Libyan	Arabic	Libyan dinar
Libia f	*libio(-a) m,f*	*árabe*	*dinar libio m*
Liechtenstein	Liechtensteiner	German	Swiss franc
Liechtenstein m	*liechtenstiense mf*	*alemán*	*franco suizo m*
Lithuania	Lithuanian	Lithuanian	Lithuanian lita
Lituania f	*lituano(-a) m,f*	*lituano*	*lita lituana f*
Luxembourg	Luxemburger	French/German	euro
Luxemburgo m	*luxemburgués(-esa) m,f*	*francés/alemán*	*euro m*
Macedonia, Republic of	Macedonian	Macedonian	dinar
Macedonia, República de f	*macedonio(-a) m,f*	*macedonio*	*dinar m*
Madagascar	Malagasy	Malagasy/French	Malagasy franc
Madagascar m	*malgache mf*	*malgache/francés*	*franco malgache m*
Malawi	Malawian	Chichewa/English	Malawian kwacha
Malawi m	*malawiano(-a) m,f/ malawí mf*	*chichewa/inglés*	*kwacha malawiano m*
Malaysia	Malaysian/Malay	Malay	Malaysian ringgit
Malasia f	*malasio(-a) m,f/ malayo(-a) m,f*	*malayo*	*ringgit de Malasia m*
Maldives	Maldivian	Dhivehi	rufiyaa
Maldivas fpl	*maldivo(-a) m,f*	*maldivo*	*rufiyaa f*
Mali	Malian	French	CFA franc
Malí m	*maliense mf*	*francés*	*franco CFA m*
Malta	Maltese	Maltese/English	Maltese pound
Malta f	*maltese mf/ maltés(-esa) m,f*	*maltés/inglés*	*libra maltesa f*
Mauritania	Mauritanian	Arabic/French	ouguiya
Mauritania f	*mauritano(-a) m,f*	*árabe/francés*	*ouguiya m*
Mauritius	Mauritian	English/French	Mauritian rupee
Mauricio m	*mauriciano(-a) m,f*	*inglés/francés*	*rupia de Mauricio f*
Mexico	Mexican	Spanish	Mexican peso
Méjico/México m	*mejicano(-a) m,f/ mexicano(-a) m,f*	*español*	*peso mexicano m*
Micronesia, Federated States of	person from the Federated States of Micronesia	English	US dollar
Micronesia, Estados Federados de	*habitante de los Estados Federados de Micronesia mf*	*inglés*	*dólar americano m*

Country/ País	Inhabitant/ Habitante	Official language(s)/ Lengua(s) oficial(es)	Currency/ Moneda
Moldova/Moldavia *Moldavia/Moldova f*	Moldovan *moldavo(-a) m,f*	Moldovan *moldavo*	Moldovan leu *leu moldavo m*
Monaco *Mónaco m*	Monegasque *monegasco(-a) m,f*	French *francés*	euro *euro m*
Mongolia *Mongolia f*	Mongolian *mongol(a) m,f*	Khalkha *mongol*	Mongol tugrik *khalkha tugrik m*
Montenegro *Montenegro m*	Montenegrin *montenegrino(-a) m,f*	Serbian *serbio m*	dinar *dinar m*
Morocco *Marruecos mpl*	Moroccan *marroquí mf*	Arabic *árabe*	dirham *dirham marroquí m*
Mozambique *Mozambique m*	Mozambican *mozambiqueño(-a) m,f*	Portuguese *portugués*	metical *metical m*
Myanmar *Mianmar m*	Burmese *burmano(-a) m,f*	Burmese *burmés*	kyat *kyat m*
Namibia *Namibia f*	Namibian *namibio(-a) m,f*	English/Afrikaans *inglés/africaans*	Namibian dollar *dólar namibio m*
Nepal *Nepal m*	Nepalese/Nepali *nepalés(-esa) m,f/nepalí mf*	Nepali *nepalí*	Nepali rupee *rupia nepalí f*
Netherlands, The *Países Bajos mpl*	Dutchman, Dutchwoman/ Netherlander *holandés(-esa) m,f/ neerlandés(-esa) m,f*	Dutch *holandés*	euro *euro m*
New Zealand *Nueva Zelanda f*	New Zealander *neozelandés(-esa) m,f*	English/Maori *inglés/maorí*	New Zealand dollar *dólar neozelandés m*
Nicaragua *Nicaragua f*	Nicaraguan *nicaragüense mf*	Spanish *español*	cordoba *córdoba m*
Niger *Niger m*	Nigerien *nigerino(-a) m,f*	French *francés*	CFA franc *franco CFA m*
Nigeria *Nigeria f*	Nigerian *nigerino(-a) m,f*	English *inglés*	naira *naira nigeriana f*
North Korea/Democratic People's Republic of Korea *Corea del Norte/ República Democrática Popular de Corea f*	North Korean *norcoreano(-a) m,f*	Korean *coreano*	won *won m*
Northern Ireland *Irlanda del Norte f*	person from Northern Ireland *norirlandés(-esa) m,f*	English *inglés*	Sterling pound *libra esterlina f*
Norway *Noruega f*	Norwegian *noruego(-a) m,f*	Norwegian *noruego*	Norwegian krone *corona noruega f*
Oman *Omán m*	Omani *omaní mf*	Arabic *árabe*	Omani rial *rial omaní m*
Pakistan *Paquistán/Pakistán*	Pakistani *paquistaní mf*	Urdu/English *urdu/inglés*	Pakistan rupee *rupia paquistaní f*
Panama *Panamá m*	Panamanian *panameño(-a) m,f*	Spanish *español*	balboa *balboa m*
Papua New Guinea *Papua Nueva Guinea f*	person from Papua New Guinea/Papuan *papuano(-a) m,f/papú mf*	English/Motu *inglés/motu*	kina *kina f*

Country/ País	Inhabitant/ Habitante	Official language(s)/ Lengua(s) oficial(es)	Currency/ Moneda
Paraguay *Paraguay m*	Paraguayan *paraguayo(-a) m,f*	Spanish *español*	guarani *guaraní m*
Peru *Perú m*	Peruvian *peruano(-a) m,f*	Spanish/Quechua *español/quechua*	nuevo sol *sol m*
Philippines *Filipinas fpl*	Filipino/Philipino *filipino(-a) m,f*	Philippine/English *filipino/inglés*	peso *peso filipino m*
Poland *Polonia f*	Pole *polonés(-esa) m,f/ polaco(-a) m,f*	Polish *polaco*	zloty *zloty m*
Portugal *Portugal m*	Portuguese *portugués(-esa) m,f*	Portuguese *portugués*	euro *euro m*
Puerto Rico *Puerto Rico m*	Puerto Rican *puertorriqueño(-a) m,f*	Spanish/English *español/inglés*	US dollar *dólar americano m*
Qatar/Katar *Qatar/Katar m*	Qatari *qatarí/katarí mf*	Arabic *árabe*	Qatar riyal *rial de Qatar m*
Romania/Rumania *Rumanía f*	Romanian/Rumanian *rumano(-a) m,f*	Romanian *rumano*	Romanian leu *leu rumano m*
Russia (Russian Federation) *Rusia (Federación Rusa) f*	Russian *ruso(-a) m,f*	Russian *ruso*	rouble *rublo m*
Rwanda *Ruanda f*	Rwandese/Rwandan *ruandés(-esa) m,f*	French/Kinyarwanda *francés/kinyaruanda*	Rwanda franc *franco ruandés m*
Saint Lucia *Santa Lucía f*	Saint Lucian *santalucense mf*	English *inglés*	East Caribbean dollar *dólar del Caribe Oriental m*
Saint Vincent and the Grenadines *San Vicente y Granadinas m*	St. Vincentian *sanvicentino(-a) m,f*	English *inglés*	East Caribbean dollar *dólar del Caribe Oriental m*
San Marino *San Marino m*	San Marinese *sanmarinense mf/ sanmarinés(-esa) m,f*	Italian *italiano*	euro *euro m*
Saudi Arabia *Arabia Saudí*	Saudi/Saudi Arabian *saudí/árabe saudita mf*	Arabic *árabe*	Saudi Arabian Riyal *rial de Arabia Saudita m*
Scotland *Escocia f*	Scot/Scotsman, Scotswoman *escocés(-esa) m,f*	English *inglés*	Sterling pound *libra esterlina f*
Senegal *Senegal m*	Senegalese *senegalés(-esa) m,f*	French *francés*	CFA franc *franco CFA m*
Seychelles *Seychelles fpl*	Seychellois *habitante de las Seychelles mf*	English/French/Creole *inglés/francés/criollo*	Seychelles rupee *rupia de Seychelles f*
Sierra Leone *Sierra Leona f*	Sierra Leonean *sierraleonense mf/ sierraleonés(-esa) m,f*	English *inglés*	leone *leone m*

Country/ País	Inhabitant/ Habitante	Official language(s)/ Lengua(s) oficial(es)	Currency/ Moneda
Singapore *Singapore/Singapur m*	**Singaporean** *singapurense mf*	**Chinese/Malay/English/Tamil** *chino/malayo/inglés/tamil*	**Singapore dollar** *dólar de Singapur m*
Slovakia (Slovak Republic) *Eslovaquia (República Eslovaca) f*	**Slovak** *eslovaco(-a) m,f*	**Slovak** *eslovaco*	**Slovak koruna** *corona eslovaca f*
Slovenia *Eslovenia f*	**Slovenian/Slovene** *esloveno(-a) m,f*	**Slovenian** *esloveno*	**tolar** *tólar m*
Somalia *Somalia f*	**Somali** *somalí mf*	**Somali** *somalí*	**Somali shilling** *chelín somalí m*
South Africa *Sudáfrica/República Sudafricana f*	**South African** *sudafricano(-a) m,f*	**Afrikaans/English** *afrikaans/inglés*	**South African rand** *rand sudafricano m*
South Korea/Republic of Korea/Korea *Corea del Sur/República de Corea/Corea f*	**South Korean** *surcoreano(-a) m,f*	**Korean** *coreano*	**won** *won m*
Spain *España f*	**Spaniard** *español(a) m,f*	**Spanish** *español*	**euro** *euro m*
Sri Lanka *Sri Lanka f*	**Sri Lankan** *srilanqués(-esa) m,f/ cingalés(-esa) m,f*	**Singhala/Tamil** *cingalés/tamil*	**Sri Lanka rupee** *rupia de Sri Lanka f*
Sudan *Sudán m*	**Sudanese** *sudanés(-esa) m,f*	**Arabic** *árabe*	**Sudanese dinar** *dinar sudanés m*
Suriname *Surinam m*	**Surinamese** *surinamés(-esa) m,f/ surinamita mf*	**Dutch** *holandés*	**Suriname guilder** *florín de Surinam m*
Swaziland *Swazilandia f*	**Swazi** *suazi mf/swazilandés (-esa) m,f*	**Siswati/English** *siswati/inglés*	**lilangeni** *lilangeni m*
Sweden *Suecia f*	**Swede** *sueco(-a) m,f*	**Swedish** *sueco*	**Swedish krona** *corona sueca f*
Switzerland *Suiza f*	**Swiss** *suizo(-a) m,f*	**French/German/Italian/Romansch** *francés/alemán/italiano/ romanche*	**Swiss franc** *franco suizo m*
Syria *Siria f*	**Syrian** *sirio(-a) m,f*	**Arabic** *árabe*	**Syrian pound** *libra siria f*
Taiwan *Taiwán m*	**Taiwanese** *taiwanés(-esa) m,f*	**Mandarin Chinese** *chino mandarín*	**Taiwan dollar** *dólar de Taiwán m*
Tajikistan *Tayikistán*	**Tajikistani** *tayiko(-a) m,f*	**Tajik** *tayiko*	**rouble** *rublo m*
Tanzania *Tanzania f*	**Tanzanian** *tanzanés(-esa) m,f/ tanzano(-a) m,f*	**Swahili/English** *suahili/inglés*	**Tanzanian shilling** *chelín de Tanzania m*
Thailand *Tailandia f*	**Thai** *tailandés(-esa) m,f*	**Thai** *tai*	**baht** *baht m*
Togo *Togo m*	**Togolese** *togolés(-esa) m,f*	**French** *francés*	**CFA franc** *franco CFA m*
Trinidad and Tobago *Trinidad y Tobago f*	**Trinidadian/Tobagoan/ Tobagodian** *trinidense mf/ habitante de Trinidad y Tobago mf/ trinitario(-a) m,f*	**English** *inglés*	**Trinidad and Tobago dollar** *dólar de Trinidad y Tobago m*

Country/ País	Inhabitant/ Habitante	Official language(s)/ Lengua(s) oficial(es)	Currency/ Moneda
Tunisia *Túnez m*	**Tunisian** *tunecino(-a) m,f*	**Arabic** *árabe*	**Tunisian dinar** *dinar tunecino m*
Turkey *Turquía f*	**Turk** *turco(-a) m,f*	**Turkish** *turco*	**Turkish lira** *lira turca f*
Turkmenistan *Turkmenistán m*	**Turkmenistani** *turkmeno(-a) m,f*	**Turkmen/Russian** *turkmeno/ruso*	**Turkmenian manat** *manat m*
Uganda *Uganda f*	**Ugandan** *ugandés(-esa) m,f*	**English** *inglés*	**New Uganda shilling** *nuevo chelín* *ugandés m*
Ukraine *Ucrania f*	**Ukrainian** *ucranio(-a) m,f/* *ucraniano(-a) m,f*	**Ukrainian** *ucraniano*	**hryvna** *hryvna m*
United Arab Emirates *Emiratos Arabes Unidos* */Unión de Emiratos* *Arabes mpl*	**Emirian** *habitante de los Emiratos* *Arabes Unidos mf*	**Arabic** *árabe*	**dirham** *dirham m*
United Kingdom *Reino Unido m*	**Briton** *británico(-a) m,f*	**English** *inglés*	**Sterling pound** *libra esterlina f*
United States of America *Estados Unidos de* *América*	**person from the United** **States/American** *estadounidense mf*	**English** *inglés*	**US dollar** *dólar americano m*
Uruguay *Uruguay m*	**Uruguayan** *uruguayo(-a) m,f*	**Spanish** *español*	**Uruguayan peso** *peso uruguayo m*
Uzbekistan *Uzbekistán m*	**Uzbekistani** *uzbeko(-a) m,f*	**Uzbek** *uzbeko*	**Uzbekistani som** *som de Uzbekistán m*
Vanuatu *Vanuatu m*	**Vanuatuan** *habitante de Vanuatu mf*	**English/French/Bislama** *inglés/francés/bislama*	**vatu** *vatu m*
Venezuela *Venezuela f*	**Venezuelan** *venezolano(-a) m,f*	**Spanish** *español*	**bolívar** *bolívar m*
Vietnam *Vietnam m*	**Vietnamese** *vietnamita mf*	**Vietnamese** *vietnamita*	**dông** *dông m*
Wales *País de Gales m*	**Welshman, Welshwoman** *galés(-esa) m,f*	**English/Welsh** *inglés/galés*	**Sterling pound** *libra esterlina f*
Yemen *Yemen m*	**Yemeni** *yemení mf*	**Arabic** *árabe*	**Yemeni riyal** *rial del Yemen m/* *dinar yemení m*
Yugoslavia, Federal **Republic of** *Yugoslavia, República* *Federal de f*	**Yugoslavian** *yugoslavo(-a) m,f*	**Serbian** *serbio*	**dinar** *dinar m*
Zaïre *Zaire m*	**Zaïrese/Zairean** *zairense mf/zaireño(-a) m,f*	**French** *francés*	**zaïre** *zaïre m*
Zambia *Zambia f*	**Zambian** *zambiano(-a) m,f*	**English** *inglés*	**kwacha** *kwacha m*
Zimbabwe *Zimbabwe/Zimbabue f*	**Zimbabwean** *zimbabuense mf/* *zimbabuo(-a) m,f*	**English** *inglés*	**Zimbabwe dollar** *dólar de Zimbabwe m*

The euro

On 1 January 2002, Spain, along with the eleven other European countries that make up the euro zone, replaced its national currency with euro notes and coinage. This single currency is valid across the twelve euro zone member countries.

The basic unit of currency is the euro (€), which is divided into 100 cents. There are seven notes with values of 5, 10, 20, 50, 100, 200 and 500 euros and eight coins with values of 1, 2, 5, 10, 20, 50 cents, 1 euro and 2 euros. The design of the euro notes is uniform throughout the euro zone. All the coins have a common face denoting the value and a national face indicating where they were produced.

One euro is worth approximately 60 pence (0.92 US dollars). £1 is worth approximately 1.66 euros and $1 is worth 1.085 euros, subject to foreign exchange fluctuations. The official conversion rate between the Spanish peseta and the euro is fixed at the rate: 1 euro = 166.386 Ptas and 1 Pta = 0.00601012 euros.

euros	pesetas
1	166.386
2	332.772
5	831.930
10	1,663.86
20	3,327.72
50	8,319.30
100	16,638.60
200	33,277.20
500	83,193.00

pesetas	euros
100	0.601012
200	1.20202
500	3.00506
1,000	6.01012
1,500	9.0518
2,000	12.0202
5,000	30.0506
10,000	60.1012
50,000	300.506

Aa

AA *abbr* (▶**average adjuster**) ajustador(a) de averías *m,f*

AAA *adj* (rating) AAA; ~ **bond** *n* bono clase AAA *m*

AAD *abbr* (▶**at a discount**) (Fin) por debajo del cambio; (S&M) con descuento

abandon *vt* (place, person) abandonar; (project, idea) renunciar a; (claim) desistir de

abandonment *n* (of complaint, option) abandono *m*; ~ **clause** *n* cláusula de abandono *f*

abate *vt* (taxes, prices, levy) reducir; (contract) extinguir

abatement *n* (of taxes, prices, levy) reducción *f*; (of contract) extinción *f*

abbreviate *vt* abreviar

abbreviation *n* abreviatura *f*

ABC *abbr* (▶**activity-based costing**) cálculo *m* de costes Esp *or* costos AmL basado en la actividad

ABCC *abbr* (▶**Association of British Chambers of Commerce**) *asociación de cámaras de comercio británicas*

ABC method *n* (of inventory management) método ABC *m*

abeyance *n*: **be in** ~ (custom, practice) haber caído en desuso; (project, activity) estar suspendido *or* en suspenso

abide by *vt* (rule, decision) atenerse a

ability *n* (talent) capacidad *f*, aptitud *f*; (faculty, power) capacidad *f*; **to the best of one's abilities** lo mejor que uno pueda; ~ **to earn** facultad para ganar; ~ **to pay** *o* **repay** capacidad de pago

able *adj* (administrator) hábil, capaz; **be** ~ **to do sth** poder hacer algo; (using a learned skill) saber hacer algo; ~ **to work** apto para el trabajo; **I am pleased to be** ~ **to inform you that...** me complace poder comunicarle que... (frml)

abnormal *adj* (level, rate) anormal, singular; (profit) extraordinario

aboard¹ *adv* a bordo

aboard² *prep* (ship, plane) a bordo de; (train, bus) en

abolish *vt* (institution, practice) abolir, suprimir; (law) abolir, derogar

abolition *n* (of institution, practice) abolición *f*, supresión *f*; (of law) abolición *f*, derogación *f*; (of trade controls) supresión *f*

abort¹ *vt* (program) cancelar, abandonar; (operation, mission, trial, launch) interrumpir

abort² *n* (of program) cancelación *f*

abortive *adj* (attempt, project, efforts) frustado

above¹ *prep* (in rank, status) por encima de; **not be** ~ **the law** no estar por encima de la ley; ~**-average** *adj* por encima de la media; ~**-board** *adj* (action, deal) legítimo; (person) sincero; ~ **par** *adj* sobre la par

above² *adv* (on top, higher up, overhead) arriba; (in text) anteriormente, más arriba; **the floor** ~ el piso de arriba; ~**-mentioned** *adj* susodicho, antes citado; ~**-named** *adj* arriba mencionado

above³ *adj* (in text) susodicho, antes citado; **the** ~ **address** la dirección arriba indicada

abreast *adv*: **be** ~ **of** (developments) mantenerse informado de; **keep** ~ **of** (conditions, legislation) mantenerse informado de *or* al corriente de

abroad *adv* (work, live) en el extranjero; (go) al extranjero

abrogate *vt* abrogar

abrogation *n* abrogación *f*

abscond *vi* fugarse

absence *n* (of person) ausencia *f*; (lack) falta *f*; **in the** ~ **of sth** (information) ante la ausencia de algo; (news) a falta de; (person) en ausencia de; **in the** ~ **of evidence to the contrary** a falta de pruebas en contra; ~ **of consideration** *n* falta de consideración *f*; ~ **without leave** *n* ausencia sin permiso *f*

absent *adj* ausente; **go** ~ **without leave** ausentarse sin permiso

absentee *n* ausente *m,f*; ~ **landlord** *n*, ~ **owner** *n* propietario(-a) *m,f* ausentista *or* absentista Esp; ~ **rate** *n* nivel *m* de ausentismo *or* absentismo Esp

absenteeism *n* ausentismo *m*, absentismo *m* Esp

absolute *adj* (trust, confidence, certainty) absoluto, pleno; (right) incuestionable; (court order, decree) definitivo; (in contract) firme; **in** ~ **terms** en términos absolutos; ~ **address** *n* dirección absoluta *f*; ~ **liability** *n* responsabilidad objetiva *f*; ~ **majority** *n* mayoría absoluta *f*; ~ **monopoly** *n* monopolio absoluto *m*; ~ **ownership** *n* propiedad total *f*; ~ **poverty** *n* miseria *f* *or* pobreza *f* absoluta; ~ **sale** *n* venta irrevocable *f*; ~ **title** *n* derecho absoluto *m*

absorb *vt* (overheads, surplus) absorber; (information) asimilar; (time) asorber, llevar

absorbing: ~ **capacity** *n* (of security market) capacidad de absorción *f*; ~ **company** *n* empresa absorbente *f*

absorption *n* (of overheads, surplus) absorción *f*; (of information) asimilación *f*; ~ **costing** *n* cálculo *m* de costes Esp *or* costos AmL de absorción, costeo por absorción *m* AmL; ~ **rate** *n* índice de absorción *m*

abstain *vi* (in election) abstenerse; ~ **from (doing) sth** abstenerse de (hacer) algo

abstention *n* abstención *f*

abstract *n* resumen *m*, extracto *m*; ~ **of accounts** *n* extracto de cuentas *m*; ~ **of record** *n* resumen de los autos *m*; ~ **of title** *n* documento que señala los antecedentes de propiedad de un inmueble desde su primer asiento registral

ABT *abbr* (▸**American Board of Trade**) Cámara de Comercio Americana *f*

abundance *n* abundancia *f*

abundant *adj* abundante

abuse¹ *n* (of authority, power, trust, confidence) abuso *m*

abuse² *vt* (authority, power) abusar de

abusive *adj* (practice) abusivo

a/c *abbr* (▸**account**) c/ (cuenta), cta. (cuenta)

AC *abbr* (▸**advanced country**) país desarrollado *m*; (▸**authorization under consideration**) autorización en trámite *f*

academic *adj* académico

ACAS *abbr* BrE (▸**Advisory, Conciliation and Arbitration Service**) ≈ IMAC (Instituto de Mediación, Arbitraje y Conciliación)

ACB *abbr* (▸**adjusted cost base** *o* **basis**) base *f* de coste Esp *or* costo AmL ajustada

Acc *abbr* (▸**accountancy**) contabilidad *f*

ACC *abbr* (▸**American Chamber of Commerce**) Cámara de Comercio Americana *f*

accede to *vt* (demand, request) acceder a; (contract) suscribir

accelerate *vti* acelerar

accelerated *adj* (amortization, depreciation, redemption, purchase) acelerado; ~ **conversion** *n* (of debentures) conversión acelerada *f*; ~ **cost recovery system** *n* sistema de recuperación acelerada de costes Esp *or* costos AmL *m*

acceleration *n* aceleración *f*; ~ **clause** *n* (for mortgage) cláusula de aceleración *f*; ~ **of maturity** *n* anticipación del vencimiento *f*; ~ **premium** *n* (HRM) prima de aceleración *f*; (Ind) prima de rendimiento *f*; ~ **principle** *n* (Econ) principio de aceleración *m*

accelerator *n* (Econ) acelerador *m*; ~ **principle** *n* (Econ) principio del acelerador *m*

accept *vt* (offer, job, payment, bid, credit card, cheque, delivery) aceptar; ~ **a bill** comprometerse a pagar una factura; ~ **cash payments only** cobrar al contado; ~ **a collect call** AmE (*cf* ▸**accept a reverse-charge call** BrE) aceptar una llamada a cobro revertido; ~ **delivery of sth** aceptar la entrega de algo; ~ **liability** aceptar la obligación; ~ **no liability** no aceptar ninguna responsabilidad; ~ **on presentation** aceptar a su presentación; ~ **a reverse-charge call** BrE (*cf* ▸**accept a collect call** AmE) aceptar una llamada a cobro revertido

acceptable *adj* (behaviour, risk, price, investment) aceptable; **of** ~ **quality** de calidad aceptable; ~ **use policy** *n* política de uso aceptable *f*

acceptance *n* (of offer, job, payment, bid, credit card, cheque, delivery) aceptación *f*; ~ **account** *n* cuenta de aceptación *f*; ~ **against documents** *n* aceptación contra documentos *f*; ~ **bill** *n* letra aceptada *f*; ~ **by intervention** *n* aceptación por intervención *f*; ~ **commission** *n* comisión de aceptación *f*; ~ **credit** *n* crédito de aceptación *m*; ~ **facility** *n* servicio financiero de aceptación *m*; ~ **fee** *n* comisión *f or* cuota *f* de aceptación; ~ **house** *n* banco de aceptación *m*; ~ **ledger** *n* libro de letras aceptadas *m*; ~ **market** *n* mercado de efectos aceptados *m*; ~ **price** *n* precio de aceptación *m*; ~ **register** *n* registro de letras aceptadas *m*; ~ **slip** *n* borderó de aceptación *m*; ~ **supra protest** *n* aceptación bajo protesta *f*; ~ **test** *n* prueba de acogida *f*; ~ **trial** *n* prueba de aceptación *f*

accepted *adj* (draft, liability, pairing) aceptado

accepting: ~ **bank** *n* banco de aceptación *m*; ~ **banker** *n* bancario(-a) de aceptación *m,f*; ~ **house** *n* casa de aceptaciones *f*

acceptor *n* (of bill) aceptante *mf*

access¹ *n* acceso *m*; **have/give** ~ **to sth** tener/dar acceso a algo; ~ **code** *n* código de acceso *m*; ~ **control** *n* control de acceso *m*; ~ **cycle** *n* ciclo de acceso *m*; ~ **provider** *n* proveedor de acceso *m*; ~ **right** *n* derecho de acceso *m*; ~ **time** *n* tiempo de acceso *m*

access² *vt* (database) acceder a

accessibility *n* (of information) accesibilidad *f*; (of place) fácil acceso *m*

accessible *adj* (file, information, place) accesible; (person) accesible, asequible

accession n (to the EU) adhesión f; (Prop) acceso m

accessorial service n servicio adicional m

accessory[1] n (extra) accesorio m; (to crime) cómplice mf

accessory[2] adj accesorio; ~ **advertising** n publicidad secundaria f

accident n accidente m; **have an** ~ tener or sufrir un accidente; **by** ~ (by chance) por casualidad; (unintentionally) sin querer; ~ **and health insurance** n seguro de accidentes y de enfermedad m; ~ **insurance** n seguro contra accidentes m; ~ **prevention** n prevención de accidentes f; ~ **risk** n riesgo de accidente m

accommodate vt (with loan) favorecer; (in office) alojar

accommodating credit n crédito m ajustado or de favor

accommodation n (compromise) arreglo m; (lodging) BrE alojamiento m; (loan, credit) crédito m; **reach an** ~ **with sb over sth** llegar a un acuerdo con alguien sobre algo; **take** ~ aceptar una garantía; ~ **acceptance** n aceptación de complacencia f; ~ **address** n dirección temporal f; ~ **agency** n agencia de alojamiento f; ~ **allowance** n asignación para vivienda f; ~ **bill** n pagaré de favor m; ~ **bureau** n oficina de alojamiento f; ~ **draft** n giro m avalado or de favor; ~ **endorsement** n endoso por aval m; ~ **maker** n librador(a) de un pagaré de favor m,f; ~ **note** n pagaré avalado m; ~ **paper** n documento de garantía m, papel avalado m; ~ **party** n firmante de favor mf; ~ **payment** n pago de deferencia m; (Fin) pago por aval m

accommodations n pl AmE alojamiento m

accommodatory credit n crédito con garantía personal m

accompanying adj (note, instructions, document) adjunto; ~ **letter** n carta de compañía f

accomplish vt (task) cumplir; (aim) conseguir

accomplishment n (of task) cumplimiento m; (of aim) consecución f

accord n acuerdo m; ~ **and satisfaction** n acuerdo m y satisfacción f

accordance n: **in** ~ **with** de acuerdo con, en conformidad con; **in** ~ **with your instructions** de acuerdo con sus instrucciones

accordingly adv (correspondingly) en consecuencia; (therefore) por lo tanto, por consiguiente, consiguientemente

according to prep (in agreement with) conforme a, de acuerdo con; (as stated by) según; ~ **to the norm** conforme a la norma; ~ **to plan** conforme al plan; ~ **to schedule** según lo previsto, de acuerdo al horario or al programa

account n (explanation) explicación f; (version) versión f; (report) informe m; (with bank, building society, shop, company) cuenta f; (invoice) BrE cuenta f, factura f; (part of budget) partida f, rubro m AmL; (on stock exchange) cada una de las quincenas el las que se divide el año en la Bolsa británica; **bring** o **call sb to** ~ **for sth** pedirle cuentas a alguien sobre algo; **buy for the** ~ (Stock) comprar a término; **hold sb to** ~ **for sth** responsabilizar a alguien de algo; **have an** ~ **with** o **at a bank** tener una cuenta en un banco; **keep (an)** ~ **of sth** llevar (la) cuenta de algo; **my** ~ mi cuenta; ~ **of** cuenta de; **on** ~ en cuenta; **on** ~ **of** debido a, por causa de; **on no** ~ en ningún caso; **open/ close/transfer an** ~ abrir/cerrar/transferir una cuenta; **put it on/charge it to my** ~ cárguelo a mi cuenta; **sell for the** ~ (Stock) vender a cuenta; **settle one's** ~ pagar or saldar su cuenta; **take** ~ **of sth** o **take sth into** ~ tener algo en cuenta; **win an** ~ conseguir una cuenta or un contrato; ~ **activity** n movimiento de la cuenta m; ~ **analysis** n análisis de cuentas m; ~ **book** n libro de cuentas m; ~ **card** n ficha de cuenta f; ~ **day** n día de cuenta m; ~ **executive** n ejecutivo(-a) de cuentas m,f; ~ **form** n estado de cuentas m; (balance sheet) balance de cuentas m; ~ **format** n formato de cuenta m; ~ **group** n grupo de cuentas m; ~ **holder** n titular de una cuenta mf; ~ **maintenance** n mantenimiento de cuenta m; ~ **management** n administración f or gestión f de una cuenta; ~ **manager** n (Bank) gestor(a) de cuentas m,f; (HRM) ejecutivo(-a) de cuentas m,f; (S&M) director(a) de cuentas m,f; ~ **market** n mercado contable m; ~ **movement** n movimiento de la cuenta m; ~ **name** n nombre de cuenta m; ~ **number** n número de cuenta m; ~**-only check** AmE, ~**-only cheque** BrE n cheque sólo para depositar m; ~ **payee** n (on cheque) tenedor(a) de cuenta m,f; ~ **period** n periodo m de contratación bursátil a crédito or de contratación bursátil a cuenta; ~ **planning** n planificación contable f; ~ **reconcilement** n, ~ **reconciliation** n conciliación de cuentas f; ~ **rendered** n cuenta pendiente de aprobación f; ~ **settled** n cuenta saldada f; ~ **statement** n estado de cuentas m; (figure itself) estado m or saldo m de cuenta; ~ **title** n denominación de una cuenta f; ~ **transaction** n transacción a or ⋯⋗

en cuenta *f*; ~ **turnover** *n* movimiento *m or* rotación *f* de la cuenta (*cf* ▸**accounts**)

accountability *n* responsabilidad *f*; ~ **in management** *n* responsabilidad *f* en la administración *or* en la gestión

accountable *adj* responsable; **be ~ to sb for sth** ser responsable ante alguien de algo; ~ **advance** *n* anticipo contable *m*; ~ **officer** *n* funcionario(-a) responsable *m,f*; ~ **receipt** *n* recibo contable *m*

accountancy *n* contabilidad *f*, contaduría *f* AmL; ~ **profession** *n* profesión contable *f*; ~ **service** *n* servicio contable *m*

accountant *n* contable *mf* Esp, contador(a) *m,f* AmL; ~ **general** *n* jefe(-a) de contabilidad *m,f*

account for *vt* (expenditure, time) dar cuentas de; (absence, mistake, success) explicar; (add up to) representar; ~ **sth to sb** darle cuentas de algo a alguien; **wages ~ 70% of the total** los sueldos representan un *or* el 70% del total; **this model accounts for 17% of the market** este modelo tiene el 17% del mercado

accounting *n* contabilidad *f*, contabilización *f*; **for ~ purposes** a efectos contables; ~ **adjustment** *n* ajuste contable *m*; ~ **analysis** *n* análisis contable *m*; ~ **balance of payments** *n* contabilidad de la balanza de pagos *f*; ~ **clerk** *n* empleado(-a) de contabilidad *m,f*; ~ **control** *n* control contable *m*; ~ **convention** *n* práctica contable *f*; ~ **costs** *n pl* costes *m pl* Esp *or* costos *m pl* AmL contables; ~ **cycle** *n* ciclo contable *m*; ~ **data** *n pl* datos contables *m pl*; ~ **department** *n* departamento de contabilidad *m*, contaduría *f*; ~ **entry** *n* asiento contable *m*; ~ **error** *n* error contable *m*; ~ **file** *n* fichero contable *m*; ~ **firm** *n* firma contable *f*; ~ **harmonization** *n* armonización contable *f*; ~ **income** *n* ingreso *m or* renta *f* contable; ~ **law** *n* ley *f* contable *or* de contabilidad; ~ **method** *n* método contable *m*; ~ **model** *n* modelo contable *m*; ~ **office** *n* (of government department) departamento *m or* oficina *f* de contabilidad, contaduría *f*; ~ **officer** *n* jefe(-a) de contabilidad *m,f*; ~ **package** *n* conjunto de programas de contabilidad *m*; ~ **period** *n* periodo contable *m*; ~ **policy** *n* política contable *f*; ~ **practice** *n* práctica contable *f*; ~ **principle** *n* principio de contabilidad *m*; ~ **procedure** *n* procedimiento de contabilidad *m*; ~ **profit** *n* beneficio contable *or* del ejercicio; ~ **rate of interest** *n* tasa *f or* tipo *m* de interés de cuenta; ~ **rate of return** *n* tasa *f or* tipo *m* de rendimiento contable; ~ **ratio** *n* (Acc) proporción contable *f*; (Fin) coeficiente contable *m*; ~ **records** *n pl* registros de contabilidad *m pl*; ~ **report** *n*

estado *m or* informe *m* contable; ~ **return** *n* beneficio contable *m*; ~ **software** *n* programas *m pl or* software *m* de contabilidad; ~ **standard** *n* norma *f* contable *or* de contabilidad; ~ **system** *n* sistema contable *m*; ~ **treatment** *n* tratamiento contable *m*; ~ **year** *n* año contable *m*; ~ **year then ended** *n* año contable finalizado

accounts *n pl* (records) cuentas *f pl*; (department) departamento de contabilidad *m*, contaduría *f*; ~ **appraisal** *n* estimación contable *f*; ~ **certification** *n* certificación de cuentas *f*; ~ **close-off** *n* bloqueo de cuentas *m*; ~ **department** *n* departamento de contabilidad *m*, contaduría *f*; ~ **payable** *n pl* cuentas a pagar *f pl*; ~ **payable ledger** *n* libro mayor de cuentas a pagar *m*; ~ **receivable** *n pl* cuentas a cobrar *f pl*; ~ **receivable ledger** *n* libro mayor de cuentas a cobrar *m*

accredit *vt* (representative, official) darle credenciales a; (agent, broker) acreditar

accreditation *n* acreditación *f*

accredited *adj* (investor) acreditado; **A~ Chartered Accountant** *n* ≈ Contable Colegiado(-a) *m,f* Esp, ≈ Contador(a) Autorizado(-a) Colegiado(-a) *m,f* AmL

accrual *n* (of interest) acumulación *f*; ~ **accounting** *n* contabilidad acumulativa *f*; ~ **basis** *n* base de acumulación *f*; ~ **concept** *n* concepto de acumulación *m*; ~ **date** *n* fecha de acumulación *f*; ~ **interest rate** *n* tasa de interés acumulado *f*; ~ **method** *n* método de acumulación *m*; ~ **principle** *n* principio de acumulación *m*

accrue *vti* (interest, profits) acumular

accrued *adj* (interest, income, dividend, charge, liability) acumulado; (asset) acumulado, devengado; ~ **interest payable** *n* intereses acumulados por pagar *m pl*; ~ **interest receivable** *n* intereses acumulados por cobrar *m pl*

acct. *abbr* (▸**account**) cta. (cuenta)

accumulate ⟦1⟧ *vt* (interest, expenses, revenue) acumular; (information, evidence) reunir, acumular; (products) acopiar ⟦2⟧ *vi* acumularse

accumulated *adj* (interest, dividend, profit, deficit, depreciation) acumulado; (information, evidence) reunido, acumulado; (products) acopiado; ~ **depletion** *n* amortización acumulada *f*; ~ **surplus** *n* excedente *m or* superávit *m* acumulado, plusvalía acumulada *f*

accumulating *adj* (fund, income) acumulativo

accumulation *n* (of interest, expenses, revenue) acumulación *f*; (of information, evidence) reunión f, acumulación f; (of products) acopio m; ~ **area** n (Stock) zona de acumulación f

accumulative adj (dividends) acumulativo

accuracy n (of figures, data, statement) exactitud f; (of judgment) justeza f; (of report, document, aim) precisión f

accurate adj (description) ajustado; (figures) exacto; (judgment) justo; (report, aim) preciso

accusation n acusación f; **bring an ~ against sb** acusar a alguien; **make an ~** hacer una acusación

accuse vt acusar; ~ **sb of (doing) sth** acusar a alguien de (hacer) algo

ACD abbr (▸**automated cash dispenser**) cajero automático m

ACE abbr (▸**Amex Commodities Exchange**) Bolsa de Contratación Amex f, Bolsa de Productos Amex f

acetate n (for projector) transparencia f

ACH abbr (▸**Automated Clearing House**) Cámara de Compensación Automatizada f

achievable adj factible

achieve vt (growth, level, objective) lograr; (ambition) realizar

achievement n (success) logro m; (of goal, ambition) realización f; ~ **quotient** n coeficiente de rendimiento m; ~ **test** n test de conocimientos específicos m

achiever n triunfador(a) m,f

acid adj ácido; ~ **rain** n lluvia ácida f; ~ **test** n prueba de fuego f; ~ **test ratio** n coeficiente de liquidez m, ratio de liquidez inmediata m

acknowledge vt (mistake, achievement, authority, right, claim) reconocer; (failure, fault) admitir, reconocer; (arrival) confirmar; (assistance, services) agradecer; ~ **receipt of sth** (letter, cheque, goods) acusar recibo de algo; ~ **receipt by letter** acusar recibo por carta

acknowledgement n (of indebtness) reconocimiento m; (of payment) acuse de recepción m; (of order) confirmación f; (on document) acuse de recibo m; (of contract) documento de aceptación m; ~ **of receipt** n (of payment) acuse de recibo m

Ackt. abbr (▸**acknowledgement (of receipt)**) acuse de recibo m

ACOP abbr (▸**approved code of practice**) código de procedimiento aprobado m

acquaint vt: ~ **sb with sth** (inform of) poner a alguien al corriente de algo; (familiarize with) familiarizar a alguien con algo

acquaintance n (person) conocido(-a) m,f; (relationship) relación f; (knowledge) conocimiento m; **make sb's ~** conocer a alguien

acquainted adj: **be ~ with sb** conocer a alguien; **be ~ with sth** (be informed of) estar al tanto or al corriente de algo; (be familiar with) estar familiarizado con algo

acquest n propiedad adquirida f

acquire vt (company, shares, knowledge, experience) adquirir; ~ **an interest** adquirir una participación

acquired adj (company, shares, knowledge, experience) adquirido; ~ **surplus** n superávit obtenido m

acquiring: ~ **authority** n (in compulsory purchase) autoridad de adquisición f; ~ **company** n (in corporate takeover) compañía adquirente f

acquisition n (action, company, takeover) adquisición f; ~ **accounting** n contabilidad de adquisiciones f; ~ **agent** n agente comprador(a) m,f; ~ **cost** n coste m Esp or costo m AmL de adquisición; ~ **financing** n financiación de compra f; ~ **policy** n política de adquisición f; ~ **price** n precio de adquisición m; ~ **value** n valor de adquisición m

acquisitive adj (company) codicioso; ~ **instinct** n instinto adquisitivo m

acquit vt (debt, duty) descargar, pagar; (accused) absolver; ~ **oneself** desenvolverse

acquittal n (of debt) descargo m; (of duty) desempeño m; (of accused) absolución f

acquittance n (confirmation) carta de pago f; (of debt) descargo m

acronym n sigla f

across-the-board[1] adj (reduction, increase) igual para todas las categorías; (change) que cubre todo

across-the-board[2] adv para todas las categorías

across-the-counter adj (purchases) bursátil; (sales) al contado

across-the-network adj a través del sistema

ACRS abbr (▸**accelerated cost recovery system**) sistema m de recuperación acelerada de costes Esp or costos AmL

ACSS abbr (▸**Automated Clearing Settlement System**) Sistema de Liquidación de Compensación Automatizado m

act[1] n acto m; (Law, Pol) ley f, acto m; **by an ~ of God** (Law) por caso fortuito, por acto de la naturaleza; ~ **of acknowledgement** n acto de reconocimiento m; ~ **of bankruptcy** n acto de quiebra m; ~ **of cession** n acto de cesión m; **A~ of Congress** n AmE ≈ Ley de las Cortes f, ≈ Ley del Congreso f; ~ **of God** n caso de fuerza mayor m; ~ **of honor** AmE, ~ **of honour** BrE n aceptación ⟶

haciendo honor a la firma; **A~ of Parliament** n BrE Ley del Parlamento f

act² vi actuar; **~ as sth** (serve as) servir de; **~ bona fide** actuar de buena fe; **~ in the capacity of** actuar en calidad de; **~ in good faith** actuar de buena fe; **~ on behalf of** actuar en nombre de; **act for** vt (represent) representar; **act on** vt (advice, suggestion) seguir; (letter) actuar sobre

ACT abbr (▸**advance corporation tax**) impuesto anticipado de sociedades m

acting adj (chairperson, head, director, allowance) interino; (partner) en funciones; **~ member** n suplente mf

action¹ n (activity) acción f; (practical measures) medidas f pl; (deed) acto m; (Law) proceso m; **an ~ against sb** un proceso contra alguien; **bring an ~ against sb** (Law) ejercitar una acción contra alguien; **be out of ~** (telephone, machine) estar fuera de servicio; **put a plan into ~** poner un plan en acción; **take ~ (against sb)** tomar medidas (contra alguien); **~ code** n (Comp) código de intervención m; **~ for cancelation** AmE, **action for cancellation** BrE n condición resolutoria f; **~ for damages** n acción por daños y perjuicios f; **~ for libel** n demanda por difamación f; **~ message** n (Comp) mensaje de intervención m; **~-oriented** adj de acción; **~ plan** n plan de acción m; **~ statement** n cláusula de decisión f

action² vt BrE (sale, transfer) poner en marcha; (claim) tramitar

actionable adj (claim) justiciable; (remark, offence, allegation) procesable

activate vt activar

active adj activo; **in ~ employment** en empleo activo; **play an ~ part in sth** tomar parte activa en algo; **~ account** n cuenta activa f; **~ bond** n título al portador de gran liquidez m; **~ business** n comercio activo m; **~ capital** n capital activo m; **~ computer** n computadora activa f AmL, ordenador activo m Esp; **~ dealing** n negociación activa f; **~ demand** n demanda activa f; **~ file** n fichero activo m; **~ financing** n financiación activa f; **~ income** n ingreso activo m; **~ investment** n inversión activa f; **~ investor** n inversor(a) activo(-a) m,f; **~ management** n administración f or gestión f activa; **~ market** n mercado activo m; **~ money** n dinero productivo m; **~ partner** n socio(-a) activo(-a) m,f; **~ securities** n pl valores activos m pl; **~ shares** n pl acciones activas f pl; **~ trader** n comerciante activo(-a) m,f; **~ trading** n negociación activa f

activist n (Econ) militante mf; (Pol) activista mf

activity n actividad f; **~ analysis** n análisis de actividades m; **~-based costing** n cálculo de costes Esp or costos AmL basado en la actividad m; **~ charges** n pl cargos por actividad m pl; **~ chart** n diagrama de actividad m; **~ rate** n nivel de actividad f; **~ ratio** n tasa de actividad f; **~ total** n total de la actividad m

actual adj (real) real; **~ address** n (Comp) dirección real f; **~ amount** n (of outlay, expenditure) cantidad real f, importe efectivo m; **~ cash value** n valor real en efectivo m; **~ cost** n coste m Esp or costo m AmL real; **~ expenditure** n gastos reales m pl; **~ instruction** n (Comp) instrucción real f; **~ investment** n inversión real f; **~ level of unemployment** n nivel real de desempleo m; **~ loss** n pérdida real f; **~ outcome** n resultado real m; **~ price** n precio real m; **~ quotation** n cotización real f; **~ stock** n existencias reales f pl; **~ tax rate** n tipo impositivo real m; **~ volume** n (of production) volumen real m

actualize vt (represent realistically) actualizar

actuals n pl disponibilidades f pl, efectivos m pl

actuarial adj (deficit, liability, loss) actuarial; **~ life expectation** n esperanza matemática de vida f

actuary n actuario(-a) m,f; **~'s valuation** n cálculo actuarial m

ACV abbr (▸**actual cash value**) valor real en efectivo m

ad n (▸**advertisement**) anuncio m; **~ button** n botón de anuncio m; **~ server** n servidor del anuncio m; **~ space** n espacio del anuncio m

A/D abbr (▸**after date**) después de fecha

Adam Smith Institute n BrE gabinete británico de estrategia económico y político

adapt vt adaptar

adaptability n adaptabilidad f

adaptable adj adaptable

adaptation n adaptación f

adaptive control n control por adaptación m

adaptor n adaptador m

AD-AS abbr (▸**aggregate demand-aggregate supply**) demanda agregada-oferta agregada f

ADC abbr (▸**analogue-to-digital converter** BrE, ▸**analog-to-digital converter** AmE) conversor de analógico a digital m

add vt (put, say, write in addition) añadir, agregar; (numbers, figures) sumar; **~ sth to sth** sumarle algo a algo; **add back** vt (sum) volver a sumar; **add in** *vt* (details, numbers, figures, statement) añadir; **add together** *vt* (numbers, figures) sumar simultáneamente; **add up** *vt* (numbers, figures) sumar

Add. *abbr* (▸**address**) dirección *f*

added-value *adj* con valor agregado

added value *n* valor agregado *m*

addendum *n* (Law) apéndice *m*; (text amendment) adición *f*

adder *n* sumador *m*

adding *n* adición *f*; ~ **machine** *n* máquina de sumar *f*, sumadora *f*

addition *n* (Acc, Comp) suma *f*; (text amendment) adición *f*; **in** ~ además; **in** ~ **to** además de; **no** ~**, no correction** sin adición, sin corrección

additional *adj* (charge, expense, pay, feature) adicional; (premium, tax) complementario; (security) suplementario; ~ **postage** *n* sobretasa postal *f*; ~ **voluntary contributions** *n pl* BrE cuotas voluntarias adicionales *f pl*

additive-free *adj* sin aditivos

add-on[1] *adj* añadido; (interest, yield) aditivo; (costs) incorporado, agregado; (Comp) (board, card) externo; (memory) externo, adicional; ~ **equipment** *n* (Comp) material complementario incorporable *m*; (Mgmnt) equipo complementario *m*; ~ **sales** *n pl* BrE *ventas subsecuentes a un cliente satisfecho*

add-on[2] *n* añadido *m*; (Comp) componente adicional *m*

address[1] *n* dirección *f*; ~ **bar** *n* barra de dirección *f*; ~ **book** *n* libro de direcciones *m*; ~ **field** *n* campo de dirección *m*; ~ **file** *n* fichero de direcciones *m*; ~ **label** *n* etiqueta postal *f*; ~ **line** *n* línea para la dirección *f*

address[2] *vt* (parcel, envelope) remitir; (speech, talk) dirigir; (meeting) dirigirse a; (issue, problem) orientar; (Law) dirigir; ~ **oneself to sth** (issue, problem) dedicarse a; ~ **complaints to sb** dirigir sus reclamaciones a alguien

addressable *adj* direccionable

addressee *n* destinatario(-a) *m,f*

addressing *n* direccionamiento *m*; ~ **machine** *n* *máquina de imprimir direcciones*

Addressograph® *n* *máquina de imprimir direcciones*

adduce *vt* (proof, reason) aducir

adequacy of coverage *n* (Ins) cobertura apropiada *f*

adequate *adj* (funds, supply, explanation) adecuado; **we didn't get** ~ **notice** no se nos avisó con la suficiente anticipación; ~ **target rate** *n* tipo *m* indicativo adecuado *or* objetivo adecuado

adequately *adv* (sufficiently) suficientemente; (well enough) de forma aceptable *or* adecuada; ~ **funded** *adj* con fondos adecuados; (Acc) adecuadamente fundado

ADG *abbr* (▸**assistant director general**) director(-a) general adjunto(-a) *m,f*

adhere to *vt* (contract) adherir a; (principle) atenerse a

adhesion *n* adhesión *f*; ~ **contract** *n* contrato de adhesión *m*

adhesive *adj* (label) adhesivo; ~ **tape** *n* cinta adhesiva *f*

ad hoc *adj* (request) ad hoc; **problems are dealt with on an** ~ **basis** los problemas se van tratando según van surgiendo; ~ **committee** *n* comisión ad hoc *f*

ad infinitum *adv* al infinito

ad interim *adj* (judgment) provisional

adjoining *adj* (room, building) contiguo

adjourn [1] *vt* (postpone) aplazar; (halt) suspender; **the meeting was** ~**ed** se levantó la sesión
[1] *vi* (court) levantar la sesión

adjournment *n* (postponement) aplazamiento *m*; (halting) suspensión *f*; ~ **debate** *n* BrE (in Parliament) debate de aplazamiento *m*

adjudge *vt* (decree) decretar; ~ **heavy damages** declarar judicialmente fuertes daños

adjudicate *vt* (auction, contract, contest, bankruptcy) adjudicar; (claim) determinar judicialmente; ~ **sb bankrupt** declarar a alguien en quiebra

adjudication *n* adjudicación *f*

adjudicator *n* adjudicador(a) *m,f*

adjunct *n* (addition) complemento *m*; (appendage) apéndice *m*; (person) ayudante *mf*

adjust *vt* (prices, wages, rates, charges, timetable) ajustar; (claim) solventar; ~ **sth downwards/upwards** BrE *o* **downward/ upward** AmE ajustar algo a la baja/al alza; ~ **(oneself) to sth** (situation) adaptarse a algo

adjustable *adj* ajustable; ~ **mortgage loan** *n* préstamo hipotecario ajustable *m*; ~ **rate mortgage** *n* hipoteca de tasa ajustable *f*

adjusted *adj* ajustado; ~ **cost base** *n*, ~ **cost basis** *n* base de coste Esp *or* costo AmL ajustada *f*; ~ **income** *n* ingreso ajustado *m*; ~ **trial balance** *n* balance de comprobación ajustado *m*

adjuster *n* (Ins) tasador(a) *m,f*

adjusting entry *n* asiento de ajuste *m*

adjustment *n* (of prices, wages, rates, charges) ajuste *m*; (to situation) adecuación *f*; (Ins) repartición *f*; ~ **account** *n* cuenta de ajuste ⋯▸

f; ~ **bond** n bono secundario m; ~ **clause** n (Ins) cláusula de finiquito f

adman n (infrml) (►**advertising man**) hombre anuncio m

admass adj (culture, society) cautivo de la publicidad

admin. abbr (►**administration**) admón. (administración)

administer vt administrar

administered adj administrado; ~ **price** n precio administrado m

administration n (of institution, business) administración f, dirección f; (of estate, fund, inheritance) administración f; (**Pol**) gobierno m, administración f; (managing body) administración f; (in insolvency law) intervención f; ~ **costs** n pl costes m pl Esp or costos m pl AmL de administración; ~ **expenses** n pl gastos de administración m pl; ~ **officer** n jefe(-a) administrativo(-a) m,f; ~ **order** n orden administrativa f

administrative adj (charge, cost, expenses, audit, board) administrativo; (overheads) de administración; **take** ~ **control of a company** tomar el control administrativo de una compañía; ~ **assistant** n auxiliar administrativo(-a) m,f; ~ **law** n derecho administrativo m; ~ **officer** n oficial administrativo(-a) m,f, administrativo(-a) m,f; ~ **staff** n pl personal administrativo m; ~ **work** n trabajo administrativo m

administrator n (of business, institution, country) administrador(a) m,f; (of deceased's estate) administrador(a) de la sucesión m,f; (in insolvency law) administrador(a) m,f, interventor(a) m,f; (Comp) (of software) gestor(a) m,f

admissibility n admisibilidad f

admissible adj admisible

admission n (to place) entrada f, admisión f; (price to enter) entrada f; (to organization) ingreso m, admisión f; (confession) confesión f; **by his/her own** ~ por su propia admisión; ~ **free** entrada gratuita; ~ **fee** n derechos de admisión m pl; ~ **of securities** n admisión de acciones, bonos y valores f; ~ **to listing** n, ~ **to quotation** n admisión a la cotización f

admit vt (to place) dejar entrar, admitir; (crime, mistake, failure) admitir, reconocer; (request, suggestion, wish) aceptar; ~ **sb to the Bar** admitir a alguien en el Colegio de Abogados

admittance n acceso m, entrada f; **no** ~ prohibida la entrada; **gain** ~ **to sth** conseguir entrar a algo

admitted company n compañía autorizada f

adopt vt (idea, strategy, stance) adoptar; (recommendation) aprobar; BrE (as candidate) elegir

adoption n (of idea, strategy, stance) adopción f; (of recommendation) aprobación f; BrE (of candidate) elección f; ~ **process** n (of product) proceso de adopción m

ADP abbr (►**automatic data processing**) PAD (proceso automático de datos)

adrail n (at railway station) panel publicitario m

adrate n tarifa publicitaria f

adrift adj a la deriva

adshel n (at bus stop) panel publicitario m

ADSL abbr (►**asymmetrical digital subscriber line**) línea digital asimétrica de abonado f

adult[1] n adulto(-a) m,f

adult[2] adj (Law) mayor de edad; ~ **fare** n tarifa de adulto f; ~ **population** n población adulta f

adulteration of proceedings n (Law) falsificación de actas f

ADV abbr (►**advice enclosed**) contiene (carta de) aviso

ad val abbr (►**ad valorem**) ad valórem, sobre el valor

ad valorem adj ad valórem, sobre el valor; ~ **duty** n arancel sobre el valor m, derecho de aduana ad valórem m; ~ **rate** n tarifa ad valórem f; ~ **tax** n impuesto ad valórem m

advance[1] n (early payment) anticipo m, adelanto m; (loan) préstamo m; (in technology) adelanto m; (of civilization, in science) progreso m; (of prices) alza m; **in** ~ por adelantado, por anticipado; **pay in** ~ pagar por adelantado or por anticipado; **thanking you in** ~ agradeciéndole de antemano; **make an** ~ **payment** anticipar un pago; **they gave me an** ~ **of £100 on my salary** me dieron un adelanto or un anticipo de 100 libras a cuenta del sueldo; ~ **account** n cuenta de anticipos f; ~ **against goods** n anticipo contra entrega de productos m; ~ **against security** n préstamo con garantía pignoraticia m; ~ **bill** n efecto anticipado m; ~ **billing** n facturación anticipada f; ~ **booking** n BrE (cf ►**advance reservation** AmE) (of hotel) reserva anticipada f; (of theatre, restaurant) venta anticipada f; ~ **booking office** n taquilla de venta anticipada f; ~ **copy** n (of book) ejemplar de anticipo m; ~ **notice** n preaviso m; ~ **on goods** n adelanto sobre mercancías m; ~ **on salary** n anticipo salarial m; ~ **on securities** n BrE anticipo sobre valores m; ~ **payment** n pago anticipado m; ~ **premium** n prima pagada por adelantado f; ~ **publicity** n publicidad anticipada f; ~**s received** n pl anticipos recibidos m pl; ~ **reservation** n

AmE (cf ▸**advance booking** BrE) (of hotel) reserva anticipada f; (of theatre, restaurant) venta anticipada; ~ **royalty payment** n pago anticipado de derechos m; ~ **security** n valor anticipado m; ~ **selling** n (of security) venta anticipada f

advance² **1** vt (money, wages) anticipar, adelantar; (loan) anticipar; (employee) ascender; (date, meeting) adelantar; (knowledge) fomentar, potenciar; (interests, cause) promover; (idea, argument) presentar, proponer; (tape) avanzar; ~ **sb sth** anticiparle or adelantarle algo a alguien **2** vi (technology, society, project) avanzar, progresar; (employee) ascender

advanced adj (software, technology, system, idea) avanzado; (training) superior; (country) desarrollado; ~ **collection** n (Tax) cobro anticipado m; **A~ Level General Certificate of Education** n examen británico a nivel de bachillerato superior, ≈ Curso de Orientación Universitaria m Esp, ≈ Selectividad f Esp; **A~ Supplementary Level General Certificate of Education** n examen británico adicional a nivel de bachillerato superior, ≈ Curso de Orientación Universitaria m Esp, ≈ Selectividad f Esp; ~ **search** n (Comp) búsqueda avanzada f

advancement n adelantamiento m, avance m

advantage n ventaja f; **have an ~ over sb** tener ventaja sobre alguien; **knowledge of German an ~** se valorarán conocimientos de alemán; **take ~ of sth/sb** aprovecharse de algo/alguien; **take ~ of an opportunity to do sth** aprovecharse de una oportunidad para hacer algo; **turn sth to one's ~** sacar provecho or partido de algo

advantageous adj (arrangement) ventajoso, favorable; **be ~ to sb** ser ventajoso or favorable para alguien

adventure n (Fin) especulación f aislada or eventual

adversary n adversario(-a) m,f

adverse adj (balance) desfavorable; (consequences, influence, effect, result) negativo, adverso; ~ **balance of trade** n balanza comercial negativa f; ~ **movement** n (in price of bonds) movimiento adverso m; ~ **opinion** n opinión f adversa or desfavorable or negativa; ~ **price movement** n evolución adversa de los precios f; ~ **trading conditions** n pl condiciones comerciales adversas f pl

adversely adv adversamente; ~ **affected** adj afectado adversamente

advert n anuncio m

advertise **1** vt (product, job) anunciar; **as ~d on TV** según anunciado en la televisión

2 vi hacer publicidad; ~ **for sb** poner un anuncio para alguien; ~ **for bids** solicitar ofertas públicamente

advertisement n anuncio m

advertiser n anunciante mf

advertising n (business) publicidad f; (advertisements) publicidad f, propaganda f; **be o work in ~** trabajar en publicidad; ~ **agency** n agencia de publicidad f; ~ **agent** n agente de publicidad mf; ~ **budget** n presupuesto publicitario m; ~ **campaign** n campaña publicitaria f; ~ **channel** n canal publicitario m; ~ **code** n código publicitario m; ~ **consultant** n consultor(a) de publicidad m,f; ~ **copy** n original del anuncio m; ~ **coverage** n cobertura publicitaria f; ~ **department** n (of magazine) departamento de publicidad m; ~ **director** n director(a) de publicidad m,f; ~ **effectiveness** n efectividad del anuncio f, eficacia publicitaria f ~ **executive** n ejecutivo(-a) de la publicidad m,f; ~ **expenditure** n, ~ **expenses** n pl gastos de publicidad m pl; ~ **gimmick** n truco publicitario m; ~ **industry** n industria de la publicidad f; ~ **jingle** n jingle publicitario m, melodía publicitaria f; ~ **man** n hombre anuncio m; ~ **manager** n gerente de publicidad mf; ~ **media** n pl medios publicitarios m pl; ~ **overkill** n exceso de medios publicitarios m; ~ **rates** n pl tarifas de publicidad f pl; ~ **reach** n alcance publicitario m; ~ **revenue** n ingresos publicitarios m pl; ~ **slogan** n eslogan publicitario m, slogan m; ~ **space** n espacio publicitario m; **A~ Standards Authority** n organización británica para la regulación de la publicidad; ~ **strategy** n estrategia publicitaria f; ~ **talk** n jerga de publicidad f; ~ **technique** n técnica publicitaria f; ~ **turnover** n facturación de publicidad f; ~ **value** n valor publicitario m; ~ **vehicle** n medio m or vehículo m publicitario; ~ **weapon** n arma publicitaria f; ~ **wearout** n saturación publicitaria f

advertorial n publireportaje m

advice n (notification) aviso m; (counsel) consejos m pl; (professional) asesoramiento m; ~ **enclosed** contiene (carta de) aviso; **give sb ~** aconsejar a alguien; **no ~** sin aviso; **a piece of ~** un consejo; **seek sb's ~** o **seek ~ from sb** consultar a alguien; **take ~ from sb** consultar a alguien; **take** o **follow sb's ~** seguir los consejos de alguien, hacerle caso a alguien; **take legal ~** asesorarse con or consultar a un abogado; **until further ~** hasta nuevo aviso; ~ **of arrival** n aviso de llegada m; ~ **of delivery** n aviso de entrega m; ~ **note** n carta de aviso f

advisable adj aconsejable, conveniente

advise ☐1 *vt* (caution, postponement)
aconsejar, recomendar; (give advice to)
aconsejar; (professionally) asesorar; (inform)
informar; (in writing) notificar; ~ **a draft**
notificar un giro; ~ **sb of sth** informar a
alguien de algo; **please ~ us of the**
dispatch of the order les rogamos nos
hagan saber *or* nos notifiquen cuando el
pedido haya sido despachado; ~ **sb to do**
sth aconsejar a alguien que haga algo; **you**
would be well ~d to see a lawyer sería
aconsejable que se asesorara con un
abogado *or* haría bien en asesorarse con un
abogado
☐2 *vi* aconsejar; (professionally) asesorar; ~
against (doing) sth desaconsejar (hacer)
algo

advised bill *n* nota de aviso *f*

adviser, **advisor** *n* consejero(-a) *m,f*;
(professional) asesor(a) *m,f*

advising bank *n* banco *m* girador *or*
ordenante

advisory *adj* (role, board, body) consultivo;
(function, group) asesor; (service, work) de
asesoramiento; **in an ~ capacity** en calidad
de asesor; ~ **committee** *n* BrE (*cf*
▸**prudential committee** AmE) comisión
asesora *f*, comité asesor *m*; **A~,**
Conciliation and Arbitration Service *n*
BrE ≈ Instituto de Mediación, Arbitraje y
Conciliación *m*

advocacy advertising *n* publicidad de
apoyo *f*

advocate¹ *n* (in Scottish legal system)
abogado(-a) *m,f*

advocate² *vt* recomendar

aerial advertising *n* publicidad aérea *f*

aerogram *n* aerograma *m*

aeroplane BrE, **airplane** AmE *n* aeronave
f, aeroplano *m*, avión *m*; ~ **banner** *n*
estandarte aéreo *m*

aerospace *adj* aeroespacial

affair *n* (matter, incident, event) asunto *m*;
(case) caso *m*; **the current state of ~s** la
situación actual; **put one's ~s in order**
poner sus asuntos en orden

affect *vt* afectar; **be ~ed** quedar afectado

affidavit *n* declaración jurada *f*

affiliate¹ *n* filial *f*; ~ **member** *n* miembro
afiliado *m*; ~ **program** AmE, ~
programme BrE *n* programa del afiliado *m*

affiliate² ☐1 *vt* afiliar
☐2 *vi* afiliarse; ~ **to sth** afiliarse a algo

affiliated *adj* (company, bank, chain) filial;
(retailer, wholesaler, trade union) afiliado; (group)
asociado; **be ~ to sth** estar afiliado a algo

affiliation *n* afiliación *f*; ~ **fee** *n* cuota de
afiliación *f*

affirmative *adj* (reply, statement) afirmativo;
~ **action** *n* AmE discriminación positiva *f*

affix *vt* (label) adherir; (stamp) pegar; (seal)
estampar; (notice, poster, bill) fijar; ~ **a seal to**
sth sellar algo

affixed *adj* (attached) adjunto; ~
document *n* anexo *m*, documento adjunto
m

affluence *n* abundancia *f*, opulencia *f*

affluent *adj* (country) próspero; (person)
acomodado, rico; **the ~ society** la sociedad
opulenta

afford *vt* permitirse (el lujo de); (advantage)
ofrecer; **I just can't ~ the time to do it** es
que no dispongo de tiempo para hacerlo; **I**
can't ~ to pay for it no tengo con qué
pagarlo, no puedo pagarlo

affordable *adj* (price) asequible

afloat *adj* (business) boyante; **keep ~**
(business) mantenerse a flote; ~ **price** *n*
precio flotante *m*

aforementioned *adj* anteriormente
mencionado

a fortiori *adv* con más razón

AFT *abbr* (▸**automatic funds transfer**)
transferencia de fondos automática *f*

after-acceptance *n*, **after-acceptation**
n aceptación a posteriori *f*

after-acquired: ~ **clause** *n* cláusula de
adquisición posterior *f*; ~ **property** *n*
propiedad de adquisición posterior *f*

after-effect *n* secuela *f*, repercusión *f*

after-hours *adj* (dealing, trading, market, price,
rally) tras el cierre, fuera de horas

afterimage *n* imagen secundaria *f*

after-market *adj* propio del mercado
secundario

after market *n* mercado secundario *m*

aftermath *n* repercusiones *f*, secuelas *f pl*;
in the ~ of sth en el periodo subsiguiente
de algo

after-profits *adj* (tax) después de
beneficios

after-sales *adj* (service) posventa; (manager)
de posventa

after-tax *adj* (dividend, income, profit) después
de impuestos

A.G. *abbr* (▸**accountant general**) jefe(-a)
de contabilidad *m,f*

against *prep* contra; ~ **all risks** a *or*
contra todo riesgo; ~ **documents** contra
entrega de documentos; **insured ~ theft**
asegurado contra robo; ~ **one's judgment**
contra su propio parecer; ~ **the law** illegal,
prohibido por (la) ley; ~ **payment** contra
pago; ~ **policy** en contra de costumbre; **the**
pound dropped to a new low ~ the dollar
la libra registró un nuevo mínimo frente al
dólar; ~ **text** contra texto

agcy *abbr* (▸agency) (office) agencia *f*; (branch) sucursal *f*, filial *f*; (department) organismo *m*; (government department) gestoría *f*

age¹ *n* (of person, animal, thing) edad *f*; (epoch) era *f*; ~ **allowance** *n* BrE (Tax) *desgravación a la tercera edad*; ~ **at entry** *n* edad de ingreso *f*; ~ **at expiry** *n* edad al vencimiento *f*; ~ **bracket** *n* grupo etario *m*; ~ **discrimination** *n* discriminación por edad *f*; ~ **distribution** *n* distribución según edad *f*; ~**-earnings profile** *n* perfil de ingresos por edad *m*; ~ **exemption** *n* exención por edad *f*; ~ **group** *n* grupo etario *m*; ~ **limit** *n* límite de edad *m*

age² ⏐1⏐ *vt* (put in date order) ordenar por antigüedad *or* por fecha; (stocks) dar antigüedad a, fechar
⏐2⏐ *vi* (deteriorate with age) deteriorarse

aged: ~ **account** *n* cuenta vencida *f*; ~ **trial balance** *n* balance de comprobación vencido *m*

ageing: ~ **of accounts receivable** *n* ordenación cronológica de las cuentas a cobrar *f*; ~ **of receivables** *n* análisis de la antigüedad de las cuentas a cobrar *m*; ~ **schedule** *n* lista *f or* relación *f* cronológica

ageism *n* discriminación por motivo de edad *f*

agency *n* (office) agencia *f*; (branch) sucursal *f*, filial *f*; (department) organismo *m*; (government department) gestoría *f*; **through the** ~ **of sb** a través de *or* por medio de alguien; ~ **account** *n* cuenta de agencia *f*; ~ **agreement** *n* contrato de representación *m*; ~ **audit** *n*, ~ **auditing** *n* auditoría de agencia *f*; ~ **bank** *n* banco representante *m*; ~ **billing** *n* facturación de agencia *f*; ~ **broker** *n* broker *mf or* intermediario(-a) *m,f* de bolsa; ~ **cost** *n* (Stock) costes *m pl* Esp *or* costos *m pl* AmL de corretaje; ~ **fee** *n* comisión *f or* cuota *f* de agencia; (paid by shipowner to agents) gasto *m* de agencia *or* de representación; ~ **fund** *n* fondo de agencia *m*; ~ **law** *n* ley de representación *f*

agenda *n* orden del día *m*, agenda *f*; **be on the** ~ estar en el orden del día *or* en la agenda; **the first item on the** ~ el primer punto del orden del día; **put sth on the** ~ poner algo en el orden del día

agent *n* (for person) agente *mf*; (for company - person) agente *mf*, representante *mf*; (- firm) agencia *f*; ~ **bank** *n* banco agente *m*; ~ **corporation** *n* compañía *f or* sociedad *f* representante

agglomeration *n* aglomeración *f*

aggravated risk *n* riesgo agravado *m*

aggregate¹ *adj* (value, sales) total, global; (income, output) total; (production) global; (risk) agregado; ~ **balance** *n* balance consolidado *m*; ~ **book value** *n* valor *m* contable

agregado *or* total contable; ~ **demand** *n* demanda *f* agregada *or* global; ~ **statement** *n* estado de cuentas global *m*; ~ **supply** *n* oferta agregada *f*

aggregate² *n* monto global *m*; **in the** ~ en total

aggregate³ *vt* agregar, globalizar

aggressive *adj* (person, company, strategy, marketing, pricing) agresivo

agio *n* agio *m*; ~ **account** *n* cuenta de agio *f*

agiotage *n* agiotaje *m*

AGM *abbr* (▸annual general meeting) asamblea *f or* junta *f* anual

agree ⏐1⏐ *vt* (price, terms) acordar; (date, details) decidir, concertar; ~ **the accounts/ the books** aceptar las cuentas/los libros; ~ **sth by consensus** consensuar algo; ~ **to do sth** (reach an agreement) quedar en hacer algo; (consent) aceptar hacer algo; ~ **that...** (be in agreement) estar de acuerdo en que...; (admit, concede) reconocer *or* admitir *or* aceptar que...
⏐2⏐ *vi* (be of same opinion) estar de acuerdo; (reach mutual understanding) ponerse de acuerdo; (consent) acceder, asentir; (statements, figures) concordar; ~ **about sth** estar de acuerdo sorbre algo, coincidir en algo; ~ **with sth/sb** estar de acuerdo con algo/ alguien; **agree on** *vt* (price, terms of sale) ponerse de acuerdo en, convenir; **agree to** *vt* (terms, conditions) aceptar

agreed *adj* (price, terms, plan, report) acordado; (value, time, place, total, sum) convenido; **as** ~ según lo convenido; ~ **takeover** *n* toma de control pactada *f*

agreement *n* (shared opinion) acuerdo *m*; (formal agreement, treaty) convenio *m*; (contract) contrato *m*; (consent) consentimiento *m*; **break/honour** BrE *o* honor AmE **an** ~ romper/respetar un acuerdo; **come to** *o* **reach an** ~ **(with sb)** llegar a un acuerdo (con alguien); **enter into an** ~ aceptar los términos de un acuerdo; **have an** ~ **(with sb)** tener un acuerdo (con alguien); **be in** ~ **(with sb)** estar de acuerdo (con alguien); **obtain sb's** ~ **(to sth)** obtener el consentimiento de alguien (para algo); **sign an** ~ firmar un acuerdo

agribusiness *n* industria agropecuaria *f*, agroindustria *f*

agricultural *adj* (land, subsidy, loan, production, cooperative, sector) agrícola; (job) agrícola, agropecuario; (policy, levy) agrario

agriculturalist *n* agricultor(a) *m,f*, agrónomo(-a) *m,f*

agriculture *n* agricultura *f*, agronomía *f*

agriculturist *n* agricultor(a) *m,f*, agrónomo(-a) *m,f*

agrifood industry *n* industria agrícola-alimentaria *f*

agrifoodstuffs n pl materias primas agrícolas f pl

agrochemical[1] adj agroquímico

agrochemical[2] n agroquímico m

agroforestry n agrosilvicultura f

agroindustry n agroindustria f

agronomist n agrónomo(-a) m,f

agronomy n agronomía f

agt abbr (▶agent) (for person) agente mf; (for company - person) agente mf, representante mf; (- firm) agencia f

agy. abbr (▶agency) (office) agencia f; (branch) sucursal f, filial f; (department) organismo m; (government department) gestoría f

ahead adv hacia adelante; **be ~ (of)** llevar ventaja (a); **get ~ (of)** adelantarse (a); **in the months ~** durante los próximos meses; **payments ~ of time** pagos por adelantado; **plan ~** planear de antemano; **she arrived a few minutes ~ of us** llegó unos minutos antes que nosotros; **you will be notified ~ of the meeting** se le hará saber antes de or con antelación a la reunión

AHS abbr (▶assistant head of section) jefe(-a) auxiliar de sección m,f

AI abbr (▶accrued interest) interés acumulado m; (▶accumulated interest) interés acumulado m; (▶artificial intelligence) IA (inteligencia artificial)

aid[1] n (help) ayuda f; (financial) ayuda f, asistencia f; **with the ~ of** con la ayuda de; **~ in kind** ayuda en especie f; **~ program** AmE, **~ programme** BrE n programa de ayuda m; **~ scheme** n plan de ayuda m

aid[2] vt ayudar; (understanding) favorecer; (company) promover; (person) asistir; **~ and abet sb** instigar y secundar a alguien

AIDA abbr (▶attention, interest, desire, action) atención, interés, deseo, acción

aide n asesor(a) m,f

aide-mémoire n (memorandum) memorándum m, ayuda memoria f; (reminder) recordatorio m

ailing adj (industry, economy) renqueante, aquejado de problemas; (bank) en dificultades

aim[1] n propósito m; **with the ~ of doing sth** con la intención or el propósito de hacer algo

aim[2] vt (criticism, product, programme) dirigir; **~ sth at sb** dirigir algo a alguien; **~ to do sth** querer or proponerse hacer algo

AIM abbr (▶Alternative Investment Market) Alternativo Mercado de Inversión m

air[1] n aire m; **by ~** por avión; **on the ~** en el aire; **~ bill (of lading)** n conocimiento de embarque aéreo m; **~ carrier** n empresa de transporte aéreo f; **~ consignment note** n carta de porte aéreo f; **~ fare** n tarifa aérea f; **~ freight** n (system) transporte aéreo m; (charge) flete (aéreo) m; (goods) carga (aérea) f; **~ lane** n ruta aérea f; **~ pollution** n contaminación del aire f; **~ rights** n (Media) derechos m pl de antena or de emisión; (Transp) derechos de vuelo m pl; **~ terminal** n terminal aérea f; **~ traffic** n tráfico aéreo m; **~-traffic control** n control de tráfico aéreo m; **~-traffic controller** n controlador(a) de tráfico aéreo m,f; **~ transport** n transporte aéreo m; **~ travel** n viajes aéreos m pl; **~ traveler** AmE, **~ traveller** BrE n pasajero(-a) de vía aérea m,f

air[2] vt (idea, proposal) dar a conocer; **~ one's opinions/views** divulgar las propias opiniones/los propios puntos de vista

airbus n aerobús m, airbus m

air-conditioned adj climatizado

air conditioning n climatización f

aircraft n aeroplano m, avión m; **~ industry** n industria aeronáutica f; **~ operator** n operador(a) aéreo(-a) m,f

aircrew n tripulación de un avión f

airline n línea aérea f

airliner n avión de pasajeros m

airmail[1] n correo aéreo m; **by ~** por correo aéreo; **~ letter** n carta por correo aéreo f; **~ paper** n papel para correo aéreo m; **~ transfer** n transferencia por correo aéreo f

airmail[2] vt enviar por correo aéreo

airplane AmE ▶**aeroplane** BrE

air-pocket stock n (infrml) acciones o valores que caen en picado al entrar en un bache

airport n aeropuerto m; **~ tax** n impuestos de aeropuerto mpl

airtight adj (container, seal) hermético

airtime n (for advertising) tiempo m de emisión or de antena; (on radio) tiempo en radio m; (on television) tiempo en TV m; **~ buyer** n comprador(a) de espacio en medios audiovisuales m,f

airway n vía aérea f

airworthiness n aeronavegabilidad f; **~ certification** n certificado de aeronavegabilidad m

airworthy adj en condiciones de vuelo

aisle n (in cinema, shop, train) pasillo m

a.k.a. abbr (▶also known as) alias, también conocido como

alarm n alarma f; **~ bell** n timbre de alarma m; **~ call** n llamada de alarma f; **~ signal** n señal de alerta f

aleatory contract n contrato aleatorio m

alert n alerta f; **be on the ~** estar sobre aviso

A level n (▸Advanced Level General Certificate of Education) *examen británico a nivel de bachillerato superior*, ≈ C.O.U. (Curso de Orientación Universitaria) Esp, ≈ Selectividad *f* Esp

algorithm n algoritmo m

algorithmic adj algorítmico

alias[1] adv alias, también conocido como

alias[2] n alias m; (Comp) seudónimo m

aliasing n ajeno m, solapamiento m; (graphics) espúreo m, aliasing m

alien[1] adj extranjero; ~ **to sth/sb** ajeno a algo/alguien; ~ **corporation** n compañía *f* or empresa *f* extranjera, sociedad anónima extranjera *f*

alien[2] n extranjero(-a) m,f

alienable adj alienable, enajenable

alienate vt alienar, enajenar

alienation n alienación *f*, enajenación *f*; ~ **effect** n efecto de alienación m

alienee n (Law) *persona que adquiere el bien o derecho enajenado*

align vt alinear

alignment n alineación *f*

alimony n pensión alimenticia *f*; ~ **income** n ingresos por pensión alimenticia m pl

all-day adj que dura todo el día; ~ **opening** n apertura ininterrumpida *f*; ~ **trading** n mercado continuo m

allegation n alegación *f*

alleged adj presunto

all-employee option scheme n BrE plan de opción para todo el personal m

alleviate vt (problem) mitigar

alleviation n (of problem) mitigación *f*

alliance n alianza *f*

allied adj (subject) relacionado, afín; ~ **industries** n pl industrias afines *f* pl; ~ **member** n (Stock) miembro aliado m; ~ **trades** n pl negocios afines m pl

alligator spread n margen de cocodrilo m

all-in adj (price) todo comprendido, todo incluido; (insurance) contra todo riesgo

all-inclusive adj (rate, price) con todo incluido, total

all-loss, all-risk adj a toda pérdida, contra todo riesgo

allocate vt (money, securities) adjudicar, consignar; (funds, resources) destinar, prorratear; (contract) adjudicar; (work) asignar, repartir; ~ **costs to the appropriate accounts** aplicar or asignar los costes Esp or costos AmL a las cuentas apropiadas

allocation n (of funds, money, duties, contracts) adjudicación *f*; (of costs, resources) asignación *f*; (of earnings) distribución *f*; (of responsibilities)

asignación *f*, distribución *f*; (of work) distribución *f*, reparto m; ~ **by tender** n adjudicación por licitación *f*; ~ **to reserves** n asignación *f* or atribución *f* or dotación *f* a reservas

allonge n (on bill of exchange) talón m

All Ordinaries Index n índice All Ordinaries m

all-or-nothing clause n BrE cláusula de todo o nada *f*

allot vt (assign) asignar; (distribute) repartir, distribuir; (Acc) consignar; (Stock) repartir

allotment n (assignment) asignación *f*; (distribution) reparto m, distribución *f*; (Acc) consignación *f*; (Stock) reparto m

allotted share n acción asignada *f*

allottee n (Stock) beneficiario(-a) m,f

all-out adj (effort) a toda potencia; ~ **strike** n huelga general *f*

allow vt (claim) admitir; (money, resources) ceder; (person, organization, action, change) autorizar; **we ~ a discount for cash** ofrecemos descuento si se paga en efectivo; ~ **sb to do sth** permitirle a alguien hacer algo or que haga algo; **please ~ two weeks for delivery** la entrega se hará dentro de un plazo de dos semanas; **allow for** vt reservar para, hacer provisión para; ~ **for a margin of error** permitir un margen de error

allowable adj (claim, deduction, exemption) admisible; (expense, refund) deducible; ~ **against tax** desgravable; ~ **business investment loss** n BrE (cf ▸**deductible business investment loss** AmE) pérdida deducible en inversiones empresariales *f*

allowance n provisión *f*, deducción *f*; (for damaged or lost goods) indemnización *f*; (Tax) desgravación *f*; (from employer) complemento m, sobresueldo m; (from state) prestación *f*; **make an ~** hacer una concesión; **make ~s** (for exceptional occurrences) hacer provisiones; ~ **for bad debts** n reserva para cuentas dudosas *f*; ~ **for depreciation** n deducción por amortización *f*; ~ **for exchange fluctuations** n provisión para fluctuaciones en el cambio *f*; ~ **for inflation** n reserva para inflación *f*; ~ **for living expenses** n provisión para gastos de mantenimiento *f*; ~ **for personal expenses** n (Tax) desgravación de gastos personales *f*; ~ **for traveling expenses** AmE, ~ **for travelling expenses** BrE n (Tax) deducción por gastos de viaje *f*; ~ **in kind** n indemnización *f* or retribución *f* en especie

allowed adj (deduction) permitido; ~ **time** n (for work) tiempo concedido m

all-risks adj todo riesgo; (insurance, cover) contra todo riesgo

all-round price n precio global m

all-savers certificate n certificado de ahorros universal m

all-sector average n (for growth) promedio de todo el sector m

All Share Index n BrE *índice del Financial Times*

all-time adj (record) histórico; **an ~ high/ low** un máximo/mínimo histórico

ALM abbr (►**asset-liability management**) GAP (gestión de activos y pasivos)

alpha adj (share, stock, position. stage) alfa; **~-test** n (Comp) prueba alfa f

alphabetical adj alfabético; **in ~ order** en orden alfabético

alphanumeric adj alfanumérico; **~ character** n carácter alfanumérico m

alt. abbr (►**altered**) mod. (modificado)

alter vt alterar

alteration n alteración f; **~s and improvements** n pl (in annual accounts) modificaciones f pl y mejoras f pl; **~ of capital** n alteración de capital f

alternate[1] adj (by turns, successive) alterno; **on ~ days** en días alternos

alternate[2] n AmE (cf ►**substitute** BrE) sustituto(-a) m,f; **~ demand** n demanda de bienes sustitutivos f

alternate[3] vt alternar

Alternate key n tecla alternativa f

alternating shifts n pl turnos alternos m pl

alternative[1] n alternativa f; **there is no ~** no hay alternativa

alternative[2] adj (plan, method) otro, diferente; (cost, funding, economic strategy) alternativo; **~ energy** n energía alternativa f; **A~ Investment Market** n Alternativo Mercado de Inversión m; **~ payee** n beneficiario(-a) alternativo(-a) m,f; **~ technology** n tecnología alternativa f

Alt key (►**Alternate key**) tecla alt (tecla alternativa)

altruism n altruismo m

always-on connection n (Comp) conexión permanente f

a.m. abbr (►**ante meridiem**) a.m. (ante merídiem)

amalgamate [1] vt (companies, activities, shares) fusionar [2] vi fusionarse

amalgamation n fusión f; **~ agreement** n contrato de fusión m

amass vt amasar

ambient adj ambiental; **~ temperature** n temperatura ambiente f

ambition n ambición f

ambitious adj (person, plan) ambicioso

amend vt (Law) enmendar, reformar; (Patents, Pol) modificar, enmendar; (Stock, Tax) corregir

amended adj (Law) enmendado, reformado; (Patents, Pol) modificado, enmendado; (Stock, Tax) corregido; **~ act** n ley reformada f; **~ prospectus** n prospecto rectificado m

amendment n (Law) enmienda f, reformación f; (Patents, Pol) modificación f, enmienda f; (Stock, Tax) corrección f

American adj americano; (US) estadounidense; **in ~ terms** (currency exchange) en términos americanos; **~ Board of Trade** n Cámara de Comercio Americana f; **~ Chamber of Commerce** n Cámara de Comercio Americana f; **~ National Standards Institute** n *instituto nacional estadounidense de normalización,* ≈ Asociación Española de Normalización y Certificación f; **~ option** n (Stock) opción a la americana f; **~ Standard Code for Information Interchange** n *código estadounidense normalizado de intercambio de información;* **~ Standards Association** n (cf ►**British Standards Institution**) *asociación estadounidense de normalización,* ≈ Asociación Española de Normalización y Certificación; **~ Stock Exchange** n bolsa estadounidense de valores

Amex abbr (►**American Stock Exchange**) bolsa estadounidense de valores; **~ Commodities Exchange** n Bolsa de Contratación Amex f, Bolsa de Productos Amex f

amicable adj (manner, settlement) amigable; (arrangement) amistoso; **reach an ~ agreement** llegar a un acuerdo amistoso

amicably adv (settle, part) por la vía amistosa

AML abbr (►**adjustable mortgage loan**) préstamo hipotecario ajustable m

amortizable adj (debt, loan) amortizable

amortization n amortización f; **~ adjustment** n ajuste de la amortización m; **~ expense** n coste m Esp or costo m AmL de amortización; **~ fund** n fondo de amortización m; **~ loan** n préstamo amortizable m; **~ method** n método de amortización m; **~ payment** n pago de amortización m; **~ reserve** n reserva de amortización f; **~ schedule** n cuadro m or plan m de amortización

amortize vt (asset) amortizar

amortized adj amortizado; **~ capital** n capital amortizado m; **~ cost** n coste m Esp or costo m AmL amortizado; **~ mortgage loan** n préstamo hipotecario amortizado m; **~ value** n valor amortizado m

amortizement n depreciación f

amount *n* (quantity) cantidad *f*; (of bill, damage) importe *m*; (of business) volumen *m*; (of loss) monto *m*; ~ **brought forward** *n*, ~ **carried forward** *n* cantidad llevada a cuenta nueva *f*, saldo a cuenta nueva *m*; ~ **charged** *n* cantidad cargada *f*; ~ **contributed** *n* suma de aportación *f*; ~ **credited to an account** *n* cantidad ingresada en una cuenta *f*; ~ **due** *n* cantidad *f* adeudada *or* a pagar; ~ **exported** *n* cantidad exportada *f*; ~ **invested** *n* suma invertida *m*; ~ **outstanding** *n* cantidad pendiente *f*; ~ **overdue** *n* cantidad no pagada al vencimiento *f*; ~ **overpaid** *n* cantidad pagada de más *f*; ~ **paid** *n* cantidad pagada *f*; ~ **paid by installments** AmE, ~ **paid by instalments** BrE *n* cantidad pagada a plazos *f*; ~ **paid out** *n* cantidad desembolsada *f*; ~ **payable** *n* cantidad pagadera *f*; ~ **payable on settlement** *n* valor pagadero a la liquidación *m*; ~ **repayable** *n* cantidad reembolsable *f*; ~ **to be made good** *n* cantidad a demostrar *f*; ~ **underpaid** *n* cantidad pagada de menos *f*

amount to *vt* (bill, debt, assets) ascender a

amt *abbr* (▸**amount**) cantidad *f*

AMT *abbr* (▸**airmail transfer**) transferencia por correo aéreo *f*

A/N *abbr* (▸**alphanumeric**) A/N (alfanumérico)

analogical *adj* analógico

analogue BrE, **analog** AmE *adj* (channel, computer, monitor) analógico

analogue-to-digital BrE, **analog-to-digital** AmE *adj* analógico a digital; ~ **converter** *n* conversor de analógico a digital *m*

analyse BrE, **analyze** AmE *vt* analizar

analyser BrE, **analyzer** AmE *n* analizador *m*

analysis *n* análisis *m*; **in the final** ~ en fin de cuentas; ~ **book** *n* libro de análisis *m*; ~ **of cost variances** *n* análisis *m* de las desviaciones del coste Esp *or* costo AmL

analyst *n* analista *mf*

analytic *adj* analítico

analytical *adj* (accounting, audit, auditing, review, training) analítico

analyze AmE ▸**analyse** BrE

analyzer AmE ▸**analyser** BrE

anchor *n* presentador(a) de noticias *m,f*

anchorman *n* presentador(a) de noticias *m,f*

anchorwoman *n* presentadora de noticias *f*

ancillary *adj* (costs, service) auxiliar; (operation) auxiliar, subsidiario; ~ **staff** *n* personal auxiliar *m*

angel *n* (infrml) promotor(a) teatral *m,f*

angle *n* (point of view) perspectiva *f*, punto de vista *m*

animatic *n* esbozo de anuncio para TV *m*

animation *n* animación *f*

ankled *adj* (jarg) (from job) despedido

annex[1] *n* AmE ▸**annexe** BrE

annex[2] *vt* anexionar

annexe BrE, **annex** AmE *n* (to building, document) anexo *m*

anniversary *n* aniversario *m*; ~ **offer** *n* oferta aniversario *f*

announce *vt* (cut, details) anunciar

announcement *n* anuncio *m*; ~ **of sale** *n* anuncio de venta *m*

annual[1] *adj* anual; **on an** ~ **basis** sobre una base anual; ~ **accounts** *n pl* cuentas anuales *f pl*; ~ **adjustment** *n* ajuste anual *m*; ~ **cash flow** *n* flujo anual de tesorería *m*; ~ **certificate** *n* (on audit) certificado anual *m*; ~ **closing** *n* cierre anual *m*; ~ **depreciation** *n* depreciación anual *f*; ~ **dividend** *n* dividendo anual *m*; ~ **earnings** *n pl* ganancias anuales *f pl*; ~ **fee** *n* cuota anual *f*; ~ **general meeting** *n* asamblea *f or* junta *f* general anual; ~ **leave** *n* vacaciones anuales *f pl*; ~ **meeting** *n* asamblea *f or* junta *f* anual; ~ **payment** *n* pago anual *m*; ~ **percentage rate** *n* tasa porcentual por año *f*; ~ **premium** *n* prima anual *f*; ~ **rate** *n* (of interest, growth) tasa anual *f*; ~ **repayment** *n* devolución anual *f*; ~ **report** *n* informe *m or* memoria *f* anual; ~ **return** *n* (from shares) rendimiento *m or* rédito *m* anual; ~ **salary review** *n* revisión salarial anual *f*; ~ **statement** *n* estado anual *m*; ~ **subscription** *n* suscripción anual *f*; ~ **turnover** *n* facturación anual *f*; ~ **wage** *n* salario anual *m*; ~ **yield** *n* interés *m or* rendimiento *m* anual

annual[2] *n* anuario *m*

annualize *vt* anualizar

annualized *adj* anualizado; ~ **percentage rate** *n* tasa porcentual por año *f*

annually *adv* anualmente

annuitant *n* beneficiario(-a) *m,f* de una anualidad *or* de una renta; (Tax) rentista *mf*

annuity *n* anualidad *f*; ~ **assurance** *n* seguro de renta vitalicia *m*; ~ **bond** *n* bono de renta vitalicia *m*; ~ **fund** *n* fondo de anualidad *m*; ~ **income** *n* renta anual *f*; ~ **insurance** *n* seguro de renta vitalicia *m*; ~ **payable in advance** *n* anualidad pagadera por anticipado *f*; ~ **payable in arrears** *n* anualidad pagadera a plazo vencido *f*; ~ **payment** *n* pago de anualidad *m*; ~ **plan** *n* plan de anualidades *m*; ~ **policy** *n* póliza de anualidades *f*

annul *vt* (contract) cancelar; (decision) anular

annulling clause *n* cláusula abrogatoria *f*

annulment *n* (of contract) cancelación *f*; (of decision) anulación *f*

annunciator board *n* AmE (Stock) tablero indicador *m*

anomaly *n* anomalía *f*

anonymity *n* anonimato *m*

anonymous *adj* anónimo; ~ **product testing** *n* prueba anónima de un producto *f*

Ansaphone® *n* Ansaphone® *m*

ANSI *abbr* (▸**American National Standards Institute**) *instituto nacional estadounidense de normalización,* ≈ AENOR (Asociación Española de Normalización y Certificación)

answer[1] *n* respuesta *f*, contestación *f*; ~ **to sth** (to question, letter, accusation) respuesta a algo; (to problem) solución de algo; **in ~ to your letter** en relación con *or* con relación a su carta; ~ **mode** *n* (Comp) modalidad de respuesta *f*, modo respuesta *m*

answer[2] [1] *vt* (person, letter) contestar; (telephone) contestar, coger Esp, atender AmL; (criticism) responder a [2] *vi* contestar, responder; **answer for** *vt* (safety of product) responder por; **answer to** *vt* (be accountable to) responder ante

answerable *adj* responsable

answerback code *n* código de respuesta *m*

answering: ~ **machine** *n* contestador *m*; ~ **service** *n* servicio de respuesta *m*

answerphone *n* contestador *m*

ante *prep* ante

antedate *vt* (document, cheque, event) antedatar

ante meridiem *adv* ante merídiem

antialiasing *n* (Comp) anti-ajeno *m*, antisolapamiento *m*, antialiasing *m*

anti-avoidance: ~ **legislation** *n* legislación antievasión *f*; ~ **rule** *n* norma contra la evasión fiscal *f*

anticipate *vt* (problem, objection, delay, need) prever; (bill, debt) anticipar; (income, inheritance) gastar de antemano

anticipated *adj* (problem, delay, need, cost, demand) previsto; (bill, debt, profit) anticipado; **as ~** según lo previsto; ~ **growth rate** *n* tasa de crecimiento prevista *f*

anticipation *n* (of profits, income) previsión *f*, anticipación *f*; **thanking you in ~ for your cooperation** agradeciendo de antemano su colaboración; ~ **equivalence** *n* equivalencia por anticipo *f*

anticipatory *adj* (response, pricing) anticipado; (purchase) de previsión; ~ **breach of contract** *n* violación

anticipadora de contrato *f*; ~ **hedge** *n* cobertura anticipada *f*

anticompetitive *adj* no competitivo

anticyclical *adj* (advertising) anticíclico

antidumping *adj* antidumping

anti-inflationary *adj*, **anti-inflation** *adj*, **anti-inflationist** *adj* antiinflacionista

antimarket *adj* antimercadista

antimonopoly laws *n pl* leyes antimonopolio *f pl*

antiquated *adj* anticuado

antirecession *adj* antirecesión

antitrust *adj* (Admin) antitrust; (Law) antimonopolista, antimonopolio; ~ **act** *n* ley antimonopolio *f*; ~ **law** *n* legislación antimonopolio *f*

antivirus software *n* programa antivirus *m*

AO *abbr* (▸**administration officer**) jefe(-a) administrativo(-a) *m,f*

AOB *abbr* (▸**any other business**) ruegos y preguntas

AOCB *abbr* (▸**any other competent business**) ruegos y preguntas

AON clause *n* BrE (▸**all-or-nothing clause**) cláusula de todo o nada *f*

AP *abbr* (▸**additional premium**) prima complementaria *f*; (▸**array processor**) procesador vectorial *m*; (▸**associated person**) BrE persona asociada *f*; (▸**Associated Press**) *agencia de noticias estadounidense*

apartment *n* AmE (*cf* ▸**flat** BrE) apartamento *m*, piso *m* Esp, departamento *m* AmL; ~ **building** *n* edificio *m* de apartamentos *or* pisos Esp *or* departamentos AmL

APC *abbr* (▸**average propensity to consume**) propensión media al consumo *f*

API *abbr* (▸**alternative participation instrument**) BrE instrumento de participación alternativa *m*; (▸**application program interface**) interfaz para programas de aplicación *m*

apiece *adv* (per item) por unidad; (per person) cada uno

apologize *vi* disculparse; ~ **to sb for sth** disculparse ante alguien por algo

apology *n* disculpa *f*, excusa *f*; **apologies from J Brown** BrE (for not attending meeting) J Brown envía sus excusas por no poder asistir; **offer one's apologies** disculparse, excusarse, presentar sus disculpas *or* excusas; **please accept my apologies** le ruego me disculpe; **send one's apologies** enviar sus excusas

apparatus *n* (equipment, system) aparato *m*

apparent *adj* aparente; **it was ~ that...** estaba claro que..., era evidente *or* obvio que...; **become** ~ hacerse patente, empezar a verse; ~ **authority** n (Law) poder aparente m; ~ **tax rate** n tipo impositivo aparente m

appeal¹ n (for funds, tenders) solicitud f; (of plan, idea, product) atractivo m; (against judicial decision) recurso m, apelación f; ~ **bond** n fianza de apelación f; ~ **court** n tribunal de apelación m; ~ **proceedings** n pl autos de apelación m pl; ~**s procedure** n procedimiento de apelación m

appeal² vi (Law) apelar; ~ **for sth** (funds) pedir or solicitar algo; **appeal against** vt (sentence, judgment) recurrir; **appeal to** vt (ask) rogar, suplicar; (attract) atraer

appear vi (come into view) aparecer; (seem) parecer; (be published) aparecer, salir; (in catalogue) figurar; (in court) comparecer; ~ **on television** aparecer en televisión, salir en or por televisión; ~ **to do sth** parecer hacer algo

appearance n (look) aspecto m; (coming into view) aparición f; (in court) comparecencia f; ~**s can be deceptive** las apariencias engañan, no hay que fiarse de las apariencias

append vt agregar, añadir; ~ **sth to sth** agregar or añadir algo a algo; (enclose) adjuntar or acompañar algo a algo; **he ~ed his signature to the document** estampó su firma al pie del documento

appendix n apéndice m

applet n applet m, programita f

appliance n dispositivo m

appliances n pl (domestic) electrodomésticos m pl

applicable adj aplicable; ~ **to sth/sb** aplicable a algo/alguien; **delete as** ~ tache lo que no corresponda; **not** ~ no pertinente

applicant n solicitante mf; ~ **for registration** n (Stock) solicitante de cotización mf

application n (request) solicitud f; (Comp), (of technique, law, funds) aplicación f; **prices on** ~ BrE solicítenos precios; **put in an** ~ **(for a job)** presentar una solicitud (de empleo); ~ **control** n (in auditing) control m de aplicación or de cumplimiento; ~ **fee** n (for share issue) cuota f or derecho m de suscripción; ~ **for admission** n solicitud de admisión f; ~ **for listing** n solicitud de cotización f; ~ **for shares** n suscripción de acciones f; ~ **for subsidies** n solicitud de subsidios f; ~ **form** n forma f or formulario m de solicitud; ~**s package** n (Comp) paquete de aplicaciones m; ~**s program** n (Comp) aplicación informática f; ~ **program interface** n interfaz para programas de aplicación; ~**s programmer** n programador(a) de aplicaciones m,f; ~ **right** n derecho de

suscripción m; ~ **server** n (Comp) servidor de aplicaciones m; ~ **service provider** n (Comp) proveedor de servicio de aplicaciones m; ~**s software** n aplicaciones informáticas f pl; ~**s terminal** n terminal de aplicaciones m

applied adj (cost, overheads, research) aplicado; ~ **economics** n economía aplicada f

apply ⌐1⌐ vt (method, knowledge, regulation) aplicar
⌐2⌐ vi (rule, criterion) aplicarse; ~ **at the office** destinar a la oficina; ~ **in person** solicitar personalmente; **please** ~ **in writing to...** diríjase por escrito a..., escriba a...; ~ **to sth/sb** (be applicable to) aplicarse a algo/ alguien; ~ **within** infórmese aquí, razón aquí; **apply for** vt (post, job, membership) solicitar; (bonds, shares, loan) suscribir

appoint vt (date, place) designar, señalar; ~ **sb (to sth)** (to post, committee) nombrar or designar a alguien (para algo)

appointed adj (agent, chairman) nombrado; **they met at the** ~ **time** se reunieron a la hora señalada; ~ **executor** n administrador(a) de herencia m,f; ~ **guardian** n (of trust) administrador(a) de herencia m,f; ~ **stockist** n distribuidor(a) designado(-a) m,f

appointee n persona nombrada f

appointment n (arrangement to meet) cita f; (of date) designación f; (of employee) nombramiento m; **by** ~ **only** sólo con cita previa; **arrange** o **make an** ~ concertar una cita; **have an** ~ tener una cita; **keep an** ~ asistir a una cita; ~**s vacant** n pl empleos vacantes m pl

apportion vt (costs, land, property, shares) prorratear; (duties, time) distribuir; ~ **budget funds** consignar fondos presupuestarios

apportioned contract n contrato adjudicado m

apportionment n (of costs) prorrateo m; (of duties, time) distribución f; ~ **rule** n (Tax) regla de prorrateo f

appraisal n (of employee, situation, project, performance) evaluación f; (of property) tasación f, avalúo m AmL; **make an** ~ **of future needs** evaluar las necesidades futuras; ~ **report** n informe de evaluación m; ~ **rights** n pl AmE (Stock) derechos de tasación m pl

appraise vt (employee, situation, project, performance) evaluar; (property) tasar, avaluar AmL

appraised value n (Fin) valor valuado m; (Prop) valor estimado m

appraiser n tasador(a) m,f, valuador(a) m,f AmL

appreciable adj apreciable

appreciate [1] *vt* (understand the significance of) apreciar; (welcome) estimar
[2] *vi* (increase in value) (**Acc**) (re)valorizarse; (**Prop, Stock**) ganar valor

appreciated surplus *n* plusvalía *f*, superávit por revalorización *m*

appreciation *n* (gratitude) agradecimiento *m*, reconocimiento *m*; (understanding) estimación *f*, valoración *f*; (increase in value) (re)valorización *f*

apprentice *n* aprendiz(a) *m,f*

apprenticeship *n* aprendizaje *m*

approach[1] *n* (method, outlook) enfoque *m*, planteamiento *m*; (offer) propuesta *f*; (request) solicitud *f*, petición *f*, pedido *m* AmL

approach[2] [1] *vi* (date) acercarse, aproximarse
[2] *vt* (problem) abordar; ~ **sb about sth** abordar a alguien sobre algo

appropriate[1] *adj* apropiado, adecuado; ~ **for sth/sb** apropiado *or* adecuado para algo/alguien

appropriate[2] *vt* (take) apropiarse de; (set aside) destinar, asignar

appropriation *n* (taking) apropiación *f*; (setting aside) asignación *f*; ~ **account** *n* cuenta *f* de consignación *or* de dotación; **A~ Act** BrE, **A~ Bill** AmE *n* Decreto de Presupuestos *m*; ~**s for contingencies** *n* dotación para contingencias *f*; ~ **of income** *n* distribución de ingresos *f*; ~ **to a reserve** *n* asignación a una reserva *f*

approval *n* (acceptance) aprobación *f*; **buy sth on** ~ comprar algo a prueba; **have/get the** ~ **of sb** tener/conseguir la aprobación de alguien; **seek sb's** ~ (**for sth**) tratar de obtener la aprobación de alguien (para algo); ~ **of the accounts** *n* aprobación de cuentas *f*; ~ **process** *n* (**Bank**) trámite de autorización *m*

approve *vt* (action, accounts, decision) aprobar

approved *adj* (device, software, decision, plan, document, price) aprobado; (premises, depository) autorizado; ~ **list** *n* (of investments) lista aprobada *f*; ~ **share** *n* acción admitida *f*

approx. *abbr* (▶**approximately**) aproximadamente

approximate[1] *adj* aproximado; ~ **price** *n* precio aproximado *m*; ~ **rate of return** *n* tasa aproximada de beneficios *f*

approximate[2] *vt* aproximarse a

approximately *adv* aproximadamente

approximation *n* aproximación *f*

appurtenant *adj* aparejado; ~ **structures** *n pl* estructuras accesorias *f pl*

APR *abbr* (▶**annual** *o* **annualized percentage rate**) tasa porcentual por año *f*

a priori *adj* a priori; ~ **statement** *n* juicio a priori *m*

APS *abbr* (▶**advanced planning system**) sistema de planificación avanzado *m*

aptitude *n* (of individual) aptitud *f*; ~ **test** *n* prueba de aptitud *f*

A/R *abbr* (▶**all risks**) todo riesgo

arb *abbr* (▶**arbiter**) árbitro(-a) *m,f*

arbiter *n* árbitro(-a) *m,f*

arbitrage *n* arbitraje *m*; ~ **bonds** *n pl* AmE bonos de arbitraje *m pl*; ~ **dealer** *n* arbitrajista *mf*; ~ **dealing** *n* operación de arbitraje *f*; ~ **house** *n* casa de arbitraje *f*; ~ **in securities** *n* BrE arbitraje de valores *m*; ~ **margin** *n* BrE margen de arbitraje *m*; ~ **stocks** *n pl* valores de arbitraje *m pl*; ~ **trader** *n* intermediario(-a) de arbitraje *m,f*; ~ **trading** *n* operación de arbitraje *f*

arbitrageur *n* arbitrajista *mf*

arbitral *adj* (award) arbitral

arbitrary *adj* (decision, assessment, income, taxation) arbitrario

arbitrate *vi* arbitrar; ~ **in sth** (dispute) arbitrar en algo

arbitration *n* arbitraje *m*; **go to** ~ recurrir *or* someterse al arbitraje; ~ **agreement** *n* acuerdo de arbitraje *m*; ~ **board** *n* junta arbitral *f*; ~ **clause** *n* cláusula de arbitraje *f*; ~ **committee** *n* comité de arbitraje *m*; ~ **proceedings** *n pl* procedimiento de arbitraje *m*; ~ **transaction** *n* transacción de arbitraje *f*; ~ **tribunal** *n* tribunal arbitral *m*

arbitrator *n* árbitro(-a) *m,f*

arcade *n* (for shopping) galería *f*

architect *n* arquitecto(-a) *m,f*; ~**'s liability** *n* responsabilidad civil del arquitecto *f*

archival storage *n* almacenamiento de archivos *m*

archive[1] *n* archivo *m*; ~ **file** *n* fichero *m*; ~ **storage** *n* almacenamiento de archivos *m*

archive[2] *vt* archivar

archivist *n* archivero(-a) *m,f*, archivista *mf*

area *n* (region) zona *f*, área *f*; (of city, building, room) zona *f*; (surface extent) superficie *f*; (of knowledge) campo *m*; **in the London** ~ en la zona *or* en el área de Londres; ~ **code** *n* AmE (**Comms**) (*cf* ▶**dialling code** BrE) prefijo *m*; ~ **of expertise** *n* (of professional) área de conocimientos especializados *f*; ~ **manager** *n* gerente de área *mf*; ~ **office** *n* oficina de zona *f*; ~ **of responsibility** *n* área de responsabilidad *f*; ~ **sales executive** *n* vendedor(a) de zona *m,f*

arguable *adj* discutible

argue [1] *vi* (disagree) discutir; (make a case) argumentar; ~ **about** *o* **over sth** discutir por algo; ~ **with sb** discutir con alguien; ~ **for/against sth** argumentar a favor de/contra de algo

2 *vt* (case) argumentar; (issue) discutir, debatir

ARI *abbr* (▸**accounting rate of interest**) tasa *f or* tipo *f* de interés de cuenta

Ariel *abbr* (▸**Automated Real-Time Investments Exchange**) Bolsa de Valores Automatizada a Tiempo Real *f*

arise *vi* (difficulty, opportunity) surgir, presentarse; ∼ **from sth** (be due to) obedecer a algo; (originate in) surgir (a raíz) de algo; **if the need** ∼**s** si fuera necesario

arm *n* brazo *m*; **at** ∼**'s length** a distancia; (Acc, Tax) en pie de igualdad; ∼**'s-length competition** *n* competencia en pie de igualdad *f*; ∼**'s-length price** *n* precio de mercado *m*; ∼**'s-length principle** *n* principio de la igualdad de oportunidades *m*; ∼**'s-length transaction** *n* transacción en igualdad de condiciones *f*; (Bank, Comms) transacción entre empresas interrelacionadas *f*

ARM *abbr* (▸**adjustable rate mortgage**) hipoteca de tasa ajustable *f*

around-the-clock[1] *adj* (*cf* ▸**round-the-clock** BrE) continuo; ∼**-the-clock service** *n* servicio de 24 horas *m*

around-the-clock[2] *adv* (*cf* ▸**round-the-clock** BrE) continuamente

ARR *abbr* (▸**accounting rate of return**) tasa *f or* tipo *m* de rendimiento contable

arrange *vt* (meeting, interview) organizar; (deal, appointment) concertar; (loan) tramitar

arrangement *n* (agreement) convenio *m*; (ordering) clasificación *f*; **by** ∼ por acuerdo; **come to an** ∼ llegar a un acuerdo; **make** ∼**s for sth** hacer los preparativos para algo; ∼ **fee** *n* gastos de gestión *m pl*

arranger *n* (Fin) facilitador(a) *m,f*

array *n* (of figures, data) matriz *f*; (of products) serie *f*; ∼ **processor** *n* procesador vectorial *m*

arrearage *n* (Fin) atrasos *m pl*; (Stock) demora en el pago *f*

arrears *n pl* (Acc) importe atrasado *m*; (Bank, Stock) deuda atrasada *f*; (Fin) morosidad *f*; (dividend or interest still owed) atrasos *m pl*; **in** ∼ en mora; **be in** ∼ tener atrasos; **fall into** *o* **get into** ∼ **with sth** atrasarse *or* retrasarse en los pagos de algo; **pay one month in** ∼ pagar con un mes de retraso; ∼ **of work** *n pl* trabajo atrasado *m*

arrest[1] *n* detención *f*; **be under** ∼ quedar detenido; **place** *o* **put sb under** ∼ detener a alguien

arrest[2] *vt* (person) detener; (inflation) contener; (decline) atajar; (progress, growth - hinder) dificultar, poner freno a; (- halt) detener

arrival *n* llegada *f*

arrive *vi* llegar

arson *n* incendio provocado *m*

art *n* arte *m*; ∼ **department** *n* (of advertising company) departamento gráfico *m*; ∼ **designer** *n* dibujante *mf*; ∼**s sponsor** *n* patrocinador(a) de arte *m,f*; ∼**s sponsorship** *n* patrocinio de arte *m*

article *n* (small object, clause) artículo *m*; (in newspaper) crónica *f*; (in newsgroup) artículo (de grupo de noticias) *m*, registro *m*; **under** ∼ **(Law)** escriturado; ∼**s of association** *n pl* estatutos *m pl*; ∼ **of consumption** *n* artículo de consumo *m*; ∼**s of incorporation** *n pl* escritura de constitución *f*; ∼**s for personal use** *n pl* (at customs) artículos de uso personal *m pl*

articled clerk *n* ≈ pasante *mf*

articulated vehicle *n* BrE vehículo articulado *m*

artificial *adj* ficticio; ∼ **barrier to entry** *n* (Imp/Exp) barrera artificial de entrada *f*; ∼ **currency** *n* moneda artificial *f*; ∼ **exchange rate** *n* tipo de cambio ficticio *m*; ∼ **intelligence** *n* inteligencia artificial *f*; ∼ **obsolescence** *n* caída en desuso artificial *f*, caducidad artificial *f*

artisan *n* artesano(-a) *m,f*; ∼ **fair** *n* feria de artesanía *f*

artistic *adj* artístico; ∼ **director** *n* (in advertising company) director(a) artístico(-a) *m,f*

artwork *n* (illustrative material) ilustraciones *f pl*

a/s *abbr* (▸**at sight**) a la vista

ASA *abbr* (▸**Advertising Standards Authority**) *organización británica para la regulación de la publicidad*; (▸**American Standards Association**) AENOR (≈ Asociación Española de Normalización y Certificación)

a.s.a.p. *abbr* (▸**as soon as possible**) lo antes posible

ascending *adj* ascendente; **in** ∼ **order** en orden ascendente

ascertain *vt* (fact) verificar, averiguar; (cost) establecer; (price) determinar

ascertainable *adj* (person, group) investigable

ascertained goods *n pl* mercancías comprobadas *f pl*

ascertainment error *n* (Comp) error de observación *m*

ASCII *abbr* (▸**American Standard Code for Information Interchange**) ASCII; ∼ **file** *n* archivo ASCII *m*

ascribe *vt*: ∼ **sth to sth/sb** atribuir algo a algo/alguien

ASE *abbr* (▸**American Stock Exchange**) *bolsa estadounidense de valores*

A-share *n* BrE acción clase A *f*

ask ⬜1 *vt* (inquire, inquire of) preguntar; (request, demand) pedir; ∼ **a question** hacer una pregunta; ∼ **sb sth** preguntarle algo a alguien; ∼ **sb for sth** pedirle algo a alguien; ∼ **sth for sth** (price) pedir algo por algo; ∼ **sb to do sth** pedirle a alguien que haga algo ⬜2 *vi* preguntar

asked and bid *adj* (buying, selling price) demandado y ofertado

asking price *n* precio *m* del vendedor *or* de venta

AS level *n* (▸Advanced Supplementary Level General Certificate of Education) *examen británico opcional que se hace por algunos alumnos interesados al cabo del primer año del bachillerato superior*

ASP *abbr* (▸application service provider) proveedor de servicio de aplicaciones *m*

aspect *n* aspecto *m*

aspiration level *n* nivel de aspiración *f*

assay mark *n* AmE (*cf* ▸hallmark BrE) marca de aleación *f*

assemblage *n* (of land) reunión *f*

assembler *n* (Comp) ensamblador *m*

assembling *n* (Comp) ensamblaje *m*

assembly *n* (meeting) reunión *f*; (group) concurrencia *f*; (parliament) asamblea *f*; (Ind) montaje *m*; ∼ **language** *n* (Comp) lenguaje ensamblador *m*; ∼ **line** *n* línea *f or* cadena *f* de montaje; ∼ **line worker** *n* trabajador(a) en cadena *m,f*; ∼ **plant** *n* planta de montaje *f*

assent *n* asentimiento *m*; BrE (of parliament) aquiescencia *f*

assert *vt* (declare) afirmar; (right, claim) hacer valer, vindicar; (authority) imponer

assertion *n* afirmación *f*

assertiveness *n* seguridad en sí mismo *f*; ∼ **training** *n* cursos *mpl or* ejercicios *mpl* en reafirmación personal

assess *vt* (value, amount) calcular; (person, performance, potential, results) evaluar; (situation) aquilatar, formarse un juicio sobre; (Tax) (penalty) imponer; (taxpayer) gravar

assessable income *n* renta imponible *f*

assessed: ∼ **tax** *n* impuesto liquidable *m*; ∼ **valuation** *n* AmE (*cf* ▸rateable value BrE) valor imponible *m*

assessing: ∼ **action** *n* acción impositiva *f*; ∼ **tax** *n* cuota liquidable *f*

assessment *n* (of value, amount) cálculo *m*; (of person, performance, potential, results) evaluación *f*; (Law) valoración *f*; (Prop) estimación *f*; (Tax) evaluación fiscal *f*; ∼ **center** AmE, ∼ **centre** BrE *n* (HRM) centro de evaluación *m*; ∼ **notice** *n* (Tax) aviso de

imposición *m*; ∼ **roll** *n* (Tax) lista de contribuyentes *f*

assessor *n* (Ins) evaluador(a) *m,f*; (Tax) asesor(a) *m,f*

asset *n* activo *m*; ∼ **account** *n* cuenta activa *f*; ∼ **allocation** *n* asignación de activos *f*; ∼-**backed** *adj* (finance, investment, securities) respaldado por activos; ∼-**based** *adj* (financing, investment) basado en activos; ∼ **coverage** *n* (Acc) garantía con activos *f*; (Stock) cobertura de activos *f*; ∼ **diversification** *n* diversificación de activos *f*; ∼ **held abroad** *n* activo exterior *m*; ∼ **management** *n* administración *f or* gestión *f* de activos; ∼ **management company** *n* compañía de gestión de activos *f*; ∼ **manager** *n* administrador(a) de activos *m,f*; ∼ **mix** *n* combinación de activos *f*; ∼ **portfolio** *n* cartera de activos *f*; ∼ **sale** *n* venta de activos *f*; ∼ **stripping** *n* desglose *m or* liquidación *f* de activos; ∼ **swap** *n* canje de activos *m*; ∼ **sweating** *n* AmE explotación del activo *f*; ∼ **turnover** *n* rotación de activos *f*; ∼ **value** *n* valor de activo *m*; ∼ **write-down** *n* amortización de un activo *f*

assets *n pl* bienes *m pl*, activos *m pl*; ∼ **and drawbacks** *n pl* activos *m pl* y devoluciones *f pl*; ∼ **and liabilities management** *n* administración de activos y pasivos *f*; ∼ **and liabilities statement** *n* balance *m* de activo y pasivo *or* de situación; ∼ **under construction** *n pl* activos *m pl* en construcción *or* en curso

assign *vt* (costs) aplicar, imputar; (transfer) ceder; (property) traspasar, transmitir

assignable *adj* (credit) transferible

assigned account *n* cuenta *f* en garantía *or* cedida en calidad de empeño

assignee *n* cesionario(-a) *m,f*; ∼ **in bankruptcy** *n* apoderado(-a) en bancarrota *m,f*

assignment *n* (mission) misión *f*; (task) función *f*, tarea *f*; (of expenditure) asignación *f*; (of income, lease, patent, rights) cesión *f*; (of debts) cesión *f*, traspaso *m*; ∼ **day** *n* día de notificación *m*; (for options) día de cesión *m*; ∼ **notice** *n* (Stock) aviso de asignación *m*

assignor *n* cedente *mf*

assimilation *n* asimilación *f*

assistance *n* ayuda *f*, asistencia *f*

assistant *n* auxiliar administrativo(-a) *m,f*, ayudante *mf*; (in shop) dependiente(-a) *m,f*; ∼ **administrator** *n* auxiliar administrativo(-a) *m,f*; ∼ **cashier** *n* BrE (*cf* ▸assistant teller AmE) cajero(-a) adjunto(-a) *m,f*; ∼ **director** *n* subdirector(a) *m,f*, director(a) adjunto(-a) *m,f*; ∼ **director general** *n* director(a) general adjunto(-a) *m,f*; ∼ **general director** *n* director(a)

adjunto(-a) *m,f*; ~ **general manager** *n*
director(a) general adjunto(-a) *m,f*,
subdirector(a) general *m,f*; ~ **head of**
section *n* jefe(-a) auxiliar de sección *m,f*; ~
manager *n* subdirector(a) *m,f*, director(a)
adjunto(-a) *m,f*; ~ **teller** *n* AmE (*cf*
▸**assistant cashier** BrE) cajero(-a)
adjunto(-a) *m,f*; ~ **to manager** *n*
asistente(-a) ejecutivo(-a) *m,f*

assisted area *n* zona de ayuda *f*

associate[1] *vt* (involve, connect) vincular;
(link in mind) asociar, relacionar; **associate**
with *vt* asociarse con

associate[2] *adj* (company) asociado; (director,
editor, manager) adjunto

associate[3] *n* miembro asociado(-a) *m,f*

associated *adj* (company, account, employer)
asociado; ~ **with sth/sb** relacionado con
algo/alguien; ~ **person** *n* BrE (Stock)
persona asociada *f*; **A~ Press** *n* agencia de
noticias estadounidense

association *n* (organization, mental link)
asociación *f*; (relationship) relación *f*; **in ~**
with sth/sb en asociación con algo/alguien;
A~ of British Chambers of Commerce
n asociación de cámaras de comercio
británicas

assortment *n* variedad *f*, colección *f*; (of
goods) surtido *m*

asst *abbr* (▸**assistant**) auxiliar
administrativo(-a) *m,f*, ayudante *mf*; (in shop)
dependiente(-a) *m,f*

assume *vt* (suppose) suponer; (duties,
responsibility, role, risk) asumir; (power) hacerse
con, tomar; (debt) hacerse cargo de

assumption *n* (supposition) presunción *f*;
(duties, responsibility, role, risk) asunción *f*; ~ **of**
mortgage *n* aceptación de hipoteca *f*

assured[1] *adj* (capital) asegurado; (income)
seguro

assured[2] *n* asegurado(-a) *m,f*

asymmetric *adj* (information) asimétrico

asymmetrical *adj* asimétrico; ~ **digital**
subscriber line *n* línea digital asimétrica
de abonado *f*

asymmetry *n* asimetría *f*

asynchronous *adj* asincrónico

at *prep* (rate, price) a; **as ~ a** fecha; ~ **sign** *n*
arroba *f*

ATC *abbr* (▸**air-traffic control**) control de
tráfico aéreo *m*

ATM *abbr* (▸**at-the-money**) al precio (de
contado); (▸**automated** *o* **automatic teller**
machine) AmE cajero *m* bancario *or*
automático; ~ **card** *n* tarjeta *f* del cajero
bancario *or* del cajero automático

atmosphere *n* (of planet) atmósfera *f*;
(feeling, mood) ambiente *m*

atomic *adj* atómico; ~ **energy** *n* energía
atómica *f*

atomistic competition *n* competencia
atomizada *f*

at-risk: ~ **amount** *n* volumen del riesgo
m; ~ **rule** *n* norma de riesgo *f*

ATS *abbr* (▸**automatic transfer service**)
servicio automático de transferencia *m*

attach *vt* (document, copy) adjuntar

attached *adj* adjunto; ~ **account** *n*
cuenta adjunta *f*; ~ **copy of letter** *n* copia
de la carta adjunta *f*

attachment *n* (to e-mail) adjunto *m*, anexo
m; (Ins) anexo *m*; ~ **bond** *n* fianza de
embargo *f*

attack[1] *n* ataque *m*

attack[2] *vt* (problem) acometer

attained age *n* edad cumplida *f*

attempt[1] *n* intento *m*

attempt[2] *vt* intentar; ~ **to do sth** tratar
de *or* intentar hacer algo

attend *vt* (meeting) asistir a; **attend to** *vt*
cumplir; ~ **to a customer** atender a un
cliente

attendance *n* asistencia *f*; ~ **bonus** *n*
prima por asistencia *f*; ~ **fees** *n pl* cuotas
de asistencia *f pl*; ~ **money** *n* cuotas de
asistencia *f pl*, dietas por asistencia *f pl*

attention *n* atención *f*; **attract/hold sb's**
~ atraer/mantener la atención de alguien;
for the ~ of (in fax) a la atención de; **pay ~**
to sth/sb prestarle atención a algo/alguien;
~ **factor** *n* (in advertising) factor de atención
m; ~**, interest, desire, action** *n* atención
f, interés *m*, deseo *m*, acción *f*; ~ **value** *n* (in
advertising) valor de atención *m*

attest *vt* (fact) atestiguar, dar fe de;
(signature) autenticar, autorizar; (prove)
atestiguar, avalar; **attest to** *vt* dar fe de,
atestiguar

attestation *n* (of fact) testimonio *m*; (of
signature) autenticación *f*, autorización *f*;
(proof) testimonio *m*, prueba *f*

at-the-money *adj* al precio (de contado);
~ **call** *n* compra a precio corriente *f*; ~
call option *n* opción de compra a precio
corriente *f*; ~ **option** *n* opción indiferente *f*;
~ **put** *n* venta al precio de mercado *f*; ~
put option *n* opción de venta a precio de
mercado *f*

attitude *n* actitud *f*; ~ **survey** *n* estudio
de actitudes *m*

attorney *n* AmE abogado(-a) *m,f*; ~**-at-law**
n AmE abogado(-a) *m,f*; ~**-in-fact** *n* AmE
apoderado(-a) *m,f*

attract *vt* (interest) suscitar; ~ **customers** *o*
business atraer clientes; ~ **sb's attention**
llamar *or* atraer la atención de alguien; **it** ⸱⸱⸱

~s a higher rate of interest devenga un interés más alto

attractive *adj* (for investors) atractivo; (in vogue) de moda; **~ offer** *n* oferta atractiva *f*; **~ terms** *n pl* condiciones atractivas *f pl*

attributable *adj* atribuible; **~ to sth/sb** atribuible a algo/alguien

attribute¹ *n* atributo *m*

attribute² *vt*: **~ sth to sth/sb** atribuir algo a algo/alguien

attribution *adj* atribución *f*

attrition *n* desgaste *m*; (HRM) bajas vegetativas *f pl*; **~ rate** *n* tasa de desgaste *f*

atypical *adj* (worker) atípico

auction¹ *n* subasta *f*, remate *m* AmL; **sell sth at** *o* **put sth up for ~** subastar algo, rematar algo AmL; **~ market** *n* mercado *m* de subasta *or* de remate AmL; **~ room** *n* sala *f* de subastas *or* de remate AmL

auction² *vt* subastar, rematar AmL; **auction off** *vt* subastar, rematar AmL

audience *n* audiencia *f*

audio *adj* (equipment, system) de sonido, de audio; **~ conference** *n*, **~ conferencing** *n* audioconferencia *f*

audiotyping *n* audiomecanografía *f*

audiovisual *adj* (equipment, display) audiovisual; **~ aids** *n pl* ayudas *f pl or* medios *m pl* audiovisuales

audit¹ *n* auditoría *f*; **~ activity** *n* BrE actividad de auditoría *f*; **~ certificate** *n* certificado de auditoría *m*; **~ file** *n* archivo de auditoría *m*; **~ group** *n* grupo de auditoría *m*; **A~ Office** *n* BrE ≈ Tribunal de Cuentas *m* Esp; **~ officer** *n* funcionario(-a) auditor(a) *m,f*; **~ report** *n* informe de auditoría *m*; **~ software** *n* aplicación informática para auditoría *f*, software de auditoría *m*; **~ standard** *n* norma de auditoría *f*; **~ team** *n* equipo de auditores *m*; **~ trail** *n* (Acc) rastreo de auditoría *m*; (Comp) verificación retrospectiva *f*; **~ window** *n* (Comp) ventana de intervención *f*

audit² *vt* (Acc) auditar; (Comp) verificar

auditability *n* auditabilidad *f*

auditable *adj* auditable

audited *adj* (statement, circulation) auditado

auditee *n* auditado(-a) *m,f*

auditing *n* auditoría *f*; **~ department** *n* departamento de auditoría *m*; **~ principle** *n* principio de auditoría *m*; **~ procedure** *n* procedimiento de auditoría *m*; **~ standard** *n* norma de auditoría *f*

auditor *n* auditor(a) *m,f*; **~'s certificate** *n* dictamen *m or* informe *m* de auditoría; **A~'s Operational Standard** *n* norma de operación del auditor *f*; **~'s opinion** *n*

opinión del auditor *f*; **~'s report** *n* informe del auditor *m*

au fait *adj* al tanto

AUP *abbr* (▸acceptable use policy) política de uso aceptable *f*

autarchy *n* autarquía *f*

autex system *n* sistema autex *m*

authenticate *vt* autenticar, autentificar

authenticated signature *n* firma *f* autentificada *or* certificada

authentification *n* autenticación *f*, autentificación *f*

author *n* autor(a) *m,f*; **~'s note** *n* nota del autor *f*; **~ royalties** *n* derechos de autor *m pl*

authoring *n* autoría *f*; **~ language** *n* lenguaje autor *m*; **~ system** *n* sistema autor *m*; **~ tool** *n* herramienta de autoría *f*

authoritarian *adj* (management) autoritario

authoritative *adj* (version) autoritativo

authorities *n pl* autoridades *f pl*

authority *n* autoridad *f*, competencia *f*; **give sb (the) ~ to do sth** autorizar a alguien para que haga algo; **have the ~ to do sth** estado autorizado para hacer algo; **have signing ~** tener autoridad para firmar; **have it on good ~ that ...** saber de buena fuente que ...; **he is an ~ on the subject** es una autoridad en la materia; **~ bond** *n* AmE obligación de organismo público *f*

authorization *n* autorización *f*; **~ center** AmE, **~ centre** BrE *n* (Bank) centro de autorización *m*; **~ code** *n* (Bank) código de autorización *m*; **~ number** *n* (Bank) número de autorización *m*

authorize *vt* (transaction, cheque) autorizar; (funds, budget) aprobar; **~ sb to do sth** autorizar a alguien para hacer algo

authorized *adj* (person, bank, bond, share, capital, credit, signature) autorizado; **be ~ to sign** tener firma autorizada; **~ agent** *n* agente autorizado(-a) *m,f*; (Law) agente oficial *mf*; **~ clerk** *n* (Stock) empleado(-a) de bolsa *m,f*; **~ dealer** *n* (Bank) agente autorizado(-a) *m,f*; (Stock) intermediario(-a) autorizado(-a) *m,f*

auto *n* AmE (*cf* ▸car BrE) coche *m*, automóvil *m*; **~ rental** *n* AmE (*cf* ▸car hire BrE) alquiler de coches *m*

autobank card *n* tarjeta de banco automático *f*

autoboot *n* (Comp) autoarranque *m*

autofeeder *n* (Comp) alimentador automático *m*

autofinancing *n* autofinanciación *f*

autoloader *n* (Comp) autocargador *m*

autologin *n* (Comp) carga automática *f*

autologon n (Comp) entrada automática al sistema f

automate vt automatizar

automated adj automatizado; ~ **cash dispenser** n BrE (cf ►**automated teller machine** AmE) cajero automático m; **A~ Clearing House** n Cámara de Compensación Automatizada f; **A~ Clearing Settlement System** n Sistema de Liquidación de Compensación Automatizado m; **A~ Real-Time Investments Exchange** n Bolsa de Valores Automatizada a Tiempo Real f; ~ **teller machine** n AmE (cf ►**automated cash dispenser** BrE) cajero automático m

automatic adj (check, control, reset) automático; ~ **adjustment point** n (for salaries) punto de ajuste automático m; ~ **call forwarding** reenvío automático m; ~ **cash dispenser** n BrE (cf ►**automatic teller machine** AmE) cajero automático m; ~ **data processing** n proceso automático de datos m; ~ **feeder** n (in office equipment) alimentador automático m; ~ **funds transfer** n transferencia de fondos automática f; ~ **reinvestment** n reinversión automática f; ~ **teller machine** n AmE (cf ►**automatic cash dispenser** BrE) cajero automático m; ~ **transfer** n transferencia automática f; ~ **transfer service** n BrE servicio automático de transferencia m; ~ **updating** n (of data) actualización automática f; ~ **withdrawal** n reembolso automático m

automation n automatización f

automobile n AmE automóvil m, coche; ~ **benefit** n AmE beneficio por automóvil m; ~ **insurance** n AmE (cf ►**car insurance** BrE) seguro de automóviles m; ~ **liability insurance** n AmE (cf ►**car liability insurance** BrE) seguro de responsabilidad civil de automóviles m

automotive industry n AmE (cf ►**car industry** BrE) industria automotriz f

autonomous adj (investment, consumption, expenditure) autónomo; ~ **work group** n grupo autónomo de trabajo m

autonomy n autonomía f

autopark n (Comp) estacionamiento automático m

autoresponder n (Comp) respondedor m or contestador m automático, autocontestador m

autorestart n (Comp) autoarranque m

autosave n (Comp) autoalmacenamiento m

autostart n (Comp) autoarranque m

auxiliary adj (equipment, memory, storage) auxiliar

av abbr (►**audiovisual**) audiovisual; ~**-commercial** n anuncio audiovisual m

av. abbr (►**average**) media f, promedio m

availability n disponibilidad f

available adj (balance, funds, time, asset) disponible; (cash) disponible, en caja; **not ~** no disponible; ~ **at short notice** disponible a corto plazo; ~ **on a current basis** disponible actualmente; **make ~** (money) poner a disposición; ~ **space** n (on hard disk) espacio aprovechable m

aval n endoso especial de garantía m

avatar n (Comp) avatar m

AVCs n pl BrE (►**additional voluntary contributions**) cuotas voluntarias adicionales f pl

average[1] adj (price, cost, wage, yield) medio, promedio; (amount, earnings, income, revenue, rate, premium) medio; (interest rate, balance) promedio; ~ **access time** n (Comp) tiempo medio de acceso m; ~ **collection period** n periodo medio de cobro m; ~ **daily balance** n saldo medio diario m; ~ **maturity** n (of a security) vencimiento medio m; ~ **propensity to consume** n propensión media al consumo f; ~ **propensity to save** n propensión media al ahorro f; ~ **tax rate** n tipo impositivo medio m; ~ **unit cost** n coste m Esp or costo m AmL unitario medio; ~ **working week** BrE, ~ **workweek** AmE n semana laborable media f

average[2] n media f, promedio m; (Acc) avería f; **above/below ~** por encima/por debajo de la media; **on ~** como promedio; **take an ~** hacer un promedio; ~ **adjuster** n ajustador(a) de averías m,f

average[3] vt (earn on average) ganar un promedio or una media de; **average down** vt promediar a la baja; **average out** vt (cost, profit) promediar; **average up** vt promediar al alza

averager n (Stock) promediador(a) m,f

averaging n promedio m; ~ **amount** n cantidad promediada f; ~ **formula** n fórmula f del promedio or del término medio

averaging-down n compra de títulos a bajo precio f

aviation n aviación f; ~ **insurance** n seguro de aviación m; ~ **risk** n riesgo de aviación m

avoid vt evitar; (Tax) eludir, evadir

avoidable adj (costs) evitable

avoidance n (of accidents) prevención f; ~ **of tax** n evasión fiscal f

award[1] vt (contract) adjudicar; (prize, grant, salary increase) conceder

award[2] n (of contract) adjudicación f; (of prize, grant, salary increase) concesión f; (prize) galardón m, premio m; (sum of money) ⋯⟶

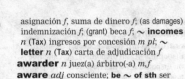

asignación *f*; suma de dinero *f*; (as damages) indemnización *f*; (grant) beca *f*; ~ **incomes** *n* (Tax) ingresos por concesión *m pl*; ~ **letter** *n* (Tax) carta de adjudicación *f*
awarder *n* juez(a) árbitro(-a) *m,f*
aware *adj* consciente; **be** ~ **of sth** ser

consciente de algo, darse cuenta de algo

away-from-home expenses *n pl* gastos por residir fuera del domicilio familiar *m pl*

AWY *abbr* (▸**airway**) vía aérea *f*

Bb

B2A *abbr* (▸**business-to-administration**) entre empresa y administración

B2B *abbr* (▸**business-to-business**) empresa a empresa, interempresas

B2B2C *abbr* (▸**business-to-business-to-consumer**) empresa a empresa a consumidor

B2C *abbr* (▸**business-to-consumer**) empresa a consumidor

B2G *abbr* (▸**business-to-government**) empresa a gobierno *or* a administración

BA *abbr* (▸**Bachelor of Arts**) ≈ licenciado(-a) en Humanidades *m,f*

Bachelor: ∼ **of Arts** *n* ≈ licenciado(-a) en Humanidades *m,f*; ∼ **of Business Administration** *n* licenciado(-a) en Administración de Empresas *m,f*; ∼ **of Commerce** *n* licenciado(-a) en Comercio *m,f*; ∼ **of Economics** *n* licenciado(-a) en Economía *m,f*; ∼ **of Laws** *n* ≈ licenciado(-a) en Derecho *m,f*; ∼ **of Science** *n* ≈ licenciado(-a) en Ciencias *m,f*; ∼ **of Science in Business Administration** *n* licenciado(-a) *m,f* en Administración de Empresas *or* en Ciencias Empresariales *m,f*; ∼ **of Science in Industrial Relations** *n* licenciado(-a) en Relaciones Laborales *m,f*

back[1] *adj* (rent, tax, interest) atrasado; ∼ **arrow** *n* (Comp) flecha de retroceso *f*; ∼ **cover** *n* contracubierta *f*; ∼ **issue** *n* (of newspaper, magazine) edición atrasada *f*, número atrasado *m*; ∼ **number** *n* (of newspaper, magazine) número atrasado *m*; ∼ **office** *n* (Admin) oficina de apoyo *f*, trastienda *f*; ∼ **order** *n* pedido *m* retrasado *or* en espera; ∼ **pay** *n* atrasos *m pl*; ∼ **payment** *n* atrasos *m pl*; (HRM, S&M) devolución *f*

back[2] *vt* (project) respaldar; **back down** *vi* (in argument) volverse atrás; **back off** *vi* retirarse; **back out** *vi* retirarse; **back out of** *vt* (contract, deal) retirarse de; **back up** *vt* (file, data) hacer una copia de seguridad de; (person, efforts) apoyar, respaldar

backbencher *n* BrE diputado(-a) de fila *m,f*

backbenches *n pl* BrE *escaños de los diputados que no son ministros*

backbench MP *n* BrE diputado(-a) de fila *m,f*

backbiting *n* maledicencia *f*

backbone *n* (Comp) eje central *m*; (of network) espina dorsal *f*, segmento principal *m*; (in broadband) cable principal *m*

back burner *n*: **put sth on the** ∼ dejar algo en suspenso por el momento

backdate *vt* (wage increase) pagar con efecto retroactivo; (cheque, contract) antedatar

backdated *adj* (wage increase) (con efecto) retroactivo; (cheque, contract) antedatado; **an increase** ∼ **to April** un aumento con retroactividad desde abril

backdating *n* entrada en vigor con efecto retroactivo *f*

backdoor *adj* (tax) encubierto, disfrazado; (financing) clandestino, secreto; (lending) indirecto; (operation) furtivo, bajo cuerda; (selling) secreto

backdrop *n* (to situation) telón de fondo *m*

backed *adj* respaldado; ∼ **bill of exchange** *n* letra de cambio avalada *f*

backend *adj* (system) en segundo plano

backer *n* promotor(a) comercial *m,f*

background *n* (of person, situation) antecedentes *m pl*; ∼ **color** AmE, ∼ **colour** BrE *n* color de fondo *m*; ∼ **information** *n* información básica *f*; ∼ **investigation** *n* (of applicant) investigación de antecedentes *f*; ∼ **paper** *n* documento de antecedentes *m*; ∼ **printing** *n* impresión sin prioridad *f*; ∼ **processing** *n* (Comp) proceso no prioritario *m*; (HRM) procesamiento de antecedentes *m*; ∼ **task** *n* (Comp) tarea secundaria *f*

backhander *n* (infrml) astilla *f* (infrml)

backing *n* respaldo *m*, apoyo *m*; (of bank-note issue) garantía *f*; ∼ **storage** *n* (Comp) almacenamiento de archivos *m*

backlog *n* (of work) acumulación *f*; ∼ **demand** *n* demanda acumulada *f*; ∼ **of orders** *n* acumulación de pedidos *f*; (Fin) cartera de pedidos atrasados *f*; ∼ **of payments** *n* cartera de pagos *f*

backlogged order *n* pedido acumulado *m*

back-pedal *vi* volverse atrás

backselling *n* retroventa *f*

backslash *n* barra inversa *f*; ∼ **key** *n* tecla de barra inversa *f*

backspace[1] *n* retroceso *m*; ∼ **key** *n* tecla de retroceso *f*

backspace[2] *vi* retroceder

backspread n (Stock) liquidación de un arbitraje f

backstop n respaldo m; ∼ **loan facility** n servicio de préstamo respaldado m

back-to-back adj (credit) subsidiario; ∼ **loan** n préstamo de contrapartida m; ∼ **placement** n colocación directa f; ∼ **transaction** n transacción de respaldo mutuo f; ∼ **transfer** n transferencia de respaldo mutuo f

backtrack vi (from plan, promise) echarse atrás

backup¹ adj (Comp) (file, copy, battery) de seguridad; (memory, facility) de apoyo; ∼ **credit line** n línea de crédito de respaldo f; ∼ **line** n (Fin) línea f de respaldo or de apoyo; ∼ **material** n material de apoyo m; ∼ **service** n (S&M) servicio de posventa m; ∼ **support** n (Stock) apoyo de reserva m; ∼ **system** n (for stock options) sistema de respaldo m; ∼ **withholding** n (Tax) retención retroactiva f

backup² n (support) respaldo m; (Comp) copia de reserva f

backward: ∼ **averaging** n promediado hacia atrás m, promedio con efecto retroactivo m; ∼ **integration** n integración regresiva f; ∼ **linkage** n vinculación hacia atrás f; ∼ **scheduling** n horario regresivo m; ∼ **vertical integration** n integración vertical decreciente f

backwardation n margen de cobertura m, prima por retraso f; ∼ **rate** n tasa de interés de la bonificación f

backwash effect n efecto backwash m

backyard n: **not in my** ∼ (jarg) en mi patio no

BACS abbr (▸**Banks Automated Clearing System**) Sistema Bancario de Compensación Automática m

bad adj (bargain, management, news, reputation) malo; (cheque) incobrable, sin fondos; (investment) malogrado; (loan) incobrable, dudoso; ∼ **buy** n mala compra f; ∼ **debt** n deuda incobrable f; ∼**-debt provision** n provisión para incobrables f; ∼**-debt recovery** n recuperación de deudas incobrables f; ∼ **debtor** n deudor moroso m; ∼ **and doubtful debt** n deuda mala y dudosa f; ∼ **paper** n (infrml) (Bank) documento incobrable m; ∼ **sector** n (Comp) sector deteriorado m; ∼ **title** n (Prop) título imperfecto m; ∼ **will** n mala voluntad f; (Acc) fondo de comercio negativo m

baggage n equipaje m; ∼ **allowance** n equipaje permitido m; ∼ **cart** n AmE (cf ▸**luggage trolley** BrE) carro de equipajes m; ∼ **handling** n carga y descarga del equipaje f; ∼ **locker** n AmE (cf ▸**left-luggage locker** BrE) taquilla para equipajes en

consigna f; ∼ **reclaim area** n zona de recogida de equipaje f

bail¹ n fianza f; **grant/refuse** ∼ **to sb** concederle/denegarle la libertad bajo fianza a alguien; **be released on** ∼ ser puesto en libertad bajo fianza; ∼ **bond** n compromiso de fianza m; (Fin, Stock) bono depositario m

bail² vt poner en libertad bajo fianza; **bail out** vt (Fin) avalar, salir fiador de; (Law) pagar una fianza a

bailee n depositario(-a) m,f

bailer n depositante mf

bailiff n (Law) agente judicial mf; (on estate) administrador(a) m,f

bailment n caución f; (Law) depósito m

bailor n fiador(a) m,f

bailout n operación de rescate f

bal. abbr (▸**balance**) balance m

balance¹ n (in accounting) balance m; (bank balance, rest of sum of money) saldo m; (difference, remainder) resto m; ∼ **in your favor** AmE o **favour** BrE saldo a su favor; ∼ **abroad** n saldo en el extranjero m; ∼ **of account** n saldo m or estado m de cuenta; ∼ **book** n libro de balances m; ∼ **brought down** n balance a cuenta nueva m; ∼ **brought forward** n balance llevado a cuenta nueva m; ∼ **carried forward** n balance a cuenta nueva m; ∼ **due** n saldo deudor m; ∼ **due to creditor** n saldo favorable al acreedor m; ∼ **due to debitor** n saldo favorable al deudor m; ∼ **of invoice** n balanza de facturación f; ∼ **item** n detalle del balance m; ∼ **on current account** n balance de una cuenta corriente m; ∼ **of payments** n balanza de pagos f; ∼ **of payments deficit** n déficit de la balanza de pagos m; ∼ **of payments surplus** n superávit de la balanza de pagos m; ∼ **of power** n proporción de fuerzas f; ∼ **sheet** n balance m; **off the** ∼ **sheet** fuera del balance general; ∼ **of trade** n balanza comercial f

balance² ⟦1⟧ vt (account) saldar; (weigh up) sopesar; ∼ **the books** (infrml) saldar las cuentas; ∼ **sth against sth** sopesar algo con algo; ∼ **sth with sth** equilibrar algo con algo
⟦2⟧ vi (accounts) cuadrar; **balance out** vt compensar

balanced adj (budget, growth, portfolio) equilibrado

balancing item n contrapartida f

bale¹ n bala f

bale² vt embalar

baling n embalaje m

ballast n lastre m

balloon n globo m; ∼ **advertising** n publicidad con globos f; ∼ **interest** n interés creciente *m*; ∼ **loan** *n* préstamo de pago total al vencimiento *m*; ∼ **note** *n* pagaré especial *m*; ∼ **payment** *n* (Bank) pago *m* especial *or* extraordinario; (Stock) pago final superior al promedio *m*; ∼ **repayment** *n* devolución en un solo pago *f*

ballot¹ *n* votación *f*; **take a ∼ on sth** someter algo a votación; ∼ **box** *n* urna electoral *f*; ∼ **paper** *n* papeleta *f*

ballot² **1** *vt* (members) invitar a votar **2** *vi* votar, acudir a las urnas

ballpark figure *n* cifra aproximada *f*

ban¹ *n* prohibición *f*; ∼ **on sth** prohibición de algo

ban² *vt* (activity) prohibir; (organization) proscribir; **the staff are ∼ned from joining a trade union** el personal tiene prohibido afiliarse a un sindicato

BAN *abbr* (▸**bond anticipation note**) vale por pronto pago de bono *m*

band *n* (range, category) banda *f*; ∼ **of fluctuation** *n* (of currency rate) banda de fluctuación *f*

B&D *abbr* (▸**bad and doubtful debt**) deuda mala y dudosa *f*

banded: ∼ **offer** *n* oferta asociada *f*; ∼ **pack** *n* (S&M) envase conjunto *m*; (of notes) fajo de billetes *m*

banding *n* (HRM) calificación *f*

bandwidth *n* amplitud de banda *f*

bank¹ *n* banco *m*; ∼ **acceptance** *n* aceptación bancaria *f*; ∼ **account** *n* cuenta bancaria *f*; ∼ **advance** *n* anticipo bancario *m*; ∼ **annuities** *n pl* anualidades bancarias *f pl*; ∼ **assets** *n* activos bancarios *m pl*; **B∼s Automated Clearing System** *n* Sistema Bancario de Compensación Automática *m*; ∼ **balance** *n* estado de cuentas *m*; ∼ **base rate** *n* tasa base bancaria *f*; ∼ **bill** *n* AmE (*cf* ▸**banknote** BrE) billete de banco *m*; (bill of exchange) pagaré bancario *m*; ∼ **bond** *n* bono bancario *m*; ∼ **branch** *n* sucursal de banco *f*; ∼ **card** *n* tarjeta bancaria *f*; ∼ **certificate** *n* certificado bancario *m*; ∼ **charges** *n pl* cargos bancarios *m pl*; ∼ **check** AmE, ∼ **cheque** BrE *n* cheque bancario *m*; ∼ **clearing** *n* compensación bancaria *f*; ∼ **clerk** *n* empleado(-a) bancario(-a) *m,f*; ∼ **code** *n* código bancario *m*; ∼ **commission** *n* comisión bancaria *f*; ∼ **credit** *n* crédito bancario *m*; ∼ **credit transfer** *n* transferencia de un crédito bancario *f*; ∼ **deposit** *n* depósito bancario *m*; ∼ **draft** *n* giro bancario *m*; ∼**-endorsed** *adj* endosado por un banco; ∼ **endorsement** *n* endoso bancario *m*; **B∼ of England** *n* banco central del Reino Unido, ≈ Banco de España *m* Esp; ∼ **examiner** *n* BrE (*cf* ▸**commissioner of banking** AmE)

inspector(a) oficial de bancos *m,f*; ∼ **facility** *n* servicio bancario *m*; ∼ **giro** *n* BrE giro bancario *m*; ∼ **group** *n* AmE (*cf* ▸**banking group** BrE) grupo bancario *m*; ∼ **guarantee** *n* garantía bancaria *f*; ∼ **holding company** *n* sociedad de control del banco *f*; ∼ **holiday** *n* BrE (*cf* ▸**legal holiday** AmE) fiesta nacional *f*; ∼ **interest** *n* interés bancario *m*; ∼ **for International Settlements** *n* Banco de Pagos Internacionales *m*; ∼ **of issue** *n* banco de emisión *m*; ∼ **lending** *n* préstamos bancarios *m pl*; ∼ **loan** *n* préstamo bancario *m*; ∼ **loan rate** *n* interés sobre préstamos de un banco *m*; ∼ **manager** *n* director(a) de banco *m,f*; ∼ **officer** *n* empleado(-a) bancario(-a) *m,f*; ∼ **overdraft** *n* descubierto *m or* sobregiro *m* bancario; ∼ **paper** *n* valores bancarios *m pl*; ∼ **rate** *n* tasa bancaria *f*; ∼ **reconciliation** *n* (re)conciliación bancaria *f*; ∼ **reserve** *n* fondo de reserva *m*; ∼ **run** *n* corrida sobre un banco *f*; ∼ **runner** *n* retirada de fondos por pánico *f*; ∼ **security** *n* garantía bancaria *f*; ∼ **service charge** *n* cargo *m or* comisión *f* por servicio bancario; ∼ **statement** *n* estado de cuenta *m*; ∼ **subsidiary** *n* subsidiaria bancaria *f*; ∼ **switching** *n* (Comp) conmutación de bancos *f*; ∼ **teller** *n* (person) cajero(-a) bancario(-a) *m*; (machine) cajero automático *m*; ∼**-to-bank lending** *n* préstamo interbancario *m*; ∼ **transaction** *n* transacción bancaria *f*; ∼ **transfer** *n* transferencia bancaria *f*; ∼ **vault** *n* cámara acorazada *f*

bank² *vt* (money) depositar, ingresar Esp; **bank on** *vt* (rely on) contar con; **bank with** *vt* tener una cuenta en

bankable *adj* (assets) descontable; ∼ **bill** *n* letra descontable *f*; ∼ **paper** *n* valores bancarios *m pl*

bankbook *n* libreta de banco *f*

banker *n* banquero(-a) *m,f*; ∼**'s acceptance** *n* aceptación bancaria *f*; ∼**'s bill** *n* letra bancaria *f*; ∼**'s check** AmE, ∼**'s cheque** BrE *n* cheque bancario *m*; ∼**'s discount** *n* descuento bancario *m*; ∼**'s draft** *n* cheque de banco *m*; ∼**'s order** *n* domiciliación bancaria de pagos *f*; ∼**'s reference** *n* referencia del banco *f*

banking *n* banca *f*; ∼ **account** *n* cuenta bancaria *f*; ∼ **activity** *n* actividad bancaria *f*; ∼ **center** AmE, ∼ **centre** BrE *n* centro bancario *m*; ∼ **charges** *n pl* cargos bancarios *m pl*; ∼ **community** *n* comunidad bancaria *f*; ∼ **group** *n* BrE (*cf* ▸**bank group** AmE) grupo bancario *m*; ∼ **hours** *n pl* horario bancario *m*; ∼ **house** *n* casa de banca *f*; ∼ **industry** *n* industria bancaria *f*; ∼ **institution** *n* institución bancaria *f*; ∼ **law** *n* ley bancaria *f*; ∼ ⋯⊳

operation n operación bancaria f; ~ **rate** n tipo de redescuento m; ~ **sector** n sector bancario m; ~ **service** n servicio bancario m

banknote n BrE (cf ▸**bank bill** AmE) billete de banco m; ~ **trading** n compraventa de billetes bancarios f

bankroll¹ n AmE (financial resources) fortuna f

bankroll² vt (infrml) financiar

bankrupt¹ adj (company, person) en bancarrota, en quiebra; **go** ~ ir a la bancarrota

bankrupt² vt hacer quebrar, llevar a la quiebra or a la bancarrota

bankrupt³ n fallido(-a) m,f

bankruptcy n bancarrota f, quiebra f; **file for** ~ presentar una solicitud de declaración de quiebra; **go into** ~ quebrar; **B~ Act** n Ley de Quiebras f; ~ **court** n tribunal de quiebras m; ~ **estate** n conjunto de bienes de una quiebra m; ~ **Law** n Ley de Quiebras f; ~ **notice** n aviso m or notificación f de quiebra; ~ **proceedings** n pl procedimiento de quiebra m

banner n (Comp) banner (publicitario) m; ~ **campaign** n campaña publicitaria en el Internet mediante banners; ~ **headline** n titular a toda página m; ~ **year** n año insignia m

bar¹ n (Comp, Media) barra f; (Law) jurado m, tribunal m; **a** ~ **to sth** un obstáculo or un impedimento para algo; **B~ Association** n AmE (cf ▸**Law Society** BrE) ≈ Colegio de Abogados m; ~ **chart** n gráfico de barras m; ~ **code** BrE (cf ▸**bar graphics** AmE) código de barras m; ~ **code scanner** n lector de código de barras m; ~ **graph** n gráfico de barras m; ~ **graphics** n pl AmE (cf ▸**bar code** BrE) código de barras m

bar² vt excluir, prohibir; ~ **sb from a place** excluir a alguien de un lugar

bare adj desnudo; ~ **contract** n contrato sin causa m; ~ **ownership** n propiedad desnuda f

bargain¹ n (agreement) convenio m; (cheap purchase) ganga f; (Stock) (deal) transacción f; **he drives a hard** ~ sabe cómo conseguir lo que quiere, es buen negociador; **into the** ~ por encima, por si fuera poco; **make a** ~ **with sb** hacer un trato or un pacto con alguien; **strike a** ~ llegar a un acuerdo; ~ **basement** n (in shop) sección de rebajas f; ~ **hunter** n cazador(a) de gangas m,f; ~ **price** n precio de oportunidad m; ~ **rate** n tarifa especial f

bargain² vi (haggle) regatear; (negotiate) negociar; ~ **with sb over sth** (over price, item) regatear con alguien por algo; **bargain down** vt (seller) negociar a la baja; **bargain for** vt (anticipate) esperar, contar con;

(negotiate) negociar; **bargain on** vt esperar, contar con

bargainer n negociador(a) m,f

bargaining n negociación f; ~ **agent** n (for union) agente negociador(a) m,f; ~ **chip** n (infrml) concesión o compromiso que se puede ofrecer en una negociación; ~ **position** n posición negociadora f; ~ **power** n poder negociador m; ~ **table** n mesa de negociaciones f; ~ **unit** n unidad de negociación f

barge n barcaza f, gabarra f

barometer n (for measuring trends) barómetro m

barratry n (fraud) baratería f

barrel n barril m; ~**s per day** n pl barriles por día m pl

barren money n deuda sin interés f

barrier n barrera f; **a** ~ **to entry/exit/trade** una barrera de entrada/de salida/al comercio

barrister n ≈ abogado(-a) m,f; ~**s' chambers** n BrE cámara f or despacho m de abogados

barter¹ **1** vt permutar, trocar **2** vi hacer trueques

barter² n trueque m, permuta f; ~ **agreement** n acuerdo m or tratado m de trueque; ~ **economy** n economía de permuta f; ~ **trade** n comercio de trueque m; ~ **transaction** n operación de trueque f

base¹ n base f; ~ **address** n (Comp) dirección de base f; ~ **amount** n (Tax) cantidad base f; ~ **capital** n capital base m; ~ **configuration** n (Comp) configuración básica f; ~ **date** n fecha base f; ~ **lending rate** n interés básico sobre préstamos m; ~ **pay** n AmE (cf ▸**basic pay** BrE) salario m or sueldo m base; ~ **pay rate** n AmE (cf ▸**basic pay rate** BrE) tipo de sueldo por hora m; ~ **period** n periodo base m; ~ **price** n precio base m; ~ **rate** n tasa base f; ~ **stock** n acciones de base f pl; ~ **wage** n AmE (cf ▸**basic wage** BrE) sueldo base m; ~ **year** n año base m

base² vt basar; ~ **a decision on sth** basar una decisión en algo; **a Tokyo-~d company** una empresa establecida en Tokio

baseband n (Comp) banda de base f

baseline n (Comp) línea de referencia f

basic adj (price) básico, base; (amount, tax, income, trend) básico; (idea) básico, fundamental; (right) fundamental; ~ **agreement** n acuerdo marco m; ~ **books** n pl (Fin) libros básicos m pl; ~ **commodity** n bien de primera necesidad m; ~ **earnings per share** n pl ganancia básica por acción f; ~ **grade** n calidad normal f; ~ **pay** n BrE (cf ▸**base pay** AmE) salario *m or* sueldo *m* base; **∼ pay rate** *n* BrE (*cf* ▸**base pay rate** AmE) tipo de sueldo por hora *m*; **∼ premium** *n* (Ins) prima base *f*; **∼ rate** *n* interés base *m*; **∼-rate tax** *n* impuesto de tipo básico *m*; **∼ rating** *n* aplicación de tarifa básica *f*; **∼ relief** *n* (Tax) desgravación básica *f*; **∼ salary** *n* salario *m or* sueldo *m* base; **∼ unit** *n* unidad de base *f*; **∼ wage** *n* BrE (*cf* ▸**base wage** AmE) sueldo base *m*

BASIC *abbr* (▸**Beginner's All-Purpose Symbolic Instruction Code**) BASIC (código de instrucciones simbólicas de carácter general para principiantes)

basics *n pl* fundamentos *m pl*; **get down to ∼** ir a lo que importa

basis *n* base *f*; **on the ∼ of sth** a base de algo; **on the ∼ that...** partiendo de la base de que...; **on a daily ∼** a base diaria; **∼ of an agreement** *n* base de un acuerdo *f*; **∼ for discussion** *n* base para la discusión *f*; **∼ point** *n* punto básico *m*

basket *n* (of currencies, goods, products) cesta *f*; **∼ purchase** *n* compra global *f*; **∼ trading** *n* negociación sobre un conjunto de valores *f*

batch *n* lote *m*; **∼ computer** *n* ordenador *m* Esp *or* computadora *f* AmL por lotes; **∼ control** *n* control de lotes *m*; **∼ file** *n* fichero secuencial *m*; **∼ job** *n* tarea por lotes *f*; **∼ processing** *n* proceso por lotes *m*; **∼ production** *n* producción en lotes *f*; **∼ size** *n* tamaño de lote *m*

bath *n* (jarg) (Stock) batacazo *m* (jarg); **take a ∼** (jarg) sufrir un batacazo

battery *n* (for computer, car) batería *f*; (for radio) pila *f*

baud *n* baudio *m*; **∼ rate** *n* velocidad media de transferencia *f*

BB *abbr* (▸**bulletin board**) (Comp) tablón de anuncios (electrónico) *m*; (▸**Bureau of the Budget**) Oficina del Presupuesto *f*

BBS *abbr* (▸**bulletin board system**) (Comp) sistema de tablón de anuncios *m*

BC *abbr* (▸**budgetary control**) control presupuestario *m*

bcc *abbr* (▸**blind carbon copy** copia *f* ciega *or* oculta *or* invisible

BCom *abbr* (▸**Bachelor of Commerce**) licenciado(-a) en Comercio *m,f*

b/d *abbr* (▸**bring down**) llevar a cuenta nueva, reabrir

b/d. *abbr* (▸**balance brought down**) balance a cuenta nueva

B/D *abbr* (▸**bank draft**) giro bancario

BDR *abbr* (▸**bearer depository receipt**) RDP (recibo de depósito del portador)

B/E *abbr* (▸**bill of entry**) conocimiento de entrada *m*, declaración de aduana *f*; (▸**bill of exchange**) letra de cambio *f*

BEA *abbr* (▸**Bureau of Economic Analysis**) departamento de análisis económico *m*

beancounter *n* (infrml) cabeza contable *f*

bear[1] *n* (Fin) bajista *mf*; **sell a ∼** vender a plazo en firme; **∼ account** *n* cuenta de especulaciones a la baja *f*; **∼ call spread** *n* margen de compra a la baja *m*; **∼ campaign** *n* campaña bajista *f*; **∼ closing** *n* cierre a la baja *m*; **∼ covering** *n* compra para cubrir ventas al descubierto *f*; **∼ hug** *n* (jarg) (corporate takeover) *compra de una sociedad por otra más grande*; **∼ market** *n* mercado *m* bajista *or* con tendencia a la baja; **∼ operation** *n* operación a la baja *f*; **∼ position** *n* posición bajista *f*; **∼ put spread** *n* margen de venta a la baja *m*; **∼ raid** *n*, **∼ raiding** *n* manipulación a la baja *f*; **∼ sale** *n* venta al descubierto *f*; **∼ speculation** *n* especulación a la baja *f*; **∼ spread** *n* diferencia a la baja *f*; **∼ transaction** *n* operación a la baja *f*

bear[2] *vt* (interest) devengar, producir; (burden, responsibility) soportar; **∼ the cost of sth** correr con el coste Esp *or* costo AmL de algo; **∼ the costs** asumir los costes Esp *or* costos AmL; **∼ a date of** tener fecha de; **∼ sth in mind** tener presente algo, tener algo en cuenta

bearer *n* portador(a) *m,f*; **∼ bill** *n* efecto al portador *m*; **∼ bond** *n* bono al portador *m*; **∼ certificate** *n* certificado al portador *m*; **∼ check** AmE, **∼ cheque** BrE *n* cheque al portador *m*; **∼ instrument** *n* instrumento al portador *m*; **∼ proxy** *n* poder al portador *m*; **∼ security** *n* título al portador *m*; **∼ share** *n* acción al portador *f*; **∼ stock** *n* acciones al portador *f pl*; **∼ warrant** *n* opción de compra al portador *f*

bearish *adj* (market) bajista; (movement, spread) a la baja; **be ∼** estar a la baja

beat *vt* (opponent) ganarle a, derrotar, vencer; (inflation) abatir; (record) batir, superar; **beat down** *vt* (price) conseguir rebajar regateando; **I managed to beat him down** conseguí que me lo dejase más barato

BEcon *abbr* (▸**Bachelor of Economics**) licenciado(-a) en Economía *m,f*

bed and breakfast deal *n* (jarg) (Stock) *venta con recompra al día siguiente para evadir impuestos*

bedroom community *n* AmE (*cf* ▸**dormitory town** BrE) ciudad dormitoria *f*

beep[1] *n* señal sonora *f*

beep[2] *vi* emitir una señal sonora

before *prep* antes de; ~ **hours** antes de horas de oficina; ~ **maturity** antes del vencimiento

beforehand *adv* por anticipado

before-hours dealing *n* negociación previa a la apertura *f*

before-tax *adj* antes de impuestos

beggar-my-neighbor policy AmE, **beggar-my-neighbour policy** BrE *n* política económica para empobrecer al vecino

begin ① *vt* (meeting, campaign) empezar, comenzar, iniciar; ~ **doing** *o* **to do sth** empezar *or* comenzar a hacer algo; ~ **work on sth** empezar *or* comenzar a trabajar en algo

② *vi* (meeting, year) empezar, comenzar, iniciarse; **to** ~ **with** para empezar

Beginner's All-Purpose Symbolic Instruction Code *n* código de instrucciones simbólicas de carácter general para principiantes *m*

beginning *n* comienzo *m*; ~ **inventory** *n* inventario *m* inicial *or* de apertura *or* de entrada

behalf: on ~ **of** *prep* de parte de, en nombre de

behavior AmE ‣**behaviour** BrE

behavioral AmE ‣**behavioural** BrE

behaviour BrE, **behavior** AmE *n* comportamiento *m*; ~ **modification** *n* modificación de la conducta *f*

behavioural BrE, **behavioral** AmE *adj* de conducta, conductual; ~ **research** *n* investigación conductista *f*; ~ **science** *n* ciencia del comportamiento *f*

belated claim *n* daño diferido *m*

bell curve *n* curva campaniforme *f*

bellwether *n* indicador de tendencia *m*

below¹ *prep* debajo de; ~ **average** *adj* por debajo de la media; ~**-market-price** *adj* inferior al precio de mercado; ~ **par** *adj* bajo la par

below² *adv* (in letter, document) abajo

below-the-line: ~ **credit** *n* (jarg) financiación mediante préstamo *f*; ~ **item** *n* partida extraordinaria *f*; ~ **revenue** *n* ingresos bajo la línea *m pl*

Bench *n* Tribunal *m*

benchmark *n* punto de referencia *m*; (test of software) banco de pruebas *m*; ~ **method** *n* método *m* de comparación *or* de comprobación; ~ **price** *n* precio de referencia *m*; ~ **reserve** *n* AmE reserva referenciada *f*; ~ **test** *n* prueba de referencia *f*

beneficial *adj* provechoso; ~ **interest** *n* intereses patrimoniales *m pl*; ~ **owner** *n* propietario(-a) beneficiario(-a) *m,f*; ~ **ownership** *n* propiedad en usufructo *f*

beneficially interested *adj* con derecho a usufructo

beneficiary *n* beneficiario(-a) *m,f*; ~ **clause** *n* cláusula de beneficiario *f*; ~ **under a trust** *n* beneficiario(-a) bajo un fideicomiso *m,f*

benefit¹ *n* beneficio *m*; (welfare) prestación *m*, subsidio *m*; (from plan, employer) prestación *f*; **for the** ~ **of sb** por el bien de alguien; **be of** ~ **to sb** beneficiar a alguien; **be on** ~**s** BrE (*cf* ‣**be on welfare** AmE) vivir de subsidios sociales; **go on** ~**s** BrE (*cf* ‣**go on welfare** AmE) recibir prestaciones de la Seguridad Social; **reap the** ~**s of sth** recoger los beneficios de algo; ~**-cost analysis** *n* análisis de beneficios y costes Esp *or* costos AmL *m*; ~ **in kind** *n* prestación en especie *f*; ~ **society** *n* AmE (*cf* ‣**friendly society** BrE) mutualidad *f*, sociedad de beneficencia *f*

benefit² ① *vt* beneficiar

② *vi* beneficiarse; ~ **from sth** sacar provecho de algo

benevolent *adj* (HRM) benévolo; (Ind,Pol) benevolente; ~**-authoritative** *adj* benevolente-autoritario; ~ **capitalism** *n* capitalismo benevolente *m*

benign *adj* (conditions) propicio; (attitude) benévolo; (influence) benéfico; ~ **neglect** *n* desatención benévola *f*, descuido benévolo *m*

bequeath *vt* legar

bequest *n* legado *m*

best¹ *adj* mejor; ~ **alternative** *n* mejor alternativa *f*; ~ **bid** *n* mejor oferta *f*; ~ **bidder** *n* mejor postor(a) *m,f*; ~**-case scenario** *n* argumento de supuesto óptimo *m*, escenario para el mejor de los casos *m*; ~ **estimate** *n* estimación óptima *f*; ~ **positioned partner** *n* socio(-a) mejor posicionado(-a) *m,f*; ~ **practical means** *n pl* medios prácticos más adecuados *m pl*; ~ **practice** *n* práctica más recomendable *f*; ~ **price** *n* mejor precio *m*

best² *n* mejor *m*; **at** ~ (price, order) al mejor

bestseller *n* (book) bestseller *m*

bet¹ *n* apuesta *f*

bet² *vti* apostar

beta *n* beta *f*; ~ **coefficient** *n* coeficiente beta de regresión *m*; ~ **factor** *n* factor beta *m*; ~ **share** *n* acción beta *f*; ~ **stock** *n* acciones beta *f pl*; ~**-test** *n* prueba beta *f*; ~ **version** *n* versión beta *f*

better¹ *adj* mejor

better² *vt* (conditions) mejorar; (chances) aumentar

betterment *n* mejora *f*, plusvalía *f*; ~ **tax** *n* impuesto sobre la plusvalía *m*

better-off *adj* (financially) de mejor posición económica

betting *n* apuestas *f pl*

b/f *abbr* (▸**brought forward**) llevado a cuenta nueva, suma y sigue

b/g *abbr* (▸**bonded goods**) mercancías *f pl* en almacén de aduanas *or* en depósito

biannual *adj* semestral

bias *n* (prejudice) prejuicio *m*

biased *adj* parcial

bid¹ *n* (at auction) oferta *f*, puja *f*; (attempt) intento *m*, tentativa *f*; **buy on ~** (Stock) comprar a precio de oferta; **make a ~** hacer una oferta; **a ~ to do sth** un intento de hacer algo; **~ bond** *n* fianza *f* de licitación *or* de la oferta; **~ closing** *n* cierre de licitación *m*; **~ opening** *n* apertura de plicas *f*; **~ price** *n* precio comprador *m*

bid² [1] *vt* (offer) ofertar; (order) mandar, ordenar

[2] *vi* (at auction) pujar, licitar; (stock) hacer una oferta; **bid for** *vt* (at auction) pujar por; (projects, contracts) licitar; **bid on** *vi* AmE ofrecer más

bidder *n* (for tender, offer) postor *m*

bidding *n* licitación *f*; **~ requirement** *n* requisito para ofertar *m*; **~ technique** *n* técnica de licitación *f*

bidding-up *n* oferta al alza *f*

bidirectional *adj* bidireccional; **~ printer** *n* impresora bidireccional *f*

biennial *adj* bienal

big *adj* (investor) grande; (customer) importante; **earn ~ money** ganar mucho dinero; **make it ~** tener un gran éxito; **think ~** ser ambicioso, planear las cosas a lo grande; **B~ Bang** *n* BrE (Stock) Big Bang *m*; **~ banks** *n pl* bancos importantes *m pl*; **~ business** *n* empresas de gran magnitud *f pl*; **be ~ business** ser un gran negocio; **the B~ Four** *n* BrE *las cuatro mayores corporaciones bancarias del Reino Unido*; **~ name** *n* personaje *mf*; **the B~ Six** *n* BrE *las seis firmas de auditoría más importantes a nivel internacional*

bilateral *adj* (agreement, aid, loan, trade) bilateral; (contact) bilateral, sinalagmático

bilateralism *n* bilateralismo *m*

bill¹ *n* (invoice) factura *f*; (banknote) AmE (*cf* ▸**note** BrE) billete de banco *m*; (in restaurant) BrE (*cf* ▸**check** AmE) cuenta *f*; (promissory note) pagaré *m*; (payable, receivable) efecto *m*; (legislation) proyecto de ley *m*, ley *f*; (advertising) cartel publicitario *m*; **take a ~** (Fin) pagar una letra; **~ book** *n* libro *m* de facturas *or* de letras; **~ broker** *n* agente de letras *mf*; **~ of costs** *n* cuenta de gastos *f*; **~ diary** *n* registro de letras *m*; **~ of entry** *n* conocimiento de embarque *m*, declaración de aduana *f*; **~ of exchange** *n* letra de cambio *f*; **~ of lading** *n* conocimiento de embarque *m*; **~ market** *n* mercado de letras *m*; **~ of materials** *n* lista de materiales *f*; **~ merchant** *n* corredor(a) de cambios *m,f*; **~ payable** *n* efecto a pagar *m*; **~ receivable** *n* efecto a cobrar *m*; **~ of sale** *n* contrato *m or* escritura *f* de venta; **~ of sight** *n* declaración provisional *f*

bill² *vt* pasarle la cuenta *or* la factura a; **~ sb for sth** pasarle a alguien la cuenta *or* la factura por algo

billback *n* AmE aporte posterior de dinero *m*, efecto como aval *m*

billboard *n* AmE (*cf* ▸**hoarding** BrE) valla publicitaria *f*

biller *n* (machine) facturador *m*

billing *n* (invoicing) facturación *f*; (in advertising) importe total de negocios *m*; **~ cycle** *n* ciclo de facturación *m*; **~ date** *n* AmE (*cf* ▸**invoice date** BrE) fecha de facturación *f*; **~ day** *n* día de facturación *m*; **~ department** *n* AmE (*cf* ▸**invoicing department** BrE) departamento de facturación *m*

billion *n* (one thousand million) mil millones *m pl*; BrE (obs) (one million million) billón *m*

BIM *abbr* (▸**British Institute of Management**) *instituto británico de gestión empresarial*

bimetallic *adj* (standard) bimetálico

bimetallism *n* bimetalismo *m*

bimonthly *adj* (every two months) bimestral; (twice a month) bimensual

binary *adj* (code, digit, number, operator, search) binario; **~-to-decimal conversion** *n* conversión binario a decimal *f*

bind *vt* (commit) obligar; (book) encuadernar, empastar; **~ oneself to sth** (agree to) comprometerse a algo

binder *n* (file, folder) carpeta *f*; AmE (Ins) póliza de seguro provisional *f*; (Prop) sujeción *f*

binding *adj* (agreement, promise, offer) vinculante; **be ~ on sb** ser vinculante para alguien

biochip *n* chip biológico *m*

biocontrol *n* biocontrol *m*

biodegradability *n* biodegradabilidad *f*

bioeconomics *n* bioeconomía *f*

bioengineering *n* ingeniería biológica *f*

biographical *adj* biográfico; **~ data** *n* datos biográficos *m pl*

biometrics *n* biometría *f*

biotope *n* biotopo *m*

bipolar *adj* bipolar; **~ transistor** *n* transistor bipolar *m*

birth certificate *n* certificado *m or* partida *f* de nacimiento

BIS *abbr* (▸**Bank for International Settlements**) BPI (Banco de Pagos Internacionales)

bisque clause *n* cláusula de modificación parcial *f*

bit *n* (Comp) bit *m*, bitio *m*; ∼ **configuration** *n* configuración binaria *f*; ∼ **density** *n* densidad en dígitos binarios *f*; ∼**s per inch** *n pl* bitios por pulgada *m pl*; ∼**s per second** *n pl* bitios por segundo *m pl*; ∼ **rate** *n* velocidad de transferencia de bitios *f*; ∼ **string** *n* cadena de bitios *f*

biweekly *adj* bisemanal

bk *abbr* (▸**bank**) banco *m*

bkg *abbr* (▸**banking**) banca *f*

B/L *abbr* (▸**bill of lading**) conocimiento de embarque *m*

black¹ *adj* negro; ∼ **books** *n pl* registro de castigos *m*; ∼ **box** *n* caja negra *f*; ∼ **capitalism** *n* capitalismo *m* salvaje *or* tardío; ∼ **economy** *n* economía *f* sumergida Esp *or* paralela AmL; **B∼ Friday** *n* viernes negro *m*; ∼ **gold** *n* oro negro *m*; ∼ **market** *n* mercado negro *m*; **buy sth on the ∼ market** comprar algo en el mercado negro; ∼ **marketeer** *n persona que comercia en el mercado negro*; **B∼ Monday** *n* lunes negro *m*; ∼ **money** *n* dinero negro *m*; **B∼ Thursday** *n* jueves negro *m*; ∼ **trading** *n* comercio clandestino *m*; **B∼ Wednesday** *n* miércoles negro *m*

black² *n* negro *m*; **be in the ∼** no estar en números rojos

black³ *vt* BrE boicotear

blackboard trading *n* operación *f* a precio puesto *or* con pizarra

blacking *n* BrE *boicoteo contra la contratación de personal no sindicalizado*

blackleg *n* BrE (infrml) esquirol *mf* (infrml)

blacklist¹ *n* lista negra *f*

blacklist² *vt* poner en la lista negra

blackmail¹ *n* chantaje *m*

blackmail² *vt* chantajear

blackout *n* (of electrical supply) apagón *m* (of radio, television) suspensión en la emisión *f*

blank¹ *adj* (cheque, form, order, credit, signature) en blanco

blank² *n* blanco *m*

blank³ *vt* (Comp) ocultar, borrar

blanket *adj* (agreement, rate, statement, recommendation) general; (ban, measure) global; (licence) de cobertura total; (bond) general, colectivo; (insurance) global, abierto; (statute) colectivo; ∼ **order** *n* orden de compra abierta *f*

blanking *n* (Comp) ocultación *f*

bleak *adj* (outlook) poco prometedor

bleed *vt* (infrml) sacar dinero a, sangrar (infrml)

bleeding-edge *adj* (research, technology) punta

blighted area *n* zona desertizada *f*

blind *adj* (faith, trust, advertisement) ciego; (carbon copy) ciego, oculto, invisible; ∼**-alley job** *n* AmE trabajo sin perspectivas de avance *m*; ∼ **test** *n* prueba a ciegas *f*

blister packaging *n* embalaje con papel de burbujas *m*

blitz¹ *n* (S&M) ataque intensivo *m*

blitz² *n* (group, target market) asediar

block¹ *n* bloque *m*; (of shares) paquete *m*; **in ∼ mode** (Comp) en modo de bloque; ∼ **averaging** *n* promedio de grupo *m*; ∼ **booking** *n* reserva en bloque *f*; ∼ **code** *n* (Comp) código de bloques *m*; ∼ **diagram** *n* (Comp) esquema funcional *m*; ∼ **funding** *n* asignación de fondos en bloque *f*; ∼ **grant** *n* subvención global *f*; ∼ **move** *n* (Comp) desplazamiento de bloque *m*; ∼ **purchase** *n* compra de un lote *f*; ∼ **stock trader** *n* intermediario(-a) por lotes *m,f*; ∼ **transfer** *n* (Comp) transferencia por bloques *f*; ∼ **vote** *n* voto en bloque *m*; ∼ **voting** *n* votación en bloque *f*

block² *vt* (funds, account, sale) bloquear, congelar; (progress, attempt) obstaculizar, impedir

blockade *n* bloqueo *m*

blockbuster *n* (infrml) éxito de taquilla *m*, bomba *f*

blocked *adj* (funds, account) bloqueado

blocking *n* (Comp) agrupación en bloque *f*; ∼ **software** *n* software de bloqueo *m*

blow¹ *n* golpe *m*; **a ∼ to sb** un golpe para alguien

blow² *vt* (infrml) (money) fundir

blowout *n* AmE venta rápida *f*

blue *adj* azul; ∼ **book** *n* AmE *informe sobre la situación financiera*; ∼ **button** *n* BrE (jarg) empleado(-a) de bolsa *m,f*; ∼ **chip** *n* (security) valor de primera clase *m*; (share) acción de primera clase *f*; ∼**-chip company** *n* compañía de acciones de primera clase *f*; ∼**-chip customer** *n* cliente de primer orden *mf*; ∼**-chip securities** *n pl* valores de primera clase *m pl*; ∼**-chip stock** *n* acciones de primer orden *f pl*; ∼**-collar worker** *n* obrero(-a) *m,f*; **B∼ Cross** *n* AmE Cruz Azul *f*; ∼ **economy** *n* BrE economía oficial *f*; ∼ **laws** *n pl* AmE *leyes de prohibición comercial en los domingos*,; ∼**-sky** *n* AmE inversión monetaria insegura *f*; ∼**-sky bargaining** *n* AmE negociación sin valor *f*; ∼**-sky law** *n* AmE legislación sobre emisión y venta de valores *f*; ∼**-sky research** *n* investigación pura *f*

blueprint *n* anteproyecto *m*

Bluetooth® *n* Bluetooth® *m, norma de la informática y las telecomunicaciones*

blurb *n* (description) reseña *f*, texto de presentación *m*; (publicity) propaganda publicitaria *f*

bn *abbr* (▸**billion**) (one thousand million) mil millones *m pl*; BrE (obs) (one million million) billón *m*

B.O. *abbr* (▸**branch office**) filial *f*, sucursal *f*

board¹ *n* (committee) consejo *m*; (Pol) comité *m*; (Comp) tablero *m*; ~ **of accounting** *n* comisión contable *f*; ~ **of arbitration** *n* comisión *f or* junta *f* de arbitraje; ~ **broker** *n* corredor(a) de bolsa con mesa *m,f*; ~ **control** *n* control del consejo *m*; ~ **of directors** *n* consejo de administración *m*; ~ **of management** *n* consejo de dirección *m*; ~ **meeting** *n* junta del consejo de administración *f*; **B~ of Trade** *n* BrE ≈ Junta de Comercio *f* Esp; ~ **of trustees** *n* consejo de fideicomisarios *m*

board² *vti* embarcar(se)

boarding *n* embarque *m*; ~ **card** *n* tarjeta de embarque *f*; ~ **gate** *n* puerta de embarque *f*; ~ **pass** *n* tarjeta de embarque *f*

boardroom *n* sala de juntas *f*; (Stock) sala de cotizaciones *f*

bodily injury *n* daño corporal *m*

body *n* (organization) organismo *m*; (of e-mail) cuerpo (del mensaje) *m*; ~ **of creditors** *n* masa de acreedores *f*; ~ **of evidence** *n* conjunto de pruebas *m*; ~ **language** *n* lenguaje *m* corporal *or* no verbal; ~ **of law** *n* cuerpo *m* legal *or* de leyes; ~ **politic** *n* cuerpo político *m*

BOGOF *abbr* (▸**buy one get one free**) se regala uno gratis

bogus *adj* (claim, complaint, document, information) falso; (company) fantasma; (bank) fraudulento; (argument) falaz

boilerplate *n* (clichéd language) cliché *m*; (standard contract text) modelo de contrato *m*

boiler room *n* AmE *cabina desde donde telefonean los especuladores ilegales de valores*

bold *n* negrita *f*; ~ **face** *n* negrita *f*; ~**-face character** *n* carácter en negrita *m*; ~ **type** *n* negrita *f*

bolster *vt* (morale) alentar, reforzar; ~ **sb's confidence** reforzar la confianza de alguien

bona fide *adj* (offer, purchaser, clause) de buena fe; (trade union) genuino

bonanza *n* (in mining) bonanza *f*

bond *n* (Fin) bono *m*, obligación *f*; (Ins) fianza *f*; **in** ~ en aduana; ~ **anticipation note** *n* vale por pronto pago de bono *m*; ~ **broker** *n* corredor(a) *m,f* de cambios *or* de comercio; ~ **capital** *n* capital de renta fija *m*; ~ **certificate** *n* certificado *m* nominativo *or* de bono; ~ **conversion** *n* conversión de renta fija *f*; ~ **creditor** *n* acreedor(a) *m,f* con caución *or* garantizado(-a) por fianza; ~ **dealer** *n* colocador(a) de bonos *m,f*; ~ **discount** *n* descuento sobre bonos *m*; ~ **financing** *n* financiación mediante emisión de obligaciones *f*; ~ **fund** *n* fondo de bonos *m*; ~ **interest** *n* interés del bono *m*; ~ **issue** *n* emisión de bonos *f*; ~ **loan** *n* préstamo hipotecario *m*; ~ **market** *n* mercado *m* de bonos *or* de obligaciones de renta fija; ~ **price** *n* precio de los bonos *m*; ~ **rate** *n* tipo de interés del bono *m*; ~ **rating** *n* clasificación de títulos *f*; ~ **sale** *n* venta de valores de renta fija *f*; ~ **switching** *n* conmutación de bonos *f*; ~ **trader** *n* intermediario(-a) de renta fija *m,f*; ~ **trading** *n* operación con bonos *f*; ~ **underwriting** *n* suscripción de bonos *f*; ~ **washing** *n* lavado de bonos *m*; ~ **yield** *n* rendimiento del bono *m*

bonded: ~ **cargo** *n* carga almacenada en depósito *f*; ~ **debt** *n* deuda garantizada con bonos *f*; ~ **goods** *n pl* mercancías *f pl* en almacén de aduanas *or* en depósito; ~ **warehouse** *n* almacén de depósito *m*

bondholder *n* obligacionista *mf*

bonding cost *n* coste *m* Esp *or* costo *m* AmL de emisión

bone of contention *n* manzana de la discordia *f*

bonus *n* (to employee) bonificación *f*; (to policyholder) prima *f*; (to shareholder) dividendo extraordinario *m*; ~ **certificate** *n* certificado de prima *m*; ~ **issue** *n* BrE (*cf* ▸**stock dividend** AmE) emisión de acciones liberadas *f*; ~ **pack** *n* envase con premio *m*; ~ **payment** *n* pago de prima *m*; ~ **scheme** *n* plan de bonificaciones *m*; ~ **share** *n* acción gratuita *f*; ~ **stock** *n* acciones gratuitas *f pl*

book¹ *n* (of cheques, tickets) talonario *m*; (Acc, Stock) libro de contabilidad *m*; (for foreign exchange market) libro *m*; (for underwriting of securities) libro de anotaciones *m*; **by the** ~ según las normas *or* las reglas; **cook the** ~**s** (infrml) falsificar las cuentas; ~ **cost** *n* coste *m* Esp *or* costo *m* AmL en libros; ~ **debt** *n* deuda contabilizada *f*; ~ **depreciation** *n* depreciación en libros *f*; ~ **entry** *n* apunte *m or* asiento *m* contable, asiento en libros *m*; ~ **inventory** *n* inventario en libros *m*; ~ **loss** *n* pérdida *f* contable *or* según libros; ~ **profit** *n* beneficio *m* aparente *or* contable *or* según libros; ~ **value** *n* valor en libros *m*

book² ⟦1⟧ *vt* (in bookkeeping) contabilizar; (reserve) reservar

····⟩

2 *vi* (reserve) hacer una reserva, reservar; ~ **early** reservar con anticipación *or* con antelación; **book in** *vi* (at hotel) firmar el registro; (at office) firmar a la entrada; **book out** *vi* (of hotel) despedirse; (of office) firmar a la salida; **book up** *vt* (hotel) reservar la totalidad de; **I'm booked up all this week** tengo toda la semana ocupada

booking *n* (in bookkeeping) contabilización *f*; (reservation) reserva *f*, reservación *f* AmL; ~ **fee** *n* cuota de reserva *f*; ~ **office** *n* despacho de billetes *m*; ~ **order** *n* orden de reserva *f*; ~ **system** *n* sistema de reserva *m*

bookkeeper *n* tenedor(a) de libros *m,f*

bookkeeping *n* contabilidad *f*, teneduría de libros *f*

bookmaker *n* corredor(a) de apuestas *m,f*

bookmark[1] *vt* (website) marcar

bookmark[2] *n* (Comp) marcador *m*

Boolean *adj* booleano; ~ **algebra** *n* álgebra de Boole *f*; ~ **search** *n* búsqueda de Boole *f*; ~ **variable** *n* variable booleana *f*

boom[1] *n* boom *m*, auge *m*

boom[2] *vi* estar en auge; **sales are ~ing** hay un boom de las ventas

boomlet *n* periodo breve de prosperidad *m*

boondoggle *n* AmE (infrml) proyecto innecesario *m*

boost[1] *n* (of confidence) refuerzo *m*, (of growth, interest rate) estímulo *m*, (of sales) aumento *m*; **give a ~ to sth** dar empuje a algo, estimular algo

boost[2] *vt* (confidence) reforzar; (growth, interest rate, economy, production) estimular; (sales) aumentar

booster training *n* capacitación *f or* formación *f* complementaria

boot[1] *n* (Comp) arranque *m*; (of car) BrE (*cf* ►**trunk** AmE) maletero *m*; ~ **disk** *n* disco de arranque *m*

boot[2] *vt* (computer) arrancar, inicializar; **boot out** *vt* (infrml) (employee) echar, poner de patitas en la calle (infrml); **boot up** *vt* (computer) arrancar, inicializar

booth *n* barraca *f*

bootstrap *vt* (Comp) cargar

boot-up *n* (Comp) arranque *m*

BOP *abbr* (►**balance of payments**) balanza de pagos *f*

border *n* (Pol) frontera *f*; ~ **control** *n* control fronterizo *m*; ~ **trade** *n* comercio fronterizo *m*; ~ **worker** *n* trabajador(a) fronterizo(-a) *m,f*

borderline case *n* caso dudoso *m*

borough *n* barrio *m*, municipio *m*; (local authority) Ayuntamiento *m*

borrow [1] *vt* (money) pedir *or* tomar prestado; (stock) pedir en préstamo; (idea)

sacar; ~ **funds** pedir fondos prestados; ~ **money from sb** pedirle dinero prestado a alguien; ~ **at call** tomar prestado a la vista; ~ **at interest** pedir prestado con intereses; ~ **long/short** pedir prestado a largo/corto plazo

2 *vi* pedir *or* solicitar préstamos; ~ **abroad** tomar un préstamo en el extranjero; ~ **in the Euromarket** tomar un préstamo en el Euromercado; ~ **interest-free** solicitar un préstamo sin intereses; ~ **on securities** pedir un préstamo sobre valores

borrowed *adj* (money, funds) prestado; (stock) a préstamo; (capital) ajeno a la sociedad

borrower *n* prestatario(-a) *m,f*; ~ **country** *n* país prestatario *m*

borrowing *n* empréstito *m*; ~ **abroad** *n* endeudamiento externo *m*, obtención de créditos en el exterior *f*; ~ **bank** *n* banco prestatario *m*; ~ **capacity** *n* capacidad de endeudamiento *f*; ~ **ceiling** *n* tope de endeudamiento *m*; ~ **cost** *n* coste *m* Esp *or* costo *m* AmL de un préstamo; ~ **fee** *n* cargo por el empréstito *m*; ~ **limit** *n* límite de endeudamiento *m*; ~ **power** *n* capacidad de endeudamiento *f*; ~ **rate** *n* tasa de préstamos *f*; ~ **requirement** *n* requisito de préstamo *m*

boss *n* (infrml) jefe(-a) *m,f*

Boston box *n*, **Boston matrix** *n* matriz de Boston *f*

BOT *abbr* BrE (►**Board of Trade**) ≈ Junta de Comercio *f* Esp

bottled-up *adj* (price increase) refrenado

bottleneck *n* cuello de botella *m*, estrangulamiento *m*; (traffic jam) embotellamiento *m*; ~ **inflation** *n* inflación de demanda *f*

bottom[1] *n* fondo *m*; (of organization) nivel inferior *m*; **the ~ has fallen out of the market** se ha derrumbado el mercado; ~ **end of the range** *n* parte más baja de la gama *f*; ~ **fisher** *n* inversor(a) de oportunidades *m,f*; ~ **price** *n* precio mínimo *m*; ~ **rung** *n* (of organization) nivel *m* básico *or* inferior

bottom[2] *vi* tocar fondo; **bottom out** *vi* (market, prices, graph) tocar fondo

bottom line *n* (of accounts) balance *m or* saldo *m* final; **the ~ line** lo esencial; **the ~ line is that we'll have to get rid of people** en cuentas resumidas *or* al fin y al cabo, tendremos que echar a gente; ~ **profit margin** *n* margen *m* de beneficio final *or* de beneficios del resultado final

bottom-up: ~ **approach to investing** *n* enfoque invertido de la inversión *m*; ~ **management** *n* dirección ascendente *f*

bought *adj* comprado; ~ **book** *n* libro de compras *m*; ~ **contract** *n* escritura de

331

bounce ⋯⋗ break ⋯

compraventa *f*; ~ **day book** *n* libro diario de compras *m*; ~ **deal** *n* emisión precolocada *f*; ~ **journal** *n* libro diario de compras *m*; ~ **ledger** *n* mayor de compras *m*

bounce[1] [1] *vt* (infrml) (cheque) rechazar; (e-mail) devolver
[2] *vi* (infrml) (cheque) ser devuelto; (e-mail) rebotar; **bounce back** *vi* recuperarse

bounce[2] *n* (of e-mail) rebote *m*; ~ **message** *n* aviso de no entrega *m*

bounced check AmE, **bounced cheque** BrE *n* (infrml) cheque devuelto *m*

boundary *n* (Prop) límite (de propiedad) *m*

bourgeois *adj* burgués

bourgeoisie *n* burguesía *f*

boutique *n* boutique *f*

box *n* (container) estuche *m*; BrE (cf ▶**check box** AmE) (on page, computer screen) casilla *f*, recuadro *m*; **think outside the** ~ pensar lateralmente; ~ **number** *n* (of printed advert) número de referencia *m*; ~ **office** *n* (of cinema, theatre) taquilla *f*; ~ **spread** *n* (Stock) margen de depósito *m*

boycott[1] *n* boicot *m*, boicoteo *m*

boycott[2] *vt* boicotear

BP deficit *n* (▶**balance of payments deficit**) déficit de la balanza de pagos *m*

bpi *abbr* (▶**bits per inch**) bpp (bitios por pulgada)

bpm *abbr* (▶**best practical means**) medios prácticos más adecuados *m pl*

BPR *abbr* (▶**business process re-engineering**) reingeniería de procesos *f*

bps *abbr* (▶**bits per second**) bps (bitios por segundo)

bracket *n* (of prices, taxes) tramo *m*

brainchild *n* (infrml) (design) creación *f*

brain drain *n* (infrml) fuga de cerebros *f* (infrml)

brainstorm[1] *n* (good idea) idea genial *f*; (confusion) frenesí *m*

brainstorm[2] *vi* tener una sesión de brainstorming

brainstorming *n* brainstorming *m*, puesta en común *f*

brains trust *n* grupo de expertos *m*, trust de cerebros *m*

branch *n* (of credit institution, bank, business) sucursal *f*, ramo *m*; (Comp) bifurcación *f*; ~ **address** *n* dirección de bifurcación *f*; ~ **banking** *n* banca con sucursales *f*; ~ **manager** *n* director(a) de sucursal *m,f*; ~ **network** *n* red de sucursales *f*; ~ **number** *n* número de sucursal *m*; ~ **office** *n* sucursal *f*, filial *f*

brand *n* (of product, service) marca *f*; ~ **acceptance** *n* aceptación de marca *f*; ~ **advertising** *n* publicidad de marca *f*; ~

association *n* asociación de marca *f*; ~ **awareness** *n* conocimiento de marca *m*; ~ **building** *n* establecimiento de marca *m*; ~ **development** *n* desarrollo de marca *m*; ~ **differentiation** *n* diferenciación de marca *f*; ~ **identification** *n* identificación de marca *f*; ~ **image** *n* imagen de marca *f*; ~ **leader** *n* marca líder *f*; ~ **loyalty** *n* lealtad a una marca *f*; ~ **management** *n* gestión de la marca *f*; ~ **manager** *n* gerente de marcas *mf*; ~ **marketing** *n* marketing de marca *m*; ~ **name** *n* nombre comercial *m*; ~ **portfolio** *n* cartera de marcas *f*; ~ **positioning** *n* posicionamiento de marca *m*; ~ **preference** *n* preferencia de marca *f*; ~ **promotion** *n* promoción de marca *f*; ~ **recognition** *n* reconocimiento de marca *m*; ~ **share** *n* cuota de marca *f*; ~ **strategy** *n* estrategia de marca *f*; ~ **switching** *n* cambio de marca *m*

branded good *n* artículo de marca *m*

brand-new *adj* flamante

brass *n* (infrml) alto ejecutivo *m*

BRC *abbr* (▶**business reply card**) tarjeta de respuesta comercial *f*

BRE *abbr* (▶**business reply envelope**) sobre *m* de respuesta comercial *or* impreso con franqueo pagado

breach[1] *n* incumplimiento *m*; **they are in** ~ **of the planning laws** están infringiendo *or* contraviniendo la ley de ordenación urbana; ~ **of confidence** *n* abuso de confianza *m*; ~ **of contract** *n* incumplimiento de contrato *m*; ~ **of duty** *n* incumplimiento del deber *m*; ~ **of security** *n* fallo de seguridad *m*; ~ **of trust** *n* abuso de confianza *m*

breach[2] *vt* (contract) incumplir; (market) abrir brecha en

bread *n* (infrml) (money) pasta *f*

bread-and-butter *adj* primordial; ~ **issue** *n* BrE (cf ▶**pocketbook issue** AmE) problema básico *m*; ~ **letter** *n* breve misiva de agradecimiento *f*; ~ **technique** *n* técnica de la venta segura *f*

breadline *n* (infrml) nivel de subsistencia *m*; **be on the** ~ vivir en la miseria

breadwinner *n* mantenedor(a) de la familia *m,f*

break[1] *n* (pause) pausa *f*; (rest) descanso *m*; (holiday) vacaciones cortas *f pl*; (change) cambio *m*; (drop in prices) bajada de precios *f*, desplome *m*; (good luck) golpe de suerte *m* (infrml); **a coffee** ~ un descanso para tomar café; **a** ~ **in the market** una baja en el mercado; **a** ~ **in the routine** un cambio de rutina; **a** ~ **with tradition** una ruptura con la tradición; **work without a** ~ trabajar sin parar *or* descansar

break² ⊡ *vt* (law) violar; (contract) incumplir, romper; (promise, word) no cumplir; (appointment) faltar a, no acudir a; (record) batir; (deadlock, impasse) salir de; (person, company) arruinar a; (pattern, continuity) romper; (news) comunicar; ~ **the ceiling** (Fin) romper el techo; (Stock) sobrepasar el límite máximo; ~ **new ground** abrir brecha; ~ **ranks** romper filas; ~ **a strike** (worker) romper una huelga; (employer) acabar con una huelga

⊡ *vi* (rest) hacer un descanso; (news, story) hacerse público; ~ **even** equilibrar; **let's** ~ **for coffee** paremos para tomar un café; **break down** ⊡ *vt* (expenses) asignar; (costs) desglosar ⊡ *vi* (machine, device) averiarse; (negotiations, relations) fracasar; **break into** *vt* (market) introducirse en; **break off** *vt* (negotiations) romper; **break up** *vi* (meeting) terminar

breakage *n* rotura *f*; ~ **clause** *n* cláusula de rotura *f*

breakaway *adj* (faction, group) disidente, escindido; ~ **union** *n* sindicato separatista *m*

breakdown *n* (malfunction) avería *f*; (failure) colapso *m*; (of negotiations) ruptura *f*, fracaso *m*; (personal) crisis nerviosa *f*; (of figures, numbers) desglose *m*; ~ **of expenses** *n* recorte de gastos *m*; ~ **of tasks** *n* descomposición del trabajo en fases *f*

break-even *adj* (point, price) de equilibrio; ~ **analysis** *n* análisis *m* del punto muerto *or* del punto crítico; ~ **level of income** *n* nivel de ingresos de punto muerto *m*; ~ **quantity** *n* (Econ) cantidad de punto muerto *f*; (Mgmnt) cantidad de paridad *f*

breaking-off *n* (of relationship) ruptura *f*

breakout *n* ruptura *f*

breakpoint *n* punto de interrupción *m*; ~ **instruction** *n* (Comp) instrucción de reenvío *f*; ~ **sale** *n* venta *f* de equilibrio *or* de rendimiento nulo

breakthrough *n* (in negotiations) avance extraordinario *m*; (in science) adelanto *m*, descubrimiento *m*

break-up *n* (of company) desmembramiento *m*; (of talks) fracaso *m*; (of political party) disolución *f*; ~**-up value** *n* valor de realización inmediata *m*

breed *vt* (confidence) producir

bribe¹ *n* soborno *m*, cohecho *m*; **take** ~**s** recibir sobornos

bribe² *vt* sobornar, cohechar

briber *n* cohechador(a) *m,f*

bribery *n* soborno *m*, cohecho *m*; ~ **and corruption** el soborno y la corrupción

bricks and mortar company *n* empresa de inmuebles *f*

bricks to clicks *n* paso de una empresa tradicional al Internet; ~ **company** *n* empresa que a dado el paso de métodos tradicionales al Internet

bridge¹ *n* puente *m*; ~ **financing** *n* financiación puente *f*; ~ **loan** *n* AmE (*cf* ▸**bridging loan** BrE) préstamo puente *m*

bridge² *vt* (differences) salvar; ~ **the gap between rich and poor** acortar la distancia entre los ricos y los pobres

bridgeware *n* programas de traspaso *m pl*

bridging: ~ **advance** *n* préstamo de transición *m*; ~ **loan** *n* BrE (*cf* ▸**bridge loan** AmE) préstamo puente *m*; ~ **software** *n* programas puente *m pl*

brief¹ *adj* (statement, summary) breve; ~ **audit** *n* auditoría limitada *f*

brief² *vt* (official, committee) informar; (lawyer) instruir; ~ **sb about** *o* **on sth** informar alguien sobre algo

brief³ *n* (document) informe *m*; (instructions) instrucciones *f pl*; (for lawyer) expediente *m*; (legal case) caso *m*; **hold a/no** ~ **for sth** abogar/no abogar por algo; **this is not part of the committee's** ~ esto no entra dentro de la competencia del comité

briefing *n* (document) informe *m*; (instructions) instrucciones *f pl*; ~ **session** *n* sesión informativa *f*

brightness *n* (Comp) reflexibilidad media *f*

bring *vt* (person) conducir; (news, object) traer; **the merger will** ~ **enormous benefits** la fusión va a traer *or* reportar enormes beneficios; ~ **charges against sb** formularle cargos a alguien, formular cargos en contra de alguien; ~ **sth into fashion** poner algo de moda; ~ **a lawsuit** *o* **an action against sb** interponer *or* iniciar una demanda *or* una acción en contra de alguien; ~ **pressure to bear on sb** ejercer presión sobre alguien; ~ **sth to bear against sb** apuntar algo contra alguien; (Law) aplicar algo contra alguien; ~ **sth to an end** terminar algo; ~ **sth to light** sacar algo a la luz; ~ **sth under control** (inflation, unemployment) poner algo bajo control; ~ **sb up to date** poner a alguien al día; ~ **sb up to date on sth** poner a alguien al tanto de algo; ~ **sth up to date** actualizar algo; **bring about** *vt* (change, reform) efectuar; **bring back** *vt* (Stock) devolver; **bring down** *vt* (prices, inflation rate) hacer bajar; (Acc) llevar a cuenta nueva, reabrir; **bring forward** *vt* (Acc) llevar a cuenta nueva; **bring in** *vt* (revenue) aportar; (customers) atraer; (regulation, system) introducir; (bill) presentar; (expert, consultant) pedir la ayuda de; (verdict) pronunciar; **bring out** *vt* (new issue) lanzar; **bring together** *vt* reunir; **bring up** *vt* (new subject) suscitar

brisk *adj* (pace) rápido; (trade) animado, activo; (demand, market) animado; (trading) ágil; **business is ~** el negocio va bien

British *adj* británico; **~ Chamber of Commerce** *n* ≈ Cámara de Comercio Española *f* Esp; **~ Institute of Management** *n* instituto británico de gestión empresarial; **~ Standards Institution** *n* (cf ►**American Standards Association**) ≈ Asociación Española de Normalización y Certificación *f*; **~ Standards Specification** *n* especificación de normas británicas; **~ Summer Time** *n* horario de verano británico *m*; **~ Telecom** *n* red nacional británica de telecomunicaciones, ≈ Compañía Telefónica Nacional de España *f*

broad *adj* amplio; **~-based** *adj* de amplia base; **~-brush** *adj* sin perfilar; **~ market** *n* mercado amplio *m*; **~ money** *n* dinero en sentido amplio *m*

broadband *n* (Comp, Media) banda ancha *f*; **~ Internet** *n* Internet de banda ancha *m*; **~ network** *n* red de banda ancha *f*

broadbanding *n* BrE (HRM) racionalización salarial *f*

broadcast[1] *n* emisión *f*

broadcast[2] *vt* (on TV) transmitir; (on radio) emitir

broadcasting *n* (TV) transmisión *f*; (radio) radiodifusión *f*

broaden *vt* (scope, horizons, interests) ampliar; **~ the tax base** ampliar la base del impuesto

broadsheet *n* BrE (newspaper) periódico de gran formato *m*

brochure *n* folleto *m*

brochureware *n* catálogos en línea *m pl*

broke[1] *adj* (infrml) sin blanca (infrml); **go ~** (infrml) arruinarse, quebrar

broke[2] *vi* (trade) operar

broken *adj* (promise, contract) roto; **~ amount** *n* (Stock) cantidad inactiva *f*; **~ lot** *n* lote suelto *m*

broker[1] *n* (Fin) broker *mf*, comisionista *mf*; (Ins) agente *mf*; (Stock) corredor(a) de bolsa *m,f*; **~'s commission** *n* comisión del corredor de bolsa *f*; **~-dealer** *n* corredor(a)-intermediario(-a) de cambio y bolsa *m,f*; **~ fund** *n* fondo del corredor de comercio *m*; **~'s loan** *n* préstamo del corredor *m*

broker[2] *vt* (deal) negociar; AmE (bonds, commodities) hacer corretaje de

brokerage *n* corretaje *m*; **~ account** *n* cuenta de corretaje *f*; **~ commission** *n*, **~ fee** *n* comisión de corretaje *f*; **~ firm** *n* empresa de intermediación *f*; **~ house** *n* firma de corretaje en bolsa *f*

broking *n* corretaje *m*; **~ house** *n* correduría de bolsa *f*

brought forward *adj* llevado a cuenta nueva, suma y sigue

brown *adj* marrón; **~ book** *n* BrE (jarg) libro marrón *m*; **~ goods** *n pl* línea marrón *f*, electrodomésticos *m pl*

brownout *n* AmE (of electric power) caída *f*

browse *vt* (document) hojear

browser *n* buscador *m*; **~ interface** *n* interfaz del buscador *m*

browsing *n* browsing *m*, exploración *f*

brush up *vt* (infrml) (experience, skill) poner al día; **brush up on** *vt* dar un repaso a (infrml), ponerse al corriente de

B/S *abbr* (►**balance sheet**) balance *m*

BSBA *abbr* (►**Bachelor of Science in Business Administration**) licenciado(-a) *m,f* en Administración de Empresas *or* en Ciencias Empresariales

BSc *abbr* (►**Bachelor of Science**) licenciado(-a) en Ciencias *m,f*

BSI *abbr* (►**British Standards Institution**) ≈ AENOR (Asociación Española de Normalización y Certificación)

BSIR *abbr* (►**Bachelor of Science in Industrial Relations**) licenciado(-a) en Relaciones Laborales *m,f*

BSS *abbr* (►**British Standards Specification**) especificación de normas británicas

BST *abbr* (►**British Summer Time**) horario de verano británico *m*

BT *abbr* (►**British Telecom**) red nacional británica de telecomunicaciones, ≈ CTNE (Compañía Telefónica Nacional de España)

bubble *n* estafa *f*; **~ memory** *n* (Comp) memoria de burbujas *f*; **~ pack** *n* (S&M) envase de burbujas *m*; **~ sort** *n* (Comp) clasificación por cribadura *f*

buck[1] *n* AmE (infrml) dólar *m*; **cost big ~s** costar mucha pasta (infrml); **make a fast** *o* **quick~** hacer dinero fácil; **pass the ~** pasar la pelota (infrml); **the ~ stops here** la responsabilidad es mía

buck[2] *vt* (system) oponerse a; **~ the market** ir en contra del mercado; **~ the trend** ir en contra de la tendencia general

bucket shop *n* agencia de viajes con precios reducidos *f*

budget[1] *n* presupuesto *m*; **come in under ~** costar menos de lo presupuestado; **go** *o* **run over ~** costar más de lo presupuestado, exceder el presupuesto; **be on a (tight) ~** tener un presupuesto muy justo; **~ account** *n* cuenta presupuestaria *f*; **~ analysis** *n* análisis presupuestario *m*; **~ appropriation** *n* crédito presupuestario *m*; (in governmental accounting) asignación ···⟩

presupuestaria *f*; ~ **ceiling** *n* techo presupuestario *m*; ~ **constraint** *n* restricción presupuestaria *f*; ~ **cut** *n* recorte presupuestario *m*; ~ **cycle** *n* ciclo presupuestario *m*; ~ **deficit** *n* déficit presupuestario *m*; ~ **equilibrium** *n* equilibrio presupuestario *m*; ~ **estimate** *n* estimación presupuestaria *f*; ~ **expenditure** *n* gasto presupuestario *m*; ~ **management** *n* gestión presupuestaria *f*; ~ **period** *n* periodo del presupuesto *m*; ~ **preparation** *n* elaboración *f or* preparación *f* del presupuesto; ~ **proposal** *n* proyecto de presupuesto *m*; ~ **surplus** *n* superávit *m* presupuestario *or* de presupuesto; ~ **year** *n* ejercicio presupuestario *m*

budget² *vt* presupuestar; **budget for** *vt* incluir en el presupuesto

budget³ *adj* (inexpensive) económico; ~ **price** *n* precio reducido *m*

Budget *n* BrE presupuesto del Estado *m*; ~ **speech** *n* BrE presentación del presupuesto *f*

budgetary *adj* (accounts, control, deficit, policy) presupuestario

budgeted *adj* (cost, income, profit) presupuestado

budgeting *n* confección *f or* elaboración *f* del presupuesto

buffer *n* (Comp) (circuit) memoria tampón *f*; (storage area) memoria intermedia *f*; ~ **area** *n* zona intermedia *f*; ~ **storage** *n* almacenamiento intermedio *m*; ~ **store** *n* memoria *f* interfaz *or* de tránsito; ~ **zone** *n* zona tapón *f*

bug *n* (in program) error *m*

build *vt* (offices) construir, edificar; (career) forjarse; (empire) levantar, construir; ~ **a company from nothing** levantar una empresa de la nada; ~ **sth into a contract** incorporar algo a un contrato; ~ **links with sth/sb** establecer vínculos con algo/alguien; **build up** 1 *vt* (firm) fomentar, fundar; (reputation) crear, conseguir 2 *vi* urbanizarse

building *n* edificio *m*; ~ **and loan association** *n* AmE banco (de crédito) hipotecario *m*; ~ **lot** *n* solar *m*; ~ **materials** *n pl* materiales de construcción *m pl*; ~ **permit** *n* AmE (*cf* ►**planning permission** BrE) permiso para construir *m*; ~ **regulations** *n pl* legislación sobre construcciones *f*; ~ **repair** *n* reparación de edificios *f*; ~ **site** *n* obra *f*; ~ **society** *n* BrE (*cf* ►**building** *o* **savings and loan association** AmE) banco (de crédito) hipotecario *m*

built-in *adj* (mechanism, feature) incorporado; (weakness, tendency) intrínseco; (check) automático; (test) integrado; ~

obsolescence *n* obsolescencia planeada *f*, caducidad programada *f*

built-up area *n* área edificada *f*, zona urbanizada *f*

bulge *n* (Stock) comba *f*

bulk *n* (main part) grueso *m*; (volume) granel *m*; **in** ~ a granel; ~ **business** *n* negocio granel *m*; ~ **buyer** *n* comprador(a) de graneles *m,f*; ~ **buying** *n* compras a granel *f pl*; ~ **commodity** *n* mercancías a granel *f pl*; ~ **discount** *n* descuento por compra a granel *m*; ~ **e-mail** *n* spam *m*, bulk e-mail *m*; ~ **goods** *n pl* artículos de mucho consumo *m pl*; ~ **mail** *n* envío postal de gran volumen *m*; ~ **order** *n* pedido a granel *m*; ~ **price** *n* precio por venta a granel *m*; ~ **shipment** *n* cargamento a granel *m*; ~ **storage** *n* almacenamiento de gran capacidad *m*

bulky *adj* (cargo, goods) voluminoso

bull *n* (Stock) alcista *mf*; **buy a** ~ comprar al alza; **go a** ~ especular al alza; ~ **account** *n* cuenta alcista *f*; ~**-and-bear bond** *n* BrE bono alcista y bajista *m*; ~ **buying** *n* compra de alcista *f*; ~ **campaign** *n* campaña alcista *f*; ~ **market** *n* mercado *m* alcista *or* al alza; ~ **operation** *n* operación al alza *f*; ~ **operator** *n* operador(a) alcista *m,f*; ~ **position** *n* posición alcista *f*; ~ **purchase** *n* compra al descubierto *f*; ~ **speculation** *n* especulación alcista *f*; ~ **speculator** *n* especulador(a) alcista *m,f*; ~ **transaction** *n* operación alcista *f*

bulldog: ~ **bond** *n* BrE *obligación en libras esterlinas emitida por una sociedad extranjera en el Reino Unido*; ~ **edition** *n* AmE edición matinal *f*; ~ **issue** *n* BrE *emisión en libras esterlinas de una sociedad extranjera en el Reino Unido*; ~ **loan** *n* BrE *crédito en libras esterlinas emitido por una sociedad extranjera en el Reino Unido*

bullet *n* (jarg) (Bank) amortización única *f*; ~ **point** *n* punto grueso *m*; ~ **repayment** *n* reembolso inmediato *m*

bulletin *n* boletín *m*; ~ **board** *n* (Comp) tablón de anuncios (electrónico) *m*; AmE (*cf* ►**noticeboard** BrE) tablón de anuncios *m*; ~ **board system** (Comp) *n* sistema de tablón de anuncios *m*

bullion *n* oro y plata en lingotes *m*; ~ **market** *n* mercado del oro y la plata *m*

bullish *adj* (market, movement, stance) alcista; (stock) en alza; (tendency) alcista, al alza

bullishness *n* alcismo *m*

bumper *adj* (crop) récord, extraordinario; (year) floreciente; (edition) extra; (pack) gigante

bunching *n* (Tax) acumulación *f*

bundled: ~ **deal** n transacción de acciones f; ~ **software** n paquete (de software) m

bundling n (S&M) agrupamiento m

bunny bond n (jarg) bono reinvertible m

buoyancy n dinamismo m

buoyant adj (supply, demand) intensivo; (market) sostenido, al alza

burden[1] n carga f; **the ~ of proof lies with the prosecution** el peso de la prueba recae en la acusación; ~ **of losses** n volumen de siniestros m; ~ **of payment** n obligación de pago f; ~ **of taxation** n carga impositiva f

burden[2] vt (with debt) cargar

bureau n oficina f; **B~ of the Budget** n Oficina del Presupuesto f; **B~ of Economic Analysis** el departamento de análisis económico m; **B~ of Labour Statistics** n BrE oficina de estadística laboral f; ~ **of standards** n (Comp) dirección de normalización f

bureaucracy n burocracia f

bureaucrat n burócrata mf

bureaucratic adj burocrático

bureaucratization n burocratización m

burglary n allanamiento de morada m, robo m

burning cost n coste m Esp or costo m AmL de pérdida neta

burnout n (HRM) agotamiento m; (Tax) extinción f

burst: ~ **advertising** n publicidad intensiva f; ~ **campaign** n campaña de saturación f; ~ **mode** n (Comp) modalidad f or modo m en ráfagas

burster n (for paper) separador m

bus n (Comp) bus m; ~ **mailing** n envío en bus m

business n (commerce) negocios m pl, comercio m; (company) negocio m; (matter, affair) asunto m, tarea f; (transactions) asuntos (a tratar) m pl; **any other (competent) ~** ruegos y preguntas; **do ~** hacer negocios; **do ~ over the phone** hacer negocios por teléfono; **do ~ with sb** comerciar con alguien; **it's been a pleasure doing ~ with you** ha sido un placer hacer negocios con usted; **get down to ~** ir al grano; **go about one's ~** ocuparse de sus propios asuntos; **go into ~** montar un negocio; **go out of ~** ir a la quiebra, quebrar; ~ **is good** el negocio anda or marcha bien; **the firm has a lot of ~ to get through** tener muchos asuntos or temas que tratar; **she's in ~ as a legal adviser** trabaja como asesora legal; **the firm has been in ~ for over 50 years** la empresa tiene más de 50 años de actividad comercial; **lose ~** perder clientes or clientela; **mix ~**

with pleasure mezclar el trabajo con la diversión; **no ~ value** sin valor comercial; **if there's no further ~...** si no hay más asuntos a tratar...; **on ~** de viaje de negocios; **set up one's own ~** montar su propio negocio; ~ **is slack** hay muy poco movimiento; ~ **transferred to** negocio trasladado a; ~ **as usual** (sign) la venta continúa en el interior

business a... ~ **account** n cuenta de negocios f; ~ **activity** n actividad comercial f; ~ **acumen** n perspicacia f empresarial or en los negocios; ~ **address** n dirección comercial f; ~ **administration** n administración de empresas f; ~ **agent** n agente de negocios mf; ~ **angel** n ángel m, inversor particular que provee capital para negocios de alto riesgo; ~ **assets** n pl capital de negocio m

c... ~ **call** n (by phone) llamada de negocios f; (in person) visita de negocios f; ~ **card** n tarjeta de visita f; ~ **center** AmE, ~ **centre** BrE n centro de negocios m; ~ **class** n clase preferente f; ~ **college** n academia de negocios f; ~ **community** n esferas empresariales f pl; ~ **computing** n computación f or informática f de gestión; ~ **concern** n empresa especulativa f, entidad comercial f; ~ **connection** n conexión comercial f; ~ **consultant** n empresólogo(-a) m,f; ~ **corporation** n corporación f or empresa f mercantil; ~ **correspondence** n correspondencia comercial f; ~ **creation** n creación comercial f; ~ **cycle** n ciclo económico m

d... ~ **day** n día laborable m; ~ **decision** n decisión comercial f; ~ **development** n desarrollo empresarial m; ~ **development manager** n director(a) de desarrollo comercial m,f

e... ~ **economics** n economía de empresa f; ~ **economist** n economista mercantil mf; ~ **enterprise** n empresa comercial f; ~ **environment** n medio comercial m; ~ **ethics** n pl ética comercial f; ~ **etiquette** n etiqueta comercial f; ~ **expenses** n pl gastos del negocio m pl; ~ **experience** n experiencia comercial f

f... ~ **failure** n quiebra comercial f; ~ **finance** n financiación comercial f; ~ **forecasting** n previsión comercial f

g... ~ **game** n juego m de empresas or de negocios

h... ~ **hours** n pl horas de comercio f pl

i... ~ **indicator** n indicador comercial m; ~ **intelligence** n información comercial f; ~ **interest** n interés comercial m; ~ **investment** n inversión empresarial f

l... ~ **law** n derecho mercantil m; ~ **lease** n arrendamiento comercial m; ~ **letter** n ⋯▸

carta *f* comercial *or* de negocios ~ **liability** *n* responsabilidad comercial *f*; ~ **loan** *n* préstamo para fines comerciales *m*; ~ **losses** *n pl* pérdidas de explotación *f pl*; ~ **lunch** *n* almuerzo de negocios *m*

(**m...**) ~ **machine** *n* máquina de oficina *f*; ~ **magnate** *n* potentado(-a) comercial *m,f*; ~ **management** *n* dirección *f or* gestión *f* de empresas; ~ **manager** *n* director(a) de empresa *m,f*; ~ **meeting** *n* encuentro de negocios *m*; ~ **model** *n* modelo comercial *m*

(**n...**) ~ **name** *n* razón social *f*

(**o...**) ~ **objective** *n* objetivo de negocios *m*; ~ **opportunity** *n* oportunidad *f* comercial *or* de negocios; ~**-oriented** *adj* empresarial, orientado hacia los negocios, de orientación comercial

(**p...**) ~ **package** *n* (Comp) paquete de gestión *m*; (Fin) paquete comercial *m*; ~ **pages** *n pl* (of newspaper) páginas de negocios *f pl*; ~ **park** *n* parque empresarial *m*; ~ **plan** *n* plan *m* comercial *or* de negocios; ~ **planning** *n* planificación *f* de la empresa *or* de negocios *f*; ~ **policy** *n* política empresarial *f*; ~ **portfolio** *n* cartera de negocios *f*; ~ **practice** *n* práctica comercial *f*; ~ **premises** *n pl* local comercial *m*; ~ **press** *n* prensa profesional *f*; ~ **process engineering** *n* reingeniería de procesos *f*; ~ **proposition** *n* propuesta de negocio *f*

(**r...**) ~ **recovery** *n* recuperación del negocio *f*; ~ **regulations** *n pl* normativa comercial *f*; ~ **reply card** *n* tarjeta de respuesta comercial *f*; ~ **reply envelope** *n* sobre *m* de respuesta comercial *or* impreso con franqueo pagado; ~ **risk** *n* riesgo comercial *m*

(**s...**) ~ **school** *n* escuela de comercio *f*; ~ **sector** *n* sector empresarial *m*; ~ **sense** *n* sentido comercial *m*; ~ **slowdown** *n* reducción de la actividad comercial *f*; ~ **start-up** *n* puesta en marcha *f*; ~ **strategist** *n* especializado(-a) en estrategias comerciales *m,f*; ~ **strategy** *n* estrategia *f* comercial *or* empresarial; ~ **stream** *n* flujo de negocio *m*; ~ **studies** *n pl* estudios empresariales *m pl*

(**t...**) ~ **tax** *n* impuesto comercial *m*; ~ **transaction** *n* transacción comercial *f*; ~ **travel** *n* viajes de negocios *m pl*; ~ **trend** *n* tendencia comercial *f*; ~ **trip** *n* viaje de negocios *m*

(**v...**) ~ **venture** *n* empresa comercial *f*

(**w...**) ~ **world** *n* mundo de los negocios *m*

(**y...**) ~ **year** *n* ejercicio anual *m*

businesslike *adj* (person, manner) formal, serio

businessman *n* empresario *m*, hombre de negocios *m*

business-to-administration *adj* entre empresa y administración

business-to-business *adj* (advertising, marketing) empresa a empresa, interempresas

business-to-business-to-consumer *adj* empresa a empresa a consumidor

business-to-consumer *adj* empresa a consumidor

business-to-government *adj* empresa a gobierno *or* a administración

businesswoman *n* empresaria *f*, mujer de negocios *f*

bust *adj*: go ~ (infrml) ir a la quiebra

bust-up acquisition *n* (of corporation) adquisición fracasada *f*

busy *adj* (person) ocupado, atareado; (schedule) apretado; AmE (*cf* ▸**engaged** BrE) (telephone line) ocupado *or* comunicando Esp; ~ **signal** *n* AmE (*cf* ▸**engaged tone** BrE) señal *m* de ocupado *or* de comunicando Esp

butterfly: ~ **effect** *n* efecto dominó *m*; ~ **spread** *n* margen de mariposa *m*

button *n* (Comp) botón *m*

buy[1] *vt* (purchase) comprar; (bribe) sobornar; (infrml) (accept as true) tragar, creer; ~ **sb sth** comprarle algo a alguien; ~ **sth for sb** comprar algo para alguien; ~ **sth for sth** (at a cost of) comprar algo por algo; ~ **sth from sb** comprarle algo a alguien; ~ **low and sell high** comprar a la baja y vender al alza; ~ **on the bad news** comprar con malas noticias; ~ **one get one free** se regala uno gratis; **buy back** *vt* recomprar; (Fin) rescatar; **buy down** *vt* (Bank) anticipar; (Prop) comprar a la baja; **buy in** *vt* (goods) aprovisionarse de; (Stock) comprar; **buy into** *vt* (company) comprar acciones de; (idea) apoyar; **buy out** *vt* (partner) comprar la parte de; **buy up** *vt* acaparar

buy[2] *n* compra *f*; **a good/bad ~** una buena/mala compra; ~ **order** *n* (Stock) orden de compra *f*; ~ **transaction** *n* (Stock) operación de compra *f*

buyback *n* rescate *m*; ~ **agreement** *n* (in international trade) acuerdo de recompra *m*; ~ **clause** *n* cláusula de retrocompra *f*; ~ **option** *n* (Stock) opción de recompra *f*

buyer *n* comprador(a) *m,f*; **at ~'s risk** a riesgo del comprador; ~ **credit** *n* crédito al consumidor *m*; ~**s' market** *n* mercado de compradores *m*; ~**'s rate** *n* tasa de compra *f*

buy-in *n* toma de posición *f*; (of securities) compra por intermediación *f*

buying *n* compra *f*; ~ **behavior** AmE, ~ **behaviour** BrE *n* comportamiento de compra *m*; ~ **commission** *n* comisión de compra *f*; ~ **habits** *n pl* usos de compra *m pl*; ~ **hedge** *n* cobertura de compra *f*; ~ **house** *n* casa compradora *f*; ~ **order** *n* orden de compra *f*; ~ **pattern** *n* modelo de

compra *m*; ~ **power** *n* poder adquisitivo *m*;
~ **price** *n* precio de compra *m*

buyout *n* (Fin) oferta de compras *f*; (Ins)
transferencia de beneficios *f*; (Stock) compra
f total *or* de control ; **the** ~ **of a partner** la
compra de la parte de un socio; ~ **proposal**
n (Stock) propuesta de compra al cien por
cien *f*

buzz *n* (infrml) (telephone call) llamada *f*;
(rumour) rumor *m*; **give sb a** ~ (infrml)

(telephone) llamar a alguien

buzzword *n* (infrml) palabra de moda *f*

by-election *n* elección parcial *f*

by-law *n* estatuto *m*

by-line *n* pie de autor *m*

by-product *n* subproducto *m*

byte *n* byte *m*, octeto *m*; ~ **mode** *n*
modalidad byte a byte *f*

Cc

c. *abbr* (▶**coupon**) cupón *m*

C2C *abbr* (▶**consumer-to-consumer**) consumidor a consumidor, entre consumidores

c/a *abbr* (▶**current account** BrE, ▶**checking account** AmE) c/c (cuenta corriente)

CA *abbr* (▶**certified accountant**) BrE (*cf* ▶**C.P.A.** AmE) censor(a) jurado(-a) de cuentas *m,f*, contador(a) público(-a) *m,f* AmL; (▶**Consumers' Association** BrE, *cf* ▶**CAC** AmE) ≈ OCU (Organización de Consumidores y Usuarios)

C/A *abbr* (▶**capital account**) cuenta de capital *f*, (▶**credit account**) cuenta de crédito *f*

CAB *abbr* (▶**Citizens' Advice Bureau**) *organización voluntaria británica que asesora legal o financieramente*

cabin *n* cabina *f*; ~ **staff** *n* personal de cabina *m*

cabinet *n* gabinete *m*, ≈ Consejo de Ministros *m*; ~ **reshuffle** *n* reorganización gubernamental *f*; ~ **security** *n* (Stock) título ministerial *m*; ~ **minister** *n* ministro(-a) del gobierno *m,f*

cable[1] *n* cable *m*; ~ **address** *n* dirección cablegráfica *f*; ~ **television** *n* televisión por cable *f*; ~ **transfer** *n* giro cablegráfico *m*

cable[2] *vt* telegrafiar

CAC *abbr* (▶**Consumers' Advisory Council** AmE, *cf* ▶**CA** BrE) ≈ OCU (Organización de Consumidores y Usuarios)

cache *n* (Comp) cache *m*; ~ **buffer** *n* antememoria *f*; ~ **memory** *n* memoria temporal *f*

c.a.d. *abbr* (▶**cash against documents**) pago contra documentación *m*

CAD *abbr* (▶**computer-aided design**) CAD (diseño asistido por computadora AmL *or* ordenador Esp); (▶**Control-Alternate-Delete**) Control-Alternar-Suprimir *m*

cadastral *adj* catastral; ~ **survey** *n* inspección catastral *f*

cadastre *n* catastro *m*

CADD *abbr* (▶**computer-aided design and drafting**) CADD (diseño y dibujo asistido por computadora AmL *or* ordenador Esp)

cadre *n* (HRM) ejecutivo *m,f*; (Pol) cuadro *m*

CAE *abbr* (▶**computer-assisted engineering**) ingeniería *f* asistida por computadora AmL *or* ordenador Esp

cage *n* (Stock) (AmE) trastienda *f*; ~ **card** *n* (Comp) tarjeta multifilar *f*

CAI *abbr* (▶**computer-aided instruction**) CAI (instrucción asistida por computadora AmL *or* ordenador Esp)

CAL *abbr* (▶**computer-aided learning**) aprendizaje *m* asistido por computadora AmL *or* ordenador Esp

calculable *adj* calculable

calculate *vt* calcular

calculated risk *n* riesgo calculado *m*

calculating machine *n* máquina calculadora *f*

calculation *n* cálculo *m*

calculator *n* calculadora *f*

calendar *n* calendario *m*; ~ **day** *n* día de calendario *m*; (in contract) día natural *f*; ~ **month** *n* mes calendario *m*; ~ **year** *n* año natural *m*

calibre BrE, **caliber** AmE *n* (of staff) calibre *m*, capacidad *f*

call[1] *n* (by telephone) llamada *f*; (visit) visita; (customer demand) demanda *f*; (Acc, Stock) obligación *f*; (Bank) petición de devolución *f*; **at** *o* **on** ~ (Fin) a la vista; **give sb a** ~ llamar (por teléfono) a alguien, telefonear a alguien; **make/receive/return a** ~ hacer/recibir/devolver una llamada; **there isn't much** ~ **for such things** hay poca demanda para esas cosas; **she has many** ~**s on her time** está muy solicitada; ~ **account** *n* cuenta *f* a la vista *or* de suscripciones pagaderas; ~ **to the Bar** *n* BrE *ceremonia de ingreso en el Colegio de Abogados*; ~ **box** *n* AmE (*cf* ▶**phone box** BrE, ▶**telephone box** BrE) cabina telefónica *f*; ~ **buyer** *n* comprador(a) de una opción de compra *m,f*; ~ **center** AmE, ~ **centre** BrE *n* centro de llamadas *m*; ~ **center agent** AmE, ~ **centre agent** BrE *n* representante de un centro de llamadas *mf*; ~ **charge** *n* cargo de llamadas *m*; ~ **date** *n* (Bank) fecha de vencimiento *f*; ~ **for bids** *n*, ~ **for tenders** *n* llamada a licitación *f*; ~ **forwarding** *n* desvío de llamada *m*; ~ **loan** *n* préstamo a la vista *m*; ~ **money** *n* dinero a la vista *m*; ~ **notice** *n* aviso de opción de compra *m*; ~ **option** *n* opción de compra *f*; ~ **option writer** *n* emisor(a) de opciones de compra *m,f*; ~ **premium** *n* prima de rescate *f*; ~ **price** *n* precio de rescate *m*; ~ **protection** *n* protección contra rescate anticipado *f*; ~ **provision** *n* provisión de rescate *f*; ~ **purchase** *n* adquisición de una opción de compra *f*; ~ **and put option** *n* opción de compra y venta *f*; ~ **queuing** *n* colocación en espera de llamadas *f*; ~ **rate** *n* tasa *f* a la vista *or* de interés sobre préstamos a corto plazo; (interest rates) tipo de interés para préstamos a la vista *m*; (of stock, shares) tasa de interés de la demanda *f*; ~ **report** *n* (Comp) informe de intervención *m*; (S&M) informe de visita *m*; ~ **spread** *n* (Stock) margen de rescate *m*; ~ **waiting** *n* llamada en espera *f*

call² *vt* (by telephone) llamar; (meeting) convocar; (strike) declarar; (demand payment of) cobrar; ~ **sb as a witness** llamar a alguien como testigo; ~ **collect** AmE (*cf* ▶**make a reverse charge call** BrE, ▶**reverse the charges** BrE) llamar a cobro revertido; ~ **on a Freefone® number** BrE (*cf* ▶**call toll-free** AmE) llamar sin pagar tasas; ~ **sb over the intercom** llamar a alguien por el intercomunicador; ~ **sb to account** pedir cuentas a alguien; ~ **securities for redemption** demandar títulos para rescate; ~ **toll-free** AmE (*cf* ▶**call on a Freefone number** BrE) llamar sin pagar tasas; **call back** *vti* (phone again) volver a llamar; (return call) llamar; **call for** *vt* (action, skill) requirir; **call in** *vi* llamar (por teléfono), telefonear; ~ **in sick** llamar para dar parte de enfermo; **call off** *vt* (meeting) suspender; (strike) suspender, desconvocar; **call out** *vt* (workers) convocar a la huelga; **call up** *vti* llamar (por teléfono)

CALL *abbr* (▶**computer-assisted language learning**) aprendizaje *m* de idiomas asistido por computadora AmL *or* ordenador Esp

callable *adj* amortizable, redimible; ~ **bond** *n* bono *m* amortizable anticipadamente *or* redimible antes del vencimiento; ~ **capital** *n* capital a la vista *m*; ~ **preferred stock** *n* AmE acciones preferentes amortizables *f pl*

call-back *n* (Comp) *opción de ser llamados en persona que se ofrece a los visitantes de un sitio*

called-away *adj* (bonds) amortizado

called security *n* título redimido *m*

called-up share capital *n* capital social exigido *m*

caller *n* persona que llama (por teléfono); ~ **display** *n* presentación visual del número llamado *m*

calling *n* (occupation) profesión *f*; ~ **card** *n* AmE (*cf* ▶**visiting card** BrE) targeta de visita *f*; ~ **cycle** *n* (S&M) ciclo de visitas *m*; ~ **program** *n* programa de llamada *m*

calumniate *vi* calumniar

calumniation *n* calumnia *f*

calumny *n* calumnia *f*

CAM *abbr* (▶**computer-aided manufacturing**) CAM (fabricación asistida por computadora AmL *or* ordenador Esp)

cambist *n* cambista de divisas *mf*

cambistry *n* cambios de divisas *m pl*

camera: **in** ~ *adv* (meeting) a puerta cerrada

camera-ready *adj* listo para fotografiar; ~**-ready copy** *n* material listo para fotografiar *m*

campaign *n* campaña *f*; **conduct a** ~ emprender una campaña; ~ **plan** *n* plan de campaña *m*

camp-on *adj* (call) en espera

canal *n* canal *m*

cancel *vt* (meeting, trip, order, option, debt) cancelar; (cheque, contract, premium) anular; **cancel out** *vt* (advantage) anular; (debt) cancelar; (deficit, loss) compensar

canceled AmE ▶**cancelled** BrE

canceling AmE ▶**cancelling** BrE

cancellation *n* (of meeting, trip, order, option, debt) cancelación *f*; (of cheque, contract, premium) anulación *f*; ~ **clause** *n* (in contract) cláusula *f* abrogatoria *or* resolutoria *or* de rescisión; ~ **fee** *n* gastos de cancelación *m pl*; ~ **notice** *n* aviso de cancelación *m*

cancelled BrE, **canceled** AmE *adj* (debt, share) cancelado; (cheque) anulado

cancelling BrE, **canceling** AmE *adj* (clause) abrogatorio, resolutorio, de rescisión

cancel order *n* orden de cancelación *f*

can crowd *n* (infrml) grupo cerrado de inversores *m*

C&D *abbr* (▶**collected and delivered**) recogido y entregado; (cheque, draft) cobrado y entregado

C&E *abbr* BrE (▶**Customs & Excise Department**) ≈ Departamento de Aduanas y Tributos *m*, ≈ Servicio de Aduanas *m*

c&f *abbr* (▶**cost and freight**) c&f (coste y flete Esp, costo y flete AmL)

C&I *abbr* (▶**cost and insurance**) coste y seguro *m* Esp, costo y seguro *m* AmL

candidacy *n* candidatura *f*

candidate *n* candidato(-a) *m,f*

candidature *n* candidatura *f*

canvass *vt* hacer una encuesta de, sondear

canvasser *n* representante comercial *mf*

cap¹ *n* (upper limit) tope *m*; **put a** ~ **on sth** poner un tope a algo; ~ **issue** *n*

(▸**capitalization issue**) emisión de acciones liberadas *f*; ∼ **rate** *n* (▸**capitalization rate**) tasa de capitalización *f*

cap² *vt* (expenditure) poner un tope a, limitar; (interest rates) poner un tope a

CAP *abbr* (▸**Common Agricultural Policy**) PAC (Política Agrícola Común)

capability *n* capacidad *f*

capacity *n* capacidad *f*; **at full** ∼ a plena capacidad; **in one's** ∼ **as sth** en su calidad de algo; **in an advisory** ∼ en calidad de asesor; ∼ **planning** *n* planificación de capacidad *f*; ∼ **to work** *n* aptitud física para el trabajo *f*; ∼ **utilization** *n* utilización de la capacidad productiva *f*

capex *abbr* (▸**capital expenditure**) gasto de capital *m*

capital *n* capital *m*; **make** ∼ **out of sth** aprovecharse de algo; ∼ **account** *n* cuenta de capital *f*; ∼ **accumulation** *n* acumulación de capital *f*; ∼ **aid** *n* capital de ayuda *m*; ∼ **allotment** *n* asignación de capital *f*; ∼ **allowance** *n* desgravación sobre bienes de capital *f*; ∼ **appreciation** *n* revalorización del capital *f*, alza de capital *m*; ∼ **asset** *n* activo fijo *m*; ∼ **base** *n* base de capital *f*; ∼ **bonus** *n* gratificación de capital *f*; ∼ **budget** *n* presupuesto de capital *m*; ∼ **budgeting** *n* presupuestación del capital *f*; ∼ **contribution** *n* aporte de capital *m*; ∼ **cost** *n* coste *m* Esp *or* costo *m* AmL de inversión; ∼ **costs** *n pl* coste *m* Esp *or* costo *m* AmL de capital; ∼ **dividend** *n* dividendo de capital *m*; ∼ **equipment** *n* equipo capital *m*; ∼ **expenditure** *n* gasto de capital *m*; ∼ **financing** *n* financiación del capital *f*; ∼ **flight** *n* evasión de divisas *f*; ∼ **fund** *n* fondo de capital *m*; ∼ **funding** *n* provisión de fondos de capital *f*; ∼ **gain(s)** *n (pl)* plusvalía *f*; **make a** ∼ **gain** producir un incremento de capital; ∼ **gains tax** *n* impuesto sobre la plusvalía *m*; ∼ **gearing** *n* BrE apalancamiento de capital *m*; ∼ **goods** *n pl* bienes de capital *m pl*; ∼ **growth** *n* crecimiento del capital *m*; ∼ **increase** *n* capitalización *f*; ∼ **inflow** *n* afluencia *f or* entrada *f* de capital; ∼ **injection** *n* inyección de capital *f*; ∼-**intensive** *adj* intensivo en capital; ∼ **investment** *n* inversión de capital *f*; ∼ **leverage** *n* (*cf* ▸**capital gearing** BrE) apalancamiento de capital *m*; ∼ **loss** *n* minusvalías *f pl*, pérdida de capital *f*; ∼ **market** *n* mercado de capitales *m*; ∼ **outflow** *n* salida de capital *f*; ∼ **outlay** *n* desembolso de capital *m*; ∼ **project** *n* proyecto de inversión *m*; ∼ **requirements** *n pl* necesidades *f pl* de financiación *or* del capital; ∼ **reserve** *n* reserva de capital *f*; ∼ **resource** *n* recurso de capital *m*; ∼ **risk** *n* riesgo del capital *m*;

∼ **shares** *n pl* acciones de capital *f pl*; ∼ **spending** *n* gasto de capital *m*; ∼ **stock** *n* BrE (*cf* ▸**equity capital** AmE) capital social en acciones *m*; ∼ **strategy** *n* estrategia de inversión *f*; ∼ **structure** *n* estructura de capital *f*; ∼ **transaction** *n* transacción de capital *f*; ∼ **transfer** *n* transferencia de capital *f*; ∼ **transfer tax** *n* BrE impuesto sobre las transferencias de capital *m*; ∼ **value** *n* valor (del) capital *m*

capitalism *n* capitalismo *m*

capitalist¹ *adj* (class, imperialism) capitalista

capitalist² *n* capitalista *mf*

capitalistic *adj* capitalista

capitalization *n* (of income, interest, reserves) capitalización *f*; ∼ **bond** *n* bono de capitalización *m*; ∼ **issue** *n* (*cf* ▸**stock dividend** AmE) emisión de acciones liberadas *f*; ∼ **rate** *n* tasa de capitalización *f*; ∼ **ratio** *n* coeficiente de capitalización *m*; ∼ **shares** *n pl* acciones de capitalización *f pl*

capitalize *vt* capitalizar; **capitalize on** *vt* sacar beneficio de, capitalizar

capitalized *adj* (interest, cost, value) capitalizado

capital letter *n* mayúscula *f*

capitation *n* capitación *f*; ∼ **tax** *n* impuesto *m* de capitación *or* por persona

captain *n* capitán *m*; ∼ **of industry** *n* capitán de empresa *m*

caption *n* (under illustration) pie *m*; (heading) encabezamiento *m*

captive *adj* cautivo; ∼ **audience** *n* audiencia cautiva *f*; ∼ **market** *n* mercado cautivo *m*

capture¹ *vt* (market) ganar; (attention, interest) captar, atraer

capture² *n* (of data) toma *f*

car *n* (automobile) coche *m*; (rail) AmE (*cf* ▸**carriage** BrE) vagón *m*; ∼ **allowance** *n* dietas de transporte *f pl*; ∼ **hire** *n* BrE (*cf* ▸**auto rental** AmE) alquiler de coches *m*; ∼-**hire operator** *n* BrE agente de coches de alquiler *mf*; ∼-**hire service** *n* BrE servicio de alquiler de coches *m*; ∼ **industry** *n* BrE (*cf* ▸**automotive industry** AmE) industria automotriz *f*; ∼ **insurance** *n* BrE (*cf* ▸**automobile insurance** AmE) seguro de automóviles *m*; ∼ **liability insurance** *n* BrE (*cf* ▸**automobile liability insurance** AmE) seguro de responsabilidad civil de automóviles *m*; ∼ **loan** *n* préstamo para automóvil *m*; ∼ **manufacturer** *n* fabricante de coches *mf*; ∼ **park** *n* BrE (*cf* ▸**parking lot** AmE) aparcamiento *m*, estacionamiento *m*; ∼ **pool** *n* consorcio de coches *m*; ∼ **registration** *n* registro de automóviles *m*; ∼ **tax** *n* impuesto sobre el automóvil *m*

CAR *abbr* (▸**compound annual rate**) TAC (tasa anual compuesta)

carat *n* (of gold) quilate *m*

carbon *n* carbón *m*; ~ **copy** *n* copia mecanográfica *f*; (in e-mail) copia carbón *f*; ~ **paper** *n* papel carbón *m*

card *n* tarjeta *f*; (index card) ficha *f*; (thin cardboard) cartulina *f*; **be on the** ~s (infrml) estar previsto; **give sb his/her** ~s BrE (infrml) poner a alguien de patitas en la calle (infrml); ~ **bin** *n* (Comp) casillero para fichas *m*; ~ **catalog** AmE, ~ **catalogue** BrE *n* caja de fichas *f*; ~ **file** *n*, ~ **index** *n* fichero *m*; ~ **issuer** *n* emisor(a) de la tarjeta *m,f*; ~ **punch** *n* perforadora de tarjetas *f*; ~ **reader** *n* lector de tarjetas *m*; ~ **sorter** *n* clasificadora de tarjetas *f*; ~ **swipe** *n* lector de tarjetas *m*

cardholder *n* titular de tarjeta de crédito *mf*; ~ **fee** *n* gastos del titular de la tarjeta *m pl*

care *n* cuidado *m*; ~ **of** casa de; **take** ~ **of sth** (be responsible for, deal with) ocuparse *or* encargarse de algo

career *n* carrera (profesional) *f*; ~ **advancement** *n* desarrollo profesional *m*; ~s **adviser** *n* consejero(-a) de salidas profesionales *m,f*, orientador(a) vocacional *m,f*; ~ **break** *n* interrupción de la carrera profesional *f*; ~ **change** *n* cambio de profesión *m*; ~ **development** *n* desarrollo profesional *m*; ~ **Development Loan** *n* BrE préstamo para el desarrollo profesional *m*; ~ **expectations** *n pl* expectativas profesionales *f pl*; ~ **goal** *n* meta profesional *f*; ~ **guidance** *n* guía de carrera *f*; ~ **ladder** *n* jerarquía profesional *f*; ~ **management** *n* gestión del desarrollo profesional *f*; ~s **officer** *n* consejero(-a) vocacional *m,f*, orientador(a) vocacional *m,f*; ~-**oriented** *adj* de orientación profesional; ~ **path** *n* trayectoria profesional *m*; ~ **planning** *n* proyecto de carrera *m*; ~ **prospects** *n pl* perspectivas de desarrollo profesional *f pl*

caret *n* signo de inserción *m*

cargo *n* carga *f*; ~ **aircraft** *n* avión *m* carguero *or* de carga; ~ **insurance** *n* seguro de mercancías *m*; ~ **liner** *n* buque de carga de línea regular *m*; ~ **plane** *n* BrE (*cf* ▸**freight plane** AmE) avión *m* carguero *or* de carga; ~ **ship** BrE, ~ **vessel** *n* BrE (*cf* ▸**freighter** AmE) barco de carga *m*, carguero *m*

caring *adj* (society) compasivo; (capitalism) benevolente

carnet *n* guía *f*; ~ **system** *n* (Imp/Exp) sistema de admisión temporal *m*

carr fwd *abbr* (▸**carriage forward**) porte debido

carriage *n* (transportation) porte *m*; (rail) BrE (*cf* ▸**car** AmE) vagón *m*; ~ **forward** porte debido; ~ **and insurance paid** porte y seguro pagados; ~ **paid** porte pagado; ~ **charge** *n* precio del acarreo *m*; ~ **expenses** *n pl* gastos de transporte *m pl*; ~ **return** *n* retorno de carro *m*

carried back *adj* arrastrado a cuentas anteriores

carried down *adj* suma y sigue, sustraído de cuenta

carried forward *adj* llevado *or* trasladado a cuenta nueva, suma y sigue

carried over *adj* llevado a cuenta nueva, suma y sigue

carrier *n* (Comp) soporte *m*; (transport company) transportista *mf*

carrot and stick *n* (infrml) (in negotiations) meta y cumplimiento

carr pd *abbr* (▸**carriage paid**) porte pagado

carry *vt* (goods, passengers) acarrear; (product, model) tener, vender; (risk) asumir; (guarantee) tener; (logo) traer; (balances) trasladar; (loss) arrastrar; ~ **information on sth/sb** llevar información sobre algo/alguien; ~ **a report** (newspaper) contener un informe; ~ **the whole department** llevar todo el peso del departamento; **carry back** *vt* traspasar al periodo anterior; **carry forward** *vt* traspasar al periodo futuro; **carry out** *vt* (order) cumplir; (plan, policy) llevar a cabo; (survey) hacer

carry-back *n* (Acc) existencias en efectivo *f pl*; (Tax) repercusión contra ejercicios anteriores *f*; ~ **loss** *n* pérdida traspasada al periodo anterior *f*, pérdidas con efecto retroactivo *f pl*; ~ **system** *n* sistema de repercusión contra ejercicios anteriores *m*

carry-forward *n* distribución en ejercicios posteriores *f*, saldo a cuenta nueva *m*; ~ **system** *n* sistema de repercusión contra ejercicios posteriores *m*

carrying: ~ **cable** *n* cable de suspensión *m*; ~ **cash** *n* efectivo útil *m*; ~ **charges** *n pl* gastos *m pl* incidentales *or* de corretaje en operaciones a crédito; ~ **cost** *n* coste *m* Esp *or* costo *m* AmL incidental; ~ **value** *n* valor neto contable *m*

carry-over *n* saldo anterior *m*; ~ **business** *n* negocio de remanente *m*; ~ **effect** *n* (Media) efecto remanencia del mensaje publicitario *m*; ~ **loss** *n* pérdida traspasada al año siguiente *f*; ~ **rate** *n* índice de remanente *m*; ~ **stocks** *n pl* remanente de mercaderías *f*

carte-blanche *n* carta blanca *f*

cartel *n* cartel *m*

cartelization *n* cartelización *f*

carve-out rule n norma establecida f

cascading adj (Comp) en cascada; ~ **style sheet** n hoja de estilo en cascada f; ~ **windows** n pl ventanas en cascada f pl

case n caso m; **argue one's own** ~ defender el propio caso; **as the** ~ **may be** según (sea) el caso; **the** ~ **for/against sth** los argumentos en pro/en contra de algo; **the** ~ **for the defence** BrE **/defense** AmE**/prosecution** la defensa/la acusación; **have a very strong** ~ (Law) tener muchas posibilidades de ganar un caso; **in any** ~ de todas formas, en cualquier caso; **in** ~ **of sth** en caso de algo; **in no/that** ~ en ningún/ese caso; **to be a** ~ **in point** servir de ejemplo; **make (out) a** ~ **(for sth)** presentar argumentos convincentes (para algo); ~ **history** n carpeta f or expediente m de antecedentes; ~ **law** n jurisprudencia f; ~ **notes** n pl expediente m; ~ **papers** n pl documentos del caso m pl; ~ **study** n estudio de caso m

CASE abbr (▶**computer-assisted software engineering**) ingeniería f de programas asistida por computadora AmL or ordenador Esp

casebound adj (book) de tapa dura, en cartoné

case-sensitive adj (Comp) receptivo

case-shift n (Comp) inversión f

cash¹ n dinero en efectivo m; (amount available immediately) liquidez f; (available capital) líquido m, dinero en metálico m; (funds) efectivo m; (legal tender) dinero m; **awash with** ~ (infrml) con sobrante de liquidez; **for** ~ al contado; **on a** ~-**received basis** previo pago al contado; **pay (in)** ~ pagar en metálico; **be short of** ~ andar justo (de dinero); ~ **account** n cuenta de caja f; ~ **advance** n anticipo en efectivo m; ~ **against documents** n pago contra documentación m; ~ **asset** n activo líquido m; ~ **balance** n saldo de caja m; ~ **before delivery** n pago m or cobro m antes de la entrega; ~ **benefit** n beneficio líquido m; ~ **bonus** n bonificación en efectivo f; (on bonds) dividendo extraordinario en efectivo m; ~ **book** n libro de caja m; ~ **box** n caja f; ~ **budget** n presupuesto de caja m; ~ **buyer** n comprador(a) al contado m,f; ~ **card** n tarjeta para cajero automático f; ~ **certificate** n certificado de caja m; ~ **collection** n acopio de efectivo m; ~ **commodity** n mercancía al contado f; ~ **contribution** n aportación dineraria f; ~ **control** n control de caja m; ~ **cow** n (jarg) fuente de ingresos f; ~ **credit** n crédito de caja m; ~ **crop** n cultivo comercial m; ~ **deficit** n déficit de caja m; ~ **desk** n caja f; ~ **discount** n descuento por pago al contado m; ~ **dispenser**, ~-**dispensing**

machine n cajero automático m; ~ **dividend** n dividendo en efectivo m; ~ **flow** n cash-flow m, flujo de caja m; ~ **flow accounting** n contabilidad del flujo de caja f; ~ **flow problem** n problema de liquidez m; ~ **holdings** n efectivo en caja m, disponibilidad en efectivo f; ~ **in advance** n pago adelantado m; ~ **in hand** n efectivo disponible m; **have** ~ **in hand** tener dinero en mano; ~ **inflow** n entrada en efectivo f; ~ **limit** n límite m de efectivo or de liquidez; ~ **machine** n BrE (cf ▶**automated teller machine** AmE) cajero automático m; ~ **management** n gestión f de caja or de liquidez; ~ **market** n mercado al contado m; ~ **office** n departamento de caja m; ~ **on delivery** n entrega contra reembolso f; ~ **outflow** n salida f de recursos líquidos or en efectivo; ~ **payment** n pago al contado m; ~-**poor** adj con efectivo insuficiente; ~ **price** n precio al contado m; ~ **purchase** n compra al contado f; ~ **receipts** n pl cobros m pl, entradas f pl de caja or de efectivo; ~ **register** n caja registradora f; ~ **requirement** n requerimiento de caja m; ~ **reserve** n reserva de efectivo f; ~-**rich** adj con sobrante de liquidez; ~ **risk** n riesgo de liquidez m; ~-**settled** adj pagado al contado; ~-**strapped** adj con falta de liquidez; ~ **surplus** n excedente de efectivo m, superávit m; ~ **surrender value** n (Ins) valor de rescate al contado m; ~ **transaction** n transacción al contado f; ~ **transfer** n transferencia f al contado or de efectivo; ~ **value** n valor en efectivo m; ~ **withdrawal** n retiro de fondos m; ~ **with order** n pago al hacer el pedido m

cash² vt (cheque) cobrar; **cash in** vt (bonds) hacer efectivo; **cash in on** vt (demand) aprovechar; **cash up** vi BrE hacer la caja

cashable adj canjeable

cash-and-carry n (shop) almacén de venta al por mayor m; (system) venta al por mayor f

cashback n servicio de retiro de fondos en una tienda

cashier n cajero(-a) m,f; ~'**s check** AmE n cheque bancario m; ~'**s department** n departamento de caja m

cashless: ~ **payment system** n sistema de pago no al contado m; ~ **society** n sociedad sin dinero f

cashpoint n BrE (cf ▶**automated teller machine** AmE) cajero automático m

cassette n casete f; ~ **tape recorder** n grabadora de casetes f

casual adj (labour, work, worker - not regular) eventual; (- seasonal) temporero

CAT *abbr* (▸**computer-assisted testing**) comprobación *f* asistida por computadora AmL *or* ordenador Esp; (▸**computer-assisted translation**) traducción *f* asistida por computadora AmL *or* ordenador Esp

catalogue[1] BrE, **catalog** AmE *n* catálogo *m*; ∼ **buying** *n* compra por catálogo *f*; ∼ **price** *n* precio de catálogo *m*

catalogue[2] BrE, **catalog** AmE *vt* catalogar

catalyst *n* catalizador *m*

catastrophe *n* catástrofe *f*; ∼ **cover** *n* cobertura contra catástrofe *f*; ∼ **reserve** *n* reserva para riesgos catastróficos *f*

catastrophic *adj* (loss) catastrófico

catch-all account *n* cuenta general *f*

catching-up hypothesis *n* hipótesis de actualización tecnológica *f*

catch line *n* (in advertising) título atrayente *m*

catch up *vi* ponerse al día

catch-up: ∼ **demand** *n* demanda adquirida *f*; ∼ **effect** *n* efecto de alcance *m*

categorization *n* clasificación *f*, categorización *f*

categorize *vt* clasificar

category *n* categoría *f*, clase *f*; ∼ **A share** *n* acción de clase A *f*

cater for *vt* atender a

catering *n* hostelería *f*, catering *m* Esp; ∼ **trade** *n* hostelería *f*

CATS *abbr* (▸**computer-assisted trading system**) sistema *m* de negociación asistido por computadora AmL *or* ordenador Esp

cats and dogs *n pl* (Stock) valores especulativos *m pl*

cause[1] *n* causa *f*; ∼ **and effect** causa y efecto; **you have no** ∼ **for complaint** *o* **to complain** no tienes motivos de queja; **there's no** ∼ **for concern** no hay por qué preocuparse; **show** ∼ (Law) fundamentar; **with (good)** ∼ con (toda la) razón; **without (good)** ∼ sin causa (justificada), sin motivo (justificado); ∼ **of action** *n* (Law) causa de acción *m*

cause[2] *vt* causar; ∼ **sb problems** causarle *or* ocasionarle problemas a alguien

caution *n* (carefulness) precaución *f*, cautela *f*; (Law) amonestación *f*; **act with** ∼ actuar con cautela *or* prudencia; **exercise extreme** ∼ extremar la precaución; **be let off with a** ∼ (Law) escapar con una amonestación; **throw** ∼ **to the winds** liarse la manta a la cabeza; ∼ **money** *n* cantidad depositada en garantía *f*

cautionary *adj* cautelar

cautious *adj* (person, approach) cauteloso; ∼ **optimism** *n* optimismo cauto *m*

caveat emptor *phr* por cuenta y riesgo del comprador

CBD *abbr* (▸**cash before delivery**) pago *m or* cobro *m* antes de la entrega

CBI *abbr* (▸**Confederation of British Industry**) ≈ CEOE (Confederación Española de Organizaciones Empresariales)

cc *abbr* (▸**carbon copy**) copia mecanográfica *f*; (in e-mail) cc (copia carbón)

CCA *abbr* (▸**current cost accounting**) contabilidad de costes Esp *or* costos AmL corrientes *f*

CCC *abbr* (▸**Commodity Credit Corporation**) Compañía de Crédito al Consumo *f*

CCI *abbr* (▸**Chamber of Commerce and Industry**) CCI (Cámara de Comercio e Industria)

CCL *abbr* (▸**customs clearance**) despacho *m* aduanero *or* de aduanas

CC/O *abbr* (▸**certificate of consignment/origin**) certificado de consignación/origen *m*

c-commerce *abbr* (▸**collaborative commerce**) comercio colaborativo *m*

CCT *abbr* (▸**common customs tariff**) tarifa exterior común *f*; (▸**compensating common tariff**) arancel común de compensación *m*

CCTV *abbr* (▸**closed-circuit television**) televisión en circuito cerrado *f*

cd *abbr* (▸**cum dividend**) con dividendo

c.d. *abbr* (▸**certificate of deposit**) c.d. (certificado de depósito)

c/d *abbr* (▸**carried down**) suma y sigue, sustraído de cuenta

CD *abbr* (▸**certificate of deposit**) CD (certificado de depósito); (▸**compact disc** BrE, ▸**compact disk** AmE) disco compacto *m*; (▸**customs declaration**) declaración de aduana *f*

CD-I *abbr* (▸**compact disc interactive** BrE, ▸**compact disk interactive** AmE) CD-I *m* (disco compacto interactivo)

CDL *abbr* (▸**Career Development Loan**) BrE préstamo para el desarrollo profesional *m*

CD-R *abbr* (▸**compact disc recordable** BrE, ▸**compact disk recordable** AmE) CD-R *m* (disco compacto registrable)

CD-ROM *abbr* (▸**compact disc read-only memory** BrE, ▸**compact disk read-only memory** AmE) CD-ROM *m* (disco compacto con memoria sólo de lectura)

CD-RW *abbr* (▸**compact disc rewritable** BrE, ▸**compact disk rewritable** AmE) CD-RW (disco compacto reescrible)

CE *abbr* (▸**Council of Europe**) CE (Consejo de Europa)

CEA *abbr* (▸**Commodity Exchange Authority**) *organismo oficial encargado de los mercados de materias primas*; (▸**Council** ⋯⋗

of Economic Advisers) Consejo *m or* Junta *f* de Asesores Económicos

cease 1 *vt* (production, publication) interrumpir, suspender; ~ **to exist** dejar de existir; ~ **to have effect** (contract) dejar de tener efecto

2 *vi* (production) interrumpirse; (work) detenerse

CEC *abbr* (▸**Commission of the European Communities**) Comisión de las Comunidades Europeas *f*

cedant *n* cedente *mf*

cede *vt* ceder

ceding company *n* compañía cedente *f*

Ceefax® *n* BrE *sistema de teletexto de la BBC*

CEIC *abbr* (▸**closed-end investment company**) sociedad de inversión cerrada *f*

ceiling *n* (upper limit) límite máximo *m*; ~ **price** *n* precio máximo *m*; ~ **rate** *n* (of futures) tasa máxima *f*, tipo máximo *m*; ~ **tax rate** *n* tipo impositivo máximo *m*

cell *n* (Comp) celda *f*; (Comms) célula *f*; ~ **organization** *n* organización celular *f*

cellphone *n* AmE (*cf* ▸**mobile phone** BrE) teléfono móvil *m*, móvil *m*

censor *vt* censurar

censorware *n* software de censura *f*

censure *vt* censurar

census *n* censo *m*

cent *n* centavo *m*

center AmE ▸**centre** BrE

central *adj* (office, planning) central; (area, location) céntrico; (problem) fundamental, principal; **play a** ~ **role** *o* **part in sth** jugar un papel primordial *or* fundamental en algo; ~ **bank** *n* banco central *m*; ~ **buying** *n* compra centralizada *f*; **C**~ **European Time** *n* hora centroeuropea *f*; ~ **government** *n* gobierno central *m*; ~ **processing unit** *n* unidad central de proceso *f*; **C**~ **Standard Time** *n* hora oficial en los estados centrales de los EE.UU. *f*

centralize *vt* centralizar

centralized *adj* (institution, money) centralizado

centrally *adv* centralmente; ~ **financed program** AmE, ~ **financed programme** BrE *n* programa *m* financiado centralmente *or* de financiación centralizada; ~ **planned economy** *n* economía de planificación centralizada *f*

centre BrE, **center** AmE *n* centro *m*; ~ **for Economic and Social Information** *n* *centro de información económica y social*, ≈ Centro de Investigaciones Sociológicas *m* Esp; ~ **spread** *n* anuncio en doble página central *m*

CEO *abbr* AmE (▸**chief executive officer**) presidente(-a) *m,f*

cert. *abbr* (▸**certificate**) certificado *m*

certificate¹ *n* certificado *m*; ~ **of consignment/origin** *n* certificado de consignación/origen *m*; ~ **of deposit** *n* certificado de depósito *m*; ~ **of incorporation** *n* certificado de organización de una sociedad *m*; ~ **of insurance** *n* certificado de seguro *m*; ~ **of origin** *n* certificado de origen *m*; ~ **of ownership** *n* certificado de propiedad *m*; ~ **of posting** *n* certificado de franqueo *m*; ~ **of quality** *n* certificado de calidad *m*; ~ **of registration** *n* (Law) certificado de registro *m*; (Patents) título de propiedad *m*; (Tax) certificado de inscripción *m*; ~ **of title** *n* certificado de título *m*; ~ **of use** *n* certificado de uso *m*; ~ **of value** *n* certificado de valor *m*; ~ **of value and origin** *n* certificado de valor y origen *m*

certificate² *vt* certificar

certification *n* certificación *f*; ~ **authority** *n* (Comp) autoridad de certificación *f*

certified *adj* (cheque, invoice, accounts, copy, statement) certificado; ~ **as a true copy** autentificado como copia fiel; ~ **accountant** *n* BrE (*cf* ▸**certified public accountant** AmE) censor(a) jurado(-a) de cuentas *m,f*, contador(a) público(-a) *m,f* AmL; ~ **declaration of origin** *n* declaración de origen certificada *f*; ~ **mail** *n* AmE (*cf* ▸**registered post** BrE) correo certificado *m*; ~ **public accountant** *n* AmE (*cf* ▸**certified accountant** BrE, ▸**chartered accountant** BrE) censor(a) jurado(-a) de cuentas *m,f* Esp, contador(a) público(-a) *m,f* AmL; ~ **true copy** *n* copia fiel y auténtica *f*

certifying officer *n* empleado(-a) diplomado(-a) *m,f*

CESI *abbr* (▸**Centre for Economic and Social Information**) *centro de información económica y social*, ≈ CIS Esp (Centro de Investigaciones Sociológicas)

cessation *n* cese *m*, cesación *f*; ~ **of interest** *n* BrE (Bank) cesación de interés *f*; ~ **of payment of premiums** *n* cesación de pago de las primas *f*

cession *n* cesión *f*; ~ **of portfolio** *n* cesión de cartera *f*

CET *abbr* (▸**Central European Time**) hora centroeuropea *f*

c/f *abbr* (▸**carried forward**) llevado *or* trasladado a cuenta nueva, suma y sigue

CF *abbr* (▸**carriage forward**) porte debido *m*

CFC *abbr* (▸**chlorofluorocarbon**) CFC (clorofluorocarbono)

CFO *abbr* (▶**chief financial officer**) director(a) de finanzas *m,f*

CFTC *abbr* (▶**Commodity Futures Trading Commission**) *agencia para la regulacion del mercado de futuros*

CGA *abbr* (▶**color/graphics adaptor** AmE, ▶**colour/graphics adaptor** BrE) CGA (adaptador color/gráficos)

CGT *abbr* (▶**capital gains tax**) impuesto sobre la plusvalía *m*

chain *n* cadena *f;* ~ **of command** *n* cadena de órdenes *f;* ~ **of distribution** *n* cadena de distribución *f;* ~ **feeding** *n* (Comp) alimentación de cadena *f;* ~ **mall** *n* AmE centro comercial de cadena *m;* ~ **production** *n* producción en serie *f;* ~**-store** *n* tienda de una cadena *f*

chair¹ *n* (of meeting, conference, company) presidente(-a) *m,f,* **be in the** ~ presidir

chair² *vt* (meeting, committee) presidir

chairman *n* presidente *m;* ~ **of the board** *n* presidente del consejo *m;* ~ **of the board of directors** *n,* ~ **of the board of management** *n* presidente *m* de la junta directiva *or* del consejo de administración; ~**'s brief** *n* informe del presidente *m;* ~ **and chief executive** *n* AmE (*cf* ▶**chairman and managing director** BrE) presidente y director ejecutivo *m;* ~ **elect** *n* presidente electo *m;* ~ **of the executive board,** ~ **of the executive committee** *n* presidente *m* de la junta directiva *or* del consejo de administración; ~ **and general manager** *n* presidente y director ejecutivo *m;* ~ **of the management board** *n* presidente de la junta directiva *m;* ~ **and managing director** *n* BrE (*cf* ▶**chairman and chief executive** AmE) presidente y director ejecutivo *m;* ~ **of the supervisory board** *n* presidente de la junta supervisora *m*

chairwoman *n* presidenta *f*

challenge¹ *n* (to rival, to one's abilities) desafío *m,* reto *m;* (to juror) recusación *f;* **issue a** ~ **to sb** desafiar *or* retar a alguien; **I like a** ~ me gusta todo lo que supone un reto *or* un desafío; **take up** *o* **accept a** ~ aceptar el reto *or* el desafío; **a serious** ~ **to her authority** un serio desafío a su autoridad

challenge² *vt* (rival) desafiar, retar; (authority, right, findings) cuestionar; (assumption, idea, theory) cuestionar, poner en entredicho *or* en duda *or* en tela de juicio; (juror) recusar; ~ **sb to do sth** desafiar a alguien a que haga algo; **this job will really** ~ **him** este trabajo realmente supondrá un reto para él

challenger *n* contendiente *m,f,* rival *m,f*

chamber *n* (for meetings, trials) cámara *f,* sala *f;* **C**~ **of Commerce** *n* Cámara de Comercio *f;* **C**~ **of Commerce and Industry** *n* Cámara de Comercio e Industria *f*

chance *n* (fate) casualidad *f,* azar *m;* (risk) riesgo *m;* (opportunity) oportunidad *f,* ocasión *f;* (likelihood) posibilidad *f,* chance *f;* **by** ~ por casualidad; **be in with a** ~ BrE (infrml) tener posibilidades; **leave nothing to** ~ no dejar nada al azar; **stand a** ~ **(of sth)** tener posibilidades (de algo); **take a** ~ correr un riesgo; **take one's** ~ aprovechar la oportunidad

Chancellor of the Exchequer *n* BrE ≈ Ministro(-a) de Economía y Hacienda *m,f* Esp

chancery *n* cancillería *f*

change¹ *n* cambio *m;* ~ **of address** *n* cambio de dirección *m;* ~ **of beneficiary** *n* cambio de beneficiario *m;* ~ **dispenser** *n* dispensador de cambio *m;* ~ **dump** *n* (Comp) volcado de modificaciones *m;* ~ **files** *n* (Comp) ficheros de movimiento *m pl;* ~ **management** *n* dirección *f or* gestión *f* del cambio; ~ **of ownership** *n* traspaso de propiedad *m*

change² *vti* cambiar; ~ **dollars into euros** cambiar dólares en euros; ~ **hands** (goods, business) cambiar de dueño

changeover *n* cambio *m*

channel¹ *n* canal *m;* **go through the proper** ~**s** canalizar debidamente, pasar por los canales debidos; **put sth through the proper** ~**s** canalizar algo debidamente; ~ **capacity** *n* capacidad de canal *f;* ~ **of communication** *n* canal de comunicación *m;* ~ **of distribution** *n* canal de distribución *m;* ~ **for orders** *n* canal de pedidos *m;* ~ **management** *n* dirección *f or* gerencia *f* de canales; ~ **of sales** *n* canal de ventas *m*

channel² *vt* canalizar; ~ **sth into sth** canalizar algo hacia algo; ~ **sth through sth** canalizar algo a través de algo

Channel Tunnel *n* Túnel del Canal de la Mancha *m*

chaos theory *n* teoría del caos *f*

chapel *n* BrE sección sindical *f*

CHAPS *abbr* BrE (▶**Clearing House Automatic Payments System**) sistema de pagos automáticos de compensación *m*

chapter *n* capítulo *m*

character *n* carácter *m;* ~ **array** *n* conjunto de caracteres *m;* ~ **card** *n* tarjeta de caracteres *f;* ~ **density** *n* densidad en caracteres *f;* ~ **file** *n* archivo de caracteres *m;* ~ **merchandising** *n* comercialización de un personaje *f;* ~ **set** *n* conjunto *m or* juego *m* de caracteres; ~ **string** *n* cadena de caracteres *f*

charge¹ *n* (financial) carga *f*, cargo *m*, gasto *m*; (commission) comisión *f*; (accusation) acusación *f*, cargo *m*; (responsibility) cargo *m*; **bring** *o* **press** ∼**s against sb** presentar cargos contra alguien; **be in** ∼ **of sth** ser responsable de algo, estar encargado de algo; **no** ∼**s for packing** embalaje gratuito; **take** ∼ **(of sth)** hacerse cargo (de algo); ∼ **account** *n* cuenta de cargo *f*; ∼ **buyer** *n* BrE (*cf* ▸**credit buyer** AmE) comprador(a) a crédito *m,f*; ∼ **card** *n* tarjeta de pago *f*; ∼ **hand** *n* capataz(a) *m,f*; ∼**s prepaid** *n pl* gastos prepagados *m pl*

charge² *vt* (person, price) cobrar; (fee, interest) cargar; ∼ **an expense to an account** cargar un gasto a una cuenta; ∼ **sth to expenses** cargar algo a la cuenta de la compañía; ∼ **sb with sth** acusar a alguien de algo

chargeable¹ *adj* (assets, capital gains) imponible; ∼ **to tax** imputable a impuestos; ∼ **staff** *n pl* personal a cargo *m*

charge-back *n* AmE cargo al usuario *m*

charge-off *n* disminución de un cargo *f*, extorno del activo *m*

charitable *adj* (donation, foundation, organization) benéfico

charity *n* organización benéfica *f*; ∼ **fundraising** *n* recaudación de fondos para beneficencia *f*

chart¹ *n* (diagram, graph) gráfico *m*; (table) tabla *f*; ∼ **of accounts** *n* cuadro de cuentas *m*, plan contable *m*

chart² *vt* (progress, changes) seguir atentamente

charter¹ *n* fletamento *m*, fletamiento *m*; (of flights) chárter *m*; ∼ **flight** *n* vuelo chárter *m*; ∼ **plane** *n* avión chárter *m*

charter² *vt* (vehicle) fletar

chartered: ∼ **accountant** BrE (*cf* ▸**certified public accountant** AmE) *n* censor(a) jurado(-a) de cuentas *m,f*, contador(a) público(-a) *m,f* AmL; ∼ **bank** *n* AmE banco registrado *m*; ∼ **financial consultant** *n* AmE consultor(a) financiero(-a) autorizado(-a) *m,f*

charterer *n* fletador(a) *m,f*

chartering *n* fletamento *m*, fletamiento *m*; ∼ **agent** *n* agente de fletes *mf*; ∼ **broker** *n* corredor(-a) fletador(-a) *m,f*

chartism *n* chartismo *m*

chartist *n* analista *mf* *or* grafista *mf* de bolsa

chat¹ *n* (Comp) charla *f*, chat *m*; ∼ **room** *n* sala de charla *f*

chat² *vi* charlar, chatear

chattels *n pl* bienes muebles *m pl*

cheap *adj* barato; ∼ **money** *n* dinero barato *m*

check¹ *vt* (facts information) comprobar, verificar; (accounts, bill) revisar, comprobar; (machine, product) inspeccionar; (quality) controlar; (passport, ticket) revisar, controlar; ∼ **items against a list** cotejar objetos con una lista; **check in** ⒈ *vt* (luggage) facturar ⒉ *vi* (for work) fichar (a la entrada); (at hotel) firmar el registro; (at airport) facturar el equipaje; **check off** *vt* AmE (*cf* ▸**tick off** BrE) marcar, ponerle visto a; **check (up) on** *vt* hacer averiguaciones sobre

check² *n* (payment method) AmE ▸**cheque** BrE; (in restaurant) AmE (*cf* ▸**bill** BrE) cuenta *f*; (test) control *m*, revisión *f*; (of machinery, equipment) inspección *f*; (verification) comprobación *f*; (stop, restraint) control *m*, freno *m*; **keep** *o* **hold in** ∼ controlar, contener; **keep a** ∼ **on** controlar, vigilar; **put a** ∼ **on** frenar; ∼ **bit** *n* (Comp) bitio de control *m*; ∼ **box** *n* AmE (*cf* ▸**box** BrE) casilla *f*, recuadro *m*; ∼ **character** *n* carácter de control *m*; ∼ **digit** *n* dígito de comprobación *m*

checkbook AmE ▸**chequebook** BrE

checker *n* verificador(a) *m,f*

check-in *n* (at airport) facturación *f*

checking account *n* AmE (*cf* ▸**current account** BrE) cuenta corriente *f*

checklist *n* lista de control *f*

check-off *n* cuota sindical *f*

checkout *n* caja *f*; ∼ **assistant** BrE, ∼ **clerk** AmE *n* cajero(-a) *m,f*

checkpoint *n* punto de control *m*

checkroom *n* AmE (*cf* ▸**left-luggage office** BrE) consigna *f*

checksum *n* (Comp) suma de verificación *f*

chemical *n* producto químico *m*; ∼ **industry** *n* industria química *f*; ∼ **works** *n* fábrica de productos químicos *f*

cheque BrE, **check** AmE *n* cheque *m*; **a** ∼ **for $500** un cheque (por valor) de 500 dólares; **a** ∼ **in favour** BrE *o* **favor** AmE **of sb** un cheque a favor de alguien; **a** ∼ **made to cash** un cheque para cobrar en efectivo; **make a** ∼ **payable to sb** extender un cheque a favor de alguien; **pay by** ∼ pagar con cheque; **a** ∼ **to the amount of** un cheque por la cantidad de *or* por valor de; ∼ **card** *n* tarjeta de cheque *f*; ∼ **clearing** *n* compensación de cheques *f*; ∼ **counterfoil** *n* matriz de cheque *f*; ∼ **issue** *n* emisión de cheques *f*; ∼ **requisition** *n* requerimiento *m or* solicitud *f* cheque; ∼ **signer** *n* firmante del cheque *mf*, girador(a) *m,f*; ∼ **stub** *n* talón de cheque *m*

chequebook BrE, **checkbook** AmE *n* chequera *f*, talonario *m*; ∼ **journalism** *n* (infrml) periodismo a golpe de talonario *m*

chief *n* jefe(-a) *m,f*; ∼ **accountant** *n* contable *m,f* Esp *or* contador(a) *m,f* AmL jefe(-a); ∼ **accounting officer** n director(a) de contabilidad m,f; ∼ **buyer** n jefe(-a) de compras m,f; ∼ **editor** n jefe(-a) de redacción m,f; ∼ **executive** n director(a) ejecutivo(-a) m,f; ∼ **executive officer** n AmE presidente(-a) m,f; ∼ **financial officer** n director(a) de finanzas m,f; ∼ **information officer** n director(a) general de información m,f, jefe(-a) de información m,f; (Comp) director(a) m,f or gerente mf de informática; ∼ **operating officer** n director(a) general (de operaciones) m,f; ∼ **supervisor** n supervisor(a) en jefe m,f; ∼ **value** n valor principal m

child n hijo(-a) m,f; ∼ **allowance** n AmE, ∼ **benefit** n BrE subsidio para familias con hijos m, asignación familiar f; ∼ **maintenance payment** n pago de la pensión alimenticia de los hijos m; ∼ **tax credit** n deducción familiar por los hijos f

childcare n puericultura f; ∼ **expense deduction** n deducción por cargas familiares f; ∼ **expenses** n gastos por cuidado de menores m pl; ∼ **facilities** n pl instalaciones de atención infantil f pl

child-centered adj AmE, **child-centred** BrE adj concebido en función del niño

children's court n Juzgado de Letras de Menores m

Chinese adj chino; ∼ **money** n BrE (jarg) pago efectuado en valores; ∼ **wall** n (Stock) pared china f

chip n (Comp) chip m, microplaqueta f; ∼-**based card** n tarjeta con circuito de memoria f; ∼ **card** n tarjeta con chip f

CHIPS abbr AmE (▸**Clearing House Interbank Payment System**) sistema de compensación y liquidación interbancario para divisas y Eurodólares

choice[1] n elección f; **have no** ∼ no tener más remedio; **a limited** ∼ una selección limitada; **make a** ∼ escoger

choice[2] adj selecto, escogido

chose n (Law) objeto en propiedad; ∼ **in action** n derecho de acción m

Christmas bonus n paga extraordinaria de Navidad f

chronic adj (unemployment) crónico

chunk vt (infrml) repartir; (Fin) despedazar; (Mgmnt) dividir

churn rate n proporción f de pérdida de clientes or de pérdida de abonados

CI&F abbr (▸**cost, insurance and freight**) CI&F (coste Esp or costo AmL, seguro y flete)

CIM abbr (▸**computer-integrated manufacture** o **manufacturing**) fabricación f or producción f integrada por computadora AmL or ordenador Esp

CIO abbr (▸**chief information officer**) director(a) general de información m,f, jefe(-a) de información m,f; (Comp) director(a) m,f or gerente mf de informática

CIP abbr (▸**carriage and insurance paid**) porte y seguro pagados

cipher n cifra f; ∼ **code** n código cifrado m

circle n círculo m; **to come full** ∼ volver al punto de partida

circuit n circuito m; (for judges) distrito judicial m; ∼ **breaker mechanism** n (Comp) mecanismo de sistema automatizado m

circular[1] adj circular; ∼ **flow** n flujo circular m; ∼ **letter** n circular f

circular[2] n circular f

circulate vt (information, news) divulgar

circulating adj (assets, capital) circulante; ∼ **medium** n instrumento de cambio m

circulation n circulación f; ∼ **breakdown** n colapso de circulación m; ∼ **department** n departamento de circulación m

circumstances n pl circunstancias f pl; **in** o **under the** ∼ dadas las circunstancias; **in** o **under no** ∼ en ningún caso; **owing to** ∼ **beyond our control** debido a circunstancias ajenas a nuestra voluntad

circumstancial evidence n prueba circunstancial f

citation n citación (judicial) f

cite vt citar, emplazar judicialmente

citizen n ciudadano(-a) m,f; **C**∼**s' Advice Bureau** n organización voluntaria británica que asesora legal o financieramente; ∼ **bonds** n pl bonos emitidos por las colectividades locales; **C**∼**'s Charter** n Carta de Derechos del Ciudadano f

citizenship n ciudadanía f

city n ciudad f; ∼ **centre** BrE n centro de la ciudad m; ∼ **hall** n AmE (cf ▸**town hall** BrE) Ayuntamiento m

City n BrE (London's financial district) City f

civil adj civil; ∼ **action** n demanda legal f, proceso civil m; ∼ **aviation** n aviación civil f; ∼ **code** n código civil m; ∼ **engineer** n ingeniero(-a) civil m,f; ∼ **law** n derecho civil m; ∼ **lawyer** n ≈ abogado(-a) civilista m,f; ∼ **penalty** n multa civil f; ∼ **rights** n pl derechos civiles m pl; **C**∼ **Rights Act** n AmE Ley de los Derechos Civiles f; ∼ **servant** n funcionario(-a) m,f; **C**∼ **Service** n BrE administración pública f; **C**∼ **Service Commission** n BrE comisión británica de funcionarios; ∼ **status** n registro civil m

claim[1] n (demand) demanda f, reclamación f; (assertion) afirmación f, pretensión f; (to right) derecho m; (for tax relief) petición f; **lay** ∼ **to sth** reivindicar algo; **put in a** ∼ presentar una reclamación; **settle a** ∼ **out of court** ···⟩

resolver una demanda de forma privada; ~**s
adjuster** *n* ajustador(a) de reclamaciones
m,f; ~**s department** *n* departamento de
reclamaciones *m*; ~ **for compensation** *n*
reclamación de compensación *f*; ~ **for
damages** *n* demanda por daños *f*; ~ **for
indemnification** *n* reclamación de
indemnización *f*; ~ **for refund** *n* solicitud
de devolución *f*; ~ **form** *n* formulario de
reclamación *m*; ~**s manager** *n* director(a)
m,f or jefe(-a) *m,f* de reclamaciones; ~
payment *n* pago de la reclamación *m*; ~**s
prevention** *n* prevención de reclamaciones
f; ~**s procedure** *n* procedimiento de
reclamación *m*; ~**s reserve** *n* reserva para
siniestros *f*; ~ **settlement** *n* liquidación *f*
de daños *or* de siniestro

claim² [1] *vt* reclamar; (right) reivindicar;
(tax deduction) solicitar; (social security benefits -
apply for) solicitar; (- receive) cobrar; (assert)
declarar(se), afirmar(se); ~ **an amount** (Tax)
exigir una cantidad; ~ **damages** (Ins) exigir
indemnización por daños; (Law) reclamar
daños y perjuicios; **you can ~ your
expenses back** puedes pedir que te
reembolsen los gastos; ~ **immunity from
tax** alegar exención fiscal; ~ **personal
exemption** reclamar una exención personal
[2] *vi* reclamar; **you can ~ on the
insurance** lo puedes reclamar por el seguro;
claim against *vt* reclamar a

claimant *n* demandante *mf*, reclamante *mf*

clarification *n* (of situation, reasons,
statement, policy) aclaración *f*

clarify *vt* (situation, reasons, statement, policy)
aclarar

class *n* clase *f*; (type) tipo *m*; (category)
categoría *f*; ~ **action** *n* acción popular *f*,
demanda colectiva *f*; ~ **war** *n* lucha de
clases *f*

class-A share *n* acción de clase A *f*

classic *adj* (example, method, strategy) clásico

classical *adj* (economics, model) clásico

classification *n* (of accounts, risks)
clasificación *f*

classified *adj* (categorized) clasificado;
(information, document) secreto, confidencial; ~
ad *n*, ~ **advertisement** *n* anuncio por
palabras *m*; ~ **directory** *n* guía clasificada
f; ~ **return** *n* (Tax) declaración clasificada *f*;
~ **stock** *n* acciones clasificadas *f pl*

classify *vt* (categorize) clasificar; (information,
document) clasificar como secreto

clause *n* cláusula *f*

clawback *n* desgravación por devolución
de impuestos *f*

Cld *abbr* (▸**cleared**) compensado

clean¹ *adj* (product, technology) limpio;
(Stock) sin garantía escrita; (Acc) sin
observaciones, sin salvedades; ~

acceptance *n* (Bank) aceptación *f* absoluta
or directa; ~ **bill** *n* letra limpia *f*; ~ **bill of
lading** *n* conocimiento de embarque limpio
m; ~ **hands** *n pl* manos limpias *f pl*,
conducta intachable *f*; ~ **letter of credit** *n*
carta *f* de crédito abierta *or* de crédito
simple; ~ **opinion** *n* (infrml) opinión *f* clara
or limpia; ~ **payment** *n* pago simple *m*; ~
record *n* historial limpio *m*; ~ **signature**
n firma clara y sin alteraciones *f*

clean² *vt* limpiar; **clean up** *vt* limpiar

cleaning-up operation *n* operación de
limpieza *f*

cleanup *n* limpieza *f*; ~ **campaign** *n*
campaña de limpieza *f*

clear¹ *adj* (explanation, instructions, idea) claro;
(profit, income) neto; (loss) líquido; (thinking)
lúcido; **in the ~** (free of debt) libre de deudas;
(not under suspicion) fuera de sospecha; (safe)
fuera de peligro; **make sth ~ (to sb)** dejar
algo claro (a alguien); **be ~ of debts** estar
libre de deudas; ~ **days** *n pl* días
completos *m pl*; ~ **title** *n* título (de
propiedad) limpio *m*

clear² [1] *vt* (cheque) compensar; (debt, funds,
securities, stock) liquidar; (wipe out, erase)
borrar; ~ **£1,000 on a deal** sacar mil libras
en una operación; ~ **customs** pasar por la
aduana; ~ **the market** equilibrar el
mercado; ~ **one's name** limpiar su nombre;
~ **sth with sb** obtener autorización de
alguien para hacer algo
[2] *vi* (cheque) ser compensado; **the cheque
took six days to ~** el cheque tardó seis días
en aparecer en cuenta; **clear up** *vt* (issue,
misunderstanding, doubts) aclarar

clearance *n* (permission) autorización *f*;
(from Customs) despacho de aduana *m*; (of
stock) liquidación *f*; **get *o* obtain ~ from sb**
conseguir *or* obtener autorización de
alguien; ~ **agent** *n* agente de despacho de
aduanas *mf*; ~ **inwards** BrE, ~ **inward** AmE
n despacho de entrada *m*; ~ **outwards** BrE,
~ **outward** AmE *n* despacho de salida *m*; ~
sale *n* liquidación *f*

cleared *adj* compensado; ~ **without
examination** (Imp/Exp) desaduanado sin
inspección; ~ **check** AmE, ~ **cheque** BrE *n*
cheque compensado *m*

clearer *n* (infrml) banco adscrito a la
*Cámara de Compensación bancaria de
Londres*

clearing *n* (of cheque) compensación *f*; (of
debt) compensación bancaria *f*; ~ **account**
n cuenta de compensación *f*; ~ **agent** *n*
agente de compensación *mf*; ~ **bank** *n*
*banco adscrito a la Cámara de Compensación
bancaria de Londres*; ~ **center** AmE, ~
centre BrE *n* centro de compensación *m*; ~
day *n* día de compensación *m*; ~ **entry** *n*

entrada en compensación *f*; ~ **house** *n*
cámara de compensación *f*; **C~ House
Automatic Payments System** *n* BrE
sistema de pagos automáticos de
compensación *m*; **C~ House Interbank
Payment System** *n* AmE *sistema de
compensación y liquidación interbancario
para divisas y Eurodólares*; ~ **system** *n*
régimen clearing *m*, sistema de
compensación *m*

clerical *adj* (personnel, staff, worker, work) de
oficina; (error) administrativo

clerk *n* oficinista *mf*, empleado(-a) *m,f*

click¹ ⊞ *vt* (key, mouse button) teclear
⊡ *vi* cliquear, hacer clic; **click on** *vt*
cliquear en, hacer clic en

click² *n* (Comp) clic *m*; **~s and mortar
company** *n* empresa que combina métodos
tradicionales con el Internet *f*; ~ **payment**
n pago al clic *m*; ~ **rate** *n* proporción de
clics *f*; ~ **stream** *n* secuencia de clics *f*

clickable *adj* (Comp) interactivo

click-through rate *n* (Comp) proporción
de clics *f*

client *n* cliente *mf*; ~ **account** *n* cuenta
de cliente *f*; ~ **base** *n* base de clientes *f*; ~
firm *n* firma cliente *f*; **~-led marketing
policy** *n* política de marketing dirigida por
el consumidor *f*; ~ **ledger** mayor de
clientes *m*; **~/server** *n* (Comp) cliente/
servidor *m*

clientele *n* clientela *f*

climb ⊞ *vi* (increase) aumentar
⊡ *vt* (stairs) subir; ~ **the promotion ladder**
subir en el escalafón; **climb down** *vi* dar
marcha atrás

climbdown *n* marcha *f or* vuelta *f* atrás

clip art *n* clip art *m*, galería de imágenes *f*

clipping *n* AmE (*cf* ▸**cutting** BrE) (from
newspaper) recorte *m*; ~ **service** *n* servicio
de documentación *m*

clock¹ *n* reloj *m*; ~ **card** *n* ficha de
control de asistencia *f*; ~ **rate** *n* (Comp)
velocidad de reloj *f*; ~ **signal** *n* (Comp)
señal de reloj *f*

clock² *vt* (speed, time) registrar, hacer;
clock in *vi* fichar (a la entrada); **clock off** *vi*
BrE (*cf* ▸**punch out** AmE) fichar (a la salida);
clock on *vi* BrE (*cf* ▸**punch in** AmE) fichar
(a la entrada); **clock out** *vi* fichar (a la salida)

clone¹ *n* clon *m*

clone² *vt* clonar

close¹ *adj* (cooperation, relationship, link,
connection) estrecho; (examination, inspection)
minucioso; **in ~ contact** en estrecho
contacto; **pay ~ attention to sth** prestar
mucha atención a algo; **work in ~
collaboration with sb** trabajar en estrecha
colaboración con alguien; ~ **company** *n*

BrE *sociedad controlada por un máximo de
cinco personas*

close² *n* cierre *m*; **buy/sell on ~** comprar/
vender al cierre; ~ **of business** *n* cierre *m*
de operaciones *or* del negocio; ~ **of the
market** *n* cierre del mercado *m*

close³ *vt* (deal, sale) cerrar; ~ **the gap**
acabar con el déficit; ~ **a position** cerrar
una posición; **close down** *vti* cerrar; **close
out** *vt* liquidar

closed *adj* cerrado; ~ **account** *n* cuenta *f*
cancelada *or* cerrada *or* saldada; ~ **circuit**
n circuito cerrado *m*; **~-circuit television**
n televisión en circuito cerrado *f*; ~
corporation *n* AmE compañía cerrada *f*; ~
economy *n* economía cerrada *f*; ~
position *n* posición cerrada *f*; ~ **question**
n pregunta cerrada *f*; ~ **season** *n* (in
broadcasting) temporada baja *f*; ~ **shop** *n*
monopolio sindical *m*; ~ **union** *n* *sindicato
de afiliación restringida o cerrada*

closed-end *adj* de capital fijo *or* limitado;
~ **fund** *n* fondo con número de acciones fijo
f; ~ **investment fund** *n* fondo de inversión
cerrado *f*; ~ **investment trust** *n* sociedad
inversora de capital limitado *f*; ~
mortgage *n* hipoteca *f* limitada *or* cerrada;
~ **mutual fund** *n* AmE sociedad de
inversión mobiliaria de capital fijo *f*

closedown *n* (of broadcasting) cierre de la
emisión *m*

closely *n* (connected, associated)
estrechamente; (examine) minuciosamente; **a
~-held corporation** una compañía
estrechamente controlada

close-out price *n* cambio de liquidación
m

closing *n* cierre *m*; **at ~** al cierre; ~
agreement *n* AmE (Tax) convenio final *m*;
~ **balance** *n* balance *m or* saldo *m* de
cierre; ~ **bid** *n* oferta definitiva *f*; ~ **date**
n fecha limite *f*; ~ **entry** *n* (Acc) asiento de
cierre *m*; ~ **inventory** *n* inventario *m* final
or de cierre; ~ **price** *n* cotización de cierre
f; ~ **purchase** *n* compra al cierre *f*; ~
quotation *n* cotización de cierre *f*; ~ **rate
method** *n* BrE (*cf* ▸**current rate method**
AmE) método del cambio de cierre *m*; ~ **sale**
n venta al cierre *f*; ~ **session** *n* sesión de
cierre *f*; ~ **statement** *n* saldo de cierre *m*;
~ **time** *n* hora de cierre *f*; ~ **trade** *n*
operación al cierre *f*; ~ **transaction** *n*
transacción de cierre *f*

closing-down costs *n pl* costes *m pl*
Esp *or* costos *m pl* AmL de clausura *or* de
liquidación

closure *n* cierre *m*

clothing *n* prendas de vestir *f pl*; ~
industry *n* industria de la confección *f*

clout n (informal) peso m, influencia f; **have** o **carry** ∼ tener peso or influencia

club class n clase club f

cluster n ramillete m; ∼ **analysis** n análisis de grupos m; ∼ **controller** n controlador(a) de grupo m,f; ∼ **sample** n muestra f por segmentos or por universos; ∼ **sampling** n muestreo m por segmentos or por universos

clustering n agrupación f

CM abbr (▶**configuration management**) gestión de la configuración f; (▶**content management**) gestión del contenido f

CMA abbr (▶**cash management account**) cuenta de administración de fondos f

cmdty abbr (▶**commodity**) (food product, raw material) bien m; (consumer good) bien de consumo m, mercancía f, producto m

CMS abbr (▶**World Bank Capital Markets System**) Sistema de Mercados de Capital del Banco Mundial m

CN abbr (▶**credit note**) nota de crédito f

C/N abbr (▶**cover note**) aviso de cobertura m

cnee abbr (▶**consignee**) consignatario m,f

cnmt abbr (▶**consignment**) remesa f

CNS abbr BrE (▶**continuous net settlement**) liquidación neta continua f

c/o abbr (▶**care of**) c/d (casa de); (▶**certificate of origin**) certificado de origen m

Co. abbr (▶**company**) Cía. (compañía); **and** ∼ y compañía

coal n carbón m; ∼ **industry** n industria del carbón f; ∼ **mining** n minería del carbón f

coalition n coalición f; ∼ **government** n gobierno de coalición m

coastal adj (trading) costero; (pollution) de las costas

coasting n cabotaje m

coaxial cable n cable coaxial m

COBOL abbr (▶**Common Business Oriented Language**) COBOL (lenguaje común orientado a la gestión y los negocios)

co-branding n el uso de los logotipos de dos empresas en un sitio para aparentar una coinversión

COD abbr (▶**cash on delivery**) entrega contra reembolso f

code¹ n código m; ∼ **of accounts** n código de cuentas m; ∼ **address** n dirección codificada f; ∼ **of arbitration** n código de arbitraje m; ∼ **box** n casilla del código f; ∼ **check** n comprobador de código m; ∼ **of conduct** n código deontológico m; ∼ **of ethics** n código de ética m; ∼ **name** n nombre codificado m; ∼ **of practice** n

código de práctica m; (Law) código de conducta m; ∼ **of procedure** n código de procedimiento m

code² vt (Comp) codificar

codec n (Comp) codificador-descodificador m

codetermination n codeterminación f, cogestión f; ∼ **rights** n pl derechos de cogestión m pl

codicil n codicilo m

coding n codificación f; ∼ **of accounts** n codificación de cuentas f; ∼ **error** n error de codificación m; ∼ **system** n sistema de codificación m

co-director n codirector(a) m,f

coefficient n coeficiente m; ∼ **of association** n coeficiente de asociación m; ∼ **of contingency** n coeficiente de contingencia m

coemption n acaparamiento de toda la oferta m

co-finance vt cofinanciar

co-financing n cofinanciación f

cognition n cognición f

cognitive n (powers, behaviour, process, learning) cognitivo; ∼ **ergonomics** n pl ergonomía cognitiva f

cohesion n cohesión f; ∼ **fund** n fondo de cohesión m

coin n moneda f

coinage n (coins) monedas f pl; (system) sistema monetario m; (minting) acuñación f

coincide vi coincidir

coinsurance n coaseguro m, coseguro m

coinsured adj coasegurado

coinsurer n coasegurador(a) m,f

col. abbr (▶**column**) columna f

COLA abbr (▶**cost-of-living adjustment**) AmE ajuste m del coste Esp or costo AmL de vida

cold adj frío; ∼ **boot** n (Comp) arranque en frío m; ∼ **call** n visita sin preparación previa f; ∼ **calling** n visitas o llamadas de venta sin cita; ∼ **canvass** n puerta a puerta f; ∼ **mailing** n envío de folletos por correo sin preparación previa; ∼ **start** n (Comp) arranque en frío m; ∼ **storage** n almacenamiento en cámara frigorífica m; **put sth into** ∼ **storage** (plan, project) dejar algo en suspenso; ∼ **type** n composición no tipográfica f

collaborate vi colaborar

collaboration n colaboración f

collaborative adj (action) colaborador; (effort) común; (work) en colaboración; ∼ **commerce** n comercio colaborativo m

collaborator n colaborador(a) m,f

collage n collage m

collapse¹ *n* (of prices, currency, market) caída en picado *f*; (of company) quiebra *f*; (of plan) fracaso *m*

collapse² *vi* (prices, currency, market) caer en picado; (company) quebrar, ir a la bancarrota; (system) derrumbarse

collapsible company *n* BrE, **collapsible corporation** *n* AmE sociedad defraudadora de impuestos *f*

collar *n* (Econ) banda *f*; (Stock) contrato de cobertura *m*

collate *vt* (compare) cotejar; (merge) intercalar

collateral *n* colateral *m*; ∼ **acceptance** *n* aceptación colateral *f*; ∼ **assignment** *n* cesión de garantía *f*; ∼ **bill** *n* cuenta *f* colateral *or* con garantía prendaria; ∼ **loan** *n* BrE (*cf* ▸**Lombard loan** AmE) empréstito con garantía *m*, préstamo *m* con caución *or* con garantía; ∼ **security** *n* garantía adicional *f*; ∼ **trust bond** *n* bono *m* con garantía prendaria *or* de garantía colateral; ∼ **trust certificate** *n* certificado con garantía prendaria *m*

collateralize *vt* garantizar

collateralized *adj* garantizado; ∼ **preferred share** *n* acción preferente con garantía prendaria *f*

collating sequence *n* (Comp) secuencia de intercalación *f*

collation *n* (comparison) cotejo *m*; (merging) intercalación *f*

collator *n* compaginadora de documentos *f*, interclasificadora *f*; ∼ **code** *n* código de cotejo *m*; ∼ **number** *n* número de cotejo *m*

colleague *n* compañero(-a) *m,f*

collect *vt* (debt, commission, premium) cobrar; (payment) recaudar; (statistics, information) reunir, recoger; ∼ **sums due** recaudar las sumas vencidas

collect call *n* AmE (*cf* ▸**reverse-charge call** BrE) llamada a cobro revertido *f*

collected and delivered *adj* recogido y entregado; (cheque, draft) cobrado y entregado

collectible *adj* cobrable

collecting: ∼ **agency** *n* banco de cobro *m*; ∼ **bank** *n* banco de cobranzas *m*; ∼ **charge** *n* cargo recaudador *m*

collection *n* (of rent, cheques, debts) cobro *m*; (of taxes, customs duties) recaudación *f*; (of premiums) cobro *m*, cobranza *f*; (of money) colecta *f*; (of objects) colección *f*; (of evidence) recopilación *f*; (of mail, refuse) recogida *f*; for ∼ al cobro; ∼ **against documents** *n* cobro contra documentación *m*; ∼ **agent** *n* (Tax) inspector(a) recaudador(a) *m,f*; ∼ **agreement** *n* (Tax) acuerdo de cobro *m*; ∼ **charge** *n* cargo por cobranza *m*; ∼ **costs**

n pl costes *m pl* Esp *or* costos *m pl* AmL de recaudación; ∼ **letter** *n* carta de cobro *f*; ∼**-only check** AmE, ∼**-only cheque** BrE *n* cheque pagadero sólo por ventanilla *m*

collective *adj* (agreement, insurance) colectivo; ∼ **bargaining** *n* negociación colectiva *f*; ∼ **bargaining agreement** *n* contrato colectivo *m*; ∼ **dismissal** *n* BrE despido colectivo *m*

collectively *adv* colectivamente

collector *n* cobrador(a) *m,f*; ∼ **of customs** *n* administrador(a) de aduanas *m,f*; ∼ **of taxes** *n* recaudador(a) de contribuciones *m,f*

collision *n* colisión *f*; ∼ **clause** *n* cláusula de colisión *f*; ∼ **coverage** *n* cobertura de colisión *f*; ∼ **insurance** *n* seguro de colisión *m*

colloquium *n* coloquio *m*

collusion *n* colusión *f*

co-locate *vt* (Comp) co-localizar

co-location *n* (Comp) colocalización *f*

colony *n* colonia *f*

colour BrE, **color** AmE *n* color *m*; ∼ **display** *n* pantalla a color *f*; ∼**/graphics adaptor** *n* adaptador color/gráficos *m*; ∼ **separation** *n* separación de colores *f*; ∼ **supplement** suplemento en color *m*

column *n* columna *f*; ∼ **centimeters** AmE, ∼ **centimetres** BrE *n pl* centímetros de columna *m pl*; ∼ **heading** *n* encabezamiento de columna *m*; ∼ **inches** *n pl* pulgadas de columna *f pl*

columnar journal *n* diario en columnas *m*

co-manager *n* codirector(a) *m,f*, director(a) adjunto(-a) *m,f*

COMB *abbr* (▸**combination**) combinación *f*

combat *vt* (unemployment, drug trafficking) combatir

combination *n* combinación *f*

combine¹ **[1]** *vt* (elements) combinar; (companies) fusionar; ∼ **sth with sth** combinar algo con algo **[2]** *vi* (elements) combinarse; (companies) fusionarse; **combine with** *vt* (company) fusionarse con

combine² *n* (of companies) asociación *f*

combined *adj* (amount, premium, mark) combinado; ∼ **balance sheet** *n* balance de situación combinado *m*; ∼ **committee** *n* comité mixto *m*; ∼ **financial statement** *n* estado financiero combinado *m*; ∼ **issue** *n* (Media) edición combinada *f*; ∼ **mark** *n* (Patents) marca mixta *f*; ∼ **statement of income** *n* cuenta de pérdidas y ganancias combinada *f*; ∼ **transport** *n* transporte combinado *m*

come *vi* venir, acudir; **come along** *vi* (progress) ir, marchar; **come before** *vt* (court, judge) comparecer ante; **come off** *vi* tener éxito; **come to** *vt* (amount to) equivaler a; (bill) ascender a

comeback *n* vuelta *f*, retorno *m*; **make** *o* **stage a** ∼ reaparecer en escena

COMEX *abbr* (▶**Commodities Exchange of New York**) *mercado de contratación de derivados de Nueva York*

comfort letter *n* carta *f* de apoyo *or* de recomendación

coming *adj* venidero

comm. *abbr* (▶**commission**) comisión *f*

command[1] *n* mandato *m*; (Comp) comando *m*; ∼ **economy** *n* economía *f* dirigida *or* planificada; ∼ **file** *n* archivo de comandos *m*; ∼ **key** *n* tecla de comando *f*; ∼ **line** *n* línea de comandos *f*

command[2] *vt* (order) mandar; (price) imponer

commencement *n* (of insurance cover, policy) inicio *m*

commensurate *adj* proporcionado; ∼ **with sth** en proporción con algo; ∼ **charge** *n* (EU) cargo proporcional *m*

comment[1] *n* comentario *m*; **no** ∼ sin comentarios; **pass** ∼ **on sth** hacer comentarios sobre algo

comment[2] *vi* hacer comentarios; ∼ **on sth** hacer comentarios sobre algo

commentary *n* comentario *m*

commerce *n* comercio *m*; ∼ **clause** *n* cláusula comercial *f*; ∼ **site** *n* (on Internet) sitio comercial *m*

commercial[1] *adj* (activity, strategy, lease, loan) comercial; **no** ∼ **value** sin valor comercial; ∼ **accounts** *n pl* cuentas de comercio *f pl*; ∼ **agent** *n* representante de comercio *mf*; ∼ **artist** *n* dibujante publicitario(-a) *m,f*; ∼ **bank** *n* banco *m* comercial *or* mercantil; ∼ **bill** *n* AmE letra de cambio comercial *f*; ∼ **break** *n* (on television, radio) cuña publicitaria *f*; ∼ **broker** *n* AmE corredor(a) de comercio *m,f*; ∼ **center** AmE, ∼ **centre** BrE *n* centro comercial *m*; ∼ **concern** *n* negocio comercial *m*; ∼ **designer** *n* diseñador(a) comercial *m,f*; ∼ **director** *n* director(a) *m,f* *or* jefe(-a) *m,f* comercial; ∼ **establishment** *n* fondo de comercio *m*; ∼ **law** *n* derecho mercantil *m*; ∼ **lawyer** *n* ≈ abogado(-a) mercantilista *m,f*; ∼ **letting** *n* BrE alquiler comercial *m*; ∼ **manager** *n* director(a) *m,f* *or* jefe(-a) *m,f* comercial; ∼ **paper** *n* papel comercial *m*; ∼ **property** *n* propiedad comercial *f*; ∼ **radio** *n* radio comercial *f*; ∼ **sample** *n* muestra comercial *f*; ∼ **target** *n* objetivo de ventas *m*; ∼ **television** *n* televisión comercial *f*; ∼ **traveler** AmE,

∼ **traveller** BrE *n* viajante de comercio *mf*; ∼ **treaty** *n* tratado comercial *m*; ∼ **vehicle** *n* vehículo comercial *m*

commercial[2] *n* anuncio *m*

commercialism *n* comercialidad *f*

commercialization *n* comercialización *f*

commercialize *vt* comercializar

commercially *adv* comercialmente; **be** ∼ **available** estar a la venta; ∼ **viable** comercialmente viable

commingling *n* mezcla *f*

commissary *n* AmE comisario *m*; ∼ **goods** *n pl* productos de economato *m pl*

commission[1] *n* comisión *f*; **a basic salary plus** ∼ un sueldo base más (la) comisión; **receive 5%** ∼ recibir el 5% de comisión *or* una comisión del 5%; **sell sth on** ∼ vender algo a comisión; ∼ **account** *n* cuenta de comisión *f*; ∼ **agent** *n* comisionista *mf*; ∼ **broker** *n* comisionista (en bolsa de comercio) *mf*; **C**∼ **of the European Communities** *n* Comisión de las Comunidades Europeas *f*; ∼ **house** *n* casa de comisiones *f*; ∼ **of inquiry** *n* comisión investigadora *f*; ∼ **merchant** *n* comisionista *mf*; ∼ **rate** *n* tasa de comisión *f*; ∼ **salesman** *n* vendedor(a) a comisión *m,f*

commission[2] *vt* (report) encargar

commissioner *n* liquidador(a) de averías *m,f*; ∼ **of banking** *n* AmE (*cf* ▶**bank examiner** BrE) inspector(a) oficial de bancos *m,f*; **C**∼**s of Customs and Excise** *n* Comisarios de Aduanas y Contribuciones Indirectas *m pl*; ∼ **of deeds** *n* funcionario(-a) notarial *m,f*; **C**∼ **of the Inland Revenue** *n* BrE inspector(a)-recaudador(a) de la Administración Fiscal *m,f*

commit *vt* (crime, error) cometer; (funds, time, resources) asignar, consignar; ∼ **sth/sb to sth** entregar algo/a alguien a algo; ∼ **sb to trial** remitir a alguien al tribunal; ∼ **oneself to (doing) sth** comprometerse a (hacer) algo

commitment *n* compromiso *m*; **meet one's** ∼**s** hacer frente a sus compromisos *or* obligaciones; **there is no** ∼ **to buy** no hay (ninguna) obligación *or* ningún compromiso de comprar; ∼ **fee** *n* comisión de compromiso *f*

committed costs *n pl* costes *m pl* Esp *or* costos *m pl* AmL obligados

committee *n* comité *m*, comisión *f*; **be on a** ∼ ser miembro de un comité *or* una comisión; ∼ **of inquiry** *n* comisión investigadora *f*; ∼ **of inspection** *n* comité de inspección *m*; ∼ **meeting** *n* reunión del comité *f*; ∼ **member** *n* miembro del comité *m*

commodity *n* (food product, raw material) bien *m*; (consumer good) bien de consumo *m*, mercancía *f*, producto *m*; ~ **broker** *n* corredor(a) *m,f* de mercancías *or* de productos *m,f*; ~ **cartel** *n* cartel de productos *m*; ~ **credit** *n* crédito de mercancía *m*; **C~ Credit Corporation** *n* AmE Compañía de Crédito al Consumo *f*; ~ **currency** *n* dinero de mercancía *m*; ~ **exchange** *n* bolsa *f* de comercio *or* de contratación; **C~ Exchange Authority** *n* organismo oficial encargado de los mercados de materias primas; **Commodities Exchange of New York** *n* mercado de contratación de derivados de Nueva York; ~ **futures** *n pl* futuros sobre productos básicos *m pl*; ~ **futures market** *n* mercado de productos a futuro; **C~ Futures Trading Commission** *n* AmE agencia para la regulación de mercados futuros; **commodities index** *n* índice de mercaderías *m*; ~ **market** *n* bolsa de contratación *f*; ~ **pricing** *n* fijación de precios de los productos básicos *f*; ~ **tax** *n* impuesto sobre mercancías *m*; ~ **trading** *n* comercio de productos *m*

common *adj* común; **by** ~ **consent** de común acuerdo; **C~ Agricultural Policy** *n* Política Agrícola Común *f*; **C~ Business Oriented Language** *n* lenguaje común orientado a la gestión y los negocios *m*; ~ **carrier** *n* empresa de transportes *f*; ~ **currency** *n* moneda común *f*; ~ **customs tariff** *n* tarifa exterior común *f*; ~ **denominator** *n* denominador común *m*; ~ **directive** *n* directiva *f or* directriz *f* común; ~ **dividend** *n* dividendo ordinario *m*; ~ **law** *n* derecho angloamericano *m*; ~**-law spouse** *n* cónyuge de hecho *mf*; ~**-law wife** *n* esposa de hecho *f*; **C~ Market** *n* (obs) mercado común *m* (obs); ~ **par value** *n* valor nominal común *m*; ~ **pricing** *n* fijación común de precios *m*; ~ **revenue** *n* ingreso habitual *m*; ~ **sense** *n* sentido común *m*; ~ **share certificate** *n* BrE (*cf* ▸**common stock certificate** AmE) certificado de acción ordinaria *m*; ~ **share dividend** *n* BrE (*cf* ▸**common stock dividend** AmE) dividendo de acción ordinaria *m*; ~ **shareholder** *n* BrE (*cf* ▸**common stockholder** AmE) accionista ordinario(-a) *m,f*; ~ **shares** *n pl* BrE (*cf* ▸**common stock** AmE) acciones ordinarias *f pl*; ~ **stock** *n* (*cf* ▸**common shares** BrE) acciones ordinarias *f pl*; ~ **stock certificate** *n* AmE (*cf* ▸**common share certificate** BrE) certificado de acción ordinaria *m*; ~ **stock dividend** *n* AmE (*cf* ▸**common share dividend** BrE) dividendo de acción ordinaria *m*; ~ **stockholder** *n* AmE (*cf* ▸**common shareholder** BrE) accionista ordinario(-a) *m,f*

Commons *n pl* BrE Cámara de los Comunes *f*

Commonwealth *n* Commonwealth *f*; ~ **Preference** *n* BrE *preferencias arancelarias para países de la Commonwealth*

comms *abbr* (▸**communications**) comunicaciones *f pl*

communal *adj* (ownership) comunal

commune *n* comuna *f*

communicate ① *vt* comunicar; ~ **sth to sth/sb** comunicar algo a algo/alguien ② *vi* comunicarse; ~ **with sb** comunicarse con alguien

communication *n* (act, message) comunicación *f*; **be in/get into** ~ **(with sb)** estar/ponerse en comunicación *or* en contacto (con alguien); ~ **barrier** *n* barrera de comunicación *f*; ~ **gap** *n* vacío de comunicación *m*; ~ **link** *n* enlace de comunicación *m*; ~ **management** *n* dirección de las comunicaciones *f*; ~ **media** *n* medios de comunicación *m pl*; ~ **mix** *n* combinación de estrategias de comunicación *f*; ~**s network** *n* red de comunicaciones *f*; ~ **objective** *n* objetivo de comunicación *m*; ~**s satellite** *n* satélite de comunicaciones *m*; ~**s skills** *n pl* técnicas de comunicación *f pl*; ~ **strategy** *n* estrategia de comunicación *f*; ~**(s) technology** *n* tecnología de la comunicación *f*; ~ **theory** *n* teoría de la comunicación *f*

communiqué *n* comunicado *m*

communism *n* comunismo *m*

communist *adj* comunista

community *n* comunidad *f*; **C~ Action** *n* (EU) Acción Comunitaria *f*; **C~ Aid** *n* (EU) Ayuda Comunitaria *f*; ~ **association** *n* asociación de vecinos *f*; **C~ budget** *n* (EU) presupuesto comunitario *m*; ~ **debt** *n* deuda conjunta *f*; **C~ goods** *n pl* (EU) productos comunitarios *m pl*; ~ **of goods** *n* comunidad de bienes *f*; **C~ imports** *n* (EU) importaciones de la Comunidad *f pl*; ~ **of interests** *n* comunidad de intereses *f*; ~ **network** *n* red comunitaria *f*; **C~ Programme** BrE *n* (EU) programa comunitario *m*; ~ **property** *n* bienes gananciales *m pl*

commutability *n* conmutabilidad *f*

commutable *adj* conmutable

commutation *n* conmutación *f*; ~ **right** *n* derecho de conmutación *m*; ~ **ticket** *n* AmE abono *m*

commute ① *vt* (sentence, punishment, payment) conmutar ② *vi* viajar todos los días (entre el lugar de residencia y el de trabajo)

commuter *n* (person) viajero(-a) abonado(-a) *m,f*; (aircraft) conmutador *m*; ∼ **airline** *n* línea aérea de cabotaje *f*; ∼ **belt** *n* cercanías *f pl*; ∼ **suburb** *n* ciudad dormitoria *f*; ∼ **tax** *n* AmE impuesto sobre los viajeros de abono *m*; ∼ **train** *n* tren de cercanías *m*

compact disc BrE, **compact disk** AmE *n* disco compacto *m*; ∼ **interactive** *n* disco compacto interactivo *m*; ∼ **recordable** *n* disco compacto registrable *m*; ∼ **read-only memory** *n* disco compacto con memoria sólo de lectura *m*; ∼ **rewritable** *n* disco compacto reescribible *m*

company *n* compañía *f*, empresa *f*; ∼ **accounts** *n pl* cuentas *f pl* empresariales *or* de la empresa; **Companies Act** *n* BrE (*cf* ▸**Companies Bill** AmE) Decreto *m or* Ley *f* de Sociedades Mercantiles; ∼ **benefits** *n pl* subsidio de la compañía *m*; **Companies Bill** *n* AmE (*cf* ▸**Companies Act** BrE) Decreto *m or* Ley *f* de Sociedades Mercantiles; ∼ **car** *n* (fringe benefit) coche de la empresa *m*; ∼ **credit card** *n* tarjeta de crédito de empresa *f*; ∼ **director** *n* director(a) de empresa *m,f*; ∼ **executive** *n* ejecutivo(-a) de la compañía *m,f*; ∼ **law** *n* derecho de sociedades *m*; ∼ **lawyer** *n* ≈ abogado(-a) mercantilista *m,f*; ∼**-level agreement** *n* BrE acuerdo del ámbito de una empresa *m*; ∼ **logo** *n* logo *m or* logotipo *m* de la compañía; ∼ **manager** *n* director(a) de la compañía *m,f*; ∼ **meeting** *n* reunión de empresa *f*; ∼ **model** *n* modelo de empresa *m*; ∼ **performance** *n* resultado de la compañía *m*; ∼ **philosophy** *n* filosofía de la empresa *f*; ∼ **policy** *n* política de la empresa *f*; ∼ **profile** *n* perfil de la empresa *m*; ∼ **seal** *n* sello de la empresa *m*; ∼ **secretary** *n* secretario(-a) *m,f* general *or* de la empresa; ∼ **strategy** *n* estrategia de la empresa *f*; ∼ **structure** *n* estructura de la empresa *f*; ∼ **tax** *n* impuesto de sociedades *m*; ∼ **town** *n ciudad cuya economía depende de una sola empresa*; ∼ **union** *n* sindicato *m* blanco AmL *or* de empresa Esp

comparability *n* comparabilidad *f*

comparable *adj* (salary, situation) comparable, equiparable; ∼ **to** *o* **with sth** comparable *or* equiparable a algo; ∼ **basis** *n* (of reporting) base comparable *f*; ∼ **worth** *n* valor comparable *m*

comparative *adj* (value, analysis, advertising) comparativo; (relative) relativo; ∼ **balance sheet** *n* balance de situación comparativo *m*; ∼ **statement** *n* balance *m or* estado *m* de situación comparativo

comparatively *adv* comparativamente

compare *vt* comparar; ∼ **sth to** *o* **with sth** comparar algo con algo

comparison *n* comparación *f*; ∼ **shopping** *n* compra comparativa *f*; ∼ **test** *n* prueba de comparación *f*

compartmentalization *n* compartimentación *f*

compartmentalize *vt* compartimentalizar

compatibility *n* compatibilidad *f*

compatible *adj* compatible

compensate *vt* compensar; (Law) indemnizar; ∼ **sb for sth** compensar a alguien por algo; ∼ **sb for damage** indemnizar a alguien por daños y perjuicios

compensating *adj* (balance, depreciation, loss) compensatorio; (error) de compensación

compensation *n* compensación *f*; **in** ∼ **for sth** en compensación por algo; ∼ **fee** *n* tarifa de compensación *f*; ∼ **for industrial injury** *n* indemnización por accidente laboral *f*; ∼ **for loss or damage** *n* compensación por pérdida o daño *f*; ∼ **fund** *n* fondo de compensación *m*; ∼ **settlement** *n* acuerdo *m* de compensación *or* de indemnización; ∼ **stocks** *n pl* BrE acciones de compensación *f pl*; ∼ **tax** *n* impuesto de compensación *m*

compensatory *adj* (damages, finance, fiscal policy) compensatorio; (levy) compensador

compete *vi* competir; **compete against** *vt* competir contra

competence *n* competencia *f*

competency of court *n* jurisdicción del tribunal *f*

competent *adj* (person) competente; ∼ **party** *n* (to contract) parte cualificada *f*

competing *adj* (bid, offer, company, product) rival

competition *n* competencia *f*; ∼ **act** *n* ley de competencia *f*; ∼ **policy** *n* política de competencia *f*

competitive *adj* (strategy, pricing, rate, trading) competitivo; (salary, pay) bueno; ∼ **advantage** *n* ventaja competitiva *f*; **have a** ∼ **advantage over sb** competir ventajosamente con alguien; ∼ **bidding** *n* licitación pública *f*; ∼ **disadvantage** *n* desventaja competitiva *f*; ∼ **edge** *n* ventaja competitiva *f*; ∼ **intelligence** *n* información sobre los competidores *f*; ∼ **tendering** *n* licitación *f or* oferta *f* competitiva

competitiveness *n* competitividad *f*

competitor *n* competidor(a) *m,f*; ∼ **analysis** *n* análisis de competidores *m*

compile *vt* compilar

compiler *n* compilador(a) *m,f*

complain *vi* quejarse; ∼ **to sb about sth** quejarse a alguien de algo

complaint *n* queja *f*; **have no cause** *o* **grounds for** ~ no tener motivo de queja; **a letter of** ~ una carta de reclamación; **make** *o* **lodge a** ~ presentar una queja por vías oficiales; ~**s procedure** *n* procedimiento de reclamación *m*

complement *n* complemento *m*

complementary *adj* (product, technology, demand) complementario

complete[1] *adj* (entire) completo, total; (finished) cumplido, ejecutado; ~ **audit** *n* auditoría *f* completa *or* total; ~ **refund** *n* reembolso total *m*

complete[2] *vt* (make entire) completar; (finish) cumplir; ~ **a sale** cerrar una venta

completed *adj* consumado, terminado

completely *adv* completamente

completeness *n* integridad *f*, totalidad *f*

completion *n* conclusión *f*, terminación *f*; BrE (in house purchase) *formalización del contrato de compraventa f*; **bring sth to** ~ terminar algo, llevar algo a término; ~ **date** *n* fecha de terminación *f*

complex *adj* (issue, decision) complicado, complejo; (transaction) complicado; ~ **trust** *n* (Law) fideicomiso complejo *m*

complexity *n* complejidad *f*

compliance *n* conformidad *f*; **in** ~ **with your wishes/the law** conforme a sus deseos/la ley; ~ **audit** *n* auditoría de cumplimiento *f*; ~ **cost** *n* coste *m* Esp *or* costo *m* AmL de cumplimiento; ~ **department** *n* departamento *m* administrativo *or* de cumplimiento; ~ **system** *n* (Tax) sistema de cumplimiento de las obligaciones tributarias *m*

complication *n* complicación *f*

complimentary *adj* (flattering) elogioso, favorable; (free) de regalo; ~ **close** *n* fórmula *f* de cortesía *or* de despedida; ~ **copy** *n* ejemplar de regalo *m*; ~ **subscription** *n* suscripción gratuita *f*

compliments slip *n* BrE hoja de cumplido *f*

comply *vi* cumplir; **comply with** *vt* cumplir con; ~ **with a clause** cumplir con una cláusula

component[1] *adj* componente; ~ **part** *n* componente *m*, parte integrante *f*

component[2] *n* componente *m*, pieza *f*; ~ **factory** *n* fábrica de componentes *f*

compose *vt* componer; (letter) redactar; **be** ~**d of sth** estar compuesto de algo

composite *adj* (currency, price, insurance, package) compuesto; (rate, depreciation) combinado; (yield) mixto; ~ **leading index** *n* índice adelantado compuesto *m*; ~ **leading indicator** *n* indicador adelantado compuesto *m*; ~ **mark** *n* (Patents) marca

mixta *f*; ~ **spread** *n* (of risk) diversificación mixta *f*

composition *n* composición *f*; (with creditors) convenio *m*

compound[1] *adj* compuesto; ~ **annual rate** *n* tasa anual compuesta *f*; ~ **duty** *n* derecho compuesto *m*; ~ **entry** *n* apunte *m* *or* asiento *m* compuesto; ~ **growth rate** *n* tasa de crecimiento compuesto *f*; ~ **interest** *n* interés compuesto *m*; ~ **journal entry** *n* asiento compuesto en el diario *m*; ~ **rate** *n* tasa compuesta *f*; ~ **yield** *n* ingreso compuesto *m*

compound[2] *vt* (problem) agravar, exacerbar; (debt) componer, concertar; (risk, difficulties) acrecentar, aumentar; (Fin, Law) capitalizar

comprehensive *adj* (report, review) completo; (agreement, budget, answer) global; (responsibility, tax reform) general; (Ins) a todo riesgo, completo; ~ **general liability insurance** *n* seguro de responsabilidad general *m*; ~ **health insurance** *n* seguro sanitario a todo riesgo *m*; ~ **insurance** *n* seguro contra todo riesgo *m*; ~ **insurance policy** *n* póliza de seguros global *f*; (automobile) póliza de seguro a todo riesgo *f*; ~ **liability insurance** *n* seguro de responsabilidad a todo riesgo *m*; ~ **personal liability insurance** *n* seguro general de responsabilidad personal *m*; ~ **policy** *n* (Ins) póliza combinada *f*

compress *vt* (file, data) comprimir

compression *n* (of file, data) compresión *f*

comprise *vt* (consist of) constar de; (cover) abarcar

comprised total loss *n* pérdida total incluida *f*

compromise[1] *n* compromiso *m*; **come to** *o* **reach a** ~ llegar a un arreglo; ~ **agreement** *n* acuerdo conciliatorio *m*; ~ **decision** *n* decisión de compromiso *f*; ~ **solution** *n* solución de compromiso *f*

compromise[2] [1] *vt* (person, organization, reputation) comprometer; ~ **oneself** ponerse en una situación comprometida [2] *vi* transigir; ~ **on sth** transigir en algo

comptroller *n* interventor(a) *m,f*, contralor(a) *m,f* AmL; **C~ Of The Currency** *n organismo estadounidense para el control y seguimiento de las actividades bancarias*; **C~ General** *n* AmE inspector(a) general *m,f*

compulsive *adj* (buying) compulsivo

compulsory *adj* (redundancy, insurance, licence) obligatorio; (deduction, liquidation) forzoso; (power) coercitivo; (regulation) coactivo, obligatorio; ~ **arbitration** *n* BrE arbitraje *m* necesario *or* obligatorio; ~ **competitive tendering** *n* BrE licitación competitiva obligatoria *f*; ~ **margin** *n* BrE ⋯▷

margen obligatorio m; ~ **purchase** n
expropiación f; **C**~ **Purchase Act** n BrE
Ley de Expropiación f; ~ **purchase order**
n orden de expropiación f; ~ **retirement** n
BrE (cf ▸**mandatory retirement** AmE)
jubilación f forzosa or obligatoria; ~
saving n BrE ahorro forzoso m; ~ **third
party insurance** n seguro obligatorio de
responsabilidad civil m

computation n cálculo m; ~ **of errors** n
cálculo de errores m

computational adj computacional; (error)
de cálculo

compute vt computar

computer n computadora f AmL,
ordenador m Esp

(**computer...a**) ~ **accounting** n
contabilidad f informatizada or
computadorizada AmL; ~ **age** n era f de las
computadoras AmL or de los ordenadores
Esp; ~-**aided** adj asistido por computadora
AmL or ordenador Esp ~-**aided design** n
diseño m asistido por computadora AmL or
ordenador Esp; ~-**aided design and
drafting** diseño m y dibujo m asistido por
computadora AmL or ordenador Esp;
~-**aided engineering** n ingeniería f
asistida por computadora AmL or ordenador
Esp; ~-**aided instruction** n instrucción f
asistida por computadora AmL or ordenador
Esp; ~-**aided language learning** n
aprendizaje m de idiomas asistido por
computadora AmL or ordenador Esp;
~-**aided learning** n aprendizaje m asistido
por computadora AmL or ordenador Esp;
~-**aided manufacturing** n fabricación f
asistida por computadora AmL or ordenador
Esp; ~ **animation** n animación f por
computadora AmL or por ordenador Esp;
~-**assisted** adj asistido por computadora
AmL or ordenador Esp; ~-**assisted
engineering** n ingeniería f asistida por
computadora AmL or ordenador Esp;
~-**assisted language learning** n
aprendizaje m de idiomas asistido por
computadora AmL or ordenador Esp;
~-**assisted learning program** n
programa m de aprendizaje asistido por
computadora AmL or ordenador Esp;
~-**assisted software engineering** n
ingeniería f de programas asistida por
computadora AmL or ordenador Esp;
~-**assisted testing** n comprobación f
asistida por computadora AmL or ordenador
Esp; ~-**assisted trading system** n sistema
m de negociación asistido por computadora
AmL or ordenador Esp; ~-**assisted
translation** n traducción f asistida por
computadora AmL or ordenador Esp

(**b...**) ~-**based** adj informatizado,
computadorizado AmL; ~-**based training** n

formación f or capacitación f por
computadora AmL or ordenador Esp

(**c...**) ~ **center** AmE, ~ **centre** BrE n centro
de procesamiento de datos m; ~ **code** n
código de calculadora m; ~
communication n teleinformática f; ~
company n empresa f de computadoras
AmL or de ordenadores Esp; ~
conferencing n teleconferencia f por
computadora AmL or ordenador Esp; ~
consultant n asesor(a) de informática m,f;
~ **control** n (of stock) control m por
computadora AmL or ordenador Esp;
~-**controlled** adj controlado por
computadora AmL or ordenador Esp; ~
crime n delito informático m

(**d...**) ~ **department** n servicio de
informática m; ~-**driven** adj dirigido por
computadora AmL or ordenador Esp

(**e...**) ~ **engineer** n ingeniero(-a)
informático(-a) m,f

(**f...**) ~ **file** n fichero m de computadora AmL
or ordenador Esp; ~ **fraud** n fraude
informático m

(**g...**) ~ **graphics** n pl infografía f, gráficos
mpl de computadora AmL or de ordenador
Esp

(**i...**) ~ **instruction** n instrucción de
máquina f; ~-**integrated manufacture** n,
~-**integrated manufacturing** n
fabricación f or producción f integrada por
computadora AmL or ordenador Esp

(**l...**) ~ **language** n lenguaje de máquina m;
~ **law** n derecho aplicable a la informática
m; ~ **leasing** n alquiler f de computadoras
AmL or de ordenadores Esp; ~ **literacy** n
competencia en la informática f; ~-**literate**
adj competente en la informática; ~ **log** n
diario de máquina m

(**m...**) ~ **map** n esquema m de la
computadora AmL or del ordenador Esp; ~
memory n memoria f de la computadora
AmL or del ordenador Esp

(**n...**) ~ **network** n red f de computadoras
AmL or de ordenadores Esp

(**o...**) ~-**operated** adj manejado por
computadora AmL or ordenador Esp; ~
operation n manejo m de la computadora
AmL or del ordenador Esp; ~ **operator** n
operador(a) informático(-a) m,f; ~ **output** n
salida f de computadora AmL or de
ordenador Esp

(**p...**) ~ **package** n paquete informático m;
~ **phobia** n fobia informática f; ~
presentation n presentación f en
computadora AmL or ordenador Esp; ~
printout n impresión f por computadora
AmL or ordenador Esp; ~ **processing** n
proceso m de computadora AmL or de
ordenador Esp; ~ **program** n programa

informático m; ~ **programmer** n programador(a) m,f de computadoras AmL or de ordenadores Esp; ~ **programming** n programación (informática) f

(**r**) ~ **return** n (Tax) declaración f por computadora AmL or ordenador Esp; ~ **room** n sala f de computadoras AmL or de ordenadores Esp; ~ **run** n ejecución f or pasada f en computadora AmL or ordenador Esp

(**s...**) ~ **science** n informática f; ~ **scientist** n especialista en informática mf; ~ **screen** n pantalla f de computadora AmL or de ordenador Esp; ~ **simulation** n simulación f por computadora AmL or ordenador Esp; ~ **software** n software m de la computadora AmL or del ordenador Esp; ~ **software licence** BrE, ~ **software license** AmE n licencia f de programas de computadora AmL or ordenador Esp; ~ **system** n sistema informático m

(**t...**) ~ **technology** n tecnología informática f; ~-**telephony integration** n integración informática-telefonía f; ~ **terminal** n terminal m de computadora AmL or de ordenador Esp; ~ **time** n tiempo de máquina m; ~ **trading** n comercio informático m

(**w...**) ~ **whizz kid** n (jarg) joven prodigio(-a) en materia de computación m,f (jarg); ~ **wizard** n experto(-a) en informática m,f

computerization n (of data, records) computerización f; (of company, department) informatización f

computerize vt (data, records) computerizar; (company, department) informatizar

computerized adj (data, records, banking) computerizado; (company, department, accounting system, file) informatizado

computing n informática f; ~ **center** AmE, ~ **centre** BrE n centro de cálculo m; ~ **company** n compañía f de computadoras AmL or de ordenadores Esp; ~ **power** n capacidad de cálculo f; ~ **room** n sala f de computadoras AmL or de ordenadores Esp; ~ **speed** n velocidad de cálculo f

con n (infrml) estafa f, timo m; ~ **artist** n (infrml) estafador(a) m,f, timador(a) m,f; ~ **man** n (infrml) estafador m, timador m

concatenation n concatenación f

conceal vt (object, fact, truth) ocultar

concealed adj (asset) oculto; (employment, unemployment) encubierto

concealment n (of information, losses) ocultación f

concentrate [1] vt concentrar; ~ **one's attention/efforts on sth** centrar la atención/las energías en algo

[2] vi concentrarse; ~ **on sth** concentrarse en algo

concentration n concentración f; ~ **banking** n banca de concentración f; ~ **of industry** n concentración industrial f

concept n concepto m; ~ **test** n prueba conceptual f

conceptual n (framework) conceptual

concern[1] n (business organization) empresa f; (affair, matter) asunto m; (anxiety) preocupación f, inquietud f; (interest) interés m; **express** ~ **about sth** expresar preocupación por algo

concern[2] vt (affect, involve) concernir, incumbir; (interest) interesar; (relate to) referirse a; (worry) preocupar, inquietar; **be** ~**ed about** o **for sth/sb** estar preocupado por algo/alguien; **as far as sth/sb is** ~**ed** por lo que se refiere a algo/alguien; **the department** ~**ed** el departamento en cuestión; **be** ~**ed in sth** estar involucrado en algo; **it** ~**s all of us** nos concierne or incumbe a todos; **it doesn't** ~ **you** no es asunto tuyo; **to whom it may** ~ a quien le interese; **be** ~**ed with sth** ocuparse de algo

concerning prep sobre, acerca de, con respecto a

concerted n (effort) concertado

concession n concesión f; **make** ~**s** hacer concesiones

concessionaire n concesionario(-a) m,f

concessional adj (terms) muy favorable; (exports) de favor

concessionary adj (rate) concedido

conciliate vt conciliar

conciliation n conciliación f; ~ **board** n junta de conciliación f; ~ **officer** n BrE funcionario(-a) de conciliación m,f; ~ **procedure** n BrE procedimiento conciliatorio m

conciliator n conciliador(a) m,f

conclude [1] vt (end) concluir; (deal) cerrar; (agreement) llegar a; ~ **that...** llegar a la conclusión de que...

[2] vi (end) concluir, terminar; **conclude from** vt llegar a la conclusión a partir de

conclusion n (of agreement) cierre m; (of contract) conclusión f; **bring a meeting to a** ~ llevar una reunión a una conclusión; **come to** o **reach a** ~ llegar a una conclusión; **come to** o **reach the** ~ **that...** llegar a la conclusión de que...; **draw a** ~ **from sth** sacar una conclusión de algo; **in** ~ en conclusión

conclusive adj conclusivo; ~ **evidence** n (Law) indicios indudables m pl

concrete adj (evidence, labour) concreto

concur vi (agree) convenir; (events, circumstances) concurrir

concurrent *adj* (events, processing) concurrente, simultáneo; (opinions, statements, conclusions) coincidente

condemn *vt* condenar

condensed *adj* (statement) condensado; (report) resumido

condition *n* (state) condición *f*, estado *m*; (stipulation) condición *f*, requisito *m*, estipulación *f*; **in good/bad** ~ en buen/mal estado; **make it a** ~ **that...** imponer como condición que...; **it was a** ~ **of the agreement that...** el acuerdo estipulaba que...; **on** ~ **that...** a condición de que...; **on the** ~ **that...** con la condición de que...; **on no** ~ bajo ningún concepto; **on one** ~ con una condición; **under existing** ~s en las circunstancias actuales; ~s **of contract** *n pl* condiciones del contrato *f pl*; ~s **of employment** *n pl* condiciones de empleo *f pl*; ~ **precedent** *n* AmE condición suspensiva *f*; ~s **of sale** *n pl* condiciones de venta *f pl*; ~ **subsequent** *n* AmE condición resolutoria *f*; ~s **of tender** *n pl* condiciones de la oferta *f pl*; ~s **of use** *n pl* condiciones de uso *f pl*

conditional *adj* (sale, endorsement acceptance, transaction) condicional; ~ **branch** *n* (Comp) bifurcación condicional *f*; ~ **clause** *n* (Law) cláusula onerosa *f*

conditionality *n* carácter condicional *m*

conditioned *adj* condicionado

condominium *n* condominio *m*

conducive *adj*: ~ **to** (growth) propicio para

conduct[1] *n* conducta *f*; ~ **money** *n* dinero de gestión *m*

conduct[2] *vt* (share sale, meeting, trade, survey) conducir

confederation *n* confederación *f*; **C**~ **of British Industry** *n* ≈ Confederación Española de Organizaciones Empresariales *f*

confer *vt* (rights) conferir

conference *n* conferencia *f*; ~ **board** *n* junta de conferencias *f*; ~ **call** *n* llamada tridireccional *f*; ~ **delegate** *n* delegado(-a) a una conferencia *m,f*; ~ **proceedings** *n pl* procedimientos de la conferencia *m pl*; ~ **report** *n* informe de la conferencia *m*; ~ **system** *n* sistema de conferencias *m*; ~ **table** *n* mesa de conferencias *f*; ~ **venue** *n* lugar de la conferencia *m*

confession *n* (of crime) confesión *f*

confidence *n* confianza *f*; ~ **game** *n* AmE (*cf* ►**confidence trick** BrE) estafa *f*, timo *m*; ~ **level** *n* nivel de confianza *m*; ~ **man** *n* estafador *m*, timador *m*; ~ **trick** *n* BrE (*cf* ►**confidence game** AmE) estafa *f*, timo *m*; ~ **trickster** *n* estafador(a) *m,f*, timador(a) *m,f*

confidential *adj* (information) confidencial; ~ **clerk** *n* empleado(-a) de confianza *m,f*; ~ **secretary** *n* secretario(-a) de confianza *m,f*

confidentiality *n* confidencialidad *f*; ~ **agreement** *n* acuerdo de confidencialidad *m*

configuration *n* configuración *f*; ~ **control** *n* control de la configuración *m*; ~ **management** *n* gestión de la configuración *f*

configure *vt* configurar

confirm *vt* (report, order, reservation) confirmar; (agreement) ratificar

confirmation *n* (of order) confirmación *f*; ~ **notice** *n* aviso de confirmación *m*

confirmed *adj* (credit, letter of credit) confirmado

confirming: ~ **bank** *n* *banco que confirma un crédito*; ~ **house** *n* casa de confirmación *f*; ~ **letter** *n* carta de confirmación *f*

confiscate *vt* confiscar, incautar

confiscation *n* confiscación *f*, incautación *f*

conflict *n* lucha *f* conflicto *m*; ~ **of interest** *n* conflicto de intereses *m*; ~ **of laws** *n* conflicto de leyes *m*

conflicting *adj* (views, versions, evidence) contradictorio; (interests) opuesto

confluence *n* (of interests) confluencia *f*

conformed copy *n* (of legal document) copia conformada *f*

conformity *n* conformidad *f*; **in** ~ **with sth** de conformidad con algo; ~ **to accounting rules** *n* conformidad con las normas contables *f*

conform to *vt* (standards) ajustarse a

confront *vt* hacer frente a

confrontation *n* confrontación *f*; (in court) careo *m*

congestion *n* (of telephone lines) sobrecarga *f*; (of market) aglomeración *f*, congestión *f*; ~ **surcharge** *n* sobretasa por acumulación *f*

conglomerate *n* conglomeración *f*, conglomerado (de empresas) *m*; ~ **diversification** *n* diversificación *f* conglomerada *or* de conglomerado; ~ **merger** *n* fusión de conglomerados *f*

congress *n* congreso *m*

Congress *n* AmE (*cf* ►**Parliament** BrE) ≈ Cortes *f pl* Esp

Congressional *adj* AmE del Congreso

Congressman *n* AmE (*cf* ►**Member of Parliament** BrE) ≈ diputado *m*, ≈ Miembro del Congreso *m*

Congresswoman *n* AmE (*cf* ►**Member of Parliament** BrE) ≈ diputada *f*, ≈ Miembro del Congreso *f*

congruence *n* congruencia *f*

congruent adj congruente; **be ~ with sth** ser congruente con algo

conjunction n conjunción f; **in ~ with sth** en conjunción con algo; **~ of circumstances** n cúmulo de circunstancias m

conjuncture n coyuntura f

connect [1] vt (attach, link) conectar; (ideas, events, people) relacionar, asociar; **~ sth to sth** conectar algo a algo; **I'm trying to ~ you** (by telephone) un momento que le comunico
[2] vi (rooms) comunicarse; **~ to the Internet** conectar al Internet; **~ with sth** (train, boat, flight) enlazar con algo, conectar con algo AmL

connected adj (ideas, events) relacionado; **be ~ to the Internet** estar conectado al Internet; **be ~ with sth** estar relacionado con algo

connecting adj (flight) de enlace; (rooms) comunicado

connection n (link) conexión f, enlace m; **get a ~ to the Internet** conectar al Internet; **have ~s** tener enchufe; **in ~ with sth** en conexión or en relación con algo; **in ~ with your order** con relación a or en relación con su pedido; **in this ~** a este respecto, con respecto a esto; **lose one's ~ to the Internet** perder la conexión al Internet; **miss one's ~** (when travelling) perder la combinación or la conexión; **~ charge** n (Comp) cuota de conexión f; **~ time** n (Comp) tiempo de conexión m

connectivity n conectividad f

cons. abbr (▸consolidated) consolidado

consecutive adj (days) consecutivo

consensus n consenso m; **~ agreement** n acuerdo unánime m

consent¹ n consentimiento m; **by mutual ~** de común acuerdo; **give/refuse one's ~** dar/negar su consentimiento

consent² vi acceder; **~ to sth** acceder a algo, consentir en algo

consequence n (result) consecuencia f; (importance) importancia f; **as a o in ~** en consecuencia; **as a o in ~ of sth** a consecuencia de algo

consequential adj (loss) consiguiente, resultante; (damage) consecuencial, indirecto; **~ effect** n (of court action) efecto resultante m

conservation n conservación f; **~ of portfolio** n conservación de cartera f

conservationist n conservacionista mf

conservatism n conservadurismo m

conservative adj (approach, estimate) cauteloso, prudente; **~ accounting** n contabilidad previsora f

Conservative adj BrE Conservador; **~ Party** n BrE Partido Conservador m

conserve vt (energy) conservar, ahorrar; (resources) proteger, conservar; (wildlife) conservar, preservar

consideration n (attention, thought) consideración f; (factor) factor m; (payment) remuneración f; (Law) causa contractual f, contraprestación f; **in ~ of sth** en consideración a algo; **a small payment in ~ of sb's services** un pequeño pago en retribución a los servicios de alguien; **take sth into ~** tener algo en cuenta; **the proposals are still under ~** todavía se están considerando las propuestas; **upon further ~** considerándolo más detenidamente

consign vt (goods) consignar

consignee n consignatario(-a) m,f

consigner ▸consignor

consignment n remesa f; **on ~** en comisión, en consignación; **~ insurance** n seguro sobre mercancías en consignación m; **~ note** n hoja de embarque f

consignor n expedidor(a) m,f, consignador(a) m,f

consistency n (regularity) uniformidad f; (coherence) coherencia f; (Mgmnt, S&M) continuidad f; **~ check** n control de conformidad m; **~ principle** n principio de uniformidad m

consistent adj (person) coherente, consecuente; (excellence, failure) constante; (denial) sistemático, constante

consistently adv (argue) coherentemente; (behave) consecuentemente, coherentemente; (claim, refuse) sistemáticamente, constantemente

consol. abbr (▸consolidated) consolidado

CONSOL abbr BrE (▸consolidated annuity) anualidad consolidada f

consolidate [1] vt (position, reputation, debts) consolidar; (companies) fusionar
[2] vi (companies) fusionarse

consolidated adj (debt, loan, figures, tax return) consolidado; **on a ~ basis** sobre bases consolidadas; **~ accounts** n pl cuentas consolidadas f pl; **~ annuity** n BrE anualidad consolidada f; **~ balance sheet** n balance (de situación) consolidado m; **~ cash flow statement** n estado de flujos de caja consolidado m; **~ financial statement** n estado financiero consolidado m; **~ fund** n BrE fondo consolidado m; **~ net profit** n beneficio neto consolidado m; **~ statement** n estado consolidado m; **~ stock** n BrE existencias consolidadas f pl; **~ tape** n (Stock) cinta consolidada f

consolidation n (of balances, funds, shares, interests) consolidación f; (of companies) fusión f; **~ loan** n préstamo de consolidación m

consortium n consorcio m; ~ **bank** n banco de consorcio m

conspectus n estudio de conjunto m; (Fin) vista f general or de conjunto

conspicuous consumption n consumo ostentoso m

constant[1] adj (price, capital, risk) constante; ~ **dollars** n dólares de poder adquisitivo constante m pl; ~**-payment loan** n préstamo de pago invariable m

constant[2] n constante f

constituent adj (company) constituyente

constitute vt constituir

constitution n constitución f; (of association, party) estatutos m pl

constitutional adj (foundation) constitucional; (strike) legal; ~ **law** n derecho constitucional m

constr abbr (▸**construction**) construcción f

constrained adj (cycle) restringido; ~ **market pricing** n AmE fijación restrictiva de precios de mercado f

constraining adj (factor) constrictor

constraint n (compulsion) coacción f; (restriction) restricción f, limitación f; **act under** ~ actuar bajo coacción; **without** ~ sin restricciones or limitaciones

construct vt construir

construction n construcción f; **under** ~ en construcción; ~ **corporation** n empresa constructora f; ~ **industry** n sector de la construcción m; ~ **loan** n préstamo inmobiliario or para la construcción; ~ **worker** n obrero(-a) de la construcción m,f

constructive adj (criticism, suggestion, advice) constructivo; ~ **delivery** n entrega implícita f; ~ **dismissal** n despido constructivo m; ~ **eviction** n desalojo constructivo m; ~ **notice** n AmE notificación sobreentendida f; ~ **receipt** n recibo implícito m; ~ **total loss** n pérdida total implícita f

consul n cónsul mf; ~ **general** n cónsul general mf

consular adj (fees) consular

consulate n consulado m

consult vt consultar

consultancy n consultoría f; ~ **work** n trabajo de asesor m

consultant n asesor(a) m,f, consejero(-a) m,f, consultor(a) m,f; ~ **engineer** n ingeniero(-a) consultor(a) m,f

consultation n consulta f; **in** ~ **with sb** en consulta con alguien

consultative adj (body, committe, group) consultivo; **in a** ~ **capacity** en capacidad de asesor or consultor

consulting: ~ **division** n división de consultoría f; ~ **engineer** n técnico(-a) asesor(a) m,f; ~ **firm** n consulting m, consultoría f, firma consultora f; ~ **service** n servicio de consultoría m

consume vt consumir

consumer n consumidor(a) m,f; ~ **acceptance** n aceptación del consumidor f; ~ **advertising** n publicidad para el consumidor f; **C~s' Advisory Council** n AmE (cf ▸**Consumers' Association** BrE) ≈ Organización de Consumidores y Usuarios f; ~ **advisory service** n servicio de asesoramiento al consumidor m; **C~s' Association** n BrE (cf ▸**Consumers' Advisory Council** AmE) ≈ Organización de Consumidores y Usuarios f; ~ **banking** n banca orientada al consumo f; ~ **behavior** AmE, ~ **behaviour** BrE n comportamiento del consumidor m; ~ **benefit** n ventaja para el consumidor f; ~ **buying power** n poder adquisitivo del consumidor m; ~ **choice** n elección f or opción f del consumidor; ~ **credit** n crédito al consumo m; ~ **demand** n demanda de consumo f; ~ **durables** n pl bienes (de consumo) duraderos m pl; ~ **expectations** n pl expectativas del consumidor f pl; ~ **expenditure** n gasto de consumo m; ~ **goods** n bienes de consumo m pl; ~ **habits** n pl hábitos m pl del consumidor or de consumo; ~ **lending** n crédito al consumidor m; ~ **loan** n préstamo al consumidor m; ~ **loyalty** n lealtad del consumidor f; ~ **magazine** n revista del consumidor f; ~ **market** n mercado de consumo m; ~ **marketing** n marketing de consumo m; ~ **nondurables** n pl bienes no duraderos m pl; ~ **organization** n organización del consumidor f; ~ **orientation** n orientación del consumo f; ~**-oriented** adj orientado al consumidor; ~ **panel** n panel de consumidores m; ~ **pattern** n modelo de consumo m; ~ **preference** n preferencia del consumidor f; ~ **pressure** n presión del consumidor f; ~ **price** n precio al consumidor m; ~ **price index** n AmE (cf ▸**retail price index** BrE) índice de precios al consumo m; ~ **product** n producto de consumo m; ~ **profile** n perfil del consumidor m; ~ **protection** n protección al consumidor f; ~ **research** n estudio de mercado m; ~ **resistance** n resistencia del consumo f; ~ **response** n respuesta del consumidor f; ~ **satisfaction** n satisfacción del consumidor f; ~ **society** n sociedad de consumo f; ~ **survey** n encuesta de consumidores f; ~ **test** n prueba del consumidor f; ~ **trend** n tendencia de consumo f

consumerism n consumismo m

consumerist *n* consumista *mf*
consumer-to-consumer *adj* consumidor a consumidor, entre consumidores
consummate *vt* consumar
consumption *n* consumo *m*; ~ **goods** *n pl* bienes de consumo *m pl*; ~ **pattern** *n* estructura del consumo *f*; ~ **per capita** *n* consumo por persona *m*; ~ **tax** *n* impuesto sobre el consumo *m*
contact *n* contacto *m*; **come into** ~ **with sth** entrar en contacto con algo; **have several** ~**s in the music business** tener varios contactos en el mundo de la música; **make** ~ **with sb** ponerse en contacto con alguien; ~ **report** *n* informe *m* de contactos *or* de visita
contain *vt* (amount, demand, inflation) contener
container *n* contáiner *m*, contenedor *m*; ~ **bill of lading** *n* conocimiento de embarque de contenedores *m*; ~ **ship** *n* buque portacontenedores *m*
containerization *n* contenedorización *f*
containerize *vt* contenedorizar
containment *n* (of credit) recorte *m*; (of demand) contención *f*
contaminate *vt* contaminar
contamination *n* contaminación *f*
contango *n* interés de aplazamiento *m*, reporte *m*; ~ **business** *n* BrE operación *f* de reporte *or* con interés de aplazamiento; ~ **day** *n* BrE día del reporte *m*; ~ **market** *n* mercado de contangos *m*
cont'd *abbr* (▶**continued**) sigue
contempt of court *n* desacato al tribunal *m*; **be in** ~ **of court** (witness) caer en rebeldía
content *n* contenido *m*; ~ **management** *n* gestión del contenido *f*; ~ **manager** *n* director(a) del contenido *m,f*; ~ **provider** *n* proveedor de contenido *f*
contents *n pl* contenido *m*
contest[1] *n* (competition) concurso *m*; (struggle, battle) lucha *f*, contienda *f*
contest[2] *vt* (will, decision) impugnar; (statement) rebatir
contestable clause *n* cláusula disputable *f*
context *n* contexto *m*; **in/out of** ~ en/ fuera de contexto; **put sth into** ~ poner algo en contexto; ~**-sensitive** *adj* sensible al contexto
contiguous *adj* contiguo
Continent *n* (mainland Europe) continente *m*
continental *adj* continental; ~ **trade** *n* comercio continental *m*
contingency *n* contingencia *f*; ~ **arrangements** *n pl* acuerdos para

imprevistos *m pl*; ~ **clause** *n* cláusula condicional *f*; ~ **fund** *n* fondo de imprevistos *m*; ~ **management** *n* dirección *f* *or* gestión *f* por contingencia; ~ **order** *n* orden de contingencia *f*; ~ **payment** *n* pago *m* contingente *or* eventual; ~ **plan** *n* plan *m* de contingencia *or* de emergencia; ~ **planning** *n* planificación *f* de contingencia *or* de emergencia; ~ **reserve** *n* reserva para contingencias *f*
contingent *adj* (cost, expenses, market, obligation) contingente; (asset) contingente, condicionado; (budget, liability) contingente, eventual; (claim) contingente, condicionado; (order) imprevisto; ~ **fee** *n* comisión por cobranza *f*
contingently *adv* eventualmente
continuation *n* continuación *f*; AmE (Law) suspensión *f*; ~ **day** *n* día de reportes *m*
continue *vti* continuar; ~ **doing** *o* **to do sth** seguir haciendo algo; ~**d sigue**; ~**d on page 96** continúa en la pág. 96
continued *adj* (success) permanente; (threat) continuo; (support) constante; ~ **bond** *n* bono de vencimiento aplazado *m*
continuing *adj* (interest, support, cost) continuo; (commitment, guarantee) permanente; ~ **professional education** *n* educación profesional permanente *f*
continuity *n* continuidad *f*; ~ **of employment** *n* BrE continuidad en el empleo *f*
continuous *adj* (process, production, audit, market) continuo; (survey) permanente; ~ **assessment** *n* evaluación continua *f*; ~ **form** *n pl* formulario continuo *m*; ~ **net settlement** *n* BrE liquidación neta continua *f*; ~ **stationery** *n* papel continuo *m*
contr. *abbr* (▶**contractor**) contratista *mf*
contra *n* contrapartida *f*; ~ **account** *n* contrapartida *f*; ~**-deal** *n* contraoferta *f*; ~ **entry** *n* contraasiento *m*
contraband *n* contrabando *m*
contrabandist *n* contrabandista *mf*
contract[1] *n* contrato *m*; (for public works) contrata *f*; **break a** ~ incumplir *or* violar un contrato; **enter into a** ~ **(with sb)** celebrar un contrato (con alguien); **exchange** ~**s** BrE (in property deal) suscribir el contrato de compraventa; **honor** AmE *o* **honour** BrE **a** ~ cumplir un contrato; **put sth out to** ~ otorgar la contrata de *or* para algo; **sign a** ~ firmar *or* suscribir un contrato; **be under** ~ **to sb** estar bajo contrato con alguien; **under the terms of your** ~ según lo establecido en su contrato; **win/lose a** ~ obtener *or* conseguir/perder un contrato; ~ **agreement** *n* acuerdo de contrato *m*; ~ **bargaining** *n* negociación de ⋯⟶

contrato *f*; ~ **of employment** *n* contrato de trabajo *m*; ~ **for the sale of goods** *n* contrato para la venta de mercancías *m*; ~ **for services** *n* contrato de servicios *m*; ~ **hire** *n* contratación *f*, salario por contrato *m*; ~ **holder** *n* portador(a) *m,f or* tenedor(a) *m,f* de contrato; ~ **of indemnity** *n* contrato de indemnización *m*; ~ **labor** AmE, ~ **labour** BrE *n* (workers) mano de obra contratada *f*; (work) trabajo contratado *m*; ~ **licence** BrE, ~ **license** AmE *n* licencia por contrato *f*; ~**s manager** *n* director(a) de contratos *m,f*; ~ **note** *n* nota de contrato *f*; ~**s officer** *n* contratista *mf*; ~ **payment** *n* pago contractual *m*; ~ **price** *n* AmE (Tax) precio contractual *m*; ~ **specifications** *n pl* especificaciones contractuales *f pl*; ~ **work** *n* trabajo bajo contrato *m*

contract² ⊡ *vt* (loan, debt, liability) contraer; (person) contratar ⊡ *vi* (growth) contraerse; ~ **(with sb) for sth** celebrar un contrato (con alguien) para algo; ~ **to do sth** comprometerse por contrato a hacer algo; **contract in** *vi* BrE suscribirse, darse de alta; **contract out** ⊡ *vt* (job, work) subcontratar ⊡ *vi* BrE (withdraw) darse de baja

contracted-in rate *n* BrE (of National Insurance) tipo concertado *m*

contracted-out rate *n* BrE (of National Insurance) tipo establecido *m*

contracting party *n* parte contratante *f*

contraction *n* contracción *f*; (of demand) contracción *f*, disminución *f*

contractor *n* contratista *mf*

contractual *adj* (liability, obligation, provision, payment) contractual

contrarian *n* (Stock) inversor(a) contracorriente *m,f*

contrast *n* contraste *m*

contribute *vt* contribuir

contributed capital *n* capital aportado *m*

contribution *n* (personal, financial) contribución *f*; **make a** ~ **to sth** hacer una contribución a algo; ~ **of capital** *n* aportación de capital *f*

contributor *n* (Tax) contribuyente *mf*; (donor) donante *mf*; (writer) colaborador(a) *m,f*; ~ **of capital** *n* capitalista *mf*

contributory *adj* (pension fund, pension plan) contributivo; ~ **negligence** *n* (Law) negligencia concurrente *f*

control¹ *n* control *m*; **beyond** *o* **outside sb's** ~ fuera del control de alguien; **owing to circumstances beyond our** ~ debido a circunstancias ajenas a nosotros; **bring sth under** ~ controlar algo; **be in** ~ **of sth** tener el control de algo; **keep/lose** ~ **(of sth)** mantener/perder el control (de algo);

government ~**s on trade** controles gubernamentales del comercio; **out of** ~ fuera de control; **inflation has got out of** ~ la inflación está fuera de control; **take** ~ tomar el control; **everything is under** ~ todo está bajo control; ~ **account** *n* cuenta de control *f*; **C**~**-Alternate-Delete** *n* (Comp) Control-Alternar-Suprimir *m*; ~ **ball** *n* (Comp) bola rodante *f*; ~ **block** *n* (Stock) bloque de control *m*; ~ **character** *n* (Comp) carácter de verificación *f*; ~ **command** *n* (Comp) comando de control *m*; ~ **cycle** *n* ciclo de control *m*; ~ **data** *n* datos de control *m pl*; ~ **group** *n* grupo de control *m*; ~ **information** *n* información·de control *f*; ~ **key** *n* (Comp) tecla de mando *f*; ~ **panel** *n* tablero de control *m*; ~ **procedure** *n* (Comp) procedimiento de control *m*; ~ **program** *n* programa de control *m*; ~ **question** *n* pregunta de control *f*; ~ **stock** *n* valores de control *m pl*

control² *vt* (demand, market, growth, expenditure) controlar; (prices, rate) controlar, regular; (inflation) controlar, contener

controllable *adj* (cost) controlable

controlled *adj* (corporation, circulation, rate) controlado; (price) controlado, regulado; (economy) dirigido; (market) intervenido; ~ **commodities** *n pl* BrE productos controlados *m pl*

controller *n* director(a) administrativo(-a) *m,f*; (financial) director(a) financiero(-a) *m,f*

controlling *n* (shareholder) mayoritario; ~ **account** *n* cuenta de mayor *f*; ~ **interest** *n* participación mayoritaria *f*

controversial *adj* controvertido

controversy *n* controversia *f*

convene *vt* (meeting) convocar

convenience *n* conveniencia *m*, comodidad *m*; **at your** ~ cuando le resulte conveniente, cuando le venga bien; **at your earliest** ~ a la mayor brevedad posible, a la brevedad; **it is provided for our customers'** ~ lo proveemos para la comodidad de nuestros clientes; ~ **bill** *n* factura de prueba *f*; ~ **food** *n* comida preparada *m pl*; ~ **goods** *n pl* artículos de consumo corriente *m pl*; ~ **product** *n* producto de conveniencia *m*; ~ **sampling** *n* muestreo aleatorio *m*; ~ **store** *n* AmE tienda de conveniencia *f*

convenor *n* (of committee) presidente(-a) *m,f*; (of meeting) organizador(a) *m,f*; (in union) representante sindical *mf*

convention *n* convención *f*

conventional *adj* (method, mortgage) convencional; (design, style) tradicional, clásico

converge *vi* (ideas, activities) converger

convergence *n* convergencia *f*

conversational *adj* conversacional; ~ **entry** *n* (Comp) entrada conversacional *f*; ~ **mode** *n* (Comp) modalidad dialogada *f*, modo conversación *m*

conversationally *adv* en modo de conversación

conversely *adv* a la inversa

conversion *n* conversión *f*; ~ **algorithm** *n* algoritmo de conversión *m*; ~ **cost** *n* coste *m* Esp *or* costo *m* AmL de transformación; ~ **date** *n* fecha de conversión *f*; ~ **factor** *n* factor de conversión *m*; ~ **issue** *n* emisión de conversión *f*; ~ **loan** *n* empréstito de conversión *m*; ~ **price** *n* precio de conversión *m*; ~ **rate** *n* tasa de conversión *f*

convert *vt* (shares, currency) convertir; ~ **sth into capital/cash** convertir algo en capital/dinero; ~ **pounds into kilos** convertir libras a *or* en kilos

convertible *adj* (bond, security, share, currency, loan) convertible

convey *vt* (goods) transportar; (person) llevar; (transmit) transmitir; (property) traspasar

conveyance *n* (transport) transporte *m*; (vehicle) vehículo *m*; (of property) traspaso *m*

conveyancing *n* redacción de escrituras de traspaso *f*

conveyor belt *n* cinta *f or* correa *f* transportadora

conviction *n* (belief) convicción *f* (Law) condena *f*; **a ~ for sth** una condena por algo

COO *abbr* (▸**chief operating officer**) DG (director general), director(a) general de operaciones *m,f*; (▸**country of origin**) país de origen *m*

cookie *n* (Comp) cookie *m*

cool down *vt* (Econ) enfriar

cooling-off period *n* periodo de reflexión *m*

co-op *abbr* (▸**cooperative**) cooperativa *f*; ~ **advertising** *n* publicidad cooperativa *f*

cooperate *vi* cooperar; ~ **with sb in doing** *o* **to do sth** cooperar con alguien para hacer algo; ~ **with sb on sth** cooperar con alguien en algo

cooperation *n* cooperación *f*; ~ **agreement** *n* acuerdo de cooperación *m*

cooperative¹ *adj* (society, marketing, attitude) de colaboración, cooperativo; (effort, venture) conjunto; ~ **bank** *n* ≈ Banco de Crédito Agrícola *m*; ~ **credit association** *n* asociación de crédito cooperativo *f*; ~ **credit institution** *n* institución de crédito cooperativo *f*

cooperative² *n* cooperativa *f*

coopetition *n* cooperación *f* y competencia *f*

coordinate *vt* coordinar

coordinated *adj* coordinado; ~ **universal time** *n* hora universal coordinada *f*

coordination *n* coordinación *f*

coordinator *n* coordinador(a) *m,f*

co-owner *n* copropietario(-a) *m,f*

co-ownership *n* copropiedad *f*

copier *n* copiadora *f*

coprocessor *n* coprocesador *m*

coproduct *n* coproducto *m*

copy¹ *n* (of document, file) copia *f*; (duplicate) duplicado *m*; (of book, newspaper) ejemplar *m*; (text) texto *m*; ~**-adaptor** *n* adaptador de copia *m*; ~ **appeal** *n* atractivo del anuncio publicitario *f*; ~ **body** *n* (of advert) cuerpo del texto *m*; ~ **brief** *n* resumen de un texto *m*; ~ **chief** *n* jefe(-a) de redacción *m,f*; ~ **claim** *n* afirmación del mensaje publicitario *f*; ~ **date** *n* fecha de redacción *f*; ~ **deadline** *n* hora límite de redacción *f*; ~ **editor** *n* editor(a) *m,f*, corrector(a) *m,f*; ~**-protected** *adj* (disk) protegido contra copia; ~ **reader** *n* corrector(a) de estilo *m,f*

copy² *vt* copiar; ~ **sth from the original** copiar algo del original; ~ **sb (in)** enviar una copia a alguien; ~ **and paste** copiar y pegar; ~ **sth to sb** enviarle una copia de algo a alguien

copyright *n* copyright *m*; **hold the ~ on sth** tener los derechos de algo; **it is in/out of ~** los derechos de autor tienen/no tienen vigencia; ~ **reserved** todos los derechos reservados; ~ **Act** *n* Ley de Derechos de Autor *f*

copywriter *n* redactor(a) de material publicitario *m,f*

copywriting *n* escritura de material publicitario *f*

cordless *adj* inalámbrico; ~ **digital telecommunications** *n pl* comunicaciones digitales inalámbricas *f pl*

core *n* (essential element) núcleo *m*; ~ **business** *n* negocio básico *m*; ~ **definition** *n* definición esencial *f*; ~ **firm** *n* compañía *f* central *or* matriz; ~ **funding** *n* financiación básica *f*; ~ **hours** *n pl* horas centrales *f pl*; ~ **inflation** *n* inflación básica *f*; ~ **inflation rate** *n* proporción de inflación básica *f*; ~ **memory** *n* (Comp) memoria de núcleos *f*; ~ **product** *n* producto básico *m*; ~ **region** *n* región central *f*; ~ **size** *n* (Comp) capacidad de la memoria de núcleos *f*; ~ **storage** *n* (Comp) memoria de núcleos *f*; ~ **time** *n* tiempo mínimo *m*; ~ **workforce** *n* mano de obra imprescindible *f*

corner¹ *n* (monopoly) monopolio *m*; ~ **shop** *n* BrE (*cf* ▸**neighborhood store** AmE) tienda de barrio *f*

corner² *vt* (market) acaparar

cornerer *n* acaparador(a) *m,f*

cornering *n* (of goods) acaparamiento *m*; (of market) monopolización *f*

cornerstone *n* piedra de toque *f*

corp. *abbr* (▸**corporation**) corp. (corporación)

corpographics *n* recolección de información sobre la cultura de empresas clientes

corporate *adj* (culture, strategy, banking, management) corporativo; ∼ **account** *n* cuenta corporativa *f*; ∼ **accountability** *n* responsabilidad corporativa *f*; ∼ **advertising** *n* publicidad corporativa *f*; ∼ **affairs** *n pl* asuntos corporativos *m pl*; ∼ **affiliate** *n* (employee) socio(-a) corporativo(-a) *m,f*; (company) corporación afiliada *f*; ∼ **assets** *n pl* activos *m pl or* bienes *m pl* sociales; ∼ **body** *n* corporación *f*; ∼ **bond** *n* AmE obligación societaria *f*; ∼ **client** *n* cliente corporativo(-a) *m,f*; ∼ **credit card** *n* tarjeta de crédito corporativa *f*; ∼ **customer** *n* cliente corporativo(-a) *m,f*; ∼ **data center** AmE, ∼ **data centre** BrE *n* centro de datos corporativo *m*, centro informático de empresa *m*; ∼ **database** *n* base de datos corporativa *f*; ∼ **debenture** *n* obligación de empresa *f*; ∼ **discount** *n* descuento corporativo *m*; ∼ **earnings** *n pl* ganancias corporativas *f pl*; ∼ **entity** *n* sociedad comercial *f*; ∼ **executive** *n* ejecutivo(-a) de empresa *m,f*; ∼ **finance** *n* finanza corporativa *f*; ∼ **financing** *n* financiación corporativa *f*; ∼ **group** *n* grupo de empresas *m*; ∼ **identity** *n* identidad corporativa *f*; ∼ **image** *n* imagen corporativa *f*; ∼ **income tax** *n* impuesto sobre la renta de sociedades *m*; ∼ **insider** *n* empleado que maneja información reservada; ∼ **investment** *n* inversión en sociedades *f*; ∼ **investor** *n* BrE inversor(a) corporativo(-a) *m,f*; ∼ **issue** *n* emisión de acciones de una compañía *f*; C∼ **Law** *n* Ley de Sociedades Mercantiles *f*; ∼ **lending** *n* empréstito corporativo *m*; ∼ **loan** *n* préstamo a una corporación *m*; ∼ **member** *n* miembro corporativo(-a) *m,f*; ∼ **model** *n* modelo corporativo *m*; ∼ **name** *n* razón social *f*; ∼ **planning** *n* planificación empresarial *f*; ∼ **raider** *n* especulador(a) corporativo(-a) *m,f*, tiburón (corporativo) *m*; ∼ **raiding** *n especulación agresiva sobre una empresa*; ∼ **seal** *n* sello de la empresa *m*; ∼ **spending** *n* gasto de sociedad *m*; ∼ **sponsorship** *n* patrocinio corporativo *m*; ∼ **structure** *n* estructura corporativa *f*; ∼ **tax** *n* impuesto (sobre la renta) de sociedades *m*; ∼ **treasurer** *n* tesorero(-a) de la empresa *m,f*, ∼ **venture capital** *n* capital de riesgo de una corporación *m*

corporation *n* corporación *f*; ∼ **tax** *n* BrE impuesto de sociedades *m*

corporatism *n* corporativismo *m*

corporeal *adj* corpóreo *m*; ∼ **hereditaments** *n pl* bienes materiales por heredar *m pl*

corpus *n* (Fin) patrimonio de un fideicomiso *m*, bienes fideicometidos *m pl*; (Law) cuerpo *m*

corr. *abbr* (▸**correspondence**) correspondencia *f*

correct¹ *adj* (answer, figures) correcto

correct² *vt* (error, defect, person) corregir; (proofs) leer

corrected invoice *n* factura rectificada *f*

correcting entry *n* contraasiento *m*

correction *n* corrección *f*; ∼ **maintenance** *n* mantenimiento de corrección *m*

corrective *n* (measures) correctivo; ∼ **action** *n* operación de corrección *f*; ∼ **subsidy** *n* subsidio *m* correctivo *or* de ajuste; ∼ **tax** *n* impuesto corrector *m*

correlate *vt* correlacionar

correlation *n* correlación *f*

correspond *vi* (tally) corresponderse; (be equivalent) corresponder; (by letter) escribirse; **correspond to** *vt* corresponder a; **correspond with** *vt* (tally with) corresponderse con; (by letter) escribirse

correspondence *n* correspondencia *f*; **enter into** ∼ **with sb** entablar correspondencia con alguien; **be in** ∼ **with sb** escribirse *or* cartearse con alguien

correspondent *n* corresponsal *mf*; ∼ **bank** *n* banca corresponsal *f*

corresponding *adj* (equivalent) correspondiente

corruption *n* corrupción *f*

corset *n* (restriction) limitación *f*, restricción *f*

cosign *vt* firmar conjuntamente

cost¹ *n* coste *m* Esp, costo *m* AmL; **at** ∼ al coste Esp, al costo AmL; **at no additional** *o* **extra** ∼ sin cargo adicional; **cover one's** ∼**s** cubrir los gastos; **cut** ∼**s** reducir (los) gastos; **pay** ∼**s** (Law) pagar las costas; ∼**s taxable to sb** costes Esp *or* costos AmL gravables a alguien; ∼ **accountant** *n* contable de costes *mf* Esp, contador(a) de costos *m,f* AmL; ∼ **accounting** *n* contabilidad *f* de costes Esp *or* de costos AmL; ∼ **allocation** *n* asignación *f or* imputación *f* de costes Esp *or* de costos AmL; ∼ **analysis** *n* análisis *m* de los costes Esp *or* de los costos AmL; ∼ **apportionment** *n* prorrateo *m* del coste Esp *or* del costo AmL; ∼ **awareness** *n* conscienciación *f* del coste Esp *or* del costo AmL; ∼ **base** *n* base *m* del coste Esp *or* del costo AmL; ∼**-benefit**

analysis *n* análisis *m* de coste-beneficio Esp *or* de costo-beneficio AmL; ~ **of borrowing** *n* coste *m* Esp *or* costo *m* AmL de un empréstito *or* de un préstamo; ~ **of capital** *n* coste *m* Esp *or* costo *m* AmL de capital; ~ **center** AmE, ~ **centre** BrE *n* centro *m* de costes Esp *or* de costos AmL; ~ **consciousness** *n* conciencia *f* del coste Esp *or* del costo AmL; ~ **control** *n* control *m* de costes Esp *or* de costos AmL; ~ **curve** *n* curva *f* de costes Esp *or* de costos AmL; ~ **distribution** *n* distribución *f* de costes Esp *or* de costos AmL; ~**-effective** *adj* eficaz en relación con el coste Esp *or* costo AmL, rentable; ~ **effectiveness** *n* relación *f* coste-eficacia Esp *or* costo-eficacia AmL, rentabilidad *f*; ~**-efficient** *adj* coste-eficiente Esp, costo-eficiente AmL; ~ **estimate** *n* estimación *f* de costes Esp *or* de costos AmL; ~ **factor** *n* factor *m* del coste Esp *or* del costo AmL; ~ **forecast** *n* previsión *f* de costes Esp *or* de costos AmL; ~ **and freight** coste *m* Esp y flete *m*, costo *m* AmL y flete *m*; ~ **of funds** *n* coste *m* Esp *or* costo *m* AmL de los fondos; ~ **and insurance** coste *m* Esp y seguro *m*, costo *m* AmL y seguro *m*; ~**, insurance and freight** *n* coste *m* Esp y seguro *m*, seguro *m* y flete *m*; ~ **of labor** AmE, ~ **of labour** BrE *n* coste *m* Esp *or* costo *m* AmL de la mano de obra; ~ **of living** *n* coste *m* Esp *or* costo *m* AmL de la vida; ~**-of-living adjustment** *n* AmE ajuste *m* del coste Esp *or* del costo AmL de vida; ~**-of-living allowance** *n* subsidio *m* por aumento del coste Esp *or* del costo AmL de vida; ~**-of-living index** *n* índice *m* del coste Esp *or* del costo AmL de la vida; ~ **method** *n* (in inventory) método *m* de coste Esp *or* de costo AmL; ~ **minimization** *n* minimización *f* de costes Esp *or* de costos AmL; ~ **overrun** *n* sobrecoste *m* Esp, sobrecosto *m* AmL; ~ **per click** *n* coste *m* Esp *or* costo *m* AmL por clic; ~ **per mille** *n* coste *m* Esp *or* costo *m* AmL por mil páginas vistas; ~ **price** *n* precio *m* de coste Esp *or* de costo AmL; ~ **pricing** *n* fijación *f* del coste Esp *or* del costo AmL *f*; ~ **reduction** *n* reducción *f* de costes Esp *or* de costos AmL; ~ **of sales** *n* coste *m* Esp *or* costo *m* AmL de ventas; ~**-sensitive** *adj* sensible al coste Esp *or* al costo AmL; ~ **structure** *n* estructura *f* del coste Esp *or* del costo AmL; ~ **variance** *n* variación *f* del coste Esp *or* del costo AmL

cost² *vt* (have as price) costar; (calculate cost of) establecer el precio de coste Esp *or* costo AmL de

costing *n* cálculo *m* de costes Esp *or* de costos AmL

costly *adj* caro, costoso

cotenancy *n* arrendamiento conjunto *m*

co-tenant finance *n* financiación coarrendataria *f*

cottage industry *n* industria familiar *f*

council *n* consejo *m* **C~ of Economic Advisers** *n* Consejo *m* or Junta *f* de Asesores Económicos; **C~ of Europe** *n* Consejo de Europa *m*; ~ **house** *n* BrE vivienda de protección oficial *f*; **C~ of Ministers** *n* (of European Union) Consejo de Ministros *m*; ~ **tax** *n* BrE contribución urbana *f*, impuesto municipal *m*

counsel¹ *n* (advice) asesoramiento *m*; (lawyer) asesor(a) legal *m,f*

counsel² *vt* (advise) asesorar

count *vt* contar; ~ **on** *vt* contar con

counter¹ *n* (in shop) mostrador *m*; (in bank, post office) ventanilla *f*

counter² *vt* (claim) oponerse a; (deficiency, trend) contrarrestar; (idea, statement) rebatir, refutar

counter- *pref* contra-

counteract *vt* contrarrestar

counterclaim *n* contrademanda *f*

counterdeal *n* operación recíproca *f*

counterfeit *n* (act) falsificación *f*; (banknote) billete falso *m*; (coin) moneda falsa *f*; ~ **copy** *n* copia falsificada *f*; ~ **goods** *n pl* (in fashion sector) imitaciones ilegales *f pl*

counterfoil *n* talón *m*

countermand *vt* revocar

countermeasure *n* contramedida *f*

counteroffer *n* contraoferta *f*

counterpack *n* contrapaquete *m*

counterpart *n* (person) homólogo(-a) *m,f*; (thing) equivalente *m*

counterparty *n* BrE contraparte *f*; ~ **capital** *n* capital de la contraparte *m*

countersign *vt* (document, authorization) refrendar

countervailing¹ *adj* (argument, tendency) compensatorio; (credit) de compensación, compensatorio; (power) compensador

countervailing² *n* compensación *f*

country *n* (nation) país *m*; (countryside) campo *m*; ~ **code** *n* (Bank) código de país *m*; ~ **of destination** *n* país de destino *m*; ~ **of origin** *n* país de origen *m*; ~ **planning** *n* ordenación rural *f*; ~ **of residence** *n* país de residencia *m*; ~**-specific** *adj* (development aid) específico del país

county *n* condado *m*; ~ **council** *n* *gobierno regional de cada condado m*; ~ **court** *n* juzgado comarcal *m*

couple *vt* juntar; ~**d with sth** junto con algo; (Comp) acoplado con algo

coupon *n* cupón *m*; ~ **bond** *n* bono al portador con cupones *m*; ~ **rate** *n* interés ⋯▸

nominal *m*; ~ **yield** *n* rendimiento del cupón *m*

courier *n* mensajero(-a) *m,f*; ~ **firm** *n* empresa de mensajería *f*; ~ **service** *n* servicio de mensajería *m*

course *n* curso *m*; **go on a** ~ ir a hacer un curso; **a** ~ **in** *or* **on sth** un curso de *or* sobre algo; **in the** ~ **of sth** en el curso de algo, durante algo; **in due** ~ a su debido tiempo; **run its** ~ seguir su curso; **take a** ~ hacer un curso; ~ **of action** *n* curso de acción *m*

courseware *n* aplicaciones para cursos de educación a distancia *f pl*

court *n* juzgado *m*, tribunal *m*; **the** ~ **is adjourned** se levanta la sesión; **appear in** ~ comparecer ante el tribunal *or* los tribunales; **go to** ~ **(over sth)** ir a juicio (por algo); **the** ~ **is now in session** la audiencia está abierta; **the** ~ **will rise** pónganse de pie; **settle out of** ~ llegar a una transacción extrajudicial; **the case was settled out of** ~ la querella se resolvió de forma privada; **take sb to** ~ demandar a alguien; ~ **of appeal** *n* tribunal de apelación *m*; ~**-appointed attorney** *n* AmE ≈ abogado de oficio; ~ **of arbitration** *n* tribunal de arbitraje *m*; ~ **case** *n* causa *f*, juicio *m*; ~ **of inquiry** *n* BrE comisión de investigación *f*; **C**~ **of Justice** *n* Tribunal de Justicia *m*; ~ **of law** *n* tribunal judicial ordinario *m*; ~ **order** *n* orden del tribunal *f*; ~ **procedure** *n* norma procesal *f*, procedimiento judicial *or* legal *m*; ~ **proceedings** *n pl* proceso *m*; ~ **of record** *n* AmE *tribunal que guarda constancia de los autos o del sumario*

covenant *n* concierto *m*, contrato *m*

covenantor *n* parte contratante *f*

cover¹ *n* cubierta *f*; (Ins) BrE (*cf* ►**coverage** AmE) cobertura *f*; (Fin) garantía *f*; **take out** ~ **against sth** asegurarse contra algo; **under separate** ~ por separado; ~ **letter** *n* AmE (*cf* ►**covering letter** BrE) carta *f* adjunta *or* de presentación; ~ **note** *n* aviso de cobertura *m*; ~ **page** *n* portada *f*; ~ **ratio** *n* proporción *f or* relación *f* de cobertura

cover² *vt* (costs, expenses, area, event) cubrir; (liabilities) hacer frente a; (eventuality) contemplar; (with insurance) cubrir, asegurar; **be** ~**ed against sth** estar asegurado contra algo; **the policy** ~**s you against all risks** esta póliza lo cubre contra todo tipo de riesgos; ~**ed by insurance** (for damage, loss) cubierto por seguro; **this legislation only** ~**s large companies** esta legislación sólo se aplica a las empresas grandes; **cover up** *vt* (fact) ocultar, tapar

coverage *n* (in media) cobertura *f*; (Ins) AmE (*cf* ►**cover** BrE) cobertura *f*; ~ **ratio** *n* ratio de cobertura *m*

covered *adj* cubierto; ~ **call option** *n* opción de compra cubierta *f*; ~ **long** *n* largo cubierto *m*; ~ **option** *n* opción con garantía *f*; ~ **position** *n* BrE posición cubierta *f*; ~ **short** *n* venta a término cubierta *f*

covering: ~ **deed** *n* acta de garantía *f*; ~ **letter** *n* BrE (*cf* ►**cover letter** AmE) carta *f* adjunta *or* de presentación; ~ **warrant** *n* certificado de cobertura *m*

cover-up *n* encubrimiento *m*

cowboy *n* (infrml) (Ind) chapucero(-a) *m,f*; ~ **economy** *n* AmE (infrml) *economía del despilfarro y la irresponsabilidad*

cp. *abbr* (►**coupon**) cupón *m*

CP *abbr* (►**commercial paper**) papel comercial *m*; (►**Community Programme** BrE) programa comunitario *m*

CPA *abbr* (►**critical path analysis**) análisis del camino crítico *m*

C.P.A. *abbr* (►**certified public accountant**) AmE (*cf* ►**CA** BrE) censor(a) jurado(-a) de cuentas *m,f* Esp, contador(a) público(-a) *m,f* AmL

CPC *abbr* (►**cost per click**) coste *m* Esp *or* costo *m* AmL por clic

CPE *abbr* (►**centrally planned economy**) economía de planificación centralizada *f*

CPI *abbr* (►**consumer price index**) AmE, *cf* ►**RPI** BrE) IPC *m* (índice de precios al consumo)

CPM *abbr* (►**cost per mille** coste *m* Esp *or* costo *m* AmL por mil páginas vistas; (►**critical path method**) método del camino crítico *m*

CPP *abbr* (►**current purchasing power**) poder adquisitivo actual *m*

CPU *abbr* (►**central processing unit**) UCP *f* (unidad central de proceso)

cr *abbr* (►**credit**) crédito *m*; (►**creditor**) acreedor(a) *m,f*

CR *abbr* (►**carriage return**) retorno de carro *m*

cracker *n* (Comp) crácker *m*, revientasistemas *m*

craft *n* (trade) oficio *m*; ~ **union** *n* gremio *m*

crash¹ *n* (Stock) crac *m*, quiebra *f*; (Comp) quiebra *f*

crash² *vi* (prices, stock market) hundirse; (shares) caer a pique; (Comp) quebrarse

crawler *n* (Comp) rastreador *m*, gateador *m*, araña *f*

CRC *abbr* (►**camera-ready copy**) material listo para fotografiar *m*

cream n (best part) flor f y nata f, crema f; **the ~ of the crop** n lo mejor de lo mejor

cream off vt BrE (infrml) (profits) llevarse, quedarse con; **~ the best of sth** (money, demand) hacerse con lo mejor de algo

create vt (product, demand, opportunity, market) crear; (problem, difficulty) crear, causar

creation n creación f

creative adj (strategy, marketing, department) creativo; **~ accounting** n contabilidad creativa f

creativity n creatividad f

credentials n pl (references) referencias f pl; (identifying papers) documentos (de identidad) m pl;

credibility n credibilidad f; **~ gap** n margen de credibilidad m

credit¹ n crédito m; **buy/sell sth on ~** comprar/vender algo a crédito; **~ account** n cuenta de crédito f; **~ adviser** n asesor(a) m,f or consejero(-a) m,f de crédito; **~ agency** n agencia de crédito f; **~ agreement** n convenio de crédito m; **~ association** n entidad de crédito f; **~ balance** n saldo positivo m; **~ bureau** n oficina de crédito f; **~ buyer** n AmE (cf ►charge buyer BrE) comprador(a) a crédito m,f; **~ card** n tarjeta de crédito f; **~-card booking** n BrE (cf ►credit-card reservation** AmE) reserva con tarjeta de crédito f; **~ card issuer** n emisor de tarjetas de crédito m; **~ card payment** n pago con tarjeta de crédito m; **~-card reservation** n AmE (cf ►credit-card booking** BrE) reserva con tarjeta de crédito f; **~ card transaction** n transacción con tarjeta de crédito f; **~ ceiling** n límite del crédito m, techo de crédito m; **C~ Clearing** n BrE compensación de créditos f; **~ column** n columna del haber f; **~ control** n control de crédito m; **~ controller** n supervisor(a) m,f de crédito or de cobro; **~ counsellor** n asesor(a) de crédito m,f; **~ crunch** n dificultades crediticias f pl; **~ department** n departamento de crédito m; **~ entry** n asiento de abono m; **~ facilities** n pl facilidades crediticias f pl; **~ freeze** n congelación de créditos f; **~ guarantee** n garantía de crédito f; **~ history** n historial del crédito m; **~ institution** n institución crediticia f; **~ instrument** n instrumento de crédito m; **~ insurance** n seguro de crédito m; **~ limit** n límite del crédito m; **~ line** n línea de crédito f; **~ loss** n pérdida de crédito f; **~ management** n gestión de crédito f; **~ market** n mercado crediticio m; **~ note** n nota de crédito f; **~ policy** n política crediticia f; **~ rating** n grado de solvencia estimado m; **~ rationing** n racionamiento del crédito m; **~ reference**

~ agency n agencia de referencias de crédito f; **~ report** n informe crediticio m; **~ requirement** n requisito de crédito m; **~ risk** n riesgo del crédito m; **~ sale** n venta a crédito f; **~ side** n haber m; **~ slip** n nota de crédito f, ficha de pago f; **~ squeeze** n estrechamiento m or restricción f del crédito; **~ standing** n solvencia f; **~ terms** n pl condiciones f pl crediticias or de crédito; **~ title** n título de crédito m; **~ transfer** n transferencia de crédito f; **~ union** n BrE cooperativa f or unión f de crédito; **~ voucher** n comprobante de crédito m

credit² vt abonar; **~ money to an account** abonar dinero en una cuenta

creditable adj fidedigno

creditor n acreedor(a) m,f; **~ account** n cuenta acreedora f; **~ country** n país acreedor m; **~ department** n departamento acreedor m; **~s' ledger** n mayor de acreedores m; **~s' meeting** n asamblea de acreedores f

creditworthiness n solvencia (económica) f

creditworthy adj solvente (económicamente)

creeping adj progresivo; **~ inflation** n inflación reptante f; **~ tender** n oferta progresiva f

crime n delito m

criminal adj (act) delictivo; (case) criminal; (bankruptcy) fraudulento; (investigation) policial; **start ~ proceedings against sb** iniciar proceso penal contra alguien; **~ code** n código penal m; **~ law** n derecho penal m; **~ lawyer** n ≈ abogado(-a) penalista m,f; **~ liability** n responsabilidad penal f; **~ negligence** n negligencia criminal f; **~ offence** n delito m; **~ record** n antecedentes penales m pl

crisis n crisis f; **a ~ of confidence** una crisis de confianza; **reach ~ point** hacer crisis; **~ management** n gestión de crisis f

criteria n pl criterios m pl

criterion n criterio m

critical adj (analysis, situation, period) crítico; **be ~ of sth/sb** criticar algo/a alguien; **~ mass** n masa crítica f; **~ path** n camino crítico m; **~ path analysis** n análisis del camino crítico m; **~ path method** n método del camino crítico m

criticize vt criticar

CRM abbr (►customer relationship management) gestión de las relaciones con los clientes f

crook n (infrml) timador(a) m,f

crop n cosecha f; **~ failure** n mala cosecha f

cross¹ *adj* cruzado; ~ **assembler** *n* (Comp) ensamblador *m* cruzado *or* de referencias cruzadas; ~ **check** *n* verificación cruzada *f*; ~**-current** *n* contracorriente *f*; ~ **default** *n* (Fin) falta de pago cruzado *f*; ~ **hedge**, ~ **hedging** *n* cobertura cruzada *f*; ~ **liability** *n* (Ins) responsabilidad cruzada *f*; ~**-licensing** *n* explotación mutua de derechos de patente *f*; ~ **merchandising** *n* BrE comercialización cruzada *f*; ~**-reference** *n* remisión *f*; ~ **section** *n* sección transversal *f*; ~**-subsidization** *n* subvención cruzada *m*; ~**-subsidy** *n* subsidio cruzado *m*

cross² *vt* (cheque) cruzar; (frontier) atravesar; ~ **international frontiers** atravesar las fronteras internacionales; ~ **a picket line** cruzar una línea de piquetes

cross³ *n* (Stock) cruce *m*

cross-border *adj* (trading, merger) transfronterizo

crossed *adj* (cheque, loan, trade) cruzado

crossposting *n* envío múltiple *m*

crowd *n* (Stock) corro *m*

crowding out *n* (of borrowing, investment) exclusión *m*

crowd out *vt* (borrowers, investors) excluir

Crown *n* BrE Corona *f*; ~ **charges** *n pl* BrE gastos de la Corona *m pl*; ~ **corporation** *n* empresa pública *f*; ~ **loan** *n* crédito de la Corona *m*; ~ **royalty** *n* derecho de la corona *m*; ~ **share** *n* participación de Estado *f*

crude *adj* (containing impurities) crudo; (device, method) rudimentario, burdo; ~ **oil** *n* crudo *m*, petróleo crudo *m*

CS *abbr* (▶**Civil Service**) administración pública *f*

CSC *abbr* (▶**Civil Service Commission**) *comisión británica de funcionarios*

CST *abbr* (▶**Central Standard Time**) hora central establecida *f*

CT *abbr* (▶**combined transport**) transporte combinado *m*

CTI *abbr* (▶**computer-telephony integration**) integración informática-telefonía *f*

CTL *abbr* (▶**constructive total loss**) pérdida total implícita *f*

CTR *abbr* (▶**click-through rate**) proporción de clics *f*

CTRL key *n* (▶**control key**) tecla CTRL *f* (tecla de mando)

CTT *abbr* (▶**capital transfer tax**) BrE impuesto sobre las transferencias de capital *m*

cul-de-sac *n* callejón sin salida *m*

culminate in *vt* (discussions) culminar en

culpability *n* culpabilidad *f*

culpable *adj* (action) culposo; (person) culpable

cultural *adj* cultural; ~ **attaché** *n* agregado(-a) cultural *m,f*; ~ **center** AmE, ~ **centre** BrE *n* centro cultural *m*; ~ **revolution** *n* revolución cultural *f*

culture *n* cultura *f*; ~ **shock** *n* choque cultural *m*

cum *prep* con; ~ **coupon** con cupón; ~ **dividend** con dividendo; ~ **rights** con derechos; ~ **warrant** con garantía; ~ **and ex** con y sin; ~**-rights period** *n* periodo con derechos *m*

cum. *abbr* (▶**cumulative**) acumulativo

cumulative *adj* (dividend, income, tax) acumulativo; ~ **preference shares** *n pl* BrE, ~ **preferred stock** *n* AmE acciones privilegiadas de dividendo acumulativo *f pl*

curator *n* (in bankruptcy) administrador(a) *m,f*

curb market *n* AmE (*cf* ▶**kerb market** BrE) bolsín *m*

curbside conference *n* AmE (*cf* ▶**kerbside conference** BrE) *discusión de técnicas de venta entre alumno e instructor*

currency *n* (money) divisa *f*; (prevalence) difusión *f*; (validity - of a bill) periodo de validez *m*; **gain** ~ (view, fashion) extenderse, ganar adeptos; **have** ~ **(as sth)** tener difusión (como algo); ~ **account** *n* cuenta en divisas *f*; ~ **at a discount** *n* divisa bajo la par *f*; ~ **at a premium** *n* divisa por encima de la par *f*; ~ **borrowing** *n* préstamo en divisas *m* ~ **cocktail** *n* variedad de monedas *f*; ~ **deposits** *n pl* depósitos en divisas *m pl*; ~ **depreciation** *n* depreciación monetaria *f*; ~ **devaluation** *n* devaluación monetaria *f*; ~ **draft** *n* giro en divisas *m*; ~ **futures** *n pl* futuros sobre divisa *m pl*; ~ **futures contract** *n* contrato sobre futuros de divisas *m*; ~ **futures market** *n* mercado de futuros en divisas *m*; ~ **holding** *n* reserva de divisas *f*; ~ **in circulation** *n* moneda de curso legal *f*; ~ **issue** *n* emisión de papel moneda *f*; ~ **market** *n* mercado de divisas *m*; ~ **mix** *n* combinación de divisas *f*; ~ **option** *n* opción sobre divisas *f*; ~ **reform** *n* reforma monetaria *f*; ~ **restriction** *n* restricción de divisas *f*; ~ **revaluation** *n* revalorización monetaria *f*; ~ **stabilization scheme** *n* esquema de estabilización monetaria *m*; ~ **standard** *n* patrón monetario *m*; ~ **swap** *n* intercambio de monedas *m*; ~ **symbol** *n* símbolo monetario *m*; ~ **unit** *n* unidad monetaria *f*; ~ **value** *n* valor monetario *m*; ~ **zone** *n* zona monetaria *f*

current¹ *adj* (situation, policy, price list) actual; (month, year) en curso; (issue) último; (licence, membership) vigente; (opinion, practice)

corriente, común, habitual; ∼ **account** *n*
BrE (*cf* ►**checking account** AmE) cuenta
corriente *f*; ∼ **affairs** *n pl* noticias de
actualidad *f*; ∼ **annuity** *n* anualidad en
curso *f*; ∼ **asset** *n* activo *m* circulante *or*
realizable; ∼ **business year** *n* ejercicio
económico actual *m*; ∼ **cost** *n* coste *m* Esp
or costo *m* AmL corriente; ∼ **cost**
accounting *n* contabilidad de costes Esp *or*
costos AmL corrientes *f*; ∼ **demand** *n*
demanda actual *f*; ∼ **dollars** *n* dólares *m pl*
corrientes *or* actuales; ∼ **expenditure** *n*
saldo corriente *m*; ∼ **fiscal year** *n* año
fiscal en curso *m*; ∼ **holdings** *n pl* valores
en cartera actuales *m pl*; ∼ **insurance** *n*
seguro en vigor *m*; ∼ **liability** *n* pasivo
corriente *m*; ∼ **market price** *n* precio
actual de mercado *m*; ∼ **market value** *n*
valor comercial actual *m*; ∼ **operating**
profit *n* beneficio corriente de explotación
m; ∼ **price** *n* precio *m* actual *or* corriente;
∼ **purchasing power** *n* poder adquisitivo
actual *m*; ∼ **rate** *n* tarifa actual *f*; (of interest)
tipo actual *m*; ∼ **rate method** *n* AmE (*cf*
►**closing rate method** BrE) método del
cambio de cierre *m*; ∼ **return** *n*
rendimiento corriente *m*; ∼ **revenues** *n pl*
ingresos corrientes *m pl*; ∼ **stock** *n* valores
ordinarios *m pl*; ∼ **value** *n* (of property) valor
constante *m*; (of investment) valor actual *m*; ∼
yield *n* rédito corriente *m*

current[2] *n* corriente *f*; ∼ **adaptor** *n* AmE
(*cf* ►**mains adaptor** BrE) adaptador *m* a la
red *or* de corriente

curriculum *n* plan de estudios *m*; ∼ **vitae**
n BrE (*cf* ►**résumé** AmE) curriculum (vitae) *m*

cursor *n* cursor *m*

curtilage *n* terreno alrededor de la casa *m*

curve *n* curva *f*

custodial account *n* cuenta de custodia *f*

custodian *n* (Law) tutor(a) *m,f*; (Stock)
custodio(-a) *m,f*; (Prop) administrador(a) *m,f*;
∼ **account** *n* cuenta de custodia *f*

custodianship account *n* cuenta de
custodia *f*

custody *n* custodia *f*; ∼ **account** *n* cuenta
de custodia *f*; ∼ **charge** *n* cargo por
custodia *m*

custom *n* (trade) clientela *f*; (habit)
costumbre *f*; ∼**-designed** *adj* a la medida
del cliente; ∼**-made** *adj* hecho de encargo;
∼ **and practice** *n* costumbres *f pl* y
prácticas *f pl*, usos *m pl* y costumbres *f pl*

customer *n* cliente *mf*; **the** ∼ **is always**
right el cliente siempre tiene razón; ∼
account *n* cuenta de cliente *f*; ∼
awareness *n* conciencia del cliente *f*; ∼
base *n* base de clientes *f*; ∼ **billing** *n*
facturación al cliente *f*; ∼ **card** *n* tarjeta de
cliente *f*; ∼ **care** *n* atención al cliente *f*; ∼

careline *n* servicio telefónico de atención al
cliente *m*; ∼ **confidence** *n* confianza del
cliente *f*; ∼**-driven** *adj* personalizado; ∼
liaison *n* enlace con el cliente *m*; ∼ **ledger**
n mayor de clientes *m*; ∼ **orientation** *n*
orientación del cliente *f*; ∼**-oriented** *adj*
orientado al cliente; ∼ **profile** *n* perfil del
cliente *m*; ∼ **profiling** *n* realización de un
perfil de cliente *m*; ∼ **records** *n pl* registro
de clientes *m*; ∼ **relations** *n pl* relaciones
con los clientes *f pl*; ∼ **relations manager**
n director(a) de atención al cliente *m,f*; ∼
relationship management *n* gestión de
las relaciones con los clientes *f*; ∼
research *n* investigación de clientes *f*; ∼
retention *n* retención de clientes *f*; ∼
service *n* servicio al cliente *m*; ∼ **service**
department *n* departamento de servicio al
cliente *m*; ∼ **service manager** *n* jefe(-a)
del servicio al cliente *m,f*; ∼ **service**
representative *n* representante del
servicio al cliente *mf*

customizable *adj* con la facilidad de ser
adaptado a medida

customize *vt* personalizar

customized *adj* (service, keyboard)
personalizado

customs *n* aduana *f*; **go through** ∼ pasar
por la aduana; **no** ∼ **value** sin valor en
aduana; ∼ **agency** *n* agencia de aduanas *f*;
∼ **arrangement** *n* acuerdo aduanero *m*; ∼
authorities *n* arancel aduanero *m*; ∼
barrier *n* barrera aduanera *f*; ∼ **check** *n*
verificación de aduana *f*; ∼ **clearance** *n*
despacho *m* aduanero *or* de aduanas; ∼
control *n* control aduanero *m*; ∼
declaration *n* declaración de aduana *f*; ∼
duties *n pl* derechos aduaneros *m pl*; **C**∼
& Excise Department *n* BrE ≈
Departamento de Aduanas y Tributos *m*, ≈
Servicio de Aduanas *m*; ∼ **inspection** *n*
inspección aduanera *f*; ∼ **officer** *n*
aduanero(-a) *m,f*, oficial(a) de aduanas *m,f*;
∼ **procedure** *n* formalidades aduaneras *f*
pl; ∼ **regulations** *n pl* disposiciones
aduaneras *m pl*; ∼ **tariff** *n* arancel
aduanero *m*; ∼ **valuation** *n* valoración en
aduana *f*; ∼ **warehouse** *n* depósito
aduanero *m*

cut[1] *vt* (price, rate) rebajar, reducir; (budget)
recortar; (level, number) reducir; (service,
workforce) hacer recortes en; (Comp) cortar; ∼
one's losses cortar por lo sano; ∼ **and**
paste cortar y pegar; **cut back** ⯅**1**⯅ *vt*
(spending, production, numbers) reducir
⯅**2**⯅ *vi* hacer economías, constreñirse; ∼
back on investments reducir las
inversiones; **cut down** *vt* (expenditure)
reducir, recortar; (consumption) reducir,
disminuir; (text) acortar

cut² *n* (reduction) reducción *f*, recorte *m*, rebaja *f*; (act of deletion) corte *m*; (deleted material) trozo omitido *m*; (share) tajada *f*, parte *f*; ∼**s in spending** recortes en los gastos; **make** ∼**s in sth** hacer recortes en algo; **take a** ∼ **in salary** aceptar un sueldo más bajo; **take** *o* **get one's** ∼ **of sth** sacar tajada de algo

cut³ *adj* cortado; ∼ **paper** (Comp) papel cortado *m*

cutback *n* cese repentino *m*

cut-off *n* cierre *m*; (Acc) cierre de libros (para inventario) *m*; ∼**-off date** *n* fecha límite *f*

cut-price *adj* (goods, travel) a precio rebajado

cut-throat competition *n* competencia intensa *f*

cutting *n* BrE (*cf* ▸**clipping** AmE) (from newspaper) recorte *m*

cutting edge *n* vanguardia *f*

cutting-edge *adj* punta, de vanguardia

cv *abbr* (▸**chief value**) valor principal *m*

CV *abbr* BrE (▸**curriculum vitae** BrE, ▸**résumé** AmE) CV *m* (curriculum (vitae))

C/V *abbr* (▸**certificate of value**) certificado de valor *m*

CVO *abbr* (▸**certificate of value and origin**) certificado de valor y origen *m*

C'vr *abbr* (▸**cover**) cubierta *f*; (Ins) BrE (*cf* ▸**coverage** AmE) cobertura *f*; (Fin) garantía *f*

CW *abbr* (▸**comparable worth**) valor comparable *m*

CWE *abbr* (▸**cleared without examination**) desaduanado sin inspección

c.w.o. *abbr* (▸**cash with order**) pago al hacer el pedido *m*

cy. *abbr* (▸**currency**) divisa *f*

cyberauction *n* cibersubasta *f*

cybercafé *n* cibercafé *m*

cybercitizen *n* ciberciudadano(-a) *m,f*

cyberconsumer *n* ciberconsumidor(a) *m,f*

cybercrime *n* cibercrimen *m*

cybercriminal *n* cibercriminal *mf*

cyberculture *n* cibercultura *f*

cyberholic *n* ciberadicto(-a) *m,f*

cyberintermediary *n* ciberintermediario *m*

cybermagazine *n* ciberrevista *f*

cybermall *n* centro comercial virtual *m*, sitio de comercio electrónico *m*

cybermarketing *n* cibermercadotecnia *f*

cybernetics *n* cibernética *f*

cyberpiracy *n* ciberpiratería *f*

cybershopping *n* compra electrónica *f*

cyberspace *n* ciberespacio *m*

cybersquatter *n* cibersquatter *mf*, ciberocupa *mf*

cybersurfer *n* internauta *mf*, cibernauta *mf*

cybrarian *n* cibertecario(-a) *m,f*, ciberbibliotecario(-a) *m,f*

cycle *n* ciclo *m*

cyclic *adj* cíclico; ∼ **code** *n* código cíclico *m*; ∼ **variation** *n* variación cíclica *f*

cyclical *adj* cíclico; ∼ **company** *n* empresa sensible a los ciclos económicos; ∼ **demand** *n* demanda cíclica *f*; ∼ **fluctuation** *n* fluctuación cíclica *f*; ∼ **shares** *n pl* BrE, ∼ **stock** *n* AmE acciones cíclicas *f pl*; ∼ **trade** *n* comercio cíclico *m*; ∼ **unemployment** *n* desempleo cíclico *m*; ∼ **variation** *n* variación cíclica *f*

Dd

D *abbr* (▶**delivered**) entregado; (▶**delivery**) entrega *f*

DA *abbr* (▶**design** *o* **drawing automation**) AD (automatización del dibujo); (▶**District Attorney**) AmE fiscal *mf*

D/A *abbr* (▶**deposit account**) cuenta *f* de ahorros *or* a plazo; (▶**digital/analogue** BrE, ▶**digital-analog** AmE) D/A (digital/analógico); (▶**documents against acceptance**) documentos contra aceptación *m pl*; (▶**days after acceptance**) días transcurridos desde la aceptación *m pl*

dabbler *n* (Stock) especulador(a) en bolsa *m,f*

daily[1] *adj* (interest, loan, limit) diario; **go about one's ~ business** ocuparse de las cosas diarias; **~ activity report** *n* informe de la actividad diaria *m*; **~ allowance** *n* dieta *f*; (Ins) indemnización diaria *f*; **~ closing balance** *n* saldo de cierre diario *m*; **~ money rate** *n* (Bank) tasa de dinero a la vista *f*; **~ newspaper** *n* diario *m*; **~ settlement** *n* (Stock) liquidación diaria *f*

daily[2] *adv* diariamente

dairy *adj* (product, produce) lácteo; **~ farm** *n* granja lechera *f*

daisy chain *n* (Stock) *cadena de compra y venta para manipular el mercado*

damage[1] *n* (to goods, property, reputation) daño *m*; **~s** *n pl* daños y perjuicios *m pl*; (compensation) indemnización *f*; **~ control** *n* control de daños *m*; **~ limitation** *n* limitación *f* de las averías *or* de los daños

damage[2] *vt* (goods, property, reputation) dañar

damaged *adj* (goods) dañado; **~ in transit** *adj* dañado *or* averiado en tránsito

dampen *vt* (growth) amortiguar; (enthusiasm) moderar; (speculation) calmar

danger *n* peligro *m*; **be in ~** correr peligro; **be in ~ of doing sth** correr el peligro de hacer algo; **a ~ to sth/sb** un peligro para algo/alguien; **~ point** *n* punto peligroso *m*; **~ sign** *n*, **~ signal** *n* señal de peligro *m*

dangerous *adj* (substance, waste, goods) peligroso

DAP *abbr* (▶**documents against payment**) documentos contra pago *m pl*

dash *n* (in typography) guión *m*

DAT *abbr* (▶**digital audiotape**) cinta de audio digital *f*

data *n* datos *m pl*; **~ acquisition** *n* captación de datos *f*; **~ bank** *n* banco de datos *m*; **~ bit** *n* bitio de datos *m*; **~ broadcasting** *n* transmisión de datos *f*; **~ bus** *n* bus de datos *m*, enlace común de datos *m*; **~ capture** *n* toma de datos *f*; **~ card** *n* ficha de datos *f*; **~ carrier** *n* soporte de datos *m*; **~ collection** *n* recogida de datos *f*; **~ communication** *n* comunicación de datos *f*; **~ communications equipment** *n* equipo de comunicación de datos *m*; **~ compression** *n* compresión de datos *f*; **~ conversion** *n* conversión de datos *f*; **~ entry** *n* entrada de datos *f*; **~ entry operator** *n* grabador(a) de datos *m,f*; **~ field** *n* campo de datos *m*; **~ file** *n* fichero de datos *m*; **~ flow** *n* flujo de datos *m*; **~ flow chart** *n* diagrama de flujo de datos *m*; **~ gathering** *n* recogida de datos *f*; **~ input** *n* introducción de datos *f*; **~ integrity** *n* integridad de los datos *f*; **~ link** *n* enlace de datos *m*; **~ management** *n* gestión de datos *f*; **~ mining** *n* explotación de datos *f*; **~ network** *n* red de datos *f*; **~ output** *n* salida de datos *f*; **~ preparation** *n* preparación de datos *f*; **~ processing** *n* proceso de datos *m*; **~ protection** *n* protección de datos *f*; **D~ Protection Act** *n* BrE Ley de Protección de Datos *f*; **~ retrieval** *n* recuperación de datos *f*; **~ security** *n* seguridad de los datos *f*; **~ set** *n* conjunto de datos *m*; **~ sharing** *n* uso compartido de datos *m*; **~ sheet** *n* hoja de datos *f*; **~ storage** *n* almacenamiento de datos *m*; **~ stream** *n* flujo de datos *m*; **~ structure** *n* estructura de datos *f*, matriz *f*; **~ transfer rate** *n* caudal de transferencia de datos *m*; **~ type** *n* tipo de datos *m*; **~ warehouse** *n* almacén de datos *m*

database *n* base de datos *f*; **~ management system** *n* sistema de gestión de base de datos *m*

datamart *n* explotación de datos *f*

dataphone *n* datáfono *m*

date[1] *n* fecha *f*; **after ~** después de fecha; **at due ~** al vencimiento; **at some future ~** en una fecha por determinar; **at a later** *o* **subsequent ~** en fecha posterior; **set** *o* **fix a ~ for sth** fijar la fecha para algo; **to ~** hasta la fecha; **~ of acquisition** *n* fecha de adquisición *f*; **~ of exercise** *n* fecha de ejercicio *f*; **~ of filing** *n* (Patents) fecha de ····✦

presentación f; ∼ **of grant** n (of shares for employees, patent) fecha de concesión f; ∼ **of invoice** n fecha de la factura f; ∼ **of issue** n fecha de emisión f; ∼**-marking** n fechado m; ∼ **of maturity** n fecha de vencimiento f; ∼ **of payment** n día de pago m; ∼ **of record** n fecha de registro f; ∼ **of registration** n fecha de registro f

date² vt (letter, cheque) fechar; **in your letter** ∼**d 15 Jan.** en su carta con fecha del 15 de enero

dated bond n bono de vencimiento fijo m

dawn raid n (shares sale) incursión al amanecer f

day n día m; ∼ **after day** día tras día; **the** ∼ **after tomorrow** pasado mañana; **all** ∼ todo el día; **the** ∼ **before** el día anterior; **the** ∼ **before yesterday** anteayer; ∼ **by day** día a día; **from** ∼ **to day** de un día para otro; **an eight-hour** ∼ una jornada de ocho horas; **pay sb by the** ∼ pagar a alguien por día(s); ∼**s after acceptance** n pl días transcurridos desde la aceptación m pl; ∼**s after date** n pl días m pl transcurridos desde la fecha or el vencimiento; ∼ **laborer** AmE, ∼ **labourer** BrE n jornalero(-a) m,f; ∼ **loan** n préstamo diario de dinero m; ∼ **off** n día libre m; **take a** ∼ **off** tomarse un día libre; **give sb a** ∼ **off** darle un día libre a alguien; ∼ **shift** n turno de día m; ∼**s to delivery** n pl días hasta la entrega m pl; ∼**s to maturity** n pl días hasta el vencimiento m pl; ∼ **trader** n operador(a) de posiciones diarias m,f

daybook n diario m; (Acc) libro m diario or de entradas y salidas

daylight saving n horario de verano f

day-to-day adj diario; ∼ **funding activity** f; ∼ **money** n dinero a la vista m

daywork n trabajo diurno m

dayworker n trabajador(a) diurno(-a) m,f

db abbr (▸**daybook**) diario m; (Acc) libro m diario or de entradas y salidas; (▸**debenture**) obligación f

Dbk abbr (▸**drawback**) reembolso de derechos m; (Imp/Exp) drawback m

DBMS abbr (▸**database management system**) SGBD (sistema de gestión de base de datos)

DCA abbr (▸**debt collection agency**) agencia de cobro de deudas f

DCE abbr (▸**data communications equipment**) equipo de comunicación de datos m

DCF abbr (▸**discounted cash flow**) flujo de efectivo descontado m

DCO abbr (▸**debt collection order**) orden de cobro de deudas f

DCom abbr (▸**Doctor of Commerce**) Doctor(a) en Comercio m,f

DComL abbr (▸**Doctor of Commercial Law**) Doctor(a) en Derecho Comercial m,f

dd abbr (▸**days after date**) días m pl transcurridos desde la fecha or el vencimiento; (▸**delivered**) entregado

DD abbr (▸**demand draft**) giro a la vista m; (▸**direct debit**) CD (cargo directo)

DDB abbr (▸**distributed database**) DDB (base de datos distribuida)

DDE abbr (▸**direct data entry**) entrada directa de datos f

DDP abbr (▸**delivered duty paid**) entregado derechos pagados

DDU abbr (▸**delivered duty unpaid**) suministrado sin impuestos

dead adj (person) muerto; (capital, money) muerto, improductivo; (account) inactivo, muerto; ∼ **key** n (on keyboard) tecla desactivada f; ∼ **letter** n carta rehusada f; ∼ **rise** n (in sales) subida sin efecto f; ∼ **stock** n (Acc) existencias inmovilizadas f pl; (S&M) capital improductivo m; ∼ **time** n tiempo muerto m

deadbeat n (S&M) mal(a) pagador(a) m,f

dead-end job n trabajo sin perspectivas de avance m

deadline n (period) plazo m; (set time) hora límite f; (set date) fecha límite f; **the** ∼ **is next Thursday** el plazo expira el próximo jueves; **meet/miss a** ∼ cumplir/no cumplir con un plazo

deadlock¹ n (stalemate) punto muerto m; (Comp) bloqueo m; **break the** ∼ encontrar una salida; **end in** o **reach (a)** ∼ acabar en or llegar a un punto muerto

deadlock² vt estancar

deal¹ n trato m, acuerdo m; **close a** ∼ cerrar un trato; **do a** ∼ **(with sb)** hacer un trato (con alguien); **it's a** ∼ trato hecho; **make a** ∼ hacer un trato; **the** ∼ **is off** se acabó el trato; **the** ∼ **is on** se ha llegado a un acuerdo

deal² vi negociar; (Stock) operar; **deal in** vt negociar en; (Stock) operar en; **deal with** vt (company) tener relaciones comerciales con; (mail, arrangements, crisis) ocuparse de

dealer n comerciante mf; (authorized) concesionario(-a) m,f; (Stock) corredor(a) de bolsa m,f, intermediario(-a) m,f; ∼ **in securities** n intermediario(-a) en valores m,f

dealership n concesión f

dealing n (on stock exchange) comercio m; ∼**s** n pl transacciones f pl; **have** ∼**s with sb** tratar con alguien∼ **was suspended in the company's shares** se suspendió la cotización en bolsa de la compañía; ∼ **floor** n suelo de operaciones *m*; ~ **restriction** *n* restricción en transacciones *f*

dear *adj* (expensive) caro; **D~ Mr Jones** Estimado Sr. Jones; **D~ Sir or Madam** Estimado/a Señor(a), Muy señor mío/señora mía; **D~ Sirs** Muy señores míos

death *n* muerte *f*; ~ **benefit** *n* (Ins) compensación por defunción *f*; (Tax) indemnización por fallecimiento *f*; ~ **certificate** *n* certificado *m or* partida *f* de defunción; ~ **duty** *n* BrE derecho de sucesión *m*; ~ **tax** *n* AmE derechos de sucesión *m pl*

debase *vt* (currency) devaluar

debasement *n* (of currency) devaluación *f*

debate¹ *n* debate *m*

debate² *vt* debatir

debenture *n* obligación *f*; ~ **bond** *n* obligación hipotecaria *f*; ~ **capital** *n* capital en obligaciones *m*; ~ **holder** *n* obligacionista *mf*; ~ **loan** *n* empréstito *m*

debit¹ *n* débito *m*, debe *m*; ~ **account** *n* cuenta deudora *f*; ~ **balance** *n* saldo deudor *m*; ~ **card** *n* tarjeta *f* de cobro automático *or* de débito; ~ **column** *n* columna del debe *f*; ~ **entry** *n* débito *m*, asiento de cargo *m*; ~ **interest** *n* interés deudor *m*; ~ **memorandum** *n* AmE memorándum de débito *m*; ~ **note** *n* nota de cargo *f*; ~ **side** *n* debe *m*

debit² *vt* adeudar, cargar; ~ **a sum to an account** cargar una suma a una cuenta, debitar una cantidad de una cuenta

debrief *vt* pedir y recibir informe de

debriefing *n* informe del ejercicio *m*

debt *n* deuda *f*; (liability) obligación *f*; **be in ~** tener deudas; **be $2,000 dollars in ~ to sb** tener una deuda de 2.000 dólares con alguien; **get into ~** endeudarse; **get out of ~** salir de deudas; **~ owed to sb** deuda debida a alguien; **repay a ~** pagar *or* saldar una deuda; **run into ~** endeudarse; **run up a ~** contraer una deuda; **~ burden** *n* peso *m or* carga *f* de la deuda; **~ capital** *n* capital de empréstito *m*; **~ certificate** *n* certificado de adeudo *m*; **~ charges** *n pl* cargos *m pl or* gastos *m pl* de la deuda; **~ collection** *n* cobro de una deuda *m*; **~ collection agency** *n* agencia de cobro de deudas *f*; **~ collection order** *n* orden de cobro de deudas *f*; **~ collector** *n* cobrador(a) de deudas *m,f*; **~ consolidation** *n* consolidación de la deuda *f*; **~ conversion** *n* conversión de la deuda *f*; **~ factoring** *n* descuento de deudas *m*; **~ financing** *n* financiación de la deuda *f*; **~ forgiveness** *n* cancelación de la deuda *f*; **~ instrument** *n* instrumento de la deuda *m*; **~ management** *n* gestión de la deuda *f*; **~ manager** *n* administrador(a) de la deuda

m,f; **~ ratio** *n* proporción de endeudamiento *f*, relación de deuda *f*; **~ recovery period** *n* periodo de recuperación de la deuda *m*; **~ relief** *n* alivio de la deuda *m*; **~ rescheduling** *n*, **~ retructuring** *n* reprogramación de la deuda *f*; **~ retirement** *n* amortización de deuda *f*, retiro de una deuda *m*; **~ service** *n* servicio de la deuda *m*; **~ swap** *n* intercambio de la deuda *m*

debtor *n* deudor(a) *m,f*; **~ department** *n* departamento deudor *m*

debug *vt* depurar

debugger *n* depurador *m*

debugging *n* depuración *f*

decade *n* década *f*

deceased¹ *adj* difunto

deceased² *n* difunto(-a) *m,f*

decedent *n* AmE difunto(-a) *m,f*; **~'s estate** *n* patrimonio sucesorio *m*

deceive *vt* engañar

decelerate *vi* ralentizarse, desacelerar

deceleration *n* ralentización *f*, desaceleración *f*

decentralization *n* descentralización *f*

decentralize *vt* descentralizar

decentralized *adj* (government, management) descentralizado

deception *n* engaño *m*

deceptive *adj* engañoso; **~ entry** *n* entrada fraudulenta *f*; **~ packaging** *n* envase engañoso *m*

decide **1** *vt* (question, issue) decidir; (outcome) determinar; **~ to do sth** decidir hacer algo, decidirse a hacer algo; **~ what/when** decidir qué/cuando **2** *vi* decidirse; **~ against sth/sb** decidirse en contra de algo/alguien; **~ against doing sth** optar por no hacer algo; **decide on** *vt* (date, venue) decidir

decimal *adj* decimal; **~ digit** *n* dígito decimal *m*; **~ notation** *n* notación decimal *f*; **~ number** *n* número decimal *m*; **~ point** *n* coma decimal *f*; **~ sorting** *n* clasificación decimal *f*; **~-to-binary conversion** *n* conversión de decimal a binario *f*

decipher *vt* descifrar

decision *n* decisión *f*; **come to** *o* **reach a ~** llegar a una decisión; **make** *o* **take a ~** tomar una decisión; **~ aids** *n* ayudas para la toma de decisión *f pl*; **~ analysis** *n* análisis de decisiones *m*; **~ maker** *n* persona que toma las decisiones *f*; **~ making** *n* toma de decisiones *f*; **~-making process** *n* proceso de decisión *m*; **~ model** *n* modelo de decisión *m*; **~ table** *n* tabla de decisión *f*; **~ theory** *n* teoría de la decisión *f*; **~ tree** *n* árbol de decisión *m*

decisive *adj* (measures, influence, factor) decisivo; (leadership) firme; (person, personality) decidido, resuelto

deck *n* (for magnetic tape) platina *f*

declaration *n* declaración *f*; ~ **of bankruptcy** *n* declaración de quiebra *or* bancarrota *f*; ~ **of dividend** *n* publicación de dividendo *f*; ~ **of entry** *n* declaración de entrada *f*; ~ **of membership** *n* declaración de adhesión *f*; ~ **of options** *n* declaración de primas *f*; ~ **of origin** *n* declaración de origen *f*; ~ **of trust** *n* declaración de fideicomiso *f*

declare *vt* (goods, income, intention) declarar; (opinion) manifestar; **the company ~d a dividend of 3%** la compañía fijó un dividendo del 3%; **nothing to ~** nada que declarar; ~ **sth on oath** declarar algo bajo juramento; ~ **oneself bankrupt** declararse en bancarrota *or* en quiebra; ~ **an option** (Stock) ejecutar una opción

declared *adj* (aim, purpose, motive) declarado; ~ **dividend** *n* dividendo declarado *m*; ~ **value for customs** *n* valor declarado en aduanas *m*

declination *n* declive *m*

decline¹ *n* (in interest rates, investments) disminución *f*; (in demand) descenso *m*, disminución *f*; **fall into** *o* **go into (a) ~** empezar a decaer; **be in ~** estar en declive *or* en decadencia; **a 3% ~ in profits** una disminución en las ganancias del 3%; **be on the ~** ir disminuyendo

decline² **1** *vi* (production) disminuir, decrecer; (interest) disminuir, decaer; (standard, quality, industry, region) decaer; (in price) bajar; ~ **in importance** perder importancia; **their shares have ~d in value** sus acciones han disminuido de valor
2 *vt* (offer) declinar

declining *adj* (industry, region) en declive, en decadencia; ~ **balance depreciation** *n* depreciación de balance decreciente *f*; ~ **balance method** *n* método de depreciación de saldos decrecientes *m*; ~ **interest rate** *n* tipo de interés en descenso *m*; ~ **market** *n* mercado bajista *m*; ~ **share** *n* acción *f* declinante *or* de índice decreciente

decode *vt* decodificar

decoder *n* decodificador *m*

decoding *n* decodificación *f*

decommission *vt* decomisar

decommissioning *n* decomisación *f*

decommitment *n* cancelación de compromiso *f*

decompartmentalization *n* descompartimentalización *f*

decompress *vt* (data, file) descomprimir

decompression *n* (of data, file) descompresión *f*

DEcon *abbr* (▸**Doctor of Economics**) Doctor(a) en Economía *m,f*

decrease¹ **1** *vi* (amount, numbers, output, effectiveness) disminuir, decrecer; (prices) bajar; (quality) disminuir, bajar; (interest) disminuir, decaer
2 *vt* (spending) disminuir, reducir

decrease² *n* disminución *f*, descenso *m*; **a 3% ~ in inflation** una reducción del 3% en el índice de inflación; **a ~ in value** una disminución del valor; ~ **of risk** *n* (Ins) reducción del riesgo *f*

decreasing *adj* (rate, tax) decreciente; ~ **order** *n* (Comp) orden decreciente *m*

decree¹ *n* decreto *m*; (Law) auto *m*, fallo *m*, sentencia *f*; **issue a ~** promulgar un decreto; ~ **absolute** *n* sentencia definitiva de divorcio *f*; ~ **of bankruptcy** *n* sentencia de bancarrota *f*; ~ **nisi** *n* sentencia condicional de divorcio *f*

decree² *vt* decretar

decruitment *n* descontratación *f*, reajuste de personal *m*

decrypt *vt* descifrar

decryption *n* descifrado *m*, desciframiento *m*

dedicated *adj* (Comp) dedicado

dedomiciling *n* desdomiciliación *f*

deduce *vt* deducir

deduct *vt* deducir, descontar; ~ **sth from sth** deducir *or* descontar algo de algo; **income tax is ~ed automatically** el impuesto sobre la renta se deduce automáticamente

deductibility *n* deducibilidad *f*; ~ **of employer contributions** *n* deducibilidad de aportación patronal *f*

deductible *adj* deducible; ~ **business investment loss** *n* AmE (*cf* ▸**allowable business investment loss** BrE) pérdida deducible en inversiones empresariales *f*

deduction *n* deducción *f*; **he earns $900 dollars a week after ~s** gana 900 dólares semanales netos; **make a ~** hacer una deducción; ~ **at source** *n* deducción en origen *f*; ~ **for business meals** *n* deducción por comidas de negocios *f*; ~ **for gifts** *n* deducción por regalos *f*; ~ **for loan losses** *n* deducción por pérdidas de créditos *f*

deductive reasoning *n* razonamiento deductivo *m*

de-duped *adj* (Comp) deduplicado

deed *n* (legal document) escritura *f*; **the ~s to the house** la escritura de la casa; ~ **of assignation** *n* escritura de cesión *f*; ~ **of conveyance** *n* escritura de traslación de dominio *f*; ~ **of covenant** *n* BrE escritura de garantía *f*; ~ **of foundation** *n* escritura fundacional *f*; ~ **in lieu of foreclosure** *n* escritura en sustitución de embargo de bienes hipotecados *f*; ~ **of partnership** *n* escritura de constitución de una sociedad colectiva *f*; ~ **of trust** *n* escritura de fideicomiso *f*

deed poll *n* BrE escritura unilateral *f*; **he changed his name by** ~ se cambió el apellido oficialmente

deem *vt* estimar; ~ **necessary** estimar necesario

de-encryption *n* descifrado *m*, desencriptación *f*

deep *adj* profundo; ~ **discount** *n* descuento considerable *m*; ~ **discount bond** *n* bono con alto descuento *m*

deep-seated *adj* (problem) profundamente arraigado

def. *abbr* (▸**deferred**) diferido, aplazado

de facto *adj, adv* de hecho; ~ **corporation** *n* sociedad *f or* empresa *f* de facto; ~ **manager** *n* gerente en funciones *mf*

defamation *n* difamación *f*

defamatory *adj* (statement, accusation, allegation) difamatorio

defame *vt* difamar

default[1] *n* (on payments) mora *f*; (Comp) asignación implícita *f*; **he won his case by** ~ ganó el juicio en rebeldía del demandado; **be in** ~ **in filing** (Tax) no haber presentado la declaración; **in** ~ **of sb** por la ausencia de alguien; **in** ~ **of sth** por falta de algo; **be in** ~ **on one's mortgage** estar en mora en los pagos de la hipoteca; ~ **bonds** *n pl* bonos *m pl* defectuosos *or* en bancarrota; ~ **device** *n* (Comp) dispositivo implícito *m*; ~ **interest** *n* interés por falta de pago *m*; ~ **judgment** *n* fallo por incomparecencia de la parte *m*; ~ **option** *n* (Comp) opción por defecto *f*; ~ **of payment** *n* falta de pago *f*; ~ **penalty** *n* AmE, ~ **surcharge** *n* BrE recargo por incumplimiento de pago *m*

default[2] *vi* no pagar; **default on** *vt* no pagar

defaulted bond *n* bono (de interés) en mora *m*

defaulter *n* (on payments) moroso(-a) *m,f*; (Law) rebelde *m,f*

defaulting witness *n* testigo que no comparece *m*

defeasance *n* abrogación *f*, anulación *f*

defeat[1] *vt* (opponent) derrotar, vencer; (hopes, plans) frustrar; (bill, amendment, motion) rechar

defeat[2] *n* (by opponent) derrota *f*; (of hopes, plans) fracaso *m*; (of bill, amendment, motion) rechazo *m*

defect *n* defecto *m*

defective *adj* defectuoso; ~ **packaging** *n* embalaje defectuoso *m*; ~ **service** *n* servicio deficiente *m*; ~ **title** *n* título de propiedad con defecto de forma *m*

defence BrE, **defense** AmE *n* defensa *f*; ~ **envelope** *n* (Fin) apartado de defensa *m*

defend *vt* (idea, cause, person) defender; ~ **oneself** (Law) defender el propio caso

defendant *n* demandado(-a) *m,f*

defense AmE ▸**defence** BrE

defensive *adj* (measure, strategy) defensivo; ~ **budgeting** *n* BrE *elaboración de un presupuesto para ponerse al nivel de la competencia*; ~ **cushion** *n* colchón defensivo *m*; ~ **securities** *n* títulos estables *m pl*; ~ **spending** *n* gasto justificado *m*

defer *vt* (payment) diferir, aplazar, postergar AmL; (debt) diferir

deferment *n*, **deferral** *n* (of payment) aplazamiento *m*

deferred *adj* (payment, tax) diferido, aplazado; (charge, dividend, income, retirement) diferido; (shares, stock) de dividendo diferido; (sentence) aplazado; ~ **account** *n* AmE cuenta diferida *f*; ~ **amount** *n* (Tax) cantidad aplazada *f*; ~ **billing** *n* facturación diferida *f*; ~ **futures** *n pl* (Stock) futuros diferidos *m pl*; ~ **income tax** *n* impuesto sobre la renta diferido *m*; ~ **interest bond** *n* bono de interés diferido *m*

deficiency *n* (shortcoming) deficiencia *f*; (shortfall) déficit *m*; (Tax) descubierto *m*; ~ **judgment** *n* fallo de deficiencia *m*; ~ **letter** *n* (Fin) carta de deficiencias *f*; (Stock) *carta de la comisión de operaciones de la bolsa pidiendo una revisión del prospecto*

deficient *adj* deficiente; ~ **tax installment** AmE, ~ **tax instalment** BrE *n* pago fraccionario incorrecto del impuesto *m*

deficit *n* déficit *m*; **make up/show a** ~ **of \$3,000** cubrir/arrojar un déficit de 3.000 dólares; ~ **balance of payments** *n* balanza de pagos deficitaria *f*; ~ **financing** *n* financiación mediante déficit *f*; ~ **spending** *n* gastos deficitarios *m pl*

define *vt* (word, situation, position) definir; (framework, limit, powers, duties) delimitar; ~**d benefit** prestación definida *f*; ~**d contribution** aportación definida *f*, aporte definido *m*

definition *n* (statement of meaning) definición *f*; (delimitation) delimitación *f*

deflate *vt* (economy, currency) deflactar

deflation *n* deflación *f*

deflationary *adj* (policy, measures, pressure) deflacionario

deforestation *n* desforestación *f*

deform *vt* deformar

deformation *n* deformación *f*

defraud *vt* (person, company) estafar; (state, tax authorities) defraudar; ∼ **sb of sth** estafarle algo a alguien

defraudation *n* fraude *m*

defray *vt* (cost, expense) sufragar

defunct *adj* (company) desaparecido, disuelto

degear *vt* (Fin) desarmonizar

degradation *n* (Envir) degradación *f*

degrade *vt* (Envir) degradar

degree *n* (of accuracy, damage, risk, fluctuation) grado *m*; (qualification) título *m*; **have a ∼ in sth from the University of Oxford** ser graduado *or* licenciado en algo por la universidad de Oxford; **in the slightest ∼** en el menor grado; **take a ∼ in law** hacer la carrera de derecho; **to a high ∼** en alto grado; **to a lesser ∼** en menor grado; **to some** *o* **a certain ∼** hasta cierto grado *or* punto; **to such a ∼ that...** hasta tal punto que..., en *or* a tal grado que...; ∼ **course** *n* licenciatura *f*

degressive tax *n* impuesto degresivo *m*

dehire *vt* AmE (worker) despedir

dehiring *n* AmE (of worker) despido *m*

deindustrialization *n* desindustrialización *f*

deinstall *vt* (Comp) desinstalar

de jure *adj*, *adv* de derecho

del. *abbr* (▶**delegation**) delegación *f*

DEL *abbr* (▶**delete key**) SUPR (tecla de borrado)

delay[1] *n* (holdup) retraso *m*, demora *f* AmL; (Comp) demora *f*; (Law) mora *f*; **without ∼** sin demora

delay[2] *vt* (decision, payment, departure) retrasar, demorar AmL

delayed *adj* (effect, reaction) retardado; ∼ **delivery** *n* entrega aplazada *f*; ∼ **price** *n* precio diferido *m*

delaying tactics *n pl* tácticas dilatorias *f pl*

del credere agent *n* agente de garantía *mf*

delegate[1] *n* delegado(-a) *m,f*; (to convention) compromisario(-a) *m,f*

delegate[2] *vt* delegar; ∼ **authority to sb** delegar la autoridad en alguien

delegation *n* delegación *f*; ∼ **of authorization** *n* delegación de autorización *f*; ∼ **of signing authority** *n* delegación de firma *f*

delete *vt* suprimir; (by crossing out) tachar; (Comp) borrar, suprimir; (debt) anular; ∼ **as applicable** táchese lo que no corresponda

delete key *n* tecla de borrado *f*

deletion *n* supresión *f*; (crossing out) tachadura *f*; (Comp) borrado *m*, supresión *f*; (of debt) cancelación *f*, eliminación *f*

delict *n* (in Scots law) agravio *m*

delimit *vt* delimitar

delinquency *n* (failure to pay) morosidad *f*

delinquent *adj* (debtor, taxpayer, account) moroso

delisting *n* suspensión de cotización *f*

deliver [1] *vt* (goods, message) entregar; (service) prestar; (speech) pronunciar; (ultimatum) dar; (warning) hacer; (judgment) dictar, pronunciar, emitir; (shares) emitir [2] *vi* (make deliveries) hacer repartos a domicilio; (do what is promised or required) cumplir; **we ∼** servicio a domicilio; ∼ **on a promise** cumplir lo prometido

deliverable *adj* (bill, security) entregable

delivered *adj* entregado; ∼ **duty paid** entregado derechos pagados; ∼ **duty unpaid** suministrado sin impuestos; ∼ **price** *n* precio entregado *m*

delivery *n* entrega *f*; (transfer) traspaso *m*; **buy for future ∼** comprar a entrega futura; **make ∼** (of currency) hacer entrega; **pay on ∼** pagar a la entrega *or* al recibo de la mercancía; **take ∼ (of sth)** aceptar entrega (de algo); ∼ **versus payment** (Stock) entrega contra reembolso; ∼ **broker** *n* intermediario(-a) de bolsa de entrega *m,f*; ∼ **charge** *n* gastos de entrega *m pl*; ∼ **date** *n* fecha de entrega *f*; ∼ **day** *n* día de entrega *m*; ∼ **month** *n* mes de entrega *m*; ∼ **note** *n* nota de entrega *f*; ∼ **order** *n* orden de entrega *f*; ∼ **period** *n* plazo de entrega *m*; ∼ **receipt** *n* recibo de entrega *m*; ∼ **service** *n* servicio de reparto *m*; ∼ **terms** *n pl* condiciones de entrega *f pl*; ∼ **time** *n* plazo de entrega *m*

delta *n* delta *m*; ∼ **factor** *n* BrE factor delta *m*; ∼ **hedging** *n* compensación triangular *f*; ∼ **shares** *n pl* BrE, ∼ **stock** *n* AmE acciones delta *f pl*

de luxe *adj* de lujo

dely *abbr* (▶**delivery**) entrega *f*

DEM *abbr* (▶**Domestic Equities Market**) Mercado Nacional de Títulos *m*

demand[1] *n* demanda *f*; **by popular ∼** a petición del público; **create a ∼ for sth** crear demanda de algo; **in ∼** solicitado; **make unrealistic ∼s of one's staff** exigir cosas poco realistas de sus empleados; **her work makes great ∼s on her time** el trabajo le absorbe gran parte del tiempo; **meet the ∼ for sth** cubrir la demanda de algo; **the ∼s of the job** las exigencias del trabajo; **on ∼** a requerimiento; **∼ account** n cuenta a la vista f; **∼ curve** n curva de demanda f; **∼ deposit** n depósito (exigible) a la vista m; **∼ draft** n giro a la vista m; **∼ forecasting** n previsión de la demanda f; **∼ function** n función de demanda f; **∼-led growth** n crecimiento arrastrado por la demanda m; **∼ money** n dinero a la vista m; **∼ note** n pagaré a la vista m; **∼-pull inflation** n inflación de demanda f

demand² vt (better pay, better conditions) reclamar; (payment) requerir; (dedication, perseverance) exigir, requerir; **this document ∼s your immediate attention** este documento requiere su atención inmediata; **∼ sth of sb** exigirle algo a alguien

demarcation n delimitación f; **∼ dispute** n BrE conflicto intergremial m

demarketing n desmarketing m

dematerialization n desmaterialización f

dematerialized adj desmaterializado

demerger n (of companies) separación f

demerit goods n pl bienes no deseables m pl

demised premises n pl local alquilado m

demo n demo m; **∼ version** n versión de demostración f

democracy n democracia f

democratic adj democrático; **∼ management** n administración f or gestión f democrática

democratically adv democráticamente

demographic adj demográfico; **∼ accounting** n contabilidad demográfica f

demographics n perfil demográfico m

demography n demografía f

demolition n demolición m; **∼ costs** n pl costes m pl Esp or costos m pl AmL de demolición

demonetization n desmonetización f

demonstrate 1 vt (appliance, product) hacer una demostración de; (need, ability, method) demostrar

2 vi (in protest) manifestarse; (in selling) hacer demostraciones; **∼ in favour** BrE o **favor** AmE **of/against sth/sb** manifestarse a favor de/en contra de algo/alguien

demonstration n demostración f; (protest) manifestación f

demoralize vt desmoralizar

demote vt bajar de categoría

demotion n descenso de categoría m

demotivate vt desanimar, desmotivar

demotivation n desánimo m, desmotivación f

demurrer n (Law) excepción de falta de acción f

demutualization n desmutualización f

demutualize vt desmutualizar

denationalization n desnacionalización f

denationalize vt desnacionalizar

denationalized adj (money) desnacionalizado

denial n (repudiation) negación f; (of request, rights) denegación f

denom. abbr (▶**denomination**) (of notes) valor nominal m

denomination n (of notes) valor nominal m

denominator n denominador m

de novo adj, adv de nuevo

densely adv densamente; **∼-populated** adj densamente poblado

density n densidad f; **∼ zoning** n AmE plan de urbanización regulando estrictamente el uso del terreno

deny vt (accusation, fact) negar; (rumour) desmentir; (request) denegar; **∼ sb sth** negarle algo a alguien

department n departamento m; **∼ head** n (in company) director(a) de departamento m,f; **∼ manager** n (in department store, shop) jefe(-a) de departamento m,f; **∼ store** n gran almacén m; **∼ store chain** n cadena de grandes almacenes f

departmental adj (account, assets, corporation) departamental; (management) por departamentos, departamental; **at ∼ level** a nivel departamental or del departamento; **∼ head** n jefe(-a) de departamento m,f; **∼ manager** n gerente mf departamental or del departamento

departmentalization n división departamental f

departure n salida f; **a ∼ from the norm** una desviación de la norma; **∼ lounge** n antesala de salida f; **∼ tax** n impuesto de salida del país; **∼ time** n hora de salida f

dependant n carga familiar f, persona a cargo f; **∼ tax credit** n deducción por carga familiar f

dependency n dependencia f; **∼ culture** n cultura de la dependencia f; **∼ theory** n teoría de la dependencia f

dependent adj dependiente; **be ∼ on sth/sb** depender de algo/alguien; **∼ child** n hijo dependiente m

depend on vt depender de

depletable resources n pl recursos agotables m pl

deplete vt (supplies, stock, funds - reduce) reducir; (- exhaust) agotar

depletion n (reduction) reducción f; (exhaustion) agotamiento m

deploy *vt* utilizar, hacer uso de

deployment *n* (of resources) utilización *f*

deponent *n* (Law) declarante *mf*

depopulation *n* despoblación *f*

deposit[1] *n* (into account) depósito *m*; (down payment - on purchase) depósito *m*; (- on property) entrega inicial *f*, entrada *f* Esp; **on ~** (en una cuenta) a plazo fijo; **put down a ~ on sth** hacer una entrega inicial *or* dar una entrada Esp para algo; **take a ~** (Stock) aceptar un depósito; **~ account** *n* cuenta *f* de ahorros *or* a plazo *f*; **~ bank** *n* banco *m* comercial *or* de depósitos; **~ bond** *n* BrE bono de depósito *m*; **~ book** *n* libreta bancaria *f*; **~ certificate** *n* certificado de depósito *m*; **~ facility** *n* servicio de depósitos financieros *m*; **~ in transit** *n* depósito en línea *m*; **~ institution** *n* institución de depósito *f*; **~ instrument** *n* instrumento de depósito *m*; **~ insurance** *n* garantía de depósitos *f*; **~ note** *n* formulario de depósito *m*; **~ passbook** *n* libreta de depósitos *f*; **~ rate** *n* tasa de depósito *f*; **~ slip** *n* recibo de depósito *m*

deposit[2] *vt* (money) depositar

deposition *n* deposición *f*, declaración *f*

depositor *n* depositante *mf*

depository *n* depositario(-a) *m,f*

depot *n* depósito *m*; **~ charges** *n pl* gastos de almacén *m pl*

depreciable *adj* (assets, cost, property) amortizable

depreciate [1] *vt* (investment, assets) amortizar; (currency) depreciar [2] *vi* (assets, shares, currency) depreciarse

depreciated *adj* (cost) amortizado, depreciado

depreciation *n* amortización *f*, depreciación *f*; **~ adjustment** *n* ajuste de amortización *m*; **~ allowance** *n* provisión por depreciación *f*; **~ expenses** *n pl* gastos de depreciación *m pl*; **~ of fixed assets** *n* depreciación de activos fijos *f*; **~ rate** *n* coeficiente de amortización *m*; **~ recapture** *n* recuperación de la depreciación *f*; **~ reserve** *n* fondo de amortización *m*; **~ schedule** *n* cuadro *m* de amortización *or* de depreciación

depressed *adj* (industry, prices, region) deprimido; (economy, market) deprimido, en crisis

depression *n* depresión *f*

deprive *vt* privar; **~ sth/sb of sth** privar algo/a alguien de algo

deprived *adj* (region) carenciado; **~ of sth** privado de algo

dept. *abbr* (▶**department**) dpto. (departamento)

deputy *n* (second-in-command) segundo(-a) *m,f*; (substitute) suplente *mf*, reemplazo *mf*; **~ chairman** *n* vicepresidente(-a) *m,f*; **~ chief executive** *n* director(a) ejecutivo(-a) adjunto(-a) *m,f*; **~ director** *n*, **~ manager** *n* director(a) adjunto(-a) *m,f*; **~ managing director** *n* director(a) ejecutivo(-a) adjunto(-a) *m,f*, subdirector(a) gerente *m,f*

derecognition *n* desreconocimiento *m*

deregulate *vt* desregular

deregulation *n* desregulación *f*

dereliction of duty *n* abandono del servicio *m*

derivation schedule *n* (Acc) tabla de deducciones *f*

derivative[1] *n* derivado *m*; **~s market** *n* (Fin) mercado de derivados *m*

derivative[2] *adj* (product) derivado; **~ instrument** *n* (Fin) instrumento derivado *m*

derived demand *n* demanda derivada *f*

derogate *vt* derogar

derogation *n* derogación *f*

derogatory stipulation *n* estipulación derogatoria *f*

descending tops *n pl* (Stock) máximos descendentes *m pl*, topes máximos *m pl*

descent *n* (Law) sucesión *f*

describe *vt* describir; **~ sth/sb as sth** describir algo/a alguien como algo

description *n* descripción *f*; **of every ~, of all ~s** de todo tipo, de toda clase

descriptive *adj* descriptivo

deselect *vt* (HRM) *despedir a una persona en formación antes de que haya acabado el programa*

desertification *n* desertificación *f*

design[1] *n* (of product, machine) diseño *m*; (drawing) diseño *m*, boceto *m*; (pattern, decoration) diseño *m*, motivo *m*, dibujo *m*; (product, model) modelo *m*; (plan) plan *m*; **by ~** deliberadamente; **have ~s on sth/sb** tener los ojos puestos en algo/alguien; **~ aids** *n pl* ayudas de diseño *f pl*; **~ automation** *n* automatización del dibujo *f*; **~ draft** *n* boceto de diseño *m*; **~ editor** *n* editor(a) de diseño *m,f*; **~ engineer** *n* ingeniero(-a) de diseño *m,f*; **~ fault** *n* defecto de diseño *m*; **D~ Registry** *n* (for intellectual property) Registro de Proyectos *m*

design[2] *vt* (product) diseñar; (course, programme) planear, estructurar; **be ~ed as sth** estar pensado como algo; **be ~ed for sth/sb** estar diseñado para algo/alguien; **be ~ed to do sth** estar diseñado para hacer algo

designate *vt* designar

designated *adj* (amount, beneficiary, property) designado; (income, surplus) previsto

designation *n* designación *f*

designer *n* diseñador(a) *m,f*; ~ **products**
n pl productos de diseño *m pl*

desire *n* deseo *m*; ~ **to purchase** *n* deseo
de comprar *m*

desk *n* escritorio *m*; ~ **clerk** *n*
empleado(-a) administrativo(-a) *m,f*; ~
planner *n* organizador(a) de escritorio *m,f*;
~ **research** *n* investigación de datos ya
existentes *f*; ~ **trader** *n* (Stock) corredor(a)
de despacho *m,f*

deskilling *n* descalificación *f*

desktop *adj* (computer) de (sobre)mesa, de
escritorio; ~ **publishing** *n* autoedición *f*; ~
unit *n* (Comp) unidad de escritorio *f*

despite *prep* a pesar de

destabilize *vt* desestabilizar

destination *n* destino *m*; ~ **airport** *n*
aeropuerto de destino *m*; ~ **marketing** *n*
marketing *m* de destino *or* de persuasión; ~
port *n* puerto de destino *m*

destruction *n* destrucción *f*

detail *n* detalle *m*, pormenor *m*; **for further**
~**s** para más información; **go into** ~**(s)**
entrar en detalles; **in** ~ detalladamente,
minuciosamente; **pay attention to** ~**(s)**
prestar atención a los detalles

detailed *adj* (account, description) detallado,
minucioso, pormenorizado; (examination)
minucioso, detenido

deteriorate *vi* deteriorarse

deterioration *n* deterioro *m*

determination *n* (in court) resolución *f*;
(Tax) determinación *f*

determine *vt* (cause) determinar; ~ **to do**
sth decidirse a hacer algo

determined *adj* decidido, resuelto; **be** ~
to do sth estar decidido a hacer algo

deterrent *n* factor disuasorio *m*

detour *n* desvío *m*

detriment *n* detrimento *m*, perjuicio *m*; **to**
the ~ **of sth/sb** en detrimento *or* perjuicio
de algo/alguien; **without** ~ **to sth/sb** sin
perjuicio a *or* para algo/alguien

detrimental *adj* perjudicial; ~ **to sth/sb**
perjudicial a *or* para algo/alguien

de-unionization *n* BrE desindicalización *f*

devaluation *n* devaluación *f*

devalue **1** *vt* devaluar
2 *vi* devaluarse

develop **1** *vt* (system, software, prototype, idea)
desarrollar; (theory, plan) desarrollar,
elaborar; (business, range) ampliar; (resources)
explotar; (land, area) urbanizar; (photograph)
revelar
2 *vi* (industry) desarrollarse; (nation, region)
desarrollarse, progresar; (problem, complication)
surgir, aparecer; (crisis) producirse,
progresar; ~ **from sth** evolucionar a partir

de algo; ~ **into sth** convertirse *or*
transformarse en algo

developed *adj* (country, market) desarrollado

developer *n* (Prop) promotor(a) *m,f*

developing *adj* (country, world, market) en
(vías de) desarrollo

development *n* (of idea, argument)
desarrollo *m*; (of situation, events) desarrollo *m*,
evolución *f*; (of land, area) urbanización *f*; (of
resources) explotación *f*; (event)
acontecimiento *m*, suceso *m*; **there have**
been new ~**s** las cosas han tomado un
nuevo rumbo; ~ **aid** *n* ayuda al desarrollo
f; ~ **area** *n* BrE área de desarrollo *f*; ~
assistance *n* ayuda al desarrollo *f*; ~
bank *n* banco de desarrollo *m*; ~ **director**
n director(a) de desarrollo *m,f*; ~ **loan** *n*
préstamo al desarrollo *m*; ~ **management**
n gerencia de desarrollo *f*; ~ **manager** *n*
director(a) de desarrollo *m,f*; ~ **plan** *n* plan
de desarrollo *m*; ~ **planning** *n* ,
planificación del desarrollo *f*; ~ **policy** *n*
política de desarrollo *f*; ~ **potential** *n*
potencial de desarrollo *m*; ~ **program** AmE,
~ **programme** BrE *n* programa de
desarrollo *m*; ~ **project** *n* proyecto de
desarrollo *m*; ~ **strategy** *n* estrategia de
desarrollo *f*

developmental *adj* en desarrollo,
evolutivo

deviation *n* desviación *f*; ~ **policy** *n*
política de desviación *f*

device *n* aparato *m*, dispositivo *m*;
~**-independent** *adj* (Comp) independiente
del tipo de dispositivo; ~ **mark** *n* (Patents)
marca del invento *f* ; ~**-specific** *adj* (Comp)
específico de un dispositivo

devise[1] *vt* (plan, method, system) idear, crear,
concebir; (machine, tool) inventar; ~ **sth to sb**
(Law) legar algo a alguien

devise[2] *n* (Law) herencia *f*

devisee *n* (Law) legatario(a) *m,f*

dft *abbr* (▶**draft** [1]) (Fin) cheque *m*

DFT *abbr* (▶**direct funds transfer**)
transferencia de fondos directa *f*

DHTML *abbr* (▶**Dynamic Hypertext**
Mark-up Language) HTML dinámico *m*
(lenguaje de referencia de hipertexto
dinámico)

diagnosis *n* diagnosis *f*

diagnostic[1] *n* diagnóstico *m*, detección de
averías *f*

diagnostic[2] *adj* (routine, message) de
diagnóstico

diagonal *adj* diagonal; ~ **spread** *n*
(Stock) diferencial diagonal *m*

dial[1] *vti* marcar, discar AmL; **dial up** *vti*
marcar, discar AmL

dial[2] *n* (of telephone) disco *m*; (of measuring instrument) cuadrante *m*; (of radio) dial *m*; ~ **tone** *n* AmE (*cf* ▶**dialling tone** BrE) tono de marcar *m*

dialling BrE, **dialing** AmE *n* marcación *f*, discado *m* AmL; ~ **code** *n* BrE (*cf* ▶**area code** AmE) prefijo *m*; ~ **tone** *n* BrE (*cf* ▶**dial tone** AmE) tono de marcar *m*

dialogue BrE, **dialog** AmE *n* diálogo *m*; ~ **box** *n* cuadro de diálogo *m*

dial-up *adj* conmutado, de marcación; ~ **access** *n* acceso conmutado *m*; ~ **connection** *n* conexión conmutada *m*

diary *n* agenda *f*; **let me check (in) my** ~ déjame consultar mi agenda

dictate *vt* (letter) dictar

dictation *n* dictado *m*; **take** ~ escribir al dictado

die *vi* morir; ~ **intestate** morir intestado

diesel[1] *n* (fuel) diesel *m*, gasóleo *m*, gasoil *m*; (vehicle) vehículo diesel *m*

diesel[2] *adj* (engine) diesel; ~ **oil** *n* gasóleo *m*, gasoil *m*

differ *vi* diferir; ~ **from sth/sb** diferenciarse *or* diferir de algo/alguien; ~ **with sb (about/on sth)** discrepar con alguien (sobre/en algo)

difference *n* diferencia *f*; **make up the** ~ **(in price)** poner la diferencia (en el precio); **a** ~ **of opinion over sth** una desavenencia sobre algo; **settle/resolve one's** ~**s** saldar/resolver sus diferencias

different *adj* diferente, distinto; ~ **from sth/sb** diferente *or* distinto de algo/alguien

differential[1] *adj* (analysis, cost, price, pricing, profit) diferencial

differential[2] *n* diferencial *m*

differentiate *vti* distinguir, diferenciar; ~ **between A and B** distinguir *or* diferenciar entre A y B; ~ **A from B** distinguir *or* diferenciar A de B

differentiated *adj* (marketing, product) diferenciado

differentiation *n* diferenciación *f*; ~ **strategy** *n* estrategia de diferenciación *f*

diffusion *n* difusión *f*

digerati *n pl* digeratos *m pl*

digit *n* dígito *m*

digital *adj* digital; ~/**analogue** BrE, **digital-analog** AmE *adj* digital/analógico; ~ **audiotape** *n* cinta de audio digital *f*; ~ **cash** *n* dinero electrónico *m*; ~ **certificate** *n* certificado digital *m*; ~ **convergence** *n* convergencia digital *f*; ~ **data** *n* datos digitales *m pl*; ~ **divide** *n* brecha digital *f*; ~ **economy** *n* economía digital *f*; ~ **marketplace** *n* mercado digital *m*; ~ **selective calling** *n* llamada selectiva digital *f*; ~ **signature** *n* firma digital *f*;

~ **sort** *n* clasificación numérica *f*; ~**-to-analogue converter** BrE, **digital-to-analog** AmE *n* convertidor de digital a analógico *m*; ~ **versatile disc** BrE, ~ **versatile disk** AmE *n* disco versátil digital *m*; ~ **videodisc** BrE, ~ **videodisk** AmE *n* disco *m* vídeo Esp *or* video AmL digital; ~ **wallet** *n* billetero electrónico *m*

digitization *n*, **digitalization** *n* digitalización *f*

digitize *vt*, **digitalize** *vt* digitalizar

dilapidation *n* dilapidación *f*

diluted *adj* (capital) desvalorizado

dilution *n* (of capital, equity) desvalorización *f*; (of labour) dilución *f*

DIM *abbr* (▶**Diploma in Industrial Management**) ≈ Diploma en Dirección de Empresa *m*

dime *n* AmE (infml) *moneda de diez centavos*

diminish ① *vi* (cost, number, amount) disminuir, reducirse; **the currency has** ~**ed in value** la moneda ha disminuido en valor *or* se ha depreciado ② *vt* (size, cost) reducir, disminuir

diminishing *adj* (amount, importance) cada vez menor; **the law of** ~ **returns** la ley de los rendimientos decrecientes; ~**-balance method** *n* método de saldo decreciente *m*

diode *n* diodo *m*

dip[1] *n* (in sales, production) caída *f*, descenso *m*

dip[2] *vi* (profits, sales, prices) bajar; **dip into** *vt* (savings, reserves) echar mano de

DipCOM *abbr* (▶**Diploma of Commerce**) ≈ Diploma en Comercio *m*

DipEcon *abbr* (▶**Diploma of Economics**) ≈ Diploma en Economía *m*

diploma *n* diploma *m*; **have** *o* **hold a** ~ **in sth** ser diplomado en algo; **D**~ **of Commerce** *n* ≈ Diploma en Comercio *m*; **D**~ **of Economics** *n* ≈ Diploma en Economía *m*; **D**~ **in Industrial Management** *n* ≈ Diploma en Dirección de Empresa *m*; **D**~ **in Public Administration** *n* ≈ Diploma en Administración Pública *m*

diplomacy *n* diplomacia *f*

diplomatic *adj* diplomático; **break off** ~ **relations** romper las relaciones diplomáticas; ~ **bag** *n* (*cf* ▶**diplomatic pouch** AmE) valija diplomática *f*; ~ **mission** *n* misión diplomática *m*; ~ **pouch** *n* AmE valija diplomática *f*; **D**~ **Service** *n* BrE Servicio Diplomático *m*

DipPA *abbr* (▶**Diploma in Public Administration**) ≈ Diploma en Administración Pública *m*

dir. *abbr* (▶**director**) gte. (gerente), director(a) *m,f*, presidente(-a) *m,f*

direct[1] *adj* (cause, consequence, flight) directo; ~ **access** *n* (Comp) acceso directo *m*;

~ **advertising** n publicidad directa f; ~ **bill of lading** n conocimiento m sin trasbordos or de embarque directo; ~ **call** n llamada directa f; ~ **clearer** n (Bank) compensador directo m; ~ **cost** n coste m Esp or costo m AmL directo; ~ **costing** n cálculo m de costes Esp or costos AmL directos; ~ **current** n corriente continua f; ~ **data entry** n entrada directa de datos f; ~ **debit** n cargo directo m; ~ **dialing** AmE, ~ **dialling** BrE n servicio automático m, discado m directo or automático AmL; ~ **discrimination** n discriminación directa f; ~ **exporting** n exportación directa f; ~ **funds transfer** n transferencia de fondos directa f; ~ **insurance** n seguro directo m; ~ **investment** n inversión directa f; ~ **labor** n AmE, ~ **labour** n BrE (workers) mano de obra directa f; (work) trabajo directo m; ~ **liability** n responsabilidad directa f; ~ **mail** n correo directo m; ~ **mailing** n venta directa por correo f; ~ **marketing** n marketing directo m; ~ **overheads** n pl gastos generales directos m pl; ~ **payment** n pago directo m; ~ **response** n respuesta directa f; ~ **response advertising** n publicidad de respuesta directa f; ~ **response marketing** n marketing de respuesta directa m; ~ **sale** n, ~ **selling** n venta directa f; ~ **tax** n impuesto directo m; ~ **taxation** n imposición directa f; ~ **yield** n ingreso m or producto m or rendimiento m directo, renta directa f

direct² vt (project, inquiry, remark, comment) dirigir; ~ **sb to do sth** ordenarle a alguien que haga algo

directed adj (interview) dirigido; ~ **verdict** n veredicto dictado por el juez m

direction n dirección f; **change** ~ cambiar de dirección; **follow** ~s seguir las instrucciones; **a lack of** ~ la falta de un norte; **a step in the right** ~ un paso en el buen camino; **under the** ~ **of sb** bajo la dirección de alguien; **work with the minimum of** ~ trabajar con el mínimo de instrucciones; ~s **for use** n pl modo de empleo m

directly adv directamente; ~ **related to sth** directamente relacionado con algo; ~ **responsible for sth** directamente responsable de algo

director n director(a) m,f, gerente mf, presidente(-a) m,f; ~'s **circular** n circular del director f; ~s' **fees** n pl honorarios de los directores m pl; ~ **of labor relations** AmE, ~ **of labour relations** BrE n director(a) de relaciones laborales m,f; **D**~ **of Public Prosecutions** n BrE ≈ Fiscal General del Estado mf; ~ **of public relations** n director(a) de relaciones públicas m,f; ~'s **report** n informe del

director m; ~s' **shares** n pl acciones del Consejo de Administración f pl

directorate n consejo de administración m

director-general n director(a) general m,f

directorship n dirección f

directory n directorio m; ~ **assistance** AmE, ~ **enquiries** n BrE (cf ▸**information** AmE) servicio de información telefónica m, información (de teléfonos) f

dirty adj (job, work, tactics) sucio; ~ **bill** n conocimiento con reservas m; ~ **bill of lading** n conocimiento de embarque con reservas m; ~ **float** n flotación f dirigida or sucia; ~ **money** n dinero negro m

dis abbr (▸**discount**) dto. (descuento)

disability n invalidez f, discapacidad f, minusvalía f; ~ **allowance** n deducción por invalidez f; ~ **annuity** n anualidad de invalidez f; ~ **benefit** n indemnización de invalidez f; ~ **insurance** n seguro de invalidez m; ~ **pension** n pensión de invalidez f

disabled adj (employee) discapacitado, minusválido; (Comp) desactivado; ~ **quota** n cuota de discapacitados f

disadvantage n desventaja f; **be at a** ~ estar en desventaja; **put sb at a** ~ poner alguien en desventaja; **to the** ~ **of sb** en detrimento de alguien

disadvantaged adj desventajado

disadvantageous adj desventajoso; **be** ~ **to sb** ser desventajoso para alguien

disaffirm vt negar

disaffirmation n negación f

disagree vi (differ in opinion) no estar de acuerdo; (figures, reports, accounts) no coincidir, discrepar; ~ **with sth** no coincidir con algo; ~ **with sb (about sth)** no estar de acuerdo con alguien (sobre algo)

disagreement n (difference of opinion) desacuerdo m; (disparity) discrepancia f; **be in** ~ **(with)** estar en desacuerdo (con)

disallow vt denegar

disallowable items n pl BrE (Tax) artículos no desgravables m pl

disallowance n denegación f

disappointing adj decepcionante

disaster n desastre m; ~ **area** n zona catastrófica f; ~ **clause** n cláusula de salvaguardia f; ~ **recovery** n (Comp) recuperación después de un desastre f

disastrous adj (consequences, results) desastroso, catastrófico; **have a** ~ **effect on sth** tener efectos desastrosos en algo

disbursable adj desembolsable

disburse vt desembolsar

d

disbursement *n* desembolso *m*

disburser *n* pagador(a) *m,f*

disbursing account *n* cuenta de pagos *f*

disc. *abbr* (▸**discount**) dto. (descuento)

discharge[1] *n* (of employee) despido *m*; (of debt, liabilities) liquidación *f*, pago *m*; (of duty) cumplimiento *m*; (of contract) extinción *f*; (of defendant) puesta en libertad *f*; ~ **of bankruptcy** *n* rehabilitación del quebrado *f*; ~ **of mortgage** *n* cancelación de una hipoteca *f*

discharge[2] *vt* (employee) despedir; (bankrupt) rehabilitar; (defendant) poner en libertad; (debt) extinguir; (duty, obligation) cumplir con; (exempt) eximir

disciplinary *adj* (action, procedure, measure, rule) disciplinario

discipline[1] *n* disciplina *f*

discipline[2] *vt* disciplinar

disclaim *vt* (deny) negar; (property, trust) renunciar a; **he** ~**ed all responsibility for the accident** negó toda responsabilidad del accidente

disclaimer *n* denegación *f*; (Ins) declinación de responsabilidad *f*; (of property, right) abandono *m*, renuncia *f*; ~ **of opinion** *n* abstención de opinión *f*

disclose *vt* revelar

disclosed reserve *n* (Acc) reserva publicada *f*

disclosure *n* (of information) revelación *f*; (Stock) descripción del riesgo *f*; ~ **requirement** *n* requisito para publicación *m*; (Stock) requisito de revelación *m*

discomfort index *n* (Econ) índice de malestar *m*

disconnect *vti* (Comp) desconectar

discontent *n* descontento *m*; ~ **in the workplace** descontento en el lugar de trabajo

discontinue *vt* (service, production, payment) suspender; (action, suit, appeal) desistir de

discount[1] *n* descuento *m*; **at a** ~ con descuento; (Fin) por debajo del cambio; **these shares are at a** ~ **to their issue price** estas acciones se cotizan por debajo de su precio de emisión; **a** ~ **for cash** un descuento por pago en efectivo *or* al contado; **give sb a 10%**~ *o* **a discount of 10%** hacerle a alguien un 10% de descuento *or* un descuento del 10%; **no** ~ sin descuento; **on a** ~ **basis** en régimen de descuentos; ~ **bill** *n* letra de descuento *f*; ~ **bond** *n* bono descontado *m*; ~ **brokerage** *n* corretaje de descuento *m*; ~ **charges** *n pl* gastos de descuento *m pl*; ~ **house** *n* AmE tienda de saldos *f*; BrE sociedad mediadora en el mercado de dinero *f*;

~ **market** *n* mercado de descuento *m*; ~ **price** *n* precio con descuento *m*; ~ **rate** *n* BrE (*cf* ▸**discount window** AmE) redescuento *m*, tasa de descuento *f*; ~ **store** *n* tienda de saldos *f*; ~ **travel** *n* viajes con descuento *m pl*; ~ **window** *n* AmE (*cf* ▸**discount rate** BrE) redescuento *m*, tasa de descuento *f*

discount[2] *vt* (bill of exchange, promissory note) descontar; (goods) rebajar; (price, debt) reducir; (amount, percentage) descontar, bonificar; (possibility) descartar; (claim, criticism) pasar por alto, no tener en cuenta

discountable *adj* descontable

discounted *adj* (bill, loan) descontado; (bond) emitido a descuento; ~ **cash flow** *n* flujo de efectivo descontado *m*; ~ **present value** *n* valor actual descontado *m*

discounting *n* descuento *m*; ~ **bank** *n* banco de descuento *m*

discourage *vt* desalentar, desanimar

discovery *n* (Law) *conjunto de actos procesales destinados a que las partes de un litigio obtengan información y pruebas sobre los hechos del litigio*

discrepancy *n* discrepancia *f*

discretion *n* discreción *f*; **at sb's** ~ a criterio *or* discreción de alguien; **use your** ~ usa tu criterio, haz lo que mejor te parezca

discretionary *adj* (account, share, cost, policy) discrecional; (period) de discreción

discriminate *vi* discriminar; ~ **against sb** discriminar a alguien; ~ **between** distinguir entre; ~ **in favor** AmE *o* **favour** BrE **of sb** dar trato de favor a alguien

discrimination *n* discriminación *f*; ~ **test** *n* (S&M) prueba de discriminación *f*

discriminatory *adj* discriminatorio

discuss *vt* hablar de; ~ **sth with sb** hablar de algo con alguien

discussion *n* discusión *f*, debate *m*; **under** ~ en estudio; ~**s with management** conversaciones con la patronal; ~ **group** *n* grupo de discusión *m*

diseconomy *n* deseconomía *f*; ~ **of scale** *n* deseconomía de escala *f*

disequilibrium *n* desequilibrio *m*

disguised unemployment *n* desempleo disfrazado *m*

dishonest *adj* deshonesto

dishonour[1] BrE, **dishonor** AmE *vt* (cheque) desatender el pago de, no pagar; (letter of credit) devolver, no pagar; (debt) no pagar; (agreement) no respetar; (promise) no cumplir, faltar a

dishonour[2] BrE, **dishonor** AmE *n* falta de pago *f*; ~ **at maturity** *n* falta de pago al vencimiento *f*

dishonoured BrE, **dishonored** AmE *adj*
(cheque) no pagado; ~ **bill** *n* letra impagada
f; ~ **bill of exchange** *n* letra de cambio no
atendida *f*

disincentive *n* desincentivo *m*; ~ **effect**
n efecto desincentivador *m*

disinflation *n* deflación *f*

disinformation *n* desinformación *f*

disintegration *n* desintegración *f*

disintermediation *n* desintermediación *f*

disinvest *vt* desinvertir

disinvestment *n* (*cf* ▸**divestment** AmE)
desinversión *f*

disinvestor *n* desinversor(a) *m,f*

disk *n* (Comp) disco *m*; ~ **communication
area** *n* zona de comunicaciones del disco *f*;
~ **drive** *n* unidad de disco *f*; ~ **operating
system** *n* sistema operativo de discos *m*; ~
pack *n* pila de discos *f*; ~ **space** *n* espacio
del disco *m*; ~ **unit** *n* unidad de discos *f*

diskette *n* disquete *m*; ~ **drive** *n*
disquetera *f*

dismantling *n* (of economic barriers)
supresión *f*

dismiss *vt* (employee) despedir; (executive)
destituir; (possibility, suggestion) descartar,
desechar; (request, petition, claim) desestimar,
rechazar; (charge, appeal) desestimar

dismissal *n* (of employee) despido *m*; (of
executive) destitución *f*; (of theory, suggestion,
request) rechazo *m*; (of charge, appeal)
desestimación *f*; ~ **procedure** *n*
procedimiento de despido *m*

disorderly *adj* (market) indeciso, inestable

disparaging *adj* (comment) despectivo; ~
copy *n* (S&M) mensaje publicitario
despectivo *m*

disparity *n* disparidad *f*

dispatch[1] *n* despacho *m*, envío *m*,
expedición *f*; ~ **department** *n*
departamento de expedición *m*; ~ **note** *n*
nota de envío *f*

dispatch[2] *vt* despachar, enviar; (Comp)
encaminar

dispatcher *n* expedidor(a) *m,f*

dispatching *n* despacho *m*, envío *m*,
expedición *f*; ~ **charge** *n* gasto de
expedición *m*

dispensation *n* dispensa *f*

dispense with *vt* hacer caso omiso de

display[1] *n* (exhibition) exposición *f*; (Comms,
Comp) representación visual *f*; **be on** ~
estar expuesto; **put sth on** ~ exponer algo;
~ **advertising** *n* publicidad de exposición
f; ~ **device** *n* unidad de representación
visual *f*; ~ **monitor** *n* monitor visualizador
m; ~ **pack** *n* paquete de exposición *f*; ~
unit *n* unidad de visualización *f*

display[2] *vt* (goods) exponer; (Comp)
visualizar

displayed price *n* precio expuesto *m*

disposable *adj* (income, capital) disponible;
(product) desechable

disposal *n* (power to use) disposición *f*; (sale)
venta *f*; **at sb's** ~ a disposición de alguien;
have sth at one's ~ disponer de algo, tener
algo a su disposición; **put sth at sb's** ~
poner algo a disposición de alguien

dispose of *vi* (get rid of) deshacerse de;
(sell) vender, enajenar; (have use of) disponer
de

disposition *n* disposición *f*

dispossess *vt* desahuciar

dispossess proceedings *n pl* (Law)
procedimiento de desahucio *m*; (Patents)
*procedimientos para la declaración de la
nulidad y caducidad de la patente*

dispute[1] *n* (boardroom, labour) conflicto *m*; **in**
~ en litigio; (with employer) en discusión; ~
procedure *n* procedimiento de resolución
de litigios *m*; ~ **resolution** *n* resolución de
disputa *f*

dispute[2] *vt* (claim) impugnar; (will) disputar

disputed tax *n* impuesto impugnado *m*

disruption *n* trastorno *m*

dissaving *n* desahorro *m*

disseminate *vt* (information, idea)
diseminar, difundir

dissemination *n* (of information, idea)
diseminación *f*, difusión *f*

dissolution *n* (of company, partnership,
parliament) disolución *f*

dissolve *vt* (company, partnership, parliament)
disolver

distancing *n* distanciamiento *m*

distilling *n* destilación *f*

distinction *n* distinción *f*; **make** *o* **draw a**
~ **(between)** hacer una distinción (entre)

distinctive *adj* distintivo

distinguished *adj* (career) eminente

distort *vt* (figures, facts) distorsionar

distortion *n* (of figures, facts) distorsión *f*

distraint *n* embargo *m*; ~ **of property** *n*
embargo de propiedad *m*

distressed property *n* propiedad
embargada *f*

distributable *adj* (profit) distribuible,
repartible

distribute *vt* (profits, dividends) repartir;
(goods, tasks, responsibilities, information)
distribuir

distributed *adj* (profit) distribuido; ~
computing *n* cálculo repartido *m*; ~
database *n* base de datos distribuida *f*; ~
system *n* (Comp) sistema distribuido *m*

distribution n (of goods, capital, dividends, profits, wealth) distribución f; ~ **center** AmE, ~ **centre** BrE n centro m distribuidor or de distribución; ~ **channel** n canal de comercialización m; ~ **costs** n pl costes m pl Esp or costos m pl AmL de distribución; ~ **list** n lista de distribución f; ~ **manager** n director(a) m,f or gerente mf or jefe(-a) m,f de distribución; ~ **network** n red de distribución f; ~ **office** n oficina de distribución f; ~ **service** n servicio de distribución m; ~ **stock** n valores de distribución m pl

distributor n distribuidor(a) m,f

district n distrito m; ~ **agreement** n acuerdo m or contrato m por distritos; **D**~ **Attorney** n AmE fiscal mf; **D**~ **Council** n BrE ≈ Ayuntamiento m Esp; ~ **court** n AmE juzgado de distrito m; ~ **manager** n gerente regional mf

disutility n desutilidad f

- **ditto** adv ídem

div. abbr (▶**dividend**) dividendo m

diverge vi divergir

divergence n divergencia f

divergent adj (thinking, marketing) divergente

diverse adj diverso

diversification n diversificación f; ~ **strategy** n estrategia de diversificación f

diversified adj (company) diversificado

diversify [1] vt (approach, investment, products, risks) diversificar
[2] vi diversificarse; **they diversified into sportswear** diversificaron su producción introduciéndose en el mercado de ropa de deporte

diversion n (for traffic) desvío m

diversity n diversidad f

divest vt: ~ **oneself of sth** deshacerse de algo

divestiture n desposeimiento m

divestment n AmE desinversión f

divide vt dividir

divided cover BrE, **divided coverage** AmE n cobertura repartida entre varias aseguradoras f

dividend n dividendo m; ~ **announcement** n anuncio de dividendo m; ~ **bond** n bono de dividendo m; ~ **coupon** n cupón de dividendo f; ~ **cover** n cobertura de dividendos f; ~ **declaration** n declaración de dividendo f; ~ **fund** n fondo de dividendo m; ~ **income** n ingreso por dividendos m; ~ **net** n dividendo neto m; ~ **payable** n dividendo m pagadero or a pagar; ~ **per share** n dividendo por acción m; ~ **reinvestment** n reinversión de dividendos f; ~ **tax** n impuesto sobre dividendos m; ~ **voucher** n comprobante

de dividendos m; ~ **warrant** n cheque en pago de dividendos m; ~ **yield** n rendimiento en dividendos m

divisibility n divisibilidad f

divisible adj divisible

division n (distribution) reparto m, división f; (department) división f, sección f, departamento m; (disagreement) desacuerdo m; ~ **head** n director(a) divisional m,f, director(a) m,f or gerente mf or jefe(-a) m,f de división; ~ **of labor** AmE, ~ **of labour** BrE n división del trabajo f; ~ **manager** n director(a) divisional m,f, director(a) m,f or gerente mf or jefe(-a) m,f de división; ~ **of powers** n división de poderes f

divisional adj (head, manager) divisional, de división; (management) por departamentos

divisionalization n divisionalización f

divorced adj divorciado

DJ abbr (▶**Dow Jones**) Dow Jones m

D/N abbr (▶**debit note**) nota de cargo f

DNS abbr (▶**domain name system**) sistema de nombre de dominio m

do. abbr (▶**ditto**) íd. (ídem)

DO abbr (▶**diesel oil**) gasóleo m, gasoil m; (▶**distribution office**) oficina de distribución f

D/O abbr (▶**delivery order**) orden de entrega f

dock[1] n (for ships) dique m, dock m; (in court of law) banquillo (de los acusados) m

dock[2] [1] vi atracar al muelle, entrar en dique
[2] vt BrE (wages, pay) reducir; **they've ~ed 15% off my salary** me han quitado el 15% del sueldo

Doctor n (title) Doctor(a) m,f; ~ **of Business Management** n Doctor(a) en Administración Empresarial m,f; ~ **of Commerce** n Doctor(a) en Comercio m,f; ~ **of Commercial Law** n Doctor(a) en Derecho Comercial m,f; ~ **of Economics** n Doctor(a) en Economía m,f; ~ **of Laws** n Doctor(a) en Derecho m,f

doctrine n doctrina f; ~ **of comparative costs** n doctrina f de los costes Esp or costos AmL comparativos; ~ **of strict compliance** n doctrina de estricta conformidad f; ~ **of substantial performance** n doctrina de cumplimiento sustancial f

document[1] n documento m; (article of incorporation, deed, by-law) escritura pública f; ~**s against acceptance** n pl documentos contra aceptación m pl; ~**s against payment** n pl documentos contra pago m pl; ~ **code** n código del documento m; ~ **feeder** n dispositivo de alimentación de documentos m; ~ **name** n nombre del documento m;

~ **rate** n velocidad de tratamiento de documentos f; ~ **reader** n lectora de documentos f; ~ **retrieval system** n sistema de recuperación de documentos m; ~**s of title** n pl documentos de propiedad m pl, títulos documentarios m pl

document² vt documentar

documentary¹ adj (evidence, fraud) documental; (credit, draft) documentario

documentary² n documental m

documentation n documentación f

dodge vt (infrml) (tax) evadir; (work, duty, responsibility) eludir, rehuir; (problem, issue) soslayar, eludir; (question) esquivar, soslayar

dog n (S&M) trinca f

dole n BrE (infrml) subsidio de desempleo m, paro m Esp; **be on the** ~ BrE (infrml) (cf ▸**be on welfare** AmE) estar cobrando subsidio de desempleo, estar en el paro Esp; **go on the** ~ BrE (infrml) (cf ▸**go on welfare** AmE) apuntarse para cobrar el subsidio de desempleo or el paro Esp; ~ **queue** n BrE número m de desempleados or de parados Esp; **join the** ~ **queue** BrE engrosar las filas del desempleo or del paro Esp

dollar n dólar m; ~ **area** n área de influencia del dólar f; ~ **balance** n saldo en dólares m; ~ **bid** n oferta de compra de dólares f; ~ **bill** n billete de un dólar m; ~ **cost averaging** n política para asegurar riesgos sobre el cambio del dólar; ~ **drain** n déficit en dólares del comercio exterior de Estados Unidos; ~ **premium** n prima del dólar f; ~ **price** n cotización del dólar f; ~ **shortage** n escasez de dólares f; ~ **sign** n signo m or símbolo m del dólar; ~ **standard** n patrón dólar m; ~ **value** n valor en dólares m

dollarization n dolarización f

domain n ámbito m, dominio m; (Comp) dominio m; ~ **name** n nombre de dominio m; ~ **name system** n sistema de nombre de dominio m

domestic adj (industry, sales, flight) nacional; (affairs, policy, market, airline) interno; (trade) interno, interior; (bank) nacional, interno; (consumption) nacional, interior; (output) interior; (waste) doméstico; ~ **agreement** n BrE acuerdo interno m; ~ **issue** n (Stock) emisión f interior or nacional

domicile n domicilio m

domiciled adj domiciliado

dominant adj (company, position) dominante

dominate vt dominar

domination n dominación f

donate vt donar

donated adj donado; ~ **stock** n acciones restituidas por los fundadores; ~ **surplus** n (Stock) superávit aportado en acciones m

donation n donación f

donee n donatario(-a) m,f; ~ **beneficiary** n beneficiario(-a) por donación m,f

dongle n (Comp) dongle m

donor n donante mf; ~ **agency** n agencia donante f; ~ **country** n país donante m

don't knows: **the** ~ n pl los que no saben m pl

door-to-door adj (selling) de puerta a puerta, a domicilio; (delivery, service) domiciliario; ~-**to-door salesman** n vendedor a domicilio m

dormant adj (account) inactivo, sin movimiento

dormitory town n BrE (cf ▸**bedroom community** AmE) ciudad dormitoria f

DOS abbr (▸**disk operating system**) DOS (sistema operativo de discos); ~ **prompt** n guía del DOS f

dossier n dossier m, expediente m, legajo m

dot n punto m; ~ **chart** n gráfico de puntos m; ~ **command** n comando puntual m; ~**s per inch** n pl puntos por pulgada m pl

dot-com n puntocom f

dot-matrix printer n impresora f matricial or de matriz de puntos

dotted line n línea punteada f

double¹ adj doble; ~ **account system** n sistema de cuenta doble m; ~-**acting** adj (machinery) de doble acción; ~-**barrelled** BrE, ~-**barreled** AmE (bond) con doble garantía; ~ **column** n doble columna f; ~ **counting** n doble contabilización f; ~ **density** n doble densidad f; ~-**digit inflation** n inflación de dos dígitos f; ~-**dipper** n AmE (jarg) persona con dos empleos f; ~ **eagle** n AmE moneda de oro de veinte dólares; ~-**edged sword** n BrE (cf ▸**whipsaw** AmE) arma de doble filo m; ~ **entry** n doble entrada f; ~-**entry accounting** n, ~-**entry book-keeping** n contabilidad por partida doble f; ~-**entry method** n método de partida doble m; ~-**figure inflation** n inflación de dos cifras f; ~-**income** adj (family, household) de doble ingreso; ~ **insurance** n doble seguro m; ~ **manning** n doble dotación de personal f; ~ **option** n (Stock) doble opción f; ~-**precision** n (Comp) de doble precisión; ~ **reduction** n doble reducción f; ~-**sided** adj (Comp) de doble cara; ~-**sided disk** n disco de dos caras m; ~ **space** n, ~ **spacing** n espacio doble m; ~-**spread advertising** n anuncio m or publicidad f a doble página; ~ **strike** n (Comp) doble tecleo m; ~ **taxation** n doble imposición f; ~ **time** n hora contada doble f

double² adv (pay, earn, cost) el doble

double³ **1** *vt* (earnings, profits) doblar, duplicar
2 *vi* (price, amount) duplicarse, doblarse
double-book *vt* BrE: **the room has been ~ed** la habitación ha sido reservada para dos personas distintas
double-check **1** *vt* (facts, information) volver a revisar
2 *vi* volver a mirar, verificar dos veces
double-click *vi* hacer doble clic
doubtful *adj* dudoso; **~ debt** *n* deuda de cobro dudoso *f*; **~ debtor** *n* deudor(a) dudoso(-a) *m,f*
dower *n* cuota vidual *f*, viudedad *f*
Dow Jones *n* Dow Jones *m*; **~ Jones index** *n* índice Dow Jones *m*; **~ Jones Industrial Average** *n* media industrial Dow Jones *f*
down¹ *adj* (direction, position) descendente; (system) fuera de funcionamiento; **be ~ on sth/sb** *(infrml)* tener manía a algo/alguien; **~ arrow** *n* (on keyboard) flecha hacia abajo *f*; **~-market** *adj* (product) de baja gama, inferior; **~ payment** *n* depósito *m or* pago *m* inicial, adelanto a cuenta *m*; **~ period** *n* cierre por reforma *m*; **~-the-line personnel** *n* personal subalterno *m*; **~ tick** *n* AmE *venta de un título a un precio inferior al de la cotización precedente*; **~ time** *n* tiempo *m* de indisponibilidad *or* de inactividad
down² *vt*: **~ tools** (strike) dejar de trabajar
downgrade *vt* (employee) bajar de categoría; (job) depreciar
downgrading *n* (of employee) reducción de categoría laboral *f*
downhill *adv*: **go ~** (business) ir cuesta abajo
download¹ **1** *vt* descargar, hacer un download de
2 *vi* hacer un download
download² *n* descarga *f*
downloadable *adj* cargable por teleproceso
downshift *vi* decidirse por un estilo de vida más tranquilo
downside *n* inconveniente *m*, desventaja *f*; **~ break-even point** *n* (Stock) punto de equilibrio descendiente *m*; **~ risk** *n* (Stock) riesgo por baja en los tipos de cambio *m*
downsize *vt* (workforce) reducir
downsizing *n* (of workforce) reducción *f*
downstream *adv* hacia abajo
downswing *n* baja *f*, descenso *m*, fase descendente *f*
downtown *n* AmE (*cf* ▸**town centre** BrE) centro de la ciudad *m*
downtrend *n* tendencia declinante *f*

downturn *n* baja *f*, descenso *m*, fase descendente *f*; (Stock) recesión *f*
downward¹ *adj* (trend, movement) descendente; **~ communication** *n* comunicación descendente *f*; **~ compatibility** *n* compatibilidad descendente *f*; **~ correction** *n* corrección a la baja *f*; **~ pressure** *n* (on currency, interest rates) presión a la baja *f*; **~ spiral** *n* (in wages, prices) espiral descendente *f*
downward² AmE, **downwards** BrE *adv* hacia abajo
dowry *n* dote *f*
DP *abbr* (▸**documents against payment**) documentos contra pago *m pl*; (▸**dynamic positioning**) localización dinámica *f*
dpi *abbr* (▸**dots per inch**) ppp (puntos por pulgada)
DPP *abbr* BrE (▸**Director of Public Prosecutions**) ≈ Fiscal General del Estado *mf*
DPR *abbr* (▸**director of public relations**) director(a) de relaciones públicas *m,f*
Dr *abbr* (▸**debtor**) Dr (deudor); (▸**Doctor**) (title) Dr (Doctor)
draft¹ *n* (Fin) cheque *m*; (preliminary version) borrador *m*; **in ~ form** en (forma de) borrador; **~ agreement** *n* proyecto de contrato *m*; **~ amendments** *n pl* enmiendas al borrador *f pl*; **~ budget** *n* borrador de presupuesto *m*; **~ clause** *n* borrador *m* de artículo *or* de cláusula; **~ contract** *n* proyecto de contrato *m*; (Law) borrador de un contrato *m*; **~ directive** *n* borrador de directiva *m*; **~ for collection** *n* letra al cobro *f*; **~ mode** *n* modo borrador *m*; **~ order** *n* borrador de decreto *m*; **~ project** *n* proyecto preliminar *m*; **~ prospectus** *n* borrador de prospecto *m*; **~ resolution** *n* proyecto de resolución *m*; **~ stage** *n* (Law) fase de redacción *f*; (Pol) fase de borrador *f*
draft² *vt* (document, contract) redactar el borrador de
drag-and-drop *vti* arrastrar y soltar
drain *n* (Comp) consumo *m*; (on resources) drenaje *m*
DRAM *abbr* (▸**dynamic random access memory**) RAM dinámica *f*
drastic *adj* (solution, measure, change, effect) drástico
draw *vt* (cheque) hacer, librar, retirar; (salary, pension) cobrar, percibir; (stock) agotar; (sketch) dibujar; (conclusion) sacar; **~ money from** *o* **out of the bank** retirar *or* sacar dinero del banco; **draw on** *vt* (resources, reserves, savings) recurrir a, hacer uso de; **draw up** *vt* (contract) redactar, preparar; (list) hacer; (agenda) establecer; (plan, will) formular; (deed) redactar; (white paper)

preparar; ~ **up a balance sheet** hacer balance; ~ **up a draft** redactar un documento; ~ **up a shortlist** redactar una lista de candidatos seleccionados; ~ **up a statement of account** redactar un estado de cuenta

drawback *n* (disadvantage) inconveniente *m*, desventaja *f*; (reimbursement) reembolso de derechos *m*; (Imp/Exp) drawback *m*; ~ **debenture** *n* certificado para reintegro *m*

draw-down *n* aprovechamiento de fondos prestados *m*

drawee *n* girado(-a) *m,f*, librado(-a) *m,f*

drawer *n* (of cheque) girador(a) *m,f*, librador(a) *m,f*

drawing *n* (on loan) retiro *m*; (of bill) extensión *f*, giro *m*; ~ **account** *n* cuenta *f* corriente *or* de depósitos a la vista; ~ **automation** *n* automatización del dibujo *f*; ~ **board** *n* tablero de dibujo *m*; ~ **facility** *n* (Fin) servicio de giro *m*; ~ **file** *n* archivo de diseño *m*; ~ **officer** *n* (Bank) jefe(-a) de cobros *m,f*; ~ **software** *n* programa de dibujo *m*

drawing up *n* (of report) elaboración *f*

drawn: ~ **bill** *n* letra de cambio emitida *f*; ~ **bond** *n* bono sorteado *m*

dress-down Friday *n un viernes cuando se permite llevar ropa informal al trabajo*

dressed return *n* (Tax) declaración falsificada *f*

drip *n* (S&M) goteo *m*

drive¹ *vt* (provide power for, operate) hacer funcionar, mover; ~ **a hard bargain** hacer un trato provechoso; ~ **sb to do sth** llevar *or* empujar a alguien a hacer algo; **drive down** *vt* (price) arrastrar hacia abajo

drive² *n* (Comp) accionamiento *m*; (concerted effort) impulso *m*; ~ **time** *n* (S&M) tiempo de conducción *m*

driver *n* (person) conductor(a) *m,f*; (software) módulo de gestión *m*; (hardware) circuito de arranque *m*; ~**'s license** AmE (*cf* ▶**driving licence** BrE) *n* permiso *m or* carnet *m* de conducir; **D~ and Vehicle Licensing Centre** *n* BrE *centro emisor de permisos de conducir y de circulación*

driving *n* (of vehicle) conducción *f*; ~ **licence** BrE (*cf* ▶**driver's license** AmE) *n* permiso *m or* carnet *m* de conducir

driving force *n* fuerza motriz *f*

drop¹ *n* (in prices, spending, orders, investments, production) caída *f*; **a** ~ **of 30% in sales** un descenso del 30% en las ventas; **take a** ~ **in salary** aceptar un sueldo más bajo

drop² ⟦1⟧ *vt* (prices) bajar, reducir; (case) abandonar; (charges) retirar; (plan, idea) abandonar, renunciar a

⟦2⟧ *vi* (prices) bajar

drop-down menu *n* menú desplegable *m*

drop-lock stock *n* (Stock) chicharros *m pl*

drop-out *n* (Comp) pérdida de información *f*

drop-shipping *n* AmE (S&M) venta directa *f*

drug *n* (medication) medicamento *m*; (narcotic) droga *f*; ~ **economy** *n* economía basada en los beneficios obtenidos por la venta de drogas legales; ~ **trade** *n* tráfico de drogas *m*, narcotráfico *m*

drum *n* (Comp) tambor *m*; ~ **plotter** *n* trazador de tambor *m*; ~ **printer** *n* impresora de tambor *f*

drummer *n* AmE (infrml) (HRM) corredor(a) de comercio *m,f*

dry *adj* seco; ~ **goods** *n pl* artículos *m pl* de corte y confección *or* de mercería; ~ **run** *n* prueba *f*

DSC *abbr* (▶**digital selective calling**) llamada selectiva digital *f*

DTML *abbr* (▶**Dynamic Text Mark-up Language**) DTML *m* (lenguaje de referencia dinámico)

DTP *abbr* (▶**desktop publishing**) autoedición *f*

dual *adj* (capacity, residence, responsibility) doble; (banking) dual; ~ **job holding** *n* pluriempleo *m*; ~ **listing** *n* cotización dual *f*; ~**-purpose fund** *n* fondo de doble finalidad *m*; ~ **skilling** *n* cualificación doble *f*, multihabilidades *f pl*

dubbing *n* doblaje *m*

dubious *adj* dudoso; ~ **account** *n* cuenta de valor dudoso *f*

dud check AmE, **dud cheque** BrE *n* (infrml) cheque sin fondos *m*

due *adj* (amount) debido; **she is** ~ **for promotion** le corresponde un ascenso; **in** ~ **course** a su debido tiempo; **the next payment is** ~ **on the fifth** el próximo pago vence el cinco; **he is** ~ **a pay increase** le corresponde un aumento de sueldo; ~ **to** (as a result of) por causa de, debido a; **the money** ~ **to them** el dinero que se les debe *or* se les adeuda; **the meeting is** ~ **to take place at four** la reunión está prevista para las cuatro; ~ **and unpaid** vencido e impagado; **with all** ~ **respect** con el debido respeto; **without** ~ **cause** sin causa justificada; ~ **bill** *n* pagaré *m*; ~ **capital** *n* capital exigible *m*; ~ **date** *n* fecha de vencimiento *f*; **the** ~ **date for payment is...** la fecha de vencimiento es...; ~ **date of filing** *n* (of tax return) fecha límite de presentación *m*; ~ **date of premium** *n* fecha de vencimiento de la prima *f*; ~ **date of renewal** *n* fecha tope de la renovación *f*; ~ **diligence** *n* debida diligencia *f*

dues *n pl* cuotas *f pl*

dull *adj* (market) flojo

dumb terminal n terminal m básico or mudo or no inteligente

dummy[1] n (figurehead) testaferro m

dummy[2] adj (company) fantasma; (employee) fantasma, inútil; (shareholder) que actúa como testaferro; ~ **run** n BrE ensayo m, prueba f

dump[1] n (Comp) volcado de memoria m; ~ **bin** n (S&M) *estantes de presentación independiente, con frecuencia para libros*

dump[2] vt (Comp) volcar

dumping n (of goods, products) competencia desleal f; (Comp) volcado m; (of waste) vertido m; ~ **standard** n norma de la competencia desleal f

dunning letter n carta de cobranza f

duopoly n duopolio m

dupe n (jarg) dupdo. (duplicado), copia f

duplex[1] adj (printing) bidireccional; (computer) en tándem

duplex[2] n AmE (cf ▸**semidetached house** BrE) casa f semiseparada or adosada

duplicate[1] adj (copy) duplicado; ~ **invoice** n (double invoice) factura por duplicado f; (copy) copia (de la factura) f

duplicate[2] n duplicado m; **in** ~ por duplicado

duplicate[3] vt (document) duplicar; (work, efforts) repetir (en forma innecesaria)

duplication n (of document) duplicación f; (of work, efforts) repetición (innecesaria) f

duplicatory adj duplicatorio

durable adj (goods) duradero

durables n pl bienes duraderos m pl

duration n duración f; ~ **of guarantee** n duración de la garantía f

duress n coacción f

Dutch auction n subasta a la baja f

dutiable adj (cargo) sujeto a derechos de aduana; ~ **goods** n pl mercancías f pl

imponibles or sujetas a aranceles

duty n (obligation) deber m, obligación f; (Tax) derecho aduanero m, derechos arancelarios m pl; **do one's** ~ **(by sb)** cumplir con su deber or obligación (para con alguien); **neglect one's duties** descuidar sus responsabilidades; **be on/off** ~ estar/no estar de servicio or de turno; **pay** ~ **on sth** pagar impuestos sobre algo; **take up one's duties** asumir sus funciones

duty-free adj (goods, shop) libre de impuestos; ~ **allowance** n BrE *cantidades autorizadas de productos libres de impuestos*

DVD abbr (▸**digital versatile disc** BrE, ▸**digital versatile disk** AmE) DVD m (disco versátil digital); (▸**digital videodisc** BrE, ▸**digital videodisk** AmE) DVD m (disco vídeo Esp or video AmL digital); ~**-audio** n DVD-audio m; ~ **drive** n unidad de DVD f; ~ **player** n lector (de) DVD m; ~**-ROM** n DVD-ROM m; ~ **video** n vídeo m Esp or video m AmL DVD

DVLC abbr BrE (▸**Driver and Vehicle Licensing Centre**) *centro emisor de permisos de conducir y de circulación*

dwindle vi (growth, demand) decaer

dynamic adj (growth, personality) dinámico; ~ **evaluation** n evaluación dinámica f; **D~ Hypertext Mark-up Language** n lenguaje de referencia de hipertexto dinámico m; ~ **hedging** n compensación dinámica f; ~ **management model** n modelo de administración dinámico m; ~ **obsolescence** n caída en desuso dinámica f; ~ **positioning** n localización dinámica f; ~ **programming** n programación dinámica f; ~ **random access memory** n RAM dinámica f; **D~ Text Mark-up Language** n lenguaje de referencia dinámico m

dynamism n dinamismo m

Ee

EA *abbr* BrE (▶**Employment Act**) *ley de empleo*

e-administration *n* administración electrónica *m pl*

eager beaver *n* (infrml) trabajador(a) *m,f* muy ambicioso(-a) y diligente *or* muy empeñoso(-a) AmL

eagle *n* AmE (ten dollars) águila *f*

e.&o.e. *abbr* (▶**errors and omissions excepted**) s.e.u.o. (salvo error u omisión)

early *adj* anticipado; **at your earliest convenience** tan pronto como le sea posible, a la brevedad; **in ~ June** a principios *or* a comienzos de junio; **we should appreciate an ~ reply** agradeceríamos una pronta respuesta; ~ **adopter** *n consumidor que compra un producto nuevo muy pronto*; ~**closing day** *n* día de cierre anticipado *m*; ~ **exercise** *n* (of option) ejercicio anticipado *m*; ~ **filing** *n* (of tax return) presentación anticipada *f*, ~ **fringe** *n* (of television schedule) franja horaria de primera hora de la tarde *f*; ~ **redemption** *n* rescate anticipado *m*, amortización anticipada *f*; ~ **redemption penalty** *n* penalización por reembolso anticipado *f*; ~ **retirement** *n* jubilación anticipada *f*; **take ~ retirement** jubilarse anticipadamente; ~ **settlement rebate** *n* bonificación por pago anticipado *f*; ~ **withdrawal penalty** *n* penalización *f or* sanción *f* por retirada anticipada

earmark *vt* (money, funds) destinar; (for promotion) repartir

earmarked *adj* (account, cheque) reservado; (tax) afectado

earn *vt* (salary, wages) ganar, cobrar; (money) ganar; (respect, reputation) ganarse; (interest) dar, devengar; ~ **a fast buck** (infrml) ganar un dinero rápido; ~ **a living** ganarse la vida

earned *adj* (income) percibido; (interest, premium) devengado; (surplus) acumulado

earner *n* (salaried person) asalariado-a *mf*; **the company's greatest export ~** el producto exportado que más dinero le da a la empresa; **you could be onto a nice little ~ there** (infrml) con eso te podrías sacar un buen dinero (infrml); **I am the main wage ~ of the family** yo soy la principal fuente de ingresos de mi familia

earnest money *n* depósito de garantía *m*

earning: ~ **capacity** *n*, ~ **power** *n* potencial de ingresos *m*; ~ **streams** *n pl* flujos de ganancias *m pl*

earnings *n pl* (of person) ingresos *m pl*; (of company) ganancias *f pl*, beneficios *m pl*, utilidades *f pl* AmL; ~ **before interest, taxes, depreciation, and amortization** *n pl* beneficios antes de intereses, impuestos, depreciación y amortización *m pl*; ~ **differential** *n* diferencial de sueldo *m*; ~ **drift** *n* inestabilidad de los salarios *f*; ~ **on assets** *n* ganancias en activos *f pl*; ~ **per share** *n* beneficio por acción *m*; ~ **period** *n* periodo de beneficios *m*; ~ **report** *n* balance de resultados *m*; ~ **yield** *n* (Fin) rendimiento de ganancias *m*; (Stock) tasa de rendimiento *f*

Easdaq *abbr* (▶**European Association of Securities Dealers Automated Quotation**) Easdaq *m* (sistema automático de cotización de la Asociación Europea de Operadores de Bolsa)

ease ⓵ *vt* (rules, restrictions) relajar; (tension) hacer disminuir, aliviar; (burden) aligerar; (transition) facilitar; (situation, economic policy) suavizar
⓶ *vi* (interest rate, prices) disminuir, bajar; (restrictions) relajarse; (tension) disminuir, decrecer; **ease off** *vi* (demand) bajar gradualmente; (tension) disminuir, decrecer

easement *n* (Law) servidumbre *f*

Eastern *adj* oriental, este; ~ **Bloc** *n* bloque del Este *m*; ~ **Europe** *n* Europa *f* Oriental *or* de Este; ~ **European Time** *n* horario de Europa Oriental *m*; ~ **Standard Time** *n* hora estándar del este *f*

easy *adj* fácil; ~ **money** *n* dinero abundante *m*; ~ **option** *n* opción fácil *f*; ~ **payments** *n pl* facilidades de pago *f pl*; ~ **terms** *n pl* facilidades de pago *f pl*

EAT *abbr* BrE (▶**Employment Appeal Tribunal**) ≈ Tribunal Constitucional *m* Esp

eat into *vt* (savings, reserves) comerse

e-bank *n* banco electrónico *m*

e-banking *n* banca electrónica *f*

e-bill *n* factura electrónica *f*

e-billing *n* facturación electrónica *f*

EBITDA *abbr* (**earnings before interest, taxes, depreciation, and amortization**) beneficios antes de intereses, impuestos, depreciación, y amortización *m pl*

e-bone *n* red troncal europea *f*

e-book *n* libro electrónico *m*

EBRD *abbr* (▸**European Bank for Reconstruction and Development**) BERD (Banco Europeo para Reconstrucción y Desarrollo)

e-broker *n* e-broker *mf*, intermediario(-a) electrónico(-a) *m,f*, agente de comercio electrónico *mf*

e-brokering *n* intermediación electrónica *f*

e-business *n* (commerce) comercio electrónico *m*; (company) negocio electrónico *m*

EC *abbr* (obs) (▸**European Community**) CE (obs) (Comunidad Europea)

e-card *n* tarjeta electrónica *f*

e-cash *n* dinero electrónico *m*

e-catalogue BrE, **e-catalog** AmE *n* catálogo electrónico *m*

ECB *abbr* (▸**European Central Bank**) BCE (Banco Central Europeo)

ECE *abbr* (▸**Economic Commission for Europe**) CEPE (Comisión Económica para Europa)

echelon *n* escalón *m*

ECLA *abbr* (▸**Economic Commission for Latin America**) CEPAL (Comisión Económica para América Latina)

ecolabelling BrE, **ecolabeling** AmE *n* etiquetado ecológico *m*, ecoetiquetado *m*

ecological *adj* ecológico

ecology *n* ecología *f*

ecomarketing *n* marketing ecológico *m*

e-commerce *n* comercio electrónico *m*; ∼ **hub** *n* hub del comercio electrónico *m*

econometric *adj* econométrico

econometrician *n* econometrista *mf*

econometrics *n* econometría *f*

economic *adj* (conditions, performance, aid) económico; ∼ **activity** *n* actividad económica *f*; ∼ **advancement** *n* avance económico *m*; ∼ **adviser** *n* asesor(a) económico(-a) *m,f*; ∼ **affairs** *n pl* asuntos económicos *m pl*; ∼ **austerity** *n* austeridad económica *f*; ∼ **boom** *n* auge *m or* boom *m* económico; ∼ **climate** *n* clima económico *m*; E∼ **Commission for Europe** *n* Comisión Económica para Europa *f*; E∼ **Commission for Latin America** *n* Comisión Económica para América Latina *f*; ∼ **conjuncture** *n* coyuntura económica *f*; ∼ **cost** *n* coste *m* Esp *or* costo *m* AmL económico; ∼ **cycle** *n* ciclo económico *m*; ∼ **efficiency** *n* eficiencia económica *f*; ∼ **forecasting** *n* previsión económica *f*; ∼ **growth** *n* crecimiento económico *m*; ∼ **indicator** *n* indicador económico *m*; ∼ **integration** *n* integración económico(-a) *f*; ∼ **migrant** *n* emigrante económico(-a) *m,f*; ∼ **mission** *n* misión económica *f*; ∼ **model** *n*

modelo económico *m*; E∼ **and Monetary Union** *n* Unión Económica y Monetaria *f*; ∼ **order quantity** *n* cantidad de orden económico *f*; ∼ **planning** *n* planificación económica *f*; ∼ **prospects** *n pl* perspectivas de la coyuntura económica *f pl*; expectativas económicas *f pl*; ∼ **rent** *n* renta diferencial *f*; ∼ **sanctions** *n pl* sanciones económicas *f pl*; ∼ **situation** *n* coyuntura *f or* situación *f* económica; ∼ **slowdown** *n* estancamiento económico *m*; ∼ **strategy** *n* estrategia económica *f*; ∼ **summit** *n* cumbre económica *f*; ∼ **theory** *n* teoría económica *f*; ∼ **trend** *n* tendencia económica *f*; ∼ **union** *n* unión económica *f*; ∼ **value** *n* valor económico *m*; ∼ **viability** *n* viabilidad económica *f*; ∼ **well-being** *n* bienestar económico *m*

economical *adj* económico; ∼ **use of resources** *n* uso económico de los recursos *m*

economically *adv* económicamente; ∼ **backward area** *n* área *f* económicamente subdesarrollada *or* retrasada económicamente

economics *n* economía *f*

economism *n* economismo *m*

economist *n* economista *mf*

economize *vti* economizar; ∼ **on sth** economizar *or* ahorrar en algo

economy *n* economía *f*; ∼ **of abundance** *n* economía de la abundancia *f*; ∼ **class** *n* clase económica *f*; ∼ **fare** *n* tarifa económica *f*; ∼ **flight** *n* vuelo económico *m*; ∼ **pack** *n* paquete económico *m*; ∼ **of scale** *n* economía de escala *f*; ∼ **of size** *n* economía *f* de escala *or* de tamaño; ∼ **size** *n* tamaño económico *m*; ∼ **ticket** *n* billete económico *m*

e-consumer *n* consumidor(a) económico(-a) *m,f*

ecosystem *n* ecosistema *m*

ecotoxicological *adj* ecotoxicológico

ECP *abbr* (▸**Eurocommercial paper**) efectos comerciales en eurodivisas *m pl*

ECPS *abbr* (▸**Environment and Consumer Protection Service**) Servicio de Protección al Consumidor y al Medio Ambiente *m*

ECR *abbr* (▸**efficient consumer response**) respuesta eficiente al consumidor *f*; (▸**Exchange Control Rate**) tasa del control de los tipos de cambio *f*

e-cruitment *n* reclutamiento en línea *f*

ECU *abbr* (obs) (▸**European Currency Unit**) ECU (obs), UCE (obs) (Unidad de Cuenta Europea)

ed. *abbr* (▸**edition**) edición *f*

Ed. *abbr* (▸**editor's note**) N.R. (nota de la redacción)

ED *abbr* (▸**Eurodollar**) ED (eurodólar)

EDF *abbr* (▸**European Development Fund**) Fondo Europeo de Desarrollo *m*

edge (advantage) ventaja *f*; **have the** ∼ **on** *o* **over sb** llevar ventaja a alguien

edge up *vi* (prices) aumentar lentamente, subir poco a poco

EDI *abbr* (▸**electronic data interchange**) intercambio electrónico de datos *m*; (▸**electronic document interchange**) intercambio electrónico de documentos *m*

edict *n* auto *m*

edit *vt* (data, document, text) editar; (newspaper) redactar; **edit out** *vt* suprimir, eliminar

edition *n* edición *f*

edit mode *n* modalidad de edición *f*, modo edición *m*

editor *n* (of text) redactor(a) *m,f*, editor(a) *m,f*; (of newspaper) director(a) *m,f*, editor(a) responsable *m,f*; (of software) editor *m*; ∼ **in chief** *n* redactor(a) jefe(-a) *m,f*; ∼**'s note** *n* nota de la redacción *f*

editorial *n* artículo de fondo *m*, editorial *m*; ∼ **advertisement** *n* anuncio de publicidad editorial *m*; ∼ **advertising** *n* publicidad de la redacción *f*; ∼ **board** *n* consejo de redacción *m*; ∼ **matter** *n* material editorial *m*; ∼ **staff** *n* redacción *f*

editorialist *n* editorialista *mf*

editorship *n* redacción *f*

EDP *abbr* (▸**electronic data processing**) PED (procesamiento electrónico de datos)

EDT *abbr* (▸**electronic data transmission**) transmisión de datos electrónica *f*

educated *adj* culto

education *n* educación *f*

educational *adj* (development) educativo; (establishment) docente, de enseñanza; (advertising) didáctico, informativo; ∼ **background** *n* antecedentes educativos *m pl*; ∼ **software** *n* software didáctico *m*

edutainment *n* entretenimiento didáctico *m*

EEC *abbr* (obs) (▸**European Economic Community**) CEE *f* (obs) (Comunidad Económica Europea)

EET *abbr* (▸**Eastern European Time**) horario de Europa Oriental *m*

effect[1] *n* efecto *m*; **come into** ∼ entrar en vigor; **in** ∼ (in reality) en realidad; (in operation) en vigor; **be of little/no** ∼ dar poco/no dar resultado; **no** ∼**s** sin efectos; **put into** ∼ poner en práctica; **take** ∼ entrar en vigencia; **take** ∼ **from...** entrar en vigor desde...; **to good** ∼ con gran efecto; **to the** ∼ **that...** en el sentido de que...; **to this** ∼

con este propósito; **with** ∼ **from...** con efecto a partir de...

effect[2] *vt* (settlement, payment, withdrawal) efectuar; (reconciliation) lograr

effective *adj* (method) eficaz, efectivo; (management, control, rate, demand) efectivo; ∼ **annual rate of interest** *n* tasa anual equivalente *f*; ∼ **date** *n* fecha de entrada en vigor *f*; ∼ **debt** *n* deuda vigente *f*; ∼ **net worth** *n* activo neto real *m*; ∼ **yield** *n* rendimiento real *m*

effectively *adv* efectivamente

effectual *adj* (demand) efectivo

efficiency *n* eficacia *f*, eficiencia *f*; **for maximum** ∼ para una eficiencia máxima; ∼ **agreement** *n* BrE acuerdo *m* or contrato *m* de eficiencia; ∼ **audit** *n* auditoría de eficiencia *f*; ∼ **engineer** *n* ingeniero(-a) en eficiencia *m,f*; ∼ **ratio** *n* proporción de eficiencia *f*; ∼ **variance** *n* variación en eficiencia *f*

efficient *adj* (person, system) eficiente; (machine) eficaz; ∼ **consumer response** *n* respuesta eficiente al consumidor *f*

e-form *n* formulario electrónico *m*

EFT *abbr* (▸**electronic funds transfer**) transferencia de fondos electrónica *f*

EFTA *abbr* (▸**European Free Trade Association**) AELC (Asociación Europea de Libre Comercio)

EFTPOS *abbr* (▸**electronic funds transfer at point of sale**) transferencia de fondos electrónica en punto de venta *f*

EFTS *abbr* (▸**electronic funds transfer system**) sistema electrónico de transferencia de fondos *m*

e.g. *abbr* (▸**for example**, ▸**exempli gratia**) p.ej. (por ejemplo)

egalitarianism *n* igualitarismo *m*

EGM *abbr* (▸**extraordinary general meeting**) junta general extraordinaria *f*

e-government *n* gobierno electrónico *m*

egress *n* salida *f*

EI *abbr* (▸**employee involvement**) implicación de los empleados *f*

EIB *abbr* (▸**European Investment Bank**) BEI (Banco Europeo de Inversiones)

eigenprice *n* precio propio *m*

EIP *abbr* (▸**electronic invoice presentation**) facturación electrónica *f*

EIS *abbr* (▸**executive information system**) sistema de información de ejecutivos *m*

eject *vt* (card, disk) expulsar

e-journal *n* diario electrónico *m*

e-lancer *n* trabajador autónomo que utiliza medios electrónicos

elapse *vi* transcurrir

elapsed time *n* tiempo transcurrido *m*

elastic *adj* (supply, demand, income) elástico

elasticity *n* (of supply, demand, substitution, anticipation, expectations) elasticidad *f*

e-learning *n* educación a distancia por Internet *f*

elect *vt* elegir; ~ **sb to the board** elegir a alguien para la junta

elected office *n* cargo elegido *m*

election *n* elección *f*; ~ **campaign** *n* campaña electoral *f*; ~ **meeting** *n* asamblea electoral *f*; ~ **result** *n* resultado electoral *m*

elective *adj* electivo; ~ **income** *n* ingresos *m pl* facultativos *or* opcionales

electoral *adj* electoral; ~ **college** *n* AmE colegio electoral *m*; ~ **register**, ~ **roll** *n* censo *m or* registro *m* electoral

electorate *n* electorado *m*

electric *adj* eléctrico; ~ **power** *n* energía eléctrica *f*; ~ **train** *n* tren eléctrico *m*

electrical *adj* eléctrico; ~ **appliance** *n* aparato eléctrico *m*; ~ **engineering** *n* ingeniería eléctrica *f*

electricity *n* electricidad *f*; ~ **consumption** *n* consumo de electricidad *m*; ~ **generation** *n* BrE (*cf* ▸**power generation** AmE) generación de electricidad *f*; ~ **industry** *n* industria de la electricidad *f*; ~ **sector** *n* sector de electricidad *m*

electrification *n* (of railways) electrificación *f*

electronic *adj* electrónico; ~ **accounting system** *n* sistema *m* de contabilidad informatizado *or* de contabilidad computadorizado AmL; ~ **bank** *n* banco electrónico *m*; ~ **banking** *n* banca electrónica *f*; ~ **banking service** *n* servicio de banca electrónica *m*; ~ **bill presentment** *n* facturación electrónica *f*; ~ **billing** *n* facturación electrónica *f*; ~ **business** *n* (commerce) comercio electrónico *m*; (company) negocio electrónico *m*; ~ **business facilitator** *n* facilitador(a) del comercio electrónico *m,f*; ~ **catalogue** BrE, ~ **catalog** AmE *n* catálogo electrónico *m*; ~ **certificate** *n* certificado electrónico *m*; ~ **commerce** *n* comercio electrónico *m*; ~ **component** *n* componente electrónico *m*; ~ **data interchange** *n* intercambio electrónico de datos *m*; ~ **data processing** *n* procesamiento electrónico de datos *m*; ~ **data transmission** *n* transmisión de datos electrónica *f*; ~ **directory** *n* directorio electrónico *m*; ~ **distance learning** *n* educación a distancia por Internet *f*; ~ **document interchange** *n* intercambio de documentos electrónicos *m*; ~ **engineer** *n* técnico(-a) electrónico(-a) *m,f*; ~ **form** *n* formulario electrónico *m*; ~ **funds**

transfer *n* transferencia de fondos electrónica *f*; ~ **funds transfer at point of sale** *n* transferencia de fondos electrónica en punto de venta *f*; ~ **funds transfer system** *n* sistema electrónico de transferencia de fondos *m*; ~ **government** *n* gobierno electrónico *m*; ~ **home banking** *n* banca domiciliaria electrónica *f*; ~ **intelligence** *n* inteligencia electrónica *f*; ~ **invoice presentation** facturación electrónica *f* ; ~ **mail** *n* correo electrónico *m*; ~ **mall** *n* central comercial electrónico *m*; ~ **marketing** *n* marketing electrónico *m*; ~ **media** *n* medios electrónicos *m pl*; ~ **messaging** *n* mensajería electrónica *f*; ~ **money** *n* dinero electrónico *m*; ~ **news gathering** *n* periodismo electrónico *m*; ~ **office** *n* oficina electrónica *f*; ~ **order form** *n* hoja de pedidos electrónica *f*; ~ **organizer** *n* agenda electrónica *f*; ~ **payment** *n* pago electrónico *m*; ~ **payment terminal** *n* terminal de pago electrónico *m*; ~ **personal organizer** *n* agenda electrónica *f*; ~ **point of sale** *n* punto de venta electrónico *m*; ~ **posting board** *n* (Stock) pantalla de precios electrónica *f*; ~ **publishing** *n* publicación electrónica *f*; ~ **shopping** *n* compra electrónica *f*; ~ **signature** *n* firma electrónica *f*; ~ **storefront** *n* escaparate electrónico *m*

electronically *adv* electrónicamente; ~ **programmable read only memory** *n* memoria sólo de lectura programable electrónicamente *f*

electronics *n* electrónica *f*; ~ **engineer** *n* técnico(-a) electrónico(-a) *m,f*

electrostatic *adj* electrostático; ~ **printer** *n* impresora electrostática *f*

electrotype *n* electrotipo *m*

element *n* (factor) elemento *m*; **an ~ of risk** un elemento de riesgo

eligibility *n* elegibilidad *f*; ~ **rule** *n* norma de la elegibilidad *f*; ~ **test** *n* prueba de capacidad *f*

eligible *adj* elegible; **be ~ for sth** (by having right) tener derecho a algo; (by meeting requirements) reunir los requisitos para algo; ~ **for tax relief** desgravable; **be ~ to do sth** reunir los requisitos para hacer algo; ~ **to adjudicate** (Law) con derecho a adjudicar; ~ **asset** *n* activo elegible *m*; ~ **bills** *n pl* BrE letras aceptables para el redescuento *f pl*; ~ **expense** *n* gasto computable *m*; ~ **paper** *n* valores negociables *m pl*

eliminate *vt* eliminar

ellipsis *n* puntos suspensivos *m pl*

EMA *abbr* (▸**European Monetary Agreement**) Tratado Monetario Europeo *m*

e-mail[1] *n* (▸**electronic mail**) (system, message) e-mail *m*, correo electrónico *m*; (on letterhead, business card) e-mail *m*; **be on ~** tener e-mail; **send sb an ~** enviarle un e-mail a alguien; **send sb sth by ~** mandarle *or* enviarle algo a alguien por e-mail; **~ account** *n* cuenta de correo electrónico *f*; **~ address** *n* dirección de correo electrónico *f*, dirección *f or* casilla *f* electrónica; **~ box** *n* buzón *m* de correo electrónico *or* de e-mail; **~ message** *n* e-mail *m*, correo electrónico *m*, mensaje de correo electrónico *m*, emilio *m* (infrml); **~ server** *n* servidor de e-mail *m*

e-mail[2] *vt* mandar *or* enviar por e-mail; **~ sb sth** mandarle *or* enviarle algo a alguien por e-mail

e-mall *n* centro comercial electrónico *m*

emancipation *n* emancipación *f*

e-marketing *n* marketing electrónico *m*

e-marketplace *n* cibermercado *m*

embargo *n* embargo *m*; **lift** *o* **end an ~** levantar un embargo; **put an ~ on sth** prohibir el comercio *or* el uso de algo

embarkation *n* (of passengers) embarque *m*

embark on *vi* (course of action) embarcarse en

embassy *n* embajada *f*

embed *vt* (Comp) intercalar

embedded *adj* (Comp) intercalado; **~ command** *n* comando integrado *m*; **~ hyperlink** *n* hiperenlace empotrado *m*; **~ option** *n* opción intercalada *f*

embezzle *vt* desfalcar

embezzlement *n* desfalco *m*

embezzler *n* desfalcador(a) *m,f*

em dash *n* cuadratín *m*

emergency *n* emergencia *f*; **in (the event of) an ~** en caso de emergencia; **~ aid** *n* ayuda de emergencia *f*; **~ exit** *n* salida de emergencia *f*; **~ powers** *n pl* poderes extraordinarios *m pl*; **~ service** *n* servicio de emergencia *m*

emerging *adj* (market, nation) emergente

EMI *abbr* (▸**European Monetary Institute**) IME (Instituto Monetario Europeo)

eminent domain *n* derecho de expropiación *m*

emission *n* (of gases) emisión *f*; **~ limit** *n* límite de emisión *m*; **~ standard** *n* estándar de emisión *m*

e-money *n* dinero electrónico *m*

emoticon *n* emoticón *m*, expreicono *m*

emotional *adj* emocional; **~ appeal** *n* (of product, advertisement) atractivo emocional *m*

emphasis *n* énfasis *m*; **lay** *o* **place** *o* **put ~ on sth** hacer hincapié *or* poner énfasis en la importancia de algo

emphasize *vt* enfatizar, poner énfasis en

emphatic *adj* categórico

empirical *adj* empírico

empirics *n* empírico *m*

employ *vt* (person, method) emplear; **the company ~s hundreds of workers** la compañía emplea a *or* da empleo a cientos de trabajadores

employable *adj* capacitado para trabajar

employed *adj* empleado; **~ capital** *n* capital en uso *m*

employee *n* empleado(-a) *m,f*; **~ association** *n* asociación de empleados *f*; **~ benefit** *n* beneficio *m or* ventaja *f* para los empleados; **~s' buyout** *n* compra de la empresa por los empleados; **~ communications** *n pl* comunicaciones con los empleados *f pl*; **~ contributions** *n pl* aportaciones de los empleados *f pl*; **~ counseling** AmE, **~ counselling** BrE *n* asesoramiento a los empleados *m*; **~ involvement** *n* implicación de los empleados *f*; **~-owned firm** *n* empresa administrada por los empleados *f*; **~ participation** *n* participación de los empleados *f*; **~ pension plan** *n* plan de pensión para los empleados *m*; **~ profit sharing** *n* participación de los empleados en los beneficios *f*; **~ rate** *n* BrE (of National Insurance) tipo de aportación de los asalariados *m*; **~ relations** *n pl* relaciones con el personal *f pl*; **~ shareholding scheme** *n* plan de participación accionaria de los empleados *m*; **~ share ownership trust** *n* trust de personal propietario de acciones; **~ stock option** *n* opción de compra de acciones para los empleados *f*

employer *n* empresario(-a) *m,f*, patrón(a) *m,f*; **~s' association** *n* asociación patronal *f*; **~'s contribution** *n* cuota patronal *f*; **~s' federation** *n* federación patronal *f*; **~'s occupational pension scheme** *n* plan de pensión laboral del empresario *m*; **~ rate** *n* (of National Insurance) porcentaje de contribución del empresario *m*, tipo de aportación del empresario *m*; **~'s return** *n* (Tax) declaración del empresario *f*; **~ taxation number** *n* número de identificación fiscal de la empresa *m*

employment *n* empleo *m*; **be in ~** tener trabajo; **be in regular ~** tener (un) trabajo fijo; **on the ~ front** en el ámbito del empleo; **seek ~** buscar empleo *or* trabajo; **take up ~ with sb** entrar a trabajar con alguien; **E~ Act** *n* BrE *ley de empleo*; **~ agency** *n* agencia de colocación *f*; **E~ Appeal Tribunal** *n* BrE ≈ Tribunal Constitucional *m* Esp;

⋯⋙

e

∼ **bureau** n agencia de colocación f; ∼ **figures** n pl cifras de empleo f pl; ∼ **law** n legislación laboral f, ley de empleo f; ∼ **offer** n oferta de empleo f; ∼ **office** n BrE oficina de empleo f; **E**∼ **Protection Act** n BrE *ley de protección del empleo*; ∼ **record** n registro de empleo m; **E**∼ **Service** n BrE ≈ Instituto Nacional de Empleo m; ∼ **situation** n situación laboral f; ∼ **tax** n impuesto sobre el empleo m; ∼ **tax credit** n desgravación fiscal del empleo f

emporium n centro comercial m

empowerment n (of women, workers) atribución de poder f, empoderamiento m

empty¹ adj (container) vacío; (seat, place) libre, desocupado; (promise) vano

empty² vt vaciar; **empty out** vt vaciar

empty³ n envase vacío m

EMS abbr (▸**European Monetary System**) SME (Sistema Monetario Europeo)

em space n espacio de la eme f

EMU abbr (▸**Economic and Monetary Union**) UME (Unión Económica y Monetaria); (▸**European Monetary Union**) UME (Unión Monetaria Europea)

emulate vt emular

emulation n (Comp) emulación f; ∼ **board** n placa de emulación f; ∼ **card** n tarjeta de emulación f; ∼ **software** n programas de emulación m pl

emulator n (Comp) emulador m

emy abbr (▸**emergency**) emergencia f

enable vt (make possible) posibilitar, permitir; (Comp) (hardware) encender; (software) activar; ∼ **sb to do sth** permitir(le) a alguien hacer algo

enabling adj (legislation) habilitante; (act, clause) de autorización

enact vt (law) promulgar; (bill) aprobar

enactment n (law) ley f; (of law) promulgación f; (of bill) aprobación f

encashable adj convertible en efectivo

encashment n cobro m en efectivo or en metálico; ∼ **schedule** n tabla de encajes f

encl. abbr (▸**enclosed**) adj. (adjunto)

enclave economy n economía aislada f

enclose vt adjuntar, remitir adjunto; **I ∼…/please find ∼d…** le remito adjunto…

enclosed adj adjunto; ∼ **document** n anexo m, documento adjunto m

encode vt codificar, cifrar

encoding n codificado m, cifrado m

encompass vt abarcar

encourage vt (person) animar, alentar; (industry, competition) fomentar; (growth) fomentar, estimular; (speculation) intensificar; ∼ **sb in sth** alentar a alguien en algo; ∼ **sb to do sth** alentar a alguien a hacer algo

encouragement n (of person) aliento m, estímulo m; (of trade) fomento m

encouraging adj alentador

encroachment n intrusión f

encroach on vt usurpar

encrypt vt cifrar, codificar

encryption n cifrado m, codificación f

encumbered adj (Law) gravado, sujeto a gravamen; **be ∼ with sth** (debt, responsibility) estar cargado or agobiado de algo

encumbrance n (Law) gravamen m

end¹ n (finish, close) fin m, final m; (purpose) fin m; **at the ∼ of the day** (finally) al fin y al cabo, a fin de cuentas; (literally) al acabar or al terminar el día; **in the ∼** al final; **put an ∼ to sth** poner fin or punto final a algo; **to this ∼** con or a este fin; **at the top ∼** (of scale) en el extremo superior; **the top ∼ of the range** lo mejor de la gama; ∼ **consumer** n consumidor(a) m,f or usuario(-a) m,f final; ∼ **of file** n fin de archivo m; ∼**-of-file mark** n marca de fin de archivo f; ∼ **of financial year** n final m de año contable or del ejercicio contable; ∼**-of-line goods** n pl artículos de fin de serie m pl; ∼ **of message** n (Comp) fin de mensaje m; ∼ **of month** n fin de mes m; ∼**-of-month account** n cuenta de periodo mensual f; ∼ **product** n producto final m; ∼ **result** n resultado final m; ∼**-of-season sale** n rebajas f pl or liquidación f de fin de temporada; ∼ **of the taxation year** n cierre del año fiscal m; ∼**-use goods** n pl bienes m pl finales or de uso final ; ∼**-use trader** n comerciante(-a) de bienes finales m,f; ∼ **user** n consumidor(a) m,f or usuario(-a) m,f final

end² **1** vt (argument, discussion) terminar, dar or poner fin a; (speculation) acabar or terminar con; (conclude) terminar, concluir **2** vi acabar, terminar, concluir

endanger vt arriesgar

endeavour¹ BrE, **endeavor** AmE n esfuerzo m, intento m; **make every ∼ to do sth** esforzarse al máximo por hacer algo, intentar hacer algo por todos los medios

endeavour² BrE, **endeavor** AmE vi esforzarse; ∼ **to do sth** esforzarse por hacer algo

ending n fin m, final m; ∼ **balance** n balance m final or de cierre; ∼ **inventory** n inventario final m

endorse vt (cheque, warrant) endosar; (employee) ayudar con un aval; (statement, decision) aprobar; (product) apoyar, promocionar

endorsee n endosatario(-a) m,f

endorsement n (of cheque, warrant, note) endoso m; (of statement, decision) aprobación f; (of product) promoción f

endorser n endosante(-a) m,f

endowment n donación f; ~ **assurance** n seguro mixto m; ~ **fund** n fondo de beneficiencia m; ~ **insurance** n seguro mixto m; ~ **mortgage** n BrE hipoteca de inversión f; ~ **policy** n poliza con seguro de vida m

energy n energía f; ~ **conservation** n conservación de la energía f; ~ **crisis** n crisis energética f; ~ **efficiency** n eficiencia de la energía f; ~ **management** n dirección f or gerencia f de energía; ~ **reserve** n reserva energética f; ~ **resources** n pl recursos energéticos m pl; ~ **source** n fuente energética f; ~ **supply** n suministro de energía m

enforce vt (claim, right) hacer valer; (law, regulation) hacer cumplir

enforceable adj ejecutable, ejecutorio

enforced adj coercitivo; ~ **collection** n cobro coercitivo m

enforcement n aplicación f or cumplimiento m de la ley; ~ **action** n acción coercitiva f; ~ **order** n orden ejecutoria f; ~ **procedure** n procedimiento ejecutorio m

engage vt (staff) contratar; **engage in** vt (campaign) emprender; (politics) dedicarse a

engaged adj BrE (cf ▶busy AmE) (telephone line) ocupado, comunicando Esp; **be** ~ **in sth** (activity) estar comprometido en algo; **be otherwise** ~ tener otro compromiso; ~ **tone** n BrE (cf ▶busy signal AmE) (on telephone) señal m de ocupado or de comunicando Esp

engagement n (appointment) compromiso m; (of staff) contratación f; **a previous** o **prior** ~ un compromiso previo

engine n motor m; ~ **of growth** n motor del crecimiento m

engineer n técnico(-a) m,f

engineering n ingeniería f; ~ **design** n diseño técnico m; ~ **firm** n firma de ingeniería f; ~ **manager** n director(a) técnico(-a) m,f, gerente de ingeniería mf; ~ **works** n taller de maquinaria m

enhance vt (value, purchasing power) aumentar; (capacity) ampliar, aumentar; (reputation, performance) mejorar; (Comp) (image) procesar

enhanced adj (quality, features) resaltado; (performance) mejorado; (Comp) (image) procesado; ~ **graphics array** n matriz de gráficos realzada f

enhancement n (of value) aumento m; (of capacity) ampliación f; (of quality, performance) mejora f

enjoin vt imponer; ~ **sth on sb** encarecerle algo a alguien; ~ **sb to do sth** encarecerle a alguien que haga algo

enlarge vt (room, office, photograph) ampliar; (membership) aumentar

enlarged adj (copy, edition) ampliado

enlargement n ampliación f; (of EU) expansión f

enquiry n consulta f; **all enquiries to...** razón...; **make enquiries about** realizar indagaciones sobre, hacer averiguaciones sobre; ~ **desk** n información f

enrichment n enriquecimiento m

enrolment BrE, **enrollment** AmE n (act) inscripción f; (number) número m de socios or de afiliados

entail¹ vt (risk) implicar, suponer, conllevar; (expense) acarrear, implicar, suponer; ~ **sth on sb** (Law) vincular algo a alguien

entail² n (Law) vínculo m

enter ☐1 vt (period, phase, negotiations, recession) entrar en; (appeal, plea, writ, complaint) presentar; (protest) elevar, formular; (market) introducirse en; (labour market) ingresar a; (data) dar entrada a, introducir; ~ **sth in the accounts** contabilizar algo; ~ **an item in the ledger** sentar una partida en el libro mayor; ~ **information onto a register** introducir información en un registro ☐2 vi entrar; **enter into** vt entrar en; (agreement) celebrar; ~ **into a contract with sb** establecer un contrato con alguien; ~ **into negotiations with sb** iniciar negociaciones con alguien

enterprise n (project, company) empresa f; (spirit of initiative) empuje m, iniciativa f; ~ **allowance** n BrE subvención de empresa f; ~ **zone** n zona de desarrollo industrial f

enterprising adj emprendedor

entertain vt (client) atender

entertainment n (of clients) entretenimiento m; ~ **allowance** n complemento para gastos de representación m; ~ **expenses** n gastos de representación m pl; ~ **industry** n sector del ocio m

enticing adj (offer) atractivo

entitle vt (book) titular; ~ **sb to sth/do sth** dar a alguien derecho a algo/a hacer algo

entitlement n derecho m

entity n entidad f

entrance n entrada f; ~ **card** n tarjeta de entrada f; ~ **examination** n examen de ingreso m; ~ **fee** n derechos de entrada m pl; ~ **ticket** n billete de entrada m

entrepôt *n* (port, town) centro de almacenaje y distribución *m*; (warehouse) depósito *m*

entrepreneur *n* empresario(-a) *m,f*

entrepreneurial *adj* (risk, spirit) empresarial

entrepreneurship *n* capacidad empresarial *f*

entry *n* (entrance) entrada *f*; (in accounts) asiento *m*; (in register) partida *f*; **make an ~ against sb** hacer un asiento contra alguien; **no ~** (on door) prohibida la entrada; (on road sign) prohibido el paso; **~ barrier** *n* (Imp/Exp) barrera de entrada *f*; **~ into force** *n* entrada en vigor *f*; **~-level job** *n* puesto de trabajo de nivel inicial *m*; **~ permit** *n* permiso de entrada *m*; **~ price** *n* precio de entrada *m*; **~ processing unit** *n* unidad de tratamiento de entradas *f*; **~ stamp** *n* (on arrival in new country) sello de entrada *m*; **~ visa** *n* visado de entrada *m*

enumerate *vt* enumerar

enumeration *n* enumeración *f*

envelope *n* (for letter) sobre *m*

environment *n* (surroundings) ambiente *m*; (Envir) medio ambiente *m*; (Comp) entorno *m*; **E~ and Consumer Protection Service** *n* Servicio de Protección al Consumidor y al Medio Ambiente *m*; **~ policy** *n* política medioambiental *f*

environmental *adj* (issues, problems, audit) medioambiental; (protection, management, analysis) del medio ambiente; (accounting) medioambiental, verde; (impact, damage, policy, conditions, control) ambiental; **E~ Health Officer** *n* BrE Director(a) de Sanidad Ambiental *m,f*; **~ lobby** *n* grupo de presión ecologista *m*; **E~ Protection Agency** *n* AmE Organismo de Protección del Medio Ambiente *m*

environmentalism *n* ambientalismo *m*

environmentalist *n* ecologista *mf*

environmentally *adv* en el aspecto ecológico; **~ friendly** *adj* (goods) ecológico, que no daña el medio ambiente; **~-sensitive area** *n*, **~-sensitive zone** *n* zona ambientalmente sensible *f*

e.o. *abbr* (▸**ex officio**) de oficio

EO *abbr* (▸**executive officer**) director(a) ejecutivo(-a) *m,f*

EOC *abbr* BrE (▸**Equal Opportunities Commission**) *comisión que promueve igualdad de oportunidades en el empleo*

EOE *abbr* (▸**European Options Exchange**) Mercado Europeo de Opciones *m*

EOF *abbr* (▸**end of file**) (Comp) FDA (fin de archivo)

eohp *abbr* (▸**except otherwise herein provided**) salvo indicación de lo contrario

EOM *abbr* (▸**end of message**) (Comp) FDM (fin de mensaje)

EOP *abbr* (▸**Equal Opportunities Policy**) política de igualdad de oportunidades *f*

EOQ *abbr* (▸**economic order quantity**) cantidad de orden económico *f*

EPA *abbr* (▸**Employment Protection Act**) BrE *ley de protección del empleo*; (▸**Environmental Protection Agency**) AmE Organismo de Protección del Medio Ambiente *f*

e-point-of-sale *n* punto de venta electrónico *m*

EPOS *abbr* (▸**electronic point of sale**) punto de venta electrónico *m*

EPROM *abbr* (▸**electronically programmable read only memory**) memoria sólo de lectura programable electrónicamente *f*; (▸**erasable programmable read only memory**) memoria sólo de lectura programable y que puede borrarse *f*

EPS *abbr* (▸**earnings per share**) BPA (beneficio por acción)

EPT *abbr* (▸**electronic payment terminal**) terminal de pago electrónico *m*

EPU *abbr* (▸**entry processing unit**) unidad de tratamiento de entradas *f*

EqPA *abbr* BrE (▸**Equal Pay Act**) Principio de Equidad en Remuneración *f*

equal *adj* igual; **all else being ~** si no intervienen otros factores, sin que lo demás se modifique; **on an ~ footing** en pie de igualdad, en iguales condiciones; **~ and opposite** igual y opuesto; **~ pay for work of equal value** BrE *a trabajo de igual valor igual remuneración*; **in ~ proportions** en iguales proporciones; **on ~ terms** en los mismos términos; **~ opportunity** *n* igualdad de oportunidades *f*; **E~ Opportunities Commission** *n* BrE *comisión que promueve la igualdad de oportunidades en el empleo*; **~ opportunity employer** *n* empresario(-a) que aplica la igualdad de oportunidades *m,f*; **~ opportunities policy** *n* política de igualdad de oportunidades *f*; **~ pay** *n* pago igual *m*; **E~ Pay Act** *n* BrE Principio de Equidad en Remuneración *m*; **~ voting rights** *n pl* igualdad de derechos de voto *f*, iguales derechos a voto *m pl*

equality *n* igualdad *f*; **~ standard** *n* estándar de igualdad *m*

equalization *n* compensación *f*; **~ fund** *n* fondo de compensación *m*; **~ payment** *n* pago de compensación *m*

equalize *vt* compensar

equalizing dividend *n* dividendo de regulación *m*

equilibrium *n* equilibrio *m*; ~ **price** *n* precio de equilibrio *m*; ~ **quantity** *n* cantidad de equilibrio *f*; ~ **wage rate** *n* tipo de salario de equilibrio *m*

equip *vt* equipar

equipment *n* (apparatus) equipo *m*; (act of equipping) equipamiento *m*; ~ **failure** *n* avería de máquina *f*; ~ **leasing** *n* arrendamiento de equipo *m*

equitable *adj* (fair) razonable; (Law) equitativo; ~ **distribution** *n* distribución equitativa *f*; ~ **lien** *n* gravamen equitativo *m*

equities *n pl* valores *m pl*; ~ **market** *n* mercado de valores *m*

equity *n* (share) acción *f*; (shareholders' interest in company) patrimonio neto *m*; (residual worth) participación en el capital *f*; (fairness) equidad *f*; **take an ~ stake** adquirir una participación; ~ **accounting** *n* contabilidad *f* del activo neto *or* del capital social; ~ **base** *n* base de recursos propios *f*; ~ **capital** *n* BrE (*cf* ►**capital stock** AmE) capital social en acciones *m*; ~ **dilution** *n* dilución del capital *f*; ~ **financing** *n* financiación por venta de valores *f*; ~ **funds** *n pl* fondos en títulos *m pl*; ~ **holder** *n* accionista ordinario(-a) *m,f*; ~ **holdings** *n pl* cartera de valores *f*; ~ **investment** *n* inversión en acciones *f*; ~ **investor** *n* inversor(-a) en acciones *m,f*; ~ **issue** *n* emisión de títulos *f*; ~ **joint venture** *n* coinversión por acciones *f*; ~ **option** *n* opción sobre el neto *f*; ~ **ownership** *n* participación en el capital social *f*; ~ **rate** *n* AmE tasa de recursos propios *f*; ~ **security** *n* pl título de participación en una sociedad *m*; ~ **share** *n* acción ordinaria *f*; ~ **turnover** *n* renovación del capital social *f*; ~ **value** *n* capital contable de la participación *m*; ~ **warrant** *n* derecho de adquisición de capital social *m*, derecho especial de suscripción de capital *m*

equivalence *n* equivalencia *f*

equivalent *n* equivalente *m*

era *n* era *f*

eradicate *vt* erradicar

erasable programmable read only memory *n* memoria sólo de lectura programable y que puede borrarse *f*

erase *vt* (Comp) borrar

erase head *n* cabeza de borrado *f*

ERC *abbr* (►**European Registry of Commerce**) Registro Europeo de Comercio *m*

e-recruitment *n* reclutamiento electrónico *m*

erect *vt* (customs barriers) levantar

e-revolution *n* revolución electrónico *f*

ergonometric *adj* ergonométrico

ergonometrics *n* ergonometría *f*

ergonomic *adj* ergonómico

ergonomically *adv* ergonómicamente; ~**-designed** *adj* (workstation) de diseño ergonómico

ergonomics *n* ergonomía *f*

ergonomist *n* ergonomista *mf*

ergophobia *n* ergofobia *f*

ERM *abbr* (►**Exchange Rate Mechanism**) MAC (mecanismo de ajuste de cambios)

erode *vt* (confidence, faith) minar, socavar; (power) erosionar; **wages have been ~ed by inflation** la inflación ha reducido el poder adquisitivo de los salarios

erosion *n* (of confidence, power, rights) menoscabo *m*, deterioro *m*; (of land) erosión *f*

err *vi* (in judgment) errar

errata *n pl* erratas *f pl*; (heading) fe de erratas *f*

erratum *n* errata *f*

erroneous *adj* erróneo

error *n* error *m*; **the letter was sent to you in ~** se le envió la carta por equivocación; **an ~ of judgment** un error de cálculo; **make an ~** cometer un error; ~ **control** *n* control de errores *m*; ~**-free** *adj* sin errores; ~ **message** *n* mensaje de error *m*; ~**s and omissions** *n pl* errores *m pl* y omisiones *f pl*; ~**s and omissions excepted** salvo error u omisión; ~ **rate** *n* tasa de error *f*; ~ **recovery** *n* recuperación de errores *f*; ~ **report** *n* lista de errores *f*

ersatz[1] *adj* sucedáneo

ersatz[2] *n* sucedáneo *m*

ES *abbr* (►**expert system**) sistema experto *m*

Esc *abbr* (►**escape key**) (on keyboard) tecla de escape *f*

escalate *vi* (prices) subir rápidamente; (costs, claims) aumentar; (dispute) intensificarse

escalation *n* (of costs) aumento *m*; (of dispute) intensificación *f*; ~ **clause** *n* (for cost increases) cláusula de revisión de precios *f*; (for wage increases) cláusula de escala móvil *f*

escalator *n* (moving staircase) escalera mecánica *f*; ~ **clause** *n* (for cost increases) cláusula de revisión de precios *f*; (for wage increases) cláusula de escala móvil *f*

escape *n* escape *m*; ~ **character** *n* (Comp) carácter de cambio de código *m*; ~ **clause** *n* cláusula de evasión *f*; ~ **key** *n* (Comp) tecla de escape *f*; ~ **sequence** *n* (Comp) secuencia de abandono *f*

escheat *n* (Law) reversión de propiedad *f*

escort[1] *n* acompañante *mf*

escort[2] *vt* (visitor) acompañar

escrow *n* (document) documento depositado en garantía *m*; (in Internet transaction) depositario *m*; **in ~** en depósito; **~ account** *n* cuenta de depósito en garantía *f*; **~ agent** *n* depositario legal de documentos *m*; **~ agreement** *n* acuerdo en plica *m*

ESF *abbr* (▸**European Social Fund**) FSE (Fondo Social Europeo)

e-sourcing *n* e-sourcing *m*, abastecimiento electrónico *m*

esp. *abbr* (▸**especially**) esp. (especialmente)

especially *adv* especialmente

espionage *n* espionaje *m*

esprit de corps *n* espíritu de equipo *m*

Esq. *abbr* (▸**esquire**) (form of address in letter writing) Sr.D. (Señor Don)

esquire *n* (form of address in letter writing) Señor Don *m*

essential[1] *adj* esencial; **previous experience ~** imprescindible tener experiencia previa; **be ~ to** *o* **for sth** ser esencial *or* imprescindible para algo; **~ commodities** *n pl* productos de primera necesidad *m pl*; **~ condition** *n* condición indispensable *f*; **~ feature** *n* característica principal *f*; **~ foodstuff** *n* producto alimenticio de primera necesidad *m*; **~ industry** *n* industria *f* esencial *or* vital

essential[2] *n* imperativo *m*, elemento esencial *m*; **a knowledge of French is an absolute ~** son indispensables conocimientos de francés

essentials *n pl* puntos *m pl* esenciales *or* fundamentales; **the bare ~** lo estrictamente necesario

est. *abbr* (▸**established**) establecido

EST *abbr* (▸**Eastern Standard Time**) hora estándar del este *f*

establish *vt* (motive, fact, criteria, procedure) establecer; (guilt, innocence) establecer, demostrar; (company) fundar; (committee, fund) instituir, crear; **~ a direct link with sb** (Comms) establecer comunicación directa con alguien; **his father ~ed him in business** su padre lo ayudó a establecerse en los negocios

established *adj* (business) sólido; (practice, tradition, brand) establecido; (image, product, market) consolidado; (fact) comprobado

establishment *n* (company, shop) establecimiento *m*; (of company) fundación *f*; (of committee) creación *f*; **~-level bargaining** *n* negociación a nivel del establecimiento *f*

Establishment *n* BrE Establishment *m*, Sistema *m*

estate *n* (land, property) propiedad *f*; (assets) patrimonio *m*; (of deceased person) sucesión *f*; (group of houses) urbanización *f*; (industrial) parque *m*; (housing estate) BrE (*cf* ▸**project** AmE) complejo de viviendas subvencionadas *m*; **~ agency** *n* BrE (*cf* ▸**real estate agency** AmE) agencia inmobiliaria *f*; **~ agent** *n* BrE (*cf* ▸**realtor** AmE) agente inmobiliario(-a) *m,f*; **~ duty** *n* derechos de sucesión *m pl*; **~ executor** *n* albacea testamentario(-a) *mf*; **~ income** *n* renta patrimonial *f*; **~ manager** *n* (of land, property) administrador(a) *m,f* de bienes; **~ planning** *n* disposiciones sucesorias *f pl*; **~ tax** *n* impuesto sobre transmisiones patrimoniales *m*

estimate[1] *vt* (value, cost, losses) estimar; (price, number, age) calcular

estimate[2] *n* (calculation) cálculo *m*; (judgment) estimación *f*; (of costs) presupuesto *m*; **at the highest/lowest ~** en la más alta/baja valoración; **at a rough ~** haciendo un cálculo aproximado; **~ of expenditure** *n* estimación de gastos *f*

estimated *adj* (value, cost, losses, revenue, tax) estimado; **~ time of arrival** *n* hora prevista de llegada *f*; **~ time of departure** *n* hora prevista de salida *f*

estimator *n* (S&M) estimador *m*

estoppel *n* (Law) impedimento legal *m*; **~ certificate** *n* certificado de impedimento legal *m*

estranged *adj* (spouse) separado

ETA *abbr* (▸**estimated time of arrival**) hora prevista de llegada *f*

e-tail *vt* vender en línea

e-tailer *n* tienda en línea *f*

e-tailing *n* venta en línea *f*

ETD *abbr* (▸**estimated time of departure**) hora prevista de salida *f*

Ethernet® *n* Ethernet® *m*

ethical *adj* (advertising, investment) ético

ethics *n pl* ética *f*

ethnic *adj* (group, origin) étnico; **~ monitoring** *n* política en contra de la discriminación racial en el proceso de selección y promoción de los empleados

e-ticketing *n* venta de billetes en línea *f*

e-trader *n* tienda en línea *f*

EU *abbr* (▸**European Union**) UE *f* (Unión Europea); **~ directive** *n* directiva de la UE *f*

EUA *abbr* (▸**European Unit of Account**) unidad europea de cuenta *f*

euro[1] *n* euro *m*; **~ area** *n*, **~ zone** *n* zona euro *f*

euro[2] *adj* europeo

Eurobank *n* Eurobanco *m*

Eurobond n eurobono m; ~ **issue** n emisión de eurobonos f; ~ **market** n mercado de eurobonos m

Eurocard® n Tarjeta Europea f

eurocentric adj eurocéntrico

eurocheque n eurocheque m

Euroclear n Cámara de Compensación de Eurobonos f

Eurocommercial paper n (Stock) efectos comerciales en eurodivisas m pl

eurocurrency n eurodivisa f; ~ **issue** n euroemisión f; ~ **loan** n préstamo en eurodivisas m; ~ **market** n mercado de eurodivisas m

Eurodollar n eurodólar m; ~ **bond** n bono en eurodólares m; ~ **deposit** n depósito de eurodólares m; ~ **future** n opción de futuro en eurodólares m; ~ **index** n índice del eurodólar m; ~ **market** n mercado del eurodólar m; ~ **rate** n tasa de eurodólares f

Euroequity n euroequidad f

Euromarket n euromercado m

Euromoney n eurodinero m, euromoneda f; ~ **deposit** n depósito euromonetario m

Euro MP (▸**European Member of Parliament**) Eurodiputado(-a) m,f, parlamentario(-a) europeo(-a) m,f

Euronet n Euronet f

European adj europeo; ~ **Association of Securities Dealers Automated Quotation** n sistema automático de cotización de la Asociación Europea de Operadores de Bolsa m; ~ **Bank for Reconstruction and Development** n Banco Europeo para Reconstrucción y Desarrollo m; ~ **Central Bank** n Banco Central Europeo m; ~ **Commission** n Comisión Europea f; ~ **Community** n (obs) Comunidad Europea f (obs); ~ **Convention on Human Rights** n Convención Europea de Derechos Humanos f; ~ **Court** n Corte Europea f, Tribunal Europeo m; ~ **Court of Justice** n Tribunal Europeo de Justicia m; ~ **Currency Unit** n (obs) Unidad de Cuenta Europea f (obs); ~ **Development Fund** n Fondo Europeo de Desarrollo m; ~ **Economic Community** n (obs) Comunidad Económica Europea f (obs); ~ **Free Trade Association** n Asociación Europea de Libre Comercio f; ~ **Investment Bank** n Banco Europeo de Inversiones m; ~ **Member of Parliament** n Eurodiputado(-a) m,f, parlamentario(-a) europeo(-a) m,f; ~ **monetary cooperation** n cooperación monetaria europea f; ~ **Monetary Fund** n Fondo Monetario Europeo m; ~ **Monetary Institute** n Instituto Monetario Europeo m; ~ **Monetary System** n Sistema Monetario Europeo m; ~ **Monetary Union** n Unión Monetaria Europea f; ~ **option** n (Stock) opción a la europea f; ~ **Options Exchange** n Mercado Europeo de Opciones m; ~ **Registry of Commerce** n Registro Europeo de Comercio m; ~ **Single Market** n Mercado Único Europeo m; ~ **Social Charter** n Carta Social Europea f; ~ **Social Fund** n Fondo Social Europeo m; ~**-style option** n (Stock) opción de tipo europeo f; ~ **terms** n pl (for currency trading) modalidad europea f; ~ **Union** n Unión Europea f; ~ **Unit of Account** n unidad europea de cuenta f

europhile adj euró filo

europhobic adj euró fobo

Europortfolio n eurocartera f

Euro-rates n pl eurotasas f pl

Eurorebel n eurorrebelde mf

Eurosceptic n euroescéptico(-a) m,f

eurosceptical adj euroescéptico

evade vt (tax) evadir; (question, issue, regulations) eludir; (obligation, responsibility) eludir, evadir

evaluate vt (ability, data, results) evaluar; (damage) calcular

evaluation n (of ability, data, results) evaluación f

evasion n (of tax, responsibility) evasión f; (evasive act) estratagema f; (evasive statement) evasiva f

evasive adj (reply) evasivo

even¹ adj (number) par; ~**-numbered** adj de numeración par; ~ **parity** n (Comp) paridad f

even² vt (situation) equilibrar; **even out** vi (prices) igualar; **even up** vt compensar

evened-out position n posición equilibrada f

evening n noche f; (before dark) tarde f; ~ **peak** n punta nocturna f; ~ **trade** n (Stock) operación próxima al cierre del mercado f

evenly adv (spread) uniformemente; (distributed, divided) equitativamente, en or a partes iguales

event n suceso n; (Comp) evento m; **at all ~s, in any ~** en todo caso; **in either ~** en cualquier caso; **in that ~** en ese caso; **in the ~** al final, llegado el momento; **in the ~ of** en caso de (que); ~**s subsequent to the closing date** hechos posteriores a la fecha de cierre

eventuality n eventualidad f

eventually adv finalmente

eventuate vi acontecer

evergreen adj de actualidad; ~ **credit** n crédito permanente m

evict vt desahuciar, desalojar

eviction *n* desahucio *m*, desalojo *m*; ∼ **order** *n* orden de desahucio *f*

evidence *n* evidencia *f*, prueba *f*; (Law) pruebas *f pl*; **give** ∼ **for/against sb** prestar declaración *or* declarar a favor de/en contra de alguien; **give** ∼ **on** *o* **under oath** declarar bajo juramento; **be in** ∼ estar bien visible; **on the** ∼ **of sth** en vista de algo; **have** ∼ **to support a claim** tener hechos que sustentan una reclamación; ∼ **of debt** *n* prueba de endeudamiento *f*; ∼ **of title** *n* escritura de propiedad *f*; ∼ **of use** *n* prueba de uso *f*

evidenciary *adj* probatorio

evident *adj* evidente

evolution *n* (of price) evolución *f*

e-wallet *n* billetero electrónico *m*

ex¹ *abbr* (**examined**) ex (revisado); (**excluding**) excepto; (**executed**) ejecutado

ex² *prep* sin; ∼ **claim** por derecho; ∼ **hypothesi** ex hipótesis

ex. *abbr* (▸**extra**) extra; (▸**example**) ej. (ejemplo)

exacerbate *vt* exacerbar

exact *adj* correcto, exacto; ∼ **interest** *n* interés *m* anual *or* a 365 días

exaggerated *adj* (report) exagerado

ex allotment *adj* sin asignación

examination *n* (test, study, investigation) examen *m*; (of accounts) revisión *f*, inspección *f*; (by customs) revisión *f*; (of passports) control *m*; (of witness) interrogatorio *m*; **under** ∼ bajo consideración

examine *vt* (document, dossier) examinar, estudiar; (application) examinar, revisar; (accounts) inspeccionar, revisionar; (witness, accused) interrogar

examiner *n* examinador(a) *m,f*; (customs) tasador(a) *m,f or* inspector(a) *m,f* de aduanas

example *n* ejemplo *m*; **for** ∼ por ejemplo

exceed *vt* (be greater than) exceder de; (limit) sobrepasar; (supply, demand, expectations) superar; (powers) excederse de, abusar de; ∼ **one's authority** excederse en el uso de su autoridad; **not** ∼**ing 30 days** que no exceda los 30 días, que no exceda de 30 días

except *prep* salvo; ∼ **as otherwise provided** salvo disposición contraria; ∼ **for** a reserva de; ∼ **otherwise herein provided** salvo indicación de lo contrario

exception *n* excepción *f*; **make an** ∼ hacer una excepción; **the** ∼ **that proves the rule** la excepción que confirma la regla; **take** ∼ **to sth** ofenderse por algo; **with the** ∼ **of sth/sb** con *or* a excepción de algo/alguien; **without** ∼ sin excepción; ∼**s clause** *n* cláusula de excepción *f*

exceptional *adj* (case, circumstances) excepcional; (expenses) extraordinario

excess *n* (immoderate degree) exceso *m*; BrE (on insurance policy) franquicia *f*; (surplus) excedente *m*, sobrante *m*; **in** ∼ **of** superior a, por encima de; **be in** ∼ **of** exceder de; ∼ **amount** *n* cantidad en exceso *f*; ∼ **baggage** *n* exceso de equipaje *m*; ∼ **capacity** *n* capacidad excedente *f*; ∼ **cash** *n* exceso *m* de efectivo *or* de liquidez; ∼ **contribution** *n* contribución excesiva *f*; ∼ **demand** *n* demanda excedente *f*, exceso de demanda *m*; ∼ **employment** *n* sobreempleo *m*; ∼ **fare** *n* suplemento *m*; ∼ **postage** *n* BrE franqueo suplementario *m*, recargo por franqueo insuficiente *m*; ∼ **profits** *n pl* beneficios extraordinarios *m pl*; ∼ **reserve** *n* reserva *f* extraordinaria *or* en exceso; ∼ **shares** *n pl* excedente de acciones *m*; ∼ **supply** *n* exceso *m* de oferta *or* de suministro

excessive *adj* (taxation) excesivo

excessively *adj* excesivamente

exchange¹ *n* (of one thing for another, foreign currency) cambio *m*; (of information) intercambio *m*; (stock exchange) bolsa *f*; (telephone) centralita *f*; (market) lonja *f*; **in** ∼ **(for sth)** a cambio (de algo); ∼ **arbitrage** *n* arbitraje de cambio *m*; ∼ **certificate** *n* certificado de cambio monetario *m*; ∼ **charge** *n* cargo por diferencia de cambios *m*; ∼ **contract** *n* contrato de cambios *m*; ∼ **of contracts** *n* intercambio de contratos *m*; ∼ **control** *n* control *m* de divisas *or* de cambios; E∼ **Control Rate** *n* tasa del control de los tipos de cambio *f*; ∼ **difference** *n* diferencia de cambio *f*; ∼ **discount** *n* descuento de cambio *m*; ∼ **fund** *n* fondo de cambio *m*; ∼ **office** *n* casa de cambio *f*; ∼ **rate** *n* tipo de cambio *m*; ∼ **rate agreement** *n* acuerdo sobre los tipos de cambio *m*; ∼ **rate fluctuation** *n* fluctuación del tipo de cambio *f*; E∼ **Rate Mechanism** *n* mecanismo de ajuste de cambios *m*; ∼ **risk** *n* riesgo de cambio *m*; ∼ **screen** *n* tablero electrónico de la bolsa *m*; ∼ **value** *n* valor de cambio *m*

exchange² *vt* (information, views) intercambiar; ∼ **contracts** BrE suscribir el contrato de compraventa; ∼ **sth for sth** cambiar algo por algo; ∼ **dollars for pesos** cambiar dólares a *or* en Esp pesos

exchanged share *n* acción intercambiada *f*

Exchequer *n* BrE ≈ Fisco *m*

excisable good *n* artículo imponible *m*

excise duty *n*, **excise tax** *n impuesto sobre consumos específicos*

excite *vt* (interest) despertar, suscitar

excl. *abbr* (▸**excluding**) excepto, (▸**exclusive**) exclusivo

exclude *vt* excluir

excluded *adj* (dividend, property, corporation, period) excluido; ∼ **consideration** *n* (Tax) remuneración excluida *f*

excluding *prep* excepto

exclusion *n* (omission) exclusión *f*; (in contract, insurance policy) apartado excluyente *m*; (Tax) exención *f*; **to the** ∼ **of sth** con la exclusión de algo; ∼ **clause** *n* cláusula *f* excluyente *or* de exoneración de culpa

exclusive *adj* (licence, monopoly, right, taxation) exclusivo; **they have the** ∼ **agency for our firm** tienen la representación exclusiva de nuestra firma; ∼ **of postage and packing** exclusivo de envío y embalaje; ∼ **of tax** exento de impuestos

exclusivity *n* (of product) exclusividad *f*

ex coupon *adj* sin cupón

ex cp. *abbr* (▸**ex coupon**) sin cupón

exculpatory *adj* eximente

exd. *abbr* (▸**examined**) ex (revisado)

ex div. *abbr* (▸**ex dividend**) ex-dividendo

ex dividend *adj* ex-dividendo; ∼ **date** *n* fecha sin dividendos *f*

exec. *abbr* (▸**executive**) ejecutivo(-a) *m,f*; (▸**executor**) albacea testamentario(-a) *m,f*

execute *vt* (plan) ejecutar, llevar a cabo; (duties) desempeñar, ejercer; (orders) ejecutar, cumplir; (sign, seal) cumplir con las formalidades de; (give legal effect to) ejecutar

executed contract *n* contrato perfeccionado *m*

execution *n* ejecución *f*; **put sth into** ∼ poner algo en marcha; ∼ **time** *n* (Comp) tiempo de ejecución *m*

executive¹ *adj* (class, grade) ejecutivo; (training, development) de ejecutivos; ∼ **advancement** *n* promoción de altos cargos *f*; ∼ **assistant** *n* auxiliar ejecutivo(-a) *m,f*; ∼ **board** *n* consejo *m* ejecutivo *or* de administración; ∼ **committee** *n* comité ejecutivo *m*; ∼ **compensation** *n* (travelling expenses) compensación a ejecutivos *f*; ∼ **director** *n* director(a) ejecutivo(-a) *m,f*; ∼ **information system** *n* sistema de información de ejecutivos *m*; ∼ **lounge** *n* salón de clase ejecutiva *m*; ∼ **manager** *n* director(a) *m,f or* gerente(-a) *m,f* ejecutivo(-a); ∼ **officer** *n* director(a) ejecutivo(-a) *m,f*; ∼ **option scheme** *n* plan de opción para los ejecutivos *m*; ∼ **perk** *n* ventaja adicional de los ejecutivos *f*; ∼ **search** *n* búsqueda ejecutiva *f*; ∼ **search firm** *n* compañía de búsqueda de ejecutivos *f*; ∼ **secretary** *n* secretario(-a) ejecutivo(-a) *m,f*; ∼ **stress** *n* estrés del ejecutivo *m*; ∼ **summary** *n* sumario ejecutivo *m*; ∼ **vice**

president *n* vicepresidente(-a) ejecutivo(-a) *m,f*

executive² *n* ejecutivo(-a) *m,f*; (Pol) ejecutivo *m*, poder ejecutivo *m*

executor *n* albacea testamentario(-a) *m,f*

executory *adj* ejecutorio

executrix *n* albacea testamentaria *f*

exempli gratia *adv* por ejemplo

ex-employee *n* ex empleado(-a) *m,f*

exempt¹ *adj* (income, period, corporation) exento; **be** ∼ **from sth** estar exento de algo; **be** ∼ **from doing sth** estar eximido de hacer algo; ∼ **from tax** exente *or* libre de impuestos; ∼ **employees** *n pl* AmE empleados exentos *m pl*

exempt² *vt* eximir; (dividend) pagar en origen; ∼ **sb from sth** eximir a alguien de algo

exempted sum *n* cantidad *f* exenta *or* eximida

exemption *n* exención *f*; **grant sb an** ∼ eximir a alguien; ∼ **certificate** *n* certificado de exención *m*; ∼ **clause** *n* cláusula de exención *f*

exercisable *adj* ejecutable

exercise¹ *vt* (right, option, power, influence) ejercer

exercise² *n* (of rights, power, authority) ejercicio *m*; (undertaking) operación *f*; ∼ **date** *n* (of right) fecha de comunicación *f*; (of option) fecha de ejecución *f*; ∼ **price** *n* precio de ejercicio *m*

exert *vt* (effect, pressure, influence, authority) ejercer

ex gratia payment *n* pago ex gratia *m*

exhaust *vt* (resources, funds, subject) agotar

exhaustive *adj* exhaustivo

exhibit¹ *n* (in court) *documento u objeto que se exhibe en un juicio como prueba*; (exhibition) AmE exposición *f*

exhibit² *vt* (goods) mostrar

exhibition *n* (of goods) exposición *f*; ∼ **center** AmE, ∼ **centre** BrE *n* centro de exposición *m*; ∼ **room** *n* sala de exposiciones *f*

EXIM *abbr* AmE (▸**export-import bank**) banco de exportaciones e importaciones *m*

existing *adj* existente, actual

exit¹ *n* salida *f*; ∼ **interview** *n* entrevista de salida *f*; ∼ **price** *n* precio de salida *m*

exit² ① *vi* salir ② *vt* salir de

ex officio *adj* de oficio; ∼**-officio member** *n* miembro ex oficio *mf*

exor *abbr* (▸**executor**) albacea testamentario(-a) *m,f*

exotic *n* (currency) exótico

exotics *n pl* (Stock) exóticas *f pl*

exp. *abbr* (►**export**¹) exportación *f*

expand **1** *vt* (company, trade) expandir, expansionar; (business) ampliar; (activities) ampliar, alargar; (influence, role) extender; (Comp) (memory) expandir; **~ UK operations** ampliar sus negocios en el RU **2** *vi* (business) expandirse, crecer; (market) expandirse, extenderse; **~ into Europe** introducirse en Europa

expandable *adj* (hardware, software) ampliable

expanding *adj* expansionario, expansivo

expansion *n* (of company, market) expansión *f*; **~ board** *n* placa de expansión *f*; **~ card** *n* tarjeta de expansión *f*; **~ slot** *n* ranura de expansión *f*; **~ strategy** *n* estrategia de expansión *f*

expansionary *adj* (fiscal policy) expansionista

expansive *adj* expansivo

ex parte *adj* de una parte; **~ application** *n* aplicación unilateral *f*

expatriate *n* expatriado(-a) *m,f*; **~ executive** *n* ejecutivo(-a) desplazado(-a) al extranjero *m,f*

expectation *n* expectativa *f*; **against** *o* **contrary to (all) ~(s)** contra todas las previsiones; **not come up to** *o* **not live up to (sb's) ~s** no ser tan bueno como se espera; **in ~ of sth** en espera de algo

expected *adj* (result, outcome) esperado; (date) esperado, previsto

expediency *n* conveniencia *f*

expedite *vt* (process, action, delivery) acelerar

expendable *adj* (goods) consumible

expendables *n pl* consumibles *m pl*

expenditure *n* gasto *m*, desembolso *m*; **~ base** *n* base del gasto *f*; **~ budget** *n* presupuesto de gastos *m*; **~ limit** *n* límite del gasto *m*; **~ tax** *n* impuesto sobre los gastos *m*

expense *n* gasto *m*; **all ~s paid** todos los gastos pagados; **at sb's ~** a expensas de alguien; (figuratively) a costa de alguien; **at the ~ of sth** a costa de algo, en detrimento de algo; **at my (own) ~** a cuenta mía; **at great/little/no ~ (to sb)** con mucho/poco/ningún gasto (para alguien); **go to great ~** meterse en mayores gastos; **~s incurred** gastos incurridos; **no ~ spared** sin reparar en gastos; **pay sb's ~s** pagar los gastos de alguien; **$400 dollars plus ~s** 400 dólares más los gastos; **put sth on ~s** cargar algo a la cuenta de la compañía; **~ account** *n* cuenta de gastos de representación *f*; **~ allowance** *n* (Tax) deducción de gastos *f*; **~ budget** *n* presupuesto de gastos *m*; **~ center** AmE, **~ centre** BrE *n* centro de gastos *m*; **~ item** *n* partida de gastos *f*

expensive *adj* caro

experience¹ *n* experiencia *f*; **know sth by** *o* **from ~** saber algo por experiencia; **speaking from ~** hablando por experiencia; **no previous ~ required** no se requiere experiencia previa

experience² *vt* (loss, setback, delay) sufrir; (difficulty) tener, encontrarse con; (change, improvement, growth) experimentar

experienced *adj* (investor, workforce) con experiencia; **be ~ in sth** tener experiencia en algo

experiment *n* experimento *m*; **do/carry out an ~** hacer/llevar a cabo un experimento

expert¹ *adj* experto; **take ~ advice** pedir una opinión cualificada; **~ at** *o* **in (doing) sth** experto *or* especialista en (hacer) algo; **~ network** *n* red de expertos *f*; **~ system** *n* sistema experto *m*; **~ witness** *n* testigo pericial *m*

expert² *n* experto-a *mf*; **an ~ at** *o* **in** *o* **on (doing) sth** un esperto/una esperta *or* un perito/una perita en (hacer) algo

expertise *n* conocimiento experto *m*

expiration *n* AmE ►**expiry** BrE

expire *vi* (visa, permit, passport) caducar, vencer; (period, contract) expirar; **~ in-the-money** llegar al vencimiento con beneficio potencial; **~ worthless** llegar al vencimiento sin valor alguno

expiry BrE, **expiration** AmE *n* vencimiento *m*, caducidad *f*; **~ of agreement** *n* vencimiento del acuerdo *m*; **~ date** *n* fecha *f* de caducidad *or* de vencimiento; **~ month** *n* mes de vencimiento *m*

ex-pit transaction *n* (Stock) transacción fuera del corro *f*

explain *vt* explicar

explanation *n* explicación *f*

explicit *adj* (contract, cost) explícito

explode *vi* (costs) dispararse

exploded view *n* vista despiezada *f*

exploit *vt* (workers, natural resources, situation) explotar

exploitation *n* (of workers, natural resources, situation) explotación *f*

exponential *adj* (function, trend) exponencial

export¹ *n* exportación *f*; **~s exceeded imports** las exportaciones sobrepasaron las importaciones; **for ~ only** reservado para exportación; **~ agent** *n* agente *mf or* comisionista *mf* de exportación; **~ control** *n* control a la exportación *m*; **~ credit** *n* crédito a la exportación *m*; **~ director** *n* director(a) *m,f or* jefe(-a) *m,f* de exportación; **~ documentation** *n* documentación de exportación *f*; **~ duty** *n* derechos de exportación *m pl*; ~ **earnings** *n pl* ingresos por exportación *m pl*; ~ **finance** *n* financiación de la exportación *f*; ~ **house** *n* casa exportadora *f*; **~-import bank** *n* AmE banco de exportaciones e importaciones *m*; ~ **invoice** *n* factura para exportación *f*; **~-led economic recovery** *n* recuperación económica inducida por la exportación *f*; **~-led growth** *n* crecimiento inducido por las exportaciones *m*; ~ **licence** BrE, ~ **license** AmE *n* permiso de exportación *m*; ~ **manager** *n* director(a) *m,f or* jefe(-a) *m,f* de exportación; ~ **market** *n* mercado de exportación *m*; ~ **marketing** *n* marketing de exportación *m*; ~ **permit** *n* licencia de exportación *f*; ~ **price** *n* precio de exportación *m*; ~ **regulations** *n pl* reglamentación de exportación *f*; ~ **sales** *n pl* exportaciones *f pl*; ~ **sales manager** *n* jefe(-a) de ventas de exportación *m,f*; ~ **sector** *n* sector de exportación *m*; ~ **subsidy** *n* subsidio a la exportación *m*; ~ **surplus** *n* excedente de exportación *m*; ~ **tax** *n* impuesto sobre la exportación *m*; ~ **turnover** *n* facturación de exportación *f*

export² *vt* exportar

exportation *n* exportación *f*

exporter *n* exportador(a) *m,f*

exporting *adj* exportador

expose *vt* (inefficiency, weakness) poner en evidencia; ~ **sth/sb to sth** exponer algo/a alguien a algo

exposed *adj* (sector) expuesto; **in an ~ position** en una posición peligrosa *f*; ~ **net asset position** *n* posición del activo líquido expuesta *f*; ~ **net liability position** *n* posición del pasivo neto arriesgada *f*

exposition *n* exposición *f*

ex post *adj, adv* ex post

ex post facto *adj, adv* de hechos posteriores

exposure *n* (publicity) publicidad *f*; (Stock) extensión del riesgo *f*

express¹ *adj* (intention, wish, term) expreso, explícito; (authority, condition, contract, warranty) expreso; (delivery, service) urgente; ~ **agency** *n* agencia de mensajería *f*

express² *vt* (view) expresar; (letter, package) mandar *or* enviar por correo exprés *or* expreso

expression *n* expresión *f*

expropriate *vt* expropiar

expropriation asset *n* activo de la expropiación *m*

expunge *vt* cancelar

ex-rights *adj* ex derecho; ~ **date** *n* fecha sin derechos *f*; ~ **period** *n* periodo sin derechos *m*

extend *vt* (payment, rules, contract, lease) prorrogar; (power) extender; (range, scope, influence, deadline) extender, ampliar; (loan) conceder; (time limit) ampliar

extended *adj* (period) prolongado, largo; (guarantee) prolongado; (range) extenso; (credit, cover) ampliado; (payment) prorrogado; ~ **term** *n* plazo alargado *m*

extendible *n* (bond) de vencimiento ajustable

extensible *adj* extensible; **eXtensible Mark-up Language** *n* lenguaje *m* de marcado ampliable *or* extensible

extension *n* (of contract) prórroga *f*; (of file name) extensión *f*; (of period) prolongación *f*, extensión *f*; (of deadline, time limit) prórroga *f*, extensión *f*; (to building) ampliación *f*; (Comms) (telephone line) extensión *f*; (telephone handset) supletorio *m*; ~ **costs** *n pl* costes *m pl* Esp *or* costos *m pl* AmL de ampliación; ~ **fee** *n* (Bank) comisión *f or* cuota *f* de renegociación

extensive *adj* (area) extenso; (knowledge) vasto, extenso, amplio; (experience) amplio; (damage) de consideración, importante, de envergadura; (selling) extensivo; **make ~ use of sth** hacer abundante uso de algo

extent *n* (of problem) alcance *m*; (of knowledge) amplitud *f*, vastedad *f*; (of insurance cover) amplitud *f*; **to a certain ~** en cierta medida; **to a large ~** en mayor medida, en gran parte; **to a lesser ~** en menor medida; **to that ~** hasta ese punto

extenuating circumstances *n pl* circunstancias atenuantes *f pl*

external *adj* (aid, influence) del exterior; (audit, cost, evidence, director) externo; (affairs, policy, debt, trade) exterior; (accountant, opinion) independiente; ~ **device** *n* (Comp) dispositivo externo *f*

externality *n* externalidad *f*

externalize *vt* externalizar

externally funded pension *n* BrE pensión no contributiva *f*

extinction *n* (Law) (of action) anulación *f*

extinguish *vt* (debt) cancelar; (obligation) cumplir con

extort *vt* extorsionar

extortion *n* extorsión *f*

extra¹ *adj* (pay, billing) extra; (postage) suplementario; (interest, dividend) extraordinario; ~ **charge** *n* recargo *m*

extra² *n* extra *m*

extract¹ *n* (excerpt) extracto *m*

extract² *vt* (information) extraer, sacar; (mineral) extraer

extraction *n* (of mineral) extracción *f*

extrajudicial *adj* extrajudicial

extrajudicially *adv* extrajudicialmente

extramarginal *adj* extramarginal

extranet *n* extranet *m*, extrared *f*

extraofficial *adj* extraoficial

extraofficially *adv* extraoficialmente

extraordinary *adj* (charge, dividend, item, expenses) extraordinario; **~ general meeting** *n* junta general extraordinaria *f*

extraterritorial *adj* extraterritorial

extravagance *n* despilfarro *m*

extreme *adj* (action, measure, urgency) extremo

extrinsic *adj* (value, motivation) extrínseco

ExW *abbr* (▸**ex-works**) ex *or* franco fábrica

ex warehouse *adj* fuera de almacén

ex-warrant *adj* sin derecho de compra

ex-works *adj* ex *or* franco fábrica; **~ price** *n* precio franco fábrica *m*

eye *n* ojo *m*; **in the ~s of the law** a los ojos de la ley; **be up to one's ~s in debt** estar cargado de deudas, deber hasta la camisa (infrml); **be up to one's ~s in work** estar hasta aquí de trabajo

eyewitness *n* testigo ocular *m*

EZ *abbr* (▸**enterprise zone**) zona de desarrollo industrial *f*

e-zine *n* revista electrónica *f*, folletín electrónico *m*

Ff

fabricate *vt* (goods) fabricar; (document, evidence) falsificar; (story, account) inventar

facade *n* (of building) fachada *f*

face[1] *n* (appearance, nature) fisionomía *f*; (aspect) aspecto *m*; **in the ~ of sth** a pesar de algo; **lose ~** desprestigiarse; **on the ~ of it** a primera vista; **save ~** guardar las apariencias; **~ amount** *n* valor nominal *m*; **~ time** *n* face-time *m*; **~ value** *n* valor nominal *m*; **at ~ value** a la par

face[2] *vt* (criticism, attacks, future) afrontar, hacer frente a; (risks) afrontar; (charges, sentence, fine) enfrentarse a; **~ the facts** afrontar los hechos; **be ~d with sth** estar *or* verse frente a *or* ante algo; **face up to** *vt* (problems, responsibilities) hacer frente a; (person) encarar a

face-to-face *adj* cara a cara, frente a frente; **~ selling** *n* venta por contacto directo *f*

face to face *adv* (meet, discuss) cara a cara, frente a frente

facilitate *vt* facilitar

facilitation *n* facilitación *f*, facilitamiento *m*

facilitator *n* facilitador(a) *m,f*

facilities *n pl* instalaciones *f pl*; **~ management** (Comp) *n* administración de los recursos informáticos *f*

facility *n* (credit) línea de crédito *f*; (Comp) instalación *f*

facing[1] *adj* opuesto; **~ matter** *n* anuncio colocado en la página opuesta al editorial; **~ page** *n* página de delante *f*

facing[2] *n* (S&M) superficie de presentación *f*

facsimile *n* facsímil *m*; **~ signature** *n* firma facsimilar *f*; **~ transaction** *n* transacción por facsímil *f*; **~ transmission** *n* transmisión facsimilar *f*

fact-finding *n* determinación de los hechos *f*; **~-finding mission** *n* misión de investigación *f*

faction *n* facción *f*

factoblig *abbr* (▶**facultative/obligatory**) (re-insurance) opcional/obligatorio

factor *n* factor *m*; **be a ~ in sth** ser un factor de algo; **~ cost** *n* coste *m* Esp *or* costo *m* AmL de los factores; **~ of production** *n* factor de producción *m*; **~ of productivity** *n* factor de productividad *m*

factorage *n* (percentage) comisión *f*

factoring *n* (of debts) factorización *f*, factoraje *m*

factory *n* fábrica *f*; **~ costs** *n pl* costes *m pl* Esp *or* costos *m pl* AmL de fabricación; **~ farming** *n* cultivo industrializado *m*; **~ floor** *n* suelo industrial *m*; **~ hand** *n* operario(-a) de fábrica *m,f*; **~ inspector** *n* inspector(a) de fábrica *m,f*; **~ overheads** *n pl* gastos *m pl* indirectos *or* generales de fábrica; **~ prices** *n pl* precios *m pl* de fábrica *or* franco fábrica *m*; **~ supplies** *n pl* materiales de fábrica *m pl*

factual *adj* fáctico; **~ error** *n* error de hecho *m*; **~ evidence** *n* prueba de los hechos *f*

facultative *adj* facultativo; **~/obligatory** *adj* (re-insurance) opcional/obligatorio

fad *n* (trend) moda pasajera *f*; (personal) manía *f*, maña *f* AmL

fail *vi* (idea, plan) fracasar, fallar; (business) quebrar; (neglect to do sth) faltar a la obligación; (break down) averiarse; **~ in one's duty** faltar al deber; **~ to deliver** (securities) no repartir; **~ to observe the law** incumplir la ley; **~ to reach agreement** no llegar a un acuerdo; **~ to receive** no recibir

failed *adj* (businessperson) fracasado; **~ delivery** *n* (Stock) entrega fallida *f*

failing institution *n* institución en quiebra *f*

fail-safe *adj* (device) de seguridad; (system) infalible, a toda prueba

failure *n* (of business, talks) fracaso *m*; (insolvency) quiebra *f*; **~ in payment** *n* falta de pago *f*; **~ rate** *n* proporción de quiebras *f*; **~ to accept** *n* falta de aceptación *f*; **~ to agree** *n* incapacidad de llegar a un acuerdo *f*; **~ to appear** *n* (in court) incomparecencia *f*; **~ to comply** *n* falta de cumplimiento *f*; **~ to deliver** *n* falta de entrega *f*

fair *adj* justo; **~ average quality** *n* calidad regular *f*; **~ business practice** *n* práctica comercial honesta *f*; **~ competition** *n* competencia leal *f*; **~ employment** *n* trabajo sin discriminación *m*; **~ market price** *n* precio justo *m*; **~ market value** *n* valor equitativo de venta *m*; **~ play** *n* juego limpio *m*; **~ presentation** *n* AmE (Acc) presentación *f* justa *or* leal; **~ rent** *n* alquiler razonable *m*; **~ representation** *n* AmE (*cf* ▶**true and fair view** BrE) (Acc) imagen fiel *f*; **~ return** *n* beneficio *m* *or* rendimiento *m* justo; **~ sample** *n* muestra ···▷

regular *f*; ~ **share** *n* reparto equitativo *m*; ~ **trade** *n* comercio equitativo *m*; ~ **wear and tear** *n* desgaste natural *m*

fait accompli *n* hecho consumado *m*

faith *n* fe *f*; **in good/bad** ~ de buena/mala fe

faithful *adj* fiel

fake¹ *n* falsificación *f*, imitación *f*

fake² *adj* (document) falso

fake³ *vt* (document, signature) falsificar; (results, evidence) falsear, amañar

fall¹ *vi* (prices) caer, descender, disminuir (government) caer; **sterling fell sharply against the dollar** la libra esterlina sufrió un fuerte descenso con respecto al dólar; ~ **foul of sth/sb** tener un enfrentamiento con algo/alguien; ~ **foul of the law** chocar con la ley; ~ **in value** depreciarse; ~ **into abeyance** caer en desuso; ~ **short of sth** (expectations, target) no alcanzar algo; ~ **within the scope of sth** estar dentro del alcance de algo; **fall apart** *vi* (plan, negotiations) fracasar; **fall away** *vi* (numbers) bajar; (trade) decaer; **fall back** *vi* (price) bajar; **fall back on** *vt* (resources) recurrir a; **fall behind** ⟦1⟧ *vi* rezagarse; ~ **behind with payments** atrasarse en los pagos ⟦2⟧ *vt* quedarse detrás de; ~ **behind schedule** retrasarse; **fall down** *vi* (plan, building) derrumbarse; (fail) fracasar; **fall off** *vi* (product, interest) decaer; (quality, service) empeorar, decaer; **fall through** *vi* fracasar, irse a pique

fall² *n* (in demand, output) caída *f*, disminución *f*; (in bank rate, production) caída *f*; (in population, foreign exchange reserves) descenso *m*; **buy on a** ~ (Stock) comprar a la baja; ~ **in price** *n* abaratamiento *m*; ~ **in value** *n* depreciación *f*

fallacy *n* falacia *f*

fallback *n* recurso de emergencia *m*; ~ **option** *n* opción *f* de base *or* de reserva; ~ **position** *n* posición de repliegue *f*

fallen angel *n* (Stock) angel caído *m*

fall guy *n* AmE (infrml) cabeza de turco *f* (infrml)

fallibility *n* falibilidad *f*

fallible *adj* falible

falling *adj* (price) descendente; **buy on a** ~ **market** (Stock) comprar en un mercado a la baja

fallout *n* (consequences) repercusiones *f pl*, consecuencias *f pl*; (disagreement) desacuerdo *m*, pelea *f* (infrml); (nuclear) radiación *f*

false *adj* (statement, accusation, passport, name) falso; ~ **advertising claim** *n* falsa afirmación publicitaria *f*; ~ **alarm** *n* falsa alarma *f*; ~ **declaration** *n* (Tax) declaración falsa *f*; ~ **economy** *n* economía falsa *f*; ~ **return** *n* (Tax) declaración falsa *f*

falsification *n* (of document, accounts, evidence) falsificación *f*

falsify *vt* (document, accounts, evidence) falsificar

falter *vi* vacilar

family *n* (of products, funds) familia *f*; ~ **allowance** *n* subsidio familiar *m*; ~ **brand** *n* marca familiar *f*; ~ **budget** *n* presupuesto familiar *m*; ~ **business** *n* negocio familiar *m*; ~ **circumstances** *n pl* circunstancias familiares *f pl*; ~ **income** *n* ingresos familiares *m pl*; ~**-size pack** *n* paquete familiar *m*

fancy accounting *n* contabilidad ficticia *f*

Fannie Mae *n* AmE (infrml) (▸**Federal National Mortgage Association**) *asociación nacional federal de hipotecas*

FAO *abbr* (▸**for the attention of**) a la atención de

FAP *abbr* (▸**fixed annual percentage**) PAF (porcentaje anual fijo)

f.a.q. *abbr* (▸**fair average quality**) calidad regular *f*

FAQ *abbr* (▸**frequently asked questions**) FAQ *f* (preguntas más frecuentes)

fare *n* (cost of travel) tarifa *f*; (ticket) billete *m*

far-flung *adj* (business empire) vasto

farm¹ *n* (small) granja *f*; (large) hacienda *f*, finca *f*, cortijo *m* Esp; ~ **laborer** AmE, ~ **labourer** BrE *n* trabajador(a) agrícola *m,f*; ~ **policy** *n* política agrícola *f*; ~ **produce** *n* producto agrícola *m*; ~ **shop** *n* BrE *tienda de productos agrícolas en una granja*; ~ **subsidy** *n* subsidio agrario *m*; ~ **surplus** *n* excedente agrícola *m*

farm² ⟦1⟧ *vi* ser agricultor(a); (with animals) ser ganadero-a ⟦2⟧ *vt* (land) cultivar, labrar; (cattle) criar; **farm out** *vt* (piece of work) subcontratar

farmer *n* agricultor(a) *m,f*; ~**s' association** *n* asociación agrícola *f*

farmhand *n* campesino(-a) *m,f*, labrador(a) *m,f*

farming *n* (of land) cultivo *m*, labranza *f*; (of animals) crianza *f*; ~ **business** *n* empresa agrícola *f*; (with animals) empresa ganadera *f*; ~ **method** *n* método de cultivo *m*; (with animals) método de explotación ganadera *m*

farmland *n* terreno de explotación agrícola *m*; (for animals) terreno de explotación ganadera *m*

far-reaching *adj* de gran alcance

far-sighted *adj* perspicaz, sagaz

farther *adv* más lejos; ~ **in** (Stock) más cerca; ~ **out** (Stock) más lejos

fashion n moda f; **in ~** de moda; **out of ~**
pasado de moda; **~ designer** n
diseñador(a) de modas m,f; **~ editor** n
director(a) de modas m,f; **~ goods** n pl
artículos de moda m pl; **~ house** n tienda
de modas f; **~ magazine** n revista de
modas f; **~ model** n modelo de moda mf; **~**
parade n desfile de modas m; **~ show** n
pase de modelos m

fast adj (rise, decline) rápido; **~ food** n
comida rápida f; **~ market** n (Stock)
mercado rápido m; **~ track** n vía rápida f;
~ tracking n ascensión f or promoción f
rápida

fast-growing adj de crecimiento rápido

fast-moving adj (article) de venta fácil; **~**
consumer goods n pl mercancías de
venta fácil f pl

fast-tracked adj de seguimiento rápido

FAT abbr (▶**file allocation table**) (Comp)
listado de archivos m

fatal error n (Comp) error grave m

fatality n víctima mf, muerto(-a) m,f

fat cat n (infrml) potentado m, pez gordo mf
(infrml)

father file n (Comp) fichero padre m

father of the chapel n BrE
representante m or enlace m sindical

fault[1] n (responsibility, blame) culpa f; (failing,
flaw) defecto m, falta f; (in machine) avería f; (in
goods) defecto m, falla f; **be at ~** ser
culpable; **find ~ with sth/sb** criticar algo/a
alguien; **no ~ of** sin culpa de; **there's a ~**
on the line hay una avería en la línea; **to a**
~ excesivamente; **~-tolerant system** n
(Comp) sistema indefectible m; **~-tree**
analysis n análisis de árbol de fallas m

fault[2] vt (person, performance, argument)
encontrar defectos a

faultless adj sin defecto

faulty adj (goods) defectuoso

favor AmE ▶**favour** BrE

favorability AmE ▶**favourability** BrE

favorable AmE ▶**favourable** BrE

favorite AmE ▶**favourite** BrE

favour[1] BrE, **favor** AmE n (approval, service)
favor m; **as a ~ (to sb)** como favor (a
alguien); **ask a ~ of sb** pedir un favor a
alguien; **do sb a ~** hacerle un favor a
alguien; **find ~ with sb** ser bien recibido
por alguien, tener buena acogida por parte
de alguien; **gain/lose ~** ganar/perder
aceptación; **66% in ~, 34% against** 66% a
favor, 34% en contra; **in ~ of (doing) sth** a
favor de (hacer) algo; **in sb's ~** a favor de
alguien; **the balance in your ~ is $5,000** el
saldo a su favor es de 5.000 dólares; **the**
cheque was made out in his ~ el cheque

fue extendido a su nombre; **show ~ to sb**
favorecer a alguien

favour[2] BrE, **favor** AmE vt (plan, course of
action, proposal, idea) estar a favor de, ser
partidario de; (be favourable to, treat
preferentially) favorecer

favourability BrE, **favorability** AmE n
favorabilidad f

favourable BrE, **favorable** AmE adj (price,
rate, conditions, variance, exchange) favorable; **~**
economic climate n clima económico
favorable m; **~ economic conditions** n pl
condiciones económicas favorables f pl; **~**
trade balance n balanza comercial
favorable f

favourite BrE, **favorite** AmE n (on Internet)
favorito m

fax[1] n (▶**facsimile**) fax m (facsímil); **~**
machine n aparato de fax m; **~**
transmission n transmisión por fax f

fax[2] vt enviar por fax

f.c. abbr (▶**for cash**) al contado

fco. abbr (▶**franco**) franco

fd abbr (▶**free delivery**) entrega gratuita a
domicilio f

f.d. abbr (▶**free dispatch**) franco de
consignación m

FDX abbr (▶**full duplex**) (Comp) dúplex m
integral or completo

feasibility n (practicability) viabilidad f;
(possibility) posibilidad f, factibilidad f; **~**
report n informe de viabilidad m; **~ study**
n, **~ survey** n estudio m de viabilidad or
de factibilidad

feasible adj (practicable) viable; (possible)
posible, factible

featherbedding n exceso de trabajadores
m, proteccionismo m

feature n característica f; (in newspaper)
crónica f; **~ article** n artículo periodístico
firmado m; **~ film** n largometraje m

fed. abbr (▶**federal**) federal; **~ funds** n pl
fondos federales m pl

Fed n AmE (▶**Federal Reserve**) Reserva
Federal f

federal adj (government, election, tribunal, aid,
funds) federal; **~ agency** n AmE agencia
federal f; **~ agency issue** n AmE (Fin)
emisión de la agencia federal; **~ agency**
security n AmE valor de la agencia federal;
~ government bond n AmE bono del
gobierno federal m; **F~ Insurance**
Contributions Act n AmE ley federal de
contribuciones de seguros; **F~ National**
Mortgage Association n AmE asociación
nacional federal de hipotecas; **F~ Reserve**
n AmE Reserva Federal f; **F~ Reserve**
Bank n AmE banco de la Reserva Federal m;
F~ Reserve Board n AmE Comisión de la ┄┄

Reserva Federal; **F~ Reserve System** *n*
AmE *sistema de la Reserva Federal que
facilita crédito a los bancos comerciales;* **~
sales tax** *n* AmE impuesto federal sobre
ventas *m*

federalism *n* federalismo *m*

federally *adv* federalmente; **~ regulated**
adj federalmente regulado; **~ regulated
exchange** *n* AmE bolsa regida por las leyes
federales *f*

federated company *n* empresa
federada *f*

federation *n* federación *f*

fee *n* (paid to professional) honorarios *m pl*; (for
membership) cuota *f*; **on payment of a small
~** pagando una pequeña suma *or* cantidad,
por una módica suma; **~-based service** *n*
servicio a comisión *m*; **~ income** *n*
honorarios *m pl*, ingreso por comisión *m*; **~
simple (absolute)** *n* (Prop) dominio
absoluto *m*, propiedad absoluta *f*; **~ split** *n*
(in accountancy firm) división de la comisión *f*,
fraccionamiento de los honorarios *m*

feed[1] *vt* (Comp) alimentar

feed[2] *n* (Comp) alimentación *f*; **~ circuit** *n*
circuito de alimentación *m*; **~ rate** *n*
velocidad de arrastre *f*

feedback *n* (reaction) intercambio de
información *m*; (Comp) feedback *m*,
retroalimentación *f*

feeder organization *n* empresa
proveedor(-a) *m,f*

feel *vt* (effects, consequences) sentir; **~ the
pinch** (infrml) pasar apuros

feelgood factor *n* sensación de bienestar
f

Fellow *n* (of association, institute) miembro *mf*

fellow-worker *n* compañero(-a) de
trabajo *m,f*

felonious *adj* criminal

ferry *n* transbordador *m*

fertilize *vt* fertilizar

fertilizer *n* fertilizante *m*

fetch *vt* (person, object) traer; (price) alcanzar

feudalism *n* feudalismo *m*

FF *abbr* (▸**form feed**) (Comp) avance de
formato *m*, salto de impreso *m*

FFI *abbr* (▸**for further instructions**) para
instrucciones adicionales

FHEx *abbr* (▸**Fridays and holidays
excepted**) salvo viernes y días festivos

FIAS *abbr* (▸**Foreign Investment
Advisory Service**) *servicio de
asesoramiento para inversiones en el
extranjero*

fiat: **~ money** *n* AmE (*cf* ▸**token money**
BrE) moneda *f* depreciada *or* fiduciaria *or*
nominal; **~ standard** *n* moneda fiduciaria *f*

fiberboard AmE ▸**fibreboard** BrE

fiberglass AmE ▸**fibreglass** BrE

fiber-optic AmE ▸**fibre-optic** BrE

fiber-optics AmE ▸**fibre-optics** BrE

fibreboard BrE, **fiberboard** AmE *n*
aglomerado *m*, cartón de pasta de madera *m*,
cartón duro *m*

fibreglass BrE, **fiberglass** AmE *n* fibra de
vidrio *f*

fibre-optic BrE, **fiber-optic** AmE *adj* de
fibra óptica; **~-optic cable** *n* cable de fibra
óptica *m*

fibre-optics BrE, **fiber-optics** AmE *n*
óptica de fibra *f*, fibra óptica *f*

f.i.c., FIC *abbr* (▸**free insurance and
carriage**) franco de seguro y porte

fictitious *adj* (name, address) ficticio, falso;
(capital) ficticio

fiddle[1] *vt* BrE (infrml) (accounts) hacer
chanchullos con (infrml); (expenses) falsear;
(result) amañar (infrml)

fiddle[2] *n* BrE (infrml) chanchullo *m* (infrml);
she's on the ~ está metida en un
chanchullo (infrml)

fidelity *n* fidelidad *f*; **~ guarantee** *n* fianza
f; **~ insurance** *n* seguro de fidelidad *m*

fiduciarily *adv* fiduciariamente

fiduciary *adj* (account, issue, currency)
fiduciario; **~ bond** *n* fianza *f*

field *n* campo *m*; **~ audit** *n* auditoría
externa *f*; **~ of endeavor** AmE, **~ of
endeavour** BrE *n* sector de actividad *m*; **~
investigator** *n* investigador(a) de campo
m,f; **~ operator** *n* operador(a) de campo
m,f; **~ research** *n* investigación de campo
f; **~ sales manager** *n* director(a) de ventas
de campo *m,f*; **~ staff** *n* personal de campo
m; **~ survey** *n* encuesta de campo *f*; **~
testing** *n* prueba sobre el terreno *f*; **~
work** *n* trabajo *m* de campo *or* en el
terreno; **~ worker** *n* *investigador que
trabaja en el terreno*

fierce *adj* (competition) fiero

FIFO *abbr* (▸**first in, first out**) PEPS
(primero en entrar, primero en salir)

fifth-generation computer *n*
computadora *f* AmL *or* ordenador *m* Esp de
quinta generación

fight *vt* (measure, proposal) combatir, oponerse
a, luchar contra; **~ a losing battle against**
librar una batalla perdida contra; **fight
back** *vi* contraatacar

figure *n* cifra *f*; **~s adjusted for seasonal
variations** cifras ajustadas a los cambios
estacionales; **inflation is now into double
~s** la inflación pasa del 10%; **your ~s are
in agreement with ours** sus cifras
concuerdan con las nuestras; **in round ~s**
en cifras redondas; **her salary is well into**

six ~s gana bastante más de 100.000 libras;
put a ~ on sth dar una cifra sobre algo

file[1] *n* (Comp) fichero *m*, archivo *m*; (folder)
carpeta *f*; (box file) clasificador *m*, archivador
m; (for card index) fichero *m*; (of a case)
expediente *m*, dossier *m*; (collection of
documents) archivo *m*; **access/copy/delete a
~** abrir/copiar/borrar un fichero *or* un
archivo; **~ not found** fichero no encontrado;
on ~ fichado, archivado; **open/close a ~**
abrir/cerrar un fichero *or* un archivo; **~
allocation table** *n* listado de archivos *m*;
~ clerk *n* AmE (*cf* ►**filing clerk** BrE)
archivero(-a) *m,f*, archivador(a) *m,f*; **~
compression** *n* compresión de fichero *f*; **~
conversion** *n* conversión de fichero *f*; **~
copy** *n* copia para archivo *f*; **~ directory** *n*
directorio de ficheros *m*; **~ extension** *n*
extensión de fichero *f*; **~ format** *n* formato
de fichero *m*; **~ management** *n* gestión de
ficheros *f*; **~ menu** *n* menú *m* de ficheros
or de archivos; **~ protection** *n* protección
f de ficheros *or* de archivos; **~ server** *n*
servidor de ficheros *m*; **~ sharing** *n*
utilización en común de ficheros *f*; **~
transfer protocol** *n* protocolo de
transferencia de archivos *m*

file[2] **[1]** *vt* (document) archivar; (charges,
complaint, application, report, tax return) presentar;
~ a claim for damages entablar una
demanda por daños y perjuicios
[2] *vi* archivar; **~ for bankruptcy** presentar
una declaración de quiebra; **file away** *vt*
archivar

filer *n* (Tax) declarante *mf*

filing *n* archivo *m*; (of application, tax return)
presentación *f*; **keep the ~ up to date**
mantener el archivo al día **~ basket** *n*
cestilla de archivo *f*; **~ cabinet** *n*
archivador *m*; **~ clerk** *n* BrE (*cf* ►**file clerk**
AmE) archivero(-a) *m,f*, archivador(a) *m,f*; **~
drawer** *n* cajón clasificador *m*; **~ system**
n sistema de archivo *m*

fill *vt* (vacancy) llenar; (position, post) ocupar,
cubrir; **fill in** *vt* (form) rellenar,
cumplimentar

filler *n* (to add bulk) relleno *m*; (article) artículo
de relleno *m*

fill-in *n* cumplimentación *f*

fill price *n* (Stock) precio de ejecución de la
compraventa *m*

film *n* BrE (*cf* ►**motion picture** AmE,
►**movie** AmE) película *f*; **~ advertising** *n*
publicidad de una película *f*; **~ industry** *n*
industria *f* cinematográfica *or* del cine;
~-maker *n* productor(a) cinematográfico(-
a) *m,f*; **~ production** *n* producción de
películas *f*; **~ rights** *n pl* derechos
cinematográficos *m pl*

filmsetter *n* máquina de componer
fotográficamente *f*

filmsetting *n* composición fotográfica *f*,
fotocomposición *f*

FILO *abbr* (►**first in, last out**) PEUS
(primero en entrar, último en salir)

filter *n* (Comp) filtro *m*

filtering *n* (Comp) filtración *f*; **~ software**
n software de filtración *m*

FIMBRA *abbr* (►**Financial
Intermediaries, Managers and Brokers
Regulatory Association**) *asociación
profesional de intermediarios, gestores y
agentes financieros*

final *adj* (accounts, balance, dividend, instalment)
final; (prospectus) definitivo; **put the ~
touch to sth** dar el toque final a algo; **~
acceptance** *n* (of goods) recepción
definitiva *f*; **~ demand** *n* última
reclamación *f*; **~ mortgage payment** *n*
liquidación de una hipoteca *f*; **~ proof** *n* (in
printing, photography) prueba final *f*; **~
warning** *n* última advertencia *f*

finalize *vt* (arrangements, plans) ultimar,
concluir; (date) fijar, concretar; **nothing's
been ~d yet** aún no se ha concretado nada

finance[1] *n* finanzas *f pl*; **F~ Act** *n* BrE Ley
de Finanzas *f*; **F~ Bill** *n* BrE proyecto de ley
financiero *m*; **~ company** *n* financiera *f*; **~
department** *n* departamento financiero *m*;
~ director *n* director(a) financiero(-a) *m,f*;
~ house *n* BrE empresa financiera *f*

finance[2] *vt* financiar; **~ directly** financiar
directamente

financial *adj* (sector, institution, crisis)
financiero; **~ accounting** *n* contabilidad
financiera *f*; **~ administration** *n*
administración *f or* gestión *f* financiera; **~
advertising** *n* publicidad financiera *f*; **~
agent** *n* agente financiero(-a) *m,f*; **~ aid** *n*
ayuda financiera *f*; **~ analysis** *n* análisis
financiero *m*; **~ appraisal** *n* evaluación
financiera *f*; **~ assistance** *n* ayuda *f or*
asistencia *f* financiera; **~ backer** *n*
promotor(a) financiero(-a) *m,f*; **~ backing**
n respaldo financiero *m*; **~ burden** *n* carga
financiera *f*; **~ capital** *n* capital financiero
m; **~ center** AmE, **~ centre** BrE *n* centro *m*
financiero *or* de finanzas; **~ circles** *n pl*
círculos financieros *m pl*; **~ climate** *n*
clima financiero *m*; **~ conglomerate** *n*
conglomerado financiero *f*; **~ control** *n*
control financiero *m*; **~ controller** *n*
director(a) financiero(-a) *m,f*; **~ director** *n*
director(a) financiero(-a) *m,f*; **~ disclosure**
n divulgación de información financiera *f*;
~ engineering *n* ingeniería financiera *f*; **~
firm** *n* firma financiera *f*; **~ flow** *n*
corriente *f or* fluctuación *f* financiera; **~
forecasts** *n pl* estimaciones *f pl or* ····⟶

previsiones f pl financieras; ∼ **future** n
futuro financiero m; ∼ **futures market** n
mercado de futuros financieros m; ∼
gearing n BrE apalancamiento financiero m;
∼ **history** n historia financiera f; ∼
incentive n incentivo financiero m; ∼
instrument n instrumento financiero m; ∼
intermediary n intermediario(-a)
financiero(-a) m,f; **F∼ Intermediaries,
Managers and Brokers Regulatory
Association** n asociación profesional de
intermediarios, gestores y agentes financieros;
∼ **involvement** n implicación financiera f;
∼ **leverage** n (cf ▸**financial gearing** BrE)
apalancamiento financiero m; ∼
management n gestión financiera f; ∼
manager n gerente financiero(-a) m,f; ∼
market n mercado financiero m; ∼
marketplace n plaza financiera f; ∼
officer n director(a) financiero(-a) m,f; ∼
package n plan de financiación m; ∼
paper n valores financieros m pl; ∼ **period**
n periodo financiero m; (Fin) ejercicio m
contable or económico; ∼ **planning** n
planificación financiera f; ∼ **policy** n
política financiera f; ∼ **position** n posición
financiera f; ∼ **reporting** n información
financiera f; ∼ **requirement** n requisito
financiero m; ∼ **review** n análisis
financiero m; ∼ **reward** n remuneración
financiera f; ∼ **risk** n riesgo financiero m;
∼ **service** n servicio financiero m; ∼
services industry n industria de servicios
financieros f; ∼ **simulation software** n
programa m or software m de simulación
financiera; ∼ **situation** n situación
financiera f; ∼ **stability** n estabilidad
financiera f; ∼ **standard** n norma
financiera f; ∼ **standing** n (of firm)
capacidad financiera f; ∼ **statement** n
balance m, estado m contable or financiero;
∼ **summary** n resumen financiero m; **F∼
Times Index** n índice del Financial Times
m; **F∼ Times Industrial Ordinary Share
Index** n índice bursátil de valores
industriales del Financial Times m; **F∼
Times Stock-Exchange 100 Share
Index** n índice Footsie m; **F∼ Times
Stock-Exchange Index** n índice bursátil
del Financial Times m; ∼ **year** n ejercicio
m económico or financiero

financially adv (sound, viable)
económicamente

financier n financista mf

financing n financiación f, financiamiento
m; ∼ **adjustment** n reajuste de
financiación m; ∼ **charges** n pl costes m pl
Esp or costos m pl AmL de financiación; ∼
expenses n pl gastos de financiación m pl;
∼ **facility** n mecanismo de financiamiento
m; ∼ **package** n paquete financiero m;

∼ **plan** n plan de financiación m; ∼ **rate** n
tasa de financiación f

find [1] vt (solution, cause, replacement)
encontrar; ∼ **the balance** conseguir un
equilibrio; ∼ **fault with sth/sb** criticar
algo/a alguien; ∼ **sth wanting** encontrar
algo deficiente
[2] vi fallar; ∼ **for/against sb** fallar a favor
de/en contra de alguien

finder's fee n honorarios del
intermediario m pl

findings n pl (of investigation, tribunal)
conclusiones f pl; (Law) laudo m

fine[1] n multa f

fine[2] vt multar; ∼ **sb for doing sth** multar
a alguien por hacer algo

fine[3] adj (distinction) sutil; (balance) delicado;
∼ **print** n (in contract) letra f pequeña or
menuda or chica AmL

fine-tune vt poner a punto

fine-tuning n puesta a punto f

finish vti terminar; ∼ **in the money**
terminar con beneficio potencial; ∼ **work**
acabar el trabajo

finished adj (article, goods) terminado

finite adj (number) finito; (resources) limitado

fire[1] n fuego m; (accident) incendio m; ∼
drill n ejercicio de contraincendio m; ∼
escape n escalera de incendios f; ∼ **exit** n
salida de incendios f; ∼ **hazard** n peligro
de incendio m; ∼ **prevention** n prevención
de incendios f; ∼ **regulations** n pl normas
en caso de incendio f pl

fire[2] vt (infrml) (staff) despedir, echar

fireproof adj incombustible

fire-resistant adj ignífugo

firewall n (Comp) pantalla cortafuegos f

firing n (infrml) (of staff) despido m, cese m

firm[1] n (organization) firma f; ∼ **signature** n
firma social f

firm[2] adj (offer, order, commitment, buyer, date,
contract) en firme; (currency, market) firme

firmness n (of market, shares) solidez f

firm up [1] vi (prices) recuperarse
[2] vt (price, date, deal) concretar, confirmar

firmware n microprogramación f

first[1] adj primero; ∼ **in**, ∼ **out** primero en
entrar, primero en salir; ∼ **in, last out**
primero en entrar, último en salir; **in the ∼
instance** en primera instancia; **make the ∼
move** hacer la primera jugada; ∼**-aid kit** n
botiquín de primeros auxilios m; ∼ **class** n
primera (clase) f; ∼**-class mail** AmE,
∼**-class post** BrE n correo preferencial m;
∼ **generation** n primera generación f;
∼**-generation computer** n computadora f
AmL or ordenador m Esp de primera
generación; ∼ **half** n (of month, year) primera
parte f; ∼**-line management** n dirección f

or gerencia *f* de primera línea; ~
mortgage *n* primera hipoteca *f*; ~
preferred stock *n* acciones de preferencia
f pl; ~ **quarter** *n* primer trimestre *m*;
~-**rate** *adj* de primera; **F**~ **World
countries** *n* países *m pl* industrializados *or*
desarrollados

first² *n* (original idea, accomplishment) primicia *f*

fiscal *adj* (policy, period, barrier) fiscal; ~
agent *n* intermediario fiscal(-a) *m,f*; ~
burden *n* carga fiscal *f*; ~ **drag** *n* traba
fiscal *f*; ~ **quarter** *n* trimestre fiscal *m*; ~
year *n* año *m or* ejercicio *m* fiscal; ~ **year
(then) ended** *n* año fiscal finalizado *m*

fiscalist *n* fiscalista *mf*

fiscally *adv* fiscalmente; ~ **opaque** *adj*
fiscalmente opaco

fit¹ *adj* apropiado, apto; **be** ~ **for sth/sb** ser
apropiado *or* apto para algo/alguien; ~ **and
proper** apto

fit² *n* (Stock) ajuste *m*

fit³ *vt* (equip) equipar; (make suitable)
capacitar; ~ **sth with sth** equipar algo con
algo; **her experience** ~**s her for this job** su
experiencia la capacita para este trabajo; **fit
out** *vt* equipar; **fit sth/sb out with sth**
equipar algo/a alguien con algo

f.i.t. *abbr* (▶**free of income tax**) exento de
impuestos sobre la renta

five *n* cinco *m*; ~ **spot** *n* AmE (infml) *billete
de cinco dólares*; ~-**year plan** *n* plan
quinquenal *m*

fix¹ *vt* (date, time, price) fijar; (appointment)
concertar; (details) concretar; (arrange)
arreglar

fix² *n* (Fin) fijo *m*

fixed *adj* (price, charge, rent, fee) fijo; (capital)
fijo, inmovilizado; (deposit) a plazo fijo; ~
annual percentage *n* porcentaje anual fijo
m; ~ **asset** *n* activo inmovilizado *m*;
(property) activo fijo *m*; ~ **disk** *n* (Comp)
disco fijo *m*; ~ **duty** *n* impuesto fijo *m*; ~
exchange rate *n* cambio fijo *m*; ~
income *n* renta fija *f*; ~-**interest loan** *n*
préstamo a interés fijo *m*; ~ **overheads** *n
pl* gastos generales fijos *m pl*; ~-**rate bond**
n bono de tipo de interés fijo *m*; ~-**rate
loan** *n* préstamo de interés fijo *m*; ~-**rate
mortgage** *n* crédito hipotecario a interés
fijo *m*; ~-**term contract** *n* contrato de
plazo fijo *m*; ~-**term deposit** *n* BrE (*cf*
▶**time deposit** AmE) depósito a plazo fijo *m*;
~-**term loan** *n* préstamo a plazo fijo *m*

fixing *n* (of prices) fijación *f*; (of costs)
determinación *f*; ~ **rate** *n* fixing *m*

fixture *n* instalación *f*; ~**s and fittings**
n pl accesorios *m pl* e instalaciones *f pl*;
(Acc) bienes *m pl* inmuebles y enseres *m pl*

F key *n* (▶**function key**) tecla de función *f*

flag¹ *n* (Comp) indicador *m*; ~ **of
convenience** *n* bandera de conveniencia *f*

flag² *vt* (Comp) indicar

flagship store *n* tienda insignia *f*

flame¹ **1** *vt* (Comp) enviar un desahogo a
2 *vi* (Comp) enviar un desahogo

flame² *n* (Comp) desahogo *m*

flash pack *n* envase con reducción de
precio en lugar destacado *m*

flat¹ *adj* (fee) fijo; (market) inactivo;
(organization) horizontal; ~ **bond** *n* título con
intereses acumulados en la cotización *m*; ~
rate *n* tipo fijo *m*; ~-**rate** *adj* (tax, bonus) de
tipo fijo; (price) a tipo fijo

flat² *n* BrE (*cf* ▶**apartment** AmE)
apartamento *m*, departamento *m* AmL, piso
m Esp

flaunt *vt* ostentar

flaw *n* (in material, plan, character) defecto *m*; (in
argument) error *m*

flawed *adj* defectuoso

fleet *n* (of company cars) parque *m*; (of ships)
flota *f*

Fleet Street *n* BrE *calle londinense famosa
por ser antiguamente el centro de la
industria periodística nacional*

flexibility *n* flexibilidad *f*

flexible *adj* (arrangement, system, approach,
pricing) flexible; ~ **exchange rate** *n* tipo de
cambio flexible *m*; ~-**payment mortgage**
n hipoteca de pagos flexibles *f*; ~ **schedule**
n, ~ **time** *n*, ~ **working hours** *n pl*
horario flexible *m*

flexitime *n* BrE (*cf* ▶**flextime** AmE) horario
flexible *m*

flexography *n* flexografía *f*

flexprice *n* precio flexible *m*

flextime *n* AmE (*cf* ▶**flexitime** BrE) horario
flexible *m*

flicker¹ *n* (of screen) parpadeo *m*

flicker² *vi* (screen) parpadear

flier *n* AmE (Stock) especulación peligrosa *f*;
take a ~ AmE especular

flight *n* (of aircraft) vuelo *m*; (fleeing) huida *f*;
~ **attendant** *n* auxiliar de vuelo *mf*; ~ **of
capital** *n* huida de capitales *f*; ~ **from the
dollar** *n* conversión del dólar con otras
divisas *f*; ~ **number** *n* número de vuelo *m*;
~ **to quality** *n* (Stock) huida hacia la
calidad *f*

flip chart *n* rotafolios *m*

flip-flop *n* (Comp) circuito biestable *m*

float¹ *n* (ready cash) dinero *m or* efectivo *m*
en caja, efectivo disponible *m*; (uncollected
cheques) cheques no canjeados *m pl*

float² *vt* (currency) flotar; (new issue, loan,
securities) emitir; (company) lanzar

floater *n* AmE (*cf* ▸**floating-rate note** BrE) obligación de interés variable *f*

floating[1] *adj* (asset, capital, stock, currency, debt) flotante; ∼ **cash reserve** *n* encaje *m* circulante *or* flotante; ∼ **exchange rate** *n* tipo de cambio flotante *m*; ∼ **interest rate** *n* tasa de interés flotante *f*; ∼**-rate loan** *n* préstamo de tasa flotante *m*; ∼**-rate note** *n* BrE (*cf* ▸**floater** AmE) obligación de interés variable *f*; ∼ **voter** *n* BrE votante indeciso(-a) *m,f*

floating[2] *n* (of currency) flotación *f*; (of new issue, loan, securities) emisión *f*; (of company) lanzamiento *m*

flood[1] *vt* (market) inundar, saturar

flood[2] *n* (of complaints, calls, letters) avalancha *f*, diluvio *m*; ∼ **insurance** *n* seguro contra riesgo de inundación *m*

floor *n* (for prices, rates) suelo *m*; (of stock exchange) parqué *m*; ∼ **broker** *n* agente auxiliar de bolsa *mf*, comisionista bursátil *mf*; ∼ **loan** *n* préstamo mínimo *m*; ∼ **manager** *n* BrE (*cf* ▸**floorwalker** AmE) (of department store) jefe(-a) de sección *m,f*; ∼ **official** *n* (Stock) empleado(-a) del parqué *m,f*; ∼ **plan** *n* plano *m*, planta *f*; ∼ **price** *n* precio mínimo *m*; ∼ **rate** *n* tasa mínima *f*; ∼ **return** *n* (Stock) rendimiento básico *m*; ∼ **space** *n* superficie habitable *f*; ∼ **trader** *n* corredor(a) de bolsa independiente *m,f*

floorwalker *n* AmE (*cf* ▸**floor manager** BrE) (of department store) jefe(-a) de sección *m,f*

flop *n* (infrml) fracaso *m* (infrml)

floppy *n* disco flexible *m*; ∼ **disk** *n* disco flexible *m*; ∼ **disk drive** *n* unidad de disco flexible *f*

flotation *n* (of currency) flotación *f*; (of new issue) emisión *f*; (of company) lanzamiento *m*

flourish *vi* (business, competition) florecer, prosperar

flow *n* (of funds, data, goods, passenger traffic) flujo *m*; (of operations) desarrollo *m*; **go with the** ∼ (infrml) ir con la corriente; ∼ **concepts** *n pl* (Stock) conceptos de flujo *m pl*; ∼ **control** *n* control de flujo *m*; ∼ **diagram** *n* diagrama de flujo *m*; ∼ **of money** *n* flujo monetario *m*

flowchart *n* diagrama de flujo *m*, flujograma *m*, organigrama *m*

fluctuate *vi* (prices, rates) fluctuar, oscilar

fluctuating *adj* (currency) fluctuante

fluctuation *n* (of prices, rates) fluctuación *f*, oscilación *f*

flurry *n* (of activity) frenesí *m*

flush[1] *adj* (margin) alineado; ∼ **left** *adj* justificado a la izquierda; ∼ **right** *adj* justificado a la derecha

flush[2] *vt* (text) justificar

flux *n* cambio continuo *m*; **be in a (state of)** ∼ estar continuamente cambiando

flyer *n* (advertisement) octavilla *f*

flying *adj* (fast) rápido; **get off to a** ∼ **start** (infrml) (business, project) empezar con muy buen pie; ∼ **picket** *n* piquete *m* móvil *or* volante; ∼ **visit** *n* visita relámpago *f*

FMG *abbr* (▸**fast-moving consumer goods**) mercancías de venta fácil *f pl*

FNMA *abbr* AmE (▸**Federal National Mortgage Association**) *asociación nacional federal de hipotecas*

fo *abbr* (▸**for orders**) a órdenes

FOC *abbr* (▸**free of charge**) libre de gastos

focal point *n* (of discussion) punto focal *m*

focus[1] *n* punto central *m*; ∼ **group** *n* grupo *m* analizado *or* estudiado

focus[2] *vt* (efforts, activities) concentrar; ∼ **attention on sth** dirigir la atención a algo; **focus on** *vt* centrarse en

fod *abbr* (▸**free of damage**) libre de daños

FOIA *abbr* AmE (▸**Freedom of Information Act**) *ley de libertad de información*

folder *n* carpeta *f*

folio *n* folio *m*

follow [1] *vt* (instructions, advice, fashion) seguir; ∼ **a similar pattern** (demand) seguir un modelo similar; ∼ **suit** seguir el ejemplo; ∼ **sth through** (project, scheme) seguir (con) algo hasta el final
[2] *vi* resultar; **as** ∼**s** como sigue; **follow up** *vt* (check) controlar; (pursue) seguir

follower *n* partidario(-a) *m,f*, seguidor(a) *m,f*

follow-up *n* (further action) seguimiento *m*; (of invoice, order) control *m*; ∼ **letter** *n* carta de seguimiento *f*

font *n* (in typography) juego de caracteres *m*; ∼ **family** *n* (in typography) familia de tipos *f*

food *n* alimento *m*; ∼ **chain** *n* cadena alimenticia *f*; ∼ **processing** *n* procesamiento de alimentos *m*; ∼ **retailing** *n* venta minorista de alimentos *f*; ∼ **store** *n* tienda de alimentación *f*

foodstuff *n* producto alimenticio *m*

footer *n* título en pie de página *m*

footing *n* base *f*; **on an equal** ∼ **(with sth/ sb)** en pie de igualdad (con algo/alguien); **on the same** ∼ en pie de igualdad; **put sth on a firm** ∼ poner algo en una base firme

footnote *n* (to document) nota a pie de página *f*; ∼ **disclosure** *n* (Acc) exposición en nota al pie *f*

Footsie *n* (▸**Financial Times Stock-Exchange 100 Share Index**) índice Footsie *m*

force¹ *vt* (action, change) provocar; ~ **sb into early retirement** obligar a alguien a una jubilación anticipada; ~ **an issue** forzar una salida; ~ **sb to do sth** obligar *or* forzar a alguien a hacer algo; **force down** *vt* (prices) hacer bajar; (interest rates) forzar el descenso de; **force up** *vt* (prices) hacer subir

force² *n* (validity) fuerza *f*; **in** ~ en vigor; **come into** ~ entrar en vigor; **put sth into** ~ poner algo en vigor

forced *adj* (labour, landing, sale) forzoso

forceful *adj* (argument) fuerte

force majeure *n* fuerza mayor *f*

forcible entry *n* (by police) toma de posesión violenta *f*

fore *n*: **come to the** ~ empezar a destacar

forecast¹ *n* previsión *f*, predicción *f*

forecast² *vt* prever

forecaster *n* previsor(a) *m,f*

forecasting *n* previsión *f*, pronóstico *m*

foreclose *vt* (loan, mortgage) ejecutar; **foreclose on** *vt* (loan, mortgage) ejecutar

foreclosure *n* procedimiento ejecutivo hipotecario *m*; ~ **sale** *n* venta por juicio hipotecario *f*

foredate *vt* antefechar

forefront *n*: **at the** ~ **of sth** (of research and development) a la vanguardia de algo

foreground¹ *n* primer plano *m*; **in the** ~ en primer plano

foreground² *adj* (Comp) preferencial; ~ **program** *n* programa de alta prioridad *m*

foreign *adj* (company, competitor, borrowing) extranjero; (capital, debt) externo; (trade) exterior; (aid) externo, exterior; ~ **account** *n* cuenta *f* extranjera *or* con el exterior; ~ **affairs** *n pl* asuntos exteriores *m pl*; ~ **agent** *n* representante en el extranjero *mf*; ~ **assets** *n pl* activos en divisas *m pl*; ~ **bill** *n* letra *f* extranjera *or* sobre el exterior; ~**-controlled** *adj* bajo control extranjero; ~ **correspondent** *n* corresponsal en el extranjero *mf*; ~ **currency** *n* divisa extranjera *f*; ~ **currency market** *n* bolsa de divisas *f*; ~ **currency transaction** *n* transacción en divisas *f*; ~ **direct investment** *n* inversión extranjera directa *f*; ~ **exchange** *n* (currency) divisas *f pl*; (action) cambio de divisas *m*; ~ **exchange broker** *n* corredor(a) de cambios *m,f*; ~ **exchange dealer** *n* cambista *mf*; ~ **exchange hedge** *n* cobertura *f or* protección *f* del cambio de divisas, seguro de cambio *m*; ~ **exchange holding** *n* participación en cambio de divisas *f*; ~ **exchange market** *n* mercado de divisas *m*; ~ **exchange office** *n* oficina de cambio *f*; ~ **exchange rate** *n* tipo de cambio extranjero *m*; ~ **exchange reserves** *n pl*

reserva de divisas *f*; ~ **exchange trader** *n* corredor(a) de divisas *m,f*; ~ **identity card** *n* BrE (*cf* ▶**alien registration card** AmE) tarjeta de identificación extranjera *f*; ~ **income** *n* ingresos procedentes del exterior *m pl*; ~ **investment** *n* inversión extranjera *f*; **F~ Investment Advisory Service** *n* servicio de asesoramiento para inversiones en el extranjero; ~ **investor** *n* inversor(a) extranjero(-a) *m,f*; **F~ Minister** *n* Ministro(-a) de Asuntos Exteriores *m,f*; ~ **national** *n* persona de nacionalidad extranjera *f*; ~ **sale** *n* venta de exportación *f*; ~ **securities** *n pl* valores extranjeros *m pl*; ~ **shares** *n pl*, ~ **stock** *n* acciones extranjeras *f pl*

foreigner *n* extranjero(-a) *m,f*

foreman *n* capataz(a) *m,f*, sobrestante *mf*

forename *n* nombre *m*

foresee *vt* prever

foreseeable *adj* (risk) previsible; **in the** ~ **future** en un futuro previsible

forestry *n* silvicultura *f*; ~ **industry** *n* industria forestal *f*

forex *abbr* (▶**foreign exchange**) (currency) divisas *f pl*; (action) cambio de divisas *m*; **F~ index** *n* índice de divisas *m*; ~ **option** *n* opción sobre divisas *f*; ~ **trading** *n* operación de compra-venta extranjera *f*

forfeit *vt* (property) perder el derecho a; (right) perder

forfeiting *n* forfeiting *m*

forfeiture *n* (loss) pérdida *f*; (confiscation) confiscación *f*; (of a debt) extinción *f*

forge *vt* (banknote, signature) falsificar; (bond, alliance) forjar; (plan) fraguar

forged *adj* (cheque) falso, falsificado; ~ **bill** AmE, ~ **note** BrE *n* billete falso *m*

forgery *n* falsificación *f*

forgivable loan *n* préstamo perdonable *m*

forgive *vt* perdonar

forgiveness of tax *n* exención del impuesto *f*

forgo *vt* privarse de, renunciar a; ~ **collection of sth** (debt) abstenerse de cobrar algo, renunciar al derecho de cobro de algo

form¹ *n* (shape, manner) forma *f*; (document) formulario *m*, impreso *m*; **fill in** *o* **out a** ~ (re)llenar un formulario *or* un impreso; **in** *o* **on** ~ en forma; **in the** ~ **of sth** en forma de algo; **off** *o* **out of** ~ en baja forma; ~ **feed** *n* avance de formato *m*, salto de impreso *m*; ~**-filling** *n* relleno *m* de formularios *or* de impresos

form² *vt* (committee, alliance, partnership, quorum) constituir; (company) formar

formal *adj* (agreement, communication) formal; ~ **notice** *n* admonición por mora *f*

formality n formalidad f; **dispense with formalities** prescindir de las formalidades; **it's just a** ∼ no es más que un trámite; **legal formalities** requisitos legales

formalization n formalización f

formalize vt formalizar

format[1] n formato m

format[2] vt (disk) formatear

formation n (of a corporation) constitución f, formación f

formatting n formateado m

former[1] (spouse) adj antiguo; ∼ **buyer** n comprador(a) anterior m,f

former[2] n primero(-a) m,f

formula n fórmula f; ∼ **funding** n financiación ponderada f; ∼ **investing** n inversión por fórmula f

formulate vt (policy) formular

formulation n (of policy) formulación f

fortnightly[1] adj BrE bimensual, quincenal

fortnightly[2] adv BrE bimensualmente, quincenalmente

fortress Europe n (jarg) fortaleza europea f, reducto europeo m

fortuitous adj (event) fortuito

forum n foro m

forward[1] adj (contract, security, price, rate) a plazo; (buying, sales, discount) a término; (cover) a futuro; (market) de futuros; (dealing) a futuros, a término; (delivery) futuro; (transaction) a vencimiento; (integration) progresivo; ∼ **average** n pago adelantado del impuesto m; ∼ **exchange** n divisas a plazo f pl; ∼ **exchange market** n mercado de futuros m; ∼ **exchange rate** n tipo de cambio a futura m; ∼**-facing staff** n personal de atención al público; ∼**-forward** adj a plazo con tipo de interés convenido; ∼**-forward currency deal** n transacción de divisas a plazo f; ∼ **planning** n planificación f a largo plazo or anticipada or de largo alcance; ∼ **slash** n barra oblicua f; ∼ **swap** n crédito recíproco futuro m, swop futuro m; ∼ **vertical integration** n integración vertical progresista f

forward[2] vt (package, document) remitir, enviar

forward-average vi adelantar el impuesto efectivo or el pago del impuesto

forwarder n expedidor(a) m,f

forwarding n (of goods) expedición f; (of letter) envío m; ∼ **address** n dirección f (a la que han de hacerse seguir las cartas); ∼ **agency** n casa de expedición f; ∼ **agent** n agente expedidor(a) m,f; ∼ **company** n empresa expedidora f; ∼ **department** n departamento de envíos m; ∼ **instruction** n instrucción de envío f

forward-looking adj (person, project) con visión de futuro

forward-thinking adj con previsión de futuro

fossil fuel n combustible fósil m

foster vt (environment, relationship) mantener; (growth) fomentar

foundation n fundación f; **be without** ∼ ser infundado, carecer de fundamento

foundations n pl cimientos m pl; **lay the** ∼ **of sth** poner los cimientos de algo

founder[1] n fundador(-a) m,f; ∼ **member** n miembro fundador(-a) m,f; ∼**s' shares** n pl acciones de los promotores f pl

founder[2] vi (plan, project) irse a pique, zozobrar

founding adj (company) fundador

four n cuatro m; ∼**-color set** AmE, ∼**-colour set** BrE n tirada en cuatricromía f; ∼ **sheet** n anuncio de 1 x 1,5 metros; ∼**-star gasoline** n AmE, ∼**-star petrol** n BrE gasolina súper f

fourth adj cuarto; ∼**-generation computer** n computadora f AmL or ordenador m Esp de cuarta generación; ∼ **market** n cuarto mercado m; ∼ **quarter** n cuarto trimestre m; **F**∼ **World** n cuarto mundo m

FOX abbr (▶**London Futures and Options Exchange**) mercado de opciones y futuros de Londres

f.p. abbr (▶**fully paid**) totalmente pagado

FPM abbr (▶**flexible-payment mortgage**) hipoteca de pagos flexibles f

fraction n fracción f

fractional adj (difference, amount) mínimo; (lot, share) fraccionario; (reserve) parcial

fragmentation n fragmentación f

fragmented adj (market, bargaining) fragmentado

frame n (Comp) encuadre m; ∼ **of mind** n estado de ánimo m; ∼ **of reference** n parámetros m pl, marco de referencia m

framework n marco m; **create a** ∼ **for negotiations** establecer un marco para las negociaciones; **within the** ∼ **of sth** dentro del marco de algo; ∼ **agreement** n acuerdo marco m

franchise n (right to sell) franquicia f; (right to vote) sufragio m, derecho al voto m; (retail outlet) franquicia f, tienda de una cadena f; ∼ **agreement** n acuerdo de franquicia m; ∼ **tax** n AmE impuesto de franquicia m

franchised dealer n BrE agente autorizado(-a) m,f, distribuidor(a) oficial m,f

franchisee n franquiciado(-a) m,f

franchising n franquicia f

franchisor n franquiciador(a) m,f

franco *adj* franco

frank¹ *adj* (discussions, approach) franco; (opinion, reply) sincero, franco

frank² *vt* (letter, parcel) franquear

franking machine *n* BrE (*cf* ▸**postage meter** AmE) máquina franqueadora *f*

fraud *n* fraude *m*

fraudulence *n* fraudulencia *f*

fraudulent *adj* (statement, entry) fraudulento

fraudulently *adv* fraudulentamente

FRB *abbr* AmE (▸**Federal Reserve Board**) *Comisión de la Reserva Federal*

free¹ *adj* (exempt) exento; (at no cost) gratuito; (unoccupied) libre; ~ **of all taxation** exento de todo impuesto; ~ **of charge** libre de gastos; ~ **and clear** AmE (title to property) no gravado; ~ **of damage** libre de daños; ~ **discharge** sin gastos de descarga; ~ **dispatch** franco de consignación; ~ **of income tax** exento de impuestos sobre la renta; ~ **insurance and carriage** franco de seguro y porte; **give ~ rein to sth/sb** dar rienda suelta a algo/alguien; ~ **admission** *n* entrada *f* gratuita *or* libre; ~ **banking** *n* banca libre *f*; ~ **circulation of goods and services** *n* libre circulación de bienes y servicios *f*; ~ **competition** *n* libre competencia *f*; ~ **delivery** *n* entrega gratuita a domicilio *f*; ~ **economy** *n* libre economía *f*; ~ **enterprise** *n* libre empresa *f*; ~ **enterprise economy** *n* economía *f* competitiva *or* de mercado *or* sin intervención; ~**-format** *adj* (Comp) de formato libre; ~ **gift** *n* regalo gratuito *m*; ~ **market** *n* mercado libre *m*; ~**-market price** *n* precio de libre mercado *m*; ~**-market system** *n* sistema de libre mercado *m*; ~ **movement of capital** *n* libre circulación de capitales *f*; ~ **movement of goods** *n* (in EU) libre circulación de mercancías *f*; ~ **movement of labor** AmE, ~ **movement of labour** BrE *n* libre circulación de mano de obra *f*; ~ **newspaper** *n* periódico gratuito *m*; ~ **and open market** *n* mercado libre y abierto *m*; ~ **port** *n* puerto franco *m*; ~ **sample** *n* muestra gratuita *f*; ~ **trade** *n* libre cambio *m*, libre comercio *m*; **F~ Trade Agreement** *n* Acuerdo de Libre Comercio *m*; ~**-trade area** *n* área de libre comercio *f*; ~**-trade zone** *n* zona *f* franca *or* de libre comercio

free² *vi* liberar; **free up** *vt* (resources) liberar; (time) dejar libre

freebie *n* regalo *m* (con fines comerciales)

freeboard *n* francobordo *m*

freedom *n* libertad *f*; ~ **of action** *n* libertad de acción *f*; ~ **of association** *n* libertad de asociación *f*; ~ **of choice** *n* libertad de elección *f*; ~ **of competition** *n* libertad de competencia *f*; ~ **of establishment** *n* libertad de establecimiento *f*; **F~ of Information Act** *n* AmE *ley de libertad de información*; ~ **of movement** *n* libre circulación *f*

freed-up *adj* (securities) liberado

Freefone® *n* BrE teléfono gratuito *m*; ~ **number** *n* BrE número exento de pago *m*

freehold *n* plena propiedad *f*; ~ **owner** *n* propietario(-a) absoluto(-a) *m,f*; ~ **property** *n* propiedad absoluta *f*

freeholder *n* propietario(-a) absoluto(-a) *m,f*

freelance *n* trabajador(a) *m,f* freelance *or* por cuenta propia; ~ **correspondent** *n* corresponsal independiente *mf*; ~ **worker** *n* trabajador(a) *m,f* freelance *or* por cuenta propia; ~ **writer** *n* escritor(a) *m,f* independiente *or* freelance

freelancer *n* trabajador(a) *m,f* freelance *or* por cuenta propia

freeload *vi* gorrear (infrml), gorronear (infrml) Esp

freeloader *n* gorrón(-ona) *m,f* (infrml) Esp

freely *adv* (without restriction) libremente; (offer) de buen grado; (spend, give, donate) a manos llenas; ~ **negotiable credit** *n* crédito negociable sin condiciones *m*

Freepost® *n* BrE *correo gratuito*

freesheet *n* BrE periódico gratuito *m*

free-standing *adj* autónomo

freeware *n* (Comp) soporte lógico de dominio público *m*

freeway *n* AmE (*cf* ▸**motorway** BrE) autopista *f*

freeze¹ *n* (of wages, prices, credit, account) congelación *f*

freeze² *vt* (wages, prices, credit, account) congelar

freezing *n* (of wages, prices, credit, account) congelación *f*

freight *n* (goods) carga *f*, mercancías *f pl*; (transportation) transporte *m*, porte *m*, flete *m* AmL; ~ **forward** portes debidos; ~ **and insurance paid** porte y seguro pagados; ~ **paid** porte pagado; ~ **aircraft** *n* avión de transporte de mercancías *m*; ~ **charges** *n pl* gastos de transporte *m pl*; ~ **forwarder** *n* agente de transportes *mf*; ~ **plane** *n* AmE (*cf* ▸**cargo plane** BrE) avión *m* carguero *or* de carga; ~ **terminal** *n* terminal de carga *f*; ~ **train** *n* AmE (*cf* ▸**goods train** BrE) tren *m* de carga *or* de mercancías; ~ **transport** *n* transporte de mercancías *m*

freighter *n* (aviation) carguero *m*; (shipping) barco de carga *m*, carguero *m*

French *adj* francés; **take ~ leave** despedirse a la francesa

frequency *n* frecuencia *f*; **∼ modulation** *n* modulación de frecuencias *f*

frequent *adj* frecuente

frequently *adv* con frecuencia, frecuentemente; **∼ asked questions** *n pl* preguntas más frecuentes *f pl*

fresh *adj* (not stale, frozen, or tinned) fresco; (supplies, stocks, initiative, evidence) nuevo; **∼ food** *n* alimentos *m pl* frescos *or* sin procesar; **∼ money** *n* dinero fresco *m*

friction *n* (discord) fricción *f*, desavenencia *f*; **∼ feed** *n* (Comp) alimentación por fricción *f*

frictional *n* (unemployment) coyuntural, friccional

frictionless *adj* (commerce, economy) sin fricción

Friday *n* viernes *m*; **∼s and holidays excepted** salvo viernes y días festivos; **∼s and holidays included** viernes y días festivos incluidos

friendly *adj* (person) simpático; (place, atmosphere) agradable; (welcome) cordial; (rivalry, competition) amistoso, amigable; (agreement, takeover) amistoso; **be on ∼ terms with sb** llevarse bien con alguien; **∼ society** *n* BrE (*cf* ▸**benefit society** AmE) mutualidad *f*, sociedad de beneficencia *f*; **∼ suit** *n* (Law) acción amigable *f*

Friends of the Earth *n pl* Amigos de la Tierra *m pl*

fringe *n* franja *f*; **live on the ∼s of society** vivir al margen de la sociedad; **∼ bank** *n* banco periférico *m*; **∼ benefit** *n* beneficio complementario *m*; **∼ market** *n* mercado *m* marginal *or* periférico; **∼ meeting** *n* reunión secundaria *f*

FRN *abbr* BrE (▸**floating-rate note**) obligación de interés variable *f*

front *n* frente *m*; **∼ cover** *n* portada *f*; **∼ desk** *n* mostrador de recepción *m*; **∼ money** *n* capital inicial para lanzar un proyecto empresarial *f*; **∼ office** *n* (administrative centre) alta dirección *f*, alta gerencia *f*; (reception) recepción *f*; (Stock) piso de remates *m*; **∼-page news** *n* noticias de primera plana *f pl*; **∼-runner** *n* cabeza de lista *mf*; **∼-running** *n* inversión anticipada en valores por parte de un corredor o agente para su uso propio

frontage *n* fachada *f*

front-end *adj* (computer) frontal; (money, payment, fee, loan) inicial; **∼ costs** *n pl* costes *m pl* Esp *or* costos *m pl* AmL de puesta en marcha; **∼ finance** *n* financiación de la puesta en marcha *f*; **∼ load** *n* (Stock) cobro inicial *m*; **∼ loading** *n* (Fin) concentración del gasto al principio de un periodo *f*

frontier *n* frontera *f*; **∼ control** *n* control fronterizo *m*

frontline *n* BrE primera línea *f*; **∼ employee** *n* empleado(-a) de primera línea *m,f*

frontman *n* (in broadcasting) presentador(a) *m,f*

frozen *adj* (asset, credit) congelado; (account, capital) bloqueado

frt *abbr* (▸**freight**) (goods) carga *f*, mercancías *f pl*; (transportation) transporte *m*, porte *m*, flete *m* AmL

frt fwd *abbr* (▸**freight forward**) portes debidos *m pl*

fruition *n* realización *f*; **bring sth to ∼** llevar algo a buen término; **come to ∼** llegar a concretarse

fruitless *adj* infructuoso

frustration *n* frustración *f*; **∼ of contract** *n* frustración de contrato *f*

FT-30 *n* (▸**Financial Times Industrial Ordinary Share Index**) índice bursátil de valores industriales del Financial Times

FTA *abbr* (▸**failure to agree**) incapacidad de llegar a un acuerdo *f*; (▸**Free Trade Agreement**) Acuerdo de Libre Comercio *m*

FT Index *n* (▸**Financial Times Index**) índice del FT *m* (índice del Financial Times)

FTP *abbr* (▸**file transfer protocol**) protocolo de transferencia de archivos *m*

FTSE *abbr* (▸**Financial Times Stock-Exchange Index**) índice bursátil del Financial Times *m*; **∼ 100** *n* (▸**Financial Times Stock-Exchange 100 Share Index**) índice Footsie *m*

FTZ *abbr* (▸**free-trade zone**) zona *f* franca *or* de libre comercio

fuel¹ *n* combustible *m*; **∼ efficiency** *n* eficiencia del combustible *f*; **∼ oil** *n* AmE gas oil *m*; BrE fuel-oil *m*; **∼ tax** *n* impuesto sobre el combustible *m*

fuel² *vt* (inflation) alimentar; **∼ an advance** estimular un avance, impulsar una subida; **∼ speculation** multiplicar las especulaciones

fulcrum *n* fulcro *m*

fulfil BrE, **fulfill** AmE *vt* (promise, contract, order) cumplir; (duty) cumplir con; (task) llevar a cabo, realizar; (need) satisfacer; (condition, requirement) satisfacer, llenar; (potential) alcanzar; (ambition) hacer realidad

fulfilment BrE, **fulfillment** AmE *n* (of duty, promise) cumplimiento *m*; **bring sth to ∼** llevar algo a cabo

full *adj* (complete) completo, total; (filled) lleno; **have a very ∼ day** tener un día muy ocupado; **in ∼** totalmente; **make ∼ use of sth** hacer uso pleno de algo; **pay the ∼ price** pagar el precio íntegro; **∼ adder** *n* (Comp) sumador completo *m*; **∼ amount** *n* importe total *m*; **∼ board** *n* pensión

completa *f*; **~-cost method** *n* método *m* de
coste Esp *or* costo AmL total, método de full-
cost *m*; **~-cost pricing** *n*, **~ costing** *n*
valoración *f* a coste Esp *or* costo AmL total;
~ cover BrE, **~ coverage** AmE *n* (Ins)
cobertura total *f*; **~ disclosure** *n*
divulgación completa *f*; **~ duplex** *n* (Comp)
dúplex *m* integral *or* completo; **~**
employment *n* pleno empleo *m*; **~**
exemption *n* exención total *f*; **~ fare** *n*
billete completo *m*; **~ member** *n* miembro
de pleno derecho *mf*; **~ name** *n* nombre *m*
y apellidos *m pl*; **~-page advertisement** *n*
anuncio a toda página *m*; **~ quotation** *n*
cotización plena *f*; **~ rate** *n* precio *m*
íntegro *or* sin descuento; **~-scale**
investigation *n* investigación sin
restricciones *f*; **~-screen** *adj* a toda
pantalla; **~ share** *n* acción con valor a la
par *f*

full-time *adj* (worker, official) a tiempo
completo; (job) de tiempo completo, de jornada
completa; **~ attendance** *n* asistencia de
jornada completa *f*; **~ employment** *n*
trabajo de tiempo completo *m*

full-timer *n* trabajador(a) a tiempo
completo *m,f*

fully *adv* totalmente; **~ comprehensive**
cover BrE, **~ comprehensive coverage**
AmE *n* cobertura total *f*; **~ comprehensive**
insurance policy *n* póliza de seguros de
cobertura total *f*; **~ distributed** *adj*
distribuido íntegramente; **~ paid** *adj*
totalmente pagado; (share, policy) cubierto; **~**
paid-up capital *n* capital totalmente
desembolsado *m*; **~ registered bond** *n*
bono debidamente registrado *m*; **~**
registered security *n* título totalmente en
regla *m*

function [1] *n* función *f*; **as a ~ of sth** como
una función de algo; **~ key** *n* (Comp) tecla
de función *f*

function [2] *vi* funcionar; **~ as sth** hacer
(las veces) de algo

functional *adj* (approach, analysis, costing,
management) funcional; **~ layout** *n*
disposición según la función *f*

functionality *n* funcionalidad *f*

functioning *n* funcionamiento *m*

fund [1] *n* fondo *m*; **no ~s** sin fondos; **lack**
the necessary ~s no tener los fondos
necesarios; **~ appropriation** *n* asignación
de fondos *f*; **~ management** *n*
administración *f or* gestión *f* de fondos; **~**
manager *n* gestor(a) de fondos *m,f*; **~s**
transfer *n* transferencia de fondos *f*

fund [2] *vt* (loan) provisionar; (debt) consolidar;

(research, organization) financiar

fundamental *adj* (problem, change, analysis)
fundamental

funded *adj* (debt, property) consolidado; **~**
pension plan *n* BrE, **~ retirement plan** *n*
AmE fondos de pensiones *m pl*

funding *n* (act) financiación *f*,
financiamiento *m*; (resources) fondos *m pl*,
recursos *m pl*; **~ agency** *n* organismo de
financiación *m*; **~ gap** *n* déficit de fondos *m*

fundraising *n* recaudación de fondos *f*

funeral expenses *n pl* gastos de
inhumación *m pl*

fungibility *n* fungibilidad *f*

fungible *adj* (asset) fungible

fungibles *n pl* bienes fungibles *m pl*

funnel *vt* (investment, resources) canalizar;
(efforts, energies) encauzar, canalizar

furniture *n* muebles *m pl*, mobiliario *m*; **~**
depot *n* depósito de muebles *m*; **~ and**
fittings *n pl* enseres *m pl*, mobiliario *m* e
instalación *f*; **~ warehouse** *n*
guardamuebles *m*

further *adj* más; **for ~ instructions** para
instrucciones adicionales

further to *prep* en respuesta a; **~ to your**
letter en respuesta a su carta; **~ to your**
telephone call en respuesta a su llamada
telefónica

fuse *vt* (merge) fusionar

fusion *n* (merger) fusión *f*

future [1] *adj* futuro

future [2] *n* futuro *m*; **in ~** en lo sucesivo, en
el futuro

futures *n pl* futuros *m pl*; **long/short in ~**
largo/corto en futuros *m*; **~ contract** *n*
contrato de futuros *m*; **~ market** *n*
mercado de futuros *m*; **~ option contract**
n contrato de opción sobre futuros *m*;
~-registered broker *n* corredor(a)
autorizado(-a) de futuros *m,f*; **~ trading** *n*
compraventa de futuros *f*; **~ transaction** *n*
transacción sobre futuros *f*

futurologist *n* futurólogo-a *m,f*

futurology *n* futurología *f*

fuzzy *adj* (image) borroso; (sound) confuso; **~**
loan *n* préstamo polivalente *m*; **~ logic** *n*
lógica difusa *f*

fwdr *abbr* (▸**forwarder**) expedidor(a) *m,f*

FY *abbr* (▸**financial year**) ejercicio *m*
económico *or* financiero; (▸**fiscal year**) año
m or ejercicio *m* fiscal

FYI *abbr* (▸**for your information**) para su
información

Gg

G2B *abbr* (▸**government-to-business**) gobierno a empresa

G2C *abbr* (▸**government-to-citizen**) gobierno a ciudadano; (▸**government-to-consumer**) gobierno a consumidor

G-7 *abbr* (▸**Group of Seven**) G-7 (Grupo de los Siete)

G-8 *abbr* (▸**Group of Eight**) G-8 (Grupo de los Ocho)

GA *abbr* (▸**general assembly**) asamblea general *f*

G/A *abbr* (▸**general average**) avería *f* común *or* gruesa

GAAP *abbr* (▸**Generally Accepted Accounting Principles**) PCGA (Principios de Contabilidad Generalmente Aceptados)

GAAS *abbr* (▸**Generally Accepted Auditing Standards**) *normativas de auditoría generalmente aceptadas*

GAB *abbr* (▸**general agreement to borrow**) acuerdo *m* general de préstamos *or* sobre créditos *m*

G/A con *abbr* (▸**general average contribution**) contribución a la avería gruesa *f*

G/A dep *abbr* (▸**general average deposit**) depósito de avería gruesa *m*

gadget *n* artilugio *m*

gag *n* mordaza *f*; ~ **order** *n* AmE (*cf* ▸**gagging order** BrE) *orden judicial de control de la información periodística*

gage AmE ▸**gauge** BrE

gagging order *n* BrE (*cf* ▸**gag order** AmE) *orden judicial de control de la información periodística*

gain¹ [1] *vt* (qualifications) obtener; (control) conseguir, obtener; (experience) adquirir; (value) aumentar de; ~ **entry to sth** conseguir acceso a algo; ~ **formal approval from sb** obtener la aprobación formal de alguien; ~ **ground** ganar terreno; ~ **momentum** empezar a avanzar; **the shares ~ed 5 points** las acciones subieron 5 enteros

[2] *vi* (obtain benefit, profit) beneficiarse, sacar provecho; **the shares have ~ed in value** las acciones han subido *or* aumentado de valor

gain² *n* (profit) beneficio *m*, ganancia *f*; (increase) aumento *m*; **substantial ~s in productivity** progresos notables en productividad; **make ~s on sth** obtener beneficios sobre algo; **heavy ~s were**

recorded on the stock exchange se registraron fuertes subidas en la bolsa

gainful *adj* (employment) retribuido, remunerado

galley *n* (in publishing) galera *f*

galloping *adj* (inflation) galopante

Gallup poll *n* sondeo de Gallup *m*

gamble *vi* jugar; ~ **on the stock exchange** jugar en bolsa

gambling *n* juego *m*; ~ **debts** *n pl* deudas de juego *f pl*

game *n* juego *m*; ~ **plan** *n* plan del juego *m*; ~ **theory** *n* teoría de juegos *f*

gamesmanship *n* *arte de jugar astutamente*

gaming *n* juego *m*

gamma *n* gamma *f*; ~ **share** *n* acción gamma *f*; ~ **stock** *n* BrE acciones gamma *f pl*

gang piecework *n* trabajo a destajo por equipos *m*

Gantt chart *n* (Comp) diagrama de Gantt *m*

GAO *abbr* AmE (▸**General Accounting Office**) ≈ Oficina General de Contabilidad *f* AmL, ≈ Tribunal de Cuentas *m* Esp

gap *n* déficit *m*, diferencia *f*; (Stock) diferencial *m*; **fill a ~ in the market** llenar un vacío *or* un hueco en el mercado; ~ **financing** *n* financiación del déficit *f*; ~ **loan** *n* crédito intermedio *m*

garbage *n* (Comp) basura *f*; (waste) AmE (*cf* ▸**rubbish** BrE) basura *m*; ~ **dump** *n* AmE (*cf* ▸**rubbish dump** BrE) vertedero (de basuras) *m*, basurero *m*, basural *m* AmL; ~**-in/garbage-out** *n* (Comp) entrada descontrolada/salida descontrolada *f*

garnish *vt* embargar

garnishee *n* depositario(-a) de bienes embargados *m,f*

garnishment *n* embargo *m*, interdicto *m*

gas *n* gas *m*; ~ **company** *n* compañía del gas *f*; ~ **industry** *n* industria del gas *f*; ~ **oil** *n* gasóleo *m*

GASB *abbr* AmE (▸**Governmental Accounting Standards Board**) ≈ Consejo Oficial de Normas Contables *m*, ≈ Junta Gubernamental de Normas Contables *f*

gasoline *n* AmE (*cf* ▸**petrol** BrE) gasolina *f*; ~ **expenses** *n pl* AmE gastos de combustible *m pl*

gasworks *n* fábrica de gas *f*

gate n (controlling admission) entrada f; (**Comp**) puerta f, portilla f, pasarela f AmL; (at airport) puerta (de embarque) f; (attendance) público m, concurrencia f, entrada f Esp; (takings) recaudación f, taquilla f

gatefold n desplegable m

gateway n puerta f

gather vt (information) reunir; (**Stock**) acumular

gathering n (meeting) reunión f; (people) concurrencia f

GATT abbr (▸**General Agreement on Tariffs and Trade**) Acuerdo GATT m (Acuerdo General sobre Aranceles y Comercio)

gauge[1] BrE, **gage** AmE n (of trends) indicio m

gauge[2] BrE, **gage** AmE vt (size, amount) calcular; (possibilities, effects) evaluar

gavel n (of auctioneer) martillo m

GAW abbr (▸**guaranteed annual wage**) salario anual garantizado m

gazump vt BrE (jarg) anular un compromiso de venta de una casa para vender a un mejor postor

gazumping n BrE (jarg) anulación de un compromiso de venta de una casa para vender a un mejor postor

Gb abbr (▸**gigabyte**) gigaocteto m

GCM abbr (▸**general clearing member**) (**Stock**) miembro compensador general m

GCR abbr (▸**general commodity rate**) tarifa general de productos f

GDP abbr (▸**gross domestic product**) PIB (producto interior bruto); ~ **per capita** n, ~ **per head** n PIB per capita m

gds abbr (▸**goods**) bienes m pl, mercancías f pl

gear vt orientar; **we are ~ing our business increasingly towards** BrE o **toward** AmE **the export market** estamos orientando nuestro negocio cada vez más hacia las exportaciones

gearing n BrE apalancamiento m; ~ **adjustment** n BrE ajuste de apalancamiento m; ~ **lease** n BrE arrendamiento ventajoso m; ~ **ratio** n BrE proporción f or relación f de apalancamiento

GEM abbr (▸**growing-equity mortgage**) hipoteca de amortización rápida f

gender n sexo m; ~ **bias** n prejuicios sexistas m pl; ~ **discrimination** n discriminación sexual f; ~ **gap** n diferencia debida al género f

general adj general; ~ **acceptance** n (of document) aceptación general f; **G~ Accounting Office** n AmE ≈ Oficina General de Contabilidad f AmL, ≈ Tribunal de Cuentas m Esp; ~ **administrative expenses** n pl gastos generales de administración m pl; **G~ Agreement on Tariffs and Trade** n Acuerdo General sobre Aranceles y Comercio m; ~ **agreement to borrow** n acuerdo general sobre créditos m; ~ **assembly** n asamblea general f; ~ **authorization** n autorización general f; ~ **average** n avería f común or gruesa; ~ **average contribution** n contribución a la avería gruesa f; ~ **average deposit** n depósito de avería gruesa m; ~ **averaging** n (of income) promedio general m; ~ **clearing member** n miembro compensador general m; **G~ Commissioners** n pl BrE (**Tax**) interventores generales m pl; ~ **commodity rate** n tarifa general de productos f; ~ **contractor** n contratista principal mf; ~ **counsel** n AmE (cf ▸**head of legal department** BrE) director(a) jurídico(-a) m,f; ~ **creditor** n acreedor(a) ordinario(-a) m,f; ~ **expenses** n pl gastos generales m pl; ~ **fund** n fondo de libre disposición m; ~ **government expenditure** n gasto general del Estado m; ~ **holiday** n asueto m or festivo m general; ~ **ledger** n libro m mayor general o mayor principal; ~ **liability insurance** n seguro de responsabilidad civil m; ~ **management** n gestión f or dirección f general; ~ **manager** n director(a) general m,f; ~ **meeting of members** n asamblea de socios f; ~ **meeting of shareholders** n junta general de accionistas f; ~ **mortgage** n hipoteca general f; ~ **mortgage bond** n bono hipotecario m, obligación con garantía hipotecaria f; ~ **obligation bond** n AmE bono de responsabilidad general m; ~ **partner** n socio(-a) colectivo(-a) m,f; ~ **price level** n nivel general de precios m; ~ **property tax** n impuesto sobre el patrimonio m; ~ **provision** n (for debts) provisión general f; ~ **reserve** n reserva visible f; ~ **service partner** n (in accountancy firm) socio(-a) de servicios generales m,f; ~ **statement** n (of accounts) estado general m; ~ **strike** n huelga general f

generalist n generalista mf

generalized adj generalizado

generally adv generalmente; **G~ Accepted Accounting Principles** n pl Principios de Contabilidad Generalmente Aceptados m pl; **G~ Accepted Auditing Standards** n pl normativas de auditoría generalmente aceptadas

general-purpose adj universal, de aplicación general

generate vt (ideas, income, profits, jobs) generar

generation n generación f; ~ **gap** n desfase entre generaciones m

generator *n* generador *m*

generic *adj* (brand, product, appeal) genérico; ~ **job title** *n* título genérico del puesto de trabajo *m*; ~ **search** *n* (on Internet) búsqueda genérica *f*

generous *adj* (Tax) generoso

genetically-modified *adj* (food) transgénico

gentleman's agreement *n* pacto de caballeros *m*

genuine *adj* (interest) sincero, genuino, verdadero; (inquiry, application) serio; (signature) auténtico; ~ **article** *n* producto auténtico *m*

geographic *adj* geográfico

geographical *adj* geográfico

geopolitical *adj* geopolítico

gestation *n* gestación *f*; ~ **period** *n* periodo de gestación *m*

get *vt* (after effort) conseguir; (obtain) obtener; **get across** *vt* hacer entender; ~ **sth across to sb** hacer entender algo a alguien; **get around** *vt* (difficulty) sortear, evitar; (rule, law) eludir el cumplimiento de; **get back** *vt* (property) recuperar; **we never got our money back** nunca nos devolvieron el dinero; **get behind** 1 *vi* atrasarse; ~ **behind with sth** atrasarse con algo 2 *vt* (campaign, project) apoyar, respaldar; **get by** *vi* arreglárselas; ~ **by on sth** arreglárselas con algo; **get down to** *vt* (business) llegar a; ~ **down to specifics** ir al grano; ~ **down to work** ponerse a trabajar; **get onto** *vt* ponerse en contacto con; **get over** *vt* hacer entender; ~ **sth over to sb** hacer entender algo a alguien; **get through** *vi* (on phone) conseguir comunicarse; ~ **through to sb** conseguir comunicarse con alguien

GGE *abbr* (▶**general government expenditure**) GGE (gasto general del Estado)

ghost *n* AmE (infrml) beneficiario(-a) gratuito(-a) *m,f*, parásito *mf* (infrml); ~ **site** *n* (on Internet) sitio fantasma *m*

ghostwriter *n* (jarg) negro(-a) *m,f* (jarg)

GIF *abbr* (▶**graphics interchange format**) GIF *m* (formato de interfaz de gráficos)

gift *n* donación *f*; ~ **by will** *n* transmisión testamentaria *f*; ~ **certificate** *n* AmE bono de regalo *m*; ~ **deed** *n* escritura de donación *f*; ~ **promotion** *n* promoción con regalo *f*; ~ **of property** *n* donación de propiedades *f*; ~ **tax** *n* impuesto sobre donaciones *m*; ~ **token** *n* vale para comprar un regalo *m*; ~ **voucher** *n* bono de regalo *m*

gigabyte *n* gigaocteto *m*

gigantomania *n* gigantomanía *f*

gigantomaniac *adj* gigantomaníaco

GIGO *abbr* (▶**garbage-in/garbage-out**) (Comp) GIGO (entrada descontrolada/salida descontrolada)

gilt *n* BrE papel del Estado *m*

gilt-edged *adj* de primerísima clase; ~ **bill of exchange** *n* letra de cambio de primera clase *f*; ~ **security** *n* valor de primer orden *m*; ~ **stock** *n* acciones de alto rendimiento *f pl*; ~ **stocks** *n pl* BrE (*cf* ▶**government securities** AmE) valores del Estado *m pl*

gimmick *n* truco *m*

Ginnie Mae *abbr* AmE (infrml) (▶**Government National Mortgage Association**) *asociación gubernamental hipotecaria*

giro *n* giro postal *m*

Girobank *n* BrE *banco especializado en giros bancarios*

give *vt* dar; **give away** *vt* regalar; **give back** *vt* (object, property) devolver; **give in** 1 *vi* ceder 2 *vt* (notice) presentar; **give in to** *vt* condescender con; **give up** 1 *vt* (job, project) dejar, renunciar a; (principle, belief) abandonar 2 *vi* rendirse; (Stock) repartirse

giveaway *n* regalo *m*

giver *n* (Stock) dador(a) *m,f*; ~ **for a call** *n* dador(a) de una opción de compra *m,f*; ~ **for a put** *n* dador(a) de una opción de venta *m,f*; ~ **for a put and call** *n* dador(a) de una opción de venta y de compra *m,f*; ~ **on stock** *n* dador(a) de capital social *m,f*

glamour: ~ **issue** *n* BrE (Stock) emisión *f* atractiva *or* de moda; ~ **stock** *n* BrE acción de moda *f*, valor de gran aceptación *m*

glare-free *adj* (screen) sin brillo

glass ceiling *n* techo de cristal *m*, tope *m*

gliding rate *n* tipo volátil *m*

glitch *n* interferencia *f*, problema técnico *m*

global *adj* (communications, marketing, strategy) global; (economy, harmonization) mundial; ~ **memory** *n* (Comp) memoria global *f*; ~ **search** *n* (of document, data) búsqueda automática *f*; ~ **system for mobiles** *n* BrE sistema global de comunicaciones móviles *f*; ~ **variable** *n* (Comp) variable común *f*; ~ **village** *n* aldea mundial *f*; ~ **warming** *n* calentamiento global *m*

globalization *n* globalización *f*

globalize *vt* globalizar

gloom *n* pesimismo *m*

glossary *n* glosario *m*

glossy[1] *adj* (infrml) (magazine) de lujo; (paper) satinado

glossy[2] *n* (infrml) revista de lujo *f*

glut *n* exceso *m*, superabundancia *f*

GM *abbr* (▸**general manager**) DG
(director general); (▸**genetically-modified**)
transgénico; (▸**gross margin**) margen bruto
m

GMT *abbr* (▸**Greenwich Mean Time**)
hora media de Greenwich *f*

GNI *abbr* (▸**gross national income**) INB
(ingreso nacional bruto)

GNMA *abbr* AmE (▸**Government National
Mortgage Association**) *asociación
gubernamental hipotecaria*

GNP *abbr* (▸**gross national product**)
PNB (producto nacional bruto)

go [1] *vi* ir; **go against** *vt* (instructions, policy,
person) oponerse a, ir en contra de; ~
against the current *o* **the tide** ir a
contracorriente; **go ahead** *vi* seguir
adelante; ~ **ahead with sth** seguir adelante
con algo; **go along with** *vt* estar de acuerdo
con; **go back on** *vt* (promise, word) faltar a;
go before *vt* (court, committee) presentarse
ante; **go down** *vi* (exchange rate) bajar;
(unemployment) disminuir; ~ **down in price**
bajar de precio; ~ **down in value** reducirse
el valor; **go over** *vt* (text, figures, work)
revisar, examinar; **go under** *vi* (company)
naufragar; **go up** *vi* (price, cost) subir,
aumentar; (unemployment) aumentar; ~ **up in
price** subir *or* aumentar de precio; ~ **up in
value** (re)valorizarse

go [2] *n* (attempt) intento *m*; **give sth a** ~ BrE
(infrml) intentar algo; **make a** ~ **of sth** (infrml)
sacar algo adelante

goal *n* (aim) meta *f*; (intention) propósito *m*; ~
congruence *n* congruencia de objetivos *f*;
~ **programming** *n* programación *f* de
metas *or* de objetivos; ~ **setting** *n*
establecimiento *m or* fijación *f* de objetivos

G-O bond *n* AmE (▸**general obligation
bond**) bono de responsabilidad general *m*

go-go fund *n* (jarg) valor de bolsa que
promete rápidos beneficios *m*

GOH *abbr* (▸**goods on hand**) mercancías
en almacén *f pl*

going *adj* (price) existente, actual; ~
concern *n* empresa en marcha *f*; ~ **rate** *n*
tarifa existente *f*; **pay above/below the** ~
rate pagar por encima/debajo de lo normal

gold *n* oro *m*; ~ **bullion** *n* oro en lingotes
m; ~ **bullion standard** *n* patrón lingote
oro *m*; ~ **card** *n* tarjeta oro *f*; ~ **exchange
standard** *n* patrón de cambio del oro *m*; ~
fixing *n* cotización diaria del oro *f*; ~
market *n* mercado del oro *m*; ~ **mine** *n*
mina de oro *f*; ~ **price** *n* precio del oro *m*;
~ **reserve** *n* reserva en oro *f*; ~ **rush** *n*
rebatiña del oro *f*; ~ **standard** *n* patrón oro
m

golden *adj* de oro; ~ **age** *n* edad de oro *f*;
~ **formula** *n* BrE fórmula de oro *f*; ~

handcuffs *n pl* (infrml) prima de
permanencia *f*; ~ **handshake** *n* (infrml)
gratificación *f* (por fin de sevicio); ~ **hello** *n*
(infrml) prima de contratación *f*; ~
parachute *n* (infrml) contrato blindado *m*; ~
rule *n* regla de oro *f*; ~ **share** *n* acción de
primera clase *f*; **G~ Triangle** *n* triángulo
dorado *m*

good [1] *adj* (quality, results, deal, investment)
bueno; **make** ~ (damage) compensar; ~
bargain *n* buen negocio *m*; ~ **credit risk** *n*
riesgo de crédito bueno *m*; ~ **faith** *n* buena
fe *f*; ~ **housekeeping** *n* buena
administración interna *f*; ~ **money** *n*
dinero de disposición inmediata *m*; ~
name *n* prestigio *m*, reputación *f*; ~ **return**
n (on investment) rendimiento alto *m*; ~**till-
canceled order** AmE, ~**till-cancelled
order** BrE *n* orden vigente hasta su
cancelación *f*; ~**till-date order** *n* orden
vigente hasta su fecha *f*; ~ **title** *n* título *m*
válido *or* de propiedad incontestable

good [2] *n* bien *m*; **for the** ~ **of sth/sb** por el
bien de algo/alguien; **we are £500 to the** ~
tenemos 500 libras de más

goods *n pl* bienes *m pl*, mercancías *f pl*;
the ~ **remain undelivered** las mercancías
todavía no se han entregado; ~ **and
chattels** *n pl* bienes muebles *m pl*; ~
depot *n* depósito de mercancías *m*; ~ **for
re-export** *n pl* bienes para la reexportación
m pl; ~ **on approval** *n pl* géneros a
condición; ~ **on hand** *n pl* mercancías en
almacén *f pl*; ~ **and services tax** *n*
impuesto sobre bienes y servicios *m*; ~
train *n* BrE (*cf* ▸**freight train** AmE) tren *m*
de carga *or* de mercancías

goodwill *n* fondo de comercio *m*

go-slow *n* BrE huelga de brazos caídos *f*

govern *vt* (rule, administer) gobernar;
(determine) determinar; (by regulations) regir

governing *adj* (party) de gobierno; (body,
principle) director

government *n* gobierno *m*; ~
accounting *n* cuentas *f pl* públicas *or* del
estado; ~ **agency** *n* dependencia del
gobierno *f*; ~ **annuity** *n* anualidades de
gobierno *f pl*, renta del Estado *f*; ~
assistance *n* ayuda del Estado *f*;
~**-backed** *adj* respaldado por el Gobierno;
~ **bond** *n* AmE bono del Estado *m*; ~
broker *n* síndico(-a) (de la bolsa) *m,f*; ~
contract *n* contrato de la administración
m; ~**-controlled** *adj* (corporation) controlado
por el gobierno, paraestatal; ~
expenditure *n* gasto *m* público *or* del
Estado; ~ **finance** *n* hacienda pública *f*;
~**-financed** *adj* financiado por el Estado;
~ **grant** *n* subvención del gobierno *f*,
donación gubernamental *f*; ~ **intervention** *n* ····>

intervención estatal *f*; ~ **investment** *n*
colocación del estado *f*; ~ **lawyer** *n* ≈
abogado(-a) del Estado *m,f*; ~ **loan** *n*
préstamo oficial *m*; **G**~ **National**
Mortgage Association *n* AmE *asociación*
gubernamental hipotecaria; ~ **obligation** *n*
AmE obligación del Estado *f*; ~**-owned** *adj*
(company) estatal; ~**-regulated** *adj* regulado
por el Estado; ~ **report** *n* informe del
gobierno *m*; ~ **securities** *n pl* AmE (*cf*
▸**gilt-edged stocks** BrE) valores del Estado
m pl; ~**-sponsored** *adj* (enterprise, project)
patrocinado por el Estado; ~ **stock** *n* BrE
títulos del Estado *m pl*; ~**-supported** *adj*
(project) apoyado por el Estado

governmental *adj* gubernamental; ~
accounting *n* contabilidad *f*
gubernamental *or* pública; **G**~
Accounting Standards Board *n* AmE ≈
Consejo Oficial de Normas Contables *m*, ≈
Junta Gubernamental de Normas Contables *f*

government-to-business *adj* gobierno
a empresa

government-to-citizen *adj* gobierno a
ciudadano

government-to-consumer *adj*
gobierno a consumidor

government-to-government *adj* de
gobierno a gobierno

governor *n* gobernador(a) *m,f*; **G**~
General *n* Gobernador(a) *m,f*

govt *abbr* (▸**government**) gobierno *m*

GP *abbr* (▸**general-purpose**) de aplicación
general

grab *vt* (attention) atraer; (chance, opportunity)
aprovechar

grace *n* (respite) gracia *f*; **five days'** ~ cinco
días de gracia; ~ **days** *n pl* días de gracia
m pl; ~ **period** *n* periodo de gracia *m*

grade[1] *n* clase *f*; **make the** ~ tener éxito;
~ **creep** *n* (HRM) escalamiento de
categorías *m*; ~ **drift** *n* (HRM) cambio de
categoría *m*; ~ **standard** *n* base estándar *f*

grade[2] *vt* clasificar; ~ **by size** (produce)
clasificar por tamaño

gradual *adj* gradual

gradualism *n* gradualismo *m*

gradually *adv* gradualmente

graduate[1] *n* (from higher education)
licenciado-a *m,f*; (from high school) AmE
bachiller *mf*; ~ **school of business** *n*
escuela superior de negocios *f*

graduate[2] [1] *vi* (from higher education)
licenciarse; (from high school) AmE terminar el
bachillerato
[2] *vt* (payments, contributions) escalonar

graduated *adj* (payment, tax, wage)
escalonado; **in** ~ **stages** en pasos
escalonados; ~ **income tax** *n* impuesto

sobre la renta escalonado *m*; ~ **interest** *n*
interés escalonado *m*; ~ **lease** *n* alquiler
progresivo *m*; ~ **payment mortgage** *n*
hipoteca de pagos proporcionales *f*; ~
pension scheme *n* plan de pensión
graduado *m*

graft[1] *n* (infrml) (bribery, corruption) chanchullos
m pl (infrml), corrupción *f*; (hard work) BrE
trabajo duro *m*

graft[2] *vi* (infrml) (use bribery) practicar
cohecho; (work hard) BrE currar (infrml)

grand[1] *adj* (overall) global; ~ **jury** *n* AmE
jurado de acusación *m*; ~ **larceny** *n* AmE
hurto mayor *m*; ~ **total** *n* total general *m*

grand[2] (infrml) BrE *n* mil libras *f pl*; AmE *n*
mil dólares *m pl*

grandfather clause *n* (infrml) cláusula de
exención *f*

grandfathering *n* (Tax) priorización *f*

granny bond *n* BrE (infrml) bono a largo
plazo *m*

grant[1] *n* subsidio *m*, subvención *f*; (Prop)
cesión *f*; **in** ~ **form** a modo de subvención;
~**-in-aid** *n* subsidio *m*

grant[2] *vt* (concession, licence, tenancy, right,
extension) conceder; (loan) otorgar; **take sb for**
~**ed** no darse cuenta de lo que vale alguien;
take sth for ~**ed** dar algo por descontado

grantee *n* beneficiario(-a) *m,f*; (Prop, Stock,
Tax) cesionario(-a) *m,f*

grantor *n* (Acc, Stock) cesionista *mf*; (Law,
Prop) otorgante *mf*

grapevine *n* medio de comunicación
oficiosa *m*; **I heard it through** *o* **on the** ~
me lo dijo un pajarito (infrml)

graph *n* grafo *m*; ~ **plotter** *n* trazador de
gráficos *m*

graphic *adj* gráfico; ~ **character** *n*
carácter gráfico *m*; ~ **data processing** *n*
proceso de datos gráficos *m*; ~ **database** *n*
base de datos gráfica *f*; ~ **design** *n* diseño
gráfico *m*; ~ **designer** *n* diseñador(a)
gráfico(-a) *m,f*; ~ **display terminal** *n*
terminal de representación gráfica *m*

graphical *adj* gráfico; ~ **editing** *n*
edición gráfica *f*; ~ **user interface** *n*
interfaz usuario gráfico *m*

graphically *adv* gráficamente

graphics *n pl* gráficos *m pl*; ~ **based**
browser *n* navegador gráfico *m*; ~ **board**
n tarjeta de gráficos *f*; ~ **file** *n* archivo
gráfico *m*; ~ **format** *n* formato gráfico *m*;
~ **interchange format** *n* formato de
interfaz de gráficos *m*; ~ **mode** *n* modo
gráfico *m*; ~ **printer** *n* impresora de
gráficos *f*

grass-roots *adj* (support, opinion, level) de las
bases; (movement) de base popular

gratis *adv* gratis

gratuitous *adj* (loan) gratuito

gratuity *n* gratificación *f*

graveyard: ~ **market** *n* mercado muerto *m*; ~ **shift** *n* (infrml) turno de media noche *m*

gray AmE ▸**grey** BrE

graze *vi* (jarg) *comer alimentos robados en una tienda mientras se está comprando*

grease *vt* (machinery) engrasar; ~ **sb's palm** untar a alguien

Great Depression *n* Gran Depresión *f*

Great Leap Forward *n* gran salto hacia adelante *m*

green *adj* verde; ~**-conscious** *adj* (consumers) con conciencia ecológica; ~ **accounting** *n* contabilidad *f* medioambiental *or* verde; ~ **ban** *n* negativa sindical a trabajar en proyectos que dañen el medio ambiente; ~ **belt** *n* zona verde *f*; ~ **card** *n* AmE (*cf* ▸**residence visa** BrE) visado de residencia *m*; ~ **currency** *n* moneda agropecuaria *f*; ~ **energy** *n* energía ecológica *f*; ~ **labeling scheme** AmE, ~ **labelling scheme** BrE *n* plan de etiquetado ecológico *m*; ~ **light** *n* (authorization) luz verde *f*; ~ **lobby** *n* grupo de presión verde *m*; **G**~ **Paper** *n* BrE Libro Verde *m*; **G**~ **Party** *n* Partido Verde *m*; ~ **revolution** *n* revolución *f* verde *or* ecológica

greenback *n* AmE billete de un dólar

greenfield *adj* de zona verde; ~ **site** *n* área no desarrollada *f*; ~ **site company** *n* empresa situada en un área no desarrollada *f*

greenhouse effect *n* efecto de invernadero *m*

greening *n* (jarg) enverdecimiento *m*

greenmail *n* AmE *táctica de comprar un gran lote de acciones de una empresa y amenazarla con una OPA para lograr revenderle dichas acciones con una fuerte prima*

greenmailer *n* inversor(a) hostil *m,f*, chantajista *mf*

Greens *n pl* (Pol) verdes *m pl*

Greenwich Mean Time *n* hora media de Greenwich *f*

greetings *n pl* saludos *m pl*

grey BrE, **gray** AmE *adj* gris; ~ **belt** *n* (infrml) área de población mayoritariamente jubilada *f*; ~ **market** *n* mercado gris *m*; ~ **Monday** *n* lunes gris *m*; ~ **society** *n* sociedad envejecida *f*

grid *n* cuadrícula *f*, matriz *f*; (Comp) parrilla *f*; ~ **structure** *n* estructura de matriz *f*; (Fin) estructura en rejilla *f*

grievance *n* agravio *m*; **air one's** ~**s** quejarse; **have a** ~ **against sb** tener queja de alguien; ~ **arbitration** *n* arbitraje de agravios *m*; ~ **procedure** *n* procedimiento de agravio *m*

gross[1] *adj* (income, amount, dividend) bruto; ~ **domestic product** *n* producto interior bruto *m*; ~ **earnings** *n pl* (of person) ingresos brutos *m pl*; (of company) beneficios brutos *m pl*, ganancias *f pl or* utilidades *f pl* AmL brutas; ~ **margin** *n* margen bruto *m*; ~ **misconduct** *n* falta grave *f*; ~ **national debt** *n* deuda pública bruta *f*; ~ **national expenditure** *n* gasto nacional bruto *m*; ~ **national income** *n* ingreso nacional bruto *m*; ~ **national product** *n* producto nacional bruto *m*; ~ **negligence** *n* culpa grave *f*; ~ **pay** *n* remuneración bruta *f*; ~ **profit** *n* beneficio bruto *m*, ganancia bruta *f*; ~ **revenue** *n* ingreso bruto *m*; ~ **sales** *n pl* ventas brutas *f pl*; ~ **savings** *n pl* ahorro bruto *m*; ~ **wage** *n* salario bruto *m*

gross[2] *vt* tener una entrada bruta de; **gross up** *vt* sumar en bruto

grossed-up dividend *n* (Fin) dividendo con adición del impuesto *m*; (Stock) dividendo pagado en bloque *m*

gross-up *n* suma *f*

ground *n* tierra *f*; **break new** *o* **fresh** ~ abrir nuevos horizontes; **gain/lose** ~ ganar/perder terreno; **get off the** ~ (plan, project) llegar a concretarse; **give** ~ ceder terreno; **on the** ~ BrE sobre el terreno; **be on dangerous** ~ pisar terreno peligroso; **stand one's** ~ mantenerse firme; ~ **control** *n* control de tierra *m*; ~ **crew** *n* personal de tierra *m*; ~ **lease** *n* arriendo *para tierras*; ~**-level** *adj* a planta baja; ~ **plan** *n* plano fundamental *m*; ~ **rent** *n* alquiler de la tierra *m*; ~ **rule** *n* norma básica *f*; ~ **zero** *n* base cero *f*

grounding cord *n* (Comp) cable de conexión a tierra *m*

groundless *adj* infundado

grounds *n pl* (for opposition, revocation) motivo *m*; **on** ~ **of expediency** en razón de la conveniencia; **on** ~ **of ill health** (retire, leave) por motivos de mala salud; ~ **for dismissal** *n pl* motivo de despido *m*

groundwork *n* trabajo *m* preliminar *or* de base

group *n* grupo *m*; ~ **accounts** *n pl* cuentas del grupo *f pl*; ~ **bonus** *n* prima por grupos *f*; ~ **chief accountant** *n* jefe(-a) contable de grupo *m,f*; ~ **contract** *n* contrato de grupo *m*; ~ **discussion** *n* discusión de grupo *f*; ~ **dynamics** *n pl* dinámica de grupo *f*; **G**~ **of Eight** *n* Grupo de los Ocho *m*; ~ **interview** *n* entrevista grupal *f*; ~ **leader** *n* jefe(-a) de grupo *m,f*, líder del grupo *mf*; **G**~ **of Seven** *n* Grupo de los Siete *m*; ~ **structure** *n* estructura de grupo *f*; ~ **training** *n* formación *f or* ⋯⋗

capacitación *f* grupal; ∼ **travel** *n* viaje en grupo *m*; ∼ **working** *n* trabajo de grupo *m*

groupage *n* grupaje *m*

grouping *n* agrupación *f*

groupware *n* (Comp) soporte lógico de grupo *m*

grow ① *vi* (company, money) crecer; (quantity, output, demand) aumentar; **the economy is ∼ing again** la economía vuelve a experimentar un periodo de crecimiento *or* de expansión
② *vt* (company) desarrollar

growing *adj* (demand, deficit) creciente; ∼**-equity mortgage** *n* hipoteca de amortización rápida *f*

growth *n* crecimiento *m*; ∼ **accounting** *n* contabilidad del crecimiento *f*; ∼ **area** *n* (of industrial activity) sector en expansión *m*; ∼ **curve** *n* curva de crecimiento *f*; ∼ **fund** *n* fondo de crecimiento *m*; ∼ **in value** *n* aumento de valor *m*; ∼ **index** *n* índice de crecimiento *m*; ∼ **industry** *n* industria en crecimiento *f*; ∼ **path** *n* senda de crecimiento *f*; ∼ **potential** *n* potencial de crecimiento *m*; ∼ **rate** *n* índice de crecimiento *m*; ∼ **stock** *n* acciones de compañía de gran futuro *f pl*; ∼ **strategy** *n* estrategia de crecimiento *f*

GSM *abbr* (▸**global system for mobiles**) BrE sistema global de comunicaciones móviles *f*

G-spool *n* (S&M) carrete G *m*

GST *abbr* (▸**goods and services tax**) impuesto sobre bienes y servicios *m*

GTC order *n* (▸**good-till-canceled order** AmE, ▸**good-till-cancelled order** BrE) orden GTC *f* (orden vigente hasta su cancelación)

GTD order *n* (▸**good-till-date order**) orden GTD *f* (orden vigente hasta su fecha)

guar. *abbr* (▸**guaranteed**) garantizado

guarantee[1] *n* garantía *f*; **carry a six-month ∼** tener una garantía de seis meses; **under ∼** bajo garantía; ∼ **agreement** *n* (Bank) acuerdo de garantía *m*; (Stock) contrato de garantía *m*; ∼ **bond** *n* fianza comercial *f*; (Stock) fianza de garantía *f*; ∼ **capital** *n* capital de garantía *m*; ∼ **deed** *n* escritura de garantía *f*; ∼ **fund** *n* fondo de

garantía *m*; ∼ **letter** *n* carta de garantía *f*; ∼ **of signature** *n* aval de la firma *m*

guarantee[2] *vt* (loan, debt) garantizar; (document) avalar; (stand surety for) afianzar

guaranteed *adj* (income, investment, delivery, price) garantizado; ∼ **annual wage** *n* salario anual garantizado *m*; ∼ **bill** *n* letra avalada *f*; ∼ **issue** *n* (Stock) emisión garantizada *f*; ∼ **letter of credit** *n* carta de crédito garantizada *f*; ∼ **liability** *n* pasivo de garantía *m*; ∼ **loan** *n* préstamo garantizado *m*; ∼ **minimum wage** *n* salario mínimo garantizado *m*

guarantor *n* avalista *mf*, garante *mf*

guard[1] *vt* (building) vigilar, custodiar; **guard against** *vt* (risk) protegerse contra

guard[2] *n* (person) guardia *mf*; (surveillance) guardia *f*; **be on ∼** estar de guardia; **be under ∼** estar bajo vigilancia; ∼ **books** *n pl* (S&M) libros de resguardo *m pl*; ∼ **duty** *n* turno de guardia *m*

guardian *n* tutor(a) *m,f*

guesstimate[1] *n* (infrml) tanteo *m*

guesstimate[2] *vt* (infrml) estimar por aproximación

guestworker *n* trabajador(a) invitado(a) *m,f*

GUI *abbr* (▸**graphical user interface**) GUI *m* (interfaz usuario gráfico)

guide *n* (manual) guía *f*; ∼ **price** *n* precio guía *m*

guideline *n* pauta *f*, directriz *f*; **lay down** *o* **issue ∼s** establecer pautas *or* directrices

guiding principle *n* principio director *m*

guild *n* gremio *m*

guilty *adj* culpable; ∼ **person** *n*, ∼ **party** *n* culpable *mf*

gun *vt* (jarg) *provocar la cesión forzada de cierta cantidad de acciones por un rival*

guru *n* gurú *mf*

gut feeling *n* (infrml) instinto *m*

gutter *n* (between pages) medianil *m*; ∼ **politics** *n* política sensacionalista *f*; ∼ **press** *n* prensa *f* amarilla *or* sensacionalista

guttersnipe *n* (jarg) *pequeño póster puesto en la calle*

Hh

habeas corpus *n* habeas corpus *m*

hack 1 *vt* (Comp) piratear

2 *vi* (Comp) entrar en un sistema sin autorización; **hack into** *vt* (Comp) piratear

hacker *n* pirata informático(-a) *m,f*; **~-proof** *adj* (system) a prueba de piratas

hacking *n* (infrml) pirateo informático *m*

haggle *vi* regatear; **~ about** *o* **over sth** regatear por algo

Hague Tribunal *n* Tribunal de la Haya *m*

half *adj* medio; **on ~-time** a media jornada; **~ adder** *n* (Comp) semisumadora *f*; **~ board** *n* media pensión *f*; **~-duplex** *adj* semiduplex; **~ fare** *n* media tarifa *f*; **~-life** *n* vida media *f*; **~ measures** *n pl* medias tintas *f pl*; **~-monthly** *adj* quincenal; **~-monthly** *adv* quincenalmente; **~ pay** *n* medio sueldo *m*; **~-price** *adj, adv* a mitad de precio; **~ year** *n* semestre *m*; **~-yearly** *adj* (dividend) semestral; **~-yearly** *adv* semestralmente

halftone *n* fotograbado a media tinta *m*

halfway[1] *adj* medio; **reach the ~ point** *o* **stage** *o* **mark** llegar a la etapa intermedia

halfway[2] *adv* a medio camino, a mitad; **meet sb ~** llegar a una solución intermedia *or* a un compromiso con alguien

hallmark *n* BrE (*cf* ▸**assay mark** AmE) marca de aleación *f*

hall test *n* prueba en sala *f*

halo *n* (jarg) (S&M) halo *m*

halve *vt* dividir en dos partes

hammer *vt* (policy) triturar, criticar; **~ home an argument** subrayar un argumento; **~ the market** machacar el mercado; **hammer out** *vt* (compromise, deal) negociar (con mucho toma y daca)

hammered *adj* (jarg) (Stock) insolvente

hammer price *n* (Stock) precio *m* de salida *or* de subasta

hamper *vt* (growth) obstaculizar

hand[1] *n* (body part, assistance) mano *f*; (worker) obrero-a *m,f*; (farmhand) péon *m*; **by ~** (on envelope) en su mano; **delivered by ~** entregado en mano; **give** *o* **lend sb a ~** echarle una mano a alguien; **have** *o* **take a ~ in sth** tomar parte en algo; **in ~** (available) disponible; (under control) bajo control; (being dealt with) entre manos; **in the ~s of sb** en las manos de alguien; **be in the ~s of a receiver** estar en manos de un liquidador *or* de un síndico *or* de un recaudador; **in the**

~s of a third party en manos de terceros; **on ~** disponible; **on the one ~** por un lado; **on the other ~** por otro lado; **put one's ~ in one's pocket** contribuir con dinero; **our ~s are tied** tenemos las manos atadas; **have sth to ~** tener algo a mano; **have the upper ~** tener ventaja

hand[2] *vt* pasar; **~ sb sth** *o* **sth to sb** pasarle algo a alguien; **hand in** *vt* (form) entregar; **~ in one's resignation** presentar su dimisión *or* su renuncia; **hand over** *vt* (money) entregar; (power, responsibility) transferir; **control of the business was handed over to...** la dirección del negocio fue puesta en manos de...

handbill *n* volante *m*

handbook *n* folleto *m*

handheld *adj* (Comp) manipulado; (S&M) en mano; **~ device** *n* computadora *f* AmL *or* ordenador *m* Esp de mano; **H~ Device Mark-up Language** *n* lenguaje *m* de referencia para computadoras AmL *or* ordenadores Esp de mano

handle *vt* (object, situation, affair) manejar; (person) tratar; (business, financial matters) encargarse de, ocuparse de, llevar; (goods, commodities) comerciar con; (stress, tension) poder soportar; **please do not ~ the goods** se ruega no tocar la mercancía; **~ large sums of money** manejar grandes sumas de dinero; **~ with care** manejar con cuidado

handling *n* (of situation) manejo *m*; (of goods) manipulación *f*; **~ allowance** *n* (Stock) descuento de transferencia *m*; **~ charges** *n pl* gastos de tramitación *m pl*

handmade *adj* hecho a mano

handout *n* (leaflet) folleto *m*; (press release) comunicado de prensa *m*; (of money, food) dádiva *m*

handover *n* entrega *f*

handpick *vt* (personnel, materials) seleccionar cuidadosamente

hands-free headset *n* dispositivo para teléfonos de manos libres *m*

handshaking *n* (Comp, Comms) establecimiento de comunicación *m*

hands-off *adj* (approach, policy) de no intervención *or* interferencia; (Comp) (operation, running) automático

hands-on *adj* (experience, session, training) práctico; (Comp) (operation, running) manual

handwritten *adj* manuscrito

Hang Seng Index *n* índice Hang Seng *m*

hang up *vi* (on phone) colgar; (from Internet) desconectar; ~ **on sb** colgarle a alguien

harbour BrE, **harbor** AmE *n* puerto *m*; ~ **authority** *n* autoridad portuaria *f*; ~ **dues** *n pl* derechos de puerto *m pl*

hard *adj* (question, subject) difícil; (task) arduo; (evidence) concluyente; (data, facts, news) concreto; **our prices are** ~ **to beat** nuestros precios son imbatibles; ~ **bargaining** *n* negociación dura *f*; ~ **cash** *n* dinero en efectivo *m*, efectivo *m*; ~ **copy** *n* copia impresa *f*; ~ **core** *n* (of shareholders) núcleo duro *m*; ~ **cost** *n* coste *m* Esp *or* costo *m* AmL gravoso; ~ **currency** *n* moneda fuerte *f*; ~ **discount** *n* descuento en efectivo *m*; ~ **disk** *n* disco duro *m*; ~ **disk drive** *n* unidad de disco duro *f*; ~ **error** *n* (Comp) error de máquina *m*; ~ **goods** *n pl* bienes de consumo duraderos *m pl*; ~ **graft** *n* trabajo duro *m*; ~ **loan** *n* préstamo en firme *m*; ~ **money** *n* dinero *m* en efectivo *or* en metálico; ~ **page-break** *n* (Comp) salto de página forzado *m*; ~ **return** *n* (Comp) retorno manual *m*; ~ **sell** *n* venta agresiva *f*

hard-and-fast *adj* (rules) estricto

hardback *adj* (book) con tapa dura

hard-boiled *adj* (attitude) duro

harden *vi* (increase in value - prices, shares) subir; (stabilize - prices, market) consolidar

hardening *n* (of prices, market) consolidación *f*

hard-headed *adj* práctico, realista

hard-hit *adj* (by loss) muy afectado

hard-hitting *adj* fuerte, muy franco

hardliner *n* partidario(-a) de la línea dura *m,f*

hard-nosed *adj* duro, intransigente

hardware *n* (Comp) hardware *m*, equipo *m*; ~ **compatibility** *n* compatibilidad de equipos *f*; ~ **configuration** *n* configuración del equipo *f*; ~ **failure** *n* fallo del equipo *m*; ~ **firm** *n* firma de componentes electrónicos *f*; ~ **requirement** *n* requerimiento de equipo *m*; ~ **security** *n* seguridad del equipo *f*; ~ **specialist** *n* especialista en equipo físico *mf*

harmonization *n* (of legislation, tariffs, excise duties) armonización *f*

harmonize *vt* (policies, plans) armonizar

harsh *adj* (competition) sin cuartel

haulage *n* transporte *m*; ~ **company** *n* compañía de transportes *f*; ~ **contractor** *n* contratista de transportes *mf*

haulier BrE, **hauler** AmE *n* (person) transportista *mf*; (company) compañía de transportes *f*

hazard *n* riesgo *m*; ~ **bonus** *n* bonificación por riesgo *f*

hazardous *adj* (substance, cargo) peligroso; ~ **chemical** *n* sustancia química peligrosa *f*

hazchem *abbr* (▶**hazardous chemical**) sustancia química peligrosa *f*

h.b. *abbr* (▶**hours of business**) horas de oficina *f pl*

HDML *abbr* (▶**Handheld Device Mark-up Language**) lenguaje *m* de referencia para computadoras AmL *or* ordenadores Esp de mano

head¹ *n* (body part) cabeza *f*; (chief) jefe(-a) *m,f*; (of page) cabecera *f*; (jarg) (headline) titular *m*; **$50 a** *o* **per** ~ 50 dólares por cabeza *or* por persona; **bring sth to a** ~ llevar algo a un punto crítico; **come to a** ~ llegar a un punto crítico; **go over sb's** ~ (in hierarchy) pasar por encima de alguien; **have a good** ~ **for business/figures** tener cabeza para los negocios/los números; ~**s will roll (for sth)** rodarán cabezas (a causa de algo); ~ **accountant** *n* contable *mf* Esp *or* contador(a) *m,f* AmL jefe(-a); ~ **buyer** *n* jefe(-a) de compras *m,f*; ~ **clerk** *n* jefe(-a) de oficina *m,f*; ~ **count** *n* recuento *m* (de personas); ~ **crash** *n* (jarg) (Comp) fractura *f* *or* rotura *f* de cabeza (jarg); ~ **of department** *n* jefe(-a) de departamento *m,f*; ~ **of the household** *n* cabeza de familia *m*; ~ **lease** *n* contrato de arrendamiento principal *m*; ~ **of legal department** *n* BrE (*cf* ▶**general counsel** AmE) director(a) jurídico *m,f*; ~ **office** *n* casa matriz *f*, oficina central *f*; ~ **of personnel** *n* director(a) de personal *m,f*; ~ **of section** *n* jefe(-a) de sección *m,f*; ~ **start** *n* ventaja *f*; **have a** ~ **start (on** *o* **over sb)** llevar(le) ventaja (a alguien); ~ **of state** *n* jefe(-a) de estado *m,f*; ~ **tax** *n* impuesto de capitación *m*

head² *vt* (department) dirigir, estar al frente de; (list, page) encabezar; **head up** *vt* dirigir, estar a la cabeza de

headed notepaper *n* papel con membrete *m*

header *n* (in text) cabecera *f*; (Comp) encabezamiento *m*

headhunt¹ ⊡ *vi* buscar ejecutivos *o* personal especializado ⊡ *vt* ofrecerle un puesto a; **he was** ~**ed by an advertising company** una empresa publicitaria le ofreció un puesto

headhunt² *n* caza de talentos *f*

headhunter *n* cazatalentos *mf*

headhunting *n* caza de talentos *f*

heading *n* (title) encabezamiento *m*, título *m*; (letterhead) membrete *m*

headline *n* (newspaper) titular *m*; ~ **rate** *n* (of inflation) proporción principal *f*

headquarter *vt* AmE establecer la sede de

headquarters *n* (of company) oficina principal *f*

headway *n* avance *m*; **make ~** hacer progresos

health *n* salud *f*; **H~ Authority** *n* BrE autoridad sanitaria *f*; **~ care** *n* atención de la salud *f*; **~ care industry** *n* sector de la atención médica *m*; **~ center** AmE, **~ centre** BrE *n* ambulatorio *m*, centro de salud *m*; **~ hazard** *n* riesgo para la salud *m*; **~ insurance** *n* seguro de enfermedad *m*; **~ officer** *n* inspector(a) de sanidad *m,f*; **~ regulation** *n* reglamento de higiene *m*, regulación sanitaria *f*; **~ risk** *n* riesgo para la salud *m*; **~ and safety** *n* seguridad *f* e higiene *f*; **H~ and Safety at Work Act** *n ley británica de higiene y seguridad en el trabajo*; **H~ and Safety Executive** *n oficina británica para la defensa de la seguridad y salud en el lugar de trabajo*; **H~ and Safety Inspectorate** *n* BrE *cuerpo de inspectores sociales*; **~ sector** *n* sector sanitario *m*

healthy *adj* (competition, market) sano; (economy, finances) próspero; (profit, surplus) sustancial

hear *vt* (case) ver; (charge) oír; **~ a case in chambers** ver una causa a puerta cerrada

hearing *n* (case) vista *f*; (session) sesión *f*

hearsay *n* testimonio de oídas *m*

heavily *adv* (concentrated) altamente; (taxed) excesivamente; **borrow ~ to meet one's obligations** contraer importantes deudas par hacer frente a sus obligaciones; **depend ~ on sth/sb** depender mucho de algo/alguien; **be ~ in debt** tener muchas deudas; **be ~ subsidized** recibir cuantiosas *or* importantes subvenciones; **~ traded** muy negociado

heavy *adj* (expenditure) cuantioso; (schedule) apretado; (demand) fuerte; (market) derrimido; **have a ~ day at work** tener un día de mucho trabajo; **a ~ fall in prices** una caída fuerte de los precios; **trading was ~ on the stock exchange today** hoy hubo mucho movimiento en la bolsa; **have a ~ workload** tener mucho trabajo; **~ advertising** *n* publicidad masiva *f*; **~ duties** *n pl* (Tax) derechos elevados *m pl*; **~ engineering** *n* ingeniería pesada *f*; **~ fuel** *n* combustible pesado *m*; **~ goods vehicle** *n* BrE vehículo para cargas pesadas *m*; **~ industry** *n* industria pesada *f*; **~ share** *n* acción cotizada a menos de un dolar *f*; **~ user** *n* usuario(-a) continuo(-a) *m,f*; **~ viewer** *n persona que ve mucha TV*

hedge¹ *n* cobertura *f*; **~ clause** *n* cláusula de protección *f*; **~ cost** *n* coste *m* Esp *or* costo *m* AmL cubierto; **~ fund** *n* fondo especulativo *m*; **~ management** *n* manipulación de la cobertura *f*; **~**

manager *n* administrador(a) de la cobertura *m,f*

hedge² *vt* proteger; **~ one's bets** cubrirse; **~ the risk** cubrir el riesgo

hedged *adj* (asset, liability) protegido

hedging *n* cobertura *f*; (Bank) hedging *m*; **~ operation** *n* operación de cobertura *f*; **~ strategy** *n* estrategia de cobertura

hefty *adj* (price, debt) fuerte

hegemony *n* hegemonía *f*

heighten *vt* (effect) destacar, realizar, acentuar; (tension, expectation) aumentar, agudizar

heir *n* heredero(-a) *m,f*; **~ to sth** heredero(-a) de algo; **~s and assigns** *n pl* herederos *m pl* y sucesores *m pl*

help *n* ayuda *f*; **~ key** *n* tecla de ayuda *f*; **~ menu** *n* menú de ayuda *m*; **~ mode** *n* modo de ayuda *m*

helpdesk *n* ayuda al usuario *f*

helpline *n* línea directa *f*

helpware *n* equipo de ayuda *m*

hereby *adv* por la presente

herein *adv* aquí dentro

hereof *adv* de aquí

hereto *adv* a esto

hereunder *adv* más abajo

heterogeneous *adj* heterogéneo

heuristic *adj* (problem solving) heurístico

heuristics *n pl* heurística *f*

HGV *abbr* BrE (▸**heavy goods vehicle**) vehículo para cargas pesadas *m*

hiccup *n* (setback) bache *m*

hidden *adj* (asset, reserve, price increase) oculto; (tax, unemployment) encubierto; (inflation) larvado; **~ agenda** *n* agenda oculta *f*; **~ file** *n* (Comp) fichero oculto *m*

hide *vt* ocultar

hierarchical *adj* jerárquico

hierarchy *n* jerarquía *f*; **~ of effects** *n* jerarquía de efectos *f*; **~ of needs** *n* jerarquía de necesidades *f*; **~ of objectives** *n* jerarquía de objetivos *f*

high¹ *adj* (interest rate, cost of living, premium) alto; (price, cost) elevado; **~ achiever** *n* persona de elevado rendimiento *f*; **~-caliber** AmE, **~-calibre** BrE *adj* (staff) de alto potencial, de gran valía; **~-class** *adj* (hotel) de primera clase; **~-cost labor** AmE, **~-cost labour** BrE *n* mano de obra *f* de coste Esp *or* costo AmL elevado; **H~ Court** *n* BrE (*cf* ▸**Supreme Court** AmE) Tribunal Supremo *m*, ≈ Audiencia Nacional *f* Esp; **H~ Court of Justice** *n* Tribunal Superior de Justicia *m*; **~ density** *n* alta densidad *f*; **~-density disk** *n* disco de alta densidad *m*; **~-end computer** *n* computadora *f* AmL *or* ordenador *m* Esp de nivel superior; **~-end** ⋯⋖

computing *n* computación *f or* informática *f* de alto nivel; ∼ **finance** *n* altas finanzas *f pl*; ∼**-flier** *n* (person) persona de buen rendimiento *f*; (Stock) *valor cuyo precio crece muy rápidamente*; ∼**-flying stock** *n* valor de altura *m*; ∼ **gearing** *n* BrE apalancamiento alto *m*; ∼**-grade bond** *n* bono de primera clase *m*; ∼**-income taxpayer** *n* contribuyente de ingresos elevados *mf*; ∼**-involvement products** *n pl* productos cuya compra debe ser muy meditada *m pl*; ∼**-level** *adj* (language, decision, design) de alto nivel; ∼ **leverage** *n* (*cf* ▸**high gearing** BrE) apalancamiento alto *m*; ∼ **office** *n* alto cargo *m*; ∼**-powered** *adj* (executive, campaign) dinámico, enérgico; (job) de alto(s) vuelo(s); ∼**-pressure selling** *n* venta agresiva *f*; ∼**-profile** *adj* prominente, de primera línea; ∼**-quality** *adj* de alta calidad; ∼ **resolution** *n* alta definición *f*; ∼**-return** *adj* de alto rendimiento; ∼**-rise** *adj* (building) alto; ∼**-risk** *adj* (venture) de alto riesgo; ∼**-season fare** *n* tarifa de temporada alta *f*; ∼**-speed** *adj* (Internet, memory, printer, train) de alta velocidad; ∼**-stream industry** *n* industria de alta tecnología *f*; ∼ **street** *n* BrE (*cf* ▸**main street** AmE) calle principal *f*; ∼**-street price** *n* BrE (*cf* ▸**main-street price** AmE) precio de calle principal *m*; ∼**-street spending** *n* BrE (*cf* ▸**main-street spending** AmE) gastos de calle principal *m pl*; ∼**-tech stock** *n* acciones de empresas de alta tecnología *f pl*; ∼ **technology** *n* alta tecnología *f*; ∼**-volume** *adj* de gran volumen; ∼**-yield** *adj*, ∼**-yielding** *adj* de alto rendimiento

high² *n* récord *m*; **reach an all-time** *o* **a record** ∼ alcanzar niveles sin precedentes; **inflation reached a new** ∼ la inflación alcanzó un nuevo récord

higher *adj* superior; ∼ **education** *n* educación superior *f*; ∼ **income bracket** *n* grupo de ingresos más altos *m*; **H∼ National Certificate** *n* BrE *certificado de estudios superiores*; **H∼ National Diploma** *n* BrE *diploma de estudios superiores*

highest *adj* (bid) más elevado; (tender) más alto; ∼ **bidder** *n* mejor postor(a) *m,f*; ∼ **price** *n* mayor precio *m*

highlight¹ *n* rasgo saliente *m*

highlight² *vt* (word, differences) destacar

highlighting *n* realce *m*

highly *adv* (trained, skilled) altamente; (competitive) sumamente, altamente; ∼**-paid** *adj* (job) muy bien pagado *or* remunerado

highs *n pl* (Stock) cotizaciones máximas *f pl*

highway *n* AmE (*cf* ▸**trunk road** BrE) carretera nacional *f*

hike¹ *n* (in price) aumento *m*

hike² *vt* (price) aumentar

hinder *vt* obstaculizar

hindrance *n* estorbo *m*

hindsight *n* percepción retrospectiva *f*; **with (the benefit of)** ∼ en retrospectiva

hinge on *vt* depender de

hint *n* (oblique reference) insinuación *f*, indirecta *f*; (clue) pista *f*; (trace) dejo *m*; (tip) consejo *m*

hire¹ *n* alquiler *m*, arriendo *m*; **for** ∼ en alquiler; **on** ∼ alquilado; ∼ **car** *n* coche de alquiler *m*; ∼ **charge** *n* alquiler *m*, arriendo *m*; ∼ **of money** *n* préstamo de capitales *m*; ∼ **purchase** *n* BrE (*cf* ▸**installment plan** AmE) compra a plazos *f*; **buy sth on** ∼**purchase** comprar algo a plazos; ∼ **purchase agreement** *n* contrato de compra a plazos *m*

hire² *vt* (building, equipment) alquilar; (staff) contratar; ∼ **and fire** contratar y despedir

histogram *n* histograma *m*

historic *adj* histórico

historical *adj* (cost) histórico; (yield) histórico, inicial; (loss) inicial

historically *adv* históricamente

history *n* (Comp) historial *m*

hit¹ *vt* (difficulty, problem) toparse con; (production) afectar a; (reach) llegar a, alcanzar; (Internet site) acceder a; ∼ **the bid** (Stock) mejorar la oferta; ∼ **the bricks** AmE (infrml) (HRM) ir a la huelga; **low-income groups are hardest** ∼ los grupos de bajos ingresos son los más afectados; ∼ **the headlines** salir en titulares; **the euro** ∼ **a new high** la cotización del euro alcanzó un nuevo récord; ∼ **the jackpot** dar en el blanco; ∼ **rock bottom** alcanzar el punto más bajo

hit² *n* (success) éxito *m*; (visit to Internet site) acceso *m*; ∼ **list** *n* (infrml) (of aims) *lista de objetivos a cubrir*; (of successes) lista *f* de éxitos *or* aciertos; ∼**-and-miss** *adj*, ∼**-or-miss** *adj* (infrml) (method) al azar; ∼ **order** *n* (Stock) orden de venta a un precio dado *f*; ∼ **rate** *n* (S&M) índice de éxito *m*; ∼**-and-run strike** *n* huelga relámpago *f*

hive off *vt* (company) privatizar parcialmente

hive-off *n* BrE (infrml) empresa derivada *f*

HLL *abbr* (▸**high-level language**) LAN (lenguaje de alto nivel)

HMC&E *abbr* BrE (▸**Her Majesty's Customs and Excise**) ≈ Servicio de Aduanas *m*

HMG *abbr* BrE (▸**Her Majesty's Government**) *el gobierno británico*

HNC *abbr* BrE (▸**Higher National Certificate**) *certificado de estudios superiores*

HND *abbr* BrE (▸**Higher National Diploma**) *diploma de estudios superiores*

H.O. *abbr* (▸**head office**) casa matriz *f*, oficina principal *f*

hoard *vt* acaparar

hoarded *adj* acaparado

hoarding *n* (of goods) acaparamiento *m*; (board for advertising) BrE (*cf* ▸**billboard** AmE) valla publicitaria *f*

HoD *abbr* (▸**head of department**) jefe(-a) de departamento *m,f*

hog cycle *n* (Econ) ciclo del cerdo *m*

hold¹ *vt* (meeting) celebrar, tener; (enquiry, survey) hacer; (conference, referendum, summit) celebrar; (shares, property) tener; (attention, interest) mantener; (post, position) tener, ocupar; (power) detentar; ~ **sth as a security** mantener algo como garantía; ~ **center** AmE *o* **centre** BrE **stage** dominar la situación; ~ **funds for a check** AmE *o* **cheque** BrE inmovilizar fondos para un cheque; ~ **one's ground** mantenerse firme; ~ **in check** (prices) controlar estrictamente, mantener a raya; ~ **sb liable** *o* **responsible for sth** hacer responsable a alguien de algo; ~ **the line, please** (on phone) no cuelgue, por favor; ~ **margins** respetar *or* mantener los márgenes; ~ **the market** *vender o comprar para mantener estable el precio*; ~ **water** estar bien fundado; **hold down** *vt* (prices, inflation) mantener bajo; (job) mantener; **hold off** *vi* retraerse; **hold out** ⏍ *vt* (prospect, possibility) ofrecer; (job) mantener ⏍ *vi* (supplies) durar; (resist) resistir; ~ **out for sth** retrasar un acuerdo con la esperanza de conseguir algo; **hold over** *vt* (meeting, decision, matter) aplazar, postergar AmE

hold² *n* (control) control *m*; (influence) influencia *f*; **get ~ of sb** localizar *or* ubicar AmL a alguien; **get ~ of sth** conseguir algo; **be on ~** (on telephone) estar en espera; (negotiations) estar en compás de espera; (project) estar aparcado *or* en suspenso; **put sth on ~** dejar algo en suspenso

holdback *n* retención *f*

holder *n* (of lease) arrendatario(-a) *m,f*; (of bond) tenedor(a) *m,f*; ~ **of record** *n* tenedor(a) registrado(-a) *m,f*

holding *n* (syndicate) consorcio *m*; (of stock, in company, bank) participación *f*; (of securities) tenencia *f*; (of bonds) cartera *f*; (of property) posesión *m*, tenencia *f*; ~ **company** *n*, ~ **corporation** *n* compañía tenedora *f*, holding *m*, sociedad de cartera *f*; ~ **gains** *n pl* beneficios de la sociedad tenedora *m pl*; ~ **pattern** *n* (jarg) compás de espera *m* (jarg), estancamiento *m* (jarg); ~ **period** *n* periodo de tenencia *m*

holdings *n pl* (Stock) valores en cartera *m pl*

holdover: ~ **effect** *n* efecto de aplazamiento *m*; ~ **tenant** *n* AmE inquilino(-a) en posesión *m,f*

holiday *n* (period of leave) BrE (*cf* ▸**vacation** AmE) vacaciones *f pl*; (public holiday) fiesta *f*, día festivo *m*; **go on ~** ir de vacaciones; **take a ~** tomarse unas vacaciones; ~ **entitlement** *n* derecho a vacaciones *m*; ~ **leave** *n* permiso de vacaciones *m*; ~ **pay** *n* paga de vacaciones *f*; ~ **period** *n* periodo de vacaciones *m*

holidaymaker *n* BrE (*cf* ▸**vacationer** AmE) veraneante *mf*

home *n* casa *f*; ~ **address** *n* dirección particular *f*; ~ **affairs** *n pl* asuntos internos *m pl*; ~ **banking** *n* (by telephone) banca telefónica *f*; ~ **buying** *n* compra de vivienda *f*; ~ **computer** *n* computadora doméstica *f* AmL, ordenador doméstico *m* Esp; ~ **consumption** *n* autoconsumo *m*; ~ **country** *n* país sede *m*; ~ **delivery** *n* entrega a domicilio *f*; ~**-grown** *adj* de origen nacional; ~ **improvement** *n* mejora de la casa *f*; ~ **improvement loan** *n* préstamo para mejoras en la vivienda *m*; ~ **loan** *n* préstamo para le vivienda; ~ **market** *n* mercado nacional *m*; ~ **page** *n* página *f* frontal *or* principal; ~ **shopping** *n* compras on-line *f pl*; ~ **telephone number** *n* número de teléfono particular *m*

homeowner *n* propietario(-a) *m,f*; ~**s' association** *n* asociación de propietarios *f*; ~**'s policy** *n* seguro sobre riesgos domésticos *m*

home-ownership *n* propiedad de casas *f*; **the increase in ~** el aumento del número de propietarios de viviendas

homework *n* trabajo a domicilio *m*

homeworker *n* trabajador(a) domiciliario(-a) *m,f*

homogeneous *adj* (market, good) homogéneo

homologation *n* homologación *f*

honeycomb slip *n* (Fin) borderó de casillas *m*; (Ins, Stock) borderó de cajetines *m*

honor AmE ▸**honour** BrE

honorarium *n* (frml) honorarios *m pl*, tarifas *f pl*

honorary *adj* (member, president) honorario; **in an ~ capacity** a título honorífico

honour¹ BrE, **honor** AmE *n* honor *m*; ~**s graduate** *n* BrE ≈ licenciado(-a) *m,f*

honour² BrE, **honor** AmE *vt* (agreement, obligation) cumplir (con); (bill, debt) satisfacer, pagar; (cheque, draft) pagar, aceptar; (credit card, signature) aceptar

hood *n* (Comp) cubierta *f*

hook *vt* (Comp) enganchar

hooking *n* (Comp) enganche *m*

hor *abbr* (▸**horizontal**) horizontal

horizon *n* horizonte *m*; **on the ~** en perspectiva; **open up new ~s** abrir nuevos horizontes *or* nuevas perspectivas

horizontal *adj* (merger, analysis, expansion) horizontal

horsepower *n* caballo (de fuerza) *m*

horse-trading *n* (infrml) intercambio de favores *m*

hospital *n* hospital *m*; **~ care insurance plan** *n* plan de seguro de hospitalización *m*; **~ expenses** *n pl* gastos de hospitalización *m pl*

host¹ *n* (Comp) servidor *m*, huésped *m*; **~ city** *n* ciudad anfitriona *f*; **~ computer** *n* servidor *m*; **~ country** *n* país anfitrión *m*; **~-driven** *adj* (Comp) centralizado

host² *vt* (Comp) hospedar, albergar

hostile *adj* hostil; **~ takeover bid** *n* oferta pública de adquisición hostil *f*

hosting *n* alojamiento *m*

hot¹ *adj* (jarg) (industrial relations) conflictivo; (infrml) (stolen) robado, mangado (infrml); **in the ~ seat** en un puesto difícil; **~ bill** *n* (infrml) efecto a la vista *m*, billete nuevo *m*; **~ card list** *n* (Bank) relación de tarjetas invalidadas *f*; **~ key** *n* (Comp) tecla activación *f*, clave directa *f*; **~ money** *n* dinero caliente *m*; **~ property** *n* (infrml) (popular product) producto de gran aceptación *m*; (person) personaje *m* taquillero (jarg) *or* de gran éxito; **~ shop** *n* (jarg) (S&M) agencia *f* creativa *or* de creación; **~ stock** *n* (jarg) (Stock) acción especulativa *f*

hotdesking *n* la práctica de no tener su propia estación de trabajo y sentarse donde sea

hotel *n* hotel *m*; **~ industry** *n* industria hotelera *f*; **~ proprietor** *n* propietario(-a) de hotel *m,f*

hotelier *n* hotelero(-a) *m,f*

hotline *n* (for public) línea directa *f*; (Pol) teléfono rojo *m*

hotlink *n* (Comp) enlace de hipertexto *m*

hotlist *n* (Comp) lista de favoritos *f*; (Bank) lista de invalidaciones *f*

hotspot *n* (Comp) zona *f* sensible *or* interactiva

hour *n* hora *f*; **be paid by the ~** cobrar por horas; **$100 an** *o* **per ~** 100 dólares por hora; **~s of business** *n pl* horas de oficina *f pl*

hourly¹ *adj* (rate, wage) por hora; (worker) por horas

hourly² *adv* (pay, charge) por hora(s)

house *n* casa *f*; (Stock) *sociedad de valores o inversión bancaria,* ≈ cámara *f*; **~ account** *n* (Stock) cuenta de empresa *f*; **~-building loan** *n* préstamo para la construcción de

vivienda *m*; **H~ of Commons** *n* BrE Cámara de los Comunes *f*, ≈ Congreso de los Diputados *m* Esp; **~ journal** *n* boletín de empresa *m*; **H~ of Lords** *n* BrE Cámara de los Lores *f*, ≈ Cámara Alta *f* Esp; **~ magazine** *n* revista de empresa *f*; **H~s of Parliament** *n pl* BrE parlamento británico, ≈ Cortes *f pl* Esp; **~ price** *n* precio de la vivienda *m*; **~ purchase** *n* compra de vivienda *f*; **H~ of Representatives** *n* AmE ≈ Congreso de los Diputados *m* Esp; **~ style** *n* (in publishing) estilo de la casa *m*

household *n* unidad familiar *f*; **~ appliances** *n pl* electrodomésticos *m pl*; **~ behavior** AmE, **~ behaviour** BrE *n* comportamiento de la unidad familiar *m*; **~ commodities** *n pl* bienes domésticos *m pl*; **~ durables** *n pl* productos duraderos para el hogar *m pl*; **~ goods** *n pl* mobiliario *m* y efectos domésticos *m pl*; **~ name** *n* nombre familiar *m*

householder *n* dueño(-a) de casa *m,f*

housing *n* (houses) viviendas *f pl*; (providing of houses) alojamiento *m*; **~ allowance** *n* asignación *f* or subsidio *m* para vivienda; **~ benefit** *n* BrE subsidio para vivienda *m* **~ bond** *n* bono de vivienda *m*; **~ development** *n* urbanización *f*; **~ estate** *n* BrE (cf ▸**housing project** AmE) complejo de viviendas subvencionadas *m*; **~ market** *n* mercado de la vivienda *m*; **~ project** *n* AmE (cf ▸**housing estate** BrE) complejo de viviendas subvencionadas *m*; **~ scheme** *n* complejo de viviendas subvencionadas *m*; **~ shortage** *n* escasez de viviendas *f*; **~ subsidy** *n* subsidio para vivienda *m*

h.p. *abbr* (▸**horsepower**) CV (caballo (de fuerza))

HP *abbr* BrE (▸**hire purchase**) compra a plazos *f*

h.q. *abbr,* **HQ** *abbr* (▸**headquarters**) (of company) oficina principal *f*

HR *abbr* (▸**human resources**) RRHH (recursos humanos)

HRD *abbr* (▸**human resource development**) DRH (desarrollo de recursos humanos)

HRM *abbr* (▸**human resource management**) RRHH (gestión de recursos humanos)

HRP *abbr* (▸**human resource planning**) PRH (planificación de los recursos humanos)

HSE *abbr* (▸**Health and Safety Executive**) *oficina británica para la defensa de la seguridad y salud en el lugar de trabajo*

HSWA *abbr* BrE (▸**Health and Safety at Work Act**) *ley de higiene y seguridad en el trabajo*

HTML *abbr* (▸**Hypertext Mark-up Language**) lenguaje HTML *m*

hub *n* (focal point) centro *m*; (Comp, Comms) concentrador *m*, hub *m*; ∼ **of activity** *n* centro de actividad *m*; ∼ **branch** *n* (Bank) sucursal de mayor actividad *f*

huckster *n* (infrml) (ad writer) AmE publicitario(-a) *m*; (salesperson, promoter) charlatán(-ana) *m,f*, mercachifle *mf*

huge *adj* (debt, order) enorme

human *adj* humano; ∼ **capital** *n* capital humano *m*; ∼ **consumption** *n* (of water) consumo humano *m*; ∼ **engineering** *n* técnica de las relaciones humanas *f*; ∼ **factors** *n pl* factores humanos *m pl*; ∼ **relations** *n pl* relaciones humanas *f pl*; ∼ **resource development** *n* desarrollo de recursos humanos *m*; ∼ **resource management** gestión de recursos humanos *f*; ∼ **resource planning** *n* planificación de los recursos humanos *f*; ∼ **resources** *n pl* recursos humanos *m pl*; ∼ **resources director** *n* director(a) de recursos humanos *m,f*; ∼ **rights** *n pl* derechos humanos *m pl*

hurdle *n* obstáculo *m*; ∼ **rate** *n* (in budgeting capital expenditures) tasa crítica de rentabilidad *f*; ∼ **rate of return** *n* tasa crítica de rendimiento *f*

hustle[1] *n* (busy activity) ajetreo *m*; (swindle) AmE (infrml) chanchullo *m* (infrml); ∼ **and bustle** *n* ajetreo *m*

hustle[2] ① *vt* AmE (infrml) (obtain aggressively) hacerse con ② *vi* AmE (infrml) (work energetically) reventarse (infrml); (swindle) hacer chanchullos (infrml), chanchullear (infrml)

hybrid *adj* (computer, annuity, auction) híbrido; (income tax) mixto

hydraulic *adj* (power) hidráulico

hydro *abbr* (▸**hydroelectric**) (power) hidroeléctrico

hydrocarbon *n* hidrocarburo *m*

hydroelectric *adj* (power) hidroeléctrico; ∼ **power station** *n* central hidroeléctrica *f*

hygiene *n* higiene *f*; ∼ **standard** *n* norma de higiene *f*

hype *n* gran promoción de lanzamiento *f*

hyperdocument *n* (Comp) hiperdocumento *m*

hyperinflation *n* hiperinflación *f*

hyperinflationist *adj* hiperinflacionista

hyperlink *n* (Comp) hiperenlace *m*

hypermarket *n* hipermercado *m*

hypermedia *adj* (Comp) multimedia

hypertext *n* (Comp) hipertexto *m*; **H**∼ **Mark-up Language** *n* lenguaje HTML *m*

hyphenation *n* guionado *m*

hypothecate *vt* hipotecar

hypothesis *n* hipótesis *f*

hypothetical *adj* (question, situation) hipotético

Ii

i *abbr* (▸**interest**) interés *m*

i2i *abbr* (▸**industry-to-industry**) entre industrias

IADB *abbr* (▸**Inter-American Development Bank**) BID (Banco Interamericano de Desarrollo)

IAP *abbr* (▸**Internet access provider**) proveedor de acceso de Internet *m*

IATA *abbr* (▸**International Air Transport Association**) IATA (Asociación Internacional de Transporte Aéreo)

IBEC *abbr* (▸**International Bank for Economic Cooperation**) IBEC (Banco Internacional para la Cooperación Económica)

ibid. *abbr* (▸**ibidem**) ibid. (ibidem)

ibidem *adv* ibidem

IBOR *abbr* (▸**interbank offered rate**) tasa ofrecida interbancaria *f*

IBRD *abbr* (▸**International Bank for Reconstruction and Development**) BIRD (Banco Internacional para la Reconstrucción y el Desarrollo)

IC *abbr* (▸**integrated circuit**) CI (circuito integrado)

iceberg company *n* (jarg) empresa mayor de lo aparente *f*

ICJ *abbr* (▸**International Court of Justice**) Tribunal Internacional de Justicia *m*

icon *n* (Comp) icono *m*

iconify *vt* (Comp) iconizar

id. *abbr* (▸**idem**) id. (ídem)

ID *abbr* (▸**identification**) identificación *f*; (▸**identifier**) identificador *m*; (▸**identity**) identidad *f*; (▸**import duty**) derechos fiscales sobre la importación *m pl*; ∼ **card** *n* (▸**identity card**) carné de identidad *m* Esp, DNI *m* (documento nacional de identidad) Esp; CI *f* (cedula de identidad) AmL; ∼ **number** *n* (Comp) número ID *m*

IDA *abbr* (▸**International Development Association**) AIF (Asociación Internacional de Fomento)

IDB *abbr* (▸**Inter-American Development Bank**) BID (Banco Interamericano de Desarrollo); (▸**interdealer broker**) BrE CI (corredor(a) intermediario(-a))

idem *adj* ídem

identification *n* identificación *f*

identifier *n* identificador *m*

identity card *n* carné de identidad *m* Esp, documento nacional de identidad *m* Esp; cedula de identidad *f* AmL

id est *adv* id est

idle *adj* (capital, cash, money) inactivo; (HRM) improductivo, ocioso; (machine, factory) parado; **be** ∼ (worker) no tener trabajo, estar sin hacer nada; **lying** ∼ (infrml) (money) inactivo; ∼ **balance** *n* saldo ocioso *m*; ∼ **capacity** *n* capacidad ociosa *f*; ∼ **cycle** *n* ciclo en vacío *m*; ∼ **time** *n* (Comp) tiempo inactivo *m*

iDTV *abbr* (▸**interactive digital TV**) TV digital interactiva *f*

i.e. *abbr* (▸**id est**) id est

if *conj* si; ∼**, as and when** si, como y cuando

IFC *abbr* (▸**International Finance Corporation**) CFI (Corporación de Finanzas Internacionales)

I/L *abbr* (▸**import licence** BrE, ▸**import license** AmE) licencia de importación *f*

illegal *adj* (practice, strike, alien, immigrant) ilegal; ∼ **character** *n* (Comp) carácter ilegal *m*; ∼ **dividend** *n* AmE dividendo ilegal *m*; ∼ **operation** *n* (Comp) operación no válida *f*; ∼ **seizure** *n* apropiación indebida *f*

illegally *adv* ilegalmente

illiquid *adj* (assets) no realizable

illusory *adj* (profit) ilusorio

illustrate *vt* ilustrar

illustrated *adj* (magazine) ilustrado

illustration *n* (picture) ilustración *f*; (example) ejemplo *m*; (explanation) aclaración *f*; **by way of** ∼ a modo de ejemplo

ill will *n* mala voluntad *f*

ILO *abbr* (▸**International Labor Organization** AmE, ▸**International Labour Organization** BrE) OIT (Organización Internacional de Trabajo)

ILOC *abbr* (▸**irrevocable letter of credit**) crédito documentario irrevocable *m*

image *n* imagen *f*; ∼ **advertising** *n* publicidad basada en la imagen *f*; ∼ **audit** *n* auditoría de imagen *f*; ∼ **file** *n* fichero de imagen *m*; ∼ **maker** *n* creador(a) de imagen *m,f*; ∼ **processing** *n* tratamiento de la imagen *m*; ∼ **projection** *n* proyección de imagen *f*

imaging *n* formación de imágenes *f*

imbalance n desequilibrio m; ~ **of trade** n desequilibrio de intercambios m

IMF abbr (▸**International Monetary Fund**) FMI (Fondo Monetario Internacional)

IMM abbr (▸**International Monetary Market**) Mercado Monetario Internacional m

immediate adj (reply, decision) inmediato; (aim, problem, need) urgente, apremiante; (cause, consequence) inmediato, directo; **take ~ action** actuar inmediatamente; **for ~ attention** para atención inmediata f; **for ~ delivery** para entrega inmediata; **the law will take ~ effect** la ley entrará en vigor inmediatamente; **with ~ possession** llave en mano; ~ **access** n (Comp) acceso directo m; ~ **family** n familia inmediata f

immigrant n inmigrante mf; ~ **worker** n trabajador(a) inmigrante m,f

immigration n inmigración f; ~ **control** n control de inmigración m; ~ **law** n ley de inmigración f; ~ **officer** n funcionario(-a) de inmigración m,f; ~ **policy** n política de inmigración f

imminent adj (danger, peril) inminente

immiseration n pobreza creciente de las clases trabajadoras

immiserizing growth n crecimiento empobrecedor del bienestar económico m

immovable adj (asset) inmueble; (capital) inmobiliario; ~ **estate** n bienes inmuebles m pl; ~ **property** n propiedad f

immunities n pl BrE exenciones f pl

immunity n inmunidad f; ~ **from taxation** n inmunidad tributaria f

immunization n inmunización f

immunize vt inmunizar

IMO abbr (▸**international money order**) giro postal internacional m

imp. abbr (▸**import**, ▸**importation**) importación f

impact¹ n (effect) impacto m; **have/make an ~ on sth/sb** tener/hacer un impacto en algo/alguien; ~ **printer** n impresora de percusión f; ~ **study** n estudio de impacto m

impact² vt tener un impacto en; **impact on** vt tener un impacto en

impair vt (currency) deteriorar; (efficiency) afectar, reducir

impaired capital n capital no respaldado por activo equivalente m

impairment n (of value) disminución f; (Tax) deterioro m, menoscabo m

impartial adj imparcial

impasse n punto muerto m, impasse m

impede vt (growth) poner un impedimento a; (progress, communications) dificultar, obstaculizar

imperfect adj (competition, market, obligation) imperfecto

impetus n impulso m

impinge on vt (affect) afectar; (encroach on) vulnerar; ~ **on sb's rights** vulnerar los derechos de alguien

implement vt (system) instrumentar; (contract) hacer efectivo; (policy, decision) poner en práctica

implementation n implementación f

implications n pl consecuencias f pl

implicit adj (cost) implícito

implied adj (acceptance, condition, term) implícito; (contract) sobreentendido, tácito; ~ **warranty** n AmE garantía implícita f

imply vt (suggest, hint) dar a entender, insinuar; (involve) implicar, suponer

import¹ n importación f; ~ **control** n control a la importación m; ~ **credit** n crédito a la importación m; ~ **duty** n derechos fiscales sobre la importación m pl; ~**-export** adj (trade, merchant) de importación y exportación; ~ **licence** BrE, ~ **license** AmE n licencia de importación f; ~ **manager** n director(a) de importación m,f; ~ **permit** n autorización de importación f; ~ **price** n precio de importación m; ~ **quota** n cuota de importaciones f; ~ **tariff** n arancel de importación m; ~ **trade** n comercio de importación m

import² vt (goods, data) importar

importance n importancia f; **attach ~ to sth** adjudicar importancia a algo

important adj importante

importation n importación f

imported adj (goods) importado, de importación

importer n importador(a) m,f

impose vt (restriction, punishment, condition) imponer; ~ **a tax on sth** gravar un impuesto sobre algo; ~ **undue hardship on sb** (on taxpayer) someter a alguien a una presión excesiva

imposition n imposición f

impound vt (possessions, assets) incautar, incautarse de

impounding n incautación f; (of ship) almacenamiento m

impoverished adj empobrecido

impression n impresión f; **make an ~ on sb** impresionar a alguien

impressive adj (increase) impresionante

imprest: ~ **account** n cuenta de anticipos f; ~ **fund** n fondo fijo m; ~ **system** n sistema de fondo fijo m

imprint n pie de imprenta m

imprison vt encarcelar

imprisonment n encarcelamiento m

improve ⓵ vt (product, design, results) mejorar; (chances) aumentar; (property, premises) hacer mejoras en ⓶ vi (situation, work) mejorar; (chances) aumentar

improvement n mejora f; **be an ∼ on sth** ser mejor que or superior a algo

impulse n impulso m; **∼ buy** n compra impulsiva f; **∼ buyer** n comprador(a) por impulso m,f; **∼ buying** n compra impulsiva f; **∼ goods** n pl artículos de compra impulsiva m pl; **∼ purchase** n compra impulsiva f

imputation n imputación f

imputed adj (cost, income, value) imputado; (interest) atribuido

IMRO abbr (▸**Investment Management Regulatory Organization**) BrE organización reguladora de gestores de inversiones

inability n incapacidad f; **∼ to work** incapacidad para trabajar

inaccuracy n inexactitud f

inaccurate adj (statement, estimate) inexacto, erróneo

inactive adj (account, bond) inactivo; (asset) sin movimiento; (stock) inmovilizado

inadvertently adv inadvertidamente

in-and-out trading n compra f y venta f del mismo valor en un día

inaugural adj (meeting, flight) inaugural

in-bond manufacturing n manufacturas en depósito f pl

inbound adj (investor) extranjero

in-box n buzón de e-mail m

Inc. abbr AmE (▸**incorporated business company**, cf ▸**Ltd** BrE) ≈ S.A. (sociedad anónima), ≈ S.A.A. (sociedad anónima por acciones), ≈ S.R.L. (sociedad de responsabilidad limitada)

incapacity n incapacidad f

ince abbr (▸**insurance**) seguro m

incentive n incentivo m; **∼ bonus** n prima de incentivo f; **∼ fee** n honorarios de incentivo m pl; **∼ payment system** n sistema de remuneración por incentivos m; **∼ plan** n plan de incentivo m; **∼ stock option** n AmE incentivo fiscal sobre opciones m

incentivize vt incentivar

incestuous share dealing n venta de acciones incestuosa f

inch n pulgada f

inchoate adj incompleto

incidence n frecuencia f, tasa f

incidental adj (expenses, charges) imprevisto; (consequence, effect) secundario; (advantage, benefit) adicional

incidentals n pl imprevistos m pl; **∼ allowance** n asignación para gastos imprevistos f

incineration n (of waste) incineración f; **∼ plant** n planta de incineración f

incl. abbr (▸**included**, ▸**including**, ▸**inclusive**) incluido

include vt incluir; (with letter) adjuntar, incluir

included adj incluido

including prep incluido; **not ∼ insurance** sin incluir el seguro; **∼ postage** franqueo incluido; **the bill came to £60 ∼ service** la cuenta ascendió a 60 libras, servicio incluido; **up to and ∼ 21st May** hasta el 21 de mayo inclusive

inclusion n inclusión f

inclusive adj incluido; (price, charge) global, todo incluido; **from the 23rd to the 27th ∼** del 23 al 27, ambos inclusive; **be ∼ of sth** incluir algo; **∼ of tax** los impuestos incluidos; **all prices are ∼ of VAT** todos los precios son con el IVA incluido

income n ingresos m pl; (unearned) renta f, ingresos m pl; **take sth into ∼** incluir algo en los ingresos; **∼ accounts** n pl cuentas f pl de ganancias or de ingresos; **∼ band** n banda de ingresos f; **∼ bond** n bono amortizable m; **∼ bracket** n tramo de renta m; **∼ debenture** n título con rendimiento m; **∼ earned overseas** n renta percibida en el extranjero f; **∼ and expenditure account** n cuenta de ingresos y gastos f; **∼ from employment** n ingresos salariales m pl; **∼ from interest** n ingresos por intereses m pl; **∼ from securities** n ingresos por valores m pl, renta de valores f; **∼ group** n grupo de ingresos m; **∼ per head** n renta per cápita f; **∼s policy** n política de rentas f; **∼ property** n AmE propiedad de explotación f; **∼ range** n banda de ingresos f; **∼ statement** n balance de resultados m; **∼ support** n BrE (obs) (social security payment) subsidio para las personas con pocos ingresos; **∼ target** n meta de ingreso f; **∼ tax** n impuesto sobre la renta m; **for ∼ tax purposes** para el impuesto sobre la renta; **∼ tax rate** n tipo del impuesto sobre la renta m; **∼ tax rate band** n banda de tipos del impuesto sobre la renta f; **∼ tax refund** n devolución del impuesto sobre la renta f; **∼ tax return** n declaración (del impuesto) sobre la renta f; **∼ threshold** n nivel de ingresos m

incoming adj (call, data) de entrada; (goods) recibido, nuevo; (order) nuevo; **∼ mail** n AmE, **∼ post** n BrE correo entrante m

in-company training *n* formación *f or* capacitación *f* interna

incompatible *adj* incompatible

incompetent *adj* (person) incompetente, inepto; (work) deficiente; (attempt) ineficaz; (Law) incapaz

incomplete *adj* incompleto

incontestable *adj* (clause) irrecusable

inconvertible *adj* (money) no convertible

incorporate *vt* (idea, plan) incorporar; (business, enterprise) constituir; ~ **sth into sth** incorporar algo a algo

incorporated *adj* incorporado; (business, enterprise) constituido; ~ **bank** *n* AmE banco por acciones *m*; ~ **business company** *n* AmE (*cf* ▸**limited (liability) company** BrE) ≈ sociedad anónima *f*, ≈ sociedad anónima por acciones *f*, ≈ sociedad de responsabilidad limitada *f*

incorporation *n* (of company) constitución *f*

incorporeal *adj* incorpóreo; ~ **hereditaments** *n pl* bienes inmateriales por heredar *m pl*; ~ **property** *n* propiedad intangible *f*

incorrect *adj* (answer, spelling) incorrecto; (statement, assessment) equivocado, erróneo

INCOTERM *abbr* (▸**International Commercial Term**) INCOTERM (cláusula comercial internacional)

increase¹ ① *vt* (trade, output) aumentar, incrementar; (production) incrementar; (number, size, supply) aumentar; ~ **profits by 2%** aumentar los beneficios en un 2% ② *vi* (trade, output, production) aumentar, incrementarse; (prices) aumentar, subir; (number, size, rate, power) aumentar; ~ **in value** aumentar de valor, revalorizarse; ~ **tenfold/twofold** aumentar diez veces/el doble

increase² *n* aumento *m*, incremento *m*; (in capital) ampliación *f*; **an ~ of 50% on** *o* **over last year** un aumento del 50% con respecto al año pasado; **on the ~** en aumento

increasing *adj* (budget deficit) creciente

increment *n* incremento *m*

incremental *adj* (spending, cash flow) incremental; (cost) marginal; (tax) adicional; (payment, scale) progresivo

incubator *n* (for startup ventures) incubadora *f*

incur *vt* (debt, liability) contraer; (expense) incurrir en; (damage, loss, injury) sufrir; (penalty, disadvantage) acarrear

incurable *adj* (depreciation) irremediable

incurred *adj* (costs, expenses) incurrido, realizado

indebted *adj* endeudado; ~ **to sb (for sth)** endeudado con alguien (por algo)

indebtedness *n* endeudamiento *m*

indefinite *adj* indefinido

indemnify *vt* (compensate) indemnizar; (insure) asegurar; ~ **sb for sth** indemnizar a alguien por *or* de algo; ~ **sb against sth** asegurar a alguien contra algo

indemnity *n* (compensation) indemnización *f*; (insurance) indemnidad *f*; ~ **fund** *n* fondo de indemnizaciones *m*

indent¹ *n* (in text) espacio *m*; (order) BrE pedido *m*, orden de compra *f*; ~ **house** *n* agencia de importación *f*

indent² ① *vt* (text) sangrar; BrE (foreign goods) realizar un pedido de compra de ② *vi* BrE ~ **for sth** encargar algo

indentation *n* (indenting) sangría *f*; (space) espacio *m*

indenture *n* contrato *m*; ~ **of apprenticeship** *n* contrato de aprendizaje *m*

independence *n* independencia *f*

independent *adj* independiente; **a person of ~ means** una persona que dispone de rentas; ~ **of sth/sb** independiente de algo/alguien; ~ **accountant** *n* contable *mf* Esp *or* contador(a) *m,f* AmL independiente; ~ **adjuster** *n* ajustador(a) independiente *m,f*; ~ **auditor** *n* auditor(a) independiente *m,f*; ~ **broker** *n* corredor(a) independiente *m,f*; ~ **expert** *n* experto(-a) independiente *m,f*; ~ **inquiry** *n* investigación independiente *f*; ~ **retailer** *n* minorista independiente *mf*; ~ **store** *n* tienda independiente *f*

independently *adv* independientemente; ~ **of sth/sb** independientemente de algo/alguien

in-depth *adj* (discussion, interview) en profundidad; (analysis) a fondo, en profundidad; (business plan) exhaustivo; (study) pormenorizado

indeterminate *adj* indeterminado

index¹ *n* índice *m*; ~ **card** *n* ficha *f*; ~**-card file** *n* fichero *m*; ~ **file** *n* archivo índice *m*; ~ **fund** *n* fondo indexado *m*; ~ **futures** *n pl* futuros sobre índices *m pl*; ~ **of industrial production** *n* índice de producción industrial *m*; ~ **of lagging indicators** *n* índice de indicadores retardados *m*; ~ **of leading indicators** *n* índice *m* de indicadores adelantados *or* anticipados; ~ **lease** *n* alquiler de referencia *m*, arrendamiento indexado *m*; ~ **linkage** *n* vinculación a un índice *f*; ~**-linked** *adj* ajustable; ~**-linked stock** *n* BrE acciones indexadas *m*; ~**-linking** *n* indización *f*; ~ **number** *n* número índice *m*; ~ **option** *n* opción índice *f*; ~ **point** *n* punto de índice *m*; ~ **price** *n* precio índice *m*

index² *vt* (prices, costs, wages) indexar, indiciar; (report) ponerle un índice a; (name) incluir en un índice; ~ **pensions to** ⋯∲

inflation indexar *or* indiciar las pensiones a la inflación

indexation *n* indexación *f*

indexed *adj* (file, loan, security) indexado; (bond) indizado

indexing *n* indexación *f*

indicated yield *n* rendimiento financiero necesario *m*

indication *n* indicio *m*; ∼ **of interest** *n* indicación de interés *f*

indicative *adj* indicativo; ∼ **of sth** indicativo de algo; ∼ **planning** *n* planificación indicativa *f*

indicator *n* indicador *m*

indict *vt* acusar; ∼ **sb for sth** acusar a alguien de algo

indictment *n* acusación *f*; **bring an** ∼ **against sb** formular cargos contra alguien

indirect *adj* (cost, tax, discrimination) indirecto

indirectly *adv* indirectamente

indiscountable *adj* no descontable

individual[1] *adj* (rights, investor) individual; ∼ **retirement account** *n* AmE cuenta de jubilación individual *f*; ∼ **retirement account rollover** *n* AmE renovación de cuenta de jubilación individual *f*; ∼ **savings account** *n* BrE *cuenta de ahorros particular libre de impuestos*

individual[2] *n* (person) individuo *m*

individualism *n* individualismo *m*

individualization *n* individualización *f*

individually *adv* individualmente

indivisibility *n* indivisibilidad *f*

indorse ▶endorse

indorsee ▶endorsee

indorsement ▶endorsement

indorser, **indorsor** ▶endorser

induce *vt* (cause) provocar, producir; ∼ **sb to do sth** inducir a alguien a hacer algo

induced draft *n* efecto inducido *m*

inducement *n* (incentive) incentivo *m*; (bribe) soborno *m*; (to break the law) incitación *f*; **offer a financial** ∼ ofrecer un incentivo monetario

induction *n* iniciación *f*; ∼ **course** *n* curso de introducción *m*

inductive *adj* (reasoning) inductivo

industrial *adj* industrial; ∼ **accident** *n* accidente *m* laboral *or* de trabajo; ∼ **action** *n* huelga *f*; **take** ∼ **action** emprender acciones laborales; ∼ **activity** *n* actividad industrial *f*; ∼ **advertising** *n* publicidad industrial *f*; ∼ **arbitration** *n* arbitraje industrial *m*; ∼ **base** *n* base industrial *f*; ∼ **center** AmE, ∼ **centre** BrE *n* centro industrial *m*; ∼ **complex** *n* complejo industrial *m*; ∼ **conflict** *n* conflicto industrial *m*; ∼ **court** *n* BrE (*cf* ▶**labor**

court AmE) tribunal laboral *m*, magistratura del trabajo *f*; ∼ **demand** *n* demanda industrial *f*; ∼ **democracy** *n* democracia industrial *f*; ∼ **disease** *n* enfermedad laboral *f*; ∼ **dispute** *n* conflicto laboral *m*; ∼ **engineer** *n* ingeniero(-a) industrial *m,f*; ∼ **engineering** *n* ingeniería industrial *f*; ∼ **equipment** *n* equipo industrial *m*; ∼ **espionage** *n* espionaje industrial *m*; ∼ **estate** *n* BrE (*cf* ▶**industrial park** AmE) zona industrial *f*; ∼ **injury** *n* accidente laboral *m*; ∼ **marketing** *n* marketing industrial *m*; ∼ **organization** *n* organización industrial *f*; ∼ **park** *n* AmE (*cf* ▶**industrial estate** BrE) zona industrial *f*; ∼ **plant** *n* planta industrial *f*; ∼ **production** *n* producción industrial *f*; ∼ **products** *n pl* productos industriales *m pl*; ∼ **relations** *n pl* relaciones industriales *f pl*; ∼ **relations manager** *n* gerente de relaciones industriales *mf*; ∼ **research** *n* investigación industrial *f*; ∼ **revolution** *n* revolución industrial *f*; ∼ **safety** *n* seguridad industrial *f*; ∼ **sector** *n* sector industrial *m*; ∼ **site** *n* enclave industrial *m*; ∼ **society** *n* sociedad industrial *f*; ∼ **strife** *n* disputas profesionales *f pl*; ∼ **tribunal** *n* BrE tribunal laboral *m*, magistratura del trabajo *f*; ∼ **union** *n* sindicato de industria *m*; ∼ **waste** *n* residuos industriales *m pl*; ∼ **zone** *n* polígono industrial *m*

industrialism *n* industrialismo *m*

industrialist *n* empresario(a) industrial *m,f*, industrialista *mf*

industrialization *n* industrialización *f*

industrialize *vt* industrializar

industrialized *adj* (nation, country) industrializado

industry *n* industria *f*; ∼ **standard** *n* norma industrial *f*; ∼**-wide agreement** *n* acuerdo sectorial *m*

industry-to-industry *adj* entre industrias

inefficiency *n* ineficiencia *f*

inefficient *adj* ineficiente

inelastic *adj* (supply, demand) inelástico

inelasticity *n* inelasticidad *f*; ∼ **of demand** *n* inelasticidad de la demanda *f*; ∼ **of supply** *n* inelasticidad de la oferta *f*

ineligible paper *n* valores no negociados *m pl*

inequality *n* desigualdad *f*

inertia *n* inercia *f*; ∼ **salesman** *n* vendedor por inercia *m*; ∼ **selling** *n* venta por inercia *f*

inertial *adv* inercial; ∼ **effect** *n* efecto inercia *m*; ∼ **inflation** *n* inflación inerte *f*

inevitable *adj* (result, outcome) inevitable

inevitably *adv* inevitablemente

infant n (Law) menor (de edad) mf; ∼
industry n industria incipiente f; ∼
mortality n mortalidad infantil f

inferior adj (goods) inferior

infession n (jarg) inflación debida a un
fallo en el sistema monetario

infinite adj infinito

infirm adj enfermo

inflate vt (figures, prices, economy) inflar

inflation n inflación f; **keep ∼ down**
mantener baja la inflación; ∼**is running at
10%** hay una inflación del 10%, la inflación
alcanza el 10%; ∼**-proof** adj resistente a la
inflación; ∼ **rate** n tasa de inflación f

inflationary adj (trend) inflacionario;
(pressure, spiral) inflacionario; (gap)
inflacionario, inflacionista

inflationist adj inflacionista

in-flight adj (entertainment, film, facilities)
durante el vuelo

inflow n (of currency) entrada f

influence[1] n influencia f

influence[2] vt (costs) influir; (decision)
influenciar

influential adj influyente

info abbr (▸**information**) información f

infoglut n exceso de información m

infomercial n telepromoción f

inform vt (advise) informar; (by letter)
informar, notificar; **keep sb ∼ed** mantener
a alguien informado

informal adj (arrangement, interview, meeting)
informal

informality n informalidad f

informant n informante mf

informatics n computación f, informática f

information n (facts, news) información f;
(telephone number service) AmE (cf ▸**directory
enquiries** BrE) servicio de información
telefónica m, información (de teléfonos) f; ∼
about o **on sth/sb** información acerca de or
sobre algo/alguien; **for further** ∼ para más
información; **for your** ∼ para su
información; **a piece of** ∼ un dato; ∼ **bit** n
(Comp) bitio de información m; ∼ **bureau** n
oficina de información f; ∼ **channel** n
canal de información f; ∼ **desk** n
información f; ∼ **flow** n circulación de la
información f; ∼ **handling** n manejo de la
información m; ∼ **highway** n autopista de
la información f, infopista f, infovía f; ∼
management n administración de
información f; ∼ **network** n red de
información f; ∼ **office** n oficina de
información f; ∼ **officer** n responsable de
información mf; ∼ **pack** n carpeta de
documentos informativos f; ∼ **processing**
n tratamiento de información f; ∼ **retrieval**
n recuperación de información f;

∼ **retrieval system** n sistema de
recuperación de información m; ∼
revolution n revolución de la información
f; ∼ **storage** n compilación de datos f; ∼
system n sistema de información m; ∼
technology n informática f; ∼
technology company n empresa de
tecnología de la información f; ∼ **theory** n
teoría de la información f; ∼ **transfer** n
transferencia de informaciones f; ∼
warfare n guerra de la información f

informative adj (advertising, labelling)
informativo

informed adj (decision, argument, public)
informado

infotainment n entretenimiento
informativo m

infotech n (▸**information technology**)
informática f

infra- pref infra-

infrastructure n infraestructura f

infringe vt infringir

infringement n infracción f

infringer n infractor(a) m,f

ingenuity n ingeniosidad f

ingot n lingote m

ingress n acceso m

inhabitant n habitante mf

inherent adj (risk, error, defect) inherente; **be
∼ in sth** ser inherente a algo

inherit vti heredar; ∼ **sth from sb** heredar
algo de alguien

inheritance n (property) herencia f; (act)
sucesión f; ∼ **tax** n impuesto m de
sucesiones or sobre herencias

inherited adj (property, audience) heredado

inhibit vt (person) inhibir, cohibir; (attempt,
growth, reaction) inhibir; ∼ **sb from doing sth**
impedirle a alguien hacer algo

inhospitable adj inhóspito

in-house adj (service, software, worker,
translator) interno; (training) en la empresa;
(system) propio; ∼ **lawyer** n ≈ abogado(-a)
de empresa m,f, asesor(a) jurídico(-a) m,f

initial[1] adj (funding, expenditure, outlay) inicial;
in the ∼ **stages** al principio; ∼
assessment n (Tax) gravamen inicial m; ∼
letter n inicial f; ∼ **public offering** n
oferta pública inicial f

initial[2] n inicial f

initial[3] vt (memo, document) inicialar, ponerle
las iniciales a

initialize vt (operating system) inicializar

initiate vt (talks) iniciar, dar comienzo a,
entablar; (plan) poner en marcha; (new
concept) introducir; (software) iniciar; ∼
proceedings against sb entablarle juicio a
alguien

initiation n (of plan, talks) inicio m, comienzo m; ~ **dues** n pl, ~ **fees** n pl cuotas de ingreso f pl

initiative n iniciativa f; **on one's own** ~ por iniciativa propia; **show great** ~ demostrar una gran iniciativa; **take the** ~ tomar la iniciativa

inject vt (funds, capital) inyectar

injection n (of funds, capital) inyección f

injunction n mandamiento judicial m; **seek/obtain an** ~ **against sb** solicitar/ obtener un mandamiento judicial en contra de alguien

injured party n parte f ofendida or perjudicada

injury n (physical) herida f, lesión f; ~ **to one's reputation** perjuicio a su reputación

ink-jet printer n impresora a chorro de tinta f

inland adj (trade) interior; (telephone service, postal rates) nacional; ~ **haulage** n desplazamiento interior m; **I~ Revenue (Office)** n BrE (cf ►Internal Revenue Service AmE) ≈ Hacienda f

inner adj interior; ~ **city** n centro de la ciudad m; **~city area** n zona del centro de la ciudad f; ~ **code** n (Tax) código interior m; ~ **pack** n envase interior m

innocent adj inocente

innovate vi innovar

innovation n innovación f; ~ **center** AmE, ~ **centre** BrE n centro de innovación m

innovative adj innovador

innovator n innovador(a) m,f, novador(a) m,f

inoperative adj (law, regulation, clause) inoperante

in-plant adj (training) en la propia fábrica

input¹ n (Comp) entrada f; (of resources) aportación f, aporte m AmL; ~ **data** n datos de entrada m pl; ~ **device** n dispositivo de entrada m; ~ **message** n mensaje de entrada m; ~**/output** n (Comp) entrada/ salida f; ~**-output analysis** n análisis de entrada/salida m

input² vt (data) introducir; ~ **information into a computer** introducir información en una computadora AmL or un ordenador Esp

inputs n pl (Comp) entradas f pl; (Econ) factores de producción m pl

inquiry n (investigation) investigación f; (Comp) interrogación f; **conduct/set up an** ~ **(into sth)** llevar a cabo/abrir una investigación (sobre algo); ~ **form** n formulario de encuesta m; ~ **program** n programa de consulta m; ~ **test** n (S&M) prueba de encuesta f

insert¹ vt (text) insertar; (advertisement) insertar, poner; (coin, token) introducir, meter

insert² n encarte m

in-service n (training, course) en horas de trabajo

inset¹ n (in map, photograph) recuadro m (dentro de una illustración o un mapa mayor); (page) encarte m

inset² vt (map, illustration) insertar (dentro de una illustración o un mapa mayor); (page, advertisement) encartar

inside¹ adj (pages) interior; ~ **information** n información privilegiada f; ~ **money** n dinero interior m

inside² n interior m; **have someone on the** ~ tener a alguien infiltrado

insider n empleado(-a) con información confidencial m,f; ~ **dealing** n abuso de información privilegiada m; ~ **report** n informe confidencial m; ~ **trading** n abuso de información privilegiada m

insoluble adj (problem) insoluble

insolvency n insolvencia f; ~ **clause** n cláusula de insolvencia f; ~ **legislation** n legislación sobre insolvencia f

insolvent adj insolvente

insource vi recurrir a fuentes internas

insourcing n recurso a fuentes internas m

inspect vt (object) revisar, examinar; (factory, premises) inspeccionar; (equipment) inspeccionar, revisar; (document) revisar

inspection n (of factory, premises, equipment) inspección f; (of document) revisión f

inspector n inspector(a) m,f; ~ **of taxes** n BrE inspector(a) de Hacienda m,f

inspectorate n cuerpo de inspectores m

inst. abbr (►instant) (obs) cte. (corriente)

install vt (software, system, network) instalar

installation n instalación f; ~ **diskette** n disquete de instalación m

installment plan n AmE (cf ►hire purchase** BrE) compra a plazos f; **buy sth on the** ~**plan** comprar algo a plazos

installment BrE, **installment** AmE n plazo m, mensualidad f; **by** o **in** ~**s** a plazos; **buy sth in** ~**s** comprar algo a plazos; ~ **base** n modalidad aplazada f; ~ **contract** n contrato m de venta a plazos or de venta en cuotas; ~ **credit** n crédito a plazos m; ~ **loan** n préstamo a plazos m; ~ **payment** n pago m aplazado or a plazos; ~ **repayment schedule** n plan de pago a plazos m

instance n (example) ejemplo m; (case) caso m; **at sb's** ~ a instancias or a petición de alguien; **for** ~ por ejemplo; **in the first** ~ en primer lugar; **in this** ~ en esta instancia

instant adj (success, results) instantáneo, inmediato; (reply) inmediato; (obs) (of current month) corriente; ~ **credit** n crédito m inmediato or instantáneo; ~ **messaging** n mensajería instantánea f

instinct *n* instinto *m*

institute[1] *vt* (post, committee) instituir; (service, system) establecer; (Law) (proceedings, action) entablar, iniciar; (inquiry) iniciar

institute[2] *n* instituto *m*

institution *n* institución *f*; ~ **of an appeal** *n* (Tax) interposición de una apelación *f*

institutional *adj* (investor, lender, advertising) institucional

institutionalize *vt* institucionalizar

in-store *adj* (promotion) en tienda; (merchandising) en tiendas

instruction *n* instrucción *f*; ~**s (for use)** instrucciones, modo de empleo; ~ **book** *n* manual de instrucciones *m*; ~ **leaflet** *n* folleto de instrucciones *m*; ~ **manual** *n* manual de instrucciones *m*; ~ **program** *n* programa de instrucción *m*

instrument *n* instrumento *m*

instrumental *adj* (capital) instrumental; **be** ~ **in (doing) sth** jugar un papel decisivo en (hacer) algo

instrumentality *n* instrumentalidad *f*

insufficient *adj* insuficiente; ~ **funds** *n pl* saldo insuficiente *m*

insulate *vt* aislar

insurability *n* asegurabilidad *f*

insurable *adj* (interest, risk, title) asegurable

insurance *n* seguro *m*; ~ **against sth** seguro contra algo; **take out** ~ hacerse *or* contratar un seguro; ~ **agent** *n* agente de seguros *mf*; ~ **broker** *n* agente *mf or* corredor(a) *m,f* de seguros; ~ **brokerage** *n*, ~ **broking** *n* correduría de seguros *f*; ~ **business** *n* sector de seguros *m*; ~ **certificate** *n* póliza de seguro *f*; ~ **claim** *n* demanda de seguro *f*; ~ **company** *n* aseguradora *f*, compañía de seguros *f*; ~ **contract** *n* contrato de seguros *m*; ~ **corporation** *n* aseguradora *f*, compañía de seguros *f*; ~ **cover** *n* BrE, ~ **coverage** *n* AmE cobertura del seguro *f*; ~ **industry** *n* sector de seguros *m*; ~ **policy** *n* póliza de seguro *f*; **take out an** ~ **policy** suscribir una póliza de seguros; ~**-poor** *adj* (business) con seguro insuficiente; ~ **premium** *n* prima de seguros *f*; ~ **report** *n* declaración de siniestro *f*; ~ **settlement** *n* liquidación del seguro *f*

insure *vt* asegurar; ~ **sth/sb against sth** asegurar algo/a alguien contra algo; **be** ~**d against all risks** estar asegurado contra todo riesgo

insured[1] *adj* (peril, liability, account) asegurado; ~ **mail** *n* AmE, ~ **post** *n* BrE correo asegurado *m*

insured[2] *n* asegurado(-a) *m,f*

insurer *n* asegurador(a) *m,f*; ~**'s claim** *n* reclamación del seguro *f*

int. *abbr* (▸**interest**) interés *m*

intake *n* (of people) número admitido *f*; (of new orders) entrada *f*; **this year's** ~ los que han ingresado *or* los que admitieron este año; **the new** ~ los nuevos

intangible *adj* (asset, good) intangible, inmaterial; (property, value, reward) intangible

integral *adj* (feature) integral, esencial; **be** ~ **to sth** ser esencial a algo; ~ **part** *n* parte integrante *f*

integrate *vt* integrar

integrated *adj* (company) integrado; ~ **circuit** *n* circuito integrado *m*; ~ **management system** *n* sistema de gestión integrado *m*; ~ **project management** *n* gestión integrada de proyectos *f*; ~ **services digital network** *n* red digital de servicios integrados *f*

integration *n* integración *f*

integrity *n* integridad *f*

intellectual *adj* intelectual; ~ **property** *n* propiedad intelectual *f*; ~ **property rights** *n pl* derechos sobre la propiedad intelectual *m pl*

intelligent *adj* (person, suggestion) inteligente; ~ **terminal** *n* terminal inteligente *m*

intensification *n* intensificación *f*

intensify [1] *vt* (effort) intensificar [2] *vi* (slowdown, competition) intensificarse

intensive *adj* (farming, training, course) intensivo

intention *n* intención *f*; **have no** ~ **of doing sth** no tener intención de hacer algo; **with the best of** ~**s** con la mejor intención

inter-account *adj* (dealing) intercontable

interaction *n* interacción *f*; ~ **matrix** *n* (Mgmnt) matriz interactiva *f*

interactive *adj* (computing, processing, mode, system) interactivo; ~ **digital TV** *n* TV digital interactiva *f*; ~ **marketing** *n* marketing interactivo *m*; ~ **Web page** *n* página web interactiva *f*; ~ **website** *n* sitio web interactivo *f*

interactivity *n* interactividad *f*

Inter-American Development Bank *n* AmE Banco Interamericano de Desarrollo *m*

interbank *adj* (rate, business, transaction) interbancario; ~ **offered rate** *n* tasa ofrecida interbancaria *f*

interchange *n* (of letters) intercambio *m*

intercommodity spread *n* margen entre los productos *m*

intercommunity *adj* (trade) intercomunitario

intercompany adj (market)
interempresarial; (profit) entre compañías

interconnection n interconexión f

intercontinental adj intercontinental

interdealer broker n BrE corredor(a)
intermediario(-a) m,f

interdelivery spread n margen entre
entregas m

interdepartmental adj
interdepartamental

interdependence n interdependencia f

interdependent adj interdependiente

interest n interés m; (stake) participación f,
intereses m pl; **act in sb's ∼(s)** actuar en
beneficio de alguien; **this bond bears 5% ∼**
este bono da or devenga un interés del 5%;
have considerable business ∼s tener
considerables participaciones en algunos
negocios; **earn/charge ∼ of o at 5%**
percibir/cobrar un interés del 5%; **have an
∼ in sth** (business) tener intereses or
participación en algo; **acquire a substantial
∼ in a company** adquirir una parte
considerable de las acciones de una
empresa; **look after one's own ∼s** velar por
sus propios intereses; **receive ∼ on an
investment** recibir el interés de una
inversión; **have a vested ∼ in sth** tener
intereses en algo; **∼ accrued** n interés m
acumulado or devengado; **∼ arrearage** n
intereses atrasados m pl; **∼-bearing** adj
con interés, con rendimiento de intereses;
∼-bearing deposits n pl depósitos que
devengan interés m pl; **∼-bearing
liabilities** n pl obligaciones que devengan
intereses f pl; **∼-bearing security** n título
con intereses m; **∼ charges** n pl (on loan)
gastos de intereses m pl; **∼ coupon** n
cupón de intereses m; **∼ earned** n intereses
recibidos m pl; **∼-free** adj sin intereses;
∼-free deposit n depósito sin intereses m;
∼-free loan n préstamo sin intereses m; **∼
group** n grupo de interés m; **∼ income** n
ingresos por interés m pl, interés devengado
m; **∼ on arrears** n interés de moratorio m;
∼ on bonds n interés sobre bonos m;
∼-only loan n préstamo con amortización
al vencimiento m; **∼ paid** n intereses
pagados m pl; **∼ payment** n pago de
intereses m; **∼ penalty** n penalización en
los intereses f; **∼ policy** n póliza con
interés asegurable f; **∼ rate** n tipo m or
tasa f de interés; **∼ rate adjustment** n
ajuste del tipo de interés m; **∼ rate ceiling**
n techo del tipo de interés m; **∼ rate
reduction** n reducción de los tipos de
interés f; **∼ rate risk** n riesgo de la tasa de
interés m; **∼ received** n interés recibido
m; **∼ relief** n desgravación de los intereses f;

∼ spread n márgenes de variación de
intereses m pl

interested n interesado; **∼ in (doing) sth**
interesado en (hacer) algo; **∼ party** n parte
interesada f

interface¹ n interfaz m or f

interface² **1** vt conectar
2 vi interconectar

interfere vi entrometerse; **∼ in sth**
entrometerse en algo; **∼ with sth** afectar (a)
algo

interference n intromisión f; (Comp)
interferencia f

inter-firm adj (comparison) entre empresas,
inter-empresas

intergovernmental adj
intergubernamental

intergroup adj (relations) intergrupal

interim¹ adj (agreement, loan, solution)
provisional; (chairman, audit, pension) interino;
(financing) temporal; **∼ accounts** n pl
cuentas f pl interinas or intermedias; **∼
certificate** n (Stock) certificado provisional
m; **∼ dividend** n dividendo a cuenta m; **∼
injunction** n interdicto m; **∼ profits** n pl
beneficios trimestrales m pl; **∼ report** n, **∼
statement** n informe provisional m; **∼
statements** n pl (Acc) estados m pl
intermedios or provisionales

interim² n intermedio n; **in the ∼** en el
ínterin

interindustry adj (trade) interindustrial,
entre industrias

interlinked adj (transactions) vinculado

interlocking: **∼ directorate** n (Law)
consejos de administración coincidentes m
pl; (Mgmnt) junta directiva vinculada f; **∼
directorship** n dirección mancomunada f

interlocutory adj interlocutorio; **∼
decree** n (Law) auto interlocutorio m

intermedia adj (comparisons) entre medios
de comunicación

intermediary¹ adj (corporation, goods)
intermediario

intermediary² n intermediario(-a) m,f

intermediate adj (stage, step, technology)
intermedio; (credit, loan, financing) a medio
plazo; **∼-term credit** n crédito a medio
plazo m

intermediation n intermediación f

intermittent adj (production) intermitente

internal adj (check, debt, financing,
communications, frontier) interno; (flight)
nacional; **∼ audit** n intervención interior
de cuentas f; **∼ market** n mercado interno
m; **∼ rate of return** n tasa de rendimiento
interna f; **I∼ Revenue Service** n AmE (cf
▶**Inland Revenue (Office)** BrE)

≈ Hacienda *f*; ~ **storage** *n* (Comp) memoria interna *f*

internalization *n* internalización *f*

internalize *vt* internalizar

internally *adv* (distribute, review) dentro de la organización; (finance) con recursos propios; ~-**funded pension** *n* pensión de financiación interna *f*; ~-**generated funds** *n pl* fondos generados internamente *m pl*

international *adj* (affairs, trade, banking, travel, agreement) internacional; **I**~ **Air Transport Association** *n* Asociación Internacional de Transporte Aéreo *f*; **I**~ **Bank for Economic Cooperation** *n* Banco Internacional para la Cooperación Económica *m*; **I**~ **Bank for Reconstruction and Development** *n* Banco Internacional para la Reconstrucción y el Desarrollo *m*; ~ **call** *n* (Comms) llamada internacional *f*; **I**~ **Commercial Term** *n* cláusula comercial internacional *f*; **I**~ **Court of Justice** *n* Tribunal Internacional de Justicia *m*; **I**~ **Development Association** *n* Asociación Internacional de Fomento *f*; ~ **direct dialing** AmE, ~ **direct dialling** BrE *n* discado internacional directo *m* AmL; ~ **driving licence** BrE, ~ **driver's license** AmE *n* carnet *m or* permiso *m* de conducir internacional; **I**~ **Finance Corporation** *n* Corporación de Finanzas Internacionales *f*; **I**~ **Labor Organization** AmE, **I**~ **Labour Organization** BrE *n* Organización Internacional de Trabajo *f*; ~ **law** *n* derecho internacional *m*; **I**~ **Monetary Fund** *n* Fondo Monetario Internacional *m*; **I**~ **Monetary Market** *n* Mercado Monetario Internacional *m*; ~ **money draft** *n* giro monetario internacional *m*; ~ **money order** *n* giro postal internacional *m*; **I**~ **Options Market** *n* Mercado Internacional de Opciones *m*; ~ **payment order** *n* orden de pago internacional *f*; ~ **relations** *n pl* relaciones internacionales *f pl*; ~ **standard** *n* norma internacional *f*; **I**~ **Standard Book Number** *n* Numeración Internacional Normalizada de Libros *f*; **I**~ **Standards Organization** *n* Organización Internacional de Normalización *f*; **I**~ **Telecommunications Union** *n* Unión Internacional de Telecomunicaciones *f*; **I**~ **Trade Organization** *n* Organización Internacional de Comercio *f*

internationalism *n* internacionalismo *m*

internationalization *n* internacionalización *f*

internationalize *vt* internacionalizar

Internet *n* Internet *m*; **be connected to the** ~ estar conectado al Internet; **on the** ~ en el Internet; **find sth on the** ~ encontrar algo en el Internet; ~ **access** *n* acceso al Internet *m*; ~ **access provider** *n* proveedor de acceso de Internet *m*; ~ **account** *n* cuenta de Internet *f*; ~ **address** *n* dirección Internet *f*; ~ **advertising** *n* publicidad en el Internet *f*; ~ **bank** *n* banco electrónico *m*; ~ **banking** *n* banca electrónica *f*; ~ **billing** *n* factura en línea *f*; ~ **business** *n* negocio Internet *m*; ~ **café** *n* cibercafé *m*; ~ **chat** *n* charla *f*, chat *m*; ~ **commerce** *n* comercio electrónico *or* en línea; ~ **company** *n* compañía de Internet *f*; ~ **conferencing** *n* conferencia por Internet *f*; ~ **connection** *n* conexión al Internet *f*; ~-**enabled** *adj* preparado para Internet; ~ **marketing** *n* marketing por la Red *m*; ~ **marketplace** *n* cibermercado *m*; ~ **number** *n* número Internet *m*; ~ **phone** *n* teléfono Internet *m*; ~ **presence** *n* presencia en Internet *f*; ~ **presence provider** *n* proveedor de espacio web *m*; ~ **protocol** *n* protocolo de Internet *m*; ~ **protocol address** *n* dirección de protocolo de Internet *m*; ~ **relay chat** *n* charla interactiva Internet *f*; ~ **revolution** *n* revolución Internet *f*; ~ **search** *n* búsqueda en el Internet *f*; ~ **security** *n* seguridad de Internet *f*; ~ **server** *n* servidor de Internet *m*; ~ **service provider** *n* proveedor de servicios Internet *m*; ~ **shopping** *n* compras on-line *f pl*; ~ **site** *n* sitio web *m*, site *f*; ~ **startup** *n* compañía Internet de nueva creación *f*; ~ **storefront** *n* escaparate electrónico *m*; ~ **telephone** *n* teléfono Internet *m*; ~ **telephony** *n* telefonía Internet *f*; ~ **transaction** *n* transacción por Internet *f*; ~ **use** *n* uso del Internet *m*; ~ **user** *n* usuario(-a) del Internet *m,f*

interoperability *n* interoperabilidad *f*

interpersonal *adj* (skills) interpersonal

interplay *n* efecto recíproco *m*

interpolation *n* interpolación *f*

interpret **1** *vt* (action, remark, sign, statistics) interpretar
2 *vi* (work as interpreter) hacer de *or* trabajar como intérprete

interpretation *n* interpretación *f*

interpreter *n* (in languages) intérprete *mf*; (in programming) interpretador *m*

interpreting *n* interpretación *f*

interrelation *n* interrelación *f*

interrogatories *n pl* (Law) interrogatorios *m pl*

interruption *n* interrupción *f*

interstate *adj* interestatal, entre estados; ~ **highway** *n* AmE carretera interestatal *f*

interval n intervalo m; **at ~s of 20 minutes** o **at 20-minute ~s** a intervalos de 20 minutos

intervene vi intervenir; **~ in sth** intervenir en algo

intervention n intervención f; **~ currency** n moneda de intervención f; **~ price** n precio de intervención m

interventionist[1] adj intervencionista

interventionist[2] n intervencionista mf

interview[1] n (for job) entrevista f; (Media) entrevista f, interviú f; **arrange an ~** concertar una entrevista; **he was called for an ~** lo citaron para una entrevista

interview[2] vt entrevistar

interviewee n entrevistado(-a) m,f

interviewer n entrevistador(a) m,f; **~ bias** n parcialidad del entrevistador f

inter vivos adv entre vivos; **~ trust** n fideicomiso entre vivos m

intestate adj intestado; **die ~** morir intestado

in-the-money adj (Stock) dentro del precio

intimidation n intimidación f

in toto adv totalmente

intra-Community adj (EU) (obs) intracomunitario (obs)

intradepartmental adj intradepartamental

intra-EU trade n comercio interior de la UE m

intragroup adj intragrupal

intramedia adj (comparisons) dentro de los medios de comunicación

intranet n intranet m

intrastate adj AmE intraestatal

intra vires adj dentro de su competencia

in-tray n bandeja f; **~ exercise** n ejercicio en curso m

intrinsic adj (value, motivation) intrínseco

introduce vt (person, bill) presentar; (legislation, tax, practice, subject) introducir; (product) lanzar, sacar

introduction n (of person, bill) presentación f; (of legislation, tax, practice, to activity, subject, book) introducción f; (Stock) nueva emisión de valores no directamente en bolsa

introductory adj (offer, stage) preliminar; (price, chapter) de introducción; (remarks) preliminar; (course) de introducción, de iniciación

intrusive adj intruso

intuitive adj (knowledge, management) intuitivo

inure [1] vt habituar; **~ sb to sth** habituar a alguien a algo
[2] vi (frml) tener efecto

inv. abbr (►**invoice**[1]) factura f

invalid adj (contract, will) inválido, no válido; (assumption, conclusion) inválido

invalidate vt invalidar

invalidation n invalidación f

invaluable adj inapreciable

invent vt inventar

invention n invención f

inventor n inventor(a) m,f

inventory[1] n (list, stocktaking) inventario m; (stock) existencias f pl; **closed for ~** AmE cerrado por inventario; **draw up an ~ of sth** hacer (un) inventario de algo; **~ allowance** n desgravación por inventario f; **~ analysis** n análisis de inventarios m; **~ book** n libro m de almacén or de inventario; **~ certificate** n certificado de inventarios m; **~ control** n control de existencias m; **~ controller** n controlador(a) de existencias m,f; **~ costing** n cálculo m de costes Esp or costos AmL de inventario; **~ financing** n financiación del inventario f; **~ management** n dirección f or gerencia f de inventario; **~ planning** n planificación del inventario f; **~ pricing** n fijación de precios del inventario f; **~ turnover** n rotación de existencias f

inventory[2] vt hacer (un) inventario de, inventariar

inverse adj inverso

inversely adv inversamente

invert vt invertir

inverted adj (scale, market) invertido; **~ commas** n pl BrE comillas f pl

invest [1] vt (money, capital, time) invertir; **~ sth in sth** invertir algo en algo
[2] vi invertir; **~ in shares/property/an annuity** invertir en acciones/propiedades/una renta anual

invested adj (money, capital, time) invertido

investee n participado m

investible adj invertible

investigate vt (question, crime) investigar; (complaint, claim, possibility) estudiar, examinar

investigating committee n comisión investigadora f

investigation n (examination) estudio m; (official) investigación f; **her claim is under ~** se está estudiando su petición; **upon closer ~** tras un examen más detenido

investigative adj investigador; **~ journalism** n periodismo de investigación m

investigatory adj (powers) indagatorio

investment n inversión f; **~ in sth** inversión en algo; **~ abroad** n inversión exterior f; **~ account** n cuenta de inversiones f; **~ activity** n actividad inversionista f; **~ advice** n notificación de inversión *f*; ∼ **adviser** *n* asesor(a) de inversiones *m,f*; (Stock) consultor(a) de inversiones *m,f*; ∼ **allowance** *n* (Tax) desgravación por inversión *f*; ∼ **analyst** *n* analista de inversiones *mf*; ∼ **appraisal** *n* evaluación de inversiones *f*; ∼ **bank** *n* AmE (*cf* ▸**merchant bank** BrE) banco de negocios *m*; ∼ **banker** *n* AmE (*cf* ▸**merchant banker** BrE) banquero(-a) comercial *m,f*; ∼ **banking** *n* AmE (*cf* ▸**merchant banking** BrE) banca de negocios *f*; ∼ **base** *n* base de inversión *f*; ∼ **budget** *n* presupuesto de inversiones *m*; ∼ **capital** *n* capital de inversión *m*; ∼ **company** *n* compañía inversionista *f*; ∼ **consultant** *n* asesor(a) de inversiones *m,f*; ∼ **contract** *n* contrato de inversión *m*; ∼ **fund** *n* fondo de inversión *m*; ∼ **grant** *n* subvención para inversiones *f*; ∼ **incentive** *n* incentivo a la inversión *m*; ∼ **income** *n* ingresos derivados de inversiones *m pl*; ∼ **loss** *n* pérdidas de inversión *f pl*; ∼ **management** *n* gestión *f or* dirección *f* de inversiones; **I**∼ **Management Regulatory Organization** BrE *n organización reguladora de gestores de inversiones*; ∼ **opportunity** *n* oportunidad de inversión *f*; ∼ **portfolio** *n* cartera de inversiones *f*; ∼ **property** *n* propiedad de inversión *f*; ∼ **revenue** *n* rédito de inversiones *m*; ∼ **savings account** *n* cuenta de ahorro para inversión *f*; ∼ **service** *n* servicio de inversión *m*; ∼ **software** *n* aplicaciones informáticas para inversión *f pl*; ∼ **tax credit** *n* bonificación tributaria a la inversión *f*; ∼ **trust** *n* compañía inversionista *f*; ∼ **yield** *n* rendimiento de la inversión *m*

investor *n* inversor(a) *m,f*, inversionista *mf*

invisible *adj* (earnings, exports, imports, trade) invisible

invisibles *n pl* partidas invisibles *f pl*

invitation *n* invitación *f*

invite *vt* (person) invitar; (suggestions) pedir, solicitar; (criticism) provocar; ∼ **sb for interview** llamar a alguien a una entrevista; ∼ **tenders** solicitar ofertas; ∼ **sb to do sth** invitar a alguien a hacer algo *or* que haga algo

invoice¹ *n* factura *f*; ∼ **book** *n* libro de facturas *m*; ∼ **clerk** *n* encargado(-a) de facturación *m,f*; ∼ **date** *n* BrE (*cf* ▸**billing date** AmE) fecha de facturación *f*; ∼**s inwards** BrE, ∼**s inward** AmE *n pl* facturas recibidas *f pl*; ∼ **payable** *n* factura a pagar *f*; ∼ **price** *n* precio de factura *m*; ∼ **receivable** *n* factura a cobrar *f*

invoice² ⟦1⟧ *vt* (goods) facturar; ∼ **sb (for sth)** pasarle a alguien factura (por algo) ⟦2⟧ *vi* facturar, hacer facturas

invoicing *n* facturación *f*; ∼ **amount** *n* volumen de facturación *m*; ∼ **department** *n* BrE (*cf* ▸**billing department** AmE) departamento de facturación *m*

invoke *vt* (law, penalty) invocar

involuntary *adj* (bankruptcy, liquidation, unemployment) involuntario

involve *vt* (work, time, expense) suponer; ∼ **sb in sth** (allow to participate) hacer participar a alguien en algo; (implicate) implicar *or* involucrar a alguien en algo; **he doesn't ∼ himself in the day-to-day running of the business** no toma parte en la gestión diaria del negocio

involvement *n* participación *f*

inward *adj* (investment, investor) extranjero; (cargo, charges) de entrada; ∼ **bill of lading** *n* conocimiento de embarque en la entrada *m*

IO *abbr* (▸**immigration officer**) funcionario(-a) de inmigración *m,f*; (▸**industrial organization**) organización industrial *f*

I/O *abbr* (▸**input/output**) (Comp) E/S (entrada/salida)

IOU *abbr* (▸**I owe you**) pagaré *m*

I owe you *n* (▸**IOU**) pagaré *m*

IP *abbr* (▸**Internet protocol**) protocolo de Internet *m*; ∼ **address** *n* dirección IP *f*

IPM *abbr* (▸**integrated project management**) gestión integrada de proyectos *f*

IPO *abbr* (▸**initial public offering**) OPI (oferta pública inicial); (▸**internationial payment order**) orden de pago internacional *m*

IR *abbr* (▸**industrial relations**) relaciones industriales *f pl*; BrE (▸**Inland Revenue**, *cf* ▸**IRS** AmE) ≈ Hacienda *f*

IRA *abbr* AmE (▸**individual retirement account**) cuenta de jubilación individual *f*; ∼ **rollover** *n* AmE renovación de cuenta de jubilación individual *f*

IRC *abbr* (▸**Internet relay chat**) charla interactiva Internet *f*

IRO *abbr* BrE (▸**Inland Revenue Office**, *cf* ▸**IRS** AmE) ≈ Hacienda *f*

IRR *abbr* (▸**internal rate of return**) TRI (tasa de rendimiento interna)

irredeemable *adj* irrescatable, no ejecutable

irreducible *adj* irreductible

irrefutable *adj* irrefutable

irregular *adj* (in shape, time) irregular; (contrary to rules) inadmisible, contrario a las normas; AmE (goods, stock) defectuoso; ∼ **market** *n* mercado irregular *m*

irregularity *n* irregularidad *f*

irrelevant *adj* (fact, detail) irrelevante; **be ∼ to sth** no tener relación *or* no tener que ver con algo; **be ∼ to sb** serle indiferente a alguien

irreparable *adj* (damage, harm) irreparable

irreplaceable *adj* irreemplazable

irrespective of *prep* con independencia de

irreversible *adj* (decision) irrevocable; (strategy) irreversible

irrevocable *adj* (decision, credit, trust fund) irrevocable; **∼ letter of credit** *n* crédito documentario irrevocable *m*

IRS *abbr* AmE (▶**Internal Revenue Service**, *cf* ▶**IR** BrE) ≈ Hacienda *f*

ISA *abbr* (▶**individual savings account**) BrE *cuenta de ahorros particular libre de impuestos*

ISBN *abbr* (▶**International Standard Book Number**) ISBN *f* (Numeración Internacional Normalizada de Libros)

ISDN *abbr* (▶**integrated services digital network**) RDSI *f* (red digital de servicios integrados)

island *n* (S&M) isla de venta *f*; **∼ display** *n mercancía expuesta fuera de los estantes en una tienda*; **∼ site** *n* anuncio fuera de espacio publicitario *m*

ISO *abbr*; (▶**incentive stock option**) AmE ISO (incentivo fiscal sobre opciones); (▶**International Standards Organization**) OIN (Organización Internacional de Normalización)

isolate *vt* aislar

isolationist *adj* aislacionista

ISP *abbr* (▶**Internet service provider**) proveedor de servicios Internet *m*

issuance *n* coste *m* Esp *or* costo *m* AmL de emisión; **∼ facility** *n* mecanismo de emisión *m*

issue¹ *n* (subject) asunto *m*, cuestión *f*; (controversy) controversia *f*; (of book) edición *f*; (copy) ejemplar *m*, número *m*; (of shares, debentures) emisión *f*; (progeny) descendientes *m pl*; **at ∼** en litigio; **take over an ∼** (Stock) hacerse cargo de una emisión; **the ∼ was undersubscribed** (Stock) la emisión no fue suscrita en su totalidad; **∼ date** *n* fecha

de emisión *f*; **∼ market** *n* mercado *m* primario *or* de emisiones; **∼ price** *n* precio de emisión *m*

issue² *vt* (shares, message) emitir; (letter of credit) abrir; (cheque, insurance policy) extender; (magazine, newspaper) editar; (prospectus) sacar; **∼ a writ against sb** dictar un auto contra alguien

issued *adj* (share, capital) emitido; **∼ and in circulation** emitido y en circulación

issuer *n* emisor(a) *m,f*

issuing *adj* (company, house) emisor; (bank) de emisión; **∼ authority** *n* (for passport) autoridad expedidora *f*

IT *abbr* (▶**income tax**) ≈ IRPF *m* (impuesto sobre la renta (de las personas físicas)); (▶**industrial tribunal**) BrE tribunal laboral *m*, magistratura del trabajo *f*; (▶**information technology**) informática *f*; **∼ company** *n* (▶**information technology company**) empresa de tecnología de la información *f*

italic *adj* en cursiva, en bastardilla

italics *n* cursiva *f*, bastardilla *f*

item *n* (in account) partida *f*; (point) punto *m*; (in shop, newspaper) artículo *m*; (detail) detalle *m*; **∼s on the agenda** *n pl* asuntos de la agenda *m pl*; **∼ of expenditure** *n* partida de gastos *f*

itemization *n* (of invoice) detalle *m*

itemize *vt* detallar

itemized *adj* (bill, invoice) detallado

iteration *n* (Comp) iteración *f*

iterative warnings *n pl* (Comp) advertencias iterativas *f pl*

itinerant *adj* (worker) itinerante; (salesperson) ambulante

itinerary *n* itinerario *m*

ITM *abbr* (▶**in-the-money**) (Stock) dentro del precio

ITO *abbr* (▶**International Trade Organization**) OIC *f* (Organización Internacional de Comercio)

ITU *abbr* (▶**International Telecommunications Union**) UIT *f* (Unión Internacional de Telecomunicaciones)

Jj

J/A *abbr* (▸**joint account**) cuenta conjunta *f*

jacket *n* (on disk) cubierta exterior *f*; (on book) camisa *f*, sobrecubierta *f*

jackpot *n* (in lottery) bote *m*, pozo *m*; **hit the** ∼ *infrml* sacarse el gordo

jack up *vt infrml* (price, rent) subir, aumentar

jam¹ *n* (of printer) atasco *m*; *infrml* (difficult situation) aprieto *m*; **be in/get into a** ∼ *infrml* estar en/meterse en un aprieto

jam² *vi* (printer) atascarse

japanization *n* japonización *f*

jargon *n* jerga *f*

Java® *n* (Comp) Java® *m*

JDI *abbr* (▸**joint declaration of interest**) declaración conjunta de interés *f*

jeopardize *vt* poner en peligro, arriesgar

jeopardy *n* peligro *m*; **put sth/sb in** ∼ poner algo/a alguien en peligro

jerque note *n* (Imp/Exp) certificado de declaración de entrada *m*

jet-lagged *adj* desfasado por el viaje

Jiffy bag® *n* sobre acolchado *m*

jingle *n* jingle (publicitario) *m*

JIT *abbr* (▸**just-in-time**) JIT (justo a tiempo) AmL, según demanda Esp; ∼ **production** *n* producción *f* justo a tiempo AmL *or* según demanda Esp

jitters *n pl infrml* mieditis *f infrml*; **get** *o* **have the** ∼ tener mieditis

jittery *adj* nervioso

jnr. *abbr* (▸**junior**) hijo *m*

job *n* (task) trabajo *m*, tarea *f*; (post) empleo *m*, trabajo *m*, puesto (de trabajo) *m*; **give sth/sb up as a bad** ∼ dejar algo/a alguien por imposible; **have a** ∼ tener trabajo; **have a** ∼ **in publishing** trabajar en una editorial; **know one's** ∼ conocer su oficio; **make a good/poor** ∼ **of sth** hacer algo bien/mal; **it's not my** ∼ (responsibility) no es asunto mío; **I'm only doing my** ∼ (duty) estoy cumpliendo con mi deber; **put sb in for a** ∼ recomendar a alguien para un puesto; **take a** ∼ aceptar un trabajo; ∼ **advertisement** *n* anuncio de empleo *m*; ∼ **application** *n* solicitud de empleo *f*; ∼ **appraisal** *n* estimación de empleo *f*, evaluación del puesto *f*; ∼ **assignment** *n* asignación *f* de empleo *or* de puestos; ∼ **breakdown** *n* (responsibilities of given post) desglose del trabajo *m*; (distribution of tasks) distribución de

trabajo *f*; ∼ **club** *n* BrE grupo de asesoramiento para desempleados; ∼ **cluster** *n* agrupación laboral *f*; ∼ **control** *n* control de trabajos *m*; ∼ **costing** *n* coste *m* Esp *or* costo *m* AmL del trabajo; ∼ **creation** *n* creación de empleos *f*; ∼ **creation scheme** *n* plan de creación de empleos *m*; ∼ **description** *n* descripción del puesto *f*; ∼ **design** *n* diseño de un puesto de trabajo *m*; ∼ **enlargement** *n* enriquecimiento *m or* expansión *f* del trabajo; ∼ **entry** *n* (Comp) entrada de trabajo *f*; ∼ **expectations** *n pl* expectativas de empleo *f pl*; ∼ **flexibility** *n* flexibilidad del puesto de trabajo *f*; ∼ **hopper** *n persona que cambia frecuentemente de trabajo*; ∼ **hopping** *n cambio frecuente de trabajo*; ∼ **hunter** *n* persona que busca empleo *f*; ∼ **hunting** *n* búsqueda de empleo *f*; ∼ **market** *n* mercado *m* laboral *or* de trabajo; ∼ **mobility** *n* movilidad *f* laboral *or* de trabajo; ∼ **offer** *n* oferta *f* de empleo *or* de trabajo; ∼ **opening** *n* vacante *f*; ∼ **opportunity** *n* oportunidad de empleo *f*; ∼ **order** *n* orden de trabajo *f*; ∼ **performance** *n* desempeño del puesto *f*, ejecución del trabajo *f*; ∼ **profile** *n* perfil del puesto *m*; ∼ **prospects** *n pl* perspectivas *f pl* laborales *or* de empleo; ∼ **queue** *n* (at printer) cola de espera de trabajos *f*; ∼**-related injury** *n* lesión laboral *f*; ∼ **requirement** *n* requisito del puesto *m*; ∼ **rotation** *n* rotación de trabajos *f*; ∼ **satisfaction** *n* satisfacción del trabajo *f*; ∼ **search** *n* búsqueda de puesto de trabajo *f*; ∼ **security** *n* seguridad del puesto de trabajo *f*; ∼ **seeker** *n* persona que busca trabajo *f*; ∼ **seeker's allowance** *n* BrE prestación por desempleo *f*; ∼ **share** *n* trabajo compartido *m*; ∼ **share scheme** *n* plan de empleo compartido *m*; ∼ **sharing** *n sistema en el cual dos personas comparten un puesto de trabajo*; ∼ **skills** *n pl* capacidad profesional *f*; ∼ **spec** *n* (infrml) detalles *m pl or* perfil *m* del puesto; ∼ **specification** *n* detalles *m pl or* perfil *m* del puesto; ∼ **stream** *n* (Comp) secuencia de entrada *f*; ∼ **study** *n* estudio laboral *m*; ∼ **title** *n* denominación del puesto *f*; ∼ **training** *n* formación *f or* capacitación *f* en el puesto de trabajo; ∼ **vacancy** *n* vacante de puesto de trabajo *f*

job-backwards *vi* (jarg) especular en contratos de futuros

jobber n (jarg) operador(a) de la bolsa m,f, corredor(a) intermediario(-a) m,f

jobbery n agiotaje m

jobbing n (on stock market) especulación f; (piecework) trabajo a destajo m; (temporary work) trabajo temporal m

Jobcentre n BrE ≈ Servicios Integrados para el Empleo m

jobless¹ adj desempleado, parado Esp

jobless² n pl desempleados m pl

job lot n saldo de artículos m

job-share vi compartir el trabajo

jobsworth n BrE (infrml) una persona oficial con poca autoridad que utiliza su poder para implantar su ley

jockey n (jarg) (Fin) maniobrero m

jogging n (jarg) (Bank) batido de las fichas para alineamiento m

join vt (firm) entrar en or a AmL; (union) afiliarse a; (EU) ingresar (en); ~ **the dole queue** BrE (infrml) unirse a la fila de gente que cobra subsidio de desempleo; ~ **forces (with sb)** unirse (a alguien); **join together** vi (companies) juntarse

joinder n incorporación f

joint adj (decision, initiative, statement) conjunto; (agreement) mutuo; (effort) colectivo; ~ **account** n cuenta conjunta f; ~ **action** n acción conjunta f; ~ **assignment** n cesión conjunta f; ~ **authorization** n autorización mancomunada f; ~ **bank account** n cuenta bancaria conjunta f; ~ **bond** n bono de deuda solidaria m; ~ **committee** n comisión mixta f, comité paritario m; ~ **consultation** n (HRM) coconsulta f; (Mgmnt) consulta f conjunta or en común or colectiva; ~ **consultative committee** n comisión f consultiva mixta or mixta obrero-patronal; ~ **custody** n custodia conjunta f; ~ **debtor** n deudor(a) solidario(-a) m,f; ~ **declaration of interest** n declaración conjunta de interés f; ~ **demand** n demanda conjunta f; ~ **designation** n designación conjunta f; ~ **director** n codirector(a) m,f; ~ **equity venture company** n empresa conjunta f; ~ **estate** n copropiedad f, propiedad mancomunada f; ~ **financing** n financiación conjunta f; ~ **heir** n coheredero(-a) m,f; ~ **holder** n tenedor(a) indiviso(-a) m,f; ~ **insurance** n seguro colectivo y conjunto m; ~ **liability** n responsabilidad f mancomunada or conjunta or solidaria; ~ **loan** n préstamo mancomunado m; ~ **management** n codirección f; ~ **manager** n cogerente m,f; ~ **occupancy** n ocupación conjunta f; ~ **operator** n cooperador(a) m,f, operador(a) conjunto(-a) m,f; ~ **owner** n copropietario(-a) m,f, codueño(-a) m,f,

condómino(-a) m,f; ~ **ownership** n copropiedad f, condominio m; ~ **partnership** n coasociación f; J~ **Photographic Experts Group** n grupo de expertos fotográficos m; ~ **representation** n representación f colectiva or conjunta; ~ **return** n (Tax) declaración conjunta sobre la renta f; ~ **and several liability** n responsabilidad solidaria f; ~ **signature** n firma conjunta f; ~ **stock company** n sociedad en comandita por acciones f; ~ **tenancy** n coarriendo m; ~ **venture** n (undertaking) coinversión f; (company) empresa conjunta f; ~-**venture company** n compañía f de coinversión or de inversión conjunta f

jointly adv mancomunadamente; ~ **liable** responsable mancomunado; ~ **and severally** mancomunada y solidariamente

joker n AmE (Law) disposición engañosa f

jot down vt anotar

journal n diario m; ~ **entry** n anotación f or apunte m or asiento m en el libro diario; ~ **voucher** n comprobante de diario m

journalize vt contabilizar

journey n viaje m; ~ **cycle** n (S&M) ciclo de viaje m

JP abbr (▸**Justice of the Peace**) juez(a) de paz m,f

JPEG abbr (▸**Joint Photographic Experts Group**) JPEG m, formato JPEG m (grupo de expertos fotográficos)

jr. abbr (▸**junior**) hijo m

judge¹ n juez(a) m,f

judge² **1** vt (case, person) juzgar; (situation) evaluar
2 vi juzgar; **judging by sth** a juzgar por algo

judgment n (sense, discernment) juicio m, criterio m; (estimation) cálculo m; (view) opinión f; (Law) fallo m, sentencia f; (in arbitration) fallo m, laudo m; (Prop) indemnización f; **against your better** ~ en contra de lo que te aconseja tu juicio; **in my** ~ a mi juicio; **pass** ~ **on sth/sb** juzgar algo/a alguien; **sit in** ~ **over sb** enjuiciar a alguien; **use one's** ~ usar su propio criterio; ~ **creditor** n AmE acreedor(a) m,f judicial or por sentencia firme; ~ **debtor** n AmE deudor(a) m,f judicial or por sentencia firme

judicature n judicatura f

judicial adj (affairs, proceedings) judicial; ~ **foreclosure** n aprobación de remate f, venta judicial f; ~ **notice** n citación judicial f; ~ **sale** n aprobación de remate f, venta judicial f

judiciary n (judges) judicatura f; (arm of government) poder judicial m

jumbo n (infrml) (aircraft) jumbo m; ~ **jet** n jumbo m; ~ **loan** n préstamo m grande or de gran cuantía; ~ **pack** n envase gigante m

jump¹ n (increase) aumento m; **a 20% ~ in profits** un aumento del 20% en las ganancias

jump² vi (increase) subir de repente; ~ **at sth** aceptar algo sin pensarlo; **prices ~ed by 10%** los precios subieron un 10%; ~ **the gun** precipitarse; ~ **to conclusions** sacar conclusiones precipitadas

jumpy adj (market) indeciso, inestable

juncture n coyuntura f; **at this ~** en esta coyuntura

junior¹ adj (official) subalterno; (position) de subalterno; (younger) más joven m; **be ~ to sb** ser subalterno de alguien, estar por debajo de alguien; ~ **creditor** n acreedor(a) en segunda instancia m,f; ~ **debt** n deuda subordinada f; ~ **issue** n AmE (Stock) emisión de deuda subordinada f; ~ **management** n subdirección f; ~ **manager** n director(a) adjunto(-a) m,f; ~ **mortgage** n AmE (cf ▸**second mortgage** BrE) hipoteca en segundo grado f, segunda hipoteca f; ~ **partner** n socio(-a) menor m,f; ~ **security** n AmE título subordinado m; ~ **share** n acción subordinada f

junior² n (in rank) subalterno(-a) m,f; (son) hijo m

junk n (discarded items) trastos m pl; (worthless items) basura f (infrml); (Acc) existencias inmovilizadas f pl; ~ **bond** n bono basura m; ~ **e-mail** n propaganda de buzón f; ~

mail n propaganda de buzón f

junket¹ n (infrml) (on public expenses for private purposes) excursión f, viaje m

junket² vi (infrml) (on public expenses for private purposes) ir de excursión

juridical adj (position) jurídico

jurisdiction n jurisdicción f; **fall outside sb's ~** salirse de la competencia de alguien; ~ **dispute** n disputa jurisdiccional f

jurisdictional adj (dispute) jurisdiccional f; ~ **strike** n huelga de competencias f

jurisprudence n jurisprudencia f

jurist n jurista mf

juror n jurado mf

jury n jurado m; ~ **trial** n juicio con jurado m

just adj (law, decision) justo; (compensation) equitable, razonable

justice n justicia f; **get ~** obtener justicia; **J~ of the Peace** n juez(a) de paz m,f

justifiable adj justificable

justification n (of action, text) justificación f; ~ **character** n (Comp) carácter de encuadramiento m

justified adj (action, text, price) justificado; **be ~ (in doing sth)** tener razón (en hacer algo)

justify vt (action, text) justificar

just-in-time adj (model, production) justo a tiempo AmL, según demanda Esp

juvenile court n tribunal de menores m

JV abbr (▸**joint venture**) (undertaking) coinversión f; (company) empresa conjunta f

Kk

kanban *n* ficha de reposición *f*

KBS *abbr* (▸**knowledge-based system**) sistema experto *m*

keep¹ *vt* (job) mantener, conservar; (receipt) guardar, conservar; (shop) tener; (accounts, register) llevar; (appointment) acudir a; (agreement) respetar; (law, promise) cumplir (con); ∼ **the change** quédese con la vuelta; ∼ **sth going** seguir adelante con algo; ∼ **sth (a) secret** mantener algo en segreto; ∼ **sb waiting** hacer esperar a alguien; **keep back** *vt* (information, facts) ocultar; (percentage) retener; (profits) guardarse, quedarse con; **keep to** *vt* (agreement, arrangement, plan) ceñirse a; (promise) cumplir (con); **keep up with** *vt* (developments) continuar con; (payments) seguir el ritmo de; (standards) atenderse a; **incomes didn't** ∼ **up with prices** los ingresos no se mantuvieron a la par de los precios

keep² *n* sustento *m*; **earn one's** ∼ ganarse el pan

kerb market *n* BrE (*cf* ▸**curb market** AmE) bolsín *m*

kerbside conference *n* BrE (*cf* ▸**curbside conference** AmE) *discusión de técnicas de venta entre alumno e instructor*

key¹ *adj* (factor, element, feature, role) clave; ∼ **currency** *n* divisa de referencia *f*; ∼ **data** *n pl* datos básicos *m pl*; ∼ **industry** *n* industria clave *f*; ∼ **point** *n* punto vital *m*; ∼ **rate** *n* (of interest) proporción clave *f*; (of wage) tarifa clave *f*; ∼ **stage** *n* fase clave *f*

key² *n* (for lock) llave *f*; (crucial element) clave *f*; **the** ∼ **to sth** la clave de algo; ∼ **money** *n* (for flat) dinero dado como señal *m*; ∼ **sequence** *n* (Comp) secuencia por clave *f*

key³ *vt* (text, data) teclear; ∼ **sth to sth** adjustar algo a algo; **key in** *vt* (text, data) teclear

keyboard *n* teclado *m*; ∼**-operated** *adj* manejado mediante teclado; ∼ **operator** *n* operador(a) de teclado *m,f*

keylock *n* (Comp) cerradura de seguridad *f*

Keynesian *adj* (economics) keynesiano

keypad *n* teclado numérico *m*

keypunch *n* perforadora de teclado *f*

keypuncher *n* perforista *mf*

keystroke *n* pulsación *f*; ∼ **rate** *n* coeficiente de pulsaciones *m*

keyword *n* palabra clave *f*; ∼ **search** *n* búsqueda de palabra clave *f*

kickback *n* (infrml) soborno *m*, cohecho *m*, comisión ilícita *f*

kickstart *vt* (process) darle el puntapié inicial a; ∼ **the economy** darle impulso a la reactivación de la economía

kiddie tax *n* AmE (infrml) *impuesto que los niños menores de 14 años deben pagar por intereses y dividendos superiores a $1000*

kill *vt* (demand) matar; (rumour, hope, enthusiasm) acabar con

killer bond *n* bono matador *m*

killing *n* (infrml) éxito financiero *m*; **make a** ∼ hacer el agosto

kind *n*: **in** ∼ (payment, benefits) en especie

kite *n* (jarg) letra *f* de colisión *or* de pelota

kiting *n* AmE circulación de cheques en descubierto *f*

knock¹ *n* (setback) golpe *m*; (infrml) (criticism) crítica *f*

knock² *vt* (infrml) (criticize) criticar; **knock down** *vt* (in auction, contract) adjudicar; (price, charge) rebajar; **knock off** *vi* (infrml) (finish work) cesar el trabajo

knockdown *adj* (price) mínimo

knocker *n* (infrml) (salesperson) vendedor(a) *m,f*; (critic) detractor(a) *m,f*

knock-for-knock *n* (jarg) (Ins) golpe por golpe

knocking copy *n* anuncio destinado a denigrar el producto de la competencia

knockoffs *n pl* (infrml) (clothing) imitaciones *f pl*

knock-on effect *n* repercusión *f*

knockout *n* (infrml) acuerdo entre los concursantes *m*; ∼ **agreement** *n* (infrml) acuerdo de competencia *m*; ∼ **competition** *n* concurso eliminatorio *m*

knowbot *n* robot de conocimiento *m*

know-how *n* know-how *m* (infrml), pericia *f*; ∼ **agreement** *n* acuerdo de asistencia técnica *m*

knowledge *n* conocimiento *m*; **it has come to my** ∼ **that...** ha llegado a mi conocimiento que...; **be common** *o* **public** ∼ ser del dominio público; **in the** ∼ **that...** a sabiendas de que...; **to my** ∼ que yo sepa; **without my** ∼ sin mi conocimiento; **have a working** ∼ **of sth** tener un conocimiento práctico de algo; ∼ **base** *n* base de conocimiento *f*; ∼**-based industry** *n* industria basada en el conocimiento *f*;

~-based system n sistema experto m; **~ economy** n economía del conocimiento f; **~ engineer** n ingeniero(-a) del conocimiento m,f; **~ engineering** n ingeniería del conocimiento f; **~-intensive** adj intensivo en conocimientos; **~ management** n gestión del conocimiento f; **~ sharing** n compartición del conocimiento f; **~ worker** n trabajador(a) del conocimiento m,f

knowledgeable adj inteligente

knowledgeware n software del conocimiento m

known adj conocido; **also ~ as** alias, también conocido como; **~ by name** conocido por su nombre; **~ loss** n (Ins) siniestro conocido m

kudos n prestigio m

k

Ll

L/A *abbr* (▶letter of authority) carta de autorización *f*; (▶Lloyd's Agent) representante de Lloyds *mf*

LAB *abbr* (▶local authority bill) certificado de la autoridad local *m*; (▶local authority bond) obligación de la administración local *f*

label¹ *n* (on goods, in computer program) etiqueta *f*; (brand name) marca *f*; (record company) sello discográfico *m*; ∼ **clause** *n* cláusula sobre etiquetas *f*; ∼ **of quality** *n* marchamo de calidad *m*

label² *vt* etiquetar

labelled BrE, **labeled** AmE *adj* etiquetado; ∼ **file** *n* fichero con etiqueta *m*

labelling BrE, **labeling** AmE *n* etiquetado *m*

labor AmE ▶**labour** BrE; ∼ **court** *n* AmE (*cf* ▶**industrial court** BrE) tribunal laboral *m*, magistratura del trabajo *f*; ∼ **union** *n* AmE (*cf* ▶**trade union** BrE) sindicato *m*

laborer AmE ▶**labourer** BrE

labour¹ BrE, **labor** AmE *n* (workforce) mano de obra *f*; (workers) obreros *m pl*; (task) tarea *f*; (work) trabajo *m*; **withdraw one's** ∼ ir a la huelga; ∼ **administration** *n* administración *f* or gestión *f* laboral; ∼ **agreement** *n* (HRM) acuerdo laboral *m*; (Ind, Law) convenio colectivo de trabajo *m*; ∼ **clause** *n* cláusula laboral *f*; ∼ **code** *n* código del trabajo *m*; ∼ **contract** *n* contrato de trabajo *m*; ∼ **costs** *n pl* coste *m* Esp or costo *m* AmL de mano de obra; ∼ **demand** *n* demanda *f* laboral or de mano de obra; ∼ **dispute** *n* conflicto *m* colectivo or laboral; ∼ **force** *n* mano de obra *f*; ∼-**intensive** *adj* (production) de alto coeficiente de mano de obra; (industry) con uso intensivo de mano de obra; ∼ **law** *n* ley laboral *f*; ∼ **market** *n* mercado *m* laboral or de trabajo; ∼ **mobility** *n* movilidad *f* laboral or de mano de obra; ∼ **movement** *n* movimiento obrero *m*; **L**∼ **Party** *n* BrE Partido Laborista *m*; ∼ **pool** *n* bolsa de trabajo *f*; ∼ **relations** *n pl* relaciones laborales *f pl*; ∼ **relations manager** *n* gerente de relaciones laborales *mf*; **L**∼ **Representation Committee** *n* comité de representación laboral; ∼-**saving** *adj* que ahorra trabajo; ∼ **shortage** *n* escasez de mano de obra *f*; ∼ **standard** *n* norma laboral *f*; ∼ **supply** *n* oferta *f* laboral or de trabajo; ∼ **troubles** *n pl* dificultades laborales *f pl*; ∼ **turnover** *n* rotación *f* de

mano de obra *or* de personal; ∼ **unrest** *n* descontento del personal *m*, inquietud laboral *f*

labour² BrE, **labor** AmE *vi* trabajar

labourer BrE, **laborer** AmE *n* operario(-a) *m,f*

laches *n* (Law) incuria *f*, negligencia en el ejercicio de un derecho *f*

lack¹ *n* falta *f*, escasez *f*, carencia *f*; **for** ∼ **of sth** por falta de algo

lack² *vt* (confidence, support) carecer de; **it** ∼**s originality** le falta originalidad

ladder *n* (scale) escala *f*; **start at the bottom of the** ∼ empezar desde abajo; **another step up the** ∼ **to sth** otro peldaño en la escalera hacia algo

lag *n* retardo *m*, retraso *m*; ∼ **response** *n* respuesta con retraso *f*

lag behind *vi* quedarse atrás

laggard *n* (jarg) (S&M) consumidor(a) conservador(a) *m,f*; (Stock) rezagado *m*

laissez-faire *n* laissez faire *m*; ∼ **economy** *n* economía liberal *f*

lame duck *n* (jarg) (company) deudor(a) insolvente *m,f*; (on stock market) especulador(a) insolvente *m,f*

LAN *abbr* (▶local area network) (Comp) RAL (red de área local)

land¹ *n* tierra *f*; (property) finca *f*, terreno *m*; (country) país *m*, nación *f*; ∼ **agent** *n* corredor(a) de fincas *m,f*; ∼ **compensation** *n* compensación de tierras *f*; ∼ **developer** *n* promotor(a) inmobiliario(-a) *m,f*; ∼ **development** *n* (Envir) explotación de la tierra *f*; (Prop) viabilización de tierras *f*; ∼ **economy** *n* economía de la tierra *f*; ∼ **grant** *n* concesión de terrenos *f*; ∼ **lease** *n* arrendamiento de tierras *m*; ∼ **office** *n* AmE (*cf* ▶**land registry** BrE) catastro *m*; ∼ **reform** *n* reforma agraria *f*; ∼ **registry** *n* BrE (*cf* ▶**land office** AmE) catastro *m*; ∼ **rent** *n* (Fin) renta de terreno *f*; (Prop) alquiler de la tierra *m*; ∼ **use** *n* utilización de la tierra *f*; ∼ **value tax** *n* impuesto sobre el valor de la tierra *m*

land² **1** *vt* (aircraft) hacer aterrizar; (passengers) desembarcar; (cargo) descargar; (job, contract) conseguir **2** *vi* (aircraft) aterrizar; (passengers) desembarcar

landed *adj* (cost) descargado; ∼ **property** *n* bienes raíces *m pl*

landfill site n vertedero m

landing card n tarjeta de desembarque f

landlord n arrendador m

landmark[1] adj (case) que hizo época, que sentó un precedente histórico

landmark[2] n punto prominente m

landowner n terrateniente mf, hacendado(-a) m,f

land-ownership n propiedad de la tierra f

landscape[1] adj (document layout) en formato horizontal or apaisado

landscape[2] n formato m horizontal or apaisado

landscape[3] vt crear una oficina de planificación abierta

language n lenguaje m; **in plain ~** (document, leaflet) en lenguaje claro; **~ barrier** n barrera f lingüística or del idioma

lapping n (Acc) falseamiento de la cuenta de clientes m

lapse[1] n (error) equivocación f; (interval) lapso m; (of contract) caducidad f; (of patent) expiración f; **~ of time** n lapso de tiempo m

lapse[2] vi (policy, contract) caducar

lapsed adj (discount, funds, option) caducado

lapsing n caducidad f

laptop n computadora f AmL or ordenador m Esp portátil, laptop m

large adj grande; (market) amplio; (order) importante; **in ~ quantities** en grandes cantidades; **~ exposure** n (Fin) gastos a gran escala m pl

largely adv en gran parte, ampliamente

large-scale adj (project, exporter, model) a gran escala; **~ integration** n (Comp) integración en gran escala f; **~ production** n producción en serie f

laser n láser m; **~ beam** n rayo láser m; **~ printer** n impresora láser f; **~ scanner** lector óptico m

lash out vi BrE (infrml) (spend) gastar un montón de dinero

last[1] adj último; **~ in, first out** último en entrar, primero en salir; **as a ~ resort** como último recurso; **~ day of trading** n último día de operaciones m; **~-minute decision** n decisión de última hora f; **~ number redial** n repetición f or marcación f automática del último número m; **~ sale** n última venta f; **~ will and testament** n testamento m

last[2] vi durar; **last out** vi (money, resources) durar

LATAG abbr (▶Latin American Trade Advisory Group) Grupo Consultor de Comercio Latinoamericano m

late[1] adj (far on in time) tarde; **at this ~ stage** a estas alturas; **be ~ for work** llegar tarde al trabajo; **in ~ April/summer** a finales or fines de abril/del verano; **be ~ with the rent** estar atrasado con el alquiler; **~ filer** n (of tax return) declarante fuera de plazo m; **~ filing** n (of tax return) presentación fuera de plazo f; **~ fringe** n AmE (Media) última franja horaria de emisión f; **~ payment** n pago tardío m

late[2] adv (arrive, leave) tarde; (work) hasta tarde

lateness n retraso m

latent adj (demand, tax) latente; **~ defect** n (Law) vicio oculto m

lateral adj lateral; **~ integration** n integración lateral f; **~ thinking** n pensamiento lateral m

latest adj (figures, estimate) último, más reciente; (fashion, model) último; **at the ~** a más tardar; **~ addition** n (to product range) novedad más reciente f; **~ date** n fecha límite f; **~ estimate** n última estimación f, estimación más reciente f

Latin American adj latinoamericano; **~ American Trade Advisory Group** n ≈ Grupo Consultor de Comercio Latinoamericano m

latitude n (of thinking) anchura f, latitud f

latter[1] adj (later) posterior, último; (of two) segundo

latter[2] n segundo(-a) m,f

launch[1] n (of product, service, campaign) lanzamiento m; (of company) fundación f; (of shares, stocks, securities) emisión f; (of film) estreno m; **~ offer** n oferta de lanzamiento f; **~ party** n (for book) fiesta de lanzamiento f

launch[2] vt (product, service, campaign, bond issue) lanzar; (company) crear, fundar; (shares, stocks, securities) emitir; (film) estrenar; (attack) emprender, lanzar

launching n (of product) lanzamiento m

launder vt (money) lavar

laundry list n AmE (jarg) lista de cuestiones por resolver f

LAUTRO abbr (▶Life Assurance and Unit Trust Regulatory Organization) BrE organización regulatoria de seguros de vida y de fondos de inversiones

law n (system, statute) ley f; (course of study) derecho m; **against the ~** en contra de la ley; **break the ~** infringir la ley; **keep within the ~** operar dentro de la ley; **pass a ~** aprobar una ley; **permitted by ~** permitido por la ley; **practise** BrE o **practice** AmE **~** ejercer (la profesión) de abogado; **required by ~** exigido por (la) ley; **as the ~ stands at present** según la legislación vigente; **study ~** estudiar derecho; **~ of** ···❯

comparative advantage *n* ley de ventaja comparativa *f*; ~ **court** *n* tribunal (de justicia) *m*; ~ **of diminishing returns** *n* ley de rendimientos decrecientes *f*; ~ **enforcement official** *n* funcionario(-a) encargado(-a) de la ejecución de la ley *m,f*; ~ **firm** *n* bufete de abogados *m*; **L~ Lords** *n pl* BrE *jueces que son miembros de la Cámara de los Lores*; ~ **and order** *n* orden público *m*; ~ **practice** *n* ejercicio del derecho *m*, abogacía *f*; ~ **report** *n* acta de proceso *f*; ~ **school** *n* facultad de derecho *f*; **L~ Society** *n* BrE (*cf* ▸**Bar Association** AmE) ≈ Colegio de Abogados *m*; ~ **of supply and demand** *n* ley de la oferta y la demanda *f*

lawful *adj* (conduct, action) lícito; (contract) válido, legal; (means) legal; (heir) legítimo

lawmaking¹ *n* legislación *f*

lawmaking² *adj* (power) legislativo

lawsuit *n* pleito *m*, causa *f*, querella *f*; **bring a ~ against sb** entablar un pleito contra alguien

lawyer *n* abogado(-a) *m,f*, letrado(-a) *m,f*; **a ~ specializing in International law** un abogado especialista en derecho internacional

lay *vt* (put, place) poner; (blame) echar; (plans) formar; ~ **the basis for sth** sentar las bases para algo; ~ **sth before sth/sb** presentar algo ante algo/alguien; ~ **a case before sb** exponer un caso ante alguien; ~ **claim to sth** demandar algo; ~ **a complaint against sb** formular *or* presentar una queja contra alguien; ~ **the emphasis on sth** poner el acento en algo; ~ **the foundations for sth** poner los cimientos de algo; **lay down** *vt* (rules) establecer; (Law) dictar; **lay off** *vt* (workers) AmE despedir; BrE *suspender temporalmente por falta de trabajo*; **lay on** *vt* (provide) proporcionar; (tax) imponer; **lay out** *vt* (money) gastar; (investment) invertir

layer *n* (of network) capa *f*

laying off *n* (of workers) AmE despido *m*; BrE *suspensión temporal por falta de trabajo*

layoff *n* (of workers) AmE despido *m*; BrE *suspensión temporal por falta de trabajo*; (period of unemployment) periodo de desempleo *m*; (Bank) depósito temporal *m*

lay official *n* (in industrial relations) funcionario(-a) no profesional *m,f*

layout *n* (of building) distribución *f*; (of town) trazado *m*, plan *m*; (of magazine, newspaper) diseño *m*, maquetación *f*; (of document) presentación *f*; ~ **character** *n* (Comp) carácter de encuadramiento *m*; ~ **chart** *n* (Mgmnt) esquema de disposición *m*

LBO *abbr* (▸**leveraged buyout**) compra apalancada *f*

l/c, L/C *abbr* (▸**letter of credit**) carta de crédito *f*

LC *abbr* (▸**label clause**) cláusula sobre etiquetas *f*

LCH *abbr* (▸**London Clearing House**) *cámara de compensación de Londres*

LDC *abbr* (▸**less-developed country**) país en desarrollo *m*

L/E *abbr* (**latest estimate**) última estimación *f*, estimación más reciente *f*

lead¹ *n* (first position) delantera *f*; (advantage) ventaja *f*; (example, leadership) ejemplo *m*; **follow** *o* **take sb's ~** seguir el ejemplo de alguien; **give (sb) a ~** dar ejemplo (a alguien); **take the ~** tomar la delantera; **take the ~ (in doing sth)** tomar la iniciativa (en hacer algo); ~ **bank** *n* banco director *m*; ~ **management** *n* gestión avanzada *f*; ~ **time** *n* (of new product) plazo de entrega *m*; (of stock) margen de tiempo *m*

lead² **1** *vt* (head, be in charge of) conducir; ~ **sb to a conclusion** llevar a alguien a una conclusión; ~ **sb to do sth** incitar *or* llevar a alguien a hacer algo; **they ~ the world in this kind of technology** son los líderes mundiales en este tipo de tecnología **2** *vi* tomar la delantera; ~ **for the defence** BrE *o* **defense** AmE llevar la defensa; **lead to** *vt* (result in) llevar a, conducir a

lead³ *n* plomo *m*; ~-**free fuel** *n* carburante sin plomo *m*; ~-**free gasoline** *n* AmE, ~-**free petrol** *n* BrE gasolina sin plomo *f*

leader *n* (person) jefe(-a) *m,f*, dirigente *mf*, líder *mf*; (in newspaper) editorial *m*; ~ **merchandising** *n* venta forzada de artículos más caros que los que están en promoción; ~ **pricing** *n* fijación de precios orientativos *f*; ~ **writer** *n* editorialista *mf*

leadership *n* liderazgo *m*

leading *adj* (brand, company) líder; **play a ~ role in sth** jugar un papel importante en algo; ~ **article** *n* (in newspaper) editorial *m*; ~ **indicator** *n* indicador anticipado *m*; ~ **line** *n* (S&M) línea principal *f*; ~ **question** *n* pregunta inductiva *f*; ~ **share** *n* valor estrella *m*

leading edge *n* vanguardia *f*

leading-edge *adj* de vanguardia, punta

leaf *n* (of chequebook) hoja *f*

leaflet *n* folleto *m*

league *n* liga *f*; **be in ~ (with sb)** estar aliado *or* confabulado (con alguien); **not be in the same ~ as sth/sb** no estar a la misma altura *or* al mismo nivel que algo/ alguien

leak¹ *n* (of information) filtración *f*; (from pipe) pérdida *f*

leak² *vt* (infrml) (information) filtrar; ~ **sth to sb** filtrar algo a alguien

lean *adj* (period) difícil; (management) reducido; (production) ajustado; **a ~er, more efficient company** una compañía más eficiente con menos personal; **~ year** *n* año *m* pobre *or* de carestía

lean-back medium *n* medio pasivo *m*

lean-forward medium *n* medio interactivo *m*

lean towards BrE, **lean toward** AmE *vt* tender hacia

leap¹ *vi* (increase suddenly) saltar; **inflation ~ed from 2% to 6%** la inflación saltó de un 2% a un 6%

leap² *n* (in prices) subida *f*; **~ year** *n* año bisiesto *m*

leapfrog *vt* saltar por encima de

leapfrogging *n* demanda alternativa de aumento de remuneraciones *f*

learning *n* (knowledge) saber *m*, conocimientos *m pl*; (act) aprendizaje *m*; **~ curve** *n* curva de aprendizaje *f*; **~ effect** *n* efecto de aprendizaje *m*

lease¹ *n* contrato de arrendamiento *m*; **get a new ~ of** BrE *o* **on** AmE **life** (person) recobrar el vigor; (business) revitalizarse; **take out a ~ on sth** arrendar algo; **~ agreement** *n* acuerdo de arrendamiento *m*; **~-lend** *n* préstamo-arriendo *m*; **~ option** *n* opción de arrendamiento *f*

lease² *vt* arrendar; **~ sth from sb** arrendar algo a alguien; **~ sth to sb** arrendar algo a alguien

leaseback *n* cesión-arrendamiento *f*; retroarriendo *m*

leased *adj* arrendado; **~ line** *n* (Comp) línea especializada *f*

leasehold *n* (contract) arrendamiento *m*; (property) propiedad arrendada *f*; **~ mortgage** *n* hipoteca sobre inmueble arrendado *f*; **~ property** *n* propiedad en arriendo *f*; **~ value** *n* valor *m* de propiedades arrendadas *or* del arrendamiento

leaseholder *n* arrendatario(-a) *m,f*

leasing *n* arrendamiento *m*, leasing *m*; **~ agreement** *n* acuerdo de arrendamiento *m*; **~ company** *n* sociedad de arrendamiento *f*; **~ corporation** *n* compañía de arrendamiento financiero *f*

leave¹ *vt* (job, profession, organization) dejar; (bequeath) legar, dejar; **~ open** (matter) dejar pendiente; **~ a space** dejar un espacio; **~ sth to sb** dejarle algo a alguien; **leave aside** *vt* dejar de lado, omitir; **leave behind** *vt* (outdistance) dejar atrás; **leave out** *vt* (omit) omitir; **leave over** *vt* posponer

leave² *n* (authorized absence) permiso *m*; **be/go on ~** estar/salir de permiso; **take one's ~** despedirse; **take a week's ~** tomarse

una semana de permiso; **~ of absence** *n* falta con permiso *f*; (HRM) ausencia con permiso *f*

LED *abbr* (▶**light-emitting diode**) diodo *m* electroluminiscente *or* emisor de luz

ledger *n* libro mayor *m*; **~ account** *n* cuenta del mayor *f*; **~ balance** *n* balance *m* *or* saldo *m* del mayor; **~ card** *n* ficha contable *f*; **~ entry** *n* asiento del mayor *m*; **~ posting** *n* pase de asientos al libro mayor *m*

left *adj* (Pol) izquierdista, de izquierdas; **~(-hand) column** *n* columna izquierda *f*; **~-luggage locker** *n* BrE (*cf* ▶**baggage locker** AmE) taquilla para equipajes en consigna *f*; **~-luggage office** *n* BrE (*cf* ▶**checkroom** AmE) consigna *f*; **~ shift** *n* (Comp) desplazamiento a la izquierda *m*; **~-wing** *adj* izquierdista, de izquierdas

left-click *vi* hacer clic utilizando el botón izquierdo del ratón; **~ on sth** hacer clic en algo utilizando el botón izquierdo del ratón

leftism *n* izquierdismo *m*

left-justify *vt* (document) justificar a la izquierda

leg *n* (Media) informante *mf*; (Stock) (of spread) tramo *m*

legacy *n* legado *m*; **~ data** *n* datos existentes *m pl*; **~ duty** *n* BrE, **~ tax** *n* AmE *impuesto sobre la renta de sucesiones*; **~ software** *n* software legado *m*; **~ system** *n* sistema legado *m*

legal *adj* (document, requirement, right) legal; (problem) jurídico, legal; (department, framework, status, liability) jurídico; (charges, expenses, fees) judicial; (owner) legítimo; **take ~ action** entablar un proceso; **be below the ~ age** no tener la edad establecida por la ley; **make sth ~** legalizar algo; **~ advice** *n* asesoramiento jurídico *f*; **take ~ advice** consultar a un abogado; **~ adviser** *n* asesor(a) legal *m,f*; **~ aid** *n* asesoramiento legal *m*; **~ consultancy** *n* asesoría jurídica *f*; **~ costs** *n pl* (awarded by court) costas judiciales *f pl*; **~ entity** *n* ente de existencia jurídica *m*, persona jurídica *f*; **~ force** *n* validez legal *f*; **~ harmonization** *n* (Law) armonización legal *f*; (Pol) armonización de legislaciones *f*; **~ holiday** *n* AmE (*cf* ▶**bank holiday** BrE) fiesta nacional *f*; **~ immunity** *n* inmunidad legal *f*; **~ name** *n* nombre legal *m*, razón social *f*; (administrative) denominación legal *f*; **~ notice** *n* notificación legal *f*; **~ obligation** *n* obligación legal *f*; **be under ~ obligation to do sth** estar obligado legalmente a hacer algo; **~ officer** *n* funcionario(-a) judicial *m,f*; **~ opinion** *n* dictamen jurídico *m*; **~ person** *n* persona jurídica *f*; **~ proceedings** *n pl* procedimiento judicial *m*; ⋯▶

~ profession n ≈ abogacía f; **~ redress** n reparación legal f; **~ representative** n representante legal mf; **~ residence** n domicilio legal m; **take ~ residence** adquirir la residencia legal; **~ separation** n separación legal f; **~ services** n pl asistencia jurídica f; **~ settlement** n acuerdo legal m; **~ suit** n proceso legal m; **~ system** n sistema legal m; **~ tender** n curso legal m; **~ transfer** n (of shares) transferencia legal f

legalistic adj legalista

legalization n legalización f

legalize vt legalizar

legally adv legalmente; **~-binding** adj de obligado cumplimiento, legalmente vinculante; **~ bound** adj legalmente obligado; **~ married** adj casado legalmente

legatee n legatario(-a) m,f

legislate vi legislar

legislation n legislación f; **bring in ~** introducir legislación

legislative adj (power) legislativo

legislature n legislatura f

leisure n ocio m; **at ~** ocioso; **read it at your ~** léalo cuando le venga bien; **~ center** AmE, **leisure centre** BrE n centro de ocio m; **~ industry** n industria f de recreación or del ocio; **~ time** n tiempo libre m

lend vt prestar; **~ sth against security** prestar algo sobre un valor; **~ one's name to sth** dar su nombre a algo; **~ sth on security** prestar algo con garantía; **~ one's support to sth** prestar su apoyo a algo; **~ sth to sb** prestarle algo a alguien; **~ weight to sth** (argument, assumption) otorgar importancia a algo

lender n prestamista mf; **~ of last resort** n prestamista de última instancia mf

lending n concesión de préstamos f; **~ at a premium** n préstamo a prima m; **~ bank** n banco de crédito m; **~ ceiling** n tope de préstamo m; **~ institution** n institución de crédito f; **~ limit** n límite m de crédito or de préstamos; **~ policy** n política de préstamos f; **~ rate** n tasa de interés de los préstamos f

length n (of line, surface) longitud f, largo m; (of list, report) extensión f; (duration) duración f; **at ~** (finally) por fin; (for a long time) extensamente, por extenso; (in detail) detenidamente, con detenimiento; **go to great ~s to do sth** hacer todo lo posible para hacer algo; **~ of service** n duración del servicio f

lengthen vt 1 vt alargar, prolongar 2 vi alargarse, prolongarse

less ^{1} adj, $pron$ menos; **~ and ~ money** cada vez menos dinero; **he earns ~ than you** gana menos que tú

less ^{2} adv menos; **~ than perfect** poco or punto menos que perfecto; **~-developed country** n país en desarrollo m; **~-favored area** AmE, **less-favoured area** BrE n área menos favorecida f

less ^{3} $prep$ menos; **his salary ~ tax** su salario menos impuestos

lessee n arrendatario(-a) m,f

lessen vt (cost, risk) reducir, disminuir

lessor n arrendador(a) m,f

let ^{1} n BrE contrato de arrendamiento m

let ^{2} vt BrE alquilar; **to ~** BrE (cf ►**for rent** AmE) se alquila; **~ sth to sb** alquilarle algo a alguien; **~ property** n propiedad alquilada f

letter n (document) carta f; (of alphabet) letra f; **have ~s after your name** tener título académico; **the ~ of the law** la letra de la ley; **to the ~** al pie de la letra; **~ of advice** n carta de aviso f; **~ of allotment** n (Stock) carta de adjudicación f; **~ of apology** n carta de disculpas f; **~ of application** n carta de solicitud f; **~ of appointment** n carta de nombramiento f; **~ of assignment** n (of business) carta de cesión f; (to job) carta de asignación f; **~ of attorney** n carta de poder f; **~ of authority** n carta de autorización f; **~ box** n BrE (cf ►**mailbox** AmE) buzón m; **~ of complaint** n carta de reclamación f; **~ of consent** n carta de aceptación f; **~ of credit** n carta de crédito f; **~ of delegation** n carta de delegación f; **~ of deposit** n carta de depósito f; **~ to the editor** n carta al director f; **~ of hypothecation** n carta f de pignoración or de hipoteca; **~ of indemnity** n carta de indemnización f; **~ of intent** n carta de intenciones f; **~ of introduction** n carta de introducción f; **~ quality** n calidad de carta f; **~-quality printer** n impresora de alta calidad f; **~ of recommendation** n carta de recomendación f; **~ of renunciation** n (in rights issue) carta de renuncia f; **~ of resignation** n carta de dimisión f; **~ stock** n acciones no cotizadas en bolsa f pl; **~ of undertaking** n carta de compromiso f

letterfoot n despedida f

letterhead n membrete m

lettering n (letters) caracteres m pl; (technique) rotulación f

letterpress n impresión tipográfica f

lettertype n tipo de letra m

letting n (act) alquiler m; (property) casa en alquiler; **~ agent** n agencia inmobiliaria (que arrienda propiedades) f

level ^{1} n (of expenditure, investment, orders) nivel m; (of consumption) grado m; **at (an)**

international ～ a nivel internacional; **on the ～** (infrml) de fiar; **be on a ～ with sth** estar a la par *or* a la altura de algo; **～ of return** *n* nivel de beneficios *m*

level² *adj* (constant) estable; **a ～ head is vital in business** la sensatez es esencial en los negocios; **～ money** *n* dinero de compensación *m*; **～ payment** *n*, **～ repayment** *n* devolución en cuotas iguales *f*

level³ *vt* (make equal) igualar; **～ criticism/ accusations at sb** dirigir críticas/ acusaciones a alguien; **level off** *vi*, **level out** *vi* (prices, growth, inflacion) estabilizarse; **level with** *vt* (infrml) ser sincero con

level-headed *adj* sensato

leverage *n* apalancamiento *m*; (influence) influencia *f*; **～ adjustment** *n* ajuste de apalancamiento *m*; **～ lease** *n* arrendamiento ventajoso *m*; **～ ratio** *n* proporción *f or* relación *f* de apalancamiento

leveraged *adj* (bid, company, stock) apalancado; **～ buyout** *n* compra apalancada *f*; **～ lease** *n* arrendamiento de deuda *m*; **～ management buy-in** *n* compra con influencia administrativa *f*; **～ management buy-out** *n* compra apalancada por ejecutivos *f*

leverage up *vi* apalancar

levy¹ *n* (tax) impuesto *m*, gravamen *m*; (Imp/Exp) contribución *f*, gravamen *m*; (taxing) exacción *f*

levy² *vt* (fine) imponer; (fee, charge) cobrar; **～ a tax** (impose) imponer un impuesto; (collect) recaudar un impuesto; **～ a new tax on imports** gravar las importaciones con un nuevo impuesto

levying *n* (of taxes) exigencia *f*, recaudación *f*

lf *abbr* (▸**line feed**) (Comp) avance *m or* salto *m* de línea

L/I *abbr* (▸**letter of indemnity**) carta de indemnización *f*

liability *n* (debt) deuda *f*; (responsibility) responsabilidad *f*; (drawback) handicap *m*; **liabilities** pasivo *m*, deudas *f pl*, obligaciones *f pl*; **deny/admit ～ for sth** negar/admitir ser responsable de algo; **be unable to meet one's liabilities** no poder hacer frente a sus obligaciones; **～ cost** *n* (Stock) coste *m* Esp *or* costo *m* AmL del pasivo; **～ insurance** *n* seguro de responsabilidad *m*; **～ ledger** *n* libro mayor del pasivo *m*; **～ management** *n* gestión del pasivo *f*; **～ manager** *n* administrador(a) de pasivos *m,f*

liable *adj* (Law) responsable; (Tax) sujeto; **～ for tax** sujeto a impuesto; **hold sb ～** responsabilizar a alguien, considerar a alguien reponsable; **～ to alteration without**

notice sujeto a cambios sin previo aviso; **～ to a penalty** sancionable

liaise with *vt* enlazar con

liaison *n* enlace *m*; **～ officer** *n* oficial de enlace *mf*

libel¹ *n* libelo *m*; **～ laws** *n pl* leyes antilibelo *f pl*; **～ proceedings** *n pl* juicio por difamación *m*; **～ suit** *n* pleito por difamación *m*

libel² *vt* difamar

libellous BrE, **libelous** AmE *adj* difamante, difamatorio

liberal *adj* liberal; **～ economics** *n* economía liberal *f*

liberalization *n* liberalización *f*

liberalize *vt* liberalizar

liberalizing *adj* liberalizador

liberty *n* libertad *f*; **at ～** libre

LIBID *abbr* (▸**London Interbank Bid Rate**) tasa de licitaciones interbancarias de Londres *f*

LIBOR *abbr* (▸**London Interbank Offered Rate**) *tasa de interés ofrecida en el mercado interbancario de Londres*

library *n* biblioteca *f*; **～ service** *n* servicio de biblioteca *m*

licence BrE, **license** AmE *n* (document) licencia *f*, permiso *m*; (permission) permiso *m*, autorización *f*; **manufacture sth under ～** fabricar algo bajo licencia; **～ holder** *n* titular de una licencia *mf*

licensable *adj* permisible

license¹ *n* AmE ▸**licence** BrE; **～ number** *n* AmE (*cf* ▸**registration number** BrE) (of vehicle) matrícula *f*, número de matrícula *m*; **～ plate** *n* AmE (*cf* ▸**numberplate** BrE) matrícula *f*

license² *vt* autorizar, otorgarle un permiso *or* una licencia a

licensed *adj* (practitioner) autorizado; **～ premises** *n* BrE establecimiento autorizado para vender bebidas acohólicas *f*

licensee *n* concesionario(-a) *m,f*; (Law) licenciatario(-a) *m,f*; (Patents) persona autorizada *f*

licensing *n* concesión de licencia *f*; **～ agreement** *n* acuerdo de licencia *m*; **～ laws** *n pl* BrE *leyes reguladoras de la venta y consumo de alcohol*

licensor *n* concedente *mf*

LICOM *abbr* (▸**London Interbank Currency Options Market**) *mercado interbancario de opciones sobre divisas de Londres*

lidding document *n* documento de liquidación *m*

lien *n* derecho de retención *m*

lieu n: **in ~ of** en lugar de, en vez de; **~ day** n día libre para compensar horas extras trabajadas

life n vida f; (of agreement) vigencia f; **inject new ~ into the economy** revitalizar la economía; **the useful ~ of a machine** la vida útil de una máquina; **~ annuitant** n rentista mf; **~ assurance** n BrE seguro de vida m; **~ assurance policy** n BrE póliza de seguro de vida f; **L~ Assurance and Unit Trust Regulatory Organization** n BrE organización regulatoria de seguros de vida y de fondos de inversiones; **~ cycle** n (of product) ciclo de vida m; **~-cycle analysis** n análisis de ciclo de vida m; **~ estate** n dominio vitalicio m, usufructo m; **~ expectancy** n (of person) esperanza de vida f; **~ imprisonment** n cadena perpetua f; **~ insurance** n seguro de vida m; **~ insurance company** n compañía de seguros de vida f; **~ insurance policy** n póliza de seguro de vida f; **~ insurer** n asegurador(a) de vida m,f; **~ insuring company** n aseguradora de vida f; **~ interest** n (Law) renta vitalicia f; **~ savings** n pl ahorro m de patrimonio or de seguridad; **~ tenancy** n derecho de arrendamiento vitalicio m, ocupación vitalicia f; **~ tenant** n inquilino(-a) vitalicio(-a) m,f

lifeboat operation n n (infrml) (Bank) operación salvavidas f

lifeless adj inanimado, muerto

lifestyle n estilo de vida m; **~ concept** n concepto de estilo de vida m; **~ merchandising** n comercialización de un estilo de vida f; **~ product** n producto que refleja el estilo de vida; **~ segmentation** n segmentación por estilos de vida f

lifetime n (of person) vida f; (of thing) vida efectiva f; **~ employment** n empleo vitalicio m; **~ guarantee** n garantía para toda la vida m

LIFFE abbr (⯈**London International Financial Futures Exchange**) bolsa de opciones y futuros de Londres

LIFO abbr (⯈**last in, first out**) UEPS (último en entrar, primero en salir)

lift[1] n (rise) alza f

lift[2] vt (sanctions) elevar, levantar; (restrictions, mortgage) levantar; **~ a leg** (Stock) cerrar un lado; **~ a short** (Stock) cerrar una posición corta

lifting n (of restrictions, laws) levantamiento m

light[1] adj (interest, trading) bajo; (lite) light; **~ industry** n industria ligera f

light[2] n luz f; **bring sth to ~** sacar algo a la luz; **cast** o **shed** o **throw ~ on sth** arrojar luz sobre algo; **come to ~** salir a la luz; **in the ~ of sth** considerando algo; **see sth/sb**

in a different o **new ~** ver algo/a alguien con otros ojos; **show sth/sb in a good/bad ~** dar a algo/alguien un buen/mal aspecto; **~-emitting diode** n diodo m electroluminiscente or emisor de luz; **~ pen** n lápiz óptico m

lightning strike n huelga f relámpago or sin previo aviso

limit[1] n límite m **a ~ of six months** un plazo máximo de seis meses; **set** o **put a ~ on sth** poner límite a algo; **within ~s** dentro de ciertos límites; **~ price** n precio límite m

limit[2] vt (risk, possibility, number, extent) limitar; (imports) restringir; **~ oneself to (doing) sth** limitarse a (hacer) algo

limited adj (knowledge, experience, risk, edition) limitado; (number, space) limitado, restringido; (market) con escaso movimiento; **~ company** n BrE (cf ⯈**incorporated business company** AmE) ≈ sociedad anónima f, ≈ sociedad anónima por acciones f, ≈ sociedad de responsabilidad limitada; **~ liability** n responsabilidad limitada f; **~ liability company** n BrE (cf ⯈**incorporated business company** AmE) ≈ sociedad anónima f, ≈ sociedad anónima por acciones f, ≈ sociedad de responsabilidad limitada; **~ order** n pedido limitado m; **~ owner** n (Law) socio(-a) comanditario(-a) m,f; (Prop) usufructuario(-a) m,f; **~ partner** n comanditario(-a) m,f; **~ partnership** n sociedad comanditaria f; **~ policy** n (Ins) póliza limitada f

line n línea f; (of waiting people) AmE (cf ⯈**queue** BrE) cola f; **bring sth into ~ (with sth)** alinear algo (con algo); **come into ~ (with sth)** ajustarse (a algo); **get a ~ on sth** (infrml) obtener información acerca de algo; **in ~ for sth** en (los puestos de) cabeza para algo; **in ~ with sth** (inflation, expectations) en línea con algo; **lay it on the ~** (infrml) hablar franca y abiertamente; **lay sth on the ~** arriesgar algo; **be/put sth on the ~** estar/ poner algo en peligro; **take a firm ~ (on sth)** tomar una postura firme (en cuanto a algo); **~ assistant** n asistente(-a) m,f or ayudante(-a) m,f de línea; **~ of attack** n línea de ataque f; **~ authority** n autoridad f lineal or de línea; **~ of business** n giro del negocio m; **~ of command** n línea jerárquica f; **~ of credit** n línea de crédito f; **~ executive** n ejecutivo(-a) de línea m,f; **~ extension** n ampliación de la gama f; **~ feed** n avance m or salto m de línea; **~ of least resistance** n línea de menor resistencia f; **~ management** n gerencia de línea f; **~ manager** n gerente de línea mf; **~ organization** n organización lineal f; **~ production** n producción en serie f; **~ space** n (in text) interlínea f; **~ spacing**

(in text) espacio entre líneas *m*; ∼ **and staff management** *n* gestión lineal y funcional *f*; ∼ **and staff organization** *n* organización de cuadros y personal subalterno *f*; ∼**-stretching** *n* extensión de la línea de productos *f*; ∼ **supervisor** *n* supervisor(a) de línea *m,f*

lineage *n* número de líneas *m*

linear *adj* (relationship, responsibility) lineal; ∼ **measure** *n* medida de longitud *f*; ∼ **programming** *n* programación lineal *f*

liner *n* buque de pasajeros *m*

lingua franca *n* lengua franca *f*

link[1] *n* enlace *m*; (bond) vínculo *m*; (relation) relación *f*; (connection) conexión *f*; **establish a** ∼ **between two incidents** establecer una conexión entre *or* relacionar dos incidentes; **forge close** ∼**s** fraguar estrechas relaciones; **have** ∼**s with sth/sb** tener vínculos con *or* estar vinculado a algo/alguien

link[2] *vt* (components) unir, enlazar; (terminals) conectar; (facts, events) relacionar

linkage *n* (connexion) conexión *f*; (device) acoplamiento *m*; (Comp) enlace *m*

lion's share *n* parte del león *f*

liquid *adj* (funds, savings, capital) líquido; (assets) líquido, disponible; (debt) vencido; ∼ **measure** *n* medida de capacidad para líquidos *f*; ∼ **ratio** *n* coeficiente de liquidez *m*

liquidate *vt* (assets, company, position, options) liquidar

liquidated *adj* (assets, company, position, options) liquidado; (debt) saldado

liquidation *n* liquidación *f*; **go into** ∼ entrar en liquidación; ∼ **dividend** *n* dividendo de liquidación *m*

liquidator *n* liquidador(a) *m,f*

liquidity *n* liquidez *f*; ∼ **crisis** *n* crisis de liquidez *f*; ∼ **preference** *n* preferencia de liquidez *f*; ∼ **problem** *n* problema de liquidez *m*; ∼ **ratio** *n* coeficiente de liquidez *m*; ∼ **squeeze** *n* iliquidez *f*

liquor store *n* AmE (*cf* ▸**off-licence** BrE) tienda de licores *f*

list[1] *n* (of names, addresses, candidates) lista *f*; (Prop) nómina *f*; (in publishing) catálogo *m*; **be high/low on the** ∼ (matter, problem) tener/no tener prioridad; **make a** ∼ hacer una lista; **be top of the** ∼ estar a la cabeza de la lista; **that's top/bottom of the** ∼ eso es lo primero/último que tenemos hacer; ∼ **broker** *n* agente de direcciones *mf*; ∼ **manager** *n* (S&M) jefe(-a) de lista *m,f*; ∼ **price** *n* precio de catálogo *m*

list[2] *vt* (names, events) listar; (securities, stocks) cotizar

listed *adj* (included in list) listado; (Stock) (securities, shares) cotizado; ∼ **on the stock**

exchange cotizado en la bolsa; ∼ **company** *n* empresa que cotiza en bolsa *f*; ∼ **option** *n* opción *f* cotizada *or* admitida a cotización

listener *n* (to radio) radioyente *mf*

listening time *n* (to radio) hora de audiencia *f*

listing *n* (putting on list) listado *m*; (on stock exchange) cotización *f*; ∼ **agent** *n* AmE, ∼ **broker** *n* BrE (Prop) agente de registros *mf*

listless *adj* (market, trading) indiferente

lite *adj* light

literal *n* errata *f*

literature *n* (promotional material) folletos *m pl*, información *f*; ∼ **search** *n* investigación de datos existentes *m*

litigant *n* litigante *mf*

litigation *n* litigio *m*; ∼ **risk** *n* riesgo de litigio *m*

litigator *n* abogado que se dedica a los litigios

little dragons *n pl* (infrml) (Asian countries) pequeños dragones *m pl*

live[1] *vi* vivir; ∼ **from hand to mouth** vivir al día; **live on** *vt* vivir de; **she** ∼**s on $175 a week** vive *or* se las arregla con 175 dólares a la semana; **the pension is scarcely enough to** ∼ **on** la pensión apenas alcanza para vivir; **live up to** *vt* (promise) cumplir; **live with** *vt* (fact, situation) aceptar

live[2] *adj* (broadcast, programme) en directo

livestock *n* animales de cría *m pl*

living *n* vida *f*; **earn** *o* **make a** ∼ ganarse la vida; **work for a** ∼ trabajar para vivir; ∼ **accommodation** *n* BrE, ∼ **accommodations** *n pl* AmE vivienda *f*; ∼ **conditions** *n pl* condiciones de vida *f pl*; ∼ **expenses** *n pl* gastos de mantenimiento *m pl*; ∼ **space** *n* espacio vital *m*; ∼ **standards** *n pl* nivel de vida *m*; ∼ **wage** *n* salario de subsistencia *m*

LLB *abbr* (▸**Bachelor of Laws**) ≈ licenciado(-a) en Derecho *m,f*

LLD *abbr* (▸**Doctor of Laws**) Doctor(a) en Derecho *m,f*

Lloyd's *n* compañía Lloyd's *f*; ∼ **Agent** *n* representante de Lloyd's *mf*; ∼ **Corporation** *n* Compañía Lloyd's *f*; ∼ **List** *n* lista de Lloyd's *f*; ∼ **of London** *n* compañía de seguros Lloyd's; ∼ **Register** *n* Registro Lloyd's *m*

LMBI *abbr* (▸**leveraged management buy-in**) compra con influencia administrativa *f*

LMBO *abbr* (▸**leveraged management buy-out**) CAPE (compra apalancada por ejecutivos)

load[1] *n* carga *f*; ∼ **factor** *n* factor de consumo *m*

load[2] *vt* (software, cargo, vehicle) cargar

loading n (surcharge) recargo m, sobreprima f (jarg); (of vehicle) carga f; ~ **agent** n agente de carga mf

loan n préstamo m, crédito m, empréstito m; **apply for a** ~ solicitar un préstamo; **approval of a** ~ aprobación de un préstamo f; **arrange a** ~ disponer un préstamo; **make a** ~ hacer un préstamo; **take a** ~ consituir un préstamo; **take a** ~ **out** disponer de un préstamo; ~ **account** n cuenta de empréstitos f; ~ **agreement** n contrato de préstamo m; ~ **application** n solicitud de préstamo f; ~ **authorization** n autorización de préstamo f; ~ **capital** n capital de empréstito m; ~ **company** n compañía prestamista f; ~ **department** n departamento de crédito m; ~ **exposure** n riesgo de préstamos m; ~ **fee** n gastos de préstamo m pl; ~ **holder** n titular de un préstamo mf; ~ **insurance** n seguro de préstamo m; ~ **loss** n pérdidas de préstamos f pl; ~ **market** n mercado de préstamos m; ~ **recipient** n receptor(a) del préstamo m,f; ~ **recovery** n recuperación de préstamo f; ~ **repayment** n devolución de préstamo f; ~ **shark** n (infrml) extorsionador(a) m,f, usurero(-a) m,f; ~ **stock** n fondos de préstamo m pl; ~ **value** n valor para préstamo m; ~ **write-off** n cancelación de préstamo f; ~ **yield** n rentabilidad del préstamo f

loanable adj prestable

lobby[1] n grupo de presión m; ~ **group** n grupo de presión m

lobby[2] [1] vt (politicians, delegates) presionar, ejercer presión sobre
[2] vi presionar, ejercer presión; ~ **for sth** presionar or ejercer presión para obtener algo

lobbying n presión f

lobbyist n miembro de un grupo de presión

local[1] adj (firm, industry, currency, election) local; ~ **area network** n (Comp) red de área local f; ~ **authority** n autoridad local f; ~ **authority bill** n certificado de la autoridad local m; ~ **authority bond** n obligación de la administración local f; ~ **call** n llamada local f; ~ **government** n administración local f; ~ **labor** n AmE, ~ **labour** n (workers) mano de obra local f; ~ **link lien** n (Comp) enlace de hipertexto local m; ~ **loop** n (Comp) bucle local m; ~ **newspaper** n periódico local m; ~ **press** n prensa local f; ~ **shop** n tienda de barrio f; ~ **tax** n impuesto m or tributo m municipal; ~ **time** n hora local f; ~ **variable** n (Comp) variable local f

local[2] n (jarg) (Stock) local m

localization n (Comp) localización f

localize vt (Comp) localizar

locate vt (business, building) situar, ubicar; (fault) localizar

location n (siting) ubicación f, emplazamiento m; (discovery of position) localización f

LOCH abbr (▸**London Options Clearing House**) cámara de compensación de opciones de Londres

lock vt (Comp) desactivar, bloquear; **lock away** vt (jarg) (Stock) guardar bajo llave; **lock in** vt (Stock) sincronizar, encerrar

locked n (market) inmovilizado

locked-in adj sin salida para poder comprar o vender; ~**-in capital** n capital retraído m; ~**-in effect** n efecto inmovilizado m; ~**-in industry** n industria cerrada f; ~**-in value** n (of shares allocated to employees) valor en posición cubierta bloqueada m

lock-in n (S&M) acuerdo exclusivo m

lockout n cierre patronal m

lock-up BrE local sin trastienda m; ~**-up option** n opción de cierre f; (in corporate takeover) opción inmovilizada f; ~**-up premises** n pl BrE local sin trastienda m

lodge [1] vt (objection, complaint) presentar; (appeal) interponer
[2] vi (reside) alojarse, hospedarse

log[1] n diario de operaciones m; ~ **file** n archivo de registro m

log[2] vt (record) registrar, anotar, tomar nota de; **log in** vi iniciar la sesión; **log off** vi terminar la sesión; **log on** vi iniciar la sesión; **log out** vi terminar la sesión

logic n lógica f; ~ **circuit** n circuito lógico m; ~ **device** n dispositivo lógico f

log-in n inicio de la sesión m

logistical adj logístico

logistically adv logísticamente

logistics n pl logística f

logo n (▸**logotype**) logotipo m

log-off n fin de la sesión m

log-on n inicio de la sesión m

logoptics n logóptica f

logotype n logotipo m

log-out n fin de la sesión m

logrolling n AmE (infrml) sistema de concesiones mutuas m

Lombard: ~ **loan** n AmE (cf ▸**collateral loan** BrE) empréstito con garantía m, préstamo m con caución or con garantía; ~ **rate** n tasa Lombard f

London n Londres; ~ **Clearing House** n cámara de compensación de Londres; ~ **Futures and Options Exchange** n mercado de opciones y futuros de Londres; ~ **Interbank Bid Rate** n tasa de licitaciones interbancarias de Londres f; ~ **Interbank**

Currency Options Market *n mercado interbancario de opciones sobre divisas de Londres*; ~ **Interbank Offered Rate** *n tasa de interés ofrecido en el mercado interbancario de Londres*; ~ **International Financial Futures Exchange** *n bolsa de opciones y futuros de Londres*; ~ **Options Clearing House** *n cámara de compensación de opciones de Londres*; ~ **School of Economics** *n Universidad londinense de estudios económicos y sociales*; ~ **Stock Exchange** *n Bolsa de Valores de Londres*; ~ **Traded Options Market** *n mercado de opciones negociadas de Londres*; ~ **weighting** *n subsidio por residir en Londres*

long *adj* largo; **go** ~ (Stock) estar largo; ~ **bond** *n* bono a largo plazo *m*; ~ **call** *n* compra al alza *f*; ~ **call position** *n* posición compradora larga *f*; ~**-distance** *adj* (telephone call) de larga distancia; **call** ~**-distance** hacer una llamada de larga distancia; ~**-established** *adj* muy arraigado; ~ **futures position** *n* posición de futuros a largo plazo *f*; ~**-haul** *adj* de largo recorrido; ~ **hedge** *n* cobertura de una posición larga *f*; ~ **lease** *n* enfiteusis *f*; ~ **list** *n* (of candidates) lista para selección *f*; ~ **position** *n* posición larga *f*; ~ **put** *n* venta al alza *f*; ~ **put position** *n* posición vendedora larga *f*; ~**-range forecast** *n* previsión a largo plazo *f*; ~**-range planning** *n* planificación *f* a largo plazo *or* de largo alcance; ~**-standing** *adj* antiguo; ~ **straddle** *n* estructura de deribados al alza *f*; ~ **ton** *n* tonelada larga *f*; ~ **wave** *n* onda larga *f*; ~ **weekend** *n* puente *m*

longer-term *adj* (option) a más largo plazo

longitudinal *adj* longitudinal

longs *n pl* (Stock) posiciones acaparadoras *f pl*

long-term *adj* (loan, gain, objective, trend) a largo plazo; ~ **bond** *n* bono a largo plazo *m*; ~ **credit** *n* crédito a largo plazo *m*; ~ **investment** *n* inversión a largo plazo *f*; ~ **financing** *n* financiación a largo plazo *f*; ~ **planning** *n* planificación *f* a largo plazo *or* de largo alcance; ~ **security** *n* obligación a largo plazo *f*; ~ **unemployed** *n pl gente que ha estado desempleada por largo tiempo*; ~ **unemployment** *n* desempleo *m or* paro *m* Esp de larga duración

look *vi* (seem) parecer; ~ **bad/good** tener mala/buena pinta; ~ **promising** tener buenas perspectivas; **look after** *vt* (customer) atender; (be responsible for) encargarse de, ocuparse de; **look at** *vt* (person, object) mirar; (possibilities) considerar, estudiar; **look for** *vt* buscar; **look forward to** *vt* tener ganas de; ~ **forward to doing sth** tener ganas de hacer algo; **look into** *vt* (matter, problem, case) investigar; (possibility) estudiar, considerar;

look out for *vt* estar en la búsqueda de; **look over** *vt* (work, contract) revisar, chequear; **look through** *vt* (work) revisar, chequear; (report) echarle un vistazo a, hojear; **look to** *vt* (attend to) ocuparse de; ~ **the future** poner la mira en el futuro; ~ **to sb for sth** contar con alguien para algo; **look up** [1] *vt* (try to find) buscar [2] *vi* (improve) mejorar; **business is** ~**ing up** los negocios van mejorando

lookup table *n* tabla de consulta *f*

loop *n* (Comp) bucle *m*; **be in/out of the** ~ estar/no estar enterado

loophole *n* vacío legal *m*

loose *adj* (page) suelto; (goods) a granel, suelto; (organization) poco rígido; (structure) flexible; **buy/sell sth** ~ comprar/vender algo suelto; ~ **change** *n* calderilla *f*, dinero suelto *m*; ~ **inserts** *n pl* (Media) encartes *m pl*

loose-leaf *adj* de hoja suelta

lorry *n* BrE (*cf* ▶**truck** AmE) camión *m*; ~ **driver** *n* BrE (*cf* ▶**teamster** AmE) camionero(-a) *m,f*, conductor(a) de camión *m,f*

lose [1] *vt* (job, right, opportunity, customers) perder; ~ **ground** (in competition) perder terreno, retroceder; **we have lost many clients to our competitors** muchos de nuestros clientes han pasado a la competencia; **their hesitation lost them the contract** la falta de decisión les costó *or* les hizo perder el contrato [2] *vi* perder; ~ **on a deal** salir perdiendo en un negocio; **lose out** *vi* salir perdiendo; ~ **out on a deal** salir perdiendo en un negocio; ~ **out to sb** perder terreno frente a alguien

loss *n* pérdida *f*; **cut one's** ~**es** reducir las pérdidas; (figuratively) cortar por lo sano; **sell sth at a** ~ vender algo con pérdida; **take a** ~ asumir una pérdida; ~ **adjuster** *n* tasador(a) de pérdidas *m,f*; ~ **carry-back** *n* traslado de pérdidas a ejercicios anteriores *m*; ~ **carry-forward** *n* traslado de pérdidas a ejercicios futuros *m*; ~**es carried forward** *n pl* pérdidas llevadas a cuenta nueva *f pl*; ~ **contingency** *n* contingencia de pérdidas *f*; ~ **of custom** *n* pérdida de la clientela *f*; ~ **of earnings** *n* pérdida de sueldo *f*; ~ **in value of assets** *n* pérdida de valor de los activos *f*; ~ **of income** *n* pérdida de ingresos *f*; ~ **leader** *n* artículo de reclamo *m*; ~ **leader pricing** *n* determinación de precios de venta con pérdida *f*; ~ **limitation** *n* limitación de la pérdida *f*; ~ **of market** *n* pérdida de mercado *f*; ~ **of pay** *n* pérdida de remuneración *f*; ~**pricing** *n* (jarg) *fijación de precios con pérdida para promover la* ⋯⟫

venta; $\sim$ **of priority** *n* pérdida de prioridad *f*; $\sim$ **provision** *n* provisión para pérdidas *f*; $\sim$**es suffered** *n pl* pérdidas sufridas *f pl*

lossmaker *n* productor(a) de pérdidas *m,f*

lossmaking *adj* deficitario

lottery *n* lotería *f*; $\sim$ **ticket** *n* boleto de lotería *m*

love money *n préstamo buscado a gente conocida para fundar una puntocom nueva*

low[1] *adj* (price, wages, productivity) bajo; (proportion) pequeño; (standard, quality) bajo, malo; **the $\sim$ end of the market** la gama baja del mercado; **the $\sim$ end of the range** el extremo bajo de la banda; $\sim$ **achiever** *n* persona *f* de bajo desempeño *or* de bajo rendimiento; $\sim$**-budget** *adj* (film) de bajo presupuesto; $\sim$**-cost** *adj* (loan) barato; $\sim$**-flier** *n* persona *f* de bajo desempeño *or* de bajo rendimiento; $\sim$**-grade** *adj* de baja calidad; $\sim$**-hanging fruit** *n ganancias que se consiguen fácilmente or sin mucho esfuerzo*; $\sim$**-income household** *n* familia con ingresos reducidos *f*; $\sim$**-income taxpayer** *n* contribuyente de bajos ingresos *mf*; $\sim$**-interest loan** *n* préstamo a bajo interés *m*; $\sim$**-key** *adj* moderado; $\sim$ **memory** *n* (Comp) memoria baja *f*; $\sim$**-paid** *adj* de bajo ingreso, mal pagado, mal remunerado; **the $\sim$-paid** los mal pagados; $\sim$ **pay** *n* ingreso *m or* salario *m* bajo; $\sim$**-polluting** *adj* poco contaminante; $\sim$**-pressure selling** *n* venta poco apremiante *f*; $\sim$**-priced** *adj* barato; $\sim$ **profile** *n* perfil discreto *m*; **keep a $\sim$ profile** tratar de pasar desapercibido; $\sim$**-profile** *adj* discreto, de perfil discreto; $\sim$**-quality goods** *n* bienes de baja calidad *m pl*; $\sim$ **return** *n* (on investment) rendimiento bajo *m*; $\sim$**-season fare** *n* tarifa de temporada baja *f*; $\sim$**-stream** *adj* (Ind) de bajo índice de operación; $\sim$**-tech** *adj* de baja tecnología; $\sim$**-yield bond** *n* bono de bajo rendimiento *m*; $\sim$**-yielding** *adj* de baja rentabilidad

low[2] *n* mínimo *m*; **inflation was at an all-time $\sim$** la inflación estaba en el punto más bajo de la historia; **the peso has dropped to a new $\sim$ against the dollar** la cotización del peso ha alcanzado un nuevo mínimo con respecto al dólar

lowballer *n* (jarg) (company) empresa con objetivos modestos de gestión *f*; (individual) inversor(a) de teoría contraria *m,f*

lower[1] *adj* (price) inferior; $\sim$ **case letter** *n* letra minúscula *f*; $\sim$ **classes** *n pl* clase baja *f*; $\sim$ **income bracket** *n* grupo de ingresos más bajos *m*; $\sim$ **quartile** *n* cuartil inferior *m*

lower[2] *vt* (price) bajar; (taxation) reducir

lowest *adj* (price) ínfimo; (bidder, tender) más bajo; $\sim$ **common denominator** *n* mínimo común denominador *m*

loyalty *n* (of customer, employee) lealtad *f*, fidelidad *f*; $\sim$ **bonus** *n* prima por lealtad *f*; $\sim$ **card** *n* tarjeta de lealtad *f*; $\sim$ **factor** *n* factor de lealtad *m*

LQ *abbr* (▶**letter quality**) calidad de carta *f*

LR *abbr* (▶**Lloyd's Register**) Registro Lloyd's *m*

LRC *abbr* (▶**Labour Representation Committee**) *comité de representación laboral*

ls *abbr* (▶**lump sum**) suma global *f*

LSE *abbr* (▶**London School of Economics**) *universidad londinense de estudios económicos y sociales*; (▶**London Stock Exchange**) *bolsa de valores de Londres*

LSI *abbr* (▶**large-scale integration**) (Comp) LSI (integración a gran escala)

Ltd *abbr* BrE (▶**limited company**, *cf* ▶**Inc.** AmE) $\approx$ S.A. (sociedad anónima), $\approx$ S.A.A. (sociedad anónima por acciones), $\approx$ S.R.L. (sociedad de responsabilidad limitada)

LTOM *abbr* (▶**London Traded Options Market**) *mercado de opciones negociadas de Londres*

LTU *abbr* (▶**long-term unemployed**) *gente que ha estado desempleada por largo tiempo*

lucky *adj* (person) afortunado; $\sim$ **break** *n* (infrml) (chance) racha de suerte *f*

lucrative *adj* lucrativo, provechoso

Luddite *n* ludita *mf*

luggage *n* equipaje *m*; $\sim$ **trolley** *n* BrE (*cf* ▶**baggage cart** AmE) carro de equipajes *m*

lull *n* calma *f*

lump *n* (contract work) destajo *m*; $\sim$ **sum** *n* suma global *f*; $\sim$**-sum contract** *n* contrato por precio global *m*; $\sim$**-sum distribution** *n* distribución global *f*; $\sim$**-sum price** *n* precio global *m*; $\sim$**-sum tax** *n* impuesto global *m*

luncheon voucher *n* (*cf* ▶**meal ticket** AmE) vale de comida *m*

lunch-hour *n* hora de comer *f*

lurk *vi* (infrml) (Comp) estar de fisgoneo *or* mironeo

lurker *n* (infrml) (Comp) mirón(-ona) *m,f*

lurking *n* (infrml) (Comp) fisgoneo *m*, mironeo *m*

luxury *adj* (goods, tax) de lujo

LV *abbr* (▶**luncheon voucher**) vale de comida *m*

LW *abbr* (▶**long wave**) OL *f* (onda larga)

Mm

M *abbr* (▸**monetary aggregates**) totales monetarios *m pl*; (▸**money**) dinero *m*; (supply) oferta monetaria *f*; BrE (▸**motorway**) autopista *f*

m/a *abbr* (▸**my account**) mi cuenta

machine *n* máquina *f*; ∼ **accounting** *n* contabilidad *f* computerizada *or* informatizada; ∼ **address** *n* (Comp) dirección de máquina *f*; ∼**-assisted translation** *n* traducción automática *f*; ∼**-based** *adj* automático; ∼ **code** *n* código de máquina *m*; ∼**-made** *adj* hecho a máquina; ∼ **operator** *n* maquinista *mf*; ∼**-readable** *adj* (code) legible por máquina; ∼ **run** *n* pasada de máquina *f*

machinery *n* (equipment) maquinaria *f*; (system) aparato *m*

macho *adj* (behaviour, attitude) machista

macro *n* (Comp) macroinstrucción *f*

macrocompany *n* macroempresa *f*

macrocomputing *n* macroinformática *f*

macrodistribution *n* macrodistribución *f*

macroeconomic *adj* (policy) macroeconómico

macroeconomics *n* macroeconomía *f*

macroenvironment *n* macroambiente *m*

macromarketing *n* macromarketing *m*

macroproject *n* macroproyecto *m*

macrosegment *n* macrosegmento *m*

macrosegmentation *n* macrosegmentación *f*

made *adj* hecho; ∼ **to last** hecho para durar; ∼ **bill** *n* (Econ) letra endosada *f*

made-to-measure *adj* hecho a medida

Madison Avenue *n* AmE *avenida neoyorkina famosa por sus agencias de publicidad*

mag *n* (infrml) (▸**magazine**) revista *f*

magazine *n* revista *f*

magistrate *n* juez(a) de primera instancia e instrucción *m,f*, magistrado(-a) *m,f*; ∼**s' court** *n* juzgado de paz *m*

magnate *n* magnate *mf*

magnetic *adj* magnético; ∼ **card** *n* ficha magnética *f*; (Comp) tarjeta magnética *f*; ∼ **core** *n* núcleo magnético *m*; ∼ **disk** *n* disco magnético *m*; ∼ **head** *n* cabeza magnética *f*; ∼ **storage** *n* memoria magnética *f*; ∼ **tape** *n* cinta magnética *f*

magnitude *n* (size) magnitud *f*; (importance) envergura *f*; ∼ **of a right** *n* (Law) amplitud de un derecho *f*

mail[1] *n* (postal system, letters) AmE (*cf* ▸**post** BrE) correo *m*; (e-mail) correo electrónico *m*, e-mail *m*; **by** ∼ AmE (*cf* ▸**by post** BrE) por correo; **it's in the** ∼ AmE (*cf* ▸**it's in the post** BrE) ya ha sido enviado *or* está en camino; **put sth in the** ∼ AmE (*cf* ▸**put sth in the post** BrE) echar algo al correo *or* al buzón **through the** ∼ AmE (*cf* ▸**through the post** BrE) por correo; ∼ **bomb** *n* (Comp) bomba e-mail *f*; ∼ **clerk** *n* AmE (*cf* ▸**postal clerk** BrE) empleado(-a) postal *m,f*; ∼ **fraud** *n fraude en una promoción por correo*; ∼ **management** *n* gestión del correo electrónico *f*; ∼ **order** *n* (activity) venta por correo *f*; (order) pedido *m* por correo *or* por correspondencia; **buy sth by** ∼ **order** comprar algo por correo; ∼ **order business** *n* (company) compañía de venta por correo *f*; (activity) venta por correo *f*; ∼ **order catalog** AmE, **mail order catalogue** BrE *n* catálogo de venta por correo *m*; ∼ **order selling** *n* venta por correo *f*; ∼ **server** *n* (Comp) servidor de correo *m*; ∼ **transfer** *n* transferencia por correo *f*

mail[2] *vt* AmE (*cf* ▸**post** BrE) enviar por correo; ∼ **sth to sb** AmE (*cf* ▸**post sth to sb** BrE) enviar algo por correo a alguien

mailbox *n* (for letters) AmE (*cf* ▸**letter box** BrE, ▸**postbox** BrE) buzón *m*; (for e-mail) buzón de correo electrónico *m*

mailing *n* (action) correo *m*; (S&M) mailing *m*; (of advertising material) envío publicitario *m*, propaganda *f or* publicidad *f* por correo; ∼ **address** *n* domicilio postal *m*; ∼ **list** *n* lista *f* de mailing *or* de direcciones

mailman *n* AmE (*cf* ▸**postman** BrE) cartero *m*

mailmerge *n* fusión *f* de correo *or* de ficheros de direcciones

mailshot *n* mailing *m*; **do a** ∼ hacer un mailing

main *adj* (road, branch, residence) principal; (office) central; ∼ **line** *n* (rail) línea principal *f*; ∼ **menu** *n* (Comp) menú principal *m*; ∼ **street** *n* AmE (*cf* ▸**high street** BrE) calle principal *f*; ∼ **street price** *n* AmE (*cf* ▸**high street price** BrE) precio de calle principal *m*; ∼ **street spending** *n* AmE (*cf* ▸**high street spending** BrE) gastos de calle ····▸

principal *m pl*; ~ **trading partner** *n* principal socio(-a) comercial *m,f*

mainframe *n* servidor *m*

mains *n pl* BrE (*cf* ▸**supply network** AmE) línea principal *f*, red de alimentación *f*; ~ **adaptor** *n* BrE (*cf* ▸**current adaptor** AmE) adaptador *m* a la red *or* de corriente

mainstay *n* (of organization, economy) pilar *m*, puntal *m*

mainstream *adj* (culture) establecido; (ideology) dominante

maintain *vt* (rate, lead, attitude) mantener; (machine) ocuparse del mantenimiento de; ~ **that...** sostener que...

maintenance *n* mantenimiento *m*; (for spouse, child) pensión alimenticia *f*; ~ **allowance** *n* pensión alimenticia *f*; ~ **charges** *n pl* gastos de conservación *m pl*; ~ **engineer** *n* ingeniero(-a) de mantenimiento *m,f*; ~ **equipment** *n* equipo de mantenimiento *m*; ~ **expenses** *n pl* gastos de mantenimiento *m pl*; ~ **fee** *n* (for keeping bank account) cargo de mantenimiento *m*; (for property) honorarios por mantenimiento *m pl*; ~ **payment** *n* pago de pensión alimenticia *m*; ~ **personnel** *n* equipo de mantenimiento *m*; ~ **schedule** *n* calendario de mantenimiento *m*; ~ **staff** *n* equipo de mantenimiento *m*

Majesty *n* Majestad *f*; **on Her** ~**'s Service** BrE al servicio de Su Majestad; **Her** ~**'s Customs and Excise** *n* BrE ≈ Servicio de Aduanas *m*; **Her** ~**'s Government** *n* BrE *el gobierno británico*

major *adj* (breakthrough, change, contribution) muy importante; (setback) serio; (road, account, currency) principal; (trend) dominante; **all** ~ **credit cards accepted** se aceptan todas las principales tarjetas de crédito; **be at a** ~ **disadvantage** estar en franca desventaja; **a** ~ **issue** un asunto de gran *or* de fundamental importancia; ~ **producer** *n* (of commodity) productor *m* principal *or* importante

majority *n* (of age, in vote) mayoría *f*; **be in the** *o* **a** ~ ser mayoría; ~ **decision** *n* decisión mayoritaria *f*; ~ **holding** *n* participación mayoritaria *f*; ~ **interest** *n* interés *m* mayoritario *or* de la mayoría; ~ **interest partner** *n* socio(-a) con participación mayoritaria *m,f*; ~ **ownership** *n* propiedad de la mayoría *f*; ~ **rule** *n* sistema mayoritario *m*, regla de la mayoría *f*; ~ **rule voting** *n* votación por el método de la mayoría *f*; ~ **shareholder** *n* accionista mayoritario(-a) *m,f*; ~ **shareholding** *n* accionariado(-a) mayoritario(-a) *m,f*; ~ **stake** *n* interés *m* mayoritario *or* de la mayoría; (Stock) paquete mayoritario *m*; ~ **stockholder** *n*

accionista mayoritario(-a) *m,f*; ~ **verdict** *n* veredicto mayoritario *m*; ~ **vote** *n* voto mayoritario *m*

make[1] *vt* (arrangements, announcement, list, will) hacer; (product) hacer, fabricar; (changes, payment) hacer, efectuar; (manufacture) manufacturar; (create) crear; ~ **it** (infrml) (suceed) llegar; ~ **a lot of money** hacer mucho dinero; ~ **or break sth/sb** ser el éxito o la ruina de algo/alguien; ~ **a profit/loss** ganar/perder dinero; ~ **a profit of $20,000** ganar *or* sacar 20.000 dólares; **make out** *vt* (list, receipt) hacer; (bill of exchange) librar; (invoice) extender; (cheque) emitir, rellenar; ~ **out a check** AmE *o* **cheque** BrE **to sb** extender un cheque a la orden de *or* a nombre de alguien; **make over** *vt* (property, money) transferir, ceder; **make sth over to sb** transferir *or* ceder algo a alguien; **make up** *vt* (team) componer; (Fin) ajustar; ~ **up one's accounts** saldar las propias cuentas; ~ **up the difference** compensar la diferencia; **make up for** *vt* (compensate) compensar; ~ **up for lost time** recuperar el tiempo perdido

make[2] *n* (brand) marca *f*

make-or-buy decision *n* decisión de fabricar o comprar *m*

maker *n* (manufacturer) fabricante *mf*; (signatory) signatario(-a) *m,f*; (of note) firmante *mf*

makeshift *adj* (arrangement) provisional; (solution) improvisado

make-up *n* (Acc) falseación *f* (infrml), manipulación contable *f*, maquillaje (de balance) *m* (jarg); ~ **pay** *n* remuneración complementaria *f*

making *n* (of profit) obtención *f*; (of paper) fabricación *f*; (of clothes) confección *f*; **be the** ~ **of sb** ser la clave del éxito de alguien; **have the** ~**s of sth** (person) tener madera de algo; (thing) tener los ingredientes para ser algo; **his problems are of his own** ~ sus problemas se los ha buscado él solito

making-up *n* (for losses, of accounts, of balance sheet) compensación *f*

maladministration *n* mala administratión *f*

malfunction[1] *n* fallo de funcionamiento *m*

malfunction[2] *vi* funcionar mal

malicious *adj* (person, remark) malicioso, malintencionado; (damage) doloso, intencional; ~ **mischief** *n* agravio malicioso *m*; ~ **prosecution** *n* demanda de mala fe *f*

maliciously *adv* con alevosía, de mala fe

malingerer *n* falso(-a) enfermo(-a) *m,f*

malingering *n* enfermedad ficticia *f*

mall *n* AmE (*cf* ▸**commercial centre** BrE) centro comercial *m*

malleable *adj* (capital) maleable

malpractice *n* negligencia profesional *f*

Malthusian *adj* maltusiano

Malthusianism *n* maltusianismo *m*

mammoth *adj* (reduction) enorme; (project, cost) gigantesco, enorme, colosal

man¹ *n* hombre *m*; **the ~ in the street** el ciudadano medio *or* de a pie; **~-day** *n* día-hombre *m*; **~-hour** *n* hora-hombre *f*; **~-year** *n* año-hombre *m*

man² *vt* (operate) atender a, manejar; (provide personnel for) dotar de personal; (ship) tripular

manage ⓵ *vt* (company, shop, office) dirigir, administrar, gerenciar AmL; (staff, team) dirigir; (land, finances, fund) administrar; **~ sb's affairs** administrar los negocios de alguien; **~ to do sth** lograr *or* poder hacer algo
⓶ *vi* dirigir, administrar; **~ on $300 a week** arreglarse *or* arreglárselas con 300 dólares a la semana

manageable *adj* (size, amount) razonable; (task, goal) posible de alcanzar

managed *adj* (currency, loan, trade) controlado; (economy) dirigido, intervenido; (account) administrado, controlado; (bond) administrativo; (costs) administrado, gestionado; (news) manipulado

management *n* (act) dirección *f*, administración *f*, gestión *f*; (handling, control) manejo *m*; (managers) directivos *m pl*; (of particular company) dirección *f*, gerencia *f*; **under new ~** bajo nueva dirección; **the ~ regrets any inconvenience caused** la dirección se disculpa por las molestias causadas; **~ accountancy** *n* contabilidad de gestión *f*; **~ accountant** *n* contable *mf* Esp *or* contador(a) *m,f* AmL de gestión; **~ accounting** *n* contabilidad de gestión *f*; **~ accounts** *n pl* cuentas de gestión *f pl*; **~ audit** *n* auditoría *f* administrativa *or* de gestión; **~ board** *n* consejo de administración *m*; **~ buy-in** *n* compra financiada de acciones de una empresa por personas ajenas a ella; **~ buyout** *n* compra por ejecutivos; **~ by crisis** *n* administración *f or* dirección *f* por crisis; **~ by exception** *n* dirección *f or* gestión *f* por excepción; **~ by objectives** *n* dirección *f or* gestión *f* por objetivos; **~ by walking around** *n* dirección por contacto directo *m*; **~ of change** *n* administración del cambio *f*; **~ chart** *n* organigrama de gestión *m*; **~ committee** *n* comité directivo *m*; **~ computing** *n* computación *f or* informática *f* de gestión; **~ consultancy** *n* consultoría de gestión *f*; **~ consultant** *n* consultor(a) en administración (de empresas) *m,f*,

consultor(a) administrativo(-a) *m,f*; **~ contract** *n* contrato *m* administrativo *or* de gestión; **~ control** control de gestión *m*; **~ expenses** *n pl* gastos de gerencia *m pl*; **~ fee** *n* (Bank) comisión de administración *f*, cuota administrativa *f*; (for managing property) honorarios de administración *m pl*; (for managing a portfolio) comisión de administración *f*; **~ game** *n* juego de la administración *m*; **~ information** *n* información *f* para la administración *or* para la dirección; **~ information system** *n* sistema de información para la gestión *m*; **~ reshuffle** *n* reorganización de la dirección *f*; **~ skill** *n* habilidad administrativa *f*; **~ staff** *n* personal *m* administrativo *or* directivo; **~ structure** *n* estructura *f* administrativa *or* directiva *or* de la gestión; **~ style** *n* estilo de gerencia *m*; **~ system** *n* sistema *m* de administración *or* de dirección; **~ team** *n* equipo *m* administrativo *or* de gestión; **~ technique** *n* técnica *f* administrativa *or* de administración; **~ theory** *n* teoría administrativa *f*; **~ trainee** *n* ejecutivo(-a) *m,f* en formación *or* en capacitación; **~ training** *n* formación *f or* capacitación *f* de mandos

manager *n* (of company, department) director(a) *m,f*, gerente *mf*; (of shop, restaurant) gerente *mf*, encargado(-a) *m,f*; (of estate, fund) administrador(a) *m,f*; (of performer, sportsperson) mánager *mf*; **~'s office** *n* oficina del gerente *f*

manageress *n* (obs) (of shop, restaurant) encargada *f*

managerial *adj* (staff, function) directivo; (style, effectiveness) administrativo; (accounting, structure) administrativo, directivo, de gestión; (prerogative) de la dirección; **~ grid** *n* cuadrícula administrativa *f*, parrilla de gestión *f*; **~ position** *n* cargo *m* ejecutivo *or* directivo *m*, puesto directivo *m*

managing *adj* (agent) administrador; **~ director** *n* director(a) *m,f* gerente *or* administrativo(-a); **~ partner** *n* socio(-a) *m,f* administrador(a) *or* director(a); **~ underwriter** *n* garante administrador(a) *m,f*

M&A *abbr* (▸**mergers and acquisitions**) fusiones *f pl* y adquisiciones *f pl*

mandarin *n* (government) mandarín *m*

mandate *n* mandato *m*

mandatory *adj* (injunction) mandatario; (sentence, accounting plans) obligatorio, preceptivo; **~ copy** *n* material publicitario obligatorio *m*; **~ quote period** *n* periodo obligatorio de cotización *m*; **~ retirement** *n* AmE (*cf* ▸**compulsory retirement** BrE) jubilación *f* forzosa *or* obligatoria

m

manifest n manifiesto m; ∼ **of cargo** n manifiesto del cargamento m; ∼ **clerk** n funcionario(-a) de manifiesto m,f

manifold n papel de copia m

manipulate vt (market, accounts) manipular

manipulation n (of market, accounts) manipulación f

manipulator n (of market, accounts) manipulador(a) m,f

man-made adj (material) sintético, artificial; (fibre) sintético

manned adj (service) dotado de personal

manning n personal m, plantilla f Esp; ∼ **level** n nivel de personal m

manpower n mano de obra f; ∼ **audit** n auditoría f de la mano de obra or de recursos humanos; ∼ **cost** n coste m Esp or costo m AmL de la mano de obra; ∼ **management** n dirección de recursos humanos f; ∼ **planning** n planificación f de la mano de obra or del potencial humano disponible; ∼ **shortage** n carencia de personal f

MANTIS abbr (▸**Market and Trading Information System**) sistema de información de la Bolsa de Valores de Londres para la ejecución automática de transacciones

manual[1] adj (labour, worker) manual

manual[2] n (for reference) manual m

manually adv manualmente

manufacture[1] vt (articles) manufacturar, fabricar; (foodstuffs) elaborar, producir; (clothes) confeccionar; ∼ **sth under licence** BrE o **license** AmE fabricar algo bajo licencia

manufacture[2] n (of articles) manufactura f, fabricación f; (of foodstuffs) elaboración f, producción f; (of clothes) confección f; (product) manufactura f

manufactured adj (articles) manufacturado, fabricado; (foodstuffs) elaborado, producido; (clothes) confeccionado; ∼ **goods** n pl productos elaborados m pl, bienes manufacturados m pl

manufacturer n fabricante mf; ∼**'s price** n precio del fabricante m; ∼**'s recommended price** n precio recomendado por el fabricante m; ∼**'s suggested retail price** n precio de venta al público sugerido por el fabricante m

manufacturing[1] adj (sector, industry) manufacturero; (process, capacity, costs, profits, rights) de fabricación; (base) industrial; (activity) fabril

manufacturing[2] n fabricación f; ∼**-based economy** n economía de carácter manufacturero f; ∼ **resource planning** n planificación de recursos de fabricación f; ∼

under licence BrE, ∼ **under license** AmE n fabricación con licencia f

manuscript n manuscrito m

map n (of city) plano m; (Comp) mapa m

mapping n (Comp) encuadre m

margin n (of profit, error, safety, on page) margen m; (Stock) cobertura f; **buy sth on** ∼ comprar algo al margen; ∼ **account** n cuenta de adelantos f; ∼ **buying** n compra al descubierto f; ∼ **call** n demanda de cobertura suplementaria f; ∼ **deposit** n depósito de garantía m; ∼ **purchase** n compra parcialmente a crédito f; ∼ **security** n valor de garantía m

marginal adj (difference, improvement) mínimo; (role, significance) menor; (cost, profit, rate) marginal; ∼ **constituency** n distrito electoral marginal m; ∼ **costing** n cálculo m de costes Esp or costos AmL diferenciales or marginales; ∼ **note** n nota marginal f; ∼ **pricing** n fijación marginal de precios f; ∼ **product** n producto marginal m; ∼ **productivity** n productividad marginal f; ∼ **propensity to invest** n propensión marginal a la inversión f; ∼ **propensity to save** n propensión marginal al ahorro f; ∼ **return on capital** n rendimiento marginal del capital m

marginalism n marginalismo m

marginalize vt marginalizar

marginally adv al margen

marine adj (accident, insurance, pollution) marítimo; ∼ **engineer** n ingeniero(-a) naval m,f

marital status n estado civil m

maritime adj (trade, loan, risk, peril, fraud) marítimo; ∼ **law** n derecho marítimo m

mark[1] vt (price) marcar; ∼ **stock** cotizar valores en bolsa; ∼ **time** hacer tiempo; ∼ **sth to the market** ajustar algo al valor del mercado; **mark down** vt (sales, goods) rebajar, reducir el precio de; **mark off** vt cancelar; **mark up** vt (prices) aumentar

mark[2] n marca f; **the cost has reached the $100,000** ∼ el coste Esp or costo AmL ha llegado a los 100.000 dólares

mark-down n reducción f

marked adj (decline, difference, improvement) marcado; (cheque) confirmado; ∼ **price** n precio marcado m; ∼**-to-market** adj ajustado al valor de mercado

market[1] n mercado m; (stock market) bolsa f; **at the** ∼ **call** según la demanda; **away from the** ∼ en sentido contrario al mercado; **come onto the** ∼ entrar en el mercado; **corner the** ∼ **(in sth)** hacerse con el mercado (de algo); **in the** ∼ **for sth** interesado en comprar algo; **no** ∼ sin mercado; **on the** ∼ en el mercado; **put sth**

on the ~ poner algo en venta; **play the ~** jugar en la Bolsa

(**market...a**) ~ **acceptance** n aceptación del mercado f; ~ **access** n acceso a los mercados m; ~ **adjustment** n ajuste del mercado m; ~ **aim** n meta comercial f; ~ **analysis** n análisis de mercado m; ~ **analyst** n analista de mercado mf; ~ **appraisal** n estimación del mercado f; ~ **awareness** n conocimiento del mercado m

(**b...**) ~ **base** n base del mercado f; ~ **behavior** AmE, ~ **behaviour** BrE n comportamiento del mercado m

(**c...**) ~ **capitalization** n capitalización de mercado f; (Stock) capitalización bursátil f; ~ **close** n cierre del mercado m; ~ **conditions** n pl condiciones del mercado f pl; ~ **confidence** n confianza del mercado f; ~ **creation** n creación de mercado f

(**d...**) ~ **day** n día de mercado m; ~ **dealing** n operación de mercado f; ~ **demand** n demanda de mercado f; ~ **development** n desarrollo de mercado m; ~ **disclosure** n información sobre el mercado f; ~ **downturn** n fase de depresión del mercado f; ~**-driven** adj impulsado por el mercado

(**e...**) ~ **economy** n economía de mercado f; ~ **entry** n entrada en el mercado f; ~ **equilibrium** n equilibrio de mercado m; ~ **evaluation** n evaluación del mercado f; ~ **expansion** n expansión del mercado f; ~ **exploration** n exploración del mercado f

(**f...**) ~ **fit** n adaptación f al mercado or a la clientela; ~ **fluctuation** n fluctuación de mercado f; ~ **forces** n pl fuerzas del mercado f pl; ~ **forecast** n perspectivas de mercado f pl, pronóstico del mercado m; ~ **fragmentation** n fragmentación del mercado f

(**g...**) ~ **gap** n brecha en el mercado f

(**h...**) ~ **hours** n pl horario del mercado m

(**i...**) ~ **index** n índice del mercado m; ~ **indicator** n indicador del mercado m; ~ **intelligence** n información sobre el mercado f

(**l...**) ~ **leader** n líder del mercado mf; (Stock) valor bursátil importante m; ~ **leadership** n liderazgo del mercado m

(**m...**) ~ **maker** n creador(a) de mercado m,f; ~ **management** n dirección f or gestión f del mercado

(**n...**) ~ **niche** n nicho de mercado m

(**o...**) ~ **objective** n objetivo de mercado m; ~ **of one** n mercado exclusivo m; M~ **and Opinion Research International** n compañía británica de sondeo de la opinión pública, ≈ Demoscopia m Esp; ~

opportunity n oportunidad de mercado f; ~**-oriented** adj orientado al mercado

(**p...**) ~ **penetration** n penetración en el mercado f; ~ **position** n posición en el mercado f; ~ **positioning** n posicionamiento en el mercado m; ~ **potential** n potencial del mercado m; ~ **presence** n presencia en el mercado f; ~ **price** n precio de mercado m; **buy sth at the ~ price** comprar algo a precio de mercado; ~ **pricing** n determinación f or fijación f de precios del mercado; ~ **profile** n perfil de mercado m; ~ **prospects** n pl perspectivas de mercado f pl; ~ **psychology** n psicología de mercado f

(**r...**) ~ **rate** n tipo de interés del mercado m; ~ **receptiveness** n receptividad del mercado f; ~ **recovery** n recuperación del mercado f; ~ **report** n informe sobre el mercado m; ~ **research** n estudio de mercado m; M~ **Research Corporation of America** n sociedad estadounidense de estudios de mercado; ~ **researcher** n investigador(a) de mercado m,f; ~ **resistance** n resistencia del mercado f; ~ **rigging** n manipulación del mercado f

(**s...**) ~ **saturation** n saturación del mercado f; ~ **sector** n sector de mercado m; ~ **segmentation** n segmentación de mercado f; ~**-sensitive** adj sensible al mercado; ~ **share** n cuota de mercado f; ~ **size** n amplitud del mercado f; ~ **skimming** n esquilmado del mercado m; ~ **slump** n caída en picado del mercado f, hundimiento del mercado m; ~ **study** n, ~ **survey** n estudio de mercado m

(**t...**) ~ **test** n, ~ **testing** n prueba de mercado f; M~ **and Trading Information System** n sistema de información de la Bolsa de Valores de Londres para la ejecución automática de transacciones; ~ **trend** n tendencia del mercado f

(**v...**) ~ **valuation** n valoración de mercado f; ~ **value** n valor m comercial or en el mercado m; ~ **view** n panorama del mercado m

(**w...**) ~ **watcher** n observador(a) del mercado m,f

market² vt comercializar

marketability n comerciabilidad f

marketable adj (goods, product) comercializable; (value) comercial; (securities) negociable; ~ **bond** n obligación ordinaria f; ~ **title** n BrE (Prop) título negociable m

marketeer n experto(-a) en marketing m,f

marketer n operador(a) de mercado m,f

marketing n marketing m, mercadotecnia f; ~ **agreement** n acuerdo comercial m; ~ **audit** n auditoría de marketing f; ~ **authorization** n autorización de ⋯▸

comercialización f; ~ **budget** n presupuesto de marketing m; ~ **campaign** n campaña de marketing f; ~ **concept** n concepto de marketing m; ~ **cost** n coste m Esp or costo m AmL de marketing; ~ **consultant** n asesor(a) de marketing m,f; ~ **department** n departamento de marketing m; ~ **director** n director(a) de marketing m,f; ~ **executive** n ejecutivo(-a) de marketing m,f; ~ **information system** n sistema de información de marketing m; ~ **manager** n director(a) de marketing m,f; ~ **mix** n mezcla de estrategias de marketing f; ~ **model** n modelo de marketing m; ~ **plan** n plan de marketing m; ~ **policy** n política comercial f; ~ **strategy** n estrategia de marketing f; ~ **team** n equipo de marketing m; ~ **tool** n herramienta de marketing f

marketplace n mercado m, plaza comercial f; (on Internet) cibermercado m; **companies must be able to compete in the** ~ las empresas deben ser capaces de competir en el mercado

marking n (Fin) marcación f

mark-up n margen m de ganancia or de beneficio; ~ **language** n (Comp) lenguaje de referencia m; ~ **pricing** n fijación f del precio al coste Esp or costo AmL medio recargado

marriage n matrimonio m; ~ **allowance** n deducción por matrimonio f; ~ **breakdown** n ruptura del matrimonio f; ~ **deduction** n deducción por matrimonio f; ~ **penalty** n recargo por matrimonio m

married adj (man, woman) casado; ~ **couples' allowance** n BrE desgravación al matrimonio f

mart n AmE (infrml) centro comercial m

Marxism n marxismo m

Marxist[1] adj marxista

Marxist[2] n marxista mf

mask vt ocultar

mass adj (advertising) de masas; (distribution, appeal, unemployment) masivo; (dismissal, risk) colectivo; ~ **communication** n comunicación de masas f; ~ **consumption** n gran consumo m; ~ **e-mail** n correo electrónico no solicitado m; ~ **mailing** n (Comp) carteo masivo m; ~-**market** adj (goods) de masas; ~ **market** n mercado de masas m; ~ **marketing** n marketing de masas m; ~ **media** n pl medios de comunicación (de masas) m pl; ~ **memory** n (Comp) memoria de masa f; ~ **production** n fabricación en serie f; ~ **storage** n (Comp) almacenamiento m masivo or de gran capacidad; ~ **storage device** n dispositivo de memoria masiva m

massage vt (figures, data, statistics) manipular

massive adj (support, increase, task) enorme, grande; (protest) masivo

mass-produce vt fabricar en serie

mast n (Comms) torre f

master n (copy) original m; ~ **budget** n presupuesto m maestro or principal; M~ **of Business Administration** n Master en Dirección y Administración de Empresas m; ~ **card** n (Comp) tarjeta maestra f; M~ **of Commerce** n Master de Comercio m; ~ **copy** n copia maestra f; ~ **disk** n disco maestro m; ~ **document** n documento maestro m; M~ **of Economics** n Master de Economía m; ~ **file** n fichero maestro m; ~ **key** n (Comp) tecla maestra f; ~ **lease** n arrendamiento principal m; ~ **owner** n propietario(-a) principal m,f; ~ **plan** n plan maestro m; ~ **policy** n AmE póliza colectiva f; M~ **of Science** n Master de Ciencias m; ~ **tape** n cinta original f

mastermind vt planear, dirigir

masthead n (in newspaper) mancheta f

MAT abbr (▸**machine-assisted translation**) traducción automática m; (▸**multiple access time**) tiempo de acceso múltiple m

match[1] vt (offer, results) igualar; (description) ajustarse a, corresponder a; (specifications) ajustarse a; **match up to** vt igualar; ~ **up to sb's expectations** colmar las esperanzas de alguien

match[2] n (in Internet search) resultado m, éxito m

matched adj (samples) emparejado; ~ **book** n libro equilibrado m; ~ **orders** n pl órdenes f pl casadas or emparejadas; ~ **sale-purchase transaction** n compra y venta coincidente f; ~ **trade** n transacción combinada de compraventa f

matching n (of product line) armonización f; ~ **grant** n subvención paralela f; ~ **principle** n (of costs with revenues) principio de equilibrio m

material[1] n material m; (substance) materia f; ~**s accounting** n contabilidad de materiales f; ~**s handling** n movimiento de materiales m; ~ **purchase** n compra de materias primas f

material[2] adj (fact, gain, needs) material; (factor, reason) importante, de peso; (evidence) sustancial; **be** ~ **to sth** ser esencial a algo; ~ **interest** n (in company) interés material m

materialism n materialismo m

materiality n (in accounting reports) importancia relativa f, materialidad f

materialize vi (idea) materializarse

materialized labour ⇢ mechanic ⋯

materialized labour BrE, ~ **labor** AmE
n mano de obra concreta *f*

maternity *n* maternidad *f*; ~ **allowance**
n bonificación por maternidad *f*; ~ **benefit**
n subsidio por maternidad *m*; ~ **leave** *n*
licencia de maternidad *m*, baja de
maternidad *f* (infrml); ~ **pay** *n* paga por
maternidad *f*; ~ **protection** *n* protección a
la maternidad *f*

matrix *n* matriz *f*; ~ **analysis** *n* análisis
matricial *m*; ~ **management** *n* dirección *f*
or gerencia *f* de la matriz; ~ **organization**
n organización *f* matriz *or* matricial; ~
printer *n* impresora matricial *f*; ~ **trading**
n intercambio de valores *m*

matter[1] *n* (affair) asunto *m*; **be a** ~ **of sth**
ser cuestión de algo; **it's a** ~ **of experience**
es sólo cuestión de experiencia; **as a** ~ **of**
course por costumbre; **as a** ~ **of fact** en
realidad; **the** ~ **is closed** el asunto está
concluido; **in the** ~ **of sth** en cuanto a algo;
the ~ **in hand** el asunto de que se trata;
take ~**s into one's own hands** tomar cartas
en el asunto

matter[2] *vi* importar; ~ **to sb** importar a
alguien

mature[1] *adj* (policy, bond, debenture) vencido;
(market) maduro; (economy) completo, maduro

mature[2] *vi* (policy, bond, debenture) vencer

matured *adj* (policy, bond, debenture, capital)
vencido

maturing: ~ **security** *n* título de
próximo vencimiento *m*; ~ **value** *n* valor
cercano a su vencimiento *m*

maturity *n* vencimiento *m*; **come to** ~
llegar al vencimiento; ~ **date** *n* fecha de
vencimiento *f*; ~ **value** *n* valor al
vencimiento *m*; ~ **yield** *n* beneficio al
vencimiento *m*

max. *abbr* (▶**maximum**) máximo

maximal *adj* (awareness) máximo

maximin *n* maximin *m*

maximization *n* maximización *f*

maximize *vt* (profit, output, efficiency, window)
maximizar

maximum[1] *adj* (capacity, price, rate)
máximo; ~ **allowable deduction** *n* (Tax)
deducción máxima permitida *f*; ~ **brand**
exposure *n* exposición máxima de la
marca *f*; ~ **load** *n* límite de carga *m*; ~
return *n* beneficio máximo *m*

maximum[2] *n* máximo *m*; **up to a** ~ **of...**
hasta un máximo de...

Mb *abbr* (▶**megabyte**) Mb (megabyte)

MBA *abbr* (▶**Master of Business**
Administration) MBA (Master en Dirección
y Administración de Empresas)

MBO *abbr* (▶**management buyout**) CPE
(compra por ejecutivos); (▶**management**

by objectives) dirección *f or* gestión *f* por
objetivos

MBS *abbr* (▶**mortgage-backed security**)
título *m or* valor *m* respaldado por una
hipoteca

m-business *n* comercio electrónico
utilizando el móvil *m*

MBWA *abbr* (▶**management by walking**
around) dirección por contacto directo *f*

mcht *abbr* (▶**merchant**) comerciante *mf*

mchy *abbr* (▶**machinery**) maquinaria *f*

MCom *abbr* (▶**Master of Commerce**)
Master de Comercio *m*

MCT *abbr* (▶**mainstream corporation**
tax) impuesto corporativo total *m*

MD *abbr* (▶**managing director**) director(a)
m,f gerente *or* administrativo(-a)

MDW *abbr* (▶**measured daywork**) jornada
controlada *f*

meal *n* comida *f*; ~ **allowance** *n* subsidio
para comida *m*; ~ **ticket** *n* AmE (*cf*
▶**luncheon voucher** BrE) vale de comida *m*

mean[1] *adj* (cost, time, value) medio; ~ **time**
between failures (Comp) *n* tiempo medio
entre averías *m*

mean[2] *n* media *f*

means[1] *n* (method, way) medio *m*; **as a** ~ **of**
sth como medio de algo; **by** ~ **of sth** por
medio de algo, mediante algo; ~ **of**
payment *n* medio de pago *m*

means[2] *n pl* (income, wealth) medios *m pl*,
recursos *m pl*; **have the** ~ **to do sth** contar
con los medios para hacer algo; **live beyond**
one's ~ vivir por encima de las
posibilidades

means-test *vt investigar los ingresos de*
una persona para determinar si tiene derecho
a ciertos subsidios

means test *n investigación de los ingresos*
de una persona para determinar si tiene
derecho a ciertos subsidios

means-tested *adj* (benefits) sujeto al
ingreso

measure[1] *n* (course of action) medida *f*;
(indicator) indicador *m*; **as a precautionary** ~
como medida precautoria; **in some** ~ en
cierta medida; **in great** *o* **large** *o* **no small**
~ en gran medida, en gran parte; **with a**
(certain) ~ **of success** con cierto éxito;
take ~**s (to do sth)** tomar medidas (para
hacer algo); ~ **of control** *n* (of prices)
medida de control *f*

measure[2] *vt* medir; ~ **sb's performance**
medir el desempeño de alguien

measured daywork *n* (in job evaluation)
jornada controlada *f*

measurement *n* (size) medida *f*; (act)
medición *f*

mechanic *n* mecánico(-a) *m,f*

mechanical *adj* (data) mecánico; ∼ **engineering** *n* ingeniería mecánica *f*

mechanism *n* mecanismo *m*

mechanization *n* mecanización *f*

mechanize *vt* mecanizar

MEcon *abbr* (▸**Master of Economics**) Master de Economía *m*

media *n pl* medios de comunicación *m pl*; ∼ **analysis** *n* análisis de los medios de comunicación *m*; ∼ **analyst** *n* analista de medios de comunicación *mf*; ∼ **buyer** *n* comprador(a) de medios de comunicación *m,f*; ∼ **buying** *n* compra de espacios en medios de comunicación *f*; ∼ **consultant** *n* asesor(a) de comunicaciones *m,f*; ∼ **coverage** *n* cobertura en los medios de comunicación *f*; give ∼ **coverage to sth** dar cobertura en los medios de comunicación a algo; ∼ **event** *n* acontecimiento mediático *m*; ∼ **fragmentation** *n* fragmentación de los medios de comunicación *f*; ∼**-independent** *adj* independiente de los medios de comunicación; ∼ **mix** *n* combinación de estrategias de medios de comunicación *f*; ∼ **plan** *n* plan de medios de comunicación *m*; ∼ **planner** *n* planificador(a) de medios de comunicación *m,f*; ∼ **planning** *n* planificación de medios *f*; ∼ **relations** *n pl* relaciones con los medios de comunicación *f pl*; ∼ **selection** *n* selección de medios de comunicación *f*; ∼ **streaming** *n* transmisión multimedia continua *f*; ∼ **studies** *n* estudios de periodismo *m pl*

median *n* mediana *f*; ∼ **amount** *n* cantidad media *f*; ∼ **rule** *n* regla de la mediana *f*

mediate ⓵ *vi* (between parties) mediar ⓶ *vt* arbitrar; ∼ **a solution** mediar para llegar a una solución

mediation *n* mediación *f*

mediator *n* mediador(a) *m,f*

medical[1] (assistance, costs, insurance) *adj* médico; **on** ∼ **grounds** por razones de salud

medical[2] *n* revisión médica *f*, examen médico *m*, chequeo *m*; **have a** ∼ someterse a una revisión médica, hacerse un chequeo

medium[1] *adj* mediano

medium[2] *n* (of communication) medio *m*; ∼ **of account** *n* instrumento de cuenta *m*; ∼ **of exchange** *n* medio de cambio *m*; ∼ **of redemption** *n* sistema de amortización *m*

medium-dated *adj* con vencimiento a medio plazo

mediums *n pl* (Stock) medios *m pl*

medium-term *adj* (loan, credit, instrument) a medio plazo; ∼ **financial strategy** *n* BrE estrategia financiera a medio plazo *f*

meet *vt* (expenses) sufragar, cubrir; (demands, debt) satisfacer; (requirements, claim, draft) atender; (targets) sostener; (deadline, quota) cumplir con; (costs) saldar; ∼ **the needs of sth/sb** responder a las necesidades de algo/alguien; ∼ **one's obligations** atender a sus obligaciones; **they failed to** ∼ **payments on their loan** no pudieron pagar las letras del préstamo; **meet with** *vt* (opposition, hostility) ser recibido con; (approval) recibir; (salesperson) reunirse con; ∼ **with failure** fracasar; ∼ **with success** tener éxito

meeting *n* reunión *f*; (face to face) careo *m*; **the** ∼ **broke up** la reunión se disolvió; **call/hold a** ∼ convocar/celebrar una reunión; **be in a** ∼ estar en una reunión, estar reunido Esp; **M**∼ **of minds** *n* mutuo acuerdo *m*; (Law) acuerdo *m or* concierto *m* de voluntades

megabucks *n pl* (infrml) pasta gansa *f* (infrml)

megabyte *n* megabyte *m*

megacorp *n* (jarg) megaempresa *f*

megacorporation *n* megaempresa *f*

member *n* (of company, union) miembro *mf*; ∼ **of the board** *n* miembro *mf* de la junta directiva *or* del consejo; ∼ **of the board of management** *n* miembro del consejo de administración *mf*; **M**∼ **of Congress** *n* AmE (*cf* ▸**Member of Parliament** BrE) ≈ diputado(-a) *m,f*, ≈ Miembro del Congreso *mf*; ∼ **corporation** *n* sociedad miembro *f*; **M**∼ **of the European Parliament** *n* Miembro del Parlamento Europeo *mf*; ∼ **firm** *n* empresa miembro *f*; **M**∼ **of Parliament** *n* BrE (*cf* ▸**Member of Congress** AmE, ▸**Congressman** AmE, ▸**Congresswoman** AmE) ≈ diputado(-a) *m,f*, ≈ Miembro del Congreso *mf*; ∼ **of the public** *n* ciudadano(-a) *m,f*; ∼ **of staff** *n* (of company) empleado(-a) *m,f*; ∼ **state** *n* estado miembro *m*

membership *n* condición de afiliación *f*; ∼ **dues** *n pl* cuota de participación *f*

memo *n* (▸**memorandum**) memorándum *m*

memorandum *n* (frml) memorándum *m*; ∼ **account** *n* cuenta en orden *f*; ∼ **of association** *n* (of trading corporation) escritura de constitución *f*; ∼ **of intent** *n* memorándum de intención *n*

memory *n* memoria *f*; ∼ **bank** *n* banco de memoria *m*; ∼ **capacity** *n* capacidad de memoria *f*; ∼ **card** *n* tarjeta de memoria *f*; ∼ **chip** *n* chip de memoria *m*; ∼ **dump** *n* vaciado de memoria *m*; ∼ **expansion card** *n* tarjeta de expansión de memoria *m*; ∼ **extension** *n* ampliación de la memoria *f*; ∼ **lapse** *n* error de memoria *m*; ∼ **operation** *n* operación de la memoria *f*; ∼ **print-out** *n* impresión de la memoria *f*; ∼**-resident** *adj* residente en memoria

menial *adj* (work) de baja categoría

mental *adj* (handicap, impairment) mental

mention *vt* mencionar; **as** ∼**ed above** según arriba se menciona; ∼ **sb in one's will** dejarle algo a alguien (en el testamento); **not to** ∼**...** por no decir nada de..., sin contar...

menu *n* menú *m*; ∼ **bar** *n* barra de menús *f*; ∼**-driven** *adj* dirigido por menú; ∼ **item** *n* elemento de menú *m*

MEP *abbr* (▸**Member of the European Parliament**) Miembro del Parlamento Europeo *mf*

mercantile *adj* (bank, agency, exchange) mercantil; (doctrine) mercantilista; ∼ **law** *n* derecho mercantil *m*

mercantilism *n* mercantilismo *m*, doctrina mercantilista *f*

merchandise *n* mercancías *f pl*; ∼ **broker** *n* corredor(a) de mercancías *m,f*; ∼ **inventory** *n* inventario de mercancías *m*

merchandiser *n* comerciante *mf*

merchandising *n* comercialización *f*; ∼ **director** *n* director(a) comercial *m,f*; ∼ **service** *n* servicio de comercialización *m*

merchant *adj* (vessel) mercante; (account, capitalism) mercantil; ∼ **bank** *n* BrE (*cf* ▸**investment bank** AmE) banco *m* mercantil *or* de negocios; ∼ **banker** *n* BrE (*cf* ▸**investment banker** AmE) banquero(-a) comercial *m,f*; ∼ **banking** *n* BrE (*cf* ▸**investment banking** AmE) banca *f* mercantil *or* de negocios; ∼ **marine** *n*, ∼ **navy** *n* marina mercante *f*; ∼ **site** *n* (on Internet) sitio comercial *m*

merchantable *adj* comercializable; ∼ **quality** *n* calidad comercial *f*; ∼ **title** *n* título negociable *m*

merge¹ [1] *vt* (companies, organizations) fusionar, unir; (programs, data) fusionar; ∼ **and purge** (jarg) *mezclar dos listas de envío quitando nombres y direcciones repetidas* [2] *vi* (companies, departments) fusionarse, unirse; **merge into** *vt* fusionarse a; **merge with** *vt* fusionarse con

merged *n* (company) fusionado

merger *n* fusión *f*; ∼ **accounting** *n* BrE (*cf* ▸**pooling of interests** AmE) contabilidad de fusiones *f*; (balance sheets) fusión de intereses *f*; ∼**s and acquisitions** *n pl* fusiones *f pl* y adquisiciones *f pl*; ∼ **arbitrage** *n* arbitraje de fusión *m*; ∼ **company** *n* compañía de fusión *f*; ∼ **expenses** *n pl* gastos de fusión *m pl*

meridian *n* meridiano *m*

merit *n* mérito *m*; **judge sth on its** ∼**s** juzgar algo por lo que vale; ∼ **increase** *n*

BrE (*cf* ▸**merit raise** AmE) aumento salarial por méritos *m*; ∼ **pay** *n* paga por mérito *f*; ∼ **raise** *n* AmE (*cf* ▸**merit increase** BrE) aumento salarial por méritos *m*

meritocracy *n* meritocracia *f*

MERM *abbr* (▸**Multilateral Exchange Rate Model**) MMTC (modelo multilateral de tipos de cambio)

mesoeconomy *n* mesoeconomía *f*

message *n* mensaje *m*; **leave a** ∼ dejar un recado; ∼ **box** *n* (Comp) cuadro de diálogo *m*; ∼ **feedback** *n* comprobación en bucle *f*; ∼ **handling** *n* manejo de mensajes *m*; ∼ **header** *n* encabezamiento de mensaje *m*; ∼ **processing program** *n* programa *m or* software *m* de proceso de mensajes; ∼ **retrieval** *n* recuperación de mensajes *f pl*; ∼ **switching** *n* conmutación de mensajes *f pl*; ∼ **window** *n* cuadro de diálogo *m*

messaging *n* mensajería *f*

messenger *n* mensajero(-a) *m,f*

metadata *n* (Comp) metadatos *m pl*

metamarketing *n* metamarketing *m*

metasearch *n* (Comp) metabúsqueda *f*; ∼ **engine** *n* metadispositivo de búsqueda *m*

meterage *n* AmE (*cf* ▸**meter rate** BrE) medición *f*

metered mail *n* AmE correspondencia con franqueo impreso *f*

meter rate *n* (tariff) tarifa según contador *f*; (measuring) BrE (*cf* ▸**meterage** AmE) medición *f*

method *n* método *m*; ∼**s engineering** *n* ingeniería de métodos *f*; ∼ **of payment** *n* método de pago *m*; ∼ **of preparation** *n* método de preparación *m*; ∼**s study** *n* estudio de métodos *m*; ∼ **of taxation** *n* método de tributación *m*

methodology *n* metodología *f*

metric *adj* métrico; **go** ∼ cambiar al sistema métrico; ∼ **system** *n* sistema métrico *m*

metricate *vi* cambiar al sistema métrico

metrication *n* adopción del sistema métrico *f*

metropolitan *adj* (area, town) metropolitano

mezzanine *adj* (debt, finance, funding) intermedio; ∼ **bracket** *n* (Stock) clasificación intermedia *f*; ∼ **level** *n* nivel de una empresa previo a la cotización en bolsa *m*

mfd *abbr* (▸**manufactured**) manufacturado, fabricado

MFN *abbr* (▸**most-favored nation** AmE, ▸**most-favoured nation** BrE) nación más favorecida *f*

M-form *n* (in job organization) forma M *f*

mfr *abbr* (▸**manufacturer**) fabricante *mf*

MGR *abbr* (▶**manager**) (of company, department) gte. (gerente) (of shop, restaurant) gte. (gerente), encargado(-a) *m,f*; (of estate, fund) administrador(a) *m,f*; (of performer, sportsperson) mánager *mf*

micro *n* micro *m*

microbrowser *n* microbuscador *m*

microchip *n* microchip *m*

microcomputer *n* microcomputadora *f* AmL, microordenador *m* Esp

microcomputing *n* microinformática *f*

microcredit *n* microcrédito *m*

microdecision *n* microdecisión *f*

microdisk *n* microdisco *m*

microeconomic *adj* microeconómico

microeconomics *n* microeconomía *f*

microelectronic *adj* microelectrónico

microelectronics *n* microelectrónica *f*

microfilm *n* microfilme *m*

micromarketing *n* micromarketing *m*

micromarketplace *n* micromercado *m*

micropayment *n* micropago *m*

microprocessor *n* microprocesador *m*

microprogram *n* microprograma *m*

microsegmentation *n* microsegmentación *f*

microtransaction *n* microtransacción *f*

midcareer plateau *n* fase de promoción bloqueada de los mandos intermedios *f*

middle *adj* central, medio; **(take) a ~ course** (hallar) un compromiso entre dos opciones opuestas; **the ~ ground** terreno neutral; **the ~ range of the market** la gama media del mercado; **~ class** *n* clase media *f*; **~-income bracket** *n* grupo de ingresos medios *m*; **~-income taxpayer** *n* contribuyente de ingresos medios *mf*; **~ management** *n* gerencia intermedia *f*, mandos intermedios *m pl*; **~ manager** *n* mando intermedio *m*; **~-strike option** *n* opción a precio medio de ejercicio *f*; **~-strike price** *n* precio medio de ejercicio *m*

middleman *n* intermediario(-a) *m,f*; **cut out the ~** eliminar al intermediario

migrant *adj* (labour, worker, status) migratorio

migration *n* emigración *f*; **~-fed unemployment** *n* desempleo alimentado por migración *m*

migratory *adj* (worker) migratorio

mile *n* milla *f*; **~s per gallon** *n pl* millas por galón *f pl*; **~s per hour** *n pl* millas por hora *f pl*

milestone *n* (significant event) hito *m*

military *adj* militar; **~ attaché** *n* agregado(-a) militar *m,f*

milk *vt* (infrml) (opportunity) aprovechar

milking strategy *n* estrategia de marketing a corto plazo para coger el máximo provecho de un artículo en el tiempo mínimo sin preocuparse de las posibilidades de ventas a largo plazo

milk round *n* BrE *reclutamiento anual de estudiantes universitarios*

mill *n* AmE (thousandth of a dollar) milésima *f*

millionaire *n* millonario(-a) *m,f*

min. *abbr* (▶**minimum**) mínimo

Mind Map® *n* Mind Map® *m*

mindset *n* modo de pensar *m*

mine *n* mina *f*

mineral *n* mineral *m*; **~-based economy** *n* economía basada en los recursos minerales *f*; **~ industry** *n* industria minera *f*; **~ resources** *n pl* recursos minerales *m pl*; **~ rights** *n pl* derechos mineros *m pl*

mini- *pref* mini-; **~-page** *n* minipágina *f*; **~-series** *n* miniserie *f*

minicomputer *n* minicomputadora *f* AmL, miniordenador *m* Esp

minimal *adj* mínimo; **~ state intervention** *n* intervención mínima del Estado *f*

minimax *n* minimax *m*; **~ principle** *n* principio del minimax *m*; **~ strategy** *n* estrategia de aproximación al minimax *f*

minimization *n* minimización *f*

minimize *vt* (cost, risk) reducir (al mínimo), minimizar; (window) minimizar

minimum[1] *adj* (amount, charge, tax) mínimo; **~ balance** *n* saldo mínimo *m*; **~ cost** *n* mínimo *m* de coste Esp *or* de costo AmL; **~ lending rate** *n* BrE tasa de préstamo mínimo *f*; **~ living wage** *n* salario mínimo vital *m*; **~ margin** *n* (Stock) margen mínimo *m*; **~ price change** *n* cambio mínimo en el precio *m*; **~ price fluctuation** *n* fluctuación mínima del precio *f*; **~ quality standard** *n* norma mínima de calidad *f*; **~ quote size** *n* cotización mínima *f*; **~ reserve requirements** *n pl* reserva mínima obligatoria *f*; **~ stock** *n* existencias mínimas *f pl*; **~ wage** *n* salario mínimo *m*

minimum[2] *n* mínimo *m*; **with a ~ of delay** con un mínimo retraso; **with a ~ of effort** con un esfuerzo mínimo; **reduce sth to a ~** reducir algo al mínimo

mining *n* minería *f*; **~ industry** *n* industria minera *f*

ministerial *adj* ministerial; **~ order** *n* BrE orden ministerial *f*

ministry *n* ministerio *m*; **M~ of Transport Test** *n* BrE *examen anual a vehículos británicos,* ≈ Inspección Técnica de Vehículos *m*

minor[1] *adj* menor; (under-age) menor de edad; **~-league** *adj* de segunda, de segundo orden, de segunda fila

minor[2] *n* (child) menor de edad *mf*

minority *n* minoría *f*; **be in a** *o* **the ~** estar en (una *or* la) minoría; **be in a ~ of one** ser una minoría de uno; **~ holding** *n* participación minoritaria *f*; **~ interest** *n* participación minoritaria *f*; **~ investment** *n* inversión minoritaria *f*; **~ shareholder** *n* accionista minoritario(-a) *m,f*; **~ shareholding** *n* accionariado(-a) minoritario *m,f*; **~ stake** *n* participación minoritaria *f*; **~ stockholder** *n* accionista minoritario(-a) *m,f*

mint[1] *n* fábrica de la moneda *f*

mint[2] *vt* (coins) acuñar; (phrase) inventar

Mint *n* Casa de la Moneda *f*

mintage *n* acuñación *f*

minus[1] *n* (symbol) menos *m*; **~ advantage** *n* (jarg) desventaja *f*; **~ balance** *n* saldo *m* negativo *or* desfavorable; **~ sign** *n* signo menos *m*; **~ tick** *n* AmE *venta de un título a precio inferior que el de su cotización inmediatamente anterior*

minus[2] *prep* menos

minute[1] *n* (of time) minuto *m*; (memorandum) nota *f*; **~ book** *n* libro de actas *m*

minute[2] *vt* (meeting) levantar (el) acta de

minutes *n pl* (of meeting) acta *f*; **take (the) ~** levantar (el) acta

minutiae *n pl* minucias *f pl*

mirror site *n* (on Internet) sitio especular *m*

MIS *abbr* (▸**management information system**) SIG (sistema de información para la gestión); (▸**marketing information system**) sistema de información de marketing *m*

misaligned rate of exchange *n* BrE tipo de cambio descentrado *m*

misalignment *n* desalineación *f*, desacuerdo *m*

misallocation *n* asignación inadecuada *f*

misapply *vt* aplicar a destino indebido

misappropriate *vt* (funds) malversar

misappropriation *n* (of funds) malversación *f*

misc. *abbr* (▸**miscellaneous**) vario

miscalculate *vti* calcular mal

miscalculation *n* error de cálculo *m*

miscarriage of justice *n* injusticia *f*

miscellaneous *adj* vario; **file it under ~** archívalo en 'varios'; **~ expenses** *n pl* gastos varios *m pl*

miscoding *n* error de programación *m*

misconduct *n* conducta desordenada *f*

misdeclaration *n* declaración incorrecta *f*

misdemeanour *n* BrE, **misdemeanor** *n* AmE delito menor *m*

misfeasance *n* (behaviour) infidelidad *f*; (act) infidencia *f*

misfile *vt* clasificar incorrectamente

misguided *adj* equivocado

mishandle *vt* (affair, case) llevar mal

mislead *vt* engañar

misleading *adj* (advertising) engañoso; (information) equívoco

mismanage *vt* (company) administrar mal; (affair, negotiations) llevar *or* dirigir mal

mismanagement *n* mala administración *f*

mismatch *n* desalineación *f*, descuadre *m*, desigualdad *f*

mismatched maturity *n* vencimiento desfasado *m*

mispricing *n* error de precios *m*

misprint *n* errata *f*

misread *vt* (situation, intention) interpretar mal, malinterpretar; (writing, word) leer mal

misrepresent *vt* (situation, event) deformar, falsear; (remarks, views) tergiversar

misrepresentation *n* distorsión *f*, deformación *f*; **~ of the facts** tergiversación de los hechos

miss *vt* (appointment, work) faltar a; (chance) perder, dejar pasar; (train, plane) perder; **~ the boat** (infml) perder el tren; **to be too good to ~** ser demasiado bueno para no aprovecharlo; **miss out** *vt* (line, paragraph) saltarse; **miss out on** *vt* perder la oportunidad de

mis-sell *vt* (pension, policy) vender falsamente

mis-selling *n* (of pension, policy) venta falsa *f*

missing *adj* (lost) extraviado; (lacking) que falta; **~ market** *n* mercado no existente *m*

mission *n* misión *f*; **~ statement** *n* formulación de la misión *f*

mistake *n* error *m*; **by ~** por equivocación, por error; **make a ~** cometer un error, equivocarse; **~ of law** *n* error de derecho *m*

mistaken *adj* (impression, idea) equivocado, falso; **~ about sth/sb** equivocado sobre algo/alguien

mistype *vt* mecanografiar mal

misunderstanding *n* malentendido *m*

misuse[1] *n* (of funds) malversación *f*; (of resources) despilfarro *m*; (of power) abuso *m*; (of tool) mal utilización *f*; (of word) mal uso *m*, uso incorrecto *m*

misuse[2] *vt* (funds) malversar; (resources) despilfarrar; (authority) abusar de; (language, tool) utilizar *or* emplear mal

mitigating circumstances *n pl* circunstancias atenuantes *f pl*

mitigation *n* atenuación *f*; **in ~** como (circunstancia) atenuante; **~ of damages** *n* minoración de la indemnización por daños y perjuicios *f*; **~ of taxes** *n* reducción impositiva *f*

mix[1] *n* mezcla *f*; (S&M) combinación de estrategias *f*

mix[2] *vt* mezclar; **~ business with pleasure** mezclar los negocios con el placer

mixed *adj* (account, credit, funds) mixto; (cost) mixto, semifijo, semivariable; (fortunes) desigual; (reception, response) tibio, poco entusiasta; **have ~ feelings (about sth/sb)** tener sentimientos encontrados (sobre algo/alguien); **~ economy** *n* economía mixta *f*; **~ farming** *n* policultivo *m*

MLM *abbr* (►**multilevel marketing**) marketing de varios niveles *m*

MLR *abbr* (►**minimum lending rate**) BrE tasa de préstamo mínimo *f*

MMF *abbr* (►**money market fund**) FIAMM (fondo de inversión en activos del mercado monetario)

MMMF *abbr* (►**money market mutual fund**) FIAMM (fondo de inversión en activos del mercado monetario)

m/o *abbr* (►**my order**) mi orden, mi pedido

MO *abbr* (►**mail order**) pedido por correo *m*; (►**money order**) orden *f or* papel *m* de pago

mobile[1] *adj* móvil; **~ communications** *n pl* comunicacions móviles *f pl*; **~ Internet** *n* Internet móvil *m*; **~ payment** *n* pago móvil *m*; **~ phone** *n*, **~ telephone** *n* BrE (*cf* ►**cellphone** AmE) teléfono móvil *m*, móvil *m*; **~ telephony** *n* telefonía móvil *f*; **~ worker** *n* trabajador(a) itinerante *m,f*

mobile[2] *n* BrE (*cf* ►**cellphone** AmE) móvil *m*

mobility *n* movilidad *f*; **~ clause** *n* BrE cláusula de movilidad *f*; **~ of labor** AmE, **~ of labour** BrE *n* movilidad *f* laboral *or* de trabajo

mode *n* (means) medio *m*; (kind) modo *m*; (Comp) modalidad *f*, modo *m*; **~ of transport** BrE, **~ of transportation** AmE *n* modo de transporte *m*

model *n* (formula, prototype, design) modelo *m*; (scale version) maqueta *f*, modelo *m*; **on the American ~** siguiendo el modelo americano, a imitación del modelo americano; **take/use sth/sb as a ~** tomar/utilizar algo/a alguien de *or* como modelo; **~ profile** *n* perfil del modelo *m*

modem *n* (►**modulator/demodulator**) módem (modulador-desmodulador); **~ link** *n* conexión de módem *f*

moderate[1] *adj* moderado; **~ income** *n* ingreso moderado *m*

moderate[2] *vt* moderar

moderated *adj* (mailing list, chat) moderado

moderator *n* (of group, meeting, newsgroup) moderador(a) *m,f*

modern *adj* moderno; **~ portfolio theory** *n* teoría moderna de la cartera *f*

modernization *n* modernización *f*

modernize *vt* modernizar

modest *adj* (increase) modesto; (recovery) moderado

modestly *adv* modestamente

modification *n* (of data, buildings) modificación *f*; **make ~s to sth** hacerle modificaciones a algo; **with such ~s as the circumstances require** con las modificaciones que las circunstancias requieran

modified *adj* (accrual, life insurance) modificado; **~ net premium** *n* prima neta modificada *f*; **~ re-buy** *n* (jarg) *hábitos de compra modificados*

modify *vt* (design, wording) modificar; (demands, proposal) moderar

modular *adj* (production, housing) modular

modularity *n* modularidad *f*

modulation *n* modulación *f*

modulator/demodulator *n* (Comp) modulador-desmodulador *m*

modus operandi *n* procedimiento *m*

MOF *abbr* (►**multioption facility**) servicio de opción múltiple *m*

MOFF *abbr* (►**multioption financing facility**) servicio de financiación de opción múltiple *m*

mold AmE ►**mould** BrE

momentum *n* impulso *m*

monetarism *n* monetarismo *m*

monetarist[1] *n* monetarista *mf*

monetarist[2] *adj* monetarista

monetary *adj* (policy, inducement) monetario; (asset) monetario, líquido; **~ ease** *n* facilidad monetaria *f*; **~ item** *n* (on balance sheet) partida monetaria *f*; **~ standard** *n* patrón monetario *m*; **~ unit** *n* unidad monetaria *f*

monetization *n* monetización *f*

money *n* dinero *m*; (currency) moneda *f*, dinero *m*; (supply) oferta monetaria *f*; **satisfaction guaranteed or your ~ back** si no queda satisfecho, le devolvemos el dinero; **earn ~** ganar dinero; **he's earning good ~** está ganando un buen sueldo, está ganando bien; **there's ~ in it** es buen negocio; **lose/make ~** perder/hacer dinero; **put ~ down** adelantar el dinero; **put ~ into sth** invertir en algo; **save/spend ~**

ahorrar/gastar dinero; **throw good ∼ after bad** seguir tirando dinero (a la basura); **have ∼ to burn** estar cargado de dinero; **∼ at call** n dinero a la vista m; **∼-back coupon** n vale de reintegro m; **∼-back guarantee** n garantía de devolución del dinero f; **∼-back offer** n oferta de reintegro f; **∼ broker** n corredor(a) de cambios m,f; **∼ in circulation** n dinero en circulación m; **∼ income** n ingresos monetarios m pl; (Tax) renta monetaria f; **∼ laundering** n blanqueo de dinero m; **∼ lender** n prestamista mf; **∼ management** n gestión del dinero f; **∼ market** n mercado de dinero m; **∼ market fund** n fondo de inversión en activos del mercado monetario m; **∼ market institution** n institución del mercado bursátil f; **∼ market instrument** n instrumento del mercado monetario m; **∼ market mutual fund** n fondo de inversión en activos del mercado monetario m; **∼ market paper** n título del mercado monetario m; **∼ market rate** n índice del mercado monetario m; **∼ market return** n rendimiento del mercado monetario m; **∼ market trader** n intermediario(-a) del mercado monetario m,f; **∼ matters** n pl asuntos monetarios m pl; **∼-off pack** n envase con cupón de descuento m; **∼ order** n orden f or papel m de pago; **∼ restraint** n restricción monetaria f; **∼-spinner** n BrE (infrml) fuente de dinero f; **∼ supply** n oferta monetaria f; **∼ transfer order** n orden de transferencia de dinero f; **∼ up front** n pago adelantado m, adelanto de dinero m

moneyed capital n capital reinvertido m

moneymaker n fuente de dinero f

moneymaking[1] adj lucrativo, rentable

moneymaking[2] n enriquecimiento m, lucro m

monies n pl sumas de dinero f pl; **∼ paid in** n pl cobros m pl; **∼ paid out** n pl pagos m pl; **∼ received** n pl dinero recibido m

monitor[1] n (Comp) monitor m; (screen) pantalla f

monitor[2] vt (process, progress) seguir, controlar; (market) controlar; (performance) supervisar; (electronically) monitorizar, monitorear

monitoring n (of process, progress) seguimiento m, control m; (electronic) monitorización f, monitoreo m; (Tax) observación f, verificación f

monochrome adj monocromo

monoeconomics n monoeconomía f

monogram n monograma m

monopolistic adj (competition) monopolístico

monopolization n acaparamiento m; **∼ of goods** n acaparamiento m de bienes or de mercancías

monopolize vt (market, industry) monopolizar; (conversation) acaparar

monopolizer n acaparador(a) m,f

monopoly n monopolio m; **have a ∼ of the market** monopolizar el mercado; **break sb's ∼** acabar con el monopolio de alguien; **Monopolies and Mergers Commission** n comisión británica de monopolios y fusiones; **∼ power** n poder monopolístico m; **∼ price** n precio de monopolio m

monopsonic adj monopsónico

monopsony n monopsonio m

monorail n monorrail m

montage n montaje m

month n mes m; **this ∼'s actuals** disponibilidades del mes en curso; **∼s after sight** n pl meses vencidos m pl; **∼-to-month tenancy** n arrendamiento m mensual or al mes or mes a mes

monthly[1] adj (rent, savings, sales, instalment) mensual; **∼ investment plan** n plan mensual de inversión m; **∼ statement** n (of account, credit card) estado mensual m

monthly[2] adv mensualmente

mood n (state of mind) humor m; (atmosphere) atmósfera f, clima m; **∼ advertising** n publicidad de ambiente f; **∼ conditioning** n condicionante del estado de ánimo m; **∼ music** n música ambiental f

moonlight vi (infrml) tener un segundo empleo (que no se declara), estar pluriempleado

moonlight economy n economía del pluriempleo f

moonlighter n (infrml) pluriempleado(-a) m,f

moonlighting n (infrml) pluriempleo m

moral adj (persuasion) moral; **∼ law** n ética f, ley moral f

morale n moral f; **boost sb's ∼** levantarle la moral a algn; **good/bad for ∼** bueno/malo para la moral; **∼ is high/low** tienen la moral alta/baja

moratorium n moratoria f

MORI abbr (▸**Market and Opinion Research International**) compañía británica de sondeo de la opinión pública, ≈ Demoscopia m Esp

mortality n mortalidad f; **∼ table** n tabla de mortalidad f

mortg. abbr (▸**mortgage**[1]) hipoteca f

mortgage[1] n hipoteca f; **pay off a ∼** terminar de pagar una hipoteca, redimir una hipoteca; **take out a ∼** conseguir una hipoteca; **∼ account** n cuenta hipotecaria f; **∼ arrears** n pl atrasos en el pago de la ⋯⟆

hipoteca *m pl*; **~-backed security** *n* título *m or* valor *m* respaldado por una hipoteca; **~ bank** *n* ≈ banco (de crédito) hipotecario *m*; **~ bond** *n* bono *m* hipotecario *or* con garantía; **~ broker** *n* corredor(a) de hipotecas *m,f*; **~ ceiling** *n* límite máximo de hipoteca *m*, tope de hipoteca *m*; **~ certificate** *n* certificado de hipoteca *m*; **~ company** *n* sociedad hipotecaria *f*; **~ credit association** *n* asociación de crédito hipotecario *f*; **~ debt** *n* deuda hipotecaria *f*; **~ discount** *n* descuento hipotecario *m*; **~ insurance** *n* seguro de hipotecas *m*; **~ lender** *n* prestamista hipotecario(-a) *m,f*; **~ life insurance** *n* AmE seguro de vida con hipoteca *m*; **~ loan** *n* préstamo hipotecario *m*; **~ loan company** *n* empresa de préstamos hipotecarios *f*; **~ market** *n* mercado hipotecario *m*; **~ payment** *n* pago *m* hipotecario *or* de hipoteca; **~ portfolio** *n* cartera hipotecaria *f*; **~ rate** *n* tasa hipotecaria *f*; **~ relief** *n* desgravación hipotecaria *f*; **~ repayment** *n* pago *m* hipotecario *or* de hipoteca; **~ statement** *n* balance hipotecario *m*

mortgage² *vt* hipotecar

mortgagee *n* acreedor(a) hipotecario(-a) *m,f*

mortgager *n*, **mortgagor** *n* deudor(a) hipotecario(-a) *m,f*

most-active list *n* (of stocks) lista de los más activos *f*

most-favored nation *n* AmE, **most-favoured nation** *n* BrE nación más favorecida *f*

MOT *abbr* (▸**Ministry of Transport Test**) examen anual a vehículos británicos; ≈ ITV (Inspección Técnica de Vehículos)

mothball *vt* (project) aparcar, archivar

motherboard *n* (Comp) placa base *f*

mothercard *n* (Comp) placa base *f*

mother of the chapel *n* BrE representant *f or* enlace *f* sindical

motif *n* motivo *m*

motion *n* (for vote) moción *f*; **the ~ was carried** la moción fue aprobada; **go through the ~s (of doing sth)** fingir (hacer algo); **propose a ~** presentar una moción; **put** *o* **set sth in ~** poner algo en marcha; **vote on a ~** votar una moción; **~ of censure** *n* moción de censura *f*; **~ picture** *n* AmE (*cf* ▸**film** BrE) película *f*; **~ picture advertising** *n* AmE publicidad de una película *f*; **~-picture industry** *n* AmE (*cf* ▸**film industry** BrE) industria *f* cinematográfica *or* del cine; **M~ Pictures Experts Group** *n* grupo de expertos de imagen en movimiento *m*

motivate *vt* (staff, decision) motivar

motivation *n* motivación *f*

motivational *adj* (analysis, research) motivacional

motivator *n* motivador *m*

motor *n* motor *m*; **~ fleet** *n* parque móvil *m*; **~ mileage allowance** *n* BrE desgravación por kilometraje *f*; **~ vehicle** *n* automóvil *m*; **~ vehicle insurance** *n* seguro de automóviles *m*

motorway *n* BrE (*cf* ▸**freeway** AmE) autopista *f*

mould¹ BrE, **mold** AmE *n* molde *m*; **break the ~** romper el molde; **be cast in the same ~** estar cortado por el mismo patrón

mould² BrE, **mold** AmE *vt* (public opinion) moldear

mount ① *vt* (campaign, event) organizar, montar; (picket) formar ② *vi* (cost) subir, elevarse

mounting *adj* (cost, expenditure) cada vez mayor, creciente

mouse *n* (Comp) ratón *m*; **by word of ~** de internauta a internauta; **~ button** *n* botón del ratón *m*; **~ driver** *n* unidad de ratón *f*; **~ mat** *n* alfombrilla para ratón *f*

movable property *n* bienes muebles *m pl*

movables *n pl* bienes muebles *m pl*

move¹ ① *vt* (employee) trasladar; (sell) vender; (propose) proponer; **we are moving offices** nos cambiamos de oficina; **~ that...** proponer que... ② *vi* (change location, premises) mudarse, cambiarse; **get sth moving** poner algo en marcha; **~ in tandem** (currencies) evolucionar simultáneamente; (Stock) moverse en serie; **the company plans to ~ into the hotel business** la compañía tiene planes de introducirse en el ramo hotelero; **~ into the money** (Stock) pasarse a opciones dentro del precio; **~ to larger premises** mudarse a un local más grande; **~ to a new job** cambiar de trabajo; **she ~d quickly to scotch the rumours** inmediatamente tomó medidas para acallar los rumores; **move in** *vi* (to new premises) mudarse, cambiarse; **move in on** *vt* (territory, business) invadir; **move out** *vi* (from old premises) mudarse, cambiarse; **move up** *vi* (prices, shares, index) subir

move² *n* (action, step) paso *m*; (measure) medida *f*; (change of premises) traslado *m*, mudanza *f*; (in currency) transferencia *f*; (Stock) jugada *f*; **make the first ~** dar el primer paso; **a good ~** una buena decisión, un paso acertado; **the next ~** el siguiente paso; **the company's ~ into electronics** la entrada de la compañía en el campo de la electrónica; **a smart ~** una maniobra inteligente

movement *n* movimiento *m*; (of price) evolución *f*; (in stock market) actividad *f*;

~ **certificate** n (Imp/Exp) certificado de movimiento m; ~ **of labor** AmE, ~ **of labour** BrE n movimiento de la mano de obra m

mover and shaker n (infrml) promotor(a) e impulsor(a) m,f

movie n AmE (cf ▸**film** BrE) película f

moving average n media móvil f

Moving Pictures Audio Layer 3 n Imagen en Movimiento nivel 3 f

MP abbr BrE (▸**Member of Parliament**) ≈ diputado(-a) m,f, ≈ Miembro del Congreso mf

MP3 n (▸**Moving Pictures Audio Layer 3**) MP3 m (Imagen en Movimiento nivel 3); ~ **file** n archivo MP3 m; ~ **phone** n teléfono MP3 m; ~ **player** n lector MP3 m

MPEG abbr (▸**Motion Pictures Experts Group**) MPEG m, formato MPEG m

mpg abbr (▸**miles per gallon**) millas por galón f pl

mph abbr (▸**miles per hour**) millas por hora f pl

MPP abbr (▸**message processing program**) programa m or software m de proceso de mensajes

MPT abbr (▸**modern portfolio theory**) teoría moderna de la cartera f

MQS abbr (▸**minimum quote size**) cotización mínima f

MRA abbr (▸**multiple regression analysis**) análisis de regresión múltiple m

MRCA abbr (▸**Market Research Corporation of America**) sociedad estadounidense de estudios de mercado

MRP abbr (▸**manufacturer's recommended price**) precio recomendado por el fabricante m; (▸**manufacturing resource planning**) planificación de recursos de fabricación f

MRR abbr (▸**minimum reserve requirements**) reserva mínima obligatoria f

m/s abbr (▸**months after sight**) meses vencidos m pl

MS abbr (▸**manuscript**) manuscrito m; (▸**member state**) estado miembro m

MSc abbr (▸**Master of Science**) Master de Ciencias m

MSRP abbr (▸**manufacturer's suggested retail price**) precio de venta al público sugerido por el fabricante m

MT abbr (▸**mail transfer**) transferencia por correo f; (▸**mean time**) TM (tiempo medio)

MTBF abbr (▸**mean time between failures**) (Comp) tiempo medio entre averías m

MTFS abbr BrE (▸**medium-term financial strategy**) estrategia financiera a medio plazo f

MTN abbr (▸**multilateral trade negotiation**) negociación comercial multilateral f

multiaccess[1] adj multiacceso

multiaccess[2] n multiacceso m

multiannual adj multianual

multibrand stategy n estrategia multimarca f

multichannel adj (strategy, distribution) multicanal, multivía

multiclient adj (survey) multicliente

multicurrency adj (loan, option) multidivisa

multidisciplinary adj multidisciplinario

multiemployer bargaining n negociación con múltiples empresarios f

multifamily adj (housing) multifamiliar

multifunctional adj multifuncional

multijobbing n multitarea f

multijurisdictional adj multijurisdiccional

multilateral adj (agreement, aid, agency) multilateral; ~ **development bank** n banco de desarrollo multilateral m; **M~ Exchange Rate Model** n modelo multilateral de tipos de cambio m; ~ **trade negotiation** n negociación comercial multilateral f

multilateralism n multilateralismo m

multilevel marketing n marketing de varios niveles m

multilingual adj multilingüe

multimedia adj multimedia; ~ **training** n formación f or capacitación f en multimedia

multimillion adj multimillonario; ~ **pound deal** n convenio multimillonario de libras m

multimodal adj (transport) multimodal

multinational[1] adj (company, bank, trading) multinacional

multinational[2] n multinacional f

multinationally adv multinacionalmente

multioption adj de opción múltiple; ~ **facility** n servicio de opción múltiple m; ~ **financing facility** n servicio de financiación de opción múltiple m

multipack n multipack m

multiplant adj (bargaining) multiplanta

multiplatform adj multiplataforma

multiple[1] adj (buyer, taxation) múltiple; ~ **access time** n (Comp) tiempo de acceso múltiple m; ~**-activity chart** n gráfico de actividades múltiples m; ~**-choice** adj de opción múltiple; ~**-choice question** n pregunta de elección múltiple f; ~**-choice test** n examen tipo test m; ~ **exchange rate** n tipo de cambio múltiple m; ····>

~ management n dirección f or gerencia f múltiple; **~-management plan** n plan de gestión múltiple m; **~ regression** n regresión múltiple f; **~-risk insurance** n seguro multirriesgo m

multiple² n múltiple m

multiplication n multiplicación f; **~ sign** n signo de multiplicar m

multiplier n multiplicador m

multiply vt multiplicar

multiprocessing n multiproceso m

multiprocessor n multiprocesador m

multiprogramming n multiprogramación f

multipurpose adj (tool, appliance) multiuso; (peripheral, software) polivalente

multiregional adj multiregional

multisector adj multisectorial

multisegmented adj (operation) multisegmentado

multiskilling n cualificación múltiple f, polivalencia f

multistage adj (tax) en etapas múltiples

multistorey adj BrE, **multistory** adj AmE (building, car park) de varios pisos

multitasking n multitarea f

multiunion adj BrE (bargaining, plant) multisindical

multiunionism n BrE multisindicalismo m

multiuser adj (system) de usuarios múltiples; (licence) de multiusuarios

multivariety store n tienda múltiple f

multiyear adj plurianual, multianual; **~ operational plan** n plan operacional plurianual m; **~ rescheduling agreement** n acuerdo reajustable plurianual m; **~ spending envelope** n partida plurianual de gastos f

municipal adj (government, body) municipal; **~ bond** n AmE bono municipal m; **~ bond offering** AmE n ofrecimiento de bono municipal m; **~ borough** n distrito municipal m, municipio m; **~ revenue bond** n AmE bono municipal que se paga por ingresos

muniment n documento de título m; **~s of title** n pl títulos m pl acreditativos or de propiedad

murder n asesinato m; (Law) homicidio m; **~ one** n AmE (infml) asesinato con premeditación m

Murphy's Law n Ley de Murphy f

must-fit n, **must-fit match** n ajuste obligatorio m

mutilated adj (cheque) mutilado; **~ note** n pagaré deteriorado m; **~ security** n valor cuya impresión no es clara

mutual adj (recognition) mutuo; **by ~ consent** de común acuerdo, por acuerdo or consentimiento mutuo; **~ agreement** n mutuo acuerdo m; **by ~ agreement** de común acuerdo, de convenio mutuo; **~ benefit** n beneficio mutuo m; **the arrangement will be to our ~ benefit** el arreglo será beneficioso para ambos; **~ border** n frontera común f; **~ company** n, **~ corporation** n compañía f or sociedad f mutua; **~ fund** n fondo mutuo m; **~ insurance** n seguro mutuo m; **~ insurance company** n compañía mutua de seguros f; **~ insurer** n aseguradora mutualista f; **M~ Offset System** n (Stock) sistema de compensación mutua m; **~ savings bank** n banco mutualista de ahorros m

mutuality n mutualidad f; **~ of contract** n reciprocidad del contrato f

mutually adv mutuamente; **the contract was ~ beneficial** el contrato era beneficioso para las dos partes; **~ binding** solidario; **~ exclusive** mutuamente excluyente

MYOP abbr (▶**multiyear operational plan**) plan operacional plurianual m

MYRA abbr (▶**multiyear rescheduling agreement**) acuerdo reajustable plurianual m

mystery shopper n (jarg) representante de una compañía que va a varias tiendas pidiendo un artículo específico para comprobar su calidad

Nn

n/a *abbr* (▸**no-account**) sin cuenta

N/A *abbr* (▸**no advice**) sin aviso; (▸**not applicable**) no pertinente, (▸**not available**) no disponible

NAFA *abbr* (▸**net acquisition of financial assets**) adquisición neta de activos financieros *f*

NAFTA *abbr* (▸**North American Free Trade Agreement**) TLC (Tratado de Libre Comercio)

naked *adj* (ambition) puro; ~ **call** *n* compra sin garantía *f*; ~ **call option** *n* opción de compra de acciones sin garantía *f*; ~ **option** *n* opción sin garantía *f*; ~ **position** *n* posición en descubierto *f*; ~ **put** *n* opción doble sin garantía *f*

name[1] *n* (of person, company) nombre *m*; **by** ~ de nombre; **by** *o* **of the** ~ **of** llamado; **clear one's** ~ probar su inocencia; **large profits, that's the** ~ **of the game** grandes ganancias, de eso se trata; **give sth/sb a bad** ~ dar mala fama a algo/alguien; **in my** ~ **and on my behalf** en mi nombre y representación; **in my** ~, **place and stead** en mi nombre y representación; **in the** ~ **of** en nombre de; **in** ~ **only** sólo de nombre; **make a** ~ **for oneself** *o* **make one's** ~ hacerse famoso; ~ **badge** *n* gafete de identificación *m*; ~ **brand** *n* nombre de marca *m*; ~ **day** *n* (on London Stock Exchange) día anterior al de liquidación *m*

name[2] *vt* (company) ponerle nombre a; (appoint) nombrar; ~ **a date for sth** fijar una fecha para algo; ~ **and shame sb** avergonzar a alguien públicamente

named *adj* (person) designado; (client) nominativo

namely *adv* a saber

nanny: ~ **software** *n* software de filtración *m*; ~ **state** *n* papá-estado *m*

narcodollars *n pl* (infrml) narcodólares *m pl* (infrml)

narrow[1] *adj* (range, view) limitado; (attitude, ideas) cerrado, intolerante; (band) estrecho; (margin) escaso, estrecho, reducido; (market) flojo, con escasez de operaciones

narrow[2] [1] *vt* (gap) estrechar; (limit) restringir, limitar

[2] *vi* (spread) estrechar; (gap) reducirse; (options, odds) reducirse; (field) restringirse; **narrow down** *vt* reducir; **narrow sth down to sth** reducir algo a algo

narrowcasting *n* (S&M) selección limitada *f*

narrowing *adj* (inflation gap) decreciente

NASD *abbr* (▸**National Association of Securities Dealers**) *asociación estadounidense de operadores de bolsa*

NASDAQ *abbr* (▸**National Association of Securities Dealers Automated Quotation**) *cotización automatizada de la asociación estadounidense de operadores de bolsa*

nat. *abbr* (▸**national**) nacional

national *adj* (bank, currency, campaign, average) nacional; (affairs) interno; **N~ Association of Securities Dealers** *n asociación estadounidense de operadores en bolsa*; **N~ Association of Securities Dealers Automated Quotation** *n cotización automatizada de la asociación estadounidense de operadores de bolsa*; **N~ Bureau of Standards** *n oficina estadounidense de normalización*; **N~ Curriculum** *n* BrE ≈ Diseño Curricular Base *m* Esp; ~ **debt** *n* BrE (*cf* ▸**public debt** AmE) deuda *f* nacional *or* pública; ~ **demand** *n* demanda nacional *f*; ~ **grid** *n red británica de suministro de electricidad*; ~ **insurance** *n* BrE ≈ Seguridad Social *f*; ~ **insurance contribution** *n* BrE aportación a la seguridad social *f*; ~ **insurance number** *n* BrE ≈ número de afiliación a la Seguridad Social *m*; ~ **interest** *n* interés nacional *m*, razón de estado *f*; **N~ Lottery** *n* Lotería Nacional *f*; ~ **minimum wage** *n* salario mínimo nacional *m*; ~ **newspaper** *n* periódico nacional *m*; ~ **press** *n* prensa nacional *f*; ~ **sales tax** *n* AmE impuesto nacional sobre ventas *m*; ~ **savings certificate** *n* BrE bono de ahorro del estado *m*; **N~ Securities Clearing Corporation** *n* AmE ≈ Corporación Nacional de Compensación de Valores *f*; **N~ Wages Council** *n consejo británico salarial*; ~ **wealth** *n* riqueza nacional *f*

nationalism *n* nacionalismo *m*

nationalization *n* nacionalización *f*

nationalize *vt* nacionalizar

nationalized *adj* (industry, enterprise, sector) nacionalizado

nationally *adv* (organized, coordinated) a escala nacional; (advertised, distributed) por todo el país, a escala nacional

nationwide¹ *adj* (campaign) a escala nacional; **a ~ network of agents** una red de agentes que cubre todo el territorio nacional

nationwide² *adv* (distribute, operate) a escala nacional

native *adj* (land, country) natal; (industry) nacional

natural *adj* (rights, price, monopoly) natural; (increase) vegetativo; **~ break** *n* interrupción natural *f*; **~ business year** *n* año comercial natural *m*; **~ capital** *n* capital constituido por tierras *m*; **~ gas** *n* gas natural *m*; **~ number** *n* (Comp) entero natural *m*; **~ person** *n* persona física *f*; **~ rate of employment** *n* tasa natural de empleo *f*; **~ rate of growth** *n* tasa natural de crecimiento *f*; **~ rate of interest** *n* tasa natural de interés *f*; **~ resources** *n pl* recursos naturales *m pl*; **~ resources management** *n* gestión de los recursos naturales *f*; **~ wastage** *n* (of workforce) bajas voluntarias (cuando luego los puestos quedan sin cubrir) *f pl*

nature *n* naturaleza *f*; **~ conservation** *n* conservación de la naturaleza *f*

NAV *abbr* (▸**net asset value**) VAN (valor de activo neto)

navigate *vi* (on Internet) navegar (en el Internet)

navigation *n* (Transp, Comp) navegación *f*; **~ aid** *n* (Comp) soporte de navegación *m*; **~ bar** *n* (Comp) barra de navegación *f*

NB *abbr* (▸**nota bene**) nota bene

NBV *abbr* (▸**no business value**) sin valor comercial

NC *abbr* (education) BrE (▸**National Curriculum**) ≈ DCB (Diseño Curricular Base) Esp

NCR *abbr* (▸**net cash requirement**) necesidades de contado *f pl*

NCS *abbr* (▸**noncallable securities**) *valores no rescatables antes de su vencimiento*

n.c.v. *abbr* (▸**no commercial value**) sin valor comercial

NCV *abbr* (▸**no customs value**) sin valor en aduana

NDP *abbr* (▸**net domestic product**) PIN (producto interior neto)

near¹ *adj* cercano, próximo; **in the ~ future** en un futuro próximo; **~-cash items** *n pl* activos líquidos *m pl*; **~ future** *n* futuro inmediato *m*; **~ letter quality** *n* calidad casi de correspondencia *f*; **~ money** *n* cuasi dinero *m*

near² *vt* acercarse a; **the project is ~ing completion** el proyecto está por acabar

nearby contracts *n pl*, **nearbys** *n pl* (jarg) contratos de futuros *m pl*

nearest month *n* mes inmediato *m*

nearly contract *n* cuasi contrato *m*

necessary *adj* necesario; **~ labor** AmE, **~ labour** BrE *n* (workers) mano de obra *f* indispensable *or* necesaria; (work) trabajo necesario *m*

necessity *n* (need) necesidad *f*; (necessary item) cosa necesaria *f*; **the bare necessities** lo indispensable, lo imprescindible; **the ~ for reform** la necesidad de una reforma; **of ~** necesariamente; **out of ~** por necesidad

need¹ *n* necesidad *f*; **~ for sth** necesidad de algo; **if ~ be** si fuera necesario; **those in ~** los necesitados; **be in (urgent) ~ of sth** necesitar algo (urgentemente); **there's no ~ to do sth** no hay necesidad de hacer algo; **~s analysis** *n* análisis de necesidades *m*; **~s test** *n* (Tax) comprobación de necesidades *f*

need² *vt* necesitar; **~ to do sth** tener que hacer algo; **our firm ~s to be more competitive** nuestra empresa debe ser más competitiva

need-to-know basis *n* base de necesidad de conocimiento *f*

needy¹ *adj* necesitado

needy² *n pl* necesitados *m pl*

negate *vt* invalidar

negative *adj* negativo; **~ cash flow** *n* cash-flow *m or* flujo de caja *m* negativo, liquidez negativa *f*; **~ feedback** *n* reacción negativa *f*, feedback negativo *m*; **~ income tax** *n* impuesto negativo sobre la renta *m*; **~ net worth** *n* valor neto negativo *m*; **~ option** *n* opción negativa *f*; **~-sum game** *n* juego de suma negativa *m*

neglect¹ *vt* (business) descuidar; (duty, obligations) desatender, faltar a, no cumplir con; **~ to do sth** omitir hacer algo; **~ to mention that...** omitir mencionar que...

neglect² *n* (lack of care) abandono *m*; (negligence) negligencia *f*; (of duty, obligations) incumplimiento *m*; **~ clause** *n* cláusula de negligencia *f*

neglected *adj* (building) abandonado; (opportunity) desaprovechado; (promise) incumplido

negligence *n* negligencia *f*, descuido *m*; **~ clause** *n* cláusula de negligencia *f*

negligent *adj* negligente

negligently *adv* negligentemente

negotiability *n* negociabilidad *f*

negotiable *adj* (bill, contract) negociable; **~ salary** ~ sueldo negociable *or* a negociar; **~ bill of exchange** *n* letra de cambio negociable *f*; **~ bill of lading** *n* conocimiento de embarque negociable *m*; **~ instrument** *n* título negociable *m*; **~ order of withdrawal** *n* orden negociable de retirada *f*; ～ **order of withdrawal account** *n* cuenta de ahorro a la vista con interés *f*

negotiate **1** *vt* (contract, settlement, bill, draft) negociar; (loan) gestionar, negociar; (difficulty) superar; ～ **sth with sb** negociar algo con alguien

2 *vi* negociar; ～ **with sb** negociar con alguien

negotiated *adj* (price, underwriting) negociado; ～ **market price** *n* precio de mercado negociado *m*

negotiating *adj* (committee, team) negociador, encargado de las negociaciones; (position) negociador; (procedure) de negociación; ～ **bank** *n banco que negocia un crédito*; ～ **machinery** *n* (in industrial relations) mecanismo de negociación *m*; ～ **table** *n* mesa de negociaciones *f*

negotiation *n* negociación *f*; **by** ～ mediante negociaciones *or* negociación; **enter into/be in** ～**s with sb** entrar en/estar en negociaciones con alguien; **the contract is still under** ～ todavía se está negociando el contrato; ～ **fee** *n* (Bank) costo de negociación *m*, gastos de tramitación *m pl*; ～ **strategy** *n* estrategia de negociación *f*

negotiator *n* negociador(a) *m,f*

neighborhood AmE ►**neighbourhood** BrE; ～ **store** *n* AmE (*cf* ►**local shop** BrE, ►**corner shop** BrE) tienda de barrio *f*

neighboring AmE ►**neighbouring** BrE

neighbourhood BrE, **neighborhood** AmE *n* vecindario *m*; ～ **effect** *n* efecto externo *m*

neighbouring BrE, **neighboring** AmE *adj* (country) vecino

neocorporatism *n* neocorporativismo *m*

neomalthusianism *n* neomaltusianismo *m*

neomercantilism *n* neomercantilismo *m*

neon sign *n* rótulo de neón *m*

nepotism *n* nepotismo *m*

nerve centre BrE, **nerve center** AmE *n* centro *m or* punto *m* neurálgico

NES *abbr* (►**not elsewhere specified**) no especificado en otro punto

nest *vt* (Comp) anidar

nest egg *n* (infrml) ahorros *m pl*

nesting *n* (Comp) anidamiento *m*

net [1] *adj* (Fin) neto; (effect, result) global; ～ **of sth** neto de algo; ～ **acquisition of financial assets** *n* adquisición neta de activos financieros *f*; ～ **acquisitions** *n pl* adquisiciones netas *f pl*; ～ **asset** *n* activo neto *m*; ～ **asset value** *n* valor de activo neto *m*; ～ **book value** *n* valor neto en libros *m*; ～ **borrowing** *n* empréstitos *m pl or* préstamos *m pl* netos; ～ **capital expenditure** *n* gasto neto de capital *m*;

～ **capital gain** *n* plusvalías netas *f pl*; ～ **capital loss** *n* minusvalías netas *f pl*; ～ **capital requirement** *n* exigencia neta del capital *f*; ～ **capital spending** *n* gasto neto de capital *m*; ～ **cash flow** *n* flujo neto de caja *m*; ～ **cash requirement** *n* necesidades de contado *f pl*; ～ **change** *n* variación neta *f*; ～ **contribution** *n* contribución neta *f*; ～ **cost** *n* coste *m* Esp *or* costo *m* AmL neto; ～ **current asset** *n* activo neto circulante *m*; ～ **debit** *n* débito neto *m*; ～ **debt** *n* deuda neta *f*; ～ **dividend** *n* dividendo neto *m*; ～ **domestic product** *n* producto interior neto *m*; ～ **earnings** *n pl* ganancias netas *f pl*; ～ **equity** *n* capital propio *m*, patrimonio neto *m*; ～ **expenditure** *n* desembolso neto *m*; ～ **federal tax** *n* AmE impuesto federal neto *m*; ～ **forward position** *n* posición futura neta *f*; ～ **gain** *n* ganancia neta *f*; ～ **income** *n* ingreso neto *m*, renta neta *f*; ～ **interest** *n* interés neto *m*; ～ **investment position** *n* posición de inversión neta *f*; ～ **listing** *n* (Prop) listado neto *m*; ～ **loss** *n* pérdida neta *f*; ～ **margin** *n* margen neto *m*; ～ **operating income** *n* beneficio de explotación neto *m*; ～ **operating loss** *n* pérdida de explotación neta *f*; ～ **operating profit** *n* beneficio neto de operación *m*; ～ **output** *n* producción neta *f*; ～ **pay** *n* salario neto *m*; ～ **premium** *n* prima neta *f*; ～ **present value** *n* valor actual neto *m*; ～ **price** *n* precio neto *m*; ～ **proceeds** *n pl* (from sale) producto neto *m*; ～ **profit** *n* beneficio neto *m*; ～ **profit margin** *n* margen de beneficio neto *m*; ～ **purchases** *n pl* compras netas *f pl*; ～ **rate** *n* (of interest on loan) tasa neta *f*; ～ **realizable value** *n* valor realizable neto *m*; ～ **receipts** *n pl* entradas netas *f pl*, ingresos netos *m pl*; ～ **recorded assets** *n pl* activos contabilizados netos *m pl*; ～ **register** *n* registro neto *m*; ～ **remittance** *n* consignación neta *f*, remesa neta *f*; ～ **sales** *n pl* ventas netas *f pl*; ～ **surplus** *n* superávit neto *m*; ～ **taxable capital gain** *n* plusvalías netas imponibles *f pl*; ～ **value** *n* valor neto *m*; ～ **weight** *n* peso neto *m*; ～ **working capital** *n* capital circulante neto *m*; ～ **worth** *n* activo neto *m*; ～ **yield** *n* (of share) rendimiento neto *m*

net² *vt* rendir; **net against** *vt* deducir de

Net *n* Internet *m*, Red *f*, Web *f*, Telaraña *f*; ～ **access** *n* acceso al Internet *m*; ～ **browser** *n* buscador *m*; ～ **economy** *n* neteconomía *f*; ～**-enabled** *adj* preparado para el Internet; ～ **generation** *n* generación Internet *f*, cibergeneración *f*; ～ **market** *n* cibermercado *m*

netcasting *n* difusión en red *f*

netiquette *n* netiqueta *f*

n

netizen n internauta mf, ciberciudadano(-a) m,f

netrepreneur n empresario(-a) de Internet m,f

netspeak n ciberlenguaje m

netsurf vti navegar

netsurfer n (person) internauta mf, navegador(a) m,f; (computer) computadora f AmL or ordenador m Esp de red

netsurfing n navegación (por la red) f

network¹ n (system) red f; (in broadcasting) cadena f; ~ **analysis** n análisis de una red m; ~ **architect** n arquitecto(-a) de red m,f; ~ **building** n construcción de red f; ~ **engineer** n ingeniero(-a) de red m,f; ~ **manager** n director(a) de red m,f; ~ **marketing** n marketing de red m; ~ **television** n AmE emisiones televisivas en cadena f pl

network² [1] vt (Comp) interconectar; (broadcast) transmitir en cadena [2] vi hacer contactos en el mundo de negocios

networking n (Comp) gestión de redes f; (making business contacts) establecimiento de contactos en el mundo de negocios; ~ **software** n programa m or software m de gestión de redes

neural network n red neural f

neurolinguistic programming n programación neurolingüística f

neutral adj neutral; ~ **to bearish** neutral a la baja

neutralism n neutralismo m

neutrality n neutralidad f

never-never n BrE (infrml) compra a crédito or a plazos f; **pay for/buy sth on the** ~ pagar/comprar algo a plazos

nevertheless adv no obstante

new adj nuevo; ~ **business** n nuevo giro m; ~ **deal** n nuevo trato m; ~ **economy** n economía nueva f; ~ **edition** n nueva edición f; ~**-for-old insurance** n seguro de valor de nuevo m; ~ **information and communications technologies** n nueva tecnología de la información y la comunicación f; ~ **issue** n (Stock) nueva emisión f; ~ **money** n dinero fresco m; ~**-product development** n desarrollo de nuevo producto m; ~ **technology** n tecnología nueva f; ~ **technology agreement** n acuerdo m or contrato m sobre nueva tecnología; ~ **world order** n nuevo orden mundial m; ~ **year** n año nuevo m

newbie n (infrml) (on Internet) novato(-a) m,f

newcomer n (to sector, market) recién llegado(-a) m,f

newly adj (elected) recientemente; ~ **industrialized country** n país recientemente industrializado m; ~ **privatized** adj de reciente privatización

news n noticias f pl; (piece of news) noticia f; **be in the** ~ estar de actualidad, ser noticia; ~ **agency** n BrE (cf ►**wire service** AmE) agencia de noticias f; ~ **bulletin** n espacio informativo m; ~ **conference** n rueda f or conferencia f de prensa; ~ **coverage** n cobertura f informativa or de noticias; ~ **editor** n redactor(a) jefe(-a) m,f; ~ **flash** n avance de noticias m; ~ **headlines** n pl titulares m pl; ~ **item** n noticia f; ~**-on-demand** n noticias f pl a petición or a solicitud; ~ **posting** n (on Internet) boletín de foro m; ~ **round-up** n resumen informativo m; ~ **server** n (on Internet) servidor de noticias m; ~ **service** n agencia de noticias f; ~ **sheet** n hoja de noticias f

newscaster n presentador(a) de noticias m,f

newsfeed n servicio electrónico de noticias m

newsgroup n foro de interés m, grupo de discusión m, newsgroup m

newsletter n (printed, e-mailed) boletín m

newspaper n periódico m, diario m; ~ **advertisement** n anuncio de periódico m; ~ **advertising** n publicidad en periódicos f; ~ **publisher** n redactor(a) jefe de un periódico m,f; ~ **syndicate** n sindicato m periodístico or de periódicos

newsroom n redacción f

New York n Nueva York f; ~ **York Futures Exchange** n mercado de futuros de Nueva York; ~ **York Mercantile Exchange** n bolsa mercantil de Nueva York; ~ **York Stock Exchange** n bolsa de Nueva York f

next-generation adj (software, computer, product) de la próxima generación

next-to-reading matter n espacio publicitario al lado de texto redaccional

NFTZ abbr (►**Non Free-Trade Zone**) zona de no libre comercio f

NGO abbr (►**nongovernmental organization**) ONG (organización no gubernamental)

NI abbr BrE (►**national insurance**) ≈ Seguridad Social f

NIC abbr (►**national insurance contribution**) aportación a la seguridad social f; (►**newly industrialized country**) país recientemente industrializado m

niche n buena posición f, colocación conveniente f; (S&M) nicho m; ~ **market** n mercado altamente especializado m; ~ **marketing** n marketing especializado m

NICT *abbr* (▸**new information and communications technologies**) nueva tecnología de la información y la comunicación *f*

night *n* noche *f*; ~ **depository** *n* depósito *m* nocturno *or* fuera de hora; ~ **letter** *n* AmE telegrama de madrugada *m*; ~ **safe** *n* depósito *m* nocturno *or* fuera de hora; ~ **shift** *n* turno de noche *m*; ~ **work** *n* trabajo nocturno *m*

Nikkei *n* Nikkei *m*; ~ **Average** *n* promedio Nikkei *m*; ~ **Index** *n* índice Nikkei *m*

nil *n* cero *m*; ~ **paid** pago nulo *m*

NIMBY *abbr* (▸**not in my backyard**) *en mi patio no* (*campaña contra el vertido de desechos tóxicos cerca de viviendas*)

nine-bond rule *n* (of New York Stock Exchange) regla de los nueve bonos *f*

ninety-nine-year lease *n contrato de arrendamiento por noventa y nueve años*

NIT *abbr* (▸**negative income tax**) impuesto negativo sobre la renta *m*

NLP *abbr* (▸**neurolinguistic programming**) programación neuro-lingüística *f*

NLQ *abbr* (▸**near letter quality**) NLQ (calidad casi de correspondencia)

NMS *abbr* (▸**normal market size**) BrE amplitud normal del mercado *f*

no. *abbr* (▸**number**) núm, n, n° (número)

no-account *adj* sin cuenta

no-claim(s) bonus *n* BrE bonificación por no tener reclamaciones *f*

no-competition pact *n* pacto de no competencia *m*

node *n* nodo *m*

no-fault *adj* sin culpa *m*; ~ **automobile insurance** AmE, ~ **car insurance** BrE *n* seguro del automóvil sin culpa *m*

no-frills *adj* (model) práctico y funcional, sin lujos; (flight) barato; (design) sencillo

no-growth *adj* sin crecimiento

noise *n* ruido *m*; ~ **emission** *n* sonoemisión *f*; ~ **insulation** *n* aislamiento del ruido *m*; ~ **level** *n* nivel del ruido *m*

no-load fund *n* AmE fondo sin gastos de gestión *m*

no-loan fund *n* fondo de inversión no proveniente de préstamo *m*

nominal *adj* (asset, price, growth) nominal; (fee, rent) simbólico; ~ **damages** *n pl* daños *m pl* nominales *or* de poca consideración; ~ **GDP** *n* valor nominal del PIB *m*; ~ **interest** *n* interés nominal *m*; ~ **interest rate** *n* tasa nominal de interés *f*; ~ **ledger** *n* libro mayor nominal *m*; ~ **quotation** *n* cotización nominal *f*; ~ **value** *n* valor nominal *m*; ~ **wage** *n* salario nominal *m*

nominate *vt* (appoint, choose) nombrar, designar; ~ **sb (for sth)** proponer a alguien (para algo)

nomination *n* (appointment, choice) nombramiento *m*, designación *f*; (proposal) propuesta *f*, postulación *f* AmL

nominee *n* candidato(-a) propuesto(-a) *m,f*, nominatario(-a) *m,f*; (Stock) sociedad interpuesta *f*; ~ **account** *n* cuenta nominal *f*; ~ **company** *n* sociedad interpuesta *f*; ~ **shareholder** *n*, ~ **stockholder** *n* accionista nominatario(-a) *m,f*

nonacceptance *n* inaceptación *f*; (of bill, note) rechazo *m*

nonaccruing *adj* (loan) no acumulable

nonadjustable *adj* (rate) no ajustable

nonagricultural *adj* (use) no agrícola

nonappearance *n* (Law) contumacia *f*

nonapproved *adj* (options) sin aprobar; ~ **pension scheme** *n* BrE plan de pensiones no aprobado *m*

non-arm's-length *adj* en desigualdad de condiciones; ~ **transaction** *n* transacción comercial sin favor *f*

nonattendance *n* ausencia *f*, no asistencia *f*

nonattributable *adj* no atribuible

nonaudit *adj* sin auditar

nonavailability *n* no disponibilidad *f*

nonbank *adj* (financial institution) no bancario; ~ **bank** *n* sociedad que realiza ciertas prácticas bancarias *f*

nonbanking *adj* (sector) no bancario

nonbasic *adj* (industry, commodity) no básico

nonbudgetary *adj* no presupuestario; ~ **total** *n* total no presupuestario *m*

nonbusiness *adj* no comercial, no empresarial; ~ **income tax** *n* impuesto sobre la renta de actividades no comerciales *m*

noncallable *adj* (bond) no redimible; ~ **securities** *n valores no rescatables antes de su vencimiento*

noncash *adj* (payment system) no al contado; (payment) no dinerario; (rewards) en especies; (self-service) sin dinero

noncheckable AmE, **nonchequable** BrE *adj* (account) sin emisión de cheques; (deposit) que no admite cheques

nonclearing *adj* (item) no compensable; (member) no liquidador

noncommercial *adj* no comercial

noncommittal *adj* (reply) evasivo, que no compromete a nada

noncompeting *adj* (group) no competidor

noncompetitive *adj* (bid) sin competencia

noncompletion *n* incumplimiento *m*

noncompliance *n* incumplimiento *m*; ∼ **with sth** incumplimiento de algo

noncompulsory *adj* voluntario; (Law) no obligatorio; ∼ **expenditure** *n* gasto no obligatorio *m*

nonconcessional *adj* no concesionario

nonconforming *adj* (use) no conforme

nonconformity *n* disconformidad *f*

nonconsolidated *adj* no consolidado

noncontestability clause *n* cláusula *f* de no disputa *or* de no objeción

noncontribution clause *n* cláusula de no contribución *f*

noncontributory *adj* (pension fund, pension plan, pension scheme) no contributivo

noncontrollable *adj* (cost) incontrolable

nonconvertible *adj* (bond) no convertible

noncooperation *n* no cooperación

noncreditable *adj* (tax) no acreditable

noncumulative *adj* (tax) no acumulativo; ∼ **preferred stock** *n* acciones privilegiadas de dividendo no acumulativo *f pl*

noncurrent *adj* (asset) fijo, inmovilizado, no circulante; (loan) vencido

noncyclical *adj* (performance) acíclico

nondebugged *adj* sin corregir los errores

nondeductibility *n* (of employer contributions) indeducibilidad *f*, no deducibilidad *f*

nondelivery *n* no entrega *f*

nondestructive *adj* (testing) no destructivo

nondisclosure *n* encubrimiento *m*

nondiscretionary *adj* (trust) no discrecional

nondiscrimination notice *n* apercibimiento *m or* notificación *f* de no discriminación

nondisturbance clause *n* cláusula de inalterabilidad *f*

nondurable *adj* (goods) no duradero

nondurables *n pl* productos perecederos *m pl*

nondutiable *adj* exento de derechos o aranceles

nonencashable *adj* (deposit) no canjeable, no liquidable

nonessential *adj* secundario, accesario, no esencial

non-EU national *n* persona no perteneciente a la UE *f*

nonexecution *n* incumplimiento *m*

nonexecutive *adj* (director) sin funciones ejecutivas

nonexempt *adj* no exento

nonfeasance *n* incumplimiento *m*; (Law) omisión *f*

nonfiler *n* (Tax) *contribuyente que no presenta declaración*

nonfiling *n* (of tax return, tax form) falta de presentación *f*

nonfinancial *adj* (reward) no financiero

Non Free-Trade Zone *n* zona de no libre comercio *f*

nonfulfilment *n* BrE, **nonfulfillment** AmE *n* (of contract) incumplimiento *m*

nonfungible goods *n pl* bienes no fungibles *m pl*

nongovernmental organization *n* organización no gubernamental *f*

noninterest *adj* (earnings) sin intereses

noninterest-bearing *adj* sin (rendimiento de) intereses, que no devenga interés; ∼ **deposit** *n* depósito que no devenga interés *m*; ∼ **securities** *n pl* acciones sin intereses *f pl*

nonintervention *n* desintermediación *f*; (Pol) no intervención *f*

nonlife insurance *n* seguro no de vida *m*

nonlinear programming *n* programación no lineal *f*

nonlisted *adj* (securities, company) no cotizado en bolsa

nonluxury *adj* (goods) no lujoso

nonmandatory *adj* (guidelines) no preceptivo

nonmanual *adj* (worker) no manual

nonmanufacturing *adj* (sector) no manufacturero

nonmarketable *adj* no negociable; ∼ **instrument** *n* instrumento no negociable *m*; ∼ **title** *n* BrE (*cf* ▸**nonmerchantable title** AmE) título *m* intransferible *or* no negociable

nonmarket sector *n* sector no comercializado *m*

nonmember *n* no socio(-a) *m,f*; ∼ **bank** *n* AmE *banco que no es miembro de la Reserva Federal*; ∼ **corporation** *n* corporación no respaldada *f*; ∼ **firm** *n* firma no reconocida *f*

nonmerchantable title *n* AmE (*cf* ▸**nonmarketable title** BrE) título *m* intransferible *or* no negociable

nonmetropolitan *adj* no metropolitano

nonmonetary *adj* (investment) no monetario; (rewards) en especies

non-negotiable *adj* (cheque) no negociable; ∼ **instrument** *n* documento *m or* instrumento *m* no negociable

nonobligatory *adj* no obligatorio

nonobservance *n* (of conditions) inobservancia *f*

nonoccupying owner *n* propietario(-a) no ocupante *m,f*

nonofficial (organization) *adj* no oficial

nonoil *adj* (country) carente de petróleo

nonoperating *adj* (expense, revenue) ajeno a la operación

nonparticipating *adj* (share, stock) no participativo

nonpayment *n* impago *m*, falta de pago *f*

nonpecuniary *adj* (returns) no pecuniario

nonpenalized *adj* (adjustment) sin recargo; ∼ **taxable income** *n* ingreso imponible sin recargo *m*

nonperformance *n* incumplimiento *m*

nonperforming *adj* (assets) improductivo; (credit) en falta de cumplimiento, en falta de ejecución, en mora; (loan) no ejecutable

nonproductive *adj* (loan) improductivo; (HRM, Mgmnt) no productivo

nonprofessional *adj* (behaviour) no profesional

nonprofit AmE ▸**non-profit-making** BrE

nonprofitable *adj* no lucrativo, sin ánimo de lucro, sin beneficio

non-profit-making BrE, **nonprofit** AmE *adj* (accounting, enterprise) no lucrativo; (company) sin fines de lucro; (association, organization) sin afán *or* ánimo de lucro

nonpublic *adj* (information) privado

nonpurpose loan *n* préstamo sin finalidad declarada *m*

nonqualifying *adj* (share, annuity, business) no habilitante; ∼ **stock option** *n* opción-bono no remunerativa *f*

nonquoted *adj* no cotizado

nonrecourse *adj* (finance) sin posibilidad de recurso; (financing) sin recursos

nonrecoverable *adj* no recuperable

nonrecurring *adj* (charge) no recurrente; ∼ **appropriation** *n* asignación extraordinaria *f*

nonrecyclable *adj* no reciclable

nonrefundable *adj* (deposit, fee, tax) no reembolsable; (Stock) no reintegrable

nonregistrant *n* no inscrito(-a) *m,f*

nonrenewable *adj* (resource) no renovable

nonresident[1] *adj* (company, bank) no residente; (tax) de no residente, de visitante

nonresident[2] *n* no residente *mf*

nonresidential *adj* (mortgage) no residencial

nonreusable *adj* no reutilizable

nonroutine *adj* (decision) no rutinario

nonscheduled *adj* no programado

nonsegregated *adj* (account) no segregado

nonstandard *adj* (mail) sin normalizar; ∼ **tax relief** *n* reducción impositiva no ordinaria *f*

nonstatutory *adj* no obligatorio

nonsterling *adj* (area) de no influencia de la libra esterlina

nonstock company *n* BrE, ∼ **corporation** *n* AmE sociedad sin acciones *f*

nonstop *adj* (flight) sin escalas

nonstore retailing *n* venta minorista directa *f*

nontariff *adj* (barrier) no arancelario

nontax *adj* (receipts) no tributario; (revenue) no tributario, libre de impuestos

nontaxable *adj* (income) no sujeto al pago de impuestos, exento del pago de impuestos; (beneficiary, obligation) no imponible; (year) no impositivo; ∼ **profitable firm** *n* compañía mercantil no imponible *f*

nontradables *n pl* no comerciables *m pl*

nontransferable *adj* intransferible

non-union *adj* (labour) no sindicado; (company) no sindicado, no sindicalizado

nonutilized *adj* (line of credit) inutilizado

nonvariable *adj* no variable

nonverbal *adj* (communication) no verbal

nonvoting *adj* (shares, stock) sin derecho de voto

nonworking *adj* (spouse) que no trabaja

non-zero-sum game *n* juego de suma no nula *m*

no-par *adj* (stock, securities) sin valor nominal

no-par-value *adj* (share) sin valor nominal

norm *n* norma *f*

normal[1] *adj* (price, rate, practice) normal; ∼ **course of business** *n* desarrollo normal de la empresa *m*; ∼ **market size** *n* BrE amplitud normal del mercado *f*; ∼ **relationship** *n* (in prices) relación normal *f*; ∼ **retirement age** *n* edad normal de jubilación *f*; ∼ **trading unit** *n* unidad normal de negociación *f*; ∼ **wear and tear** *n* uso *m* y desgaste *m* normales

normal[2] *n* normal *m*; above/below ∼ por encima/por debajo de lo normal; when things get back to ∼ cuando todo vuelva a la normalidad

normalcy *n* AmE, **normality** *n* BrE normalidad *f*

normative *adj* (economics, forecasting) normativo

North American Free Trade Agreement *n* Tratado de Libre Comercio *m*

North Sea gas *n* gas del Mar del Norte *m*

nosedive[1] *n* caída en picado *f*; **prices took a ~ yesterday** ayer los precios cayeron en picado

nosedive[2] *vi* (prices) caer en picado; (reputation, popularity) sufrir un bajón

no-show *n* (infrml) *pasajero que no se presenta a un vuelo*

no-strike *adj* (agreement, deal) de no ir a la huelga; (clause) de no declaración de huelga

nostro account *n* (Bank) cuenta nostro *f*

nota bene *phr* nota bene

notarize *vt* otorgar ante notario

notary public *n* notario(-a) *m,f*

note[1] *n* (record, message) nota *f*; BrE (banknote) (*cf* ▸**bill**[1] AmE) billete (de banco) *m*; **go on one's ~** AmE ayudar a alguien con un aval; **keep a ~ of sth** llevar nota de algo; **make a ~ (of sth)** tomar nota (de algo); **take ~s** tomar apuntes; **~s to the accounts** notas a las cuentas; **~s to the financial statements** anexo *or* memoria *or* notas a los estados financieros; **~ issue** *n* (Bank) emisión fiduciaria *f*; **~-issuing bank** *n* banco emisor *m*; **~ payable** *n* documento por pagar *m*; **~ receivable** *n* documento por cobrar *m*

note[2] *vt* (information, details) anotar, apuntar; **~ that...** observar *or* notar que...

notebook *n* cuaderno *m*; (Comp) computadora *f* AmL *or* ordenador *m* Esp portátil

notepad *n* (paper) bloc de notas *m*; (computer) computadora *f* AmL *or* ordenador *m* Esp portátil

notice[1] *n* aviso *m*; (of termination of employment) aviso *m or* notificación *f* de despido; (Ins) declaración *f*; **at short ~** con poca antelación; **at 2 days' ~** con un preaviso de 2 días; **bring sth to sb's ~** hacer observar algo a alguien; **come to sb's ~** llegar al conocimiento de alguien; **escape (sb's) ~** pasar inadvertido; **give ~ to sb** notificar a alguien; **she was given her ~** la despidieron; **hand in one's ~** presentar su renuncia *or* dimisión; **put up a ~** poner un aviso *or* un letrero; **until further ~** hasta nuevo aviso; **without prior ~** sin previo aviso; **work one's ~** BrE trabajar el tiempo de preaviso (desde la renuncia hasta la fecha acordada); **~ account** *n* cuenta sujeta a preaviso *f*; **~ of appeal** *n* (Tax) aviso de recurso *m*; **~ of assessment** *n* (Tax) aviso de imposición *m*; **~ of assignment** *n* notificación de ejercicio *f*; **~ of call** *n* aviso de opción de compra *m*; **~ of cancellation** *n* notificación de cancelación *f*; **~ of default** *n* aviso de falta de pago *m*; **~ of dishonor** AmE, **~ of dishonour** BrE *n* aviso *m* de rechazo *or* de falta de aceptación; **~ of intention** *n* aviso de intención *m*, carta de

intenciones *f*; **~ of objection** *n* (Tax) aviso de objeción *m*; **~ of original assessment** *n* (Tax) aviso de imposición inicial *m*; **~ period** *n* (after dismissal, resignation) periodo de notificación *m*; **~ of reassessment** *n* (Tax) aviso de reevaluación *m*; **~ of revocation** *n* (of option) aviso de anulación *m*; **~ to quit** *n* aviso de desocupar *m*; **give ~ to quit** dar aviso de desalojo *or* de expulsión

notice[2] *vt* notar

noticeboard *n* BrE (*cf* ▸**bulletin board** AmE) tablón de anuncios *m*

notification *n* notificación *f*

notify *vt* notificar; **~ sb of sth** dar aviso a alguien de algo, notificar algo a alguien

notional *adj* (rent) nocional

notwithstanding *prep* no obstante (frml); **~ any other provision** independientemente de cualquier otra disposición

novation *n* novación *f*

novelty *n* novedad *f*; **~ value** *n* valor de novedad *m*

NOW account *n* (▸**negotiable order of withdrawal account**) cuenta de ahorro a la vista con interés *f*

no-win situation *n* situación sin salida *f*

np *abbr* (▸**net proceeds**) producto neto *m*

n.p.v. *abbr* (▸**no-par-value**) sin valor nominal

NPV *abbr* (▸**net present value**) VAN (valor actual neto)

NSF *abbr* (▸**not sufficient funds**) fondos insuficientes *m pl*; **~ check** AmE, **~ cheque** BrE *n* cheque *m* con fondos insuficientes

nspf *abbr* (▸**not specially provided for**) no específicamente dispuesto

nuclear *adj* nuclear; **~ energy** *n* energía nuclear *f*; **~ industry** *n* industria nuclear *f*; **~ plant** *n* planta nuclear *f*; **~ power** energía nuclear *f*; **~ power station** *n* central de energía nuclear *f*; **~ reactor** *n* reactor nuclear *m*

nugatory payment *n* pago nulo *m*

nuisance *n* perjuicio *m*; **~ tax** *n* impuesto burocrático *m*

null *adj* nulo; **~ and void** nulo; **declare sth ~ and void** declarar nulo algo; **render sth ~ and void** anular *or* invalidar algo

number[1] *n* número *m*; **~ crunching** *n* (infrml) cálculo complejo; **~ one priority** *n* prioridad principal *f*

number[2] *vt* (assign a number to) numerar; **~ consecutively** numerar consecutivamente

numbered account *n* cuenta numerada *f*

numbering *n* numeración *f*

numberplate *n* BrE (*cf* ▸**license plate** AmE) matrícula *f*

numeric *adj* numérico; ∼ **character** *n* carácter numérico *m*; ∼ **keypad** *n* teclado numérico *m*

numerical *adj* (control, filing, flexibility) numérico

NVD *abbr* (▶**no value declared**) sin declaración de valor

NWC *abbr* (▶**National Wages Council**) consejo británico salarial

NYFE *abbr* (▶**New York Futures Exchange**) mercado de futuros de Nueva York

NYMEX *abbr* (▶**New York Mercantile Exchange**) bolsa mercantil de Nueva York

NYSE *abbr* (▶**New York Stock Exchange**) bolsa de Nueva York *f*

Oo

oa *abbr* (▸**overall¹**) global

OA *abbr* (▸**office automation**) AO (automatización de oficinas), ofimática *f*, buromática *f*

O&M *abbr* (▸**organization and methods**) organización *f* y métodos *mpl*

O.A.P. *abbr* BrE (▸**old age pensioner**) pensionista *mf*

oath *n* juramento *m*; **take the ∼** (Law) jurar; **under ∼** bajo juramento; **put sb under ∼** tomarle juramento *or* juramentar a alguien

obey *vt* (person, instructions) obedecer

obiter dictum *n* (Law) juicio no vinculante *m*

object¹ *n* (thing) objeto *m*; (aim) objetivo *m*; **fail/succeed in one's ∼** fracasar/triunfar en su objetivo; **money is no ∼** el dinero no les preocupa; **with the ∼ of doing sth** con el propósito de hacer algo

object² *vi* oponerse; **object to** *vt* (proposal) oponerse a, poner reparos a; **∼ to an assessment** (Tax) poner objeciones a una imposición

objection *n* objeción *f*; **make/raise/voice an ∼** hacer/poner/expresar una objeción; **no ∼s** sin objeciones; **∼ overruled/ sustained** objeción denegada/justificada; **∼ to an assessment** (Tax) objeción a una imposición

objective¹ *adj* (evaluation, indicator, selling) objetivo; **∼ budgeting** *n* elaboración objetiva de presupuesto *f*

objective² *n* objetivo *m*; **∼-setting** *n* determinación *f or* fijación *f* de objetivos

obligate *vt* obligar; **∼ sb to do sth** obligar a alguien a hacer algo; **be/feel ∼d (to do sth)** estar/sentirse obligado (a hacer algo); **be/feel ∼d to sb** estar/sentirse en deuda con alguien

obligation *n* (duty, requirement) obligación *f*; (financial commitment) compromiso *m*; **the company was unable to meet its ∼s** la compañía no pudo hacer frente a sus compromisos; **no ∼ to buy** sin obligación de comprar; **be under an ∼ to do sth** estar obligado a hacer algo; **be under no ∼** no estar obligado; **without ∼** sin compromiso; **∼ bond** *n* bono con obligación *m*

obligatory *adj* obligatorio

oblige *vt* obligar; **∼ sb by doing sth** complacer a alguien haciendo algo; **∼ sb to do sth** obligar a alguien a hacer algo

obligee *n* tenedor(a) de una obligación *m,f*

obligor *n* obligado(-a) *m,f*

observance *n* (of a rule) cumplimiento *m*; (of the law) acatamiento *m*

observation *n* observación *f*; **∼ test** *n* prueba de observación *f*

observe *vt* (watch, comment) observar; (the law) acatar

obsolescence *n* obsolescencia *f*; (S&M) caída en desuso *f*

obsolescent *adj* que se está volviendo obsoleto

obsolete *adj* (machinery) obsoleto; (ideas, approach) anticuado, obsoleto

obstruct *vt* (physically) obstruir; (plan, progress) obstaculizar, dificultar

obtain *vt* obtener; **∼ sth by fraud** obtener algo fraudulentamente; **∼ permission in writing** obtener permiso por escrito

OBU *abbr* (▸**offshore banking unit**) oficina bancaria ultramarina *f*

o/c *abbr* (▸**overcharge²**) recargo *m*, cobro excesivo *m*; (Acc) importe en demasía *m*

OCC *abbr* AmE (▸**Options Clearing Corporation**) *cámara de compensación de opciones*

occupancy *n* ocupación *f*; **∼ cost** *n* coste *m* Esp *or* costo *m* AmL de ocupación; **∼ level** *n* nivel de ocupación *m*

occupant *n* (of post) titular *mf*; (of house, building) ocupante *mf*; (tenant) inquilino(-a) *m,f*

occupation *n* (work) ocupación *f*, profesión *f*; (of house, building) ocupación *f*

occupational *adj* (mobility) laboral; (illness, disease) profesional; (health) ocupacional; (accident) de trabajo; (analysis) ocupacional, de ocupaciones; (hazard) laboral, ocupacional; **∼ pension scheme** *n* BrE plan de jubilación profesional *m*; **∼ safety and health** *n* seguridad *f* y salud *f* en el trabajo

occupier *n* ocupante *mf*; (tenant) inquilino(-a) *m,f*

occupy *vt* (offices, post, space) ocupar; (time) llevar, ocupar

OCO order *n* (▸**one-cancels-the-other order**) orden condicionada *f*

OCR *abbr* (▸**optical character reader**) lector óptico de caracteres *m*; (▸**optical**

character recognition) reconocimiento óptico de caracteres *m*

O/D *abbr* (▸**overdraft**) descubierto *m*, sobregiro *m*; (▸**overdrawn**) en descubierto, sobregirado

odd *adj* (number) impar; ∼ **change** *n* cambio sobrante *m*; ∼ **jobs** *n pl* trabajos diversos *m pl*; ∼**-job man** *n* factótum *m*, hombre que hace de todo *m*; ∼**-lot** *n* (Stock) paquete de menos de 100 acciones *m*, pequeño lote *m*; ∼ **man out** *n* excepción *f*; ∼ **one** *n* (of pair) impar *mf*; ∼ **size** *n* (in production) tamaño especial *m*; ∼**-value pricing** *n* fijación de precios de valor poco corriente *f*

oddment *n* artículo *m* suelto *or* de saldo

oddments *n pl* retales *m pl*

OECD *abbr* (▸**Organization for Economic Cooperation and Development**) OCDE (Organización para la Cooperación y Desarrollo Económicos)

OEIC *abbr* (▸**open-ended** BrE *o* **open-end** AmE **investment company**) sociedad *f* de inversión abierta *or* de inversión con cartera variable

off *adj* (not switched on) apagado

off-balance-sheet *adj* (commitment, financing) fuera del balance general

offence BrE, **offense** AmE *n* (breach of the law) infracción *f*; (crime) delito *m*; (insult) ofensa *f*; **cause** *o* **give** ∼ **to sb** ofender a alguien; **commit an** ∼ cometer una infracción; **take** ∼ **at sth** ofenderse *or* sentirse ofendido por algo

offensive¹ *adj* (remark, strategy) ofensivo

offensive² *n* ofensiva *f*; **launch an** ∼ **against sth/sb** lanzar una ofensiva contra algo/alguien; **be on/take the** ∼ estar/ ponerse a la ofensiva

offer¹ *vt* (job, help) ofrecer; (product) ofertar; (objection) objetar; (idea, solution) proponer, sugerir; (excuse) presentar; (oportunity) brindar, ofrecer; **she is someone with a lot to** ∼ es una persona con mucho que ofrecer; ∼ **one's services** ofrecer sus servicios; ∼ **to do sth** ofrecer a hacer algo

offer² *n* oferta *f*; **that's my final** ∼ esa es mi última oferta; **make an** ∼ presentar una oferta; **make sb an** ∼ **they can't refuse** hacerle una oferta muy tentadora a alguien; **on** ∼ en oferta; **or nearest** ∼ u oferta más próxima; **under** ∼ (house) en oferta; ∼ **for sale** *n* oferta de venta *f*; ∼ **price** *n* precio de oferta *m*; ∼ **wanted** *n* solicitud de oferta *f*

offeree *n* receptor(a) de una oferta *m,f*

offering *n* (of bribe) ofrecimiento *m*; ∼ **date** *n* (of new issue) fecha de oferta *f*; ∼ **price** *n* precio de oferta *m*

off-exchange instrument *n* instrumento fuera de la bolsa de valores *m*

offhand buying *n* compra directa *f*

office *n* (room) oficina *f*, despacho *m*; (building, set of rooms) oficina *f*, oficinas *f pl*; (staff) oficina *f*; (of lawyer) bufete *m*, despacho *m*; (of architect) estudio *m*; (of doctor) AmE consultorio *m*, consulta *f*; (post, position) cargo *m*; ∼ **for sale** se vende oficina; **for** ∼ **use only** sólo para uso interno; **come into** ∼ (incumbent) asumir un cargo; **be in/out of** ∼ estar en el poder/fuera del poder; **leave** ∼ dejar el cargo; **take** ∼ tomar posesión del cargo; ∼ **automation** *n* automatización de oficinas *f*, ofimática *f*, buromática *f*; ∼ **block** *n* BrE edificio de oficinas *m*; ∼ **boy** *n* botones *m*, ordenanza *m*, recadero *m*; ∼ **building** *n* edificio de oficinas *m*; ∼ **equipment** *n* equipo de oficina *m*; ∼ **expenses** *n pl* gastos de oficina *m pl*; **O∼ of Fair Trading** *n* ≈ Departamento de Control de Prácticas Comerciales *m*, ≈ Oficina de Protección al Consumidor *f*; ∼ **hours** *n pl* horas de oficina *f pl*; **in** *o* **during** ∼ **hours** en horas de oficina; **out of** *o* **outside** ∼ **hours** fuera de las horas de oficina; **O∼ of International Trade** *n* Oficina de Comercio Internacional *f*; ∼ **job** *n* puesto de oficinista *m*; ∼ **management** *n* dirección *f or* gerencia *f or* organización *f* de oficina; ∼ **manager** *n* director(a) *m,f or* jefe(-a) *m,f* de oficina; ∼ **planning** *n* planificación de la oficina *f*; ∼ **premises** *n pl* local para oficina *m*; ∼ **routine** *n* rutina de oficina *f*; ∼ **space** *n* espacio para oficina *m*; ∼ **staff** *n pl* personal de oficina *m*; ∼ **supplies** *n pl* materiales de oficina *m pl*; ∼ **technology** *n* tecnología de oficina *f*; **O∼ of Telecommunications** *n* BrE *oficina de telecomunicaciones*; ∼ **work** *n* trabajo de oficina *m*; ∼ **worker** *n* oficinista *mf*, empleado(-a) de oficina *m,f*

officer *n* (in government service) funcionario(-a) *m,f*; (of union, party) dirigente *mf*; (of club) directivo(-a) *m,f*; ∼**'s check** AmE, ∼**'s cheque** BrE *n* cheque de caja *m*; ∼ **of the court** *n* funcionario(-a) de tribunales *m,f*

official¹ *adj* (statement, document, figures) oficial; (strike) oficial, legal; ∼ **action** *n* BrE (HRM) acción oficial *f*; ∼ **exchange rate** *n* tipo oficial de cambio *m*; ∼ **list** *n* (Stock) cotización oficial *f*; ∼ **quotation** *n* cotización oficial *f*; ∼ **receiver** *n* síndico(-a) *m,f*; ∼ **valuer** *n* tasador(a) oficial *m,f*

official² *n* (in government service) funcionario(-a) *m,f*; (of union, party) dirigente *mf*

officialese *n* argot burocrático *m*

officially *adv* oficialmente

off-licence n BrE (cf ▸**liquor store** AmE, ▸**package store** AmE) tienda de licores f

off-limits adj (de acceso) prohibido; ~ **area** n área fuera de límites f

offline[1] adj (equipment, system) autónomo, fuera de línea, no acoplado al sistema; (working, processing, storage) fuera de línea; ~ **browser** n buscador fuera de línea m

offline[2] adv (read, write, work) fuera de línea; **go** ~ desconectarse

offload vt (responsibility, work) descargar

off-peak adj (travel, fare, tariff, demand) fuera de las horas punta Esp, fuera de las horas pico AmL; (off-season) de temporada baja

off-period adjustments n pl (Acc) ajustes después del periodo de cierre m pl

off-prime adj (Econ) de segundo orden

off-profile return n (Tax) declaración atípica f

off-sale date n fecha de retirada de la venta f

off-season[1] adj de temporada baja

off-season[2] n temporada f baja or inactiva

offset[1] vt (costs, loss, shortfall) compensar; (in printing) imprimir en offset; ~ **sth against sth** deducir algo de algo

offset[2] n (compensation) compensación f; (in printing) offset m; ~ **account** n cuenta de compensación f

offsetting n compensación f; ~ **entry** n partida compensatoria f, asiento compensatorio m; ~ **transaction** n transacción compensatoria f

offshore adj (investment, trust) extranjero; (banking) ultramarino, offshore; (placement) internacional; (dollars) de ultramar; (competition) offshore; (drilling) costero; ~ **bank** n banco offshore m; ~ **banking unit** n oficina bancaria ultramarina f; ~ **center** AmE, ~ **centre** BrE n centro de ultramar m, centro financiero internacional m; ~ **funds** n pl fondos colocados en paraísos fiscales m pl

off-site adj (cost) de instalación exterior

off-the-board adj (Stock) fuera de cotización

off-the-job training n formación f or capacitación f fuera del puesto de trabajo

off-the-peg BrE, **off-the-rack** AmE adj (clothes) de confección

off-the-record adj (remark) fuera de acta, sin carácter oficial

off-the-shelf adj (goods) de confección; ~ **company** n empresa de conveniencia f

OFT abbr (▸**Office of Fair Trading**) ≈ Departamento de Control de Prácticas Comerciales m, ≈ Oficina de Protección al Consumidor f

Oftel abbr (▸**Office of Telecommunications**) BrE oficina de telecomunicaciones

OHMS abbr BrE (▸**On Her Majesty's Service**) al servicio de Su Majestad

oil n petróleo m; ~ **analyst** n analista petrolífero(-a) m,f; ~ **company** n compañía petrolera f; ~ **crisis** n crisis del petróleo f; ~ **deposit** n estrato de petróleo m; ~ **exporting country** n país exportador de petróleo m; ~ **field** n campo petrolífero m; ~ **glut** n saturación del petróleo f; ~ **industry** n industria petrolera f; ~ **pipeline** n oleoducto m; ~ **platform** n plataforma petrolífera f; ~ **price** n precio del petróleo m; ~**-producing country** n país productor de petróleo m; ~ **refinery** n refinería de petróleo f; ~**-rich** adj rico en petróleo; ~ **rig** n plataforma petrolífera f, torre de perforación f; ~ **shortage** n escasez de petróleo f; ~ **spill** n, ~ **spillage** n vertido de petróleo m; ~ **tanker** n petrolero m

OIT abbr (▸**Office of International Trade**) Oficina de Comercio Internacional f

old adj (person, object, rivalry) viejo; (custom, tradition) viejo, antiguo; (problem, job, law) antiguo; ~ **economy** n vieja economía f

old age n vejez f; ~ **pension** n pensión de jubilación f; ~ **pensioner** n BrE pensionista mf

old-established adj antiguo

old-fashioned adj anticuado

oligopolistic adj oligopolístico

oligopoly n oligopolio m

oligopsony n oligopsonio m

OM abbr (▸**options market**) mercado de opciones m

Ombudsman n (Pol) defensor del pueblo m; (Stock) Defensor del Accionista m

omission n omisión f

omit[1] vt omitir; ~ **to do sth** omitir hacer algo

omitted dividend n dividendo omitido m

omnibus survey n encuesta ómnibus f

on adj (not switched off) conectado

on-board adj (Comp) interno

on-demand bond n bono a la demanda m

one adj (stating number) un(a); (single) único; ~**-bank holding company** n casa matriz de banco único f; ~**-cent sale** n AmE venta ínfima f; ~**-minute manager** n directivo(-a) de corta vida m,f

one-cancels-the-other order n orden condicionada f

one-for-one adj (price relationship) uno por uno

one-off adj único; ~ **cash gift** n donación en metálico realizada sólo en una ocasión f

onerous *adj* (contract) leonino

one-stop: ∼ **shop** *n* ventanilla única *f*; ∼ shopping *n* compras en un mismo sitio *f pl*; ∼ **shopping center** AmE, ∼ **shopping centre** BrE *n* centro comercial *m*

one-time *adj* (event, fee) único; ∼ **buyer** *n* comprador(a) de una sola vez *m,f*

one-to-one *adj* (discussion) mano a mano; (contact) personal; (correlation) de uno a uno; (marketing) personalizado; **on a** ∼ **basis** de uno a uno; ∼**-to-one straddle** *n* opción doble uno a uno *f*

one-way *adj* (Comp) de una dirección; ∼ **protection** *n* (Stock) protección unidireccional *f*

ongoing *adj* en curso; ∼ **concern** *n* asunto en marcha *m*

on-lending *n* represtamo *m*

online¹ *adj* (help, access, ordering, banking) en línea; (mode) conectado; **be** ∼ (user) estar conectado *or* en línea; ∼ **advertisement** *n* publicidad en línea *f*; ∼ **advertising** *n* publicidad en línea *f*; ∼ **bookstore** *n* ciberlibrería *f*; ∼ **business** *n* comercio en línea *m*; ∼ **catalog** AmE, ∼ **catalogue** BrE *n* catálogo en línea *m* ∼ **community** *n* cibercomunidad *f*; ∼ **customer** *n* ciberconsumidor(a) *m,f*; ∼ **data service** *n* servicio de datos directo *m*; ∼ **database** *n* base de datos en línea *f*; ∼ **government** *n* gobierno electrónico *m*; ∼ **journal** *n* (magazine) revista electrónica *f*; ∼ **learning** *n* (education) educación a distancia por Internet *f*; (training) formación *f or* capacitación *f* en línea; ∼ **marketplace** *n* cibermercado *m*; ∼ **order form** *n* hoja de pedido electrónica *f*; ∼ **payment** *n* pago en línea *m*; ∼ **presence** *n* presencia en Internet *f*, alojamiento web *m*; ∼ **procurement** *n* adquisición *f* en línea *or* electrónica; ∼ **purchase** *n* compra en línea *f*; ∼ **recruitment** *n* reclutamiento en línea *m*; ∼ **sale** *n* venta en línea *f*; ∼ **selling** *n* venta en línea *f*; ∼ **service provider** *n* proveedor de servicios Internet *m*; ∼ **shop** *n* tienda *f* online *or* en línea; ∼ **shopper** *n* ciberconsumidor(a) *m,f*; ∼ **shopping** *n* compra en línea *f*; ∼ **system** *n* sistema en línea *m*; ∼ **trainer** *n* encargado(-a) *m,f* de formación en línea *or* de capacitación en línea; ∼ **training** *n* formación *f or* capacitación *f* en línea

online² *adv* (search, shop, bank, buy) en línea; **go** ∼ conectar al Internet

o.n.o. *abbr* (▶**or nearest offer**) u oferta más próxima

on-pack *adj* en el envase; ∼ **price reduction** *n reducción de precio anunciada sobre el envase*

on-sale date *n* fecha de puesta a la venta *f*

on-screen *adj* (help) en pantalla

onset *n* comienzo *m*, inicio *m*

onshore *adj* (banking) en territorio nacional

on-site manager *n* jefe(-a) de obra *m,f*

on-target earnings *n pl* sueldo base más comisión *m*

on-the-job training *n* formación *f or* capacitación *f* en la empresa

on-the-record *adj* (remark) con carácter oficioso

on-the-spot reporter *n reportero desplazado al lugar de los hechos*

onward *adj* (flight) de conexión; ∼ **clearing** *n* (Bank) compensación progresiva *f*

o/o *abbr* (▶**order of**) orden de

o.p. *abbr* (▶**out-of-print**) agotado

OPEC *abbr* (▶**Organization of Petroleum Exporting Countries**) OPEP (Organización de los Países Exportadores de Petróleo)

open¹ *adj* (file, document, shop, government) abierto; (meeting, session) a puertas abiertas, abierto al público en general; (membership) abierto al público; (trial) público; **let's leave the date** ∼ no concretemos la fecha todavía; **have/keep an** ∼ **mind (about** *o* **on sth)** tener/mantener una mente abierta (sobre algo); ∼ **on the print** (Stock) abierto en imprenta; ∼ **to buy** disponible para la compra; **lay oneself** ∼ **to criticism** exponerse a ser objeto de críticas; ∼ **to debate** abierto a debate; ∼ **to several interpretations** susceptible de diversas interpretaciones; **be** ∼ **to offers** estar abierto a considerar ofertas; ∼ **account** *n* cuenta comercial *f*; ∼ **bid** *n* licitación abierta *f*; ∼ **check** AmE, ∼ **cheque** BrE *n* cheque *m* abierto *or* libre *or* no cruzado; ∼ **competition** *n* competencia abierta *f*; ∼ **contract** *n* contrato abierto *m*; ∼ **credit** *n* crédito *m* abierto *or* al descubierto; ∼**-door policy** *n* política de puertas abiertas *f*; ∼ **economy** *n* economía abierta *f*; ∼**-end** *adj* AmE (*cf* ▶∼**-ended** BrE) sin límite; ∼**-end contract** *n* AmE (*cf* ▶∼**-ended contract** BrE) contrato *m* de suministro abierto *or* sin límites preestablecidos; ∼**-end fund** *n* AmE (*cf* ▶∼**-ended fund** BrE) fondo de inversión de capital variable *m*; ∼**-end investment company** *n* AmE (*cf* ▶∼**-ended investment company** BrE) sociedad *f* de inversión abierta *or* de inversión con cartera variable; ∼**-end management company** *n* AmE (*cf* ▶∼**-ended management company** BrE) sociedad de gestión abierta *f*; ∼**-ended** *adj* BrE (*cf* ▶∼**-end** AmE) sin límite; ∼**-ended contract** *n* BrE (*cf* ▶∼**-end contract** AmE) contrato *m* de suministro abierto *or* sin límites preestablecidos; ∼**-ended fund** *n* BrE (*cf* ▶∼**-end fund** AmE) fondo de inversión de capital variable *m*; **∼-ended investment company** *n* BrE (*cf* ▸**∼-end investment company** AmE) sociedad *f* de inversión abierta *o* de inversión con cartera variable; **∼ house** *n* puertas abiertas *f pl*; **∼ learning** *n* enseñanza abierta *f*; **∼ letter** *n* carta abierta *f*; **∼ letter of credit** *n* carta de crédito sin condiciones *f*; **∼ market** *n* mercado abierto *m*; **buy/sell securities on the ∼ market** comprar/vender valores en el mercado abierto *or* libre; **∼ market rate** *n* cotización del mercado libre *f*; **∼ market trading** *n* comercio en mercado libre *m*; **∼ network** *n* red de datos abierta *f*; **∼ order** *n* orden abierta *f*; **∼-plan** *adj* (office) de plan abierto; **∼ policy** *n* póliza *f* abierta *or* flotante; **∼ position** *n* (Stock) posición abierta *f*; **∼ price** *n* precio abierto *m*; **∼ question** *n* cuestión pendiente *f*, punto sin resolver *m*; **∼ shop** *n* empresa *f* con sindicación voluntaria *or* que no exige sindicación; **∼ space** *n* espacio abierto *m*; **∼ systems interconnection** *n* (Comp) interconexión de sistemas abiertos *f*; **∼ tendering** *n* licitación abierta *f*; **∼ ticket** *n* billete abierto *m*; **∼ trading** *n* transacción en posición abierta *f*; **∼ union** *n* sindicato abierto *m*; **O∼ University** *n* BrE *universidad a distancia británica* , ≈ Universidad Nacional de Educación a Distancia *m* Esp

open[2] *vt* (shop, branch, file, dossier) abrir; (meeting) abrir, dar comienzo a; (debate) abrir, iniciar; (negotiations, talks) entablar; **∼ an account with sb** abrir una cuenta con alguien; **∼ the door to sth** abrir las puertas a algo; **∼ a (long/short) position** abrir una posición (larga/corta); **open up** *vt* (business, factory, shop) abrir; (opportunities) explorar; **∼ up the market to competition** abrir el mercado a la competencia

opening *n* (of meeting, trade, tenders) apertura *f*; (job vacancy) vacante *f*; (opportunity) oportunidad *f*; **at the ∼** (Stock) a la apertura; **late ∼ till 8 pm on Thursdays** los jueves abierto hasta las 8; **∼ balance** *n* balance *m or* saldo *m* de apertura; **∼ bid** *n* oferta de apertura *f*; **∼ date** *n* fecha de apertura *f*; **∼ hours** *n pl* horario de apertura *m*; **∼ inventory** *n* inventario inicial *m*; **∼ position** *n* (Stock) posición de apertura *f*; **∼ price** *n* precio de apertura *m*; **∼ quotation** *n* cotización de apertura *f*

opening-up *n* (Stock) apertura al comercio *f*

operate [1] *vt* (business) dirigir, llevar; (machine) manejar; (policy, system) aplicar, tener; (public service) ofrecer
[2] *vi* (company) operar; (person) trabajar; (machine) funcionar; (factor) intervenir, actuar; (rules, laws) regir; **∼ in tandem**

trabajar en equipo; **we ∼ out of our own house** trabajamos *or* operamos desde nuestro domicilio; **he ∼s from a base in Madrid** tiene su base de operaciones en Madrid

operating *adj* (cost, profit, loss, income) de explotación; (capital) de explotación, de operación; (cycle) de operación; (expenditure) de operaciones, de funcionamiento; (interest, capacity) operativo; **∼ account** *n* (Bank) cuenta de operación *f*, (Ind) cuenta de explotación *f*, **∼ gearing** *n* BrE, **∼ leverage** *n* apalancamiento operativo *m*; **∼ system** *n* (Comp) sistema operativo *m*

operation *n* (activity, business) operación *f*; (functioning) funcionamiento *m*; (of machine) manejo *m*; (of system) uso *m*; **be in ∼** (machine) estar en funcionamiento; (system) regir; **come into ∼** entrar en funcionamiento; **bring** *o* **put sth into ∼** poner algo en funcionamiento; **∼s analysis** *n* análisis de las operaciones *m*; **∼s audit** *n* auditoría *f* operacional *or* de operaciones; **∼ code** *n* (Comp) código de orden *m*; **∼s department** *n* (of brokerage firm) departamento de operaciones *m*; **∼s director** *n* director(a) *m,f or* gerente *mf* de operaciones; **∼ field** *n* (Comp) campo de operación *m*; **∼s management** *n* dirección *f or* gerencia *f* de operaciones; **∼s manager** *n* director(a) de operaciones *m,f*; **∼s research** *n* investigación de operaciones *f*

operational *adj* (planning, control, margin) operacional; (balance, staff) operativo; (analysis, audit) operativo, operacional, de operaciones; (budget) de operaciones; **∼ environment** *n* (Comp) condiciones de funcionamiento *f pl*; **∼ investment** *n* (in buildings, equipment) inversión de explotación *f*; **∼ manager** *n* director(a) *m,f or* gerente *mf* de operaciones; **∼ research** *n* investigación operacional *f*

operative[1] *adj* (rules, measures) en vigor, en vigencia; **become ∼** entrar en vigor *or* en vigencia

operative[2] *n* operativo(-a) *m,f*

operator *n* (of computer, switchboard) operador(a) *m,f*; (of equipment) operario(-a) *m,f*; (company) empresa *f*, compañía *f*

opinion *n* opinión *f*; (Law) dictamen *m*; **ask sb's ∼** pedirle su opinión a alguien; **get a second ∼** consultarlo con otro especialista; **have a high/low ∼ of sth/sb** tener buena/mala opinión de algo/alguien; **in my ∼** en mi opinión; **that's a matter of ∼** es cuestión de opinión; **be of the ∼ that...** opinar que...; **∼ leader** *n* líder de opinión *m*; **∼ poll** *n* encuesta de opinión *f*; **∼ polling** *n* sondeo de opinión *m*; **∼ survey** *n* encuesta de opinión *f*; **∼ of title** *n* dictamen de propiedad *m*, opinión de título *f*

opportunism n oportunismo m

opportunist n oportunista mf

opportunistic adj (behaviour) oportunista

opportunity n oportunidad f, ocasión f; **at the earliest** o **first ∼** a la primera oportunidad; **give sb the ∼ to do sth** darle a alguien la oportunidad de hacer algo; **an ideal/unique ∼** una oportunidad ideal/ única; **take the ∼ to do sth** aprovechar la ocasión para hacer algo; **∼ cost** n coste m Esp or costo m AmL de oportunidad

oppose vt (be against) oponerse a, estar en contra de; (resist) combatir, luchar contra; **be ∼d to sth** oponerse a algo, estar en contra de algo; **as ∼d to sth/sb** a diferencia de algo/alguien

opposing adj (viewpoint, faction) contrario, opuesto; (vote) contrapuesto

opposite adj (opinion, view) opuesto; (page) de enfrente, contiguo; **∼ number** n (in another organization) homólogo(-a) m,f

opposition n (resistance, parliamentary) oposición f; (rivals, competitors) competencia f; **in ∼ (to)** (as opponent) en contra (de); (as competitor) en competencia (con); **∼ party** n partido de la oposición m

opt vi optar; **∼ to do sth** optar por hacer algo; **opt for** vt optar por; **opt out** vi BrE optar por independizarse (del control de los gobiernos locales); **∼out of sth** retractarse de algo; **∼ out of doing sth** optar por no hacer algo

optical adj óptico; **∼ character reader** n lector óptico de caracteres m; **∼ character recognition** n reconocimiento óptico de caracteres m; **∼ pen** n lápiz óptico m; **∼ scanner** n explorador óptico m; **∼ wand** n lápiz óptico m

optimal adj (rate, tariff, taxation) óptimo

optimality n optimalidad f

optimization n optimización f

optimize vt optimizar

optimum adj (capacity) óptimo

opt-in adj (e-mail, marketing) opt-in, con el permiso previo del receptor

option n opción f; **the best ∼ is to...** la mejor opción es...; **the cheapest ∼ is to...** la alternativa más barata es...; **the easy** o **soft ∼** la opción más fácil; **have an ∼ on sth** tener una opción de compra en algo; **have no ∼ but to...** no tener otra opción sino...; **keep** o **leave one's ∼s open** no descartar ninguna posibilidad; **the only ∼ is to...** la única alternativa es...; **take an ∼** hacer uso de una opción de compra; **∼ account** n cuenta opcional f; **∼ bargain** n negocio a prima m, transacción en el mercado de opciones f; **∼ buyer** n comprador(a) de opciones m,f; **∼ class** n clase de opción f;

O∼s Clearing Corporation n AmE cámara de compensación de opciones; **∼ contract** n contrato de opciones m; **∼ exercise** n ejercicio de la opción m; **∼ holder** n tenedor(a) de una opción m,f; **∼s market** n mercado de opciones m; **∼ premium** n prima de opción f; **∼ price** n precio de opción m; **∼ pricing formula** n fórmula para valorar opciones f; **∼ seller** n AmE vendedor(a) de opciones m,f; **∼ spread** n diferencial de opciones m; **∼ writer** n emisor(a) de una opción m,f

optional adj (accessory) opcional; (feature) facultativo; (course, item) optativo; **an ∼ extra** un extra que no viene incluido en el precio

OR abbr (▸**operational research**) investigación operacional f; (▸**operations research**) investigación de operaciones f

oracle n oráculo m

oral adj (contract) oral

orange goods n pl productos de duración de vida media

ord. abbr (▸**order**) (command, instruction) orden f; (sequence, proper arrangement) orden m; (for stock) pedido m

order[1] n (command, instruction) orden f; (sequence, proper arrangement) orden m; (for stock) pedido m; (by court) mandamiento m; **by ∼** por orden de; **for ∼s** a órdenes m; **in ∼ of importance** por orden de importancia; **in ∼ of priority** en orden de prioridad; **in the ∼ specified** en el orden señalado; **my ∼** mi orden, mi pedido; **∼ of** orden de; **of** o **in the ∼ of** del orden de; **costs of** o **in the ∼ of £5,000** costes Esp or costos AmL del orden de 5.000 libras; **on ∼** pedido; **on the ∼s of sb** por orden de alguien; **out of ∼** adj (not functioning) averiado; (infrml) (inappropriate) fuera de lugar; **pay to the ∼ of John Smith** páguese a la orden de John Smith; **place an ∼ for sth** hacer un pedido de algo; **put in ∼** poner en orden; **put one's affairs in ∼** poner sus asuntos en orden; **put into ∼** ordenar; **take ∼s** (for goods) aceptar pedidos; **(made) to ∼** (hecho) de encargo; **be in perfect working ∼** funcionar perfectamente; **∼ acceptance** n aceptación del pedido f; **∼ blank** n formulario de pedido m; **∼ book** n libro de pedidos m; **∼ card** n tarjeta de pedido f; **∼ entry** n entrada de pedido f; **∼ flow pattern** n tendencia del flujo de pedidos f; **∼ form** n hoja de pedido f; **∼s in hand** n pl cartera de pedidos f; **∼ number** n número de pedido m; **∼ on hand** n pedido en existencia m; **∼ quantity** n cantidad de pedido f; **∼ to pay** n orden de pago f

order² vt (action, dismissal) ordenar; (goods) pedir, encargar; **∼ sb to do sth** ordenar a alguien que haga algo

orderly adj (market) tranquilo

ordinal adj ordinal; **∼ data entry** n (Comp) entrada de datos ordinal f

ordinance n ordenanza f

ordinary adj (interest, account, loss) ordinario; **the ∼ course of business** la marcha normal de los negocios; **∼ general meeting** n (of shareholders) junta general ordinaria f; **∼ share** n acción ordinaria f; **∼ shareholder** n, **∼ stockholder** n accionista ordinario(-a) m,f

ore n (deposit) mena f, mineral m

org abbr (**▸organization**) (company) organización f

organic adj (farming, foodstuffs, growth) orgánico

organicity n organicidad f

organigram n organigrama m

organization n (action, group) organización f; (order, system) método m, sistema m; **∼ behavior** AmE, **∼ behaviour** BrE n comportamiento de la organización m; **∼ chart** n organigrama m; **∼ cost** n coste m Esp or costo m AmL de organización; **∼ culture** n cultura de organización f; **∼ development** n desarrollo de la organización m; **O∼ for Economic Cooperation and Development** n Organización para la Cooperación y Desarrollo Económicos f; **∼ and methods** n organización f y métodos m pl; **O∼ of Petroleum Exporting Countries** n Organización de los Países Exportadores de Petróleo f; **∼ planning** n planificación de la organización f; **∼ structure** n estructura de la organización f; **∼ theory** n teoría de la organización f; **O∼ for Trade Co-operation** n Organización para la Cooperación Comercial f

organizational adj (change, psychology, effectiveness) organizacional; (unit) organizacional, de organización; (behaviour) de la organización; (theory, size) organizativo; **∼ fit** n ajuste de organizaciones m

organize vt (event, activity, strike) organizar; (ideas) ordenar

organized adj (market, labour) organizado; **∼ crime** n crimen organizado m

organizer n (notebook) agenda f or organizador m personal; (Comp) agenda electrónica f; (person) organizador(a) m,f

orientation n orientación f; **∼ course** n curso de orientación m

origin n origen m; **∼ and destination study** n estudio de origen y destino m

original¹ adj (invoice, order, cost, owner) original; **∼ address** n (Comp) dirección de origen f; **∼ assessment** n (Tax) imposición original f; **∼ document** n documento de origen m; **∼ entry** n (in bookkeeping) registro cronológico m; **∼ margin** n margen original m; **∼ maturity** n vencimiento original m

original² n original m

originate ① vi (practice, idea) originarse ② vt (idea, style) crear

originating document n documento originario m

originator n (Bank) emisor(a) m,f

OS abbr (**▸operating system**) (Comp) SO (sistema operativo)

OSA abbr (**▸overseas sterling area**) área internacional de dominio de la libra esterlina f

OSI abbr (**▸open systems interconnection**) (Comp) OSI (interconexión de sistemas abiertos)

OSP abbr (**▸online service provider**) proveedor de servicios Internet m

OT abbr (**▸overtime**) horas f pl extra or extraordinarias

OTC abbr (**▸Organization for Trade Co-operation**) Organización para la Cooperación Comercial f; (**▸over-the-counter**) no registrado en bolsa; **∼ option** n opción OTC f

OTCM abbr (**▸over-the-counter market**) mercado de valores extrabursátil m

OTE abbr (**▸on-target earnings**) sueldo base más comisión m

other adj otro; **∼ assets** n pl otros activos m pl; **∼ beneficiary** n otro(-a) beneficiario(-a) m,f; **∼ income** n otros ingresos m pl; **∼ receivables** n pl (on balance sheet) otros efectos por cobrar m pl

OTS abbr BrE (**▸Overseas Trade Statistics**) estadísticas del comercio exterior

OU abbr BrE (**▸Open University**) universidad a distancia británica, ≈ UNED (Universidad Nacional de Educación a Distancia) Esp

out adv fuera; (on strike) en huelga; **the manager is ∼** el director no está; **the bill is ∼ by £5** se han equivocado en cinco libras en la cuenta; **be ∼ for sth** (infrml) buscar algo; **have it ∼ with sb** resolver un problema hablando seriamente con alguien; **a report is ∼ today** un informe publicado hoy; **the secret is ∼** el secreto se ha descubierto; **be ∼ to do sth** estar decidido a hacer algo; **he's ∼ to** o **at lunch** ha salido a comer

outage n corte m, apagón m

outbid vt (at auction) hacer mejor oferta que, sobrepujar

out-box *n* (for e-mail) buzón de envío *m*

outcome *n* (result) resultado *m*; (consequences) consecuencias *f pl*

outcry *n* estruendo *m*; ~ **market** *n* mercado de subasta *m*

outdated *adj* (idea, product) anticuado

outdo *vt* (rival) superar, ganarle a; (result, achievement) mejorar, superar

outdoor *adj* (advertising) exterior

outer *adj* exterior; ~ **code** *n* (Comp) código exterior *m*; ~ **pack** *n* envase exterior *m*

outflow *n* (of funds) salida *f*

outgoing *adj* (president) saliente; (invoice) enviado; ~ **call** *n* llamada al exterior *f*; ~ **mail** *n*, ~ **post** *n* BrE correo saliente *m*

outgoings *n pl* desembolso *m*

outlaw *vt* proscribir

outlay *n* desembolso *m*

outlet *n* (for selling) punto de venta *m*; (for waste) salida *f*; ~ **store** *n* tienda de venta al público *f*

outline[1] *n* esquema *m*; **in** ~ en líneas generales; **describe sth in broad** ~ describir algo en líneas generales

outline[2] *vt* (plan, situation) esbozar

outlook *n* (attitude) punto de vista *m*; (prospects) perspectivas *f pl*; **the economic** ~ **for the next year** las perspectivas económicas para el año próximo

outmanoeuvre BrE, **outmaneuver** AmE *vt* superar en estrategia a

out-of-court *adj* (settlement) extrajudicial

out-of-favour BrE, **out-of-favor** AmE *adj* (industry) caído en desgracia; (stock) sin demanda

out-of-pocket expenses *n pl* desembolsos varios *m pl*

out-of-print *adj* agotado

out-of-state *adj* (corporation) extraterritorial

out-of-the-money *adj* (call, put) con pérdida potencial; ~ **option** *n* opción con precio diferente al de mercado *f*

out-of-town *adj* (centre, shop, store) a las afueras

out-of-work *adj* sin trabajo

outpace *vt* dejar atrás

outperform *vt* superar

outperformance *n* resultado superior *m*

outplacement *n* *orientación vocacional pagada por una empresa, principalmente para los ejecutivos que han sido despedidos*; ~ **agency** *n* *agencia que ayuda a las personas despedidas a salir de la empresa y colocarse*

output[1] *n* (of factory) producción *m*; (of worker, machine) rendimiento *m*; (Comp) salida *f*;

increase industrial ~ incrementar la producción industrial; ~ **bonus** *n* incentivo por productividad *m*; ~ **data** *n* datos de salida *m pl*; ~ **device** *n* (Comp) dispositivo de salida *m*; ~ **file** *n* archivo de salida *m*; ~ **per head** *n* producto per cápita *m*; ~ **per hour** *n* producción por hora *f*

output[2] *vt* (data, text) extraer; (to printer) imprimir

outright *adj* (ownership) incondicional; ~ **gift** *n* donación propiamente dicha *f*

outset *n* comienzo *m*; **at/from the** ~ al/ desde el comienzo

outside[1] *n* exterior *m*; **at the** ~ como máximo; **bring in a consultant from (the)** ~ traer a un asesor independiente *or* de fuera; **be on the** ~ **looking in** estar dejado de lado

outside[2] *adj* (finance, money) exterior; (interference, pressure) externo; (chance, possibility) remoto; **she has a lot of** ~ **interests** tiene muchos intereses al margen de su trabajo; ~ **broadcast** *n* emisión de exteriores *f*; ~ **call** *n* llamada *f* afuera *or* desde fuera; ~ **director** *n* director(a) externo(a) *m,f*; ~ **line** *n* (telephone) línea externa *f*

outside[3] *prep* fuera de; **that's** ~ **our jurisdiction** eso queda fuera de nuestra jurisdicción; ~ **office hours** fuera de las horas de oficina; **it's** ~ **my price range** está fuera de mi presupuesto; ~ **the reference of sth** más allá de la referencia de algo

outsider *n* forastero(-a) *m,f*; (in field) profano(-a) *m,f*; (in organization) intruso(-a) *m,f*; ~ **broker** *n* broker *mf or* intermediario(-a) *m,f* independiente

outsource [1] *vt* enviar a fuentes externas, recurrir a fuentes externas para [2] *vi* recurrir a fuentes externas

outsourcing *n* recurso a fuentes externas *m*

outstanding[1] *adj* (amount, matter, obligation) pendiente; (ability) extraordinario, excepcional; (achievement) destacado; **we have work still** ~ tenemos trabajo pendiente; ~ **accounts** *n pl* cuentas pendientes *f pl*; ~ **advance** *n* anticipo pendiente *m*; ~ **balance** *n* saldo pendiente *m*, déficit *m*; ~ **commitment** *n* compromiso *m or* obligación *f* pendiente; ~ **credits** *n pl* créditos pendientes *m pl*; ~ **debt** *n* deuda pendiente de pago *f*; ~ **entry** *n* entrada *f or* ingreso *m* pendiente; ~ **item** *n* partida pendiente *f*; ~ **loan** *n* préstamo pendiente *m*; ~ **order** *n* pedido sin entregar *m*; ~ **payment** *n* pago atrasado *m*

outstanding[2] *n* montón insoluto *m*, pago pendiente *m*

out-tray *n* bandeja de salida *f*

O

outvote vt (other board-members) emitir más votos que

outward adj (journey) de ida; ~ **leg** n trayecto de ida m; ~ **payment** n pago externo m

outward-looking adj (approach) abierto

outweigh vt superar en valor a

outwork n trabajo a domicilio m

outworker n trabajador(a) domiciliario(-a) m,f

overaccumulation n sobreacumulación f

over-achiever n persona de rendimiento superior a lo esperado

overage n (Fin) superávit m; ~ **loan** n préstamo para cubrir posibles excesos de costes

overall¹ adj (result, reduction, cost, deficit, demand) global; ~ **rate of return** n tasa global de beneficio f

overall² adv generalmente

overbid vt ofrecer más que

overbooked adj reservado con exceso

overbooking n overbooking m, sobrecontratación f, sobreventa f

overbought adj sobrecomprado

overcapacity n supercapacidad f

overcapitalization n sobrecapitalización f

overcapitalized adj sobrecapitalizado

overcautious adj demasiado cauto or cauteloso

overcharge¹ ⓵ vt cobrarle de más a; ~ **sb for sth** cobrarle de más a alguien por algo; **we were ~d (by) £50** nos cobraron cincuenta libras de más ⓶ vi cobrar de más

overcharge² n recargo m, cobro excesivo m; (Acc) importe en demasía m

overcome vt superar

overcommitment n exceso de compromisos m

overcompensation n compensación excesiva f

overconsumption n exceso de consumo m

overdependence n sobredependencia f

overdiversification n diversificación excesiva f

overdraft n descubierto m, sobregiro m; **have an ~ of £500 o a £500 ~** tener un descubierto or un sobregiro de 500 libras, estar sobregirado en 500 libras; ~ **facility** n facilidad de sobregiro f

overdraw vt (account) dejar en descubierto

overdrawn adj (account, amount) en descubierto; (person) sobregirado; **be ~ by £500 o be £500 ~** tener un descubierto or

un sobregiro de 500 libras, estar sobregirado en 500 libras

overdue adj (cheque) vencido; **payment is now ~** el plazo ha vencido y se requiere pago inmediato; **you're ~ for promotion** hace tiempo que te deberían haber ascendido

overemployment n exceso de empleo m

overestimate vt sobreestimar

overexploitation n sobreexplotación f

overextended adj (financial resources) sobreextendido

overfunding n provisión f or captación f excesiva de fondos

overhang n (Stock) exceso de oferta m

overhaul¹ vt (machine, system) revisar, poner a punto

overhaul² n (of machine, system) revisión f, puesta a punto f

overhead adj (costs) indirecto, general; (charges) indirecto, general; ~ **capital** n capital social fijo m; ~ **projector** n proyector de acetatos m; ~ **transparency** n transparencia f

overheads n pl gastos m pl indirectos or generales; ~ **recovery** n recuperación f de gastos indirectos or de gastos generales

overheated adj (machine, economy) recalentado

overheating n recalentamiento m

overindebtedness n sobreendeudamiento m

overinsured adj sobreasegurado

overissue n exceso de emisión m

overkill n (infrml) exceso de medios m, desbordamiento m

overlap n superposición f

overlay n (guide) alza m

overleaf adv a la vuelta; **see ~** véase a la vuelta

overman vt dotar de exceso de personal

overmanned adj (factory, office) con demasiado personal; **be ~** tener demasiado personal

overmanning n exceso de personal m

overnight adj (deposit, loan, travel) nocturno; (money) nocturno, a un día; ~ **repo** n (Stock) repo a un día m; ~ **security** n (Stock) valor a un día m

overpaid adj pagado en exceso

overpass vt exceder

overpay vt (deliberately) pagarle demasiado or en exceso a; (in error) pagarle de más a

overpayment n pago en exceso m

overplacing n sobrecolocación f

overprice vt fijar un precio excesivo para

overpriced *adj* de precio excesivo; **this product is** ~ este producto tiene un precio demasiado alto

overprint *n* sobreimpresión *f*

overproduce *vt* sobreproducir

overproduction *n* superproducción *f*

overprovision *n* provisión en exceso *f*

overrate *vt* sobreestimar, sobrevalorar

overrepresent *vt* (in market) sobrerrepresentar

overrepresentation *n* (in market) sobrerrepresentación *f*

override¹ *vt* (decision, recommendation, order) invalidar, anular; (wishes, advice) hacer caso omiso de; (program) cancelar

override² *n* (in device, machine) anulación de automatismo *f*; (HRM) compensación extraordinaria a un vendedor *f*

overriding *adj* (importance, need, consideration) primordial; (priority, authority) absoluto; (interest) dominante; (influence) preponderante; ~ **commission** *n* sobrecomisión *f*

overrule *vt* (decision, verdict) anular, invalidar; (objection) rechazar, no admitir; **I was ~d by my superiors** la decisión de mis superiores anuló *or* invalidó la mía

overrun¹ *vt* (budget) rebasar

overrun² *n* (of budget) rebasamiento *m*; (of production) exceso *m*

oversaving *n* exceso de ahorro *m*

overseas *adj* (trade, market) exterior; (aid) exterior, externo; (asset) extranjero, en el exterior; (investor, customer, visitor, tourism) extranjero; (branch) en el exterior; (department) de ultramar; ~ **agent** *n* agente exterior *mf*; ~ **sterling area** *n* área internacional de dominio de la libra esterlina *f*; **O~ Trade Statistics** *n pl* BrE *estadísticas de comercio exterior*

oversee *vt* supervisar

overseer *n* capataz *mf*

oversell *vt* (sell too much of) sobrevender; (promote excessively) exagerar los méritos de

overselling *n* propaganda excesiva *f*

overshoot *vt* (target, budget) exceder, rebasar

oversight *n* descuido *m*

oversold *adj* (market) saturado

overspend¹ ① *vi* gastar en exceso ② *vt* gastar en exceso; ~ **a budget** pasarse del presupuesto

overspend² *n* déficit presupuestario

overspent *adj* (Acc) agotado

overspill *n* excedente de población *m*; ~ **town** *n* ciudad satélite *f*

overstaffed *adj* con exceso de personal; **be ~** tener exceso de personal

overstaffing *n* exceso de personal *m*

overstep *vt* sobrepasar, rebasar, pasarse de; ~ **the mark** pasarse de la raya

overstimulate *vt* sobreestimular

overstretch *vt* (resources) estirar al máximo

oversubscribed *adj* cubierto en exceso, sobresuscrito

oversubscription *n* (of shares) exceso de peticiones de suscripción *m*

oversupply *n* oferta excesiva *f*

overtax¹ *vt* hacer pagar impuestos excesivos

overtax² *n* tributación excesiva *f*

overtaxation *n* imposición excesiva *f*

over-the-counter *adj* (dealings) no registrado en bolsa; ~ **market** *n* mercado de valores extrabursátil *m*; ~ **option** *n* opción extrabursátil *f*; ~ **retailing** *n* venta minorista *f*; ~ **trading** *n* AmE *comercio legal de acciones sin cotización oficial*

overtime *n* horas *f pl* extra *or* extraordinarias; **work** ~ hacer horas extra; ~ **ban** *n* prohibición de tiempo extra *f*; ~ **pay** *n* paga *f* por horas extra *or* por horas extraordinarias

overtrading *n* (Econ) exceso *m* de comercialización *or* de inversión; (Stock) sobreinversión *f*

overurbanization *n* sobreurbanización *f*

overuse¹ *n* superutilización *f*

overuse² *vt* abusar de, usar demasiado

overvaluation *n* sobrevaloración *f*

overvalue *vt* sobrevalorar

overvalued *adj* (currency) sobrevalorado

overview *n* descripción general *f*

overwrite *vt* (Comp) (write on top) superponer; (delete) borrar

overwriting *n* (Stock) suscripción *f*

owe *vt* deber, adeudar; ~ **sb sth** *o* **sth to sb** deberle algo a alguien; ~ **sb for sth** deberle algo a alguien

owing *adj* que se debe *or* se adeuda; **the money still** ~ el dinero que aún se debe *or* se adeuda; **I have some leave** ~ **to me** me deben unos días de vacaciones

owing to *prep* debido a

own¹ *adj* propio; ~ **brand** *n* marca propia *f*; ~ **label** *n* etiqueta propia *f*

own² *vt* (property) tener, ser dueño de, poseer

owner *n* dueño(-a) *m,f*, propietario(-a) *m,f*; (of patent) titular *mf*; **at** ~**'s risk** bajo la responsabilidad del dueño; ~**-manager** *n* gerente-propietario(-a) *m,f*; ~ **occupation** *n* tenencia por el propietario *f*; ~**-occupied home** *n* casa ocupada por su propietario *f*; ~**-occupier** *n* propietario(-a)-ocupante *m,f*; ~**-operator** *n* explotador(a) *m,f*

ownership *n* derecho de propiedad *m*;
under new ~ nuevo propietario; **~ form** *n*
AmE formulario de propiedad *m*; **~ rights** *n*
pl derechos de propiedad *m pl*

ozone *n* ozono *m*; **~ depletion** *n*
agotamiento del ozono *m*; **~-friendly** *adj*
(product) que no daña la capa de ozono; **~
layer** *n* capa de ozono *f*

Pp

p. *abbr* (▸**page**) p (página), pág. (página)

P2P *abbr* (▸**path-to-profitability**) *plan comercial del inicio de un negocio que exige un rendimiento de la inversión*; (▸**peer-to-peer**) (Comp) de par a par

p.a. *abbr* (▸**per annum**) por año

PA *abbr* (▸**personal assistant**) ayudante(-a) *m,f or* secretario(-a) *m,f* personal; (▸**power of attorney**) poder notarial *m*; (▸**Press Association**) *asociación británica de prensa*; (▸**public address system**) sistema altavoces *m*

PABX *abbr* BrE (▸**private automatic branch exchange**) centralita automática privada unida a la red pública *f*

pace *n* (of change) ritmo *m*; (of trend) velocidad *f*; **keep ~ with sth** (developments, progress) mantenerse al tanto de algo; **set the ~** marcar la pauta; **speed up the ~ of reform** acelerar el ritmo de las reformas

pacesetter *n* persona que marca la pauta *f*

pacify *vt* (shareholders) apaciguar

pack¹ *n* embalaje *m*; **~ shot** *n* (in advertising) *plano macro sobre el producto*

pack² *vt* (put into container) envasar; (make packets with) empaquetar; (for transport) embalar; (data) comprimir; **~ a jury** formar un jurado tendencioso

package¹ *n* paquete *m*; **~ code** *n* código del envase *m*; **~ deal** *n* (economic measures) conjunto de medidas económicas *m*; (agreement) acuerdo global *m*; (workers' demands) paquete de reivindicaciones *m*; (holiday) vacaciones organizadas *f pl*; **~ design** *n* diseño *m* del envase *or* de la envoltura; **~ holiday** *n* BrE vacaciones organizadas *f pl*; **~ mortgage** *n* hipoteca *para financiar la compra del inmueble y su mobiliario*; **~ store** *n* AmE (*cf* ▸**off-licence** BrE) tienda de licores; **~ tour** *n* viaje organizado *m*; **~ tour operator** *n* agente de viajes organizados *mf*, touroperador(a) *m,f*

package² *vt* embalar, empaquetar

packaged goods *n pl* mercancía empaquetada *f*

packaging *n* (packing) embalaje *m*; (wrapping) envoltorio *m*; (presentation) presentación *f*; **~ cost** *n* coste *m* Esp *or* costo *m* AmL de embalaje

packer *n* embalador(a) *m,f*

packet *n* (container) paquete *m*; (considerable sum) BrE (infrml) dineral *m*; **cost/earn** *o* **make a ~** BrE (infrml) costar/ganar un dineral; **~ switching** *n* (Comp) conmutación de paquetes *f*

packing *n* empaquetado *m*; **~ company** *n* compañía empaquetadora *f*; **~ costs** *n pl* gastos de embalaje *m pl*; **~ density** *n* (of data) densidad de almacenamiento *f*; **~ slip** *n* albarán *m*

Pac-Man®: **~ defence** BrE, **~ defense** AmE *n* (in corporate mergers and acquisitions) defensa comecocos *f*; **~ strategy** *n* estrategia Pac-Man *f*

pact *n* pacto *m*

pad¹ *n* (Comp) (for mouse) almohadilla *f*; (of paper) bloc *m*

pad² *vt* (report, speech) rellenar, meter paja en (infrml); **pad out** *vt* (report, speech) rellenar, meter paja en (infrml)

page¹ *n* página *f*; **~ break** *n* cambio de página *m*; **~ exposure** *n* índice de lectura de la página impresa *m*; **~-jacking** *n* (Comp) *apropiación del contenido de un sitio web para incorporarlo a otro, especialmente uno que contenga material ofensivo*; **~ length** *n* longitud de página *f*; **~ number** *n* número de página *m*; **~ proofs** *n pl* pruebas de página *f pl*; **~ rate** *n* tarifa por página *f*; **~ setting** *n* composición de página *f*; **~ traffic** *n* BrE (jarg) *estimación del número total de lectores de una publicación*

page² *vt* (using pager) llamar por el busca; (using loudspeaker) llamar por el altavoz; (Comp) paginar

pager *n* busca *m*

paginate *vt* paginar

pagination *n* paginación *f*

paging device *n* (pager) busca *m*; (for paginating) dispositivo de paginación *m*

paid *adj* (amount, dividend) pagado; (employment) remunerado; (employee) a sueldo; **be ~ in cash** cobrar al contado; **~ on delivery** pago a la entrega; **~ by the piece** pagado por unidad; **~ by piece rate** pagado por pieza; **be ~ a rate of** recibir una proporción de; **~ holidays** *n pl* BrE (*cf* ▸**paid vacations** AmE) vacaciones remuneradas *f pl*; **~ instrument** *n* instrumento liberado *m*; **~ leave** *n* permiso pagado *m*; **~ vacations** *n* AmE (*cf* ▸**paid holidays** BrE) vacaciones remuneradas *f pl*

paid-in capital *n* capital cubierto *m*

paid-out capital n capital desembolsado m

paid-up adj (shares) liberado; (capital) desembolsado; ~ **addition** n (Ins) adquisición pagada f; ~ **member** n BrE miembro que ha pagado su cuota m

paired adj (shares) pareado

pallet n paleta f

palmtop n computadora f AmL or ordenador m Esp agenda

PAL/SECAM technology n tecnología PAL/SECAM f

pamphlet n octavilla f, panfleto m

Pan American Tracing and Reservations System n (for air travel) sistema panamericano de localización y reservas

P&L abbr (▶profit and loss) pérdidas y ganancias f pl; ~ **account** n BrE, ~ **statement** n AmE cuenta de pérdidas y ganancias f

p&p abbr (▶postage and packing) gastos de franqueo y empaquetado

P&S abbr (▶purchase and sale) compra y venta f; ~ **statement** n declaración de compra y venta f

panel n (Comp) plantilla f; ~ **data** n (S&M) datos del panel m pl; ~ **of experts** n grupo de expertos m; ~ **testing** n (S&M) prueba de panel f

pan-European adj paneuropeo

panic n pánico m; ~ **buying** n (S&M) compra provocada por el pánico m; ~ **selling** n (S&M) venta provocada por el pánico m

PANTRAC abbr (▶Pan American Tracing and Reservations System) (for air travel) sistema panamericano de localización y reservas

paper n (material) papel m; (newspaper) periódico m; (infrml) (bills, securities) efectos m pl, valores m pl; **a piece** o **sheet of** ~ una hoja de papel; **put a proposal down on** ~ poner una propuesta por escrito; **it seems simple enough on** ~ en teoría parece sencillo; **this agreement/contract is not worth the** ~ **it's written on** este acuerdo/contrato es papel mojado or no tiene el menor valor; ~ **feed** n (Comp) alimentación del papel f; ~ **feeder** n (Comp) alimentador de papel m; ~ **gold** n papel oro m; ~ **industry** n industria papelera f; ~ **loss** n pérdida potencial f; ~ **mill** n fábrica de papel f; ~ **money** n papel moneda m; ~ **profit** n beneficio no realizado m; ~ **qualifications** n pl documentos de titulación m pl; ~ **shredder** n destructora de documentos f; ~ **stacker** n (Comp) recogedor de papel m; ~ **tape** n (Comp)

cinta de papel f; ~ **track** n (Comp) pista para el papel f

paperback n libro en rústica m; **come out in** ~ salir en rústica; ~ **rights** n pl derechos de reedición (en rústica) m pl

paperclip n clip m, sujetapapeles m

paperless adj (certificates of deposit) por computadora AmL, por ordenador Esp; ~ **entry** n entrada sin dinero f; ~ **office** n oficina electrónica f; ~ **trading** n transacción sin papel f

paperwork n papeleo m

par n par f; **above/below** ~ por encima/por debajo de la par; **at** ~ a la par; ~ **for the course** lo normal, lo habitual; **be on a** ~ **with sth/sb** estar en pie de igualdad con algo/alguien; ~ **bond** n bono con valor a la par m; ~ **stock** n acciones a la par f pl; ~ **trading** n cambio a la par m; ~ **value** n valor a la par m; ~ **value share** n acción con valor a la par f; ~ **value stock** n acciones con valor a la par f pl

paradigm n paradigma m

paragraph n (text subdivision) párrafo m, apartado m; (symbol) símbolo de punto y aparte m; **new** ~ punto y aparte; ~ **mark** n símbolo de punto y aparte m

paralegal¹ adj paralegal

paralegal² n AmE asistente de abogado mf

parallel¹ adj (trading, import, loan) paralelo; (currency) no oficial; ~ **access** n (Comp) acceso en paralelo m; ~ **interface** n interfaz paralelo m; ~ **pricing** n fijación de precios no oficial f; ~ **printer** n impresora en paralelo f; ~ **processing** n (Comp) procesamiento en paralelo m

parallel² n paralelo m; **draw a** ~ **between** establecer un paralelo entre; **in** ~ paralelamente

parameter n parámetro m; ~**-driven software** n programa accionado por parámetros m

parametric adj paramétrico; ~ **programming** n programación paramétrica f

parcel¹ n (package) BrE paquete m; (of land) parcela f; ~ **post** n BrE servicio de paquetes postales m

parcel² vt (package) BrE empaquetar; **parcel out** vt (land) parcelar

parent n (Comp) padre m; ~ **bank** n banca matriz f; ~ **company** n compañía f or empresa f matriz; ~ **dividends** n pl dividendos de la empresa matriz m pl

parenthesis n (inserted phrase) paréntesis m; (punctuation mark) AmE (cf ▶round bracket BrE) paréntesis m; **in parentheses** entre paréntesis

pari passu adv igualmente

parity *n* paridad *f*; ~ **bit** *n* (Comp) bitio de paridad *m*; ~ **bond** *n* bono de paridad *m*; ~ **check** *n* (Comp) control de paridad *m*; ~ **clause** *n* (Ins) cláusula sobre paridad *f*; ~ **of exchange** *n* paridad de tipo de cambio *f*; ~ **price** *n* precio de paridad *m*; ~ **pricing** *n* fijación de precios de paridad *f*; ~ **ratio** *n* relación de paridad *f*

park *n* parque *m*

park-and-ride *n* *sistema de transporte público entre aparcamientos en las afueras y el centro de una ciudad*

parking *n* estacionamiento *m*; ~ **lot** *n* AmE (*cf* ▸**car park** BrE) aparcamiento *m*, estacionamiento *m*

parliament *n* parlamento *m*

Parliament *n* BrE (*cf* ▸**Congress** AmE) ≈ Cortes *f pl* Esp

parliamentary *adj* (procedure, vote) parlamentario; ~ **appropriation** *n* asignación parlamentaria *f*

part *n* (section, measure) parte *f*; (component) pieza *f*; (spare part) repuesto *m*, pieza de recambio *f*; (role) papel *m*; (of publication) fascículo *m*; **the better** *o* **best** ~ **of sth** la mayor parte de algo; **for the most** ~ por lo general, en general; **for my** ~ por mi parte; **in** ~ en parte; **in great** ~ en gran parte; **have no** ~ **in sth** no tener parte en algo; **it was an error on my** ~ fue un error por mi parte; **be** ~ **and parcel of sth** formar parte de algo; **play an important** ~ **in sth** desempeñar un papel importante en algo; **take** ~ **in sth** tomar parte en algo; ~**-cancellation** *n* cancelación parcial *f*; ~ **exchange** *n*: parte del pago *f*; **offer sth in** ~ **exchange** ofrecer algo como parte del pago; ~ **payment** *n* pago parcial *m*; **in** ~ **payment** a cuenta

partial *adj* (acceptance, delivery, loss, payment) parcial; ~ **release** *n* (Prop) redención parcial *f*; ~/**total loss** *n* pérdida total/parcial *f*; ~ **withdrawal** *n* (Stock) reembolso parcial *m*; ~ **write-off** *n* amortización parcial *f*

partially *adv* (partly) parcialmente; (with bias) con parcialidad

participant *n* participante *mf*

participate *vi* participar; ~ **in sth** participar en algo

participating *adj* (interest) preferente; ~ **bond** *n* obligación preferente *f*; ~ **preference share** *n* acción preferente con participación *f*; ~ **preferred stock** *n* AmE acciones privilegiadas *f pl*

participation *n* participación *f*; ~ **in a transaction** participación en una transacción; ~ **agreement** *n* acuerdo de participación *m*; ~ **loan** *n* préstamo de participación *m*, crédito sindicado *m*; ~ **rate** *n* nivel de participación *f*

participative *adj* (management, leadership, budgeting) participativo

particularity *n* particularidad *f*

particulars *n pl* (details) detalles *m pl*; (personal details) coordenadas *f pl*, información personal *f*; ~ **of sale** *n pl* descripción de la propiedad en venta *f*

partition *n* (of office) repartición *f*; (Comp) partición *f*, segmentación *m*; (Law, Prop) reparto *m*

partly *adv* parcialmente; ~**-finished goods** *n pl* productos *m pl* semiacabados *or* semielaborados *or* en procesos; ~**-paid share** *n* acción pagada parcialmente *f*

partner *n* socio(-a) *m,f*; **take a** ~ tomar un socio

partnership *n* (commercial) sociedad *f* personal *or* de responsabilidad ilimitada; (relationship) asociación *f*; **he aspires to a** ~ **in the firm** aspira a ser socio de la empresa; **go into** ~ **with sb** asociarse con alguien; ~ **agreement** *n* contrato de sociedad *m*

part-time[1] *adj* (employee, worker, job) a tiempo parcial

part-time[2] *adv* (work) a tiempo parcial

part-timer *n* (infrml) trabajador(a) a tiempo parcial *m,f*

party *n* (person or organization involved) parte *f*; (political) partido *m*; (group) grupo *m*; (social event) fiesta *f*; ~ **to an agreement/contract** parte de un acuerdo/contrato; ~ **line** *n* (telephone service) línea compartida *f*, línea telefónica común *f*; (policy stance) consignas partidarias *f pl*; ~ **ticket** *n* (for group) billete de grupo *m*; ~ **wall** *n* pared medianera *f*

pass *vt* (law, measure, motion, budget) aprobar; (resolution) adoptar; (comment, remark) hacer; (forged banknotes) pasar; ~ **a dividend** (Fin) omitir un dividendo; ~ **for press** meter en máquina, pasar a la prensa; ~ **judgment** pronunciar una sentencia; ~ **the proofs** pasar las pruebas; ~ **sentence** pronunciar una sentencia condenatoria; **pass on** *vt* (information, message) comunicar; (cost to the customer) trasladar; **pass over** *vt* (for promotion) pasarle por encima a; (fact, detail) pasar por alto; (remark, behaviour) pasar por alto, dejar pasar; ~ **sth over in silence** dejar algo de lado en silencio

passed *adj* (dividend) impagado, no repartido, omitido

passenger *n* pasajero(-a) *m,f*; ~ **care** *n* atención a los pasajeros *f*; ~ **list** *n* lista de pasajeros *f*; ~ **lounge** *n* sala de pasajeros *f*; ~ **service** *n* servicio de viajeros *m*; ~ **throughput** *n* flujo de pasajeros *m*

passer-by *n* transeúnte *mf*

passive *adj* (income, loss, investor, trust) pasivo; (bond) sin intereses

passport *n* pasaporte *m*; ~ **control** *n* control de pasaportes *m*; ~ **holder** *n* titular del pasaporte *mf*

pass-through *adj* (loan) de transferencia; (security) subrogado

password *n* (Comp) contraseña *f*; ~ **protected** *adaj* protegido por contraseña

past *adj* (week, month, year) último; (occasion) anterior; ~ **service benefit** *n* prestaciones por servicios pretéritos *f*

past-due claim *n* reclamación vencida *f*

paste *vt* (in word-processed document) pegar

pasteboard *n* cartón *m*

paste-up *n* modelado *m*; (Media, S&M) montaje de originales *m*

PA system *n* (▸**public address system**) sistema altavoces *m*

pat. *abbr* (▸**patent**) patente *f*; ~ **pend.** *abbr* (▸**patent pending**) patente en trámite

patch *n* (Comp) ajuste *m*; (territory) territorio *m*; **go through/hit a bad** ~ pasar por/tener una mala racha; **not be a** ~ **on sth/sb** no tener comparación con algo/alguien

patchy *adj* (performance) irregular, con altibajos; (results, response) irregular; (coverage) incompleto

patent¹ *n* patente *f*; ~ **applied for** patente solicitada; ~ **pending** patente en trámite; **take out a** ~ sacar una patente; **take out a** ~ **on sth** patentar algo; ~ **agent** *n* agente de patentes *mf*; **P**~ **and Trademark Office** *n* AmE (*cf* ▸**Patent Office** BrE) Registro de patentes y marcas *m*; ~ **application** *n* aplicación de una patente *f*; ~ **certificate** *n* certificado de patente *m*; ~ **infringement** *n* uso indebido de patente *m*, violación de patente *f*; ~ **life** *n* duración *f or* vigencia *f* de una patente; **P**~ **Office** *n* BrE (*cf* ▸**Patent and Trademark Office** AmE) Registro de la propiedad industrial *m*; ~ **protection** *n* protección de patentes *f*; ~ **rights** *n pl*, ~ **royalties** *n pl* derechos de patente *m pl*; ~ **trading** *n* comercio de patentes *m*

patent² *vt* patentar

patentability *n* patentabilidad *f*

patentable *adj* (invention) patentable

paternalism *n* paternalismo *m*

paternity leave *n* licencia de paternidad *m*

path *n* camino *m*; **the** ~ **to success** el camino al éxito; ~**-goal theory** *n* teoría de los medios y las metas *f*; ~**-to-profitability** *n* plan comercial del inicio de un negocio que exige un rendimiento de la inversión

patrimonial *adj* (industry) patrimonial

pattern *n* pauta *f*; (Comp) patrón *m*; ~ **agreement** *n* acuerdo *m or* contrato *m* modelo

pave *vt*: ~ **the way for sth/sb** preparar el terreno para algo/alguien

pawn¹ *n* prenda *f*; **place sth in** ~ empeñar algo, dejar algo en prenda; **redeem sth from** ~ desempeñar algo; ~ **ticket** *n* papeleta de empeño *f*

pawn² *vt* empeñar, dejar en prenda

pawnbroker *n* prestamista sobre prenda *mf*

pawned stock *n* capital fiado *m*

pawnshop *n* casa de empeño *f*

pay¹ *n* (of employee) sueldo *m*; (of manual worker) paga *f*, salario *m*; (for one day) jornal *m*; **in the** ~ **of sb** a sueldo de alguien; ~ **bargaining** *n* negociaciones de sueldo *f pl*; ~ **check** AmE, **pay cheque** BrE *n* cheque *m* de la paga *or* del sueldo; ~ **claim** *n* reclamación salarial *f*; ~ **comparability** *n* comparabilidad de pagos *f*; ~ **and conditions** *n pl* sueldo *m* y condiciones *f pl*; ~ **differential** *n* diferencial de pago *m*; ~ **cut** *n* recorte de sueldo *m*; ~ **dispute** *n* disputa salarial *f*; ~ **envelope** *n* AmE (*cf* ▸**pay packet** BrE) sobre de la paga *m*; ~ **freeze** *n* congelación de salarios; ~ **in lieu of notice** *n* compensación en lugar de preaviso *f*; ~ **increase** *n* aumento de sueldo *m*; ~ **negotiations** *n pl* negociaciones de sueldo *f pl*; ~ **packet** *n* BrE (*cf* ▸**pay envelope** AmE) sobre de la paga *m*; ~ **policy** *n* política de pagos *f*; ~ **raise** *n* AmE (*cf* ▸**pay rise** BrE) aumento de sueldo *m*; **get a** ~ **raise** conseguir un aumento de sueldo; ~ **review** *n* revisión *f* salarial *or* del salario; ~ **rise** *n* BrE (*cf* ▸**pay raise** AmE) aumento de sueldo *m*; **get a** ~ **rise** conseguir un aumento de sueldo; ~ **round** *n* serie de negociaciones salariales *f*; ~ **settlement** *n* acuerdo salarial *m*; ~ **slip** *n* nómina *f*; ~ **statement** *n* estado de los salarios *m*; ~ **station** *n* AmE (*cf* ▸**payphone** BrE) teléfono público *m*; ~ **talks** *n pl* negociaciones salariales *f pl*; ~ **TV** *n* televisión pagada *f*

pay² 1 *vt* (employee, creditor, tradesperson) pagarle a; (bill, debt) pagar, saldar; (tax, rent, instalment) pagar; (amount, fees, expenses) pagar, abonar; (settle) finiquitar; ~ **attention (to)** prestar atención (a); ~ **a call on sb** hacerle una visita a alguien; ~ **cash** pagar al contado Esp *or* de contado AmL; ~ **sth (to sb) for sth** pagar(le) algo (a alguien) por algo; **this account** ~**s 8% interest** esta cuenta da *or* produce un interés del 8%; ~ **top dollar** AmE *o* **pay top whack** BrE (infrml) **for sth** pagar mucho *or* el máximo por algo; ~ **sb a visit** hacerle una visita a alguien

2 *vi* (person) pagar; (work, activity) pagarse; ∼ **by check** AmE *o* **cheque** BrE pagar con cheque; ∼ **by giro** pagar por giro; ∼ **by the hour** pagar por hora; ∼ **by installments** AmE *o* **instalments** BrE pagar a plazos; ∼ **in cash** pagar al contado Esp *or* de contado AmL; ∼ **in full** pagar totalmente *or* por completo; ∼ **in kind** pagar en especie; ∼ **in ready cash** pagar en efectivo; ∼ **in specie** pagar en especie; ∼ **quarterly** pagar trimestralmente; ∼ **over the odds (for sth)** pagar demasiado (por algo); ∼ **to the order of** pagar a la orden de; ∼ **weekly/yearly** pagar semanalmente/anualmente; **pay back** *vt* (money) devolver, reintegrar; (loan, mortgage) pagar; **pay in** **1** *vt* (money) depositar, ingresar Esp **2** *vi* BrE hacer un depósito *or* un ingreso Esp; **pay off** **1** *vt* (loan, mortgage) amortizar; (debt) pagar, saldar, cancelar, liquidar; (creditor) pagarle a; (employee) liquidarle el sueldo a (al despedirlo) **2** *vi* (hard work, effort) valer la pena, tener su compensación; **pay out** **1** *vt* (dividend, compensation) pagar; (spend) desembolsar **2** *vi* (insurance company) pagar

payable *adj* pagadero; ∼ **after notice** pagadero después del aviso; ∼ **at maturity** pagadero al vencimiento; ∼ **in advance** pagadero anticipadamente; ∼ **monthly in arrears** pagadero mensualmente a plazo vencido; ∼ **on** (date) pagadero en; ∼ **on demand** pagadero a la vista; ∼ **to the bearer** pagadero al portador; **make sth** ∼ **to sb** hacer algo pagadero a alguien; ∼ **dividend** *n* dividendo a pagar *m*

payables at year-end *n pl* AmE efectos a pagar al cierre del ejercicio *m pl*

pay-as-you-earn *n* BrE, **pay-as-you-go** *n* AmE *sistema de retención de impuestos en la fuente de la renta de trabajo*

payback *n* (HRM) devolución *f*; (Mgmnt) recuperación *f*; ∼ **method** *n* método *m* de pago *or* de restituir; ∼ **period** *n* (Acc, HRM) periodo *m* *or* plazo *m* de recuperación; (S&M) plazo de amortización *m*; ∼ **provision** *n* provisión de pago *f*

payday *n* día de paga *m*

PAYE *abbr* BrE (▸**pay-as-you-earn**) *sistema de retención de impuestos en la fuente de la renta de trabajo*

payee *n* beneficiario(-a) *m,f*

payer *n* pagador(a) *m,f*

paying *adj* (bank) pagador; ∼ **agent** *n* (Tax) agente de pagos *mf*; ∼ **guest** *n* huésped *mf*

paying-in slip *n* BrE, **pay-in slip** *n* AmE papeleta de ingreso *f* Esp, formulario para depósitos *m* AmL

paymaster *n* pagador *m*

payment *n* (of debt, money, wage) pago *m*; (instalment) plazo *m*, cuota *f* AmL; (into account) depósito *m*, ingreso *m* Esp; (reward, thanks) pago *m*, recompensa *f*; ∼ **for sth** pago por algo; **keep up** ∼**s on one's mortgage** estar al día en el pago de la hipoteca; **make a** ∼ hacer un pago; ∼ **made to sb** pago en favor de alguien; ∼ **authorization** *n* autorización de pago *f*; ∼ **bond** *n* fianza de pago *f*; ∼ **by results** *n* pago *m* por resultados *or* según resultados; ∼ **commitment** *n* obligación *f* *or* compromiso *m* de pago; ∼ **date** *n* fecha *f* *or* día *m* de pago; ∼ **guarantee** *n* garantía de pago *f*; ∼ **holiday** *n* *acuerdo que permite un periodo durante el cual no hay que pagar la mensualidad*; ∼ **in arrears** *n* pago atrasado *m*; ∼ **in full on allotment** *n* liberación de acciones en adjudicación *f*; ∼ **in kind** *n* pago en especie *m*; ∼**-in-kind bond** *n* bono de pago en especie *m*; ∼ **method** *n* método de pago *m*; ∼ **on account** *n* pago en cuenta *m*; ∼ **order** *n* orden de pago *f*; ∼ **processing** *n* procesamiento de pagos *m*; ∼ **request** *n* demanda de pagar *f*; ∼ **requisition** *n* requerimiento de pago *m*; ∼ **terms** *n pl* condiciones de pago *f pl*; ∼ **transfer** *n* transferencia de pago *f*; ∼ **type** *n* forma de pago *f*

payoff *n* (result) resultado final *m*; (benefit) beneficio *m*; (reward) retribución *f*

payola *n* AmE (infrml) soborno *m* Esp

payout *n* pago *m*; (Bank) amortización *f*

pay-per-click *n* pago por clic *m*

pay-per-view *n* televisión a la carta *f*, pago por visión *m*; ∼ **TV** *n* televisión de pago *f*

payphone *n* BrE (*cf* ▸**pay station** AmE) teléfono público *m*

payroll *n* nómina *f*; **be on the** ∼ estar en nómina; ∼ **department** *n* departamento de nóminas *m*

pay-self check AmE, **pay-self cheque** BrE *n* cheque nominativo *m*

PBR *abbr* (▸**payment by results**) pago *m* por resultados *or* según resultados

PBS *abbr* (▸**Public Broadcasting Services**) *cadena pública estadounidense de radiodifusión*

p.c. *abbr* (▸**per cent**) p.c. (por ciento)

PC *abbr* (▸**personal computer**) PC (ordenador personal Esp, computadora personal AmL); ∼**-based** *adj* basado en PC; ∼**-compatibility** *n* compatibilidad del PC *f*

P/C *abbr* (▸**petty cash**) caja chica *f*

p.c.m. *abbr* (▸**per calendar month**) por mes

pd *abbr* (▸**paid**) pagado

PD *abbr* (▸**postdated**) postfechado

PDA *abbr* (▸**personal digital assistant**) auxiliar digital personal *m*

PDF *abbr* (▸**portable document format**) formato PDF *m* (formato de documento transferible)

PDM *abbr* (▸**physical distribution management**) gerencia *f or* gestión *f* de la distribución física

PDO *abbr* (▸**protected designation of origin**) DOP *f* (Denominación de Origen Protegida)

peaceful *adj* (protest, picketing) pacífico, no violento

peak¹ *n* (highest level) punto máximo *m*; (on graph) pico *m*; (of career) apogeo *m*, cúspide *f*; ∼ **hour** *n* hora *f* punta Esp *or* pico AmL; ∼ **level** *n* nivel máximo *m*; ∼ **period** *n* hora *f* punta Esp *or* pico AmL; ∼ **rate** *n* tarifa alta *f*; ∼ **season** *n* temporada alta *f*; ∼ **time** *n* (Media) hora de máxima audiencia *f*

peak² *vi* alcanzar el máximo

pecuniary *adj* (benefit) pecuniario

pedestrian *n* peatón(-tona) *m,f*; ∼ **mall** AmE, ∼ **precinct** BrE *n* zona peatonal *f*

pedlar *n* BrE (*cf* ▸**huckster** AmE) vendedor(a) ambulante *m,f*

peer *n* (equal) par *mf*, igual *mf*; (contemporary) coetáneo(-a) *m,f*; (lord) par *m*, lord *m*; ∼ **group** *n* grupo paritario *m*; ∼ **(group) pressure** *n* presión que ejerce el grupo paritario *m*; ∼ **review** *n* crítica por los pares *f*; ∼**-to-peer** *adj* (network) de par a par

peg *vt* (currency, prices) vincular; ∼ **the exchange** fijar el cambio

pegged *adj* (price) fijo, estable; (exchange rate) fijo

pegging *n* fijación *f*; ∼ **device** *n* dispositivo *m* de estabilización artificial de precios *or* de fijación de precios

penalize *vt* castigar

penalty *n* (punishment) pena *f*, castigo *m*; (fine) multa *f*; (disadvantage) desventaja *f*; **pay the** ∼ **(for sth/for doing sth)** pagar (algo/el haber hecho algo); ∼ **clause** *n* cláusula *f* punitiva *or* de penalización; ∼ **for breach of contract** *n* penalización por incumplimiento de contrato *f*; ∼ **for late tax payment** *n* recargo por pago fuera de plazo *m*; ∼ **for noncompliance** *n* penalización por incumplimiento *f*; ∼ **rate** *n* tasa de penalización *f*

pen-based computer *n* computadora *f* AmL *or* ordenador *m* Esp con registrador gráfico

pending¹ *adj* pendiente, por resolver; ∼ **business** *n* negocios pendientes *m pl*; ∼ **tray** *n* cartera de asuntos pendientes *f*

pending² *prep* en espera de

pendulum arbitration *n* arbitraje pendular *m*

penetrate *vt* (market) penetrar en; (organization) infiltrarse en

penetration *n* penetración *f*; ∼ **pricing** *n* fijación de precios de penetración *f*; ∼ **rate** *n* índice de penetración *f*

pennant *n* (Stock) gallardete *m*

penny *n* (currency unit) BrE penique *m*; AmE centavo *m*; (small sum) céntimo *m*, centavo *m*; **count the pennies** mirar el dinero *or* la plata AmL (infrml); **she hasn't a** ∼ **to her name** no tiene un céntimo, no tiene donde caerse muerta (infrml); **in for a** ∼, **in for a pound** BrE de perdidos, al río; **you'll pay back every** ∼ **you owe me** me pagarás hasta el último céntimo; **cost/be worth a pretty** ∼ costar/valer un dineral; **be** ∼ **wise and pound foolish** gastar a manos llenas y hacer economías en nimiedades; **he's worth every** ∼ vale su peso en oro; ∼ **share** *n* BrE acción con valor muy bajo *f*; ∼ **stock** *n* AmE acciones con valor inferior a un dólar *f pl*

pension *n* pensión *f*; (on retirement) jubilación *f*, pensión *f*; **be on** *o* **draw a** ∼ cobrar una pensión; ∼ **charges** *n pl* aportaciones *f pl* a fondos de pensiones *or* a sistemas complementarios de pensiones; ∼ **contributions** *n pl* cuotas a la Seguridad Social *f pl*; ∼ **costs** *n pl* costes *m pl* Esp *or* costos *m pl* AmL de pensiones; ∼ **fund** *n* fondo de pensiones *m*; ∼**-holder** *n* beneficiario(-a) de una pensión *m,f*; ∼ **income** *n* ingresos por pensión *m pl*; ∼ **liabilities** *n pl* obligaciones de jubilación *f pl*; ∼ **payment** *n* pago de la pensión *m*; ∼ **plan** *n*, ∼ **scheme** *n* BrE plan de pensiones *m*

pensionable *adj* (age) de jubilación; (earnings, employment) sometido a descuentos de jubilación

pensioner *n* jubilado(-a) *m,f*

pent-up *adj* (demand) contenido, reprimido; (energy) acumulado

peon *n* AmE (jarg) (HRM) peón *m*

people-intensive *adj* con alta participación de gente, intensivo en cuanto a gente

PEP *abbr* BrE (▸**Personal Equity Plan**) Plan Personal de Compra de Acciones *m*

per *prep* por; **as** ∼ según; **as** ∼ **from** por indicación de; ∼ **annum** por año; ∼ **calendar month** por mes; ∼ **day** por día; ∼ **head** por cabeza; ∼ **month** por mes; ∼ **person** por persona; ∼ **share** por acción; ∼ **year** por año; ∼ **contract basis** *n* base según contrato *f*; ∼ **diem allowance** *n* dieta *f*; ∼ **kilometer rate** AmE, ∼ **kilometre rate** BrE *n* tarifa por kilómetro *f*

PER *abbr* (▶**price-earnings ratio**) ratio precio-beneficio *m*

per capita *adj* (debt, income) per cápita

perceived benefit *n* beneficio percibido *m*

per cent[1] *n* porcentaje *m*; **a half ∼ o a half of one ∼** un cero coma cinco por ciento; (on stock exchange) un medio punto por ciento

per cent[2] *adj* por ciento; **a five ∼ discount** un descuento del cinco por ciento, un cinco por ciento de descuento

per cent[3] *adv* por ciento; **profits are up (by) twenty ∼** los beneficios han aumentado (en) un veinte por ciento

percentage[1] *n* porcentaje *m*; **get a ∼ of the profits** recibir un tanto por ciento *or* un porcentaje de los beneficios; **∼ of capital held** *n* porcentaje de capital retenido *m*; **∼-of-completion method** *n* método de porcentaje de obra ejecutada *m*; **∼-of-sales method** *n* método de porcentaje de ventas *m*

percentage[2] *adj* (change, increase, interest) porcentual; **in ∼ terms** en tantos porciento; **∼ point** *n* punto porcentual *m*

percentagewise *adv* a modo de porcentaje

percentile *n* percentil *m*

perfect[1] *adj* (competition, market, monopoly, substitute) perfecto; **∼ hedge** *n* (Stock) cobertura perfecta *f*; **∼ price discrimination** *n* discriminación perfecta de precios *f*

perfect[2] *vt* perfeccionar

perfected security *n* título perfeccionado *m*

perform [1] *vt* (function) desempeñar, hacer, cumplir; (role) desempeñar; (task) ejecutar, llevar a cabo [2] *vi* (worker, company, stocks) rendir; (economy) marchar

performance *n* (of employee) desempeño *m*, rendimiento *m*; (of company) resultados *m pl*; (of stocks) rendimiento *m*; (of machine) comportamiento *m*, performance *m* AmL; (of function, duty) ejercicio *m*, desempeño *m*; (of task) ejecución *f*, realización *f*; **∼ against objectives** *n* actuación *f or* desarrollo *m* por objetivos; **∼ appraisal** *n* evaluación del desempeño *f*; **∼ budgeting** *n* presupuestación de ejecución *f*; **∼ evaluation** *n* evaluación del desempeño *f*; **∼ guarantee** *n* (S&M) garantía de rendimiento *f*; (Stock) garantía de actuación *f*; **∼ indicator** *n* indicador de rendimientos; (of employee) indicador de desempeño *m*; (of company) indicador de resultados *m*; **∼ management** *n* gestión de desempeño *f*; **∼ marketing** *n* marketing de rendimiento *m*; **∼ measurement** *n* medición *f* de ejecución

or del rendimiento; **∼ monitoring** *n* control de actuación *m*, supervisión del desempeño *f*; **∼ rating** *n* (of investment) valoración de la actuación *f*; **∼-related indicator** *n* indicador relacionado con los resultados *m*; **∼-related pay** *n* remuneración según rendimiento *f*; **∼ review** *n* (of employee) evaluación de rendlimiento *f*; (of company) análisis de resultados *m*; **∼ stock** *n* acciones de alto rendimiento *f pl*; **∼ target** *n* meta *f* de desempeño *or* de rendimiento; **∼ testing** *n* prueba *f* de desempeño *or* de rendimiento

performer *n* (Econ) ejecutante *mf*

performing rights *n pl* (Media) derechos de interpretación *m pl*; (Law) derechos de ejecución *m pl*

peril *n* riesgo *m*; **∼ point** *n* punto de riesgo *m*

perimeter advertising *n* publicidad de perímetro *f*

period *n* (interval, length of time) periodo *m*; (when specifying a time limit) plazo *m*; (epoch) época *f*; **for the ∼ of** para el periodo de; **over the ∼ of** durante el periodo de; **over a ∼ of time** durante un periodo de tiempo; **within a two-month ∼** dentro de un plazo de dos meses; **∼ cost** *n* coste *m* Esp *or* costo *m* AmL del periodo; **∼ of grace** *n* plazo de gracia *m*; **∼ of notice** *n* (after dismissal, resignation) periodo de notificación *m*; **∼ of payment** *n* periodo de pago *m*

periodgram *n* gráfico cronológico *m*

periodic *adj* (amounts, charges) periódico

periodical[1] *adj* periódico

periodical[2] *n* revista *f*

peripheral[1] *adj* periférico; **∼ computer** *n* computadora periférica *f* AmL, ordenador periférico *m* Esp; **∼ device** *n* dispositivo periférico *m*; **∼ equipment** *n* equipo periférico *m*; **∼ worker** *n* trabajador(a) periférico(-a) *m,f*

peripheral[2] *n* periférico *m*

periphery firm *n* empresa periférica *f*

perishable *adj* (goods, fish, fruit) perecedero

perishables *n pl* perecederos *m pl*

perjury *n* perjurio *m*; **commit ∼** cometer perjurio

perk *n* (infrml) beneficio extra *m*, extra *m*; **a ∼ of the job** (infrml) un privilegio *or* beneficio del puesto

permanent *adj* (employment, contract, residence) permanente; (address, job) permanente, fijo; **∼ exhibition** BrE, **∼ exhibit** AmE *n* exposición permanente *f*; **∼ financing** *n* financiación a largo plazo *f*; **∼ income bearing share** *n* acción productora de renta permanente *f*; **∼ staff** *n* empleados fijos *m pl*, personal permanente *m*

permissible *adj* (error) permitido

permission *n* permiso *m*; **give sb ∼ to do sth** darle permiso a alguien para hacer algo; **∼ marketing** *n* marketing con permiso previo *m*

permit[1] *vt* permitir; **∼ sb to do sth** permitirle a alguien hacer algo

permit[2] *n* permiso *m*; **∼ bond** *n* garantía de licencia *f*; **∼-free** *adj* exento de licencia

permitted *adj* (quantity) permitido

permutation *n* permutación *f*

perpendicular *adj* perpendicular; **∼ spread** *n* (Stock) diferencial perpendicular *m*

perpetual *adj* (bond, lease) perpetuo; **∼ preferred share** *n* acción preferente sin vencimiento *f*

perpetuity *n* perpetuidad *f*; **in ∼** a perpetuidad

per pro *prep*, **per procurationem** *prep* por poder, por autorización, por orden

perquisite *n* beneficio extra *m*, extra *m*

per se *adv* por sí mismo

persistent *adj* (demand) persistente, (salesperson) insistente, persistente

person *n* persona *f*; **∼-day** *n* día-hombre *m*; **∼-job fit** *n* adecuación entre una persona y su trabajo; **∼-to-person call** *n* AmE llamada de persona a persona *f*

personal *adj* (expenses, credit, guarantee) personal; **no ∼ calls are allowed** no se permite hacer llamadas particulares; **a letter marked '∼'** una carta marcada 'personal'; **a ∼ matter** un asunto privado *or* personal; **for ∼ reasons** por razones personales; **∼ allowance** *n* BrE (*cf* ▶**personal exemption** AmE) deducción personal *f*; **∼ assistant** *n* ayudante(-a) *m,f* *or* secretario(-a) *m,f* personal; **∼ banking service** *n* servicio bancario personal *m*; **∼ benefit** *n* (Tax) subsidio personal *m*; **∼ computer** *n* computadora *f* AmL *or* ordenador *m* Esp personal; **∼ digital assistant** *n* auxiliar personal digital *m*; **∼ disposable income** *n* ingreso personal disponible *m*; **∼ effects** *n pl* efectos personales *m pl*; **P∼ Equity Plan** *n* BrE Plan Personal de Compra de Acciones *m*; **∼ exemption** *n* AmE (*cf* ▶**personal allowance** BrE) deducción personal *f*; **∼ financial planning software** *n* software de planificación financiera personal *m*; **∼ identification number** *n* número de identificación personal *m*; **∼ income** *n* renta personal *f*; **∼ injury** *n* lesión personal *f*; **∼ liability** *n* responsabilidad personal *f*; **∼ loan** *n* préstamo personal *m*; **∼ particulars** *n pl* datos personales *m pl*; **∼ pension scheme** *n* BrE plan personal de jubilación *m*; **∼ property** *n* inmuebles personales *m pl*; **∼ savings** *n pl* ahorros personales *m pl*; **∼ secretary** *n* secretario(-a) personal *m,f*; **∼ selling** *n* venta personal *f*; **∼ share** *n* acción nominativa *f*; **∼ wealth** *n* patrimonio personal *m*; **∼ Web page** *n* página web personal *f*

personality *n* personalidad *f*; **∼ promotion** *n* BrE (jarg) *promoción que utiliza a personas famosas*

personalization *n* personalización *f*

personalized *adj* (cheque, letter) personalizado

personally *adv* personalmente; **∼ liable** *o* **responsible** personalmente responsable

personnel *n* (staff) personal *m*; (department) departamento de personal *m*; (field) administración *f or* gestión *f* de personal; **∼ department** *n* departamento de personal *m*; **∼ director** *n* director(a) de personal *m,f*; **∼ file** *n* archivo de personal *m*; **∼-intensive** *adj* con alta ocupación de personal; **∼ management** *n* administración *f or* gestión *f* del personal; **∼ manager** *n* director(a) *m,f or* gerente *mf* de personal; **∼ officer** *n* jefe(-a) de personal *m,f*; **∼ policy** *n* política de personal *f*

perspective *n* perspectiva *f*; **be in ∼** estar en perspectiva; **get sth in/out of ∼** considerar/no considerar algo objetivamente; **keep things in ∼** ver el asunto en su justa medida; **put sth in (its right/true) ∼** poner algo en su justa medida

persuade *vt* convencer, persuadir; **∼ sb to do sth** persuadir a alguien para que haga algo *or* de hacer algo

persuasion *n* persuasión *f*

persuasive *adj* persuasivo

PERT *abbr* (▶**programme evaluation and review technique**) técnica de evaluación y revisión del programa *f*

pertaining to *prep* correspondiente a

pertain to *vt* corresponder a, pertenecer a

pertinence *n* pertinencia *f*; **∼ chart** *n* gráfico *m or* organigrama *m* de correspondencia; **∼ tree** *n* árbol de correspondencia *m*

pessimist *n* pesimista *mf*

pessimistic *adj* (outlook) pesimista

pesticide *n* pesticida *m*

Peter principle *n* (HRM) principio de Peter *m*

petition[1] *n* (written document) petición *f*; (Law) demanda *f*; **file *o* lodge a ∼** presentar una demanda; **a ∼ for divorce** una demanda de divorcio; **sign a ∼** firmar una petición

petition[2] *vt* elevar una petición a, peticionar AmL; **petition for** *vt* (divorce) presentar una demanda de

petitioner n peticionario(-a) m,f; (Law) demandante m,f

petrobond n petrobono m

petrocurrency n petrodivisa f

petrodollar n petrodólar m

petrol n BrE (cf ►**gasoline** AmE) gasolina f

petroleum n petróleo m; ~ **industry** n sector del petróleo m

petty adj (expenses, regulations) menor; (details) insignificante, nimio; (attitude) mezquino; ~ **official** n funcionario(-a) de bajo nivel m,f

petty cash n caja chica f; ~ **book** n libro de caja chica m; ~ **fund** n fondo de caja chica m; ~ **voucher** n comprobante de caja chica m

PFI abbr (►**private finance initiative**) proyecto dónde el sector privado se encarga de la construcción y la financiación de algo y luego el gobierno paga por el servicio, así evitando los costes de primer establecimiento

pg. abbr (►**page**) p (página), pág. (página)

PG abbr (►**paying guest**) huésped mf

PGI abbr (►**protected geographic indication**) IGP f (indicación geográfica protegida)

phantom adj (income, share, tax, capital) ficticio

pharmaceutical adj farmacéutico; ~ **industry** n industria farmacéutica f

pharmaceuticals n pl productos farmacéuticos m pl

phase[1] n fase f; ~ **zero** n fase cero f

phase[2] vt (construction, development) escalonar, realizar por etapas; (coordinate) sincronizar; **phase in** vt (technology, service, system) introducir or colocar progresivamente; **phase out** vt (technology, service, system) eliminar progresivamente or por fases

phased adj (increase) progresivo, gradual; (distribution) por fases

philosophy n filosofía f

phone[1] n teléfono m; **answer the** ~ contestar el teléfono; **by** ~ por teléfono; **be on the** ~ (speaking) estar hablando por teléfono; (subscribe) BrE tener teléfono; **you're wanted on the** ~ te llaman por teléfono; **over the** ~ por teléfono; ~ **banking** n banca telefónica f; ~ **bill** n factura telefónica f; ~ **book** n guía f telefónica or de teléfonos; ~ **booking** n BrE (cf ►**phone reservation** AmE) reserva por teléfono f; ~ **booth** AmE, ~ **box** BrE (cf ►**call box** AmE) cabina telefónica f; ~ **call** n llamada telefónica f; ~ **company** n compañía telefónica f; ~ **directory** n guía f telefónica or de teléfonos; ~ **line** n línea telefónica f; ~ **link** n enlace telefónico m; ~ **message** n mensaje telefónico m; ~ **number** n número de teléfono m; ~ **reservation** n AmE (cf ►**phone booking** BrE) reserva por teléfono f; ~ **tap** n intervención telefónica f; ~ **tapping** n intervención de un teléfono f; ~ **voucher** n tarjeta prepagada f

phone[2] [1] vt (person, place, number) llamar (por teléfono); (order) hacer por teléfono [2] vi llamar (por teléfono), telefonear; ~ **for sth** llamar para pedir algo; **phone back** vti (call again) volver a llamar; (return call) llamar; **phone in** vi llamar (por teléfono), telefonear; ~ **in sick** llamar para dar parte de enfermo; **phone out** vi llamar al exterior; **phone up** vti llamar (por teléfono)

phonecard n tarjeta telefónica f

phone-in n programa de llamadas m; ~ **poll** n registro telefónico m; ~ **program** AmE, ~ **programme** BrE n programa de llamadas m

photo n foto f; ~ **call** n fotollamada f

photocopiable adj fotocopiable

photocopier n fotocopiadora f

photocopy[1] n fotocopia f

photocopy[2] vt fotocopiar

photogravure n fotograbado m

phreakage n piratería de líneas telefónicas f

physical adj (commodity, depreciation, deterioration, injury) físico; ~ **assets** n pl activos m pl físicos or materiales or tangibles; ~ **barrier** n (for trade) barrera física f; ~ **collateral** n garantías materiales f pl; ~ **distribution management** n gerencia f or gestión f de la distribución física; ~ **handicap** n, ~ **impairment** n minusvalía física f; ~ **inventory** n inventario físico m; ~ **market** n mercado físico m

pick[1] vt (team) seleccionar; **pick up** [1] vt (bargain) conseguir; (cargo) recoger; ~ **up the tab** (infrml) comprometerse a pagar una factura [2] vi (prices, sales) subir, repuntar; (economy, business) repuntar

pick[2] n (choice) elección f, derecho de elección m; **the** ~ **of sth** lo mejor de algo; **take your** ~ elige or escoge el/la que quieras

picket[1] n (group) piquete m; (individual) miembro de un piquete; ~ **line** n piquete m

picket[2] [1] vt formar un piquete frente a, piquetear AmL [2] vi tomar parte en un piquete, piquetear AmL

picketing n formación de piquetes f

pickup bond n bono con alto interés y pronto vencimiento m

pictogram n pictograma m

pictorial *adj* (presentation) gráfico, ilustrado

picture *n* (illustration) ilustración *f*; (photograph) foto *f*; (on TV) imagen *f*; (by artist) cuadro *m*; (situation) panorama *m*; **put sb in the ~** poner a alguien al tanto (de la situación); **~ caption** *n* pie de ilustración *m*

piece *n* (part of sth broken, torn, cut, divided) pedazo *m*, trozo *m*; (component) pieza *f*, parte *f*; (coin) moneda *f*, pieza *f*; **a ~ of advice** un consejo; **a ~ of information** un dato; **a ~ of legislation** una ley; **~ rate** *n* precio *m* unitario *or* por pieza; **~ wage** *n* salario a destajo *m*

piecework *n* trabajo a destajo *m*; **~ system** *n* sistema de pago a destajo *m*

pieceworker *n* destajista *mf*, trabajador(a) a destajo *m,f*

pie chart *n* gráfico circular *m*

piggyback *adj* (loan, legislation) concatenado

PIK bond *abbr* (►**payment-in-kind bond**) bono de pago en especie *m*

piker *n* (jarg) (Stock) oportunista *mf*

pilot¹ *adj* (scheme, study, project, production) piloto; **~ launch** *n* lanzamiento piloto *m*; **~ run** *n* ensayo piloto *m*

pilot² *n* (broadcast) piloto *m*

pin *n* (of paper feeder) diente *m*; **~ money** *n* dinero para gastos personales *m*

PIN *abbr* (►**personal identification number**) número de identificación personal *m*

pink *adj* rosa, rosado AmL; **~ paper** *n* BrE (Pol) borrador *m*; **~ pound** *n* BrE *el poder adquisitivo de la comunidad homosexual*; **~ sheet market** *n* AmE mercado bursátil informal *m*; **~ sheets** *n pl publicación diaria de la oficina estadounidense de cotizaciones que contiene una relación actualizada del mercado extrabursátil*; **~ slip** *n* AmE notificación de despido *f*

pioneer¹ *n* pionero(-a) *m,f*; **~ product** *n* producto pionero *m*

pioneer² *vt* promover

pip *n* (jarg) (Stock) pipo *m* (jarg)

pipeline *n* (Ind) tubería *f*; (Comms) cable coaxial *m*; **be in the ~** (order) estar tramitándose; (change, proposal) estar preparándose

piracy *n* piratería *f*

pirate *adj* (copy, radio) pirata

pirated *adj* (product) pirateado

pit *n* (Stock) lonja de transacciones *f*

pitch *n* (by salesperson) palabrería de vendedor *m*; (in market) puesto *m*; (Comp) espaciado *m*

pitfall *n* hueco *m*

pixel *n* pixel *m*

pkg. *abbr* (►**package¹**) paquete *m*

PKI *abbr* (►**public key infrastructure**) infraestructura de claves públicas *f*

pkt. *abbr* (►**packet**) paquete *m*

P/L *abbr* (►**partial loss**) pérdida parcial *f*

placard *n* cartel *m*

place¹ *n* lugar *m*, sitio *m*; (job) puesto *m*; (in contest) puesto *m*, lugar *m*; **when the new accounting system is in ~** cuando se haya implementado el nuevo sistema de contabilidad; **the new manager is not yet in ~** el nuevo director aún no ha entrado en funciones *or* no ha asumido el cargo; **take ~** tener lugar; **~ of abode** *n* residencia *f*; **~ of birth** *n* lugar de nacimiento *m*; **~ of business** *n* (office) oficina *f*; (shop) comercio *n*; **~ of employment** *n* lugar de empleo *m*; **~ of origin** *n* lugar de origen *m*; **~ of payment** *n* lugar de pago *m*; **~ of residence** *n* residencia *f*; **~ of work** *n* (company, organization, building) lugar de trabajo *m*

place² *vt* (shares, money, goods) colocar; (deposit) hacer; (advertisement) poner; (phone call) pedir; **~ an embargo on sth** poner embargo a algo; **~ emphasis on sth** poner énfasis sobre algo; **~ a hold on an account** constituir una custodia en una cuenta; **~ sb in custody** poner a alguien bajo custodia; **~ sth in trust** dar algo en fideicomiso; **~ an order (with)** hacer un pedido (a); **~ a question on the agenda** incluir un asunto en el orden del día; **~ sb under guardianship** poner a alguien bajo tutela; **they ~d her with a Boston firm** la colocaron *or* le encontraron trabajo en una empresa de Boston

placement *n* (work experience) prácticas en una empresa *f pl*; (of bonds) colocación *f*; **~ test** *n* contrato de empleo a prueba *m*

PLACO *abbr* (►**Planning Committee**) comité de planificación *m*

plaintiff *n* demandante *mf*

plan¹ *n* (scheme) plan *m*; (diagram, map) plano *m*; **draw up** *o* **make ~s** hacer planes; **go according to ~** salir conforme estaba planeado, salir según el plan; **a ~ of action** un plan de acción

plan² **1** *vt* (journey, itinerary) planear, programar; (economy, strategies) planificar; **~ to do sth** pensar hacer algo **2** *vi* hacer planes; **~ ahead** planear las cosas de antemano; **~ for the future** hacer planes para el futuro

plane *n* (aircraft) BrE (*cf* ►**airplane** AmE) avión *m*; (surface) plano *m*

plank *n* (of policy) elemento fundamental *m*

planned *adj* (obsolescence) planificado; (economy) dirigido; (capacity) planificado, planeado

planning *n* planificación *f*; ~ **approval** *n* AmE (*cf* ▸**planning permission** BrE) permiso de construcción *m*; ~ **authority** *n* organismo de planificación *m*; ~ **commission** *n* comisión de planificación *f*; ~ **committee** *n* comité de planificación *m*; ~ **department** *n* departamento de planificación *m*; ~ **permission** *n* BrE (*cf* ▸**planning approval** AmE) permiso de construcción *m*; ~ **restriction** *n* restricción de planificación *f*, limitación a la urbanización *f*

plant *n* (fixed assets) equipo *m*, instalación *f*; (factory) planta *f*, fábrica *f*; ~ **capacity** *n* capacidad de planta *f*; ~ **hire** *n* alquiler de planta *m*; ~ **maintenance** *n* mantenimiento de las instalaciones *m*; ~ **management** *n* dirección *f* or gerencia *f* de fábrica; ~ **manager** *n* director(a) *m,f* or gerente *mf* de fábrica

plantation *n* plantación *f*

plastic[1] *n* (substance) plástico *m*; (credit cards) (infrml) plástico *m* (infrml); **pay by** ~ pagar con tarjeta

plastic[2] *adj* de plástico

plastics *n pl* plásticos *m pl*; ~ **industry** *n* industria del plástico *f*

platform *n* plataforma *f*; (for trains) andén *m*

play[1] *vt* jugar; ~ **(sth) by ear** improvisar (algo); ~ **the market** especular; ~ **a role** *o* **part in sth** desempeñar un papel en algo; **play down** *vt* (importance) minimizar; (risk, achievement) quitarle *or* restarle importancia a, minimizar; **play on** *vt* (fears, generosity) aprovecharse de, explotar

play[2] *n* juego *m*; **bring sth/come into** ~ poner algo/entrar en juego; **make a** ~ **for sth** tratar de lograr algo; ~ **book** *n* AmE (of company) manual de actuación *m*

playback *n* repetición *f*

player *n* (in negotiations) participante *mf*

plc *abbr* BrE (▸**public limited company**) ≈ S.A. (sociedad anónima), ≈ S.A.A. (sociedad anónima por acciones)

plea *n* alegato *m*; **enter a** ~ **of guilty/not guilty** declararse culpable/inocente; ~ **bargain** *n* convenio entre el acusado y el fiscal para tratar de evitar que se dicte la pena máxima

plead [1] *vt* (give as excuse) alegar; (argue) defender; ~ **sb's case** hablar en favor de alguien; (Law) llevar el caso de alguien; ~ **ignorance** alegar ignorancia [2] *vi* suplicar, rogar; ~ **guilty/not guilty** declararse culpable/inocente

pleading *n* alegación *f*, alegato *m*

pleasant *adj* agradable; ~ **working environment** *n* ambiente de trabajo agradable *m*

please *adv* por favor; ~ **forward** despachar por favor; ~ **let us know which date suits** por favor, háganos saber que fecha le conviene; ~ **reply** se ruega respuesta; ~ **submit your quotations** por favor, expongan sus presupuestos; ~ **fax your confirmation** por favor, envíe su confirmación por fax

pledge[1] *n* (promise) promesa *f*; (token, pawned object) prenda *f*; (of money) cantidad prometida *f*, donativo prometido *m*; (collateral) garantía *f*, aval *m*; **keep a** ~ cumplir una promesa, cumplir con su palabra; **make a** ~ **to do sth** prometer hacer algo

pledge[2] *vt* (support, funds) prometer

plenary *adj* (parliamentary session) plenario

plentiful *adj* abundante; **a** ~ **supply of sth** una abundancia de algo

plenum *n* sesión plenaria *f*

plinth *n* zócalo *m*

plot[1] *n* (of land) solar *m*, terreno *m*, parcela *f*; (on graph) línea *f*; ~ **book** *n* AmE registro agrario *m*

plot[2] *vt* (curve, graph) trazar

plotter *n* (Comp) trazador *m*

plotting *n* trazado *m*; ~ **board** *n* (Comp) tablero de dibujo *m*; ~ **pen** *n* (Comp) lápiz trazador *m*; ~ **table** *n* tablero cuadriculado *m*

ploughback BrE, **plowback** AmE *n* reinversión *f*

plough back BrE, **plow back** AmE *vt* (profits) reinvertir

PLR *abbr* (▸**public lending right**) derecho a empréstito público *m*

plug[1] *n* (electrical) enchufe *f*; (in advertising) (infrml) propaganda *f*; **give sth a** ~ (infrml) hacerle propaganda a algo; **pull the** ~ **on sth** (infrml) terminar con algo; ~**-and-play** *n* plug and play *m*, equipo de enchufar y usar *m*

plug[2] *vt* (infrml) hacerle propaganda a; ~ **and play** enchufar y usar; **plug in** *vt* (Comp) enchufar

plug-in *n* unidad enchufable *f*

plummet *vi* (prices, income) caer en picado, desplomarse, irse a pique

plunge[1] *n* (of price, value) caída *f*; (speculation) especulación fuerte *f*; **shares took a** ~ las acciones se fueron a pique *or* cayeron en picado; **take the** ~ arriesgarse

plunge[2] *vi* (price, output) caer en picado, irse a pique; (speculate) arriesgar grandes sumas

plunger *n* (Stock) especulador(a) fuerte *m,f*

pluralism *n* pluralismo *m*

plus[1] *n* (advantage) pro *m*, ventaja *f*

plus[2] *adj* (point) positivo, a favor; **the work will cost £10,000** ~ la obra le costará unas 10.000 libras como mínimo; **on the** ~ **side** ···▷

entre las ventajas or los pros; ~ **sign** n signo de suma m

plus³ prep más; **2 ~ 5 equals 7** 2 más 5 son 7; **£50 per hour ~ expenses** cincuenta libras por hora más gastos; ~ **the fact that...** además de que...

plus⁴ conj además de que

plywood n contrachapado m

p.m. abbr (▸**per month**) por mes; (▸**post meridiem**) de la tarde

PN abbr, **P/N** abbr (▸**promissory note**) pagaré m

p.o. abbr (▸**postal order**) BrE giro postal m

PO abbr (▸**Patent Office**) BrE Registro de la propiedad industrial m; (▸**Post Office**) servicio nacional de correo británico, ≈ Correos m, ≈ Dirección General de Correos y Telégrafos f; ~ **Box** n Apdo. (apartado postal or de correos)

P.O. abbr (▸**purchase order**) O/C (orden de compra)

poach vt (staff, ideas) robar

poaching n (of staff, ideas) robo m

pocket n (of consumer) bolsillo m; **be £100 in ~** haber ganado 100 libras; **be in sb's ~** estar controlado por alguien; **have sb in one's ~** tener a alguien en el bolsillo; **prices to suit every ~** precios para todos los bolsillos; **end up out of ~** terminar perdiendo dinero; ~ **calculator** n calculadora de bolsillo f; ~ **computer** n computadora f AmL or ordenador m Esp de bolsillo; ~ **envelope** n sobre de bolsillo m

pocketbook issue n AmE (cf ▸**bread-and-butter issue** BrE) problema básico m

POD abbr (▸**paid on delivery**) pago a la entrega; (▸**proof of debt**) comprobante de deuda m; (▸**proof of delivery**) prueba de entrega f

point¹ n (dot, item, place, on scale, in contest) punto m; (in time) momento m; (decimal) coma f, punto decimal m AmL; (on index of share prices) entero m; (in real estate, commercial lending) ficha m; **make a ~ of doing sth** asegurarse de hacer algo; **make the ~ that...** observar que...; ~ **of departure** n punto de partida m; ~ **of entry** (into country) punto de entrada m; ~ **of export** n punto de exportación m; ~ **of law** n cuestión de derecho f; ~ **of no return** n momento a partir del cual ya no se puede volver atrás m; ~ **of origin** n punto de origen m; ~ **of presence** n (on Internet) punto de presencia m; ~ **price** n (of options) precio del punto m; ~ **of sale** n punto de venta m; ~**-of-sale advertising** n publicidad en los puntos de venta f; ~**-of-sale material** n material de punto de venta m; ~**-of-sale promotion** n promoción en el punto de venta f; ~**-of-sale terminal** n

terminal en punto de venta m; ~ **of view** n punto de vista m

point² vi señalar; ~ **and click** (Comp) señalar con el puntero y hacer clic; **point to** vt (indicate) indicar; (with cursor) señalar con el puntero

pointer n (Comp) (presentation aid) puntero m; (on dial) aguja f; (clue) pista f; (tip) idea f, sugerencia f

poison n tóxico m; ~ **pill** n AmE (jarg) en adquisiciones públicas, la estrategia por parte de la empresa objetivo de desacreditar el valor de sus acciones para no hacerlas atractivas al comprador

polarization n polarización f

police n policía f; ~ **force** n policía f; ~ **record** n antecedentes penales m pl

policy n (plan) política f; (insurance) póliza f; **company ~ on advertising** la política de la compañía en materia de publicidad; **this government has no ~ on wages** este gobierno no tiene una política salarial or de salarios; **take out a ~** hacerse una póliza; **it is government ~ to reduce inflation** la reducción de la inflación es una de las directrices de la política gubernamental; ~ **of the big stick** n (infrml) política f de fuerza or del garrote; ~ **dividend** n dividendo de una póliza m; ~ **formulation** n formulación de una política f; ~ **statement** n declaración de política f

policyholder n tomador(a) de seguro m,f

policymaker n persona que establece la política

policymaking n establecimiento de la política m

political adj (issue, change, situation, climate) político; ~ **contribution** n contribución política f; ~ **co-operation** n cooperación política f; ~ **correctness** n progresismo ideológico m; ~ **donation** n donación política f; ~ **economy** n economía política f; ~ **fund** n fondo político m; ~ **institution** n institución política f; ~ **levy** n BrE impuesto político m; ~ **party** n partido político m; ~ **system** n régimen político m; ~ **union** n unión política f

politically adv políticamente; ~ **correct** adj políticamente correcto

politician n político(-a) m,f

politicize vt politizar

politics n política f

poll¹ n (opinion poll) encuesta f, sondeo m; (ballot) votación f; **conduct a ~** encuestar; **go to the ~s** acudir a las urnas; ~ **tax** n BrE (obs) capitación f, impuesto per cápita m

poll² vt (question) sondear, encuestar; (obtain in ballot) obtener; (cast in ballot) emitir; (Comp) interrogar

polling *n* (questioning) interrogación *f*; (voting) votación *f*; (of network, modem) invitación a emitir *f*; ~ **booth** *n* cabina electoral *f*; ~ **day** *n* día de elecciones *m*; ~ **station** *n* colegio electoral *m*

pollutant *n* contaminante *f*

pollute *vt* contaminar

polluter *n* contaminador(a) *m,f*; ~ **pays principle** *n* principio de 'el que contamine paga (por la limpieza)'

pollution *n* contaminación *f*, polución *f*; ~ **charge** *n* carga de polución *f*; ~ **control** *n* control de la contaminación *m*; ~ **monitoring** *n* control de la contaminación *m*; ~ **tax** *n* impuesto por contaminación *m*

pony *n* AmE (jarg) plagio *m*

pool¹ *n* (of money) fondo (común) *m*; (of resources) reserva *f*; (cartel, of secretaries) pool *m*; (of vehicles) parque móvil *m*;

pool² *vt* (resources, ideas) aunar, juntar

pooling *n* (Econ) pooling *m*; ~ **arrangements** *n pl* acuerdos de fondo común *m pl*; ~ **of interests** *n* AmE (*cf* ►**merger accounting** BrE) contabilidad de fusiones *f*; (balance sheets) fusión de intereses *f*

poor *adj* (person, demand) pobre; (quality) malo; (servicio) deficiente; **a ~ return on one's investment** un bajo rendimiento de su inversión

POP *abbr* (►**point of presence**) (on Internet) punto de presencia *m*

pop-down menu *n* menú descendente *m*

popular *adj* (price, press, capitalism) popular; (opinion) general; **by ~ demand** *o* **request** a petición del público

popularity *n* popularidad *f*; ~ **rating** *n* índice de popularidad *m*

population *n* población *f*; ~ **census** *n* censo *m* demográfico *or* de población; ~ **count** *n* recuento de población *m*; ~ **density** *n* densidad de población *f*; ~ **explosion** *n* explosión demográfica *f*; ~ **statistics** *n pl* estadística demográfica *f*

populist¹ *adj* populista

populist² *n* populista *mf*

pop-up *n* (jarg) *folleto que cobra relieve al abrirlo*; ~ **menu** *n* menú emergente *m*

pork *n* AmE (infrml) favores políticos *m pl*; ~ **barrel** *n* AmE (infrml) legislación con fines electorales *f*; ~ **chop** *n* AmE (infrml) enchufismo sindical *m*

port¹ *n* (for shipping) puerto *m*; (Comp) puerta *f*

port² *vt* (Comp) transferir

portability *n* (Comp) transportabilidad *f*

portable *adj* (hardware) portátil; (software) transferible; ~ **computer** *n* computadora *f* AmL *or* ordenador *m* Esp portátil, laptop *m*; ~ **document format** *n* formato PDF *m*, formato de documento transferible *m*;

~ **video player** *n* proyector *m* de video AmL *or* vídeo Esp portátil

portal *n* portal *m*

portfolio *n* (Fin) cartera (de valores) *f*; (Pol) cartera *f*; (case) portafolio(s) *m*, cartera *f*; (samples of work) carpeta de trabajos *f*; ~ **dividend** *n* dividendo de cartera de valores *m*; ~ **income** *n* ingresos en cartera *m pl*; ~ **insurance** *n* seguro de cartera *m*; ~ **investment** *n* inversión de cartera *f*; ~ **management** *n* administración *f or* gerencia *f or* gestión *f* de carteras; ~ **manager** *n* gestor(a) de la cartera de valores *m,f*; ~ **selection** *n* selección de cartera *f*; ~ **split** *n* división de cartera de valores *f*; ~ **switching** *n* intercambio de cartera *m*; ~ **theory** *n* teoría de la cartera de valores *f*; ~ **transfer** *n* cesión de cartera *f*

porting *n* (of software) transferencia *f*

portion *n* (of dividend, amount) parte *f*

portrait¹ *adj* en formato vertical

portrait² *n* (format) formato vertical *m*

POS *abbr* (►**point of sale**) punto de venta *m*; ~ **advertising** *n* publicidad en los puntos de venta *f*; ~ **terminal** *n* terminal PV *m* (terminal en punto de venta)

pose *vt* (threat) representar; (problem, question) plantear

position¹ *n* (location) posición *f*; (circumstances) situación *f*; (job) empleo *m*, puesto *m*; (stance, point of view) postura *f*, posición *f*; ~ **closed** BrE ventanilla cerrada; **be in a/no ~ to do sth** estar/no estar en condiciones de hacer algo; **be in an awkward ~** estar en una situación delicada; **take a ~** (Stock) tomar posición; ~ **account** *n* cuenta de posición *f*; ~ **of authority** *n* posición de autoridad *f*; ~ **paper** *n* (Pol) documento de situación *f*; ~ **trader** *n* operador(a) de posición *m,f*; ~ **trading** *n* negociación de posiciones *f*

position² *vt* posicionar

positional *adj* posicional

positioning *n* posición *f*, posicionamiento *m*; ~ **theory** *n* (S&M) teoría posicional *f*

positive *adj* (attitude, response) positivo; (criticism) constructivo; (proof) definitivo; (decisive) catergórico; (sure) seguro; **be ~ about sth/that...** estar seguro de algo/de que...; ~ **cash-flow** *n* cash-flow positivo *m*, flujo de caja positivo *m*; ~ **confirmation** *n* (in auditing) confirmación positiva *f*; ~ **discrimination** *n* discriminación positiva *f*; ~ **feedback** *n* reacción positiva *f*; ~ **gearing** *n* BrE, ~ **leverage** *n* apalancamiento positivo *m*; ~**-sum game** *n* juego de suma positiva *m*

possession *n* (ownership) posesión *f*; (object owned) bien *m*; **gain ~ of sth** conseguir la posesión de algo; **be in ~ of sth** estar en ⋯⟶

posesión de algo; **take ~ of sth** tomar
posesión de algo

possibility *n* posibilidad *f*

possible *adj* posible; **as soon as ~** lo
antes posible

post¹ *n* (postal system, letters) BrE (*cf* ▸**mail**
AmE) correo *m*; (e-mail) correo electrónico *m*,
e-mail *m*; (job) puesto *m*; (important position)
cargo *m*; **by ~** BrE (*cf* ▸**by mail** AmE) por
correo; **it's in the ~** BrE (*cf* ▸**it's in the
mail** AmE) ya ha sido enviado *or* está en
camino; **put sth in the ~** BrE (*cf* ▸**put sth
in the mail** AmE) echar algo al correo *or* al
buzón; **take up a ~** (important position) tomar
posesión de *or* asumir un cargo; **take up
one's ~** (job) entrar en funciones; **through
the ~** BrE (*cf* ▸**through the mail** AmE) por
correo

post² *vt* (letter, parcel) BrE (*cf* ▸**mail** AmE)
enviar por correo; (employee) destinar,
mandar; (meeting) anunciar; (list, notice) poner,
fijar; (sales, receipts) anotar; (in newsgroup)
anunciar, poner una nota de; **~ an entry**
anotar (una entrada), apuntar; **keep sb ~ed
(about sth)** tener *or* mantener a alguien al
corriente (de algo); **the company ~ed
losses of two million dollars** la compañía
registró pérdidas de dos millones de dólares;
~ margin (open position by selling option)
contabilizar el margen; **~ no bills** prohibido
fijar carteles; **~ sth to sb** BrE (*cf* ▸**mail sth
to sb** AmE) enviar algo por correo a alguien;
post up *vt* (list, notice) poner, fijar; (account)
poner al día

post- *pref* post-, pos-; **~audit** *n*
intervención a posteriori *f*; **~balance-
sheet event** *n* acontecimiento *m or* hecho
m posterior al balance general;
~bankruptcy *adj* posterior a la quiebra;
~closing trial balance *n* balance de
situación *m*; **~Communist** *adj*
poscomunista; **~election** *adj* posterior a la
elección; **~industrial society** *n* sociedad
posindustrial *f*; **~peak** *adj* después del
punto máximo; **~purchase** *adj* poscompra;
~sales service *n* servicio de posventa *m*;
~war *adj* (period) de posguerra; **~war
boom** *n* auge de posguerra *m*

postage *n* franqueo *m*; **~ due** portes
debidos; **~ paid** con franqueo pagado; **~
certificate** *n* certificado de franqueo *m*;
~-due stamp *n* franqueo en destino *m*; **~
meter** *n* AmE, (*cf* ▸**franking machine** BrE)
franqueadora *f*; **~ and packing** *n pl* gastos
de franqueo y empaquetado *m pl*; **~ rate** *n*
tarifa postal *f*; **~ stamp** *n* sello (de correos) *m*

postal *adj* postal; **~ address** *n* dirección
postal *f*; **~ ballot** *n* BrE (election) votación
por correo *f*; (form) voto por correo *m*; **~
clerk** *n* BrE (*cf* ▸**mail clerk** AmE)
empleado(-a) postal *m,f*; **~ code** *n* BrE (*cf*

▸**zip code** AmE) código postal *m*; **~ money
order** AmE, **~ order** BrE *n* giro postal *m*; **~
service** *n* servicio de correos *m*; **~ vote** *n*
(election) votación por correo *f*; (form) voto por
correo *m*; **~ worker** *n* empleado(-a) de
correos *m,f*

postbox *n* BrE (*cf* ▸**mailbox** AmE) buzón *m*

postcode *n* BrE (*cf* ▸**zip code** AmE) código
postal *m*

postdate *vt* posfechar

postdated *adj* (cheque) posfechado

posted price *n* precio de cotización *m*

poster *n* cartel *m*; **~ advertising** *n*
pancartas publicitarias *f pl*; **~ campaign** *n*
campaña de pancartas publicitarias *f*

postgraduate *n* posgraduado(-a) *m,f*

posting *n* (of entries) pase de asientos *m*;
(appointment) destino *m*; (civil procedure) aviso
público *m*; (commercial procedure) inscripción *f*;
~ error *n* error *m* de pase *or* de
transcripción

Post-it® *n* etiqueta de quita y pon *f*

postman *n* BrE (*cf* ▸**mailman** AmE) cartero
m

postmark¹ *n* matasellos *m*; **date as ~**
según fecha del matasellos

postmark² *vt* (letter, parcel) matasellar; **it's
~ed Tokyo** lleva matasellos de Tokyo

postmaster *n* (person) administrador de
correos *m*; (for e-mail) jefe de correos *m*

post meridiem *adv* de la tarde

Post Office *n* (service) *servicio nacional de
correo británico*, ≈ Correos *m*, ≈ Dirección
General de Correos y Telégrafos *f*; (place)
oficina de correos *f*; **~ Office Box** *n* BrE
apartado *m* postal *or* de correos; **~ Office
Giro** *n* BrE giro postal *m*

postpaid *adj* de franqueo pagado

postpone *vt* aplazar, posponer, postergar
AmL; **~ tax payment** aplazar el pago de
impuestos

postscript *n* posdata *f*

potential¹ *adj* (danger, improvement, failure)
potencial, posible; (income, demand, user)
potencial; (buyer, profit) posible

potential² *n* potencial *m*; **she never
achieved her full ~** no llegó a desarrollar
plenamente su potencial; **have ~** tener
potencial; **have the ~ to do sth** tener (el)
potencial para hacer algo

potentially *adv* potencialmente

pound *n* (currency) libra (esterlina) *f*; (weight)
libra *f*; **~ sterling** *n* BrE libra esterlina

poverty *n* pobreza *f*; **~ line** *n* umbral de
pobreza *m*; **~ trap** *n* trampa de la pobreza *f*

power¹ *n* (control, influence, authority) poder *m*;
(political) poderío *m*, poder *m*; (nation, of
machine) potencia *f*; (physical strength, force)

fuerza *f*; (of wind, sun) potencia *f*, fuerza *f*; (source of energy) energía *f*; (electricity) electricidad *f*; **come to** ~ llegar al poder; **do everything in one's** ~ **to do sth** hacer todo en su poder para hacer algo; **have the** ~ **to do sth** tener autoridad para hacer algo; **in** ~ (government) en el poder; ~ **on** con tensión eléctrica; **the** ~**s that be** los que mandan; ~ **of appointment** *n* facultad para efectuar nombramientos *f*; ~ **of attorney** *n* poder notarial *m*; ~ **failure** *n* corte de corriente *m*, caída de tensión *f*; ~ **generation** *n* AmE (*cf* ▸**electricity generation** BrE) generación de electricidad *f*; ~ **industries** *n pl* industrias energéticas *f pl*; ~ **politics** *n* política de fuerza *f*; ~ **of recourse** *n* poder para pleitos *m*; ~ **of sale** *n* facultad de vender *f*, poder de venta *m*; ~ **struggle** *n* lucha por el poder *f*; ~ **surge** *n* subida de tensión *f*

power² *vt* (Comp) encender; (Ind) impulsar

powerful *adj* poderoso

powers *n pl* (Law) competencias *f pl*

pp *abbr* (▸**per pro, per procurationem**,) p.p. (por poder), p.a. (por autorización), p.o. (por orden); (▸**postpaid**) de franqueo pagado

pp. *abbr* (**pages**) págs. (páginas)

p.p. *abbr*, **Ppd** *abbr* (▸**prepaid**) pagado por adelantado

PPF *abbr*(▸**project preparation facility**) SPP (servicio de preparación de proyectos)

PPI *abbr* (▸**producer price index**) índice de precios a la producción *m*

PPP *abbr* (▸**private patients plan**) plan de pacientes privados *m*; (▸**profit and performance planning**) planificación de beneficios y rendimientos *f*; (▸**public-private partnership**) sociedad entre el sector público y el privado *f*

PPV *abbr* (▸**pay-per-view**) televisión a la carta *f*, pago por visión *m*

pr. *abbr* (▸**price**) precio *m*

PR *abbr* (▸**public relations**) relaciones públicas *f pl*

PRA *abbr* (▸**purchase and resale agreement**) compromiso de compra y reventa *m*

practical *adj* (use, politics) práctico

practice¹ *n* (repetition, implementation) práctica *f*; (custom, procedure) costumbre *f*; (of profession) ejercicio *m*; (of doctor) consultorio *m*, consulta *f*; (of lawyer) bufete *m*; (of accountant) estudio contable *m*; **it is common** ~ es práctica habitual; **in** ~ en la práctica; **be in** ~ (as doctor) ejercer de médico; (as lawyer) ejercer de abogado; (in use) practicarse; **put sth into** ~ poner algo en práctica; **set up in** ~ **(as a doctor/lawyer)** empezar a ejercer (de médico/abogado)

practice² *vt* AmE ▸**practise** BrE

practise BrE, **practice** AmE **1** *vt* (skill) practicar; (medicine) ejercer; ~ **law** ejercer de *or* como abogado, ejercer la abogacía **2** *vi* (professionally) ejercer; ~ **as a doctor/ lawyer** ejercer de médico/abogado

pragmatic *adj* pragmático

pragmatically *adv* pragmáticamente

preacquisition profits *n pl* beneficios de preadquisición *m pl*

preamble *n* (to agreement, contract) preámbulo *m*

pre-approach *n* enfoque previo *m*

pre-arranged *adj* preestablecido

pre-assessing *n* (Tax) pretributación *f*

pre-audit *n* intervención a priori *f*

pre-authorized *adj* (cheque, payment) preautorizado

pre-bankruptcy *n* prequiebra *f*

pre-bill *n* factura proforma *f*

precarious *adj* precario

precaution *n* precaución *f*; **as a** ~ por *or* como precaución; **take** ~**s (against sth)** tomar precauciones (contra algo)

precautionary *adj* (measure) preventivo, de precaución; (saving) preventivo

precede *vt* preceder

precedence *n n* precedencia *f*; **give sth/ sb** ~ **(over sth/sb)** darle precedencia a algo/alguien (sobre algo/alguien); **take** ~ **(over sth/sb)** tener precedencia (sobre algo/ alguien)

precedent *n* precedente *m*; **break with** ~ romper con la costumbre; **create** *o* **set a** ~ **(for sth)** sentar precedente (para algo)

preceding *adj* (day, year) anterior; (page, paragraph, chapter) anterior, precedente

precious *adj* (object) precioso, valiosísimo

precision engineering *n* ingeniería de precisión *f*

preclosing *n* cierre anticipado *m*

preclude *vt* (possibility) excluir; ~ **sb from doing sth** impedirle a alguien hacer algo

precoded *adj* precodificado

precompute *vt* (interest in instalment loans) precalcular

preconception *n* prejuicio *m*

precondition *n* condición previa *f*

predate *vt* (precede) ser anterior a; (document, letter) antedatar, poner una fecha anterior en

predator *n* depredador(a) *m,f*, predador(a) *m,f*

predatory *adj* (company) buitre; (competition) desleal; ~ **pricing** *n* fijación de precios depredadores *f*

p

predecessor n (person) predecesor(a) m,f; (company) compañía predecesora f

predetermine vt predeterminar

predetermined adj (price) predeterminado

predict vt predecir

predictable adj (result, outcome) previsible; ∼ **life** n (of business asset) vida f estimable or previsible

pre-eminent adj preeminente

pre-emption n derecho m preferente or de prioridad; ∼ **right** n derecho de prioridad m

pre-emptive adj (right, bid) preferente

pre-emptor n AmE comprador(a) por derecho de prioridad m,f

pre-empt spot n anuncio reservado de antemano a tarifa reducida m

pre-entry n registro previo m

pre-existing adj (use) preexistente

pref. abbr (▸preference) preferencia f

prefabricated adj (house) prefabricado

prefer vt preferir; ∼ **charges (against sb)** presentar cargos (contra alguien); ∼ **sth to sth** preferir algo a algo; ∼ **to do sth** preferir hacer algo

preference n preferencia f; in ∼ to sth/sb en lugar de algo/alguien; give ∼ to sth/sb dar preferencia a algo/alguien; ∼ **dividend** n BrE (cf ▸preferred dividend AmE) dividendo m preferente or privilegiado; ∼ **settings** n pl (Comp) calibraciones personales f pl; ∼ **shares** n pl BrE (cf ▸preferred stock AmE) acciones f pl preferentes or privilegiadas

preferential adj (tariff, trade, terms, rate) preferencial, preferente; (creditor, debt) privilegiado; give ∼ **treatment to sth/sb** dar trato preferencial a algo/alguien

preferred adj (creditor, debt) privilegiado; (beneficiary, risk) preferente; (rate) preferencial; (position) preferido; ∼ **dividend** n AmE (cf ▸preference dividend BrE) dividendo m preferente or privilegiado; ∼ **stock** n AmE (cf ▸preference shares BrE) acciones f pl preferentes or privilegiadas

prefinancing credit n crédito de prefinanciación m

prejudice n (bias) prejuicio m; (damage) perjuicio m; have a ∼ against/in favour BrE o favor AmE of sth/sb estar predispuesto contra/a favor de algo/alguien; without ∼ sin perjuicio de los derechos de los firmantes

prejudicial adj perjudicial

prelease vt prearrendar

preliminary adj (examination, remarks, measures, expenses) preliminar; ∼ **day** n (Stock) día previo m; ∼ **estimate** n cálculo anticipado m; ∼ **investigation** n (Law) instrucción f; ∼ **project** n anteproyecto m; ∼ **prospectus** n prospecto de emisión preliminar m

premature adj prematuro

premier borrower n BrE prestatario(-a) de primera clase m,f

premise n premisa f; on the ∼ that... sobre la base de que...

premises n pl local m; they were escorted off the ∼ se les hizo salir del local

premium[1] n (bonus, insurance premium) prima f; (surcharge) recargo m; be at a ∼ (Stock) estar sobre la par; (be scarce) escasear; the shares are at a 20% ∼ las acciones están a un 20% sobre la par; when time is at a ∼ cuando el tiempo apremia; put a ∼ on sth/sb concederle mucha importancia a algo/alguien; ∼ **bond** n bono de prima m; ∼ **loan** n préstamo con primas m; ∼ **price** n precio de incentivo m; ∼ **payment** n pago de prima m; ∼ **pricing** n fijación de precios de incentivo f; ∼ **quotations** n pl cotizaciones con prima f pl; ∼ **reserve** n reserva de primas f

premium[2] adj (product) de calidad superior; ∼ **offer** n super oferta f

Premium Bond BrE n bono del Estado que permite ganar dinero participando en sorteos mensuales

prenuptial adj (contract, agreement) prematrimonial

pre-owned adj AmE (vehicle) seminuevo

prepackaged adj, **prepacked** adj (goods) (pre)empaquetado

prepaid adj (advertisement, insertion, letter of credit) pagado por adelantado; (interest) cobrado por adelantado; (envelope) con franqueo pagado; (postage, charges) pagado; (expenses) anticipado, pagado por anticipado

preparation n preparación f; be in ∼ estar en preparación; in ∼ for sth como preparación para algo; make ∼s for sth hacer preparativos para algo

prepare [1] vt (make ready) preparar; (report) redactar; ∼ **the ground** o **way (for sth)** preparar el terreno (para algo); ∼ **a return** (Tax) preparar una declaración
[2] vi prepararse; ∼ **for sth** prepararse para algo; ∼ **to do sth** prepararse para hacer algo

prepared adj (ready) listo; (speech, statement) preparado; be ∼ **to do sth** (willing) estar dispuesto a hacer algo

prepayment n pago m anticipado or por adelantado m; ∼ **clause** n cláusula de pago anticipado f; ∼ **penalty** n penalización por pago anticipado f; ∼ **privilege** n privilegio de pago anticipado m

pre-production *adj* (expenditure) previo a la producción

prerecorded *adj* grabado (de antemano); ～ **broadcast** *n* transmisión en diferido *f*

prerequisite *n* requisito esencial *m*

preretiree *n* prejubilado(-a) *m,f*

preretirement pension *n* pensión de prejubilación *f*

prerogative *n* prerrogativa *f*

pres. *abbr* (▸**president**) presidente *m,f*

presale *n* preventa *f*; ～ **order** *n* orden de venta anticipada *f*; ～**s service** *n* servicio de preventa *m*

prescribe *vt* (order, require) prescribir; (recommend) recomendar

prescribed *adj* (contract, price, share) prescrito; (form, information) reglamentario; (rate) preestablecido; (time) previsto

prescription *n* (ordering) prescripción *f*

prescriptive right *n* derecho legal por prescripción *m*

preselect *vt* (S&M) preseleccionar

presence *n* presencia *f*

present[1] *adj* (at scene) presente; (situation, salary, address) actual; **among those** ～ entre los presentes; **at the** ～ **time** *o* **moment** en este momento; **in the** ～ **state of affairs** en la situación actual; ～ **value** *n* valor *m* descontado *or* presente; ～ **value method** *n* método *m* del valor descontado *or* presente

present[2] *n* (current time) presente *m*; (gift) regalo *m*; **at** ～ en este momento, actualmente; **for the** ～ por ahora, por el momento

present[3] *vt* (report, proposal) presentar; (argument) exponer; (threat) constituir; ～ **a check** AmE *o* **cheque** BrE **for payment** presentar un cheque al cobro; ～ **a draft for acceptance** presentar una letra para su aceptación; ～ **sth fairly** (in auditing) presentar algo razonablemente

presentation *n* (of document, bill, proposal) presentación *f*; (display) presentación *f*, demostración *f*; **have good** ～ **skills** tener un don para presentaciones; **on** ～ **of this voucher** presentando *or* al presentar este vale; ～ **copy** *n* ejemplar gratuito *m*; ～ **pack** *n* paquete de presentación *m*; ～ **software** *n* software de presentación *m*

presenter *n* BrE (Media) presentador(a) *m,f*

preservation *n* (of habitat) conservación *f*; ～ **order** *n* orden de preservación *f*

preservative *n* conservante *m*; **no** ～**s** sin conservantes; **no** ～**s or additives** sin conservantes ni aditivos

preserve *vt* conservar

preserved foods *n pl* alimentos en conserva *m pl*

preset *adj* predefinido

presettlement *n* preacuerdo *m*

president *n* (of state, society) presidente(-a) *m,f*; AmE (of bank, corporation) director(a) *m,f*, presidente(-a) *m,f*

presidential *adj* presidencial

preside over *vt* (meeting) presidir

presiding judge *n* juez(a) de turno *m,f*

presidium *n* (HRM) junta permanente *f*; (Pol) presidio *m*

press[1] *n* (Media) prensa *f*; **get a good/bad** ～ tener buena/mala prensa; **go to** ～ ir a imprenta; ～ **advertisement** *n* anuncio en prensa *m*; ～ **advertising** *n* publicidad en la prensa *f*; ～ **agency** *n* agencia de prensa *f*; **P**～ **Association** *n* BrE *asociación británica de prensa*; ～ **briefing** *n* informe de prensa *m*; ～ **campaign** *n* campaña de prensa *f*; ～ **clipping** *n* AmE (*cf* ▸**press cutting** BrE) recorte de prensa *m*; ～ **conference** *n* rueda de prensa *f*; ～ **copy** *n* ejemplar para reseña publicitaria *m*; ～ **coverage** *n* cobertura periodística *f*; ～ **cutting** *n* BrE (*cf* ▸**press clipping** AmE) recorte de prensa *m*; ～ **date** *n* fecha de publicación *f*; ～ **edition** *n* edición de prensa *f*; ～ **kit** *n* información para la prensa *f*; ～ **officer** *n* agregado(-a) *m,f or* oficial(a) *m,f* de prensa; ～ **pack** *n* paquete informativo *m*; ～ **pass** *n* acreditación de prensa *f*; ～ **photographer** *n* fotógrafo(-a) de prensa *m,f*; ～ **relations** *n pl* relaciones con la prensa *f pl*; ～ **release** *n* boletín *m or* comunicado *m* de prensa; ～ **statement** *n* declaración a la prensa *f*

press[2] [1] *vt* (button, key) pulsar; ～ **charges (against sb)** presentar cargos (contra alguien); **I** ～**ed him for an answer** insistí en que me diera una respuesta; ～ **any key** pulsar cualquier tecla; ～ **the point** insistir en el tema; **they** ～**ed him to change his policy** ejercieron presión sobre él para que cambiara de política

[2] *vi* (urge, pressurize) presionar; ～ **for changes** presionar para que haya cambios; **press ahead, press on** *vi* seguir adelante; ～ **ahead** *o* **on with sth** seguir adelante con algo

pressure[1] *n* presión *f*; **bring** ～ **to bear on sb (to do sth)** ejercer presión sobre alguien (para que haga algo); **put** ～ **on sb (to do sth)** presionar a alguien (para que haga algo); **take the** ～ **off** aliviar la presión; **be under a lot of** ～ **at work** tener muchas presiones en el trabajo; **the** ～ **of work** la presión del trabajo; **work under** ～ trabajar bajo presión; ～ **group** *n* grupo de presión *m*; ～ **selling** *n* venta bajo presión *f*

pressure[2] *vt*, **pressurize** *vt* BrE presionar; **feel** ～**d** sentirse presionado; ⋯⋗

~ **sb into doing sth** o **to do sth** presionar a alguien para que haga algo

prestige n prestigio m; ~ **advertising** n publicidad de prestigio f; ~ **goods** n pl artículos suntuarios m pl; ~ **pricing** n fijación de precios de prestigio f

prestigious adj prestigioso

presumption n presunción f

presumptive tax n impuesto en régimen de evaluación global

pretax adj (profit, income) bruto, antes de impuestos; (earnings, yield) antes de impuestos

pretest n preencuesta f

pretesting n prueba preliminar f; ~ **copy** n mensaje publicitario de preencuesta m

pretreatment n (of waste) tratamiento preliminar m

prevail vi (common sense, justice) prevalecer, imponerse; (attitude) preponderar, predominar, reinar; (situation) reinar, imperar

prevailing adj (trend, view) imperante, preponderante; (uncertainty) reinante; **in the ~ economic climate** en el actual clima económico; ~ **market price** n precio en vigor en el mercado m; ~ **party** n (Law) parte predominante f

prevent vt (hinder) impedir; (forestall) prevenir; ~ **sb from doing sth** impedir que alguien haga algo, impedirle a alguien hacer algo

prevention n prevención f

preventive adj (maintenance) preventivo; (detention) preventivo, provisional

preview vt (document) previsualizar

previous adj (year, occasion, attempt, page) anterior; (experience, knowledge) previo; ~ **to sth** anterior a algo; ~ **engagement** n compromiso previo m; ~ **history** n historial previo m

previously adv antes; ~**-mentioned** adj antes citado

price[1] n precio m; (of shares) cotización f, precio m; **at a ~ of** a un precio de; **go up/ down in** ~ subir/bajar de precio; ~**s can go down as well as up** los precios pueden tanto bajar como subir; ~**s have been marked down** los precios han sido ajustados a la baja; ~ **on application** precio en aplicación; **put a ~ on sth** poner precio a algo; ~**/sale for the account** precio/venta para la cuenta; **the** ~ **has weakened further** el precio se ha debilitado más; ~ **bracket** n categoría de precio f; ~ **ceiling** n precio límite m; ~ **change** n cambio de precios m; P~ **Commission** n BrE comisión de política de precios; ~ **competitiveness** n competitividad de los precios f; ~ **control** n

control de precios m; ~ **cut** n, ~ **cutting** n recorte de precios m; ~ **deregulation** n desregulación de precios f; ~ **determination** n determinación de precios f; ~ **differential** n margen entre los precios m; ~**-earnings ratio** n ratio precio-beneficio m; ~ **ex-works** n precio en fábrica m; ~ **fixing** n fijación de precios f; (illegal) manipulación de precios f; ~ **floor** n precio mínimo m; ~ **freeze** n congelación de precios f, ~ **gap** n desajuste de precios m; ~**s and incomes policy** n política de ingresos y precios f; ~ **increase** n subida de precios f; ~ **index** n índice de precios m; ~ **inflation** n inflación de precios f; ~ **level** n nivel de precios m; ~ **limit** n límite de precio m; ~ **list** n lista de precios f; ~ **maintenance** n mantenimiento de los precios m; ~ **mechanism** n mecanismo de precios m; ~ **offered** n precio ofrecido m; ~**-performance ratio** n razón de comportamiento de los precios m; ~**s policy** n política de precios f; ~ **pressure** n presión de los precios f; ~ **protection** n (Stock) protección del precio f; ~ **quotation list** n lista de precios efectivos f; ~ **range** n escala de precios f; **it's out of my ~ range** cuesta más de lo que puedo pagar; ~ **reduction** n rebaja (de precios) f; ~ **regulation** n control de precios m; ~ **rigging** n chanchullo m; ~ **scanner** n lector óptico de precios m; ~**-sensitive** adj sensible al precio; ~ **setting** n fijación de precios f; ~ **spread** n dispersión de precios f, ~ **stability** n estabilidad de precios f; ~ **sticker** n etiqueta de precio f; ~ **structure** n estructura de precios f; ~ **support** n mantenimiento de precios m; ~ **tag** n (label) etiqueta del precio f; (figuratively) precio m; ~ **trend** n tendencia del precio f; ~ **undercutting** n venta a un precio más barato f; ~ **variance** n variación del precio f; ~ **war** n guerra de precios f

price[2] vt (fix price of) fijar el precio de; (mark price on) ponerle el precio a; **all items must be clearly ~d** todos los artículos deben llevar el precio claramente indicado; **competitively/reasonably ~d** con un precio razonable; **they have ~d themselves out of the market** han subido tanto los precios que se han quedado sin compradores

pricey adj (infrml) caro

pricing n (calculation) cálculo de precios m; (fixing) fijación de precios f; ~ **arrangement** n acuerdo sobre fijación de precios m; ~ **model** n modelo de valoración m; ~ **policy** n política de precios f; ~ **review** n revisión de precios f; ~ **strategy** n estrategia de precios f; ~ **tactic** n táctica de fijación de precios f

pricing-down n rebaja de precios f

pricing-up n fijación de precios más altos f
prima facie evidence n prueba
presunta f
primarily adv primeramente
primary adj (resource, industry, sector)
primario; (offering) primario, de emisión;
(activities) primario, principal; (capital, deficit)
principal; **be of ∼ importance** ser de una
importancia primordial; **∼ commodity** n
bien de primera necesidad m, mercancía
básica f; **∼ dealer** n corredor(a) de
mercado primario m,f; **∼ distribution** n
(Stock) primera emisión f; **∼ issue** n
(Stock) emisión primaria f; **∼ reserve** n
reserva primaria f
prime¹ adj (cause, factor) principal; (example,
opportunity) excelente; (costs) básico; (location,
site) de primer orden; (property) de primera;
∼ borrower n AmE prestatario(-a) de
primera clase m,f; **∼ entry** n (Acc) entrada
principal f; **∼ lending rate** n AmE tasa de
préstamo preferencial f; **∼ paper** n papel
de primera línea m; **∼ position** n (in the
market) posición de primera línea f; **∼ rate
(of interest)** n BrE (cf ▸prime AmE) tasa de
interés preferencial f; **∼-rate loan** n
préstamo a interés preferencial m; **∼ time**
n (in broadcasting) hora de máxima audiencia f
prime² n AmE (cf ▸prime rate BrE) tasa de
interés preferencial f
prime³ vt (brief) preparar
Prime Minister n BrE primer(a)
ministro(-a) m,f, ≈ Presidente(-a) del
Gobierno m,f
principal¹ adj (asset, customer, residence)
principal; **∼ accounting system** n
sistema de contabilidad principal m; **∼
business** n negocio principal m; **∼
business address** n domicilio social m; **∼
place of business** n domicilio social m; **∼
shareholder** n, **∼ stockholder** n
accionista principal mf; **∼ sum** n principal
m
principal² n principal m, capital m
principally adv fundamentalmente
principle n principio m; **on ∼** de
principio; **∼ of accrual** n principio de
acumulación m
print¹ vt imprimir; (publish) publicar, editar;
print out vt imprimir
print² n (lettering) letra f; **in ∼** (published)
publicado; (available) a la venta; **out of ∼**
agotado; **∼ bar** n línea de linotipia f; **∼
driver** n unidad de impresión f; **∼ line** n
línea de impresión f; **∼ media** n material
impreso m; **∼ preview** n borrador de
impresión m; **∼ run** n tirada f
printed adj impreso; **∼ in bold type**
impreso en negrita; **∼ form** n impreso m;
∼ matter n impresos m pl

printer n (device) impresora f; (person)
impresor(a) m,f; (company) imprenta f; **∼
port** n puerta de impresora f
printing n (amount printed) tirada f; (process)
impresión f; **∼ press** n prensa de imprimir
f; **∼ speed** n velocidad de impresión f; **∼
unit** n unidad de impresión f; **∼ works** n
imprenta f
printout n impresión f
prior adj (knowledge, engagement) previo;
(period) anterior; **∼ to sth** previo a algo;
without ∼ notice sin previo aviso; **∼
charge** n cargo previo m; **∼-preferred
stock** n acciones preferidas a otras de igual
clase f pl
prioritize vt (task) dar prioridad a,
priorizar
priority n prioridad f; **get one's priorities
right** saber cuáles son sus prioridades; **give
∼ to sth** dar prioridad a algo; **have o take
∼ (over sth)** tener prioridad (sobre algo); **∼
allocation** n (of shares) adjudicación
prioritaria f; **∼ date** n fecha f prioritaria
or de prioridad; **∼ mail** n AmE (cf ▸priority
post BrE) correo de pronta expedición m; **∼-
payment instrument** n instrumento de
pago prioritario m; **∼ post** n BrE (cf
▸priority mail AmE) correo de pronta
expedición m; **∼ right** n derecho de
prioridad m; **∼ share** n acción de
preferencia f
privacy n intimidad f; **∼ law** n ley de
protección de la intimidad f; **∼ policy** n
política de protección de los datos
personales f; **∼ statement** n declaración de
la confidencialidad f
private adj (matter) privado, confidencial;
(conversation, institution, capital) privado; (letter,
income) personal; **sell sth by ∼ agreement**
vender algo mediante acuerdo privado; **in ∼**
en privado; **be in ∼ practice** (doctor) ejercer
la medicina privada; AmE (lawyer) ocuparse
de asuntos civiles; **∼ account** n cuenta
particular f; **∼ arrangement** n acuerdo
privado m; (Law) contrato privado m; **∼
automatic branch exchange** n BrE
centralita automática privada unida a la red
pública f; **∼ bank** n banco privado m; **∼
banking** n banca privada f; **∼ brand** n
marca privada f; **∼ company** n compañía
privada f; **∼ enterprise** n empresa privada
f; **∼ finance initiative** n proyecto dónde el
sector privado se encarga de la construcción y
la financiación de algo y luego el gobierno
paga por el servicio, así evitando los costes de
primer establecimiento; **∼ good** n bien
privado m; **∼ health scheme** n BrE plan
privado de seguro médico m; **∼ hearing** n
(Law) vista a puerta cerrada f; **∼ hospital**
n hospital privado m; **∼ household**
n hogar privado m, vivienda privada f;

⸱⸱⸱⸴

p

~ individual n persona privada f; **~
investment** n inversión privada f; **~
investor** n (Stock) inversor(a) privado(-a) m,f; **~
issue** n (Stock) emisión privada f; **~
ledger** n libro mayor privado m; **~ lender**
n prestamista privado(-a) m,f; **~ limited
company** n ≈ sociedad limitada f; **~
limited partnership** n sociedad limitada
sin cotización en bolsa f; **~ means** n pl
fortuna personal f, rentas f pl; **~ office** n
despacho privado m, oficina privada f; **~
patient** n paciente privado(-a) m,f; **~
patients plan** n plan de pacientes privados
m; **~ property** n propiedad privada f; **~
prosecution** n querella f; **~ school** n
colegio privado m, escuela privada f; **~
secretary** n secretario(-a) m,f particular or
personal; **~ sector** n sector privado m

privatization n privatización f; **~
program** AmE, **~ programme** BrE n
programa de privatización m

privatize vt privatizar

privatized adj (company) privatizado

privilege n (special right) privilegio m;
(honour) privilegio m, honor m; AmE (Stock)
contrato de opción m; **~ leave** n permiso
privilegiado m

privileged adj (position) privilegiado;
(information, document) confidencial

Privy Council n BrE Consejo de la Corona
m

prize n premio m; **~ bond** n bono m de
premio

pro- pref pro(-); **he's very ~European** es
muy pro-Europa

PRO abbr (▸public relations officer)
encargado(-a) de relaciones públicas m,f

proactive adj (strategy) proactivo

probability n probabilidad f; **in all ~** con
toda probabilidad; **~ theory** n teoría de la
probabilidad f

probable adj probable

probate¹ n (process) legalización f; (will)
testamento legalizado m; **grant sb ~**
declarar a alguien legítimo albacea; **~
court** n tribunal de sucesiones m; **~ price**
n (Stock) precio de homologación m

probate² vt (will) autenticar, legalizar

probation n (for employee) prueba f, periodo
de prueba m; (for criminal) libertad condicional
f; **on ~** (employee) en prueba; (criminal) en
libertad condicional; **~ period** n (for
employee) periodo de prueba m; (for criminal)
periodo de libertad condicional f

probationary adj de prueba; **~
employee** n empleado(-a) a prueba m,f; **~
period** n (for employee) periodo de prueba m;
(for criminal) periodo de libertad condicional f

probationer n (employee) empleado(-a) a
prueba m,f, (criminal) persona en libertad
condicional f

probe¹ ⟦1⟧ vt (finances) investigar; (public
opinion) sondear
⟦2⟧ vi investigar; **~ into sb's business
affairs** investigar las actividades financieras
de alguien

probe² n investigación f

problem n problema m; **cause sb ~s**
causarle or ocasionarle problemas a
alguien; **~ analysis** n análisis del
problema m; **~ assessment** n evaluación
del problema f; **~ customer** n cliente
problema mf; **~ determination** n (Comp)
determinación del problema f; **~ solving** n
resolución de problemas f

procedural adj (agreement, issue) de
procedimiento

procedure n procedimiento m; **a ~ for
the avoidance of disputes** un
procedimiento para evitar disputas; **the ~
to be followed in such cases** el
procedimiento a seguir en tales casos

proceed vi (work) avanzar; **~ against sb**
(Law) demandar a alguien; **everything is
~ing according to plan** todo marcha
conforme al plan; **~ to do sth** pasar a hacer
algo; **let us ~ to the next item on the
agenda** pasemos al siguiente punto del
orden del día; **~ with sth** seguir adelante
con algo

proceedings n pl (Law) proceso m;
(events) acto m; (measures) medidas f pl;
(minutes) actas f pl

proceeds n pl ganancias f pl; (of sales)
producto m

process¹ n (series of actions, lawsuit) proceso
m; (method) proceso m procedimiento m; **be
in ~** estar en proceso; **in the ~** al hacerlo;
be in the ~ of doing sth estar haciendo
algo; **~ analysis** n análisis de procesos m;
~ chart n diagrama de procedimientos m;
~ control n control de procesos m; **~
costing** n cálculo m de costes Esp or costos
AmL de proceso; **~ engineering** n técnica
de fabricación f; **~ industry** n industria de
procesado f

process² vt (data) procesar; (raw materials,
waste) procesar, tratar; (applications) dar curso
a, ocuparse de, procesar; (order) tramitar,
ocuparse de; (candidates) atender

processed food n producto alimenticio
elaborado m

processing n (of cheques, data)
procesamiento f; (of order, application)
tramitación f; (of raw materials, waste)
tratamiento f, procesamiento f; **~ fee** n
gastos de procesamiento m pl; **~ plant** n

planta de procesado *f*; ~ **profits** *n pl*
beneficios de fabricación *m pl*

processor *n* (Comp) procesador *m*

procuration fee *n* comisión de
prestamista *f*

procurement *n* obtención *f*; ~ **agent** *n*
agente de compras *mf*; ~ **costs** *n pl* costes
m pl Esp *or* costos *m pl* AmL de
abastecimiento *or* de compras; ~
department *n* departamento de compras *m*;
~ **manager** *n* gerente *mf or* jefe(-a) *m,f* de
compras

produce[1] *vt* (manufactured goods) producir,
fabricar; (reaction) producir, causar; (effect)
surtir, producir; (document) presentar;
(evidence, proof) presentar, aportar; (for cinema,
television) producir, realizar; (for theatre) poner
en escena

produce[2] *n* productos (alimenticios) *m pl*;
~ **of Spain** producto de *or* producido en
España

producer *n* (manufacturer) fabricante *mf*,
productor(a) *m,f*; (of film, TV programme, play)
productor(a) *m,f*, realizador(a) *m,f*; (theatre,
radio director) director(a) de escena *m,f*; ~
advertising *n* publicidad del productor *f*;
~'s **brand** *n* marca del productor *f*; ~'s
goods *n pl* bienes de producción *m pl*; ~
price *n* precio al productor *m*; ~ **price
index** *n* índice de precios a la producción *m*

product *n* producto *m*; ~ **acceptance** *n*
aceptación del producto *f*; ~ **adaptation** *n*
adaptación del producto *f*; ~ **advertising** *n*
publicidad del producto *f*; ~ **analysis** *n*
análisis del producto *m*; ~ **awareness** *n*
conocimiento del producto *m*; ~ **benefits**
n pl beneficios del producto *m pl*; ~
bundling *n* agrupamiento de productos *m*;
~ **classification** *n* clasificación de
productos *f*; ~ **compatibility** *n*
compatibilidad de productos *f*; ~ **cost** *n*
coste *m* Esp *or* costo *m* AmL del producto; ~
costing *n* cálculo *m* de costes Esp *or* costos
AmL del producto; (price setting) fijación del
precio *f*; ~ **cycle** *n* ciclo del producto *m*; ~
design *n* diseño de producto *m*; ~
development *n* desarrollo del producto *m*;
~ **diversification** *n* diversificación de
productos *f*; ~ **engineer** *n* ingeniero(-a) de
producto *m,f*; ~ **engineering** *n* ingeniería
de producto *f*; ~ **evaluation** *n* evaluación
del producto *f*; ~ **feature** *n* característica
del producto *f*; ~ **image** *n* imagen del
producto *f*; ~ **knowledge** *n* conocimiento
del producto *m*; ~ **launch** *n* lanzamiento
del producto *m*; ~ **liability** *n*
responsabilidad civil (del fabricante) *f*; ~
licence BrE, ~ **license** AmE *n* licencia de
producto *f*; ~ **life** *n* vida de un producto *f*;
~ **life cycle** *n* ciclo de vida de un producto
m; ~ **life expectancy** *n* esperanza de vida

de un producto *f*; ~ **line** *n* abanico de
productos *m*; ~ **management** *n* dirección *f*
or gerencia *f* del producto; ~ **manager** *n*
jefe(-a) del producto *m,f*; ~ **marketing** *n*
marketing del producto *m*; ~ **mix** *n*
combinación *f or* mezcla *f* de estrategias de
productos; ~ **performance** *n* rendimiento
del producto *m*; ~ **placement** *n*
emplazamiento *m*, posicionamiento del
producto *m*; ~ **planning** *n* planificación de
los productos *f*; ~ **portfolio** *n* cartera de
productos *f*; ~ **positioning** *n*
posicionamiento del producto *m*; ~ **profile**
n perfil del producto *m*; ~ **profitability** *n*
rentabilidad del producto *f*; ~ **promotion** *n*
promoción de un producto *f*; ~ **range** *n*
gama de productos *f*; ~ **research** *n*
investigación del producto *f*; ~ **research
and development** *n* investigación y
desarrollo del producto *f*; ~ **safety** *n*
seguridad del producto *f*; ~ **testing** *n*
prueba del producto *f*

production *n* (of manufactured goods)
producción *f*, fabricación *f*; (of coal, grain, film,
TV programme, play) producción *f*; (theatre, radio)
dirección *f*; (showing) presentación *f*; **go into/
out of** ~ empezar a/dejar de producirse; **on
~ of sth** al presentar algo; **put sth into ~**
poner algo en producción; ~ **bonus** *n*
prima de producción *f*; ~ **capacity** *n*
capacidad de producción *f*; ~ **company** *n*
empresa productora *f*; ~ **control** *n* control
de producción *m*; ~ **cost** *n* coste *m* Esp *or*
costo *m* AmL de producción; ~ **department**
n departamento de producción *m*; ~
engineering *n* ingeniería de producción *f*;
~ **goods** *n pl* bienes de producción *m pl*;
~ **line** *n* cadena de producción *f*; ~
management *n* administración *f or*
gestión *f* de la producción; ~ **manager** *n*
director(a) *m,f or* gerente *mf* de producción;
~ **planning** *n* planificación de la
producción *f*; ~ **process** *n* proceso de
producción *m*; ~ **rate** *n* índice de
producción *m*; ~ **run** *n* fase de ejecución *f*;
~ **schedule** *n* programa de producción *m*;
~ **standard** *n* norma de producción *f*; ~
technique *n* técnica de producción *f*; ~
time *n* periodo de producción *m*; ~ **worker**
n obrero(-a) manual *m,f*

productive *adj* (capital, workforce, land)
productivo; (meeting) fructífero,
productivo

productivity *n* productividad *f*; ~
agreement *n* acuerdo de productividad *m*;
~ **bargaining** *n* negociación sobre la
productividad *f*; ~ **bonus** *n* bono de
productividad *m*; ~ **campaign** *n*, ~ **drive**
n campaña de productividad *f*; ~ **gains**
n pl beneficios de productividad *m pl*; ~
measurement *n* medición de la   ····⟩

productividad *f*; ~ **tool** *n* software de
productividad *m*

profession *n* profesión *f*; **a lawyer by ~**
un abogado de profesión; **the medical ~**
(doctors) el cuerpo médico

professional¹ *adj* (status, service,
qualifications, ethics, staff) profesional; **take ~**
advice asesorarse con un profesional;
~ **body** *n* organismo profesional *m*; ~
fees *n pl* honorarios profesionales *m pl*; ~
liability *n* responsabilidad profesional *f*; ~
secret *n* secreto profesional *m*

professional² *n* profesional *mf*

professionalism *n* profesionalismo *m*

professionalization *n*
profesionalización *f*

profile *n* perfil *m*; **an accurate consumer**
~ un perfil fiable del consumidor tipo; **keep**
a low ~ procurar pasar desapercibido;
raise the ~ of sth/sb atraer la atención a
algo/alguien

profit *n* beneficio *m*, ganancia *f*; **at a ~ of**
con beneficio de; **do sth for ~** hacer algo
con fines lucrativos; ~ **for the financial**
year beneficio del ejercicio; ~ **for the year**
after tax beneficio anual *or* del ejercicio
después de impuestos; **they're interested in**
a quick ~ les interesan las ganancias
rápidas; **make a ~** producir un beneficio;
make a ~ of £20 sacar un beneficio de 20
libras; **this service does not operate at a**
~ este servicio no es rentable; **sell sth at a**
~ vender algo con beneficios; ~**s**
surpassed forecasts in the first quarter los
beneficios superaron las previsiones en el
primer trimestre; **take ~s** realizar
beneficios; ~ **before tax** *n* beneficio antes
de impuestos *m*; ~ **breakdown** *n*
distribución de los beneficios *f*; ~ **carried**
forward *n* beneficio a cuenta nueva *m*; ~
ceiling *n* beneficio máximo *m*; ~ **center**
AmE, ~ **centre** BrE *n* centro de beneficios *m*;
~ **center accounting** AmE, ~ **centre**
accounting BrE *n* contabilidad de un centro
de beneficio *f*; ~ **forecast** *n* previsión de
beneficios *f*; ~ **and loss** *n* pérdidas *f pl* y
ganancias *f pl*; ~ **and loss account** *n* BrE,
~ **and loss statement** *n* AmE cuenta de
pérdidas y ganancias *f*; ~**-making** *adj* con
ánimo de lucro; ~**-making enterprise** *n*
empresa rentable *f*; ~ **margin** *n* margen de
beneficio *m*; (S&M) margen de ganancia *m*;
~ **maximization** *n* optimización de las
ganancias *f*, maximización de beneficios *f*; ~
motive *n* motivo de ganancias *m*; ~
optimization *n* optimización de beneficios
f; ~ **performance** *n* beneficios obtenidos
m pl; (Fin) resultado de beneficios *m*; ~ **and**
performance planning *n* planificación de
beneficios y rendimientos *f*; ~ **planning** *n*
planificación de beneficios *f*; ~ **potential** *n*

potencial de beneficio *m*; ~ **projection** *n*
proyección de beneficios *f*; ~**-related pay** *n*
remuneración vinculada a los beneficios *f*;
~ **sharing** *n* participación *f* en las
ganancias *or* en los beneficios; ~**-sharing**
plan AmE, ~**-sharing scheme** BrE *n* plan
de participación en los beneficios *m*; ~
squeeze *n* reducción *f* de las ganancias *or*
de márgenes en los beneficios; ~ **taking** *n*
(Econ) realización de beneficios *f*; (Fin)
retirada de dividendos *f*; ~ **target** *n*
objetivo de beneficios *m*; ~**s tax** *n* impuesto
sobre beneficios *m*; ~ **test** *n* análisis *m or*
comprobación *f* de beneficios

profitability *n* rentabilidad *f*; ~ **analysis**
n análisis de la rentabilidad *m*; ~ **ratio** *n*
proporción *f or* relación *f* de rentabilidad

profitable *adj* (company, investment)
lucrativo, rentable; (day) provechoso

profiteer *n* especulador(a) *m,f*

profiteering *n* especulación *f*

pro forma *adj* (invoice, balance sheet, return)
pro forma

program¹ *n* (Comp) programa *m*; AmE
(schedule, plan, on television or radio)
►**programme** BrE; ~ **analyst** *n* analista de
programas *mf*; ~ **bug** *n* error del programa
m; ~ **file** *n* archivo *m or* fichero *m* de
programa; ~ **flow** *n* desarrollo del
programa *m*; ~ **language** *n* lenguaje de
programación *m*; ~ **library** *n* biblioteca de
programas *f*; ~ **package** *n* conjunto *m or*
paquete *m* de programas; ~ **testing** *n*
prueba del programa *f*; ~ **trading** *n*
contratación *f* automática por ordenador Esp
or computadora AmL

program² *vt* (Comp) programar

programmable *adj* programable; ~
function *n* función programable *f*

programme BrE, **program** AmE *n* (schedule,
plan, on television or radio) programa *m*; ~
budgeting *n* elaboración de presupuestos
de programas *f*; ~ **evaluation plan** *n* plan
de evaluación del programa *m*; ~
evaluation and review technique *n*
técnica de evaluación y revisión del
programa *f*; ~ **planning** *n* programación *f*;
~ **structure** *n* estructura del programa *f*

programmed *adj* (instruction, learning,
management) programado

programming *n* programación *f*; ~ **aid** *n*
ayuda a la programación *f*; ~ **language** *n*
lenguaje de programación *m*

progress¹ *n* (advancement) progreso *m*; (of
situation, events) desarrollo *m*, evolución *f*; **in ~**
en marcha; **make quick ~** hacer rápidos
progresos; ~ **chaser** *n* BrE *encargado de*
supervisar el cumplimiento de un programa
de trabajo; ~ **control** *n* control *m* de
avance *or* de progreso; ~ **payment** *n* pago

escalonado *m*; ~ **report** *n* informe sobre el progreso de un trabajo *m*

progress[2] *vi* (work, technology, person) progresar, avanzar, adelantar

progressive *adj* (deterioration, tax, obsolescence, scale) progresivo; (attitude, measure) progresista

progressively *adv* progresivamente

prohibit *vt* (forbid) prohibir; (prevent) impedir; ~ **sb from doing sth** (forbid) prohibirle a alguien hacer algo; (prevent) impedir que alguien haga algo, impedirle a alguien hacer algo

prohibited *adj* (goods) prohibido

prohibition *n* prohibición *f*, ~ **notice** *n* apercibimiento *m or* notificación *f* de prohibición

prohibitive *adj* (cost, price) prohibitivo

project[1] *n* (scheme) proyecto *m*; (housing project) AmE (*cf* ►**estate** BrE) complejo de viviendas subvencionadas *m*; ~ **agent** *n* agente de proyecto *mf*; ~ **analysis** *n* análisis de proyectos *m*; ~ **appraisal** *n* evaluación de proyectos *f*; ~ **approval** *n* aprobación del proyecto *f*; ~ **assessment** *n* evaluación *f or* valoración *f* de proyecto; ~ **design** *n* diseño de proyecto *m*; ~ **engineer** *n* ingeniero(-a) de proyectos *m,f*; ~ **financing** *n* financiación de un proyecto *f*; ~ **leader** *n* director(a) *m,f or* jefe(-a) *m,f* de proyecto; ~ **management** *n* dirección *f or* gestión *f* de proyectos; ~ **manager** *n* director(a) *m,f or* jefe(-a) *m,f* de proyecto; ~ **planning** *n* planificación de un proyecto *f*; ~ **sponsor** *n* patrocinador(a) de un proyecto *m,f*; ~ **preparation facility** *n* servicio de preparación de proyectos *m*

project[2] *vt* (image) proyectar; (expenditure, costs, trends) hacer una proyección de, extrapolar; (forecast) pronosticar

projected *adj* (balance sheet) previsto

projection *n* proyección *f*

projective *adj* (test) de proyección

proletarianization *n* proletarización *f*

proletariat *n* proletariado *m*

proliferate *vi* proliferar

prolong *vt* prolongar

prominent *adj* prominente

promise[1] *n* promesa *f*; **make/break/keep a** ~ hacer/faltar a/cumplir una promesa; **show great** ~ ser muy prometidor; ~ **to pay** *n* promesa de pago; ~ **to sell** *n* promesa de vender

promise[2] *vt* prometer; ~ **sb sth** *o* **sth to sb** prometerle algo a alguien; ~ **to do sth** prometer hacer algo

promising *adj* prometidor; **look** ~ tener buenas perspectivas

promissory note *n* pagaré *m*; **make a** ~ extender un pagaré

promo *abbr* (jarg) (►**promotion**) (of product, service) promoción *f*

promotary company *n* AmE compañía promotora *f*

promote *vt* (employee) ascender; (public employee) ascender, promover; (product, service) promocionar; (research, good relations) promover, fomentar, potenciar; (free trade) promover, fomentar; (efficiency) promover; (growth) estimular; **be** ~**d** (employee) ser ascendido

promoter *n* promotor(a) *m,f*

promotion *n* (of employee) ascenso *m*; (of public employee) ascenso *m*, promoción *f*; (publicity) promoción *f*, publicidad *f*, propaganda *f*; (publicity campaign) promoción *f*, campaña *f* publicitaria *or* de promoción; (of research, trade) promoción *f*, fomento *m*; **gain** *o* **win** ~ conseguir el ascenso; ~ **cost** *n* costes *m pl* Esp *or* costos *m pl* AmL de promoción; ~ **ladder** *n* escala de promoción *f*; ~**s manager** *n* jefe(-a) de promoción *m,f*; ~ **mix** *n* combinación de estrategias de promoción *f*; ~ **prospects** *n pl* perspectivas de ascenso *f pl*

promotional *adj* (allowance, budget, exercise, sample, video) promocional; (campaign) publicitario, de promoción; (material, literature) de promoción; ~ **mix** *n* combinación de estrategias promocionales *f*; ~ **site** *n* (on Internet) sitio web promocional *m*

prompt[1] *adj* (delivery, reply) rápido, pronto; (payment) pronto; **be** ~ **in one's payments** pagar puntualmente; ~ **payment would be appreciated** se agradece la prontitud en el pago; ~ **note** *n* (Fin) aviso inmediato *m*

prompt[2] *vt* (give rise to) incitar; ~ **sb to do sth** mover *or* inducir a alguien a hacer algo

prompt[3] *n* (Comp) aviso *m*

pronounce *vt* (judgment, sentence) pronunciar, dictar; ~ **a judicial decree** dictar un auto

proof *n* prueba *f*; **at** ~ **stage** (before printing) en fase de pruebas; ~ **of debt** *n* comprobante de deuda *m*; ~ **of delivery** *n* prueba de entrega *f*; ~ **of identity** *n* documentación *f*; ~ **of loss** *n* prueba del siniestro *f*; ~ **of postage** *n* comprobante de envío *m*; ~ **of ownership** *n* (of registered shares) prueba de pertenencia *f*; ~ **of purchase** *n* comprobante de compra *m*; ~ **of title** *n* prueba de propiedad *f*

proofread *vt* corregir las pruebas de

proofreader *n* corrector(a) de pruebas *m,f*

proofs *n pl* (in publishing) pruebas *f pl*

propensity *n* propensión *f*; ~ **to consume** *n* propensión a consumir *f*; ~ **to invest** *n* propensión a invertir *f*; ~ **to save** *n* ⸳⸳⸳⸼

propensión a ahorrar *f*; **~ to work** *n*
propensión al trabajo *f*

property *n* (possessions) propiedad *f*;
(buildings, land) propiedades *f pl*, bienes *m pl*
raíces *or* inmuebles; (building) inmueble *m*;
(piece of land) terreno *m*, solar *m*, parcela *f*; (in
advertising) producto de gran aceptación *m*; **~
bond** *n* bono de propiedad *m*; **~ company**
n sociedad inmobiliaria *f*; **~ developer** *n*
promotor(a) inmobiliario(-a) *m,f*; **~
development** *n* ampliación de la propiedad
f; **~ development project** *n* proyecto de
explotación de la propiedad *m*; **~ held in
joint names** *n* propiedad mancomunada *f*;
~ income *n* renta de la propiedad *f*; **~
insurance** *n* seguro inmobiliario *m*; **~
management** *n* gestión inmobiliaria *f*; **~
market** *n* mercado *m* inmobiliario *or* de
bienes raíces *or* de propiedades; **~ owner** *n*
propietario(-a); **~ rights** *n pl* derechos de la
propiedad *m pl*; **~ speculator** *n*
especulador(a) inmobiliario(-a) *m,f*; **~ tax** *n*
impuesto sobre la propiedad inmobiliaria *m*

proportion *n* (ratio, proper relation)
proporción *f*; (part) parte *f*, porcentaje *m*; **as
a ~ of sth** como proporción de algo; **a high
o large ~ of small companies went bust**
un alto porcentaje de compañías pequeñas
se fueron a pique; **in ~ to sth** en proporción
a algo

proportional *adj* (tax, income tax)
proporcional; **~ representation** *n*
representación proporcional *f*

proportionality *n* proporcionalidad *f*

proportionate *adj* proporcionado

proportionately *adv* proporcionalmente

proposal *n* propuesta *f*; **put *o* make a ~
to sb** hacerle una propuesta a alguien; **our
~ still stands** nuestra proposición sigue en
pie

propose *vt* (motion) presentar, proponer,
(amendment) proponer; **~ doing *o* to do sth**
pensar hacer algo; **I ~ that the meeting be
adjourned** propongo que se levante la sesión

proposer *n* proponente *mf*

proposition *n* proposición *f*, propuesta *f*;
**the company has made a highly attractive
~** la compañía ha hecho una proposición
que no se puede rechazar; **it's not a viable
~** no es una proposición viable

proprietary *adj* (device, software, drug) de
marca registrada, patentado; (product) de
marca; (interest, insurance) patrimonial; (brand)
comercial; (name, system) propietario; (rights)
de la propiedad; **~ company** *n* (in Australia,
South Africa) sociedad anónima *f*

proprietor *n* propietario(-a) *m,f*

proprietorship *n* derecho de propiedad *m*

prop up *vt* (currency) entibar, respaldar

pro rata¹ *adj* (payment, charge) prorrateado;
on a ~ basis a prorrata

pro rata² *adv* a prorrata

prorate¹ *n* AmE prorrata *f*

prorate² *vt* AmE prorratear

pros and cons *n pl* pros *m pl* y contras
m pl

prosecute ① *vt* (person) procesar;
(application) proseguir; **~ sb for forgery**
procesar a alguien por falsificación
② *vi* (bring legal action) iniciar procedimiento
criminal, interponer una acción judicial; (be
prosecutor) llevar la acusación

prosecuting attorney AmE,
prosecuting counsel BrE *n* fiscal *mf*

prosecution *n* (bringing to trial)
interposición de una acción judicial *f*; (case)
proceso *m*, juicio *m*; (prosecuting side)
acusación *f*; (of campaign) prosecución *f*; **bring
a ~ against sb** interponer una acción
judicial contra alguien; **~ case** *n* acusación
f; **~ witness** *n* testigo *mf* de cargo *or* de la
acusación

prosecutor *n* fiscal *mf*; (in private
prosecution) abogado(-a) *m,f* de *or* por la
acusación

prospect *n* (possibility) posibilidad *f*; (situation
envisaged) perspectiva *f*; (hope) expectativa *f*;
(potential buyer) cliente potencial *m*; **have little
~ of success** tener pocas expectativas de
éxito; **the job has no ~s** el puesto no tiene
perspectivas; **a young executive with ~s**
un joven ejecutivo con perspectivas de
futuro *or* con porvenir

prospecting *n* prospección *f*

prospective *adj* (buyer, customer) posible

prospector *n* explorador(a) *m,f*

prospectus *n* prospecto *m*; (for share issue)
folleto explicativo *m*

prosperity *n* prosperidad *f*; **~ indicator**
n indicador de prosperidad *m*

prosperous *adj* próspero

protect *vt* (rights, interests) proteger; **~
oneself (against *o* from sth)** protegerse
(contra *or* de algo)

protected *adj* protegido; **~ designation
of origin** *n* Denominación de Origen
Protegida *f*; **~ geographic indication** *n*
indicación geográfica protegida *f*

protection *n* protección *f*

protectionism *n* proteccionismo *m*

protectionist¹ *adj* proteccionista

protectionist² *n* proteccionista *mf*

protective *adj* (headgear, covering, attitude)
protector; (clothing) de protección; (tariffs,
duties) proteccionista; **~ custody** *n*
detención de una persona para su propia
protección; **~ safety screen** *n* pantalla
protectora de seguridad *f*

pro tem[1] *adj* interino

pro tem[2] *adv* por el momento

protest[1] *n* (dissent, complaint) protesta *f*; (demonstration) manifestación de protesta *f*; **in ~ (at** *o* **against sth)** en señal de protesta (por *or* contra algo); **lodge a ~** presentar una protesta; **make** *o* **stage a ~ about** *o* **against sth** protestar contra algo; **under ~** bajo protesta; **~ strike** *n* huelga de protesta *f*; **~ vote** *n* voto de protesta *m*

protest[2] ⟦**1**⟧ *vi* protestar; **~ against** *o* **about** *o* **at sth** protestar contra *or* acerca de *or* por algo; **~ to sb** presentar una protesta ante alguien

⟦**2**⟧ *vt* AmE (decision, action) protestar (contra)

protocol *n* protocolo *m*

prototype *n* prototipo *m*

prototyping *n* creación de prototipos

prove ⟦**1**⟧ *vt* (theory, statement, system) probar; (innocence) probar, demostrar; (will) comprobar, verificar; (debt) justificar; **~ sb's identity** verificar la identidad de alguien; **~ one's** *o* **the point** *o* **case** demostrar que se está en lo cierto; **~ sb right/wrong** demostrar que alguien tiene razón/está equivocado; **~ sth right/wrong** demostrar que algo es/no es cierto

⟦**2**⟧ *vi* (turn out) resultar; **~ right/wrong** resultar acertado/equivocado

proven *adj* (experience, ability) probado, comprobado; **a ~ track record** un historial probado

provide *vt* proveer; (assistance) proporcionar; (capital) aportar; **~ the base for sth** estipular las bases para algo; **~ sth for** *o* **to sth/sb** proporcionarle algo a algo/ alguien; **~ a market for sth** proporcionar un mercado para algo; **~ sb with sth** proporcionarle algo a alguien; **provide against** *vt* tomar precauciones contra; **provide for** *vt* (person) mantener; **not ~ for** no condicionado para; **not specially ~ for** no específicamente dispuesto

provided (that) *conj* siempre que, siempre y cuando

provident fund *n* fondo de previsión *m*

provider *n* proveedor(a) *m,f*

province *n* BrE provincia *f*; (self-governing) ≈ Comunidad Autónoma *f* Esp

provincial *adj* provincial

provision *n* (of funding) provisión *f*; (of services) prestación *f*; (preparatory arrangments) previsiones *f pl*; (stipulation) disposición *f*; **make ~ for sth** (financially) apartar fondos para algo; **make ~ for the future** hacer previsiones para el futuro; **the present law makes no ~ for this** la ley actual no contempla este caso; **under the ~s of the agreement** según las disposiciones del acuerdo; **with the ~ that...** con la condición

de que...; **~ for bad debts** *n* provisión para pérdidas *f*; **~ for contingency** *n* provisión para riesgos y gastos *f*

provisional *adj* (acceptance, invoice, insurance policy) provisional

provisionally *adv* provisionalmente

proviso *n* condición *f*; **with the ~ that...** con la condición de que...

prox. *abbr* (▶**proximo**) pmo. (próximo)

proximo *adv* próximo

proxy *n* (authorization, document) poder *m*; (person) representante *mf*, apoderado(-a) *m,f*; **by ~** por poder; **~ statement** *n* información que debe ser suministrada a los accionistas por quien solicita de éstos poderes para representarlos en la asamblea de accionistas; **~ vote** *n* voto por poder *m*

proxyholder *n* apoderado(-a) *m,f*

PRP *abbr* (▶**performance-related pay**) remuneración según rendimiento *f*; (▶**profit-related pay**) remuneración vinculada a los beneficios *f*

prudent *adj* (person, policy, approach) prudente

prudential *adj* prudencial; **~ committee** *n* AmE (*cf* ▶**advisory committee** BrE) comisión asesora *f*, comité asesor *m*; **~ consideration** *n* (Bank) retribución prudencial *f*

prudently *adv* prudentemente

pruning *n* reducción *f*, recorte *m*

P.S. *abbr* (▶**personal secretary**) secretario(-a) personal *m,f*; (▶**postscript**) P.D. (posdata)

PSBR *abbr* (▶**public sector borrowing requirement**) necesidades *f pl* crediticias del sector público *or* de préstamo del sector público

PSE *abbr* (▶**public sector employment**) empleo en el sector público *m*; (▶**public service employment**) empleo en el servicio público *m*

psychographics *n pl* psicográficos *m pl*

psychological *adj* (test, profile, price) psicológico

psychology *n* psicología *f*

psychometric *adj* (test, testing) psicométrico

psychometrics *n pl* psicometría *f*

PTL *abbr* (▶**partial/total loss**) pérdida total/parcial *f*

public[1] *adj* (affairs, amenities, consumption) público; **be in the ~ eye** ser objeto de la atención pública; **go ~** (company) salir a bolsa; (journalist, newspaper) hacer revelaciones; **it wouldn't be in the ~ interest** no beneficiaría a la ciudadanía; **be ~ knowledge** ser bien conocido; **make sth ~** hacer algo público; **be ~ property** ser del ⸱⸱⸱⟩

dominio público; ～ **access** *n* (to information) acceso público *m*; ～ **accounting** *n* contabilidad pública *f*; **P～ Accounts Committee** *n* comisión del gasto público *f*; ～ **address system** *n* sistema altavoces *m*; ～ **administration** *n* administración pública *f*; ～ **authorities** *n pl* poderes públicos *m pl*; ～ **body** *n* organismo público *m*; **P～ Broadcasting Services** *n pl* *cadena pública estadounidense de radiodifusión*; ～ **company** *n* compañía pública *f*, empresa que cotiza en bolsa *f*; ～ **corporation** *n* sociedad pública *f*; ～ **debt** *n* AmE (*cf* ▶**national debt** BrE) deuda pública *f*; ～ **distribution** *n* (of securities) distribución pública *f*; ～ **domain** *n* dominio público *m*; **be in the** ～ **domain** ser del dominio público; ～ **domain software** *n* programas de dominio público *m pl*; ～ **enterprise** *n* empresa pública *f*; ～ **expenditure** *n* gasto público *m*; ～ **finances** *n pl* finanzas públicas *f pl*; ～ **funds** *n pl* fondos públicos *m pl*; ～ **good** *n* bien público *m*; ～ **health** *n* salud pública *f*; ～ **holiday** *n* fiesta oficial *f*; ～ **interest company** *n* compañía *f* con intereses públicos *or* de interés público; ～ **investor** *n* inversor(a) público(-a) *m,f*; ～ **invitation to bid** *n* invitación pública a ofertar *f*; ～ **issue** *n* (Stock) emisión pública *f*; ～ **key infrastructure** *n* infraestructura de claves públicas *f*; ～ **lending right** *n* derecho a empréstito público *m*; ～ **limited company** *n* BrE ≈ sociedad anónima *f*, ≈ sociedad anónima por acciones *f*; ～ **limited partnership** *n* sociedad limitada con cotización en bolsa *f*; ～ **monies** *n pl* erario público *m*; ～ **offering** *n* oferta pública de venta *f*; ～ **opinion** *n* opinión pública *f*; ～ **ownership** *n* propiedad pública *f*; **come under** ～ **ownership** quedar bajo propiedad pública; ～/**private key encryption** *n* encriptación de clave pública/privada *f*; ～**-private partnership** *n* sociedad entre el sector público y el privado *f*; ～ **prosecutor** *n* acusador(a) público(-a) *m,f*, fiscal *mf*; ～ **purse** *n* tesoro público *m*; **P～ Record Office** *n* BrE ≈ Archivo Nacional *m* Esp, ≈ Oficina de Registro *f* Esp; ～ **relations** *n pl* relaciones públicas *f pl*; ～ **relations agency** *n* agencia de relaciones públicas *f*; ～ **relations consultancy** *n* asesoría de relaciones públicas *f*; ～ **relations consultant** *n* asesor(a) de relaciones públicas *m,f*; ～ **relations officer** *n* encargado(-a) de relaciones públicas *m,f*; ～ **sector** *n* sector público *m*; ～ **sector borrowing requirement** *n* necesidades *f pl* crediticias del sector público *or* de préstamo del sector público; ～ **sector company** *n* empresa pública *f*; ～ **sector employment** *n* empleo en el sector público *m*; ～ **sector**

pay *n* sueldos del sector público *m pl*; ～ **service** *n* servicio público *m*; ～ **service body** *n* organismo de servicio público *m*; ～ **service contract** *n* contrato de servicio público *m*; ～ **service corporation** *n* AmE empresa de servicios públicos *f*; ～ **service employment** *n* empleo en el servicio público *m*; ～ **spending** *n* gasto público *m*; ～ **transport** BrE, ～ **transportation** AmE *n* transporte público *m*; ～ **treasury** *n* erario público *m*; ～ **use** *n* uso público *m*; ～ **utility (company)** *n* empresa de servicios públicos *f*; ～ **warning** *n* advertencia pública *f*; ～ **welfare** *n* asistencia *f or* beneficencia *f* pública; ～ **works** *n pl* obras públicas *f pl*; ～ **works program** AmE, ～ **works programme** BrE *n* programa de obras públicas *m*

public² *n* público *m*; **the** ～ **at large** el público en general; **in** ～ en público; **open to the** ～ abierto al público (en general)

publication *n* publicación *f*; ～ **date** *n* fecha de publicación *f*

publicity *n* publicidad *f*; **attract a lot of** ～ atraer gran publicidad; ～ **budget** *n* presupuesto publicitario *m*; ～ **campaign** *n* campaña publicitaria *f*; ～ **department** *n* departamento de publicidad *m*; ～ **expenses** *n pl* gastos publicitarios *m pl*; ～ **man** *n* publicista *m*; ～ **manager** *n* director(a) de publicidad *m,f*; ～ **material** *n* material publicitario *m*; ～ **stunt** *n* truco publicitario *m*

publicize *vt* (product, service) promocionar, publicitar; (make public) hacer público

publicly *adv* (admit, criticize) públicamente, en público; ～ **funded** *adj* financiado con dineros públicos; ～**-listed company** *n* compañía que cotiza en bolsa *f*; ～**-traded company** *n* empresa de gestión pública *f*; ～**-traded share** *n* acción negociada públicamente *f*

publish *vt* (book, newspaper) publicar, editar; (accounts, article) publicar; (make known) hacer público, divulgar

published *adj* (accounts, price, information) publicado; ～ **monthly** de publicación mensual

publisher *n* (company) editorial *f*, casa editorial *f*; (person) editor(a) *m,f*

publishing *n* (business) mundo editorial *m*; (of book) publicación *f*; **be** *o* **work in** ～ trabajar en una editorial; ～ **director** *n* director(a) editorial *m,f*; ～ **house** *n* casa editorial *f*

PUF *abbr* (▶**purchase underwriting facility**) servicio de compra de suscripciones *m*

pull¹ *vt* (customers, audience) atraer; (withdraw) retirar; (proof) imprimir; ～ **the carpet** *o* **rug**

(out) from under sb fastidiarle los planes a alguien; ~ **strings** o **wires** AmE tocar resortes; ~ **the strings** tener la sartén por el mango; **pull down** vt (inflation) frenar; **pull in** vt (investments, customers, audience) atraer; **pull off** vt (infrml) (achieve) lograr; **pull out** vi (withdraw from deal) echarse atrás; **pull out of** vt (negotiations) retirarse de

pull² n (influence) influencia f; (jarg) (in publishing) primera prueba f; ~ **of prices** n tirón de los precios m; ~ **technology** n técnica de extracción f

pull-down menu n menú desplegable m

pulse n (Comp) impulso m

pump vt bombear; ~ **funds into sth** inyectar or invertir fondos en algo

pump priming n (jarg) (of the economy) reactivación (estimulada) f

punch¹ vt (card) fichar; ~ **the time clock** fichar; **punch in** vi AmE (cf ▸**clock on** BrE) fichar (a la entrada); **punch out** vi AmE (cf ▸**clock off** BrE) fichar (a la salida)

punch² n (device) perforadora f; ~ **card** n tarjeta perforada f

punched card n tarjeta perforada f

punctual adj punctual

punctuality n puntualidad f

punitive adj (interest rate, fine) leonino, excesivamente gravoso; ~ **damages** n pl daños punitivos m pl

punt n (jarg) (speculation) inversión en bolsa de valores con muy poca probabilidad de dar beneficios

punter n BrE (infrml) (customer) cliente mf; (better) apostador(a) m,f

pupil n (Law) pasante mf

pupillage n (Law) pasantería f

purchase¹ n adquisición f, compra f; **make a** ~ hacer una compra; **no** ~ **necessary** sin obligación de compra; ~ **acquisition** n adquisición por compra f; ~ **of assets** n compra de activos f; ~ **book** n libro de compras m; ~ **contract** n contrato de compra m; ~ **cost** n (of assets) precio de compra m; ~ **credit** n crédito para comprar m; ~ **decision** n decisión de compra f; ~ **for settlement** n (Stock) compra en liquidación f; ~ **fund** n fondo de compras m; ~ **group** n grupo de compras m; ~ **invoice** n factura de compra f; ~**s journal** n diario de compras m; ~ **ledger** n libro mayor de compras m; ~ **method** n método de compra m; ~ **order** n orden de compra f; ~ **price** n precio de compra m; ~ **price method** n método de precio de compra m; ~ **and resale agreement** n compromiso de compra y reventa m; ~ **underwriting facility** n servicio de compra de suscripciones m

purchase² vt adquirir, comprar; ~ **sth from sb** comprarle algo a alguien

purchasing n compra f; ~ **company** n compañía adquirente f; ~ **costs** n pl costes m pl Esp or costos m pl AmL de compras; ~ **department** n departamento de compras m; ~ **hedge** n cobertura de compra f; ~ **manager** n director(a) de compras m,f; ~ **officer** n funcionario(-a) de compras m,f; ~ **power** n poder adquisitivo m

pure adj (inflation, monopoly, capitalism) puro; (profit) neto; (competition) perfecto; (interest rate) absoluto; ~ **play** n (Comp) nueva puntocom que sólo funciona a través del Internet; (Stock) empresa especializada f; ~ **player** n nueva puntocom que sólo funciona a través del Internet

purification n depuración f; ~ **plant** n planta depuradora f

purify vt depurar

purpose n (intention, reason) propósito m, intención f, objeto m; **for a** ~ por alguna razón; **for commercial** ~s para usos comerciales; **for this** ~ para este fin; **on** ~ a propósito; **it serves no useful** ~ no sirve para nada; **to good** ~ con resultado positivo; **to no/little** ~ sin resultado positivo; ~**-built** adj construido con propósitos específicos; ~ **loan** n préstamo específico respaldado m

purse strings n pl presupuesto m; **hold** o **control the** ~ administrar el dinero

pursuant to prep de conformidad con, con arreglo a; ~ **to article** de conformidad con el artículo

pursue vt (policy, plan) seguir (con); (claim) seguir adelante (con); (research) continuar con, proseguir; (profession) ejercer, dedicarse al ejercicio de; ~ **a career in Law** dedicarse a la abogacía; **I have decided not to** ~ **the matter further** he decidido no continuar con este tema

push¹ vt (promote) promocionar; (button) apretar, pulsar; ~ **sb to the limit** llevar a alguien hasta el límite; ~ **one's luck** (infrml) tentar a la suerte; ~ **sb to the wall** acorralar a alguien; **push ahead** vi seguir adelante; ~ **ahead with sth** seguir adelante con algo; **push back** vt (event, date) posponer, aplazar, postergar AmL; **push down** vt (prices) hacer bajar; **push for** vt presionar para; **push through** vt (legislation) hacer aprobar; **push up** vt (prices) hacer subir

push² n (for sales) campaña f; **at a** ~ en el peor de los casos; **if/when it comes to the** ~ llegado el caso; **get the** ~ BrE (infrml) ser despedido; **give sb the** ~ BrE (infrml) poner a alguien de patitas en la calle (infrml); **when** ~ **comes to shove** cuando llega la hora de la ⤳

P

verdad; ∼-**button telephone** n teléfono de botones m; ∼ **incentive** n (in advertising) incentivo de empuje m; ∼ **money** n incentivo de ventas m; ∼/**pull strategy** n estrategia de tira y afloja f; ∼ **technology** n técnica de búsqueda f

put[1] vt poner; **put about** vt (story, rumour) hacer correr; **put it about that...** hacer correr la voz de que...; **put across** vt (idea, message) comunicar; **put aside** vt (money) guardar, ahorrar; (goods, time) reservar; (differences, quarrel) dejar de lado; **put away** vt (money) guardar, ahorrar; (imprison) encarcelar; **put back** vt (event, date) posponer, aplazar, postergar AmL; **put by** vt (money) ahorrar; **put down** vt (sum) entregar, dejar (en depósito); (deposit) dejar; (motion) presentar; (telephone) colgar; (write down) escribir; **put forward** vt (theory, plan) presentar, proponer; (suggestion) hacer, presentar; (candidate) proponer, postular AmL; (trip, meeting) adelantar; **put in** vt (claim, request, tender) presentar; ∼ **in a 50-hour week** trabajar cincuenta horas por semana; **put in for** vt solicitar; **put off** vt (meeting, visit, decision) aplazar, posponer, postergar AmL; (discourage) desanimar; **put sb off** (postpone appointment with) decirle a alguien que no venga; **put on** vt (exhibition) organizar; **I'll put her on** (connect by telephone) le paso con ella; **put out** vt (statement) publicar; (broadcast) transmitir; (money) prestar; (calculation, estimate) causar un

desajuste en; **they put the work out to contract** subcontrataron el trabajo; **the contract is being ∼ out to tender** se va a sacar el contrato a licitación or a concurso; **put through** vt (reform) llevar a cabo; (deal) cerrar; (telephone call) pasar; **she put me through to the manager** me comunicó or me pasó con el gerente; **put together** vt (team) formar; **put up** vt (price, fare) aumentar; (money, capital) poner, aportar; (building) levantar; (notice) poner; (candidate) proponer, postular AmL; **put sb up as** o **for sth** proponer a alguien como or para algo

put[2] n opción de venta f; ∼ **bond** n bono con opción de venta m; ∼ **and call** n operación con dobles primas f; ∼ **option** n opción de venta f; ∼ **premium** n prima de venta f; ∼ **purchase** n adquisición de una opción de venta f; ∼**'s strike** n ejercicio de una opción de venta m; ∼ **writer** n vendedor(a) de una opción de venta m,f

put-through n (Stock) colocación privada f

p.v. abbr (▸**par value**) valor a la par m

PVP abbr (▸**portable video player**) proyector m de video AmL or vídeo Esp portátil

pyramid[1] n pirámide f; ∼ **hierarchy** n jerarquía piramidal f; ∼ **selling** n venta piramidal f

pyramid[2] vi acumular

pyramidal adj piramidal

PYT abbr (▸**payment**) pago m

Qq

QC *abbr* (▸**quality circle**) círculo de calidad *m*; (▸**quality control**) control de calidad *m*; (▸**Queen's Counsel**) consejero(-a) de la Reina *m,f*

qnty *abbr* (▸**quantity**) ctdad (cantidad)

qtr *abbr* (▸**quarter**) (fourth) cuarto *m*; (three months) trimestre *m*

qty *abbr* (▸**quantity**) ctdad (cantidad)

quadripartite *adj* (agreement) cuadripartito

quadruplicate *adj* cuadruplicado; **in ~** en cuadruplicado

qualification *n* (educational) título *m*; (skill, necessary attribute) requisito *m*; (eligibility) derecho *m*; (reservation) reserva *f*; (to accounts) salvedad *f*, reparo *m*; **have the right ~s for the job** cumplir todos los requisitos para el puesto, estar debidamente cualificado para el puesto; **without ~** sin reserva; **~ shares** *n pl* acciones entregadas en garantía *f pl*

qualified *adj* (personnel) cualificado; (doctor, teacher, engineer) titulado; (competent) capacitado; (approval, opinion, report) con reservas; (acceptance) condicionado; (borrowing, investment, majority) calificado; **be ~ to do sth** estar capacitado para hacer algo; (eligible) reunir los requisitos necesarios para hacer algo; **~ accountant** *n* contable *m,f* Esp autorizado(-a) *or* diplomado(-a), contador(a) *m,f* AmL autorizado(-a) *or* diplomado(-a)

qualify ① *vt* (certify as competent) capacitar; (entitle) dar derecho a; (statement) matizar; **~ sb for sth/to do sth** capacitar a alguien para algo/para hacer algo ② *vi* (professionally) sacar el título; (be entitled) tener derecho; (meet requirements) reunir los requisitos; (count) contar; **~ as sth** (professionally) sacar el título de algo; (count) contar como algo; **~ for sth/to do sth** (be entitled) tener derecho a algo/a hacer algo; **~ for sth** (meet requirements) cumplir *or* reunir los requisitos para algo

qualifying *adj* (annuity, share) habilitante; (period) estipulado como requisito; **a ~ remark** una matización, una precisión

qualitative *adj* (analysis, research) cualitativo

qualitatively *adv* cualitativamente

quality *n* calidad *f*; **~ assessment** *n* valoración de la calidad *f*; **~ asset** *n* activo de calidad *m*; **~ assurance** *n* garantía *f* de calidad; **~ certificate** *n* certificado de calidad *m*; **~ circle** *n* círculo de calidad *f*; **~ control** *n* control de calidad *m*; **~ controller** *n* inspector(a) de calidad *m,f*; **~ engineer** *n* ingeniero(-a) de calidad *m,f*; **~ engineering** *n* ingeniería de calidad *f*; **~ good** *n* producto de calidad *m*; **~ label** *n* etiqueta de calidad *f*; **~ of life** *n* calidad de vida *f*; **~ management** *n* dirección de calidad *f*; **~ market** *n* mercado de calidad *m*; **~ newspaper** *n* periódico de calidad *m*; **~-price ratio** *n* relación calidad-precio *f*; **~ standard** *n* norma de calidad *f*; **~ of working life** *n* calidad de vida en el trabajo *f*

Quango *abbr* BrE (▸**quasi-autonomous non-governmental-organization**) *organización no gubernamental que funciona como órgano consultivo*

quantifiable *adj* cuantificable

quantification *n* cuantificación *f*

quantify *vt* cuantificar

quantitative *adj* (analysis, methodology, research) cuantitativo

quantitatively *adv* cuantitativamente

quantity *n* cantidad *f*; **in ~** en grandes cantidades; **~ buyer** *n* comprador(a) de cantidad *m,f*; **~ discount** *n* descuento por cantidad *m*; **~ surveyor** *n* aparejador(-a) *m,f*

quantum *n* cuanto *m*

quarter *n* (fourth) cuarto *m*; (three months) trimestre *m*; **~-end** *n* fin de trimestre *m*; **~-page advertisement** *n* anuncio de un cuarto de página *m*

quartering *n* (jarg) (in industrial relations) penalización por falta de puntualidad *f*

quarterly[1] *adj* (dividend, instalment) trimestral

quarterly[2] *adv* trimestralmente

quarterly[3] *n* (publication) trimestral *m*

quartile *n* cuartil *m*; **~ deviation** *n* rango semiintercuartílico *m*

quash *vt* (writ, sentence, order) abolir, anular

quasi *adv* cuasi; **~-autonomous non-governmental-organization** *n* BrE *organización no gubernamental que funciona como órgano consultivo*; **~-contract** *n* cuasi contrato *m*; **~-independence** *n* cuasi independencia *f*; **~-money** *n* activo casi líquido *m*, cuasi-dinero *m*; **~-monopoly** *n* cuasi monopolio *m*

q

queen *n* reina *f*; **Q~'s Counsel** *n* BrE consejero(-a) de la Reina *m,f*

query[1] *n* (question) pregunta *f*, consulta *f*; (doubt) duda *f*; **answer a ~** aclarar una duda; **I have a ~** tengo una duda, quisiera hacer una pregunta; **raise** *o* **put a ~** poner una pregunta sobre la mesa; **~ language** *n* (Comp) lenguaje *m* de consulta *or* de interrogación; **~ mode** *n* (Comp) modo *m* de consulta *or* de interrogación; **~ window** *n* (Comp) ventana *m* de consulta *or* de interrogación

query[2] *vt* (statement) cuestionar; AmE (ask) preguntar

question *n* (inquiry) pregunta *f*; (issue) cuestión *f*; **answer a ~** responder a una pregunta; **ask a ~** hacer una pregunta; **be beyond ~** estar fuera de toda duda; **bring** *o* **call sth into ~** poner algo en duda; **in ~** en cuestión; **there is no ~ of...** no se ha planteado siquiera la posibilidad de que...; **be out of the ~** ser impensable; **put the ~** someter una moción a votación; **without ~** sin lugar a duda; **~ mark** *n* signo de interrogación *m*; **a ~ mark hangs over his future** su futuro está en el aire; **~ time** *n* BrE *sesión de interpelaciones dirigidas al primer ministro*

questionnaire *n* cuestionario *m*

queue[1] *n* (of people) BrE (*cf* ▶**line** AmE) cola *f*; (Comp) cola *f*, fila en espera *f*; (of telephone calls) cola (de llamadas) *f*

queue[2] *vi* (people) BrE (*cf* ▶**wait in line** AmE) hacer cola; **queue up** *vi* BrE (*cf* ▶**wait in line** AmE) hacer cola

queueing *n* (Comp, Comms) puesta en cola *m*; **~ system** *n* sistema de colas *m*

quick *adj* (method, calculation, question) rápido; (asset) líquido, realizable; (sale) fácil; **he'd like a ~ word with you** quiere hablar contigo un momento; **~-buck artist** *n* AmE (jarg) oportunista *mf*; **~ fix** *n* (infrml) arreglo rápido *m*; **~ ratio** *n* (Acc) proporción *f or* ratio *m* de liquidez inmediata

quid *n* BrE (infrml) libra *f*; **be ~s in** BrE (infrml) sacar ganancia

quid pro quo *n* compensación *f*

quiet *adj* (business) tranquilo; (market) inactivo, poco animado; **a ~ day on the stock exchange** un día muy tranquilo en la Bolsa

quit [1] *vt* (job) dejar; (premises, town) dejar, irse de; (Comp) salir de [2] *vi* (stop) parar; (give in) abandonar; (resign) renunciar; (Comp) salir; **~ while you're ahead** retírate ahora que vas ganando; **receive notice to ~** recibir una notificación de desahucio

quitclaim *n* finiquito *m*

quit rate *n* tasa *f* de abandono del empleo *or* de dimisión del empleo

quondam *adj* otrora

quorate *adj* BrE con quórum; **the meeting isn't ~** no hay quórum en la reunión

quorum *n* quórum *m*; **form a ~** tener quórum

quota *n* cuota *f*; **above ~** por encima de la cuota; **~ fixing** *n* fijación de cuotas *f*; **~ sampling** *n* muestreo por cuotas *m*; **~ system** *n* sistema de cuotas *m*

quotable *adj* cotizable

quotation *n* (on stock market) cotización *f*; (estimate) presupuesto *m*; **ask for a ~** pedir un presupuesto; **give sb a ~** darle *or* hacerle un presupuesto a alguien; **~ board** *n* (Stock) tablero de cotización *m*; **~ marks** *n pl* comillas *f pl*

quote[1] *n* (estimate) presupuesto *m*; (on stock market) cotización *f*; **ask for a ~** pedir un presupuesto; **give sb a ~** darle *or* hacerle un presupuesto a alguien; **in** *o* **between ~s** entre comillas; **~ value** *n* valor de cotización *m*

quote[2] *vt* (on stock market) cotizar; (price) dar, ofrecer; (date) proponer; (reference number) indicar; (example) dar; (instance) citar

quoted *adj* (securities, shares) cotizado; (company) cotizado en bolsa; (price) de cotización

quotient *n* cociente *m*

QWERTY keyboard *n* teclado QWERTY *m*

QWL *abbr* (▶**quality of working life**) calidad de vida en el trabajo *f*

Rr

R/A *abbr* (▸**refer to acceptor**) referir *or* remitir al aceptante

race *n* raza *f*; ∼ **discrimination** *n* discriminación racial *f*; **R∼ Relations Act** *n ley de relaciones interraciales*

racial *adj* racial; ∼ **discrimination** *n* discriminación racial *f*

rack *n* (for letters, documents) organizador *m*; (for luggage) rejilla *f*, portaequipajes *m*; (Comp) casillero *m*; **go to ∼ and ruin** (infrml) venirse abajo

racket *n* (infrml) chanchullo *m*

racketeering *n* crimen organizado *m*

radar *n* radar *m*; ∼ **alert** *n* (Stock) vigilancia activa *f*

radiation *n* radiación *f*

radical *adj* radical

radio *n* (broadcasting, medium) radio *f*; (set) radio *f or m* AmL; **on the ∼** en la radio; ∼ **advertising** *n* publicidad en la radio *f*; ∼ **audience** *n* audiencia de radio *f*; ∼ **broadcast** *n* emisión de radio *f*; ∼ **commercial** *n* anuncio comercial en la radio *m*; ∼ **program** AmE, ∼ **programme** BrE *n* programa de radio *m*; ∼ **station** *n* emisora de radio *f*

radiotelegram *n* radiotelegrama *m*

radiotelegraphy *n* radiotelegrafía *f*

radiotelephone *n* radioteléfono *m*

radiotelephony *n* radiotelefonía *f*

raft *n* (of policies, measures) serie *f*

rag *n* (infrml) periodicucho *m* (infrml); ∼ **trade** *n* (infrml) industria de la confección *f*

ragged *adj* desigual, desordenado, irregular

raid[1] *n* (takeover attempt) operación de tiburoneo *f*; (by police) redada *f*

raid[2] *vt* (house, building) hacer una redada en; AmE (personnel, executives) llevarse, robar; ∼ **a company** absorber una compañía de manera hostil; ∼ **the market** (jarg) especular en el mercado

raider *n* tiburón *m*

rail *n* (for train) riel *m*; (railway) ferrocarril *m*; ∼**-air link** *n* enlace rail-avión *m*; ∼ **link** *n* conexión ferroviaria *f*; ∼ **network** *n* red ferroviaria *f*; ∼ **strike** *n* huelga ferroviaria *f*; ∼ **system** *n* sistema ferroviario *m*; ∼ **transport** BrE, ∼ **transportation** AmE *n* transporte por ferrocarril *m*; ∼ **traveler**

AmE, ∼ **traveller** BrE *n* viajero(-a) de ferrocarril *m,f*

railcar *n* AmE (*cf* ▸**railway carriage** BrE, ▸**railway coach** BrE) vagón *m* de ferrocarril *or* de tren

railhead *n* cabeza de línea *f*

railroad *n* AmE (*cf* ▸**railway** BrE) ferrocarril *m*; ∼ **network** *n* AmE (*cf* ▸**railway network** BrE) red de ferrocarriles *f*; ∼ **service** *n* AmE (*cf* ▸**railway service** BrE) servicio de ferrocarril *m*; ∼ **station** *n* AmE (*cf* ▸**railway station** BrE, ▸**train station** BrE) estación de ferrocarril *f*; ∼ **system** *n* (*cf* ▸**railway system** BrE) red de ferrocarriles *f*; ∼ **timetable** *n* AmE (*cf* ▸**railway timetable** BrE) horario de trenes *m*

railway *n* BrE (*cf* ▸**railroad** AmE) ferrocarril *m*; ∼ **carriage** *n* BrE, ∼ **coach** *n* BrE (*cf* ▸**railcar** AmE) vagón *m* de ferrocarril *or* de tren; ∼ **network** *n* (*cf* ▸**railroad network** AmE) red de ferrocarriles *f*; ∼ **service** *n* BrE (*cf* ▸**railroad service** AmE) servicio de ferrocarril *m*; ∼ **station** *n* BrE (*cf* ▸**railroad station** AmE) estación de ferrocarril *f*; ∼ **system** *n* (*cf* ▸**railroad system** AmE) red de ferrocarriles *f*; ∼ **timetable** *n* BrE (*cf* ▸**railroad timetable** AmE) horario de trenes *m*

rainforest *n* selva tropical *f*

rainmaker *n* AmE (jarg) *abogado que atrae a nuevos clientes para su despacho*

raise[1] *vt* (price, salary) subir, aumentar; (consciousness, awarenesss) aumentar, acrecentar; (standing, reputation) aumentar; (standard) mejorar; (money, funds) recaudar; (cheque) extender; (capital) reunir; (tax) imponer; (invoice) preparar; (embargo) levantar; (objection, question) plantear; (subject) sacar; (fears, doubt) suscitar, dar lugar a; ∼ **a loan (against sth)** conseguir *or* obtener un préstamo poniendo algo como garantía

raise[2] *n* AmE (*cf* ▸**rise** BrE) (in pay) aumento *m*

rake in *vt* (infrml) recoger; **they're raking it in** se están forrando (infrml)

rake-off *n* (infrml) tajada *f* (infrml); **take** *o* **get a ∼ from sth** sacar tajada de algo

rally[1] *n* (of market, prices) recuperación *f*

rally[2] [1] *vi* (currency, prices) recuperarse; (market) reactivarse, recuperarse [2] *vt* (support) conseguir

RAM *abbr* (▸**random access memory**) RAM *f* (memoria de acceso aleatorio); ∼ **disk** *n* disco de RAM *m*

ramp *n* (slope) rampa *f*; BrE (infrml) (swindle) engaño *m*, estafa *f*

R&D *abbr* (▸**research and development**) I&D (investigación y desarrollo); ∼ **expenditure** *n* gastos de I&D *m pl*

random *adj* (check, sample, variation) aleatorio; (selection, sampling) al azar; **at** ∼ aleatoriamente, al azar; ∼ **access** *n* acceso aleatorio *m*; ∼ **access memory** *n* memoria de acceso aleatorio *f*; ∼ **channel** *n* canal probabilístico *m*; ∼ **number** *n* número aleatorio *m*; ∼**-number generator** *n* generador de números aleatorios *m*; ∼ **observation method** *n* método de observación aleatoria *m*; ∼ **walk theory** *n* teoría del camino aleatorio *f*

randomization *n* aleatorización *f*

randomize *vt* randomizar

randomly *adv* aleatoriamente

range[1] *n* (of products, prices, options) ámbito *m*; (scope) ámbito *m*, campo *m*; (Stock) banda *f*; (Tax) abanico *m*

range[2] *vi* (extend) extenderse; (numbers) oscilar; ∼ **from sth to sth** *o* **between sth and sth** oscilar entre algo y algo

rank[1] *n* (status) categoría *f*; **close** ∼**s** cerrar filas; **pull** ∼ **(on sb)** hacer valer sus privilegios (con alguien); ∼**-and-file** *n* personal del nivel más bajo *m*

rank[2] [1] *vt* clasificar
[2] *vi* clasificarse, figurar; **rank above** *vt* figurar por encima de; **rank after** *vt* figurar después de; **rank below** *vt* figurar por debajo de

ranking *n* clasificación *f*; ∼ **in order of seniority** *n* clasificación por antigüedad *f*

rapid *adj* (growth, turnover) rápido; ∼ **transit system** *n* AmE sistema de tránsito rápido *m*

raster *n* (Comp) trama *f*

ratchet effect *n* efecto *m* palanca *or* de trinquete

rate[1] *n* (speed) velocidad *f*; (rhythm) ritmo *m*; (level, ratio) razón *f*; (price, charge) tarifa *f*; **at a** ∼**of 10,000 euros a month** a razón de 10,000 euros mensuales; **the work is paid at a** ∼**of $20 per hour** el trabajo se paga a (razón de) 20 dólares por hora; **at the top** ∼ (Tax) al tipo más alto; **a high/low hourly** ∼ **of pay** una paga por hora alta/baja; **take the** ∼ (Stock) aceptar el porcentaje; ∼ **of adoption** *n* tasa de adopción *f*; ∼ **asked** *n* (Stock) coeficiente solicitado *m*; ∼ **ceiling** *n* tasa tope *f*; ∼ **cutting** *n* recorte de precios *m*; ∼ **of decay** *n* (of options) índice de decadencia *m*; ∼ **of depreciation** *n* tipo de depreciación *m*; ∼ **of discount** *n* tipo de descuento *m*; ∼ **of exchange** *n* tipo de

cambio *m*; ∼ **of exploitation** *n* proporción de explotación *f*; ∼ **fixing** *n* fijación de tarifas *f*; ∼ **floor** *n* tipo mínimo *m*; ∼ **for the job** *n* precio según el trabajo *m*; ∼ **of increase** *n* tasa de incremento *f*; ∼ **of interest** *n* tasa de interés *f*; ∼ **of relief** *n* (Tax) tipo de la deducción *m*; ∼ **resetter** *n* mecanismo de puesta a cero del tipo *m*; ∼ **of return** *n* tasa de rendimiento *f*; ∼ **of return on capital employed** *n* tasa de rendimiento del capital invertido *f*; ∼ **of surplus value** *n* tasa de valor superávit *f*; ∼ **of tax** *n*, ∼ **of taxation** *n* tipo impositivo *m*; ∼ **variance** *n* varianza de tipo *f*; ∼ **war** *n* guerra de tarifas *f*

rate[2] *vt* (rank, regard) estimar, valorar; (classify) clasificar; (merit) merecer

rateable value *n* BrE (obs) (*cf* ▸**assessed valuation** AmE) valor catastral *m*

ratification *n* (of treaty) ratificación *f*

ratify *vt* (treaty) ratificar

rating *n* (classification) clasificación *f*; (Fin) tarificación *f*; ∼ **agency** *n* organismo de clasificación (de valores) *m*; ∼ **scale** *n* escala de valoración *f*

ratings *n pl* índice de audiencia *m*; **go up in the** ∼ subir en los niveles de popularidad

ratio *n* (proportion) proporción *f*, ratio *m*, relación *f*; (coefficient) coeficiente *m*; **in a** ∼ **of two to one** en una proporción *or* relación de dos a uno; **in inverse/direct** ∼ **to sth** en razón inversa/directa a algo, de forma inversamente/directamente proporcional a algo; ∼ **spread** *n* compra o venta de opciones en proporciones diferentes

ration *vt* racionar

rational *adj* (expectations, decision) racional; (management) racionalizado

rationale *n* razones *f pl*; **the** ∼ **behind a decision** la base lógica detrás de una decisión

rationalization *n* racionalización *f*; ∼ **program** AmE, ∼ **programme** BrE *n* programa de racionalización *m*

rationalize *vt* racionalizar

rationing *n* racionamiento *m*

rat race *n* (infrml) carrera de la vida moderna *f*

raw *adj* (data) bruto, no procesado; ∼ **materials** *n pl* materias primas *f pl*

RCH *abbr* (▸**Recognized Clearing House**) Cámara de Compensación Autorizada *f*

rcvd *abbr* (▸**received**) recibido

Rd. *abbr* (▸**road**) carretera *f*

RD *abbr* (▸**refer to drawer**) RD (dirigirse al librador); (▸**reserve deposit**) depósito de reserva *m*

RDB *abbr* (▸**relational database**) BDR (base de datos relacional)

re. *abbr* (▸**regarding**) acerca de, con referencia a, en cuanto a

RE *abbr* (▸**Royal Exchange**) Bolsa de Valores de Londres

reach¹ *vt* (destination, limit, audience) llegar a; (stage, figure, agreement, compromise) llegar a, alcanzar; (contact) contactar con, ponerse en contacto con; ~ **a total of** alcanzar un total de

reach² *n* alcance *m*

reachback *n* (Tax) retroactividad *f*

react *vi* reaccionar; ~ **well under stress** reaccionar bien estando bajo tensión

reaction *n* reacción *f*; ~ **time** *n* tiempo de reacción *m*

reactionary¹ *adj* reaccionario

reactionary² *n* reaccionario(-a) *m,f*

reactivate *vt* (software) reactivar

reactivation *n* reactivación

reactive *adj* (strategy) reactivo

read¹ *vt* (book, words, program) leer; (sign, mood, situation) interpretar; (proofs) corregir; **take sth as read** (assume) dar algo por sentado; (minutes) dar algo por leído; ~ **the tape** (Stock) leer la cinta; **read over** *vt*, **read through** *vt* leer; **read up on** *vt* estudiar, investigar

read² *n* lectura *f*; ~ **head** *n* cabeza de lectura *f*; ~ **notification** *n* confirmación de lectura *f*; ~**-only memory** *n* memoria de sólo lectura *f*; ~**/write** *n* lector/escritor *m*; ~**-write head** *n* cabeza lectora-grabadora *f*

readable *adj* legible

reader *n* (person) lector(a) *m,f*; (device) lector *m*

readership *n* (of newspaper, book) número de lectores *m*; ~ **profile** *n* perfil de los lectores *m*

readjustment *n* reajuste *m*

ReadMe file *n* fichero de lectura *m*

readvertise ⨍1⨍ *vt* (post, item) anunciar de nuevo
⨍2⨍ *vi* volver a poner un anuncio

ready *adj* listo; **get** ~ **(for sth/to do sth)** prepararse (para algo/para hacer algo); **get** *o* **make sth** ~ preparar algo; **a** ~ **market for sth** un mercado muy receptivo para algo; **be** ~ **to do sth** (prepared) estar listo para hacer algo; (willing) estar dispuesto a hacer algo; ~ **to hand** a mano; ~ **cash** *n*, ~ **money** *n* dinero *m* en efectivo *or* en metálico; ~ **reckoner** *n* baremo *m*

ready-to-wear *adj* (clothes) de confección

reaffirm *vt* reafirmar

reafforestation *n* BrE reforestación *f*, repoblación forestal *f*

real *adj* (reason, name) verdadero; (cost, earnings, growth) real; **in** ~ **terms** en términos reales; ~ **address** *n* (Comp) dirección real *f*; ~ **asset** *n* activo inmobiliario *m*; ~ **exchange rate** *n* tasa de cambio real *f*; ~ **interest rate** *n* tasa de interés real *f*; ~ **number** *n* número real *m*; ~ **rate of return** *n* tasa real de rendimiento *f*; ~ **storage** *n* memoria real *f*; ~ **time** *n* tiempo real *m*; ~**-time chat** *n* charla en tiempo real *f*; ~**-time transmission** *n* transmisión en tiempo real *f*

real estate *n* bienes *m pl* inmuebles *or* raíces; ~ **agency** *n* AmE (*cf* ▸**estate agency** BrE) agencia inmobiliaria *f*; ~ **company** *n* AmE empresa *f or* sociedad *f* inmobiliaria; ~ **funds** *n pl* AmE fondos inmobiliarios *m pl*; ~ **investment** *n* AmE inversión inmobiliaria *f*; ~ **investment trust** *n* AmE consorcio de inversiones inmobiliarias *m*; ~ **market** *n* AmE mercado *m* inmobiliario *or* de bienes raíces *or* de propiedades

realign *vt* (currencies, positions) realinear; (salaries) reajustar

realignment *n* (of currencies, positions) realineamento *m*; (of salaries) reajuste *m*

realism *n* realismo *m*

realistic *adj* realista

realizable *adj* (assets, property, plan) realizable; (ambition) alcanzable

realization *n* (of assets, plan) realización *f*

realize *vt* (assets) realizar; (profit) producir; (ambition) hacer realidad; (goal) conseguir; (potential) desarrollar; (plan) llevar a cabo; (become aware of) darse cuenta de

realized *adj* (gains, losses) realizado

reallocate *vt* (redistribute) redistribuir; (reassign) reasignar

reallocation *n* (redistribution) redistribución *f*; (reassignation) reasignación *f*

reallowance *n* doble bonificación *f*, doble compensación *f*

Realpolitik *n* política real *f*

realtor *n* AmE (*cf* ▸**estate agent** BrE) agente inmobiliario(-a) *m,f*

reap *vt* (benefits) recoger; ~ **the rewards** disfrutar las gratificaciones

reapply *vi* volver a presentarse; ~ **for a job** volver a presentarse para un trabajo

reappoint *vt* volver a nombrar

reappointment *n* nuevo nombramiento *m*

reappraisal *n* revaluación *f*

reappraise *vt* revaluar

reason *n* razón *f*; **by** ~ **of sth** en virtud de algo; **do anything within** ~ hacer cualquier cosa dentro de lo razonable; **the** ~ **for sth/ for doing sth** la razón *or* el motivo de algo/ para hacer algo; **for** ~**s best known to**

⋯⟩

herself por razones *or* motivos que sólo ella conoce; **for health** ∼s por razones *or* motivos de salud; **for no** ∼ por ninguna razón; **listen to** *o* **see** ∼ atender a razones; **make sb see** ∼ hacer entrar en razón a alguien; **it stands to** ∼ es lógico; **with (good)** ∼ con razón

reasonable *adj* (offer, request, expense, person) razonable; (price, sum) razonable, moderado

reasonably *adv* razonablemente

reasoned *adj* razonado

reasoning *n* razonamiento *m*

reassess *vt* (chances, situation, issue) volver a estudiar, reexaminar; (Tax) reevaluar

reassessment *n* (of chances, situation, issue) nuevo estudio *m*, reexaminación *f*; (Tax) reevaluación fiscal *f*

reassign *vt* (funds) reasignar

reassignment *n* reasignación *f*

rebase *vt* establecer una nueva base para

rebate *n* (of money paid) reembolso *m*; (discount) bonificación *f*, rebaja *f*

reboot *vt* reinicializar

rebooting *n* reiniciación *f*

rebrand *vt* cambiar la marca de

rebranding *n* cambio de marca *m*

rebuild *vt* (building, economy) reconstruir; (trust, faith) volver a cimentar, restablecer; (stocks) reponer

rebuy *vt* recomprar

recalculate *vt* recalcular

recall[1] *n* (of product) retirada *f*; (of option) recompra *f*; (memory) memoria *f*; ∼ **test** *n* test de respuesta *m*

recall[2] *vt* (product) retirar; (option) recomprar

recapitalization *n* recapitalización *f*

recapitalize *vt* recapitalizar

recapturable *adj* (depreciation) recuperable

recapture *vt* recuperar; (debt) refundir; (Acc) recobrar

recast *vt* (system, project) reestructurar; (text) volver a escribir *or* redactar

recede *vi* (prospect) desvanecerse; (danger) alejarse

receipt[1] *n* (document) recibo *m*; (act) recibo *m*, recepción *f*; **acknowledge** ∼ **of sth** acusar recibo de algo; **be in** ∼ **of sth** (letter, payment) estar en posesión de algo; **make out a** ∼ extender un recibo; **on** ∼ **of sth** a la recepción de algo; ∼ **book** *n* talonario de recibos *m*; ∼ **for payment** *n* resguardo de un pago *m*; ∼ **of goods** *n* recepción de mercancías *f*; ∼ **slip** *n* justificante *m*; ∼ **stamp** *n* sello de recibo *m*

receipt[2] *vt* (bill, invoice) poner el sello de 'pagado' en

receipts *n pl* ingresos *m pl*, entradas *f pl*; ∼ **and payments account** *n* cuenta de cobros y pagos *f*

receivable *adj* a *or* por cobrar; ∼ **basis** *n* base de cuentas a cobrar *f*

receivables *n pl* cuentas a cobrar *f pl*

receive [1] *vt* (letter, visit) recibir; (answer) obtener; (payment) recibir, cobrar, percibir; (stolen goods) comerciar con; (proposal, news, idea) recibir, acoger; ∼ **sth against payment** recibir algo contra pago; ∼**d with thanks the sum of £30** recibí (conforme) la suma de 30 libras

[2] *vi* comerciar con mercancía robada

receiver *n* (in bankruptcy) síndico(-a) *m,f*, depositario(-a) judicial *m,f*; (addressee) destinatario(-a) *m,f*, consignatario(-a) *m,f*; (part of telephone) auricular *m*; (for radio, television signals) receptor *m*; (of stolen goods) comerciante de mercancía robada *mf*; **at** ∼**'s risk** por cuenta y riesgo del receptor; **call in the** ∼s solicitar la suspensión de pagos; **be in the hands of the** ∼s estar en suspensión de pagos; **pick up** *o* **lift the** ∼ levantar el auricular; **put down** *o* **replace the** ∼ colgar el auricular; ∼ **and manager** *n* (in bankruptcy) síndico(-a) *m,f* or depositario(-a) *m,f* y administrador(a) *m,f*

receivership *n* administración judicial *f*; **go into** ∼ pasar a administración judicial; **put into** ∼ poner en manos de la administración judicial

receiving *adj* (bank, station) receptor; (office) de recepción

reception *n* (place, social event, for radio or television) recepción *f*; (response, reaction) recibimiento *m*, acogida *f*; **I'll meet you at** *o* **in** ∼ te veo en recepción; ∼ **area** *n* área de recepción *f*; ∼ **committee** *n* comité de bienvenida *m*; ∼ **desk** *n* recepción *f*

receptionist *n* recepcionista *mf*

recession *n* recesión *f*; **be in/go into a** ∼ estar/entrar en recesión

recessionary *adj* (phase, gap) de recesión

recipient *n* (of letter) destinatario(-a) *m,f*; (of allowance) beneficiario(-a) *m,f*; ∼ **bank** *n* banco receptor *m*

reciprocal *adj* (agreement, trade) recíproco; (buying) bilateral; ∼ **taxation agreement** *n* acuerdo de imposición recíproca *m*

reciprocally *adv* a título de reciprocidad

reciprocity *n* reciprocidad *f*

reckon *vt* calcular; **reckon up** *vt* sumar, calcular

reckoning *n* (calculation) cálculos *m pl*; (opinion) opinión *f*; **by my** ∼ según mis cálculos; **in the final** ∼ en el momento de la verdad; **in my** ∼ a mi opinión, a mi juicio; **a time of** ∼ un momento de hacer cuentas

reclaim *vt* (rights) reclamar, reivindicar; (land) reclamar; (luggage) recoger; **I filled in a form to ~ tax** llené un formulario para que me devolvieran parte de los impuestos

reclamation *n* (of rights) reivindicación *f*; (of land) rescate *f*; (of cargo, waste) recuperación *f*; (of luggage) recogida *f*

reclassification *n* reclasificación *f*; **~ entry** *n* (Acc) asiento de reclasificación *m*

reclassify *vt* reclasificar

recognition *n* reconocimiento *m*; **the union is fighting for ~** el sindicato está luchando por obtener el reconocimiento oficial; **in ~ of sth** en reconocimiento de algo; **~ test** *n* (S&M) prueba de reconocimiento *f*

recognize *vt* (rights, union) reconocer; **~ the gravity of the situation** reconocer *or* admitir la gravedad de la situación; **~ the need for change** reconocer que es necesario cambiar

recognized *adj* (union, body) reconocido; **R~ Clearing House** *n* Cámara de Compensación Autorizada *f*; **~ investment exchange** *n* bolsa de inversión reconocida *f*

recommend *vt* recomendar; **~ doing sth** recomendar *or* aconsejar hacer algo; **~ sb for a job** recomendar a alguien para un puesto; **a plan with nothing to ~ it** un plan sin atractivos

recommendation *n* recomendación *f*; **on sb's ~** por recomendación de alguien

recommended retail price *n* precio de venta al público *m*

recommissioned *adj* vuelto al servicio

recompense[1] *vt* (for damage, loss) indemnizar, compensar; (for efforts) recompensar

recompense[2] *n* (for damage, loss) indemnización *f*, compensación *f*; (for efforts) recompensación *f*

recompilation *n* recopilación *f*

recompile *vt* recopilar

reconcile *vt* (accounts, figures, theories) conciliar; (enemies, factions) reconciliar

reconciliation *n* (of accounts, ideas, aims) conciliación *f*; (of people) reconciliación *f*; **~ account** *n* cuenta de conciliación *f*; **~ statement** *n* estado de conciliación *m*; **~ table** *n* cuadro de conciliación *m*

recondition *vt* reacondicionar

reconfiguration *n* reconfiguración *f*

reconfigure *vt* reconfigurar

reconnaissance survey *n* estudio preliminar *m*

reconsider [1] *vt* reconsiderar; **~ an assessment** (Tax) reconsiderar una liquidación
    [2] *vi* recapacitar

reconstruct *vt* (company) reestructurar, reconstruir

reconstruction *n* (of company) reestructuración *f*, reconstrucción *f*

reconversion *n* reconversión *f*

reconvert *vt* reconvertir

reconveyance *n* restitución *f*

record[1] *n* (document) documento *m*; (list) registro *m*; (file) archivo *m*; (dossier) expediente *m*; (minutes) acta *f*; (note) nota *f*; (of criminal) antecedentes (penales) *m pl*; (best achievement) récord *m*; (musical) disco *m*; **according to our ~s** según nuestros datos; **beat/break a ~** batir/superar un récord; **(just) for the ~** para que conste; **please keep this copy for your ~s** conserve esta copia para su información; **make/keep a ~ of sth** hacer/llevar un registro de algo; **it is a matter of ~ that...** hay constancia de que...; **off the ~** extraoficialmente; **on ~** registrado; **put sth on ~** hacer constar algo; **put** *o* **set the ~ straight** dejar *or* poner las cosas claras; **let the ~ show that...** que conste en acta que...; **~-breaking** *adj* (results, sales, profits) sin precedentes; **~ card** *n* ficha *f*; **~ company** *n* casa discográfica *f*; **~ date** *n* fecha de registro *f*; **~ format** *n* formato de registro *m*; **~ keeper** *n* archivador(a) *m,f*, archivero(-a) *m,f*, archivista *mf*; **~ key** *n* clave de registro *f*; **~s management** *n* dirección *f or* gerencia *f* de registros

record[2] *adj* (results, sales, profits) sin precedentes; **in ~ time** en un tiempo récord

record[3] *vt* (write down) anotar; (in minutes) hacer constar; (register) registrar; (programme, CD) grabar; **the minutes ~ that...** consta en el acta que...; **~ a meeting** registrar una reunión

recorded *adj* (amount, information) registrado; (fact) del que se tiene constancia; (music, programme) grabado; **~ delivery** *n* BrE (obs) correo certificado con acuso de recibo *m*

recoup *vt* (costs) recuperar; (losses) resarcirse de

recourse *n* recurso *m*; **have ~ to sth/sb** recurrir a algo/alguien; **without ~ to sth** sin recurrir a algo; **~ loan** *n* préstamo con aval *m*

recover [1] *vt* (investment, lead, position, metal) recuperar
    [2] *vi* (economy, industry) recuperarse, repuntar, reactivarse

recoverable *adj* (cost, error, material) recuperable

recovery *n* (of market, data, expenses) recuperación *f*; (of debts) cobro *m*; (of economy, industry) recuperación *f*, repunte *m*, reactivación *f*; (in profits, prices) mejora *f*, ····⟶

repunte m; (reacquisition) reactivación f; ~ **plan** n plan de rehabilitación m; ~ **scheme** n BrE programa de recuperación m; ~ **vehicle** n vehículo recuperador m

recreation n (leisure) esparcimiento m; (pastime) forma de esparcimiento f, pasatiempo m

recreational adj (facility) recreativo

recruit[1] vt reclutar, contratar

recruit[2] n recluta mf

recruitment n (of staff) contratación m; ~ **advertising** n publicidad de contratación f; ~ **agency** n agencia de colocaciones f, oficina f de empleo or de trabajo; ~ **bonus** n bonificación por contratación f; ~ **consultant** n asesor(a) de selección m,f; ~ **manager** n gerente de contratación mf

rectification n rectificación f

rectify vt rectificar

recto n recto m, anverso m

recyclable adj reciclable

recycle vt reciclar

recycled adj (paper) reciclado

recycling n reciclaje m

red[1] adj rojo; **R~ Book** n AmE (infrml) (Fin) Libro Rojo m; ~ **clause** n cláusula roja f; ~ **goods** n pl (jarg) bienes de rápido consumo y pronta reposición; ~ **herring** n folleto informativo de una nueva emisión m; ~**-herring prospectus** n prospecto preliminar m; ~ **tape** n trámites burocráticos m pl

red[2] n rojo m; **be in/out of the** ~ estar en/no estar en números rojos

red. abbr (▶redeemable) reembolsable

redeem vt (debt, mortgage) pagar, liquidar; (coupon) canjear; (from pawnshop) desempeñar; (fault, error) compensar; (good name) rescatar

redeemable adj (shares, stock) rescatable; (bond) amortizable; ~ **preference share** n acción preferente amortizable f

redeemed adj (share, debenture) rescatado

redelivery n devolución f, retorno m

redemption n (of debt) liquidación f, cancelación f, amortización f; (of promissory note) cancelación f; (of coupon) canje m; ~ **before due date** n reembolso anticipado m, amortización antes del vencimiento f; ~ **bond** n bono de amortización m; ~ **call** n aviso de amortización m; ~ **date** n fecha f de amortización or de vencimiento; ~ **fee** n tasa de amortización f; ~ **fund** n fondo de rescate m; ~ **premium** n prima f de amortización or de rescate; ~ **price** n precio de rescate m; ~ **table** n cuadro de amortización m; ~ **value** n valor de rescate m; ~ **yield** n rendimiento de una acción en la fecha de rescate

redeploy vt (redistribute) redistribuir; (staff) reorganizar

redeployment n (redistribution) redistribución f; (of staff) reorganización f

redeposit vt redepositar

redesign vt rediseñar

redevelop vt reorganizar

redevelopment n reorganización f

redirect vt (letter, parcel) enviar a una nueva dirección

rediscount n redescuento m; ~ **rate** n tipo de redescuento m

rediscountable adj redescontable

rediscounter n redescontador m

rediscounting n redescuento m

redistribute vt redistribuir

redistribution n redistribución f

redlining n (jarg) negación de hipotecas sobre terrenos o propiedades

redraft[1] vt volver a redactar

redraft[2] n (of document) nuevo borrador m; (Bank) giro renovado m

redress[1] n reparación f; **have no** ~ no tener derecho a ningún tipo de compensación; **seek** ~ **through the courts** tratar de obtener reparación or compensación judicial

redress[2] vt (error, wrong) reparar, enmendar; ~ **the balance** restablecer el equilibrio

reduce vt (number, amount, investment, image) reducir; (prices, taxes, rent) reducir, bajar; (expenses) mermar, recortar; (goods) rebajar

reduced adj (rate, fare, tax) reducido; **buy sth at a** ~ **price** comprar algo a precio reducido; ~ **lead time** n tiempo de entrega reducido m

reduction n (in numbers, size, spending, capital) reducción f; (in prices, charges) rebaja f; (in interest rates) recorte m; **a 5%** ~ **o a** ~ **of 5%** una rebaja or un descuento del 5%

redundancy n (superfluity) redundancia f; BrE (loss of job) despido m; ~ **benefit** n BrE indemnización por despido f; ~ **check** n (Comp) verificación por redundancia f; ~ **consultation** n BrE consulta por despido colectivo f; ~ **letter** n BrE carta de despido f; ~ **pay** n BrE compensación por despido f; ~ **payment** n BrE compensación por despido f; ~ **procedure** n BrE procedimiento de despido m

redundant adj (not needed, outdated) redundante; BrE (employee) despedido; **make** ~ BrE (staff) cesar, despedir, echar

re-educate vt reeducar

reel n carrete m; ~**-fed** adj con carrete colocado

re-elect vt reelegir

re-election n reelección f; **stand for ~** volver a presentarse como candidato

re-embark vi reembarcarse

re-emphasize vt volver a insistir en

re-employ vt volver a emplear

re-employment n reempleo m

re-endorsement n reendoso m

re-engage vt (employee) volver a contratar

re-engineer vt reconfigurar

re-engineering n reingeniería f

re-enter vt (data) reintroducir por teclado

re-establish vt (order, custom, contact) restablecer

re-establishment n restablecimiento m

re-evaluate vt revaluar

re-evaluation n (of assets) revaluación f

re-examination n reexamen m

re-examine vt reexaminar

re-export[1] vt reexportar

re-export[2] n reexportación f

re-exportation n reexportación f

re-exporter n reexportador(a) m,f

ref. abbr (▸**reference**) referencia f; **your ~** su referencia

refer vt (to source of information) remitir; (to place) enviar, mandar; **~ sth back to sb** remitir algo a alguien; **~ a proposal to the board** remitir una propuesta a la junta; **~ to acceptor** referir or remitir al aceptante; **~ to drawer** devolver al librador; **refer to** vt (mention) hacer referencia a, aludir a; (allude to) referirse a; (apply to, concern) atañer a; (consult) consultar, remitirse a; **I ~ to your letter of 18th March** con relación a su carta del 18 de marzo

referee n (for job) referencia f; **act as a ~ for sb** hacer de referencia para alguien

reference n referencia f; **by ~ to sth** con respecto a algo; **for future ~** para referencia futura; **have excellent ~s** (from previous employer) tener referencias excelentes; **in ~ to sth** en lo que afecta a algo; **make (a) ~ to sth** hacer referencia a algo; **take up ~s** (from previous employer) pedir referencias; **with ~ to sth** con referencia a algo, en cuanto a algo; **your ~** su referencia; **~ book** n libro de consulta m; **~ currency** n divisa de referencia f; **~ file** n fichero de referencias m; **~ group** n grupo de referencia m; **~ level** n nivel de referencia m; **~ material** n material de referencia m; **~ number** n número de referencia m; **~ point** n punto de referencia m

referendum n referéndum m; **hold a ~ (on sth)** celebrar un referéndum (sobre algo)

referral n remisión f

referring to prep referido a

refinance vt refinanciar

refinance credit n crédito de refinanciación m

refinancing n refinanciación f; **~ risk** n riesgo relacionado con la refinanciación m

refine vt (Internet search) refinar; (design, style) pulir, perfeccionar

refined adj (technique, analysis) refinado

refinery n refinería f

refining n refinación f

reflate [1] vt (economy) reflacionar [2] vi experimentar una reflación

reflation n reflación f

reflationary adv reactivador

reflect vt (situation, feeling, mood) reflejar; **be ~ed in sth** reflejarse en algo

refloat vt (company) reflotar

refloating n reflotamiento m

refocusing AmE, **refocussing** BrE n nuevo enfoque m

reforestation n (cf ▸**reafforestation** BrE) reforestatión f, repoblación forestal f

reform[1] n reforma; **~ package** n paquete de reformas m; **~ program** AmE, **~ programme** BrE n programa de reforma m

reform[2] vt reformar

reformat vt (disk) reformatear

refresh vt (Comp) regenerar

refresher n BrE (Law) honorarios adicionales m pl; **~ course** n curso de actualización m

refresh rate adj (Comp) velocidad de regeneración f

refuel [1] vt (plane, ship) reabastecer de combustible; (speculation) intensificar [2] vi (plane, ship) repostar, reabastecerse de combustible

refugee n refugiado(-a) m,f; **~ capital** n capital errante m

refund[1] n (of expenses, deposit) reembolso m; (of tax) devolución f; **full cash ~ if not satisfied** le devolvemos el importe total si no queda satisfecho; **no ~s** no se admiten devoluciones; **~ slip** n recibo de reintegro m

refund[2] vt (payment) devolver, reintegrar; (expenses, postage) reembolsar; **they wouldn't ~ me the full amount** no quisieron devolverme el importe total

refundable adj (deposit, tax credit) reembolsable

refurbish vt renovar, reacondicionar

refurbishment n renovación f, reacondicionamiento m

refusal n (of offer) rechazo m; (of permission, request) denegación f; (to do sth) negativa f; **give sb first ~** darle a alguien la primera opción (de compra); **their ~ to help** su negativa a ayudar

refuse[1] [1] *vt* (offer) rehusar, rechazar;
(permission) denegar; **~ acceptance of a
draft** rechazar *or* rehusar la aceptación de
una letra; **~ sb sth** negarle algo a alguien;
~ to do sth negarse a hacer algo
[2] *vi* negarse

refuse[2] *n*, residuos *m pl*, desperdicios
m pl; **~ collection** *n* recogida de basuras *f*;
~ disposal *n* evacuación de residuos *f*

regard[1] *n* (esteem) estima *f*; (consideration)
consideración *f*; **have a high ~ for sb** tener
a alguien en gran estima; **in this/that ~** en
este/ese respecto; **in *o* with ~ to sth/sb** con
respecto a algo/alguien

regard[2] *vt* considerar; **as ~s sth/sb** en *or*
por lo que se refiere a algo/alguien

regarding *prep* acerca de, con referencia
a, en cuanto a

regd. *abbr* (▶**registered**) registrado

regime *n* régimen *m*

region *n* región *f*; **in the ~ of sth**
(approximately) alrededor de algo

regional *adj* (market, development, trend)
regional; (press) regional, de provincia; **~
manager** *n* director(a) regional *m,f*; **~
office** *n* oficina regional *f*

regionally *adv* regionalmente

register[1] *n* (book, in computer) registro *m*;
(Stock) registrador *m*; (cash register) caja
(registradora) *f*; **~ of companies** *n*
registro mercantil *m*; **R~ of Members** *n*
registro de accionistas *m*; **~ office** *n* BrE
registro civil *m*

register[2] [1] *vt* (letter, package) mandar
certificado; (business name) registrar; (death,
birth) inscribir, registrar; (ship, car)
matricular; (complaint) presentar; (protest)
hacer constar; **~ a high** (Stock) registrar un
alza
[2] *vi* (enrol) inscribirse; (at hotel) registrarse

registered[1] *adj* (bond, proprietor, user)
registrado; (title) registrado, nominativo;
(representative) autorizado; **~ unemployed**
registrado desempleado; **~ address** *n*
domicilio social *m*; **~ broker** *n* corredor(a)
titulado(-a) *m,f*; **~ charity** *n* institución
benéfica registrada *f*; **~ company** *n*
sociedad legalmente constituida *f*; **R~
International Exchange** *n* Bolsa
Internacional Oficial de Valores *f*; **~ letter**
n carta certificada *f*; **~ office** *n* domicilio
social *m*; **~ options broker** *n* broker *mf or*
intermediario(-a) *m,f* de opciones
registrado(-a); **~ options trader** *n*
operador(a) de opciones autorizado(-a) *m,f*;
~ owner *n* (of bond) propietario(-a) nominal
m,f; **~ post** *n* BrE (*cf* ▶**certified mail** AmE)
correo certificado *m*; **~ share** *n* acción
nominativa *f*; **~ shareholder** *n*,

~ stockholder *n* accionista nominativo(-a)
m,f; **~ trademark** *n* marca registrada *f*

registrant *n* (of securities) registrador(a) *m,f*

registrar *n* (public official) *funcionario
encargado de llevar los registros de
nacimientos, defunciones, etc*; (of company)
secretario(-a) *m,f*; **~ of transfers** *n*
registrador(a) de transferencias *m,f*

registration *n* (of company name, trademark)
registro *m*; (enrolment) inscripción *f*,
matrícula *f*; **~ fee** *n* (Stock) derechos de
certificación *m pl*; **~ form** *n* boletín de
suscripción *m*; **~ number** *n* BrE (*cf*
▶**license number** AmE) (of vehicle) matrícula
f, número de matrícula *m*; **~ office** *n*
oficina de registro *f*

registry *n* registro *m*; **~ of deeds** *n*
registro *m* de escrituras *or* de la propiedad;
~ office *n* BrE registro civil *m*; **~ of
shipping** *n* registro de navegación *m*

regression *n* regresión *f*; **~ analysis** *n*
análisis de regresión *m*; **~ coefficient** *n*
coeficiente de regresión *m*

regressive *adj* (taxation) regresivo

regroup [1] *vt* reagrupar
[2] *vi* reagruparse

regular *adj* (payments, service, expenditure)
regular; (size, model) normal; (customer)
habitual; (meeting) ordinario; **at ~ intervals**
(in time) con regularidad; (in space) a
intervalos regulares; **be in ~ employment**
tener empleo fijo; **keep ~ hours** seguir un
horario regular; **on a ~ basis** con
regularidad, regularmente; **the ~ staff** el
personal permanente

regulate *vt* regular

regulated *adj* (company, industry, market)
regulado; **~ agreement** *n* BrE acuerdo
regulado *m*; **~ commodity** *n* producto
básico controlado *m*

regulation *n* (rule) norma *f*, regla *f*; (control)
regulación *f*; (policing) regulación *f*,
reglamentación *f*; (adjustment) reglaje *m*,
regulación *f*; **it's against (the) ~s** va contra
el reglamento

regulator *n* (mechanism) regulador *m*;
(person, body) *persona u organismo que regula
una institución*

regulatory *adj* (authority, body, measure)
regulador; **~ agency** *n* organismo con
potestad normativa *m*

rehabilitate *vt* (reputation, company)
rehabilitar

rehabilitation *n* rehabilitación *f*

rehire *vt* emplear de nuevo

rehypothecation *n* constitución de
segundas hipotecas *f*

reimburse *vt* reembolsar

reimbursement *n* reembolso *m*

reimbursing bank *n* banco reembolsador *m*

reimport[1] *vt* reimportar

reimport[2] *n* reimportación *f*

reimportation *n* reimportación *f*

reimpose *vt* volver a imponer

rein *n* rienda *f*; **give free ~ to sth** dar rienda suelta a algo; **give free ~ to sb** darle carta blanca a alguien; **keep a tight ~ on expenses** llevar un estricto control de los gastos

reinforce *vt* (effect, impact) reforzar

reinforcement *n* reforzamiento *m*, refuerzo *m*

reinfusion *n* (Fin) reintroducción *f*

reinitiate *vt* reiniciar

reinstate *vt* (employee) reintegrar, reincorporar; (official) restituir *or* rehabilitar en el cargo; (law) reinstaurar; (service) restablecer; (text) volver a incluir

reinstatement *n* (of employee) reintegro *m*, reincorporación *f*; (of official) restitución *f* *or* rehabilitación *f* en el cargo; (of public employee, insurance) reposición *f*; (of law) reinstauración *f*; (of service) restablecimiento *m*

reinsurance *n* reaseguro *m*; **~ company** *n* compañía reaseguradora *f*

reinsure *vt* reasegurar

reinvent *vt* reinventar; **~ the wheel** reinventar la rueda

reinvest *vt* reinvertir

reinvestment *n* reinversión *f*; **~ rate** *n* tipo de reinversión *m*

reinvoice *vt* volver a facturar

reissue[1] *vt* (shares) emitir de nuevo; (book) reeditar

reissue[2] *n* (of shares) nueva emisión *f*; (of book) nueva edición *f*, reedición *f*

REIT *abbr* AmE (▸real estate investment trust) consorcio de inversiones inmobiliarias *m*

reiterate *vt* reiterar

reject[1] *vt* rechazar

reject[2] *n* artículo defectuoso *m*; **~ bin** *n* almacén de rechazos *m*

rejection *n* rechazo *m*; **I sent off ten applications and I've had three ~s** mandé diez solicitudes y he recibido tres respuestas negativas; **~ letter** *n* carta de rechazo *f*

related *adj* (idea, subject, person, group) relacionado; **~ party** *n* parte interesada *f*

relation *n* (connection) relación *f*; **in ~ to sth** en relación con algo

relational database *n* base de datos relacional *f*

relationship *n* (connection) relación *f*; (kinship) parentesco *m*; **~ marketing** *n* marketing de relaciones *m*

relative *adj* relativo; **~ to sth** relativo a algo; **~ error** *n* error relativo *m*; **~ market share** *n* cuota de mercado relativa *f*; **~ price** *n* precio relativo *m*; **~ price level** *n* nivel de precios relativo *m*; **~ surplus value** *n* valor añadido relativo *m*

relatively *adv* relativamente

relativities *n pl* proporciones relativas *f pl*

relaunch[1] *n* relanzamiento *m*

relaunch[2] *vt* relanzar

relax *vt* (rules) relajar

relaxation *n* (of rules) relajación *f*

release[1] *n* (of software, product) lanzamiento *m*; (of funds, personnel, right) cesión *f*; (of prisoner) puesta en libertad *f*, liberación *f*; **he negotiated his ~ from the contract** gestionó que se le condonaran las obligaciones emanadas del contrato; **~ date** *n* (for shares allocated to employees) fecha de liberación *f*; **~ on bail** *n* libertad bajo fianza *f*; **~ to market** *n* lanzamiento al mercado *m*

release[2] *vt* (funds, personnel, right) ceder; (version of software, product) publicar; (information, figures, statement, report) hacer público, dar a conocer; (prisoner) poner en libertad, liberar; **they ~d him from the contract** le condonaron las obligaciones emanadas del contrato; **~ sb on bail** poner en libertad *or* liberar a alguien bajo fianza

relevance *n* pertinencia *f*

relevant *adj* (document, facts, authority) pertinente; **~ to sth/sb** pertinente a algo/ alguien

reliability *n* (of source, data, machine) fiabilidad *f*; (of worker) formalidad *f*, responsabilidad *f*; **~ test** *n* prueba de fiabilidad *f*

reliable *adj* (information) fidedigno; (source) fidedigno, solvente; (witness, machine) fiable; (worker) responsable, de confianza

reliance *n* (dependence) dependencia *f*; (trust) confianza *f*; **~ on sth/sb** (dependence) dependencia de algo/alguien; (trust) confianza en algo/alguien

relief *n* (Tax) desgravación *f*; (replacement) relevo *m*; (aid) ayuda *f*, auxilio *m* (*de emergencia*); (from worry) alivio *m*; (redress) desagravio *m*; **~ on business assets** *n* deducción sobre activos empresariales *f*; **~ shift** *n* turno de relevo *m*

relieve *vt* (tension) aliviar, relajar; (driver) relevar; **~ sb of responsibility for sth** eximir a alguien de la responsabilidad de algo

religious *adj* (organization) religioso

relinquish *vt* (power, freedom) renunciar a

reload *vt* (software) recargar

relocatable *adj* (area of memory)
relocalizable; ~ **address** *n* (Comp)
dirección reubicable *f*

relocate ⃞1 *vt* (factory, office) trasladar
⃞2 *vi* (company, person) trasladarse

relocation *n* (of company, person) traslado
m; (Comp) relocalización *f*; ~ **allowance** *n*
prima de traslado *f*; ~ **expenses** *n pl*
gastos de traslado *m pl*; ~ **package** *n*
indemnización por traslado *f*

reluctant *adj* reacio; ~ **to do sth** reacio a
hacer algo

rely on *vt* (trust, have confidence) confiar en;
(be dependent) basarse en; ~ **sb to do sth**
confiar en alguien para hacer algo

remailer *n* sistema de remitente *m*

remain *vi* (continue to be) seguir, continuar;
(stay) quedarse, permanecer; (be left) quedar

remainder[1] *n* resto *m*

remainder[2] *vt* (books) saldar

remainderman *n* (Fin) proprietario(-a)
desnudo(-a) *m,f*

remainders *n pl* (goods) artículos no
vendidos *m pl*; (books) restos de edición *m pl*

remake *n* nueva versión *f*

remand[1] *n* (to lower court) AmE remisión *f*;
be on ~ estar detenido

remand[2] *vt* (to lower court) AmE remitir; ~
sb in custody poner a alguien en prisión
preventiva; ~ **sb on bail** dejar a alguien en
libertad bajo fianza

remapping *n* remapeo *m*, reproyección *f*

remargining *n* nueva colocación de
fondos *f*

remarket *vt* recomercializar

remarketing *n* marketing de nuevo
lanzamiento *m*

remarks *n pl* (section heading) observaciones
f pl

remedy[1] *n* (solution) solución *f*; (Law)
(method) recurso *m*, remedio *m*; (redress)
reparación *f*; **seek** ~ **for sth** exigir
reparación por algo

remedy[2] *vt* solucionar

reminder *n* (requesting payment) recordatorio
de pago *m*; ~ **advertising** *n* publicidad
recordatoria *f*

remise *n* entrega *f*

remission *n* (of charges) exoneración *f*; (of
tax) remisión *f*

remit[1] *vt* (money, goods, payment) remitir,
enviar; (fine, debt, sentence) perdonar,
condonar; (efforts) moderar; (vigilance) aflojar;
~ **a case to a lower court** remitir un caso
a un tribunal inferior

remit[2] *n* BrE (instructions) instrucciones *f pl*;
(area of authority) competencia *f*, atribuciones
f pl; **fall within/outside sb's** ~ estar/no
estar dentro de las atribuciones *or*
competencia de alguien; **have no** ~ **to do**
sth no tener instrucciones de hacer algo;
the commission's ~ **is to examine...** el
cometido de la comisión es investigar...

remittal *n* (of sentence, debt) renuncia *f*

remittance *n* (sum) remesa *f*, envío *m* (de
dinero); (act of paying) pago *m*; ~ **account** *n*
cuenta de remesa *m*; ~ **advice** *n*
notificación de envío *f*; ~ **slip** *n* aviso de
remesa *m*

remnants *n pl* remanentes *m pl*

remote *adj* (place, possibility, hope) remoto;
(Comp) a distancia, remoto; ~ **access** *n*
acceso a distancia *m*; ~ **batch processing**
n proceso por lotes a distancia *m*; ~
control *n* (method) control remoto *m*; (device)
telemando *m*, mando a distancia *m*;
~**-controlled** *adj* controlado a distancia; ~
maintenance *n* mantenimiento a distancia
m; ~ **payment** *n* telepago *m*; ~ **printing** *n*
teleimpresión *f*; ~ **processing** *n*
procesamiento remoto *m*; ~ **support** *n*
ayuda a distancia *f*

removal *n* (of threat, problem, tariff barriers)
eliminación *f*; (of text) supresión *f*; (dismissal)
remoción *f*; (to new premises) traslado *m*; (to
new home) BrE mudanza *f*; ~ **allowance** *n*
bonificación por traslado *f*; ~ **expenses**
n pl gastos de traslado *m pl*

remove *vt* (restrictions, threat, obstacle)
eliminar; (problem, difficulty) eliminar, acabar
con; (doubt, suspicion) disipar; (text) suprimir;
~ **sb from sth** destituir a alguien de algo;
'not to be ~**d'** no es para llevar

remuneration *n* remuneración *f*; ~
package *n* paquete de remuneración *m*

rename *vt* renombrar

render *vt* (assistance) prestar; ~ **an account**
presentar una factura; ~ **a contract invalid**
o **void** invalidar un contrato; ~ **sth null and**
void anular algo; **for services** ~**ed** por
servicios prestados

renege on *vt* (commitment, agreement)
incumplir

renegociation *n* renegociación *f*

renegotiate *vt* renegociar

renew *vt* (contract, lease, passport, subscription)
renovar, (efforts, attempts) reanudar

renewable *adj* (contract, lease, bill of
exchange, energy, resources) renovable

renewal *n* (of contract, lease, passport,
subscription) renovación *f*; ~ **option** *n* (of
leasehold contract) opción de renovación *f*

renounce *vt* renunciar a

renovate *vt* (building) renovar

renovation *n* (of building) renovación *f*

renown *n* renombre *m*

renowned *adj* renombrado

rent[1] *n* alquiler *m*; **for ~** AmE (*cf* ►**to let** BrE) se alquila; **pay the ~** pagar el alquiler; **~ allowance** *n* subsidio para el pago de alquiler *m*; **~ arrears** *n pl* atrasos de alquiler *m pl*; **~ collector** *n* cobrador(a) de alquileres *m,f*; **~ control** *n* control de alquileres *m*; **~-free** *adj* sin pago de alquiler; **~-free period** *n* periodo de ocupación gratuita *m*; **~ freeze** *n* congelación de alquileres *f*; **~ per calendar month** *n* BrE alquiler por mes de calendario *m*; **~ rebate** *n* devolución del alquiler *f*; **~ receipt** *n* recibo del alquiler *m*

rent[2] [1] *vt* (from owner, to tenant) alquilar [2] *vi* (tenant) alquilar

rentable *adj* (area) arrendable

rental *n* alquiler *m*; **~ agreement** *n* acuerdo de arrendamiento *m*; **~ cost** *n* coste *m* Esp *or* costo *m* AmL de arrendamiento; **~ income** *n* renta por arrendamiento *f*; **~ payment** *n* pago del alquiler *m*; **~ period** *n* periodo del alquiler *m*; **~ rate** *n* tarifa de arrendamiento *f*, tipo de alquiler *m*; **~ right** *n* derecho de arrendamiento *m*; **~ term** *n* periodo del alquiler *m*; **~ value** *n* valor de arrendamiento *m*

renter *n* inquilino(-a) *m,f*

rentier *n* rentista *mf*

reorder[1] *vt* (goods, supplies) volver a pedir *or* encargar; (files, paragraphs) reorganizar, volver a ordenar

reorder[2] *n* segundo pedido *m*; **~ form** *n* solicitud de un nuevo pedido *f*; **~ point** *n* punto de reaprovisionamiento *m*

reorganization *n* reorganización *f*

reorganize [1] *vt* (company) reorganizar [2] *vi* reorganizarse

rep *abbr* (►**sales representative**) representante (comercial) *mf*, viajante *mf*

rep. *abbr* (►**representative**) delegado(-a) *m,f*, representante *mf*, representativo(-a) *m,f*

repack *vt* reempaquetar

repackage *vt* (goods, pay offer) reformular; (personality, client) actualizar la imagen de; (product line) actualizar *or* modernizar (la presentación de); (rewrap) volver a embalar, reembalar

repackaging *n* (of personality, client) actualización de la imagen *f*; (of product line) actualización *f*, modernización *f*

repair[1] *vt* reparar

repair[2] *n* arreglo *m*, reparación *f*; **in good ~** en buen estado

repairman *n* técnico *m*

reparation *n* (amends) reparación *f*; (Fin) indemnización *f*; **demand ~ for sth** exigir reparación por algo; **make ~ to sb for sth** indemnizar a alguien por algo; **~ for damage** *n* indemnización por daños *f*

repatriate *vt* (capital, funds, profits) repatriar; **~ foreign earnings** hacer ingresar al país beneficios percibidos en el extranjero

repatriation *n* (of capital, funds, profits) repatriación *f*

repay *vt* (money) devolver; (loan) devolver, reintegrar; (debt) pagar; (person) reembolsar

repayable *adj* reembolsable; **~ on demand** *adj* exigible sin previo aviso

repayment *n* (act of repaying) pago *m*; (instalment) plazo *m*, cuota *f* AmL; (recompense) pago *m*, recompensa *f*; **~ over 2 years** amortización a 2 años; **~ claim** *n* reclamación de devolución *f*; **~ mortgage** *n* préstamo hipotecario en el que se va amortizando el capital al mismo tiempo que se pagan los intereses; **~ options** *n pl* posibilidades de pago *f pl*; **~ schedule** *n* plan de amortización *m*; **~ term** *n* periodo *m* de pago *or* de reembolso

repeal[1] *vt* abrogar

repeal[2] *n* abrogación *f*

repeat[1] *vt* repetir

repeat[2] *n* repetición *f*; **~ business** *n* negocio que se repite *m*; **~ buying** *n* compra repetida *f*; **~ demand** *n* demanda persistente *f*; **~ purchase** *n* compra persistente *f*; **~ rate** *n* índice de repetición *m*; **~ sales** *n pl* ventas repetidas *f pl*

repeated *adj* (instances, warnings, attempts) repetido, reiterado; (requests, demands) reiterado; (criticism, insistence) constante

repeater loan *n* préstamo reincidente *m*

repercussion *n* repercusión *f*

repertoire *n* repertorio *m*

repetitive *adj* repetitivo; **~ strain injury** *n* lesión por fatiga crónica *f*

replace *vt* (act as replacement for) sustituir, reemplazar; (change) cambiar; (put back) volver a poner *or* colocar; **~ the receiver** colgar el auricular

replaceable *ad* reemplazable, sustituible; **~ good** *n* bien fungible *m*

replacement *n* (act) sustitución *f*, reemplazo *m*; (person) sustituto(-a) *m,f*; (spare part) repuesto *m*; **~ bond** *n* bono de renovación *m*; **~ capital** *n* capital *m* de reemplazos *or* de reposiciones *m*; **~ cost** *n* coste *m* Esp *or* costo *m* AmL de reposición *or* de sustitución; **~ market** *n* mercado de intercambio *m*; **~ part** *n* pieza de repuesto *f*; **~ price** *n* precio de sustitución *m*; **~ ratio** *n* tasa de reposición *f*; **~ technology** *n* ┅┅┈┊

tecnología sustituta *f*; ∼ **value** *n* valor de reposición *m*

replay *vt* (Comp) repetir

replenish *vt* (stocks) reponer

replica *n* réplica *f*

reply[1] *n* (answer) respuesta *f*, contestación *f*; (reaction) reacción *f*, respuesta *f*; **in ∼ to your letter** en respuesta a su carta; **I phoned her but there was no ∼** la llamé pero no contestó nadie *or* nadie cogió el teléfono; **∼ paid** *n* respuesta pagada *f*; **∼-paid card** *n* cupón de respuesta pagada *m*; **∼-paid envelope** *n* BrE sobre a franquear en destino *m*

reply[2] *vti* responder, contestar; **∼ to sth** contestar algo, responder a algo; **∼ to sb** responderle *or* contestarle a alguien

repo *abbr* (▸**repurchase agreement**) repo (pacto de recompra)

report[1] *n* (account, evaluation) informe *m*; (piece of news) noticia *f*; (in newspaper) reportaje *m*, crónica *f*; (annual report) memoria *f*; ∼ **file** *n* fichero de edición *m*; ∼ **form** *n* formato de informe *m*; ∼ **generation** *n* generación de estados *f*; ∼ **terminal** *n* terminal de información *m*

report[2] [1] *vt* (provide account of) informar de *or* sobre; (accident) informar de, dar parte de; (crime) denunciar, dar parte de, reportar AmL; **as ∼ed** según se anuncia; ∼ **one's conclusions** informar de sus conclusiones; ∼ **one's findings to sb** informar a alguien de sus resultados; **many companies ∼ed increased profits** muchas empresas anunciaron un incremento en sus beneficios; ∼ **sb to sb** denunciar *or* reportar AmL a alguien a alguien; ∼ **sth to sb** dar parte de algo a alguien [2] *vi* (journalist) informar; (committee) presentar un informe; (present oneself) presentarse, reportarse AmL; ∼ **for work** presentarse al trabajo; ∼ **sick** dar parte de enfermo; ∼ **to reception** presentarse en recepción; **report back** *vi* presentar un informe; ∼ **back to sb** presentar un informe a alguien; **report to** *vt* estar bajo las órdenes de, reportar a

reporting *n* (Acc) informe *m*, presentación *f*; (Fin) producción de estados *f*; (of income) declaración *f*; (of event, story) cobertura *f*; ∼ **currency** *n* moneda en que se expresa un *estado financiero*; ∼ **period** *n* periodo de declaración *m*; ∼ **requirement** *n* requisito de la declaración *m*; ∼ **restrictions** *n pl* restricciones informativas *f pl*; ∼ **standard** *n* norma para hacer los informes *f*; ∼ **system** *n* sistema de informes *m*

reposition *vt* reposicionar

repositioning *n* reposicionamiento *m*

repository *n* depósito *m*

repossess *vt* embargar

repossession *n* embargo *m*; ∼ **order** *n* orden de embargo *f*

represent[1] *vt* (client) representar; (company) ser representante *or* agente de; (describe) presentar; ∼ **a radical change in policy** representar *or* constituir un radical cambio de política

represent[2] *vt* (cheque) volver a presentar

representation *n* representación *f*; **make ∼s (to sb)** quejarse (a alguien)

representative[1] *n* (agent, sales rep) representante *mf*; (in US politics) diputado(-a) *m,f*

representative[2] *adj* (sample) representativo; **be ∼ of sth** ser representativo de algo; ∼ **firm** *n* empresa *f* representativa *or* tipo

reprivatization *n* reprivatización *f*

reprivatize *vt* reprivatizar

reprocess *vt* reprocesar

reprocessing *n* reprocesado *m*; ∼ **plant** *n* planta de reprocesado *f*

reproduction *n* reproducción *f*; ∼ **rate** *n* tasa de reproducción *f*

reprogram *vt* reprogramar

reprographics *n* reprografía *f*

rept *abbr* (▸**receipt**) recibo *m*

republish *vt* reeditar

repudiate *vt* (charge, accusation) rechazar, negar; (liability, debt) negarse a reconocer

repurchase[1] *n* recompra *f*; ∼ **agreement** *n* pacto de recompra *m*; ∼ **rate** *n* tasa de recompra *f*

repurchase[2] *vt* (debt) recomprar

repurchased *adj* (share) recomprado

reputable *adj* (company, dealer, professional) serio, de confianza, acreditado

reputation *n* reputación *f*; **have a ∼ for getting results** tener fama de obtener unos resultados excelentes; **have a good/bad ∼** tener buena/mala reputación; **he certainly lives up to his ∼** realmente se merece la reputación que tiene

request[1] *n* petición *f*; **at the ∼ of sb** a petición de alguien; **by popular ∼** por demanda popular; **make a ∼** hacer una petición; **make a ∼ for sth** pedir algo; **make a ∼ to the appropriate authority** presentar una petición en las instancias adecuadas; **price lists available on ∼** solicite nuestras listas de precios

request[2] *vt* (help, loan) pedir, solicitar; **as ∼ed** (in letter) conforme a su petición

require *vt* (need) necesitar; (call for) requerir, exigir; ∼ **sb to do sth** requerir que alguien haga algo; ∼ **sth of sb** exigir algo de alguien

required *adj* (amount, action) necesario; ∼ **rate of return** *n* tasa de rendimiento requerida *f*; ∼ **reserve** *n* (Bank) reserva obligatoria *f*

requirement *n* (need) necesidad *f*; (demand, condition) requisito *m*; **meet sb's** ∼**s** satifacer las necesidades de alguien; **you must satisfy these** ∼**s** debe llenar *or* satifacer estos requisitos

requisite *adj* necesario, requerido; **lack the** ∼ **experience** no tener la experiencia necesaria

reroute *vt* desviar

rerun¹ *vt* (computer program) reejecutar; (film, series) reponer

rerun² *n* (of computer program) reejecución *f*; (of film, series) reposición *f*; (repetion) repetición *f*

resale *n* reventa *f*; **'not for** ∼**'** prohibida la venta; ∼ **price** *n* precio de reventa *m*; ∼ **price maintenance** *n* mantenimiento del precio de reventa *m*; ∼ **value** *n* valor de reventa *m*

reschedule *vt* (loan) reestructurar; (debt, repayments) renegociar; (project, work) volver a planificar; (meeting - change time) cambiar la hora de; (- change date) cambiar la fecha de

rescheduling *n* (of loan) reestructuración *f*; ∼ **of debt** *n* reajuste del calendario de la deuda *m*

rescind *vt* (contract) rescindir, anular; (order, ruling) revocar; (law) derogar, abolir

rescission *n* (of contract) rescisión *f*, anulación *f*; (of order, ruling) revocación *f*; (of law) derogación *f*, abolición *f*

rescription *n* rescripción *f*

rescue¹ *n* rescate *m*; **come to** *o* **go to sb's** ∼ acudir en ayuda de alguien; ∼ **package** *n* paquete de medidas de salvamento *m*

rescue² *vt* rescatar, salvar; **the bank** ∼**d the company from bankruptcy** el banco salvó a la empresa de la quiebra

research¹ *n* investigación *f*; **carry out** *o* **do** ∼ llevar a cabo *or* hacer una investigación; ∼ **into** *o* **on sth** investigación sobre algo; **a piece of** ∼ un trabajo de investigación; ∼ **budget** *n* presupuesto para la investigación *m*; ∼ **and development** *n* investigación *f* y desarrollo *m*; ∼ **director** *n* director(a) de investigación *m,f*; ∼ **grant** *n* beca de investigación *f*; ∼**-intensive** *adj* con investigación intensiva; ∼ **laboratory** *n* laboratorio de investigación *m*; ∼**-oriented** *adj* orientado a la investigación; ∼ **program** AmE, ∼ **programme** BrE *n* programa de investigación *m*; ∼ **team** *n* equipo de investigación *m*; ∼ **worker** *n* investigador(a) *m,f*

research² **1** *vt* (causes, problem) investigar, estudiar; ∼ **a book** documentarse para escribir un libro **2** *vi* investigar; ∼ **into sth** investigar algo

researcher *n* investigador(a) *m,f*

resell *vt* revender

reseller *n* revendedor(a) *m,f*; ∼ **market** *n* mercado de reventa *m*

reservable *adj* (day) reservable

reservation *n* (of room, seat) AmE (*cf* ▸**booking** BrE) reserva *f*, reservación *f* AmL; (doubt, qualification) reserva *f* **have (one's)** ∼**s about sth/sb** tener sus reservas acerca de algo/alguien; **make a** ∼ hacer una reserva; **without** ∼ sin reservas; ∼ **counter** *n* mostrador de reservas *m*; ∼ **form** *n* formulario de reserva *m*; ∼ **price** *n* AmE (*cf* ▸**reserve price** BrE) (at auction) precio mínimo *m*; ∼ **system** *n* sistema de reserva *m*

reserve¹ *n* reserva *f*; **keep sth in** ∼ guardar algo en reserva; **without** ∼ sin reservas; ∼ **account** *n* cuenta de reserva *f*; ∼ **assets** *n pl* activos de reserva *m pl*; ∼ **currency** *n* moneda de reserva *f*; ∼ **deposit** *n* depósito de reserva *m*; ∼ **fund** *n* fondo de reserva *m*; ∼ **price** *n* BrE (*cf* ▸**reservation price** AmE) (at auction) precio mínimo *m*; ∼ **requirement** *n* requisito de reserva *m*; ∼ **stock** *n* existencias de reserva *f pl*

reserve² *vt* (seat, room) reservar; ∼ **judgment** reservarse la opinión; ∼ **the right to do sth** reservarse el derecho de hacer algo; **the management** ∼**s the right to refuse admission** la gerencia se reserva el derecho de admisión; **all rights** ∼**d** reservados todos los derechos

reset¹ *vt* (clock, counter) poner a cero; (computer) reinicializar

reset² *n* (Comp) reinicialización *f*

resettlement *n* reasentamiento *m*

reshuffle¹ *vt* (management) reorganizar; (responsibilities) redistribuir; (cabinet) remodelar

reshuffle² *n* (of management) reorganización *f*; (of cabinet) remodelación *f*

residence *n* residencia *f*; ∼ **permit** *n* permiso de residencia *m*; ∼ **status** *n* situación de residencia *f*; ∼ **visa** *n* BrE (*cf* ▸**green card** AmE) visado de residencia *m*

residency *n* residencia *f*

resident¹ *adj* residente; **the country in which you are ordinarily** ∼ el país del que es residente habitual; ∼ **alien** *n* extranjero residente *m*; ∼ **manager** *n* director(a) residente *m,f*; ∼ **population** *n* población residente *f*; ∼ **taxpayer** *n* contribuyente residente *mf*

r

resident² n (of country) residente mf; (of district) vecino(-a) m,f; (of building) residente mf, vecino(-a) m,f

residential adj (accommodation, area) residencial; (conference, course) con alojamiento para los asistentes

residual adj (value, cost, lender, error) residual

residuary adj (estate, legatee) residual

residue n (remnant) residuo m; (Fin) resto m

resign ⟦1⟧ vi dimitir, renunciar; ~ **from sth** dimitir de algo
⟦2⟧ vt (position) dimitir de, renunciar a

resignation n dimisión f, renuncia f; **accept sb's** ~ aceptar la dimisión de alguien; **tender one's** ~ presentar su dimisión; ~ **letter** n carta de renuncia f

resilience n (of person) capacidad de recuperación f, resistencia f; (Econ) elasticidad f

resistance n resistencia f; **meet with** ~ **(from sth/sb)** encontrar resistencia (por parte de algo/alguien); **put up** ~ oponer resistencia; **take** o **follow the line** o **path of least** ~ seguir el camino más fácil; ~ **to change** resistencia al cambio; ~ **level** n (Stock) nivel de resistencia m

resistant adj resistente

resize vt (window) redimensionar

resizing n (Comp) redimensionamiento m

reskill ⟦1⟧ vt reciclar
⟦2⟧ vi reciclarse

reskilling n reciclaje profesional m

resolution n (of problem, difficulty) solución f; (of screen) resolución f, definición f; (decision) determinación f, propósito m; (proposal) moción f; (of US legislature) resolución f; (resoluteness) resolución f, determinación f; **adopt** o **pass a** ~ aprobar una moción

resolve¹ vt (problem, difficulty) resolver; (differences) saldar, resolver; (doubt, misunderstanding) aclarar; ~ **that...** acordar que...; ~ **to do sth** resolver or decidir hacer algo

resolve² n (resoluteness) resolución f, determinación f; (decision) decisión f, determinación m

resolved adj resuelto

resort n (recourse) recurso m; **as a last** ~ como último recurso

resort to vt recurrir a

resource¹ n recurso m; ~ **allocation** n adjudicación f or asignación f or distribución f de recursos; ~ **appraisal** n evaluación f or valoración f de recursos; ~ **management** n dirección f or gerencia f or gestión f de recursos; ~ **sharing** n (Comp) compartimiento de recursos m

resource² vt (department, organization) proveer los recursos or los fondos necesarios para; (provide staff for) emplear a personal para

respect¹ n (esteem) respeto m; (way, aspect) respecto m; **in** ~ **of sth** con respecto a algo; **in all** ~**s** o **in every** ~ desde todo punto de vista; **in this** ~ en cuanto a esto; **with** ~ **to your enquiry...** por lo que respecta a su consulta...

respect² vt respetar

respectable adj (amount, profit) respetable, considerable, importante; (performance) digno, aceptable

respectively adv respectivamente

respite n (Law) prórroga f

respondent n (to market research survey) entrevistado(-a) m,f; (Law) demandado(-a) m,f; (in appeal) apelado(-a) m,f

response n (answer) respuesta f, contestación f; (reaction) reacción f, respuesta f; **in** ~ **to your enquiry** en contestación a su pregunta; ~ **projection** n proyección de la respuesta f; ~ **rate** n porcentaje de respuesta m

responsibility n responsabilidad f; **deny all** ~ **in the matter** negar toda responsabilidad en el asunto; **a position of great** ~ un puesto de mucha responsabilidad; **take** ~ **for sth** asumir la responsabilidad de algo; **take on more** ~ asumir más responsabilidades; ~ **accounting** n contabilidad de responsabilidad f; ~ **center** AmE, ~ **centre** BrE n centro de responsabilidad m

responsible adj (accountable, in charge) responsable; (worker, attitude) responsable, formal; (job) de responsabilidad; ~ **for sth/sb** responsable de algo/alguien; **hold sb** ~ **for sth** responsabilizar or hacer responsable a alguien de algo; ~ **in the law** responsable ante la ley; ~ **to sb** responsable ante alguien

responsive adj que responde positivamente

rest¹ n (remainder) resto m; (break, relaxation) descanso m; ~ **account** n cuenta de saldo f; ~ **fund** n fondo sobrante m; **R**~ **of the World** n resto del mundo m

rest² ⟦1⟧ vi (relax) descansar; ~ **assured that...** tenga la seguridad de que...; **let the matter** ~ dejar el asunto; **the prosecution/defence** BrE o **defense** AmE ~**s** ha terminado el alegato del fiscal/de la defensa
⟦2⟧ vt (cause to relax) descansar; ~ **one's case** terminar su alegato; **rest on** vt basarse en; **rest with** vt recaer sobre

restart¹ vt (system, hardware) reanudar, rearrancar

restart² n (Comp) reanudación f, rearranque m; ~ **program** n programa de rearranque m

restate vt (argument, opinion) repetir; (theory, position) replantear

restock ① vi renovar existencias; ~ **with sth** renovar existencias de algo
② vt (shop, shelves) reaprovisionar

restoration n (of file, directory, building) restauración f

restore vt (file, directory, building) restaurar; (goods, property) restituir; (money) restituir, reintegrar; (links, communications) restablecer; (confidence) devolver; ~ **law and order** restablecer el orden público

restrained adj (Law) embargado

restraint n (self-control) compostura f, circunspección f; (restriction) limitación f, restricción f; ~ **of trade** n limitación al libre comercio f

restrict vt (numbers) limitar; (power, freedom, access) restringir, limitar; (imports) restringir

restricted adj (number) limitado; (power, freedom) limitado, restringido; (document, information) confidencial; ~ **account** n cuenta inactiva por falta de margen f, cuenta restringida f; ~ **credit** n crédito restringido m; ~ **market** n mercado restringido m; ~ **surplus** n AmE (cf ▸**undistributable reserve** BrE) excedente restringido m, plusvalía restringida f

restriction n restricción f; **there are ~s on imports** las importaciones están restringidas; **place ~s on sth** imponer restricciones a algo; **subject to ~s** sujeto a restricciones; **without ~s** sin restricciones; ~ **of credit** n restricción crediticia f

restrictive adj (policy) represivo; ~ **monetary policy** n política monetaria restrictiva f; ~ **practice** n práctica restrictiva f

restructure vt reestructurar

restructured adj (loan) reestructurado

restructuring n reestructuración f; ~ **of industry** n reestructuración industrial f

restyle vt remodelar

resubmit n (plan, proposal) presentar de nuevo

result¹ n resultado m; **as a ~** como consecuencia or resultado; **with the ~ that...** con el resultado de que...; **get ~s** conseguir resultados; ~**-driven** adj incentivado por resultados

result² vi resultar; **result from** vt resultar de; **result in** vt venir a parar en

results n pl (trading figures) resultados m pl

resume ① vt (work) reanudar; (post) reasumir, volver a asumir
② vi (negoatiations, work) reanudarse

résumé n AmE (cf ▸**curriculum vitae** BrE) CV m, curriculum vitae m

resurgence n (in prices) resurgimiento m

retail¹ n venta f al por menor or al detalle; ~ **bank** n banco minorista m; ~ **banking** n banca f minorista or al por menor; ~ **broker** n intermediario(-a) de bolsa minorista m,f; ~ **business** n comercio al por menor m; ~ **center** AmE, ~ **centre** BrE n centro m comercial or de venta al por menor; ~ **chain** n cadena de tiendas f; ~ **cooperative** n cooperativa de minoristas f; ~ **deposit** n (Stock) depósito al por menor m; ~ **deposits** n pl (Bank) depósitos de clientes particulares m pl; ~ **floorspace** n superficie minorista f; ~ **giant** n gigante del comercio por menor m; ~ **house** n casa minorista f; ~ **investor** n inversor(a) minorista m,f; ~ **management** n gestión f minorista or al por menor; ~ **margin** n margen del minorista m; ~ **network** n red de minoristas f; ~ **offer** n oferta minorista f; ~ **outlet** n punto de venta al por menor m; ~ **park** n parque comercial m; ~ **price** n precio m al por menor or de venta al publico; ~ **price index** n BrE (cf ▸**consumer price index** AmE) índice de precios al consumo m; ~ **price maintenance** n mantenimiento de los precios al por menor m; ~ **sales** n pl ventas al por menor f pl; ~ **sector** n sector al por menor f; ~ **site** n (on Internet) sitio al por menor f; ~ **trade** n comercio al por menor m; ~ **trader** n comerciante al por menor mf; ~ **warehouse** n almacén para minoristas m

retail² ① vt vender al por menor or al detalle
② vi venderse al por menor or al detalle; **it ~s for $80** su precio al público es de 80 dólares, se vende al por menor a 80 dólares

retail³ adv al por menor, al detalle

retailer n minorista mf, detallista mf

retailing n venta f al por menor or al detalle

retain vt (property, money) quedarse con; (shares, authority, power, information) retener; (employ) contratar; ~ **sb's services** contratar los servicios de alguien

retainage n retención f

retained adj (earnings, profits) retenido; (income) acumulado

retainer n anticipo m, iguala f; **be on a ~** recibir un anticipo or una iguala

retaliation n represalias f pl; **in ~ (for sth)** como represalia (por algo)

retaliatory adj de represalia; **take ~ measures** o **action** tomar represalias

retendering n reoferta f

retention n (of property, money) retención f;
(of system, law) mantenimiento m,
conservación f; ~ **date** n fecha de
conservación f; ~ **on wages** n retención
sobre el sueldo f

rethink¹ n reconsideración f; **we need to
have a** ~ necesitamos reconsiderarlo

rethink² vt reconsiderar

retire [1] vt (shares, bonds) redimir; (from job)
jubilar
[2] vi (stop working) jubilarse, retirarse;
(withdraw) retirarse; ~ **from business**
retirarse del negocio; ~ **on a pension**
jubilarse con pensión

retired adj jubilado; ~ **person** n
jubilado(-a) m,f, persona jubilada f

retiree n (frml) jubilado(-a) m,f

retirement n (from job) jubilación f, retiro
m; (of debt) redención f; **come out of** ~
volver al trabajo; **go into** ~ jubilarse,
retirarse; **take early** ~ coger la jubilación
anticipada; ~ **age** n edad de jubilación f; ~
annuity policy n BrE póliza de jubilación f;
~ **fund** n fondo de retiros m; ~ **income** n
jubilación f; ~ **pension** n pensión de
jubilación f; ~ **plan** n plan de jubilación m;
~ **savings plan** n plan de ahorro para
pensión m; ~ **scheme** n BrE plan de
jubilaciones m

retouch vt retocar

retract vt (offer, statement, allegation) retirar

retractable adj (bond) amortizable antes
del vencimiento, retractable

retraction n (of evidence, statement)
retractación f

retrain [1] vt reciclar, recapacitar,
reconvertir
[2] vi reciclarse

retraining n reciclaje m; ~ **course** n
curso de reciclaje m

retranslation n (of foreign currency)
reconversión f

retrench [1] vi economizar, hacer
economías; ~ **on sth** economizar or hacer
economías en algo
[2] vt (expenses, personnel) reducir

retrenchment n reducción f or
racionalización f de gastos

retrieval n (of object, data) recuperación f;
(of situation, mistake) reparación f, remedio m;
~ **time** n (Comp) tiempo de recuperación m

retrieve vt (object, data, file) recuperar;
(situation) salvar; (loss, damage) reparar

retroactive adj (adjustment, classification,
financing) retroactivo

retrogress vi retroceder

retrogression n retrogresión f

retrospective adj (claim, pay)
retrospectivo

return¹ [1] vt (package, goods, visit, favour)
devolver; (profit, income) producir, dar; (verdict)
emitir; ~ **an amount overpaid** devolver una
cantidad pagada de más; ~ **sb's call**
devolverle la llamada a alguien; **she** ~**ed
the letter to the file** volvió a poner la carta
en el archivo; ~ **to sender** devolver al
remitente
[2] vi (to place) volver, regresar; (to former
activity, state) volver

return² n (profit) rendimiento m; (tax return)
declaración f; (to owner, of thing bought)
devolución f; (to place) regreso m, vuelta f,
retorno m; (to former activity, state) vuelta f,
retorno m; **by** ~ (of post) BrE o **by** ~ **mail**
AmE a vuelta de correo; **in** ~ (for sth) a
cambio (de algo); ~ **address** n remite m; ~
fare n BrE tarifa de ida y vuelta f; ~ **flight**
n vuelo de vuelta m; ~ **key** n tecla de
interlineación f; ~ **leg** n trayecto de vuelta
m; ~ **on assets** n rendimiento m or
rentabilidad f de los activos m; ~ **on
capital** n rendimiento m del or sobre el
capital; ~ **on capital employed** n
rendimiento del capital invertido m; ~ **on
equity** n rendimiento sobre el patrimonio
m; ~ **on invested capital** n rendimiento
sobre capital invertido m; ~ **on
investment** n rendimiento de la inversión
m; ~ **on net assets** n beneficio sobre
activos netos m; ~ **on real estate** n
rendimiento de los bienes inmuebles m; ~
on sales n rendimiento de ventas m; ~
ticket n BrE (cf ▸**round-trip ticket** AmE)
billete de ida y vuelta m; ~ **trip** (BrE, cf
▸**round trip** AmE) viaje de ida y vuelta m

returnable adj (deposit) reembolsable,
reintegrable; (bottle) retornable; ~ **goods**
n pl mercancías restituibles f pl

returned adj (goods, cheque) devuelto; ~
empty n envase vacío devuelto m

retype vt reintroducir por teclado

reusable adj (pack) reutilizable

reuse vt reutilizar

revalorization n revalorización f

revaluate vt ajustar al precio del mercado

revaluation n (of currency) revalorización f,
revaluación f; (of assets) revalorización f,
actualización f; (of exchange rate) revaluación
f; ~ **reserve** n reserva de revalorización f

revalue vt revalorar, revalorizar

revamp¹ n (of product, image) modernización f

revamp² vt (product, image) modernizar

revealed preference n preferencia
manifiesta f

revenue n ingresos m pl, entradas f pl;
(Tax) rentas públicas f pl; ~ **allocation** n
(Tax) destino de los impuestos f; ~ **center**
AmE, ~ **centre** BrE n centro de ingresos m;
~ **curve** n curva de ingresos f;

~ **department** n AmE departamento fiscal m; ~ **earner** n receptor(a) de ingresos m,f; ~ **and expenses** n pl (Acc) ingresos m pl y gastos m pl; ~ **guarantee** n (Tax) garantía fiscal f; ~ **loss** n (Acc) pérdida de beneficios m; ~ **office** n (Tax) oficina de recaudación de impuestos f; ~ **stream** n flujo de ingresos m

reversal n (inversion) inversión f; (of trend, policy) cambio m completo or total; (of court decision) revocación f; (of entries) reposición f, retrocesión f; **a ~ of roles** un intercambio de papeles

reverse¹ adj (trend) inverso, contrario; **in ~ order** en orden inverso; ~ **channel** n (Comp) canal de retorno m; ~-**charge call** n BrE (cf ▸**collect call** AmE) llamada a cobro revertido f; **make a ~-charge call** BrE (cf ▸**call collect** AmE) llamar a cobro revertido; ~ **discrimination** n AmE discriminación positiva f; ~ **engineering** n ingeniería invertida f, retroingeniería f; ~ **gearing** BrE n, ~ **leverage** n apalancamiento m inverso or negativo; ~ **mortgage** n hipoteca inversa con renta vitalicia f; ~ **printing** n (Comp) impresión inversa f; ~ **repurchase** n recompra inversa f; ~ **split** n (Fin) división inversa f; ~ **takeover** n fusión inversa f; ~ **video** n video m AmL or vídeo m Esp inverso; ~ **yield gap** n exceso de rendimiento sobre la deuda m

reverse² n (of picture, paper) reverso m, dorso m; (of coin) reverso m; **endorse a check** AmE o **cheque** BrE **on the ~** endosar un cheque al dorso

reverse³ vt (roles, positions, trend, order, process) invertir; (policy) cambiar radicalmente; (verdict, decision, ruling) revocar; (Acc) (entry) anular; ~ **the charges** BrE (cf ▸**call collect** AmE) llamar a cobro revertido; ~ **a swap** (Stock) revertir un pase

reverse-engineer vt aplicar un proceso de retroingeniería a

reversible adj (annuity) reversible

reversing entry n (Acc) contraasiento m

reversionary adj (bonus) reversionario; (review, annuity) reversible

review¹ n (reconsideration) revisión f; (report, summary) resumen m, publicación f; (magazine) revista f, reseña f; **salary under ~** el sueldo está en estudio; **working methods are under ~** los métodos de trabajo están siendo reexaminados; **my salary comes up for ~ next month** el mes que viene me toca la revisión salarial; ~ **board** n junta de revisión f; ~ **body** n organismo de revisión m

review² vt (salary) reajustar; (policy, case) reconsiderar, examinar; (situation, prospects) examinar, estudiar

revise vt (policy, plan, figures, estimate) modificar; (proofs) corregir, revisar; ~ **costs upwards/downwards** BrE o **upward/ downward** AmE ajustar or revisar los costes Esp or costos AmL al alza/a la baja

revised adj (version, edition, figures) revisado; ~ **net income** n ingreso neto revisado m

revision n (alteration) modificación f

revisionism n revisionismo m

revitalization n revitalización f

revitalize vt revitalizar

revival n (of economy) restablecimiento m; (of demand) recuperación f; **a ~ of interest in sth** un renovado interés por algo

revive ① vt (economy) reactivar; (hope, interest) hacer renacer, reavivar; (law, claim) restablecer

② vi (industry, trade) reactivarse; (hope, interest) renacer, resurgir

revocable adj (trust, credit, letter of credit) revocable

revocation n revocación f

revoke vt revocar

revolutionary adj revolucionario

revolutionize vt evolucionar

revolving adj (credit) rotativo, renovable; ~ **fund** n fondo renovable m; (in governmental accounting) fondo rotatorio m; ~ **letter of credit** n carta de crédito renovable f; ~ **line of credit** n línea de crédito renovable f; ~ **underwriting facility** n compromiso de aseguramiento continuado m

reward¹ n recompensa f; **as a** o **in ~ for sth** en recompensa por algo; ~ **card** n tarjeta de lealtad f

reward² vt recompensar; ~ **sb for (doing) sth** recompensar a alguien por (hacer) algo

rewarding adj (job, experience) gratificante

rewind vt (cassette, tape) rebobinar

rewrite¹ vt reescribir

rewrite² n nueva versión f

rhetoric n retórica f

rich adj rico; **get ~** hacerse rico

rider n (appended statement) cláusula adicional f; (condition) condición f; (Law) recomendación f (del jurado); **we should like to add a ~ to the previous remarks** quisiéramos añadir algo a los anteriores comentarios

RIE abbr (▸**recognized investment exchange**) bolsa de inversión reconocida f; (▸**Registered International Exchange**) Bolsa Internacional Oficial de Valores f

riff money n (jarg) dinero extra m

rig¹ n control monetario m

rig² *vt* (prices, market, votes) manipular

rigging *n* (of prices, market, votes) manipulación *f*

right¹ *n* (entitlement) derecho *m*; (share issue) ampliación de capital *m*; (in politics) derecha *f*; (what is correct) bien *m*; **as of** *or* **by ~** por derecho; **give sb the ~ to do sth** otorgar a alguien el derecho a hacer algo; **be in the ~** tener razón; **in its own ~** por derecho propio; **all ~s reserved** reservados todos los derechos; **be within one's ~s (to do sth)** estar en su derecho (de hacer algo); **~ of appeal** *n* derecho de apelación *m*; **with no ~ of appeal** sin derecho a apelar; **~ of combination** *n* derecho de combinación *m*; **~s of conversion** *n pl* derechos de conversión *m pl*; **~ of entry** *n* derecho de entrada *m*; **~ of establishment** *n* derecho de establecimiento *m*; **~ of first refusal** *n* primera opción *f*; **~s holder** *n* titular (de derechos) *mf*; **~s issue** *n* emisión *de acciones con derechos preferentes de suscripción para los accionistas existentes*; **~ of offset** *n* (Bank) derecho de cancelación *m*; **~-of-way** *n* servidumbre de paso *f*; **~ of recovery** *n* derecho de recuperación *m*; **~ of redemption** *n* derecho *m* de redención *or* de retracto; **~ of redress** *n* derecho de compensación *m*; **~ of reply** *n* derecho de réplica *m*; **~ of resale** *n* derecho de reventa *m*; **~ of residence** *n* derecho de residencia *m*; **~ of return** *n* derecho de devolución *m*; **~ shift** *n* desplazamiento a la derecha *m*; **~ to associate** *n* derecho de asociación *m*; **~ to know** *n* derecho a saber *m*; **~ to strike** *n* derecho a la huelga *m*; **~ to vote** *n* derecho de voto *m*; **~ to work** *n* derecho *m* a trabajar *or* al trabajo; **~ to work state** *n* AmE *estado que prohíbe la filiación sindical obligatoria para acceder a un puesto de trabajo*

right² *adj* (answer) correcto; (size, tool, attitude, word) adecuado, apropiado; (just, moral) justo; (right-hand) derecho; **be ~** tener razón; **be ~ to do sth** *o* **in doing sth** tener razón en hacer algo; **if the price is ~** si el precio es razonable; **at the ~ time** en el momento oportuno; **~(-hand) column** *n* columna derecha *f*; **~-wing** *adj* de derechas

right³ *vt* (injustice) reparar; **~ a wrong** reparar un daño

right-click ① *vi* pulsar el botón derecho, hacer clic con el botón derecho ② *vt* hacer clic en algo con el botón derecho

rightful *adj* (owner, heir) legítimo

right-justify *vt* (document) justificar a la derecha

ring¹ *n* (group of people) red *f*; (group of companies) cártel *m*; (Stock) corro *m*; (of telephone) sonido *m*; **give sb a ~** BrE llamar (por teléfono) a alguien, telefonear a alguien; **~ road** *n* carretera de circunvalación *f*

ring² ① *vt* BrE (person, place, number) llamar (por teléfono) ② *vi* (telephone, alarm) sonar; (use telephone) BrE llamar (por teléfono), telefonear; **~ for sth/sb** llamar algo/a alguien; **ring back** *vti* BrE (ring again) volver a llamar; (return call) llamar; **ring in** *vi* BrE llamar (por teléfono), telefonear; **~ in sick** llamar para dar parte de enfermo; **ring out** *vi* BrE llamar al exterior; **ring up** *vti* BrE llamar (por teléfono)

ringfence *vi* reservar fondos

ringfencing *n* reserva de fondos *f*

ringing out *n* AmE (jarg) liquidación de contratos antes del vencimiento *f*

ringtone *n* tonalidad *f or* tono *m* de llamada

riparian rights *n pl* derechos ribereños *m pl*

ripple effect *n* efecto residual *m*

rise¹ *n* (in prices, interest rates) aumento *m*, subida *f*; (in number, amount, exports) aumento *m*; (in unemployment) crecimiento *m*; (in pay) BrE (*cf* ►**raise** AmE) aumento *m*; (in living standards) mejora *f*; (advancement) ascenso *m*, ascensión *f*; **buy for** *or* **on a ~** comprar al alza; **the ~ and fall of sth/sb** el auge y (la) caída de algo/alguien; **give ~ to sth** (belief, speculation) dar origen *or* lugar a algo; (problem, dispute) ocasionar *or* causar algo; (idea, interest) suscitar algo; **be given a ~** BrE recibir un aumento; **a ~ in wages** BrE un aumento salarial; **be on the ~** ir en aumento, estar aumentando

rise² *vi* (price) subir, aumentar; (number, amount, wage) aumentar; BrE (court, parliament) levantar la sesión; **the euro rose slightly against the dollar** el euro subió ligeramente en relación con el dólar; **the price has ~n by $200/8%** el precio ha subido *or* aumentado 200 dólares en un 8%; **~ in price** subir *or* aumentar de precio; **~ in line with inflation** (prices, benefits) aumentar a tono con la inflación; **the property has ~n in value** la propiedad se ha (re)valorizado; **~ to the challenge** aceptar el reto; **~ to the occasion** ponerse a la altura de las circunstancias

rising *adj* (prices, interest rates) en alza, en aumento; (number, rate, cost, inflation, unemployment) creciente; (trend) al alza, alcista; **~ bottom** *n* (jarg) (Stock) precio al alza *m*

risk¹ *n* riesgo *m*; **at ~** en peligro; **at the ~ of doing sth** a riesgo de hacer algo; **at one's own ~** por su cuenta y riesgo, bajo su propia responsabilidad; **be a good/bad ~** constituir un riesgo aceptable/inaceptable; **be insured for all ~s** estar asegurado

risk ⋯⋗ roll out ⋯⋗

contra *or* a Esp todo riesgo; **run the ~ of doing sth** arriesgarse a *or* correr el riesgo de hacer algo; **spread the ~** diversificar las inversiones para minimizar los riesgos; **take a ~** arriesgarse; **~ analysis** *n* análisis de riesgos *m*; **~ assessment** *n* estimación de riesgos *f*; **~ aversion** *n* aversión al riesgo *f*; **~-avoiding capital** *n* capital libre de riesgo *m*; **~-based premium** *n* prima basada en riesgos *f*; **~ capital** *n* capital riesgo *m*; **~ exposure** *n* (Acc) exposición al riesgo *f*; **~ factor** *n* factor de riesgo *m*; **~-free** *adj* libre de riesgo; **~ management** *n* administración *f or* dirección *f* de riesgos; **~ manager** *n* gestor(a) *m,f or* gerente *mf* de riesgos; **~ monitoring** *n* control *m or* supervisión *f* del riesgo; **~-oriented** *adj* con disposición al riesgo; **~ package** *n* paquete de riesgo *m*; **~ position** *n* posición de riesgo *f*; **~ premium** *n* prima del riesgo *f*; **~ profile** *n* perfil de riesgo *m*; **~ weighting** *n* subsidio del riesgo *m*

risk² *vt* (put in danger) arriesgar, poner en peligro; (expose oneself to) arriesgarse a, correr el riesgo de; **~ doing sth** arriesgarse a *or* correr el riesgo de hacer algo

riskless *adj* (transaction) exento de riesgo

risky *adj* (investment, plan) arriesgado, riesgoso AmL; (asset) de riesgo

rival¹ *n* rival *mf*

rival² *adj* (brand) rival

rival³ *vt* rivalizar con

ROA *abbr* (▸return on assets) rentabilidad *f or* rendimiento *m* de los activos

road *n* carretera *f*; **by ~** por carretera; **be on the ~** (sales rep) estar viajante; (exhibition) estar de gira; **~ haulage company** *n* compañía de transporte por carretera *f*; **~ tax** *n* impuesto por el uso de carreteras *m*; **~ toll** *n* peaje *m*; **~ traffic** *n* circulación *f* vial *or* por carretera

roadside *n* borde de la carretera *m*; **~ site** *n* (for advertising poster) valla publicitaria en carretera *f*

roadworthy *adj* (vehicle) apto para circular

rob *vt* (bank) asaltar, atacar, robar; (person) robarle a; **~ sb of sth** (steal) robarle algo a alguien; (deprive) privar a alguien de algo; **~ the till** robar la caja

robber *n* ladrón(-ona) *m,f*

robbery *n* robo *m*, asalto *m*

robot *n* robot *m*; **~ salesperson** *n* vendedor(a) robotizado(-a) *m,f*

robotics *n* robótica *f*

robotize *vt* robotizar

robust *adj* (economy, company) fuerte

ROC *abbr* (▸return on capital) rendimiento *m* del capital *or* sobre el capital

ROCE *abbr* (▸return on capital employed) rendimiento del capital invertido *m*

rock *vt* (weaken, destabilize) estremecer; **~ the boat** (infrml) desestabilizar una situación

rock-bottom *n* punto más bajo posible *m*; **hit** *o* **reach** *o* **touch ~** tocar fondo; **rock-bottom price** *n* precio más bajo posible *m*

rocket *vi* (price) dispararse, ponerse por las nubes

rocket scientist *n* (jarg) (Stock) creador(a) de valores innovadores *m,f*

rocks *n pl*: **be on the ~** estar sin blanca (infrml), estar sin un centavo

ROE *abbr* (▸return on equity) rendimiento sobre el patrimonio *m*

ROG *abbr* (▸receipt of goods) recepción de mercancías *f*

ROI *abbr* (▸return on investment) rendimiento de la inversión *m*

ROIC *abbr* (▸return on invested capital) rendimiento sobre capital invertido *m*

role *n* rol *m*; **~ conflict** *n* conflicto de papeles *m*; **~ model** *n* modelo de conducta *m*; **~-playing** *n* juegos de rol *m pl*

roll-back *n* AmE (of price) bajada *f*

roll back *vt* AmE (prices, wages) bajar, reducir

roll-down *n* (Stock) renovación a la baja *f*

rolled-up income *n* (Tax) ingreso obtenido por un cambio de posición *m*

roller swap *n* (Fin) intercambio rotativo *m*

rolling *adj* (plan) renovable; (programme) de renovación, de rotación; **~ options positions** *n pl* posiciones de las opciones renovables *f pl*; **~ rate** *n* tipo renovable *m*; **~-rate note** *n* documento de tipo renovable *m*; **~ settlement** *n* sistema por el cual un inversor puede efectuar el pago días después de la compra *o* venta de valores; **~ strikes** *n pl* huelgas alternativas *f pl*

rolling-down *n* (Stock) cambio a una posición más baja *m*

rolling-in *n* (Stock) cambio de una posición *m*

rolling-out *n* (Stock) abandono de una posición *m*

rolling-up *n* (Stock) cambio a una posición más alta *m*

roll-out *n* introducción de un producto en un mercado de prueba antes del lanzamiento general

roll out *vt* introducir un producto en un mercado de prueba antes del lanzamiento general

rollover n (of interest) renovación f; (of loan, repayments) refinanciación f; (Bank) crédito flotante m; ~ **credit** n crédito refinanciable m; ~ **credit facility** n línea de crédito con interés variable f; ~ **loan** n préstamo con tipo variable m; ~ **order** n (Stock) orden de renovar al vencimiento f; ~ **relief** n (Tax) deducción por refinanciación f

roll over vt (interest) renovar; (loan, repayments) refinanciar

roll-up n subida f

ROM abbr (►**read only memory**) memoria de sólo lectura f

Roman law n derecho romano m

room n (in house, building) habitación f; (for meeting, reception) sala f; ~ **service** n servicio de habitaciones m; ~ **temperature** n temperatura ambiente f

root n (Comp) raíz f; ~ **directory** n directorio raíz m; ~ **segment** n segmento de base m

RORCE abbr (►**rate of return on capital employed**) tasa de rendimiento del capital invertido f

roster n lista f

rosy adj (prospects) halagüeño

rotate [1] vt (employees) cambiar de puesto periódicamente, hacer rotar [2] vi (take turns) turnarse, rotarse

rotating shift n turno rotativo m

rotation n rotación; **in** ~ por turno; ~ **clause** n cláusula de rotación f

rotogravure n huecograbado m

rough[1] adj (calculation, estimate, guide) aproximado; **make things** ~ **for sb** ponerle las cosas difíciles a alguien; ~ **draft** n primer borrador m

rough[2] n (draft) borrador m

rough out n (draft) preparar en borrador

round[1] adj redondo; **in** ~ **numbers** o **figures** en números redondos; ~ **bracket** n BrE (cf ►**parenthesis** AmE) paréntesis m; ~ **lot** n AmE (Stock) unidad de contratación f; ~ **robin** n (letter) circular f; ~ **table** n mesa redonda f; ~ **trip** n (AmE, cf ►**return trip** BrE) viaje de ida y vuelta m; ~**trip ticket** n AmE (cf ►**return ticket** BrE) billete de ida y vuelta m

round[2] n (of discussions, talks) ronda f; (of tax cuts) serie f

round[3] vt (number) redondear; **round down** vt (price, total) redondear (por defecto); **round off** vt (meeting) concluir; (number) redondear; **round up** vt (price, total) redondear (por exceso); (summarize) hacer un resumen de

roundabout n BrE (cf ►**traffic circle** AmE) rotonda f

roundhouse n rotonda f

rounding error n error de redondeo m

round-the-clock[1] adj BrE continuo; ~**-the-clock service** n BrE servicio de 24 horas m

round-the-clock[2] adv BrE continuamente

roundtripping n (infrml) (Bank) pelota f, peloteo m

round-up vt (summary) resumen m, síntesis f

route[1] n ruta f; **en** ~ en ruta

route[2] vt (Comp) encaminar

routeing BrE, **routing** AmE n encaminamiento m

router n (Comp) encaminador m

routine[1] adj (duties) rutinario; (check, maintenance) de rutina

routine[2] n rutina f; **as a matter of** ~ por rutina

routing AmE ►**routeing** BrE

row n (of figures) fila f

ROW abbr (►**Rest of the World**) resto del mundo m

royal adj (decree) real; **R**~ **Exchange** n BrE Bolsa de Valores de Londres; **R**~ **Mint** n BrE ≈ Casa de la Moneda f Esp

royalties n pl (of author) derechos de autor m pl, royalties m pl AmL

RP abbr (►**repurchase agreement**) repo (pacto de recompra)

RPI abbr (►**retail price index** BrE, cf ►**CPI** AmE) IPC m (índice de precios al consumo)

RPM abbr (►**resale price maintenance**) mantenimiento del precio de reventa m; (►**retail price maintenance**) mantenimiento de los precios al por menor m

RR abbr (►**rate resetter**) mecanismo de puesta a cero del tipo m

RRA abbr (►**Race Relations Act**) ley de relaciones interraciales

RRP abbr (►**recommended retail price**) P.V.P. m (precio de venta al público)

RRR abbr (►**real rate of return**) tasa real de rendimiento f

RSI abbr (►**repetitive strain injury**) lesión por fatiga crónica f

RSVP abbr (►**please reply**) S.R.C. (se ruega contestación)

RT abbr (►**radiotelephony**) radiotelefonía f

RTM abbr (►**release to market**) lanzamiento al mercado m

rubber n (substance) goma f; ~ **check** AmE, ~ **cheque** BrE n (infrml) cheque sin fondos m

rubber-stamp vt (paper, invoice) sellar; (decision, proposal, application) autorizar

rubber stamp n (device) sello de goma m; (approval) visto bueno m

rubbish n BrE (cf ►**garbage** AmE) basura m; ~ **dump** n BrE (cf ►**garbage dump**

AmE) vertedero (de basuras) *m*, basurero *m*, basural *m* AmL

RUF *abbr* (▸**revolving underwriting facility**) CAC (compromiso de aseguramiento continuado)

ruin[1] *n* ruina *f*; **his career was in ～s** su carrera estaba arruinada; **he's heading for financial ～** va derecho a la ruina *or* a la bancarrota

ruin[2] *vt* (career) arruinar; (plans) arruinar, echar por tierra; (hopes) destruir, echar por tierra

rule[1] *n* (regulation, principle) regla *f*, norma *f*; (guideline) pauta *f*; (ruling) fallo *m*; (government) gobierno *m*; **against the ～s** prohibido; **as a ～** por lo general, generalmente; **bend o stretch the ～s** apartarse un poco de las reglas; **break the ～s** infringir las reglas *or* normas; **go under the ～** AmE (jarg) someterse al reglamento; **observe the ～s** observar *or* acatar las reglas *or* normas; **work to ～** hacer huelga de celo; **～ book** *n* libro de normas *m*; **～s of fair practice** *n pl* código de conducta *m*; **～ of law** *n* imperio de la ley *m*; **～s and regulations** *n pl* normas *f pl* y reglamentos *m pl*; **～ of thumb** *n* regla general *f*

rule[2] [1] *vt* (country) gobernar, administrar; **the committee ～d that...** la comisión dictaminó que...

[2] *vi* (govern) gobernar; (provide legal ruling) fallar, resolver; **～ on/against/in favor** AmE *o* **favour** BrE **of sth/sb** fallar *or* resolver en/en contra de/a favor de algo/alguien; **rule out** *vt* excluir

ruled *adj* (paper) rayado

ruling[1] *adj* (principle, factor, class) dominante; **～ price** *n* precio *m* corriente *or* que rige

ruling[2] *n* fallo *m*, resolución *f*; **give a ～ in favor** AmE *o* **favour** BrE **of sb** fallar en favor de alguien, pronunciar un fallo favorable a alguien

rumour BrE, **rumor** AmE *n* rumor *m*; **～ has it that...** hay rumores de que...

run[1] [1] *vt* (business, organization, department) dirigir, llevar; (computer program) pasar, ejecutar; (tests, survey) realizar, llevar a cabo; (machine) hacer funcionar; **～ an errand** hacer un recado; **we need someone to ～ the financial side of the business** necesitamos alguien que se encargue *or* se ocupe del aspecto financiero del negocio; **～ the show** llevar la voz cantante

[2] *vi* (for public office) presentarse; **inflation is ～ning at 2%** la tasa de inflación es del 2%; **the work is ～ning six months behind schedule** el trabajo lleva seis meses de retraso; **the contract ～s for a year** el contrato es válido por un año *or* vence al cabo de un año; **～ foul of the authorities**

(Tax) topar con las autoridades fiscales; **～ low** escasear; **～ short of sth** estar escaso de algo; **run at** *vt* lanzarse sobre; **run back** *vi* (Stock) retroceder; **run down** [1] *vt* (production) ir restringiendo; (stocks, supplies) agotar; (staff, services) ir recortando *or* reduciendo; (liquid assets) disminuir [2] *vi* (stocks, supplies) agotarse; (business, factory) venirse abajo; **run into** *vt* (opposition, problem) toparse *or* tropezar con, encontrar; **～ into debt** entrar en pérdidas; **the cost runs into millions of dollars** el coste Esp *or* costo AmL asciende a millones de dólares; **run off** *vt* (copies) tirar; (photocopies) sacar; (drain) desaguar; **run on** *vi* (in time) prolongarse; (in proofreading) unir líneas; **run out** *vi* (supplies, stock) acabarse, agotarse; (lease, policy) vencer, caducar; **run out of** *vt* quedarse sin; **run over** [1] *vt* (main points, arrangements) repasar, volver sobre [2] *vi* (in time) excederse *or* pasarse del tiempo previsto; **run through** *vt* (use up) gastarse; (squander) derrochar, despilfarrar; (main points, arrangements) repasar, volver sobre; **run to** *vt* (suffice for) alcanzar para; **the report runs to 614 pages** el informe ocupa 614 páginas; **run up** *vt* (account, total, debts) ir acumulando; (overdraft) dejar acumular; (deficit) aumentar; (surplus) manejar

run[2] *n* (series) serie *f*; (print run) tirada *f*; (tendency, direction) corriente *f*; (Comp) pasada *f*; **in the long ～** a la larga; **a ～ on the banks** una corrida bancaria, un pánico bancario; **a ～ on sterling** una fuerte presión sobre la libra *m*; **～ time** *n* (of program) tiempo de proceso *m*

runaway *adj* (inflation) galopante, desenfrenado; (spending) desmedido; (success) clamoroso, arrollador; **try to curb ～ prices** tratar de frenar los precios que se disparan

runner *n* mensajero(-a) *m,f*

running *n* (management) gestión *f*, dirección *f*; (of machine) funcionamiento *m*, marcha *f*; **be in/out of the ～ (for sth)** tener/no tener posibilidades (de conseguir algo); **～ cable** *n* cable de suspensión *m*; **～ costs** *n pl* costes *m pl* Esp *or* costos *m pl* AmL de operación; **～ expenses** *n pl* gastos de mantenimiento *m pl*; **～ interest** *n* interés corriente *m*; **～ number** *n* número consecutivo *m*; **～ total** *n* total *m* actualizado *or* hasta la fecha

running-ahead *n compra y venta ilegal de un valor por cuenta del propio intermediario antes de gestionarla para un cliente*

running-in period *n* periodo de rodaje *m*

runoff *n* (Ind) desagüe *m*; AmE (Pol) segunda vuelta *f*

run-of-the-mill *adj* común y corriente

run-on *adj* (text) unido al párrafo anterior

run-up n (Stock) alza de precios f; **in the ∼ to sth** (elections) en el período previo a algo

runway n pista de salida f

rural adj (area, community, sector, tourism) rural; **R∼ Development Area** n BrE zona de desarrollo rural f

rush¹ ⓵ vt (job) hacer a todo correr or a la(s) carrera(s); (person) meterle prisa a, apurar; **∼ sb into signing a contract** meterle prisa a alguien para que firme un contrato; **∼ sb sth** o **sth to sb** remitirle or enviarle algo a alguien con la mayor brevedad (posible)

⓶ vi ir de prisa; **∼ into (doing) sth** hacer algo sin pensarlo bien; **rush out** vt (report, book) sacar rápidamente

rush² n (haste) prisa f, apuro m AmL; (sudden demand) demanda f **∼ hour** n hora f pico AmL or punta Esp; **∼ job** n trabajo urgente m; **∼ order** n pedido urgente m

rusty adj (out-of-practice) falto de prática

Ss

s.a.a.r. *abbr* (▸**seasonally-adjusted annual rate**) tipo anual con ajuste estacional *m*

sack¹ *vt* (infrml) (staff) cesar, despedir, echar

sack² *n* (infrml) despido *m*; **get the ~** (infrml) ser despedido; **give sb the ~** (infrml) cesar *or* despedir *or* echar a alguien

SAD *abbr* (▸**single administrative document**) documento administrativo simple *m*

s.a.e. *abbr* BrE (▸**self-addressed** *o* ▸**stamped-addressed envelope**, *cf* ▸**s.a.s.e.** AmE) *sobre sellado con la dirección del remitente*

SAF *abbr* (▸**structural adjustment facility**) (Fin) mecanismo de ajuste estructural *m*

safe¹ *adj* (asset, investment) seguro; **a ~ bet** una apuesta segura; **in ~ hands** en buenas manos; **play (it) ~** ser precavido, no correr riesgos; **(just) to be on the ~ side** por si acaso, para mayor seguridad; **~ hedge** *n* protección segura *f*

safe² *n* caja fuerte *f*; **~ deposit** *n* depósito en caja de seguridad *m*; **~-deposit box** *n* caja de seguridad *f*; **~-deposit vault** *n* cámara acorazada *f*, bóveda de seguridad *f* AmL

safeguard¹ *n* salvaguardia *f*; **~ against sth** salvaguardia contra algo; **as a ~** como medida preventiva

safeguard² *vt* (assets) salvaguardar; **safeguard against** *vt* (inflation) salvaguardarse contra

safekeeping *n* (of assets) custodia *f*; **give sth to sb for ~** darle algo a alguien para mayor seguridad

safety *n* seguridad *f*; **~ belt** *n* cinturón de seguridad *m*; **~ check** *n* inspección de seguridad *f*; **~-deposit box** *n* caja de seguridad *f*; **~ engineer** *n* ingeniero(-a) de seguridad *m,f*; **~ hazard** *n* riesgo de seguridad *m*; **~ limits** *n pl* límites de seguridad *m pl*; **~ management** *n* dirección *f or* gerencia *f* de seguridad; **~ margin** *n* margen de seguridad *m*; **~ measure** *n* medida de seguridad *f*; **~ net** *n* protección *f*; **~ officer** *n* empleado(-a) de seguridad *m,f*; **~ precaution** *n* medida de seguridad *f*; **~ regulation** *n* norma de seguridad *f*; **~ requirement** *n* requisito de seguridad *m*; **~ standard** *n* norma de seguridad *f*; **~ vault** *n* cámara acorazada *f*,

bóveda de seguridad *f* AmL; **~ violation** *n* violación de la seguridad *f*

sag¹ *vi* (prices, rates) caer, bajar; (production) decaer

sag² *n* (in prices, profits) caída *f*, baja *f*

sagging *adj* (profits, sales) decreciente, disminuido

sail *vi* navegar; **~ close to the wind** ir *o* andar por un terreno peligroso; **he ~ed through the interview** la entrevista le resultó muy fácil

salability AmE *see* ▸**saleability** BrE

salable AmE ▸**saleable** BrE

salableness AmE ▸**saleable** BrE

salariat *n* asalariados *m pl*

salaried *adj* (employee, staff) asalariado

salary *n* salario *m*, sueldo *m*; **'~ to be negotiated'** sueldo negociable; **~ base** *n* base salarial *f*; **~ deduction** *n* deducción salarial *f*; **~ earner** *n* asalariado(-a) *m,f*; **~ increase** *n* incremento salarial *m*; **~ range** *n* nivel de ingresos *m*; **~ rate** *n* índice salarial *m*; **~ review** *n* revisión *f* salarial *or* del salario; **~ scale** *n* escala *f* de salarios *or* de sueldos; **~ structure** *n* estructura salarial *f*

sale *n* venta *f*; (at reduced price) rebaja *f*; **buy sth at a ~/in the ~s** comprar algo en una liquidación/en las rebajas; **for ~** en venta; (sign) se vende; **hold** *o* **have a ~** tener rebajas; **make a ~** hacer una venta; **be on ~** BrE estar a la venta; AmE estar rebajado *or* en liquidación; **put sth up for ~** poner algo en venta; **~ or return** BrE *acuerdo de venta que permite al comprador devolver la mercancía que no vende*; **~ subject to safe arrival** venta condicionada a una llegada sin problemas; **work in ~s** trabajar en ventas

(**sale...a**) **~s activity** *n* actividad de ventas *f*; **~s agent** *n* agente de ventas *mf*; **~s analysis** *n* análisis de ventas *m*; **~s analyst** *n* analista de ventas *mf*; **~s appeal** *n* atractivo de las ventas *m*; **~s area** *n* (in shop) zona de ventas *f*

(**b...**) **~s book** *n* libro de ventas *m*; **~s budget** *n* presupuesto de ventas *m*; **~ by tender** *n* venta mediante licitación pública *f*

(**c...**) **~s call** *n* visita de venta *f*; **~s campaign** *n* campaña de ventas *f*; **~s charge** *n* (Stock) cargo por ventas *m*; **~s clerk** *n* AmE (*cf* ▸**shop assistant** BrE) dependiente(-a) de tienda *m,f*; ⋯⟶

~**s commission** n comisión de venta f; ~**s conference** n conferencia de ventas f; ~**s contract** n contrato de venta m

d... ~**s department** n departamento de ventas m; ~**s director** n director(a) de ventas m,f; ~**s discount** n descuento de venta m; ~**s drive** n promoción de ventas f

e... ~**s executive** n ejecutivo(-a) de ventas m,f

f... ~**s figures** n pl cifras de ventas f pl; ~**s force** n personal de ventas m; ~**s force automation** n automatización del personal de ventas f; ~**s forecast** n previsión de ventas f

g... ~ **goods** n pl artículos de liquidación m pl; ~ **of goods** n venta f de bienes or de mercancías

i... ~**s incentive** n incentivo m a la venta or de ventas; ~**s invoice** n factura de ventas f; ~ **item** n artículo de liquidación m

l... ~**s leaflet** n folleto publicitario m; ~ **and leaseback** n venta con acuerdo de alquiler f; ~**s ledger** n libro mayor de ventas m; ~**s letter** n carta de venta f; ~**s literature** n folleto publicitario m

m... ~**s management** n dirección f or gerencia f de ventas; ~**s manager** n director(a) m,f or gerente mf or jefe(-a) m,f de ventas; ~**s maximization** n maximización de las ventas f; ~**s meeting** n reunión de ventas f; ~**s mix** n mezcla de estrategias de ventas f

n... ~**s network** n red de ventas f

o... ~**s offensive** n ofensiva comercial f; ~**s office** n oficina de ventas f; ~ **on approval** n venta a prueba f; ~**s opportunity** n oportunidad de ventas f

p... ~**s personnel** n personal de ventas m; ~**s pitch** n rollo publicitario m; ~**s planning** n planificación de las ventas f; ~**s policy** n política de ventas f; ~**s portfolio** n cartera de ventas f; ~**s potential** n potencial de ventas m; ~**s presentation** n presentación comercial f; ~ **price** n (normal price) precio de venta m; (reduced price) precio rebajado m; ~ **proceeds** n pl ingresos de venta m pl; ~**s projection** n proyección de ventas f; ~**s promotion** n promoción de ventas f

q... ~**s quota** n cupo de ventas m

r... ~**s ratio** n proporción f or relación f de ventas; ~**s receipt** n recibo de ventas m; ~**s record** n registro de ventas m; ~**s rep** n (infrml), ~**s representative** n representante (comercial) mf, viajante mf; ~**s resistance** n resistencia a la venta f; ~**s returns** n devoluciones de ventas f pl; ~**s revenue** n ingresos por ventas m pl

s... ~**s slip** n AmE recibo de caja f; ~**s slump** n bajada de las ventas f

t... ~**s talk** n jerga de vendedor f; ~**s target** n objetivo de ventas m; ~**s tax** n impuesto sobre las ventas m; ~**s technique** n técnica de ventas f; ~**s territory** n territorio de ventas m; ~**s test** n prueba de ventas f; ~**s tool** n herramienta de ventas f; ~**s-type lease** n alquiler tipo venta m

v... ~ **value** n valor de venta m; ~**s value** n importe de las ventas m; ~**s volume** n cifra f or volumen m de ventas

saleability BrE, **salability** AmE n facilidad de venta f

saleable BrE, **salable** AmE adj vendible

saleableness BrE, **salableness** AmE n facilidad de venta f

salesman n (in shop) vendedor m, dependiente m; (representative) representante (comercial) m

salesmanship n arte de vender m

salesperson n (in shop) vendedor(a) m,f, dependiente(-a) m,f; (representative) representante (comercial) mf

saleswoman n (in shop) vendedora f, dependienta f; (representative) representante (comercial) f

salt vt (jarg) (memo) falsificar

salvage¹ n (rescue) salvamento m; (goods saved) objetos salvados m pl; (compensation) derecho de salvamento m; ~ **loss** n pérdida de salvamento f; ~ **value** n valor residual m

salvage² vt salvar

same adj mismo; (size) igual

same-day adj (delivery) en el día; (value) del mismo día

sample¹ n muestra f; **take a** ~ tomar una muestra; ~ **book** n muestrario m; ~ **card** n ficha para muestras f; ~ **data** n datos de muestra m pl; ~ **study** n estudio de muestra m; ~ **survey** n encuesta por muestreo f

sample² vt (opinion) hacer un muestreo de

sampling n muestreo m; ~ **offer** n oferta de muestras f

samurai bond n bono samurai m

sanction¹ n sanción f; **give one's** ~ **to sth** dar su aprobación a algo; **impose** ~**s on sb** imponer sanciones contra alguien; **lift** ~**s** levantar sanciones

sanction² n (action, initiative) sancionar; (injustice) consentir, tolerar

S&FA abbr (▸**shipping and forwarding agent**) agente de transportes marítimos mf

S&L abbr AmE (▸**savings and loan association**) ≈ banco (de crédito) hipotecario m

sandwich: ~ **board** n cartelón m; ~ **course** n curso académico con periodo de prácticas; ~ **lease** n (infrml) arrendamiento por un subarrendatario m

s.a.s.e. *abbr* AmE (▸**self-addressed stamped envelope**, *cf* ▸**s.a.e.** BrE) *sobre sellado con la dirección del remitente*

satellite *n* satélite *m*; ~ **broadcasting** *n* transmisión por vía satélite *f*; ~ **communications** *n pl* telecomunicaciones por satélite *f pl*; ~ **computer** *n* computadora satélite *f* AmL, ordenador auxiliar *m* Esp; ~ **dish** *n* antena parabólica *f*; ~ **technology** *n* tecnología de retransmisión vía satélite *f*; ~ **television** *n* televisión por satélite *f*; ~ **town** *n* ciudad satélite *f*

satisfaction *n* (contentment) satisfacción *f*; (of terms, conditions, claim) cumplimiento *m*; (of debt) pago *m*; ~ **guaranteed or your money back** si no queda satisfecho, le devolvemos el dinero; **in** ~ **of sth** en pago de algo

satisfactory *adj* satisfactorio

satisfied *adj* satisfecho; **another** ~ **customer** otro cliente satisfecho; **if you are not completely** ~ **with your purchase...** si no queda plenamente satisfecho con su compra...

satisfy *vt* (customer, need, demand) satisfacer; (requirements) llenar, reunir; (debt) saldar, liquidar, satisfacer; ~ **sb of sth** convencer a alguien de algo

saturate *vt* (economy, market) saturar

saturation *n* (of economy, market) saturación *f*; ~ **campaign** *n* campaña de saturación *f*; ~ **point** *n* punto de saturación *m*; **reach** ~ **point** alcanzar el punto de saturación

save *vt* **1** (money, space) ahorrar; (trouble, expense) ahorrar, evitar; (data) guardar **2** *vi* (put money aside) ahorrar; **save up** *vti* ahorrar; ~ **for sth/to buy sth** ahorrar para algo/para comprar algo

save-as-you-earn *n* BrE *plan de ahorro mediante descuentos en el sueldo*

saver *n* ahorrador(a) *m,f*

saving *n* ahorro *m*; **a** ~ **on travel costs** un ahorro en los gastos de viaje; **make a huge** ~ **on sth** ahorrarse una fortuna en algo

savings *n pl* ahorros *m pl*; ~ **account** *n* cuenta de ahorros *f*; ~ **bank** *n* caja de ahorros *f*; ~ **bond** *n* bono de ahorro *m*; ~ **book** *n* cartilla *f or* libreta *f* de ahorros; ~ **certificate** *n* certificado de ahorro *m*; ~ **deposit** *n* depósito de ahorro *m*; ~ **institution** *n* BrE (*cf* ▸**thrift institution** AmE) entidad *f or* institución *f* de ahorro y préstamo; ~**-linked** *adj* ligado al ahorro; ~ **and loan association** *n* AmE (*cf* ▸**building society** BrE) banco (de crédito) hipotecario *m*; ~ **passbook** *n* cartilla *f or* libreta *f* de ahorros; ~ **plan** *n* plan de ahorro *m*

say *n* voz *f* y voto *m*; **he has no** ~ **in the matter** no tiene ni voz ni voto en el asunto; **have one's** ~ expresar su opinión; **have**

the final ~ **(in sth)** tener la última palabra (en algo)

SAYE *abbr* BrE (▸**save-as-you-earn**) *plan de ahorro mediante descuentos en el sueldo*

SBA *abbr* (▸**small business administration**) administración *f or* dirección *f* de la pequeña empresa

scab *n* (infrml) (strikebreaker) esquirol *mf* (infrml)

scalability *n* escalabilidad *f*

scalable *adj* (solution, product) escalable

scale[1] *n* escala *f*; **on an international** ~ a escala internacional; **on a large/small** ~ a gran/pequeña escala; **on a** ~ **of 1 to 10** en una escala del 1 al 10; **on a worldwide** ~ a escala mundial; **to** ~ a escala; **draw/make sth to** ~ dibujar/hacer algo a escala; **'not to** ~**'** no está a escala; ~ **of charges** *n* escala de cargos *f*; ~ **of commission** *n* escala de la comisión *f*; ~ **model** *n* maqueta a escala *f*

scale[2] *vt* escalar; ~ **the ladder** escalar posiciones; **scale down** *vt* (model, drawing) reducir (a escala); (operation, investment) recortar *or* disminuir proporcionalmente; **scale up** *vt* (model, drawing) agrandar (a escala); (operation, investment) ampliar

scalp[1] *vt* AmE (infrml) (stocks, securities, tickets) revender (a precio inflado)

scalp[2] *n* AmE (infrml) operación rápida de bolsa con idea de beneficio *f*

scalper *n* AmE (infrml) (Stock) especulador(a) a muy corto plazo *m,f*; (of tickets) (*cf* ▸**(ticket) tout** BrE) revendedor(a) *m,f* (a precio inflado)

scalping *n* AmE (infrml) (Stock) especulación a muy corto plazo *f*; (of tickets) (*cf* ▸**(ticket) touting** BrE) reventa *f* (a precio inflado)

scam *n* (infrml) chanchullo *m* (infrml)

scan[1] *n* (Comp) exploración *f*; ~ **area** *n* superficie de exploración *f*

scan[2] *vt* (electronically) explorar; (statement, report) examinar

scandal *n* escándalo *m*

scanner *n* escáner *m*

scanning *n* (Comp) exploración *f*

scant *adj* (attention, coverage) escaso

scapegoat *n* (infrml) (*cf* ▸**fall guy** AmE) cabeza de turco *f* (infrml)

scarce *adj* (goods, resources) escaso

scarcity *n* escasez *f*; ~ **value** *n* valor de escasez *m*

scatter diagram, **scattergram** *n* diagrama de dispersión *m*

scavenger sale *n* (infrml) venta de embargo *f*

SCC *abbr* (▸**Spanish Chamber of Commerce**) Cámara de Comercio Española *f*

S

SCE *abbr* (▸**supply chain execution**)
ejecución de la cadena de suministros *f*

scenario *n* (possible outcome) escenario *m*;
(of film) guión *m*

scepticism BrE, **skepticism** AmE *n*
escepticismo *m*

schedule[1] *n* (plan) programa *m*, calendario
m; (timetable) horario *m*; (appendix) anexo *m*,
apéndice *m*; **be two months ahead of/
behind** ~ llevar dos meses de adelanto/
retraso con respecto a lo previsto; **on** ~
(work) conforme al programa; (train, flight)
puntual, a tiempo, a la hora prevista; **have a
very tight** ~ tener un programa muy
apretado; ~ **of charges** *n* (Law) pliego de
cargos *m*; ~ **of prices** *n* lista de precios *f*,
tarifa *f*; ~ **of repayments** *n* calendario de
pagos *m*

schedule[2] *vt* programar; **as** ~**d** según lo
programado; **the new model is** ~**d for
introduction this autumn** el lanzamiento del
nuevo modelo está previsto para el otoño;
the conference is ~**d to take place in
August** la conferencia está planeada para el
mes de agosto

scheduled *adj* (meeting, visit) previsto,
programado; (flight, service) regular; (price)
listado; **at the** ~ **time** a la hora prevista *or*
programada

scheduling *n* (planning) organización *f*,
planeamiento *m*; (of television, radio programmes)
programación *f*; (Comp) planificación *f*

schematic *adj* esquemático

scheme *n* (project) BrE plan *m*; (design)
esquema *m*; (underhand) ardid *m*

Schengen Agreement *n* Acuerdo de
Schengen *m*

science park *n* parque científico *m*

scientific *adj* (research, management,
programming) científico

scientist *n* científico(-a) *m,f*

SCM *abbr* (▸**supply chain management**)
gestión de la cadena de suministros *f*

scoop[1] *n* (news story) primicia informativa
f; (Fin) pelotazo *m*

scoop[2] *vt* (profit, news story) sacar

scope *n* (of law, regulations, reform, agreement)
alcance *m*; (of influence) ámbito *m*, esfera *f*; (of
investigation, activities) campo *m*; (opportunity,
room) posibilidades *f pl*; **there is still** ~ **for
improvement** aún se pueden mejorar las
cosas

scorched-earth policy *n* política de la
tierra quemada *f*

score[1] *n* (in test) puntuación *f*, puntuaje *m*
AmL; **on that** ~ a ese respecto

score[2] *vt* (in test) sacar; ~ **good viewer
ratings** conseguir un gran número de

telespectadores; ~ **an instant success with
sth** apuntarse un triunfo con algo

SCP *abbr* (▸**sterling commercial paper**)
papel comercial en libras esterlinas *m*; ~
market *n* mercado de papel comercial en
libras esterlinas *m*

scrambled *adj* (message) cifrado

scrap[1] *vt* (idea) desechar, descartar; (plan)
abandonar; (regulation) abolir; (vehicle,
machinery) desguazar

scrap[2] *n* (small piece) pedazo *m*; (metal waste)
chatarra *f*; **they haven't got a** ~ **of
evidence** no tienen ninguna prueba; ~
metal *n* chatarra *f*; ~ **paper** *n* papel de
borrador *m*

scrape together *vt* (money) reunir a
duras penas

scrapheap *n* montón de chatarra *m*; **find
oneself on the** ~ verse sin trabajo y sin
perspectivas de futuro

scratch *n* (Comp) tachadura *m*; ~ **area** *n*
(Comp) zona de trabajo *f*; ~ **disk** *n* disco de
trabajo *m*; ~ **file** *n* (Comp) fichero
transitorio *m*; ~ **pad** *n* (Comp) cuaderno de
anotaciones *m*

scratching *n* (countersignature) visado *m*

screen[1] *n* (of monitor, in cinema) pantalla *f*;
(partition) mampara *f*; ~ **advertising** *n*
publicidad en los cines *f*; ~ **copy** *n* copia de
la pantalla *f*; ~ **driver** *n* unidad de pantalla
f; ~ **dump** *n* vaciado de pantalla *m*; ~
editor *n* editor de pantalla *m*; ~ **rights**
n pl derechos cinematográficos *m pl*

screen[2] *vt* (candidates) filtrar, seleccionar;
(on television) emitir; (in cinema) proyectar,
seleccionar; **screen out** *vt* filtrar

screening *n* (of candidates) selección *f*; (on
television) emisión *f*; (in cinema) proyección *f*;
~ **board** *n* consejo de selección *m*; ~
process *n* proceso de selección *m*

screensaver *n* salvapantallas *m*

screenshot *n* ajuste de pantalla *m*

scrimp *vi* escatimar; ~ **on sth** escatimar
en algo; ~ **and save** apretarse el cinturón

scrip *n* (Stock) vale canjeable *m*; ~
certificate *n* certificado de dividendo
diferido *m*; ~ **dividend** *n* dividendo en
acciones *m*; ~ **issue** *n* BrE (cf ▸**stock
dividend** AmE) emisión de acciones
liberadas *f*

script *n* guión *m*

scroll[1] *vt* [1] (Comp) pasar
[2] *vi* pasar las páginas; **scroll down** [1] *vi*
pasar hacia delante, desplazarse hacia abajo
[2] *vt* pasar hacia delante, desplazar hacia
abajo; **scroll up** [1] *vi* pasar hacia atrás,
desplazarse hacia arriba. [2] *vt* pasar hacia
atrás, desplazar hacia arribe

scroll[2] *n* desplazamiento en pantalla *m*; ∼ **arrow** *n* flecha (de barra) de desplazamiento *f*; ∼ **bar** *n* barra de desplazamiento *f*

scrolling *n* desplazamiento en pantalla *m*; ∼ **down** *n* desplazamiento hacia abajo *m*; ∼ **up** *n* desplazamiento hacia arriba *m*

S/D *abbr* (▸**sight draft**) efecto *m* or letra *f* a la vista

SDA *abbr* BrE (▸**Sex Discrimination Act**) *ley de discriminación sexual*

SEA *abbr* (▸**Single European Act**) AUE (Acta Única Europea)

seal[1] *n* sello *m*; **set the** ∼ **on sth** dar el remate a algo; ∼ **of approval** *n* visto bueno *m*; ∼ **of quality** *n* sello de calidad *m*

seal[2] *vt* (envelope, parcel) cerrar; (document) sellar

sealed *adj* (envelope, parcel) cerrado; **in a** ∼ **envelope** en sobre cerrado; ∼ **tender** *n* oferta en pliego cerrado *f*

sealing wax *n* lacre *m*

seaport *n* puerto marítimo *m* or de mar

SEAQ *abbr* BrE (▸**Stock Exchange Automated Quotation**) *sistema de cotización automatizada del mercado de valores*; ∼ **International** *n* BrE *sistema de cotización automatizada de la bolsa internacional*

search[1] ① *vt* (records, files) buscar en; (building, luggage) registrar; (person) cachear ② *vi* buscar; ∼ **for sth/sb** buscar algo/a alguien

search[2] *n* búsqueda *f*; (of building) registro *m*; (for title) investigación *f*; ∼ **engine** *n* (Comp) motor de búsqueda *m*; ∼ **key** *n* (Comp) clave de búsqueda *f*; ∼ **and seizure** *n* búsqueda *f* y captura *f*; ∼ **warrant** *n* orden de registro *f*

season *n* (of year) estación *f*; (for activity, event) temporada *f*; **off** *o* **out of** ∼ fuera de temporada; ∼ **ticket** *n* (*cf* ▸**commutation ticket** AmE) abono *m*; ∼ **ticket holder** *n* poseedor(a) de un abono *m,f*

seasonal *adj* (adjustment, variation, demand) estacional; ∼ **unemployment** *n* desempleo estacional *m*; ∼ **worker** *n* temporero(-a) *m,f*

seasonality *n* (of demand) estacionalidad *f*

seasonally *adv* según la estación; ∼**-adjusted** *adj* (figures, unemployment figures) desestacionalizado; ∼**-adjusted annual rate** *n* tipo anual con ajuste estacional *m*

seasoned *adj* (worker) experimentado; (loan) acreditado, periódico, temporal; ∼ **CD** *n* certificado de depósito acreditado *m*

seat *n* asiento *m*; (in plane, bus) plaza *f*; (in theatre) localidad *f*; (in Parliament) escaño *m*

SEATS *abbr* BrE (▸**Stock Exchange Alternative Trading Service**) *sistema operativo de cotizaciones*

sec. *abbr* (▸**secretary**) secretario(-a) *m,f*

SEC *abbr* AmE (▸**Securities and Exchange Commission**, *cf* ▸**SIB** BrE) *comisión de vigilancia del mercado de valores*, ≈ CNMV Esp (Comisión Nacional del Mercado de Valores)

SECAL *abbr* (▸**sector adjustment loan**) *préstamo de ajuste del sector m*

second[1] *adj* segundo; **the** ∼ **half of the year** la segunda parte del año; **get one's** ∼ **wind** volver a recuperar las fuerzas; ∼**-class citizen** *n* ciudadano(-a) de segunda clase *m,f*; ∼**-class mail** *n* AmE (*cf* ▸**second-class post** BrE) correo ordinario *m*; ∼**-class paper** *n* (Fin) título de segunda categoría *m*; ∼**-class post** *n* BrE (*cf* ▸**second-class mail** AmE) correo ordinario *m*; ∼ **debenture** *n* segunda obligación *f*; ∼ **generation** *n* segunda generación *f*; ∼**-generation product** *n* producto de segunda generación *m*; ∼**-grade** *adj* de segundo grado; ∼**-hand** *adj* (goods) de segunda mano, seminuevo; ∼**-hand market** *n* mercado de segunda mano *m*; ∼ **home** *n* segunda residencia *f*; ∼ **mortgage** *n* BrE (*cf* ▸**junior mortgage** AmE) hipoteca en segundo grado *f*, segunda hipoteca *f*; ∼ **offence** *n* BrE, ∼ **offense** AmE *n* reincidencia *m*; ∼ **quarter** *n* segundo trimestre *m*; ∼ **reading** *n* (of bill, directive) segunda lectura *f*; ∼ **residence** *n* segunda residencia *f*; **S**∼ **World countries** *n* países de economía planificada *m pl*

second[2] *n* (of time) segundo *m*; (substandard product) artículo con defectos de fábrica *m*

second[3] *vt* (motion) apoyar, secundar

second[4] *vt* (employee) trasladar temporalmente; ∼ **sb to sth** trasladar a alguien temporalmente a algo

secondary *adj* (road, income, product) secundario; (industry) derivado; (strike, action, picketing) de solidaridad, de apoyo; ∼ **activities** *n pl* actividades secundarias *f pl*; ∼ **bank** *n* banco secundario *m*; ∼ **distribution** *n* (of shares) reventa fraccionada *f*; ∼ **education** *n* educación secundaria *f*; ∼ **labor market** AmE, ∼ **labour market** BrE *n* mercado *m* laboral secundario *or* de trabajo secundario; ∼ **legislation** *n* legislación secundaria *f*; ∼ **market** *n* mercado secundario *m*; ∼ **offering** *n* colocación en el mercado secundario *f*; ∼ **sector** *n* sector secundario *m*

second-best[1] *n* (substitute) sustituto *m*; (worse alternative) inferior *m*; **settle for** ∼ conformarse con lo inferior

S

second-best² *adj* (next after best) segundo mejor; (worse) inferior; **come off ~** quedar en segundo lugar

seconder *n persona que secunda o apoya una moción o propuesta*

second-guess *vt* anticiparse a

secondly *adv* en segundo lugar

secondment *n* traslado temporal *m*

second-to-none *adj* no inferior a nadie

secrecy *n* secreto *m*

secret¹ *adj* (payment, funds, clause) secreto; (reserve) oculto; **~ ballot** *n* votación secreta *f*

secret² *n* secreto

secretarial *adj* (job, work) de secretario(a); (course, skills) de secretariado; **~ staff** *n* personal de secretaría *m*

secretariat *n* secretaría *f*; (government) secretariado *m*

secretary *n* secretario(-a) *m,f*; **S~ of State** *n* (BrE) Secretario(-a) de Estado *m,f*; (AmE) ministro(-a) de asuntos exteriores *m,f*

section *n* (of organization, newspaper) sección *f*; (of machine, book) parte *f*; (of public opinion) sector *m*; **~ manager** *n* gerente de área *mf*

sector¹ *n* sector *m*; **the private/public ~** el sector privado/público; **~ adjustment loan** *n* préstamo de ajuste del sector *m*; **~ analysis** *n* análisis sectorial *m*; **~ investment and maintenance loan** *n* préstamo sectorial de inversión y mantenimiento *m*; **~-specific aid** *n* ayuda a sectores específicos *f*

sector² *vt* (disk) sectorizar

sectoral *adj* (strategy) sectorial

sectorial manager *n* director(a) sectorial *m,f*

secure¹ *adj* (investment, job, line, payment) seguro; **~ electronic transaction** *n* transacción electrónica segura *f*; **S~ Sockets Layer** *n* capa de conexiones seguras *f*

secure² *vt* (agreement, contract) conseguir; (job, support) conseguir, obtener; (loan) garantizar; (price) asegurar; **~ a debt by mortgage** garantizar una deuda con una hipoteca; **~ new orders** conseguir nuevos pedidos

secured *adj* (loan, advance, debenture, debt) garantizado; (credit) garantizado, cubierto; (creditor) garantizado, asegurado; (bond) hipotecario, con garantía

securities *n pl* valores *m pl*, títulos *m pl*, obligaciones *f pl*; **~ wanted** se necesitan valores; **~ account** *n* cuenta de valores *f*; **~ analysis** *n* análisis de valores *m*; **~ borrowing** *n* préstamo en valores *m*; **~ business** *n* operaciones con valores *f pl*; **~ dealer** *n* corredor(a) de valores *m,f*; **~ dealing** *n* operaciones de valores *f pl*;

~ department *n* departamento de valores *m*; **~ exchange** *n* bolsa *f* de comercio *or* de valores; **S~ and Exchange Commission** *n* AmE (*cf* ▶**Securities and Investments Board** BrE) *comisión de vigilancia del mercado de valores*, ≈ Comisión Nacional del Mercado de Valores Esp; **~ house** *n* casa de valores *f*; **S~ and Investments Board** *n* BrE (*cf* ▶**Securities and Exchange Commission** AmE) *comisión de vigilancia del mercado de valores*, ≈ Comisión Nacional del Mercado de Valores *f* Esp; **~ listing** *n* cotización de valores *f*; **~ loan** *n* préstamo de valores entre operadores *m*; **~ market** *n* bolsa *f* de comercio *or* de valores; **~ portfolio** *n* cartera de títulos *f*; **~ tax** *n* impuesto sobre valores *m*; **~ transaction** *n* transacción de títulos *f*

securitization *n* titulización *f*, aseguración *f*

securitize *vt* titulizar, asegurar

security *n* (safety) seguridad *f*; (department) departamento de seguridad *m*; (collateral) colateral *m*; (for loan) prenda *f*, fianza *f*; (guarantee) garantía *f*; **stand ~ for sb** salir garante *or* fiador de alguien; **~ backup** *n* (Comp) copia de respaldo *f*; **~ breach** *n* fallo de seguridad *m*; **~ copy** *n* copia de seguridad *f*; **~ guard** *n* guarda jurado(-a) *m,f*; **~ interest** *n* interés de garantía *m*; **~ leak** *n* falla *f or* fuga *f* de seguridad; **~ margin** *n* margen de seguridad *m*; **~ measure** *n* medida de seguridad *f*; **~ risk** *n* riesgo para la seguridad *m*; **~ service** *n* servicio de seguridad *m*; **~ of tenure** *n* tenencia asegurada *f*

seed *n* (of idea) germinación *f*; **~ capital** *n* capital generador *m*; **~ money** *n* dinero generador *m*

seek *vt* (advice) pedir; (approval) solicitar; (help, employment) buscar; (solution, explanation) tratar de encontrar, buscar; (reconciliation) buscar, tratar de lograr; **~ redress** exigir compensación

seepage *n* infiltración *f*

segment¹ *n* segmento *m*; **~ information** *n* información segmentada *f*; **~ margin** *n* margen de segmento *m*; **~ profit** *n* beneficio de segmento *m*

segment² *vt* segmentar

segmentation *n* segmentación *f*; **~ strategy** *n* estrategia de segmentación *f*

segmented *adj* segmentado

segregate *vt* segregar

segregated *adj* segregado

segregation *n* segregación *f*; (of duties) separación *f*

seize *vt* (assets, property) confiscar; (impound) embargar; (cargo, contraband) confiscar, decomisar

seizure *n* (of property) confiscación *f*; (impoundment) embargo *m*; (of cargo, contraband) confiscación *f*, decomiso *m*

select[1] *vt* seleccionar

select[2] *adj* (group) selecto; ~ **committee** *n* BrE comisión especial *f*

selected *adj* seleccionado

selection *n* (choice) selección *f*; (range) surtido *m*; ~ **board** *n* consejo de selección *m*

selective *adj* (distribution, selling) selectivo; ~ **employment tax** *n* impuesto selectivo sobre el empleo *m*; ~ **hedge** *n* cobertura selectiva *f*

selector *n* (Comms) selector *m*; ~ **channel** *n* (Comp) canal selector *m*

self- *pref* auto-; ~**actualization** *n* autoactualización *f*; ~**addressed envelope** BrE, ~**addressed stamped envelope** AmE *n* sobre sellado con la *dirección del remitente*; ~**adhesive** *adj* autoadhesivo; ~**adjusting** *adj* autoajustable; ~**amortizing** *adj* (mortgage) autoamortizable; ~**appointed** *adj* autoproclamado; ~**appraisal** *n* autoevaluación *f*; ~**assessment** *n* BrE (Tax) autoliquidación *f*; ~**catering** *adj* (apartment, holiday) sin servicio de comidas; ~**contained** *adj* autónomo; ~**drive hire** *n* alquiler de vehículo sin conductor *m*; ~**employed person** *n*, ~**employed worker** *n* trabajador(a) *m,f* autónomo(-a) *or* por cuenta propia; ~**employment** *n* autoempleo *m*, trabajo por cuenta propia *m*; ~**employment income** *n* ingresos del trabajo por cuenta propia *m pl*; ~**finance** *vt* autofinanciar; ~**financing** *n* autofinanciación *f*; ~**financing** *adj* autofinanciado; ~**fulfilling prophecy** *n* profecía de cumplimiento inevitable *f*; ~**funded** *adj* autofinanciado; ~**generated** *adj* (funds) autogenerado; ~**governing** *adj* (nation) autónomo; (organization, institution) autoregulado; ~**government** *n* autogobierno *m*, autonomía *f*; ~**help** *n* autoayuda *f*; ~**image** *n* autoimagen *f*; ~**insurance** *n* autoseguro *m*; ~**interest** *n* interés (personal) *m*; ~**liquidator** *n* oferta que, a *pesar de tener un precio muy atractivo, cubre los gastos publicitarios*; ~**loading** *adj* autocargador; ~**made** *adj* (man, woman) que ha alcanzado su posición gracias a sus propios esfuerzos; ~**management** *n* autodirección *f*, autogestión *f*; ~**motivated** *adj* automotivado; ~**motivation** *n* automotivación *f*; ~**regulating organization** *n* BrE organización

autorregulada *f*; ~**regulation** *n* autorregulación *f*; ~**regulatory organization** *n* organización autorreguladora *f*; ~**restraint** *n* autodominio *m*; ~**selection** *n* autoselección *f*; ~**service** *n* autoservicio *m*; ~**service application** *n* (Comp) aplicación de autoservicio *f*; ~**service banking** *n* banca *f* automatizada *or* de autoservicio; ~**service economy** *n* economía de autoservicio *f*; ~**service shop** BrE, ~**service store** AmE *n* tienda de autoservicio *f*; ~**start** *n* (Comp) autoarranque *m*; ~**starter** *n* (Comp) arrancador automático *m*; (person) persona *f* dinámica *or* emprendedora; ~**styled** *adj* supuesto; ~**sufficiency** *n* autosuficiencia *f*, autoabastecimiento *m* ; ~**sufficient** *adj* (country) autosuficiente, autárquico; (economy) autárquico; (person) independiente; ~**supporting** *adj* (person) económicamente independiente; (organization) autofinanciado; (debt) rentable; ~**sustained** *adj* (growth) autosostenido; ~**taught person** *n* autodidacta *mf*

sell [1] *vt* vender; ~ sth for sth vender algo en *or* por algo; **be sold on sth/sb** entusiasmarse por algo/alguien; ~ **sth to sb**, ~ **sb sth** venderle algo a alguien; **you have to ~ yourself at an interview** tienes que convencer en una entrevista de que eres el mejor [2] *vi* (person, company) vender; (product, range) venderse; **the badges ~ at 50p each** las chapas se venden a 50 peniques cada una; ~ **directly to the public** vender directamente al público; **sell back** *vt* revender; **sell forward** *vt* vender a futuro; **sell off** *vt* liquidar, saldar; **sell on** *vt* BrE revender; **sell out** [1] *vi* (stock, tickets) agotarse; (dispose of holding) vender *or* liquidar el negocio; (be traitor) venderse; **we've sold out of printers** no nos quedan impresoras, se nos han agotado las impresoras [2] *vt* (stock) agotar; (article) vender todas las existencias de; (shares, holding) vender; **sell up** [1] *vi* vender el negocio [2] *vt* (business) liquidar, vender

sell-by date *n* (on food) fecha de caducidad *f*

seller *n* vendedor(a) *m,f*; **be a good/poor ~** (product) venderse bien/mal; ~**s' market** *n* mercado de vendedores *m*; ~**'s option** *n* prima de opción a vender *f*

sell-in *n* venta inicial *f*

selling *n* venta *f*; ~ **agent** *n* intermediario(-a) de ventas *m,f*; ~ **concession** *n* descuento de venta *m*; ~ **expenses** *n pl* gastos *m pl* de comercialización *or* de venta; ~ **hedge** *n* cobertura de venta *f*; ~ **point** *n* *característica especial que se utiliza para la* ⋯⟩

venta de un producto; ∼ **price** *n* precio de venta *m*; ∼ **rate** *n* cambio de venta *m*; ∼ **space** *n* espacio de ventas *m*

selling-short *n* venta en descubierto *f*

sell-off *n* venta precipitada *f*

sellout *n* (infrml) (in theatre, cinema) éxito de taquilla *m*; (betrayal) traición *f*

sell-side *adj* (application, system) del lado vendedor

semiannual *adj* (dividend) semianual

semiblack market *n* mercado seminegro *m*

semicolon *n* punto y coma *m*

semiconductor *n* semiconductor *m*

semidetached house *n* BrE (*cf* ▸**duplex²** AmE) casa *f* adosada *or* semiseparada

semidisplay *adj* (advertising) semiintensivo

semidurable *adj* (goods) semiperecedero

semifinished *adj* (goods) semimanufacturado, semiterminado; (product) semimanufacturado, semielaborado

semifixed *adj* (cost) semifijo

semi-industrialized *adj* (country) semiindustrializado

seminar *n* seminario *m*

semiprivate *adj* (bank) semiprivado

semiprocessed *adj* (product) semielaborado

semirigid *n* (receptacle) semirrígido

semiskilled *adj* (worker) semicalificado; (work) para persona semicalificada

semistructured *adj* semiestructurado

semivariable *adj* (costs, expenses) semivariable

Senate *n* AmE Cámara Alta *f*

send *vt* (letter, parcel, messenger) mandar, enviar; ∼ **away for sth** *o* **off for sth** escribir pidiendo algo; ∼ **sth by fax** enviar algo por fax; ∼ **sth by mail** AmE *o* **post** BrE enviar algo por correo; ∼ **sth by parcel post** BrE enviar algo por paquete postal; ∼ **an order by wire** enviar una orden por telegrama; ∼ **sb for sth** mandar a alguien a buscar algo; **the news sent prices soaring** la noticia hizo disparar los precios; ∼ **sb sth** *o* ∼ **sth to sb** mandarle *or* enviarle algo a alguien; ∼ **sth under plain cover** enviar algo con la mayor discreción; ∼ **sth via an agent** mandar algo mediante un representante; ∼ **a written request** enviar una petición por escrito; **send back** *vt* (purchase) devolver, mandar de vuelta; **send for** *vt* (catalogue, application form) pedir; (goods) encargar, pedir; **send in** *vt* (application) mandar, enviar; **send off** *vt* (letter, parcel, goods) despachar, mandar, enviar; **send on** *vt* (letter) remitir; **send out** *vt* (leaflets) mandar, enviar

sender *n* (on envelope) remitente *mf*

senior¹ *adj* (in hierarchy) superior, de categoría superior; (in length of service) más antiguo; ∼ **auditor** *n* auditor(a) principal *m,f*; ∼ **citizen** *n* persona de la tercera edad *f*; ∼ **civil servant** *n* funcionario(-a) con antigüedad *m,f*; ∼ **clerk** *n* administrativo(-a) superior *m,f*; (Law) jefe(-a) administrativo(-a) *m,f*; ∼ **debt** *n* deuda principal *f*; ∼ **executive** *n* alto(-a) ejecutivo(-a) *m,f*; ∼ **issue** *n* (Stock) emisión prioritaria *f*; ∼ **loan** *n* préstamo *m* principal *or* prioritario; ∼ **management** *n* administración *f or* dirección *f* superior; ∼ **manager** *n* director(a) principal *m,f*; ∼ **officer** *n* funcionario(-a) de rango superior *m,f*; ∼ **security** *n* título de garantía preferente *m*; ∼ **vice president** *n* AmE vicepresidente(-a) *m,f* principal *or* adjunto(-a)

senior² *n* superior *mf*

seniority *n* antigüedad *f*; ∼ **bonus** *n*, ∼ **premium** *n* prima por antigüedad *f*; ∼ **principle** *n* principio de antigüedad *m*

sense *n* (physical faculty, common sense, awareness) sentido *m*; (impression) sensación *f*; (meaning) sentido *m*, significado *m*; **make** ∼ tener sentido; **make** ∼ **of sth** descifrar algo; **talk** ∼ hablar con juicio; ∼ **of responsibility** *n* sentido de responsabilidad *m*; ∼ **of security** *n* sensación de seguridad *f*

sensitive *adj* (market, zone) sensible; (document, information) confidencial; (topic, issue) delicado

sensitivity *n* sensibilidad *f*; ∼ **analysis** *n* análisis de sensibilidad *m*; ∼ **training** *n* capacitación *f or* formación *f* de sensibilidad

sensitize *vt* sensibilizar

sensory *adj* (deprivation, overload) sensorial

sentence¹ *n* (Law) sentencia *f*; **pass** ∼ **(on sb)** dictar *or* pronunciar sentencia (contra alguien)

sentence² *vt* (Law) sentenciar, condenar

separate *adj* (bank account, tax return) separado; (residence) por separado; **ask for** ∼ **bills** pedir cuentas individuales; **that is a** ∼ **issue** eso es una cuestión aparte; **(send sth) under** ∼ **cover** (enviar algo) por separado; ∼ **customer** *n* (Stock) cliente por derecho propio *m*

separately *adv* separadamente

separation *n* separación *f*; ∼ **agreement** *n* acuerdo de separación *m*

separator *n* (Comp) separador *m*

sequence *n* (of events, actions) sucesión *f*, serie *f*; (order) secuencia *f*; **in** ∼ en sucesión; ∼ **error** *n* error de secuencia *m*; ∼ **number** *n* número de secuencia *m*

sequential *adj* (access, analysis, number) secuencial

sequestration *n* (of property) secuestro *m*

sequestrator *n* (of property) depositario(-a) *m,f,*

serial *adj* (access, processing, adaptor) en serie; ~ **bond** *n* bono de vencimiento escalonado *m*; ~ **number** *n* número de orden *m*; ~**parallel** *adj* serial-paralelo; ~ **port** *n* puerta en serie *f*; ~ **printer** *n* impresora en serie *f*; ~ **reader** *n* lector en serie *m*

series *n* serie *f*

serious *adj* (injury, illness, accident, crime) grave; **S~ Fraud Office** *n* BrE (Law) brigada anticorrupción *f*, (Stock) *oficina de delitos monetarios graves*

SERPS *abbr* BrE (▷**State Earnings Related Pension Scheme**) *plan estatal de pensiones*

serve [1] *vt* (food, drink) servir; (company) servir a; (customer) atender; (community, area) abastecer; (summons, notice, order) entregar; (market) abastecer, servir; (apprenticeship) hacer; (sentence) cumplir; ~ **counternotice** presentar un contrainforme; ~ **the purpose** servir para el caso; **it ~s no useful purpose** no sirve para nada (útil); ~ **sb with a warrant** notificar a alguien una orden de detención *or* una orden de registro [2] *vi* (distribute food, drink) servir; (in shop) BrE atender; ~ **on a committee** ser miembro de una comisión

server *n* (Comp) servidor *m*

service[1] *n* servicio *m*; (overhaul, maintenance) revisión *f*, servicio *m* AmL; **at sb's ~** al servicio de alguien; ~**s for business** servicios para negocios; **for ~s rendered** por servicios prestados; ~ **not included** servicio no incluido; **be of ~ to sb** serle útil a alguien; **offer one's ~s** ofrecer sus servicios; **be out of ~** (telephone, machine) estar fuera de servicio; **we no longer require your ~s** ya no precisamos sus servicios; ~ **agreement** *n* contrato de mantenimiento *m*, acuerdo de servicio *m*; ~ **bureau** *n* centro de servicios informáticos *m*; ~ **card** *n* (Comp) tarjeta de servicio *f*; ~ **charge** *n* (in restaurant) servicio *m*; (in banking) comisión *f*; (for accommodation) gastos *m pl* comunes *or* de comunidad Esp; (for office) gastos de mantenimiento *m pl*; ~ **company** *n* compañía de servicios *f*; ~ **contract** *n* contrato de servicios *m*; ~ **delivery** *n* prestación de servicios *f*; ~ **department** *n* departamento de servicios *m*; ~ **economy** *n* economía de servicios *f*; ~ **engineer** *n* ingeniero(-a) *m,f* de funcionamiento *or* de reparaciones; ~ **enterprise** *n* empresa de servicios *f*; ~ **entrance** *n* AmE (*cf* ▷**trade entrance** BrE) entrada de servicio *f*; ~ **fee** *n* tasa de servicio *f*; ~ **handbook** *n* guía de

servicios *f*; ~ **industry** *n* industria de servicios *f*; ~ **level agreement** *n* acuerdo del nivel se servicio *m*; ~ **manual** *n* manual de mantenimiento *m*; ~ **mark** *n* marca de servicios *f*; ~ **sector** *n* sector de servicios *m*; ~ **sector job** *n* trabajo en el sector de servicios *m*; ~ **station** *n* estación de servicio *f*

service[2] *vt* (debt, loan) pagar los intereses de, revisar; (vehicle) hacerle una revisión *or* un servicio a AmL; (machine, appliance) hacerle el mantenimiento a

session *n* sesión *f*; **be in ~** estar reunido

set[1] *n* (of rules, instructions) serie *f*; (of tools) juego *m*; (Comp) conjunto *m*; **in ~s of** en series de; ~ **of accounts** *n* grupo de cuentas *m*; ~ **of bills** *n* juego de facturas *m*; ~ **of claims** *n* (Patents) expediente de reclamaciones *m*; ~ **of measures** *n* conjunto de medidas *m*; ~ **of notes** *n* (Fin) juego de facturas *m*; ~ **of options** *n* (Stock) conjunto de opciones *m*

set[2] *vt* (date, time, price, bail) fijar, acordar; (agenda) establecer, acordar; (task) asignar; (precedent) sentar; (rules, conditions) establecer, imponer; (record, standard, target, value) establecer; (fashion) dictar, imponer; (type) componer; ~ **a good example** dar un buen ejemplo; ~ **a new high** establecer un nuevo máximo; ~ **sth in motion** poner algo en marcha; ~ **the pace** dar la pauta; ~ **parameters** fijar los parámetros; ~ **a price-point** fijar un precio; ~ **sb to work** poner a alguien a trabajar; **set about** *vt* (task) acometer; ~ **about doing sth** ponerse a hacer algo; **set against** *vt* (balance, compare) comparar con; ~ **against other offers, your company's estimate...** comparada con otros presupuestos, la oferta de su compañía...; **these costs can be ~ against your total income** estos gastos pueden deducirse de sus ingresos; **set aside** *vt* (goods) guardar, apartar, reservar; (time) dejar; (money) guardar, ahorrar; (task, project) dejar (de lado); (rules) prescindir de; (judgment, verdict) anular; **set down** *vt* (write down) escribir; (rule, condition) establecer, fijar; ~ **sth down in writing** poner algo por escrito; **set forth** *vt* (argument, theory) exponer; (aims, policy, proposition) presentar; **set off** *vt* (losses) compensar; **set sth off against sth** deducir algo de algo; ~ **off a debit against a credit** compensar un débito a cuenta de un crédito; **set out** [1] *vt* (goods, argument, theory, conditions) exponer [2] *vi* (start) empezar; ~ **out to do sth** proponerse hacer algo; **I didn't ~ out with that intention** no empecé con esa intención; **set up** [1] *vt* (business) montar; (meeting) convocar a, llamar a; (interview) concertar; (committee, commission) crear; (inquiry) abrir; (claim) presentar; (type)

S

componer; (Comp) (start) arrancar; (install) montar; **set oneself up as sth** establecerse como algo [2] *vi* (in business) establecerse; **~ up on one's own account** establecerse por cuenta propia

set³ *adj* (wage, price) fijo; (resolved) resuelto; **be ~ on doing sth** estar resuelto a hacer algo

SET *abbr* (▸**secure electronic transaction**) transacción electrónica segura *f*

setback *n* revés *m*; **suffer a ~** sufrir un revés

set-off *n* (Bank) compensación *f*

settings *n pl* (Comp) posicionamientos *m pl*

setting-up costs *n pl* costes *m pl* Esp *or* costos *m pl* AmL de primer establecimiento

settle [1] *vt* (price, terms, time) acordar, fijar; (dispute) resolver; (bill, account) pagar; (debt) saldar, liquidar; **~ the figure** (of compensation) fijar la cifra; **~ sth in cash** liquidar algo en metálico; **~ old scores** (infml) ajustar cuentas pendientes [2] *vi* (in job, in country) establecerse

settlement *n* (agreement) acuerdo *m*, convenio *m*; (of account, bill) pago *m*; (of debt, security, bond) liquidación *f*; (of dispute) (re)solución *f*; (of country) colonización; **in ~ of sth** (debt) en pago de algo; **reach a ~ with sb** llegar a un acuerdo con alguien; **sell for the ~** vender a término; **~ account** *n* cuenta de liquidación *f*; **~ date** *n* (of security) fecha de liquidación *f*; **~ day** *n* día de liquidación *m*; **~s department** *n* departamento de liquidaciones *m*; **~ discount** *n* descuento de liquidación *m*; **~ draft** *n* letra de liquidación *f*; **~ in full** *n* pago íntegro *m*; **~ per contra** *n* compensación de deudas *f*; **~ price** *n* precio de liquidación *m*; **~ to the market** *n* liquidación a precios de mercado *f*; **~ transaction** *n* transacción de liquidación *f*

settlor *n* BrE (Law) fideicomitente *m*

set-up *n* (situation, arrangement) sistema *m*, organización *f*; (Comp) preparación *f*; **~ CD-ROM** *n* CD-ROM de instalación *m*; **~ costs** *n pl* costes *m pl* Esp *or* costos *m pl* AmL de primer establecimiento; **~ program** *n* (Comp) programa de instalación *m*

sever *vt* (communications) cortar; **~ links with sb** romper relaciones con alguien

severally *adv* por separado

severance *n* (of relations, links) ruptura *f*; (dismissal) despido *m*; **~ pay** *n* compensación por despido *f*

sewage *n* aguas residuales *f pl*; **~ treatment** *n* depuración de aguas residuales *m*

sew up *vt* (infml) (deal) arreglar; **have the market sewn up** dominar el mercado

Sex Discrimination Act *n* BrE *ley de discriminación sexual*

sexual *adj* sexual; **~ discrimination** *n* discriminación *f* sexual *or* por sexo; **~ division of labor** AmE, **~ division of labour** BrE *n* división del trabajo por sexos *f*; **~ harassment** *n* acoso sexual *m*; **~ stereotyping** *n* estereotipia de los sexos *f*

sexy *adj* (product) seductor

SFA *abbr* (▸**sales force automation**) automatización del personal de ventas *f*

SFO *abbr* (▸**Serious Fraud Office**) BrE (Law) brigada anticorrupción *f*; (Stock) *oficina de delitos monetarios graves*

sgd *abbr* (▸**signed**) firmado

SGML *abbr* (▸**Standard Generalized Mark-up Language**) SGML *m* (Lenguaje Estandarizado y Generalizado de Marcado)

sh *abbr* (▸**share**) acción *f*

shade [1] *vt* reducir ligeramente [2] *vi* bajar ligeramente

shadow¹ *n* sombra *f*; **S~ Cabinet** *n* BrE gabinete *m* de la oposición; **S~ Chancellor** *n* BrE *portavoz para asuntos económicos del partido de la oposición*; **~ economy** *n* economía paralela *f*; **~ price** *n* precio contable *m*

shadow² *vt* (currency) proteger

shady *adj* fuera de la ley; **~ dealing** *n* actividad clandestina *f*

shake *vt* (courage, nerve) hacer flaquear; (faith) debilitar; (person) impresionar, afectar; **the scandal has ~n the financial world** el escándalo ha conmocionado al mundo de las finanzas; **shake out** *vt* (company) reorganizar, racionalizar; (staff) reducir; **shake up** *vt* (industry, personnel) reorganizar totalmente

shakedown *n* AmE (infml) exacción de dinero *f*

shake-out *n* reorganización *f*, racionalización *f*

shake-up *n* reorganización *f*

shaky *adj* (currency, goverment) débil; (theory, start) flojo

shallow *adj* (market) superficial

sham¹ *adj* (dividend) ficticio

sham² *n* farsa *f*

shape¹ *n* (visible form) forma *f*; (general nature) configuración *f*; **knock** *o* **lick** *o* **whip sth/sb into ~** (team, new recruits) poner algo/a alguien a punto *or* en forma; **the ~ of the future** la configuración del futuro; **the ~ of things to come** la forma de las cosas por venir; **the ~ of the world economy** la configuración de la economía mundial; **take ~** (idea) cobrar forma

shape² *vt* (events) determinar; (ideas) formar; (options price) configurar; **shape up** *vi* (project) tomar forma; (plan) desarrollarse; (improve) entrar en vereda (infrml)

share¹ *n* (portion) parte *f*; (held by shareholder) acción *f*; (held by partner) participación *f*; **have a ~ in a business** tener una participación en un negocio; **~ allotment** *n* reparto de acciones *m*; **~ capital** *n* capital *m* accionario *or* en acciones; **~ certificate** *n* BrE (*cf* ▸**stock certificate** AmE) bono social *m*; **~ dividend** *n* dividendo de una acción *m*; **~ index** *n* índice *m* bursátil *or* de cotización de acciones en bolsa *m*; **~ issue for cash** *n* emisión de acciones al contado *f*; **~ of the market** *n* cuota de mercado *f*; **~ option** *n* opción *f* sobre acciones *or* de compra de acciones; **~ option scheme** *n* BrE plan de opción de acciones *m*; **~ ownership** *n* titularidad de acciones *f*; **~ participation scheme** *n* BrE plan de participación de acciones *m*; **~ portfolio** *n* cartera de acciones *f*; **~ premium** *n* BrE prima de emisión *f*; **~ price** *n* cotización de acciones *f*; **~ redemption** *n* rescate de una acción *m*; **~ register** *n* registro de acciones *m*; **~ scheme** *n* BrE (for company employees) plan de adquisición de acciones *m*; **~ split** *n* partición de acciones *f*; **~ transfer** *n* transferencia de participación *f*

share² *vt* compartir; **share in** *vt* compartir, participar de; **share out** *vt* (profits) repartir, distribuir

shared *adj* (database, ownership, monopoly) compartido

shareholder *n* accionista *mf*; **~'s auditor** *n* comisario(-a) *m,f*; **~'s equity** *n* capital *m* contable *or* de los accionistas; **~s' meeting** *n* reunión *f or* junta *f* de accionistas

shareholding *n* participación accionaria *f*

shareware *n* programas compartidos *m pl*, soporte lógico del dominio público *m pl*

shark watcher *n* (jarg) *empresa especializada en la pronta detección de intentos de absorción*

sharp *adj* (rise, fall) brusco; (person, move) astuto; (protest) severo, encarnizado; **~ movement** *n* (of option price) movimiento rápido *m*

sharply *adv* (drop, fall, increase) bruscamente

shed *vt* (workers, stock) desprenderse de; **~ light on sth** aclarar algo

sheet *n* hoja *f*; **~ feeder** *n* alimentador de hojas *m*

shelf *n* (on wall) estante *n*, anaquel *n*; (in cupboard, bookcase) estante *n*; **(buy sth) off the ~** (comprar algo) de confección; **~ display** *n* exposición en estantes *f*; **~ filler** *n* *persona que repone mercancía en los estantes de una tienda*; **~ life** *n* (of product) duración de vida *f*, vida en estantería *f*; **~ price** *n* *precio de un producto puesto en la estantería*; **~ registration** *n* AmE (Stock) registro automático *m*; **~ space** *n* espacio en estante *m*; **~ warmer** *n* artículo sin venta *m*

shell: **~ company** BrE, **~ corporation** AmE *n* corporación que existe para mantener acciones en otras compañías*; **~ operation** *n* *adquisición de una empresa que aunque ha cesado actividades cotiza en bolsa*

shell out (infrml) **1** *vt* (money) soltar (infrml), desembolsar
2 *vi* soltar (la mosca) (infrml)

shelter¹ *n* (Tax) refugio *m*

shelter² *vi* (Tax) sustraerse

sheltered *adj* (employment, industry) protegido

shelve *vt* (plan) archivar, aparcar

shield *vt* proteger

shift¹ *n* (of workers) turno *m*; (in demand, consumption) desplazamiento *m*; (in demand curve, supply curve) desviación *f*; (in emphasis) cambio *m*; **~ key** *n* (Comp) tecla de mayúsculas *f*; **~ work** *n* trabajo por turnos *m*; **~ worker** *n* trabajador(a) por turnos *m,f*

shift² **1** *vt* (sell) vender; (transfer) traspasar, trasferir; (tax burden) repercutir
2 *vi* (position, attitude) cambiar

ship¹ *n* buque *m*

ship² *vt* (send) enviar, despachar; (send by sea) enviar *or* mandar por barco; (take on board) embarcar

shipbroker *n* agente marítimo(-a) *m,f*

shipbuilder *n* constructor(a) de naves *m,f*

shipbuilding *n* construcción naval *f*

shipment *n* (act) embarque *m*; (goods) envío *m*; **ready for ~** listo para embarcar

shipowner *n* armador(a) *m,f*

shipper *n* cargador(a) *m,f*, expedidor(a) *m,f*, fletador(a) *m,f*

shipping *n* (act) despacho *m*, embarque *m*, envío *m*; (ships) navegación *f*; **~ agency** *n* agencia de transporte marítimo *f*; **~ agent** *n* consignatario(-a) de buques *m,f*; **~ bill** *n* certificado *m or* factura *f* de embarque; **~ and forwarding agent** *n* agente de transportes marítimos *mf*; **~ line** *n* compañía *f or* línea *f* de navegación

shirker *n* (infrml) haragán(-ana) *m,f*

shoot¹ *n* (jarg) (filming session) rodaje *m*

shoot² *vt* (film) rodar; **shoot up** *vt* (prices) dispararse

shooting *n* (filming) rodaje *m*

shop¹ *n* (commercial outlet) BrE (*cf* ▸**store** AmE) tienda *f*; (advertising agency) taller *m*; **~ assistant** *n* BrE (*cf* ▸**sales clerk** AmE) ⋯⟶

dependiente(-a) de tienda *m,f*; ~ **floor** *n* fábrica *f*, taller *m*; **~-floor agreement** *n* BrE acuerdo de fábrica *m*; **~-floor bargaining** *n* BrE negociación en la fábrica *f*; ~ **front** *n* BrE (*cf* ▸**storefront** AmE) fachada *f* (de una tienda); ~ **steward** *n* representante sindical *mf*; ~ **unit** *n* BrE unidad de venta *f*; ~ **window** *n* BrE (*cf* ▸**store window** AmE) escaparate *m*

shop² *vi* hacer compras; ~ **for sth** buscar algo (en las tiendas); **go ~ping** ir de compras; **shop around** *vi* comparar precios

shopaholic *n* (infrml) adicto(-a) a las compras *m,f*

shopkeeper *n* BrE (*cf* ▸**storeowner** AmE) tendero(-a) *m,f*

shoplift *vi* robar en las tiendas

shoplifter *n* ladrón(-ona) *m,f* (que roba en las tiendas)

shoplifting *n* hurto *m* (en las tiendas)

shopper *n* comprador(a) *m,f*

shopping *n* compra *f*; **do the ~** hacer la compra; ~ **basket** *n* cesta de la compra *f*; ~ **cart** *n* AmE (*cf* ▸**shopping trolley** BrE) carrito de la compra *m*; ~ **center** AmE, **centre** BrE *n* centro comercial *m*; ~ **list** *n* lista de compras *f*; ~ **mall** *n* AmE, ~ **precinct** BrE *n* centro comercial *m*; ~ **street** *n* calle comercial *f*; ~ **trolley** *n* BrE (*cf* ▸**shopping cart** AmE) carrito de la compra *m*

shop-soiled *adj* deteriorado

shore up *vt* (share price) sostener, apuntalar; (argument, case) reforzar, apoyar

short¹ *adj* corto; **at ~ notice** con poca antelación; **be in ~ supply** escasear; ~ **of money/time** corto de dinero/tiempo; **be ~ of staff** no tener suficiente personal; ~ **account** *n* cuenta en descubierto *f*; ~ **bill** *n* letra a corto plazo *f*; ~ **call** *n* compra a corto *f*; ~ **covering** *n* cobertura de posición faltante *f*; ~ **delivery** *n* entrega de mercancía incompleta *f*; ~ **futures position** *n* posición corta sobre futuros *f*; **~-handed** *adj* falto de mano de obra; **~-haul** *adj* de corto recorrido; ~ **hedge** *n* cobertura de una posición corta *f*; ~ **market** *n* mercado a corto plazo *m*; ~ **option position** *n* posición corta sobre una opción *f*; **~-range** *adj* (planning) de corto alcance; ~ **run** *n* corto plazo *m*; **~-run** *adj* a corto plazo; ~ **sale** *n* venta al descubierto *f*; ~ **seller** *n* vendedor(a) al descubierto *m,f*; ~ **selling** *n* venta a corto *f*; **~-sighted** *adj* (decision) con poca visión de futuro; **~-staffed** *adj* con poco personal, falto de personal; ~ **time** *n* jornada reducida *f*; **be on ~ time** trabajar jornadas reducidas

short² *adv* (sell) al descubierto; **fall ~ of sth** no alcanzar algo; **go** *o* **run ~ (of sth)** andar escaso (de algo)

short³ *n* corto *m*; **in ~** en resumen, resumiendo; **a ~ in a currency** un déficit en una divisa

shortage *n* (of cash, stock, manpower) escasez *f*

short-change *vt* (in shop) darle mal el cambio a; (deprive of due) no ser justo con

short-circuit *vt* (system, process) evitar parte de, acortar tomando un atajo

shortcoming *n* deficiencia *f*

shorten *vt* acortar; ~ **the odds** aumentar las posibilidades; ~ **the working week** reducir la jornada laboral

shorter-term *adj* (liability, option) a más corto plazo

shortfall *n* déficit *m*, insuficiencia *f*; **a ~ of 7% in revenues** un déficit de 7% en los ingresos

shorthand *n* taquigrafía *f*; ~ **typist** *n* estenotipista *mf*, taquimecanógrafo(-a) *m,f*

shortlist¹ *n* lista de seleccionados *f*

shortlist² *vt* preseleccionar

shortlived *adj* efímero

shorts *n pl* BrE (Stock) posiciones cortas *f pl*

short-term *adj* (bond, loan, objective, planning) a corto plazo; ~ **advance** *n* anticipo a corto plazo *m*; ~ **contract** *n* contrato a corto plazo *m*; ~ **credit** *n* crédito a corto plazo *m*; ~ **debt** *n* deuda a corto plazo *f*; ~ **deposit** *n* depósito a corto plazo *m*; ~ **interest rate** *n* tipo de interés a corto plazo *m*; ~ **investment asset** *n* activo líquido a corto plazo *m*; ~ **investment portfolio** *n* cartera de inversiones a corto plazo *f*; ~ **liabilities** *n pl* obligaciones a corto plazo *f pl*; ~ **money market** *n* mercado monetario a corto plazo *m*; ~ **security** *n* obligación a corto plazo *f*; ~ **worker** *n* trabajador(a) temporal *m,f*

shoulder *vt* (blame, responsibility) cargar con

show¹ *vt* (profit, loss, passport) mostrar, enseñar; (interest, enthusiasm) demostrar, mostrar; (truth, importance) demostrar; (film) dar, proyectar; (programme) dar, emitir; ~ **a balance of** presentar un balance de; ~ **one's hand** (infrml) poner las cartas sobre la mesa; ~ **sb sth** *o* ~ **sth to sb** mostrale algo a alguien; **show around** *vt* llevar a visitar; **show in** *vt* hacer pasar; **show out** *vt* acompañar a la puerta; **show round** *vt* BrE llevar a visitar

show² *n* (exhibition) exposición *f*; (display) demostración *f*; (stage production) espectáculo *m*; **for ~** para impresionar; **make a ~ of (doing) sth** hacer gran alarde de (hacer) algo; **on ~** expuesto; **run the ~** llevar la voz

cantante; **vote by a ~ of hands** votar a
mano alzada; **~ business** n mundo del
espectáculo m; **~ flat** n BrE piso modelo m
Esp; **~ house** n casa modelo f

showcase¹ n vitrina f

showcase² vt exhibir

showdown n confrontación f

showpiece n (of collection) obra maestra f

showroom n sala de exposición f (de
artículos a venta)

showthrough n traspaso de la imagen de
una página a otra

shr abbr (▶**share**) acción f

shred vt (documents) triturar

shredder n (for documents) trituradora f

shrink [1] vi (amount, number) reducirse,
disminuir, verse reducido
[2] vt (costs) reducir, recortar

shrinkage n (of amount, number) reducción
m; (stock losses) fugas f pl, pérdidas f pl

shrinking adj (market) retraído; (profits) en
disminución

shrink-wrap¹ vt envasar or empaquetar
al calor

shrink-wrap² n, **shrink-wrapping** n
envasado al calor m

shs abbr (▶**shares**) acciones f pl

shunter n (Stock) derivador m

shunting n (Stock) comercio triangular m

shut vti (factory, business) cerrar; **shut down**
vti (factory, business) cerrar; **shut off** vt (water,
electricity) cortar; **shut up** [1] vt (office) cerrar;
~ up shop liquidar un negocio [2] vi (close
business) cerrar

shutdown n (of factory, business, computer)
cierre m; (Stock) cierre patronal m; **~ price**
n precio de liquidación m

shutter n (outside window) postigo m,
persiana f; (inside window) postigo m,
contraventana f; **put up the ~s** BrE (infrml)
bajar la cortina, cerrar el negocio

shuttle n (flight) puente aéreo m; (bus, train
service) servicio (regular) de enlace m; **~
service** n (by air) puente aéreo m; (by bus,
train) servicio de enlace m;

shyster n (infrml) picapleitos mf

SIB abbr BrE (▶**Securities and
Investments Board**, cf ▶**SEC** AmE)
comisión de vigilancia del mercado de
valores, ≈ CNMV Esp (Comisión Nacional
del Mercado de Valores)

sick adj enfermo; **off ~** ausente por
enfermedad, incapacitado; **~ building
syndrome** n síndrome del edificio enfermo
m; **~ leave** n permiso por enfermedad m;
~ pay n salario que se percibe mientras se
está con permiso por enfermedad

sickness n enfermedad f; **~ benefit** n
subsidio de enfermedad m; **~ insurance** n
seguro de enfermedad m

sick-out n (jarg) ausencia por enfermedad f

side n lado m; **keep one's ~ of the bargain**
atender a su parte del trato; **my brother
deals with that ~ of the business** mi
hermano se ocupa de esa parte or de ese
aspecto del negocio; **he repairs cars on the
~** arregla coches como trabajo extra; **it's a
little on the expensive ~** es un poco caro;
take ~s (with sb) tomar partido (por
alguien); **'this ~ up'** este lado hacia arriba;
~ effect n efecto colateral m; **~ issue** n
cuestión secundaria f

sidehead n subtítulo m

sideline¹ n actividad suplementaria f; **~
job** n trabajo secundario m

sideline² vt marginar

sidestep vt esquivar

sidetrack¹ n AmE (cf ▶**siding** BrE)
apartadero m, vía muerta f

sidetrack² vt distraer

sideways market n mercado lateral m

side with vt ponerse del lado de; **~ sb
against sb** ponerse del lado de alguien en
contra de alguien

siding n BrE (cf ▶**sidetrack** AmE)
apartadero m, vía muerta f

siege economy n economía de asedio f

sifting sort n (Comp) clasificación por
cribadura f

sight n vista f; **at ~** a la vista; **there's no
end in ~** no se ve el final; **raise/lower one's
~s** aspirar a más/a menos; **set one's ~s on
sth** tener la vista puesta en algo; **he bought
the goods ~ unseen** compró los artículos
sin haberlos visto antes; **~ bill** n efecto m
or letra f a la vista; **~ deposit** n depósito a
la vista m; **~ draft** n efecto m or letra f a la
vista

sign¹ n (indication) señal f, indicio m; (notice)
letrero m, cartel m; (road sign) señal (vial) f;
(symbol) símbolo m; (in mathematics) signo m;
~s of improvement señales or indicios de
mejoría; **all the ~s are that...** todo parece
indicar que...

sign² [1] vt (cheque, contract, petition) firmar;
~ one's name firmar
[2] vi firmar; **~ for sth** firmar el recibí de
algo; **~ here, please** firme aquí, por favor;
~ on the dotted line (on form) firmar sobre
la línea de puntos; **sign in** vi firmar el
registro (al llegar); **sign off** vi (Media)
concluir la emisión; **sign on** vi BrE anotarse
para recibir el seguro de desempleo; **sign out**
vi firmar el registro (al salir); **sign up** vi (for
course) inscribirse, matricularse

signal *n* señal *f*; ~ **jamming** *n* interferencias *f pl*; ~ **light** *n* indicador luminoso *m*

signaling AmE, **signalling** BrE *n* señalización *f*

signatory *n* firmante *mf*, signatario(-a) *m,f*; **the signatories to the agreement** los firmantes *or* los signatarios del acuerdo

signature *n* firma *f*; **for ~** para firmar; **put one's ~ to sth** firmar algo; ~ **card** *n* (Bank) tarjeta de firma *f*; ~ **file** *n* (Comp) archivo de firma *m*; ~ **loan** *n* préstamo sin garantía *m*

signed *adj* firmado

significant *adj* (change, quantity, advantage) importante, considerable; (contribution, date, fact, remark) significativo

signify *vt* (mean) significar; (indicate) expresar

signing *n* firma *f*; ~ **officer** *n* director(a) con firma autorizada *m,f*; ~ **slip** *n* ficha *f or* hoja *f* de firmas

signpost¹ *n* poste indicador *m*

signpost² *vt* (point to) señalar; (draw attention to) destacar

silent *adj* silencioso; **the ~ majority** la mayoría silenciosa; ~ **partner** *n* AmE (*cf* ▸**sleeping partner** BrE) socio(-a) comanditario(-a) inactivo(-a) *m,f*

silicon chip *n* chip de silicio *m*

silver *n* plata *f*; ~ **ring** *n* (jarg) (Fin) anillo de plata *m*; ~ **standard** *n* patrón plata *m*; ~ **surfer** *n* (Comp) (infrml) internauta mayor *mf*

SIM *abbr* (▸**sector investment and maintenance loan**) préstamo sectorial de inversión y mantenimiento *m*; (▸**subscriber identity module**) SIM *m* (módulo de identidad del abonado); ~ **card** *n* tarjeta SIM *f*

simple *adj* (contract, interest, yield, majority) simple

simplex *adj* (transmission) unidireccional

simplified *adj* simplificado

simplify *vt* simplificar

simulate *vt* simular

simulation *n* simulación *f*; ~ **model** *n* modelo de simulación *m*

simulcast *abbr* (**simultaneous broadcast**) transmisión simultánea *f*

simultaneous *adj* (translation) simultáneo; ~ **broadcast** *n* transmisión simultánea *f*; ~ **payments clause** *n* cláusula de pagos simultáneos *f*

sincerity *n* sinceridad *f*

synchronized *adj* sincronizado

sinecure *n* prebenda *f*, sinecura *f*

sine die *adv* sin fijar fecha

single *adj* (just one) solo; (for one person) individual; (unmarried) soltero; **in 0 with ~ spacing** a un espacio; ~ **administrative document** *n* documento administrativo simple *m*; ~ **capacity** *n* capacidad única *f*; ~ **capacity trading** *n* *restricción de actividades a los intermediarios*; ~ **commission** *n* comisión única *f*; ~ **currency** *n* divisa *f or* moneda *f* única; ~ **density** *n* densidad simple *f*; ~**-employer bargaining** *n* BrE negociación con un empresario individual *f*; ~**-entry book-keeping** *n* contabilidad por partida simple *f*; ~**-entry visa** *n* visado para una sola entrada *m*; **S~ European Act** *n* Acta Única Europea *f*; ~ **European currency** *n* moneda única europea *f*; ~**-family dwelling** *n*, ~**-family home** *n*, ~**-family house** *n* vivienda unifamiliar *f*; ~**-figure** *adj* (inflation) de menos del 10%, por debajo del 10%; ~ **figures** *n pl* cifras de un solo dígito *f pl*; ~ **labor market** AmE, ~ **labour market** BrE *n* mercado *m* único laboral *or* único de trabajo; **S~ Market** *n* mercado único *m*; ~ **parent** *n* (mother) madre soltera *f*; (father) padre soltero *m*; ~**-parent family** *n* familia monoparental *f*; ~ **payment** *n* pago global *m*; ~ **person** *n* soltero(-a) *m,f*; ~**-person household** *n* vivienda unipersonal *f*; ~ **precision** *n* (Comp) precisión simple *f*; ~ **premium** *n* prima única *f*; ~ **room** *n* habitación individual *f*; ~**-room supplement** *n* suplemento por habitación individual *m*; ~**-sheet feeder** *n* alimentador de papel manual *m*; ~**-sided** *adj* de una cara; ~**-sided disk** *n* disco de una cara *m*; ~**-sided double density** *n* doble densidad por una cara; ~**-sided single density** *n* baja densidad por una cara *f*; ~ **status** *n* categoría única *f*; ~ **ticket** *n* billete *m* sencillo *or* de ida; ~ **union agreement** *n* BrE acuerdo con un solo sindicato *m*

single out *vt* seleccionar

singly *adv* individualmente

sink [1] *vt* (plan, business) hacer hundir, hacer naufragar, acabar con; ~ **sth in 0 into sth** (invest) invertir algo en algo [2] *vi* (price, value) caer a pique; (output, morale) decaer, bajar; **she has sunk in my estimation** ha bajado en mi estima; **the pound has sunk to an all-time low** la libra ha alcanzado el nivel más bajo en la historia

sinking fund *n* fondo de amortización *m*

sister: ~ **company** *n* sociedad hermana *f*; ~ **ship** *n* buque gemelo *m*

sit *vi* (parliament) reunirse en sesión parlamentaria, sesionar AmL; ~ **in judgment over sb** enjuiciar a alguien; ~ **on the fence** (infrml) no comprometerse; ~ **tight** no moverse; **sit in** *vi* (attend) asistir; (as protest) hacer una sentada; **sit in on** *vt* asistir a (como oyente/observador); **sit on** *vt* (committee, jury) formar parte de, ser miembro de; (information, document) mantener oculto; (application, claim) no dar trámite a, retener; (plan, proposal) rechazar

sit. *abbr* (▸**situation**) puesto *m*

SITC *abbr* (▸**Standard International Trade Classification**) Clasificación Normativa para el Comercio Internacional *f*

sit-down strike *n* huelga de brazos caídos *f*

site¹ *n* (location) emplazamiento *m*; (piece of land) terreno *m*, solar *m*; (building site) obra *f*; (on Internet) sitio *m*; **on** ~ in situ; ~ **audit** *n* auditoría en la sede de la empresa *f*; ~ **directory** *n* (Comp) guía de sitios web *f*; ~ **engineer** *n* ingeniero(-a) de obra *m,f*; ~ **foreman** *n* capataz(a) a pie de obra *m,f*; ~ **licence** BrE, ~ **license** AmE *n* (Comp) licencia *f* de instalación *or* de uso; ~ **manager** *n* jefe(-a) de obra *m,f*; ~ **map** *n* (Comp) mapa de sitio *f*; ~ **plan** *n* plano del terreno *m*; ~ **planning** *n* (Comp) planificación de las instalaciones *f*

site² *vt* (building, factory) situar, ubicar, emplazar

sit-in *n* sentada *f*, huelga de ocupación *f*

siting *n* emplazamiento *m*

sitrep *abbr* (▸**situation report**) informe de la situación *m*

sits. vac. *abbr* BrE (▸**situations vacant**) puestos vacantes *m pl*

sitting tenant *n* BrE inquilino(-a) en posesión *m,f*

situation *n* (circumstances, position) situación *f*; (job) empleo *m*; **a crisis** ~ una (situación de) crisis; **have the** ~ **in hand** tener la situación bajo control; **save the** ~ salvar la situación; ~ **report** *n* informe de la situación *m*; ~**s vacant** *n pl* BrE puestos vacantes *m pl*

situational marketing *n* marketing de situación *m*

six-monthly *adj* semestral

sizable AmE ▸**sizeable** BrE

size¹ *n* (dimensions) tamaño *m*; (of problem, task, operation) magnitud *f*, envergadura *f*; (of clothing) talla *f*; (of shoes, gloves) número *m*

size² *vt* (Comp) dimensionar; **size up** *vt* (infrml) (problem) evaluar

sizeable BrE, **sizable** AmE *adj* (fortune, investment, quantity) considerable; (building, property) de proporciones considerables; (problem, risk) importante, considerable

skeleton *n* (of report) esquema *f*, esbozo *m*; ~ **contract** *n* contrato marco *m*; ~ **service** *n* servicio mínimo *m*; ~ **staff** *n* personal reducido *m*

skepticism AmE ▸**scepticism** BrE

sketch¹ *n* esbozo *m*, esquema *f*, bosquejo *m*

sketch² *vt* (idea, situation) esbozar, bosquejar

skew *vt* (facts, results) presentar de manera sesgada

skill *n* habilidad *f*; **her** ~**s as a negotiator** su habilidad para negociar; ~ **at** *o* **in (doing) sth** habilidad para (hacer) algo; ~**s analysis** *n* análisis por aptitudes *m*; ~ **differential** *n* diferencial de habilidad *m*; ~**-intensive** *adj* con uso intensivo de personal cualificado

skilled *adj* (worker, union) cualificado; (work) especializado; (labour) especializado; (negotiator) hábil, experto

skimming *n* substracción de ganancias *f*

skimp on *vt* escatimar

skip¹ *vt* (meeting) faltar a; (payment) omitir; (Comp) saltar; ~ **the details** saltarse los detalles

skip² *n* (Comp) salto *m*; ~**-payment privilege** *n* privilegio de omisión de pago *m*

sky *n* cielo *m*; **the** ~**'s the limit** no hay límite

skyrocket *vi* (infrml) (prices, costs) dispararse

SLA *abbr* (▸**service level agreement**) acuerdo del nivel de servicio *m*

slack¹ *adj* (business, period) flojo; (worker) negligente; ~ **fill** *n* (S&M) presentación engañosa de un producto *f*

slack² *n* (Econ) exceso de oferta agregada *m*, oferta desanimada *f*; (of business) paralización *f*; **take the** ~ (infrml) rebajar el exceso de oferta agregada

slacken [1] *vi* (trade, demand) decaer, disminuir; (rate, effort, recovery) disminuir [2] *vt* (speed) reducir; ~ **the reins** aflojar las riendas; **slacken off** *vi* (worker) aflojar el ritmo de trabajo; (business, demand) disminuir

slack off *vi* (worker) aflojar el ritmo de trabajo; (business, demand) disminuir

slander¹ *n* calumnia *f*; ~ **action** *n* demanda por calumnia *f*

slander² *vt* calumniar

slanderous *adj* calumnioso

slant¹ *n* (point of view) enfoque *m*; (bias) sesgo *m*; **give a new** ~ **on sth** darle a algo un aspecto nuevo

slant² *vt* (account, report) darle un sesgo a; (give bias to) presentar tendenciosamente

slapdash *adj* (work) chapucero (infrml)

slash¹ *vt* (prices, taxes) rebajar drásticamente; (budget) recortar drásticamente; **'prices** ~**ed'** espectaculares rebajas

slash² *n* barra (oblicua) *f*

slate¹ *n* AmE (Pol) lista de candidatos *f*

slate² *vt* (criticize) poner por los suelos; (Pol) AmE (for post) designar

sleaze *n* sordidez *f*

sleeper *n* (success story) éxito inesperado *m*; (poor selling product) artículo sin venta *m*

sleeping *adj* (economy) dormido; ~ **beauty** *n* (jarg) empresa pequeña que atrae la atención de las grandes corporaciones; ~ **partner** *n* BrE (cf ▸**silent partner** AmE) socio(-a) comanditario(-a) inactivo(-a) *m,f*

slice *n* (of money, business, territory) parte *f*; (of market) cuota *f*

slick¹ *adj* (salesperson) astuto; (performance) muy logrado

slick² *n* (of oil) mancha *f*

slide¹ *vi* (prices) bajar

slide² *n* diapositiva *f*; ~ **projector** *n* proyector de diapositivas *m*

sliding *adj* (scale, parity) móvil; ~ **wage scale** *n* escala móvil de salarios *f*, escala salarial móvil *f*

slim down *vt* (workforce) reconvertir

slimline *adj* de trazo fino

slip¹ *n* borderó, resguardo *m*

slip² *vi* (standards, service) decaer, empeorar; (production) decaer, bajar; **slip back** *vi* (production) decaer, bajar

slog¹ *n* (infrml) trabajo duro *m*

slog² *vi* (infrml) sudar tinta; **slog away at** *vi* (infrml) romperse la espalda trabajando en

slogan *n* eslogan *m*, slogan *m*

slope *n* inclinación *f*, declive *m*

slot *n* (opening) ranura *f*; (job) puesto *m*; (on radio, television) espacio *m*; ~ **machine** *n* (for tickets) expendedora automática *f*

slot in *vt* (Comp) insertar; **I can slot you in at 3 this afternoon** le puedo hacer un hueco este tarde a las 3

slow¹ *adj* (rise, decline) lento; **business is** ~ no hay mucho movimiento (en el negocio); **make** ~ **progress** avanzar lentamente; **be** ~ **off the mark** tardar en actuar; **be** ~ **to do sth** tardar en hacer algo; ~**-moving goods** *n pl* artículos de venta difícil *m pl*; ~ **payer** *n* pagador(a) moroso(-a) *m,f*, moroso(-a) *m,f*

slow² 1 *vt* ralentizar 2 *vi* ralentizarse; **slow down** 1 *vt* ralentizar 2 *vi* ralentizarse

slowdown *n* (slackening off) ralentización *f*; (industrial action) huelga de brazos caídos *f*

sluggish *adj* (demand) débil; (market) inactivo; (growth) lento; (economy) deprimido

sluggishness *n* (of demand) debilidad *f*; (of trading) ritmo lento *m*; (of market) atonía *f*

sluice-gate price *n* (jarg) precio de compuerta *m*

slump¹ *n* (in prices, sales) baja *f* or caída *f* repentina; (economic) depresión *f*; (Stock) caída en picado *f*

slump² *vi* caer en picado

slumpflation *n* (jarg) depresión con inflación *f*

slush fund *n* fondo para sobornos *m*

small *adj* pequeño; ~ **ads** *n pl* pequeños anuncios *m pl*; ~ **business** *n* pequeña empresa *f*; ~ **business administration** *n* administración *f* or dirección *f* de la pequeña empresa; ~ **change** *n* calderilla *f*, cambio *m*, suelto *m*; ~ **claims court** *n* BrE *tribunal que conoce de causas de mínima cuantía*; ~ **denomination** *n* (of banknote) baja denominación *f*; ~ **employer** *n* pequeño(-a) empresario(-a) *m,f*; ~ **firm** *n* empresa pequeña *f*; ~ **investor** *n* pequeño(-a) inversionista *m,f*; ~ **and medium-size enterprise** *n* pequeña y mediana empresa *f*; ~ **and medium-sized manufacturing companies** *n pl* pequeñas y medianas empresas industriales *f pl*; ~ **print** *n* (in contract) letra *f* pequeña or menuda or chica AmL; ~ **speculator** *n* pequeño(-a) especulador(a) *m,f*

smalls *n pl* pequeños anuncios *m pl*

smart *adj* (businessperson) listo, vivo; (answer, comment) inteligente, agudo; (trick) hábil; (appearance, clothes) elegante; ~ **card** *n* tarjeta inteligente *f*; ~ **money** *n* dinero rápido *m*; ~ **set** *n* gente selecta *f*; ~ **terminal** *n* terminal inteligente *m*

SME *abbr* (▸**small and medium-size enterprise**) PYME (pequeña y mediana empresa)

smelt *vt* fundir

smiley *n* (Comp) smiley *m*

smooth *vt* (fluctuations) atenuar; **smooth out** *vt* (difficulties, problems) resolver, allanar

smoothly *adv* sin problemas, sin complicaciones

smooth-running *adj* que funciona bien

SMS *abbr* (▸**synchronous digital hierarchy management subnetwork**) SMS (subred de gestión de jerarquía digital síncrona); ~ **message** *n* mensaje SMS *m*, texto *m*

smuggle *vt* contrabandear, pasar de contrabando; ~ **sth through customs** pasar algo de contrabando por la aduana

smuggled *adj* (goods) de contrabando

smuggler *n* contrabandista *mf*

smuggling *n* contrabando *m*

snag *n* (infrml) dificultad imprevista *f*

snail mail *n* (infrml) correo *m* normal or por caracol

snake *n* (Econ) (EU) serpiente *f*

snap *adj* (strike) rápido; **make a ~ decision** tomar una decisión rápida

snap up *vt* (offer) no dejar escapar; (bargain) llevarse

snatch *vt* (opportunity) no dejar pasar

sneak preview *n* anticipo no oficial *m*, preestreno *m*

sneeze at *vt* despreciar

sniffer *n* (Comp) husmeador *m*, sabueso *m*

SNIG *abbr* (▶**sustained noninflationary growth**) crecimiento sostenido no inflacionario *m*

snowball *vi* aumentar con rapidez

snugging *n* ajuste *m*

s.o. *abbr* (▶**seller's option**) prima de opción a vender *f*

SO *abbr* (▶**senior officer**) funcionario(-a) de rango superior *m,f*

soar *vi* (prices, costs) dispararse

soaring *adj* (inflation) galopante; (currency) en alza

social *adj* social; **~ accounting** *n* contabilidad social *f*; **~ adjustment cost** *n* coste *m* Esp *or* costo *m* AmL de ajuste social; **~ analysis** *n* análisis social *m*; **~ capital** *n* capital social *m*; **~ category** *n* categoría social *f*; **S~ Charter** *n* Carta Social *f*; **~ class** *n* clase social *f*; **S~ Contract** *n* Contrato Social *m*; **~ cost** *n* coste *m* Esp *or* costo *m* AmL social; **~ credit** *n* crédito social *m*; **~ democracy** *n* democracia social *f*, socialdemocracia *f*; **~ exclusion** *n* exclusión *f or* marginación *f* social; **~ good** *n* bien social *m*; **~ insurance** *n* AmE seguro social *m*; **~ overhead capital** *n* capital para infraestructura social *m*; **~ ownership** *n* cooperativa *f*; **~ policy** *n* política social *f*; **~ secretary** *n* secretario(-a) de asuntos sociales *m,f*; **~ security** *n* BrE seguridad social *f*; **~ security benefit** *n* BrE subsidio de la seguridad social *m*; **~ security contribution** *n* BrE cuota de la seguridad social *f*; **~-security recipient** *n* BrE (*cf* ▶**welfare recipient** AmE) beneficiario(-a) de asistencia social *m,f*; **~ services** *n pl* BrE servicios sociales *m pl*; **~ spending** *n* gastos de previsión social *m pl*; **~ standing** *n* posición social *f*; **~ status** *n* estatus social *m*; **~ studies** *n pl* estudios sociales *m pl*; **~ welfare** *n* bienestar social *m*; **~ work** *n* asistencia social *f*; **~ worker** *n* asistente(-a) social *m,f*

socialism *n* socialismo *m*

socialist¹ *adj* socialista

socialist² *n* socialista *mf*

socialite *n* persona mundana *f*

socialization *n* socialización *f*

society *n* sociedad *f*; **S~ for Worldwide Interbank Financial**

Telecommunications *n* Sociedad Internacional de Telecomunicaciones Financieras *f*

sociocultural *adj* sociocultural

socioeconomic *adj* (group, status, climate) socioeconómico

sociological *adj* sociológico

sociometric *adj* sociométrico

sociometry *n* sociometría *f*

socioprofessional *adj* (class) socioprofesional

sociotechnical *adj* (system) sociotécnico

soft *adj* (money, currency) débil, blando; (loan, credit) blando; (market) flojo; (cost) suave; **~ commodities** *n pl* bienes de consumo perecederos *m pl*; **~ copy** *n* imagen de pantalla *f*; **~-cover book** *n* libro en rústica *m*; **~ funding** *n* financiación en condiciones favorables *f*; **~ goods** *n pl* (perishables) bienes de consumo perecederos *m pl*; (cloth) géneros textiles *m pl*; **~ job** *n* trabajito cómodo *m* (infrml), chollo *m* Esp (infrml); **~ keyboard** *n* (Comp) teclado en función programable *m*; **~ option** *n* camino fácil *m*; **~ sectoring** *n* (Comp) sectorización lógica *f*; **~ sell** *n* venta blanda *or* por persuasión; **~ target** *n* blanco fácil *m*; **~ technology** *n* tecnología flexible *f*

soften up *vt* (client) ablandar

soft-pedal *vt* (infrml) (subject, issue) restarle importancia a, minimizar

software *n* software *m*; **~ application** *n* aplicación de software *f*; **~ company** *n* empresa de programación *f*; **~ developer** *n* desarollador(a) *m,f* de software *or* de programas; **~-driven** *adj* gestionado por programa; **~ engineer** *n* ingeniero(-a) de programación *m,f*; **~ engineering** *n* ingeniería de programas *f*; **~ error** *n* error de programa *m*; **~ house** *n* empresa productora de programas *f*; **~ language** *n* lenguaje de programación *m*; **~ package** *n* paquete de programas *m*; **~ release** *n* versión de un programa *f*; **~ rot** *n* corrupción de un programa *f*

soiled *adj* (goods) dañado

solar *adj* solar; **~ energy** *n* energía solar *f*; **~ power** *n* potencia solar *f*

sold daybook *n* diario de ventas *m*

sole *adj* solo, único; **with the ~ object of doing sth** con el único objeto de hacer algo; **~ agency** *n* representación exclusiva *f*; **~ agent** *n* representante *m,f* único(-a) *or* exclusivo(-a); **~ bargaining agent** *n* BrE agente exclusivo(-a) de negociación *m,f*; **~ bargaining rights** *n pl* BrE derechos exclusivos de negociación *m pl*; **~ inventor** *n* inventor(a) único(-a) *m,f*; **~ legatee** *n* legatario(-a) único(-a) *m,f*; **~ owner** *n* ⋯⟩

dueño(-a) único(-a) *m,f*; ~ **proprietor** *n* empresario(-a) individual *m,f*, proprietario(-a) único(-a) *m,f*; ~ **proprietorship** *n* empresa individual *f*; ~ **trader** *n* comerciante individual *mf*

solicitation *n* solicitación *f*

solicitor *n* ≈ abogado(-a) *m,f*, ≈ notario(-a) *m,f*; (for bureaucratic transactions) ≈ procurador(a) *m,f*

solid *adj* (offer) en firme; (commitment) firme; (business, argument, reason) sólido; (work) concienzudo; (support, vote, agreement) unánime; **on ~ ground** sobre una base sólida

solidarity *n* solidaridad *f*

solus position *n* espacio aislado *m*

solution *n* solución *f*; **find a ~** encontrar una solución; **the ~ to all your problems** la solución a todos sus problemas

solve *vt* (problem) resolver, solucionar; (conflict) solucionar; (crime) esclarecer

solvency *n* solvencia *f*; ~ **margin** *n* margen de solvencia *m*; ~ **ratio** *n* índice *m or* coeficiente *m or* proporción *f* de solvencia

solvent *adj* (company, person) solvente; (debt) solvente, exigible

s.o.p. *abbr* (▸**standard operating procedure**) reglas permanentes del servicio *f pl*

sophisticated *adj* (market) sofisticado; (machine, system) complejo

sophistication *n* (of market) sofisticación *f*; (of machine, system) complejidad *f*

sort¹ *n* (type) tipo *m*, clase *f*; (Comp) clasificación *f*; ~ **code** *n* (Bank) número de sucursal *m*; ~ **file** *n* fichero de clasificación *m*; ~ **key** *n* clave de clasificación *f*

sort² *vt* (papers, letters) clasificar; (fix) arreglar; **sort out** *vt* (papers) ordenar, poner en orden; (desk, room) ordenar; (finances) organizar; (problem, dispute) solucionar; (misunderstanding, muddle) aclarar; (date) BrE fijar; (deal, compromise) BrE llegar a; **sort through** *vt* (papers, files) revisar

sorter *n* (person) clasificador(a) *m,f*; (machine) clasificadora *f*

sorting *n* clasificación *f*; ~ **office** *n* oficina de clasificación del correo *f*

sought-after *adj* solicitado

sound¹ *n* sonido *m*; ~ **card** *n* (Comp) tarjeta de sonido *f*; ~ **check** *n* prueba de sonido *f*; ~ **effects** *n pl* efectos especiales sonoros *m pl*; ~ **insulation** *n* aislamiento sonoro *m*; ~ **pick-up** *n* captación *f*, fonocaptor *m*; ~ **track** *n* banda de sonido *f*

sound² *adj* (business, basis, argument) sólido; (advice, decision) sensato; (colleague, staff) responsable, formal; (currency) solvente;

being of ~ **mind** en pleno uso de sus facultades mentales; **on a ~ footing** sobre una base sólida; **put the economy back on a ~ footing** sanear la economía

sound³ *vt* (alarm) dar; **the chairman ~ed a note of warning in his speech** en su discurso, el presidente llamó a la cautela; **sound out** *vt* tantear, sondear

sounding board *n* (for ideas) caja de resonancia *f*

soundness certificate *n* certificado de solvencia *m*

source *n* (of funds, capital, income, information) fuente *f*; **tax will be deducted at ~** los impuestos se descontarán directamente del sueldo; ~ **address** *n* (Comp) dirección de origen *f*; ~ **code** *n* (Comp) código fuente *m*; ~ **computer** *n* computadora *f* AmL or ordenador *m* Esp fuente; ~ **data** *n* datos de fuente *m pl*; ~ **disk** *n* disco de origen *m*; ~ **document** *n* documento fuente *m*; ~ **file** *n* archivo fuente *m*; ~ **language** *n* lenguaje fuente *m*; ~ **program** *n* programa fuente *m*

sovereign *adj* (loan, borrower) supremo

space *n* espacio *m*; ~ **bar** *n* (Comp) espaciador *m*, barra espaciadora *f*; ~ **broker** *n* corredor(a) de espacio publicitario *m,f*; ~ **buying** *n* compra de espacios publicitarios *f*; ~ **rates** *n pl* tarifa por espacio publicitario *f*

spaceman economy *n* economía del despilfarro y la irresponsabilidad

spam¹ *n* (Comp) spam *m*, correo basura *m*

spam² *vt* (Comp) enviar spam a

spamdexing *n* (Comp) spamdexing *m*

spammer *n* (Comp) spammer *mf*, enviador(a) de correo basura *m,f*

spamming *n* (Comp) spamming *m*, envío de spam *m*

span *n* (of time) lapso *m*; ~ **of control** *n* área de control *f*

Spanish *adj* español; ~ **Chamber of Commerce** *n* Cámara de Comercio Española *f*; ~**-speaking world** *n* mundo hispanohablante *m*

spare¹ *adj* (not in use) de más; (in case of need) de repuesto; **if you've got a ~ minute** si tienes un minuto (libre); ~ **capacity** *n* capacidad *f* excedente *or* sobrante; ~ **part** *n* repuesto *m*; ~ **time** *n* tiempo libre *m*

spare² *vt* (keep from using) escatimar; (do without) prescindir de; ~ **no effort** no escatimar *or* ahorrar esfuerzos; ~ **no expense** no reparar en gastos; **if you can ~ the time** si tienes *or* dispones de tiempo

spares *n pl* repuestos *m pl*

spark off *vt* (infrml) causar

sparse *adj* (population) esparso, poco denso

sparsely *adv* (populated) escasamente

spate *n* aguacero *m*

speaker *n* (lecturer) conferenciante *mf*, conferencista *mf* AmL; (in public) orador(a) *m,f*; (at conference) ponente *mf*

spearhead[1] *n* (of campaign) punta de lanza *f*

spearhead[2] *vt* (campaign) encabezar, ser la punta de lanza de

spec *n* (infrml) (specification) especificación *f*; **on ~** por especulación; (apply for job) en plan aleatorio; **buy sth on ~** comprar algo para especular

special *adj* (arrangements, circumstances, purchase) especial; **~ accounts** *n pl* cuentas especiales *f pl*; **~ clearing** *n* BrE compensación especial *f*; **~ commissioner** *n* BrE (Tax) interventor(a) especial *m,f*; **~ delivery** *n* correo *m* exprés *or* expreso; **~ drawing rights** *n pl* derechos especiales de giro *m pl*; **~ feature** *n* particularidad *f*, característica especial *f*; **~ offer** *n* oferta especial *f* **sell sth on ~ offer** ofertar algo; **~ pleading** *n* argucias *f pl*; **~ purpose allotment** *n* asignación para un fin concreto *f*; **~ tax rate** *n* tipo impositivo especial *m*

specialist[1] *n* especialista *mf*

specialist[2] *adj* (knowledge, information) especializado

speciality BrE, **specialty** AmE *n* especialidad *f*; **~ advertising** *n* publicidad especializada *f*; **~ goods** *n pl* artículos *m pl* especializados *or* de calidad; **~ retailer** *n* minorista especializado(-a) *m,f*; **~ selling** *n* venta especializada *f*; **~ trade** *n* comercio especializado *m*

specialization *n* especialización *f*

specialize *vi* especializarse; **~ in sth** especializarse en algo

specialized *adj* especializado

specialty AmE ►**speciality** BrE

specie *n* dinero contante *m*; **in ~** (payment) en especie

specific *adj* (amount, payment, provision) específico; **~ duty** *n* (Imp/Exp, Tax) derecho específico *m*; **~ performance** *n* (Law) ejecución forzosa *f*, cumplimiento forzado *m*

specification *n* especificación *f*; **the ~s for the new machinery** las especificaciones para la nueva maquinaria; **made to one's ~s** hecho según sus especificaciones; **~ of goods** *n* (Patents) descripción de los productos *f*; **~ of services** *n* (Patents) descripción de los servicios *f*

specifics *n pl* productos específicos *m pl*

specified *adj* (person, purpose, percentage) especificado; **not elsewhere ~** no especificado en otro punto

specify *vt* especificar

specimen *n* (of work, handwriting) muestra *f*; (individual item) espécimen *m*; **~ copy** *n* ejemplar de muestra *m*; **~ invoice** *n* factura de muestra *f*; **~ signature** *n* muestra de firma *f*

speculate *vi* especular; **~ in sth** especular en algo; **~ on the market** jugar a la bolsa

speculation *n* especulación *f*

speculative *adj* (buying, trading, fund) especulativo; **~ application** *n* solicitud de trabajo especulativa *f*

speculator *n* especulador(a) *m,f*

speech *n* (faculty) habla *f*; (oration) discurso *m*; **make a ~** pronunciar un discurso; **~ processing** *n* procesador de sonido *m*; **~ recognition** *n* reconocimiento de la voz *m*; **~ recognition software** *n* software de reconocimiento de la voz *m*

speed *n* velocidad *f*

speed up [1] *vt* (work, production, process) acelerar; (person) meterle prisa a, apurar [2] *vi* (work, production, process) acelerarse; (person) darse prisa, apurarse

speed-up *n* (in production) aumento *m*

spellchecker *n*, **spellcheck** *n* corrector ortográfico *m*

spend [1] *vt* (money) gastar; **~ sth on sth** gastar algo en algo; **~ a lot of time on (doing) sth** dedicar mucho tiempo a (hacer) algo [2] *vi* gastar

spending *n* gastos *m pl*; **go on a ~ spree** salir a gastar dinero; **~ cut** *n* recorte presupuestario *m*; **~ level** *n* nivel de gasto *m*; **~ money** *n* dinero para pequeños gastos *m*; **~ pattern** *n* pauta de gastos *f*; **~ power** *n* poder adquisitivo *m*; **~ surge** *n* oleada de gastos *f*

spendthrift *adj* pródigo, derrochador

sphere *n* esfera *f*; **in a limited ~** en un campo limitado; **~ of activity** *n* campo *m* *or* esfera *f* de actividad; **~ of influence** *n* esfera de influencia *f*

spiel *n* (infrml) charla *f*

spike[1] *n* (jarg) (Stock) clavo *m*

spike[2] *vt* BrE (infrml) (discard, reject) descartar

spillage *n* vertido *m*

spillover *n* desbordamiento *m*; **~ effect** *n* efecto indirecto *m*

spill over *vi* desbordarse

spin *vt* darle un sesgo a; **spin off** *vt* derivar

spin[1] *n* interpretación *f*; **put a positive ~ on sth** darle un sesgo positivo a algo; **~ doctor** *n* *asesor político que manipula los medios de comunicación*; **~ doctoring** *n* *manipulación de los medios de comunicación por los asesores políticos*

spin-off n (product) producto derivado m; (result) resultado indirecto m; ~ **benefit** n beneficio indirecto m; ~ **product** n producto derivado m

spiral¹ n (of prices) espiral f

spiral² vi (unemployment) escalar; (prices) dispararse

spiralling inflation n espiral de inflación f

spirit n espíritu m; ~ **of enterprise** n espíritu de empresa m

splash n (excitement) revuelo m; **do a front-page ~ on sth** poner algo a toda plana en la primera página; **make a ~** causar un revuelo or una sensación; ~ **screen** n (Comp) pantalla de desviación f

splash out vi derrochar dinero; ~ **on sth** derrochar dinero en algo, permitirse el lujo de comprar algo

splintered adj (authority) fraccionado

splinter group n grupo escindido m

split¹ adj dividido; **be ~ three ways** estar dividido en tres; ~ **decision** n decisión no unánime f; ~ **offering** n (Stock) emisión escalonada de obligaciones f; ~ **run** n (jarg) uso de anuncios ligeramente diferentes en distintas ediciones de un mismo periódico; ~ **screen** n (Comp) pantalla dividida f; **~-second timing** n cronometraje muy exacto m; ~ **shift** n jornada laboral partida f

split² 1 vt (money, cost) dividir; (group, party) dividir, escindir; ~ **the difference** repartirse la diferencia (a partes iguales) 2 vi (group, party) dividirse, escindirse; **split up** vi (group, party) dividirse, escindirse

split³ n (distribution) división f; (in political party) escisión f

split-off n reparto de acciones m

splitting spread n opción de compra o venta divisible f

spoil vt (ruin) arruinar; (invalidate) anular

spoilage n chatarra f

spoiled AmE ▶**spoilt** BrE

spoils system n AmE sistema de recompensas m

spoilt BrE, **spoiled** AmE adj (ballot paper) anulado

spokesperson n portavoz mf

sponsor¹ n (of programme) patrocinador(a) m,f; (of sporting event) patrocinador(a) m,f, espónsor mf, sponsor mf; (for the arts) mecenas mf; (of bill, motion) proponente mf; (guarantor) fiador(a) m,f

sponsor² vt (programme, event) patrocinar, auspiciar; (research) subvencionar, financiar; (applicant, application) apoyar, respaldar; (bill, motion) presentar, proponer

sponsored adj (event, book, television) patrocinado

sponsorship n (financing) patrocinio m, auspicio m; (of sporting event) patrocinio m, esponsorización f; (of the arts) mecenazgo m; (of application) respaldo m; (of bill, motion) respaldo m, apoyo m

spontaneous adj espontáneo; ~ **combustion** n combustión espontánea f; ~ **recall** n recuerdo espontáneo m

spool¹ n (Comp) bobina f; ~ **file** n fichero de espera m

spool² vt (Comp) bobinar

spooling n (Comp) bobinado m, spooling m

spoon-feed vt (infrml) (with information) darle de comer con cuchara a

sporadic adj esporádico; ~ **maintenance** n mantenimiento esporádico m

spot¹ adj (price, rate, market, position) al contado; (delivery, quotation) al contado; **sell ~** vender al contado; ~ **business** n venta inmediata f; ~ **cash** n dinero contante m; ~ **commodity** n producto al contado m; ~ **credit** n crédito m disponible de inmediato or spot; ~ **currency market** n mercado de divisas al contado m; ~ **exchange rate** n tipo de cambio al contado m

spot² n (time on radio, television) espacio m; **on the ~** en el acto

spot-check vt comprobar al azar

spot check n comprobación al azar f

spotlight¹ n (piece of equipment) foco m; (attention) foco de atención m; **be in the ~** ser el centro de la atención; **turn** o **put the ~ on sth** centrarse en algo

spotlight² vt (difficulties, problems) poner de relieve, destacar

spouse n consorte mf, cónyuge mf; **~'s allowance** n deducción por la esposa f

spread¹ n (of idea) difusión f; (of opinion) abanico m; (of chain of stores) extensión f; (Fin) margen m, diferencial m; (S&M) diferencia entre el precio de oferta y demanda f; **it was advertised in a double-page ~** venía anunciado a doble página; ~ **effect** n (Econ) efecto de propagación m; ~ **order** n (Stock) orden de compraventa a crédito f; ~ **position** n (Stock) posición diferencial de compraventa f; ~ **risk** n (Stock) riesgo relacionado con el margen m; ~ **trading** n (Stock) operación con margen f

spread² 1 vt (repayments, risks) espaciar; (cost) repartir; (information, news) difundir, propagar, divulgar; (influence) extender; (rumour) hacer correr, difundir; (idea) diseminar, divulgar, difundir 2 vi (influence) extenderse; (idea) diseminarse, divulgarse

spreading n difusión f; ~ **agreement** n (Stock) acuerdo sobre margen m

spreadover *n* horario escalonado *m*; ~ **working** *n* trabajo escalonado *m*

spreadsheet *n* hoja de cálculo *f*; ~ **program** *n* hoja electrónica *f*

spurt *n* arranque *m*; **put on a** ~ (infrml) acelerar

squander *vt* (money) despilfarrar, derrochar; (fortune) dilapidar; (opportunity, time) desaprovechar, desperdiciar

square¹ *adj* cuadrado; ~ **brackets** *n pl* corchetes *m pl*; ~ **foot** *n* pie cuadrado *m*; ~ **mile** *n* milla cuadrada *f*; **S~ Mile** *n centro financiero en Londres*, City *f*

square² ① *vt* (debts, accounts) pagar, saldar; (facts, principles) conciliar; ~ **sth with sb** (settle) arreglar algo con alguien; ~ **sth with sth** (reconcile) conciliar algo con algo ② *vi* (ideas, arguments) concordar; ~ **with sth** concordar *or* cuadrar con algo

squatter *n* ocupante ilegal *mf*, ocupa *mf* Esp; ~**'s rights** *n pl* derechos del ocupante ilegal *m pl*

squeeze¹ *n* (on prices) restricción *f*

squeeze² *vt* (prices) restringir; ~ **the bears** (infrml) (Stock) restringir a los bajistas; ~ **the shorts** (jarg) (Stock) apretar a los cortos

SRO *abbr* (►**self-regulating organization**) organización autorregulada *f*; (►**self-regulatory organization**) organización autorreguladora *f*

SSAP *abbr* (►**Statement of Standard Accounting Practice**) declaración sobre las normas de práctica contable *f*

SSD *abbr* (►**single-sided disk**) disco de una cara *m*

SSDD *abbr* (►**single-sided double density**) doble densidad por una cara *f*

SSL *abbr* (►**Secure Sockets Layer**) capa de conexiones seguras *f*

SSP *abbr* (►**statutory sick pay**) subsidio de enfermedad obligatorio *m*; (►**storage services provider**) proveedor de servicios de almacenamiento *m*

SSSD *abbr* (►**single-sided single density**) baja densidad por una cara *f*

St. *abbr* (►**street**) c/ (calle)

stability *n* estabilidad *f*; ~ **and growth pact** *n* pacto de estabilidad y crecimiento *m*

stabilization *n* estabilización *f*; ~ **fund** *n* fondo de estabilización *m*; ~ **policy** *n* política de estabilización *f*

stabilize ① *vt* estabilizar ② *vi* estabilizarse

stabilized *adj* (price) estabilizado

stabilizer *n* estabilizador *m*

stable *adj* (market, economy, currency) estable

stack¹ *n* (of data) pila *f*; (chimney) chimenea *f*

stack² *vt* (merchandise) apilar

stacking *n* apilamiento *m*

staff¹ *n* personal *m*, empleados *m pl*; ~ **appraisal** *n* evaluación del personal *f*; ~ **audit** *n* auditoría de personal *f*; ~ **canteen** *n* restaurante para los empleados *m*; ~ **commitment** *n* compromiso del personal *m*; ~ **costs** *n pl* costes *m* Esp *or* costos *m* AmL del personal; ~ **cutback** *n* reducción de personal *f*; ~ **development** *n* desarrollo del personal *m*; ~ **management** *n* dirección *f or* gerencia *f* del personal; ~ **member** *n* empleado(-a) *m,f*; ~ **mobility** *n* movilidad del personal *f*; ~ **organization** *n* organización del personal *f*; ~ **planning** *n* planificación del personal *f*; ~ **representative** *n* representante del personal *mf*; ~ **resourcing** *n* contratación *f* y gestión *f* del personal; ~ **training** *n* capacitación *f or* formación *f* de personal; ~ **transfer** *n* transferencia de personal *f*; ~ **turnover** *n* rotación de personal *f*; ~ **welfare fund** *n* fondo de previsión del personal *m*

staff² *vt* (office) dotar de personal; **staff up** *vi* aumentar el personal

staffed *adj* dotado de personal

staffer *n* empleado(-a) *m,f* de planta *or* de plantilla Esp

staffing *n* dotación de personal *f*; ~ **level** *n* dotación de personal *f*, nivel de empleo de personal *m*

stag *n* (Stock) especulador(a) *m,f*, ciervo *m*

stage¹ *n* (phase) etapa *f*, fase *f*; (scene) escenario *m*; **at some** ~ en algún momento; **at this** ~ en este momento, a estas alturas; **in** ~s por etapas; ~ **payment** *n* pago escalonado *m*

stage² *vt* (conference) organizar; ~ **a go-slow** (jarg) organizar una huelga de celo; ~ **a strike** *o* **walkout** organizar una huelga

staged agreement *n* BrE contrato por etapas *m*

stagflation *n* estanflación *f*, stagflación *f*

stagger *vt* (payments, shifts, holidays) escalonar

staggered *adj* (payments, shifts, holidays) escalonado; ~ **working hours** *n pl* horario escalonado *m*

staggering *n* (of payments, shifts, holidays) escalonamiento *m*

stagnant *adj* estancado

stagnate *vi* estancarse

stagnation *n* estagnación *f*, estancamiento *f*

stake¹ *n* (in company) participación *f*, intereses *m pl*; (bet) apuesta *f*; **at** ~ en juego; **the** ~**s are high** los riesgos son altos; **a 60%** ·····>

~ in the company una participación en la empresa del 60%

stake² *vt* (money) jugarse; **I'm prepared to ~ my reputation on it** estoy dispuesto a jugarme mi reputación

stakeholder *n* (shareholder) accionista *mf*; (interested party) interesado(-a) *m,f*; **~ economy** *n* economía participativa *f*; **~ pension** *n* tipo de pensión complementaria *para personas de bajos ingresos*; **~ society** *n* sociedad participativa *f*

stale *adj* (market) desanimado; (cheque) no presentado a tiempo al cobro; (ideas) trasnochado; (person) cansado; **I'm getting ~ in this job** me estoy anquilosando en este trabajo

stalemate *n* estancamiento *m*, punto muerto *m*; **reach (a) ~** estancarse, llegar a un punto muerto

stalemated *adj* (talks) estancado

stamp¹ *n* (postage) sello *m*, estampilla *f* AmL; (device) sello *m*; **~ duty** *n* BrE sellado fiscal *m*; **~ pad** *n* tampón para sellos *m*

stamp² *vt* (letter, parcel) franquear, ponerle sellos *or* estampillas AmL a; (passport, ticket) sellar; **~ the date** (on form) estampar la fecha; **she ~ed her personal style on the company** dejó su impronta *or* sello en la compañía; **stamp out** *vt* (inflation) eliminar

stamped-addressed envelope *n* BrE (*cf* **▸self-addressed stamped envelope** AmE) *sobre sellado con la dirección del remitente*

stampede *n* pánico *m*

stance *n* (on issue) postura *f*; **take a tough ~ on sth** adoptar un postura firme (con) respecto a algo

stand¹ ⟨1⟩ *vi* (offer, price, bid) mantenerse; (law, agreement) seguir vigente *or* en vigor; **~ as guarantor for sb** servir como garante de alguien; **~ at a discount** mantenerse en descuento; **~ at a premium** mantenerse una prima de emisión; **receipts ~ at $150,000** el total recaudado asciende a 150.000 dólares; **unemployment ~s at 6%** el desempleo alcanza el 6%; **~ firm** mantenerse firme, no retroceder; **~ firm in the belief that...** mantenerse firme en la creencia de que...; **~ for election** presentarse para la elección; **~ good** (sale) resultar aceptable; **~ to win/lose** tener la posibilidad de ganar/estar en peligro de perder.

⟨2⟩ *vt* (withstand) soportar, resistir; **~ the acid test of competition** pasar la prueba de fuego de la competencia; **~ the cost of sth** sufragar los gastos de algo; **~ a good chance of doing sth** tener muchas posibilidades de hacer algo; **~ a loss** asumir una pérdida; **~ one's ground** mantenerse en sus trece; **~ surety for sb** prestar una fianza a alguien; **stand by** ⟨1⟩ *vi* (remain uninvolved) mantenerse al margen; (be on alert) estar a la espectativa ⟨2⟩ *vt* (promise) mantener; (decision) atenerse a; (person) apoyar, no abandonar; **stand down** *vi* (relinquish position) retirarse; (resign) renunciar, dimitir; (witness) abandonar el estrado; **stand for** *vt* (initials, abbreviation, symbol) significar; **stand in for** *vt* sustituir; **stand off** *vt* dejar sin trabajo; **stand out for** *vt* insistir en; **stand over** *vi* quedar pendiente; **stand up** *vi* (argument) convencer; **the case did not ~ up in court** la acusación no se mantuvo en el tribunal; **stand up for** *vt* defender

stand² *n* (for goods) expositor *m*; (at exhibition) stand *m*; **make a ~ against sth/sb** oponer resitencia a algo/alguien; **take a ~ on sth** adoptar un postura con respecto a algo

stand-alone *adj* (computer, system) autónomo; **~ cost** *n* BrE coste *m* Esp *or* costo *m* AmL autónomo

standard¹ *adj* (size) estándar, normal; (procedure) habitual; (reaction) típico, normal; (weight, measure) oficial; **it is ~ practice to do so** es la práctica habitual; **~ agreement** *n* acuerdo estándar *m*; **~ commodity** *n* mercancía estándar *f*; **~ cost** *n* coste *m* Esp estándar *or* normalizado, costo *m* AmL estándar *or* normalizado; **~ costing** *n* determinación *f* de costes Esp *or* costos AmL estándar; **~ deduction** *n* deducción *f* estándar *or* global; **~ deviation** *n* desviación típica *f*; **~ error** *n* error típico *m*; **S~ Generalized Mark-up Language** *n* Lenguaje Estandarizado y Generalizado de Marcado *m*; **~ grade** *n* tipo normalizado *m*; **S~ International Trade Classification** *n* Clasificación Normativa para el Comercio Internacional *f*; **~ letter** *n* carta estándar *f*; **~ operating procedure** *n* reglas permanentes del servicio *f pl*; **~ price** *n* precio estándar *m*; **~ rate of interest** *n* BrE tipo de interés vigente *m*; **~-rate tax** *n* impuesto de tipo estándar *m*; **~-rated** *adj* (VAT) gravado con la tarifa vigente; **~-size** *adj* de talla estándar; **~ Spending Assessment** *n* tasa de gastos estándar *f*; **~ tax** *n* impuesto de tipo normal *m*; **~ time** *n* hora legal *f*

standard² *n* (level) nivel *m*; (quality) calidad *f*; (norm) norma *f*; (yardstick) criterio *m*; (of measurement) patrón *m*; **set a ~** establecer un nivel; **be up to ~** ser del nivel requerido; **~ of equalization** *n* norma de compensación *f*; **~ of living** *n* nivel de vida *m*; **~ and practice** *n* norma y uso *f*

standardization *n* estandarización *f*, normalización *f*; **~ agreement** *n* acuerdo de normalización *m*

standardize *vt* estandarizar, normalizar; (Law) uniformar

standby[1] *n* (thing) recurso *m*, repuesto *m*; (person) reserva *f*; **on ~** (passenger) en lista de espera; (computer) en reposo

standby[2] *adj* (generator, equipment) de emergencia, de reserva; (passenger) stand-by; **be on ~ duty** estar de guardia; **~ agreement** *n* acuerdo contingente *m*; **~ credit** *n* crédito *m* de disposición inmediata *or* de reserva; **~ facility** *n* línea de disposición inmediata *f*; **~ line of credit** *n* línea de crédito de contingencia *f*; **~ loan** *n* préstamo contingente *m*; **~ ticket** *n* billete en lista de espera *m*

stand-in *n* suplente *mf*, sustituto(-a) *m,f*

standing[1] *n* (position) posición *f*; (prestige) prestigio *m*; **an agreement of long ~** un acuerdo que lleva en vigencia mucho tiempo

standing[2] *adj* (agreement, authorization, deposit) permanente; **~ advance** *n* anticipo fijo *m*; **~ committee** *n* comité permanente *m*; (of European Parliament) comisión permanente *f*; **~ order** *n* BrE orden permanente de pago *f*

standoff *n* punto muerto *m*

stands *n pl* (Stock) tenderetes *m pl*

standstill *n* punto muerto *m*; **negotiations are at a ~** las negociaciones están en un punto muerto; **bring sth to a ~** (activity, production) paralizar algo; (vehicle, machine) parar algo; **~ agreement** *n* moratoria *f*

staple[1] *adj* (food) básico; (industry, product) principal; **~ commodity** *n* bien de primera necesidad *m*

staple[2] *n* (basic food) alimento básico *m*; (main product) producto principal *m*; (raw material) materia prima *f*; (for fastening paper) grapa *f*; **~ gun** *n* grapadora *f*

staple[3] *vt* grapar

stapler *n* grapadora *f*

star *n* (in sky, celebrity, symbol) estrella *f*; (asterisk) asterisco *m*; **~ network** *n* (Comp) red en estrella *f*; **~ product** *n* producto estrella *m*

start[1] *n* (beginning) principio *m*; (of machine, peripheral) arranque *m*; **get off to a good/bad ~** tener un comienzo bueno/malo; **make a ~ on sth** empezar algo; **make a fresh** *o* **new ~** empezar *or* comenzar de nuevo; **~ bit** *n* (Comp) bitio de inicio *m*

start[2] [1] *vt* (company) abrir, montar, poner; (organization) fundar (negotiations, journey, conversation) empezar, comenzar, iniciar; (job, course) empezar, comenzar; **~ an entry** abrir un asiento contable, registrar una escritura; **~ sth from scratch** empezar algo desde cero; **his father ~ed him in his own business** su padre le montó *or* le puso un negocio; **~ proceedings** abrir un expediente; **~ doing** *o* **to do sth** empezar a hacer algo; **I ~ work at eight** empiezo *or* entro a trabajar a las ocho; **~ sb off as sth** iniciar a alguien en algo

[2] *vi* (meeting) empezar, comenzar, iniciarse; **prices ~ at $30** cuestan a partir de 30 dólares; **~ in business** iniciarse en los negocios; **start on** *vt* empezar (con); **I'll start you on some filing** primero te voy a poner a archivar; **start up** [1] *vt* (company) montar, poner en marcha; (engine, machinery) arrancar, poner en marcha; (discussion) empezar; (conversation) entablar
[2] *vi* (begin business) empezar

starter home *n* primera vivienda *f*

starting *adj* (salary, wage, price) inicial; **~ point** *n* punto de partida *m*

start-up *n* (of business) puesta en marcha *f*; (of machine) arranque *m*; (company) empresa de nueva creación *f*; **~ capital** *n* capital de arranque *m*; **~ costs** *n pl* costes *m pl* Esp *or* costos *m pl* AmL de puesta en marcha

state[1] *n* estado *m*; **in a bad ~ of repair** en malas condiciones; **in a ~ of neglect** descuidado; **~ of affairs** *n* estado de cosas *m*; **~ aid** *n* ayuda estatal *f*; **~-aided** *adj* subvencionado por el Estado; **~-of-the-art** *adj* de vanguardia, moderno, vanguardista; (technology) punta; **~ bonds** *n* bonos del estado *m pl*; **~ control** *n* control *m* estatal *or* del Estado; **~ controlled** *adj* (company) controlado por el Estado; **S~ Earnings Related Pension Scheme** *n* BrE *plan estatal de pensiones*; **~ of emergency** *n* estado de emergencia *m*; **~ enterprise** *n* empresa estatal *f*; **~ intervention** *n* intervención estatal *f*; **~-owned** *adj* (bank, enterprise) estatal; **~ ownership** *n* propriedad estatal *f*; **~ pension** *n* pensión del Estado *f*; **~ of play** *n* situación *f*; **~-run** *adj* estatal; **~ subsidy** *n* subsidio estatal *m*

state[2] *vt* (facts, case) exponer; (problem) plantear, exponer; (name, address - in writing) escribir; (- orally) decir; **as ~d above** como se indica más arriba; **as ~d in the minutes** como figura *or* consta en las actas; **~ sth categorically** exponer algo categóricamente; **~ the obvious** exponer lo obvio; **he clearly ~d that...** dijo *or* manifestó claramente que...; **the contract ~s that...** el contrato establece *or* estipula que...

stated *adj* (amount, sum) indicado, establecido; (date, time) señalado, indicado; (capital, value) declarado; **their ~ intention/goal** la intención/el objetivo que han expresado

stateless *adj* apátrida, sin patria; **~ currency** *n* moneda sin respaldo estatal *f*

statement n (declaration) declaración f; (bank statement) estado m or extracto m de cuenta; (Acc) balance m, estado contable m, memoria f; (Comp) instrucción f; **as per ~** como está establecido; **make a ~** hacer una declaración; **put out a ~** publicar una declaración; **~ of account** n estado de cuenta m; **~ of affairs** n (in bankruptcy) balance de liquidación m; **~ of assets and liabilities** n estado de activos y pasivos m; **~ of earnings** n AmE estado de ganancias m; **~ of financial position** n estado de posición financiera m; **~ of income** n AmE estado de resultados m; **~ of income and expenses** n estado de ingresos y gastos m; **~ of objectives** n declaración de objetivos f; **S~ of Standard Accounting Practice** n declaración sobre las normas de práctica contable f; **~ of terms and conditions** n declaración de condiciones f

static adj (output, prices) estático

station n (railway) estación f; (radio) emisora f; **~ break** n AmE espacio publicitario m, pausa para la publicidad f

stationary adj estacionario

stationer n papelero(-a) m, f

stationery n papelería f, artículos de escritorio m pl

statistical adj estadístico; **~ software** n software de estadística m

statistician n estadístico(-a) m,f

statistics¹ n (subject) estadística f

statistics² n pl (figures) estadísticas f pl

status n (standing) estatus m; (state) situación f; (Comp) estado m; (Law) estado legal m; **~ bar** n (Comp) barra de estado f; **~ information** n información de prestigio f; **~ inquiry** n (Fin) petición de informes sobre créditos f; **~ line** n (Comp) línea de condición f; **~ report** n informe de la situación m; **~ seeker** n persona que busca cierta posición social f; **~ symbol** n símbolo de prestigio m

status quo n statu quo m

statute n ley parlamentaria f; **~ book** n códigos de leyes m; **~ law** n derecho escrito m; **~ of limitations** n ley de prescripción f

statutory adj estatutario; **have ~ effect** tener efecto legal; **~ accounts** n pl cuentas f pl estatutarias or obligatorias; **~ audit** n auditoría de cuentas obligatoria f, auditoría legal f; **~ authority** n autoridad competente f; **~ body** n organismo legal m; **~ books** n pl libros legales m pl; **~ company** n empresa pública creada por ley f; **~ expenditure** n gasto estatutario m, gastos reglamentarios m pl; **~ holiday** n fiesta f legal or oficial; **~ instrument** n instrumento legal m; **~ meeting** n junta constitutiva f; **~ merger** n absorción de

una compañía amparada por la ley f; **~ minimum wage** n salario mínimo legal m; **~ notice** n notificación legal f; **~ obligation** n obligación legal f; **~ power** n poder legal m; **~ requirement** n requisito legal m; **~ right** n BrE derecho legal m; **~ sick pay** n BrE subsidio de enfermedad obligatorio m; **~ tax rate** n tipo impositivo legal m

stave off vt (disaster) evitar; (danger, threat) conjurar

stay¹ [1] vi quedarse; **~ in the money** permanecer en un valor [2] vt (sentence) suspender; **stay out** vi (on strike) seguir en huelga

stay² n (Law) suspensión f; **~ of execution** n suspensión del cumplimiento de sentencia f

staying power n resistencia f

stay-in strike n huelga de brazos caídos f

stay-out strike n huelga de ausencia en el puesto de trabajo f

stck abbr (▶stock) (share) acción f, valor m; (capital shares) acciones f pl, valores m pl; (of shop, business) existencias f pl

stcks abbr (▶stocks) (capital shares) acciones f pl, valores m pl; (of shop, business) existencias f pl

Std abbr (▶standard) (size) estándar, normal; (weight, measure) estándar, oficial

STD abbr (▶subscriber trunk dialling BrE) selección automática a distancia del abonado f

steadily adv (constantly, gradually) regularmente, a un ritmo constante; (incessantly) sin parar; **prices were ~ rising/ falling** los precios estaban subiendo/bajando a un ritmo constante

steady adj (improvement, decline, increase) constante; (growth) constante, sostenido; (prices) estable; (job) fijo, estable; (income) regular, fijo; (worker) serio, formal; **the pound remained ~ against the dollar** la libra permaneció estable or sin cambio frente al dólar; **~-state economy** n economía constante f

steadying factor n factor estabilizador m

steamroller vt (opposition) aplastar; **~ sb into sth** imponerle a alguien algo; **they ~ed the plan through the committee** aplastando a la oposición, hicieron que la comisión aprobara el plan

steamroller tactics n pl tácticas f pl dictatoriales or avasalladoras

steel n acero m; **~ industry** n industria del acero f

steelworker n obrero(-a) de acería m,f

steelworks n acería f

steep *adj* (increase, decline) considerable, pronunciado, marcado; (price) excesivo

steepen *vi* (curve) pronunciar

steeply *adv* (increase, decline) considerablemente, marcadamente; **prices rose** ∼ los precios dispararon

steering *n* dirección *f*; ∼ **committee** *n* comité directivo *m*

stem *vt* (decline) detener, poner freno a; **stem from** *vt* provenir de

stenographer *n* estenógrafo(-a) *m,f*, taquígrafo(-a) *m,f*

stenography *n* estenografía *f*, taquigrafía *f*

step¹ *n* (pace, move) paso *m*; (measure) medida *f*; (degree in scale) peldaño *m*, escalón *m*; **a great** ∼ **forward** un gran paso adelante; **keep in** ∼ **with one's competitors** ir al mismo ritmo que los competidores; **move up a** ∼ **in the salary scale** ascender un peldaño en la escala salarial; **take** ∼**s (to do sth)** tomar medidas (para hacer algo); ∼**s method** *n* (Comp) método de pasos *m*

step² *vi* pisar; ∼ **this way, please** pase por aquí, por favor; ∼ **over the mark** saltarse las normas; **step back** *vi* distanciarse; ∼ **back from sth** distanciarse de algo; **step down** *vi* renunciar, dimitir; **step in** *vi* intervenir; **step up** *vt* (exports) aumentar; (production, campaign) intensificar

step-by-step *adj* (instructions, program, operation) paso a paso

stepped *adj* escalonado

stepped-up basis *n* (Tax) base gradual *f*

step-up *n* (in expenditure, investment) aumento *m*; (in campaign) intensificación *f*; ∼ **loan** *n* préstamo ampliado *m*

sterilization *n* (Fin) esterilización *f*

sterling *n* libra (esterlina) *f*; S∼ **Area** *n* zona de la libra esterlina *f*; ∼ **balance** *n* reserva en libras esterlinas *f*; ∼ **commercial paper** *n* papel comercial en libras esterlinas *m*

steward *n* (on plane) auxiliar de vuelo *mf*; (on ship) camarero(-a) *m,f*; (of estate) administrador(a) *m,f*; (of club) director(a) administrativo(-a) *m,f*

stick *vt* (attach, glue) pegar; '∼ **no bills'** prohibido pegar carteles; **stick to** *vt* (principles) mantener, no apartarse de; (rules) ceñirse a, atenerse a; (agreement) cumplir con, respetar; (subject, facts) ceñirse a; ∼ **to one's original plan** seguir con su plan original

sticker *n* pegatina *f*

stickiness *n* (of website) poder atractivo de un sitio que capta los visitantes

sticking point *n* punto de retención *m*

stick-on label *n* etiqueta adhesiva *f*

sticky *adj* (texture, surface) pegajoso; (problem, issue) peliagudo; (situation) difícil; (price) rígido; ∼ **deal** *n* (Stock) operación difícil *f*; ∼ **label** *n* etiqueta adhesiva *f*; ∼ **tape** *n* cinta adhesiva *f*

stiff *adj* (competition, terms, conditions) duro; (penalty) fuerte, severo

stimulate *vt* (investment, sales, demand) estimular, potenciar, promover

stimulating *adj* (discussion, environment) estimulante

stimulative *adj* (measure) estimulante

stimulus *n* estímulo *m*; **be a** ∼ **for exports** ser un estímulo para las exportaciones

stint *n* periodo *m*

stipulate *vt* estipular

stipulation *n* condición *f*, estipulación *f*; **with the** ∼ **that...** con la condición de que...

stk *abbr* (▶**stock**) (share) acción *f*, valor *m*; (capital shares) acciones *f pl*, valores *m pl*

stk. *abbr* (▶**stock exchange**) bolsa (de valores) *f*

stks *abbr* (**stocks**) (capital shares) acciones *f pl*, valores *m pl*

stock¹ *n* (of shop, business) existencias *f pl*; (supply) reserva *f*; (share) acción *f*, valor *m*; (capital shares) acciones *f pl*, valores *m pl*; (government securities) bonos *m pl or* papel *m* del Estado; (reputation) reputación *f*; (livestock) ganado *m*; **be in** ∼ (product) estar en existencia; **be out of** ∼ (product) estar agotado; **be out of** ∼ **of sth** (shop) no tener algo en existencias; **put** *o* **take** ∼ **in sth** AmE dar crédito a algo; **take** ∼ (carry out inventory) hacer inventario; (review situation) hacer un balance; **while** ∼**s last** mientras duren las existencias; ∼ **card** *n* ficha de existencias *f*; ∼ **certificate** *n* AmE (*cf* ▶**share certificate** BrE) bono social *m*; ∼ **company** *n*, ∼ **corporation** *n* sociedad anónima *f*; ∼ **contract** *n* contrato bursátil *m*; ∼ **control** *n* BrE control de existencias *m*; ∼ **controller** *n* BrE controlador(a) de existencias *m,f*; ∼ **dividend** *n* (payment) dividendo en acciones *m*; (issue of stock) AmE (*cf* ▶**bonus issue** BrE) emisión de acciones liberadas *f*; ∼ **exchange** *n* bolsa (de valores) *f*; **on the** ∼ **exchange** en la bolsa; ∼**-exchange** *adj* bursátil; S∼ **Exchange Alternative Trading Service** *n* BrE *sistema operativo de cotizaciones*; S∼ **Exchange Automated Quotation** *n* BrE *sistema de cotización automatizada del mercado de valores*; S∼ **Exchange Automated Quotation International** *n* BrE *sistema de cotización automatizada de la bolsa internacional*; S∼ **Exchange Commission** *n* AmE *consejo de inversiones de acciones, bonos y valores*, ≈ Comisión Nacional del

S

Mercado de Valores *f* Esp; **S∼ Exchange Daily Official List** *n* BrE *boletín de la bolsa*; **∼ exchange list** *n* lista de valores cotizados *f*; **∼ exchange price index** *n* índice de precios de la Bolsa de Valores *m*; **∼ exchange quotation** *n* cotización del mercado de valores *f*; **∼ exchange transaction** *n* operación *f* bursátil *or* de bolsa; **∼ in** *n* existencias en almacén *f pl*; **∼ in hand** *n* inventario *m*, existencias (disponibles) *f pl*; **∼ index futures market** *n* mercado de futuros sobre acciones *m*; **∼ index option** *n* opción sobre el índice bursátil *f*; **∼ issue** *n* emisión de acciones *f*; **∼ line** *n* gama de productos *f*; **∼ list** *n* (of shares) boletín de cotizaciones en bolsa *f*; (of inventory) lista de existencias *f*; **∼ management** *n* gestión de almacén *f*; **∼ market** *n* mercado de valores *f*; **the ∼ market made solid ground** el mercado de valores se consolidó; **∼-market** *adj* bursátil; **∼ market capitalization** *n* capitalización del mercado de valores *f*; **∼ market collapse** *n* colapso del mercado de valores *m*; **∼ market cycle** *n* ciclo del mercado de valores *m*; **∼ market index** *n* índice *m* bursátil *or* del mercado de valores; **∼ market price index** *n* índice de precios del mercado de valores *m*; **∼ option** *n* opción de compra de acciones *f*; **∼ ownership** *n* titularidad de acciones *f*; **∼ portfolio** *n* cartera de valores *f*; **∼ price index** *n* índice *m* bursátil *or* de cotización de valores; **∼ purchase warrant** *n* certificado para compra de valores *m*; **∼ quotation** *n* cotización de acciones *f*; **∼ register** *n* registro de acciones *m*; **∼ rotation** *n* rotación de existencias *f*; **∼ sheet** *n* hoja de almacén *f*; **∼ shortage** *n* mermas de las existencias *f pl*; **∼ split** *n* AmE (*cf* ▸**bonus issue** BrE) emisión de acciones liberadas *f*; **∼ swap** *n* intercambio de acciones *m*; **∼ turnover** *n* (inventory) rotación de existencias *f*; (shares) rotación de títulos *f*; **∼ valuation** *n* valoración de existencias *f*; **∼ yield** *n* rendimiento bursátil *m*

stock² *vt* vender

stockbroker *n* corredor(a) de bolsa *m,f*, broker *mf*

stockbrokerage firm *n* sociedad de intermediación bursátil *f*

stockbroking *n* corretaje de bolsa *m*

stockholder *n* accionista *mf*; **∼s' equity** *n* valor neto *m*, capital social *m*; **∼ of record** *n* AmE accionista registrado(-a) *m,f*

stockholding *n* accionariado *m*

stockist *n* BrE distribuidor(a) *m,f*

stockjobber *n* corredor(a) *m,f or* intermediario(-a) *m,f* de bolsa

stockjobbery *n* especulación bursátil *f*

stockman *n* AmE (*cf* ▸**storeman** BrE) almacenista *mf*, jefe(-a) de almacén *m,f*

stockpile¹ *n* reservas *f pl*

stockpile² *vt* almacenar

stockpiling *n* almacenamiento *m*

stocktake *vi* hacer un inventario

stocktaking *n* inventario *m*; **closed for ∼** cerrado por inventario; **∼ sale** *n* venta posbalance *f*; **∼ value** *n* valor de inventario *m*

stop¹ **1** *vt* (Comp) parar; (decline, inflation) detener, parar; (bankruptcy proceedings) detener; (production, payment) suspender; (cheque) bloquear *or* suspender el pago de; (subscription) cancelar; **∼ sb's allowance** interrumpir el subsidio de alguien; **the boss ∼ped £30 out of my wages** BrE el jefe me descontó *or* me retuvo 30 libras del sueldo; **∼ a stock** suspender un capital en acciones; **∼ work** dejar *or* terminar de trabajar **2** *vi* (Comp) pararse

stop² *n* (halt) pausa *f*, alto *m*; **bring sth to a ∼** (conversation, proceedings) poner fin a *or* interrumpir algo; **come to a ∼** (production, conversation) interrumpirse; **put a ∼ on a check** AmE *o* **cheque** BrE dar orden de no pagar un cheque; **put a ∼ to sth** (malpractice) poner fin a *or* acabar con algo; **∼ bit** *n* (Comp) bitio de detención *m*; **∼ order** *n* orden de bloqueo *f*; **∼ payment order** *n* orden de suspensión de pagos *f*; **∼ signal** *n* señal de parada *f*; **∼ time** *n* (Comp) tiempo de parada *m*

stop-and-go AmE ▸**stop-go** BrE

stopgap *n* recurso provisional *m*; **∼ measure** *n* medida provisional *f*

stop-go BrE, **stop-and-go** AmE *adj* (policy) de stop and go, de frena y avanza; **∼ cycle of inflation** *n* ciclo de inflación de alternancias de recesión-expansión *m*

stoppage *n* (in production) interrupción *f*; (industrial action) huelga *f*; (cancellation) suspensión *f*; (from wages) BrE retención *f*

stopped *adj* (cheque, bonds) bloqueado; (payment) retenido; (stock) congelado

stopper *n* (S&M) tope *m*

stopwatch *n* cronómetro *m*; **∼ studies** *n pl* estudios cronometrados *m pl*

storage *n* almacenamiento *m*, almacenaje *m*; (Comp) (action) almacenamiento *m*; (place) memoria *f*; **put sth in(to) ∼** poner algo en depósito *or* almacén; **∼ allocation** *n* (Comp) asignación de almacenamiento *f*; **∼ area** *n* área de almacenamiento *f*; **∼ capacity** *n* capacidad de almacenamiento *f*; (Comp) capacidad de memoria *f*; **∼ charges** *n pl* gastos de almacenaje *m pl*; **∼ device** *n* (Comp) dispositivo de almacenamiento *m*;

∼ **dump** n (Comp) volcado de la memoria
m; ∼ **facility** n instalación de
almacenamiento f; ∼ **field** n (Comp) campo
de almacenamiento m; ∼ **map** n (Comp)
topograma de la memoria m; ∼ **medium** n
(Comp) medio de almacenamiento m; ∼
requirements n pl (Comp) necesidades de
memoria f pl; ∼ **services provider** n
(Comp) proveedor de servicios de
almacenamiento m

store¹ n (warehouse) almacén m; (stock,
supply) reserva f; AmE (cf ▸**shop** BrE) tienda
f; ∼ **accounting** n contabilidad de almacén
f; ∼ **audit** n auditoría f de almacén or de
existencias; ∼ **brand** n AmE marca
comercial f; ∼ **card** n tarjeta de crédito de
una tienda específica f; ∼ **group** n grupo de
tiendas m; ∼ **window** n AmE (cf ▸**shop
window** BrE) escaparate m

store² vt (data, goods) almacenar

storefront AmE n (cf ▸**shop front** BrE)
fachada f (de una tienda)

storehouse n almacén m

storekeeper n (storeman) almacenista mf,
jefe(-a) m,f de almacén; AmE (storeowner)
tendero(-a) m,f

storeman n BrE (cf ▸**warehouseman**
AmE, ▸**stockman** AmE) almacenista mf,
jefe(-a) m,f de almacén

storeowner n AmE (cf ▸**shopkeeper** BrE)
tendero(-a) m,f

storeroom n depósito m

storey BrE, **story** AmE n piso m, planta f

storyboard n guión gráfico m

straddle n especulación mixta f; ∼ **buyer**
n comprador(a) con opción de compra o
venta m,f; ∼ **combination** n combinación
de opción de compra y venta f; ∼ **seller** n
vendedor(a) con opción de compra y venta
m,f

straight adj (question, investment, loan)
directo; (bond) ordinario; (denial, refusal)
rotundo, categórico; ∼ **bill of lading** n
conocimiento de embarque no traspasable
m; ∼-**line depreciation** n amortización
anual uniforme f, amortización lineal f;
∼-**line method** n método m lineal or de
cuotas constantes or de la línea recta;
∼-**line method of depreciation** n método
m de amortización anual uniforme or de
amortización lineal

straighten out vt (problem) resolver,
arreglar; (confusion, misunderstanding) aclarar;
straighten things out arreglar las cosas

straightforward adj (simple) sencillo;
(frank) directo, sincero

straights market n mercado nominativo
m

strained adj (relations) tenso

stranded goods n pl artículos de
naufragio m pl

strangle n posición de compraventa de
opciones a distintos precios

stranglehold n poder m, dominio m;
have a ∼ **on the market** dominar
totalmente el mercado

strap n compra strap f; ∼ **option** n opción
strap f

strapline n (in newspaper) titular grande m;
(on Internet) banner m

strapped adj: **be** ∼ **for cash** (infrml) estar
en apuros económicos

stratagem n ardid m

strategic adj (alliance, plan, planning)
estratégico; ∼ **business unit** n unidad
estratégica de negocio f; ∼ **fit** n ajuste
estratégico m; ∼ **interdependence** n
interdependencia estratégica f; ∼
management accounting n contabilidad f
de dirección estratégica or de gestión
estratégica; ∼ **partnership** n sociedad
colectiva estratégica f

strategist n estratega mf

strategy n estrategia f; ∼ **formulation** n
formulación de una estrategia f; ∼
implementation n implementación
estratégica f

stratification n estratificación f

stratified adj (sampling) estratificado

straw: ∼ **boss** n AmE (infrml) ayudante de
capataz m; ∼ **poll** n, ∼ **vote** n votación de
tanteo f

streaker n (Bank) bono de cupón cero m

stream n (of data) flujo m; **be/come on** ∼
estar/entrar en funcionamiento; **go
against/with the** ∼ ir contra/con la
corriente

streamer n (in newspaper) titular en
bandera m; (Comp) cinta de serpentina m,
streamer m

streaming media n pl medios por
caudales m pl

streamline vt racionalizar

streamlining n racionalización f

street n calle f; ∼ **book** n registro de
valores gestionados m; ∼ **dealing** n venta
de valores no oficial f; ∼ **price** n precio m
tras el cierre or fuera de horas; ∼ **trader**
BrE, ∼ **vendor** AmE n comerciante m,f or
vendedor(a) m,f callejero(-a)

strength n (of currency, economy) solidez f; (of
market) fuerza f; (of material) resistencia f;
(strong point) virtud f, punto fuerte m; (number)
número m; **be at full** ∼ tener todo el
personal trabajando; **be below** ∼ estar
corto de personal; **bring sth up to full** ∼
llevar algo al nivel deseado; **go from** ∼ **to**
∼ ir viento en popa; **the** ∼ **of the**   ⸱⸱⸱⸥

workforce has fallen by 50% el número de los trabajadores ha descendido en un 50%; **we employed her on the ~ of his recommendation** la contratamos basándonos en su recomendación; **be up to full ~** estar al nivel deseado; **~s, weaknesses, opportunities and threats analysis** n análisis de las fuerzas, debilidades, oportunidades y amenazas m

strengthen [1] vt (support, opposition) aumentar, acrecentar; (position) fortalecer, afianzar, consolidar
[2] vi (support, opposition) aumentar, acrecentarse; (prices) afianzarse; (currency, economy) fortalecerse

strengthening n (of currency) fortalecimiento m; (prices) afianzamiento m

stress[1] n (pressure) estrés m, tensión f; (emphasis) énfasis m; **learn how to cope with ~** aprender a sobrellevar el estrés; **lay great ~ on punctuality** dar mucha importancia a la puntualidad; **be under great ~** estar muy estresado; **perform well under ~** trabajar bien bajo presión; **~ management** n combate del estrés m; **~-related** adj (illness) provocado por or relacionado con el estrés

stress[2] vt (pressurize) estresar, agobiar; (emphasize) enfatizar, recalcar; **stress out** vt estresar, agobiar

stressful adj (life, job) estresante

strict adj estricto; **~ adherence to a contract** estricta adhesión al contrato; **reply in the ~est confidence** se garantiza absoluta reserva; **under ~ instructions** bajo instrucciones precisas; **in ~est secrecy** en el más absoluto secreto; **on the ~ understanding that...** bajo la condición rigurosa de que...; **~ cost price** n precio m de coste Esp or costo AmL estricto; **~ foreclosure** n ejecución hipotecaria forzosa f; **~ time limit** n plazo perentorio m

strife n conflictos m pl; **industrial ~** conflictos laborales; **~-ridden** adj (period) conflictivo

strike[1] n huelga f; **break a ~** boicotear una huelga, esquirolear (infrml); **come out on** BrE o **go (out) on ~** ir a la huelga; **be on ~** estar en huelga; **the ~ has been called off** se canceló la huelga; **~ action** n medida de huelga f; **~ ballot** n votación de huelga f; **~ benefits** n pl subsidio de huelga m; **~ clause** n cláusula de huelga f; **~ committee** n comité de huelga m; **~ fund** n fondo de huelga m; **~ notice** n aviso de huelga m; **~ pay** n paga de huelga f; **~ price** n (Stock) precio de ejercicio m; **~ rate** n (jarg) (S&M) índice de eficacia m; **~ threat** n amenaza de huelga f; **~ vote** n votación de huelga f; **~ yield** n (Stock) rendimiento del ejercicio m

strike[2] [1] vi hacer huelga; **~ in sympathy** hacer huelga por simpatía or por solidaridad
[2] vt (oil, gold) encontrar, dar con; **~ a balance** hacer balance; **~ a deal** hacer un trato, llegar a un acuerdo; **~ it rich** (infrml) hacerse rico; **strike off** vt (delete) tachar; (disqualify) prohibirle el ejercicio de la profesión a; **~ sb off the list** borrar a alguien de la lista

strikebound adj paralizado por la huelga

strikebreaker n esquirol mf (infrml)

strikebreaking n esquirolismo m (infrml)

strikeover n (Comp) doble pulsación f

striker n huelguista mf

string n (Comp) cadena f; **no ~s attached** sin condiciones, sin cortapisas

stringent adj (measures, programme) estricto; **~ money market** n mercado monetario restrictivo m

stringently adv estrictamente

strip[1] n (coupon) cupón m; (of land) franja f; **~ bond** n strip m; **~ development** n desarrollo por zonas m

strip[2] vt (room, building) vaciar; **~ a company of its assets** vaciar una compañía, vender el activo de una compañía

stripped adj (bond, security) sin cupón

strong adj (currency, indication) fuerte; (economy) fuerte, pujante; (reputation) sólido; (leadership, principles, support) firme; (protest) enérgico; (argument, evidence) de peso, convincente

strongarm adj (methods) de mano dura; **use ~ tactics** hacer uso de la fuerza

strongbox n caja fuerte f

strongly adv fuertemente

strongroom n cámara acorazada f

structural adj (model, change) estructural; **~ adjustment** n ajuste estructural m; **~ adjustment facility** n mecanismo de ajuste estructural m; **~ engineering** n ingeniería estructural f

structure[1] n estructura f

structure[2] vt estructurar

structured adj (interview, programming) estructurado

structuring n estructuración f

struggle n lucha f

stub n (of cheque) talón m AmL, matriz f Esp; (of receipt) resguardo m, talón m

student n estudiante mf; **~ loan** n préstamo de estudiante m

studio n estudio m

study[1] n estudio m; **~ day** n día de estudio m; **~ group** n grupo de estudios m; **~ trip** n viaje de estudios m

study[2] vt estudiar

stumbling block *n* atolladero *m*

stump up *vt* BrE (infrml) aflojar (infrml)

stunt¹ *n* (for publicity) ardid publicitario *m*; ∼ **advertising** *n* anuncio sensacionalista *m*

stunt² *vt* atrofiar

style *n* (of management) estilo *m*; ∼ **sheet** *n* hoja de estilo *f*

stylist *n* estilista *mf*

stylize *vt* estilizar

stylus *n* (pen-based device) estilete *m*

stymie *vt* (infrml) obstruir

sub *n* BrE (infrml) (▸**sub-editor**) secretario(-a) de redacción *m,f*

subactivity *n* subactividad *f*

subagent *n* subagente *mf*

suballotment *n* subasignación *f*

subchapter *n* apartado *m*, subcapítulo *m*

subcommittee *n* subcomité *m*, subcomisión *f*

subcompact *adj* subcompacto

subcontract¹ *vt* subcontratar

subcontract² *n* subcontrato *m*

subcontracting *n* subcontratación *f*

subcontractor *n* subcontratista *mf*

subcustody *n* (Fin) subcustodia *f*

subdirectory *n* subdirectorio *m*

subdivide *vt* subdividir

subdivision *n* subdivisión *f*

subdued *adj* (prices) moderado

sub-edit *vt* BrE (book, proofs) corregir, revisar; (newspaper) revisar y compaginar

sub-editor *n* BrE secretario(-a) de redacción *m,f*

subemployment *n* subempleo *m*

subentry *n* subentrada *f*

subfile *n* subarchivo *m*

subgroup *n* subgrupo *m*

subhead *n*, **subheading** *n* subtítulo *m*

subholding company *n* subholding *m*

subject¹ *n* (topic) tema *m*; (studied) asignatura *f*; (of investigation) sujeto *m*; (person) súbdito(-a) *m,f*; **change the** ∼ cambiar de tema; **on the** ∼ **of sth** en *or* sobre el tema de algo; **while we're on the** ∼**...** mientras hablamos del tema...; ∼ **filing** *n* archivo por materias *m*; ∼ **index** *n* índice de materias *m*; ∼ **matter** *n* contenido *m*; ∼ **search** *n* búsqueda por campo *f*

subject² *adj* sujeto; **be** ∼ **to sth** (approval, change, taxation) estar sujeto a algo; ∼ **to mortgage** sujeto a hipoteca; ∼ **to price controls** (products) sujeto a controles de precio; ∼ **to quota** sometido a contingente

subjective *adj* subjetivo; ∼ **perception** *n* percepción subjetiva *f*

sub judice *adj* pendiente de resolución judicial

sublet¹ *vti*, **sublease** *vti* subarrendar

sublet² *n*, **sublease** *n* subarriendo *m*

subletter *n* subarrendatario(-a) *m,f*

sublicence BrE, **sublicense** AmE *n* subconcesión *f*, sublicencia *f*

subliminal *adj* (advertising, response, image, perception) subliminal

submanager *n* director(a) adjunto(-a) *m,f*

submarginal *n* submarginal *m*

submission *n* (plan, proposal) propuesta *f*; (report) informe *m*; (presentation) presentación *f*; (Law) alegato *m*; ∼ **of bids** *n* presentación de ofertas *f*

submit *vt* (proposal) presentar; (claim, application) someter; ∼ **a dispute to arbitration** someter un litigio a arbitraje; ∼ **a plan to sb for approval** presentarle un plan a alguien para su aprobación

submortgage *n* hipoteca con garantía de otra hipoteca *f*

suboffice *n* suboficina *f*

suboptimization *n* suboptimización *f*

subordinate¹ *adj* subalterno

subordinate² *n* subalterno(-a) *m,f*, subordinado(-a) *m,f*

subordinate³ *vt* subordinar; ∼ **sth to sth** subordinar algo a algo

subordinated *adj* (asset, loan) subordinado

subordination *n* subordinación *f*; ∼ **agreement** *n* acuerdo de subordinación *m*; ∼ **interest** *n* interés de subordinación *m*

subparagraph *n* subinciso *m*

subpoena¹ *n* citación *f*

subpoena² *vt* citar; ∼ **sb to testify** citar a alguien para testificar

sub-post office *n* BrE estafeta de correos *f*

subprogram *n* subprograma *m*, subrutina *f*

subrogation *n* subrogación *f*; ∼ **clause** *n* cláusula de subrogación *f*

subroutine *n* subrutina *f*

subscribe ⟦1⟧ *vt* (donate) donar, (sign) suscribir; **the share issue was heavily** ∼**d** hubo muchas solicitudes de compra de acciones ⟦2⟧ *vi* (for loan, shares) suscribir; (to magazine, newspaper) suscribirse; (to TV, Internet service) abonarse; ∼ **for shares in a company** suscribir acciones en una empresa; ∼ **to an issue** suscribir una emisión

subscribed *adj* (capital) suscrito

subscriber *n* (for shares, to magazine, newspaper) suscriptor(a) *m,f*; (to TV, telephone, Internet service) abonado(-a) *m,f*; ∼ **identity module** *n* módulo de identidad del abonado *m*; ∼ **trunk dialling** BrE *n* selección automática a distancia del abonado *f*

S

subscribing option n facultad de suscribir f

subscript n subíndice m

subscription n (for shares, to magazine, newspaper) suscripción f; (to TV, Internet service) abono m; **take out a ~** (for shares, to magazine, newspaper) suscribirse a; (to TV, Internet service) abonarse a; **~ form** n formulario de suscripción m; **~-free ISP** n proveedor de servicios Internet gratis m; **~ price** n precio de suscripción m; **~ ratio** n proporción de suscripción f; **~ warrant** n certificado de suscripción m

subsector n subsector m

subsequent adj (events, developments) posterior, subsiguiente; **~ event** n hecho posterior m, suceso subsecuente m

subset n subconjunto m

subshare n acción subdividida f

subsidiarity n subsidiaridad f

subsidiary¹ adj (company, bank) filial; (payment, loan) subsidiario; (income) adicional, extra; (role) secundario; **~ account** n cuenta f auxiliar or subsidiaria, subcuenta f; **~ accounting record** n libro auxiliar m, registro contable auxiliar m; **~ accounting system** n sistema de contabilidad auxiliar m; **~ ledger** n libro mayor auxiliar m

subsidiary² n filial f

subsidization n subvención f

subsidize vt (company, project) subvencionar, subsidiar AmL

subsidized adj (prices, exports, travel) subvencionado, subsidiado AmL

subsidy n subvención f, subsidio m

subsistence n subsistencia f; **~ allowance** n dieta f; **~ economy** n economía de subsistencia f; **~ farming** n cultivo de subsistencia m; **~ level** n nivel de subsistencia m; **live at ~ level** vivir a un nivel de subsistencia; **~ wage** n salario de subsistencia m

substance n sustancia f

substandard adj inferior al nivel medio

substantial adj (amount, income, interest, loan) considerable, importante; (changes, difference, risk) sustancial; (contribution) importante

substantially adv (considerably) de manera sustancial or considerable; (basically) básicamente, sustancialmente

substantiate vt (rumour, story, statement) confirmar, corroborar; (accusation, claim) probar

substantive adj (evidence, proof, research) sustantivo, de peso; (change) sustancial; (issue) fundamental; (motion) BrE con enmiendas; **~ law** n derecho sustantivo m

substitute¹ adj sustitutivo; **~ goods** n pl bienes de sustitución m pl

substitute² n (thing) sucedáneo m; (person) BrE (cf ▸**alternate** AmE) sustituto(-a) m,f; **accept no ~s** no acepte imitaciones

substitute³ vt sustituir; **~ A for B** sustituir B por A

substituted adj (share) sustituido

substitution n sustitución f; **~ law** n ley de reemplazo f

substructure n infraestructura f

subtenancy n subarriendo m

subtenant n subarrendatario(-a) m,f

subtotal n subtotal m

subtract vt restar; **~ sth from sth** restar algo de algo

suburb n barrio m

subway n (railway) AmE (cf ▸**underground** BrE, ▸**tube** BrE) metro m; (for pedestrians) BrE paso subterráneo m

succeed vi tener éxito, acertar, triunfar

succeeding adj (weeks, months) subsiguiente; **~ account** n cuenta siguiente f

success n éxito m; **be a ~** (person, thing) tener éxito; **make a ~ of sth** tener éxito en algo; **~ story** n historia de éxito f

successful adj exitoso; **the ~ candidate** el candidato elegido; **be ~ in sth** tener éxito en algo; **be ~ in doing sth** lograr hacer algo con éxito; **a ~ outcome** (to negotiations) un resultado óptimo; **~ bidder** n (at auction) adjudicatario(-a) m,f

succession n sucesión f; **~ law** n derecho de sucesión m

successive adj (days, weeks) consecutivo; (governments) sucesivo

successor n sucesor(a) m,f; (assignee) causahabiente m

sue ⓵ vt demandar; **~ sb for infringement of patent** demandar a alguien por violar una patente; **~ sb for libel** demandar a alguien por libelo ⓶ vi entablar una demanda, poner pleito Esp; **~ for damages** demandar por daños perjuicios

suffer ⓵ vt (loss, consequences, damage, setback) sufrir ⓶ vi (person) sufrir; (business, performance) verse afectado

sufficient adj suficiente, bastante; **not ~ funds** fondos insuficientes

suggest vt (propose) sugerir, proponer; (indicate) indicar; (evoke) sugerir

suggested retail price n precio al por menor sugerido m

suggestion n sugerencia f; **make a ~** hacer una sugerencia; **put a ~ before a**

committee exponer una sugerencia ante un comité; **there is no ∼ of corruption** no hay sombra de corrupción; **∼ box** n buzón de sugerencias m

suit[1] vt (be convenient for) convenirle a; **Tuesday/four o'clock would ∼ me better** me convendría más el martes/a las cuatro

suit[2] n (Law) juicio m, pleito m

suitability n (for job) idoneidad f

suitable adj (appropriate) apropiado, adecuado; (acceptable, proper) apropiado (convenient) conveniente; **the most ∼ person for the job** la persona más indicada para el trabajo

sulphur BrE, **sulfur** AmE n azufre m; **∼ emission** n emisión de azufre f

sum n suma f; **this ∼ does not appear in the accounts** esta cantidad no figura en las cuentas; **do one's ∼s** hacer las cuentas; **the ∼ of £200** la suma de 200 libras; **∼ advanced** n anticipo m; **∼ assured** n suma asegurada f

summarize vti resumir; **to ∼** en resumen

summary[1] n resumen m

summary[2] adj (dismissal) inmediato; (trial, judgment) sumario; (account, description) breve, corto; (report, statement) resumido; **∼ application** n (Law) ejecución rápida f

summer n verano m; **∼ recess** n (of Parliament) receso estival m

summit n (meeting) cumbre f; **∼ conference** n cumbre f, conferencia cumbre f

summons[1] n citación f; **take out a ∼ against sb** citar a alguien, mandar una citación a alguien

summons[2] vt citar

sumptuary adj (law) suntuario

sum up [1] vt (discussion, report) resumir; (person, situation) hacerse una idea de [2] vi recapitular; **to ∼** en resumen

Sunday n domingo m; **∼s and holidays excepted** salvo domingos y días festivos; **∼ trading** n comercio dominical m

sundries n pl varios m pl

sundry adj (articles, expenses) vario; **∼ accounts** n pl cuentas f pl diversas or de varios

sunk adj (capital) amortizado; (cost) hundido

sunrise industry n industria f incipiente or en los albores

sunset: **∼ act** n ley a punto de ser retirada f; **∼ industry** n industria consolidada f; **∼ law** n AmE (jarg) *ley que require que los entes administrativos justifiquen periódicamente ante la legislatura los motivos de su existencia*; **∼ provision** n *disposición que especifica una fecha de expiración*; **∼ report** n informe a punto de caducar m

sunshine law n AmE ley de transparencia f

super- pref super

superannuate vt jubilar

superannuation n jubilación f; **∼ contribution** n contribución por jubilación f; **∼ fund** n fondo de pensiones m; **∼ scheme** n BrE plan de jubilación m

supercomputer n supercomputadora f AmL, superordenador m Esp

superficial adj superficial; **∼ loss** n pérdida superficial f

superhighway n AmE autopista f

superimposed adj (tax) superpuesto

superintendent n (of maintenance, hostel) encargado(-a) m,f; (of building) AmE portero(-a) m,f; (of institution) director(a) m,f; **S∼ of Bankruptcy** n interventor(a) m,f or contralor(a) m,f AmL de quiebras, supervisor(a) de quiebras m,f

superior[1] adj superior; **of ∼ quality** de calidad superior; **be ∼ to sth/sb** ser superior a algo/alguien

superior[2] n superior mf

superiority n superioridad f

supermarket n supermercado m

supernormal adj (profit) superior a lo normal

supernumerary n supernumerario m

superposed adj (tax) superpuesto

superpower n superpotencia f

super-saver n superahorrador m

superscript n índice superior m

supersede vt substituir, suplantar

supersite n *espacio para carteles de gran tamaño*

superstore n hipermercado m

superstructure n superestructura f

super-video-graphics array n conjunto m de gráficos de supervídeo AmL or supervídeo Esp

supervise vt supervisar

supervision n supervisión f, control m

supervisor n supervisor(a) m,f

supervisory adj (management, personnel, board) de supervisión; (duties, post) de supervisor; **in a ∼ capacity** en capacidad de supervisor

supplement[1] n (extra charge) recargo m; (appendix) apéndice m; (separate publication) suplemento m; (insert) separata f

supplement[2] vt (income) complementar; (report) completar

supplemental adj suplementario

supplementaries n pl suplementarios m pl

supplementary *adj* (cost, budget, period) suplementario; (agreement, reserve) complementario; ∼ **entry** *n* (Acc) asiento contable suplementario *m*; ∼ **pension scheme** *n* BrE plan de pensiones suplementario *m*

supplier *n* proveedor(a) *m,f*; ∼ **credit** *n* crédito de suministrador *m*

supplies *n pl* existencias *f pl*

supply[1] *n* (provision) suministro *m*; (stock) existencias *f pl*; (reserve) reservas *f pl*; **be in plentiful/short** ∼ abundar/escasear; ∼ **chain** *n* cadena de suministros *f*; ∼ **chain execution** *n* ejecución de la cadena de suministros *f*; ∼ **chain management** *n* gestión de la cadena de suministros *f*; ∼ **curve** *n* curva de oferta *f*; ∼ **and demand** *n* oferta *f* y demanda *f*; ∼ **function** *n* función de oferta *f*; ∼ **network** *n* AmE (*cf* ▶**mains** BrE) red de alimentación *f*, línea principal *f*; ∼ **price** *n* precio de oferta *m*; ∼ **shock** *n* choque de oferta *m*; ∼ **side economics** *n* economía de oferta *f*

supply[2] *vt* (goods) suministrar, abastecer, proveer; (retailer, manufacturer) abastecer; (electricity, gas) suministrar; (evidence, information) proporcionar, facilitar; (demand, need) satisfacer; (deficiency) suplir; ∼ **collateral** aportar una garantía; ∼ **goods on trust** suministrar bienes a crédito; ∼ **references** dar referencias; ∼ **the shortfall** reparar el déficit; ∼ **sb with sth** abastecer a alguien de algo, suministrarle algo a alguien

support[1] *n* apoyo *m*; (person) sostén *m*; **in** ∼ **of sth/sb** en apoyo de algo/alguien; ∼ **activities** *n pl* actividades de apoyo *f pl*; ∼ **hotline** *n* línea directa de consulta *f*; ∼ **level** *n* nivel de apoyo *m*; ∼ **price** *n* (for commodities) precio *m* de apoyo *or* (de) sostén; ∼ **service** *n* servicio de apoyo *m*; ∼ **staff** *n* personal de apoyo *m*; ∼ **system** *n* sistema de apoyo *m*

support[2] *vt* (person, cause, motion) apoyar; (price, growth) mantener, sostener; (dependant) mantener; (explanation, theory) respaldar, confirmar, sustentar; **a move to** ∼ **the dollar** una medida para mantener la cotización del dólar

supported *adj* (with maintenance) con servicio de mantenimiento; (with IT backup) con apoyo técnico

supporter *n* partidario(-a) *m,f*

supporting *adj* (documents, evidence) acreditativo; (purchases) secundario

suppress *vt* (facts, evidence, truth) ocultar; (Comp) suprimir

suppressed *adj* (inflation) contenido

supra *adv* supra

supranational *adj* supranacional

supraorganization *n* supraorganización *f*

Supreme Court *n* AmE (*cf* ▶**High Court** BrE) Corte Suprema *f*, Tribunal Supremo *m*, ≈ Audiencia Nacional *f* Esp

surcharge[1] *n* recargo *m*; **impose a** ∼ **on sth** aplicar un recargo a algo

surcharge[2] *vt* aplicar un recargo a

surety *n* (security) fianza *f*; (person) fiador(a) *m,f*; **offer £100 as (a)** ∼ ofrecer 100 libras de fianza; **stand** ∼ **for sb** ser fiador de alguien; ∼ **in cash** *n* fianza en efectivo *f*

surf *vti* (on Internet) navegar

surface *n* superficie *f*; **by** ∼ **mail** por correo marítimo o terrestre; ∼ **area** *n* superficie *f*, área *f*

surfer *n* (on Internet) internauta *mf*, navegante *mf*

surfing *n* (on Internet) navegación *f*, travesía por Internet *mf*

surge[1] *n* (in demand, sales) aumento repentino *m*

surge[2] *vi* (demand, sales, popularity) aumentar vertiginosamente

surpass *vt* exceder, superar

surplus *n* (of stock, produce) excedente *m*; (of funds) superávit *m*; **in** ∼ en excedente; **in financial** ∼ en situación de excedente financiero; **a** ∼ **of assets over liabilities** un excedente del activo sobre el pasivo; ∼ **dividend** *n* dividendo extraordinario *m*; ∼ **reserve** *n* reserva del excedente *f*; ∼ **value** *n* valor *m* de la plusvalía *or* del excedente

surprise *n* sorpresa *f*; ∼ **function** *n* (Econ) función sorpresa *f*

surrender[1] *n* (of document, passport, foreign exchange) entrega *f*; (of rights) renuncia *f*; (of patent) cesión *f*; (Law) dejación *f*; **for** ∼ (security) para rescate; ∼ **charge** *n* coste *m* Esp *or* costo *m* AmL de rescate; ∼ **of property** *n* cesión de bienes *f*; ∼ **value** *n* valor de rescate *m*

surrender[2] *vt* (document, ticket) entregar; (right, claim) renunciar a

surtax *n* impuesto adicional *m*, sobretasa *f*

surveillance *n* vigilancia *f*

survey[1] *n* (of land) inspección *f*; (of building) inspección *f*, peritaje *m*, peritación *f*; (written report on building) informe del perito *m*, peritaje *m*, peritación *f*; (poll) encuesta *f*, sondeo *m*; (investigation) estudio *m*; (overall view) visión *f* general *or* de conjunto; **carry out** *o* **conduct a** ∼ **a** (investigation) llevar a cabo *or* hacer un estudio; (poll) llevar a cabo *or* hacer una encuesta *or* un sondeo; ∼ **fee** *n* (for finance house) honorarios de inspección *m pl*; ∼ **fees** *n pl* (for surveying property) gastos de peritación *m pl*

survey[2] *vt* (situation, plan, prospects) examinar, analizar; (group) encuestar, hacer un sondeo de; (building) inspeccionar, llevar a cabo un peritaje de; (land, region - measure) medir; (- inspect) inspeccionar, reconocer

surveyor *n* (of land) agrimensor(a) *m,f*, topógrafo(-a) *m,f*; (of building) inspector(a) *m,f*

survival *n* supervivencia *f*; **the ∼ of the fittest** la ley del más fuerte; **∼ process** *n* (of firms) proceso de supervivencia *m*; **∼ strategy** *n* estrategia de supervivencia *f*

survive *vi* sobrevivir

surviving *adj* (company, spouse) superviviente

survivor *n* superviviente *mf*; **∼ policy** *n* (Ins) póliza para los beneficiarios *f*

survivorship *n* supervivencia *f*; **∼ account** *n* cuenta de supervivencia *f*; **∼ clause** *n* AmE cláusula de supervivencia *f*; **∼ insurance** *n* seguro de supervivencia *m*

susceptible *adj* susceptible

suspect[1] *vt* (person) sospechar de; (sincerity, motives) tener dudas acerca de

suspect[2] *n* sospechoso(-a) *m,f*

suspect[3] *adj* (package) sospechoso; (document, evidence) de dudosa autenticidad

suspend *vt* (payment, work, trading, member) suspender; (judgment, decision) posponer

suspended sentence *n* condena condicional *f*

suspense: **∼ account** *n* cuenta transitoria *f*; **∼ balance** *n* saldo transitorio *m*; **∼ entry** *n* partida en suspenso *f*

suspension *n* (cessation, banning) suspensión *f*; (deferment) aplazamiento *m*; **∼ file** *n* archivo de hamaca *m*; **∼ of trading** *n* suspensión de operaciones *f*

sustain *vt* (damage, loss, injury, defeat) sufrir; (objection) admitir; (claim) apoyar, respaldar

sustainable *adj* (development, growth, level, rate) sostenible

sustained *adj* (efforts) sostenido, continuo; **∼ noninflationary growth** *n* crecimiento sostenido no inflacionario *m*

SVGA *abbr* (▶**super-video-graphics array**) SVGA (conjunto de gráficos de supervideo AmL *or* supervídeo Esp)

swamp *vt* inundar; **be ∼ed by debts** estar agobiado de deudas; **be ∼ed with work** estar inundado *or* agobiado de trabajo

swap[1] *n*, **swop** *n* (exchange of liabilities) swap *m*, permuta financiera *f*; (interest rate instrument) crédito recíproco *m*, swap *m*; (infrml) (exchange) cambio *m*, trueque *m*; **∼ market** *n* mercado *m* de créditos recíprocos *or* de swaps; **∼ option** *n* opción sobre permuta financiera *f*

swap[2], **swop** [1] *vt* intercambiar; **∼ sth for sth** cambiar algo por algo

[2] *vi* hacer un intercambio

swaption *n*, **swoption** *n* intercambio *m*

swatch *n* muestrario *m*

sway *vt* (outcome) influir en

swear *vi* (Law) prestar juramento; **∼ on affidavit** declarar bajo juramento

sweated *adj* (labour) explotado; **∼ goods** *n pl bienes fabricados por mano de obra explotada*

sweatshop *n empresa que explota al personal*

sweeping *adj* (changes) radical

sweetener *n* (infrml) (bribe) astilla *f* (infrml)

sweetheart contract *n* convenio colectivo favorable al empresario *m*

swell *vt* (accounts, coffers) inflar

SWIFT *abbr* (▶**Society for Worldwide Interbank Financial Telecommunications**) SITF (Sociedad Internacional de Telecomunicaciones Financieras)

swindle[1] *n* estafa *f*

swindle[2] *vt* estafar

swindler *n* estafador(a) *m,f*

swing[1] *vt* (infrml) (manage) arreglar; **∼ a deal** conseguir un trato; **if you want that job, I think I can ∼ it** si quieres ese puesto, creo que puedo arreglarlo

swing[2] *n* (shift) cambio *m*; (Pol) viraje *m*; **the ∼s of the market** las fluctuaciones del mercado; **∼ credits** *n pl* créditos recíprocos al descubierto *m pl*; **∼ loan** *n* préstamo puente *m*, préstamo recíproco al descubierto *m*; **∼ shift** *n* AmE turno de tarde *m*; **∼ voter** *n* votante indeciso(-a) *m,f*

swingeing *adj* BrE (cuts, increases) salvaje; (criticism, attack) durísimo, feroz

swipe *vt* (credit card) pasar (por un lector de tarjetas)

switch[1] *n* (device) interruptor *m*; (program) desvío *m*; (shift, change) cambio *m*; (exchange) intercambio *m*; **∼ dealing** *n* transacción de arbitraje *f*; **∼ selling** *n* BrE (S&M) *venta forzada de artículos más caros que los artículos en promoción*; (Stock) venta de un valor para comprar otro con mejor perspectiva; **∼ trading** *n* comercio *m* triangular *or* circular; (Stock) negociación rotativa *f*

switch[2] [1] *vt* (change) cambiar de; (exchange) intercambiar; **the price tags have been ∼ed** han intercambiado las etiquetas de precio; **∼ production to Oxford** trasladar la producción a la planta de Oxford; **∼ roles (with each other)** intercambiarse los papeles

[2] *vi* (from one thing to another) cambiar; **∼ to modern methods** pasarse a métodos modernos; **switch around** *vi* (exchange ⋯⋮

positions, roles) cambiar; **switch off** $\boxed{1}$ *vt*
(machine) apagar $\boxed{2}$ *vi* (machine) apagarse;
switch on $\boxed{1}$ *vt* (machine) encender, prender
AmL $\boxed{2}$ *vi* (machine) encenderse, prenderse
AmL; **switch over** *vt* (exchange positions, roles)
cambiar; **switch over to** *vt* cambiar a

switchboard *n* (for telephones) centralita *f*;
(Comp) tablero de distribución *m*; (electrical)
cuadro repartidor *m*; ∼ **operator** *n*
telefonista *mf*

switcher *n cliente que no se mantiene fiel a
un determinado minorista de Internet*

switching *n* (Comp) conmutación *f*; (Fin)
cambio de posición *m*; (Stock) venta de
títulos sin reinversión inmediata *f*; ∼ **cost**
n coste *m* Esp *or* costo *m* AmL de cambiar
proveedor

switching-in rate *n* tipo más cercano *m*

switching-out rate *n* tipo más alejado *m*

switchover *n* cambio *m*

swop ▸**swap**

swoption ▸**swaption**

sworn *adj* (statement) jurado; ∼ **broker** *n*
(Stock) corredor(a) jurado *m,f*

SWOT analysis *abbr* (▸**strengths,
weaknesses, opportunities and threats
analysis**) análisis de las fuerzas,
debilidades, oportunidades y amenazas *m*

symbiotic *adj* (marketing) simbiótico

symbol *n* símbolo *m*

symbolic *adj* simbólico *f*; **be ∼ of sth**
simbolizar algo

sympathetic *adj* (understanding)
comprensivo; (response, view) favorable;
(environment, atmosphere) cordial; **be ∼ to sth**
(to request, demand) mostrarse favorable a
algo; (to cause) simpatizar con algo

sympathizer *n* simpatizante *mf*

sympathy *n* simpatía *f*; **go out in ∼ with
sb** (strikers) ir a la huelga en solidaridad con
alguien; ∼ **action** *n* acción *f* por simpatía
or por solidaridad; ∼ **strike** *n* huelga de
solidaridad *f*

symposium *n* simposio *m*

sync *abbr* (▸**synchronization**)
sincronización *f*; **out of ∼** no sincronizado

synchronization *n* sincronización *f*

synchronous *adj* síncrono; ∼ **digital
hierarchy management subnetwork** *n*
subred de gestión de jerarquía digital
síncrona *f*

syndicalism *n* sindicalismo *m*

syndicate[1] *n* (group, cartel) agrupación *f* (of
banks) consorcio *m*, sindicato *m*; (of investors)
sindicato *m*; (Media) agencia de distribución
periodística *f*; ∼ **manager** *n* (for corporate
financing) gestor(a) del sindicato *m,f*

syndicate[2] *vt* (loan) sindicar; (column, article,
interview) distribuir (a diferentes medios de
comunicación)

syndicated *adj* (column, loan, swap)
sindicado

syndication *n* (Bank) formación de un
consorcio *f*; (Media) distribución *f* (a diferentes
medios de comunicación); (Comp) *la compra y
publicación de material de un proveedor de
contenido para sitios web*

synergism *n* sinergismo *m*

synergy *n* sinergía *f*

synetics *n pl método de resolver problemas
recurriendo a la creatividad*

synopsis *n* sinopsis *f*

syntax *n* sintaxis *f*; ∼ **error** *n* error de
sintaxis *m*

synthesis *n* síntesis *f*

synthetic *adj* (bond) sintético; (incentive)
artificial

system *n* sistema *m*; ∼ **administrator** *n*
(Comp) administrador(a) del sistema *m,f*; ∼**s
analysis** *n* análisis de sistemas *m*; ∼**s
analyst** *n* analista de sistemas *mf*; ∼**s
design** *n* diseño de sistemas *m*; ∼
development *n* desarrollo del sistema *m*;
∼ **disk** *n* disco de sistema *m*; ∼**s
engineering** *n* ingeniería de sistemas *f*; ∼
error *n* error de sistema *m*; ∼ **failure** *n*
fallo del sistema *m*; ∼**s management** *n*
dirección *f or* gestión *f* de sistemas; ∼**s
planning** *n* planificación de sistemas *f*; ∼**s
programmer** *n* programador(a) de sistemas
m,f; ∼**s programming** *n* programación de
sistemas *f*; ∼**-provider** *n* sistema-proveedor
m; ∼ **requirement** *n* requerimiento de
sistema *m*; ∼**s software** *n* software del
sistema *m*; ∼ **of taxation** *n* sistema
impositivo *m*; ∼**s theory** *n* teoría de
sistemas *f*

systematic *adj* (risk, sampling) sistemático
∼ **cost basis** *n* base *f* sistemática del coste
Esp *or* costo AmL

systematize *vt* sistematizar

Tt

t. *abbr* (▸**tare**) T. (tara)

TA *abbr* (▸**technical assistant**) asistente(-a) técnico(-a) *m,f*; (▸**telegraphic address**) dirección telegráfica *f*; (▸**training agency**) agencia *f* de capacitación *or* de formación; (▸**transactional analysis**) análisis *m* transaccional *or* de transacción

tab¹ *n* (Comp) tabulador *m*; (account, bill) (infrml) cuenta *f*; **keep ∼s on sth/sb** (infrml) vigilar algo/a alguien; **pick up the ∼** (infrml) pagar la cuenta; **set the ∼s** establecer los márgenes; **∼ key** *n* tecla de tabulación *f*; **∼ setting** *n* posición de tabulación *f*

tab² *vt* tabular

table¹ *n* (Comp) listado *m*; (in document) cuadro *m*, tabla *f*; **put proposals on the ∼** ofrecer propuestas para discusión; **∼ of contents** *n* índice de materias *m*; **∼ of par values** *n* (Stock) tabla de valores nominales *f*

table² *vt* (submit) BrE presentar; (postpone) AmE posponer, diferir; (data) presentar en forma de tabula, tabular; **∼ an amendment** (BrE) someter a aprobación una enmienda; (AmE) aplazar la discusión de una enmienda

tabloid *n* tabloide *m*; **∼ press** *n* prensa *f* amarilla *or* sensacionalista

tabular *adj* (report) tabular; **in ∼ form** en forma de tabla

tabulate *vt* (results, data) presentar en forma de tabla, tabular; (insert tabs in) tabular; **in ∼d form** en forma de tabla

tabulating machine *n* máquina tabuladora *f*

tabulation *n* tabulación *f*; **∼ character** *n* carácter de tabulación *m*

tabulator *n* tabulador *m*

T-account *n* (Acc) cuenta contable tipo T *f*; (Bank) cuenta T *f*

tacit *adj* (knowledge, renewal) tácito; (acceptance) implícito; **by ∼ agreement** por acuerdo tácito

tackle *vt* (problem) abordar, afrontar

tactic *n* táctica *f*

tactical *adj* (plan, planning, pricing) táctico

tactile *adj* táctil; **∼ keyboard** *n* teclado táctil *m*

tag¹ *n* etiqueta *f*; **∼ reader** *n* lector de etiquetas *m*

tag² *vt* (article, product) etiquetar, ponerle una etiqueta a; (criminal) controlar por medios electrónicos; (Comp) codificar

tagboard *n* AmE cuadro repartidor *m*

tagline *n* eslogan *m*

tail *n* cola *f*; **the ∼ end of the season** el final de la estación

tail away *vi* (income) ir disminuyendo *or* mermando; (interest) ir decayendo

tailgating *n* (Stock) oferta fraudulenta *f*

tailor¹ *n* sastre *mf*; **∼-made** *adj* hecho a medida; **∼-made contract** *n* contrato a medida *m*

tailor² *vt* (clothing) confeccionar; (adapt) adaptar

tailoring *n* adaptación especial *f*

tailspin *n* (infrml) caída en picado *f*; **go into a ∼** (economy, business) caer en picado

taint *vt* (meat, water) contaminar; (name, reputation) mancillar, deshonrar

take¹ **1** *vt* (earn) hacer, sacar; (buy, order) llevarse; (newspaper) comprar; (sample, steps, measures) tomar; (survey) hacer; (one's profit) aceptar; **we took over $10,000** hicimos *or* sacamos más de 10.000 dólares; **I'll ∼ this pair** (me) llevo este par

2 *vi* (succeed) tener éxito; **take away** *vt* restar; **take sth away from sth** restar algo de algo; **take back** *vt* (return to shop) devolver; (accept back) aceptar la devolución de; (employee) volver a emplear; (statement) retirar; **take down** *vt* (address, details) apuntar, anotar; **∼ down in shorthand** taquigrafiar; **take in** *vt* (information) asimilar; (corrections, amendments) incluir; (areas, topics) incluir, abarcar; (deceive) engañar; **∼ in extra work** aceptar trabajo extra; **take off** **1** *vt* (deduct) descontar; **they take $15 off if you pay cash** te descuentan 15 dólares si pagas en efectivo; **take the day/afternoon off** tomarse el día/la tarde libre; **take the phone off the hook** descolgar el teléfono **2** *vi* (business) despegar; (career) tomar vuelo; **take on** *vt* (staff) contratar; (client) aceptar, tomar; (competitor) enfrentarse a; (work) encargarse de, hacerse cargo de; (responsibility, role) asumir; (merchandise) cargar; **take out** *vt* (money) sacar, retirar; (insurance) sacar; (mortgage) conseguir; (patent) obtener; **∼ out an injunction** obtener un mandamiento judicial; **take over** **1** *vt* (assume control of) tomar control de; (company) absorber; (responsibility, role) asumir; (job) hacerse cargo de **2** *vi* (assume control) tomar control; **he hopes his son will ∼ over when he retires** espera que su hijo se haga cargo ⋯▸

cuando se jubile; **the night shift** ∼s **over at eleven** los del turno de la noche toman el relevo a las once; ∼ **over from sb** sustituir a alguien; (in shift work) relevar a alguien; **take up** vt (offer, suggestion, challenge) aceptar; (stand, stance) adoptar; (issue, point) volver a; (time) llevar; (space) ocupar; (shares) tomar; (option) suscribir; **he took up a job in a factory** se puso a trabajar en una fábrica; **we'll** ∼ **you up on your offer** aceptamos su oferta; **when she took up her new role as director** cuando asumió sus funciones de directora

take² n (earnings) ingresos m pl, recaudación f; (share) parte f; (commission) comisión f; **be on the** ∼ (infrml) dejarse sobornar

takeback bargaining n negociación revocable f

take-home pay n sueldo neto m

takeoff n despegue m

take-out loan n hipoteca de pago fijo f

takeover n absorción f, adquisición f; ∼ **bid** n oferta pública de adquisición f, oferta pública de compra f; ∼ **merger** n adquisición mayoritaria de las acciones de una sociedad por otra f

taker n tomador(a) m,f; ∼ **of a rate** n comprador(a) de una cuota m,f

takers-in n pl (Stock) compradores m pl, suscriptores m pl

takeup n (of shares) adquisición f; (of Treasury bills) suscripción f; ∼ **rate** n (of shares) tarifa aceptada f

talk¹ **1** vi hablar; ∼ **about sth/sb** hablar de algo/alguien; ∼ **to sb** hablar con alguien **2** vt hablar de; **we're** ∼**ing big money here** (infrml) estamos hablando de mucho dinero; ∼ **business** hablar de negocios; ∼ **sb into/out of doing sth** convencer a alguien de que haga/de que no haga algo; ∼ **nonsense** decir tonterías; ∼ **sense** hablar con sentido; ∼ **shop** (infrml) hablar del oficio or del trabajo; **talk around** vt (persuade) convencer; ∼ **around a problem** dar vueltas alrededor de un problema; **talk over** vt (problem, issue) discutir, hablar de; **talk up** vt (shares) inflar el valor de; **they** ∼**ed her up to $500** le hicieron subir la oferta a 500 dólares

talk² n (conversation) conversación f; (lecture) charla f; (rumour) rumor m; **be all** ∼ **(and no action)** hablar mucho y no hacer nada; **break off** ∼s suspender las conversaciones; **give a** ∼ **about** o **on sth** dar una charla sobre algo; **have a** ∼ **with sb** tener una conversación con alguien; **have** o **hold** ∼s mantener or sostener conversaciones; **it's just** ∼ es pura palabrería; **there is** ∼ **of his retiring** corre la voz de que se va a jubilar

talking heads n pl (jarg) bustos parlantes m pl

tally¹ n cuenta f; **keep a** ∼ **of sth** llevar la cuenta de algo; ∼ **register** n registro de cuentas m; ∼**-roll** n rollo de papel de máquina de calcular m; ∼ **sheet** n hoja de registro f

tally² vi (amounts, totals, versions) coincidir, concordar, cuadrar

tallyman n vendedor a crédito m

talon n (Stock) talón m

tamper-proof adj a prueba de destrozos

tamper with vt (equipment, controls) tocar, andar con (infrml); (document, figures) alterar; (jury, witness) sobornar

tandem account n cuenta doble f

tangible adj (assets, wealth) tangible; ∼ **fixed assets** n pl inmovilizado material m; ∼ **personal property** n bienes tangibles personales m pl

tangibles n pl activos tangibles m pl

tank n tanque m; (on truck) cisterna f

tanker n buque cisterna m

tap¹ n (Stock) tap f; ∼ **bill** n valor continuo m; ∼ **issue** n emisión a goteo f; ∼ **stocks** n pl BrE acciones estabilizadoras del mercado f pl

tap² vt (market) pulsar; (resources) desviar; (telephone) intervenir; ∼ **the market for sth** tantear el mercado en busca de algo

tape¹ n (magnetic) cinta f; (adhesive) cinta adhesiva f; **have sth on** ∼ tener algo grabado; ∼ **cartridge** n cargador de cinta magnética m; ∼ **drive** n unidad de cinta f; ∼ **feed** n alimentación de cinta f; ∼ **file** n fichero registrado en cinta m; ∼ **library** n biblioteca de cintas f; ∼ **measure** n cinta métrica f; ∼ **punch** n perforadora de cinta f; ∼ **recorder** n grabadora f; ∼ **recording** n grabación en cinta f

tape² vt (record) grabar; (stick) pegar con cinta adhesiva; (fasten) sujetar con cinta adhesiva

taper vt (tax relief) segmentar; **taper off** vi disminuir gradualmente

tape-record vt grabar

tare n tara f; ∼ **weight** n peso de tara f, taraje m

target¹ n objetivo m; **above/below** ∼ por encima/debajo del objetivo previsto; **achieve** o **meet one's** ∼ conseguir su objetivo; **be on** ∼ ir de acuerdo a lo previsto; **reach one's** ∼ alcanzar or lograr su objetivo; **set oneself a** ∼ figarse un objetivo; ∼ **audience** n público objetivo m; ∼ **buyer** n comprador(a) objetivo(-a) m,f; ∼ **company** n empresa objetivo f; ∼ **computer** n computadora destinataria f AmL, ordenador destinatario m Esp; ∼ **date** n fecha propuesta *f*; ~ **field** *n* (Comp) campo de referencia *m*; ~ **group** *n* grupo objetivo *m*; ~ **language** *n* lenguaje objeto *m*; ~ **market** *n* mercado objetivo *m*; ~ **marketing** *n* marketing de objetivos *m*; ~ **price** *n* precio indicativo *m*; ~ **pricing** *n* fijación de precios indicativos *f*; ~ **rate** *n* tipo objetivo *m*; ~ **segment** *n* segmento objetivo *m*; ~ **setting** *n* determinación *f or* fijación *f* de objetivos; ~ **zone** *n* (for exchange rates) zona meta *f*

target² *vt* (advertising, campaign) dirigir; (group) apuntar a

targeted campaign *n* campaña dirigida a un público concreto

targeting *n* fijación de objetivos *f*

tariff *n* (Tax) arancel *m*; (customs) tarifa aduanera *f*; (of prices) BrE tarifa *f*; ~ **agreement** *n* acuerdo aduanero *m*; ~ **barrier** *n* barrera arancelaria *f*; ~ **protection** *n* protección arancelaria *f*; ~ **quota** *n* cuota de tarifa *f*; ~ **rate** *n* tipo de arancel *f*; ~ **schedule** *n* programa de tarifas *m*; ~ **system** *n* sistema arancelario *m*; ~ **wall** *n* barrera arancelaria *f*; ~ **war** *n* guerra de tarifas *f*

taring *n* determinación de la tara *f*

task *n* tarea *f*; ~ **force** *n* equipo operativo *m*, grupo de trabajo *m*; ~ **initiation** *n* comienzo de una tarea *m*; ~ **management** *n* gestión *f or* dirección *f* de tarea; ~ **scheduling** *n* programación de tareas *f*; ~ **setting** *n* determinación de tareas *f*; ~ **work** *n* destajo *m*

tax¹ *n* (individual charge) impuesto *m*; (in general) impuestos *m pl*; **after** ~ después de deducir los impuestos; **before** ~ antes de deducir los impuestos; **free of** ~ libre de impuestos; ~ **on goods/services** impuesto sobre mercancías/servicios; **pay one's** ~**es** pagar los impuestos; **pay £3,000 in** ~ pagar 3.000 libras de *or* en impuestos; **put** *o* **place a** ~ **on sth** gravar algo con un impuesto

(**tax...a**) ~ **abatement** *n* reducción del tipo impositivo *f*; ~ **adjustment** *n* ajuste *m or* reajuste *m* impositivo; ~ **administration** *n* administración tributaria *f*; ~ **advantage** *n* ventaja fiscal *f*; ~ **adviser** *n* asesor(a) *m,f or* consejero(-a) *m,f* fiscal; ~ **allowance** *n* desgravación fiscal *f*; ~ **arrears** *n pl* impuestos *m pl* atrasados *or* vencidos; ~ **assessment** *n* determinación del impuesto *f*, estimación *f* de la base imponible; ~ **audit** *n* auditoría *f or* intervención *f* fiscal; ~ **avoidance** *n* elusión legal de impuestos *f*

(**b...**) ~ **band** *n* banda fiscal *f*; ~ **barrier** *n* barrera fiscal *f*; ~ **base** *n* base *f* imponible *or* impositiva; ~ **base broadening** *n* ampliación de la base impositiva *f*; ~

benefit *n* beneficio fiscal *m*; ~ **bill** *n* cuota tributaria *f*; ~ **bracket** *n* categoría impositiva *f*; ~ **break** *n* amnistía fiscal *f*; ~ **buoyancy** *n* elasticidad tributaria *f*; ~ **burden** *n* carga fiscal *f*

(**c...**) ~ **claim** *n* reclamación fiscal *f*; ~ **code** *n* código *m* impositivo *or* fiscal; ~ **collection** *n* recaudación de impuestos *f*; ~ **collector** *n* recaudador(a) de impuestos *m,f*; ~ **concession** *n* concesión fiscal *f*; ~ **consultant** *n* asesor(a) fiscal *m,f*; ~ **cost** *n* coste *m* Esp *or* costo *m* AmL fiscal; ~ **credit** *n* bonificación fiscal *f*, crédito tributario *m*; ~ **cut** *n* reducción de impuestos *f*

(**d...**) ~ **debtor** *n* deudor(a) fiscal *m,f*; ~ **deducted at source** *n* impuesto retenido en origen *f*; ~**deductible** *adj* deducible a efectos impositivos; ~ **deductibility** *n* posibilidad de deducción fiscal *f*; ~ **deduction** *n* deducción impositiva *f*; ~ **deferral** *n* aplazamiento del pago de impuestos *m*; ~ **disc** *n* BrE (on car) pegatina del impuesto de circulación *f*; ~ **district** *n* BrE distrito fiscal *m*; ~ **dodger** *n* (infrml) defraudador(a) de impuestos *m,f*; ~ **dodging** *n* evasión fiscal *f*

(**e...**) ~**-efficient** *adj* eficiente desde el punto de vista fiscal; ~**-efficient investment** *n* inversión que genera beneficios fiscales *f*; ~ **equalization** *n* equiparación fiscal *f*; ~ **equalization account** *n* cuenta de liquidación de impuestos *f*; ~ **equalization scheme** *n* BrE plan de liquidación fiscal *m*; ~ **evader** *n* evasor(a) de impuestos *m,f*; ~ **evasion** *n* evasión *f* fiscal *or* de impuestos; ~**-exempt** *adj* (goods) exento de impuestos; (corporation) exento de tributación; **T**~**-Exempt Special Savings Account** *n* BrE *cuenta de ahorros especial exenta de impuestos*; ~ **exemption** *n* exención fiscal *f*; ~ **exile** *n* (situation) exilio fiscal *m*; (person) *exiliado por motivos fiscales*; ~ **expert** *n* experto(-a) fiscal *m,f*

(**f...**) ~ **form** *n* formulario de Hacienda *m*; ~ **fraud** *n* fraude fiscal *m*; ~**-free** *adj* (allowance, benefit) libre de impuestos

(**g...**) ~ **guidelines** *n pl* directrices fiscales *f pl*

(**h...**) ~ **harmonization** *n* armonización fiscal *f*; ~ **haven** *n* paraíso fiscal *m*; ~ **holiday** *n* franquicia fiscal *f*, tregua tributaria *f*

(**i...**) ~ **incentive** *n* incentivo fiscal *m*; ~ **increase** *n* aumento de los impuestos *m*; **T**~ **Information Registry** *n* Registro de Información Fiscal *m*; ~ **inspector** *n* inspector(a) de Hacienda *m,f*; ~ **installment** AmE, **tax instalment** BrE *n* pago fraccionario del impuesto *m*

⟮**l...**⟯ ～ **law** n derecho fiscal m; ～ **lawyer** n ≈ abogado(-a) tributarista m,f; ～ **liability** n cuota líquida f, deuda f fiscal or impositiva; ～ **loophole** n discriminación f or exención f fiscal

⟮**o...**⟯ ～ **offset** n crédito por impuestos pagados m

⟮**p...**⟯ ～ **package** n conjunto de medidas fiscales m; ～**-paid income** n ingresos después de impuestos m pl; ～ **payable** n deuda tributaria f; ～ **proposals** n pl propuestas fiscales f pl; ～ **provision** n provisión f fiscal or para impuestos, reserva para impuestos f

⟮**r...**⟯ ～ **rate** n tipo m impositivo or del impuesto; ～ **rate schedule** n tarifa del impuesto f; ～ **rebate** n devolución de impuestos f; ～ **receipts** n pl ingresos m pl fiscales or tributarios, recaudación tributaria f; ～ **record** n registro fiscal m; ～ **reduction** n reducción impositiva f; ～ **reform** n reforma fiscal f; ～ **refund** n devolución del impuesto f; ～ **relief** n desgravación (fiscal) f; ～ **relief at source** n BrE desgravación fiscal en origen f; ～ **return** n declaración sobre la renta f; ～ **return form** n formulario m or impreso m de declaración sobre la renta; ～ **revenue** n ingresos m pl fiscales or tributarios, recaudación tributaria f

⟮**s...**⟯ ～ **shelter** n refugio fiscal m; ～ **software** n software para el tratamiento de datos fiscales m; ～ **system** n sistema m fiscal or impositivo or tributario

⟮**t...**⟯ ～ **threshold** n nivel de tributación m, umbral impositivo m

⟮**u...**⟯ ～ **umbrella** n cobertura fiscal m; ～ **unit** n unidad impositiva f

⟮**w...**⟯ ～ **withholding** n retención fiscal f; ～ **write-off** n amortización fiscal f

⟮**y...**⟯ ～ **year** n año m or ejercicio m fiscal; ～ **yield** n recaudación tributaria f, rendimiento fiscal m

tax² vt (company, goods, earnings) gravar; (costs, bill) tasar; **we're being ～ed too highly** nos están cobrando demasiado en impuestos; **my income is ～ed at source** mis ingresos ya vienen con los impuestos descontados

taxable adj (income, allowance) gravable, imponible; (profit) gravable; (dividend, benefit, quota) imponible; (sale) sujeto a impuesto; ～ **capital** n capital imponible m; ～ **capital gains** n pl ganancias imponibles del capital f pl; ～ **social security benefits** n pl prestaciones imponibles de la seguridad social f pl; ～ **value** n BrE (cf ▸**assessed valuation** AmE) valor imponible m; ～ **year** n ejercicio fiscal m

taxation n (taxes) impuestos m pl; (system) sistema m fiscal or tributario; (act) fijación de impuestos f; **reduce/increase ～** reducir/aumentar los impuestos; ～ **authorities** n pl autoridades fiscales f pl; ～ **period** n periodo fiscal m; ～ **system** n sistema m fiscal or tributario; ～ **year** n ejercicio fiscal m

taxflation n inflación fiscal f

taxman n (person) recaudador m; (tax authorities) (infml) Hacienda f, fisco m

taxpayer n contribuyente mf; ～ **number** n número m de identificación fiscal or de identificación tributaria

T-bill n AmE (▸**treasury bill**) letra del Tesoro f; ～ **futures** n pl AmE futuros sobre letras del Tesoro m pl

TDED abbr (▸**Trade Data Elements Directory**) anuario de datos comerciales m

TDI abbr (▸**trade data interchange**) intercambio de datos comerciales m

team n equipo m; **it was a ～ effort** fue un trabajo de equipo; **they make a good ～** forman un buen equipo; ～ **briefing** n sesión informativa para el equipo f; ～ **building** n formación de equipo f; ～ **leader** n jefe(-a) m,f or líder mf del equipo; ～ **member** n miembro de equipo m,f; ～ **spirit** n espíritu de equipo m; ～ **theory** n teoría de equipo f

teamster n AmE (cf ▸**lorry driver** BrE) camionero(-a) m,f conductor(a) de camión m,f; **T～s Union** n sindicato americano de camioneros y trabajadores del sector automovilístico

team up vi asociarse, unirse; ～ **with sb** asociarse con alguien

teamwork n trabajo en equipo m

tear n desgarrón m, rasgón m; ～**-proof** adj a prueba de desgarro; ～ **strip** n tira de rasgado f

tear-off adj recortable; ～**-calendar** n calendario de taco m; ～**-coupon** n cupón para arrancar m; ～**-portion** n (of chequebook) parte recortable f

teaser n publicidad de intriga f; ～ **ad** n publicidad de intriga f; ～ **campaign** n campaña publicitaria de intriga f; ～ **rate** n (Fin) tasa provocadora f

teasing n uso de campañas de intriga m

techMARK n mercado especializado de acciones de nuevas tecnologías

technical adj (analysis, progress, data) técnico; **for ～ reasons** por motivos técnicos; ～ **adviser** n consejero(-a) técnico(-a) m,f; ～ **assistance** n asistencia técnica f; ～ **assistant** n asistente(-a) técnico(-a) m,f; ～ **college** n escuela politécnica f; ～ **consultant** n asesor(a)

técnico(-a) *m,f*; ~ **director** *n* director(a)

técnico(-a) *m,f*; ~ **help** *n* ayuda técnica *f*; ~ **hitch** *n* fallo técnico *m*; ~ **manager** *n* director(a) *m,f or* gerente *m,f* técnico(-a); ~ **market** *n* (Stock) mercado técnico *m*; ~ **mastery** *n* dominio técnico *m*; ~ **point** *n* cuestión de forma *f*; ~ **rally** *n* (Stock) recuperación técnica *f*; ~ **salesperson** *n* vendedor(a) técnico(-a) *m,f*; ~ **sign** *n* (Stock) signo técnico *m*; ~ **standard** *n* (of product safety) norma técnica *f*; ~ **support** *n* (Comp) apoyo técnico *m*; (Ind) asistencia técnica *f*; ~ **term** *n* tecnicismo *m*, término técnico *m*

technicality *n* tecnicidad *f*

technique *n* técnica *f*

technocracy *n* tecnocracia *f*

technocrat *n* tecnócrata *mf*

technocratic *adj* tecnocrático

technological *adj* (change, progress, innovation, obsolescence) tecnológico; ~ **forecast** *n* pronóstico tecnológico *m*; ~ **forecasting** *n* predicción tecnológica *f*; ~ **gap** *n* (Econ) brecha tecnológica *f*; (Ind) vacío tecnológico *m*; ~ **park** *n* parque tecnológico *m*

technologically *adv* (advanced) tecnológicamente

technology *n* tecnología *f*; ~**-based industry** *n* industria tecnológica *f*; ~ **cooperation** *n* cooperación tecnológica *f*; ~ **and market interface** *n* interacción tecnología-mercado *f*; ~ **park** *n* parque tecnológico *m*; ~ **stocks** *n pl* acciones de nuevas tecnologías *f pl*; ~ **transfer** *n* transferencia de tecnología *f*; ~ **watch** *n* vigilancia tecnológica *f*

technostructure *n* tecnoestructura *f*

teenage *adj* de adolescentes *m*; ~ **market** *n* mercado de los adolescentes *m*

teething troubles *n pl*, **teething problems** *n pl* problemas iniciales *m pl*

tel. *abbr* (▸**telephone**) teléf (teléfono)

telebanking *n* telebanca *f*

telecommunicate *vt* transmitir por telecomunicaciones

telecommunication network *n* red de telecomunicaciones *f*

telecommunications *n pl* telecomunicaciones *f pl*; ~ **company** *n* compañía de telecomunicaciones *f*; ~ **industry** *n* industria de las telecomunicaciones *f*

telecommute *vi* trabajar a domicilio *or* a distancia

telecommuter *n* trabajador(a) *m,f* domiciliario(-a) *or* a distancia

telecommuting *n* trabajo *m* a domicilio *or* a distancia

teleconference *n* teleconferencia *f*

teleconferencing *n* teleconferencia *f*

telecottage *n* centro rural de telecomunicación *m* (*usado por teletrabajadores*)

telegraphic *adj* telegráfico; ~ **address** *n* dirección telegráfica *f*; ~ **money order** *n* giro telegráfico *m*; ~ **transfer** *n* transferencia *f* telegráfica *or* cablegráfica

telelearning *n* educación en línea *f*

telemarket *n* telemarket *m*

telemarketing *n* telemarketing *m*

telematics *n* telemática *f*

teleordering *n* telepedido *m*

telepayment *n* telepago *m*

telephone[1] *n* teléfono *m*; **answer the** ~ contestar el teléfono; **by** ~ por teléfono; **be on the** ~ (speaking) estar hablando por teléfono; (subscribe) BrE tener teléfono; **you're wanted on the** ~ te llaman por teléfono; **over the** ~ por teléfono; ~ **answering service** *n* servicio de respuesta telefónica *m*; ~ **banking** *n* banca telefónica *f*; ~ **bill** *n* factura telefónica *f*; ~ **book** *n* guía *f* telefónica *or* de teléfonos; ~ **booking** *n* BrE (*cf* ▸**telephone reservation** AmE) reserva por teléfono *f*; ~ **booth** *n* AmE, ~ **box** BrE *n* (*cf* ▸**call box** AmE) cabina telefónica *f*; ~ **call** *n* llamada telefónica *f*; ~ **company** *n* compañía telefónica *f*; ~ **directory** *n* guía *f* telefónica *or* de teléfonos; ~ **exchange** *n* central telefónica *f*; ~ **extension** *n* extensión telefónica *f*; ~ **interviewing** *n* entrevistas telefónicas *f pl*; ~ **line** *n* línea telefónica *f*; ~ **message** *n* mensaje telefónico *m*; ~ **number** *n* número de teléfono *m*; ~ **operator** *n* telefonista *mf*; ~ **receiver** *n* auricular (telefónico) *m*; ~ **reservation** *n* AmE (*cf* ▸**telephone booking** BrE) reserva por teléfono *f*; ~ **sale** *n* venta por teléfono *f*; ~ **selling** *n* venta telefónica *f*; ~ **subscriber** *n* abonado(-a) telefónico(-a) *m,f*; ~ **support** *n* apoyo por teléfono *m*; ~ **tap** *n* intervención telefónica *f*; ~ **tapping** *n* intervención de un teléfono *f*

telephone[2] [1] *vt* (person, place, number) llamar (por teléfono); (order) hacer por teléfono
[2] *vi* llamar (por teléfono), telefonear; ~ **for sth/sb** llamar algo/a alguien

telephonic *adj* telefónico

telephony *n* telefonía *f*

teleprinter *n* teleimpresora *f*

teleprocessing *n* teleproceso *m*

telerecording *n* teleregistro *m*

telesales *n* BrE televentas *f pl*; ~ **person** *n* BrE vendedor(a) de televentas *m,f*

teleshopping *n* compra telefónica *f*, telecompra *f*

Teletex Output of Price Information by Computer n *información bursátil por videotexto de la Bolsa de Valores de Londres*

teletext® n teletexto m

teletraining n formación f or capacitación f en línea

teletypewriter n terminal teleescritor m

televise vt televisar

television n (medium, industry) televisión f; (set) televisor m, televisión f; ~ **advertising** n publicidad televisiva f; ~ **announcer** n locutor(a) de televisión m,f; ~ **audience** n telespectadores m pl; ~ **channel** n canal m or cadena f de televisión; ~ **commercial** n anuncio comercial televisivo m; ~ **coverage** n cobertura televisiva f; ~ **network** n cadena de televisión f; ~ **program** AmE, ~ **programme** BrE n programa de televisión m; ~ **screen** n pantalla de televisión f; ~ **set** n televisor m, televisión f; ~ **viewer** n telespectador(a) m,f

televisual adj BrE televisivo; ~ **audience data** n BrE datos sobre la audiencia televisiva m pl

telework n teletrabajo m

teleworker n teletrabajador(a) m,f

teleworking n teletrabajo m

telewriter n telecopiadora f

telewriting n teletranscripción f

telex¹ n télex m; **send a** ~ enviar or mandar un télex; ~ **machine** n teletranscriptor m

telex² [1] vt enviar por télex [2] vi enviar un télex

teller n (Bank) cajero(-a) m,f

tel. no. abbr (▸**telephone number**) teléf. (número de teléfono)

temp¹ n empleado(-a) eventual m,f, temporero(-a) m,f; ~ **agency** n agencia de trabajo temporal f

temp² vi hacer trabajo eventual or temporal

temping n trabajo f eventual or temporal; ~ **agency** n agencia de trabajo temporal f

template n plantilla f

temporal adj temporal; ~ **method** n (of currency translation) método temporal m

temporary¹ adj (accommodation, arrangement) temporal, temporario AmL, provisional; (job, employment, staff) eventual, temporal, temporario AmL; (status) temporal, temporario AmL; (measure) provisional; ~ **residence** n residencia temporal f; ~ **residence permit** n permiso de residencia temporal m; ~ **residence visa** n visado de residencia temporal m; ~ **resident** n residente temporal mf

temporary² n empleado(-a) eventual m,f, temporero(-a) m,f

tenancy n arriendo m, arrendamiento m, inquilinato m; ~ **agreement** n contrato m de alquiler o de arriendo

tenant n arrendatario(-a) m,f, inquilino(-a) m,f

tend vi (have tendency, be inclined) tender; **prices are** ~**ing downwards** BrE o **downward** AmE los precios tienden a la baja; ~ **to sth/sb** ocuparse de algo/alguien; ~ **to do sth** tender a hacer algo; ~ **towards** BrE o **toward sth** AmE inclinarse por algo

tendency n tendencia f; ~ **to do sth** tendencia a hacer algo; ~ **towards** BrE o **toward** AmE **sth** tendencia hacia algo

tender¹ n (offer) oferta f; (currency) moneda de curso legal f; **put in** o **submit a** ~ **for sth** presentarse a concurso or a una licitación para algo; **put sth out to** o **up for** ~ sacar algo a concurso or a licitación; ~ **documents** n pl pliegos de propuesta m pl; ~ **offer** n (Stock) oferta pública de adquisición f; ~ **to contract** n licitación f, propuesta de contrato f; (Law) concurso m

tender² [1] vt (resignation, apologies) presentar, ofrecer; ~ **money in discharge of debt** ofrecer dinero para saldar una deuda; ~ **notice** proponer una convocatoria [2] vi presentarse a concurso or a una licitación; ~ **for a contract** presentarse a concurso or a una licitación para un contrato

tendering n licitación f

tenement n vivienda f

Ten-Forty n AmE *título del estado rescatable a 10 años y pagadero a 40 años*

tenor n contenido m; ~ **bill** n letra de cambio f

tentative adj (plan, arrangement) provisional; (offer) tentativo

tenure n (of office, post) ejercicio m, ocupación f; (of property, land) tenencia f, ocupación f; **have security of** ~ tener estabilidad en el cargo

tenured adj (post, staff) permanente

term n (word) término m; (period) periodo m; (of loan) vencimiento m; (time to due date) plazo m; (of government, treaty, patent) duración f; (at school, university) trimestre m; **in the short/ medium/long** ~ a corto/medio/largo plazo; ~ **bond** n bono a plazo fijo m; ~ **certificate** n certificado a plazo m; ~ **deposit** n depósito a plazo m; ~ **draft** n letra de cambio al vencimiento f; ~ **insurance** n seguro temporal m; ~ **loan** n préstamo a plazo m; ~ **of office** n incumbencia f; ~ **of payment** n plazo de devolución m

terminable adj rescindible

terminal[1] *n* (Comp) terminal *m*; (at airport) terminal *f*; (railway station) estación terminal *f*; ~ **computer** *n* computadora *f* AmL *or* ordenador *m* Esp terminal; ~ **emulator** *n* emulador de terminal *m*; ~ **operator** *n* operador(a) de terminal *m,f*; ~ **screen** *n* pantalla terminal *f*; ~ **user** *n* usuario(-a) de terminal *m,f*

terminal[2] *adj* (price, bonus) final; (decline) irreversible; (loss) al cierre

terminate [1] *vt* (contract) poner término a; (discussion) poner fin a; (employee) AmE despedir; ~ **a fund** (Fin) agotar una provisión; ~ **sb's employment** rescindir el contrato a alguien
[2] *vi* (lease) terminarse

termination *n* (of contract) rescisión *f*; (of policy) vencimiento *m*; ~ **benefits** *n pl* indemnización por despido *f*; ~ **clause** *n* cláusula *f* resolutoria *or* de rescisión; ~ **of employment** *n* baja *f*, cese *m*; ~ **with notice** *n* BrE cese con preaviso *m*, despido con notificación *m*; ~ **papers** *n pl* documentos de rescisión *m pl*; ~ **payment** *n* finiquito *m*; ~ **of tenancy** *n* fin del contrato de arrendamiento *m*

terminology *n* terminología *f*

terms *n pl* (of shipment, tender, trade) condiciones *f pl*; **in** ~ **of sth** en cuanto a algo; **in real** ~ en cifras reales; **in relative** ~ en términos relativos; **offer easy** ~ ofrecer facilidades de pago; **not on any** ~ bajo ningún concepto; **be on good/bad** ~ **with sb** estar en buenas/malas relaciones con alguien, llevarse bien/mal con alguien; **under the** ~ **of the contract** según los términos del contrato; ~ **of acceptance** *n pl* condiciones de aceptación *f pl*; ~ **and conditions** *n pl* (of policy, arrangement) plazos *m pl* y condiciones *f pl*; (of issue) modalidades *f pl*; ~ **of employment** *n pl* condiciones de empleo *f pl*; ~ **of payment** *n pl* condiciones de pago *f pl*; ~ **of reference** *n pl* (of study) ámbito *m*; (of committee - aim) cometido *m*; (- area of responsibility) competencia *f*; (- instructions) mandato *m*; ~ **of sale** *n pl* condiciones de venta *f pl*

terotechnology *n* terotecnología *f*

terrestrial *adj* (broadcasting) terrestre

territory *n* (land) territorio *m*; (of salesperson, agent) área *f*; **go with the** ~ ser un gaje del oficio

terrorism *n* terrorismo *m*

tertiary *adj* (sector, product, activities) terciario; (education) superior, de nivel terciario

TESSA *abbr* BrE (▶**Tax-Exempt Special Savings Account**) *cuenta de ahorros especial exenta de impuestos*

test[1] *n* prueba *f*; **put sth to the** ~ poner algo a prueba; **stand the** ~ **of time** resistir el paso del tiempo; ~ **area** *n* zona de pruebas *f*; ~ **audit** *n* auditoría de prueba *f*; ~ **bed** *n* banco de pruebas *m*; ~ **bench** *n* banco de ensayos *m*; ~ **case** *n caso que sienta jurisprudencia*; ~ **drive** *n* prueba de carretera *f*; ~ **equipment** *n* equipo de prueba *m*; ~ **mailing** *n envío de folletos por correo a un grupo reducido de gente para hacer una prueba*; ~ **market** *n* mercado de prueba *m*; ~ **problem** *n* problema de ensayo *m*; ~ **run** *n* ejecución de prueba *f*; ~ **town** *n* ciudad de prueba *f*

test[2] *vt* (product) probar, poner a prueba; (knowledge, skill) evaluar; (hypothesis) comprobar; (commitment) poner a prueba; (student) examinar, hacerle una prueba a; ~ **sth on animals** probar algo en animales; **test out** *vt* (product) probar, poner a prueba; (theory) poner en práctica

testamentary *adj* (debt, trust) testamentario

testdeck *n* (Comp) paquete de prueba *m*

test-drive *vt* probar (en carretera)

tester *n* (of product) probador(a) *m,f*; (of quality) controlador(a) *m,f*; (sample) frasco de muestra *m*

testify *vi* testificar, declarar

testimonial *n* recomendación *f*; ~ **advertisement** *n* anuncio testimonial *m*

testimony *n* declaración *f*, testimonio *m*; **give** ~ prestar declaración

testing *n* (of products) pruebas *f pl*; ~ **ground** *n* terreno de pruebas *n*; **a** ~ **ground for new ideas** un terreno de pruebas para ideas nuevas; ~ **procedure** *n* procedimiento de prueba *m*

test-market [1] *vt* (product) hacer una prueba de mercado de
[2] *vi* realizar pruebas en el mercado

text[1] *n* texto *m*; ~ **in full** texto completo; ~ **editing** *n* edición de texto *f*; ~ **editor** *n* editor de textos *m*; ~ **message** *n* mensaje texto *m*, texto *m*; ~ **mode** *n* modalidad textual *f*, modo texto *m*

text[2] *vt* enviarle un texto a

textbook *n* libro de texto *m*; ~ **case** *n* caso modelo *m*; ~ **operation** *n* operación modelo *f*

textile *n* textil *m*; ~ **industry** *n* industria textil *f*; ~ **trade** *n* comercio textil *m*

thank *vt* agradecer; ~ **sb for sth** darle las gracias a alguien por algo, agradecerle algo a alguien; ~**ing you in advance** *o* **in anticipation** gracias anticipadas *or* por anticipado

thank-you n gracias f pl; ~ **letter** n carta de agradecimiento f; ~ **note** n breve misiva de agradecimiento f

theft n robo m; ~ **risk** n riesgo de robo m

theft-proof adj a prueba de robo

theme n tema m; ~ **advertising** n publicidad temática f; ~ **park** n parque de atracciones m; ~ **tune** n tema musical m

theoretical adj teórico; ~ **capacity** n capacidad teórica f

theory n teoría f; **in** ~ en teoría; ~ **of comparative costs** n teoría f de costes Esp or costos AmL comparativos

thermal adj térmico; ~ **energy** n energía térmica f

thin adj (profits) magro, escaso; (market) flojo; (excuse, argument) pobre, poco convincente; (response, attendance) escaso; (crowd, audience) poco numeroso; ~ **capitalization** n (Acc) capitalización escasa f

think vti pensar; ~ **the unthinkable** pensar lo impensable

thinking n pensamiento m

think-tank n (infrml) grupo de expertos m

third adj tercero; ~ **country** n tercer país m; ~ **currency** n tercera moneda f; ~ **force** n (Pol) tercera potencia f; ~ **market** n tercer mercado m; ~ **person** n tercera persona f; ~ **quarter** n tercer trimestre m; ~ **way** n (Pol) tercera vía f

third-class adj (ticket) de tercera clase; ~ **mail** n AmE correo con tarifa económica m

third-generation adj (computer) de tercera generación

third party n tercero m, tercera persona f; ~ **credibility** n credibilidad de un tercero f; ~ **insurance** n seguro m contra terceros or de responsabilidad civil Esp; ~ **intervention** n intervención de un tercero f; ~ **liability** n responsabilidad civil de terceros f; ~ **risk** n riesgo de terceros m; ~ **sale** n venta de terceros f

third-rate adj de poca calidad

Third World n Tercer Mundo m; ~ **country** n país del Tercer Mundo m

thrash out vt (problem) discutir a fondo; (policy) llegar a un acuerdo sobre

threat n amenaza f; ~ **effect** n efecto amenazador m

three n tres m; ~-**month bond** n bono a tres meses m; ~-**months' rate** n tasa trimestral f, trimensualidad f; ~-**way call** n llamada tridireccional f; ~-**way split** n división en tercios f

threshold n umbral m; (Tax) nivel m; ~ **agreement** n acuerdo umbral m; ~ **amount** n cantidad mínima perceptible f; ~ **level** n nivel de umbral m; ~ **point** n (Stock) punto de umbral m; ~ **price** n

precio umbral m; ~ **rate** n tarifa mínima f; ~ **value** n (Comp) valor de umbral m; ~ **worker** n AmE trabajador(a) no cualificado(-a) m,f

thrift n economía f; ~ **institution** n AmE (cf ▸**savings institution** BrE) entidad f or institución f de ahorro y préstamo

thrive vi (business, town) prosperar

thriving adj próspero

through[1] prep por; ~ **the agency of sb** a través de or por medio de alguien

through[2] adj (train, route) directo; **you're** ~ BrE (connected on telephone) hable; ~ **charge** n, ~ **rate** n tarifa hasta destino f

throughput n (production) producción f; (efficiency, performance) rendimiento total m; (Acc) contribución marginal bruta f, productividad f; (Comp) (capacity) caudal de proceso y transferencia m

throughway n AmE (cf ▸**motorway** BrE) autopista f

throw vt (switch, lever) darle a; ~ **one's money around** despilfarrar or derrochar el dinero; **you can't solve the problem by** ~**ing money at it** el problema no lo vas a resolver gastando dinero sin ton ni son; ~ **oneself into a task** meterse de lleno en una tarea; ~ **sb out of work** echar a alguien del trabajo; **throw away** vt (money) malgastar, despilfarrar, tirar; (opportunity) desaprovechar, desperdiciar; (advantage) desperdiciar; **throw out** vt (bill, proposal) rechazar; (calculations, arrangements) desbaratar; (suggestion) hacer; (idea) proponer; **throw up** vt (results) arrojar, dar; (facts, discrepancies) relevar (la existencia de), poner en evidencia; (demand) producir; (job) dejar

tick[1] n (Stock) punto básico m, valor mínimo de variación m; (mark) visto m, tic m; (credit) BrE (infrml) crédito m; **buy sth on** ~ BrE (infrml) comprar algo (de) fiado (infrml); ~ **mark** n punteo m

tick[2] vt (name, answer) marcar (con un visto); ~ **the appropriate box** ponga un visto en or marque la casilla correspondiente; **tick off** vt BrE (cf ▸**check off** AmE) marcar, ponerle visto a; **tick over** vi (business) ir tirando; **tick up** vt (Bank) tildar

ticker n (Stock) tablero automático de cotizaciones m; ~ **tape** n cinta de teletipo f

ticket n (for bus, train) boleto m AmL, billete m Esp; (for plane) pasaje m AmL, billete m Esp; (for cinema, theatre) entrada f; (for baggage, coat) ticket m; (label) etiqueta f; (parking fine) multa f; (Stock) resguardo m; (Pol) lista f; ~ **agency** n (for theatre) agencia de localidades f; ~ **collector** n revisor(a) m,f; ~ **day** n (on London Stock Exchange) día anterior al de liquidación m; ~ **office** n taquilla f; ~ **tout** n BrE (cf ▸**scalper** AmE) revendedor(a) m,f (a precio inflado); ~ **touting** n BrE (cf ►**scalping** AmE) reventa f (a precio inflado)

tickler file n (Bank) archivo de vencimientos m

tidal power n energía maremotriz f

tide over vt sacar de apuros; **I've lent her £100 to tide her over till she gets paid** le he prestado 100 libras para que se arregle hasta que le paguen

tie[1] vt (fasten, restrict) atar; **she's ~d by her job** el trabajo la tiene atada; **you have to ~ them down to a definite date** tienes que hacer que se comprometa a una fecha concreta; **the contract ~s us to a strict timetable** el contrato nos obliga a cumplir un horario estricto; ~ **sth to sth** (make conditional) condicionar algo a algo; ~ **sth to** o **with sth** (link) relacionar or ligar algo con algo; **tie in with** vt concordar con, cuadrar con; **tie up** vt (capital, assets) inmovilizar; (production, project) paralizar, parar; (deal) cerrar; (arrangements) finalizar; **I'll be even more ~d up tomorrow** mañana voy a estar aún más ocupado or atareado; **all our money is ~d up in property** todo nuestro dinero está invertido or metido en bienes raíces; ~ **up loose ends** atar cabos sueltos; **she's ~d up with a customer at the moment** en este momento está ocupada atendiendo a un cliente

tie[2] n (bond) atadura f

tied adj (loan) atado; (aid) vinculado, condicionado

tied-up adj (capital) inmovilizado

tie-in n conexión f; ~ **advertising** n anuncio colectivo m; ~ **display** n promoción conjunta f; ~ **promotion** n promoción combinada f; ~ **sale** n venta acoplada f

tiger economy n economía emergente f

tight adj (margin) estrecho; (schedule) apretado; (security) estricto; (control) estricto, riguroso; (budget) ajustado; (market) escaso; (money) caro; (fiscal policy, monetary policy) restrictivo; **keep a ~ rein on sb** atar corto a alguien; **keep a ~ rein on sth** controlar algo rigurosamente; **run a ~ ship** ser muy eficiente

tighten vt (credit controls, rules) endurecer; ~ **the monetary reins** intensificar las restricciones monetarias; ~ **one's belt** apretarse el cinturón; **tighten up** vi poner condiciones más estrictas; **tighten up on** vt volverse más estricto con

tightening-up n (of rules) endurecimiento m

till n caja f; ~ **money** n dinero en caja m; ~ **receipt** n recibo de caja f

tilt vt: ~ **the balance** inclinar la balanza

time[1] n tiempo m; (period of hours) rato m; (by clock) hora m; (instance, occasion) vez f; **be**

ahead of one's ~ anticiparse a época; **at the appointed ~** a la hora fijada; **at a given ~** en un tiempo determinado; **at a given ~ in the future** en un tiempo futuro; **at the present ~** en la actualidad; **at some ~ in the future** en algún momento futuro; **be behind the ~s** (idea) ser anticuado, estar desfasado; (person) ser un anticuado; **by the specified ~** dentro del plazo especificado; ~**s are hard** estos son malos tiempos or tiempos difíciles; **keep up** o **move with the ~s** ir con los tiempos, mantenerse al día; ~ **is money** el tiempo es oro; **on ~** a tiempo; **be on ~ and a half** cobrar la jornada y media; **this ~ next week** dentro de una semana; **with ~ to spare** con tiempo de sobra; ~ **after sight** n plazo después de la vista m; ~**-barred** adj prescrito; ~ **bill** n letra a plazo f; ~ **card** n ficha de control f, tarjeta f reloj or de fichar; ~ **clock** n reloj de control de asistencia m; ~ **constraint** n restricción de tiempo f; ~**-consuming** adj que requiere mucho tiempo; ~ **deposit** n AmE (cf ►**fixed-term deposit** BrE) depósito a plazo fijo m; ~ **frame** n marco temporal m, periodo de tiempo m; ~ **horizon** n fecha límite f; ~**-keeping** n control m or cronometración f de tiempo; ~ **lag** n desfase cronológico m; ~ **limit** n plazo m; ~ **management** n dirección f or gerencia f de los horarios de trabajo; ~ **and methods study** n estudio de tiempo y métodos m; ~ **and motion study** n estudio m de desplazamientos y tiempos or de tiempo y movimientos; ~ **off** n tiempo libre m; ~ **off work** n tiempo libre fuera del trabajo m; ~ **policy** n (Ins) póliza con vencimiento fijo f; ~ **premium** n (Stock) prima debida por el periodo corrido del seguro f; ~ **pressure** n apremio m; ~ **rate** n pago por horas m, remuneración por unidad de tiempo f; ~**-saving** adj que ahorra tiempo; ~ **segment** n franja horaria f; ~ **sheet** n hoja de asistencia f; ~ **slot** n cuota de tiempo f; ~ **span** n periodo m; ~ **spread** n (Stock) margen de tiempo m, diferencial horizontal m; ~ **to market** n plazo de comercialización m; ~ **value** n (of options) valor tiempo m; ~ **zone** n huso horario m

time[2] vt (worker) tomarle el tiempo a; (choose time of) prever

timed backup n (Comp) copia de seguridad temporizada f

timekeeper n medidor(a) de intervalos de tiempo m,f; **be a good/bad ~** BrE (worker) ser puntual/impuntual

timely adj oportuno

timeout n compás de espera m (jarg)

timer n reloj (automático) m

timescale n escala de tiempo f

timeshare n multipropiedad f; ~ **developer** n promotor(a) de multipropiedades m,f; ~ **property** n multipropiedad f

timesharing n (Comp) tiempo compartido m; (Prop) multipropiedad f; **on a ~ basis** en multipropiedad

timetable[1] n (Transp) horario m; (schedule, programme) agenda f

timetable[2] vt programar

timing n (measuring) cálculo de tiempo m, cronometraje m

TINA abbr (▶**there is no alternative**) no hay alternativa

tin shares n pl acciones de mala calidad f pl

tip[1] n (gratuity) propina f; (helpful hint) consejo (práctico) m; (Bank) extratipo m; (for waste) BrE vertedero (de basuras) m, basurero m, basural m AmL; **the ~ of the iceberg** la punta del iceberg

tip[2] [1] vt (give gratuity to) darle (una) propina a; ~ **the scales** inclinar la balanza [2] vi (give gratuity) dar propina; **tip off** vt avisarle a, darle un chivatazo a Esp (infrml)

tip-in n (in newspaper, magazine) encarte m

tip-off n soplo m (infrml), chivatazo m Esp (infrml)

tipping point n punto crítico cuando el 20% de negocios de una impresa se hace a través del Internet

title n título m; (right of ownership) derecho m, titularidad f; (document) título de propiedad m; ~ **deed** n título de propiedad m; ~ **page** n página de portada f; ~ **to the goods** n título sobre los bienes m

titular adj (head, leader) nominal

TL abbr (▶**total loss**) pérdida total f

TLI abbr (▶**transferable loan instrument**) instrumento de préstamo transferible m

TLO abbr (▶**total loss only**) sólo pérdida total

TMO abbr (▶**telegraphic money order**) giro telegráfico m

TNC abbr (▶**transnational corporation**) TNC f (corporación transnacional), multinacional f

TOB abbr (▶**takeover bid**) OPA f (oferta pública de adquisición), OPC f (oferta pública de compra)

toehold n punto de apoyo m; **get a ~ in the market** asentarse en el mercado, conseguir un punto de apoyo en el mercado; ~ **purchase** n toma de posición menor al 5 por ciento

toggle[1] n (Comp) interruptor m, palanca basculante f; ~ **switch** n interruptor m basculante or de palanca

toggle[2] vi (Comp) bascular

token[1] n (indication) señal f; (coin) ficha f; (voucher) BrE vale m; (Comp) contraseña f; **in ~ of sth** en señal de algo; **a small ~ of my gratitude** una pequeña muestra de mi agradecimiento

token[2] adj (payment, fine, strike, gesture) simbólico; **the ~ woman on the committee** la mujer que pusieron en el comité para aparentar igualdad; ~ **money** n BrE (cf ▶**fiat money** AmE) moneda f despreciada or fiduciaria; ~ **stoppage** n suspensión simbólica f

tokenism n formulismo m

tolerance n tolerancia f; ~ **level** n nivel de tolerancia m

toll n (on road) peaje m; **take its ~ on sth** tener un efecto grave sobre algo; ~ **call** n AmE (cf ▶**trunk call** BrE) llamada interurbana f, conferencia f Esp; ~**-free** adj libre de gastos or de peaje; ~**-free call** n AmE llamada libre de tasas f; ~**-free number** n AmE número exento de pago m; ~ **motorway** n BrE (cf ▶**turnpike** AmE) autopista de peaje f

tollbooth n cabina de peaje f

tollbridge n puente de peaje m

tombstone n (Stock) anuncio de emisión sindicada m, tombstone m; ~ **ad** n (Fin) esquela f

tom/next abbr (▶**from tomorrow to the next business day**) el próximo día hábil a partir de mañana

tomorrow adv, n mañana; **from ~ to the next business day** el próximo día hábil a partir de mañana; **they were spending money like there was no ~** estaban gastando dinero a troche y moche; ~ **week** de aquí a una semana

toner n (for photocopier, printer) tóner m

tontine n tontina f

tool n herramienta f; ~**s** utillaje m; ~ **bar** n (Comp) barra de trabajo f; ~**s of the trade** n herramientas del trabajo f pl

top[1] n (highest part) parte f superior or de arriba; (of page) parte superior f; (of organization) cúpula f; **at the ~ of one's profession** en la cumbre de su profesión; **buy at the ~ of the market** comprar a precio alto; **get ~ billing** ser primero de cartel; **come out on ~** salir ganando; **the ~ end of the range** la parte alta de la gama; **from ~ to bottom** de arriba abajo; **the ~ of the league** la cabeza de la liga; **life at the ~** la vida en la cumbre; **her name is at the ~ of the list** es la primera de la lista; **off the ~ of one's head** sin pensarlo; **there's VAT on ~** además or encima hay que agregarle el IVA; **be on ~ of one's work** tener el trabajo al día; **get on ~ of the situation** controlar la situación; **be o go over the ~**

(infrml) pasarse; **the ~ of the tree** (infrml) la máxima categoría jerárquica; **work one's way to the ~** llegar hasta arriba trabajando; **~ copy** *n* copia original *f*; **~ executive** *n* alto(-a) ejecutivo(-a) *m,f*; **~-flight** *adj* sobresaliente, de primera categoría; **~-heavy** *adj* sobredimensionado; **the company is ~-heavy** la empresa tiene demasiados altos ejecutivos; **~-level** *adj* de alto nivel; **~-level efficiency** *n* eficiencia de más alto nivel *f*; **~ level talks** *n pl* conversaciones de alto nivel *f pl*; **~ management** *n* alta dirección *f*; **~ price** *n* precio máximo *m*; **~ quality** *n* alta calidad *f*; **~-of-the-range** *adj* de gama alta; **~-rank product** *n* producto de primera categoría *m* ; **~-ranking** *adj* de primera categoría; **~-ranking official** *n* alto(-a) funcionario(-a) *m,f*; **~ rate of tax** *n* tipo máximo del impuesto *m*; **~-rated** *adj* escogido; **~ salaries review body** *n* BrE organismo de revisión de los salarios más altos *m*; **~-secret** *adj* confidencial, de alto secreto

top² *vt* (offer, achievement) superar; (list) encabezar; **exports ~ped the £80 million mark** las exportaciones superaron los 80 millones de libras; **top out** *vi* (rate, price, cost) cotizar al máximo; (demand, consumption) tocar techo, alcanzar el punto más alto *or* las cotas más altas; **top up** *vt* (income, capital) suplementar; (savings) reponer

top-down *adj* verticalista; (Comp) descendente, arriba-abajo; **~ approach to investing** *n* enfoque descendente de la inversión *m*; **~ management** *n* gestión vertical *f*

TOPIC *abbr* (▶**Teletex Output of Price Information by Computer**) *información bursátil por videotexto de la Bolsa de Valores de Londres*

topping out *n* valor techo *m*

topping-up clause *n* cláusula de relleno *f*

top-up: **~ card** *n* tarjeta telefónica prepagada *f*; **~ deduction** *n* deducción ampliada *f*; **~ insurance** *n* seguro extra *m*; **~ loan** *n* crédito para complementar uno anterior

tort *n* (in England and Wales) acto ilícito civil *m*; **~ liability** *n* responsabilidad por lesión jurídica *f*

tortfeasor *n* injuriador(a) *m,f*

total¹ *adj* (amount, number, cost, assets, income, revenue) total; (failure) rotundo, absoluto; **~ capitalization** *n* capitalización total *f*; **~ current spending** *n* gasto corriente total *m*; **~ estimates** *n pl* estimaciones totales *f pl*; **~ liability** *n* pasivo total *m*; **~ loss** *n* pérdida total *f*; **~ loss only** *n* sólo pérdida total; **~ public debt** *n* deuda pública total

f; **~ public expenditure** *n*, **~ public spending** *n* gasto público total *m*; **~ quality** *n* calidad total *f*; **~ quality control** *n* control de calidad total *m*; **~ quality management** *n* gestión de calidad total *f*; **~ quality marketing** *n* marketing de calidad total *m*; **~ sales** *n pl* ventas totales *f pl*; **~ votes cast** *n pl* total de votos emitidos *m*

total² *n* total *m*; **in ~** en total; **~ to date** *n* total a la fecha *m*

total³ *vt* (amount to) ascender *or* elevarse a un total de; (add up) sumar, totalizar

totality *n* totalidad *f*

totalizator *n* totalizador *m*

totalize *vt* totalizar

tot up *vt* (infrml) sumar

touch¹ *n* (communication) contacto *m*; **at the ~ of a button** con sólo tocar un botón; **it's ~ and go whether they'll succeed** no es nada seguro que vayan a tener éxito; **I'll be in ~** (by phoning) ya te llamaré; (by writing) ya te escribiré; **get in ~ with sb** ponerse en contacto con alguien; **keep in ~ with sb** (acquaintance, contact) mantenerse en contacto con alguien; **keep in ~ with sth** (new developments) mantenerse al corriente de algo; **be out of ~ with sth** (new developments) no estar al corriente de algo; **the personal/professional ~** el toque personal/profesional; **put the final** *o* **finishing ~/~es to sth** darle el último toque/los últimos toques a algo; **put sb in ~ with sb** poner a alguien en contacto con alguien; **~-activated** *adj* activado por el tacto; **~ key** *n* tecla de contacto *f*; **~ screen** *n* pantalla táctil *f*; **~-sensitive** *adj* sensible al tacto; **~-sensitive screen** *n* pantalla sensible al tacto *f*; **~-tone phone** *n* teléfono con teclado *m*

touch² *vt* (physically, interfere with) tocar; (affect) afectar; **~ sb for money** BrE (infrml) darle un sablazo a alguien (infrml); **sales ~ed rock bottom in June** las ventas tocaron fondo en junio; **touch off** *vt* (argument) provocar

touchpad *n* (Comp) almohadilla de toque *f*, placa sensible al tacto *f*

touch-type *vi* mecanografiar al tacto *or* sin mirar al teclado

tough *adj* (conditions, terms, legislation, stance) duro; (policy, discipline) duro, de mano dura; (boss) severo, exigente, estricto; (negotiator) implacable; (competitor) serio; (decision, question) difícil, peliagudo; (material, fabric) resistente, fuerte; **be/get ~ (with sb)** ponerse duro (con alguien); **take a ~ line with sb** mostrarse severo con alguien; **be ~ on sb** (strict) ser duro *or* severo con alguien; ····⟩

(unfair) ser injusto para con alguien; **have a ~ time** pasarlo muy mal

tough out *vt* (infrml) aguantar; **tough it out** no transigir, no ceder

tour *n* (Leis) gira *f*; (of building) visita *f*; (of town) recorrido turístico *m*; **~ of inspection** *n* recorrido de inspección *m*; **~ operator** *n* touroperador(a) *m,f*

tourism *n* turismo *m*

tourist *n* turista *mf*; **~ attraction** *n* atracción turística *f*; **T~ Board** *n* BrE Cámara de Turismo *f*; **~ class** *n* clase turista *f*; **~ fare** *n* tarifa turista *f*; **~ information office** *n* oficina de información turística *f*; **~ season** *n* estación turística *f*; **~ tax** *n* impuesto para turistas *m*; **~ trade** *n* industria turística *f*; **~ visa** *n* visado turístico *m*

tout¹ [1] *vt* (wares) ofrecer; (idea, product) promocionar; (tickets) BrE (*cf* ►**scalp** AmE) revender (a precio inflado) [2] *vi* buscar clientes; **~ for custom** *o* **business** buscar clientes

tout² *n* (person looking for business) *persona que busca clientes*; (ticket seller) BrE (*cf* ►**scalper** AmE) revendedor(a) *m,f* (a precio inflado)

touting *n* (of tickets) BrE (*cf* ►**scalping** AmE) reventa *f* (a precio inflado)

tow¹ *vt* remolcar

tow² *n* remolque *m*

towage *n* remolque *m*; **~ charges** *n pl* derechos de remolque *m pl*

towaway zone *n* AmE *zona de donde se permite llevar a grúa los coches mal aparcados*

town *n* ciudad *f*; **~-centre** *n* BrE centro de la ciudad *m*; **~ councillor** BrE, **~ councilor** AmE *n* concejal *mf*; **~ and country planning** *n* BrE planificación urbana y rural *f*; **~ hall** *n* BrE (*cf* ►**city hall** AmE) Ayuntamiento *m*; **~ planner** *n* urbanista *mf*; **~ planning** *n* urbanismo *m*

toxic *adj* (waste) tóxico

toxicity *n* toxicidad *f*

toxicological *adj* toxicológico

TP *abbr* (►**teleprocessing**) teleproceso *m*

TQM *abbr* (►**total quality management**) gestión de calidad total *f*

tr. *abbr* (►**transfer**) transferencia *f*

trace *vt* (payment, call) localizar, rastrear

traceable *adj* (cost) identificable

track¹ *n* (mark) pista *f*, huellas *f pl*; (railway) vía *f*; (Comp) pista *f*; **keep/lose ~ of sth/sb** seguir/perder la pista de algo/alguien; **the project is back on ~** el proyecto ha vuelto a ponerse al día; **be on the right/wrong ~** ir por buen/mal camino; **~ record** *n*

antecedentes *m pl*, historial *m*; **have a good ~ record** tener buenos antecedentes

track² *vt* (sales, costs, expenses, spending) seguir; **track down** *vt* localizar

trackball *n* (Comp) bola rodante *f*

tracker fund *n* fondo (de inversión) en índices *m*

tracking *n* (of sales, costs, expenses, spending) seguimiento *m*; **~ system** *n* sistema de seguimiento *m*

tract house *n* AmE casa construida en serie *f*

tractor-fed *adj* (Comp) con arrastre de dientes

tractor feed *n* (Comp) alimentación por arrastre *f*

trade¹ *n* (buying, selling) comercio *m*; (business, industry) industria *f*; (skilled occupation) oficio *m*; **by ~** de oficio; **do a brisk** *o* **roaring ~ (in sth)** hacer un negocio redondo (en algo); **~ in industrial goods** el negocio de bienes industriales; **learn a ~** aprender un oficio; **offer discounts to the ~** ofrecer descuentos al ramo; **~ is picking up** cada vez hay más movimiento en los comercios; **~ acceptance** *n* aceptación comercial *f*; **~ account** *n* cuenta comercial *f*; **~ agreement** *n* acuerdo *m or* convenio *m* comercial; **~ association** *n* asociación comercial *f*; **~ balance** *n* balanza *f or* saldo *m* comercial; **~ barrier** *n* barrera comercial *f*; **~ bill** *n* letra comercial *f*; **~ book** *n* libro comercial *m*; **~ channel** *n* canal comercial *m*; **~ creation** *n* creación comercial *f*; **~ credit** *n* crédito comercial *m*; **~ creditor** *n* acreedor(a) comercial *m,f*; **~ cycle** *n* ciclo comercial *m*; **T~ Data Elements Directory** *n* anuario de datos comerciales *m*; **~ data interchange** *n* intercambio de datos comerciales *m*; **~ date** *n* (Stock) fecha de operación *f*; **~ debtor** *n* deudor(a) comercial *m,f*; **~ deficit** *n* déficit comercial *m*; **~ description** *n* descripción comercial *f*; **T~ Descriptions Act** *n* BrE *ley sobre descripciones comerciales*; **~ directory** *n* directorio comercial *m*; **~ discount** *n* descuento comercial *m*; **~ embargo** *n* embargo comercial *m*; **~ entrance** *n* BrE (*cf* ►**service entrance** AmE) entrada de servicio *f*; **~ exhibition** *n* exposición comercial *f*; **~ facilitation** *n* facilitación comercial *f*; **~ fair** *n* feria *f* comercial *or* de muestras; **~ figures** *n pl* cifras comerciales *f pl*; **~ financing** *n* financiación del comercio *f*; **~ flow** *n* flujo comercial *m*; **~ gap** *n* déficit de la balanza comercial *m*; **~ imbalance** *n* desequilibrio comercial *m*; **~ journal** *n* diario comercial *m*; **~ magazine** *n* revista comercial *f*; **~ mission** *n* misión comercial *f*; **~ name** *n* razón social *f*;

(Patents) marca comercial *f*; ~
organization *n* organización comercial *f*;
~ **paperback** *n* publicación comercial *f*; ~
policy *n* política comercial *f*; ~ **practice** *n*
práctica comercial *f*; ~ **press** *n* prensa
comercial *f*; ~ **price** *n* precio al por mayor
m; ~ **promotion** *n* fomento del comercio *m*;
~ **publication** *n* publicación comercial *f*;
~ **register** *n* registro de comercio *m*; ~
regulation *n* ordenanza comercial *f*;
~**-related** *adj* relacionado con el comercio;
~ **representative** *n* representante de
comercio *mf*; ~ **restriction** *n* restricción al
comercio *f*; ~ **return** *n* rendimiento
comercial *m*; ~ **route** *n* ruta comercial *f*; ~
sanction *n* sanción comercial *f*; ~ **secret**
n secreto de fabricación *m*; ~ **show** *n*
exposición comercial *f*; ~ **strategy** *n*
estrategia comercial *f*; ~ **surplus** *n* balanza
comercial favorable *f*, superávit de la
balanza comercial *m*; ~ **talks** *n pl*
conferencias comerciales *f pl*; ~ **terms** *n pl*
condiciones de venta *f pl*; ~ **ticket** *n* marca
comercial *f*; ~ **union** *n* BrE (*cf* ▸**labor
union** AmE) sindicato *m*; **T~s Union
Congress** *n confederación de los sindicatos
británicos*; ~ **union dues** *n pl* BrE cuotas
sindicales *f pl*; ~ **union membership** *n* BrE
afiliación *f* sindical *or* a un sindicato; ~
union representative *n* BrE delegado(-a)
sindical *m,f*; ~ **unionism** *n* BrE
sindicalismo *m*; ~ **volume** *n* volumen
comercial *m*; ~ **war** *n* guerra comercial *f*

trade² **1** *vi* comerciar; ~ **as sth** trabajar
como algo; **their shares are now trading at
£30** sus acciones están a 30 libras; ~ **at a
profit/loss** comerciar con ganacias/pérdidas;
cease trading cerrar, dejar de comerciar; ~
in stocks and bonds negociar con valores y
bonos; ~ **on one's own account** comerciar
por cuenta propia; ~ **under the name of
sth** comerciar bajo nombre de algo; ~ **with
sb** comerciar con alguien; ~ **within the
European Union** negociar dentro de la
Unión Europea
2 *vt* intercambiar; ~ **raw materials for
manufactured goods** cambiar materias
primas por bienes manufacturados; **trade
down** *vi* comprar o vender bienes más
baratos que nunca; **trade in** *vt* (old model for
new) dar como parte del pago; **trade sth in
for sth** dar algo como parte del pago de algo;
trade off **1** *vi* llegar a una solución de
compromiso **2** *vt* sacrificar; ~ **off market
share against profit margins** compensar
cuota de mercado con márgenes de
beneficio; ~ **off one thing for another**
cambiar una cosa por otra; **trade up** *vi
vender un bien para comprar otro de mayor
valor*

tradeability *n* comerciabilidad *f*

tradeable *adj* comerciable; ~
promissory note *n* pagaré negociable *m*
traded *adj* (option) negociado
trade-in *n* (article) artículo usado aceptado
como parte del pago *m*; (transaction)
*transacción por la cual se da un artículo
usado como parte del pago*
trademark *n* (symbol, name) marca *f*
registrada *or* de fábrica; (distinctive
characteristic) sello característico *m*
trade-off *n* equilibrio *m*; **a ~ between
growth and profitability** un compromiso
entre el crecimiento y la rentabilidad
trader *n* comerciante *mf*; (large-scale)
almacenista *mf*; (shopkeeper) negociante *mf*;
(on stock exchange) corredor(a) de bolsa *m,f*,
intermediario(-a) *m,f*; ~ **in securities** *n*
intermediario(-a) en títulos *m,f*
tradesman *n* (shopkeeper) (obs)
comerciante *m*, tendero *m*; (deliveryman)
proveedor *m*; (repairman) BrE *electricista,
fontanero etc que trabaja a domicilio*; ~**'s
entrance** *n* entrada de servicio *f*
tradespeople *n pl* (shopkeepers) (obs)
comerciantes *m pl*, tenderos *m pl*; (deliverers
of goods) proveedores *m pl*; (repairers) BrE
*electricistas, fontaneros etc que trabajan a
domicilio*
trading *n* (in goods) comercio *m*; (on stock
exchange) contratación *f*, operaciones
(bursátiles) *f pl*; ~ **was brisk on the Stock
Exchange today** hoy hay habido un
mercado muy activo en la Bolsa; ~ **finishes
at 4** la Bolsa cierra a las cuatro; **in the final
hour of** ~ en la última hora de mercado; ~
account *n* cuenta *f* de beneficios brutos *or*
de beneficios en bruto; ~ **activity** *n*
actividad de compraventa *f*; ~ **area** *n*
(territory) zona comercial *f*; (shop) zona de
comercio *f*; ~ **authorization** *n* autorización
de comercio *f*; ~ **bloc** *n* bloque comercial
m; ~ **company** *n* sociedad comercial *f*; ~
debts *n pl* deudas comerciales *f pl*; ~ **desk**
n corro de contratación *m*; ~ **estate** *n* BrE
zona industrial *f*; ~ **floor** *n* parqué de
operaciones *m*; ~ **hours** *n pl* horario de
contratación *m*; ~ **income** *n* beneficio
bruto *m*; ~ **losses** *n pl* pérdidas del
ejercicio *f pl*; ~ **member** *n* (of exchange)
socio(-a) activo(-a) *m,f*; ~ **name** *n* nombre
comercial *m*; ~ **operation** *n* operación
comercial *f*; ~ **partner** *n* socio(-a)
comercial *m,f*; ~ **pattern** *n* modelo de
negociación *m*; ~ **pit** *n* (Stock) parqué de
operaciones *m*; ~ **portfolio** *n* (of investments)
cartera comercial *f*; ~ **post** *n
establecimiento comercial en un lugar poco
poblado*; (Stock) puesto de operaciones *m*; ~
range *n* (of commodities, securities) banda de
fluctuación de precios *f*; ~ **room** *n* cámara ⋯▸

de comercio *f*; ~ **security** *n* efecto negociable *m*; ~ **session** *n* sesión de contratación *f*; ~ **stamp** *n* cupón *m*; ~ **standard** *n* norma comercial *f*; **T~ Standards Office** *n* AmE *departamento de normas comerciales*; ~ **volume** *n* volumen de contratación *m*; ~ **year** *n* año comercial *m*

trading-up *n* venta a precios superiores *f*

tradition *n* tradición *f*

traditional *adj* tradicional

traffic *n* (vehicles) tráfico *m*, circulación *f*, (of ships, on network, trafficking) tráfico *m*; (of aircraft) tráfico aéreo *m*; (goods, people transported) tránsito *m*, movimiento *m*; (pedestrians) AmE tránsito de peatones *m*; (paying customers) AmE clientela *f*; ~ **builder** *n* (S&M) *promoción destinada a estimular el flujo de personas en un establecimiento*; ~ **circle** *n* AmE (*cf* ▸**roundabout** BrE) rotonda *f*; ~ **congestion** *n* congestión del tráfico *f*; ~ **control** *n* control de tráfico *m*; ~ **count** *n* (S&M) recuento de circulación *m*; ~ **department** *n* (S&M) departamento de expedición *m*; ~ **jam** *n* atasco *m*, embotellamiento de tráfico *m*; ~ **manager** *n* (on website) organizador(a) del tráfico *m,f*; ~ **planning** *n* (S&M) (of work) gestión de los flujos de trabajo *f*; (of advertising) planificación de los anuncios según la audiencia *f*

traffic in *vt* comerciar en, traficar en

trafficker *n* traficante *mf*

trail *vt* (broadcast) arrastrar

trailblazing *adj* precursor

trailer *n* (for equipment) remolque *m*; (live-in vehicle) AmE caravana *f*; (in cinema, on TV) avance(s) *m* (*pl*), tráiler *m* Esp

train[1] *n* tren *m*; ~ **fare** *n* tarifa ferroviaria *f*; ~ **station** *n* BrE (*cf* ▸**railroad station** AmE) estación de ferrocarril *f*; ~ **timetable** *n* horario de trenes *m*

train[2] [1] *vt* (employee, worker) capacitar, formar; **they are being ~ed to use the machine** les están enseñando a usar la máquina [2] *vi* estudiar; ~ **as/to be a lawyer** estudiar abogacía/para abogado

trainee *n* persona en prácticas *f*; (apprentice) aprendiz *mf*; (Law) pasante *mf*; ~ **civil servant** *n* funcionario(-a) en prácticas *m,f*; ~ **manager** *n* *empleado haciendo prácticas de gerencia*; ~ **programmer** *n* programador(a) *m,f* aprendiz(a) *or* en prácticas

traineeship *n* *puesto remunerado en el cual se recibe capacitación práctica*; (Law) pasantía *f*

trainer *n* proveedor(a) *m,f* de capacitación *or* de formación

training *n* capacitación *f*, formación *f*; ~ **will be given to all staff** todo el personal recibirá capacitación *or* formación; ~ **agency** *n* BrE agencia *f* de capacitación *or* de formación; ~ **center** AmE, ~ **centre** BrE *n* centro *m* de capacitación *or* de formación; ~ **course** *n* curso *m* de capacitación *or* de formación; ~ **manager** *n* gerente *mf* de capacitación *or* de formación; ~ **needs** *n pl* necesidades *f pl* de capacitación *or* de formación; ~ **officer** *n* responsable *mf* de capacitación *or* de formación; ~ **program** AmE, ~ **programme** BrE *n* programa *m* de capacitación *or* de formación; ~ **scheme** *n* BrE plan *m* de capacitación *or* de formación; ~ **of trainers** *n* capacitación de proveedores de capacitación *f*, formación de proveedores de formación *f*

tranche *n* (of debt) tramo *m*, porción *f*; (of shares) bloque *m*, paquete *m*; (of capital) parte *f*

transact [1] *vt* gestionar, negociar; ~ **business (with sb)** negociar (con alguien), hacer negocios (con alguien); ~ **a deal** gestionar un trato [2] *vi* (company, bank) negociar, llevar a cabo transacciones comerciales

transaction *n* (deal) transacción *f*, operación *f*; (act of transacting) negociación *f*; **make a ~** hacer una transacción; ~ **cost** *n* coste *m* Esp *or* costo *m* AmL de las transacciones; ~ **date** *n* fecha de operación *f*; ~ **fee** *n* gastos de transacción *m pl*; ~ **file** *n* fichero de movimientos *m*; ~ **management** *n* gestión de transacciones *f*; ~ **management software** *n* software de gestión de transacciones *m*; ~ **processing** *n* proceso de transacción *m*; ~ **risk** *n* riesgo de la transacción *m*; ~ **status** *n* situación de transacción *f*; ~ **tax** *n* impuesto sobre transacciones *m*

transactional *adj* transaccional; ~ **analysis** *n* análisis *m* transaccional *or* de transacción; ~ **site** *n* sitio web de transacciones *m*

transcode *vt* transcodificar

transcoder *n* transcodificador *m*

transcribe *vt* transcribir

transcriber *n* aparato de transcripción *m*

transcript *n* transcripción *f*

transcription *n* transcripción *f*

transducer *n* transductor *m*

transeuropean *adj* (network) transeuropeo

transfer[1] *n* (of accounts, assets, funds, power) transferencia *f*; (of property) transferencia *f*, traspaso *m*, transmisión *f*; (of responsibilities) traspaso *m*; (of employee) traslado *m*; (of passenger) transbordo *m*; (of technology) transmisión *f*; **she applied for a ~** solicitó el traslado; **he's a ~ from another branch**

lo han trasladado de otra sucursal; ~
account n cuenta de transferencia f; ~
address n (Comp) dirección de transferencia
f; ~ **deed** n escritura de transmisión f; ~
earnings n pl ingresos de transferencia m pl;
~ **fee** n (for sports player) traspaso m; ~ **fees** n
pl (Law) derechos de transferencia m pl;
(Prop) honorarios de traspaso m pl; ~
income n renta de transferencia f; ~ **order**
n orden de transferencia f; ~ **payment** n
pago de transferencia m; ~ **price** n precio de
cesión m; ~ **pricing** n fijación del precio de
transferencias f; ~ **rate** n velocidad de
transferencia f; ~ **register** n (Stock) registro
de transferencias m; ~ **tax** n impuesto sobre
transmisiones patrimoniales m

transfer² ⟦1⟧ vt (property, right) transferir,
traspasar; (funds, account) transferir; (call)
pasar; (employee) trasladar; ~ **by wire**
transferir por cable; **he ~red the money to
his current** BrE o **checking** AmE **account**
transfirió el dinero a su cuenta corriente; ~
ownership of sth transferir la propiedad de
algo; **can you ~ me to Sales?** ¿me puede
comunicar or poner Esp con Ventas?
⟦2⟧ vi (company, employee) trasladarse

transferability n (of registered shares)
transmisibilidad f

transferable adj (options, stock, securities,
credit, ticket) transferible; **not ~**
intransferible; ~ **loan certificate** n
certificado de préstamo transferible m; ~
loan instrument n instrumento de
préstamo transferible m

transferee n beneficiario(-a) de una
transferencia m,f; ~ **company** n compañía
cesionaria f

transferor n BrE (Bank) transferidor m; (of
inheritance rights) cesionista mf; ~ **company**
n empresa cedente f

transferred adj (share) transferido; ~
charge call n conferencia a cobro
revertido f

transform vt transformar

transformation n transformación f; ~
industry n industria de transformación f

transient adj (worker, medium) transitorio

transire n permiso aduanero de retirada de
mercancías

transit n tránsito m; **in ~** en tránsito; ~
card n (in airline travel) tarjeta de tránsito f;
~ **credit** n crédito en tránsito m; ~
document n documento de tránsito m; ~
lounge n sala de tránsito f; ~ **market** n
mercado de tránsito m; ~ **passenger** n
pasajero(-a) en tránsito m,f

transition n transición f; ~ **period** n
periodo de transición m

transitional adj (stage, period, government)
de transición

transitory adj transitorio

translate vt (word, text, program, language)
traducir

translation n (of word, text, program, language)
traducción f; ~ **differential** n diferencial
de traducción m; ~ **program** n programa
traductor m; ~ **rate** n (Fin), tasa de
conversión f

translator n (person) traductor(a) m,f;
(program) programa de traducción m; ~**'s
note** n nota del traductor f

transmission n (conveyance, vehicle
mechanism) transmisión f; (broadcasting)
transmisión f, emisión f

transmit vt (data) transmitir; (broadcast)
transmitir, emitir

transmittal letter n carta de envío f

transmitter n (for radio, TV) transmisor m

transmitting adj transmisor; ~ **station**
n estación emisora f

transnational adj (corporation)
transnacional

transparency n (of material, behaviour, for
overhead projector) transparencia f; (Acc)
claridad f

transparent adj transparente

transport¹ n (movement, vehicle) BrE (cf
▶**transportation** AmE) transporte m;
(shipment) AmE remesa f; **salesperson
required: own ~ essential** se necesita
vendedor: vehículo propio imprescindible;
~ **advertising** n BrE publicidad en medios
de transporte f; ~ **agent** n BrE agente de
transportes mf; ~ **insurance** n BrE seguro
de transportes m; ~ **link** n BrE enlace de
transporte m; ~ **service** n BrE servicio de
transporte m; ~ **system** n BrE sistema de
transporte m

transport² vt transportar; ~ **by air**
transportar por avión

transportable adj transportable

transportation n (movement, vehicle) AmE
(cf ▶**transport** BrE) transporte m

transposal n trasposición f

transpose vt trasponer

transposition n trasposición f; ~ **error** n
error de trasposición m

transverse adj transversal

trashy adj (infrml) (goods) de baja calidad

travel¹ vi viajar

travel² n viajes m pl; ~ **agency** n agencia
de viajes f; ~ **agent** n agente de viajes mf;
~ **allowance** n dietas de viaje f pl, viáticos
m pl AmL; ~ **document** n documentación
de viaje f; ~ **expense claim** n reclamación
de gastos de viaje f; ~ **expenses** n pl
gastos de viaje m pl; ~ **insurance** n seguro
de viaje m; ~ **restriction** n restricción de ····⟶

recorrido *f*; ~ **service** *n* servicio de viajes *m*; ~ **voucher** *n* bono de viaje *m*

travelator *n* BrE cinta transbordadora *f*, pasillo rodante *m*

traveller BrE, **traveler** AmE *n* viajero(-a) *m,f*; ~'s **cheque** BrE, **traveler's check** AmE *n* cheque de viajero *m*

travelling BrE, **traveling** AmE *n* viajes *m pl*; ~ **allowance** *n* dietas de viaje *f pl*, viáticos *m pl* AmL; ~ **expenses** *n pl* dietas de viaje *f pl*, viáticos *m pl* AmL; ~ **salesman** *n* viajante de comercio *mf*

traversable *adj* (Law) contradictorio

traverse[1] *vt* (Law) contradecir

traverse[2] *n* (Law) contradicción *f*

treasurer *n* tesorero(-a) *m,f*; ~ **check** AmE, ~ **cheque** BrE *n* cheque de tesorería *m*; ~'s **report** *n* informe del tesorero *m*

treasury *n* fisco *m*

Treasury *n* Tesoro *m*; BrE (*cf* ▶**Treasury Department** AmE) Tesoro *m*, ≈ Hacienda Pública *f*, ≈ Ministerio de Economía y Hacienda *m* Esp; ~ **bill** *n* letra del Tesoro *f*; ~ **bill futures** *n pl* futuros sobre letras del Tesoro *m pl*; ~ **bill rate** *n* cotización de las letras del Tesoro *f*; ~ **bill tender** *n* oferta de letras del Tesoro *f*; ~ **Board** *n* Consejo Económico *m*; ~ **bond** *n* AmE bono del Tesoro *m*; ~ **Department** *n* AmE (*cf* ▶**Treasury** BrE) Departamento del Tesoro *m*, ≈ Hacienda Pública *f*, ≈ Ministerio de Economía y Hacienda *m* Esp; ~ **note** *n* pagaré del Tesoro *m*; ~ **stock** *n* BrE autocartera *f*, bono del Tesoro *m*; AmE acciones *f pl* rescatadas *or* propias readquiridas

treat *vt* tratar; ~ **sewage** *o* **wastewater** depurar las aguas residuales

treatment *n* (of person, object) trato *m*; (of subject, idea, waste) tratamiento *m*

treaty *n* tratado *m*; **enter into a** ~ suscribir un tratado; **sell sth by private** ~ vender algo mediante acuerdo privado; **T**~ **of Rome** *n* Tratado de Roma *m*; ~ **shopping** *n* aprovechamiento de las ventajas fiscales concedidas a terceros países, a través de filiales en estos

treble[1] *adj* triple

treble[2] [1] *vt* triplicar [2] *vi* triplicarse

tree *n* árbol *m*; ~ **diagram** *n* diagrama de árbol *f*, árbol *m*; ~ **structure** *n* estructura en árbol *f*

trend *n* tendencia *f*; **set the** ~ **(in sth)** marcar la pauta (en lo que respecta a algo); **a** ~ **towards** BrE *o* **toward** AmE **centralization** una tendencia a *or* hacia la centralización; **an upward/downward** ~ una tendencia alcista *or* al alza/bajista *or* a

la baja; ~ **analysis** *n* análisis de tendencias *m*; ~ **reversal** *n* reversión de tendencia *f*

trendsetter *n persona que inicia una moda*

trendsetting *adj* que inicia una moda

trespass[1] *vi entrar sin autorización en propiedad ajena*

trespass[2] *n entrada sin autorización en propiedad ajena*

trespasser *n* intruso(-a) *m,f*; '~s **will be prosecuted**' prohibido el paso

trespassing *n entrada sin autorización en propiedad ajena*; '**no** ~' prohibido el paso

trial *n* (in court) juicio *m*; (test) prueba *f*; **give sth/sb a** ~ poner algo/a alguien a prueba; **go on** *o* **stand** ~ **for sth** ser procesado por algo; **if the case goes to** ~ si el caso va a juicio; **on** ~ (being tested) a prueba; **undergo** ~**s** ser sometido a prueba; ~ **balance** *n* balance de comprobación *m*; ~ **by jury** *n* juicio con *or* por jurado *m*; ~ **court** *n* tribunal de primera instancia *m*; ~ **and error** *n* ensayo *m* y error *m*; ~**-and-error method** *n* método de tanteo *m*; ~ **examiner** *n* instructor(a) *m,f*; ~ **jury** *n* jurado ordinario *m*; ~ **offer** *n* oferta de prueba *f*; ~ **order** *n* pedido de prueba *m*; ~ **period** *n* periodo de prueba *m*; ~ **purchase** *n* compra de prueba *f*; ~ **run** *n* pasada de comprobación *f*; ~ **subscriber** *n* abonado(-a) a prueba *m,f*; ~ **subscription** *n* suscripción de prueba *f*; ~**s and tribulations** *n pl* tribulaciones *f pl*

triangular *adj* (merger, operation) triangular

triangulation *n* triangulación *f*

tribunal *n* tribunal *m* ~ **of enquiry** *n* tribunal de consulta *m*

trick[1] *vt* engañar, embaucar; ~ **sb into doing sth** engañar a alguien para que haga algo; ~ **sb out of sth** birarle algo a alguien

trick[2] *n* trampa *f*, ardid *m*; **the** ~**s of the trade** (infrml) los gajes del oficio

trickle-down theory *n* teoría de la filtración *f*

trifling *adj* insignificante

trigger[1] *n* (of machine) disparador *m*; **be a** ~ **for sth** provocar algo; ~ **mechanism** *n* mecanismo del disparador *m*; ~ **point** *n* punto de provocación *m*; ~ **price** *n* precio de intervención *m*

trigger[2] *vt* (cost, reaction, response) provocar; (alarm) accionar

trim[1] *vt* (budget, spending) recortar; (workforce) reducir; ~ **the investment program** AmE *o* **programme** BrE recortar el programa de inversión

trim[2] *n* (condition) estado *m*, condiciones *f pl*; (good condition) buen estado *m*, buenas condiciones *f pl*; **in good** ~ en buen estado

trip *n* viaje *m*

tripack *n* envasado triple *m*

tripartism *n* tripartismo *m*

triple[1] *adj* triple

triple[2] [1] *vt* triplicar
[2] *vi* triplicarse

triple-A *adj* (rating) triple A; **~ bond** *n* bono clase AAA *m* **~-rated borrower** *n* prestatario con calificación triple A *m*

triplicate *adj* triplicado; **in ~** por triplicado

troika *n* troika *f*

trouble[1] *n* (problems) problemas *f pl*; (problem) problema *f*; (effort) molestia *f*; (unrest) conflicto *m*; **be in ~** estar en apuros; **get into ~** meterse en un lío; **get out of ~** salir de apuros; **go to a lot of ~** tomarse muchas molestias; **~-free** *adj* sin problemas; **~ spot** *n* foco de perturbaciones *m*

trouble[2] *vt* (worry) preocupar; (bother) molestar

troubled *adj* (region, industry) aquejado de problemas; (period) conflictivo

troublemaker *n* alborotador(a) *m,f*

troubleshoot *vi* (Comp) buscar averías

troubleshooter *n* (HRM) investigador(a) de conflictos laborales *m,f*; (Comp) localizador(a) *m,f* de fallas AmL *or* de fallos Esp

troubleshooting *n* (HRM) investigación de conflictos laborales *f*; (Comp) localización *f* y corrección *f* de fallas AmL *or* de fallos Esp

trough[1] *n* (on graph, curve, in cycle) depresión *f*

trough[2] *vi* llegar al punto más bajo

truck *n* AmE (*cf* ▸**lorry** BrE) camión *m*

trucking *n* AmE transporte por carretera *m*

true *adj* (story, account) verídico; (purpose) verdadero; (faithful) fiel; **be ~** (be consistent with fact, reality) ser cierto, ser verdad; **~ to sample** conforme a la muestra; **~ copy** *n* copia fiel *f*; **~ and fair** *adj* (audit) verdadero y equitativo; **~ and fair view** *n* BrE (*cf* ▸**fair representation** AmE) imagen fiel *f*; **~ lease** *n* arrendamiento real *m*; **~ owner** *n* propietario(-a) legítimo(-a) *m,f*, titular verdadero(-a) *m,f*

truncate *vt* truncar

truncation *n* truncamiento *m*

trunk *n* (box) baúl *m*; (of car) AmE (*cf* ▸**boot** BrE) maletero *m*; **~ call** *n* BrE (obs) (*cf* ▸**toll call** AmE) llamada interurbana *f*, conferencia *f* Esp; **~ line** *n* (for telephone) línea interurbana *f*; (on railway) línea troncal *f*; **~ road** *n* BrE (*cf* ▸**highway** AmE) carretera nacional *f*

trust[1] *n* (confidence, faith) confianza *f*; (institution) fundación *f*; (monopoly group) trust *m*, cartel *m*; (money, property) fondo de inversiones *m*; (custody) fideicomiso *m*; **hold sth in ~ for sb** mantener algo en fideicomiso para alguien; **on ~** (without verification) bajo palabra; (on credit) a crédito; **sell sth on ~** vender algo a crédito; **a position of ~** un puesto de confianza *or* de responsabilidad; **put one's ~ in sth/sb** confiar en algo/alguien; **take sth on ~** creer algo sin tener pruebas; **~ account** *n* cuenta de fideicomiso *f*; **~ agreement** *n* acuerdo de fideicomiso *m*; **~ company** *n* (corporation) compañía fiduciaria *f*; (bank) banco fiduciario *m*; **~ deed** *n* escritura fiduciaria *f*; **~ fund** *n* fondo *m* fiduciario *or* de fideicomiso; **~ instrument** *n* escritura fiduciaria *f*; **~ unit** *n* unidad fiduciaria *f*

trust[2] *vt* confiar en, tener confianza en

trustbuster *n* AmE (infrml) *funcionario encargado de aplicar la legislación antimonopolista*

trustbusting *n* AmE (infrml) desmontaje de un trust *m*

trusted third party *n* tercero de confianza *m*

trustee *n* (of money, property) fiduciario(-a) *m,f*, fideicomisario(-a) *m,f*; (of bankrupt) síndico(-a) *m,f*; (of institution) miembro del consejo de administración *m*; **~ in bankruptcy** *n* síndico(-a) en quiebra *m,f*

trusteeship *n* (of money, property) fideicomiso *m*; (Stock) fiduciaría *f*; (of institution) puesto en el consejo de administración *m*

trustify *vt* trustificar

trustworthiness *n* (of data) exactitud *f*; (of person) honradez *f*

trustworthy *adj* (data) exacto; (account, witness) fidedigno; (colleague) digno de confianza

truth *n* (quality, condition) verdad *f*; (of story) veracidad *f* **~ in lending** *n* AmE declaración veraz de los términos del préstamo *f*, veracidad en contratos de préstamo *f*

truthful *adj* (person) que dice la verdad, veraz, sincero; (testimony) veraz, verídico; (answer) veraz

truthfulness *n* veracidad *f*

tryout *n* prueba de aptitud *f*

try out *vt* poner a prueba

TS *abbr* (▸**timesharing**) tiempo compartido *m*

TT *abbr* (▸**technology transfer**) transferencia de tecnología *f*; (▸**telegraphic transfer**) transferencia *f* telegráfica *or* cablegráfica; (▸**timetable**) horario *m*

TTC *abbr* (▸**tender to contract**) licitación *f*, propuesta de contrato *f*; (Law) concurso *m*

tube *n* BrE (infrml) (*cf* ▸**subway** AmE) metro *m*

TUC *abbr* (▸**Trades Union Congress**) *confederación de los sindicatos británicos*

tug-of-war n tira y afloja m

tuning n adaptación f

tunnel n túnel m

turf war n guerra de territorios f

turn¹ n (rotation) vuelta f; (change of direction) vuelta f, giro m; (bend, turning) curva f; (place in sequence) turno m; (Stock) ganancia del intermediario f; **do sb a good** ~ hacerle un favor a alguien; **this dramatic** ~ **of events** este dramático giro de los acontecimientos; **be on the** ~ (events, situation) estar cambiando; **take a** ~ **for the better/worse** empezar a mejorar/empeorar

turn² 1 vt (profit) sacar; (inventory, merchandise) AmE darle salida a; ~ **one's attention to sth** dirigir la atención hacia algo 2 vi (luck) cambiar; (merchandise) AmE venderse; **turn around** 1 vt (company, economy) sanear; ~ **orders around within 24 hours** despachar los pedidos en 24 horas 2 vi (luck, economy) cambiar completamente, dar or pegar un vuelco; (trend) invertirse; **turn away** vt rechazar; **we can't afford to** ~ **away business** no podemos permitirnos el lujo de rechazar trabajo; **turn down** 1 vt (offer, application) rechazar; (job, candidate) rechazar, no aceptar; **they** ~ed **him down for the job** no le dieron el puesto; **her request for a loan was** ~ed **down** le negaron el préstamo 2 vi (sales) desplomarse; **turn in** vt (work, report) entregar; (profit) realizar; ~ **in a good performance** (company) tener buenos resultados; **turn off** vt apagar; **turn on** vt encender; **turn out** vt (goods) sacar, producir; **turn over** vt (document) entregar; **she** ~ed **the company over to her son** puso la empresa a nombre de su hijo; **we** ~ed **over $8 million last year** facturamos 8 millones de dólares el año pasado; **stock is** ~ed **over very rapidly** la rotación de las existencias es muy rápida

turnabout n cambio completo m

turnaround, turnround BrE n (of orders) procesamiento m; (Fin) cambio de posición m; (in trend) vuelco m; ~ **period** n periodo de respuesta m; ~ **time** n (Comp) tiempo m de devolución or respuesta

turning point n punto decisivo m

turnkey adj (system, project) llave en mano; (solution) llaves en mano; ~ **contract** n contrato de montaje llave en mano m

turnout n concurrencia f

turnover n (of business, sales) facturación f; (of stock) rotación f; (of staff) movimiento m; ~ **rate** n índice de rotación de existencias m; ~ **ratio** n proporción de rotación f; ~ **tax** n impuesto m sobre el volumen de ventas or sobre el tráfico de empresas

turnpike n AmE (cf ▸**toll motorway** BrE) autopista de peaje f

turnround BrE ▸**turnaround**

TV abbr (▸**television**) TV (televisión)

tweak vt reajustar, retocar

twenty-four n veinticuatro m; ~-**four hour service** n servicio de 24 horas m; ~-**four hour trading** n comercio las 24 horas del día m; (Stock) operaciones bursátiles las 24 horas del día f pl

twice adv dos veces; ~-**a-week** adj bisemanal

twilight shift n BrE turno vespertino m

twin room n habitación doble f

twisting n (jarg) (Fin) inducción a operaciones innecesarias f

two n dos m; ~ **bits** n pl AmE (infrml) moneda de 25 centavos; ~-**color** AmE, ~-**colour** BrE adj a dos colores; ~-**digit inflation** n inflación de dos dígitos f; ~-**sided** adj (Comp) de dos caras; ~-**tier bargaining** n negociación en dos niveles f; ~-**tier system** n sistema de dos niveles m; ~-**tier wage structure** n estructura salarial de dos niveles f; ~-**way** adj (agreement) bilateral; (street) de doble sentido; (traffic) en ambas direcciones; (Comp) de dos direcciones; ~-**way split** n división en dos f

txt msg n (▸**text message**) texto m

tycoon n magnate mf

type¹ n (sort, kind) tipo m; (typical example) tipo m, ejemplo típico m; (characters) tipo (de imprenta) m; (printing blocks) tipos (de imprenta) m pl; **in large/small** ~ en caracteres grandes/pequeños, en letra grande/pequeña; ~ **area** n zona tipo f; ~ **font** n fuente de tipos f

type² vt mecanografiar; **type in** vt (word) teclear; (password, data) introducir; **type out** vt mecanografiar; **type up** vt pasar a máquina

typebar n línea de linotipia f

typeface n tipo (de letra) m, letra f

typeset vt componer

typesetter n (person) cajista mf; (machine) máquina de componer f

typesetting n composición (tipográfica) f

typewrite vt mecanografiar

typewriter n máquina de escribir f

typewritten adj mecanografiado, escrito a máquina

typical adj típico

typically adv típicamente

typify vt tipificar

typing n mecanografía f; ~ **error** n error mecanográfico m; ~ **pool** n (typists) mecanógrafos m pl; (department) servicio de mecanografía m; ~ **service** n servicio mecanográfico *m*; ~ **speed** *n* velocidad mecanográfica *f*

typist *n* mecanógrafo(-a) *m,f*

typo *n* (infrml) errata *f*, error tipográfico *m*

typographer *n* tipógrafo(-a) *m,f*

typographic, **typographical** *adj* tipográfico; ~ **error** *n* errata *f*, error tipográfico *m*

typological *adj* (analysis) tipológico

typology *n* tipología *f*

Uu

U/a *abbr* (►**underwriting account**) cuenta de subscripción de seguros *f*

UBR *abbr* (►**Uniform Business Rate**) *tipo empresarial uniforme*

U-hypothesis *n* (of income distribution) hipótesis U *f*

UK-incorporated *adj* incorporado al R.U.

UKTA *abbr* (►**United Kingdom Trade Agency**) *agencia comercial del Reino Unido*

ult. *abbr* (obs) (►**ultimo**) pdo. (pasado)

ultimate *adj* (aim, goal, destination, consumer) final; ~ **risk** *n* (Bank) riesgo máximo *m*

ultimatum *n* ultimátum *m*; **give sb an** ~ darle un ultimátum a alguien

ultimo *adj* (obs) pasado

ultraportable *adj* (laptop, device) ultra-portátil

ultravires *adj* antiestatutario; ~ **borrowing** *n* empréstito ultra vires *m*; ~ **activities** *n pl* actividades que sobrepasan sus atribuciones *f pl*

umbrella *n* paraguas *m*; **under the** ~ **of sth** bajo la protección de algo; ~ **fund** *n* fondo de contingencia *m*; ~ **group** *n* grupo paraguas *m*; ~ **project** *n* proyecto que sirve de marco para otros *m*

UMTS *abbr* (►**Universal Mobile Telecommunication System**) UMTS *m* (sistema universal de telecomunicaciones móviles)

UN *abbr* (►**United Nations**) ONU *f* (Organización de las Naciones Unidas)

UNA *abbr* (►**United Nations Association**) ANU *f* (Asociación de las Naciones Unidas)

unabridged *adj* íntegro; **complete and** ~ versión íntegra

unacceptable *adj* (terms, conditions) inadmisible; (conduct, standard) inaceptable, inadmisible

unaccepted *adj* (bill) inaceptado

unaccompanied *adj* (baggage) no acompañado

unaccounted for *adj* inexplicado

unacknowledged *adj* no reconocido; **my letter went** ~ no acusaron recibo de mi carta

unadjusted *adj* (figures, statistics) desajustado; **in** ~ **figures** en cifras desajustadas

unadvertised *adj* no anunciado

unaffiliated *adj* (union) no afiliado

unalienable *adj* inalienable

unallocated *adj* no asignado

unallotted *adj* (shares) no distribuido

unaltered *adj* (share price) inalterado

unamortized *adj* (discount, premium) no amortizado

unanimity *n* unanimidad *f*

unanimous *adj* (decision) unánime; ~ **in sth** unánime en algo

unanimously *adv* (vote) unánimemente; (elect) por unanimidad

unanticipated *adj* imprevisto

unappropriated *adj* (profit) no asignado; (surplus) disponible

unapproved *adj* (funds) desaprobado

unassailable *adj* (argument) irrefutable, irrebatible; (reputation) incuestionable; (right) inalienable; (position) invulnerable

unassessed *adj* no evaluado

unassignable *adj* intransferible

unassured *adj* no asegurado

unattainable *adj* (objective) inalcanzable

unattended *adj* (production, luggage) desatendido

unaudited *adj* no auditado

unauthenticated *adj* (signature) no autentificado

unauthorized *adj* (shares, signature) no autorizado

unavailability *n* falta de disponibilidad *f*

unavailable *adj* indisponible; (Comp) no disponible; **he's** ~ **at the moment** en este momento no le puede atender; **it's** ~ no se puede obtener

unavoidable *adj* (costs) inevitable

unavoidably *adv* inevitablemente; **I was** ~ **delayed** no he podido evitar el retraso

unbacked *adj* (Bank) no respaldado

unbalanced *adj* (account) no conciliado; (report) tendencioso, partidista; (growth) desequilibrado

unbiased *adj* (opinion, report) imparcial, objetivo; (person) ecuánime, imparcial

unblock *vt* (account) desbloquear

unbounded *adj* (risk) no vinculado

unbranded *adj* (goods) sin marca

unbundle *vt* facturar separadamente

unbundling *n* desglose *m*

unbusinesslike *adj* anticomercial

uncallable *adj* (loan) no denunciable

uncalled capital *n* capital (suscrito y) no desembolsado *m*

uncancelled BrE, **uncanceled** AmE *adj* (debt) activo

uncashed *adj* (cheque) no cobrado

unchanged *adj* inmodificado, sin modificar

uncheck *vt* AmE (*cf* ▸**untick** BrE) (box) desactivar

unchecked[1] *adj* (figures) no cotejado; (spread, advance) libre, sin obstáculos; (baggage) no comprobado; ∼ **inflationary economy** *n* economía inflacionista no controlada *f*

unchecked[2] *adv* libremente, sin restricción

unclaimed *adj* (balance, deposit, letter, right) no reclamado

uncleared *adj* (cheque) no compensado; (goods) no despachado por aduanas

uncollectable *adj* (account, taxes) incobrable

uncollected *adj* (funds) no cobrado, no recaudado

uncommitted *adj* (funds) disponible; (resources) no comprometido

uncompromising *adj* inflexible

unconditional *adj* (acceptance, remission) incondicional

unconditionally *adv* sin condiciones, incondicionalmente

unconfirmed *adj* (credit, letter of credit) no confirmado

unconsidered *adj* (remark, course of action) precipitado, irreflexivo; (ignored) sin reconocimiento

unconsolidated *adj* no consolidado; **on an ∼ basis** con carácter no consolidado

unconstitutional *adj* inconstitucional

unconverted *adj* no convertido

uncorrected *adj* sin corregir

uncorroborated *adj* no confirmado, no corroborado

uncovered *adj* (amount, advance) en descubierto; (balance) descubierto; (cheque) sin (provisión de) fondos; (loan) sin garantía; ∼ **bear** *n* especulador(a) a la baja sin provisión de fondos *m,f*; ∼ **call** *n* opción de compra sin cobertura *f*; ∼ **option** *n* opción sin cubrir *f*; ∼ **put** *n* opción de venta sin cobertura *f*

uncrossed *adj* (cheque) no cruzado, sin cruzar

uncurbed *adj* (competition) libre

uncurtailed *adj* (competition, rights) sin restricciones

undamaged *adj* indemne

undamped *adj* (demand) no disminuido

undated *adj* sin fecha

undecided *adj* (person) indeciso; (question, issue) pendiente, no resuelto

undelete *vt* restituir

undeliverable *adj* (cheque) intransferible, no librable

undelivered *adj* no entregado al destinatario; **if ∼ please return to sender** si no se entrega al destinatario, por favor devuélvase al remitente

undeniable *adj* innegable

undependable *adj* informal

undepreciated *adj* (cost) no depreciado; ∼ **capital cost** *n* gastos de instalación no amortizados *m pl*

undepressed *adj* (Stock) no deprimido

underabsorb *vt* (costs, expenses) absorber de forma insuficiente

underabsorption *n* (of costs, expenses) absorción insuficiente *f*

underachieve *vi* rendir por debajo de su capacidad o del nivel exigido

underachiever *n* persona que no rinde al nivel de su capacidad o al nivel exigido

underapplied *adj* (overheads) subutilizado

underassess *vt* (Acc) liquidar de forma insuficiente

underassessment *n* (Tax) infravaloración de la renta a efectos fiscales

underbid [1] *vt* hacer una oferta más baja que [2] *vi* hacer una oferta más baja

undercapacity *n* subcapacidad *f*

undercapitalized *adj* descapitalizado, infracapitalizado, subcapitalizado

undercharge [1] *vt* cobrarle de menos a [2] *vi* cobrar de menos

underclass *n* subclase *f*

underconsumption *n* subconsumo *m*

undercover *adj* (audit, payment) secreto

undercut *vt* ofrecer precios más bajos que

undercutting *n* oferta a bajo precio *f*

underdeclaration *n* (Tax) declaración insuficiente *f*

underdeveloped *adj* (country) subdesarrollado

underdevelopment *n* subdesarrollo *m*

underemployed *adj* (person) subempleado; (resources, plant, space) infrautilizado; (capacity) subutilizado

underemployment *n* (of workforce) subempleo *m*; (of resources, amenities) infrautilización *f*

underestimate[1] *vt* (difficulty, importance) subestimar; (person) subestimar, menospreciar; **they ∼d the cost by $5,000** calcularon el coste Esp *or* costo AmL en 5.000 dólares menos de lo que correspondía

underestimate² *n* cálculo demasiado bajo *m*

underestimation *n* subestimación *f*, infravaloración *f*

underevaluation *n* evaluación modesta *f*

underfinanced *adj* sin suficientes fondos

underfund *vt* infradotar, no dotar *or* no proveer de suficientes fondos a

undergo *vt* (change, transformation) sufrir; **the company has undergone several changes of ownership** la compañía ha cambiado de manos varias veces; **the new system is ∼ing trials** se está probando el nuevo sistema

undergraduate *n* estudiante universitario(-a) *m,f*

underground¹ *n* (BrE, *cf* ▶**subway** AmE) metro *m*

underground² *adj* (newspaper, organization) clandestino; (economy) clandestino, sumergido; (employment) sumergido

underhanded, **underhand** BrE *adj* (person) solapado; (method, trick) poco limpio; (dealings) poco limpio, turbio

underinsured *adj* asegurado por menos del valor real

underinvest *vti* subinvertir

underinvestment *n* subinversión *f*

underlessee *n* subarrendatario(-a) *m,f*

underline *vt* (word, mistake, importance) subrayar

underling *n* subordinado(-a) *m,f*

underlining *n* subrayado *m*

underlying *adj* (trend, rate, cause, inflation) subyacente; (debt) precedente; **∼ net assets** *n pl* activos netos subsidiarios *m pl*

undermanned *adj* falto de personal, con menos personal del necesario

undermanning *n* falta de personal *f*

undermargined *adj* (account) submarginal

undermentioned *adj* abajo mencionado

underperform *vi* tener bajo rendimiento

underperforming *adj* pobre

underpin *vt* (currency) apuntalar; (system) sostener; (argument, claim) respaldar, sustentar

underpopulated *adj* poco poblado

underprice *vt* ponerle un precio demasiado bajo a

underpriced *adj* con precio demasiado bajo; **it's ∼ at $10** a 10 dólares está demasiado barato

underprivileged *adj* desfavorecido

underproduction *n* producción deficitaria *f*, subproducción *f*

underquote *vt* ofrecer a precio inferior

underrate *vt* subestimar

underreport *vt* dar pocos informes sobre

underrepresent *vt* representar insuficientemente

underrun *n* (Fin) diferencia entre dinero solicitado y obtenido *f*; **∼ costs** *n pl* costes *m pl* Esp *or* costos *m pl* AmL inferiores a los previstos

underscore *vt* (text, fact, need) subrayar

undersecretary *n* (Pol) subsecretario, -a *mf*

undersell *vt* (competitor) vender más barato que; **∼ oneself** malvenderse; **we are never undersold** vendemos más barato que nadie

underselling *n* venta a un precio más bajo *f*

undersigned *n mf* abajofirmante; **I, the ∼, declare that** el abajofirmante declara que

underspend ① *vt* (budget) gastar por debajo de
② *vi* gastar menos de lo presupuestado

underspending *n* (of budget) gasto por debajo del presupuesto *m*

understaffed *adj* (office, project) con personal insuficiente; **we're very ∼** estamos muy escasos *or* faltos de personal

understaffing *n* escasez *f or* falta *f* de personal *f*

understand *vti* entender

understanding *n* (grasp) entendimiento *m*; (interpretation) interpretación *f*; (agreement) acuerdo *m*; **come to an ∼ (with sb)** llegar a un acuerdo (con alguien); **on the ∼ that...** a condición de que...

understatement *n* (Tax) subestimación *f*; **∼ of income** *n* subestimación de la renta *f*

undersubscribed *adj* suscrito de forma insuficiente

undertake *vt* (reponsibility) asumir; (obligation) contraer; (task) emprender, acometer; **∼ to do sth** comprometerse a hacer algo

undertaking *n* (venture) empresa *f*, tarea *f*; (contract) compromiso *m*; **give an ∼ (that...)** comprometerse (a que...); **a written ∼** un compromiso por escrito

undertax *vt* gravar con un impuesto más bajo del establecido

under-the-counter *adj* (deal) poco limpio; (sale) bajo mano; **∼ goods** *n pl* mercancías que se compran/venden ilícitamente *f pl*

under the counter *adv* bajo mano

undertrade *vt* abaratar

undertrading *n* abaratamiento *m*

underuse *vt* infrautilizar

underutilize *vt* (resources) infrautilizar

undervaluation *n* infravaloración *f*, subvaloración *f*

undervalue[1] *vt* (goods, stock) subvalorar; (currency) subvalorar, subvaluar

undervalue[2] *n* (of shares) subestimación *f*

undervalued *adj* (goods, stock) subvalorado; (currency) subvalorado, subvaluado

underway *adj* en marcha; **be/get** ∼ estar/ponerse en marcha; **get a meeting** ∼ dar comienzo a una reunión

underweight *adj* que no tiene el peso requerido; **it's two kilos** ∼ le faltan dos kilos

underwrite *vt* (Ins) asegurar; (project, venture) financiar; (proposal, measures) apoyar, avalar; ∼ **a share issue** garantizar la colocación de una emisión de acciones

underwriter *n* (Ins) (person) asegurador(a) *m,f*; (company) empresa aseguradora *f*; (on second insurance) reasegurador(a) *m,f*; (on stock exchange) suscriptor(a) *m,f*

underwriting *n* (Ins) reaseguro *m*; (Stock) subscripción *f*; ∼ **account** *n* cuenta de subscripción de seguros *f*; ∼ **agreement** *n* acuerdo de suscripción *m*; ∼ **commission** *n* comisión de suscripción *f*; ∼ **fee** *n* comisión de garantía *f*

underwritten *adj* suscrito

undeveloped *adj* (resources, region) sin explotar

undifferentiated *adj* (marketing) no diferenciado; (products) indiferenciado

undischarged *adj* (bankrupt) no rehabilitado; (debt) no liquidado, sin pagar; (duty) no cumplido; (commitment) no librado, no pagado

undisclosed *adj* no revelado

undiscovered *adj* (not found) no descubierto; (not known) desconocido

undisposed of *adj* (stock) no vendido

undistributable *adj* (capital) no distribuible; ∼ **reserve** *n* BrE (*cf* ▸**restricted surplus** AmE) reserva no distribuible *f*, plusvalía restringida *f*

undistributed *adj* (allotment, balance, income, profit) no distribuido

undivided *adj* (profits) sin repartir; (property) no repartido

undo *vt* (put right) reparar, enmendar; (cancel out) anular; ∼ **the damage** reparar el daño

undocumented *adj* (worker) indocumentado, sin documentación

undue *adj* (hardship) indebido; ∼ **influence** *n* coacción *f*

unduly *adv* excesivamente

unearned *adj* (increment) no ganado; (premium) no ganado, no cobrado; (dividend, interest) no devengado; ∼ **income** *n* rentas *f pl*

UN-ECLA *abbr* (▸**United Nations Economic Commission for Latin America**) CEPAL (Comisión Económica para América Latina)

uneconomic *adj* antieconómico

unemployable *adj* inempleable

unemployed[1] *adj* desempleado, parado Esp; **be** ∼ estar en el paro Esp

unemployed[2] *n pl* desempleados *m pl*, parados Esp *m pl*

unemployment *n* desempleo *m*, paro *m* Esp; ∼ **benefit** *n* BrE (*cf* ▸**unemployment compensation** AmE) subsidio de desempleo *m*; **U**∼ **Benefit Office** *n* oficina británica para cobrar el subsidio de desempleo, ≈ oficina del paro *f* (infrml) Esp; ∼ **compensation** *n* AmE (*cf* ▸**unemployment benefit** BrE) subsidio de desempleo *m*; ∼ **figures** *n pl* cifras de desempleo *f pl*; ∼ **insurance** *n* seguro de desempleo *f*; ∼ **rate** *n* índice *m or* tasa *f* de desempleo; ∼ **statistics** *n pl* estadísticas de desempleo *f pl*

unencumbered *adj* (estate) libre de gravamen; (balance) sin cargas

unendorsed *adj* no endosado, no garantizado

unenforceable *adj* (contract) no ejecutable

unequal *adj* (exchange, trade) desigual

uneven *adj* (trend) irregular; (peformance, quality, lot) desigual

unexchangeable *adj* incambiable

unexecuted *adj* no ejecutado

unexpended *adj* (balance) no gastado

unexpired *adj* (lease) no caducado; (cost) no vencido

unexplained *adj* inexplicado

unfailing *adj* (source, supply) inagotable; (interest, support) constante

unfair *adj* (treatment, criticism, decision) injusto; (dismissal) injustificado; (competition) desleal; (trade) sucio; **that gives him an** ∼ **advantage** eso lo coloca en una injusta situación de ventaja; ∼ **labor practice** AmE, ∼ **labour practice** BrE *n* práctica laboral injusta *f*; ∼ **trading practice** *n* práctica de negocio sucio *f*

unfavourable BrE, **unfavorable** AmE *adj* (difference, exchange, balance of trade) desfavorable

unfavourably BrE, **unfavorably** AmE *adv* (regard, react) desfavorablemente

unfeasible *adj* irrealizable

unfilled *adj* (vacancy) no cubierto

u

unfinished *adj* sin terminar, inacabado; **we have some ∼ business to deal with** tenemos unos asuntos pendientes que tratar

unfit *adj* (physically) incapacitado; (incapable) incapaz; **∼ for human consumption** no apto para el consumo; **he was ∼ for the job** no estaba capacitado para el trabajo; **the doctor declared him ∼ for work** el médico dictaminó que estaba incapacitado para trabajar

unforeseeable *adj* imprevisible

unforeseen *adj* (problem) imprevisto

unformatted *adj* sin formatear

unfreeze *vt* (wages, prices) descongelar; (account) desbloquear, descongelar

unfriendly *adj* poco amistoso; **∼ takeover attempt** *n*, **∼ takeover bid** *n* intento de absorción hostil *m*

unfulfilled *adj* (order) no despachado

unfunded *adj* (borrowing, pension) no consolidado; (debt) flotante

ungeared balance sheet *n* balance de situación mal estructurado *m*

ungraded *adj* no clasificado

unhedged *adj* sin cobertura

unidimensional *adj* unidimensional

UNIDO *abbr* (▸**United Nations Industrial Development Organization**) ONUDI (Organización de las Naciones Unidas para el Desarrollo Industrial)

unification *n* unificación *f*

unified *adj* (credit) unificado

uniform *adj* (accounting) uniforme; (price) uniforme, constante; **U∼ Business Rate** *n* *tipo empresarial uniforme*; **U∼ Commercial Code** *n* Código Uniforme de Comercio *m*; **∼ practice code** *n* AmE (Stock) código de procedimiento uniforme *m*; **U∼ Resource Locator** *n* localizador uniforme de recursos *m*

uniformity *n* uniformidad *f*

unify *vt* (methods, procedures) unificar

unilateral *adj* (agreement, measure, regulation) unilateral

unilaterally *adv* unilateralmente

unimpaired *adj* (capital) libre de cargas *or* de gravámenes

unimpeachable *adj* (contract, evidence) irreprochable; (data) irrefutable, fidedigno

unimpressive *adj* (performance) mediocre

unincorporated *adj* (business, company) no incorporado

uninfected *adj* (Comp) no infectado

uninstall *vt* (software) desinstalar

uninstallation *n* (of software) desinstalación *f*

uninsurable *adj* no asegurable

uninsured *adj* no asegurado

unintended *adj* (consequences, effects) no buscado, no planificado; (investment) no planificado

uninterruptible *adj* ininterrumpible

uninvested *adj* no invertido

union *n* (act, state) unión *f*; (trade union) sindicato *m*; **join a ∼** afiliarse a un sindicato; **∼ affiliation** *n* afiliación *f* sindical *or* a un sindicato; **∼ agreement** *n* acuerdo *m or* contrato *m* sindical; **∼ dues** *n pl* cuota del sindicato *f*; **∼ member** *n* sindicalista *mf*; **∼ membership** *n* afiliación *f* sindical *or* a un sindicato; **∼ movement** *n* movimiento sindical *m*; **∼ officer** *n* dirigente sindical *mf*; **∼ official** *n* empleado(-a) sindical *m,f*; **∼ representative** *n* representante sindical *mf*; **∼ rights** *n pl* derechos sindicales *m pl*; **∼ rule** *n* norma sindical *f*; **∼ shop** *n* taller agremiado *m*

unionization *n* sindicalización *f*

unionized *adj* sindicado

unique *adj* único; **∼ reference number** *n* folio único de referencia *m*; **∼ selling proposition** *n*, **∼ selling point** *n* proposición única de venta *f*; **∼ visitor** *n* (to website) visitante unico(-a) *m,f*

unissuable *adj* (note) no emisible

unissued *adj* (capital, stock) no emitido; **∼ Treasury share** *n* bono del Tesoro en cartera *m*

unit *n* unidad *f*; **the plant manufactures 10,000 ∼s a month** la planta produce 10.000 unidades al mes; **∼ cost** *n* coste *m* Esp *or* costo *m* AmL unitario; **∼ of currency** *n* unidad monetaria *f*; **∼ holder** *n* (Stock) tenedor(a) unitario(-a) *m,f*; **∼ labor cost** AmE, **∼ labour cost** BrE *n* coste *m* Esp *or* costo *m* AmL unitario del trabajo; **∼ of measurement** *n* unidad de medida *f*; **∼ price** *n* precio *m* unitario *or* por pieza; **∼ pricing** *n* fijación de precios por unidad *f*; **∼ of trading** *n* unidad de negociación *f*; **∼ trust** *n* sociedad inversora por obligaciones *f*; **∼ value** *n* valor unitario *m*; **∼ value index** *n* índice de valor unitario *m*

unitary *adj* unitario

United Kingdom *n* Reino Unido *m*; **∼ Kingdom Trade Agency** *n* agencia *comercial del Reino Unido*

United Nations *n pl* Naciones Unidas *f pl*; **∼ Nations Association** *n* Asociación de las Naciones Unidas *f*; **∼ Nations Economic Commission for Latin America** *n* Comisión Económica para América Latina *f*; **∼ Nations Industrial Development Organization** *n* Organización de las Naciones Unidas para el Desarrollo Industrial *f*; **∼ Nations**

Organization *n* Organización de las Naciones Unidas *f*

United States *n pl* Estados Unidos *m pl*; ∼ **States Mint** *n casa de la moneda de los Estados Unidos*; ∼ **States Postal Office** *n correos de los Estados Unidos*; ∼ **States Postal Service** *n servicio postal de los Estados Unidos*

unity *n* unidad *f*

universal *adj* (general) general; (worldwide, all-purpose) universal; ∼ **agent** *n* apoderado(-a) general *m,f*; ∼ **bank** *n* banco universal *m*; ∼ **life insurance** *n* seguro de vida universal *m*; ∼ **life-policy** *n* póliza de seguro de vida universal *f*; **U**∼ **Mobile Telecommunication System** *n* sistema universal de telecomunicaciones móviles *m*; **U**∼ **Postal Union** *n* Unión Postal Universal *f*; ∼ **serial bus** *n* (Comp) bus serial universal *m*; ∼ **time coordinated** hora universal coordinada *f*

universalism *n* universalismo *m*

universe *n* (S&M) universo *m*

university *n* universidad *f*

unjustified *adj* (criticism, threat) injustificado; (text) no justificado

unknown[1] *adj* desconocido; ∼ **at this address** desconocido en esta dirección; **an** ∼ **quantity** una incógnita

unknown[2] *n* incógnita *f*

unlawful *adj* (act, picketing) ilegal; ∼ **trespass** *n entrada sin autorización en propiedad ajena*

unlawfully *adv* ilegalmente

unless *conj* a no ser que, a menos que; ∼ **otherwise agreed** salvo que se acuerde lo contrario; ∼ **otherwise provided** a menos que se disponga lo contrario; ∼ **otherwise specified** si no se especifica lo contrario

unleveraged *adj* no apalancado

unlicensed *adj* sin licencia; ∼ **broker** *n* corredor(a) de bolsa sin licencia *m,f*

unlimited *adj* (supply, powers, liability) ilimitado; (securities, accounts) sin límite; ∼ **company** *n* sociedad ilimitada *f*

unlisted *adj* (company, security) sin cotización oficial, no cotizado en la bolsa; (share, market) sin cotización oficial; (name, item) no incluido en la lista; (telephone number) AmE no incluido en la guía telefónica; **U**∼ **Securities Market** *n mercado de valores no cotizados*; ∼ **trader** *n* intermediario(-a) de valores sin cotización *m,f*; ∼ **trading** *n* operación con valores no cotizados *f*

unload *vt* (ship, cargo) descargar; (shares, goods) deshacerse de; ∼ **sth on sb** endosarle *or* encargarle algo a alguien (infrml)

unlock *vt* (file, keyboard) desbloquear; (funds) liberar

unmanageable *adj* (object) inmanejable; (person) ingobernable;

unmanufactured materials *n pl* materias primas *f pl*

unmarketable *adj* invendible

unmatched *adj* (Stock) desequilibrado

unmatured *adj* (coupon) no devengado; (debt) no vencido

unmortgaged *adj* no hipotecado, libre de hipotecas

unnamed *adj* (disk, file) innominado

unnegotiable *adj* innegociable

unnumbered *adj* (page) sin numerar

UNO *abbr* (▸**United Nations Organization**) ONU (Organización de las Naciones Unidas)

unofficial *adj* (meeting, member, report) no oficial, extraoficial; (result, announcement) no oficial, oficioso; (action, strike) no oficial; **in an** ∼ **capacity** con carácter extraoficial

unpack *vt* desembalar

unpaid *adj* (cheque) impagado, no pagado; (bill, tax) impagado; (dividend) no pagado; (work, worker) no retribuido; (leave) sin sueldo; (debt) pendiente, no liquidado; (capital) no desembolsado

unpalatable *adj* (fact, idea, truth) desagradable

unpatented *adj* no patentado

unplanned *adj* (expenditure, visit) imprevisto; (Econ) no planificado

unpostable *adj* (Acc) no registrable

unprecedented *adj* sin precedentes

unpredictable *adj* imprevisible

unprejudiced *adj* (impartial) imparcial; (not bigoted) sin prejuicios

unprepared *adj* (speech) improvisado; **be** ∼ **for sth** (not ready) no estar preparado para algo; (not expecting) no esperar algo

unpresented *adj* (cheque) no presentado, sin cobrar

unpriced *adj* sin precio

unprocessable *adj* (Comp) no procesable

unprocessed *adj* (Comp) sin procesar

unproductive *adj* (capital, business, mine) improductivo; (labour) no productivo; (discussion, meeting) infructuoso, que no conduce a nada

unprofessional *adj* (conduct) poco profesional

unprofitable *adj* (business) no rentable; (meeting) infructuoso, inútil

unprogrammed *adj* no programado

unpromising *adj* poco prometedor

unprompted *adj* (response) espontáneo

unprotested *adj* (Fin) no protestado

unpublished *adj* inédito, no publicado

u

unpunctual *adj* impuntual, poco puntual

unqualified *adj* (staff) no calificado; (accountant) sin titulación *or* título; (approval, agreement) incondicional, sin restricciones; (acceptance) sin salvedades; **the campaign was an ~ success/failure** la campaña fue un éxito/fracaso rotundo

unquestionable *adj* (authority) indiscutible; (evidence) irrefutable, incuestionable

unquoted *adj* (company, shares, securities) sin cotización oficial, no cotizado en la bolsa

unread *adj* (e-mail, message) no leído

unrealistic *adj* (expectations, target) poco realista

unrealistically *adv* de manera poco realista

unrealized *adj* (profit, gains, losses) no realizado; (potential, talent) sin explotar; (ambition, dream) que no se ha realizado *or* cumplido

unreasonable *adj* (demand, price) excesivo, poco razonable; (person, conduct, attitude) poco razonable, irrazonable

unreceipted *adj* (invoice) sin acuse de recibo

unrecoverable *adj* (Comp) irrecuperable

unredeemable *adj* (bond, debenture) no amortizable

unredeemed *adj* (pledge, bond) no redimido

unregistered *adj* (labour, stock, trademark) no registrado; **~ person** *n* (Tax) persona sin registrar *f*

unreliable *adj* (person) informal; (information) poco fidedigno

unremunerative *adj* poco remunerador

unrepealed *adj* no revocado

unreported *adj* no comunicado

unrequired *adj* (dividend) no exigido

unresolved *adj* (problem, dispute) no resuelto

unresponsive *adj* (market) insensible

unrest *n* descontento *m*, malestar *m*; (violent) disturbios *m pl*

unrestricted *adj* (authority, power, growth) ilimitado; (letter of credit) ilimitado, sin restricción; (quota) sin restricciones; (access) no restringido

unrewarding *adj* (task) ingrato, poco gratificante; (experience, discussion) infructuoso, poco fructífero

unrivalled BrE, **unrivaled** AmE *adj* incomparable, inigualable

unsafe *adj* inseguro; **~ paper** *n* (Fin) documento inseguro *m*

unsaleable BrE, **unsalable** AmE *adj* invendible

unsatisfied *adj* (demand) insatisfecho

unscheduled *adj* no programado

unscramble *vt* descifrar

unscreened *adj* no protegido

unseat *vt* (government) derribar, derrocar; **~ the board** destituir al consejo

unsecured *adj* (stock) no garantizado, sin garantía; (loan, bond) sin garantía; (overdraft) no garantizado; (creditor) no garantizado, no asegurado; (credit) descubierto; (debt) quirografario

unsettle *vt* (plans) alterar; (situation) desestabilizar

unsettled *adj* (issue, question, dispute) pendiente (de resolución), sin resolver; (debt, account) pendiente, sin saldar; (period) agitado

unsettling *adj* (news, prospect) inquietante; (effect) desestabilizador

unship *vt* (goods) desembarcar

unsigned *adj* sin firmar

unskilled *adj* (worker) no cualificado; (work) no especializado

unsocial hours *n pl* BrE horario fuera de lo normal *m*

unsold *adj* (goods) no vendido

unsolicited *adj* (goods, services, testimonial) no solicitado; (application) no pedido; **~ bulk e-mail** *n* spam *m*; **~ mail** *n* propaganda que se recibe por correo

unsorted *adj* sin clasificar

unsound *adj* (argument, position) poco sólido; (case) rebatible, impugnable; (risk) poco seguro

unspent *adj* no gastado; **~ cash balance** *n* saldo de caja no utilizado *m*

unstable *adj* (prices) variable; (government, equilibrium) inestable

unstamped *adj* (debenture) sin sellar

unstructured *adj* (interview) no estructurado

unsubsidized *adj* no subvencionado

unsubstantiated *adj* sin confirmar

unsuccessful *adj* (attempt) infructuoso, fallido, vano; **be ~** no tener éxito; **be ~ in doing sth** no lograr hacer algo; **the ~ outcome of the talks** el fracaso de las negociaciones

unsuitable *adj* (candidate) poco idóneo; (time) inconveniente

unsuited *adj* no apto

unsupported *adj* (claim, statement, allegation) sin pruebas que lo corroboren *or* respalden; (Comp) (without maintenance) sin servicio de mantenimiento; (without IT backup) sin apoyo técnico

unsustainable *adj* (development) insostenible

unsystematic *adj* poco sistemático

untapped *adj* (resources, market) sin explotar

untargeted *adj* indeterminado

untaxed *adj* libre de impuestos

untested *adj* (product, device) no probado, no puesto a prueba; (theory) no verificado *or* probado

untick *vt* BrE (*cf* ►**uncheck** AmE) (box) desactivar

untied *adj* (aid) no condicionado

untimely *adj* (announcement) inoportuno; (arrival) inoportuno, intempestivo

untrained *adj* (staff) falto de formación *or* capacitación

untransferable *adj* intransferible

untried *adj* (method) no probado; (person) no puesto a prueba; (accused person) no procesado; (case) no sometido a juicio

unused *adj* (part, credit, relief) no utilizado

unusual *adj* inusual; ~ **item** *n* partida inusual *f*

unvalued policy *n* (Ins) póliza en blanco *f*

unverified *adj* no verificado

unvouched for *adj* no garantizado

unwaged *n pl* BrE no asalariados *m pl*, personas sin trabajo remunerado *f pl*

unwanted *adj* (object) superfluo

unweighted *adj* (index, figures) sin compensación

unworkable *adj* (solution, plan) impracticable, no viable

unwritten *adj* (rule) no escrito, sobreentendido; (agreement) no escrito; (constitution, law) basado en el derecho consuetudinario

unzip *vt* (file) descomprimir

up¹ *adv* arriba; **prices are 5% ~** *o* **~ (by) 5% on last month** los precios han aumentado un 5% con respecto al mes pasado; **from $25 ~** a partir de 25 dólares; **'this side ~'** este lado hacia arriba; **it's a step ~ for me** para mí es un paso adelante; **she's not ~ to the job** no puede con el trabajo (infrml); **it's not ~ to me to decide** no soy yo quien tiene que decidir; **be ~ to one's neck in work** (infrml) estar hasta la coronilla de trabajo (infrml); **be ~ to scratch** (infrml) ser del nivel requerido

up² *adj* (infrml) (Comp) (functioning) en funcionamiento; **~ and running** listo y en marcha

up³ *vt* (prices, costs) aumentar, subir; (bid, offer) aumentar, superar

up-and-coming *adj* joven y prometedor

updatable *adj* actualizable

update¹ *vt* (manual, report, information) poner al día, actualizar; (skills) poner al día; (machinery, technology) poner al día,

modernizar; **~ sb on sth** poner a alguien al corriente *or* al tanto de algo

update² *n* actualización *f*; **give sb an ~ on sth** poner a alguien al corriente *or* al tanto de algo

updating *n* actualización *f*

up-front *adj* (cost, commitment) inicial; (payment) por adelantado; (person, statement) franco, abierto

up front *adv* (pay) por adelantado; **they want the money ~** quieren el dinero por adelantado

upgrade¹ *n* (of employee) ascenso *m*; (of job) aumento de categoría *m*; (of salaries) aumento *m*, mejora *f*; (improvement) mejora *f*; (of computer hardware) ampliación *f*; (of software) nueva versión *f*

upgrade² *vt* (modernize) modernizar; (improve) mejorar; (employee) ascender; (job) realzar; (salaries) aumentar, mejorar; (facilities) mejorar; (service) elevar el nivel de prestaciones de; (computer hardware) ampliar; (computer memory) aumentar; (software) instalar una nueva versión de

upgradeable *adj* (Comp) ampliable

upgrading *n* (improvement) mejoramiento; (Comp) evolución *f*; **the ~ of a loan** el aumento de la cuantía de un préstamo

uphold *vt* (decision, verdict) confirmar

upkeep *n* (running, maintenance) mantenimiento *m*; (costs) gastos de mantenimiento *m pl*

upload *vt* (data) cargar

upmarket¹ *adj* (product, service) de alta calidad; (goods) de primera calidad

upmarket² *adv*: **go** *o* **move ~** subir de categoría

upper *adj* (ranks, echelons) superior, más elevado; **~ cap** *n* (on tax relief) tope máximo *m*; **~ case** *n* caja alta *f*; **~ case letter** *n* letra mayúscula *f*; **~ income bracket** *n* ingresos superiores *m pl*; **~ limit** *n* (on value of shares) límite superior *m*; **~ quartile** *n* cuartil superior *m*

ups and downs *n pl* altibajos *m pl*

upselling *n* venta de un producto más avanzado o caro de lo que ha pedido un cliente

upset price *n* AmE (at auction sale) precio mínimo *m*

upside *n* ventaja *f*

upsize *vt* (company) ampliar con incremento de personal

upsizing *n* (of company) ampliación con incremento de personal *f*

upstairs market *n* AmE transacción al margen de la bolsa *f*

upstream¹ *adv* a contracorriente; **go ~** ir a contracorriente

upstream² *adj* (industry) abastecedor; (float) contracorriente; ~ **direct marketing** *n* marketing directo a contracorriente *m*; ~ **loan** *n préstamo de una subsidiaria a la empresa matriz*

upsurge *n* (in demand, production) aumento *m*

upswing *n* (in demand, production) alza *f*

uptick *n* (Stock) *operación a precio más alto que una anterior*

uptime *n* (Comp) tiempo *m* productivo *or* de operación

up-to-date *adj* (figures, information, report) al día, actualizado; (method) más actual; **be ~ (with sth)** estar al día *or* al corriente (de algo); **bring sb ~** poner a alguien al día; **bring sth ~** actualizar algo; **keep sth/sb ~** mantener algo/a alguien al día; **the most ~ equipment** el equipo más avanzado

up-to-sample *adj* conforme a los resultados de la muestra

up-to-the-minute *adj* (information) al instante; (technology) del momento

uptrend *n* tendencia al alza *f*

upturn *n* (in demand, production) repunte *m*, mejora *f*; **an ~ in the economy** un repunte en la economía

UPU *abbr* (▸**Universal Postal Union**) UPU (Unión Postal Universal)

upward¹ *adj* (movement) ascendente; **give an ~ thrust to interest rates** subir los tipos de interés; ~ **compatibility** *n* (Comp) compatibilidad ascendente *f*; ~ **mobility** *n* movilidad social ascendente *f*; ~ **pressure** *n* (on budget) presión ascendente *f*; ~ **revision** *n* (of prices) revisión al alza *f*; ~ **spiral** *n* (in wages, prices) espiral ascendente *f*; ~ **trend** *n* (Stock) tendencia *f* alcista *or* al alza

upward² *adv* AmE ▸**upwards** BrE

upwardly mobile *adj* de movimiento social ascendente

upwards BrE, **upward** AmE *adv* (move) hacia arriba; ~ **of 30 years/$100** más de 30 años/100 dólares; **revise an estimate ~** revisar un presupuesto al alza

urban *adj* (area, centre) urbano; ~ **planning** *n* urbanismo *m*; ~ **planner** *n* urbanista *mf*; ~ **renewal** *n* remodelación urbana *f*; ~ **sprawl** *n* extensión urbana *f*

urbanization *n* urbanización *f*

urbanize *vt* urbanizar

urge *vt* exhortar; ~ **sb to do sth** exhortar a alguien a hacer algo

urgency *n* (of situation, problem) urgencia *f*; **treat sth as a matter of ~** tratar algo con la mayor urgencia

urgent *adj* (matter, case, letter) urgente; **be in ~ need of sth** necesitar algo urgentemente

urgently *adv* urgentemente, con urgencia; **'staff ~ needed'** se necesita personal con urgencia

URL *abbr* (▸**Uniform Resource Locator**) URL *m* (localizador uniforme de recursos)

URN *abbr* (▸**unique reference number**) folio único de referencia *m*

u/s *abbr* (▸**unsorted**) sin clasificar

US *abbr* (▸**United States**) EE.UU. (Estados Unidos); ~ **federal finance** *n finanzas federales de los Estados Unidos*; ~ **federal government paper** *n papel del gobierno federal de los Estados Unidos*; ~ **Treasury bond market** *n mercado de bonos del Tesoro de los Estados Unidos*; ~ **Treasury market** *n mercado del Tesoro de los Estados Unidos*

usability *n* (Comp) funcionalidad *f*

usable *adj* utilizable

usance *n* plazo de pago de una letra internacional *m*; **at thirty days' ~** en un plazo de treinta días; ~ **bill** *n* letra a plazo *f*; ~ **credit** *n* crédito a plazos *m*

USB *abbr* (▸**universal serial bus**) (Comp) USB *m* (bus serial universal)

use¹ *n* (of machine, method) uso *m*, empleo *m*, utilización *f*; (application, function) uso *m*; **come into ~** empezar a utilizarse; **go out of ~** dejar de utilizarse; **have the ~ of sb's office** poder usar la oficina de alguien; **be in ~** (machine) estar funcionando *or* en funcionamiento; (method) emplearse, usarse; **instructions for ~** instrucciones, modo de empleo; **make ~ of sth** hacer uso de algo; **be (of) ~ to sb** serle útil *or* de utilidad a alguien, servirle a alguien

use² *vt* (for task, purpose) usar; (avail oneself of) utilizar, usar, hacer uso de; **use up** *vt* (supplies) agotar

used *adj* (second-hand) usado, de segunda mano; ~ **assets** *n pl* bienes de segunda mano *m pl*

useful *adj* (invention, tool, advice, information) útil; (experience) útil, provechoso; **come in ~** BrE ser útil, venir bien; ~ **economic life** *n* vida económica útil *f*; ~ **life** *n* (of asset, machine) vida útil *f*

user *n* usuario(-a) *m,f*; ~ **attitude** *n* actitud del usuario *f*; ~ **charge** *n* aportación *f or* pago *m* del usuario; ~ **cost** *n* coste *m* Esp *or* costo *m* AmL de uso; ~ **fee** *n* cuota del usuario *m*; ~**-friendliness** *n* facilidad *f* de uso *or* de manejo; ~**-friendly** *adj* de uso fácil; ~ **group** *n* grupo de usuarios *m*; ~ **guide** *n* guía de usuario *f*; ~ **interface** *n* interfaz de usuario *m*; ~ **network** *n* red de usuarios *m*; ~**-oriented** *adj* orientado al usuario; ~ **profile** *n* perfil del usuario *m*; ~ **strategy** *n* estrategia de usuario *f*; ~ **support** *n* asistencia a los usuarios *f*, apoyo técnico para usuarios *f*; ~**-unfriendly** *adj* difícil de usar

username *n* (Comp) nombre de usuario

USM *abbr* (▸**United States Mint**) *casa de la moneda de los Estados Unidos*; (▸**Unlisted Securities Market**) *mercado de valores no cotizados*

USP *abbr* (▸**unique selling proposition** *o* **point**) proposición única de venta *f*

USPO *abbr* (▸**United States Postal Office**) *correos de los Estados Unidos*

USPS *abbr* (▸**United States Postal Service**) *servicio postal de los Estados Unidos*

usual *adj* (method, response, comment) acostumbrado, habitual, usual; (place, time, route) de siempre, de costumbre; **as** ~ como de costumbre, como siempre; **'business as** ~**'** estamos abiertos; **on the** ~ **terms** en condiciones normales; **with the** ~ **proviso** con los requisitos establecidos; ~ **first name** *n* nombre habitual *m*

usufruct *n* usufructo *m*

usufructuary *n* usufructuador(a) *m,f*, usufructuario(-a) *m,f*

usurer *n* usurero(-a) *m,f*

usurious *adj* (capital) usurario

usury *n* usura *f*

UTC *abbr* (▸**universal time coordinated**, ▸**coordinated universal time**) HUC (hora universal coordinada)

utilitarian *adj* (practical) utilitario

utilitarianism *n* utilitarismo *m*

utility *n* (usefulness) utilidad *f*; (public service) empresa de servicio público *f*; ~ **company** *n* empresa de servicio público *f*; ~ **function** *n* función de utilidad *f*; ~ **program** *n* programa de utilidades *m*; **utilities sector** *n* sector de servicios públicos *m*

utilization *n* utilización *f*; (of natural resources) empleo *m*; ~ **percent** *n* porcentaje de utilización *m*

utilize *vt* utilizar; (natural resources) emplear

utilized *adj* (capacity) utilizado, aprovechado

utmost¹ *adj* (greatest) mayor, sumo; **with the** ~ **care** con sumo cuidado; **of the** ~ **importance** de la mayor importancia; ~ **good faith** *n* principio de buena fe *m*

utmost² *n* máximo *m*; **do one's** ~ **(to do sth)** hacer todo lo posible (por hacer algo); **to the** ~ al máximo

UVI *abbr* (▸**unit value index**) índice de valor unitario *m*

U/W *abbr* (▸**underwriter**) (person) asegurador(a) *m,f*; (company) empresa aseguradora *f*; (on second insurance) reasegurador(a) *m,f*; (on stock exchange) suscriptor(a) *m,f*

u

Vv

vacancy *n* (job) vacante *f*; (in hotel) habitación libre *f*; **fill a** ~ cubrir una vacante; **a** ~ **exists for an electrician** se necesita *or* se busca electricista; **'vacancies'** (jobs) 'ofertas de trabajo'; (rooms) 'hay habitaciones'; **'no vacancies'** 'completo'

vacant *adj* (post) vacante; (building, premises) desocupado, vacío; (land) inocupado; (hotel room) libre; ~ **lot** *n* solar desocupado *m*; ~ **possession** *n derecho del comprador de encontrar la vivienda libre una vez escriturada*

vacation *n* AmE (*cf* ▶**holiday** BrE) vacaciones *f pl*; **go on** ~ ir de vacaciones; **take a** ~ tomarse unas vacaciones; ~ **entitlement** *n* derecho a vacaciones *m*; ~ **leave** *n* permiso de vacaciones *m*; ~ **pay** *n* paga de vacaciones *f*; ~ **period** *n* periodo de vacaciones *m*

vacationer *n* AmE (*cf* ▶**holidaymaker** BrE) veraneante *mf*

vacuum *n* vacío *m*; ~-**packed** *adj* envasado al vacío; ~ **packaging** *n* envase vacío *m*

valid *adj* (contract, passport, argument) válido; (excuse, criticism) legítimo, válido; (Law) (document) vigente

validate *vt* (contract, document, claim) validar; (theory) dar validez a, validar; (Law) legalizar

validation *n* (of contract, document, theory) validación *f*; (Law) legalización *f*

validity *n* validez *f*; ~ **period** *n* plazo de validez *m*

valorization *n* valorización *f*

valorize *vt* (goods) tasar

valuable *adj* (asset, resource, advice) valioso; (time) precioso

valuables *n pl* artículos de valor *m pl*

valuation *n* (of property) evaluación *f*, peritaje *m*; (of inventory, stocks) evaluación *f*; (of shares) tasación *f*; **make a** ~ **of sth** hacer una evaluación de algo; ~ **allowance** *n* descuento *m*; (Acc) bonificación *f*; ~ **basis** *n* base de valoración *f*; ~ **clause** *n* (Ins) cláusula de valoración *f*; ~ **price** *n* precio de valoración *m*; ~ **report** *n* tasación *f*, avalúo *f* AmL

value¹ *n* valor *m*; ~ **for money** una buena relación calidad-precio; **that's good** ~ **(for money)** está muy bien de precio; **gain** *o* **increase in** ~ aumentar de valor, revalorizarse; **go down in** ~ disminuir de

valor; **lose (in)** ~ depreciarse; **no** ~ **declared** sin declaración de valor; **goods to the** ~ **of £500** mercancías por un valor de 500 libras; ~-**added** *n* valor *m* agregado *or* añadido Esp; ~-**added network** *n* red de valor agregado *f*; ~-**added reseller** *n* (Comp) revendedor de valor agregado *m*; ~-**added service** *n* servicio de valor agregado *m*; **V**~ **Added Tax** *n* BrE impuesto *m* sobre el valor agregado AmL *or* añadido Esp; ~ **analysis** *n* análisis del valor *m*; ~ **at cost** *n* valor *m* al coste Esp *or* al costo AmL; ~ **date** *n* fecha de valor *f*; ~ **engineering** *n* estudio de los componentes de un artículo *m*; ~ **judgment** *n* juicio de valor *m*; ~ **position** *n* (Stock) posición de precio *f*; ~ **test** *n* (Tax) prueba de valor *f*

value² *vt* (assets, property, business) tasar, valorar, avaluar AmL; (opinion, advice) valorar, apreciar; ~ **sth at sth** tasar *or* valorar *or* avaluar AmL algo en algo

valued *adj* (client) apreciado; ~ **policy** *n* (Ins) póliza de valor declarado *f*

valueless *adj* sin valor

VAN *abbr* (▶**value-added network**) red de valor agregado *f*

vanguard *n* vanguardia *f*; **in the** ~ a la vanguardia

vapourware BrE, **vaporware** AmE *n* programas vapor *m pl*

VAR *abbr* (Comp) (▶**value-added reseller**) revendedor de valor agregado *m*

variability *n* variabilidad *f*

variable¹ *adj* (capital, charge, costs, expenses) variable; ~ **interest rate** *n* tasa de interés variable *f*; ~ **lending rate** *n* tasa de préstamo variable *f*; ~ **rate** *n* tasa variable *f*; ~-**rate mortgage** *n* hipoteca de tasa variable *f*

variable² *n* variable *f*

variance *n* discrepancia *f*, desacuerdo *m*; (in statistics) varianza *f*; (Acc) desviación *f*; **be at** ~ **with sb** discrepar con *or* de alguien; **be at** ~ **with sth** discrepar de algo; ~ **analysis** *n* análisis de desviaciones *m*

variation *n* (fluctuation, change, permutation) variación *f*; (difference) diferencias *f pl*

varied *adj* variado

variety *n* (diversity) variedad *f*; **a large/wide** ~ **of colours** una gran variedad de colores; **for a** ~ **of reasons** por varias razones

variometer *n* variómetro *m*

vary 1 *vt* (routine) variar, cambiar; (terms) modificar

2 *vi* variar; ~ **from sth** desviarse *or* apartarse de algo; **the price varies from week to week** el precio varía de una semana a la otra; **vary with sth** variar según algo

varying *adj* (amounts) variable; **with ~ degrees of success** con mayor o menor éxito

vast *adj* (size, wealth) inmenso, enorme; (sum) enorme; (range) muy extenso, amplísimo; (experience, knowledge) vasto

VAT *abbr* BrE (▶**Value Added Tax**) IVA *m* (impuesto sobre el valor agregado AmL *or* añadido Esp); ~ **payment** *n* BrE pago del IVA *m*; ~ **registered trader** *n* BrE comerciante que repercute IVA *mf*; ~ **registration number** *n* BrE número de inscripción del IVA *m*; ~ **return** *n* BrE declaración del IVA *f*

vault *n* (of bank) cámara acorazada *f*, bóveda de seguridad *f* AmL; ~ **cash** *n* efectivo en caja *m*; ~ **reserve** *n* AmE reserva en banco central *f*

VC *abbr* (▶**valuation clause**) cláusula de valoración *f*; (▶**variable charge**) cargo variable *m*; (▶**venture capital**) capital-riesgo *m*; (▶**venture capitalist**) capitalista de riesgo *mf*

VCR *abbr* (▶**videocassette recorder**) video AmL *m*, vídeo *m* Esp

VDT *abbr* (▶**video** o **visual display terminal** AmE, *cf* ▶**VDU** BrE) UDV *f* (unidad de despliegue visual)

VDU *abbr* (▶**visual display unit**) (*cf* ▶**VDT** AmE) UDV *f* (unidad de despliegue visual)

vector *n* vector *m*

veer *vi* (vehicle, opinion, conversation) virar, desviarse; ~**off** o **away from the subject** desviarse del tema

vega *n* (Stock) vega *m*

vehicle *n* vehículo *m*; ~ **hire** *n*, ~ **leasing** *n* alquiler de vehículos *m*

velocity *n* velocidad *f*; ~ **of circulation** *n* (Fin) velocidad de circulación *f*

velvet *n* (Fin) ganancia especulativa *f*

vendee *n* cesionario(-a) *m,f*

vending *n* venta *f*, distribución *f*; ~ **machine** *n* máquina expendedora *f*

vendor *n* vendedor(a) *m,f*; ~ **company** *n* empresa vendedora *f*; ~**-financed** *adj* financiado por el vendedor; ~ **rating** *n* calificación de proveedores *f*

ventilate *vt* (subject, argument) ventilar, airear

ventilation *n* ventilación *f*

venture *vt* (money) arriesgar; (opinion, guess) aventurar; **venture on** *vt* (project) aventurarse en

venture[1] *n* operación *f*, empresa *f*; (Fin) especulación eventual *f*; (Ins) riesgo *m*; ~ **capital** *n* capital-riesgo *m*; ~ **capital company** *n* compañía de capital-riesgo *f*; ~ **capital corporation** *n* corporación de capital-riesgo *f*; ~ **capitalist** *n* capitalista de riesgo *mf*; ~ **management** *n* administración del riesgo *f*; ~ **team** *n* (S&M) equipo encargado de un nuevo producto *m*

venue *n* (for meeting, conference) lugar *m*

VER *abbr* (▶**voluntary export restraint**) contención voluntaria a la exportación *f*

verbal *adj* (agreement, communication, offer, warning) verbal

verbatim[1] *adv* palabra por palabra

verbatim[2] *adj* literal, textual

verdict *n* (Law) veredicto *m* (opinion) juicio *m*; **bring in** o **return a ~** (jury) emitir un veredicto; **deliver a ~** (magistrate) pronunciar sentencia, fallar; **give one's ~ on sth/sb** dar su opinion sobre algo/alguien; **a ~ of guilty/not guilty** veredicto de culpabilidad/ inocencia

verge *n* borde *m*; **be on the ~ of an agreement** estar al punto de llegar a un acuerdo, estar a las puertas de un acuerdo; **be on the ~ of bankruptcy/ruin** estar al borde de la bancarrota/ruina

verifiable *adj* verificable

verification *n* (checking) verificación *f*; (confirmation) confirmación *f*, corroboración *f*; ~ **of accounts** *n* verificación de cuentas *f*; ~ **phase** *n* etapa *f* or fase *f* de verificación

verify *vt* (check) verificar; (confirm) confirmar, corroborar

versatile *adj* (person, tool, material) versátil

versatility *n* versatilidad *f*

version *n* versión *f*; ~ **control** *n* (Comp) gestión de versiones *f*

verso *n* (of page) dorso *m*, verso *m*

versus *prep* frente a, en oposición a; (Law) contra

vert *abbr* (▶**vertical**) vert (vertical)

vertical *adj* vertical; ~ **integration** *n* integración vertical *f*; ~ **market** *n* mercado vertical *m*; ~ **merger** *n* fusión vertical *f*; ~ **organization** *n* organización vertical *f*; ~ **planning** *n* planificación vertical *f*; ~ **portal** *n* portal vertical *m*; ~ **spread** *n* diferencial vertical *m*

very high frequency *n* frecuencia muy alta *f*

very important person *n* persona muy destacada *f*

vest *vt* investir; ~ **sb with sth** (authority) investir a alguien de algo

vested *adj* (rights) inalienable; ~ **benefits** *n pl* beneficios otorgados *m pl*; ~ **interest** *n* (Fin, Law) derecho adquirido *m*; (personal stake) interés (personal) *m*; **have a** ~ **interest in sth** tener un interés personal en algo; ~ **interests** *n pl* intereses creados *m pl*

vet *vt* (applicant) someter a investigación; (application, proposal) examinar, investigar

veterinary *adj* (certificate, controls) veterinario

veto¹ *n* veto *m*; **have a** ~ tener derecho de veto; **put a** ~ **on sth** vetar algo; **use** *o* **exercise one's** ~ ejercer el veto

veto² *vt* vetar

vetting *n* (of application, proposal) examinación *f*, investigación *f*

vexed *adj* (question, subject, issue) polémico, controvertido

VGA *abbr* (▸**video graphics adaptor**) VGA (adaptador de gráficos de video AmL *or* vídeo Esp, adaptador videográfico); ~ **card** *n* tarjeta VGA *f*

VHF *abbr* (▸**very high frequency**) VHF (frecuencia muy alta)

via *prep* (by way of) por; (by means of) por medio de

viability *n* viabilidad *f*

viable *adj* viable

vicarious *adjn* indirecto; ~ **liability** *n* responsabilidad civil subsidiaria *f*

vice-chairman *n*, **vice-president** *n* vicepresidente(-a) *m,f*

vice-secretary *n* vicesecretario(-a) *m,f*

vice versa *adv* viceversa

vicious *adj* (circle, cycle) vicioso

victim *n* víctima *f*

victimization *n* persecución *f*

victimize *vt* victimizar

victualling *n* abastecimiento *m*

video¹ *n* video *m* AmL, vídeo *m* Esp; ~ **camera** *n* videocámara *f*; ~ **card** *n* tarjeta *f* de video AmL *or* de vídeo Esp; ~ **conference** *n n* videoconferencia *f*; ~ **conference over IP** *n n* videoconferencia por IP *f*; ~ **conferencing** *n* videoconferencia *f*, ~ **disc** BrE, ~ **disk** AmE *n* videodisco *m*; ~ **display** *n* pantalla *f* de video AmL *or* de vídeo Esp; ~ **display terminal** *n* AmE (*cf* ▸**visual display unit** BrE) unidad de despliegue visual *f*; ~ **graphics adaptor** *n* adaptador *m* de gráficos de video AmL *or* vídeo Esp, adaptador videográfico *m*; ~ **graphics array** *n* matriz *f* de video AmL *or* vídeo Esp gráfico; ~**-mail** *n* videocorreo *m*; ~**-on-demand** *n* video *m* AmL *or* vídeo *m* Esp a

petición *or* a la carta; ~ **piracy** *n* videopiratería *f*; ~**-RAM** *n* video *m* AmL *or* vídeo *m* Esp RAM; ~ **recorder** *n* aparato *m* de video AmL *or* de vídeo Esp; ~ **terminal** *n* terminal *m* de video AmL *or* de vídeo Esp; ~ **webcast** *n* emisión por la Red *f*

video² *vt* grabar en video AmL *or* vídeo Esp

videocassette *n* videocasete *m*; ~ **recorder** *n* aparato *m* de video AmL *or* de vídeo Esp; ~ **recording** *n* grabación en videocasete *f*

videophone *n* videoteléfono *m*

videosurveillance *n* vigilancia *f* por video AmL *or* por vídeo Esp

videotape¹ *n* cinta *f* de video AmL *or* de vídeo Esp; ~ **recorder** *n* aparato *m* de video AmL *or* de vídeo Esp; ~ **recording** *n* grabación *f* en video AmL *or* en video Esp

videotape² *vt* grabar en video AmL *or* en video Esp

videotex *n* videotex *m* Esp, videotexto *m* Esp, videtex *m* AmL

vie *vi* competir; **we were vying with two other companies for the contract** competíamos con otras dos compañías por el contrato

view¹ *n* (opinion, attitude) opinión *f*, parecer *m*; **in my** ~ en mi opinión; **in** ~ **of sth** en vista de algo; **have sth in** ~ tener algo en mente; **take a different** ~ adoptar una postura diferente; **take a gloomy** ~ **of the situation** tener una opinión pesimista de la situación; **with a** ~ **to doing sth** con miras a hacer algo; ~ **screen** *n* videopantalla *f*

view² **[1]** *vt* (accounts) examinar; (property, TV programme) ver; (regard) ver, considerar; (Comp) visionar **[2]** *vi* ver la televisión

viewdata *n pl* videodatos *m pl*

viewed page *n* (on Internet) página *f* visitada *or* vista

viewer *n* (of television) telespectador(a) *m,f*; (Comp) espectador(a) *m,f*

viewing *n* (of property) visita *f*; '~ **by appointment only'** sólo visitas concertadas previamente; ~ **figures** *n pl* niveles de audiencia *m pl*; ~ **habits** *n pl* hábitos televisivos *m pl*; ~ **public** *n* telespectadores *m pl*; ~ **room** *n* sala de visionado *f*

viewpoint *n* punto de vista *m*

vignette *n* viñeta *f*

violate *vt* (agreement, law, right) violar

violation *n* (of agreement, law, right) violación *f*; **in** ~ **of sth** en violación de algo

VIP *abbr* (▸**very important person**) VIP *mf* (persona muy destacada)

viral marketing *n* (Comp) marketing viral *m*

virtual *adj* (Comp) virtual; ∼ **bank** *n* banco electrónico *m*; ∼ **community** *n* comunidad virtual *f*; ∼ **coupon** *n* vale electrónico *m*; ∼ **environment** *n* entorno virtual *m*; ∼ **learning** *n* educación en línea *f*; ∼ **mall** *n* centro comercial virtual *m*; ∼ **marketplace** *n* mercado virtual *m*; ∼ **office** *n* oficina virtual *f*; ∼ **private network** *n* red privada virtual *f*; ∼ **reality** *n* realidad virtual *f*; ∼ **reality modelling language** BrE, ∼ **reality modeling language** AmE *n* lenguaje de modelación de realidad virtual *m*; ∼ **shopping cart** *n* cesta virtual *f*; ∼ **store** *n* tienda *f* virtual or electrónica, cibertienda *f*; ∼ **storefront** *n* escaparate virtual *m*; ∼ **ticketing** *n* venta de billetes electrónica *f*

virtue *n* virtud *f*; **by** ∼ **of sth** en virtud de algo

virus *n* virus *m*; ∼ **checker** *n* programa *m* or software *m* antivirus; ∼**-free** *adj* sin virus

visa *n* visado *m*

vis-à-vis *prep* con respecto a

viscosity *n* viscosidad *f*

viscous *adj* (supply, demand) viscoso

visible *adj* (export, import, trade balance) visible

visibles *n pl* visibles *m pl*

vision *n* visión *f*

visit[1] *n* (to person, place, website) visita *f*

visit[2] *vt* (person, place, website) visitar

visitation *n* inspección *f*

visiting *adj* visitante; ∼ **card** *n* BrE (*cf* ▸**calling card** AmE) tarjeta de visita *f*

visitor *n* (to person, place, website) visitante *mf*; ∼**'s tax** *n* impuesto de no residente *m*

visual *adj* (appeal, impact) visual; ∼ **aids** *n pl* material visual *m*; ∼ **arts** *n pl* artes visuales *m pl*; ∼ **display terminal** *n* AmE, ∼ **display unit** *n* BrE unidad de despliegue visual *f*

visuals *n pl* elementos visuales *m pl*

vital *adj* (equipment, supplies) esencial, fundamental; (factor, issue) decisivo, de vital importancia; **a matter of** ∼ **importance** un asunto de vital importancia; **it is absolutely** ∼ **that it is kept secret** es imprescindible mantenerlo en secreto; **be** ∼ **to sth/sb** ser de vital importancia para algo/alguien

vitiate *vt* (contract, agreement) viciar

viz *adv* a saber

VLR *abbr* (▸**variable lending rate**) tasa de préstamo variable *m*

v-mail *abbr* (▸**video-mail**) videocorreo *m*

vocation *n* vocación *f*

vocational *adj* profesional; ∼ **guidance** *n* orientación profesional *f*; ∼ **training** *n* formación profesional *f*

VOD *abbr* (▸**video-on-demand**) video *m* AmL or vídeo *m* Esp a petición or a la carta

vogue *n* moda *f*; **be in** ∼ estar de moda or en boga; **come into/go out of** ∼ ponerse/pasar de moda

voice[1] *n* voz *f*; **the workers want a** ∼ **in management decisions** los trabajadores quieren participar en las decisiones de la dirección; ∼**-activated** *adj* activado por la voz; ∼ **mail** *n* audiomensajería *f*; ∼ **mailbox** *n* buzón telefónico *m*; ∼ **message** *n* mensaje vocal *m*; ∼ **messaging** *n* mensajería vocal *f*; ∼**-over** *n* voz en off *f*; ∼ **recognition** *n* reconocimiento de la voz *m*; ∼ **recognition software** *n* software de reconocimiento de la voz *m*

voice[2] *vt* (opinion, concern, anger) expresar

void[1] *adj* (invalid) nulo, inválido; **make sth** ∼ anular or invalidar algo; **to be** ∼ **of sth** estar desprovisto or falto de algo; ∼ **contract** *n* contrato nulo *m*; ∼ **policy** *n* póliza nula *f*

void[2] *vt* (contract, agreement, cheque) anular, invalidar

voidable *adj* anulable

voidance *n* anulación *f*

vol. *abbr* (▸**volume**) volumen *m*

volatile *adj* (situation, market) inestable, volátil; (capital) volátil, fugaz

volatility *n* volatilidad *f*

voltage *n* voltaje *m*; ∼ **regulator** *n* regulador de voltaje *m*

volume *n* (amount) cantidad *f*, volumen *m*; (of business, orders, sales, sound) volumen *m*; (book) tomo *m*, volumen *m*; ∼ **deleted** *n* (Stock) volumen borrado *m*; ∼ **discount** *n* descuento por volumen *m*; ∼ **mailing** *n* envío masivo de correo *m*; ∼ **trading** *n* (Stock) contratación por volumen *f*

voluntarism *n* voluntarismo *m*

voluntary *adj* (attendance, compliance, arbitration, group) voluntario; (organization) de beneficencia; ∼ **bankruptcy** *n* bancarrota voluntaria *f*; ∼ **contributions** *n pl* BrE (to National Insurance) aportaciones *f pl* or cuotas *f pl* voluntarias; ∼ **controls** *n pl* controles voluntarios *m pl*; ∼ **export restraint** *n* contención voluntaria a la exportación *f*; ∼ **liquidation** *n* liquidación voluntaria *f*; **go into** ∼ **liquidation** hacer liquidación voluntaria; ∼ **redundancy** *n* BrE baja incentivada *f*; ∼ **unemployment** *n* desempleo *m* or paro *m* Esp voluntario; ∼ **winding-up** *n* liquidación voluntaria *f*; ∼ **work** *n* trabajo voluntario *m*; ∼ **worker** *n* voluntario(-a) *m,f*

volunteer[1] *n* voluntario(-a) *m,f*; ∼ **development worker** *n* cooperante para el desarrollo *mf*

volunteer² **1** *vt* (information, services) ofrecer

2 *vi* ofrecerse; ~ **for sth** ofrecerse para algo; ~ **to do sth** ofrecerse a hacer algo

vortal *n* (Comp) vortal *m*, portal vertical *m*

vote¹ *n* (ballot cast) voto *m*, sufragio *m*; (total votes cast) votos *m pl*; (act of voting) votación *f*; (right to vote) sufragio *m*, derecho *m* de *or* al voto; **call for a** ~ pedir una votación; **cast one's** ~ emitir su voto; **decide the matter by a** ~ decidir el asunto por votación; **give sb/gain the** ~ conceder a alguien/conseguir el derecho de *or* al voto; **put sth to the** ~ someter algo a votación; **take a** ~ **on sth** someter algo a votación; **the** ~ **was 12 to 4 in favour** BrE *o* **favor** AmE el resultado de la votación fue de 12 votos a favor y 4 en contra; **win by 2** ~**s** ganar por dos votos; ~ **against** *n* voto en contra *m*; ~ **of confidence** *n* voto de confianza *m*; ~ **in favor** AmE, ~ **in favour** BrE *n* voto a favor *m*; ~ **netting** *n* rendimiento en votos *m*; ~ **of no confidence** *n* voto de censura *m*

vote² **1** *vt* (support, choose) votar, votar por; (elect) elegir por votación; **we** ~**d her treasurer** la elegimos tesorera por votación; ~ **sb into office** votar por *or* a alguien para un cargo; **he was** ~**d onto the board** fue elegido por votación para integrar la junta; ~ **sb out of office** votar para reemplazar a alguien en su cargo

2 *vi* votar; ~ **against sth** votar en contra de algo; ~ **by a show of hands** BrE votar a mano alzada; ~ **for sb** votar por *or* a alguien; ~ **for sth** votar en favor de algo; ~ **on sth** someter algo a votación; **we** ~**d to continue the strike** votamos que continuase

la huelga; **members** ~**d to increase subscriptions** los socios votaron por aumentar la cuota; **vote down** *vt* (bill, proposal) rechazar (por votación); **vote in** *vt* elegir (por votación); **vote out** *vt* no reelegir; **vote through** *vt* (bill, proposal) aprobar (por votación)

voter *n* votante *m,f*; ~ **turnout** *n* número de votantes *m*

voting *n* votación *f*; ~ **booth** *n* cabina *f* electoral *or* para votar; ~ **paper** *n* papeleta (de voto) *f*; ~ **procedures** *n pl* mecanismos de votación *m pl*; ~ **right** *n* derecho de voto *m*; ~ **security** *n* valor con derecho de voto *m*; ~ **share** *n* acción con derecho de voto *f*; ~ **stock** *n* acciones con derecho de voto *f pl*

voucher *n* (receipt) comprobante *m*; (cash substitute) vale *m*

vouch mark *n* (Acc) prueba testimonial *f*

VP *abbr* (►**vice-president**) VP (vicepresidente)

VPN *abbr* (►**virtual private network**) red privada virtual *f*

VRAM *abbr* (►**video-RAM**) VRAM *m* (video *m* AmL *or* vídeo *m* Esp RAM)

VRML *abbr* (►**virtual reality modelling language** BrE, ►**virtual reality modeling language** AmE) VRML *m* (lenguaje de modelación de realidad virtual)

VTR *abbr* (►**videotape recording**) VTR (grabación en video AmL *or* en vídeo Esp)

vulnerable *adj* vulnerable

vulture fund *n* fondo buitre *m*

Ww

wage[1] *n* salario *m*, sueldo *m*; (paid daily) jornal *m*; **~s** paga *f*; **earn a good ~** ganar bien, ganar un buen sueldo; **be on a low ~** ganar poco, tener un salario bajo; **~ agreement** *n* convenio salarial *m*; **~-and-price guidelines** *n pl* directrices de salarios y precios *f pl*; **~ arbitration** *n* arbitraje salarial *m*; **~ bracket** *n* categoría salarial *f*; **~ ceiling** *n* límite superior de salario *m*; **~ claim** *n* reclamación salarial *f*; **~ control** *n* regulación salarial *f*; **~ cost** *n* coste *m* Esp *or* costo *m* AmL salarial; **~ demand** *n* demanda salarial *f*; **~ differentials** *n pl* diferenciales de salarios *m pl*; **~ drift** *n* deriva *f or* desviación *f* salarial; **~ earner** *n* asalariado(-a) *m,f*; **~ explosion** *n* explosión salarial *f*; **~ freeze** *n* congelación salarial *f*; **~ gap** *n* diferencial de salarios *m*; **~ incentive** *n* incentivo salarial *m*; **~ increase** *n* aumento salarial *m*; **~ indexation** *n* indización salarial *f*; **~ inflation** *n* inflación de salarios *f*; **~ lag** *n* desfase salarial *m*; **~ level** *n* nivel de sueldo *m*; **~ negotiations** *n pl* negociaciones salariales *f pl*; **~ policy** *n* política salarial *f*; **~-price inflation spiral** *n* espiral inflacionista de salarios y precios *f*; **~-price spiral** *n* espiral salarios-precios *f*; **~ restraint** *n* moderación salarial *f*; **~ round** *n* serie de negociaciones salariales *f*; **~ scale** *n* escala *f* de salarios *or* de sueldos; **~ settlement** *n* liquidación salarial *f*; **~ spread** *n* escala *f* de salarios *or* de sueldos; **~ structure** *n* estructura de los salarios *f*; **~ subsidy** *n* subsidio salarial *m*; **~-tax spiral** *n* espiral del impuesto sobre los salarios *f*; **~ theory** *n* teoría salarial *f*

wage[2] *vt* (war) hacer; **~ a campaign against sth** hacer (una) campaña contra algo; **~ war on inflation** luchar contra *or* hacerle la guerra a la inflación

waged *n pl* BrE asalariados *m pl*

wager[1] *n* apuesta *f*

wager[2] *vt* apostar

wait[1] *vti* esperar; **~ in line** AmE (*cf* ►**queue up** BrE) hacer cola; **wait for** *vt* esperar

wait[2] *n* espera *f*; **~ days** *n pl* días de espera *m pl*; **~ list** *n* AmE lista de espera *f*

wait-and-see policy *n* política de seguir los acontecimientos *f*

waiter *n* BrE (Stock) camarero *m*

waiting *adj* (period, time) de espera; **play a ~ game** retrasarse a propósito *or* deliberadamente; **~ list** *n* lista de espera *f*

waive *vt* (right, privilege) renunciar a; (rule) no aplicar; (condition) no exigir; (Tax) eximir

waiver *n* (of rule) no aplicación *f*, exención *f*; (of payment) exoneración *f*; (of claim, right) renuncia *f*; (Tax) exención *f*; (document) documento de renuncia *m*; **~ clause** *n* cláusula de renuncia *f*

walkout *n* huelga laboral *f*

walkover *n* (infrml) victoria fácil *f*

wall *n* (freestanding) muro *m*; (of building, room) pared *f*; (barrier) barrera *f*; **go to the ~** (infrml) (company, business) irse a pique (infrml)

wallflower *n* (jarg) acción de escasa aceptación *f*

Wall Street Crash *n colapso de la bolsa de Wall Street*

Wall-Streeter *n* persona que trabaja en Wall Street *f*

WAN *abbr* (►**wide area network**) red de área extendida *f*

wane *vi* (interest, popularity) decaer, disminuir, declinar; **support for the strike has ~d** la huelga ha perdido apoyo

wangle *vt* (infrml) (job) agenciarse (infrml), arreglárselas para conseguir; **he ~d his way onto the committee** se las arregló para entrar en el comité

want *n* (requirement, need) necesidad *f*; (lack) falta *f*; (penury) miseria *f*, indigencia *f*; **~ ad** *n* AmE anuncio clasificado *m*

WAP *abbr* (►**wireless application protocol**) WAP *m* (protocolo de aplicación sin cables *or* de aplicación inalámbrica); **~ phone** *n* teléfono WAP *m*; **~ portal** *n* portal WAP *m*; **~ server** *n* servidor WAP *m*; **~ technology** *n* tecnología WAP *f*; **~ user** *n* usuario(-a) WAP *m,f*

war *n* guerra *f*; **wage ~ on sth** hacerle la guerra a algo; **~ babies** *n pl* (jarg) *bonos y valores de empresas relacionadas con la defensa*; **~ chest** *n fondos destinados a un fin especial*

ward off *vt* (attack) rechazar

warehouse[1] *n* almacén *m*; **~ charges** *n pl* gastos de almacenaje *m pl*; **~ supervisor** *n* supervisor(a) de almacén *m,f*

warehouse[2] *vt* almacenar

warehouseman n AmE (cf ▸storeman
BrE) almacenista mf, guarda mf or jefe(-a)
m,f de almacén

warehousing n almacenamiento m

warez n pl (infrml) software pirateado m

warm adj caliente; ~ **restart** n (Comp)
arranque en caliente m

warm-up n calentamiento m; ~ **session** n
sesión de calentamiento f

warn vt advertir; ~ **sb about** o **of sth**
advertir a alguien de algo, prevenir a
alguien contra algo; ~ **sb against sth/sb**
prevenir a alguien contra algo/alguien; ~
sb against doing sth advertir a alguien que
no haga algo; ~ **sb that...** advertir a alguien
que...

warning n (advice, threat) advertencia f;
(notificación) aviso m; **she was given an
official** ~ la amonestaron oficialmente;
without ~ sin previo aviso; ~ **device** n
dispositivo de alerta m; ~ **indicator** n
indicador de aviso m; ~ **list** n (Bank) lista
de alerta f; ~ **sign** n señal de peligro f

warrant¹ n (receipt) comprobante m;
(guarantee) garantía f; (authorization)
autorización legal f; (negotiable security)
warrant m; (voucher) vale m; ~ **of attorney**
n poder m; ~ **discounting** n descuento con
certificado m; ~ **for payment** n mandato
de pago m; ~ **holder** n (for buying shares)
titular de un certificado mf; ~ **issue** n
emisión garantizada f

warrant² vt (guarantee) garantizar; (justify)
justificar

warranted adj garantizado; (Ins)
comprobado

warrantee n beneficiario(-a) de un aval
m,f

warranter n garante mf

warranty n garantía f; **be under** ~ estar
en garantía; ~ **card** n tarjeta de garantía f;
~ **of title** n garantía de propiedad f

wash sale n (Stock) transacción ficticia f,
venta aparente f

WASP abbr (▸wireless application
service provider) proveedor de servicios
WAP m

wastage n (loss) pérdida f; (waste)
desperdicio m, despilfarro m

waste¹ n (of fuel, materials) desperdicio m,
derroche m; (refuse) residuos m pl, desechos
m pl; **a** ~ **of effort** un esfuerzo inútil; **it's a**
~ **of money** es tirar el dinero; **a** ~ **of time**
una pérdida de tiempo; ~ **disposal** n
eliminación de desperdicios f; ~ **dumping**
n vertido de desperdicios m; ~
management n gestión de los residuos f;
~ **paper** n papelote m; ~ **product** n
desperdicio m; ~ **recycling** n reciclado de

residuos m; ~ **treatment** n tratamiento de
los residuos m; ~**-water treatment** n
depuración de aguas residuales m

waste² vt (money, electricity) despilfarrar,
derrochar; (time) perder; (space)
desaprovechar, desperdiciar; (opportunity)
desperdiciar; (talents, efforts) desperdiciar,
malgastar

wasteful adj (method, process)
antieconómico; (expenditure) no rentable;
(person) despilfarrador, derrochador

wasteland n tierra baldía f, yermo m

wasting asset n (Acc) activo consumible
m; (Stock) activo no renovable m

watch¹ [1] vt (value of shares) vigilar; (film,
programme) mirar, ver; (television) ver, mirar;
~ **one's back** estar alerta; **the staff are
always** ~**ing the clock** los empleados están
siempre pendientes del reloj; **investors are**
~**ing the situation with interest** los
inversores están siguiendo la situación
muy de cerca; ~ **one's step** tener cuidado;
I've got to ~ **the time** tengo que estar
atento a la hora; **we'll have to** ~ **what we
spend** tendremos que mirar (mucho) lo que
gastamos
[2] vi (look on) mirar; (pay attention) prestar
atención; **watch for** vt esperar; **watch out
for** vt (exercise caution with) tener cuidado con;
(look carefully for) prestar atención a

watch² n (observation) vigilancia f; **keep a
close** ~ **on sth/sb** vigilar algo/a alguien
atentamente

watchdog n (person) guardián(-ana) m,f;
(organization) organismo de control m; ~
committee n comité de vigilancia m; (Pol)
comité de control m

watcher n observador(a) m,f

watchlist n (Stock) lista de control f

watchman n vigilante mf

watchword n (motto) lema m, consigna f;
(password) contraseña f

water n agua f; **not hold** ~ (excuse, theory)
no tener fundamento; **be in/get into hot** ~
estar/meterse en un apuro; **keep one's head
above** ~ mantenerse a flote; **pour** o **throw
cold** ~ **over sth** ponerle trabas a algo;
spend money like ~ gastar dinero como si
fuera agua; **test the** ~ tantear el terreno; ~
company n compañía de agua f; ~
damage n daño por agua f; ~**-generated**
adj (electricity) hidrogenerado; ~ **pollution** n
contaminación del agua f; ~ **power** n
energía hidráulica f; ~ **purification** n
depuración del agua f; ~ **supply** n
suministro de agua m; ~ **transportation** n
transporte por agua m; ~ **treatment** n
tratamiento del agua m

watered adj (capital) inflado, desvalorizado;
(stock) mojado

watermark *n* (on banknote) filigrana *f*

watermarked *adj* (banknote) filigranado

waterproof *adj* (packing) impermeable; (paper) a prueba de humedad

watertight *adj* (seal, container) hermético; (method, plan) infalible; (argument) irrebatible, sin fisuras; (contract, law) sin lagunas *or* vacíos

wave *n* onda *f*; **make ∼s** hacer olas, causar problemas; **∼ power** *n* potencia de onda *f*

wavelength *n* longitud de onda *f*; **be on the same ∼** estar en la misma onda

waybill *n* carta de porte *f*

ways and means *n pl* medios *m pl*, métodos *m pl*; **∼ and means committee** *n* AmE *comité gubernamental que supervisa las decisiones y la legislación en materia de finanzas*

WB *abbr* (▸**waybill**) carta de porte *f*

WBT *abbr* (▸**Web-based training**) formación *f or* capacitación *f* en línea

w.c. *abbr* (▸**without charge**) gratis, sin cargo

wd. *abbr* (▸**warranted**) garantizado

W/d *abbr* (▸**warranted**) (Ins) comprobado

weak *adj* (market) débil

weaken ⊡ *vt* (currency, economy, government, power) debilitar ⊡ *vi* (currency) caer; **the pound has ∼ed against the dollar** la libra ha caído frente al dólar

weakest link theory *n* teoría de que el hilo se rompe por lo más delgado

weakness *n* debilidad *f*

wealth *n* (money) riqueza *f*; (affluence) opulencia *f*; (large quantity) abundancia *f*; **a ∼ of information/opportunities** una abundancia de información/oportunidades; **∼ creation** *n* creación de riqueza *f*; **∼ distribution** *n* distribución de la riqueza *f*; **W∼ of Nations** *n* riqueza de las naciones *f*; **∼ tax** *n* impuesto sobre el patrimonio *m*

wear and tear *n* desgaste natural *m*

wearout factor *n* factor de desgaste *m*

weather¹ *n* tiempo *m*; **∼ permitting** si el tiempo lo permite; **∼ report** *n* boletín meteorológico *m*

weather² *vt* (crisis, scandal) sobrellevar, capear; (recession) capear

Web *n* Web *f*, Red *f*; **∼ ad broker** *n* intermediario(-a) de publicidad en línea *m,f*; **∼ address** *n* dirección Internet *f*; **∼ advertising** *n* publicidad *f* en línea *or* en la Red; **∼ application** *n* aplicación web *f*; **∼-assisted selling** *n* venta asistida por la Red *f*; **∼ authoring** *n* creación de páginas web *f*; **∼ authoring program** *n* programa de creación de páginas web *m*; **∼-based application** *n* aplicación web *f*; **∼-based**

training *n* formación *f or* capacitación *f* en línea; **∼ broker** *n* intermediario(-a) de publicidad en línea *m,f*; **∼ browser** *n* navegador (de Internet) *m*; **∼ call centre** BrE, **∼ call center** AmE *n* centro de llamadas en el Internet *m*; **∼ chat** *n* charla (en línea) *f*; **∼ client** *n* cliente web *mf*; **∼ commerce** *n* comercio en línea *m*, cibercomercio *m*; **∼ content** *n* contenido *m* de la Red *or* de la Web; **∼ content developer** *n* programador(a) de contenidos de la Web *m,f*; **∼ content management** *n* gestión del contenido de la Web *f*; **∼ design** *n* diseño de sitios web *m*; **∼ designer** *n* diseñador(a) de sitios web *m,f*; **∼ developer** *n* desarrollador(a) web *m,f*; **∼ document** *n* documento de Web *m*; **∼ farm** *n* servicio de alojamiento web a través de servidores múltiples; **∼ front-end** *n* interfaz usuario-web *m*; **∼ hosting** *n* alojamiento web *m*; **∼ hosting server** *n* servidor de alojamiento web *m*; **∼ media broker** *n* intermediario(-a) de publicidad en línea *m,f*; **∼ page** *n* página web *f*; **∼ phone** *n* teléfono Internet *m*; **∼ presence** *n* presencia en Internet *f*; **∼-ready** *adj* preparado para Internet; **∼ ring** *n* anillo web *m*; **∼ search** *n* búsqueda en el Internet *f*; **∼ server** *n* servidor web *m*; **∼ session** *n* sesión de Internet *f*; **∼ shop** *n* tienda *f* electrónica *or* en línea; **∼ space** *n* espacio web *m*; **∼ space provider** *n* proveedor de espacios web *m*; **∼ telephony** *n* telefonía Internet *f*; **∼ tutor** *n* proveedor(a) *m,f* de formación en línea *or* de capacitación en línea

webcam *n* webcam *m*

webcast¹ *n* emisión *f* por la Red *or* por Internet

webcast² *vt* transmitir por la Red

webcasting *n* difusión *f* por la Red *or* por Internet

web-enable *vt* preparar para la Web

web-enabled application *n* aplicación web *f*

webification *n* conversión en formato web *f*

webify *vt* (information, text page, file) convertir en formato web

webinar *n* seminario on-line *m*

webmaster *n* administrador(a) de Web *m,f*, webmaster *mf*

website *n* website *m*, sitio web *m*; **∼ hosting** *n* alojamiento web *m*; **∼ plan** *n* mapa de un sitio web *f*

web-surf *vi* navegar

web-surfing *n* navegación *f*, travesía por Internet *f*

webzine *n* revista *f* web *or* electrónica, ciberrevista *f*

weed out *vt* (errors, items) eliminar; (applicants) eliminar, descartar

week *n* semana *f*; **£500 a** *o* **per** ~ 500 libras semanales *or* por semana; **a five-day/ 35 hour** ~ una semana (laboral) de cinco días/35 horas; **a** ~ **in advance** una semana por adelantado; **pay sb by the** ~ pagar a alguien semanalmente; ~ **order** *n* (Stock) orden para una semana *f*

weekday *n* día *m* laborable *or* de semana; **on** ~s entre semana, los días de semana

weekend *n* fin de semana *m*; **have a long** ~ hacer puente

weekly[1] *adj* (wage, rent, return) semanal

weekly[2] *adv* semanalmente

w.e.f. *abbr* (▸**with effect from**) con efecto a partir de

weigh [1] *vt* (load) pesar; (factors, arguments, evidence) sopesar

[2] *vi* (load) pesar; **your inexperience will** ~ **against you** tu falta de experiencia será un factor en tu contra; **this** ~**ed heavily in her favour** BrE *o* **favor** AmE esto la favoreció enormemente; **weigh up** *vt* (situation) considerar, ponderar; ~ **up the pros and cons** sopesar los pros y los contras

weight[1] *n* peso *m*; **add** *o* **lend** ~ **to sth** darle más peso a algo; **his opinions carry no** ~ sus opiniones no tienen peso; **pull one's** ~ hacer su parte; **throw one's** ~ **behind sth** apoyar algo con dedicación; ~ **limit** *n* peso máximo autorizado *m*; ~**s and measures** *n pl* pesos *m pl* y medidas *f pl*

weight[2] *vt* (option positions) ponderar

weighted *adj* (average, index, distribution) ponderado; ~ **average cost** *n* coste *m* Esp *or* costo *m* AmL medio ponderado

weighting *n* ponderación *f*

welcome[1] *adj* (guest) bienvenido; (change, news) grato; **the extra money will be most** ~ el dinero extra vendrá muy bien

welcome[2] *n* bienvenida *f*; **the proposal got a frosty** ~ **from the union** la propuesta tuvo una fría acogida por parte del sindicato; ~ **message** *n* (Comp) mensaje de bienvenida *m*; ~ **page** *n* (Comp) página de bienvenida *m*; ~ **speech** *n* discurso de bienvenida *m*

welcome[3] *vt* (visitor, delegation) darle la bienvenida a; ~ **the opportunity to do sth** agradecer la oportunidad de hacer algo

welfare *n* (well-being) bienestar *m*; (state aid) asistencia *f*; (payment) prestaciones sociales *f pl*; **be on** ~ AmE (*cf* ▸**be on benefits** *o* **the dole** BrE) vivir de subsidios sociales; **go on** ~ AmE (*cf* ▸**go on benefits** *o* **the dole** BrE) recibir prestaciones de la Seguridad Social; ~ **agency** *n* oficina de bienestar social *f*; ~ **benefit** *n* subsidio de bienestar social *m*; ~ **department** *n* departamento

de bienestar social *m*; ~ **economics** *n* economía del bienestar *f*; ~ **fund** *n* fondo de bienestar *m*; ~ **legislation** *n* legislación social *f*; ~ **payment** *n* asistencia *f or* prestación *f* social; ~ **recipient** *n* AmE (*cf* ▸**social-security recipient** BrE) beneficiario(-a) de asistencia social *m,f*; ~ **service** *n* servicio de bienestar social *m*; ~ **state** *n* estado del bienestar *m*; ~ **trap** *n* trampa del bienestar *f*; ~ **worker** *n* asistente social *mf*

welfarist *n* defensor(a) del estado del bienestar *m,f*

well *adv* bien; ~**-balanced** *adj* equilibrado; ~**-educated** *adj* culto, instruido; ~**-established** *adj* consolidado; ~**-grounded** *adj* bien fundado; ~**-informed** *adj* bien informado; ~**-known** *adj* conocido; ~**-meaning** *adj* bienintencionado; ~**-motivated** *adj* bien motivado; ~ **off** *adj* en buena posición; ~**-packaged** *adj* bien embalado; ~**-paid** *adj* bien pagado; ~**-placed** *adj* bien situado; ~**-positioned** *adj* bien colocado; ~**-stocked** *adj* bien surtido

wellhead: ~ **cost** *n* (in oil industry) coste *m* Esp *or* costo *m* AmL en pozo; ~ **price** *n* precio en la cabeza de pozo *m*

Weltanschauung *n* concepción global *f*

western *adj* oeste, del oeste, occidental; **W**~ **European Union** *n* Unión Europea Occidental *f*; ~**-style** *adj* de estilo occidental

westernized *adj* occidentalizado; **become** ~ occidentalizarse

wet *adj* (goods, stock) líquido

wetware *n* (infml) (Comp) (developers) desarrolladores *m pl*; (users) usuarios *m pl*

WEU *abbr* (▸**Western European Union**) UEO (Unión Europea Occidental)

W formation *n* (Stock) configuración en W *f*

WFSE *abbr* (▸**World Federation of Stock Exchanges**) *federación mundial de bolsas*

WFTU *abbr* (▸**World Federation of Trade Unions**) *federación mundial de sindicatos*

WFUNA *abbr* (▸**World Federation of United Nations Associations**) FMANU (Federación Mundial de Asociaciones de las Naciones Unidas)

wgt *abbr* (▸**weight**) peso *m*

what you see is what you get *n* lo que ves es lo que (ob)tienes, *programa que muestra por pantalla el documento tal y como será impreso*

wheel *n* rueda *f*; **with her at the** ~, **the company...** con ella en frente, la compañía...; **set** *o* **put (the)** ~**s in motion**

poner las cosas en marcha; **∼s of government** n pl maquinaria administrativa f; **∼s within wheels** n pl entresijos m pl

wheel and deal vi (infrml) trapichear (infrml)

wheeler-dealer n (infrml) trapichero(-a) m,f (infrml)

wheeling and dealing n (infrml) trapicheos m pl (infrml)

whereas conj (while, on the other hand) mientras que, en tanto que; (Law) (since) considerando que, por cuanto; **∼ clauses** n pl considerandos m pl

whiplash n (Stock) latigazo m

whipsaw¹ n AmE (cf ▸**double-edged sword** BrE) arma de doble filo m

whipsaw² vt AmE (Stock) perder por partida doble

whipsawed adj AmE (Stock) con pérdidas por partida doble

whistle n (of factory) sirena f; **blow the ∼ on sb** delatar a alguien; **blow the ∼ on sth** revelar algo; **∼-blower** n (infrml) empleado que informa sobre actividades ilícitas en su empresa; **∼-blowing** n (infrml) revelación de actividades ilícitas en el organismo en el que se trabaja

white adj blanco; **∼-collar crime** n delito de guante blanco m; **∼-collar job** n puesto de trabajo de oficina m; **∼-collar union** n sindicato de empleados m; **∼-collar worker** n administrativo(-a) m,f, empleado(-a) de oficina m,f, oficinista mf; **∼ goods** n pl electrodomésticos m pl; **∼ information** n información financiera f; **∼ knight** n (infrml) (in takeover) persona respetuosa f; **∼ land** n (jarg) terreno sin calificar m; **∼ market** n mercado legalizado m; **∼ noise** n ruido blanco m; **W∼ Paper** n BrE Libro Blanco m

whiteboard n pizarra f vileda® or blanca

whitewash vt (infrml) encubrir

whittle away vt (funds, resources) ir mermando; (influence) ir reduciendo or disminuyendo; (rights) ir menoscabando

whittle away at vt ir minando or socavando

whittle down vt (costs, commissions) reducir poco a poco; **we've ∼d the applicants down to five** hemos reducido el número de candidatos a cinco

whizz kid n (infrml) chico(-a) prodigio m,f, joven promesa mf

whole¹ adj entero; **∼ life insurance** n seguro de vida entera m; **∼ life insurance policy** n póliza de vida entera f; **∼ years** n pl años completos m pl

whole² n todo m; **the situation has to be seen as a ∼** hay que enfocar la situación

como un todo or de manera global; **the business is to be sold as a ∼** el negocio se va a vender como una unidad; **this affects the industry as a ∼** esto afecta a la industria en general; **on the ∼** en general

wholesale¹ adj al por mayor; (rejection) en bloque; **∼ cuts in the budget** recortes radicales or drásticos en el presupuesto; **∼ bank** n banco mayorista m; **∼ banking** n banca f mayorista or al por mayor or al mayoreo AmL; **∼ business** n comercio al por mayor m; **∼ cooperative** n cooperativa de mayoristas f; **∼ dealer** n comerciante mayorista mf; **∼ delivery** n entrega al por mayor f; **∼ goods** n pl mercancías al por mayor f pl; **∼ manufacture** n confección f al por mayor or al mayoreo AmL; **∼ market** n mercado al por mayor m; **∼ merchant** n comerciante al por mayor mf; **∼ price** n precio al por mayor m; **∼ price index** n índice de precios al por mayor m; **∼ price inflation** n inflación de los precios al por mayor f; **∼ trade** n comercio al por mayor m; **∼ trader** n negociante al por mayor mf

wholesale² adv (buy, sell) al por mayor; **they rejected the proposals ∼** rechazaron las propuestas en bloque

wholesale³ n venta al por mayor f; **by ∼** al por mayor

wholesale⁴ ① vt vender al por mayor ② vi venderse al por mayor

wholesaler n mayorista mf

wholesaling n venta al por mayor f

wholly adv totalmente, completamente; **∼ dependent** totalmente dependiente; **∼ and exclusively** total y exclusivamente; **∼-owned** adj (corporation, subsidiary) en propiedad absoluta

whse abbr (▸**warehouse**) almacén m

whys and wherefores n pl los porqués m pl

wide adj (in dimension) ancho; (experience, coverage, powers) amplio; (variety) grande; (selection, area) amplio, extenso; **be ∼ of the mark** ser muy erróneo; **∼ area network** n red de área extendida f; **∼ monetary base** n base monetaria extendida f; **∼ opening** n (Stock) diferencial desusadamente amplio m; **∼ range** n amplia gama f; **∼-ranging** adj de amplia cobertura

widely adv (vary) mucho; **these products are now ∼ available** estos productos se consiguen con facilidad ahora; **a ∼-held view** una opinión muy extendida; **∼ recognized** ampliamente reconocido; **a ∼-used brand of detergent** una marca de detergente muy usada

w

widen *vt* (gap, tax base, range, debate, scope) ampliar; (interests) diversificar; (road, entrance) ensanchar

widening *n* (of influence) ampliación *f*, aumento *m*; (of road, entrance) ensanchamiento *m*

widespread *adj* difundido

widow *n* viuda *f*; ~'**s bereavement allowance** *n* deducción por viudedad *f*; ~-**and-orphan stock** *n* acción defensiva *f*; ~'**s pension** *n* viudedad *f*

widower *n* viudo *m*

width *n* anchura *f*

wild card *n* (Comp) comodín *m*

wildcat *adj* (project, speculation) arriesgado; (venture) descabellado; ~ **drilling** *n* perforación exploratoria *f*; ~ **strike** *n* huelga salvaje *f*

wilful BrE, **willful** AmE *adj* (misconduct, neglect) intencionado, deliberado; (damage) causado con premeditación; ~ **default** *n* incumplimiento voluntario *f*; ~ **misrepresentation of facts** *n* desfiguración voluntaria de los hechos *f*

will *n* testamento *m*; **make a** ~ hacer testamento

willful AmE ►**wilful** BrE

win¹ ① *vt* (customers, prize) ganar; (contract) conseguir; (promotion, pay increase) conseguir, obtener; (support) conseguir, ganarse; **they've won business from their competitors** le han quitado clientes a la competencia; ~ **sb's favor** AmE *o* **favour** BrE ganarse *or* obtener el favor de alguien; ~ **one's spurs** dar pruebas de sus aptitudes
② *vi* ganar; **win back** *vt* recuperar; **win over** *vt* convencer

win² *n* victoria *f*

wind *n* viento *m*; **find out/know which way the** ~ **is blowing** averiguar/saber por dónde van los tiros (infrml); **get** ~ **of sth** enterarse de algo; **in the** ~ en el ambiente; **take the** ~ **out of sb's sails** desanimar a alguien; ~**s of change** *n pl* vientos de cambio *m pl*; ~ **power** *n* fuerza del viento *f*

wind down ① *vt* (company) terminar gradualmente; (production, trade) reducir paulatinamente
② *vi* (activity) llegar a su fin

windfall *n* sorpresa caída del cielo *f*; ~ **benefit** *n* beneficio *m* imprevisto *or* inesperado; ~ **gain** *n* ganancia imprevista *f*; ~ **loss** *n* pérdida inesperada *f*; ~ **profit** *n* ganancia inesperada *f*; ~ **profits tax** *n* impuesto sobre beneficios extraordinarios *m*; ~ **tax** *n* impuesto extraordinario *m*

winding-up *n* (of corporation) liquidación *f*, disolución *f*; (of meeting) conclusión *f*, finalización *f*; ~ **arrangements** *n pl*

acuerdos de disolución *m pl*; ~ **order** *n* orden de disolución *f*; ~ **sale** *n* venta de liquidación *f*

window *n* (of building, on computer screen) ventana *f*; (of shop) escaparate *m*; (of sales counter, envelope) ventanilla *f*; **go out (of) the** ~ (plans) venirse abajo, desbaratarse; **put sth in the** ~ poner algo en el escaparate; ~ **display** *n* escaparate *m*; ~-**dressing** *n* (in annual accounts) alteración falaz de un balance *f*, manipulación de la contabilidad *f*; ~ **envelope** *n* sobre con ventanilla *m*; ~ **of opportunity** *n* ventana de oportunidad *f*; ~ **sticker** *n* cinta adhesiva para las ventanas *f*

window-shop *vi* mirar los escaparates; **go** ~**ping** ir a mirar los escaparates

wind up ① *vt* (meeting) concluir, finalizar; (company) cerrar, liquidar; (partnership) liquidar
② *vi* (project) concluir, terminar

wine *n* vino *m*; ~ **industry** *n* industria vinícola *f*; ~ **list** *n* carta de vinos *f*; ~ **merchant** *n* vinatero(-a) *m,f*; ~-**producing area** *n* área vinícola *f*

winner *n* (person) ganador(a) *m,f*; (product, idea) éxito *m*; **they reckon they're onto a** ~ **with their latest idea** creen que su última idea va a ser un exitazo (infrml); ~ **takes all** todo para el ganador

winning *adj* (candidate) ganador; ~ **streak** *n* (infrml) racha de triunfos *f*

winnings *n pl* ganancias *f pl*

win-win *adj* (situation) donde se gana de todas maneras

wipe *vt* (tape, disk) borrar; ~ **sth from a tape** borrar algo de una cinta; ~ **the slate clean** hacer borrón y cuenta nueva; **wipe out** *vt* (deficit) cancelar; (lead, advantage) eliminar

wire *n* (for electricity, telecommunications) cable *m*; (infrml) (telegram) telegrama *m*; **down to the** ~ hasta el último momento; ~-**house** *n* (infrml) *correduría en la que las sucursales están conectadas con la sed principal mediante cables telefónicos y telegráficos*; ~ **service** *n* AmE (*cf* ►**news agency** BrE) agencia de noticias *f*; ~ **transfer** *n* giro telegráfico *m*

wired *n* (population, homes) conectado

wireless *adj* inalámbrico; ~ **application protocol** *n* protocolo *m* de aplicación sin cables *or* de aplicación inalámbrica; ~ **application server** *n* servidor WAP *m*; ~ **application service provider** *n* proveedor de servicios WAP *m*; ~ **commerce** *n* comercio sin cables *m*; ~ **e-commerce** *n* comercio electrónico sin cables *m*; ~ **Internet** *n* Internet sin cables *m*; ~ **portal** *n* portal sin cables *m*; ~ **Web** *n* Internet sin cables *m*

wiretapping n escucha telefónica f

wish list n lista de deseos f

withdraw [1] vt (funding, support, service, application, motion, charges) retirar; (offer) rescindir; (permission) cancelar; (product) retirar de la venta; (coin, note) retirar de la circulación; (demand) renunciar a; (statement, allegation) retirar, retractarse de; ~ **money (from an account)** retirar or sacar dinero (de una cuenta)
[2] vi (from business activity) retirarse

withdrawal n (of funding, support, capital) retirada f, retiro m AmL; (of application, candidate, appeal) retirada f; (of product) retirada de la venta f; (of coins, notes) retirada de la circulación f; ~ **warrant** dinero or fondos m; ~ **from stocks** n retirada de existencias f; ~ **notice** n aviso m de retirada or retiro m AmL de fondos; ~ **slip** n resguardo de reintegro m Esp, recibo de retiro de fondos m AmL; ~ **warrant** n autorización para retirar fondos f

withhold vt (payment, funds) retener; (consent, permission, assistance) negar; (information) denegar

withholding n (of securities, taxes) retención fraudulenta f; ~ **tax** n AmE impuesto retenido m

within prep dentro de; ~ **the allotted time frame** dentro del tiempo permitido; **keep** ~ **the law** mantenerse dentro la ley; ~ **a period of** en un periodo de; ~ **prescribed limits** dentro de los límites prescritos; ~ **the prescribed time** dentro del plazo fijado; ~ **sb's reach** al alcance de alguien; ~ **a week** dentro de una semana

without prep sin; ~ **charge** gratis, sin cargo; ~ **engagement** sin compromiso; ~ **a hitch** sin ningún tropiezo; ~ **any liability on our part** sin ninguna responsabilidad por nuestra parte; ~ **obligation** sin obligación; ~ **prejudice** sin prejuicio; ~ **previous warning** sin advertencia previa; ~ **privileges** sin privilegios; ~ **respite** (from work) sin respiro; ~ **warning** sin aviso

with-profits endowment assurance n seguro dotal con beneficios m

witness¹ n (person) testigo mf; (evidence) testimonio m; **in** ~ **whereof** en fe or en testimonio de lo cual; ~ **for the defence** BrE, ~ **for the defense** AmE n testigo mf de descargo or de la defensa; ~ **for the prosecution** n testigo de cargo mf

witness² vt (signature) atestiguar; (will) atestiguar la firma de; (document) firmar como testigo; (change, event) ser testigo de; (crime, accident) presenciar, ser testigo de

wizard n (Comp) experto(-a) m,f

wobbly adj (recovery) tambaleante

wolf n (jarg) (Stock) seductor m

wood n (material) madera f; (area of trees) bosque m; **be out of the** ~**s** estar a salvo

woodland n zona forestal f

word n palabra f; **a** ~ **of advice** un consejo; **break one's** ~ faltar a su palabra; **give one's** ~ dar su palabra; **go back on one's** ~ faltar a su palabra; **have a** ~ **with sb about sth** hablar de algo con alguien; **keep one's** ~ cumplir su palabra; **put in a** ~ **for sb** decir unas palabras en favor de alguien; **take sb at his/her** ~ tomarle la palabra a alguien; **a** ~ **of warning** una advertencia; ~ **count** n recuento de palabras m; ~**-of-mouth advertising** n publicidad boca a boca f; ~**-of-mouth marketing** n marketing boca a boca m; ~**s per minute** n pl palabras por minuto f pl; ~ **processing** n tratamiento m or procesamiento m de textos; ~**-processing center** AmE, ~**-processing centre** BrE n centro de tratamiento de textos m; ~**-processing software** n software de procesamiento de textos m; ~**-processing system** n sistema de procesamiento de textos m; ~ **processor** n procesador de textos m; ~ **wrap** n salto de línea m

wording n (of contract, letter, paragraph) redacción f; (of message, note) términos m pl; (of question) formulación f

work¹ n (labour, tasks, output) trabajo m; (employment) trabajo m, empleo m; (of machine) marcha f; (product, single item) obra f; **at** ~ (person) en el trabajo; (influence) en juego; **get (down) to** o **go to** o **set to** ~ **(on sth)** empezar a trabajar (en algo); **go to** ~ ir a trabajar or al trabajo; **be in** ~ tener trabajo; **be out of** ~ estar sin trabajo; **put** o **set sb to** ~ poner a alguien a trabajar; **start/finish** ~ **at seven** entrar a trabajar or al trabajo/ salir del trabajo a las siete; ~ **backlog** n volumen de trabajo pendiente m; ~ **classification** n clasificación laboral f; ~ **cycle** n ciclo de trabajo m; ~ **ethic** n ética del trabajo f; ~ **experience** n experiencia laboral f; ~ **flow** n flujo de trabajo m; (Comp) flujo de operaciones m; ~ **history** n historial laboral m; ~**-in-process** AmE, ~**-in-progress** BrE n trabajo en curso m; ~**-life balance** n equilibrio entre la vida profesional y privada m; ~ **permit** n permiso de trabajo m; ~ **plan** n plan de trabajo m; ~ **prospects** n pl perspectivas de trabajo f pl; ~ **sampling** n muestreo del trabajo m; ~ **schedule** n horario de trabajo m; ~ **stoppage** n interrupción del trabajo f; ~ **study** n estudio de trabajo m

work² [1] vi (person) trabajar; (machine, system) funcionar; (plan, measures) surtir efecto; ~ **against/in favor** AmE o **favour** BrE **of sth/sb** obrar en contra de/a favor de algo/alguien; ~ **alongside each other**

⋯▶

trabajar codo con codo; ~ **alternate weekends** trabajar fines de semana alternos; ~ **as part of a team** trabajar como parte de un equipo; ~ **closely with sb** trabajar en estrecha colaboración con alguien; ~ **for sb** trabajar para alguien; ~ **for a living** trabajar para ganarse la vida; ~ **full time** trabajar a tiempo completo; ~ **hard** trabajar mucho or duro; ~ **in the media** trabajar en medios de comunicación; ~ **in partnership with sb** trabajar en sociedad con alguien; ~ **in shifts** trabajar por turnos; ~ **in tandem with sb** trabajar a medias con alguien; ~ **overtime** trabajar horas extras; ~ **to a very tight schedule** trabajar en un horario muy preciso; ~ **together** trabajar juntos, colaborar; ~ **unsocial hours** trabajar en horarios insociables; **we ~ a 35 hour week** nuestra semana laboral es de 35 horas. 2 *vt* (person) hacer trabajar; (machine) hacer funcionar; (patent) explotar; **work off** *vt* (debt) amortizar, pagar (trabajando); **work on** *vt* trabajar en; **work out** 1 *vt* (percentage, probability) calcular; (solution) idear, encontrar; (plan) elaborar, idear; (procedure) idear, desarrollar; (settlement) lograr; (terms, details) concretar 2 *vi* (turn out) salir, resultar; ~ **out well/badly** salir or resultar bien/mal; **work out at** *vt* (bill) (venir a) sumar; **it ~s out at $75 a gram/a head** sale (a) 75 dólares el gramo/por cabeza; **the complete package ~s out at £420** el paquete completo sale 420 libras or sale por 420 libras Esp

workable *adj* (arrangement, solution, plan) factible, viable

workaholic *n* adicto(-a) al trabajo *m,f*

workday *n* AmE (*cf* ►**working day** BrE) (weekday) día *m* laborable or de trabajo; (part spent at work) jornada laboral *f*

worker *n* trabajador(a) *m,f,* operario(-a) *m,f,* obrero(-a) *m,f;* ~ **buy-out** *n* compra por los trabajadores *f;* ~**s' collective** *n* colectivo de trabajadores *m;* ~**s' compensation** *n* compensación a los trabajadores *f;* ~**s' compensation insurance** *n* seguro de compensaciones laborales *m;* ~ **involvement** *n* implicación *f* de los empleados or de los trabajadores; ~ **representation** *n* representación de los trabajadores *f*

workforce *n* (of company) personal *m,* planta laboral *f;* (of country) población activa *f*

working *n* (functioning) funcionamiento *m;* (gainful employment) trabajo *m;* ~ **account** *n* cuenta de trabajo *f;* ~ **area** *n* (in office) zona de trabajo *f;* ~ **asset** *n* activo circulante *m;* ~ **capital** *n* capital circulante *m;* ~ **conditions** *n pl* condiciones de trabajo *f pl;* ~ **control** *n* control efectivo *m;* ~ **copy** *n* borrador *m;* ~ **day** *n* BrE (*cf* ►**workday**

AmE) (weekday) día *m* laborable or de trabajo; (part spent at work) jornada laboral *f;* ~ **environment** *n* ambiente laboral *m;* ~ **group** *n* grupo de trabajo *m;* ~ **holiday** *n* BrE (*cf* ►**working vacation** AmE) vacaciones en las que se realiza algún trabajo *f pl;* ~ **hours** *n pl* horas de trabajo *f pl;* ~ **hypothesis** *n* hipótesis de trabajo *f;* ~ **life** *n* vida *f* activa or laboral; ~ **paper** *n* documento de trabajo *m;* ~ **party** *n* grupo de trabajo *m;* ~ **pattern** *n* norma *f* or pauta *f* de trabajo; ~ **population** *n* población activa *f;* ~ **practice** *n* práctica laboral *f;* ~ **ratio** *n* coeficiente de explotación *m;* ~ **time** *n,* ~ **timetable** *n* horario de trabajo *m;* ~ **vacation** *n* AmE (*cf* ►**working holiday** BrE) vacaciones en las que se realiza algún trabajo *f pl;* ~ **week** *n* BrE (*cf* ►**workweek** AmE) semana laborable *f*

working-class *adj* (person) de clase obrera or trabajadora; (area) obrero

working class *n* clase *f* obrera or trabajadora

workload *n* cantidad de trabajo *f*

workmate *n* compañero(-a) de trabajo *m,f*

workplace *n* lugar de trabajo *m;* ~ **bargaining** *n* negociación en el lugar de trabajo *f;* ~ **shadowing** *n* formación *f* or capacitación *f* mediante observación (que consiste en seguir y observar a alguien en el puesto)

works *n* (factory) fábrica *f;* ~ **committee** *n* BrE comité de empresa *m;* ~ **council** *n* BrE comité de trabajadores *m;* ~ **manager** *n* director *m* or gerente *mf* de fábrica

work-share *vi* compartir el trabajo

work-sharing *n* sistema en el cual dos personas comparten un puesto de trabajo

worksheet *n* hoja de trabajo *f;* (Comp) hoja de programación *f*

workshop *n* taller *m*

workspace *n* área de trabajo *f*

workstation *n* estación de trabajo *f*

work-to-rule *n* huelga de celo *f*

workweek *n* AmE (*cf* ►**working week** BrE) semana laborable *f*

world *n* mundo *m;* **all over the ~** en todo el mundo; **their views are ~s apart** sus opiniones son totalmente opuestas; **the ~ of finance** el mundo de las finanzas; **W~ Bank** *n* Banco Mundial *m;* ~ **beater** *n* producto de primera *m;* ~**-beating** *adj* (product) de primera; ~**-class** *adj* de talla mundial; ~ **consumption** *n* consumo mundial *m;* ~ **debt** *n* deuda mundial *f;* ~ **economy** *n* economía mundial *f;* ~ **exports** *n pl* exportaciones mundiales *f pl;* ~**-famous** *adj* mundialmente famoso, de fama mundial; **W~ Federation of Stock Exchanges** *n* federación mundial de bolsas;

W∼ Federation of Trade Unions n *federación mundial de sindicatos*; **W∼ Federation of United Nations Associations** n Federación Mundial de Asociaciones de las Naciones Unidas f; **∼ inflation** n inflación mundial f; **∼ leader** n líder mundial mf; **∼ market** n mercado mundial m; **∼ price** n precio mundial m; **∼ trade** n comercio mundial m; **W∼ Trade Center** AmE, **W∼ Trade Centre** BrE n centro del comercio mundial m; **W∼ Trade Organization** n Organización Mundial del Comercio f; **∼ Wide Web** n Telaraña mundial f

worldwide¹ adj mundial, universal

worldwide² adv por todo el mundo

worm n (Comp) gusano m

WORM abbr (▸write-once-read-many) escritura única lectura múltiple f

worse adj peor; **get ∼** empeorar

worsen 1 vi (conditions, prospects) empeorar 2 vt empeorar

worse off adj (citizens, worker) en peor situación económica; **I'm £30 a month ∼** tengo 30 libras menos al mes; **I ended up $50 ∼** o **∼ by $50** salí perdiendo 50 dólares

worst adj peor; **∼-case projection** n proyección del peor caso posible f; **∼-case scenario** n escenario para el peor de los casos m

worth¹ n (monetary) valor m; (merit) mérito m, valía f

worth² adj con un valor de, que vale; **be ∼ £5** valer 5 libras, tener un valor de 5 libras; **not be ∼ a bean** (infrml) no valer un duro (infrml) Esp; **∼ goods ∼ £5,000** mercancías por valor de 5.000 libras; **he must be ∼ about £2 million** debe tener unos 2 millones de libras; **be ∼ a mint** (infrml) valer un potosí; **not be ∼ a penny** (infrml) no valer un duro (infrml) Esp

worthless adj (cheque) sin valor

worthwhile adj (enterprise, project) que vale la pena

wp abbr (▸without prejudice) sin prejuicio

WP abbr (▸weather permitting) si el tiempo lo permite; (▸word processor) WP (procesador de textos)

W/P abbr (▸working party) grupo de trabajo m

wpm abbr (▸words per minute) ppm (palabras por minuto)

wrap¹ vt (parcel) envolver; **wrap up** vt (parcel) envolver; (order, sale) conseguir; (deal) cerrar; (meeting) dar fin a

wrap² n (wrapper, wrapping) envoltorio m; **keep sth under ∼s** (infrml) mantener algo en secreto; **take the ∼s off sth** (infrml) sacar algo a la luz

wraparound n (Comp) (of memory) renovación f; (of text) retorno de cursor m; **∼ annuity** n anualidad f cruzada or protegida

wrapper n (for newspaper, book) faja f; (dustjacket) sobrecubierta f, camisa f; (for food) envoltorio m, envoltura f

wrapping n envoltorio m, envoltura f

wrap-up n AmE resumen m

wreck vt arruinar

wrinkle n (infrml) (Stock) característica nueva f

writ n orden f or mandato m judicial; **issue a ∼ (against sb)** expedir una orden or un mandato (contra alguien); **serve a ∼ on sb** notificarle una orden or un mandato a alguien; **∼ of attachment** n mandamiento de embargo m; **∼ of error** n auto de casación m; **∼ of sequestration** n auto de embargo m; **∼ of subpoena** n auto de requerimiento m

writable adj (Comp) registrable

write 1 vt escribir; (report, article) redactar; (cheque) extender; (option) emitir; **∼ a stock option** suscribir una opción de compra de acciones; **∼ sth to disk** traspasar algo a un disco 2 vi escribir; **write against** vt (Stock) reajustar con referencia a; **write an option against sth** vender una opción sobre algo; **write back** vi contestar por carta; **write down** vt (name, details, number) anotar, apuntar; (asset) amortizar, reducir el valor contable de, depreciar; **write off** 1 vt (entry) cancelar; (project, career) dar por perdido; **∼ off a debt** borrar como incobrable una deuda; **∼ sth off to bad debts** pasar algo a cuentas incobrables 2 vi amortizar; **write up** vt (asset) actualizar, poner al corriente, revalorizar

write-down n (of asset) depreciación f

write-off n cancelación f

write-once-read-many n escritura única lectura múltiple f

write-protect vt proteger de escritura

writer n (Stock) emisor(a) m,f

write-up n (of asset) revaluación f; (report) artículo m, reportaje m

writing n escritura f; **in ∼** por escrito; **the ∼ was on the wall for the company** la compañía tenía los días contados

writing-down allowance n descuento con rebaja de valor m

written adj (evidence, warning) escrito; (agreement, offer, statement) por escrito; **∼ call** n (Stock) opción de compra emitida f; **∼ option** n (Stock) opción emitida f; **∼ put** n (Stock) opción de venta emitida f

written-down *adj* (value) amortizado

wrong *adj* falso, incorrecto; **be in the** ∼ **job** haberse equivocado de profesión; **you have the** ∼ **number** se ha equivocado de número; ∼ **connection** *n* (on telephone) falsa llamada *f*

wrongdoing *n* comisión *f* de un delito *or* de una falta

wrong-foot *vt* agarrar *or* pillar desprevenido

wrongful *adj* (accusation) injusto *m*; (arrest) ilegal; (dismissal) improcedente

wrongly *adv* (believe, assume)

equivocadamente; (accuse) injustamente; (spell) mal, incorrectamente

wt. *abbr* (▸**weight**) peso *m*

WTC *abbr* (▸**World Trade Center** AmE, ▸**World Trade Centre** BrE) centro del comercio mundial *m*

WTO *abbr* (▸**World Trade Organization**) OMC *f* (Organización Mundial del Comercio)

WWW *abbr* (▸**World Wide Web**) Telaraña mundial *f*

WYSIWYG *abbr* (▸**what you see is what you get**) WYSIWYG (lo que ves es lo que (ob)tienes)

X *abbr* (▸**telephone extension**) extensión telefónica *f*

xc. *abbr* (▸**ex coupon**) sin cupón

x-d. *abbr* (▸**ex dividend**) sin dividendo

xerographic *adj* xerográfico

Xerox®¹ *n* (copy) xerocopia *f*

Xerox®² *vt* fotocopiar, xerografiar

x-interest *n* interés x *m*

XML *n* (▸**eXtensible Mark-up Language**) XML *m* (lenguaje de marcado ampliable *or* extensible)

x-pri *abbr* (▸**without privileges**) sin privilegios

yankee bond *n* AmE bono yanqui *m*

yankees *n pl* (jarg) títulos estadounidenses *m pl*, yanquis *m pl*

yardstick *n* (for measuring performance) criterio *f*

year *n* año *m*; **it costs $500 a** ∼ cuesta 500 dólares al año; **in the** ∼ **of** en el año de; ∼ **then ended** año que acaba de finalizar; ∼ **to date** año *or* ejercicio hasta la fecha; **the** ∼ **under review** el año a examen; ∼ **of acquisition** *n* año de adquisición *m*; ∼ **of assessment** *n* (Tax) año fiscal *m*; ∼ **of averaging** *n* (Tax) año del promedio *m*; ∼ **end** *n* fin de año *m* ; ∼**-end** *adj* (report) de fin de año; ∼**-end adjustment** *n* ajuste de cierre de ejercicio *m*, regularización *f*; ∼**-end audit** *n* auditoría de cierre de ejercicio *f*; ∼**-end dividend** *n* dividendo

complementario de fin de año *m*; ∼ **of issue** *n* año de emisión *m*

yearly¹ *adj* anual

yearly² *adv* anualmente

year-on-year *adj* (decline) anual

year-to-year *adj* anual

yellow *adj* amarillo; **Y**∼ **Book** *n* BrE libro amarillo *m*; ∼**-dog contract** *n* AmE *contrato con renuncia a la afiliación sindical*; ∼**-dog fund** *n* AmE *previsión para los obreros sin filiación sindical*; ∼ **goods** *n pl* (jarg) productos de la línea amarilla *m pl*; **Y**∼ **Pages**® *n pl* Páginas Amarillas® *f pl*; ∼ **sheets** *n pl* AmE *publicación diaria de la oficina nacional de cotizaciones*; ∼ **strip** *n* (Stock) cobertura amarilla *f*

yield¹ *n* rendimiento *m*; (of tax) producto *m*; ∼ **curve** *n* curva de rendimiento *f*;

∼ **equivalence** *n* equivalencia de rendimiento; ∼ **gap** *n* diferencial de rendimiento *m*; ∼ **maintenance** *n* mantenimiento de rendimientos *m*; ∼ **to call** *n* rendimiento sobre pedido *m*; ∼ **to maturity** *n* rendimiento al vencimiento *m*; ∼ **to worst** *n* rendimiento a la baja *m*; ∼ **variance** *n* variación de rendimiento *f*

yield² *vt* (Fin) rendir; (results) dar, arrojar; (crop, fruit, mineral, oil) producir; (position, territory) ceder; **these bonds** ∼ **9.2%** estos bonos rinden *or* dan un (interés del) 9.2%

young *adj* joven; ∼ **upwardly mobile professional** *n* joven profesional con ambiciones *mf*

Yours faithfully *adv*, **Yours sincerely**

adv (as letter-ending) le saluda atentamente

youth *n* juventud *f*; ∼ **market** *n* mercado de jóvenes *m*; ∼ **training** *n* BrE aprendizaje juvenil *m*

yo-yo *vi* (infrml) fluctuar

yo-yo stock *n* (infrml) acciones de fluctuación volátil *f pl*

yr *abbr* (▸**year**) año *m*

YT *abbr* BrE (▸**youth training**) aprendizaje juvenil *m*

YTM *abbr* (▸**yield to maturity**) rendimiento al vencimiento *m*

yuppie *n* (infrml) (▸**young upwardly mobile professional**) yuppie *mf* (joven profesional con ambiciones)

Zz

zap *vt* (Comp) borrar

zero¹ *n* cero *m*; ∼**-base budget** *n* presupuesto base cero *m*; ∼**-coupon bond** *n* bono cupón cero *m*; ∼ **growth** *n* crecimiento cero *m*; ∼ **inflation** *n* inflación cero *f*; ∼ **rate** *n* (of VAT) tipo cero *m*; ∼**-rated** *adj* (goods, item) no sujeto al IVA; **be** ∼**-rated for VAT** ser tipo cero para el IVA

zero² *vt* (instrument, meter) poner en *or* a cero; **zero in on** *vt* (issue, problem) centrarse en, concentrar la atención en *or* sobre

zip¹ *vt* (file) comprimir

zip² *n* (Comp) compresión *f*; ∼ **code** *n* AmE (*cf* ▸**postal code** *o* **postcode** BrE) código postal *m*; ∼ **file** *n* archivo comprimido *m*

zonal *adj* zonal; ∼ **distribution** *n* distribución por zonas *f*

zone¹ *n* (area) zona *f*; (district) AmE distrito *m*

zone² *vt* dividir en *or* por zonas

zoning *n* división por zonas *f*

zoom *n* (Comp) zoom *m*, ampliación *f*

zoom in *vi* hacer un zoom in; ∼ **on sth/sb** hacer un zoom in sobre algo/alguien

zoom out *vi* hacer un zoom out

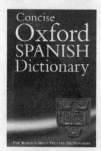
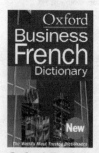